D0578266

. . . The Author of a *Gazette* (in the Opinion of the
Learned) ought to be qualified with an extensive
Acquaintance with Languages, a great Easiness and
Command of Writing and Relating things cleanly
and intelligibly, and in few Words; he should be able
to speak of War both by Land and Sea; be well
acquainted with Geography, with the History of the
Time, with the several Interests of Princes and States,
the Secrets of Courts, and the Manners and Customs
of all Nations. Men thus accomplish'd are very rare
in this remote part of the World; and it would be well
if the Writer of these Papers could make up among
his Friends what is wanting in himself. . . .

B. FRANKLIN

FROM FRANKLIN'S FIRST APPEAL FOR CONTRIBUTIONS TO HIS
PENNSYLVANIA GAZETTE, SEPTEMBER 25—OCTOBER 2, 1729.

The Saturday Evening

POST

Treasury

SELECTED FROM
THE COMPLETE FILES
BY ROGER BUTTERFIELD AND
THE EDITORS OF THE SATURDAY EVENING POST

SIMON AND SCHUSTER • NEW YORK

COPYRIGHT © 1954 BY CURTIS PUBLISHING COMPANY
ALL RIGHTS RESERVED
INCLUDING THE RIGHT OF REPRODUCTION
IN WHOLE OR IN PART IN ANY FORM
PUBLISHED BY SIMON AND SCHUSTER
A GULF+WESTERN COMPANY
ROCKEFELLER CENTER, 630 FIFTH AVENUE
NEW YORK, NEW YORK 10020

ISBN 0-671-63400-3
ISBN 0-671-22842-0 PBK.

18 19 20 21 22 23 24 25

1 2 3 4 5 6 7 8 9 10 Pbk.

ACKNOWLEDGMENTS

THE MAN WHO COULD NOT BE CORNERED. Copyright, 1898, by the Curtis Publishing Co. Reprinted by permission of the Estate of George Horace Lorimer.

THE SERGEANT'S PRIVATE MADHOUSE. Copyright, 1899, by the Curtis Publishing Co. Reprinted from *Wounds in the Rain* by Stephen Crane, by permission of the publisher, Alfred A. Knopf, Inc. Copyright, 1900, 1926, by Alfred A. Knopf, Inc.

THE PASSING OF "THIRD FLOOR BACK." Reprinted by permission of Dodd, Mead & Company. Copyright, 1904, by Jerome K. Jerome. Canadian permission courtesy A. P. Watt & Son in behalf of Hurst and Blackett, Ltd.

THE RANSOM OF RED CHIEF. Copyright, 1907, by the Curtis Publishing Co. Republished in *Whirligigs*, by O. Henry. Copyright, 1910, by Doubleday & Company, Inc.

THE GREAT PANCAKE RECORD. Copyright, 1907, by the Curtis Publishing Co. Copyright, 1908, by Dodd, Mead & Company, 1910, by Little, Brown and Company, 1938, by Owen Johnson. From *The Prodigious Hickey* by Owen Johnson, courtesy of Little, Brown and Company.

A PIECE OF STEAK. Copyright, 1909, by the Curtis Publishing Co. Reprinted by permission of Charmian K. London.

SAD DAYS AT OLD SIWASH. Copyright, 1909, by the Curtis Publishing Co. Copyright, 1911, by Little, Brown and Company. Copyright, 1939, by Clara Lynn Fitch.

THE BOLT FROM THE BLUE. Copyright, 1910, by the Curtis Publishing Co. Reprinted by permission of Dodd, Mead & Company from *The Innocence of Father Brown*, by G. K. Chesterton. Copyright, 1911, by Dodd, Mead & Company. Canadian permission courtesy A. P. Watt & Son in behalf of Miss D. E. Collins and Messrs. Cassell & Co., Ltd.

WORDS AND MUSIC. Copyright, 1911, by the Curtis Publishing Co. Reprinted by permission of Mrs. Irvin S. Cobb.

ALIBI IKE. Copyright, 1915, by the Curtis Publishing Co. Reprinted from *How to Write Short Stories*, by Ring Lardner. Copyright, 1924, by Charles Scribner's Sons, Copyright, 1952, by Ellis A. Lardner; used by permission of the publishers.

CONSIDER THE LIZARD. Copyright, 1913, by the Curtis Publishing Co. Reprinted by permission of Houghton Mifflin Company.

A LITTLE TOWN CALLED ST. MONTIGNIES ST. CHRISTOPHE. Copyright, 1914, by the Curtis Publishing Co. Reprinted by permission of Mrs. Irvin S. Cobb.

IN ALSACE. Copyright, 1915, by the Curtis Publishing Co. Reprinted from *Fighting France*, by Edith Wharton; used by permission of the publishers, Charles Scribner's Sons.

TURN ABOUT. Copyright, 1932, by William Faulkner. Reprinted by permission of Random House, Inc.

A VICTORY DANCE. Copyright, 1920, by the Curtis Publishing Co. Reprinted from *Collected Poems*, by Alfred Noyes, published by J. B. Lippincott Co.

PERSHING AT THE FRONT. Copyright, 1927, by the Curtis Publishing Co. From the book, *Lyric Laughter*. Copyright, 1939, by E. P. Dutton & Co., Inc.

SPEAKING OF OPERATIONS. Copyright, 1915, by the Curtis Publishing Co. Reprinted by permission of Mrs. Irvin S. Cobb.

TUTT AND MR. TUTT—IN WITNESS WHEREOF. Reprinted from *Tut, Tut! Mr. Tutt*, by Arthur Train. Copyright, 1921, by the Curtis Publishing Co., 1923, by Charles Scribner's Sons, 1950, by Helen C. Train; used by permission of the publishers.

TACT. Copyright, 1922, by the Curtis Publishing Co. Republished 1947 by Alfred A. Knopf, Inc., in the volume *Mrs. Egg and Other Americans*, and copyrighted in the name of Alice Baldwin Beer.

BABYLON REVISITED. Reprinted from *Taps at Reveille* by F. Scott Fitzgerald. Copyright, 1931, by the Curtis Publishing Co., 1935, by Charles Scribner's Sons; used by permission of the publishers.

LIGHTNING NEVER STRIKES TWICE. From *Married People*. Copyright, 1936, 1937, by Mary Roberts Rinehart. Reprinted by permission of Rinehart & Co., Inc.

MONEY. Copyright, 1936, by the Curtis Publishing Co. Reprinted by permission of Carl Van Vechten, Literary Executor to Miss Stein.

DYGARTSBUSH. Copyright, 1937, by the Curtis Publishing Co. Courtesy Little, Brown and Company and the Atlantic Monthly Press.

THE CHILD BY TIGER. Copyright, 1937, by Maxwell Perkins as Executor. Reprinted by permission of Harper & Brothers.

WINNING IS MORE FUN THAN LOSING. Copyright, 1936, by the Curtis Publishing Co. Reprinted by permission of the author.

HARK! HARK! THE PARI-MUTUELS BARK! Copyright, 1936, by the Curtis Publishing Co. Reprinted from *I'm a Stranger Here Myself*. Copyright, 1938, by Ogden Nash, by permission of Little, Brown and Company.

VERMONT PRAISE. Copyright, 1946, by the Curtis Publishing Co. Republished by the Macmillan Company in *Collected Poems—New and Enlarged Edition*, by Robert P. Tristram Coffin.

A BALLAD OF ANTHOLOGIES. Copyright, 1941, by the Curtis Publishing Co. Republished by Viking Press in *Stones From a Glass House*, by Phyllis McGinley.

The following stories are all copyrighted by the Curtis Publishing Co. in the respective years shown: CARRIE NATION AND KANSAS, ©1901; THE NICKELODEONS, ©1907; THE MISHAPS OF GENTLE JANE, ©1904; THE HARD-ROCK MAN, ©1908; THE FIRST BIRDMAN, ©1910; WHO'S WHO—AND WHY: W. CHURCHILL, ©1912; WHO'S WHO—AND WHY: ROOSEVELT II, ©1913; BEYOND THE BRIDGE, ©1920; THREE POEMS, ©1928; THE TERRIBLE SHYNESS OF ORVIE STONE, ©1933; TUGBOAT ANNIE, ©1931; ROOM TO BREATHE IN, ©1933; EVERYBODY OUT, ©1934; WILDFIRE, ©1935; THE DEVIL AND DANIEL WEBSTER, ©1936; HUNDRED-TONGUED CHARLEY, THE GREAT SILENT ORATOR, ©1936; PULL, PULL TOGETHER, ©1937; THE HUNTING OF THE HAGGIS, ©1939; MY FATHER WAS THE MOST WRETCHEDLY UNHAPPY MAN I EVER KNEW, ©1941; THE ATOM GIVES UP, ©1940; CITY IN PRISON, ©1943; HOW THE BRITISH SANK THE "SCHARNHORST," ©1944; THE IMMORTAL HARPY, ©1944; SOLID CITIZEN, ©1944; THE LAST NIGHT, ©1943; A FEW KIND WORDS FOR UNCLE SAM, ©1948; IS THERE A LIFE AFTER FORTY?, ©1947; NOTE ON DANGER B, ©1947; THE MURDERER, ©1946; THE COLONEL SAVED THE DAY, ©1950; OLD IRONPUSS, ©1951; THE ORDEAL OF JUDGE MEDINA, ©1950; DEATH ON M-24, ©1952; THE SECRET INGREDIENT, ©1952; I GREW UP WITH EISENHOWER, ©1952; THE DEVIL IN THE DESERT, ©1950; FLORIDA LOAFING, ©1924; SCATTERGOOD BAINES —INVADER, ©1917; by the Curtis Publishing Co.

LIBRARY OF CONGRESS CATALOG CARD NUMBER: 54-8651
MANUFACTURED IN THE UNITED STATES OF AMERICA

TABLE OF CONTENTS

In January 1969, *The Saturday Evening Post* closed its doors forever. For the millions of Americans who grew up on its stories and whose memories are filled with kaleidoscopic visions of its covers, this was one of the saddest signs of the changing times.

The text of this commemorative edition of *The Saturday Evening Post Treasury* is the same as that of the original, published in 1954. Even the introduction is unchanged. The book was planned at a time when the magazine was at its peak of importance and influence. It represented all we most admired and wanted most to remember about *The Saturday Evening Post*. It still does.

THE PUBLISHER

INTRODUCTION

THE SATURDAY EVENING POST is America's oldest magazine, but its great period of growth and influence has all been within a modern lifetime. It was on its last legs when Cyrus H. K. Curtis bought it for $1,000 in 1897. The former owner had just died and there was not enough cash on hand to print another issue. On the week The Curtis Publishing Company agreed to take it over, the *Post* had sixteen pages filled with Victorian prose and verse; the featured serial was something called "Won at Last, by the Author of 'A Terrible Penalty, His Dearest Sin, Miss Forrister's Land Steward,' etc., etc." There were five tiny advertisements, one from a Philadelphia wig maker, one from the Philadelphia and Reading Railway giving its suburban train schedules, two for patent medicines and one for Columbia bicycles. The illustrations consisted of a lady with a bustle and two views of a man's bald head, all tucked away among the ads. The paid circulation was less than 2,300 copies a week and advertising revenue for the entire year of 1897 was less than $7,000.

Under Curtis and his inspired choice as editor, George Horace Lorimer, the *Post* was completely reborn. Lorimer's idea was to put out a nickel weekly that would compete closely with the newspapers in price and outdo the most expensive monthlies in the quantity and quality of its reading matter, as well as in its printed appearance. "The *Post*," he announced in an early issue, "promises twice as much as any other magazine, and it will try to give twice as much as it promises." At first he had to go to the established stars of the writing world—Stephen Crane, Bret Harte, Rudyard Kipling, Marie Corelli, Joel Chandler Harris—and ask them,

Cyrus H. K. Curtis

George Horace Lorimer

July 28, 1906

June 20, 1903

please, to write for his refurbished weekly. The lavish financial backing which Curtis gave him (out of the profits of *The Ladies' Home Journal*) enabled him to pay top prices from the beginning. He inaugurated the policy, which was revolutionary at the time and which the *Post* has followed ever since, of returning a decision on most manuscripts within seventy-two hours, and of paying promptly on acceptance. He also ran little ads, like this:

GOOD SHORT STORIES

bring good prices. The *Post* will pay well for cleverly written, unpublished stories of from 3,000 to 5,000 words. Address "Literary Editor, The Saturday Evening Post, Philadelphia, Pa."

His enterprise got results; very soon the writers were flocking to him. New and significant names are scattered through the turn-of-the-century issues of the *Post*: Willa Cather, Owen Wister, Zona Gale, James Branch Cabell, Theodore Dreiser, Agnes Repplier. Frank Norris' *The Pit* was a *Post* serial in 1902. Jack London's smash hit, *The Call of the Wild,* was serialized in 1903. Joseph Conrad contributed a four-parter, *Gaspar Ruiz,* in 1906. Popular story writers like Montague Glass (Potash and Perlmutter), George Randolph Chester (Get-Rich-Quick Wallingford) and Peter B. Kyne (Cappy Ricks) turned up in the "slush pile," which is office slang for the unsolicited manuscripts. In time the

August 18, 1906

Post became the greatest market for writing talent the world had ever seen, and it still is; more than 175,000 manuscripts now cross its editors' desks each year.

As early as September 1899 Lorimer could boast that "the *Post* editorial page has been called the strongest ever published." It was strong for Theodore Roosevelt and hard on the Republican Old Guard; after the convention of 1912 it remarked bitterly, "The Republican party, born of an aspiration for liberty, seems to have become the most dependable refuge for oppression." It published some startling attacks on Andrew Carnegie and John D. Rockefeller, and expressed admiration for Eugene V. Debs and his "hard-headed, hard-working, clear-thinking" Socialist followers. But it never went overboard for Socialism itself, and after 1917 its favorite targets were the Russian Bolsheviki ("a foul crew") and the American "Pinkies" and "nut-sundae Socialists" who tried to act like them. In 1920 it decided that "party politics is a dreary old show" and urged Americans to elect a non-partisan businessman, preferably Herbert Hoover, as President. This wish came true eight years later but the ensuing depression and the New Deal of Franklin Roosevelt were never fully accepted by the *Post,* or by a large number of its readers. In 1952 it again found a Presidential candidate it could endorse with enthusiasm: General Dwight D. Eisenhower.

The *Post*'s circulation multiplied fifteen times during the first year of the Curtis-Lorimer regime, tripled again in the second, doubled in the third, passed one million a week in 1909, two million in 1913 and three million—after setbacks during World

"Samuel! You're not going to another lodge meeting!"

The Congressman's Headache

"Not so fast buddy; we're havin' another one on you!"

Mr. Tutt

Tugboat Annie

Little Orvie

War I and the depression—in 1937. (These are full-year averages.)
When the *Post*'s present editor, Ben Hibbs, arrived in 1942, a
drastic face-lifting and infusion of new ideas which he adminis-
tered started another upward march. The four million a week mark
was passed in 1949 and present sales are nearing five million. All
in all, more people have bought more copies of the *Post* than of
any other magazine ever published, or now being published, in
the world.

This is an impressive statistic but it does not tell all. During
these later years the *Post* has faced terrific competition from picture magazines, digests, news weeklies, television and various
other forms of armchair entertainment. Its editors have risked
everything, including an advertising revenue of $85,000,000 a
year, on the basic appeal of the written word. The risk has paid
off. Today the *Post* is printing more items of reading matter, it is
being read by more people, and it is being read more thoroughly
than ever before. This is good news for those who have been
worrying about the reading interests of the American people.

There is more good news in the contents of this book. Here
are examples of the kind of reading that has caught and held the
Post's vast audience: thirty-five stories, twenty-five articles and
eleven poems from the all-time pages of the *Post,* plus three selections from its predecessor, the *Pennsylvania Gazette.* Some of
the best short fiction of the last fifty years is here, along with
some of the funniest. A number of the *Post*'s own characters—
Hungry Smeed, the Siwash boys, Tutt and Mr. Tutt, Ma Egg,
Little Orvie, Tugboat Annie, Mr. Glencannon—are present. There
is a baseball story by Ring Lardner and a lynching story by
Thomas Wolfe. There are stories of war, of divorce, of kids and
family life, of prize-fighting, murder and the old West. Every
now and then someone makes the rash statement that the *Post*
prints only formula fiction. But no formula could be stretched to
fit such *Post* originals as William Faulkner's "Turn About," F.
Scott Fitzgerald's "Babylon Revisited," O. Henry's "The Ransom of Red Chief," and Stephen Vincent Benét's "The Devil
and Daniel Webster," to name only four of the stories in this
collection.

The articles reprinted here were chosen because they are fresh
and readable and because, in most cases, they make a definite

contribution to history. Take just one of them, "The Colonel Saves the Day," by Harold H. Martin, a *Post* associate editor. Researched under gunfire in Korea, during the first southward rush of the Communists in the summer of 1950, it was immediately made recommended reading at West Point as a classic study of command in battle. The *Post* has had first-rate reporting in its pages since the start of the present century. Read the 1907 piece by Joseph Medill Patterson called "The Nickelodeons"; I doubt if there is available anywhere else a more fascinating, more clear-cut account of the beginnings of the American movie industry. This article was written, incidentally, by a young man who shortly afterward became a co-editor of the Chicago *Tribune*; still later he founded and ran the New York *Daily News*. But he never lost his lifelong love of sitting, sometimes with his shoes off and his feet among the peanut shells, in little out-of-the-way movie houses.

Though primarily a magazine of words the *Post* for more than fifty years has been giving its customers a variety of good things to look at. The artists who have illustrated its stories include most of the great names in that field: Frederic Remington, Harrison Fisher, N. C. Wyeth, Charles Dana Gibson, Rollin Kirby, Charles Livingston Bull, Tony Sarg, Art Young, Norman Rockwell, Frederick R. Gruger, Anton Otto Fischer, Robert Riggs, and many more. Its covers are a national institution in themselves— a picture gallery of American life that has given enjoyment to millions. In this book there is a special section where seventy memorable *Post* covers are reproduced in their original colors. There is also a pictorial section on advertising, and the black-and-white decorations which appear throughout the book are adapted from *Post* illustrations by Frederick E. Banbery.

The idea of including a favorite *Post* serial was considered hopefully and abandoned with regret, since it would have taken from seventy-five to one hundred of the pages available, and that seemed out of proportion. If a choice could have been made, it might have gone to Harry Leon Wilson's *Ruggles of Red Gap* (1914) or Emerson Hough's *The Covered Wagon* (1922) or Frances Noyes Hart's *The Bellamy Trial* (1927) or Nordhoff and Hall's *Men Against the Sea* (1933) or Ethel Vance's *Escape* (1939) or Adria Locke Langley's *A Lion Is in the Streets* (1944). All of these ranked especially high in reader response. Among

N. C. Wyeth

Norman Rockwell

Charles Livingston Bull

XV

non-fiction serials Whittaker Chambers' *I Was the Witness* (1952, published in book form as *Witness*) gave the *Post* its greatest single circulation boost in history. Bing Crosby and Pete Martin's *Call Me Lucky* and Charles A. Lindbergh's *The Spirit of Saint Louis,* both published in 1953, were close runners-up.

Working editors are traditionally wary of the backward look, and this anthology was never intended to be a nosegay of past glories. In choosing its contents the same high standards have been applied which govern each new issue of the *Post*: Is the piece entertaining? Is it well written? Does it add something to knowledge, either as an example of what Americans have liked to read, or because of the information it contains?

Nothing has been included because of a famous author or a popularity that is beyond recall. Much that was good, but merely good, has been weeded out. The result is a book which is not only rich in reading pleasure, but also a permanent part of the literature of our times.

—ROGER BUTTERFIELD

PROBABLY THERE IS not an American alive who does not recognize the cover of *The Saturday Evening Post*. That is one of the aims of the editors—to make their magazine easy to know. But *Post* covers are more than a trademark. Taking them all together they form a unique pictorial history of the experiences, amusements, and foibles of the American people themselves. For more than half a century the *Post's* cover has been a mirror held up to American life.

On this and the following pages there are reproduced seventy covers from all ages of the *Post*. From them the reader can chart the development of the modern magazine cover. The first full-page cover, in 1899, merely presented a picture to illustrate a story inside the magazine. Then the cover freed itself of the contents and became something pleasant to look at, like a pretty girl. (This kind of cover still pulls readers for some magazines, but not for the *Post*.) Then came the "symbol" cover, notably the famous *Post* cherub created by J. C. Leyendecker. Then the vignettes which fitted best with two-color printing, like the delightful genre scenes of Robert Robinson. And finally, the painting which fills a page and tells a story by itself. Today's *Post* covers are mostly of this type. Outstanding examples are Norman Rockwell's "Thanksgiving" (page 32) and George Hughes' "Boy in Tux" (page 25).

THE SATURDAY EVENING
POST
JANUARY 15, 1949   15¢

WHAT THE COAL MINERS SAY
ABOUT JOHN L. LEWIS
By John Bartlow Martin

A New Leslie Ford Mystery

All Europe is on our Side of the Question, as far as Applause and good Wishes can carry them.~~Those who live under arbitrary Power do nevertheless approve of Liberty, and wish for it; they almost despair of recovering it in Europe;~~~'tis a Common Observation here, that our Cause is *the Cause of all Mankind*, and that we are fighting for their Liberty in defending our own.

Benj.~Franklin 1777

B. Franklin's birthday, on January 17, is celebrated every year by the *Post* with this cover and a quotation. The painting is by the late John Atherton.

THE SATURDAY EVENING POST

MARCH 9, '29

5c. The Copy
10c. in Canada

Samuel M. Vauclain—William Hazlett Upson—James Warner Bellah
Wesley Stout—Eleanor Mercein—Samuel Crowther—Booth Tarkington

This Rockwell painting of an old family doctor and a little girl's "sick" doll
is perhaps the best-remembered of all *Post* covers.

THE SATURDAY EVENING POST

An Illust___ ___ Weekly
Founded A°. D°. ___ ___ Benj. Franklin

OCTOBER 3, 1936 **5cts. THE COPY**

THE DOUBLE RIDE
By Francis Wallace

GOVERNMENT-RUN-EVERYTHING By John Raymond McCarl

A close runner-up in the affections of *Post* readers was this tense scene in a smalltown butcher shop, painted by Leslie Thrasher.

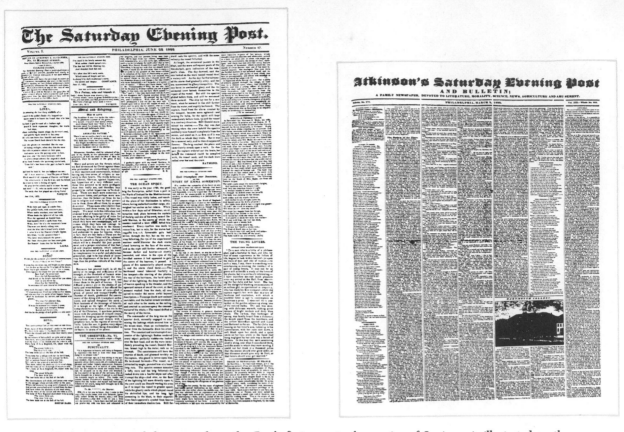

The EVOLUTION of the cover, from the *Post*'s first year to the coming of Lorimer, is illustrated on these pages. In 1821 the cover was simply filled with type. Then a few tiny pictures began to appear. In the 1874 issue at upper right the cover was given over to an installment of *East Lynne* with a picture of the

villain and his mustache. At lower left is the cover as it looked when Curtis bought the *Post*, and the first typographic changes he made. The first full-page cover, in two colors, was published by Lorimer in 1899. The *Post*'s distinctive heading type, unchanged for nearly forty years, first appeared in 1903.

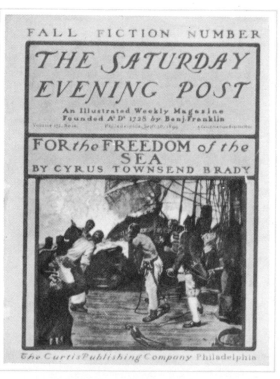

THE SATURDAY EVENING POST

An Illustrated Magazine Founded A.D. Franklin

APRIL 13, 1907   5c. THE COPY

THE CURTIS PUBLISHING COMPANY, PHILADELPHIA

COVER GIRLS were standard fare on the *Post* in the earlier years of the century. Charles Dana Gibson, Harrison Fisher, Coles Phillips, and Neysa McMein were among the experts who provided them. But the *Post* has never relied on sex appeal, and today it finds that a complicated cover story centering around a domestic situation sells more copies than a mere pretty girl.

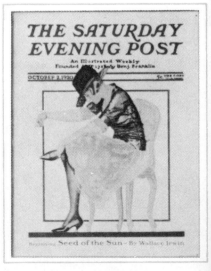

BATHING BEAUTIES are cover girls with fewer clothes on, and the *Post* has had its share of them. The first ones wore stockings and lots of skirt. With the advent of modern beach styles the *Post* has usually subordinated legs to a story theme, as in the cover at upper right. But easily the most popular of all its bathing covers was the fat lady puffing on the water wings.

THE POST CHERUB made his first wistful appearance on the New Year's cover for 1908. For more than thirty years after that he was the nation's best-known symbol of another calendar change. In addition he often portrayed some aspect of the nation's history. In 1920, for instance, he dragged the wooden camel of prohibition; in 1931 he was forging his way out of the depression; in 1940 he wore a gas mask.

THE SATURDAY EVENING POST

An Illustrated Weekly Magazine
Founded A.D. 1728 by Benj. Franklin

JULY 27, 1907   FIVE CENTS THE COPY

THE CURTIS PUBLISHING COMPANY, PHILADELPHIA

Early example of a "clinch" cover. *Post* has rarely used this theme.

THE SATURDAY
EVENING POST

An Illustrated Weekly
Founded A.D. 1728 by Benj. Franklin

DEC. 22, 1917   5cts. THE COPY

CHRISTMAS 1917

This 1917 cover was forerunner of a famous drawing by Bill Mauldin.

THE INNOCENT PLEASURES of an older America are captured for all time in the holiday covers on this page, all drawn by the great J. C. Leyendecker. Opposite, a modern *Post* artist, Amos Sewell, handles the Halloween theme. His drawing is more polished, his story more subtle, but the nostalgia is the same.

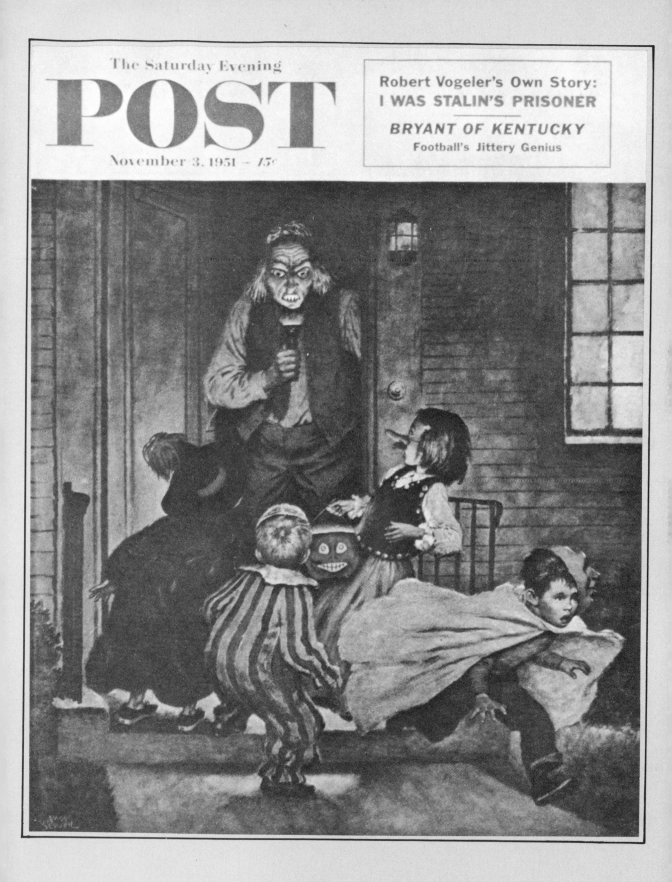

FIFTY YEARS OF AUTOMOBILE lore and history have been faithfully recorded on the covers of the *Post*. In the two examples at upper left the family buggy still had a right-hand drive. Rockwell's "Excuse My Dust" cover was a smash hit of 1920 and a wonderful free ad for the Model T—Henry Ford himself could have posed as the driver. Next to it is shown a modern tourist court about to close up shop. The two covers below might be captioned "How the Traffic Cop Has Changed."

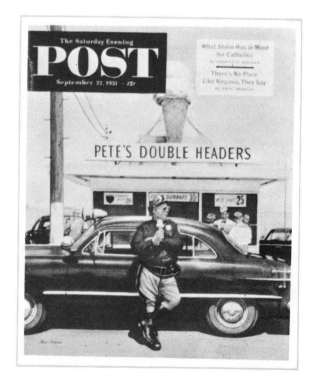

15

THE SATURDAY EVENING POST

An Illus   kly
Founded   Franklin

MARCH 15, 1913   5c. THE COPY

CRACKERS
10¢ a lb.

Beginning
John Barleycorn—By Jack London

LIFE IN AMERICA has always been the number-one theme of the *Post*'s cover artists. Robert Robinson, who painted most of these, specialized in cracker-barrel types and their political debates. Uncle Ezra at the art show, and the fat man at the movies. The early earphone radio cover is by Norman Rockwell.

The Saturday Evening
POST
October 11, 1952 · 15¢

THE CASE FOR THE REPUBLICANS
By Congressman Walter H. Judd

A FOOTBALL COACH SAYS:
**I'M THROUGH WITH
HIGH-SCHOOL FOOTBALL**

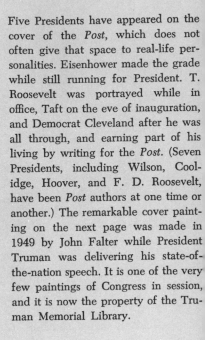

Norman
Rockwell

Five Presidents have appeared on the cover of the *Post*, which does not often give that space to real-life personalities. Eisenhower made the grade while still running for President. T. Roosevelt was portrayed while in office, Taft on the eve of inauguration, and Democrat Cleveland after he was all through, and earning part of his living by writing for the *Post*. (Seven Presidents, including Wilson, Coolidge, Hoover, and F. D. Roosevelt, have been *Post* authors at one time or another.) The remarkable cover painting on the next page was made in 1949 by John Falter while President Truman was delivering his state-of-the-nation speech. It is one of the very few paintings of Congress in session, and it is now the property of the Truman Memorial Library.

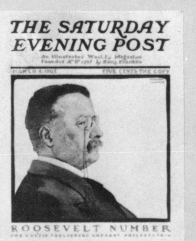

THE SATURDAY EVENING

POST

JANUARY 7, 1950   15¢

How You Can Survive an A-Bomb Blast

Why We Lost China
By Joseph Alsop

SEE PAGE 3

WORLD WAR II on the cover of the *Post* was sometimes grave, sometimes comic, and never terribly depressing. The paratrooper and Navy lookout above were part of a series by Mead Schaeffer on United States fighting men. The South Seas baseball argument and Rockwell's Rosie the Riveter, below, were strictly for laughs. At the right, Kenneth Stuart gives an idea of paperhanger Hitler's troubles in 1943.

THE `SATURDAY EVENING

POST

MAY 19, 1945   10¢

A New
Western Serial
By LUKE SHORT

A Soldier's Slant on
Compulsory Training

This wartime look at New York's Park Avenue and Grand Central Station is
a good example of John Falter's fine city-scene covers.

"Willie's Return," by Rockwell, ended the wartime saga of a favorite *Post* character. This painting was shown at the Metropolitan.

THE SATURDAY EVENING

POST

NOVEMBER 18, 1950   15¢

24

KIDS OF ALL AGES are the favorite cover subjects of most *Post* readers today. The coonskin chorus dates back to the nineteen-twenties, of course, but the rest are dedicated to the current crop of adolescents. Their activities fascinate their parents, and that makes them good material for *Post* cover artists.

The Saturday Evening

POST

October 13, 1951 — 15¢

No More Football For Us!
By Father Guthrie,
PRESIDENT, GEORGETOWN UNIVERSITY

THEY'RE RULING CHINA BY MASS MURDER
By Peggy Durdin

John Clymer

Typical of John Clymer's covers is this picture of Western school kids.

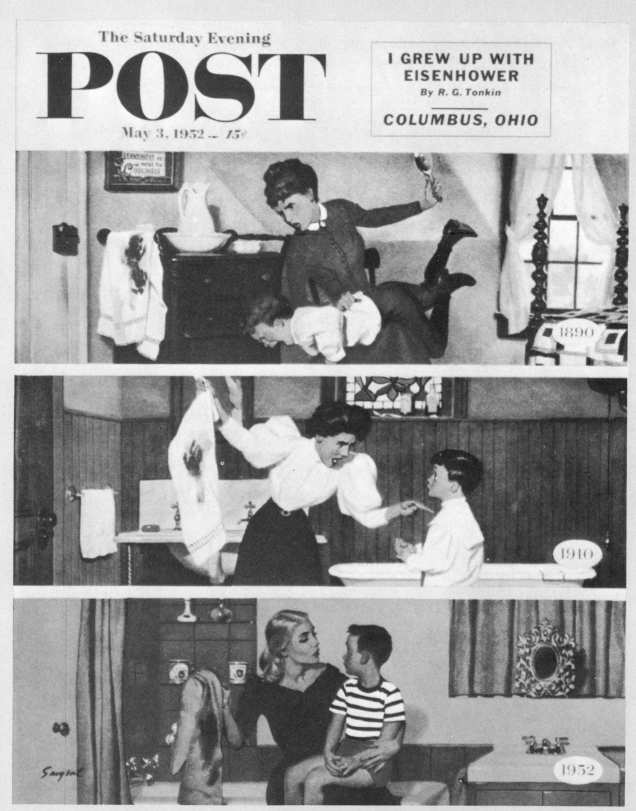

Richard Sargent painted this morality tale about boys and dirty towels.

THE FADS of this century, and some a lot older, have been pictured on *Post* covers. The phrenologist below was a part of a Rockwell series on oldtime America. The dieting cover next to it is as modern as the nearest cafeteria. The kitchen full of dirty dishes, on the next pages, was an extremely popular recent *Post* cover.

THE SATURDAY EVENING

POST

JANUARY 8, 1949   15¢

THE U-BOAT MYSTERY
OF SCAPA FLOW
By Burke Wilkinson

I Was Blind But Now I See
By Major Robert P. Steptoe

THE SATURDAY EVENING
POST

MARCH 6, 1948   15¢

A NEW HORNBLOWER
NOVELETTE
By C. S. FORESTER

A Faint Blueprint for Peace
By MARTIN SOMMERS

Three Norman Rockwell covers complete this section. In "Gossip," above, he drew himself twice (second and third from the end).

All the characters in this baseball cover were drawn from real life, as were the people in Rockwell's "Thanksgiving," next page.

REPRIEVE FOR JEMMY AND JAMES

by Benjamin Franklin

IN THE FALL of 1729 a twenty-three-year-old printer named Benjamin Franklin became part owner of a Philadelphia newspaper that bore the forbidding title of *The Universal Instructor in All Arts and Sciences and Pennsylvania Gazette.* This publication had been started the year before by Franklin's onetime boss, Samuel Keimer, who tried to make it popular by reprinting an encyclopedia in one-page installments. Franklin dropped this cumbersome feature at once, shortened the name to *Pennsylvania Gazette*, and filled its columns with lively news, editorials and advertising. In his first number he set forth some standards of editorship which could well apply to the present-day *Post* or any other magazine. (See frontispiece.) Although he modestly pleaded for contributions from his friends, Franklin himself was the *Gazette*'s best bet as a writer and reporter. His nose for news, his never-failing sense of humor, and his steady assertion of the rights and dignity of the press—at a time when "freedom of the press" was unknown either as a phrase or an idea—are illustrated in the three items reprinted here. Franklin died in 1790, ripe in years and laden with honors; his *Gazette* lived on until 1815. Six years later, on August 4, 1821, the first number of *The Saturday Evening Post* was issued from the *Gazette*'s old print shop by a firm which had acquired the assets and types of Franklin's long-time partner, David Hall. This line of succession from Franklin's famous newspaper became both an inspiration and a useful promotion asset to the *Post* after Curtis bought the magazine in 1897.

JANUARY 13-20, 1730

We think our Readers will not be displeased to have the following remarkable Transaction related to them in this particular Manner.

WEDNESDAY THE 14th Instant, being the Day appointed for the Execution of *James Prouse* and *James Mitchel* for Burglary, suitable Preparations were accordingly made. The tender Youth of one of them (who was but about 19) and the supposed Innocence of the other as to the Fact for which they were condemned, had induced the Judges (upon the application of some compassionate People) to recommend them to His Honour's known Clemency: but several Malefactors having been already pardoned, and every Body being sensible, that, considering the great Increase of Vagrants and idle Persons, by the late large Importation of such from several parts of *Europe*, it was becoming necessary for the common Good to make some Examples, there was but little Reason to hope that either, and less that both of them might escape the Punishment justly due to Crimes of that enormous Nature. About 1 o'clock the Bell began to Toll, and a numerous Croud of People was gathered near the Prison, to see these unhappy young Men brought forth to suffer. While their Irons were taken off, and their Arms were binding, *Prouse* cry'd immoderately; but *Mitchel* (who had himself all along behaved with unusual Forti-

tude) endeavoured in a friendly tender Manner to comfort him: *Do not cry, Jemmy*; (says he) *In an Hour or two it will be over with us, and we shall both be easy.* They were then placed in a Cart, together with a Coffin for each of them, and led thro' the Town to the Place of Execution: *Prouse* appear'd extreamly dejected, but *Mitchel* seemed to support himself with a becoming manly Constancy: When they arriv'd at the fatal Tree, they were told that it was expected they should make some Confession of their Crimes, and say something by Way of Exhortation to the People. *Prouse* was at length with some Difficulty prevailed on to speak; he said, his Confession had been taken in Writing the Evening before; he acknowledged the Fact for which he was to die, but said, that *Greyer* who had sworn against him was the Person that persuaded him to it; and declared that he had never wronged any Man beside Mr. *Sheed*, and his Master. *Mitchel* being desired to speak, reply'd with a sober compos'd Countenance, *What should you have me to say? I am innocent of the Fact.* He was then told, that it did not appear well in him to persist in asserting his Innocence; that he had had a fair Trial, and was found guilty by twelve honest and good

Men. He only answer'd, *I am innocent; and it will appear so before God*; and sat down. Then they were both bid to stand up, and the Ropes were order'd to be thrown over the Beam; when the Sheriff took a Paper out of his Pocket and began to read. The poor Wretches, whose Souls were at that Time fill'd with the immediate Terrors of approaching Death, having nothing else before their Eyes, and being without the least Apprehension or Hope of a Reprieve, took but little Notice of what was read; or it seems imagined it to be some previous Matter of Form, as a Warrant for their Execution or the like, 'till they heard the Words PITY and MERCY [*And whereas the said* James Prouse *and* James Mitchel *have been recommended to me as proper Objects of Pity and Mercy.*] Immediately *Mitchel* fell into the most violent Agony; and having only said, *God bless the Governor,* he swooned away in the Cart. Suitable Means were used to recover him; and when he came a little to himself, he added; *I have been a great Sinner; I have been guilty of almost every Crime; Sabbath-breaking in particular, which led me into ill Company; but Theft I never was guilty of. God bless the Governor; and God Almighty's Name be praised*; and then swooned again. *Prouse* likewise seemed to be overwhelmed with Joy, but did not swoon. All the Way back to the Prison, *Mitchel* lean'd against his Coffin, being unable to support himself, and shed Tears in abundance. He who went out to die with a large share of Resolution and Fortitude, returned in the most dispirited Manner imaginable; being utterly over-power'd by the Force of that sudden Turn of excessive Joy, for which he had been in now Way prepared. The Concern that appeared in every Face while these Criminals were leading to Execution, and the Joy that diffused it self thro' the whole Multitude, so visible in their Countenances upon the mention of a Reprieve, seems to be a pleasing Instance, and no small Argument of the general laudable Humanity even of our common People, who were unanimous in their loud Acclamation of *God bless the Governor for his Mercy.*

APOLOGY FOR PRINTERS

JUNE 3-10, 1731

BEING FREQUENTLY censur'd and condemn'd by different Persons for printing Things which they say ought not to be printed, I have sometimes thought it might be necessary to make a standing Apology for my self, and to publish it once a Year, to be read upon all Occasions of that Nature. Much Business has hitherto hindered the Execution of this Design; but having very lately given extraordinary Offence by printing an Advertisement with a certain *N.B.* at the End of it, I find an Apology more particularly requisite at this Juncture, tho's it happens when I have not yet Leisure to write such a thing in its proper Form, and can only in a loose manner throw those Considerations together which should have been the Substance of it.

I request all who are angry with me on any Account of printing things they don't like, calmly to consider these following Particulars.

That the Opinions of Men are almost as various as their Faces; an Observation general enough to become a common Proverb. So many Men so many Minds.

That the business of Printing has chiefly to do with Mens Opinions; most things that are printed tending to promote some, or oppose others.

That hence arises the peculiar Unhappiness of that Business, which other Callings are in now way liable to; they who follow Printing being scarce able to do any thing in their way of getting a Living, which shall not probably give Offence to some, and perhaps to many; whereas the Smith, the Shoemaker, the Carpenter, or the Man of many another Trade, may work indifferently for People of all Persuasions, without offending any of them: and the Merchant may buy and sell with Jews, Turks, Hereticks and Infidels of all sorts, and get Money by every one of them, without giving Offence to the most Orthodox, of any sort; or suffering the least Censure or Ill-will on the Account from any Man whatever. . . .

That it is unreasonable to imagine Printers approve of every thing they print, and to censure them on any particular thing accordingly; since in the way of their Business they print such great variety of things opposite and contradictory. It is likewise as unreasonable what some assert, *That Printers ought not to print any Thing but what they approve*; since if all of that Business should make such a Resolution, and abide by it, an End would thereby be put to Free Writing, and the World would afterwards have nothing to read but what happen'd to be the Opinions of Printers.

That if all Printers were determin'd not to print any thing till they were sure it would offend no body, there would be very little printed. . . .

I come now to the particular Case of the *N.B.* above-mention'd, about which there has been more Clamour against me, than ever before on any other Account.—In the Hurry of other Business an Advertisement was brought to me to be printed; it signified that such a Ship lying at such a Wharff, would sail for the *Barbadoes* in which a Time, and that Freighters and Passengers might agree with the Captain at such a Place; so far is what's common: But at the Bottom this odd Thing was added, N.B. *No Sea-Hens nor Black Gowns will be admitted on any Terms.* I printed it, and receiv'd my Money; and the Advertisement was stuck up around Town as usual. I had not so much Curiosity at that Time as to enquire the Meaning of it, nor did I in the least imagine it would give so much Offence. Several good Men are very angry with me on this Occasion; they are pleas'd to say I have too much Sense to do such things ignorantly; that if they were Printers they would not have done such a thing on any Consideration; that it could proceed from nothing but my abundant Malice against Religion and the Clergy: They therefore declare they will not take any more of my Papers, nor have any farther Dealings with me; but will hinder me of all the Custom they can. All this is very hard!

I believe it had been better if I had refused to print the said Advertisement. However, 'tis done and cannot be revok'd. I have only the following few Particulars to offer, some of them in my Behalf, by way of Mitigation, and some not much to the Purpose; but I desire none of them may be read when the Reader is not in a very good Humour.

That I really did it without the least Malice, and imagin'd the *N.B.* was plac'd there only to make the Advertisement star'd at, and more generally read.

That I never saw the Word *Sea-Hens* before in my Life; nor have I yet ask'd the meaning of it; and tho's I had certainly known that *Black Gowns* in that Place signified the Clergy of the Church of *England,* yet I have that confidence in the generous good Temper of such of them as I know, to be well satisfied such a trifling mention of their Habit gives them no Disturbance.

That most of the Clergy in this and the neighbouring Provinces, are my Customers, and some of them my very good Friends; and I must be very malicious indeed, or very stupid, to print this thing for a small Profit, if I had thought it would have given them just Cause for Offence. . . .

That I got Five Shillings by it.

That none who are angry with me would have given me so much to let it alone. . . .

And lastly, that I have printed above a Thousand Advertisements which made not the least mention of *Sea-Hens* or *Black Gowns*; and this being the first Offence, I have the more Reason to expect Foregiveness. . . .

I consider the Variety of Humours among Men and despair of pleasing every Body; yet I shall not therefore leave off Printing. I shall continue my Business. I shall not burn my Press and melt my Letters.

ADVENTURE WITH A TAR BARREL

SEPTEMBER 9-23, 1731

THURSDAY LAST, a certain P-----r ['tis not customary to give Names at length on these Occasions] walking carefully in clean Cloaths over some Barrels of Tar on Carpenter's Wharff, the head of one of them unluckily gave way, and let a Leg of him in above his Knee. Whether he was upon the Catch at that time, we cannot say, but 'tis certain he caught a *Tar-tar.* 'Twas observ'd he sprung out again right briskly, verifying the common Saying, *As Nimble as a* Bee *in a Tarbarrel.* You must know there are several sorts of *Bees*: 'tis true he was no *Honey Bee,* nor yet a *Humble Bee,* but a *Boo bee* he may be allow'd to be, namely *B.F.* N.B. *We hope the Gentleman will excuse this Freedom.*

THE BLACK CAT

by *Edgar A. Poe*

IN THE YEARS before the Civil War the *Post* cut loose from its Philadelphia background and became a national weekly, achieving a prosperous but not record-breaking circulation of 90,000 a week. Its chief appeal to readers was its fiction and poetry, but it also carried detailed news summaries and some forceful editorials. It published special correspondence from places like Milan, Basle, Paris and Bombay, and it was one of the first weeklies to print a full account of the California gold excitement in late 1848. Among the leading authors who contributed to it were Harriet Beecher Stowe, James Fenimore Cooper, Bayard Taylor, Timothy Shay Arthur of "Ten Nights in a Bar Room" fame, Lydia Sigourney and James K. Paulding. But only one of the hundreds of tales it printed in this period remains of interest today— Edgar Allan Poe's "The Black Cat," which ran on page one complete, in the issue for August 19, 1843. Poe was a popular writer and the *Post* was proud of getting his story. "The Black Cat," commented the editor, "is written in that vein of his which no other writer can imitate. . . . For our own part, we are bound to give the *pas* to all black cats, henceforth and forever; and to treat them with obsequeous [sic] consideration. Cruelty to animals is a sin which deserves a punishment as severe as Mr. Poe has inflicted upon his hero."

FOR THE MOST WILD, yet most homely narrative which I am about to pen, I neither expect nor solicit belief. Mad indeed would I be to expect it, in a case where my very senses reject their own evidence. Yet, mad am I not—and very surely do I not dream. But to-morrow I die, and to-day I would unburthen my soul. My immediate purpose is to place before the world, plainly, succinctly, and without comment, a series of mere household events. In their consequences, these events have terrified—have tortured—have destroyed me. Yet I will not attempt to expound them. To me, they have presented little but Horror—to many they will seem less terrible than *barroques*. Hereafter, perhaps, some intellect may be found which will reduce my phantasm to the common-place—some intellect more calm, more logical, and far less excitable than my own, which will perceive, in the circumstances I detail with awe, nothing more than an ordinary succession of very natural causes and effects.

From my infancy I was noted for the docility and humanity of my disposition. My tenderness of heart was even so conspicuous as to make me the jest of my companions. I was especially fond of animals, and was indulged by my parents with a great variety of pets. With these I spent most of my time, and never was so happy as when feeding and caressing them. This peculiarity of character grew with my growth, and, in my manhood, I derived from it one of my principal sources of pleasure. To those who have cherished an affection for a faithful and sagacious dog, I need hardly be at the trouble of explaining the nature or the intensity of the gratification thus derivable. There is something in the unselfish and self-sacrificing love of a brute, which goes directly to the heart of him who has had frequent occasion to test the paltry friendship and gossamer fidelity of mere *Man*.

I married early, and was happy to find in my wife a disposition not uncongenial with my own. Observing my partiality for domestic pets, she lost no opportunity of procuring those of the most agreeable kind. We had birds, gold-fish, a fine dog, rabbits, a small monkey and *a cat*.

This latter was a remarkably large and beautiful animal, entirely black, and sagacious to an astonishing degree. In speaking of her intelligence, my wife, who at heart was not a little tinctured with superstition, made frequent allusion to the ancient popular notion, which regarded all black cats as witches in disguise. Not that she was ever *serious* upon this point—and I mention the matter at all for no better reason than that it happens, just now, to be remembered.

Pluto—this was the cat's name—was my favorite pet and playmate. I alone fed him, and he attended me wherever I went about the house. It was even with difficulty that I could prevent him from following me through the streets.

Our friendship lasted, in this manner, for several years, during which my general temperament and character—through the instrumentality of the Fiend Intemperance had—(I blush to confess it) experienced a radical alteration for the worse. I grew, day by day, more moody, more irritable, more regardless of the feelings of others. I suffered myself to use intemperate language to my wife. At length, I even offered her personal violence. My pets, of course, were made to feel the change in my disposition. I not only neglected but ill-used them. For Pluto, however, I still retained sufficient regard to restrain me from maltreating him, as I made no scruple of maltreating the rabbits, the monkey, or even the dog, when by accident, or through affection, they came in my way. But my disease grew upon me—for what disease is like Alcohol?—and at length even Pluto, who was now becoming old, and consequently somewhat peevish—even Pluto began to experience the effects of my ill temper.

One night, returning home, much intoxicated, from one of my haunts about town, I fancied that the cat avoided my presence. I seized him; when, in his fright at my violence, he inflicted a slight wound upon my hand with his teeth. The fury of a demon instantly possessed me. I knew myself no longer. My original soul seemed, at once, to take its flight from my body; and a more than fiendish malevolence, gin-nurtured, thrilled every fibre of my frame. I took from my waistcoat-pocket a pen-knife, opened it, grasped the poor beast by the throat, and deliberately cut one of the eyes from the socket! I blush, I burn, I shudder, while I pen the damnable atrocity.

When reason returned with the morning—when I had slept off the fumes of the night's debauch—I experienced a sentiment half of horror, half of remorse, for the crime of which I had been guilty; but it was, at best, a feeble and equivocal feeling, and the soul remained untouched. I again plunged into excess, and soon drowned in wine all memory of the deed.

In the meantime the cat slowly recovered. The socket of the lost eye presented, it is true, a frightful appearance, but he no longer appeared to suffer any pain. He went about the house as usual, but, as might be expected, fled in extreme terror at my approach. I had so much of my old heart left, as to be, at first, grieved by this evident dislike on the part of a creature which had once so loved me. But this feeling soon gave place to irritation. And then came, as if to my final and irrevocable overthrow, the spirit of PERVERSE-NESS. Of this spirit philosophy takes no account. Phrenology finds no place for it among its organs. Yet I am not more sure that my soul lives, than I am that perverseness is one of the primitive impulses of the human heart—one of the indivisible primary faculties, or sentiments, which give direction to the character of Man. Who has not, a hundred times, found himself committing a vile or a silly action, for no other reason than because he knows he should *not*? Have we not a perpetual inclination, in the teeth of our best judgment, to violate that which is *Law*, merely because we understand it to be such? This spirit of perverseness, I say, came to my final overthrow. It was this unfathomable longing of the soul *to vex itself*—to offer violence to its own nature—to do wrong for the wrong's sake only—that urged me to continue and finally to consummate the injury I had inflicted upon the unoffending brute. One morning, in cool blood, I slipped a noose about its neck and hung it to the limb of a tree;—hung it with the tears streaming from my eyes, and with the bitterest remorse at my heart; —hung it *because* I knew that it had loved me, and *because* I felt it had given me no reason of offence;—hung it *because* I knew that in so doing I was committing a sin—a deadly sin that would so jeopardize my immortal soul as to place it— if such a thing were possible—even beyond the reach of the infinite mercy of the Most Merciful and Most Terrible God.

On the night of the day on which this cruel deed was done, I was aroused from sleep by the cry of fire. The curtains of my bed were in flames. The whole house was blazing. It was with great difficulty that my wife, a servant, and myself, made our escape from the conflagration. The destruction was complete. My entire worldly wealth was swallowed up, and I resigned myself thenceforward to despair.

I am above the weakness of seeking to establish a sequence of cause and effect, between the disaster and the atrocity. But I am detailing a chain of facts—and wish not to leave even a possible link imperfect. On the day succeeding the fire, I visited the ruins. The walls, with one exception, had fallen in. This exception was found in a compartment wall, not very thick, which stood about the middle of the house, and against which had rested the head of my bed. The plastering had here, in great measure, resisted the action of the fire—a fact which I attributed to its having been recently spread. About this wall a dense crowd were collected, and many persons seemed to be examining a particular portion of it with very minute and eager attention. The words "strange!" "singular!" and other similar expressions, excited my curiosity. I approached and saw, as if graven in *bas relief* upon the white surface, the figure of a gigantic *cat*. The impression was given with an accuracy truly marvellous. There had been a rope about the animal's neck.

When I first beheld this apparition—for I could scarcely regard it as less—my wonder and my terror were extreme. But at length reflection came to my aid. The cat, I remembered, had been hung in a garden adjacent to the house. Upon the alarm of fire, this garden had been immediately filled by the crowd—by some one of whom the animal must have been cut from the tree and thrown, through an open window, into my chamber. This had probably been done with the view of arousing me from sleep. The falling of other walls had compressed the victim of my cruelty into the substance of the freshly-spread plaster; the lime of which, with the flames, and the *ammonia* from the carcass, had then accomplished the portraiture as I saw it.

Although I thus readily accounted to my reason, if not altogether to my conscience, for the startling fact just detailed, it did not the less fail to make a deep impression upon my fancy. For months I could not rid myself of the phantasm of the cat; and, during this period, there came back into my spirit a half-sentiment that seemed, but was not, remorse. I went so far as to regret the loss of the animal, and to look about me, among the vile haunts which I now habitually frequented, for another pet of the same species, and of somewhat similar appearance, with which to supply its place.

One night as I sat, half stupified, in a den of more than infamy, my attention was suddenly drawn to some black object, reposing upon the head of one of the immense hogsheads of Gin, or of Rum, which constituted the chief furniture of the apartment. I had been looking steadily at the top of this hogshead for some minutes, and what now caused me surprise was the fact that I had not sooner perceived the object thereupon. I approached it, and touched it with my hand. It was a black cat—a very large one—fully as large as Pluto, and closely resembling him in every respect but one. Pluto had not a white hair upon any portion of his body; but this cat had a large, although indefinite splotch of white, covering nearly the whole region of the breast.

Upon my touching him, he immediately arose, purred loudly, rubbed against my hand, and appeared delighted with my notice. This, then, was the very creature of which I was in search. I at once offered to purchase it of the landlord; but this person made no claim to it—knew nothing of it—had never seen it before.

I continued my caresses, and, when I prepared to go home, the animal evinced a disposition to accompany me. I permitted it to do so; occasionally stooping and patting it as I proceeded. When it reached the house it domesticated itself at once, and became immediately a great favorite with my wife.

For my own part, I soon found a dislike to it arising within me. This was just the reverse of what I had anticipated; but—I know not how or why it was—its evident fondness for myself rather disgusted and annoyed. By slow degrees, these feelings of disgust and annoyance rose into the bitterness of hatred. I avoided the creature; a certain sense of shame, and the remembrance of my former deed of cruelty, preventing me from physically abusing it. I did not, for some weeks, strike, or otherwise violently ill use it; but gradually—very gradually—I came to look upon it with unutterable loathing, and to flee silently from its odious presence, as from the breath of a pestilence.

What added, no doubt, to my hatred of the beast, was the discovery, on the morning after I brought it home, that, like Pluto, it also had been deprived of one of its eyes. This circumstance, however, only endeared it to my wife, who, as I have already said, possessed, in a high degree, that humanity of feeling which had once been my distinguishing trait, and the source of many of my simplest and purest pleasures.

With my aversion to this cat, however, its partiality for myself seemed to increase. It followed my footsteps with a pertinacity which it would be difficult to make the reader comprehend. Whenever I sat, it would crouch beneath my chair, or spring upon my knees, covering me with its loathsome caresses. If I arose to walk, it would get between my feet and thus nearly throw me down, or, fastening its long and sharp claws in my dress, clamber, in this manner, to my breast. At such times, although I longed to destroy it with a blow, I was yet withheld from so doing, partly by a memory of my former crime, but chiefly—let me confess it at once—by absolute *dread* of the beast.

This dread was not exactly a dread of physical evil—and yet I should be at a loss how otherwise to define it. I am almost ashamed to own—yes, even in this felon's cell, I am almost ashamed to own—that the terror and horror with which the animal inspired me, had been heightened by one of the merest chimeras it would be possible to conceive. My wife had called my attention, more than once, to the character of the mark of white hair, of which I have spoken, and which constituted the sole visible difference between the strange beast and the one I had destroyed. The reader will remember that this mark, although large, had been originally very indefinite; but, by slow degrees—degrees nearly imperceptible, and which for a long time my Reason struggled to reject as fanciful—it had, at length, assumed a rigorous distinctness of outline. It was now the representation of an object that I shudder to name—and for this, above all, I loathed, and dreaded, and would have rid myself of the monster *had I dared*—it was now, I say, the image of a hideous—of a ghastly thing—of the GALLOWS! —oh, mournful and terrible engine of Horror and of Crime—of Agony and of Death!

And now was I indeed wretched beyond the wretchedness of mere Humanity. And *a brute beast*—whose fellow I had contemptuously destroyed—*a brute beast* to work out for *me*—for me a man, fashioned in the image of the High God—so much of insufferable wo! Alas! neither by day nor by night knew I the blessing of Rest any more! During the former the creature left me no moment alone; and, in the latter, I started, hourly, from dreams of unutterable fear, to find the hot breath of *the thing* upon my face, and its vast weight—an incarnate Night-Mare that I had no power to shake off—incumbent eternally upon my *heart*!

Beneath the pressure of torments such as these, the feeble remnant of the good within me succumbed. Evil thoughts became my sole intimates —the darkest and most evil of thoughts. The moodiness of my usual temper increased to hatred of all things and of all mankind; while, from the sudden, frequent, and ungovernable outbursts of a fury to which I now blindly abandoned myself, my uncomplaining wife, alas! was the most usual and the most patient of sufferers.

One day she accompanied me, upon some household errand, into the cellar of the old building which our poverty compelled us to inhabit. The cat followed me down the steep stairs, and, nearly throwing me headlong, exasperated me to madness. Uplifting an axe, and forgetting, in my wrath, the childish dread which had hitherto stayed my hand, I aimed a blow at the animal which, of course, would have proved instantly fatal had it descended as I wished. But this blow was arrested by the hand of my wife. Goaded, by the interference, into a rage more than demoniacal, I withdrew my arm from her grasp and buried the axe in her brain. She fell dead upon the spot, without a groan.

This hideous murder accomplished, I set myself forthwith, and with entire deliberation, to the task of concealing the body. I knew that I could not remove it from the house, either by day or by night, without the risk of being observed by the neighbours. Many projects entered my mind. At one period I thought of cutting the corpse into minute fragments, and destroying them by fire. At another, I resolved to dig a grave for it in the floor of the cellar. Again, I deliberated about casting it in the well in the yard—about packing it in a box, as if merchandise, with the usual arrangements, and so getting a porter to take it from the house. Finally, I hit upon what I considered a far better expedient than either of these. I determined to wall it up in the cellar—as the monks of the middle ages are recorded to have walled up their victims.

For a purpose such as this the cellar was admirably adapted. Its walls were loosely constructed, and had lately been plastered throughout with a rough plaster, which the dampness of the atmosphere had prevented from hardening. Moreover, in one of the walls was a projection, caused by a false chimney, or fireplace, that had been filled, or walled up, and made to resemble the rest of the cellar. I made no doubt that I could readily displace the bricks at this point, insert the corpse, and wall the whole up as before, so that no eye could detect any thing suspicious.

And in this calculation I was not deceived. By means of a crow-bar I easily dislodged the bricks, and, having carefully deposited the body against the inner wall, I propped it in that position, while, with little trouble, I re-laid the whole structure as it originally stood. Having procured mortar, sand, and hair, with every possible precaution, I prepared a plaster which could not be distinguished from the old, and with this I very carefully went over the new brick-work. When I had finished, I felt satisfied that all was right. The wall did not present the slightest appearance of having been disturbed. The rubbish on the floor was picked up with the minutest care. I looked around triumphantly, and said to myself—"Here at least, then, my labor has not been in vain."

My next step was to look for the beast which had been the cause of so much wretchedness; for I had, at length, firmly resolved to put it to death. Had I been able to meet with it, at the moment, there could have been no doubt of its fate; but it appeared that the crafty animal had been alarmed at the violence of my previous anger, and forebore to present itself in my present mood. It is impossible to describe, or to imagine, the deep, the blissful sense of relief which the absence of the detested creature occasioned in my bosom. It did not make its appearance during the night— and thus for one night at least, since its introduction into the house, I soundly and tranquilly slept;

aye, *slept* even with the burden of murder upon my soul!

The second and the third day passed and still my tormentor came not. Once again I breathed as a freeman. The monster, in terror, had fled the premises forever! I should behold it no more! My happiness was supreme! The guilt of my dark deed disturbed me but little. Some few inquiries had been made, but these had been readily answered. Even a search had been instituted—but of course nothing was to be discovered. I looked upon my future felicity as secured.

Upon the fourth day of the assassination, a party of the police came, very unexpectedly, into the house, and proceeded again to make rigorous investigation of the premises. Secure, however, in the inscrutability of my place of concealment, I felt no embarrassment whatever. The officers bade me accompany them in their search. They left no nook or corner unexplored. At length, for the third or fourth time, they descended into the cellar. I quivered not in a muscle. My heart beat calmly as that of one who slumbers in innocence. I walked the cellar from end to end. I folded my arms upon my bosom and roamed easily to and fro. The police were thoroughly satisfied and prepared to depart. The glee at my heart was too strong to be restrained. I burned to say if but one word, by way of triumph, and to render doubly sure their assurance of my guiltlessness.

"Gentlemen," I said at last, as the party ascended the steps, "I delight to have allayed your suspicions. I wish you all health, and a little more courtesy. By the bye, gentlemen, this—this is a very well constructed house." [In the rabid desire to say something easily, I scarcely knew what I uttered at all.]—"I may say an *excellently* well constructed house. These walls—are you going, gentlemen?—these walls are solidly put together;" and here, through the mere phrensy of bravado, I rapped heavily, with a cane which I held in my hand, upon that very portion of the brick-work behind which stood the ghastly corpse of the wife of my bosom.

But may God shield and deliver me from the fangs of the Arch Fiend! No sooner had the reverberation of my blows sunk into silence, than I was answered by a voice from within the tomb! —by a cry, at first muffled and broken, like the sobbing of a child, and then quickly swelling into one long, loud, and continuous scream, utterly anomalous and inhuman—a howl—a wailing shriek, half of horror and half of triumph, such as might have arisen only out of hell, conjointly from the throats of the damned in their agony and of the demons that exult in the damnation!

Of my own thoughts it is folly to speak. Swooning, I staggered to the opposite wall. For one instant the party upon the stairs remained motionless, through extremity of terror and of awe. In the next, a dozen stout arms were toiling at the wall. It fell bodily. The corpse, already greatly decayed and clotted with gore, stood erect before the eyes of the spectators. Upon its head, with red extended mouth and solitary eye of fire, sat the hideous beast whose craft had seduced me into murder, and whose informing voice had consigned me to the hangman. I had walled the monster up within the tomb!

ASSASSINATION OF PRESIDENT LINCOLN

Probable Murder of Mr. Seward

THE POLITICAL BITTERNESS which led up to the Civil War seriously damaged the *Post*'s circulation and led to a general change of policy. Henry Peterson, who became director in 1846 and part owner in 1848, was an able writer with strong pro-Union views. He took an enthusiastic part in the Republican party's first national convention, held in Philadelphia in 1856. But some of his editorials angered Southern subscribers, and the *Post* was denounced in Southern newspapers. Peterson's business partner became alarmed and when Lincoln was running for President in 1860, the *Post* did not mention the campaign in its editorial columns. Even after the war started in 1861 it remained cautious, though always on the Union side so far as the fighting was concerned. Toward the end of the war it printed some interesting reports from Washington and the military hospitals by Jane Swisshelm, a crusading lady journalist who was the Dorothy Thompson of her time.

When the great news story of the century occurred, the *Post* showed excellent judgment by reprinting in their stark simplicity the Government's "official gazettes" and the original Associated Press account, just as they came off the wires from Washington. And on its editorial page it was once more outspoken: "Never did such a pang of horror convulse the heart of the American people as when the news spread rapidly through the length and breadth of the loyal states that President Lincoln had been vilely murdered. . . . We feel as if all other feelings were swept aside by the single demand for JUSTICE—as if the voice of Mercy in our heart had been stilled forever by the same ball which silenced the tongue and deadened the thoughtful brain of its most powerful advocate."

APRIL 22, 1865

OFFICIAL GAZETTE.

WASHINGTON, April 15—1:30, A.M.—MAJOR-GENERAL DIX:—This evening, about 9:30 P.M., at Ford's Theatre, the President, while sitting in his private box with Mrs. Lincoln, Miss Harris, and Major Rathbone, was shot by an assassin who suddenly entered the box and approached behind the President.

The assassin then leaped upon the stage brandishing a large dagger or knife, and made his escape in the rear of the theatre.

The pistol ball entered the back of the President's head and penetrated nearly through the head. The wound is mortal. The President has been insensible ever since it was inflicted, and is now dying.

About the same hour, an assassin, whether the same or another, entered Mr. Seward's house, and, under pretence of having a prescription, was shown to the Secretary's sick chamber. The Secretary was in bed, a nurse and Miss Seward with

him. The assassin immediately rushed to the bed, inflicting one or two stabs on the throat and two on the face. It is hoped the wounds may not be mortal. My apprehension is that they will prove fatal.

The noise alarmed Mr. Frederick Seward, who was in an adjoining room, and hastened to the door of his father's room, where he met the assassin who inflicted upon him one or more dangerous wounds. The recovery of Frederick Seward is doubtful.

It is not probable that the President will live through the night.

General Grant and wife were advertised to be at the theatre this evening, but he started to Burlington at 6 o'clock, P.M. At a cabinet meeting, at which General Grant was present, to-day, the subject of the state of the country and the prospects of a speedy peace were discussed.

The President was very cheerful and hopeful,

He spoke very kindly of Gen. Lee and others of the Confederacy, and the establishment of the government of Virginia.

All the members of the Cabinet, except Mr. Seward, are now in attendance upon the President. I have seen Mr. Seward, but he and Frederick were both unconscious.

EDWIN M. STANTON,
Secretary of War.

WASHINGTON, April 15, 2:30 A.M. The President is still alive, but is growing weaker. The ball is lodged in his brain, three inches from where it entered the skull. He remains insensible, and his condition is utterly hopeless. The Vice President has been to see him, but all company except the Cabinet, his family, and a few friends, are rigidly excluded.

Large crowds still continue in the street as near to the house as the line of guards will allow.

SECOND OFFICIAL GAZETTE.

WASHINGTON, APRIL 15, 3 A.M. MAJOR-GENERAL DIX, New York.—The President still breathes, but is quite insensible, as he has been ever since he was shot. He evidently did not see the person who shot him, but was looking on the stage, as he was approached behind.

Mr. Seward has rallied, and it is hoped may live. Frederick Seward's condition is very critical. The attendant who was present was stabbed through the lungs, and is not expected to live. The wounds of Major Seward are not serious.

Investigation strongly indicates J. Wilkes Booth as the assassin of the President. Whether it was the same or a different person that attempted to murder Mr. Seward remains in doubt.

Chief Justice Carter is engaged in taking the evidence. Every exertion has been made to prevent the escape of the murderer. His horse has been found in the road near Washington.

EDWIN M. STANTON,
Secretary of War.

THIRD OFFICIAL GAZETTE.

WASHINGTON, April 15, 4:10, A.M. MAJOR-GENERAL DIX, New York.

The President continues insensible and is sinking.

Secretary Seward remains without change.

Frederick Seward's skull is fractured in two places, besides a severe cut upon the head. The attendant is still alive, but hopeless. Major Seward's wounds are not dangerous.

It is now ascertained, with reasonable certainty, that two assassins were engaged in the horrible crime, J. Wilkes Booth being the one that shot the President. The other is a companion of his, whose name is not known. The deception is so clean that he can hardly escape.

It appears from a letter found in Booth's trunk, that the murder was planned before the 4th of March, but fell through then because the accomplice backed out until "Richmond could be heard from."

Booth and his accomplice were at the livery stable at six o'clock last evening, and left there about ten o'clock, or shortly before that hour. It would seem that for several days they have been seeking their chance, but for some unknown reason it was not carried into effect until last night. One of them has evidently made his way to Baltimore; the other has not yet been traced.

EDWIN M. STANTON,
Secretary of War.

WASHINGTON, APRIL 15, 1865.
MAJOR-GENERAL DIX:

Abraham Lincoln died this morning at 22 minutes after 7 o'clock.

EDWIN M. STANTON,
Secretary of War.

ASSOCIATED PRESS ACCOUNT.

WASHINGTON, April 14.—President Lincoln and his wife, together with other friends, this evening visited Ford's Theatre for the purpose of witnessing the performance of the "American Cousin."

It was announced in the papers that General Grant would also be present, but that gentleman instead took the late train of cars for New Jersey.

The theatre was densely crowded, and every body seemed delighted with the scene before them.

During the third act, and while there was a temporary pause for one of the actors to enter, the sharp report of a pistol was heard, which merely attracted attention, but suggested nothing serious, until a man rushed to the front of the President's box waving a long dagger in his right hand and exclaiming, "*Sic Semper Tyrannis!*" and immediately leaped from the box, which was of the second tier, to the stage beneath, and ran across to the opposite side, thus making his escape, amid the bewilderment of the audience, from the rear of the theatre, and, mounting a horse, fled.

The screams of Mrs. Lincoln first disclosed the fact to the audience that the President had been shot, then all present rose to their feet, rushing toward the stage, many exclaiming, "Hang him! hang him!"

The excitement was one of the wildest possible description, and of course there was an abrupt termination of the theatrical performance.

There was a rush towards the Presidential box, when cries were heard, "Stand back!" "Give him air!" "Has any one stimulants?"

On a hasty examination, it was found that the President had been shot through the head above and back of the temporal bone, and that some of the brain was oozing out.

He was removed to a private house opposite to the theatre, and the Surgeon General of the Army and other surgeons were sent for to attend to his condition.

On an examination of the private box, blood was discovered on the back of the cushioned rocking-chair on which the President had been sitting, also on the partition and on the floor. A common single-barreled pocket pistol was found on the carpet.

A military guard was placed in front of the private residence to which the President had been conveyed.

An immense crowd gathered in front of it, all deeply anxious to learn the condition of the President. It had been previously announced that the wound was mortal, but all hoped otherwise. The shock to the community was terrible.

At midnight the Cabinet, with Messrs. Sumner, Colfax, and Farnsworth, Judge Carter, Governor Oglesby, Gen. Meigs, Col. Hay, and a few personal friends, with Surgeon General Barnes and his medical associates, were around his bedside.

MIDNIGHT.—The President was in a state of *syncope*, totally insensible and breathing hardly, the blood oozing from the wound at the back of his head.

The surgeons were exhausting every possible effort of medical skill, but all hope was gone.

The parting of his family with the dying President is too sad for description.

The President and Mrs. Lincoln did not start to the theatre till fifteen minutes after 8 o'clock. Speaker Colfax was at the White House at the time, and the President stated to him that he was going, although Mrs. Lincoln had not been well, because the papers had advertised that General Grant and they were to be present, and as General Grant had gone north, he did not wish the audience to be disappointed.

The President went with apparent reluctance, and urged Mr. Colfax to go with him; but that gentleman had made other engagements, and, with Mr. Ashmun, of Massachusetts, bade him good-bye.

The entire city to-night presented a scene of wild excitement, accompanied by violent expressions of indignation and the profoundest sorrow. Many shed tears.

The military authorities have despatched patrols in every direction, in order, if possible, to arrest the assassin, while the Metropolitan Police are alike vigilant for the same purpose.

The attack both at the theatre and at Secretary Seward's house took place at about the same hour, (ten o'clock,) thus showing a preconcerted plan to assassinate those gentlemen. Some evidences of the guilt of the party who attacked the President are in possession of the police.

Vice-President Johnson is in the city, and his hotel quarters are guarded by troops.

We learn that General Grant received intelligence of this sad calamity soon after midnight, when at Walnut street wharf, Philadelphia, on his way to Burlington, N. J.

GOOD-BY, JIM

by James Whitcomb Riley

FOR SEVERAL DECADES after the war the *Post* slipped deeper into the doldrums. It refused to compete with picture weeklies like *Harper*'s and *Leslie*'s, or the trashy *New York Ledger* and *Police Gazette*. In 1874 it serialized Mrs. Henry Wood's *East Lynne; or, The Elopement*, which was a success, and thereafter it relied heavily on English lady authors for its fiction. Its editorial page degenerated into discussions of spring gardening and "The Abuses of Fame"; its news column dwindled to clippings from the newspapers about fossil butterflies, carnivorous plants and "A Dog with a Cork Leg."

After Curtis bought the magazine he installed William George Jordan as his first editor. Jordan had been on the staff of the first big Curtis success, *The Ladies' Home Journal*. He improved the *Post*'s typography and hired good illustrators, but his editorial approach was more than a little old-fashioned. One of his ideas was to print what he called "The Best Poems in the World" on full pages with handsome special drawings. James Whitcomb Riley's "Good-by, Jim" (also known as "The Old Man and Jim") was one of these. It was first read by Riley himself at a testimonial party in the Grand Opera House in Indianapolis in 1888.

AUGUST 13, 1898

I

Old man never had much to say,
  'Ceptin' to Jim—
And Jim was the wildest boy he had—
  And the old man jes' wrapped up in him!
Never heerd him speak but once
Er twice in my life—and first time was
When the War broke out, and Jim he went,
The old man backin' him, fer three months.
An' all 'at I heard the old man say
Was, jes' as we turned to start away—
      "Well; good-by, Jim:
        Take keer of yourse'f!"

II

'Peared like he was more satisfied
  Jes' lookin' at Jim
And likin' him all to hisse'f like, see?
  'Cause he was jes' wrapped up in him!
And over and over I mind the day
The old man come and stood round in the way
While he was drillin', a-watchin' Jim—
And down at the depot a-heerin' him say—
      "Well; good-by, Jim:
        Take keer of yourse'f!"

III

Never was nothin' about the farm
  Disting'ished Jim—
Neighbors all ust to wonder why
  The old man 'peared wrapped up in him.
But when Cap. Biggler, he writ back
'At Jim was the bravest boy we had
In the whole dern rigiment, white er black,
And his fightin' good as his farmin' bad—
'At he had led with a bullet clean
Bored through his thigh, and carried the flag
Through the bloodiest battle you ever seen—
The old man wound up a letter to him
'At Cap. read to us, 'at said, "Tell Jim
      Good-by:
        And take keer of hisse'f."

44

IV

Jim come back jes' long enough
   To take the whim
'At he'd like to go back in cavalry—
   And the old man jes' wrapped up in him!—
Jim 'lowed 'at he'd had sich luck afore,
Guessed he'd tackle her three years more.
And the old man gave him a colt he'd raised
And follered him over to Camp Ben Wade,
And laid round fer a week or so,
Watchin' Jim on dress-parade—
Tel finally he rid away,
And last he heerd was the old man say—
     "Well; good-by, Jim:
      Take keer of yourse'f!"

V

Tuk the papers, the old man did,
   A-watchin' fer Jim—
Fully believin' he'd make his mark
   Some way—jes' wrapped up in him!
And many a time the word 'u'd come
'At stirred him up like the tap of a drum—
At Petersburg, for instance, where
Jim rid right into the cannons there,
And tuk 'em, and p'inted 'em t'other way,
And socked it home to the boys in gray,
As they skooted for timber, and on and on—
Jim a Lieutenant, and one arm gone,
And the old man's words in his mind all day—
     "Well; good-by, Jim:
      Take keer of yourse'f!"

VI

Think of a private, now, perhaps,
   We'll say like Jim,
'At's clumb clean up to the shoulder-straps—
   And the old man jes' wrapped up in him!
Think of him—with the war plum' through,
And the glorious old Red-White-and-Blue
A-laughin' the news down over Jim,
And the old man, bendin' over him—
The Surgeon turnin' away with tears
'At hadn't leaked fer years and years—
As the hand of the dyin' boy clung to
His father's, the old voice in his ears—
     "Well; good-by, Jim:
      Take keer of yourse'f!"

THE MAN WHO COULD NOT
BE CORNERED

by George Horace Lorimer

GEORGE HORACE LORIMER was a reporter on the *Boston Post* in 1898 when he read a news item about the new management of *The Saturday Evening Post*. He immediately wired publisher Curtis to ask for a job. To his surprise Curtis made an appointment with him a few days later in the lobby of a Boston hotel. They talked for about ten minutes and Lorimer was hired then and there as "literary editor" of the *Post* at $40 a week. Before the year was over Lorimer was virtually running the magazine outside the editorial page, and when Curtis lost patience with editor Jordan and fired him, Lorimer moved into the top job on a temporary basis. Curtis had announced he was going to Europe to ask a seasoned magazine man—George Sherburne Hardy—to edit the *Post*. But Lorimer worked so fast and so well that no new editor was needed for the next thirty-seven years.

Lorimer was thirty-one when he came to the *Post*. Like Henry Luce of *Time* and Dewitt Wallace of *Reader's Digest,* he was the son of a clergyman. But Lorimer grew up in a time when business dominated the American scene and his first ambition was to be a successful businessman. He had spent only one year at Yale when, so the story goes, Philip D. Armour, the Chicago packing king, met him on the street and remarked, "Give up that nonsense and come with me. I'll make you a millionaire."

Lorimer worked eight years for Armour and rose to be head of the canning department at a salary of $5,000 a year. Then he decided to strike out for himself in the wholesale grocery business, and went broke trying to develop a formula for liquid coffee extract. About this time he began to realize that journalism was his real profession; though he had been married for several years, he went back to college for a while and then turned to reporting as a deliberate preparation for something bigger. He and Curtis were in perfect accord about the *Post*: both visualized it as the special magazine of business and businessmen. But most of the writing that was being done about business in the late 1890's was either unlimited bootlicking or unlimited muckraking. Lorimer himself had to establish the pattern he wanted other writers to follow.

He did it first in the fine piece of reporting which is reprinted here; this is the first item under Lorimer's name in the *Post*'s vast index file of authors. Later on he used his association with Armour and Chicago in a series of short stories, "Letters from a Self-Made Merchant to His Son." These began in the *Post* August 3, 1901, and were the magazine's first big fiction hit in the twentieth century.

AUGUST 27, 1898

I

FOR WEEKS, the wheat pit had been a storm-centre. Day after day a dull rumble and roar, rising and falling monotonously, as when the surf booms in on a distant beach, had come down to passers-by in the street below. Men hurrying along about their business had stopped as their ears caught the sound, looked up curiously at the great plate-glass windows, and joined the jostling crowd that was pushing in through the wide doors beneath the gray stone tower.

It was April when the storm began to gather, December when it burst. At first a little thing of gusts and flurries, it scarce flawed the surface of the market; but week by week it gathered strength until it broke a cyclone that swept men from their feet and shook the foundations of trade.

It began in April, when a young man placed a careless order for a hundred thousand bushels of May wheat; and now it was December, and the young man's little holding had swelled to millions. For that first wheat he had paid some seventy cents a bushel. Then the price had dropped and dropped until he could have bought September wheat at sixty-four. And buy he did, five hundred thousand bushels of it, and kept on buying. And, as his holdings grew, his horizon widened, until he was dazzled by the prospect that he saw before him.

Wheat mounted higher, slowly at first, and then by leaps and bounds; for Europe was hungry and must have bread. The young man transferred his holdings to the December delivery, and bought and bought. Already he owned more wheat than was in all the elevators in Chicago. And now, unless the men who had sold it to him discovered their plight in time to bring grain from the West before January first, he could run the price up to a dollar, two dollars, whatever he wished. These "shorts" must fill their contracts then or pay him the difference between that final price and the one at which they had sold. To keep them ignorant of their danger until it was too late to get wheat to Chicago was the game.

Well the young man played it. The price kept rising, but there were little breaks between to lull suspicion. On December fifth, it was ninety-five and one-half cents, and all the blame was laid on hungry Europe. For the young man kept himself modestly in the background, and there was nothing but a number on a broker's books to tell who owned millions of wheat.

Old hands, who had weathered many a hard storm, began to suspect something besides Europe. They sniffed and smelt Armour, Pillsbury, Pierpont Morgan, or a New York syndicate in the market, quietly pocketed their losses, and made all snug and tight against dirty weather.

The wheat-pit of the Chicago Board of Trade, that hub whose spokes radiate to the markets of the world, and which regulates the movement of prices for grain, is a circular arena of steps on which a few hundred brokers can find standing space and face each other. Around it, scattered over the floor of the great trading chamber, are smaller pits where other grains and provisions are dealt in. Even on calm days, when the pulse of the market is slow, this is not a quiet place. In the pits there is the constant clamor of buying

and selling for future delivery; about the long rows of sample tables on the floor are quieter groups, offering and bidding on cash grain. In and out, among the men in the pits and on the floor, dart messengers, bawling the names of brokers for whom they have telegrams, and sharp above all the tumult comes the clatter of a hundred instruments, ticking out orders and carrying away quotations. From a spacious gallery, a dozen country visitors look down at the shouting, gesticulating men and wonder what it all means.

But on the ninth of last December, long before the hour for trading to begin, the crowd filled the wheat-pit to the brim, and, overflowing down the circular steps, spread out dense on the surrounding floor. The other pits were half deserted, the floor bare, except for the messengers hurrying back and forth. Above, in the gallery, the seats were filled, the aisles were choked with curious men and women. They kept rising to their feet, like people at a circus, and peering down at the waiting crowd.

As the hands of the clock crept toward the trading hour, the laughing chat of the sightseers died down and the men in the pits, who had been conversing in low tones, gravely, earnestly, became silent. Every face reflected a fierce eagerness to grasp more in the great struggle which was coming, or a half-terror lest the rest of a dwindling fortune should be swallowed up. For in that range of thirty cents, from sixty-five to ninety-five, men had made millions, had lost millions, and now a new force, an unknown quantity, loomed up large before them. For overnight that vague uneasiness which, through all the early winter, had been growing, had crystallized into panic.

Only a minute more! Every eye was on the clock, every ear alert for the clash of the gong. Only the clacking of the tireless instruments and the shrill cries of the messengers echoed from the lofty ceiling.

It came with a clang and a mighty roar. The crowd crushed together until the men in the pit were lifted from their feet. The wriggling, writhing, swaying mass bristled with wildly waving arms until it looked a monster with a thousand tentacles. Men, with faces reddened and distorted, howled and raved, now shaking clenched fists across the pit, now signaling frantically with crooked fingers.

To the people in the gallery, craning their necks in breathless eagerness to see, the meaning of this madness was not clear. But they knew that men were being made and ruined in those few minutes, and that was enough. They saw the hands on the indicator, which some days moved by eighths and some days scarce at all, flying around wildly, like the arrow on a wheel of fortune stopping not for eighths and quarters, but leaping halves and cents at a whirl. From 101½ to 109 it moved, and the highest mark that wheat had made in six years had been reached. Farther and higher the panic-stricken shorts might have driven it had not the echo of the tumult come to the young man in his office half a mile away. As yet it was not time for these big figures. Settling day was three weeks off, and there were big fish in the net who might break its meshes were they too soon lifted above water.

Into the frantic crowd, where fifty sought to buy what one would sell, his brokers came and doled out wheat until the panic was appeased and the clamor quieted.

II

WHILE THE EXCITEMENT WAS WILDEST, a sharp-eyed lad, clutching tight in one hand a slip of white paper, detached himself from the outer fringe of traders and dodged across the floor to the door. Down the stairs he went, taking them three at a time, and out into La Salle Street. A short block he ran, turned into the Home Insurance building, and, breathless, burst into an office on the first floor.

To a door in the front of this office, which gave admission to a small private apartment, the lad hurried and handed his slip of paper to an older youth, who was hovering about with the anxious air of one momentarily expecting a summons from some unexpected quarter. Armed with this slip, the youth opened the door.

Within, seated before a wide oak writing-desk, sat a man of medium height, snugly stout. His large head, set deep down into a strong neck, was perfectly bald except for a thin thatch of light-colored hair, which covered the base of his brain and climbed up over his ears and down his face on either side in closely-cropped whiskers. A high and well-shaped forehead, square, determined jaws, and keen, gray eyes, restless, darting and incisive, stamped his as an unusual and powerful personality. The eyes were his most distinguishing feature. They compelled a certain docile respect at all times, submission and fear when their owner wished it. Yet, withal, they were kindly eyes—eyes that could twinkle with fun or express depths of sympathy.

This man was Philip D. Armour, on whom perhaps some fifty thousand people are dependent for a living. Philip D. Armour is Armour & Company, who are the largest packers of meats in the world. And Armour & Company is the Armour Elevator Company, whose warehouses dot the West and line the Chicago river; and the Armour Refrigerator Line, whose rolling-stock is on all lines, East and West, North and South; and half a dozen other vast enterprises. Last of all, Philip D. Armour is "the old man." Not disrespectfully, but as the badge of his authority, is the term used.

This man began life with a country-school education. But he made up in Scotch pluck and persistence, and Yankee ingenuity and shrewdness, his natural and only inheritance, what he lacked in special equipment for life. From gold-hunting in the West, he drifted into the grain business, and thence, in a modest way, into packing provisions in Milwaukee. From Milwaukee to Chicago is but a step, and he took it.

Year by year the scope of his operations broadened. Tumble-down sheds and ramshackle shanties gave way to big brick buildings whose clustering stacks vomited forth smoke day and night. Armour & Company had become the foremost concern of its kind in the world.

Meanwhile, as the Armour Elevator Company, the head of the house had been broadening out in another direction. First of all, Mr. Armour is a merchant and warehouseman, but he has been known to speculate occasionally—in fact, all the unexplained vagaries of the market are laid at his door.

Mr. Armour is simple in his habits. At six o'clock every morning he is up, and an hour later in his office, listening to telegrams and skimming over important correspondence before passing it along to his department heads, glancing at market reports, asking quick questions and receiving careful answers. He seldom leaves his desk before five, and then it is to drive back to his unpretentious house on Prairie Avenue and pass the evening until nine in his library, when he goes to bed.

His men are notoriously well paid. Half of them tell the time by watches that the "old man" has given them, and the other half wear suits for which the bills have been sent to him. And besides his daily charities, a million and more of his money has gone into the twin institutions which bear his name. But while his left hand may give his right attends strictly to business.

III

MR. ARMOUR UNFOLDED the little white slip, and peered over the top of his glasses at the column of penciled figures and the comment scrawled beneath. His face expressed nothing.

He had been expecting something of this sort and quietly preparing for it. For the "old man" had a little business secret, too—a secret which the sharper traders had already guessed, and which he was soon to share with the rest of the world.

For once, the shrewd old speculator had been caught on the wrong side of the market. All through the fall he had been feeling pessimistic about wheat, and all through the fall he had been selling, until the aggregate which he stood committed to deliver before the first day of January had mounted into millions of bushels. And the bins in that long string of elevators along the foul river were well-nigh bare of contract-grade wheat.

But Mr. Armour possesses the saving virtue of the speculator. He can smell out an error in judgment, or a change in conditions, and take the other side with the rapidity of a flash of lightning jumping from cloud to cloud. It was late in the deal when there had come to him a suspicion that he was fairly cornered—too late unless he could accomplish the seemingly impossible. Another man must have thrown up his hands and submitted to being held up. Mr. Armour turned to fight.

It was not the money only, though no man, no matter how great his wealth, can be careless of a loss of a million dollars and more, according as the fancy of an opponent dictates. But the fierce pride of the merchant was involved—the pride of the man who had made the name of the house the synonym for success; the pride of the veteran who had stood a victor at the forks while his opponents passed under the yoke.

When he had been younger, and even in these later years of unshakable strength, there had been men of boldness and wealth who had boasted that they would break "old Armour"; that they would paint their trademarks on his yellow wagons. But after these storms had blown off to sea the rock had still been there. Armour bore no malice toward them. More than once, when some great structure of speculation had collapsed, wrecking the work of months in an hour, the head of the corner had hurried breathless to his office, and it was Armour who had saved the market from utter collapse and the man from utter ruin.

And then there were the little fellows, who, in venturing beyond their strength, had been sucked down and under. How this crowd would yelp with delight at the spectacle of the "old man" beaten at his game by a boy—and a Harvard graduate at that. For now the fight was in the open; the old man and the young man were face to face.

It was at one of the downtown clubs that the latter's secret had been discovered. Day after day there had been hasty calls for Joseph Leiter at the telephone, and the young man had talked a dozen times a morning to a mysterious someone. Even club men have that pardonable human failing—curiosity. It was discovered that the mysterious someone was the broker who was making those heavy purchases for a number on his books. Club men can put two and two together. The number became a name.

IV

IT IS A SOURCE OF STRENGTH to Mr. Armour that he is as little deceived by flattery as he is moved by abuse. He appraises men and events at their exact value.

"No man," he is fond of saying, "is stronger than his weakest point." So he probes for that weakest point, and, once he has found it, he knows his man.

Nature and chance had combined to make Leiter's position well-nigh unassailable. Drought and wet and blight had wasted the wheat-fields of Europe; except America, the great grain-producing countries had nothing to sell; the hungry had been calling across the Atlantic for bread until the grain bins in Chicago were half empty. Leiter himself had been hurrying grain away to any port far enough removed to have it out of reach on delivery day.

But there was still wheat, plenty of it, in the West and Northwest. And if Armour could get enough of it to Chicago in time the corner would be broken.

Here again Nature sided with Leiter. Even if the grain could be scraped together, it would be impossible for the railroads alone to transport it to Chicago in that brief space. Part of it must come down by boat from Duluth.

Winter comes early on those Northern lakes. In December the last blur of trailing smoke fades from the horizon, and the vast space becomes a solitude—a stretch of white, darkened with patches of steel-blue water, silent, save for the sharp snap and crack of grinding and shifting ice. Already the harbors were ice-bound, and the narrow straits of Sault Ste. Marie, through which a steamer must steer its course to Lake Michigan, becoming locked fast against attack.

In the rear of the office at 205 La Salle Street, center wires over which every way-station in the United States, every capital in Europe, every corner of the world can be reached. Within an hour after Mr. Armour had decided where he stood, ordinary business had been side-tracked, and the operators were busy sending a constantly increasing pile of telegrams marked "rush."

Armour was calling for wheat. To every "impossible," he returned a "must." Day and night he, was in the saddle, directing, watching every detail of the fierce struggle against time and the elements.

When Mr. Armour is in a hurry, there is a note in his voice which makes men hurry. When he says a thing can be done, there is a persuasiveness in his blunt logic that moves others to his way of thinking. As his telegrams were delivered, they woke up men all over the West—agents and brokers in the large cities; buyers and warehousemen at the lonely prairie stations; and farmers in Minnesota, Montana, Kansas, Nebraska, the Dakotas, and even far-off Manitoba. They started long trains of empty cars rattling across the endless prairie stretches to the stations where the loaded wagons, creaking and groaning tire-deep through the black mud, were converging and dumping the clean, sound grain. They routed out steamboat men from snug little groceries and saloons, where they had started to doze away the long winter beside squat, red-hot baseburners, and sent them aboard deserted steamers that were tied up to the wharves.

They moved a fleet of tugboats down Lake Superior, and kept them stirring back and forth in endless procession through the straits during the long, still nights, when the sharp cold bound together the cakes of ice washing about in their wake. In the harbor at Duluth there were other tugboats puffing back and forth until the fleet should be loaded to the water-line. And what steam could not do, dynamite accomplished. For while the old man in Chicago might believe in his destiny, he knew that dynamite would help it through the zero weather.

Now began the race. Long trains of loaded cars bumped in quick succession across the Western lines. Some were headed for Chicago; the rest poured their freight into the holds of the mighty fleet that had been gathering. From Duluth to Sault Ste. Marie, and thence down Lake Michigan, the steamers were strung out, booming along under every pound of steam. And in the midst of it all sat Armour, coaxing, planning, ordering and keeping the whole deal, from farmers to fleet, within the scope of his all-comprehending eye. Until the danger was past, nothing

was too big, nothing too small, for his personal attention.

V

ON DECEMBER TENTH the reporters found out the young man and made him talk. Something of what was going on in the West he knew, but he was flushed with the glory of what he had done, proud of the big game he had played and had not yet lost, even if his victory were to be incomplete.

"Am I in this wheat deal?" he asked, leaning back in his chair and looking about with the assurance of the young man for whom life has been a round of ready-made successes. "Well, I should remark. Without any desire to boast, I might say we are controlling the biggest individual line of wheat in the country."

On December thirteenth, the price dropped from 105 to 97½, but there were other forces at work now. For the next day it was reported that stocks of wheat in storage had increased 1,356,-000 bushels in two days, and the last cargoes of 3,654,000 bushels were arriving from Duluth.

All the tracks in the acres of railroad yards were stuffed and choked with cars; the enormous elevators could make room for no such extra tonnage. In the end, a fleet of one hundred and thirty-four vessels had to be pressed into service to store the surplus wheat through the winter.

It really looked as if Mr. Leiter had not counted on having all this wheat delivered to him, when, twenty-four hours later, his father came hurrying on from the East. He, too, seemed rather impressed with the bigness of it all.

"I am much pleased that my son has broadened out into a first-class merchant," he said; and then he started out to borrow money to pay for the wheat which Armour was delivering to him. And there was need, for that day saw 500,000 bushels added to the stocks, 2,500,000 bushels tendered on the son's contracts, and 3,000,000 bushels more reported on the way to Chicago.

On December thirtieth, Leiter had 8,000,000 bushels of cash wheat; Armour had filled all his contracts, and was selling out a surplus that he had on hand.

On the last day of the year a crowd gathered on 'Change to see the end of the December deal; but it had already ended—ended when, a few days before, Armour had delivered the last bushel which was due on his contracts, and left Leiter alone, with his glory and his wheat.

THE SERGEANT'S PRIVATE MADHOUSE

by Stephen Crane

ON ITS EDITORIAL PAGE in 1898 the *Post* suggested that American authors should give thanks to President McKinley, who had provided them with a new and exciting theme by declaring for war against Spain. At that moment Stephen Crane was in Cuba as a war correspondent for the New York *World*. As soon as he returned to the United States he began writing short stories based on his experiences; three of these appeared in the *Post* during the later months of 1899.

In 1895, when he was only twenty-four, Crane had achieved national fame with his powerful Civil War novel, *The Red Badge of Courage.* But his earlier book, *Maggie, a Girl of the Streets*, was attacked as immoral and had to be printed privately. During and after his Cuban service false rumors spread that he was suffering from venereal disease and could only write under the influence of drugs and alcohol. The fact was, he had always been tubercular and his insistence on sharing the lot of the front-line Marines at Cuzco and other battles broke his health permanently. Disgusted by the stories that were told about him here, he moved in 1899 to England, where he and his wife spent their last Christmas together with friends such as the Joseph Conrads, H. G. Wells and Henry James. He died in June 1900 in a German sanitarium. He was still six months short of twenty-nine.

SEPTEMBER 30, 1899

THE MOONLIGHT was almost steady blue flame, and all this radiance was lavished out upon a still, lifeless wilderness of stunted trees and cactus plants. The shadows lay upon the ground, pools of black and sharply outlined, resembling substances, fabrics, and not shadows at all. From afar came the sound of the sea coughing among the hollows in the coral rocks.

The land was very empty; one could easily imagine that Cuba was a simple, vast solitude; one could wonder at the moon taking all the trouble of this splendid illumination. There was no wind; nothing seemed to live.

But in a particular, large group of shadows lay an outpost of some forty United States marines. If it had been possible to approach them from any direction without encountering one of their sentries, one could have gone stumbling among sleeping men, and men who sat waiting, their blankets tented over their heads; one would have been in among them before one's mind could have decided whether they were men or devils. If a marine moved, he took the care and the time of one who walks across a death-chamber. The Lieutenant in command reached for his watch, and the nickel chain gave forth the slightest tinkling sound. He could see the glisten in five or six pairs of eyes that turned to regard him. His Sergeant lay near him, and he bent his face down to whisper: "Who's on post behind the big cactus bush?"

"Dryden," rejoined the Sergeant just over his breath.

After a pause the Lieutenant murmured: "He's got too many nerves. I shouldn't have put him there." The Sergeant asked if he should crawl down and look into affairs at Dryden's post. The young officer nodded assent, and the Sergeant, softly cocking his rifle, went away on his hands and knees. The Lieutenant, with his back to a dwarf tree, sat watching the Sergeant's progress for the few moments that he could see him moving from one shadow to another. Afterward the officer waited to hear Dryden's quick but low-voiced challenge; but time passed, and no sound came from the direction of the post behind the cactus bush.

The Sergeant, as he came nearer and nearer to this cactus bush—a number of peculiarly dignified columns throwing shadows of inky darkness—had slowed his pace, for he did not wish to trifle with the feelings of the sentry. He was expecting his stern hail, and was ready with the immediate answer which turns away wrath. He was not made anxious by the fact that he could not as yet see Dryden, for he knew that the man would be hidden in a way practiced by sentry marines since the time when two men had been killed by a disease of excessive confidence on picket. Indeed, as the Sergeant went still nearer he became more and more angry. Dryden was evidently a most proper sentry.

Finally he arrived at a point where he could see him seated in the shadow, staring into the bushes ahead of him, his rifle ready on his knee. The Sergeant in his rage longed for the peaceful precincts of the Washington Marine Barracks, where there would have been no situation to prevent the most complete non-commissioned oratory. He felt indecent in his capacity of a man able to creep up to the back of a G Company member on guard duty. Never mind; in the morning, back at camp——

But suddenly he felt afraid. There was something wrong with Dryden. He remembered old tales of comrades creeping out to find a picket seated against a tree, perhaps upright enough, but stone dead. The Sergeant paused and gave the inscrutable back of the sentry a long stare. Dubious, he again moved forward. At three paces he hissed like a little snake. Dryden did not show a sign of hearing. At last the Sergeant was in a position from which he was able to reach out and touch Dryden on the arm. Whereupon was turned to him the face of a man livid with mad fright. The Sergeant grabbed him by the wrist and with discreet fury shook him. "Here! Pull yourself together!"

Dryden paid no heed, but turned his wild face from the newcomer to the ground in front. "Don't you see 'em, Sergeant? Don't you see 'em?"

"Where?" whispered the Sergeant.

"Ahead and a little on the right flank. A reg'lar skirmish line. Don't you see 'em?"

"Naw," whispered the Sergeant.

Dryden began to shake. He began moving one hand from his head to his knee, and from his knee to his head rapidly, in a way that is without explanation. "I don't dare fire," he wept. "If I do they'll see me, and oh, how they'll pepper me!"

The Sergeant, lying on his belly, understood one thing. Dryden had gone mad. Dryden was the March Hare. The old man gulped down his uproarious emotions as well as he was able, and used the most simple device. "Go," he said, "and tell the Lieutenant, while I cover your post for you."

"No! They'd see me! And they'd pepper me! Oh, how they'd pepper me!"

The Sergeant was face to face with the biggest situation of his life. In the first place, he knew that at night a large or a small force of Spanish guerrillas was never more than easy rifle-range from any marine outpost, both sides maintaining a secrecy as absolute as possible in regard to their real position and strength. Everything was on a watch-spring foundation. A loud word might be paid for by a night attack which would involve five hundred men who needed their sleep, not to speak of some of them who would need their lives. The slip of a foot and the rolling of a pint of gravel might go from consequence to consequence until various crews went to general quarters on their ships in the harbor, their batteries booming as the swift searchlight flashed through the foliage. Men would get killed—notably the Sergeant and Dryden—and the outposts would be cut off, and the whole night would be one pitiless turmoil. And so Sergeant George H. Peasley began to run his private madhouse behind the cactus bush.

"Dryden," said the Sergeant, "you do as I told you, and go tell the Lieutenant."

"I don't dare move," shivered the man. "They'll see me if I move; they'll see me. They're almost up now. Let's hide——"

"Well, then you stay here a moment and I'll go and——"

Dryden turned upon him a look so tigerish that the old man felt his hair move. "Don't you stir!" he hissed. "You want to give me away? You want them to see me? Don't you stir!" The Sergeant decided not to stir.

He became aware of the slow wheeling of eternity, its majestic incomprehensibility of movement. Seconds, moments, were quaint little things, tangible as toys, and there were billions of them, all alike.

"Dryden," he whispered at the end of a century, in which, curiously, he had never joined the marine corps at all, but had taken to another walk of life and prospered greatly in it—"Dryden, this is all foolishness!"

He thought of the expedient of smashing the man over the head with his rifle, but Dryden was so supernaturally alert that there surely would issue some small scuffle, and there could be not even the fraction of a scuffle. The Sergeant relapsed into the contemplation of another century. His patient had one fine virtue. He was in such terror of the phantom skirmish line that his voice never went above a whisper, whereas his delusion might have expressed itself in coyote yells and shots from his rifle. The Sergeant, shuddering, had visions of how it might have been—the mad private leaping into the air and howling and shooting at his friends, and making them the centre of the enemy's eager attention. This, to his mind, would have been conventional conduct for a maniac. The trembling victim of an idea was somewhat puzzling. The Sergeant decided that from time to time he would reason with his patient. "Look here, Dryden, you don't see any real Spaniards. You've been drinking or—something. Now——"

But Dryden only glared him into silence. Dryden was inspired with such a profound contempt of him that it had become hatred. "Don't you stir!" And it was clear that if the Sergeant did stir the mad private would introduce calamity. "Now," said Peasley to himself, "if those guerrillas *should* take a crack at us to-night, they'd find a lunatic asylum in front, and it would be astonishing."

The silence of the night was broken by the quick, low voice of a sentry to the left some distance. The breathless stillness brought an effect to the words as if they had been spoken in one's ear.

"Halt! Who's there? Halt, or I'll fire!" Bang!

At the moment of sudden attack, particularly at night, it is improbable that a man registers much detail of either thought or action. He may afterward say: "I was here." He may say: "I was there"; "I did this"; "I did that." But there remains a great incoherency because of the tumultuous thought which seethes through the head.

"Is this defeat?" At night in a wilderness, and against skillful foes half seen, one does not trouble to ask if it is also death. Defeat is death, then, save for the miraculous ones. But the exaggerating, magnifying first thought subsides in the ordered mind of the soldier, and he knows, soon, what he is doing, and how much of it. The Sergeant's immediate impulse had been to squeeze close to the ground and listen—listen; above all else, listen. But the next moment he grabbed his private asylum by the scruff of its neck, jerked it to its feet, and started to retreat upon the main outpost.

To the left, rifle-flashes were bursting from the shadows. To the rear, the Lieutenant was giving some hoarse order or caution. Through the air swept some Spanish bullets, very high, as if they had been fired at a man in a tree. The private asylum came on so hastily that the Sergeant found he could remove his grip, and soon they were in the midst of the men of the outpost. Here there was no occasion for enlightening the Lieutenant. In the first place, such surprises require statement, question and answer. It is impossible to

get a grossly original and fantastic idea through a man's head in less than one minute of rapid talk, and the Sergeant knew that the Lieutenant could not spare the minute. He himself had no minute to devote to anything but the business of the outpost. And the madman disappeared from his ken, and he forgot about him.

It was a long night, and the little fight was as long as the night. It was heartbreaking work. The forty marines lay in an irregular oval. From all sides the Mauser bullets sang low and swift. The occupation of the Americans was to prevent a rush, and to this end they potted carefully at the flash of a Mauser—save when they got excited for a moment, in which case their magazines rattled like a great Waterbury watch. Then they settled again to a systematic potting.

The enemy were not of the regular Spanish forces, but of a corps of guerrillas, native-born Cubans, who preferred the flag of Spain. They were all men who knew the craft of the woods and were all recruited from the district. They fought more like red Indians than any people but the red Indians themselves. Each seemed to possess an individuality, a fighting individuality, which is only found in the highest order of irregular soldier. Personally, they were as distinct as possible, but through equality of knowledge and experience they arrived at concert of action. So long as they operated in the wilderness they were formidable troops. It mattered little whether it was daylight or dark, they were mainly invisible. They had schooled from the Cubans insurgent to Spain. As the Cubans fought the Spanish troops, so would these particular Spanish troops fight the Americans. It was wisdom.

The marines thoroughly understood the game. They must lie close and fight until daylight, when the guerrillas would promptly go away. They had withstood other nights of this kind, and now their principal emotion was a sort of frantic annoyance.

Back at the main camp, whenever the roaring volleys lulled, the men in the trenches could hear their comrades of the outpost and the guerrillas pattering away interminably. The moonlight faded and left an equal darkness upon the wilderness. A man could barely see the comrade at his side. Sometimes guerrillas crept so close that the flame from their rifles seemed to scorch the faces of the marines, and the reports sounded as if within two or three inches of their very noses. If a pause came, one could hear the guerrillas gabbling to each other in a kind of delirium. The Lieutenant was praying that the ammunition would last. Everybody was praying for daylight.

A black hour came finally when the men were

not fit to have their troubles increase. The enemy made a wild attack on one portion of the oval which was held by about fifteen men. The remainder of the force was busy enough, and the fifteen were naturally left to their devices. Amid the whirl of it, a loud voice suddenly broke out in song:

"The minstrel boy to the war has gone,
    In the ranks of death you'll find him;
His father's sword he has girded on,
    And his wild harp slung behind him."

"Who the deuce is that?" demanded the Lieutenant from a throat full of smoke. There was almost a full stop of the firing. The Americans were puzzled. Practical ones muttered that the fool should have a bayonet-hilt shoved down his throat. Others felt a thrill at the strangeness of the thing. Perhaps it was a sign!

"While shepherds watched their flocks by night,
    All seated on the ground,
The angel of the Lord came down,
    And glory shone around."

This croak was as lugubrious as a coffin. "Who is it? Who is it?" snapped the Lieutenant. "Stop him, somebody!"

"It's Dryden, sir," said old Sergeant Peasley as he felt around in the darkness for his madhouse. "I can't find him—yet."

"Please, oh, please—oh, do not let me fall!
    You're—gurgh-ugh—"

The Sergeant had pounced upon him.

The singing had had an effect upon the Spaniards. At first they had fired frenziedly at the voice, but they soon ceased, perhaps from sheer amazement. Both sides took a spell of meditation.

The Sergeant was having some difficulty with his charge. "Here, you, grab 'im! Take 'im by the throat! Be quiet, you idiot!"

One of the fifteen men who had been hard pressed called out, "We've only got about one clip apiece, Lieutenant. If they come again——"

The Lieutenant crawled to and fro among his men, taking clips of cartridges from those who had many. He came upon the Sergeant and his madhouse. He felt Dryden's belt and found it simply stuffed with ammunition. He examined Dryden's rifle and found in it a full clip. The madhouse had not fired a shot. The Lieutenant

distributed these valuable prizes among the fifteen men. As they gratefully took them, one said, "If they had come again hard enough they would have had us, sir—maybe."

But the Spaniards did not come again. At the first indication of daybreak they fired their customary good-by volley. The marines lay tight while the slow dawn crept over the land. Finally the Lieutenant arose among them, and he was a bewildered man, but very angry. "Now, where is that idiot, Sergeant?"

"Here he is, sir," said the old man cheerfully. He was seated on the ground beside the recumbent Dryden, who, with an innocent smile on his face, was sound asleep.

"Wake him up," said the Lieutenant briefly.

The Sergeant shook the sleeper. "Here, Minstrel Boy, turn out. The Lieutenant wants you."

Dryden climbed to his feet and saluted the officer with a dazed and childish air. "Yes, sir."

The Lieutenant was obviously having difficulty in governing his feelings, but he managed to say with calmness: "You seem to be fond of singing, Dryden? Sergeant, see if he has any whiskey on him."

"Sir?" said the madhouse, stupefied. "Singing—fond of singing?"

Here the Sergeant interposed gently, and he and the Lieutenant held palaver apart from the others. The marines, hitching more comfortably their almost empty belts, spoke with grins of the madhouse. "Well, the Minstrel Boy made 'em clear out. They couldn't stand it. But—I wouldn't want to be in his boots. He'll see fireworks when the old man interviews him on the uses of grand opera in modern warfare. How do you think he managed to smuggle a bottle along without us finding it out?"

When the weary outpost was relieved and marched back to camp, the men could not rest until they had told a tale of the voice in the wilderness. In the meantime the Sergeant took Dryden aboard a ship, and to those who assumed charge of the man he defined him as "the most useful crazy man in the service of the United States."

CARRIE NATION AND KANSAS
by William Allen White

One of the first writers Lorimer wanted for the *Post* was William Allen White, the "boy editor" of Emporia, Kansas. At the age of twenty-eight White had caused a national sensation with his editorial, "What's the Matter with Kansas?" (There was nothing the matter, he concluded, that a general cleanup of crackpot politicians couldn't cure.) In November 1899 Lorimer asked White to write some editorials for the *Post* but White wrote back: "I have gotten in a rut here in Emporia running a country daily by day, and writing short stories by night, so that I don't think that I can think of anything interesting to readers of the *Post*." But White soon became a prolific *Post* writer, producing some of the magazine's best on-the-spot reporting, stories, and even editorials. In one of the latter, published March 30, 1901, he had something interesting to say about a perennial American worry: juvenile delinquency. "The American custom of allowing boys and girls absolute liberty in their courtship, of allowing love-making 'at all hours,' is responsible for much that is disagreeable in society," wrote White, who was just beginning to raise his own family. "With all this frank and undisguised discussion before them of matters once tabooed, young people are turned into the front parlor alone to spend evenings, and when the talk runs into swamps, the world in the back parlor is astonished. . . . It is pretty nearly a question whether the chaperon or the sheriff shall step in, and regulate or control the Sunday-night performance in the parlor."

APRIL 6, 1901

On a winter's morning in Chicago a short little woman, with motherly face and rotund figure, clad in black alpaca, and not too warmly wrapped, came from a cheap Dearborn Street tavern and set out walking to see the town. The woman was Mrs. Caroline Nation, Crusader, of Medicine Lodge, Kansas.

She wandered with rather unstable purpose, and a hooting, indolent rabble followed her with curiosity. She had been well advertised. For several weeks before she came to Chicago Mrs. Nation's name had been occupying a "preferred position" in the American newspapers, and so when she began her morning's journey over the big city to purify it, the mob at her heels was ready for miracles or a fight, or both. For many hours she trudged the streets, leading the multitude. She went into saloons and pleaded with barkeepers. She prayed on the streets; she exhorted; she laughed and cried and wrought herself up to a pitch of excitement wherein nothing matters much. Then she went to find the Mayor. She hoped to argue into him what she believed to be moral courage. He heard that she was coming and fled from his office. When Mrs. Nation entered the Chicago City Hall, in the mob that came after her were a few disciples—perhaps half a dozen—and a few half-hearted sympathizers; then there came loafers, pickpockets, criminals, a few young gentlemen with nothing better to do, a few emotional people swept away from sedentary pursuits by the hypnosis of mob spirit, and a cloud of witnesses for the newspapers. Mrs. Nation was clearly conscious of the presence of her escort—and proud of it.

Thus, at the head of this hooting throng, Carrie Nation entered the Chicago City Hall. When she found that she could not scold the Mayor, the crusader mounted a wide, black-walnut railing in the great anteroom to the Mayor's office. There she stood with hair disheveled, with wild, glowing eyes, with radiant face reflecting hysteria, and began to harangue the crowd. She waved her arms; her voice creaked with excitement, her hands beat the air. At first the throng was silent, then it began to titter, then to laugh, and then to jeer and howl.

And then a centurion hustled her away. The mad scene was cut short. The mob began to surge out of the great room; women shrieked; the crush was merciless. The maelstrom caught Mrs. Nation. It whirled her around and around. Her hands that were raised to gesticulate it held im-

55

potently above her head. The roars, imprecations and laughter engulfed her frenzied babble. A city official standing near a policeman said: "Here, officer, protect that woman; she'll be killed."

The policeman watched Mrs. Nation pirouetting and laughed:

"Aw, let her get out the way she came in."

On the sidewalk she lifted up a few glorias before she went away in an elevated train, and the crowd scattered.

This is Mrs. Nation, and broadly and with the exaggeration that a crowd gets in a great city where contrasts are broader and deeper, this is the world she is working in. This picture may represent the scene on the drop curtain at the play. Now let the fiddlers thrum their strings, the cornets groan, the little man in the tinshop arrange his wares, the band strike up its overture and the play begin.

It seems a simple matter to gauge Mrs. Nation's power. Her hysteria multiplied by her inefficiency and divided by her lawlessness should give the desired result. But the quotient thus obtained is small; it is nil. And this woman's power is great. What unknown quantity has entered the equation to change it? Where is the secret of popular error about her? To answer this question it is necessary to go back to fundamentals.

It is unimportant to chronicle the fact that Mrs. Nation was born in Kentucky and to follow her life as it led her through Missouri and Oklahoma into Kansas. But it is well to note in passing that her first husband, whom she probably married for love and whose wrongs she has never forgotten, died a drunkard. Often these hidden springs in the human heart move with tremendous power. After marrying David Nation she settled down to make a comfortable home for herself and her husband, and to live out her life in the fear of the Lord.

She has but one mental output. For years she has been considering the evils of the liquor traffic. She has acted when Nature would stand the strain no longer in a primitive way—with savage music! In Medicine Lodge she used to get out a hand-organ through which perforated paper sheets are passed, and sitting on a prominent corner of the town, she would grind out dolorous temperance songs to the citizens. In time they came to give her about as much notice as one gives to the water-plug on a corner. Another form of self-relief was to haunt the local jail and constabulary and pray with the prisoners, who usually voted her a nuisance.

These two vents became monotonous. So she hiked out in Barber County in a buggy on a temperance mission. Nearly a year ago she struck the village of Kiowa. She stoned two joints. It was her first smashing. The world never heard of it. The local papers contained only humorous references to it. Everybody knew Mrs. Nation down there. But she was imbued through and through with a hatred for the saloon. There came an awful pressure of conviction as to the futility of her life, the maddening conclusion that she had made no impress, that her song and jail and prayer methods were methods of guilty puerility. She probably accused herself of rank cowardice. She finally laid hold of the territory, which is just across the line from all of us, where irresponsibility reigns. Mrs. Nation carried into that land hatred and a determination to destroy. Then she set out for Wichita from Barber County, literally with an apron full of rocks, and when she got to Wichita her courage failed. She prayed one night in the saloons instead of smashing. But courage came to her again, and the next morning she sallied out, keyed up, hilariously irresponsible, anarchistic. She smashed the finest bar in the town; she was taken to the police station, fat, double-chinned, and laughing outlandishly.

In that trip to the station she got over into the Land of Responsibility again. In palliation of her offense she quoted law at the officer who arrested her. Then the W. C. T. U. women heard of it and rushed down to see her. They congratulated her. Then she began to see that her best defense was to claim that she had started a war. To give her act State significance she wrote a note to the Governor. She dreaded being put in jail.

Mrs. Nation was a local character when she came to Wichita. The Topeka correspondents wanted Eastern papers to take a story about her joint-smashing. The Eastern papers wouldn't. They didn't know Mrs. Nation. They didn't care anything about her. Then an artist stepped to the wire, not a sign and house painter, but an engraver, who etched in these words into the query for a story: "Mrs. Nation has sent for Jerry Simpson to act as her attorney." The Eastern papers then were anxious. They knew Jerry Simpson. They answered, "Send stuff." Then it spread. Such is the influence of art on great events.

Telegrams began to pour in on Mrs. Nation. She became vain, ingloriously vain. When she got out of jail she had no idea of smashing joints further, until she found that she could take on the clairvoyant state of irresponsibility. She gathered a few followers. There was to be a general joint smashing at six o'clock one evening. Being irresponsible and headstrong, Mrs. Nation broke the agreement and began her smashing at five o'clock.

When she was arrested again she came down the street hysterical and wabbly, and bowing right and left to the multitude.

She turned to a reporter and said: "How many do you think are following me now?"

"A thousand," he answered.

"Isn't it fine?" she exclaimed, glowing. She was rational then. When she breaks out, as she occasionally does, against her friends as well as against the joint-keepers, she is irrational. She can work herself up to the blind passion sometimes, and sometimes she cannot. She collapsed one night in Topeka; but cowardice leaves her when she is rhapsodical; she is as fearful as any one when this excitation is not upon her, and she cannot induce it.

She is a deeply pious woman and has re-read the Bible so many times that Biblical quirks and tropes and metaphors put a wholesome bark on her conversation. She is argumentative, and given to much wrangling. Like many persons of limited mental capacity she is sure of her distinctions between right and wrong. Therefore she has been free to act without restraint. The person who spends valuable time toying with the equities of a circumstance, trying to locate and mark out the boundaries of exact justice before proceeding, is unlikely to follow the strenuous life. With Mrs. Nation, "Be sure you are right, then go ahead," translated, means, "Interpret your Bible and then get your hatchet." This absolute confidence in one's correct reading of the Scriptures generates the faith that stores up courage of great voltage. This faith of a little child sustained Joan of Arc; it guided Peter the Hermit. It sustained John Brown at Harper's Ferry. It is often misdirected faith; frequently it destroys those who hold it; certainly it is blind, and those who nurse this faith are probably mentally diseased. But some way—perhaps in God's own way—this faith moves mountains, often mountains that seem to be highly necessary and almost respectable. But when they have moved, in their stead men find still waters and green pastures that are altogether good and lovely.

To understand Mrs. Nation, it is necessary to know something of her legal environment. And this brings the subject of the legal prohibition of the liquor traffic in Kansas fairly up for consideration. Briefly, the story of the prohibition of liquor selling in Kansas is this: Twenty-four years ago, after four years of temperance agitation, beginning with a Francis Murphy blue ribbon revival, the people of Kansas, by a reasonably substantial majority, adopted an amendment to the State Constitution which prohibited the sale of alcoholic liquor as a beverage in Kansas. This amendment was enforced from time to time by legislative enactment. There is no doubt that the farmers, who compose the majority of the citizens of Kansas, favor the prohibitory law; and yet there is also no question that the law is laxly enforced in many parts of the State. In certain of the larger towns the law is absolutely disregarded, and a system of monthly fines is imposed —amounting, in effect, to a license—upon the liquor dealers. On the other hand, again, this is the fact, that less liquor is consumed in Kansas, reckoning by the old "per capita" method, than in any non-prohibition State. There are, of course, joints of a kind in every Kansas town; but they are sporadic: they move from one livery stable box-stall, to another, from one abandoned building to another, from one shack to another, as the town officers discover them. No business man frequents them; no young man can afford to be seen in their vicinity. The fixtures are primitive: a cigar box full of salt for the beer; a plug-tobacco box full of sawdust to spit in; a limp towel; a number of unwashed, thumb-marked tumblers to drink from, and three or four backless, spavined chairs to sit upon. Save in a half dozen of the larger Kansas towns the "gilded palace of sin," which used to agitate the temperance orator in the blue ribbon days, is extinct, and hundreds of young men have grown to manhood in Kansas without ever seeing a Kansas saloon.

This was the condition which confronted Mrs. Nation six months ago when she left home with her hatchet. She set out to destroy the saloons. In her lexicon, "to destroy" means "to smash." She smashed, and fame discovered her. Since then the story is a repetition almost daily of the same incident: she goes forth; she finds her prey; she attacks it. She is arrested, put in jail and released the next day, and goes forth again. The mob follows her: she mounts steps and stands in patrol wagons, and scolds and preaches and laughs and cries, and exhibits for a time all the symptoms of acute hysteria. Then she becomes quiet, indulges herself in remarkably lucid and effective Biblical repartee with those who talk with her, and in these normal moments she is an earnest, shrewd, sharp-tongued woman with some little fatalistic philosophy and no little fund of a merry kind of wit. The Nations are well-to-do. She can afford the luxury of saloon smashing. She dresses as most elderly ladies dress, and is not entirely devoid of pride in a pleasing personal appearance.

For she is not a sexless creature—she is a woman to the core.

So much for this St. Georgiana. Now for her dragon. Commonly he is known as the Rum Fiend, familiarly as the Saloon. The saloon is an evil. It may be deemed a necessary evil by those who feel bound to apologize for it; but it can have no defenders. Even where it is licensed, protected by law, under restrictions which narrow its iniquities to moderate and expedient vice, the saloon, personified by its devotees, may be characterized by no adjective more flattering than miscreant. At its highest estate it is an outlaw, and the greatest legal distinction the saloon has achieved after a century of fighting for statutory recognition is to be branded generically by the United States Supreme Court as a nuisance. Its purposes are all venal. It is in business to promote violence and crime; to injure the public health; to dissipate the public wealth in taxes that support the criminal court; to burden our charities; to corrupt the civic morals. The saloon is incarnate calamity. Because its work is slow and indirect, people often fail to see how it kills and maims men and tortures women like a malicious spirit.

Now the Kansas statutes, as aforementioned, recognize the saloon for what it is. The State Constitution forbids the saloon to enter the State, under penalty of the law. The saloon-keeper who enters Kansas to ply his trade does so upon terms of exact equality with the pickpocket and the chicken thief. In his traffic he has no rights, and by no ordinance or intrigue or sentiment or understanding can he have any traffic rights, however meagre or limited, in Kansas, that the law-abiding citizen is bound to respect. And in the face of this legal proscription, when the saloon-keeper does hang out his sign in Kansas he must arrange a liaison with the officers of the law, who are supported by a local public sentiment which the saloon-keeper has corrupted.

He pays a monthly fine in police court and is not molested. Citizens who concern themselves to maintain law and order complain in vain to the prosecuting attorney. At least one man may be smuggled into the jury-room from a saloon-corrupted community who regards his oath in a Pickwickian sense. Legal redress is almost impossible—or was, before Mrs. Nation came to town.

In the Kansas towns where the saloon dominated, the citizen who stood for law enforcement stood as powerless as a wooden Indian. And the joint was growing bolder and bolder. It was moving from the little towns, where foreign colonies controlled the public sentiment, to the suburbs of the county seat, and it was coming nearer and nearer to the main street. A sort of locomotor ataxia was creeping over the morals of the State. Last spring a dozen towns that had been "dry" for a generation elected "wet" city administrations. The saloon infection was spreading. Saloon-keepers became more and more insolent. Brewers from Kansas City and St. Louis began to take an interest in the situation. They slipped in elaborate bar fixtures where they dared. The joint became a saloon and the devil was having a merry time withal. The whole growth of the evil was incendiary, lawless, riotous. The lawlessness of the Kansas joint bred Mrs. Nation's mob. Kansas planted the joint and reaped the hatchet. When the glass-breaking, liquor-spilling, frantic mob laughed at law, the laughter was an echo. The brewers who started the lawless Kansas saloons laughed first at law—always a dangerous and generally an expensive experiment. Between the two outlaws there is little choice. The joint is bad. The mob is bad. As they say at the vaudeville, "both are equally as worse as each." When the two negatives met they formed a positive—an object-lesson. It was respect for law, taught probably by some sort of an unconscious *reductio ad absurdum*.

The local effect in Kansas of the Nation joint smashing was the sudden development of enthusiastic moral courage to demand the enforcement of the prohibitory law. Public sentiment crystallized over night. The State Legislature which assembled while Mrs. Nation was smashing reflected that public sentiment with unusual clearness and accuracy. Laws were passed making the possession of a Government liquor license or of a bar and saloon fixtures *prima facie* evidence of the illegal intent of the owner or holder of them; also making it possible to enjoin any one found with saloon fixtures in his possession against continuing in the saloon business, under penalty of punishment for contempt of court, without benefit of jury; and further, a law was enacted giving the prosecuting attorney inquisitorial rights. Under this law he may summon any citizen, who is required to testify whether or not he bought liquor at certain places and of certain persons. There can be no longer the least excuse for officers or citizens winking at violations of the prohibitory law in Kansas. All this the woman with the hatchet has done—by indirection. For she set out to defy the law and she has strengthened the law.

That much is certain: it may be set down in the balanced book of this hatchet account as net profit. But has not Mrs. Nation made a larger investment which shall return in a far more exceeding and eternal weight of glory? God moves in a mysterious way. This is true whether one thinks of God as an omnipotent, omniscient personality, even as the orthodox God, or whether one feels that God is only a "stream of tendency." But God moves and moves forward. And when one considers what poor sticks of men have carried God's banner—the insane, the brutal, the ignorant, the lame and the halt and the blind, but always the brave—one pauses before condemning even the most despised of creatures as unfit for the work. Did the savage veneration of the insane arise from the possible fact that too many of those who seemed mad and were stoned to death have proved that they were prophets? Are not inflamed nerves supersensitive to waves of feeling that precede great moral changes?

Is it altogether impossible that this frantic, brawling, hysterical woman in the Kansas jail, brave, indomitable, consecrated to her God, may be a prophetess whose signs and wonders shall be read and known of man by the light of another day?

And then again, perhaps this woman's work is but a ripple on the billow of the passing wave of events. Perhaps she has been advertised beyond her deserts; perhaps she will soon move beyond the lime-light of publicity and fade into oblivion; perhaps she is one of the million whose lives are hopelessly dead—innocuous, stale, "bitter with hard bondage in mortar, and in brick, and in all manner of service."

THE PASSING
OF "THIRD FLOOR BACK"

by Jerome K. Jerome

ONE NIGHT in London author Jerome Klapka Jerome happened to notice "a stooping figure, passing down a foggy street, pausing every now and then to glance up at a door." He followed but never got a look at the man's face. "It was his clothes that worried me. There was nothing out of the way about them. I could not make out why they seemed remarkable. I lost him at a corner, where the fog hung thick. . . . I could not get him out of my mind, and gradually he grew out of those curious clothes of his." He grew into the stranger of Jerome's famous *Post* story, "The Passing of 'Third Floor Back.'" (This was the original title, later changed to "The Passing of the Third Floor Back.") The story grew into a play, which had a long success in London and New York. On the stage the people in the boarding house became mere symbols labeled Cheat, Slut, Painted Lady, and so on, each converted by a mysterious stranger into something resembling their better selves. The original story is more realistic, and more interesting.

NOVEMBER 19, 1904

THE NEIGHBORHOOD of Bloomsbury Square toward four o'clock of a November afternoon is not so crowded as to secure to the stranger, of appearance anything out of the common, immunity from observation. Tibb's boy, screaming at the top of his voice that she was his honey, stopped suddenly, stepped backward on to the toes of a voluble young lady wheeling a perambulator, remained deaf, apparently, to the somewhat personal remarks of the voluble young lady. Not until he had reached the next corner—and then more as a soliloquy than as information to the street—did Tibb's boy recover sufficient interest in his own affairs to remark that he was her bee. The voluble young lady herself, following some half a dozen yards behind, forgot her wrongs in contemplation of the stranger's back. There was this that was peculiar about the stranger's back: that instead of being flat it presented a decided curve. "It ain't a 'ump, and it don't look like kervitcher of the spine," observed the voluble young lady to herself. "Blimy if I don't believe 'e's taking 'ome 'is washing up 'is back."

The constable at the corner, trying to seem busy doing nothing, noticed the stranger's approach with gathering interest. "That's an odd sort of a walk of yours, young man," thought the constable; "you take care you don't fall down and tumble over yourself."

"Thought he was a young man," murmured the constable, the stranger having passed him. "He had a young face, right enough."

The daylight was fading. The stranger, finding it impossible to read the name of the street upon the corner house, turned back.

"Why, 'tis a young man," the constable told himself; "a mere boy."

"I beg your pardon," said the stranger, "but would you mind telling me my way to Bloomsbury Square."

"This is Bloomsbury Square," explained the constable; "leastways, round the corner is. What number might you be wanting?"

The stranger took from the ticket pocket of his tightly-buttoned overcoat a piece of paper, unfolded it and read it out: "Mrs. Pennycherry. Number forty-eight."

"Round to the left," instructed the constable; "fourth house. Been recommended there?"

"By—by a friend," replied the stranger. "Thank you very much."

"A-ha," muttered the constable to himself; "guess you won't be calling him that by the end of the week, young man."

"Funny," added the constable, gazing after the retreating figure of the stranger. "Seen plenty of the other sex as looked young behind and old in front. This cove looks young in front and old behind. Guess he'll look old all round if he stops long at Mother Pennycherry's: stingy old cat."

Constables whose beat included Bloomsbury

Square had their reasons for not liking Mrs. Pennycherry. Indeed, it might have been difficult to discover any human being with reasons for liking that sharp-featured lady. Maybe the keeping of second-rate boarding-houses in the neighborhood of Bloomsbury does not tend to develop the virtues of generosity and amiability.

Meanwhile the stranger, proceeding upon his way, had rung the bell of number forty-eight. Mrs. Pennycherry, peeping from the area and catching a glimpse, above the railings, of a handsome, if somewhat effeminate, masculine face, hastened to readjust her widow's cap before the looking-glass while directing Mary Jane to show the stranger, should he prove a problematical boarder, into the dining-room, and to light the gas.

"And don't start gossiping, and don't you take it upon yourself to answer questions. Say I'll be up in a minute," were Mrs. Pennycherry's further instructions; "and mind you hide your hands as much as you can."

"What are you grinning at?" demanded Mrs. Pennycherry a couple of minutes later of the dingy Mary Jane.

"Wasn't grinning," explained the meek Mary Jane; "was only smiling to myself."

"What at?"

"Dunno," admitted Mary Jane. But still she went on smiling.

"What's he like, then?" demanded Mrs. Pennycherry.

" 'E ain't the usual sort," was Mary Jane's opinion.

"Praise be for that!" ejaculated Mrs. Pennycherry piously.

"Says 'e's been recommended by a friend."

"By whom?"

"By a friend. 'E didn't say no more."

Mrs. Pennycherry pondered. "He's not the funny sort, is he?"

Not that sort at all. Mary Jane was sure of it.

Mrs. Pennycherry ascended the stairs still pondering. As she entered the room the stranger rose and bowed. Nothing could have been simpler than the stranger's bow, yet there came with it to Mrs. Pennycherry a rush of old sensations long forgotten. For one brief moment Mrs. Pennycherry saw herself an amiable, well-bred lady, widow of a solicitor; a visitor had called to see her. It was but a momentary fancy. The next instant reality reasserted itself. Mrs. Pennycherry, a lodging-house keeper, existing precariously upon a daily round of petty meannesses, was prepared for contest with a possible new boarder, who, fortunately, looked an inexperienced young gentleman.

"Some one has recommended me to you," began Mrs. Pennycherry. "May I ask who?"

But the stranger waved the question aside as immaterial.

"You might not remember him," he smiled. "He thought that I should do well to pass here the few months I am given to be in London. You can take me in?"

Mrs. Pennycherry thought that she should be able to take the stranger in.

"A room to sleep in," explained the stranger; "any room with food and drink sufficient for a man is all that I require."

"For breakfast," began Mrs. Pennycherry, "I give——"

"What is right and proper, I am convinced," interrupted the stranger. "Pray, do not trouble to go into detail, Mrs. Pennycherry. With whatever it is I shall be content."

Mrs. Pennycherry, puzzled, shot a quick glance at the stranger, but his face, though the gentle eyes were smiling, was frank and serious.

"At all events, you will see the room," suggested Mrs. Pennycherry, "before we discuss terms."

"Certainly," agreed the stranger. "I am a little tired and shall be glad to rest there."

Mrs. Pennycherry led the way upward; on the landing of the third floor paused for a moment undecided, then opened the door of the back bedroom.

"It is very comfortable," commented the stranger.

"For this room," stated Mrs. Pennycherry, "together with full board, consisting of——"

"Of everything needful. It goes without saying," again interrupted the stranger, with his quiet, grave smile.

"I have generally asked," continued Mrs. Pennycherry, "four pounds a week. To you"—Mrs. Pennycherry's voice, unknown to her, took to itself the note of aggressive generosity—"seeing you have been recommended here, say three pound ten."

"Dear lady," said the stranger, "that is kind of you. As you have divined, I am not a rich man. If it be not imposing upon you I accept your reduction with gratitude."

Again Mrs. Pennycherry, familiar with the satirical method, shot a suspicious glance upon the stranger, but not a line was there upon that smooth, fair face to which a sneer could for a moment have clung. Clearly he was as simple as he looked.

"Gas, of course, extra."

"Of course," agreed the stranger.

"Coals——"

"We shall not quarrel," for the third time the stranger interrupted. "You have been very considerate to me as it is. I feel, Mrs. Pennycherry, I can leave myself entirely in your hands."

The stranger appeared anxious to be alone. Mrs. Pennycherry, having put a match to the stranger's fire, turned to depart. And at this point it was that Mrs. Pennycherry, the holder hitherto of an unbroken record for sanity, behaved in a manner she herself, five minutes earlier in her career, would have deemed impossible—that no living soul who had ever known her would have believed, even had Mrs. Pennycherry gone down upon her knees and sworn it to them.

"Did I say three pound ten?" demanded Mrs. Pennycherry of the stranger, her hand upon the door. She spoke crossly. She was feeling cross, with the stranger, with herself—particularly with herself.

"You were kind enough to reduce it to that amount," replied the stranger; "but if upon reflection you find yourself unable——"

"I was making a mistake," said Mrs. Pennycherry; "it should have been two pound ten."

"I cannot—I will not accept such sacrifice," exclaimed the stranger; "the three pound ten I can well afford."

"Two pound ten are my terms," snapped Mrs. Pennycherry. "If you are bent on paying more you can go elsewhere. You'll find plenty to oblige you."

Her vehemence must have impressed the stranger. "We will not contend further," he smiled. "I was merely afraid that in the goodness of your heart——"

"Oh, it isn't as good as all that," growled Mrs. Pennycherry.

"I am not so sure," returned the stranger. "I am somewhat suspicious of you. But willful woman must, I suppose, have her way."

The stranger held out his hand, and to Mrs. Pennycherry, at that moment, it seemed the most natural thing in the world to take it as if it had been the hand of an old friend, and to end the interview with a pleasant laugh—though laughing was an exercise not often indulged in by Mrs. Pennycherry. Mary Jane was standing by the window, her hands folded in front of her, when Mrs. Pennycherry reëntered the kitchen. By standing close to the window one caught a glimpse of the trees in Bloomsbury Square, and through their bare branches of the sky beyond.

"There's nothing much to do for the next half-hour till cook comes back. I'll see to the door if you'd like a run out," suggested Mrs. Pennycherry.

"It would be nice," agreed the girl, so soon as she had recovered power of speech; "it's just the time of day I like."

"Don't be longer than the half-hour," added Mrs. Pennycherry.

Forty-eight Bloomsbury Square, assembled after dinner in the drawing-room, discussed the stranger with that freedom and frankness characteristic of forty-eight Bloomsbury Square toward the absent.

"Not what I call a smart young man," was the opinion of Augustus Longcord, who was something in the city.

"Thpeaking for mythelf," commented his partner Isidore, "hav'n'th any uthe for the thmart young man. Too many of him ath it ith."

"Must be pretty smart if he's one too many for you," laughed his partner. There was this to be said for the repartee of forty-eight Bloomsbury Square: it was simple of construction and easy of comprehension.

"Well, it made me feel good just looking at him," declared Miss Kite, the highly colored. "It was his clothes, I suppose—made me think of Noah and the ark."

"It would be clothes that would make you think—if anything," drawled the languid Miss Devine. She was a tall, handsome girl, engaged at the moment in the futile efforts to recline with elegance and comfort combined upon a horsehair sofa. Miss Kite, by reason of having secured the only easy chair, was unpopular that evening; so that Miss Devine's remark received from the rest of the company more approbation than perhaps it merited.

"Is that intended to be clever, dear, or only rude?" Miss Kite requested to be informed.

"Both," claimed Miss Devine.

"Myself, I must confess," shouted the tall young lady's father, commonly called the Colonel, "I found him a fool."

"I noticed you seemed to be getting on very well together," purred his wife, a plump, smiling little lady.

"Possibly we were," retorted the Colonel; "Fate has accustomed me to the society of fools."

"Isn't it a pity to start quarreling immediately after dinner, you two," suggested their thoughtful daughter from the sofa. "You'll have nothing left to amuse you for the rest of the evening."

"He didn't strike me as a conversationalist," said the lady who was cousin to a baronet; "but he did pass the vegetables before he helped himself. A little thing like that shows breeding."

"Or that he didn't know you, and thought maybe you'd leave him half a spoonful," laughed Augustus the wit.

"What I can't make out about him," shouted the Colonel—— The stranger entered the room.

The Colonel, securing the evening paper, retired into a corner. The highly-colored Kite, reaching down from the mantelpiece a paper fan, held it coyly before her face. Miss Devine sat upright on the horsehair sofa and rearranged her skirts.

"Know anything?" demanded Augustus of the stranger, breaking the somewhat remarkable silence.

The stranger evidently did not understand. It was necessary for Augustus, the witty, to advance further into that odd silence.

"What's going to pull off the Lincoln Handicap? Tell me and I'll go out straight and put my shirt upon it."

"I think you would act unwisely," smiled the stranger; "I am not an authority upon the subject."

"Not! Why, they told me you were Captain Spy, of the Sporting Life, in disguise."

It would have been difficult for a joke to fall more flat. Nobody laughed, though why Mr. Augustus Longcord could not understand, and maybe none of his audience could have told him, for at forty-eight Bloomsbury Square Mr. Augustus Longcord passed as a humorist. The stranger himself appeared unaware that he was being made fun of.

"You have been misinformed," assured him the stranger.

"I beg your pardon," said Mr. Augustus Longcord.

"It is nothing," replied the stranger in his sweet, low voice, and passed on.

"Well, what about this theatre," demanded Mr. Longcord of his friend and partner; "do you want to go, or don't you?" Mr. Longcord was feeling irritable.

"Got the ticketh—may ath well," thought Isidore.

"D——n stupid piece, I'm told."

"Motht of them thupid, more or leth. Pity to wathte the ticketh," argued Isidore, and the pair went out.

"Are you staying long in London?" asked Miss Kite, raising her practiced eyes toward the stranger.

"Not long," answered the stranger. "At least, I do not know. It depends."

An unusual quiet had invaded the drawing-room of forty-eight Bloomsbury Square, generally noisy with strident voices about this hour. The Colonel remained engrossed in his paper. Mrs. Devine sat with her plump, white hands folded on her lap, whether asleep or not it was impos-

sible to say. The lady who was cousin to a baronet had shifted her chair beneath the gasolier, her eyes bent on her everlasting crochet work. The languid Miss Devine had crossed to the piano, where she sat fingering softly the tuneless keys, her back to the cold, barely-furnished room.

"Sit down," commanded saucily Miss Kite, indicating with her fan the vacant seat beside her. "Tell me about yourself. You interest me." Miss Kite adopted a pretty, authoritative air toward all youthful-looking members of the opposite sex. It harmonized with the peach complexion and the golden hair, and fitted her about as well.

"I am glad of that," answered the stranger, taking the chair suggested. "I do so wish to interest you."

"You're a very bold boy." Miss Kite lowered her fan for the purpose of glancing archly over the edge of it, and for the first time encountered the eyes of the stranger looking into hers. And then it was that Miss Kite experienced precisely the same curious sensation that an hour or so ago had troubled Mrs. Pennycherry when the stranger had first bowed to her. It seemed to Miss Kite that she was no longer the Miss Kite that, had she risen and looked into it, the fly-blown cheval glass over the marble mantelpiece would, she knew, have presented to her view: but quite another Miss Kite—a cheerful, bright-eyed lady, verging on middle age, yet still good-looking in spite of her faded complexion and somewhat thin brown locks. Miss Kite felt a pang of jealousy shoot through her; this middle-aged Miss Kite seemed, on the whole, a more attractive lady. There was a wholesomeness, a broad-mindedness about her that instinctively drew one toward her. Not hampered, as Miss Kite herself was, by the necessity of appearing to be somewhere between eighteen and twenty-two, this other Miss Kite could talk sensibly, even brilliantly—one felt it. A thoroughly "nice" woman this other Miss Kite; the real Miss Kite, though envious, was bound to admit it. Miss Kite wished to goodness she had never seen the woman. The glimpse of her had rendered Miss Kite dissatisfied with herself.

"I am not a boy," explained the stranger, "and I had no intention of being bold."

"I know," replied Miss Kite. "It was a silly remark. Whatever induced me to make it I can't think. Getting foolish in my old age, I suppose."

The stranger laughed. "Surely, you are not old."

"I'm thirty-nine," snapped out Miss Kite. "You don't call it young?"

"I think it a beautiful age," insisted the stranger, "young enough not to have lost the strength of youth, old enough to have learned sympathy."

"Oh, I dare say," returned Miss Kite, "any age you'd think beautiful. I'm going to bed." Miss Kite rose. The paper fan had, somehow, got itself broken. She threw the fragments into the fire.

"It is early yet," pleaded the stranger. "I was looking forward to a talk with you."

"Well, you'll be able to look forward to it," retorted Miss Kite. "Good-night."

The truth was, Miss Kite was impatient to have a look at herself in the glass, in her own room, with the door shut. The vision of that other Miss Kite—the clean-looking lady of the pale face and the brown hair—had been so vivid Miss Kite wondered whether temporary forgetfulness might not have fallen upon her while dressing for dinner that evening.

The stranger, left to his own devices, strolled toward the loo-table, seeking something to read.

"You seem to have frightened away Miss Kite," remarked the lady who was cousin to a baronet.

"It seems so," admitted the stranger.

"My cousin, Sir William Bosster," observed the crocheting lady, "who married old Lord Egham's niece—you never met the Eghams?"

"Hitherto," replied the stranger, "I have not had that pleasure."

"A charming family. Cannot understand— my cousin, Sir William, I mean, cannot understand my remaining here. 'My dear Emily'— he says the same thing every time he sees me— 'My dear Emily, how can you exist among the sort of people one meets with in a boarding-house?' But they amuse me."

"A sense of humor," agreed the stranger, "was always of advantage."

"Our family on my mother's side," continued Sir William's cousin in her placid monotone, "was connected with the Tatton-Joneses, who, when King George the Fourth——" Sir William's cousin, needing another reel of cotton, glanced up, and met the stranger's gaze.

"I'm sure I don't know why I'm telling you all this," she said in an irritable tone. "It can't possibly interest you."

"Everything connected with you interests me," gravely the stranger assured her.

"It is very kind of you to say so," sighed Sir William's cousin, but without conviction. "I am afraid sometimes I bore people."

The polite stranger refrained from contradiction.

"You see," continued the poor lady, "I really am of good family."

"Dear lady," said the stranger, "your gentle face, your gentle voice, your gentle bearing, all proclaim it."

She looked without flinching into the stranger's eyes, and gradually a smile banished the reigning dullness of her features.

"How foolish of me." She spoke rather to herself than to the stranger. "Why, of course, people —people whose opinion is worth troubling about —judge of you by what you are, not by what you go about saying you are."

The stranger remained silent.

"I am the widow of a provincial doctor, with an income of just £230 per annum," she argued. "The sensible thing for me to do is to make the best of it, and to worry myself about those high and mighty relations of mine as little as they have ever worried themselves about me."

The stranger appeared unable to think of anything worth saying.

"I have other connections," remembered Sir William's cousin; "those of my poor husband, to whom, instead of being the 'poor relation,' I could be the fairy god-mamma. They are my people— or would be," added Sir William's cousin tartly, "if I wasn't a vulgar snob."

She flushed the instant she had said the words, and, rising, commenced preparations for a hurried departure.

"Now, it seems I am driving you away," sighed the stranger.

"Having been called a 'vulgar snob'," retorted the lady with some heat, "I think it about time I went."

"The words were your own," the stranger reminded her.

"Whatever I may have thought," remarked the indignant dame, "no lady—least of all, in the presence of a total stranger—would have called herself——" The poor dame paused bewildered. "There is something very curious the matter with me this evening that I cannot understand," she explained. "I seem quite unable to avoid insulting myself."

Still surrounded by bewilderment, she wished the stranger good-night, hoping that when next they met she would be more herself. The stranger, hoping so, opened the door and closed it again behind her.

"Tell me," laughed Miss Devine, who, by sheer force of talent, was contriving to wring harmony from the reluctant piano. "How did you manage to do it?"

"How did I do what?" inquired the stranger.

"Contrive to get rid so quickly of those two old frumps?"

"How well you play!" observed the stranger. "I knew you had genius for music the moment I saw you."

"How could you tell?"

"It is written so clearly in your face."

The girl laughed, well pleased. "You seem to have lost no time in studying my face."

"It is a beautiful and interesting face," observed the stranger.

She swung round sharply on the stool and their eyes met.

"You can read faces?"

"Yes."

"Tell me, what else do you read in mine?"

"Frankness, courage, tenderness."

"Ah, yes, all the virtues. Perhaps. We will take them for granted." It was odd how serious the girl had suddenly become. "Tell me the reverse side."

"I see no reverse side," replied the stranger. "I see but a fair girl bursting into noble womanhood."

"And nothing else? You read no trace of greed, of vanity, of sordidness, of——" An angry laugh escaped her lips. "And you are a reader of faces!"

"A reader of faces." The stranger smiled. "Do you know what is written upon yours at this very moment? A love of truth that is almost fierce, scorn of lies, scorn of hypocrisy, the desire for all things pure, contempt of all things that are contemptible—especially of such things as are contemptible in woman. Tell me, do I read aright?"

I wonder, thought the girl, is that why those two others both hurried from the room? Does every one feel ashamed of the littleness that is in them when looked at by those clear, believing eyes of yours?

The idea occurred to her: "Papa seemed to have a good deal to say to you during dinner. Tell me, what were you talking about?"

"The military-looking gentleman upon my left? We talked about your mother principally."

"I am sorry," returned the girl, wishful now she had not asked the question. "I was hoping he might have chosen another topic for the first evening!"

"He did try one or two," admitted the stranger; "but I have been about the world so little. I was glad when he talked to me about himself. I feel we shall be friends. He spoke so nicely, too, about Mrs. Devine."

"Indeed," commented the girl.

"He told me he had been married for twenty years and had never regretted it but once!"

Her black eyes flashed upon him, but, meeting his, the suspicion died from them. She turned aside to hide her smile.

"So he regretted it once?"

"Only once," explained the stranger; "a passing irritable mood. It was so frank of him to admit it. He told me—I think he has taken a liking to me. Indeed, he hinted as much. He said he did not often get an opportunity of talking to a man like myself. He told me that he and your mother, when they travel together, are always mistaken for a honeymoon couple. Some of the experiences he related to me were really quite amusing." The stranger laughed at recollection of them. "That even here, in this place, they are generally referred to as 'Darby and Joan.' "

"Yes," said the girl, "that is true. Mr. Longcord gave them that name the second evening after our arrival. It was considered clever—but rather obvious, I thought myself."

"Nothing, so it seems to me," said the stranger, "is more beautiful than the love that has weathered the storms of life. The sweet, tender blossom that flowers in the heart of the young—in hearts such as yours—that, too, is beautiful. The love of the young for the young, that is the beginning of life. But the love of the old for the old, that is the beginning of—of things longer."

"You seem to find all things beautiful," the girl grumbled.

"But are not all things beautiful?" demanded the stranger.

The Colonel had finished his paper. "You two are engaged in a very absorbing conversation," observed the Colonel, approaching them.

"We were discussing Darbies and Joans," explained his daughter. "How beautiful is the love that has weathered the storms of life!"

"Ah!" smiled the Colonel, "that is hardly fair. My friend has been repeating to cynical youth the confessions of an amorous husband's affection for his middle-aged and somewhat——" The Colonel in playful mood laid his hand upon the stranger's shoulder, an action that necessitated his looking straight into the stranger's eyes. The Colonel drew himself up stiffly and turned scarlet.

Somebody was calling the Colonel a cad. Not only that, but was explaining quite clearly, so that the Colonel could see it for himself, why he was a cad.

"That you and your wife lead a cat-and-dog existence is a disgrace to both of you. At least, you might have the decency to try to hide it from the world, not make a jest of your shame to every passing stranger. You are a cad, sir: a cad!"

Who was daring to say these things? Not the stranger: his lips had not moved. Besides, it was not his voice. Indeed, it sounded much more like the voice of the Colonel himself. The Colonel looked from the stranger to his daughter, from his daughter back to the stranger. Clearly, they had not heard the voice—a mere hallucination. The Colonel breathed again.

Yet the impression remaining was not to be

shaken off. Undoubtedly it was bad taste to have joked to the stranger upon such a subject. No gentleman would have done so.

But, then, no gentleman would have permitted such a jest to be possible. No gentleman would be forever wrangling with his wife—certainly never in public. However irritating the woman, a gentleman would have exercised self-control.

Mrs. Devine had risen, was coming slowly across the room. Fear laid hold of the Colonel. She was going to address some exasperating remark to him—he could see it in her eye—which would irritate him into savage retort. Even this prize idiot of a stranger would understand why boarding-house wits had dubbed them "Darby and Joan," would grasp the fact that the gallant Colonel had thought it amusing, in conversation with a table acquaintance, to hold his own wife up to ridicule.

"My dear," cried the Colonel, hurrying to speak first, "does not this room strike you as cold? Let me fetch you a shawl."

It was useless: the Colonel felt it. It had been too long the custom of both of them to preface with politeness their deadliest insults to each other. She came on, thinking of a suitable reply: suitable from her point of view, that is. In another moment the truth would be out. A wild, fantastic possibility flashed through the Colonel's brain. If to him, why not to her?

"Letitia," cried the Colonel—and the tone of his voice surprised her into silence—"I want you to look closely at our friend. Does he not remind you of some one? Look hard."

Mrs. Devine, so urged, looked at the stranger long and hard. "Yes," she murmured, turning to her husband, "he does. Who is it?"

"I cannot fix it," replied the Colonel. "I thought that maybe you would remember."

"It will come to me," mused Mrs. Devine. "It is some one—years ago, when I was a girl—in Devonshire. Thank you, if it isn't troubling you, Harry. I left it in the dining-room."

It was, as Mr. Augustus Longcord explained to his partner Isidore, the colossal foolishness of the stranger that was the cause of all the trouble. "Give me a man who can take care of himself— or thinks he can," declared Augustus Longcord, "and I am prepared to give a good account of myself. But when a helpless baby refuses even to look at what you call your figures, tells you that your mere word is sufficient for him, and hands you over his check-book to fill up for yourself— well, it isn't playing the game."

"Auguthuth," was the curt comment of his partner, "you're a fool."

"All right, my boy, you try," suggested Augustus.

"Jutht what I mean to do," asserted his partner.

"Well," demanded Augustus, one evening later, meeting Isidore ascending the stairs after a long talk with the stranger in the dining-room with the door shut.

"Oh, don't arth me," retorted Isidore; "thilly ath, thath what he ith."

"What did he say?"

"What did he thay! Talked about the Jewth: what a grand rathe they were—how people mithjudged them: all that thort of rot. Thaid thome of the motht honorable men he had ever met had been Jewth. Thought I wath one of 'em!"

"Well, did you get anything out of him?"

"Get anything out of him! Of courthe not. Couldn't very well thell the whole rathe, ath it were, for a couple of hundred poundth, after that. Didn't theem worth it."

There were many things Bloomsbury Square came gradually to the conclusion were not worth the doing—snatching at the gravy, pouncing out of one's turn upon the vegetables and helping one's self to more than one's fair share; manœuvring for the easy chair; sitting on the evening paper, while pretending not to have seen it—all suchlike tiresome bits of business. For the little one made out of it, really, it was not worth the bother. Grumbling everlastingly at one's food; grumbling everlastingly at most things; abusing Pennycherry behind her back; abusing, for a change, one's fellow-boarders; squabbling with one's fellow-boarders about nothing in particular; sneering at one's fellow-boarders; talking scandal of one's fellow-boarders; making senseless jokes about one's fellow-boarders; talking big about one's self, nobody believing one—all suchlike vulgarities. Other boarding-houses might indulge in them; forty-eight Bloomsbury Square had its dignity to consider.

The truth is, forty-eight Bloomsbury Square was coming to a very good opinion of itself; for the which not Bloomsbury Square so much as the stranger must be blamed. The stranger had arrived at forty-eight Bloomsbury Square with the preconceived idea—where obtained from Heaven knows—that its seemingly commonplace, meanminded, coarse-fibred occupants were in reality ladies and gentlemen of the first water; and time and observation had apparently only strengthened this absurd idea. The natural result was, forty-eight Bloomsbury Square was coming round to the stranger's opinion of itself.

Mrs. Pennycherry the stranger would persist in regarding as a lady born and bred, compelled by circumstances over which she had no control to fill an arduous but honorable position in middle-class society—a sort of foster mother, to whom was due the thanks and gratitude of her promiscuous family; and this view of herself Mrs. Pennycherry now clung to with obstinate conviction. There were disadvantages attaching, but these Mrs. Pennycherry appeared prepared to suffer cheerfully. A lady born and bred cannot charge other ladies and gentlemen for coals and candles they have never burned; a foster mother cannot palm off upon her children New Zealand mutton for Southdown. A mere lodging-house keeper can play these tricks and pocket the profits. But a lady feels she cannot: Mrs. Pennycherry felt she could not.

To the stranger Miss Kite was a witty and delightful conversationalist of most attractive personality. Miss Kite had one failing: it was lack of vanity. She was unaware of her own delicate and refined beauty. If Miss Kite could only see herself with his, the stranger's, eyes, the modesty that rendered her distrustful of her natural charms would fall from her. The stranger was so sure of it Miss Kite determined to put it to the test. One evening, an hour before dinner, there entered the drawing-room, when the stranger only was there, and before the gas was lighted, a pleasant, good-looking lady, somewhat pale, with neatly-arranged brown hair, who demanded of the stranger if he knew her. All her body was trembling, and her voice seemed inclined to run away from her and become a sob. But when the stranger, looking straight into her eyes, told her that from the likeness he thought she must be Miss Kite's younger sister, but much prettier, it became a laugh instead; and that evening the golden-haired Miss Kite disappeared, never to show her highly-colored face again; and what, perhaps, more than all else, might have impressed some former habitué of forty-eight Bloomsbury Square with awe was that no one in the house made even a passing inquiry concerning her.

Sir William's cousin the stranger thought an acquisition to any boarding-house. A lady of high-class family, there was nothing outward or visible, perhaps, to tell you that she was of high-class family. She herself, naturally, would not mention the fact; yet somehow you felt it. Unconsciously, she set a high-class tone, diffused an atmosphere of gentle manners. Not that the stranger had said this in so many words: Sir William's cousin gathered that he thought it, and felt herself in agreement with him.

For Mr. Longcord and his partner, as representatives of the best type of business men, the stranger had a great respect: with what unfortunate results to themselves has been noted. The curious thing is that the firm appeared content with the price they had paid for the stranger's good opinion—had even, it was rumored, acquired a taste for honest men's respect that in the long run was likely to cost them dear. But we all have our pet extravagances.

The Colonel and Mrs. Devine both suffered a good deal at first from the necessity imposed upon them of learning, somewhat late in life, new tricks. In the privacy of their own apartment they condoled with one another.

"Tomfool nonsense," grumbled the Colonel, "you and I starting billing and cooing at our age!"

"What I object to," said Mrs. Devine, "is the feeling that somehow I am being made to do it."

"The idea that a man and his wife cannot have their little joke together for fear of what some impertinent jackanapes may think of them; it's ridiculous!" the Colonel exploded.

"Even when he isn't there," said Mrs. Devine, "I seem to see him looking at me with those vexing eyes of his. Really, the man quite haunts me."

"I have met him somewhere," mused the Colonel; "I'll swear I've met him somewhere. I wish to goodness he would go."

A hundred things a day the Colonel wanted to say to Mrs. Devine, a hundred things a day Mrs. Devine would have liked to observe to the Colonel. But by the time the opportunity occurred—when nobody else was by to hear—all interest in saying them was gone.

"Women will be women," was the sentiment with which the Colonel consoled himself. "A man must bear with them—must never forget that he is a gentleman."

"Oh, well, I suppose they're all alike," laughed Mrs. Devine to herself, having arrived at that stage of despair when one seeks refuge in cheerfulness. "What's the use of putting one's self out—it does no good, and only upsets one."

There is a certain satisfaction in feeling you are bearing with heroic resignation the irritating follies of others. Colonel and Mrs. Devine came to enjoy the luxury of much self-approbation.

But the person seriously annoyed by the stranger's bigoted belief in the innate goodness of every one he came across was the languid, handsome Miss Devine. The stranger would have it that Miss Devine was a double-souled, high-minded young woman, something midway between a Flora Macdonald and a Joan of Arc. Miss Devine, on the contrary, knew herself to be a sleek, luxury-loving animal, quite willing to sell herself to the bidder who could offer her the finest clothes, the richest foods, the most sumptuous surroundings. Such a bidder was at hand in the person of a retired bookmaker, a somewhat greasy old gentleman, but exceedingly rich and undoubtedly fond.

Miss Devine, having made up her mind that the thing had got to be done, was anxious that it should be done quickly. And here it was that the stranger's ridiculous opinion of her not only irritated but inconvenienced her. Under the very eyes of a person—however foolish—convinced you are possessed of all the highest attributes of your sex it is difficult to behave as though actuated by only the basest motives. A dozen times had Miss Devine determined to end the matter by formal acceptance of her elderly admirer's large and flabby hand; and a dozen times—the vision intervening of the stranger's grave, believing eyes —had Miss Devine refused a decided answer. The stranger would one day depart. Indeed, he had said himself, he was but a passing traveler. When he was gone it would be easier. So she thought at the time.

One afternoon the stranger entered the room where she was standing by the window, looking out upon the bare branches of the trees in Bloomsbury Square. She remembered afterward it was just such another foggy afternoon as the afternoon of the stranger's arrival three months before. No one else was in the room. The stranger closed the door and came toward her with that curious, quick, leaping step of his. His long coat was tightly buttoned, and in his hands he carried his old felt hat, and the massive, knotted stick that was almost a staff.

"I have come to say good-by," explained the stranger; "I am going."

"I shall not see you again?" asked the girl.

"I cannot say," replied the stranger. "But you will think of me?"

"Yes," she answered with a smile, "I can promise that."

"And I shall always remember you," promised the stranger, "and I wish you every joy—the joy of love, the joy of a happy marriage."

The girl winced. "Love and marriage are not always the same thing," she said.

"Not always," agreed the stranger; "but in your case they will be one."

She looked at him.

"Do you think I have not noticed?" smiled the stranger, "a gallant, handsome lad, and clever. You love him and he loves you. I could not have gone away without knowing it was well with you."

Her gaze wandered toward the fading light.

"Ah, yes, I love him," she answered petulantly. "Your eyes can see clearly enough when they want to. But one does not live on love in our world. I will tell you the man I am going to marry if you care to know." She would not meet his eyes. She kept her gaze still fixed upon the dingy trees, the mist beyond, and spoke rapidly and vehemently: "The man who can give me all my soul's desire—money and the things that money can buy. You think me a woman. I'm only a pig. He is moist, and breathes like a porpoise; with cunning in place of a brain, and the rest of him mere stomach. But he is good enough for me."

She hoped this would shock the stranger, and that now, perhaps, he would go. It irritated her to hear him only laugh.

"No," he said, "you will not marry him."

"Who will stop me?" she cried angrily.

"Your better self."

His voice had a strange ring of authority, compelling her to turn and look upon his face. Yes, it was true, the fancy that from the very first had haunted her. She had met him, talked to him— in silent country roads, in crowded city streets: where was it? And always in talking with him her spirit had been lifted up: she had been—what he had always thought her.

"There are those," continued the stranger— and for the first time she saw that he was of a noble presence, that his gentle, childlike eyes could also command—"whose better selves lie slain by their own hand and trouble them no more. But yours, my child, you have let grow too strong; it will ever be your master. You must obey. Flee from it and it will follow you: you cannot escape it. Insult it and it will chastise you with burning shame, with stinging self-reproach, from day to day." The sternness faded from the beautiful face, the tenderness crept back. He laid his hand upon the young girl's shoulder. "You will marry your lover," he smiled. "With him you will walk the way of sunlight and of shadow."

And the girl, looking up into the strong, calm face, knew that it would be so—that the power of resisting her better self had passed away from her forever.

"Now," said the stranger, "come to the door with me. Leave-takings are but wasted sadness. Let me pass out quietly. Close the door softly behind me."

She thought that perhaps he would turn his face again, but she saw no more of him than the odd roundness of his back under the tightly-buttoned coat before he faded into the gathering fog. Then softly she closed the door.

THE RANSOM OF RED CHIEF

by O. Henry

THE PEN NAME O. Henry concealed a personal story as romantic as anything that ever appeared in magazine fiction. The real name of this author was William Sidney Porter; he was born in North Carolina and went to Texas to work as a cowboy and bank cashier in Austin, where he eloped with a seventeen-year-old girl and then moved on to Houston to become a successful newspaper columnist. In 1897 a shortage was discovered in his Austin bank accounts and he was ordered to come back and explain. The shortage was small and the bank had been loosely managed; it is quite likely he would have been cleared if he had gone back and faced the music. But instead he fled like a guilty man to Honduras, where he lived with refugee American outlaws and let them pay some of his expenses. His wife's fatal illness brought him back to the States, and in 1898 he was sentenced to five years in the Federal penitentiary at Columbus, Ohio. As soon as he was released on parole he went to New York and immediately found himself as a short-story writer. In 1904 he sold sixty-five stories to various magazines; the next year he sold fifty. "The Ransom of Red Chief" was his only *Post* story, but that was not the *Post*'s fault. Lorimer wanted him to write more and advanced him payment for at least two. Soon afterward O. Henry turned up, pleading that he was in dire financial straits and that *Cosmopolitan* had offered him more than the *Post* for his next stories, which were still unwritten. Lorimer let him go and *Cosmopolitan* paid off the *Post*. But O. Henry never wrote a more delightful story than this one.

JULY 6, 1907

IT LOOKED like a good thing: but wait till I tell you. We were down South, in Alabama —Bill Driscoll and myself—when this kidnaping idea struck us. It was, as Bill afterward expressed it, "during a moment of temporary mental apparition"; but we didn't find that out till later.

There was a town down there, as flat as a flannel-cake, and called Summit, of course. It contained inhabitants of as undeleterious and self-satisfied a class of peasantry as ever clustered around a Maypole.

Bill and me had a joint capital of about six hundred dollars, and we needed just two thousand dollars more to pull off a fraudulent townlot scheme in Western Illinois with. We talked it over on the front steps of the hotel. Philoprogenitiveness, says we, is strong in semi-rural communities; therefore, and for other reasons, a kidnaping project ought to do better there than in the radius of newspapers that send reporters out in plain clothes to stir up talk about such things. We knew that Summit couldn't get after us with anything stronger than constables and, maybe, some lackadaisical bloodhounds and a diatribe or two in the Weekly Farmers' Budget. So, it looked good.

We selected for our victim the only child of a prominent citizen named Ebenezer Dorset. The father was respectable and tight, a mortgage fancier and a stern, upright collection-plate passer and forecloser. The kid was a boy of ten, with bas-relief freckles, and hair the color of the cover of the magazine you buy at the news-stand when you want to catch a train. Bill and me figured that Ebenezer would melt down for a ransom of two thousand dollars to a cent. But wait till I tell you.

About two miles from Summit was a little mountain, covered with a dense cedar brake. On the rear elevation of this mountain was a cave. There we stored provisions.

One evening after sundown, we drove in a buggy past old Dorset's house. The kid was in the street, throwing rocks at a kitten on the opposite fence.

"Hey, little boy!" says Bill, "would you like to have a bag of candy and a nice ride?"

The boy catches Bill neatly in the eye with a piece of brick.

"That will cost the old man an extra five hundred dollars," says Bill, climbing over the wheel.

That boy put up a fight like a welter-weight cinnamon bear; but, at last, we got him down in the bottom of the buggy and drove away. We took him up to the cave, and I hitched the horse in the cedar brake. After dark I drove the buggy to the little village, three miles away, where we had hired it, and walked back to the mountain.

Bill was pasting court-plaster over the scratches and bruises on his features. There was a fire burning behind the big rock at the entrance of the cave, and the boy was watching a pot of boiling coffee, with two buzzard tail-feathers stuck in his red hair. He points a stick at me when I come up, and says:

"Ha! cursed paleface, do you dare to enter the camp of Red Chief, the terror of the plains?"

"He's all right now," says Bill, rolling up his trousers and examining some bruises on his shins. "We're playing Indian. We're making Buffalo Bill's show look like magic-lantern views of Palestine in the town hall. I'm Old Hank, the Trapper, Red Chief's captive, and I'm to be scalped at daybreak. By Geronimo! that kid can kick hard."

Yes, sir, that boy seemed to be having the time of his life. The fun of camping out in a cave had made him forget that he was a captive himself. He immediately christened me Snake-eye, the Spy, and announced that, when his braves returned from the warpath, I was to be broiled at the stake at the rising of the sun.

Then we had supper; and he filled his mouth full of bacon and bread and gravy, and began to talk. He made a during-dinner speech something like this:

"I like this fine. I never camped out before; but I had a pet 'possum once, and I was nine last birthday. I hate to go to school. Rats ate up sixteen of Jimmy Talbot's aunt's speckled hen's eggs. Are there any real Indians in these woods? I want some more gravy. Does the trees moving make the wind blow? We had five puppies. What makes your nose so red, Hank? My father has lots of money. Are the stars hot? I whipped Ed Walker twice, Saturday. I don't like girls. You dassent catch toads unless with a string. Do oxen make any noise? Why are oranges round? Have you got beds to sleep on in this cave? Amos Murray has got six toes. A parrot can talk, but a monkey or a fish can't. How many does it take to make twelve?"

Every few minutes he would remember that he was a pesky redskin, and pick up his stick rifle and tiptoe to the mouth of the cave to rubber for the scouts of the hated paleface. Now and then he would let out a war-whoop that made Old Hank, the Trapper, shiver. That boy had Bill terrorized from the start.

"Red Chief," says I to the kid, "would you like to go home?"

"Aw, what for?" says he. "I don't have any fun at home. I hate to go to school. I like to camp out. You won't take me back home again, Snake-eye, will you?"

"Not right away," says I. "We'll stay here in the cave a while."

"All right!" says he. "That'll be fine. I never had such fun in all my life."

We went to bed about eleven o'clock. We spread down some wide blankets and quilts and put Red Chief between us. We weren't afraid he'd run away. He kept us awake for three hours, jumping up and reaching for his rifle and screeching: "Hist! pard," in mine and Bill's ears, as the fancied crackle of a twig or the rustle of a leaf revealed to his young imagination the stealthy approach of the outlaw band. At last, I fell into a troubled sleep, and dreamed that I had been kidnaped and chained to a tree by a ferocious pirate with red hair.

Just at daybreak, I was awakened by a series of awful screams from Bill. They weren't yells, or howls, or shouts, or whoops, or yawps, such as you'd expect from a manly set of vocal organs— they were simply indecent, terrifying, humiliating screams, such as women emit when they see ghosts or caterpillars. It's an awful thing to hear a strong, desperate, fat man scream incontinently in a cave at daybreak.

I jumped up to see what the matter was. Red Chief was sitting on Bill's chest, with one hand twined in Bill's hair. In the other he had the sharp case-knife we used for slicing bacon; and he was industriously and realistically trying to take Bill's scalp, according to the sentence that had been pronounced upon him the evening before.

I got the knife away from the kid and made him lie down again. But, from that moment, Bill's spirit was broken. He laid down on his side of the bed, but he never closed an eye again in sleep as long as that boy was with us. I dozed off for a while, but along toward sun-up I remembered that Red Chief had said I was to be burned at the stake at the rising of the sun. I wasn't nervous or afraid; but I sat up and lit my pipe and leaned against a rock.

"What you getting up so soon for, Sam?" asked Bill.

"Me?" says I. "Oh, I got a kind of a pain in my shoulder. I thought sitting up would rest it."

"You're a liar!" says Bill. "You're afraid. You was to be burned at sunrise, and you was afraid he'd do it. And he would, too, if he could find a match. Ain't it awful, Sam? Do you think anybody will pay out money to get a little imp like that back home?"

"Sure," said I. "A rowdy kid like that is just the kind that parents dote on. Now, you and the Chief get up and cook breakfast, while I go up on the top of this mountain and reconnoitre."

I went up on the peak of the little mountain and ran my eye over the contiguous vicinity. Over toward Summit I expected to see the sturdy yeomanry of the village armed with scythes and pitchforks beating the countryside for the dastardly kidnapers. But what I saw was a peaceful landscape dotted with one man plowing with a dun mule. Nobody was dragging the creek; no couriers dashed hither and yon, bringing tidings of no news to the distracted parents. There was a sylvan attitude of somnolent sleepiness pervading that section of the external outward surface of Alabama that lay exposed to my view. "Perhaps," says I to myself, "it has not yet been discovered that the wolves have borne away the tender lambkin from the fold. Heaven help the wolves!" says I, and I went down the mountain to breakfast.

When I got to the cave I found Bill backed up against the side of it, breathing hard, and the boy threatening to smash him with a rock half as big as a cocoanut.

"He put a red-hot boiled potato down my back," explained Bill, "and then mashed it with his foot; and I boxed his ears. Have you got a gun about you, Sam?"

I took the rock away from the boy and kind of patched up the argument. "I'll fix you," says the kid to Bill. "No man ever yet struck the Red Chief but what he got paid for it. You better beware!"

After breakfast the kid takes a piece of leather with strings wrapped around it out of his pocket and goes outside the cave unwinding it.

"What's he up to now?" says Bill, anxiously. "You don't think he'll run away, do you, Sam?"

"No fear of it," says I. "He don't seem to be much of a home body. But we've got to fix up some plan about the ransom. There don't seem to be much excitement around Summit on account of his disappearance; but maybe they haven't realized yet that he's gone. His folks may think he's spending the night with Aunt Jane or one of the neighbors. Anyhow, he'll be missed to-day. To-night we must get a message to his father demanding the two thousand dollars for his return."

Just then we heard a kind of war-whoop, such as David might have emitted when he knocked out the champion Goliath. It was a sling that Red Chief had pulled out of his pocket, and he was whirling it around his head.

I dodged, and heard a heavy thud and a kind of a sigh from Bill, like a horse gives out when you take his saddle off. A niggerhead rock the size of an egg had caught Bill just behind his left ear. He loosened himself all over and fell in the fire across the frying-pan of hot water for washing the dishes. I dragged him out and poured cold water on his head for half an hour.

By and by, Bill sits up and feels behind his ear and says: "Sam, do you know who my favorite Biblical character is?"

"Take it easy," says I. "You'll come to your senses presently."

"King Herod," says he. "You won't go away and leave me here alone, will you, Sam?"

I went out and caught that boy and shook him until his freckles rattled.

"If you don't behave," says I, "I'll take you straight home. Now, are you going to be good, or not?"

"I was only funning," says he sullenly. "I didn't mean to hurt Old Hank. But what did he hit me for? I'll behave, Snake-eye, if you won't send me home, and if you'll let me play the Black Scout to-day."

"I don't know the game," says I. "That's for you and Mr. Bill to decide. He's your playmate for the day. I'm going away for a while, on business. Now, you come in and make friends with him and say you are sorry for hurting him, or home you go, at once."

I made him and Bill shake hands, and then I took Bill aside and told him I was going to Poplar Cove, a little village three miles from the cave, and find out what I could about how the kidnapping had been regarded in Summit. Also, I thought it best to send a peremptory letter to old man Dorset that day, demanding the ransom and dictating how it should be paid.

"You know, Sam," says Bill, "I've stood by you without batting an eye in earthquakes, fire and flood—in poker games, dynamite outrages, police raids, train robberies and cyclones. I never lost my nerve yet till we kidnaped that two-legged skyrocket of a kid. He's got me going. You won't leave me long with him, will you, Sam?"

"I'll be back some time this afternoon," says I. "You must keep the boy amused and quiet till I return. And now we'll write the letter to old Dorset."

Bill and I got paper and pencil and worked on the letter while Red Chief, with a blanket wrapped around him, strutted up and down, guarding the mouth of the cave. Bill begged me tearfully to make the ransom fifteen hundred dollars instead of two thousand. "I ain't attempting," says he, "to decry the celebrated moral aspect of parental affection, but we're dealing with humans, and it ain't human for anybody to give up two thousand dollars for that forty-pound chunk of freckled wildcat. I'm willing to take a chance at fifteen hundred dollars. You can charge the difference up to me."

So, to relieve Bill, I acceded, and we collaborated a letter that ran this way:

Ebenezer Dorset, Esq.:

We have your boy concealed in a place far from Summit. It is useless for you or the most skillful detectives to attempt to find him. Absolutely, the only terms on which you can have him restored to you are these: We demand fifteen hundred dollars in large bills for his return; the money to be left at midnight to-night at the same spot and in the same box as your reply—as hereinafter described. If you agree to these terms, send your answer in writing by a solitary messenger to-night at half-past eight o'clock. After crossing Owl Creek, on the road to Poplar Cove, there are three large trees about a hundred yards apart, close to the fence of the wheat field on the right-hand side. At the bottom of the fence-post, opposite the third tree, will be found a small pasteboard box.

The messenger will place the answer in this box and return immediately to Summit.

If you attempt any treachery or fail to comply with our demand as stated, you will never see your boy again.

If you pay the money as demanded, he will be returned to you safe and well within three hours. These terms are final, and if you do not accede to them no further communication will be attempted.

TWO DESPERATE MEN.

I addressed this letter to Dorset, and put it in my pocket. As I was about to start, the kid comes up to me and says: "Aw, Snake-eye, you said I could play the Black Scout while you was gone."

"Play it, of course," says I. "Mr. Bill will play with you. What kind of a game is it?"

"I'm the Black Scout," says Red Chief, "and I have to ride to the stockade to warn the settlers that the Indians are coming. I'm tired of playing Indian myself. I want to be the Black Scout."

"All right," says I. "It sounds harmless to me. I guess Mr. Bill will help you foil the pesky savages."

"What am I to do?" asks Bill, looking at the kid, suspicious.

"You are the hoss," says the Black Scout. "Get down on your hands and knees. How can I ride to the stockade without a hoss?"

"You'd better keep him interested," said I, "till we get the scheme going. Loosen up."

Bill gets down on his all fours, and a look comes in his eye like a rabbit's when you catch it in a trap.

"How far is it to the stockade, kid?" he asks, in a husky manner of voice.

"Ninety miles," says the Black Scout. "And you have to hump yourself to get there on time. Whoa, now!"

The Black Scout jumps on Bill's back and digs his heels in his side.

"For Heaven's sake," says Bill, "hurry back, Sam, as soon as you can. I wish we hadn't made the ransom more than a thousand. Say, you quit kicking me or I'll get up and warm you good."

I walked over to Poplar Cove and sat around the postoffice and store, talking with the chaw-bacons that came in to trade. One whiskerando says that he hears Summit is all upset on account of Elder Ebenezer Dorset's boy having been lost or stolen. That was all I wanted to know. I bought some smoking tobacco, referred casually to the price of black-eyed peas, posted my letter surreptitiously, and came away. The postmaster said the mail-carrier would come by in an hour to take the mail on to Summit.

When I got back to the cave Bill and the boy were not to be found. I explored the vicinity of the cave, and risked a yodel or two, but there was no response.

So I lighted my pipe and sat down on a mossy bank to await developments.

In about half an hour I heard the bushes rustle, and Bill wabbled out into the little glade in front of the cave. Behind him was the kid, stepping softly like a scout, with a broad grin on his face. Bill stopped, took off his hat and wiped his face with a red handkerchief. The kid stopped about eight feet behind him.

"Sam," says Bill, "I suppose you'll think I'm a renegade, but I couldn't help it. I'm a grown person with masculine proclivities and habits of self-defense, but there is a time when all systems of egotism and predominance fail. The boy is gone. I have sent him home. All is off. There was martyrs in old times," goes on Bill, "that suffered death rather than give up the particular graft they enjoyed. None of 'em ever was subjugated to such supernatural tortures as I have been. I tried to be faithful to our articles of depredation; but there came a limit."

"What's the trouble, Bill?" I asks him.

"I was rode," says Bill, "the ninety miles to the stockade, not barring an inch. Then, when the settlers was rescued, I was given oats. Sand ain't a palatable substitute. And then, for an hour I had to try to explain to him why there was nothin' in holes, how a road can run both ways and what makes the grass green. I tell you, Sam, a human can only stand so much. I takes him by the neck of his clothes and drags him down the mountain. On the way he kicks my legs black-and-blue from the knees down; and I've got to have two or three bites on my thumb and hand cauterized.

"But he's gone"—continues Bill—"gone home. I showed him the road to Summit and kicked him about eight feet nearer there at one kick. I'm sorry we lose the ransom; but it was either that or Bill Driscoll to the madhouse."

Bill is puffing and blowing, but there is a look of ineffable peace and growing content on his rose-pink features.

"Bill," says I, "there isn't any heart disease in your family, is there?"

"No," says Bill, "nothing chronic except malaria and accidents. Why?"

"Then you might turn around," says I, "and have a look behind you."

Bill turns and sees the boy, and loses his complexion and sits down plump on the ground and begins to pluck aimlessly at grass and little sticks. For an hour I was afraid for his mind. And then I told him that my scheme was to put the whole job through immediately and that we would get the ransom and be off with it by midnight if old Dorset fell in with our proposition. So Bill braced up enough to give the kid a weak sort of a smile and a promise to play the Russian in a Japanese war with him as soon as he felt a little better.

I had a scheme for collecting that ransom without danger of being caught by counterplots that ought to commend itself to professional kidnapers. The tree under which the answer was to be left—and the money later on—was close to the road fence with big, bare fields on all sides. If a gang of constables should be watching for any one to come for the note they could see him a long way off crossing the fields or in the road. But, no, sirree! At half-past eight I was up in that tree, as well hidden as a tree toad, waiting for the messenger to arrive.

Exactly on time, a half-grown boy rides up the road on a bicycle, locates the pasteboard box at the foot of the fence-post, slips a folded piece of paper into it and pedals away again back toward Summit.

I waited an hour and then concluded the thing was square. I slid down the tree, got the note, slipped along the fence till I struck the woods, and was back at the cave in another half an hour. I opened the note, got near the lantern and read it to Bill. It was written with a pen in a crabbed hand, and the sum and substance of it was this:

Two Desperate Men.

Gentlemen: I received your letter to-day by post, in regard to the ransom you ask for the return of my son. I think you are a little high in your demands, and I hereby make you a counter-proposition, which I am inclined to believe you will accept. You bring Johnny home and pay me two hundred and fifty dollars in cash, and I agree to take him off your hands. You had better come at night, for the neighbors believe he is lost, and I couldn't be responsible for what they would do to anybody they saw bringing him back. Very respectfully,

EBENEZER DORSET.

"Great pirates of Penzance!" says I; "of all the impudent ——"

But I glanced at Bill, and hesitated. He had the most appealing look in his eyes I ever saw on the face of a dumb or a talking brute.

"Sam," says he, "what's two hundred and fifty dollars, after all? We've got the money. One more night of this kid will send me to a bed in Bedlam. Besides being a thorough gentleman, I think Mr. Dorset is a spendthrift for making us such a liberal offer. You ain't going to let the chance go, are you?"

"Tell you the truth, Bill," says I, "this little he ewe lamb has somewhat got on my nerves, too. We'll take him home, pay the ransom and make our get-away."

We took him home that night. We got him to go by telling him that his father had bought a silver-mounted rifle and a pair of moccasins for him, and we were going to hunt bears the next day.

It was just twelve o'clock when we knocked at Ebenezer's front door. Just at the moment when I should have been abstracting the fifteen hundred dollars from the box under the tree, according to the original proposition, Bill was counting out two hundred and fifty dollars into Dorset's hand.

When the kid found out we were going to

leave him at home he started up a howl like a calliope and fastened himself as tight as a leech to Bill's leg. His father peeled him away gradually, like a porous plaster.

"How long can you hold him?" asks Bill.

"I am not as strong as I used to be," says old Dorset, "but I think I can promise you ten minutes."

"Enough," says Bill. "In ten minutes I shall cross the Central, Southern and Middle Western States, and be legging it trippingly for the Canadian border."

And, as dark as it was, and as fat as Bill was, and as good a runner as I am, he was a good mile and a half out of Summit before I could catch up with him.

THE GREAT PANCAKE RECORD

by Owen Johnson

THE *Post*'s FAMOUS Lawrenceville stories began with this saga of Hungry Smeed and ran through the years 1907 to 1910. Their author was an old Lawrenceville boy who founded and edited the Lawrenceville *Literary Magazine* and was graduated from Yale in 1901. Ten years later he did a bit of campus muckraking in his novel, *Stover at Yale*. But his Lawrenceville tales of the Tennessee Shad, Turkey Reiter, the Varmint, the Gutter Pup and the rest were written in a sunnier spirit; to many readers they can never grow old. Owen Johnson continued to write stories and serials for the *Post* until 1934; he died January 27, 1952.

NOVEMBER 16, 1907

LITTLE SMEED STOOD APART, in the obscure shelter of the station, waiting to take his place on the stage which would carry him to the great new boarding-school. He was frail and undersized, with a long, pointed nose and vacant eyes that stupidly assisted the wide mouth to make up a famished face. The scarred bag in his hand hung from one clasp, the premature trousers were at half-mast, while pink polka-dots blazed from the cuffs of his nervous sleeves.

By the wheels of the stage "Fire Crackers" Glendenning and "Jock" Hasbrouck, veterans of the Kennedy House, sporting the varsity initials on their sweaters and caps, were busily engaged in cross-examining the new boys who clambered timidly to their places on top. Presently, Fire Crackers, perceiving Smeed, hailed him.

"Hello, over there—what's your name?"

"Smeed, sir."

"Smeed what?"

"Johnnie Smeed."

The questioner looked him over with disfavor and said aggressively:

"You're not for the Kennedy?"

"No, sir."

"What house?"

"The Dickinson, sir."

"The Dickinson, eh? That's a good one," said Fire Crackers with a laugh, and turning to his companion he added: "Say, Jock, won't the old Turkey be wild when he gets this one?"

Little Smeed, uncomprehending of the judgment that had been passed, stowed his bag inside and clambered up to a place on the top. Jimmy, at the reins, gave a warning shout. The horses, stirred by the whip, churned obediently through the sideways of Trenton.

Lounging on the stage were half a dozen new-comers, six well-assorted types, from the well-groomed stripling of the city to the aggressive, big-limbed animal from the West, all profoundly under the sway of the two old boys who sat on the box with Jimmy and rattled on with quiet superiority. The coach left the outskirts of the city and rolled into the white highway that leads to Lawrenceville. The known world departed for Smeed. He gazed fearfully ahead, waiting the first glimpse of the new continent.

Suddenly Fire Crackers turned and, scanning the embarrassed group, singled out the strong Westerner with an approving glance.

"You're for the Kennedy?"

The boy, stirring uneasily, blurted out:

"Yes, sir."

"What's your name?"

"Tom Walsh."

"How old are you?"

"Eighteen."

"What do you weigh?"

"One hundred and seventy."

"Stripped?"

"What? Oh, no, sir—regular way."

"You've played a good deal of football?"

"Yes, sir."

Hasbrouck took up the questioning with a critical appreciation.

"What position?"

"Guard and tackle."

"You know Bill Stevens?"

"Yes, sir."

"He spoke about you; said you played on the Military Academy. You'll try for the varsity?"

"I guess so."

Hasbrouck turned to Fire Crackers in solemn conclave.

"He ought to stand up against Turkey if he

knows anything about the game. If we get a good end we ought to give that Dickinson crowd the fight of their lives."

"There's a fellow came from Montclair they say is pretty good," Fire Crackers said, with solicitous gravity. "The line'll be all right if we can get some good halves. That's where the Dickinson has it on us."

Smeed listened in awe to the two statesmen studying out the chances of the Kennedy eleven for the house championship, realizing suddenly that there were strange and sacred purposes about his new life of which he had no conception. Then, absorbed by the fantasy of the trip and the strange unfolding world into which he was jogging, he forgot the lords of the Kennedy, forgot his fellows in ignorance, forgot that he didn't play football and was only a stripling, forgot everything but the fascination of awaiting the moment when the great school would rise out of the distance and fix itself indelibly in his memory.

"There's the water-tower," said Jimmy, extending the whip; "you'll see the school from the top of the hill."

Little Smeed craned forward with a sudden thumping of his heart. In the distance, a mile away, a cluster of brick and tile sprang out of the green, like a herd of red deer surprised in the forest. Groups of boys began to show on the roadside. Strange greetings were flung back and forth.

"Hello-oo, Fire Crackers!"

"How-de-do, Saphead!"

"Oh, there, Jock Hasbrouck!"

"Oh, you Morning Glory!"

"Oh, you Kennedys, we're going to lick you!"

"Yes you are, Dickinson!"

The coach passed down the shaded vault of the village street, turned into the campus, passed the ivy-clad house of the head master and rolled around a circle of well-trimmed lawn, past the long, low Upper House where the Fourth Form gazed at them in senior superiority; past the great brown masses of Memorial Hall and the pointed chapel, around to where the houses were ranged in red, extended bodies. Little Smeed felt an abject sinking of the heart at this sudden exposure to the thousand eyes fastened upon him from the wide esplanade of the Upper, from the steps of Memorial, from house, windows and stoops, from the shade of apple trees and along the road.

All at once the stage stopped and Jimmy cried: "Dickinson."

At one end of the red-brick building, overrun with cool vines, a group of boys were lolling in flannels and light jerseys. A chorus went up.

"Hello, Fire Crackers!"

"Hello, Jock!"

"Hello, you Hickey boy!"

"Hello, Turkey; see what we've brought you!"

Smeed dropped to the ground amid a sudden hush.

"Fare," said Jimmy aggressively.

Smeed dug into his pocket and tendered the necessary coin. The coach squeaked away, while from the top Fire Cracker's exulting voice returned in insolent exultation:

"Hard luck, Dickinson! Hard luck, you Turkey!"

Little Smeed, his hat askew, his collar rolled up, his bag at his feet, stood in the road, alone in the world, miserable and thoroughly frightened. One path led to the silent, hostile group on the steps, another went in safety to the master's entrance. He picked up his bag hastily.

"Hello, you—over there!"

Smeed understood it was a command. He turned submissively and approached with embarrassed steps. Face to face with these superior beings, tanned and muscular, stretched in Olympian attitudes, he realized all at once the hopelessness of his ever hoping to associate with such demi-gods. Still he stood, shifting from foot to foot, eying the steps, waiting for the solemn ordeal of examination and classification to be over.

"Well, Hungry—what's your name?"

Smeed comprehended that the future was decided, and that to the grave he would go down as "Hungry" Smeed. With a sigh of relief he answered:

"Smeed—John Smeed."

"Sir!"

"Sir."

"How old?"

"Fifteen."

"Sir!!"

"Sir."

"What do you weigh?"

"One hundred and six—sir!"

A grim silence succeeded this depressing information. Then some one in the back, as a mere matter of form, asked:

"Never played football?"

"No, sir."

"Baseball?"

"No, sir."

"Anything on the track?"

"No, sir."

"Sing?"

"No, sir," said Smeed humbly.

"Do anything at all?" his questioner asked.

Little Smeed glanced at the eaves where the swallows were swaying and then down at the soft couch of green at his feet and answered faintly:

"No, sir—I'm afraid not."

Another silence came, then some one said, in a voice of deepest conviction:

"A dead loss!"

Smeed went sadly into the house.

At the door he lingered long enough to hear the chorus burst out:

"A fine football team we'll have!"

"It's a put-up job!"

"They don't want us to win the championship again—that's it!"

"I say, we ought to kick."

Then, after a little, the same deep voice:

"A dead loss!"

II

WITH EACH SUCCEEDING WEEK "Hungry" Smeed comprehended more fully the enormity of his offense in doing nothing and weighing one hundred and six pounds. He saw the new boys arrive, pass through the fire of christening, give respectable weights and go forth to the gridiron to be whipped into shape by Turkey and the Butcher, who played on the school eleven. Smeed humbly and thankfully went down each afternoon to the practice, carrying the sweaters and shin-guards, like the grateful little beast of burden that he was. He watched his juniors, Spider and Red Dog, rolling in the mud or flung gloriously under an avalanche of bodies; but then, they weighed over one hundred and thirty, while he was still at one hundred and six—a dead loss! The fever of house loyalty invaded him; he even came to look with resentment on the Faculty and to repeat secretly to himself that they never would have unloaded him on the Dickinson if they hadn't been willing to stoop to any methods to prevent the House again securing the championship.

The fact that the Dickinson, in an extraordinary manner, finally won by the closest of margins, consoled Smeed but a little while. There were no more sweaters to carry, or pails of barley water to fetch, or guard to be mounted on the old rail-fence, to make certain that the spies from the Davis and Kennedy did not surprise the secret plays which Hickey and Slugger Jones had craftily evolved.

With the long winter months he felt more keenly his obscurity and the hopelessness of ever leaving a mark on the great desert of school life that would bring honor to the Dickinson. He resented even the lack of the mild hazing the other boys received—he was too insignificant to be so honored. He was only a "dead loss," good for nothing but to squeeze through his recitations, to sleep enormously, and to eat like a glutton with a hunger that could never be satisfied, little suspecting the future that lay in this famine of his stomach.

For it was written in the inscrutable fates that "Hungry" Smeed should leave a name that would go down imperishably to decades of schoolboys, when Dibbles' touchdown against Princeton and Kofer's home run should be only tinkling sounds. So it happened, and the agent of this divine destiny was Hickey.

The president of the House, by virtue of muscle and the necessary authority to suppress all insubordination, was Turkey Reiter, broad of shoulder, freckled and battling of face, but the spirit of the Dickinson was Hickey. Hickey it was, lank of figure and keen of feature, bustling of gait and drawling of speech, with face as innocent as a choir-boy's, who planned the revolts against the masters, organized the midnight feasts and the painting of water-towers. His genius lived in the nicknames of the Egghead, Beauty Sawtelle, Morning Glory, Red Dog, Wash Simmons and the Coffee Cooler, which he had bestowed on his comrades with unfailing felicity.

It so happened that, examinations being still in the threatening distance, Hickey's fertile brain was unoccupied with methods of facilitating his scholarly progress by homely inventions that allowed formulas and dates to be concealed in the palm and disappear obligingly up the sleeve on the approach of the Natural Enemy. Moreover, Hickey and Hickey's friends were in straitened circumstances, with all credit gone at the Jigger Shop, and the appetite for jiggers in an acute stage of deprivation.

In this keenly sensitive, famished state of his imagination, Hickey suddenly became aware of a fact fraught with possibilities. Hungry Smeed had an appetite distinguished and remarkable even in that company of aching voids.

No sooner had this pregnant idea become his property than Hickey confided his hopes to "Doc" Macnooder, his chum and partner in plans that were dark and mysterious. Macnooder saw in a flash the glorious and lucrative possibilities. A very short series of tests sufficed to convince the twain that in little Smeed they had a phenomenon who needed only to be properly launched to pass into history.

Accordingly, on a certain muddy morning in March, Hickey and Doc Macnooder, with Smeed in tow, stole into the Jigger Shop at an hour in defiance of regulations and fraught with delightful risks of detection.

Half drug-store, half confectioner's, the Jigger Shop was the property of Doctor Furnell, whose chief interest in life consisted in a devotion to the theory of the millennium, to the lengthy expounding of which an impoverished boy would sometimes listen in the vain hope of establishing a larger credit. On every-day occasions the shop was under the charge of "Al," a creature without heart or pity, who knew the exact financial status of each of the four hundred odd boys, even to the amount and date of his allowance. Al made no errors, his sympathies were deaf to the call, and he never (like the doctor) committed the mistake of returning too much change.

This watch-dog of the jigger was tilted back, near a farther window, the parted tow hair falling doglike over his eyes, absorbed in the reading of Spenser's Faerie Queene, an abnormal taste which made him absolutely incomprehensible to the boyish mind. At the sound of the stolen entrance, Al put down the volume and started mechanically to rise. Then, recognizing his visitors, he returned to his chair, saying wearily:

"Nothing doing, Hickey."

"Guess again," said Hickey cheerily. "We're not asking you to hang us up this time, Al."

"You haven't got any money," said Al, the recorder of allowances; "not unless you stole it."

"Al, we don't come to take your hard-earned money, but to do you good," put in Macnooder impudently. "We're bringing you a little sporting proposition."

"Have you come to pay up that account of yours?" said Al. "If not, run along, you Macnooder; don't waste my time with your wildcat schemes."

"Al, this is a sporting proposition," took up Hickey.

"Has *he* any money?" said Al, who suddenly remembered that Smeed was not yet under suspicion.

"See here, Al," said Macnooder, "we'll back Smeed to eat the jiggers against you—for the crowd!"

"Where's your money?"

"Here," said Hickey; "this goes up if we lose." He produced a gold watch of Smeed's, and was about to tender it when he withdrew it with a sudden caution. "On the condition, if we win I get it back and you won't hold it up against my account."

"All right. Let's see it."

The watch was given to Al, who looked it over, grunted in approval and then looked at little Smeed.

"Now, Al," said Macnooder softly, "give us a gambling chance; he's only a runt."

Al considered, and Al was wise. The proposition came often and he had never lost. A jigger is unlike any other ice cream; it is dipped from the creamy tin by a cone-shaped scoop called a jigger, which gives it an unusual and peculiar flavor. Since those days the original jigger has been contaminated and made ridiculous by offensive alliances with upstart syrups, meringues and macaroons with absurd titles; but then the boy went to the simple jigger as the sturdy Roman went to the cold waters of the Tiber. A double jigger fills a large soda-glass when ten cents has been laid on the counter, and two such glasses quench all desire in the normal appetite.

"If he can eat twelve double jiggers," Al said slowly, "I'll set them up and the jiggers for youse. Otherwise, I'll hold the watch."

At this there was a protest from the backers of the champion, with the result that the limit was reduced to ten.

"Is it a go?" Al said, turning to Smeed, who had waited modestly in the background.

"Sure," he answered with calm certainty.

"You've got nerve, you have," said Al with a scornful smile, scooping up the first jiggers and shoving the glass to him. "Ten doubles is the record in these parts, young fellow!"

Then little Smeed, methodically, and without apparent pain, ate the ten doubles.

III

CONOVER'S WAS NOT in the catalogue that anxious parents study, but then catalogues are like epitaphs in a cemetery. Next to the Jigger Shop, Conover's was quite the most important institution in the school. In a little white, Colonial cottage, Conover, veteran of the late war, and Mrs. Conover, still in active service, supplied pancakes and maple syrup on a cash basis, two dollars credit to second-year boys in good repute. Conover's, too, had its traditions. Twenty-six pancakes, large and thick, in one continuous sitting, was the record, five years old, standing to the credit of Guzzler Wilkins, which succeeding classes had attacked in vain. Wily Conover, to stimulate such profitable tests, had solemnly pledged himself to the delivery of free pancakes to all comers during that day on which any boy, at one continuous sitting, unaided, should succeed in swallowing the awful number of thirty-two. Conover was not considered a prodigal.

This deed of heroic accomplishment and public benefaction was the true goal of Hickey's planning. The test of the Jigger Shop was but a preliminary trying out. With medical caution, Doc Macnooder refused to permit Smeed to go beyond the ten doubles, holding very wisely that the jigger record could wait for a further day. The amazed Al was sworn to secrecy.

It was Wednesday, and the following Saturday was decided upon for the supreme test at Conover's. Smeed at once was subjected to a graduated system of starvation. Thursday he was hungry, but Friday he was so ravenous that a watch was instituted on all his movements.

The next morning the Dickinson House, let into the secret, accompanied Smeed to Conover's. If there was even a possibility of free pancakes, the House intended to be satisfied before the deluge broke. Great was the astonishment at Conover's at the arrival of the procession.

"Mr. Conover," said Hickey in the quality of manager, "we're going after that pancake record."

"Mr. Wilkins' record?" said Conover, seeking vainly the champion in the crowd.

"No—after that record of *yours,*" answered Hickey. "Thirty-two pancakes—we're here to get free pancakes to-day—that's what we're here for."

"So, boys, so," said Conover, smiling pleasantly; "and you want to begin now?"

"Right off the bat."

"Well, where is he?"

Little Smeed, famished to the point of tears, was thrust forward. Conover, who was expecting something on the lines of a buffalo, smiled confidently.

"So, boys, so," he said, leading the way with alacrity. "I guess we're ready too."

"Thirty-two pancakes, Conover—and we get 'em free!"

"That's right," answered Conover, secure in his knowledge of boyish capacity. "If that little boy there can eat thirty-two I'll make them all day free to the school. That's what I said, and what I say now."

Hickey and Doc Macnooder whispered the last instructions in Smeed's ear.

"Cut out the syrup."

"Loosen your belt."

"Eat slowly."

In a low room, with the white rafters impending over his head, beside a basement window flanked with geraniums, little Smeed sat down to battle for the honor of the Dickinson and the record of the school. Directly under his eyes, carved on the wooden table, a name challenged him, standing out of the numerous initials—Guzzler Wilkins.

"Turkey, you keep count," said Hickey. "Macnooder and I'll watch the pancakes."

"Regulation size, Conover," cried the cautious Red Dog; "no doubling now. All fair and aboveboard."

"All right, Hickey, all right," said Conover, leering wickedly from the door; "if that little grasshopper can do it, you'll get the cakes."

"Now, Hungry," said Turkey, clapping Smeed on the shoulder. "Here is where you get your chance. Remember it's for the Dickinson."

Smeed heard in ecstasy; it was just the way Turkey talked to the eleven on the eve of a match. He nodded his head with a grim little shake and smiled nervously at the twenty-odd Dickinsonians who formed around him a pit of expectant and hungry boyhood from the floor to the ceiling.

"All ready," sang out Hickey from the doorway.

"Six pancakes!"

"Six it is," replied Turkey, chalking up a monster 6 on the slate that swung from the rafters. The pancakes placed before the ravenous Smeed vanished like snowflakes on a July lawn.

A cheer went up, mingled with cries of caution.

"Not so fast."

"Take your time."

"Don't let them be too hot."

"Not too hot, Hickey."

Macnooder was instructed to watch carefully over the temperature as well as the dimensions.

"Ready again," came the cry.

"Ready—how many?"

"Six more."

"Six it is," said Turkey, adding a second figure to the score. "Six and six are twelve."

The second batch went the way of the first.

"Why, that boy is starving," said Conover, opening his eyes.

"Sure he is," said Hickey. "He's eating way back in last week—he hasn't had a thing for ten days."

"Six more," cried Macnooder.

"Six it is," answered Turkey. "Six and twelve is eighteen."

"Eat them one at a time, Hungry."

"No, let him alone."

"He knows best."

"Not too fast, Hungry, not too fast."

"Eighteen for Hungry, eighteen. Hurrah!"

"Thirty-two is a long ways to go," said Conover, gazing apprehensively at the little David who had come so impudently into his domain; "fourteen pancakes is a lot."

"Shut up, Conover."

"No trying to influence him there."

"Don't listen to him, Hungry."

"He's only trying to get you nervous."

"Fourteen more, Hungry—fourteen more."

"Ready again," sang out Macnooder.

"Ready here."

"Three pancakes."

"Three it is," responded Turkey. "Eighteen and three is twenty-one."

But a storm of protest arose.

"Here, that's not fair!"

"I say, Turkey, don't let them do that."

"I say, Hickey, it's twice as hard that way."

"Oh, go on."

"Sure it is."

"Of course it is."

"Don't you know that you can't drink a glass of beer if you take it with a teaspoon?"

"That's right, Red Dog; right! Six at a time."

"Six at a time!"

A hurried consultation was now held and the reasoning approved. Macnooder was charged with the responsibility of seeing to the number as well as the temperature and dimensions.

Meanwhile Smeed had eaten the pancakes.

"Coming again!"

"All ready here."

"Six pancakes!"

"Six," said Turkey; "twenty-one and six is twenty-seven."

"That'll beat Guzzler Wilkins."

"So it will."

"Five more makes thirty-two."

"Easy, Hungry, easy."

"Hungry's done it; he's done it."

"Twenty-seven and the record!"

"Hurrah!"

At this point Smeed looked about anxiously.

"It's pretty dry," he said, speaking for the first time.

Instantly there was a panic. Smeed was reaching his limit—a groan went up.

"Oh, Hungry."

"Only five more."

"Give him some water."

"Water, you loon; do you want to end him?"

"Why?"

"Water'll swell up the pancakes, crazy."

"No water, no water."

Hickey approached his man with anxiety.

"What is it, Hungry? Anything wrong?" he said tenderly.

"No, only it's a little dry," said Smeed unmoved. "I'm all right, but I'd like just a drop of syrup now."

The syrup was discussed, approved and voted.

"You're sure you're all right," said Hickey.

"Oh, yes."

Conover, in the last ditch, said carefully:

"I don't want no fits around here."

A cry of protest greeted him.

"Well, son, that boy can't stand much more.

That's just like the Guzzler. He was taken short and we had to work over him for an hour."

"Conover, shut up."

"Conover, you're beaten."

"Conover, that's an old game."

"Get out."

"Shut up."

"Fair play."

"Fair play! Fair play!"

A new interruption came from the kitchen. Macnooder claimed that Mrs. Conover was doubling the size of the cakes. The dish was brought. There was no doubt about it. The cakes were swollen. Pandemonium broke loose. Conover capitulated, the cakes were rejected.

"Don't be feezed by that," said Turkey warningly to Smeed.

"I'm not," said Smeed.

"All ready," came Macnooder's cry.

"Six pancakes!"

"Ready here."

"Regulation size?"

"Regulation."

"Six it is," said Turkey at the slate. "Six and twenty-seven is thirty-three."

"Wait a moment," sang out the Butcher. "He has only to eat thirty-two."

"That's so—take one off."

"Give him five, Hickey—five only."

"If Hungry says he can eat six," said Hickey firmly, "he can. We're out for big things. Can you do it, Hungry?"

"Of course."

A cheer that brought two Davis House boys running in greeted the disappearance of the thirty-third. Then everything was forgotten in the amazement of the deed.

"Please, I'd like to go on," said Smeed.

"Oh, Hungry, can you do it?"

"Really?"

"You're goin' on?"

"Holy cats!"

"How'll you take them?" said Hickey anxiously.

"I'll try another six," said Smeed thoughtfully, "and then we'll see."

Conover, vanquished and convinced, no longer thought to intimidate him with horrid suggestions.

"Mr. Smeed," he said, giving him his hand in admiration, "you go ahead; you make a great record."

"Six more," cried Macnooder.

"Six it is," said Turkey in an awed voice; "six and thirty-three makes thirty-nine!"

Mrs. Conover and Macnooder, no longer antagonists, came in from the kitchen to watch the great spectacle. Little Smeed alone, calm and unconscious, with the light of a great ambition on his forehead, ate steadily, without vacillation.

"Gee, what a stride!"

"By Jiminy, where does he put it?" said Conover, staring helplessly.

"Holy cats!"

"Thirty-nine—thirty-nine pancakes—gee!!!"

"Hungry," said Turkey entreatingly, "do you think you could eat another—make it an even forty?"

"Three more," said Smeed, pounding the table with a new authority. This time no voice rose in remonstrance. They were in the presence of a master.

"Pancakes coming."

"Bring them in!"

"Three more."

"Three it is," said Turkey faintly. "Thirty-nine and three makes forty-two—forty-two. Gee!"

In profound silence the three pancakes passed regularly from the plate down the throat of little Smeed. Forty-two pancakes!

"Three more," said Smeed.

Doc Macnooder rushed in hysterically.

"Hungry, go the limit—the limit! If anything happens I'll bleed you."

"Shut up, Doc!"

"Get out, you wild man!"

Macnooder was sent ignominiously back into the kitchen, with the curses of the Dickinson, and Smeed assured of their unfaltering protection.

"Three more," came the cry from the chastened Macnooder.

"Three it is," said Turkey. "Forty-two and three makes—forty-five."

"Holy cats!"

Still little Smeed, without appreciable abatement of hunger, continued to eat. A sense of impending calamity and alarm began to spread. Forty-five pancakes, and still eating! It might turn into a tragedy.

"Say, bub—say, now," said Turkey, gazing anxiously down into the pointed face, "you've done enough—don't get rash."

"I'll stop when it's time," said Smeed; "bring 'em on now, one at a time."

"Forty-six, forty-seven, forty-eight, forty-nine!" Suddenly, at the moment when they expected him to go on forever, little Smeed stopped, gazed at his plate, then at the fiftieth pancake, and said:

"That's all."

Forty-nine pancakes! Then, and only then, did they return to a realization of what had happened. They cheered Smeed, they sang his praises, they cheered again, and then they cried in a mighty chorus: "Pancakes, Conover, pancakes!"

Twenty minutes later, Red Dog and the Egghead, fed to bursting, rolled out of Conover's, spreading the uproarious news.

"Free pancakes! Free pancakes!"

The nearest houses, the Davis and the Rouse, heard and came with a rush.

Red Dog and the Egghead staggered down into the village and over to the circle of houses, throwing out their arms like returning bacchanalians.

"Free pancakes!"

"Hungry Smeed's broken the record!"

"Pancakes at Conover's—free pancakes!"

The word jumped from house to house, the campus was emptied in a trice. The road became choked with the hungry stream that struggled, fought, laughed and shouted as it stormed to Conover's.

"Free pancakes! Free pancakes!"

"Hurrah for Smeed!"

"Hurrah for Hungry Smeed!!"

THE NICKELODEONS
by *Joseph Medill Patterson*

THE MOVIES WERE young indeed when the *Post* published this article about them by Joseph Medill Patterson, aged twenty-eight, who thought they had an important future as "the university of the poor." In 1906 Patterson had startled his rich Chicago family by joining the Socialist party and writing a carefully documented article for the *Post* titled "The Socialist Machine" (September 29, 1906). But in 1910 he was through with Socialism and became co-editor of the Chicago *Tribune* with his cousin, Robert R. McCormick. After World War I, in which he served as a front-line artillery officer, he founded the enormously successful New York *Daily News*, which was patterned after the tabloid *Daily Mirror* of London. He also tried his hand at magazine publishing, but *Liberty*, which he started in 1924 as a rival of the *Post*, lost $14 million before he gave it up. From then to his death in 1946 he devoted himself entirely to the *News*, and especially to its editorial page, where he often reviewed movies in a manner all his own.

NOVEMBER 23, 1907

THREE YEARS AGO there was not a nickelodeon, or five-cent theatre devoted to moving-picture shows, in America. To-day there are between four and five thousand running and solvent, and the number is still increasing rapidly. This is the boom time in the moving-picture business. Everybody is making money—manufacturers, renters, jobbers, exhibitors. Overproduction looms up as a certainty of the near future; but now, as one press-agent said enthusiastically, "this line is a Klondike."

The nickelodeon is tapping an entirely new stratum of people, is developing into theatregoers a section of population that formerly knew and cared little about the drama as a fact in life. That is why "this line is a Klondike" just at present.

Incredible as it may seem, over two million people on the average attend the nickelodeons *every day of the year,* and a third of these are children.

Let us prove up this estimate. The agent for the biggest firm of film renters in the country told me that the average expense of running a nickelodeon was from $175 to $200 a week, divided as follows:

Wage of manager	$25
Wage of operator	20
Wage of doorman	15
Wage of porter or musician	12
Rent of films (two reels changed twice a week)	50
Rent of projecting machine	10
Rent of building	40
Music, printing, "campaign contributions," etc.	18
Total	$190

Merely to meet expenses, then, the average nickelodeon must have a weekly attendance of 4000. This gives all the nickelodeons 16,000,000 a week, or over 2,000,000 a day. Two million people a day are needed before profits can begin, and the two million are forthcoming. It is a big thing, this new enterprise.

The nickelodeon is usually a tiny theatre, containing 199 seats, giving from twelve to eighteen performances a day, seven days a week. Its walls are painted red. The seats are ordinary kitchen chairs, not fastened. The only break in the red color scheme is made by half a dozen signs, in black and white,

and sometimes, but not always,

STAY AS LONG AS YOU LIKE

The spectatorium is one story high, twenty-five feet wide and about seventy feet deep. Last year or the year before it was probably a second-hand clothier's, a pawnshop or cigar store. Now, the counter has been ripped out, there is a ticket-seller's booth where the show-window was, an automatic musical barker somewhere up in the air thunders its noise down on the passersby, and the little store has been converted into a theatre-let. Not a theatre, mind you, for theatres must take out theatrical licenses at $500 a year. Theatres seat two hundred or more people. Nickelodeons seat 199, and take out amusement licenses. This is the general rule.

But sometimes nickelodeon proprietors in favorable locations take out theatrical licenses and put in 800 or 1000 seats. In Philadelphia there is, perhaps, the largest nickelodeon in America. It is said to pay not only the theatrical license, but also $30,000 a year ground rent and a handsome profit.

To-day there is cutthroat competition between the little nickelodeon owners, and they are beginning to compete each other out of existence. Already consolidation has set in. Film-renting firms are quietly beginning to pick up, here and there, a few nickelodeons of their own; presumably they will make better rates and give prompter service to their own theatrelets than to those belonging to outsiders. The tendency is clearly toward fewer, bigger, cleaner five-cent theatres and more expensive shows. Hard as this may be on the little showman who is forced out, it is good for the public, who will, in consequence, get more for their money.

The character of the attendance varies with the locality, but, whatever the locality, children make up about thirty-three per cent of the crowds. For some reason, young women from sixteen to thirty years old are rarely in evidence, but many middle-aged and old women are steady patrons, who never, when a new film is to be shown, miss the opening.

In cosmopolitan city districts the foreigners attend in larger proportion than the English-speakers. This is doubtless because the foreigners, shut out as they are by their alien tongues from much of the life about them, can yet perfectly understand the pantomime of the moving pictures.

As might be expected, the Latin races patronize the shows more consistently than Jews, Irish or Americans. Sailors of all races are devotees. Most of the shows have musical accompaniments. The enterprising manager usually engages a human pianist with instructions to play Eliza-crossing-the-ice when the scene is shuddery, and fast ragtime in a comic kid chase. Where there is little competition, however, the manager merely presses the button and starts the automatic going, which is as apt as not to bellow out, I'd Rather Two-Step Than Waltz, Bill, just as the angel rises from the brave little hero-cripple's corpse.

The moving pictures were used as chasers in vaudeville houses for several years before the advent of the nickelodeon. The cinematograph or vitagraph or biograph or kinetoscope (there are seventy-odd names for the same machine)

was invented in 1888–1889. Mr. Edison is said to have contributed most toward it, though several other inventors claim part of the credit.

The first very successful pictures were those of the Corbett-Fitzsimmons fight at Carson City, Nevada, in 1897. These films were shown all over the country to immense crowds and an enormous sum of money was made by the exhibitors.

The Jeffries-Sharkey fight of twenty-five rounds at Coney Island, in November, 1899, was another popular success. The contest being at night, artificial light was necessary, and 500 arc lamps were placed above the ring. Four cameras were used. While one was snapping the fighters, a second was being focused at them, a third was being reloaded, and a fourth was held in reserve in case of breakdown. Over seven miles of film were exposed and 198,000 pictures, each 2 by 3 inches, were taken. This fight was taken at the rate of thirty pictures to the second.

The 500 arc lamps above the ring generated a temperature of about 115 degrees for the gladiators to fight in. When the event was concluded, Mr. Jeffries was overheard to remark that for no amount of money would he ever again in his life fight in such heat, pictures or no pictures. And he never has.

Since that mighty fight, manufacturers have learned a good deal about cheapening their process. Pictures instead of being 2 by 3 inches are now ⅝ by 1⅛ inches, and are taken sixteen instead of thirty to the second, for the illusion to the eye of continuous motion is as perfect at one rate as the other.

By means of a ratchet each separate picture is made to pause a twentieth of a second before the magic-lantern lens, throwing an enlargement to life size upon the screen. Then, while the revolving shutter obscures the lens, one picture is dropped and another substituted, to make in turn its twentieth of a second display.

The films are, as a rule, exhibited at the rate at which they are taken, though chase scenes are usually thrown faster, and horse races, fire-engines and fast-moving automobiles slower, than the life-speed.

Within the past year an automatic process to color films has been discovered by a French firm. The pigments are applied by means of a four-color machine stencil. Beyond this bare fact, the process remains a secret of the inventors. The stencil must do its work with extraordinary accuracy, for any minute error in the application of color to outline made upon the ⅝ by 1⅛ inches print is magnified 200 times when thrown upon the screen by the magnifying lens. The remarkable thing about this automatic colorer is that it applies the pigment in slightly different outline to each successive print of a film 700 feet long. Colored films sell for about fifty per cent more than black and whites. Tinted films—browns, blues, oranges, violets, greens and so forth—are made by washing, and sell at but one per cent over the straight price.

The films are obtained in various ways. "Straight" shows, where the interest depends on the dramatist's imagination and the setting, are merely playlets acted out before the rapid-fire camera. Each manufacturing firm owns a studio with property-room, dressing-rooms and a completely-equipped stage. The actors are experienced professionals of just below the first rank, who are content to make from $18 to $25 a week. In France a class of moving-picture specialists has grown up who work only for the cameras, but in this country most of the artists who play in the film studios in the daytime play also behind the footlights at night.

The studio manager orders rehearsals continued until his people have their parts "face-perfect," then he gives the word, the lens is focused, the cast works rapidly for twenty minutes while the long strip of celluloid whirs through the camera, and the performance is preserved in living, dynamic embalmment (if the phrase may be permitted) for decades to come.

Eccentric scenes, such as a chalk marking the outlines of a coat upon a piece of cloth, the scissors cutting to the lines, the needle sewing, all automatically without human help, often require a week to take. The process is ingenious. First the scissors and chalk are laid upon the edge of the cloth. The picture is taken. The camera is stopped, the scissors are moved a quarter of an inch into the cloth, the chalk is drawn a quarter of an inch over the cloth. The camera is opened again and another picture is taken showing the quarter-inch cut and quarter-inch mark. The camera is closed, another quarter inch is cut and chalked; another exposure is made. When these pictures so slowly obtained are run off rapidly, the illusion of fast self-action on the part of the scissors, chalk and needle is produced.

Sometimes in a nickelodeon you can see on the screen a building completely wrecked in five minutes. Such a film was obtained by focusing a camera at the building, and taking every salient move of the wreckers for the space, perhaps, of a fortnight. When these separate prints, obtained at varying intervals, some of them perhaps a whole day apart, are run together continuously, the appearance is of a mighty stone building being pulled to pieces like a house of blocks.

Such eccentric pictures were in high demand a couple of years ago, but now the straight-story show is running them out. The plots are improving every year in dramatic technique. Manufacturing firms pay from $5 to $25 for good stories suitable for film presentation, and it is astonishing how many sound dramatic ideas are submitted by people of insufficient education to render their thoughts into English suitable for the legitimate stage.

The moving-picture actors are becoming excellent pantomimists, which is natural, for they cannot rely on the playwright's lines to make their meanings. I remember particularly a performance I saw near Spring Street on the Bowery, where the pantomime seemed to me in nowise inferior to that of Mademoiselle Pilar-Morin, the French pantomimist.

The nickelodeon spectators readily distinguish between good and bad acting, though they do not mark their pleasure or displeasure audibly, except very rarely, in a comedy scene, by a suppressed giggle. During the excellent show of which I have spoken, the men, women and children maintained a steady stare of fascination at the changing figures on the scene, and toward the climax, when forgiveness was cruelly denied, lips were parted and eyes filled with tears. It was as much a tribute to the actors as the loudest bravos ever shouted in the Metropolitan Opera House.

To-day a consistent plot is demanded. There must be, as in the drama, exposition, development, climax and dénouement. The most popular films run from fifteen to twenty minutes and are from five hundred to eight hundred feet long. One studio manager said: "The people want a story. We run to comics generally; they seem to take best. So-and-so, however, lean more to melodrama. When we started we used to give just flashes—an engine chasing to a fire, a base-runner sliding home, a charge of cavalry. Now, for instance, if we want to work in a horse race it has to be as a scene in the life of the jockey, who is the hero of the piece—we've got to give them a story; they won't take anything else—a story with plenty of action. You can't show large conversation, you know, on the screen. More story, larger story, better story with plenty of action—that is our tendency."

Civilization, all through the history of mankind, has been chiefly the property of the upper classes, but during the past century civilization has been permeating steadily downward. The leaders of this democratic movement have been general education, universal suffrage, cheap periodicals and cheap travel. To-day the moving-picture machine cannot be overlooked as an effective protagonist of democracy. For through it the drama, always a big fact in the lives of the people at the top, is now becoming a big fact in the lives of the people at the bottom. Two million of them a day have so found a new interest in life.

The prosperous Westerners, who take their week or fortnight, fall and spring, in New York, pay two dollars and a half for a seat at a problem play, a melodrama, a comedy or a show-girl show in a Broadway theatre. The stokers who have driven the Deutschland or the Lusitania from Europe pay five cents for a seat at a problem play, a melodrama, a comedy or a show-girl show in a Bowery nickelodeon. What is the difference?

The stokers, sitting on the hard, wooden chairs of the nickelodeon, experience the same emotional flux and counter-flux (more intense is their experience, for they are not as blasé) as the prosperous Westerners in their red plush orchestra chairs, uptown.

The sentient life of the half-civilized beings at the bottom has been enlarged and altered, by the introduction of the dramatic motif, to resemble more closely the sentient life of the civilized beings at the top.

Take an analogous case. Is aimless travel "beneficial" or not? It is amusing, certainly; and, therefore, the aristocrats who could afford it have always traveled aimlessly. But now, says the Democratic Movement, the grand tour shall no longer be restricted to the aristocracy. Jump on the rural trolley-car, Mr. Workingman, and make a grand tour yourself. Don't care, Mr. Workingman, whether it is "beneficial" or not. Do it because it is amusing; just as the aristocrats do.

The film makers cover the whole gamut of dramatic attractions. The extremes in the film world are as far apart as the extremes in the theatrical world—as far apart, let us say, as The Master Builder and The Gay White Way.

If you look up the moving-picture advertisements in any vaudeville trade paper you cannot help being struck with this fact. For instance, in a current number, one firm offers the following variety of attractions:

Romany's Revenge (very dramatic)	300	feet
Johnny's Run (comic kid chase)	300	"
Roof to Cellar (absorbing comedy)	782	"
Wizard's World (fantastic comedy)	350	"
Sailor's Return (highly dramatic)	535	"
A Mother's Sin (beautiful, dramatic and moral) . . .	392	"
Knight Errant (old historical drama)	421	"
Village Fire Brigade (big laugh)	325	"
Catch the Kid (a scream) . .	270	"
The Coroner's Mistake (comic ghost story)	430	"
Fatal Hand (dramatic) . . .	432	"

Another firm advertises in huge type, in the trade papers:

LIFE AND PASSION OF CHRIST

Five Parts, Thirty-nine Pictures, 3114 feet . . . Price,	$373.68
Extra for coloring	125.10

The presentation by the picture machines of the Passion Play in this country was undertaken with considerable hesitation. The films had been shown in France to huge crowds, but here, so little were even professional students of American lower-class taste able to gauge it in advance, that the presenters feared the Passion Play might be boycotted, if not, indeed, in some places, mobbed. On the contrary, it has been the biggest success ever known to the business.

Last year incidents leading up to the murder of Stanford White were shown, succeeded enormously for a very few weeks, then flattened out completely and were withdrawn. Film people are as much at sea about what their crowds will like as the managers in the "legitimate."

Although the gourdlike growth of the nickelodeon business as a factor in the conscious life of Americans is not yet appreciated, already a good many people are disturbed by what they do know of the thing.

Those who are "interested in the poor" are wondering whether the five-cent theatre is a good influence, and asking themselves gravely whether it should be encouraged or checked (with the help of the police).

Is the theatre a "good" or a "bad" influence? The adjectives don't fit the case. Neither do they fit the case of the nickelodeon, which is merely the theatre democratized.

Take the case of the Passion Play, for instance. Is it irreverent to portray the Passion, Crucifixion, Resurrection and Ascension in a vaudeville theatre over a darkened stage where half an hour before a couple of painted, short-skirted girls were doing a "sister-act"? What is the motive which draws crowds of poor people to nickelodeons to see the Birth in the Manger flashed magic-lanternwise upon a white cloth? Curiosity? Mere mocking curiosity, perhaps? I cannot answer.

Neither could I say what it is that, every fifth year, draws our plutocrats to Oberammergau, where at the cost, from first to last, of thousands of dollars and days of time, they view a similar spectacle presented in a sunny Bavarian setting.

It is reasonable, however, to believe that the same feelings, whatever they are, which drew our rich to Oberammergau draw our poor to the nickelodeons. Whether the powerful emotional reactions produced in the spectator by the Passion Play are "beneficial" or not is as far beyond decision as the question whether a man or an oyster is happier. The man is more, feels more, than the oyster. The beholder of the Passion Play is more, feels more, than the non-beholder.

Whether for weal or woe, humanity has ceaselessly striven to complicate life, to diversify and make subtle the emotions, to create and gratify the new and artificial spiritual wants, to know more and feel more both of good and evil, to attain a greater degree of self-consciousness; just

as the one fundamental instinct of the youth, which most systems of education have been vainly organized to eradicate, is to find out what the man knows.

In this eternal struggle for more self-consciousness, the moving-picture machine, uncouth instrument though it be, has enlisted itself on especial behalf of the least enlightened, those who are below the reach even of the yellow journals. For although in the prosperous vaudeville houses the machine is but a toy, a "chaser," in the nickelodeons it is the central, absorbing fact, which strengthens, widens, vivifies subjective life; which teaches living other than living through the senses alone. Already, perhaps, touching him at the psychological moment, it has awakened to his first, groping, necessary discontent the spirit of an artist of the future, who otherwise would have remained mute and motionless.

The nickelodeons are merely an extension course in civilization, teaching both its "badness" and its "goodness." They have come in obedience to the law of supply and demand; and they will stay as long as the slums stay, for in the slums they are the fittest and must survive.

THE MISHAPS OF GENTLE JANE

by Carolyn Wells

CAROLYN WELLS ONCE described herself as a "jack-in-the-box brain completely surrounded by books." Her rhymed and acid wit was known to readers of *Puck*, *The Lark* and *Punch* of London before Lorimer lured her to the *Post*. Her *Nonsense Anthology*, published in 1902, is still a classic. Later she became a prolific producer of mystery novels. In a poignant *Post* article of 1933 she described her thoughts when her doctors told her she had just two more years to live, because of a serious heart condition. But she lived for nine years more, writing most of the time.

FEBRUARY 13, 1904

THE RUDE CANNIBALS

Cannibals, exceeding rude,
Once cooked Gentle Jane for food.
Though a nature mild she had,
Gentle Jane got boiling mad.

THE CURIOUS CROWD

Gentle Jane, with no one nigh her,
Touched a live electric wire.
As the crowd around her flocked,
Gentle Jane seemed rather shocked.

THE LACONIC LIGHTNING

Gentle Jane at midnight's hour
Dreamed she heard a thunder-shower;
Waking from her pleasant sleep,
Jane was struck all of a heap.

THE SHIPWRECK

Gentle Jane once chanced to be
In a fearful storm at sea;
As she viewed the raging main,
Jane's heart sank, and so did Jane.

THE HARD-ROCK MAN

by Fred R. Bechdolt

"THE HARD ROCK MAN" was the first in a notable series of *Post* reports on the men who did the nation's toughest physical jobs—the tunnel borers, skyscraper builders, pile drivers, borax hunters and others who drifted from coast to coast and border to border doing dangerous work for premium pay, and spending their money as recklessly as they made it. Strictly factual except as to personal names, these articles were written with a rugged masculine sympathy and a keen eye for historical detail. Their author was a West Coast newspaperman who had just finished work on the *Post*'s first series about prison life. He continued to write stories and articles, mostly about the West, until shortly before his death.

NOVEMBER 7, 1908

THEY were building a new railroad from the Mississippi to the Pacific. They had built from both ends; for two years each track had lengthened daily, and daily the unspanned interval had decreased. Thus they had stretched the steel bands across prairies and deserts and mountain ranges until at last, up in the heart of a wilderness of snow-covered peaks, where the waters part their seaward ways in a cloud-hung gorge, there remained to be overcome the last obstacle. Between the track ends a lump of granite rose two thousand feet. Where the climbing cañons boxed, its base was two miles thick; its sheer walls gave no hope for compromise by engineering feat of loop or switchback; it blocked the way, implacable, grim. The road's builders set about the only course, a straight attack, a tunnel through the granite. As soon as they were ready to begin this they cried for help.

The cry was raised in half a dozen cities. It was blazoned in long letters on handbills, which read:

WANTED 200 MEN FOR HARD ROCK
WORK SNOWSLIDE TUNNEL
Drill Runners $3.00 a Day. Muckers $2.00
a Day. FARE FREE!

These were posted in those parts of the half-dozen cities where their call would meet response. Answering the cry, reckless men with muscles of iron came to rend away the living rock. From time to time, during the next two years, the call was repeated; the handbills were posted at brief intervals.

One morning The Hard-Rock Man read the one at the entrance to the ten-cent lodging-house where he had slept, and knew that he had judged rightly when, on the strength of a ten-line Northern newspaper item, he had left his job on a Government breakwater down in the Gulf of Mexico. He was a loose-limbed man; his shoulders stooped, though they were very broad; where his black shirt opened from his thick, corded neck his chest showed, hairy; his hand, caressing the black bowl of an old bulldog brier pipe, was huge and gnarled and brown; his loose denim overalls failed entirely to conceal his bulging thigh muscles; his hat was black, sweat-stained, without shape. Clothes nor hat nor clumsy shoes could blot out a suggestion of alert strength that came from every line in his figure; his jaw was heavy, and above it, like blued smallpox pits, showed powder scars.

He had followed hard-rock work since he was a man grown; he had toiled underground in many different places. He liked it. This handbill summoned him to his calling, confirmed what he had heard and read when he got sick of the soft Gulf breezes. He read it through, then rapped his pipe-bowl on the wall beside it and made his way, though slowly, with the air of one who has a definite purpose, along the crowded sidewalk. It was a mean street, flanked by mean wooden buildings, from many of whose fire-escapes soiled garments hung; open saloon doors gave forth the odor of stale beer on sawdust, dingy signs of cheap lodging-houses overhung the sidewalk, and at intervals the tarnished three balls of a pawnbroker.

The people who gave way to the bulk of The Hard-Rock Man as he passed among them were as shabby as the street. He noticed neither men nor surroundings; his eye was on the signs as though he were searching for one among them. Finally he found it—hung over an employment office. He entered the place.

It was a dingy little room, by the side of the door a bench, facing it a counter topped by a wire netting, in the netting an arched window. On the bench a half-dozen men sat, rough-garbed, huge-limbed, silent. He took his place among them and waited his turn at the window. Finally it came, and he stood with his elbow crowded into its aperture, his face on his huge, brown hand looking straight into the eyes of a sallow clerk.

"I want to ship to Snowslide," he said.

The clerk looked at him and guessed wrong— "Laborer?" he asked.

"Naw—runner." The bass voice came scornful from the big chest.

The other accepted the emendation listlessly. "All right," he yawned. "Name?" When he had gotten it he handed The Hard-Rock Man a slip of blue paper bearing a number, and received in exchange a dollar. "We ship at 4:30," he sighed. "Give this to our man at the depot."

At 4:28 The Hard-Rock Man gave up the blue slip and boarded an emigrant coach near the front of the train. He dropped his heavy roll of blankets to the top of a pile on the floor beside the door, and found among the hard, wooden-backed seats one which was vacant. When the train pulled out a few moments later the car was full of men like himself, and the rumble of their deep voices rose with the roar of the wheels. He looked among the hard, rugged faces. Some were flecked, like his, with the blue of burned powder; others were twisted and marked by ragged scars. Stern lines of endurance cut them all, and with these lines on many were the deeper furrows of dissipation.

The majority had the long upper lip and the gray-blurred eyes of the Irish-American who follows "public works." Their bodies were big boned, big muscled, and the hands, gripping the arms of the seats or laid on the seat-backs before them, upraised to tilt back sweat-stained hats from seamed foreheads, or clenched in potent gestures, were heavy, gnarled, marked by great, swelling veins. Searching, he saw a face he knew, a thin face, a grizzle of beard beneath the chin, one eye gone. He rose and made his way down the aisle and, without a word of apology or of warning, he shoved his bulk into the seat which this passenger occupied alone. The one-eyed man

whirled upon him, and as quickly moved aside to give him room.

"Where the —— ye been?" he demanded.

"Galveston breakwater," growled The Hard-Rock Man. "What kind av a job is this here?"

"I dunno; the company's doin' the wurrk wit' no contract; Murphy's superintendent, Gunnysack Murphy, an' he has a dozen av his ould gang wit' him frum the Chicago ditch; Tom Ryan's walker at the west portal—the wan we're shippin' fer."

"Tom Ryan? He never pulled hard rock."

"Never that I hear tell of; but he can drive men. An', man, d'ye remember him on that soft-ground job down in Alabama? He could make a steam shovel climb a tree."

The Hard-Rock Man was fumbling in his pocket for his pipe. He brought it forth empty. "Got the makin's av a smoke?" he demanded; "I'm clean." The one-eyed man tossed into his lap a package of black tobacco. "I blowed meself in El Paso," The Hard-Rock Man continued; "had to beat it to Seattle. I bummed enough there to ship on."

The other grinned so that it puckered odd wrinkles around his empty eye-socket. "I come from Denver," he chuckled, "after a lovely week, wit' three dollars an' six bits to start on, an' landed in Seattle wit' two av ut left. I lost me hat goin' over Marshall Pass. Man—talk av wind, it like to blowed the hair aff me head."

The train was rocking with speed; around them rose the roar of heavy voices. Some one thrust a quart bottle of whisky between them; they drank, gaspingly, as though it were water and they were parched, and handed it back; they talked of their work, of tunnels long since driven, of jobs on which they had toiled together in far places; the drink began to warm within them, their voices grew louder, they argued.

" 'Twas the engineer's fault, I tell ye"—the one-eyed man hammered the seat-cushion with his fist—"fifty feet aff, they was, an' the two headin's clost together ——"

"I tell ye, no," growled The Hard-Rock Man. "Wasn't I workin' at the north portal that day— an' had been fer two months. An' fer three days back we'd heard the beat av their drills every shift. An' Old Johnson knew it. What did he care? Him gettin' more a yard than a conthractor iver got. There was men dyin' like flies that winter, frum the bad ground and the lung fever, an' most av the time us goin' a hundred foot ahead av the timbers. What did he care how clost we was? The beat av their drills in our ears, I tell ye! The headin' boss went to the walker that marnin'—I heard him say ut—an' he swore he'd not take in his shift again. Nor did he. They shot the other side just before noon. I was leanin' over the bench for a piece of the fourteen-foot steel, an' I thought some one had come up behind an' kicked me on over—till I come to meself in a dump-car wit' two dead men on top av me. Naw, 'twas ——"

He whirled, a belligerent fist upraised, as a big hand gripped his shoulder, and paused with the fist in air.

"I thought ye was growin' grass a year back," he cried. "Some one tould me ye'd died on that White Pass an' Yukon job."

"Who the —— told ye that?" The newcomer was tall and gaunt and his face was lean, with a skin like leather. He sat on the arm of the seat and took from the hand of the one-eyed man a plug of chewing tobacco. He told of the rock on White Pass where the snow lies deep far into the summer, and of the rock in the Copper River country, where black-fir forests fringe blue-green glaciers, and the ice lies beneath the surface of the earth from year's-end to year's-end. And then the three of them talked of the living rock where palmettos grow and winter breezes are soft and warm.

The train climbed slowly up a steep grade. About them men laughed and sang and cursed; and, now and then, there was a fight; and some slept huddled on the wooden seats. The air was blue with the reek of the black pipes. The window-panes fogged before the haze. Occasionally, a brakeman hurried through, slamming the door behind him. None others came to them, nor did any of them leave the car. It was midnight when they arrived at the last stop, where the cañon boxed at the granite wall of the mountain, and they climbed out into the cool, clean night.

A lean-faced Scotchman sorted them out on the platform and billeted them to their bunk-houses. They picked their ways, through camp litter and among material piles, to a group of long, low buildings on the mountainside. In one of these The Hard-Rock Man paused and looked about him. Its interior was lined on three sides by rows of bunks two high; in the middle of the long, board-walled room stood a heater-stove, about it a number of lines, on these, steaming socks and undergarments; a single incandescent gave dim light near the stove; from the shadows beyond its yellow rays came the gasping breathing of many sleeping men. He found an empty bunk which suited him, threw down his heavy blanket-roll, unwrapped and spread the bedding, kicked off his shoes and outer garments and went at once to his rest, as one who has at last found home.

The next morning he rose with sixty others. On all sides huge, half-clad bodies lurched from the timbered bunks; great, hairy limbs thrust themselves into coarse garments; about a steaming sink near the stove a dozen giants soused their shaggy heads in running water. The Hard-Rock Man drew on a suit of tattered oilskins and a "squam" hat, stamped his feet into a pair of heavy rubber boots and went to face his shift boss. He found the foreman, in the office off the bunk-room, lowering his shaggy brows over his time-book, which looked as out of place in his thick fingers as did the pencil he held. When The Hard-Rock Man entered he raised his eyes over the edge of the little book; they were the steel-gray eyes of the fighting Irishman.

"Weren't ye on Butcher Preston's shift in that East River job?" he asked. The Hard-Rock Man nodded. "I remember ye," the shift boss went on; "ye was carried up the ladder the afternoon the river come in on ye."

A triangle clanged over at the cook-house; huge feet stamped toward the door of the bunk-room. "Ye'll take a column machine," said the boss; "I'm short av men in the headin'." He bent again to his time-book. The Hard-Rock Man started for the door.

"Say," the other called—The Hard-Rock Man stopped on the threshold—"whatever came of Butcher Preston, annyhow?"

The Hard-Rock Man tilted back his "squam" hat to scratch his head. "Seems to me I remember hearin' of him," he said. "Oh, yes, he's got a gang on that borax road goin' into Death Valley —soft-ground work," he added.

They breakfasted in the cook-house, sixty at one long table. They sat on benches; the food lay before them in great tin pans; the coffee steamed in tin cups; the clash of their knives and the champ of their jaws were terrific.

They streamed out into the sunshiny morning. Before them the camp lay—a litter of unpainted, wooden buildings; a tall-stacked, red power-house; a long, gray dump, thrusting itself from the black tunnel-mouth down along the cañon-bed; lumber-piles along the upper dump; among the quarters heaps of tin cans, glistening in the sunshine; on either side the mountains, sheer-walled, black with mantling hemlocks, scarred by snowslides and by granite cliffs, frowned heavily upon the desecration.

The shift picked their way across the dump, a black-clad company of giants. They gathered at the blacksmith-shop platform, where two "nipper-boys" loaded the sharpened steel on a string of muck-cars. The long drills clanged as they fell; within the shop hammers clanked and red flakes flew from beside a flaming forge; on the platform the men lit their pipes; many of the runners carried with them huge monkey-wrenches; here and there a black-garbed giant bore a macelike chuck-wrench. The shift boss hurried up behind them, his watch in his hand. "All in!" he shouted, still at a distance. They clambered into the string of dump-cars, a brake was released, and, as the train started down the grade, an electric locomotive coupled on behind. It lurched forward and rumbled into blackness, then flew through dense gloom; dripping walls echoed with fearful loudness the roar of the wheels; dank air swept by, a steady gale. The Hard-Rock Man, leaning forward where he crouched in the gritty car, took deep breaths and it tasted good to him. Ahead came a glimmer of light; the engine uncoupled; the train hurtled beneath a string of incandescent lamps toward a menacing mass of timbers and a sheer rock wall—near, nearer—there was a jolt of lessened speed—some one had thrown himself upon the brake lever—the sixty men leaped out. Meeting them, as they clambered up the bench, sixty others, oilskin-clad, their faces black with oil, hurried toward the portal—the outgoing shift.

They fell upon their toil in the centre of the mountain; over their heads two thousand feet of living rock. From its seams water dripped upon them; its walls gleamed moist in the lamplight. In this chamber fourteen air drills bellowed and thundered. The granite shook with their reverberations; and men made signs for speech.

It was a cavern, some fifty feet long, filled with madly-toiling men and these plunging, air-driven engines. It menaced—above, beside, beneath—with terrible action and terrific din. Down its middle stretched a plank runway and along this, steadily, without ceasing, a line of sweating men wheeled barrows of broken rock—the "muck." From the vents of the drills half-frozen air rose foglike; and through this mist the incandescents on roof and sides showed huge and yellow.

Nearest the portal was the "jumbo," a great, movable platform through which the "muckers" dumped their barrow-loads to cars beneath. Then came the bench, a fourteen-foot rock wall, extending half-way from the tunnel floor to its ceiling. On its summit six tripod drills worked in a series of staccato explosions. Here the overhead timbering stopped, and the fifty-foot interval of bare, granite roof began; then the heading, the extreme front of the great bore, the van of the attack upon the mountain.

Clamped on columns of iron, eight great Burley machines pounded the face of the heading. Theirs was the bulk of the mighty roar of the place, the depth of the pulsing thunder. Two on a column, one four feet above the other, the columns a scant three feet apart, they battered the living rock; from their whistling vents the escaping air came in frozen chunks and thick, gray fog. Among them, under the plunging steel drills, so close to the dashing chucks that it seemed these must tear their faces, The Hard-Rock Man and the seven other runners bent and straightened. As they toiled the machines spat oil upon them, and the holes in the heading's breast spurted gritty muck, until their features grew black.

At times a drill stuck obstinately at a slip or fault in the rock, and when this happened the runner fell fiercely upon it, beating it with an iron bar, as though it were a living thing, his face aflame with passion, opening his mouth to curses which fell silent in the din of troubled sounds.

Where he crouched at the foot of his column The Hard-Rock Man was directly beneath the upper machine, less than three feet from the machine beside him, whose frozen exhaust struck his cheek. From the thunder of these engines he picked the bellowing of his own, and segregated this into its thousand sounds, hearkening to each of these to see that it rang true. His face was set to intentness, and it was the face of a man who is happy in his work.

Behind him on the muck-heap a "nipper-boy" lay fast asleep.

At noon came a half-hour interval, and lunch. They brought in the food on the muck-train and its advent was followed by a stampede from heading and bench. Sixty oilskin-clad, dripping men hurled themselves upon the cars, a fighting, rending mass. They surged like milling cattle. One, lighter than the rest, was forced upward by the pressure of those about him and thrown bodily among the food. Hardly was the struggle over—a brief interval of fierce eating followed that it seemed no interval at all—and they were back at their machines.

At two o'clock The Hard-Rock Man's fourteen-foot steel ran to an end in his last hole. He shut off the air, loosed the great chuck nuts, cranked back the feed screw, freed his machine a bit at the column, and turned it to one side. Then he drew forth the steel and his helper carried it away. The helper returned from the "jumbo" and the two of them unclamped the machine, loaded it on a barrow and wheeled it across the long gangway. After this they blew out the hole. They did this with the compressed air. The Hard-Rock Man coupled to the wire-wrapped hose which had fed his machine a one-inch iron pipe; the helper turned on the air from the standpipe; The Hard-Rock Man ran the iron pipe into each hole, raising it, lowering it, raising it again. It shrieked and bellowed terrifically, weirdly, and the muck flew from the holes in showers.

The heading boss stood amid the ruin of torn-down columns, where other runners were removing their raffle, two boxes of warmed giant-powder at his feet; on each box lay a bundle of nitro exploders, tipped with three-foot, thin, wire strands. To him The Hard-Rock Man went.

"Ten sticks," yelled the boss; it had grown so quiet with the cessation of machines that a man could make his voice heard. The Hard-Rock Man took ten for each of his holes. He slipped the smooth, warm, yellow cylinders down, one after another, ramming each with a long, wooden loading rod. The top one he slit with his pocket-knife, placing in the slit an exploder whose wire trailed from the rim of the hole. Then he tamped down the charge with loose, fine muck. The other runners did the same thing. The boss tied the exploder wires one to another, so that all the holes were connected; then coupled the wires at each end of the round to the wires of an electric-light circuit, which remained broken three hundred feet out toward the portal. By this time the place was clear of barrows and tools, and the men were leaving.

Some one took down the string of incandescents and bore them away in a glowing bundle, and there remained now the boss, The Hard-Rock Man, and the one-eyed man who had traveled up with him on the train the day before. They bore flickering candles, and by their light swiftly examined each foot of the wire circuit to see that it was properly coupled. Then they, too, went. One hundred yards out from the bench they joined the rest of the shift who stood, sombre shadows among the deeper, mantling shades.

"All out!" yelled the boss. There was no answer.

"Ready!" he yelled, and raised a long pole. On its end dangled a wire, the one strand necessary to connect the broken shooting-circuit.

"Fire!" He let the wire drop into its place. There came a faint shiver of air; away up in the blackness a red flash; the roar of the rending dynamite followed; then a gust of wind which blew out their candles.

"All in!" They followed the boss toward the heading. Pungent reek of dynamite met their nostrils as they approached the bench. They clambered up its face into a thick, blue fog. Some one coughed; then others. A man near The Hard-Rock Man gasped and staggered, his hand to his forehead; he fell and lay on the rock. Others, in distress, fought their way among the smoke

wreaths, whose gases sent the blood pumping through every artery in their bodies until every capillary throbbed painfully. On top of the bench was a chaos of rock, broken away from the face of the heading. In the clearing smoke-mists they toiled, cleaning away the débris for the erection of their columns. It was four o'clock before they had the ground uncovered for their mounting. Then the new shift came in to take their places, and they went out into the clean, white light of a sunny afternoon, dripping, black with oil, weary.

After two days of this The Hard-Rock Man went to the commissary and got new boots, oil-skins and tobacco, which were charged against his wages.

A month later he and his fellows went on "graveyard" shift. "Graveyard" is the interval between twelve, midnight, and eight in the morning. It was pleasant—after the work started; until that time it was dreary indeed. The men rose at eleven in the evening; ate their breakfast by the light of lamps in the cook-house, then found their ways to the tunnel-mouth in cold darkness. A month later they worked from four in the afternoon until midnight.

They handled the giant-powder with fearful recklessness. They did all their work in this same spirit. They did not fear death; they had become too familiar with it. Sometimes it showed itself grimly, taking toll from their number, making some who saw it in action tremble for a few moments. Always it did this when the move was not expected; and always it came suddenly, from an unlooked-for direction. It got the most reverence for its power when, coming in the shape of some cataclysm, it wrought havoc in the heading and delayed the work, as it did the afternoon when Paddy Shelton vanished utterly.

Paddy Shelton ran a machine on the column to the right of The Hard-Rock Man. They had shot two hours before and were "mucking" out, to set up the columns. All of them toiled feverishly with pick or shovel.

Paddy Shelton was hacking away with a pick —thud, thud––thud, thud!—the strokes came rapidly in pairs. He was a bent little man, and his body bowed over the pick like the body of a gnome. The muck was stubborn; The Hard-Rock Man sweated at the handle of a number two shovel.

"Might as well shovel nails," he shouted into the ear of his helper. "Get me another 'muck stick.' " The helper left his side; he went on with his work.

Thud, thud—thud, thud, thud. Paddy Shelton was at it harder and faster than ever. The Hard-

Rock Man's shovel stuck, tangled in broken rock. He stopped and leaned on its handle; he watched Paddy Shelton. Then he tossed the shovel from him, and turned to hurry his helper in the search for another. As he turned, a great, red wave wrapped and lifted him. There was a roar in his ears and it did not go for days.

When he awoke in the company hospital the surgeon was picking particles of rock from his back. Seven others were in the ward with him, racked with pain of broken bones and seared with burns. And eight others had been found—that is to say, enough of them had been found—for burial. Of Paddy Shelton they had found nothing; and so they surmised that his pick-point must have struck a stick of dynamite which in some manner had failed to explode with the shot.

They buried the eight on the mountainside above the cook-house. They had a little cemetery there. Its graves were marked by wooden head-boards; on these penciled legends of name, and sometimes other data—usually only name. They lay beneath the shadowing branches of black hemlocks. They were bare, without grass or flowers or any mark of care, these graves, and none visited them, save to add to their number. The Hard-Rock Man and some of the older "runners" used to gather nights round the bunk-house stove and "drive tunnel," as they called reminiscence at Snowslide.

Then they would drift from the past to the future, and some of them would read newspaper items of prospective public works. One night a man told of the New York subway—he had just come from that job. It was the tail of the winter. The snow was turning gray on the mountains, and there was warmth in the air, afternoons, warmth that stirred the blood of The Hard-Rock Man. This night he felt the stirring strongly and knew what it meant. He resolved to keep his next paycheck. He had worked nine months and he had nothing. Playtime came once each month at Snowslide—five days of it. The first day of the month was "drag day," when a man might draw his time-slip, which was negotiable; and the fifth day of the month was pay-day, when, if he had not "dragged," he got his check. For getting the time-slip he forfeited the right to go back to work for a week. The Hard-Rock Man, like most of the older "runners," had always "dragged."

Down in the stream-bed, beneath the level of the long, gray dump, was a row of unpainted, wooden buildings, flamboyant with colored canvas signs. Each sign proclaimed the name of a saloon; and each saloon had a piano, a dance hall and gambling tables. During the most of the month they were quiet places. The bartenders blinked behind their unvarnished bars; white wrappings shrouded the gambling tables; dust gathered on the silent pianos.

One day before "drag day" the round-hatted, pasty-faced, "tin-horn" gamblers came. "Drag day" a pianist materialized in each saloon. At nine o'clock that morning the deserters from the "graveyard" shift began to straggle in, and the beady-eyed, shiny-haired bartenders began to move, while the proprietors, by the bar-ends, began cashing the time-slips, each knowing that in a few days the money thus given out would be back again in his safe.

At intervals the dice clicked; between these intervals the dealers, still listless, made their peculiar sort of music, shuffling together with the long, white fingers of one hand two stacks of chips, which fell into one with a clicking sound. The pianos thumped, now and then.

At five o'clock in the afternoon the daymen began to come, and with them some of the night-shift. The dice rolled steadily; the pianos were hideous; the men of Snowslide played.

Each month The Hard-Rock Man had played for one week. And each month had seen the wages of his toil go from him. He had never regretted it. Now he was restless, and with the restlessness came dissatisfaction. He was on the "graveyard" shift, which made it worse, for no man ever gets entirely reconciled to going to work at midnight. He began to grumble to himself about the food, the tools; the slips and faults in the rock made him ugly, he bickered with his helper and cursed those about him. One night he fought over a chuck-wrench with one of the "bench runners," and they rolled together over the fourteen-foot rock wall, carrying with them a box of giant powder. When he had untangled his feet from the exploder wires The Hard-Rock Man looked up into the face of the heading boss. It was aflame with anger:

"Ye might av blowed up the whole shift an' held back the wurrk fer hours!" the foreman yelled, shaking his fist.

The Hard-Rock Man growled: "I got three meals a day afore I ever seen ye."

The next day was "drag day." He departed while the morning was young, his heavy roll of blankets on his back; and two weeks later he was in New York. He was toiling again in the depths of another tunnel, beneath the level of a crowded street, again gouging away the earth, that progress might find a straight path, unchecked; doing his part, as his instinct told him, as he could no more help doing than the capitalist can help using his money to beget more works and more power, or the thinker can help using his brains—all toward the same ultimate purpose.

Several months after The Hard-Rock Man had left trains were passing through the Snowslide tunnel, and they always stopped at the west portal before entering the black hole. While they stopped passengers gathered on the platforms to gaze down the cañon over the mountain-peaks. Sometimes the eyes of these groups would fall on the litter of ruins beneath the black-topped hemlocks down by the stream-bed. Often, the question would come to the porter, the same question—What was that place which had been? And who were the men who had lived there? And the porter, who, of course, had to know all things about the country, was able to tell them but little of the place—save that it had been a construction town. Of the men who had toiled there, and had played and had gone, he was able to tell them nothing.

SAD DAYS AT OLD SIWASH

by George Fitch

"YES, SIR, it's been seven years now since old Siwash College has been beaten in football. . . . We've shut out Hopkinsville seven times— pushed them off the field, off the earth, into the hospitals and into the discard. We've beaten six State universities by an average of seven touchdowns, two goal kicks, a rib, three jawbones and four new kinds of yells. We put such a crimp into old Muggledorfer that her Faculty suddenly decided that football developed the toes and teeth at the expense of the intellect and they took up intercollegiate beanbags instead. And in all those seven years we've never really been scared but once . . ." Thus opened the first of George Fitch's Siwash stories, which began in 1908 and continued to delight *Post* readers until 1913. Their author was an alumnus (1897) of Knox College at Galesburg, Illinois, and Knox has proudly claimed the honor of being the original Siwash. Fitch was editor of the Peoria *Herald-Transcript* when he began writing about Siwash; later he became active in the Progressive party and was elected to the Illinois House of Representatives. He died in 1915 at the age of thirty-eight.

DECEMBER 18, 1909

HONEST, Bill, sometimes, when I sit down in these sober, plug-away days—when we are kind to the poor dumb policeman and don't dare wear straw hats after the first of September—and think about the good old college times, I wonder how we ever had the nerve to imitate insanity the way we did. Here I am, rubbing noses with thirty, outgrowing my belts every year, and sitting eight hours at a desk without exploding. Am I the chap who climbed up sixty feet of waterspout a few short years ago and persuaded the clapper of the college bell to come down with me? Here you are all worn smooth on top and proprietor of an overflow meeting in the nursery. In about ten minutes you'll be tearing your coat-tails out of my hands because you have to go back home before the eldest kid asks for a story. Are you the loafer who spent all one night getting a profane parrot into the cold-air pipes of the college chapel? Maybe you think you are, but I don't believe it. If I were to tip this table over on you now you'd get mad and go home instead of handing me a volume of George Barr Mc-Cutcheon in the watch-pocket. You're not the good old lunatic you used to be, and neither am I.

And yet it's no time at all since you and I were back at Siwash College, making a dear playmate out of trouble from morning till night. I wonder what it is in college that makes a fellow want to stick his finger into conventions and customs and manners, to say nothing of the revised statutes, and stir the whole mess 'round and 'round! When you're in college, college life seems big and all the rest of the world so small that what you want to do as a student seems to be the only important thing in life—no matter if what you want to do is only to put a free-lunch sign over the First Methodist Church. What does the college student care for the U. S. A., the planet or the solar system? Why, at Siwash, I remember the biggest man in the world was Ole Skjarsen. Next to him was Coach Bost, then Rogers, captain of the football team, and then Jensen, the quarter. After him came Frankling, of the Alfalfa Delts, whose father shopped and bought railroads instead of gloves; then came Prexy, and after him the President of the United States and a few scattered celebrities, tailing down to the Mayor of Jonesville and its leading citizens—mere nobodies.

That's how important the outside world seemed to us. Is it any wonder that when we wanted to go downtown in pajamas and plug hats we paddled right along? Or that when we wanted to steal a couple of actors and tie them in a barn, while two of us took their places, we did not hesitate to do so? We felt perfectly free to do just what we pleased. The college understood us, and what the world thought never entered our heads.

There was Rearick, for instance. He was the smartest man in our class. Took scholarship prizes as carelessly as a policeman takes peanuts from a Dago stand. Since then he's gone up so fast that every time I see him I insult him by congratulating him on getting the place he's just been promoted from. But what was Rearick's hobby at Siwash? Stealing hatpins. He had four hundred hatpins when he graduated, and he never could see anything wrong in it. Guess he's got them yet. Perkins is in Congress already. He out-debated the whole Northwest and wrote pieces on subjects so heavy that you could break up coal with them. But I never saw him so earnest in debate as he was the night he got old Bill Morrison drunk and drove his hack for him all evening. He told me he had driven every hack in town but Bill's, and that Bill had baffled him for two years. It cost him four dollars to turn the trick, but he was happier after it than he was when he won the Siwash-Muggledorfer debate. Said he was ready to graduate now—college held nothing further for him. Perkins' brains weren't addled, because he has been working them double shift ever since. He just had the college microbe, that's all. It gets into your gray matter and makes you enjoy things turned inside out. You remember "Prince" Hogboom's funeral, don't you?

What year was it? Why, ninety-ump-teen. What? That's right, you got out the year before. I remember they held your diploma until you paid for the library cornerstone that your class stole and cut up into paperweights. Well, by not staying the next year you missed the most unsuccessful funeral that was ever held in the history of Siwash or anywhere else. It was one of the very few funerals on record in which the corpse succeeded in licking the mourners. I've got a small scar from it now. You may think you're going home to that valuable baby of yours, but you are not. You'll hear me out.

In this spring of umpty-steen it seemed as if only one ambition in the world was worth achieving—that was to get out of classes. Most of us had used up our cuts long ago. The Faculty is never any too patient in the spring, anyhow, and a lot of us were on the ragged edge. I remember feeling very confidently that if I went up before that brain trust in the Faculty room once more and tried to explain how it was that I was giving absent treatment to my beloved studies, said Faculty would take the college away from me and wouldn't let me play with it never no more. And that's an awful distressing fear to hang over a man who loves and enjoys everything connected with a college except the few trifling recitations which take up his time and interfere with his plans. It hung over five of us who were trying to plan some way of going over to Hambletonian College to see our baseball team wear deep paths around their diamond. We were certain to win, and as the Hambletonians hadn't found this out there was a legitimate profit to be made from

our knowledge—profit we yearned for and needed frightfully. That was why we murdered Hogboom.

It happened one evening when we were sitting on the front porch of the Eta Bita Pi house. That was the least expensive thing we could do. We had been discussing girls and baseball and spring suits, and the comparative excellence of the wheat cakes at the Union Lunch Counter and Jim's place. But whatever we talked about ran into money in the end and we had to change the subject. There's mighty little a poor man can talk about in spring in college, I can tell you. We discussed around for an hour or two, bumping into the dollar mark in every direction, and finally got so depressed that we shut up and sat around with our heads in our hands. That seemed to be about the only thing to do that didn't require money.

"We'll have to do something desperate to get to that game," said Hogboom at last. Hogboom was a Senior. He ranked "sublime" in football, "excellent" in baseball, "good" in mandolin, "fair" in dancing, and from there down in Greek, Latin and Mathematics.

"Intelligent boy," said Bunk Bailey pleasantly; "tell us what it must be. Desperate things done to order, day or night, with care and thoroughness. Trot out your desperate thing and get me an axe. I'll do it."

"Well," said Hogboom, "I don't know but it seems to me that if one of us was to die maybe the Faculty would take a day off and we could go over to Hambletonian without getting cuts."

"Fine scheme; get me a gun, Hogboom." "Do you prefer drowning or lynching?" "Kill him quick, somebody." "Look pleasant, please, while the operator is working." "What do you charge for dying?" Oh, we guyed him good and plenty, which is a way they have at old Harvard and middle-aged Siwash and Infant South Dakota University and wherever two students are gathered together anywhere in the U. S. A.

Hogboom only grinned. "Prattle away all you please," he said, "but I mean it. I've got magnificent facilities for dying just now. I'll consider a proposition to die for the benefit of the cause if you fellows will agree to keep me in cigarettes and pie while I'm dead."

"Done," says I, "and in embalming fluid, too. But just demonstrate this theorem, Hoggy, old boy. How extensively are you going to die?"

"Just enough to get a holiday," said Hogboom. "You see, I happen to have a chum in the telegraph office in Weeping Water, where I live. Now if I were to go home to spend Sunday and you fellows were to receive a telegram that I had been kicked to death by an automobile, would you have sense enough to show it to Prexy?"

"We would," we remarked, beginning to get intelligent.

"And, after he had confirmed the sad news by telegram, would you have sense enough left to suggest that college dismiss on Tuesday and hold a memorial meeting?"

"We would," we chuckled.

"And would you have foresight enough to suggest that it be held in the morning so that you could rush away to Weeping Water in the afternoon to attend the funeral?"

"Yes, indeed," we said, so mildly that the cop two blocks away strolled down to see what was up.

"And then would you be diplomatic enough to produce a telegram saying that the report was false, just too late to start the afternoon classes?"

"You bet!" we whooped, pounding Hogboom with great joy. Then we sat down as unconcernedly as if we were planning to go to the vaudeville the next afternoon and arranged the details of Hogboom's assassination. As I was remarking, positively nothing looks serious to a college boy until after he has done it.

That was on Friday night. On Saturday we killed Hogboom. That is, he killed himself. He got permission to go home over Sunday and retired to an upper back room in our house, very unostentatiously. He had already written to his operator chum, who had attended college just long enough to take away his respect for death, the integrity of the telegraph service and practically everything else. The result was that at nine o'clock that evening a messenger boy rang our bell and handed in a telegram. It was brief and terrible. Wilbur Hogboom had been submerged in the Weeping Water River while trying to abduct a catfish from his happy home and had only just been hauled out entirely extinct.

It was an awful shock to us. We had expected him to be shot. We read it solemnly and then tiptoed up to Hogboom with it. He turned pale when he saw the yellow slip.

"What is it?" he asked hurriedly. "How did it happen?"

"You were drowned, Hoggy, old boy," Wilkins said. "Drowned in your little old Weeping Water River. They have got you now and you're all damp and drippy, and your best girl is having one hysteric after another. Don't you think you ought to throw that cigarette away and show some respect to yourself? We've all quit playing cards and are going to bed early in your honor."

"Well, I'm not," said Hogboom. "It's the first time I have ever been dead, and I'm going to stay up all night and see how I feel. Another thing, I'm going down and telephone the news to Prexy myself. I've had nothing but hard words out of him all my college course, and if he can't think up something nice to say on an occasion like this I'm going to give him up."

Hogboom called up Prexy and in a shaking voice read him the telegram. We sat around, choking each other to preserve the peace, and listened to the following cross section of a dialogue—telephone talk is so interesting when you just get one hemisphere of it.

"Hello! That you, Doctor? This is the Eta Bita Pi House. I've some very sad news to tell you. Hogboom was drowned today in the Weeping Water River. We've just had a telegram—Yes, quite dead—No chance of a mistake, I'm afraid—Yes, they recovered him—We're all broken up—Oh, yes, he was a fine fellow—We loved him deeply—I'm glad you thought so much of him—He was always so frank in his admiration of you—Yes, he was honorable—Yes, and brilliant, too—Of course, we valued him for his good fellowship, but, as you say, he was also an earnest boy—It's awful—Yes, a fine athlete—I wish he could hear you say that, Doctor—No, I'm afraid we can't fill his place—Yes, it is a loss to the college—I guess you just address telegram to his folks at Weeping Water—That's how we're sending ours—Good-night—Yes, a fine fellow—Good-night."

Hogboom hung up the 'phone and went upstairs, where he lay for an hour or two with his face full of pillows. The rest of us weren't so gay. We could see the humor of the thing all right, but the awful fact that we were murderers was beginning to hang over our heads. It was easy enough to kill Hogboom, but now that he was dead the future looked tolerably complicated. Suppose something happened? Suppose he didn't stay dead? There's no peace for a murderer, anyway. We didn't sleep much that night.

The next day it was worse. We sat around and entertained callers all day. Half a hundred students called and brought enough woe to fit out a Democratic headquarters on Presidential election night. They all had something nice to say of Hoggy. We sat around and mourned and gloomed and agreed with them until we were ready to yell with disgust.

Hogboom was the most disgracefully lively corpse I ever saw. He insisted on sitting at the head of the stairs where he could hear every good word that was said of him, and the things he demanded of us during the day would have driven a stone saint to crime. Four times we went downtown for pie; three times for cigarettes; once for all the Sunday newspapers, and once for ice cream. As I told you, it was May, the time of the year when street-car fare is a problem of financial magnitude. We had to borrow money from the cook before night. Hoggy had us helpless, and he was taking a mean and contemptible advantage of the fact that he was a corpse. Half a dozen times we were on the verge of letting him come to life. It would have served him right.

Old Siwash was just naturally submerged in sorrow when Monday morning came. The campus dripped with sadness. The Faculty oozed regret at every pore. We loyal friends of Hogboom were looked on as the chief mourners and it was up to us to fill the part. We did our best. We talked with the soft pedal on. We went without cigarettes. We wiped our eyes whenever we got an audience. Time after time we told the sad story and exhibited the telegram. By noon more particulars began to come in. Prexy got an answer to his telegram of condolence. The funeral, the telegram said, would be on Tuesday afternoon. There was great and universal grief in Weeping Water, where Hogboom had been held in reverent esteem. Hoggy's chum in the telegraph office simply laid himself out on that telegram. Prexy read it to me himself and wiped his eyes while he did it. He was a nice, sympathetic man, Prexy was, when he wasn't discussing cuts or scholarship.

Getting the memorial meeting was so easy we hated to take it. The Faculty met to pass resolutions Monday afternoon, and when our delegation arrived they treated us like brothers. It was just like entering the camp of the enemy under a flag of truce. Many a time I've gone in on that same carpet, but never with such a feeling of holy calm. "They would, of course, hold the memorial meeting," said Prexy. They had in fact decided on this already. They would, of course, dismiss college all day. It was, perhaps, best to hold the memorial in the morning if so many of us were going out to Weeping Water. It was nice so many of us could go. Prexy was going. So was the mathematics professor, old "Ichthyosaurus" James, a very fine old ruin; whom Hogboom hated with a frenzy worthy of a better cause, but who, it seemed, had worked up a great regard for Hogboom through having him for three years in the same trigonometry class.

We went out of Faculty meeting men and equals with the professors. They walked down to the corner with us, I remember, and I talked with Cander, the Polykon professor, who had always seemed to me to be the embodiment of Comanche cruelty and cunning. We talked of Hogboom all the way to the corner. Wonderful how deeply the Faculty loved the boy; and with what Spartan firmness they had concealed all indications of it through his career!

When Monday night came we began to breathe more easily. Of course there was some kind of a deluge coming when Hogboom appeared, but that was his affair. We didn't propose to monkey with the resurrection at all. He could do his own explaining. To tell the truth, we were pretty sore at Hogboom. He was making a regular Roman holiday out of his demise. It kept four men busy running errands for him. We had to retail him every compliment that we had heard during the day, especially if it came from the Faculty. We had to describe in detail the effect of the news upon six or seven girls, for all of whom Hogboom had a tender regard. He insisted upon arranging the funeral and vetoed our plans as fast as we made them. He was as domineering and ugly as if he was the only man who had ever met a tragic end. He acted as if he had a monopoly. We hated him cordially by Monday night, but we were helpless. Hoggy claimed that being dead was a nerve-wearing and exhausting business, and that if he didn't get the respect due to him as a corpse he would put on his plug hat and a plush curtain and walk up the main street of Jonesville. And as he was a football man and a blamed fool combined we didn't see any way of preventing him.

However, everything looked promising. We had made all the necessary arrangements. The students were to meet in chapel at nine o'clock in the morning and eulogize Hogboom for an hour, after which college was to be dismissed for the day in order that unlimited mourning could be indulged in. There were to be speeches by the Faculty and by students. Maxwell, the human textbook, was to make the address for the Senior class. We chuckled when we thought how he was toiling over it. Noddy Pierce, of our crowd, was to talk about Hogboom as a brother; Rogers, of the football team, was to make a few grief-saturated remarks. So was Perkins. Every one was confidently expecting Perkins to make the effort of his life and swamp the chapel in sobdrops. He was in the secret and he afterward said that he would rather try to write a Shakespearean tragedy offhand than to write another funeral oration about a man whom he knew was at that moment sitting in a pair of pajamas in an upper room half a mile away and yelling for pie.

As a matter of fact, there were so many in the secret that we were dead afraid that it would explode. We had to put the baseball team on so that they would be prepared to go over to Hambletonian at noon. The game had been called off, of course, and Hambletonian had been telegraphed. But I was secretary of the Athletic Club and had done the telegraphing. So I addressed the telegram to my aunt in New Jersey. It puzzled the dear old lady for months, I guess, because she kept writing to me about it. We had to tell all the fellows in the frat house and every one of the conspirators let in a friend or two. There were about fifty students who weren't as soggy with grief as they should have been by Monday night.

I blame Hogboom entirely for what happened. He started it when he insisted that he be smuggled into the chapel to hear his own funeral orations. We argued half the Monday night with him, but it was no use. He simply demanded it. If all dead men are as disagreeable as Hogboom was, no undertaker's job for me. He was the limit. He put on a blue bathrobe and got as far as the door on his promenade downtown before we gave in and promised to do anything he wanted. We had to break into the chapel and stow him away in a little grilled alcove in the attic on the side of the auditorium where he could hear everything. Sounds uncomfortable, but don't imagine it was. That nervy slavedriver made us lug over two dozen sofa pillows, a rug or two, a bottle of moisture and three pies to while away the time with. That was where we first began to think of revenge. We got it, too—only we got it the way Samson did when he jerked the columns out from under the roof and furnished the material for a general funeral, with himself in the leading rôle.

By the time we got Hogboom planted in his luxurious nest, about three A. M., we were ready to do anything. Some of us were for giving the whole snap away, but Pierce and Perkins and Rogers objected. They wanted to deliver their speeches at the meeting. If we would leave it to them, they said, they would see that justice was ladled out.

The whole college and most of the town were at the memorial meeting. It was a grand and tear-spangled occasion. There were three grades of emotion plainly visible. There was the resigned and almost pleased expression of the students who weren't in on the deal and who saw a vacation looming up for that afternoon; the grieved and sympathetic sorrow of the Faculty who were attempting to mourn for what they had always called a general school nuisance; and there was the phenomenally solemn woe of the conspirators, who were spreading it on good and thick.

The Faculty spoke first. Beats all how much of a hypocrite a good man can be when he feels it to be his duty. There was Bates, the Latin prof. He had struggled with Hogboom three years and had often expressed the firm opinion that, if

Hoggy were removed from this world by a masterpiece of justice of some sort, the general tone of civilization would go up fifty per cent. Yet Bates got up that morning and cried—yes, sir, actually cried. Cried into a large pocket handkerchief that wasn't watertight, either. That's more than Hoggy would ever have done for him. And Prexy was so sympathetic and spoke so beautifully of young soldiers getting drawn aside by Fate on their way to the battle, and all that sort of thing, that you would have thought he had spent the last three years loving Hogboom— whereas he had spent most of the time trying to get some good excuse for rooting him out of school. You know how Faculties always dislike a good football player. I think, myself, they are jealous of his fame.

Maxwell made a telling address for the Senior class. He and Hoggy had always disagreed, but it was all over now; and the way he laid it on was simply wonderful. I thought of Hoggy up there behind the grilling, swelling with pride and satisfaction as Maxwell told how brave, how tender, how affectionate and how honorable he was, and I wished I was dead, too. Being dead with a string to it is one of the finest things that can happen to a man if he can just hang around and listen to people.

Pierce got up. He was the college silver-tongue, and we settled back to listen to him. Previous speakers had made Hoggy out about as fine as Sir Philip Sidney, but they were amateurs. Here was where Hoggy went up beside A. Lincoln and Alexander if Pierce was anywhere near himself.

There is no denying that Pierce started out magnificently. But pretty soon I began to have an uneasy feeling that something was wrong. He was eloquent enough, but it seemed to me that he was handling the deceased a little too strenuously. You know how you can damn a man in nine ways and then pull all the stingers out with a "but" at the end of it. That was what Pierce was doing. "What if Hogboom was, in a way, fond of his ease?" he thundered. "What if the spirit of good fellowship linked arms with him when lessons were waiting, and led him to the pool hall? He may have been dilatory in his college duties; he may have wasted his allowance on pool and billiards instead of in missionary contributions. He may have owed money—yes, a lot of money. He may, indeed, have been a little selfish—which one of us isn't? He may have frittered away time for which his parents were spending the fruit of their early toil—but youth, friends, is a golden age when life runs riot, and he is only half a man who stops to think of petty prudence."

That was all very well to say about Rameses or Julius Cæsar or some other deceased who is pretty well seasoned, but I'll tell you it made the college gasp, coming when it did. It sounded sacrilegious and to me it sounded as if some one who was noted as an orator was going to get thumped by the late Mr. Hogboom about the next day. I perspired a lot from nervousness as Pierce rumbled on, first praising the departed and then landing on him with both oratorical feet. When he finally sat down and mopped his forehead the whole school gave one of those long breaths that you let go of when you have just come up from a dive under cold water.

Rogers followed Pierce. Rogers wasn't much of a talker, but he surpassed even his own record that day in falling over himself. When he tried to illustrate how thoughtful and generous Hogboom was he blundered into the story of the time Hoggy bet all of his money on a baseball game at Muggledorfer, and of how he walked home with his chum and carried the latter's coat and grip all the way. That made the Faculty wriggle, I can tell you. He illustrated the pluck of the deceased by telling how Hogboom, as a Freshman, dug all night alone to rescue a man imprisoned in a sewer, spurred on by his cries—though, Rogers explained in his halting way, it afterward turned out that this was only the famous "sewer racket" which is worked on every green Freshman, and that the cries for help came from a Sophomore who was alternately smoking a pipe and yelling into a drain across the road. Still, Rogers said, it illustrated Hogboom's nobility of spirit. In his blundering fashion he went on to explain some more of Hoggy's good points, and by the time he sat down there wasn't a shred of the latter's reputation left intact. The whole school was grinning uncomfortably, and the Faculty was acting as if it was sitting, individually and collectively, on seventeen great gross of red-hot pins.

By this time we conspirators were divided between holy joy and a fear that the thing was going to be overdone. It was plain to be seen that the Faculty wasn't going to stand for much more loving frankness. Pierce whispered to Tad Perkins, Hogboom's chum, and the worst victim of his posthumous whims, to draw it mild and go slow. Perkins was to make the last talk, and we trembled in our shoes when he got up.

We needn't have feared for Perkins. He was as smooth as a Tammany orator. He praised Hogboom so pathetically that the chapel began to show acres of white handkerchiefs again. Very gently he talked over his career, his bravery and his achievements. Then just as poetically and gently he glided on into the biggest lie that has

been told since Ananias short-circuited retribution with his unholy tale.

"What fills up the heart and the throat, fellows," he swung along, "is not the loss we have sustained; not the irreparable injury to all our college activities; not even the vacant chair that must sit mutely eloquent beside us this year. It's something worse than that. Perhaps I should not be telling this. It's known to but a few of his most intimate friends. The saddest thing of all is the fact that back in Weeping Water there is a girl—a lovely girl—who will never smile again."

Phew! You could just feel the feminine side of the chapel stiffen—Hogboom was the worst fusser in college. He was chronically in love with no less than four girls and was devoted to dozens at a time. We had reason to believe that he was at that time engaged to two, and spring was only half over at that. This was the best of all; our revenge was complete.

"A girl," Perkins purred on, "who has grown up with him from childhood; who whispered her promise to him while yet in short dresses; who sat at home and waited and dreamed while her knight fought his way to glory in college; who treasured his vows and wore his ring and ——"

" 'Tain't so, you blamed idiot!" came a hoarse voice from above. If the chapel had been stormed by Comanches there couldn't have been more of a commotion. A thousand pairs of eyes focused themselves on the grill. It sagged in and then disappeared with a crash. The towsled head of Hogboom came out of the opening.

"I'll fix you for that, Tad Perkins," he yelled. "I'll get even with you if it takes me the rest of my life. I ain't engaged to any Weeping Water girl. You know it, you liar! I've had enough of this ——" You couldn't hear any more for the shrieks. When a supposedly dead man sticks his head out of a jog in the ceiling and offers to fight his Mark Antony it is bound to create some commotion. Even the professors turned white. As for the girls—great smelling salts, what a cinch! They fainted in windrows. Some of us carried out as many as six, and you had better believe we were fastidious in our choice, too.

There had never been such a sensation since Siwash was invented. Between the panic-stricken, the dazed, the hilarious, the indignant and the guilty wretches like myself, who were wondering how in thunder there was going to be any explaining done, that chapel was just as coherent as a madhouse. And then Hogboom himself burst in a side door, and it took seven of us to prevent him from reducing Perkins to a paste and frescoing him all over the chapel walls. Everybody was rattled but Prexy. I think Prexy's circulation was principally ice water. When the row was over he got up and blandly announced that classes would take up immediately and that the Faculty would meet in extra-extraordinary session that noon.

How did we get out of it? Well, if you want to catch the last car, old man, I'll have to hit the high spots on the sequel. Of course, it was a tremendous scandal—a chapel meeting breaking up in a fight. We all stood to be expelled, and some of the Faculty were sorry they couldn't hang us, I guess, from the way they talked. But in the end it blew over because there wasn't much of anything to hang on any one. The telegrams were all traced to the agent at Weeping Water, and he identified the sender as a long, short, thick, stout, agricultural-looking man in a plug hat, or words to that effect. What's more, he declared it wasn't his duty to chase around town confirming messages—he was paid to send them. Hogboom had a harder time, but he, too, explained that he had come home from Weeping Water a day late, owing to a slight attack of appendicitis, and that when he found himself late for chapel he had climbed up into the balcony through a side door to hear the chapel talk, of which he was very fond,

and had found, to his amazement, that he was being reviled by his friends under the supposition that he was dead and unable to defend himself. Nobody believed Hogboom, but nobody could suggest any proof of his villainy—so the Faculty gave him an extra five-thousand-word oration by way of punishment, and he made Perkins write it in two nights by threats of making a clean breast. Poor Hoggy came out of it pretty badly. I think it broke both of his engagements, and what between explaining to the Faculty and studying to make a good showing and redeem himself, he didn't have time to work up another before Commencement—while the rest of us lived in mortal terror of exposure and didn't enjoy ourselves a bit all through May, though it was some comfort to reflect on what would have happened if the scheme had worked—for Hambletonian beat us to a frazzle that afternoon.

That's what we got for monkeying with a solemn subject. But, pshaw! Who cares in college? What a student can do is limited only by what he can think up. Did I ever tell you what we did to the Eastern Investigator? Take another cigar. It isn't late yet.

A PIECE OF STEAK

by Jack London

JACK LONDON WAS thirty-three when " A Piece of Steak" was published; at the time he was probably the best-known and highest-paid writer in the world. His own life exceeded the farthest bounds of fiction. The illegitimate son of an itinerant astrologer and a runaway Midwest farm girl, he had been a newsboy, cannery worker, oyster pirate, seal hunter, prizefighter, gold miner, tramp and Socialist soapbox orator with two jail terms on his record before he turned to writing. His first story ran in the *Overland Monthly* in 1899, but his first big success, *The Call of the Wild*, was a *Post* serial in 1903. London wrote many short stories for the *Post* after that and his autobiographical novel, *John Barleycorn*, was serialized by Lorimer in 1913. In eighteen years he turned out fifty books and earned a million dollars, but there was nothing left at the end. He died in 1916, officially from uremic poisoning, but probably from a deliberate overdose of sleeping tablets. His full life story was colorfully told in *Sailor on Horseback* by Irving Stone, which ran in the *Post* in 1938.

NOVEMBER 20, 1909

WITH THE LAST MORSEL of bread Tom King wiped his plate clean of the last particle of flour gravy and chewed the resulting mouthful in a slow and meditative way. When he arose from the table he was oppressed by the feeling that he was distinctly hungry. Yet he alone had eaten. The two children in the other room had been sent early to bed in order that in sleep they might forget they had gone supperless. His wife had touched nothing, and had sat silently and watched him with solicitous eyes. She was a thin, worn woman of the working class, though signs of an earlier prettiness were not wanting in her face. The flour for the gravy she had borrowed from the neighbor across the hall. The last two ha'pennies had gone to buy the bread.

He sat down by the window on a rickety chair that protested under his weight, and quite mechanically he put his pipe in his mouth and dipped into the side pocket of his coat. The absence of any tobacco made him aware of his action and, with a scowl for his forgetfulness, he put the pipe away. His movements were slow, almost hulking, as though he were burdened by the heavy weight of his muscles. He was a solid-bodied, stolid-looking man, and his appearance did not suffer from being overprepossessing. His rough clothes were old and slouchy. The uppers of his shoes were too weak to carry the heavy resoling that was itself of no recent date. And his cotton shirt, a cheap, two-shilling affair, showed a frayed collar and ineradicable paint stains.

But it was Tom King's face that advertised him unmistakably for what he was. It was the face of a typical prizefighter; of one who had put in long years of service in the squared ring and, by that means, developed and emphasized all the marks of the fighting beast. It was distinctly a lowering countenance, and, that no feature of it might escape notice, it was clean-shaven. The lips were shapeless and constituted a mouth harsh to excess, that was like a gash in his face. The jaw was aggressive, brutal, heavy. The eyes, slow of movement and heavy-lidded, were almost expressionless under the shaggy, indrawn brows. Sheer animal that he was, the eyes were the most animal-like feature about him. They were sleepy, lion-like—the eyes of a fighting animal. The forehead slanted quickly back to the hair, which, clipped close, showed every bump of the villainous-looking head. A nose, twice broken and moulded variously by countless blows, and a cauliflower ear, permanently swollen and distorted to twice its size, completed his adornment, while the beard, fresh-shaven as it was, sprouted in the skin and gave the face a blue-black stain.

Altogether, it was the face of a man to be afraid of in a dark alley or lonely place. And yet Tom King was not a criminal, nor had he ever done anything criminal. Outside of brawls, common to his walk in life, he had harmed no one. Nor had he ever been known to pick a quarrel. He was a professional, and all the fighting brutishness of him was reserved for his professional appearances. Outside the ring he was slow-going, easy-natured, and, in his younger days when money was flush, too open-handed for his own good. He bore no grudges and had few enemies. Fighting was a business with him. In the ring he struck to hurt, struck to maim, struck to destroy; but there was no animus in it. It was a plain business proposition. Audiences assembled and paid for the spectacle of men knocking each other out. The winner took the big end of the purse. When Tom King faced the Woolloomoolloo Gouger, twenty years before, he knew that the Gouger's jaw was only four months healed after having been broken in a Newcastle bout. And he had played for that jaw and broken it again in the ninth round, not because he bore the Gouger any ill will, but because that was the surest way to put the Gouger out and win the big end of the purse. Nor had the Gouger borne him any ill will for it. It was the game, and both knew the game and played it.

Tom King had never been a talker, and he sat by the window, morosely silent, staring at his hands. The veins stood out on the backs of the hands, large and swollen; and the knuckles, smashed and battered and malformed, testified to the use to which they had been put. He had never heard that a man's life was the life of his arteries, but well he knew the meaning of those big, upstanding veins. His heart had pumped too much blood through them at top pressure. They no longer did the work. He had stretched the elasticity out of them, and with their distention had passed his endurance. He tired easily now. No longer could he do a fast twenty rounds, hammer and tongs, fight, fight, fight, from gong to gong, with fierce rally on top of fierce rally, beaten to the ropes and in turn beating his opponent to the ropes, and rallying fiercest and fastest of all in that last, twentieth round, with the house on its feet and yelling, himself rushing, striking, ducking, raining showers of blows upon showers of blows and receiving showers of blows in return, and all the time the heart faithfully pumping the surging blood through the adequate veins. The veins, swollen at the time, had always shrunk down again, though not quite—each time, imperceptibly at first, remaining just a trifle larger than before. He stared at them and at his battered knuckles, and, for the moment, caught a vision of the youthful excellence of those hands before the first knuckle had been smashed on the head of Benny Jones, otherwise known as the Welsh Terror.

The impression of his hunger came back on him.

"Blimey, but couldn't I go a piece of steak!" he muttered aloud, clenching his huge fists and spitting out a smothered oath.

"I tried both Burke's an' Sawley's," his wife said half apologetically.

"An' they wouldn't?" he demanded.

"Not a ha'penny. Burke said ——" She faltered.

"G'wan! Wot 'd he say?"

"As how 'e was thinkin' Sandel ud do ye tonight, an' as how yer score was comfortable big as it was."

Tom King grunted, but did not reply. He was busy thinking of the bull terrier he had kept in his younger days to which he had fed steaks without end. Burke would have given him credit for a thousand steaks—then. But times had changed. Tom King was getting old; and old men, fighting before second-rate clubs, couldn't expect to run bills of any size with the tradesmen.

He had got up in the morning with a longing for a piece of steak, and the longing had not abated. He had not had a fair training for this fight. It was a drought year in Australia, times were hard and even the most irregular work was difficult to find. He had had no sparring partner and his food had not been of the best nor always sufficient. He had done a few days' navvy work when he could get it, and he had run around the Domain in the early mornings to get his legs in shape. But it was hard training without a partner and with a wife and two kiddies that must be fed. Credit with the tradesmen had undergone very slight expansion when he was matched with Sandel. The secretary of the Gayety Club had advanced him three pounds—the loser's end of the purse—and beyond that had refused to go. Now and again he had managed to borrow a few shillings from old pals, who would have lent more only that it was a drought year and they were hard put themselves. No—and there was no use in disguising the fact—his training had not been satisfactory. He should have had better food and no worries. Besides, when a man is forty it is harder to get into condition than when he is twenty.

"What time is it, Lizzie?" he asked.

His wife went across the hall to inquire and came back.

"Quarter before eight."

"They'll be startin' the first bout in a few minutes," he said. "Only a try-out. Then there's a four-round spar 'tween Dealer Wells an' Gridley, an' a ten-round go 'tween Starlight an' some sailor bloke. I don't come on for over an hour."

At the end of another silent ten minutes he rose to his feet.

"Truth is, Lizzie, I ain't had proper trainin'."

He reached for his hat and started for the door. He did not offer to kiss her—he never did on going out—but on this night she dared to kiss him, throwing her arms around him and compelling him to bend down to her face. She looked quite small against the massive bulk of the man.

"Good luck, Tom," she said. "You gotter do 'im."

"Ay, I gotter do 'im," he repeated. "That's all there is to it. I jus' gotter do 'im."

He laughed with an attempt at heartiness, while she pressed more closely against him. Across her shoulders he looked around the bare room. It was all he had in the world, with the rent overdue, and her and the kiddies. And he was leaving it to go out into the night to get meat for his mate and cubs—not like a modern workingman going to his machine grind, but in the old, primitive, royal, animal way, by fighting for it.

"I gotter do 'im," he repeated, this time a hint of desperation in his voice. "If it's a win it's thirty quid—an' I can pay all that's owin', with a lump o' money left over. If it's a lose I get naught—not even a penny for me to ride home on the train. The secretary's give all that's comin' from a loser's end. Good-by, old woman. I'll come straight home if it's a win."

"An' I'll be waitin' up," she called to him along the hall.

It was a full two miles to the Gayety, and as he walked along he remembered how in his palmy days—he had once been the heavyweight champion of New South Wales—he would have ridden in a cab to the fight, and how, most likely, some heavy backer would have paid for the cab and ridden with him. There were Tommy Burns and that Yankee nigger, Jack Johnson—they rode about in motor cars. And he walked! And, as any man knew, a hard two miles was not the best preliminary to a fight. He was an old un, and the world did not wag well with old uns. He was good for nothing now except navvy work, and his broken nose and swollen ear were against him even in that. He found himself wishing that he had learned a trade. It would have been better in the long run. But no one had told him, and he knew, deep down in his heart, that he would not have listened if they had. It had been so easy. Big money—sharp, glorious fights—periods of rest and loafing in between—a following of eager flatterers, the slaps on the back, the shakes of the hand, the toffs glad to buy him a drink for the privilege of five minutes' talk—and the glory of it, the yelling houses, the whirlwind finish, the referee's "King wins!" and his name in the sporting columns next day.

Those had been times! But he realized now, in his slow, ruminating way, that it was the old uns he had been putting away. He was Youth, rising; and they were Age, sinking. No wonder it had been easy—they with their swollen veins and battered knuckles and weary in the bones of them from the long battles they had already fought. He remembered the time he put out old Stowsher Bill, at Rush-Cutters Bay, in the eighteenth round, and how old Bill had cried afterward in the dressing-room like a baby. Perhaps old Bill's rent had been overdue. Perhaps he'd had at home a missus an' a couple of kiddies. And perhaps Bill, that very day of the fight, had had a hungering for a piece of steak. Bill had fought game and taken incredible punishment. He could see now, after he had gone through the mill himself, that Stowsher Bill had fought for a bigger stake, that night twenty years ago, than had young Tom King, who had fought for glory and easy money. No wonder Stowsher Bill had cried afterward in the dressing-rom.

Well, a man had only so many fights in him, to begin with. It was the iron law of the game. One man might have a hundred hard fights in him, another man only twenty; each, according to the make of him and the quality of his fiber, had a definite number, and when he had fought them he was done. Yes, he had had more fights in him than most of them, and he had had far more than his share of the hard, grueling fights—the kind that worked the heart and lungs to bursting, that took the elastic out of the arteries and made hard knots of muscle out of youth's sleek suppleness, that wore out nerve and stamina and made brain and bones weary from excess of effort and endurance overwrought. Yes, he had done better than all of them. There was none of his old fighting partners left. He was the last of the old guard. He had seen them all finished, and he had had a hand in finishing some of them.

They had tried him out against the old uns, and one after another he had put them away—laughing when, like old Stowsher Bill, they cried in the dressing-room. And now he was an old un, and they tried out the youngsters on him. There was that bloke, Sandel. He had come over from New Zealand with a record behind him. But nobody in Australia knew anything about him, so they put him up against old Tom King. If Sandel made a showing he would be given better men to fight, with bigger purses to win; so it was to be depended upon that he would put up a fierce battle. He had everything to win by it—money and glory and career; and Tom King was the grizzled old chopping-block that guarded the highway to fame and fortune. And he had nothing to win except thirty quid, to pay to the landlord and the tradesmen. And, as Tom King thus ruminated, there came to his stolid vision the form of Youth, glorious Youth, rising exultant and invincible, supple of muscle and silken of skin, with heart and lungs that had never been tired and torn and that laughed at limitation of effort. Yes, Youth was the Nemesis. It destroyed the old uns and recked not that, in so doing, it destroyed itself. It enlarged its arteries and smashed its knuckles, and was in turn destroyed by Youth. For Youth was ever youthful. It was only Age that grew older.

At Castlereagh Street he turned to the left, and three blocks along came to the Gayety. A crowd of young larrikins hanging outside the door made respectful way for him, and he heard one say to another: "That's 'im! That's Tom King!"

Inside, on the way to his dressing-room, he encountered the secretary, a keen-eyed, shrewd-faced young man who shook his hand.

"How are you feelin', Tom?" he asked.

"Fit as a fiddle," King answered, though he knew that he lied, and that if he had a quid he would give it right there for a good piece of steak.

When he emerged from the dressing-room, his seconds behind him, and came down the aisle to the squared ring in the center of the hall, a burst of greeting and applause went up from the waiting crowd. He acknowledged salutations right and left, though few of the faces did he know. Most of them were the faces of kiddies unborn when he was winning his first laurels in the squared ring. He leaped lightly to the raised platform and ducked through the ropes to his corner, where he sat down on a folding stool. Jack Ball, the referee, came over and shook his hand. Ball was a broken-down pugilist who for over ten years had not entered the ring as a principal. King was glad that he had him for referee. They were both old uns. If he should rough it with Sandel a bit beyond the rules he knew Ball could be depended upon to pass it by.

Aspiring young heavyweights, one after another, were climbing into the ring and being presented to the audience by the referee. Also, he issued their challenges for them.

"Young Pronto," Ball announced, "from North Sydney, challenges the winner for fifty pounds side bet."

The audience applauded, and applauded again as Sandel himself sprang through the ropes and sat down in his corner. Tom King looked across the ring at him curiously, for in a few minutes they would be locked together in merciless combat, each trying with all the force of him to knock the other into unconsciousness. But little could he see, for Sandel, like himself, had trousers and

sweater on over his ring costume. His face was strongly handsome, crowned with a curly mop of yellow hair, while his thick, muscular neck hinted at bodily magnificence.

Young Pronto went to one corner and then the other, shaking hands with the principals and dropping down out of the ring. The challenges went on. Ever Youth climbed through the ropes —Youth unknown, but insatiable—crying out to mankind that with strength and skill it would match issues with the winner. A few years before, in his own heyday of invincibleness, Tom King would have been amused and bored by these preliminaries. But now he sat fascinated, unable to shake the vision of Youth from his eyes. Always were these youngsters rising up in the boxing game, springing through the ropes and shouting their defiance; and always were the old uns going down before them. They climbed to success over the bodies of the old uns. And ever they came, more and more youngsters—Youth unquenchable and irresistible—and ever they put the old uns away, themselves becoming old uns and traveling the same downward path, while behind them, ever pressing on them, was Youth eternal —the new babies, grown lusty and dragging their elders down, with behind them more babies to the end of time—Youth that must have its will and that will never die.

King glanced over to the press box and nodded to Morgan, of the Sportsman, and Corbett, of the Referee. Then he held out his hands, while Sid Sullivan and Charley Bates, his seconds, slipped on his gloves and laced them tight, closely watched by one of Sandel's seconds, who first examined critically the tapes on King's knuckles. A second of his own was in Sandel's corner, performing a like office. Sandel's trousers were pulled off and, as he stood up, his sweater was skinned off over his head. And Tom King, looking, saw Youth incarnate, deep-chested, heavy-thewed, with muscles that slipped and slid like live things under the white satin skin. The whole body was acrawl with life, and Tom King knew that it was a life that had never oozed its freshness out through the aching pores during the long fights wherein Youth paid its toll and departed not quite so young as when it entered.

The two men advanced to meet each other and, as the gong sounded and the seconds clattered out of the ring with the folding stools, they shook hands with each other and instantly took their fighting attitudes. And instantly, like a mechanism of steel and springs balanced on a hair trigger, Sandel was in and out and in again, landing a left to the eyes, a right to the ribs, ducking a counter, dancing lightly away and dancing menacingly back again. He was swift and clever. It was a dazzling exhibition. The house yelled its approbation. But King was not dazzled. He had fought too many fights and too many youngsters. He knew the blows for what they were—too quick and too deft to be dangerous. Evidently Sandel was going to rush things from the start. It was to be expected. It was the way of Youth, expending its splendor and excellence in wild insurgence and furious onslaught, overwhelming opposition with its own unlimited glory of strength and desire.

Sandel was in and out, here, there and everywhere, light-footed and eager-hearted, a living wonder of white flesh and stinging muscle that wove itself into a dazzling fabric of attack, slipping and leaping like a flying shuttle from action to action through a thousand actions, all of them centered upon the destruction of Tom King, who stood between him and fortune. And Tom King patiently endured. He knew his business, and he knew Youth now that Youth was no longer his. There was nothing to do till the other lost some of his steam, was his thought, and he grinned to himself as he deliberately ducked so as to receive a heavy blow on the top of his head. It was a wicked thing to do, yet eminently fair according to the rules of the boxing game. A man was supposed to take care of his own knuckles, and if he insisted on hitting an opponent on the top of the head he did so at his own peril. King could have ducked lower and let the blow whiz harmlessly past, but he remembered his own early fights and how he smashed his first knuckle on the head of the Welsh Terror. He was but playing the game. That duck had accounted for one of Sandel's knuckles. Not that Sandel would mind it now. He would go on, superbly regardless, hitting as hard as ever throughout the fight. But later on, when the long ring battles had begun to tell, he would regret that knuckle and look back and remember how he smashed it on Tom King's head.

The first round was all Sandel's, and he had the house yelling with the rapidity of his whirlwind rushes. He overwhelmed King with avalanches of punches, and King did nothing. He never struck once, contenting himself with covering up, blocking and ducking and clinching to avoid punishment. He occasionally feinted, shook his head when the weight of a punch landed, and moved stolidly about, never leaping or springing or wasting an ounce of strength. Sandel must foam the froth of Youth away before discreet Age could dare to retaliate. All King's movements were slow and methodical, and his heavy-lidded, slow-moving eyes gave him the appearance of being half asleep or dazed. Yet they were eyes that saw everything, that had been trained to see everything through all his twenty years and odd in the ring. They were eyes that did not blink or waver before an impending blow, but that coolly saw and measured distance.

Seated in his corner for the minute's rest at the end of the round, he lay back with outstretched legs, his arms resting on the right angle of the ropes, his chest and abdomen heaving frankly and deeply as he gulped down the air driven by the towels of his seconds. He listened with closed eyes to the voices of the house. "Why don't yeh fight, Tom?" many were crying. "Yeh ain't afraid of 'im, are yeh?"

"Muscle-bound," he heard a man on a front seat comment. "He can't move quicker. Two to one on Sandel, in quids."

The gong struck and the two men advanced from their corners. Sandel came forward fully three-quarters of the distance, eager to begin again; but King was content to advance the shorter distance. It was in line with his policy of economy. He had not been well trained and he had not had enough to eat, and every step counted. Besides, he had already walked two miles to the ringside. It was a repetition of the first round, with Sandel attacking like a whirlwind and with the audience indignantly demanding why King did not fight. Beyond feinting and several slowly-delivered and ineffectual blows he did nothing save block and stall and clinch. Sandel wanted to make the pace fast, while King, out of his wisdom, refused to accommodate him. He grinned with a certain wistful pathos in his ring-battered countenance, and went on cherishing his strength with the jealousy of which only Age is capable. Sandel was Youth, and he threw his strength away with the munificent abandon of Youth. To King belonged the ring generalship, the wisdom bred of long, aching fights. He watched with cool eyes and head, moving slowly and waiting for Sandel's froth to foam away. To the majority of the onlookers it seemed as though King was hopelessly outclassed, and they voiced their opinion in offers of three to one on Sandel. But there were wise ones, a few, who knew King of old time and who covered what they considered easy money.

The third round began as usual, one-sided, with Sandel doing all the leading and delivering all the punishment. A half-minute had passed when Sandel, overconfident, left an opening. King's eyes and right arm flashed in the same instant. It was his first real blow—a hook, with the twisted arch of the arm to make it rigid, and with all the weight of the half-pivoted body behind it.

It was like a sleepy-seeming lion suddenly thrusting out a lightning paw. Sandel, caught on the side of the jaw, was felled like a bullock. The audience gasped and murmured awe-stricken applause. The man was not muscle-bound, after all, and he could drive a blow like a triphammer.

Sandel was shaken. He rolled over and attempted to rise, but the sharp yells from his seconds to take the count restrained him. He knelt on one knee, ready to rise, and waited, while the referee stood over him, counting the seconds loudly in his ear. At the ninth he rose in fighting attitude, and Tom King, facing him, knew regret that the blow had not been an inch nearer the point of the jaw. That would have been a knockout, and he could have carried the thirty quid home to the missus and the kiddies.

The round continued to the end of its three minutes, Sandel for the first time respectful of his opponent and King slow of movement and sleepy-eyed as ever. As the round neared its close King, warned of the fact by sight of the seconds crouching outside ready for the spring in through the ropes, worked the fight around to his own corner. And when the gong struck he sat down immediately on the waiting stool, while Sandel had to walk all the way across the diagonal of the square to his own corner. It was a little thing, but it was the sum of little things that counted. Sandel was compelled to walk that many more steps, to give up that much energy and to lose a part of the precious minute of rest. At the beginning of every round King loafed slowly out from his corner, forcing his opponent to advance the greater distance. The end of every round found the fight manœuvered by King into his own corner so that he could immediately sit down.

Two more rounds went by, in which King was parsimonious of effort and Sandel prodigal. The latter's attempt to force a fast pace made King uncomfortable, for a fair percentage of the multitudinous blows showered upon him went home. Yet King persisted in his dogged slowness, despite the crying of the young hotheads for him to go in and fight. Again, in the sixth round, Sandel was careless, again Tom King's fearful right flashed out to the jaw, and again Sandel took the nine seconds' count.

By the seventh round Sandel's pink of condition was gone and he settled down to what he knew was to be the hardest fight in his experience. Tom King was an old un, but a better old un than he had ever encountered—an old un who never lost his head, who was remarkably able at defense, whose blows had the impact of a knotted club and who had a knockout in either hand. Nevertheless, Tom King dared not hit often. He never forgot his battered knuckles, and knew that every hit must count if the knuckles were to last out the fight. As he sat in his corner, glancing across at his opponent, the thought came to him that the sum of his wisdom and Sandel's youth would constitute a world's champion heavyweight. But that was the trouble. Sandel would never become a world champion. He lacked the wisdom, and the only way for him to get it was to buy it with Youth; and when wisdom was his, Youth would have been spent in buying it.

King took every advantage he knew. He never missed an opportunity to clinch, and in effecting most of the clinches his shoulder drove stiffly into the other's rib. In the philosophy of the ring a shoulder was as good as a punch so far as damage was concerned, and a great deal better so far as concerned expenditure of effort. Also, in the clinches King rested his weight on his opponent and was loth to let go. This compelled the interference of the referee, who tore them apart, always assisted by Sandel, who had not yet learned to rest. He could not refrain from using those glorious flying arms and writhing muscles of his, and when the other rushed into a clinch, striking shoulder against ribs and with head resting under Sandel's left arm, Sandel almost invariably swung his right behind his own back and into the projecting face. It was a clever stroke, much admired by the audience, but it was not dangerous, and was, therefore, just that much wasted strength. But Sandel was tireless and unaware of limitations, and King grinned and doggedly endured.

Sandel developed a fierce right to the body, which made it appear that King was taking an enormous amount of punishment, and it was only the old ringsters who appreciated the deft touch of King's left glove to the other's biceps just before the impact of the blow. It was true, the blow landed each time; but each time it was robbed of its power by that touch on the biceps. In the ninth round, three times inside a minute, King's right hooked its twisted arch to the jaw; and three times Sandel's body, heavy as it was, was leveled to the mat. Each time he took the nine seconds allowed him and rose to his feet, shaken and jarred, but still strong. He had lost much of his speed and he wasted less effort. He was fighting grimly; but he continued to draw upon his chief asset, which was Youth. King's chief asset was experience. As his vitality had dimmed and his vigor abated he had replaced them with cunning, with wisdom born of the long fights and with a careful shepherding of strength. Not alone had he learned never to make a superfluous movement, but he had learned how to seduce an opponent into throwing his strength away. Again and again, by feint of foot and hand and body he continued to inveigle Sandel into leaping back, ducking or countering. King rested, but he never permitted Sandel to rest. It was the strategy of Age.

Early in the tenth round King began stopping the other's rushes with straight lefts to the face, and Sandel, grown wary, responded by drawing the left, then by ducking it and delivering his right in a swinging hook to the side of the head. It was too high up to be vitally effective; but when first it landed King knew the old, familiar descent of the black veil of unconsciousness across his mind. For the instant, or for the slightest fraction of an instant rather, he ceased. In the one moment he saw his opponent ducking out of his field of vision and the background of white, watching faces; in the next moment he again saw his opponent and the background of faces. It was as if he had slept for a time and just opened his eyes again, and yet the interval of unconsciousness was so microscopically short that there had been no time for him to fall. The audience saw him totter and his knees give, and then saw him recover and tuck his chin deeper into the shelter of his left shoulder.

Several times Sandel repeated the blow, keeping King partially dazed, and then the latter worked out his defense, which was also a counter. Feinting with his left he took a half-step backward, at the same time uppercutting with the whole strength of his right. So accurately was it timed that it landed squarely on Sandel's face in the full, downward sweep of the duck, and Sandel lifted in the air and curled backward, striking the mat on his head and shoulders. Twice King achieved this, then turned loose and hammered his opponent to the ropes. He gave Sandel no chance to rest or to set himself, but smashed blow in upon blow till the house rose to its feet and the air was filled with an unbroken roar of applause. But Sandel's strength and endurance were superb, and he continued to stay on his feet. A knockout seemed certain, and a captain of police, appalled at the dreadful punishment, arose by the ringside to stop the fight. The gong struck for the end of the round and Sandel staggered to his corner, protesting to the captain that he was sound and strong. To prove it he threw two back air springs, and the police captain gave in.

Tom King, leaning back in his corner and breathing hard, was disappointed. If the fight had been stopped the referee, perforce, would have rendered him the decision and the purse would have been his. Unlike Sandel, he was not fighting for glory or career, but for thirty quid. And now Sandel would recuperate in the minute of rest.

Youth will be served—this saying flashed into King's mind, and he remembered the first time he had heard it, the night when he had put away Stowsher Bill. The toff who had bought him a drink after the fight and patted him on the shoulder had used those words. Youth will be served! The toff was right. And on that night in the long ago he had been Youth. Tonight Youth sat in the opposite corner. As for himself, he had been fighting for half an hour now, and he was an old man. Had he fought like Sandel he would not have lasted fifteen minutes. But the point was that he did not recuperate. Those upstanding arteries and that sorely-tried heart would not enable him to gather strength in the intervals between the rounds. And he had not had sufficient strength in him to begin with. His legs were heavy under him and beginning to cramp. He should not have walked those two miles to the fight. And there was the steak which he had got up longing for that morning. A great and terrible hatred rose up in him for the butchers who had refused him credit. It was hard for an old man to go into a fight without enough to eat. And a piece of steak was such a little thing, a few pennies at best; yet it meant thirty quid to him.

With the gong that opened the eleventh round Sandel rushed, making a show of freshness which he did not really possess. King knew it for what it was—a bluff as old as the game itself. He clinched to save himself, then, going free, allowed Sandel to get set. This was what King desired. He feinted with his left, drew the answering duck and swinging upward hook, then made the half-step backward, delivered the uppercut full to the face and crumpled Sandel over to the mat. After that he never let him rest, receiving punishment himself, but inflicting far more, smashing Sandel to the ropes, hooking and driving all manner of blows into him, tearing away from his clinches or punching him out of attempted clinches, and ever, when Sandel would have fallen, catching him with one uplifting hand and with the other immediately smashing him into the ropes where he could not fall.

The house by this time had gone mad, and it was his house, nearly every voice yelling: "Go it, Tom!" "Get 'im! Get 'im!" "You've got 'im, Tom! You've got 'im!" It was to be a whirlwind finish, and that was what a ringside audience paid to see.

And Tom King, who for half an hour had conserved his strength, now expended it prodigally in the one great effort he knew he had in him. It was his one chance—now or not at all. His strength was waning fast, and his hope was that before the last of it ebbed out of him he would have beaten his opponent down for the count. And as he continued to strike and force, coolly estimating the weight of his blows and the quality of the damage wrought, he realized how hard a man Sandel was to knock out. Stamina and endurance were his to an extreme degree, and they were the virgin stamina and endurance of Youth. Sandel was certainly a coming man. He had it in him. Only out of such rugged fiber were successful fighters fashioned.

Sandel was reeling and staggering, but Tom King's legs were cramping and his knuckles going back on him. Yet he steeled himself to strike the fierce blows, every one of which brought anguish to his tortured hands. Though now he was receiving practically no punishment he was weakening as rapidly as the other. His blows went home, but there was no longer the weight behind them, and each blow was the result of a severe effort of will. His legs were like lead, and they dragged visibly under him; while Sandel's backers, cheered by this symptom, began calling encouragement to their man.

King was spurred to a burst of effort. He delivered two blows in succession—a left, a trifle too high, to the solar plexus, and a right cross to the jaw. They were not heavy blows, yet so weak and dazed was Sandel that he went down and lay quivering. The referee stood over him, shouting the count of the fatal seconds in his ear. If before the tenth second was called he did not rise the fight was lost. The house stood in hushed silence. King rested on trembling legs. A mortal dizziness was upon him, and before his eyes the sea of faces sagged and swayed, while to his ears, as from a remote distance, came the count of the referee. Yet he looked upon the fight as his. It was impossible that a man so punished could rise.

Only Youth could rise, and Sandel rose. At the fourth second he rolled over on his face and groped blindly for the ropes. By the seventh second he had dragged himself to his knee, where he rested, his head rolling groggily on his shoulders. As the referee cried "Nine!" Sandel stood upright, in proper stalling position, his left arm wrapped about his face, his right wrapped about his stomach. Thus were his vital points guarded, while he lurched forward toward King in the hope of effecting a clinch and gaining more time.

At the instant Sandel arose King was at him, but the two blows he delivered were muffled on the stalled arms. The next moment Sandel was in the clinch and holding on desperately while the referee strove to drag the two men apart. King helped to force himself free. He knew the rapidity with which Youth recovered and he knew that Sandel was his if he could prevent that recovery. One stiff punch would do it. Sandel was his, indubitably his. He had outgeneraled him, outfought him, outpointed him. Sandel reeled out of the clinch, balanced on the hairline between defeat or survival. One good blow would topple him over and down and out. And Tom King, in a flash of bitterness, remembered the piece of steak and wished that he had it then behind that necessary punch he must deliver. He nerved himself for the blow, but it was not heavy enough nor swift enough. Sandel swayed but did not fall, staggering back to the ropes and holding on. King staggered after him and, with a pang like that of dissolution, delivered another blow. But his body had deserted him. All that was left of him was a fighting intelligence that was dimmed and clouded from exhaustion. The blow that was aimed for the jaw struck no higher than the shoulder. He had willed the blow higher, but the tired muscles had not been able to obey. And from the impact of the blow Tom King himself reeled back and nearly fell. Once again he strove. This time his punch missed altogether, and, from absolute weakness, he fell against Sandel and clinched, holding on to him to save himself from sinking to the floor.

King did not attempt to free himself. He had shot his bolt. He was gone. And Youth had been served. Even in the clinch he could feel Sandel growing stronger against him. When the referee thrust them apart, there, before his eyes, he saw Youth recuperate. From instant to instant Sandel grew stronger. His punches, weak and futile at first, became stiff and accurate. Tom King's bleared eyes saw the gloved fist driving at his jaw and he willed to guard it by interposing his arm. He saw the danger, willed the act; but the arm was too heavy. It seemed burdened with a hundredweight of lead. It would not lift itself, and he strove to lift it with his soul. Then the gloved fist landed home. He experienced a sharp snap that was like an electric spark and, simultaneously, the veil of blackness enveloped him.

When he opened his eyes again he was in his corner, and he heard the yelling of the audience like the roar of the surf at Bondi Beach. A wet sponge was being pressed against the base of his brain and Sid Sullivan was blowing cold water in a refreshing spray over his face and chest. His gloves had already been removed and Sandel, bending over him, was shaking his hand. He bore no ill will toward the man who had put him out, and he returned the grip with a heartiness that made his battered knuckles protest. Then Sandel stepped to the center of the ring and the audience hushed its pandemonium to hear him accept young Pronto's challenge and offer to increase the side bet to one hundred pounds. King looked on apathetically while his seconds mopped the streaming water from him, dried his face and prepared him to leave the ring. He felt hungry. It was not the ordinary, gnawing kind, but a great faintness, a palpitation at the pit of the stomach that communicated itself to all his body. He remembered back into the fight to the moment when he had Sandel swaying and tottering on the hairline balance of defeat. Ah, that piece of steak would have done it! He had lacked just that for the decisive blow, and he had lost. It was all because of the piece of steak.

His seconds were half-supporting him as they helped him through the ropes. He tore free from them, ducked through the ropes unaided and leaped heavily to the floor, following on their heels as they forced a passage for him down the crowded center aisle. Leaving the dressing-room for the street, in the entrance to the hall, some young fellow spoke to him.

"W'y didn't yuh go in an' get 'im when yuh 'ad 'im?" the young fellow asked.

"Aw, go to hell!" said Tom King, and passed down the steps to the sidewalk.

The doors of the public house at the corner were swinging wide, and he saw the lights and the smiling barmaids, heard the many voices discussing the fight and the prosperous chink of money on the bar. Somebody called to him to have a drink. He hesitated perceptibly, then refused and went on his way.

He had not a copper in his pocket and the two-mile walk home seemed very long. He was certainly getting old. Crossing the Domain he sat down suddenly on a bench, unnerved by the thought of the missus sitting up for him, waiting to learn the outcome of the fight. That was harder than any knockout, and it seemed almost impossible to face.

He felt weak and sore, and the pain of his smashed knuckles warned him that, even if he could find a job at navvy work, it would be a week before he could grip a pick handle or a shovel. The hunger palpitation at the pit of the stomach was sickening. His wretchedness overwhelmed him, and into his eyes came an unwonted moisture. He covered his face with his hands and, as he cried, he remembered Stowsher Bill and how he had served him that night in the long ago. Poor old Stowsher Bill! He could understand now why Bill had cried in the dressing-room.

THE BOLT FROM THE BLUE

by G. K. Chesterton

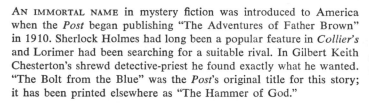

AN IMMORTAL NAME in mystery fiction was introduced to America when the *Post* began publishing "The Adventures of Father Brown" in 1910. Sherlock Holmes had long been a popular feature in *Collier's* and Lorimer had been searching for a suitable rival. In Gilbert Keith Chesterton's shrewd detective-priest he found exactly what he wanted. "The Bolt from the Blue" was the *Post*'s original title for this story; it has been printed elsewhere as "The Hammer of God."

NOVEMBER 5, 1910

THE LITTLE VILLAGE of Bohun Beacon was perched on a hill so steep that the tall spire of its church seemed only like the peak of a small mountain. At the foot of the church stood a smithy, generally red with fires and always littered with hammers and scraps of iron. Opposite to this, over a rude cross of cobbled paths, was the Blue Boar, the only inn of the place. It was upon this crossway, in the lifting of a leaden and silver daybreak, that two brothers met in the street and spoke, though one was beginning the day and the other finishing it. The Reverend and Honorable Wilfred Bohun was very devout and was making his way to some austere exercises of prayer or contemplation at dawn. Colonel the Honorable Norman Bohun, his elder brother, was by no means devout and was sitting in evening dress on the bench outside the Blue Boar, drinking what the philosophic observer was free to regard either as his last glass on Tuesday or his first on Wednesday. The Colonel was not particular.

The Bohuns were one of the very few aristocratic families really dating from the Middle Ages, and their pennon had really seen Palestine. But it is a great mistake to suppose that such houses stand high in chivalric tradition. Few except the poor preserve traditions. Aristocrats live, not in traditions but in fashions. They catch the novelty of each succeeding generation, generally in its most vulgar form. The Bohuns had been Mohawks under Queen Anne and Mashers under Queen Victoria. But, like more than one of the really ancient houses, they had rotted in the last two centuries into mere drunkards and dandy degenerates till, on the top of twenty tales of fashion and folly, there had even come a whisper of insanity. Certainly there was something hardly human about the Colonel's wolfish pursuit of pleasure; and his chronic resolution not to go home till morning had a touch of the hideous clarity of insomnia. He was a tall, fine animal, elderly but with hair still startlingly yellow. He would have looked merely blond and leonine but his blue eyes were sunk so deep in his face that they looked black. They were a little too close together. He had very long yellow mustaches, on each side of them a fold or furrow from nostril to jaw, so that a sneer seemed cut into his face. Over his evening clothes he wore a curious, pale yellow coat that looked more like a very light dressing-gown than an overcoat, and on the back of his head was stuck a soft felt hat of a bright green color, evidently some Oriental curiosity caught up at random. He was proud of appearing in such incongruous attires; proud of the fact that he always made them look congruous.

His brother, the curate, had also the yellow hair and the elegance, but he was buttoned up to the chin in black and his face was clean-shaven, cultivated and a little nervous. He seemed to live for nothing but his religion. But there were some who said—notably the blacksmith, who was a Presbyterian—that it was a love of Gothic architecture rather than of God, and that his haunting of the church like a ghost was only another and purer turn of the almost morbid thirst for beauty which sent his brother raging after women and wine. This charge was doubtful, while the man's practical piety was indubitable. Indeed, the charge was mostly an ignorant misunderstanding of the love of solitude and secret prayer, and was founded on his being often found kneeling, not before the altar but in peculiar places, in the crypts or gallery or even in the belfry. He was at the moment about to enter the church, through the yard of the smithy, but stopped and frowned a little as he saw his brother's cavernous eyes staring in the same direction. On the hypothesis that the Colonel was interested in the church he did not waste any speculations. There only remained the blacksmith's shop and, though the blacksmith was a Puritan and none of his people, Wilfred Bohun had heard some scandals about a

111

beautiful and rather celebrated wife. He flung a suspicious look across the shed.

"Good morning, Wilfred," the Colonel said; "like a good landlord I am watching sleeplessly over my people. I am going to call on the blacksmith."

Wilfred looked down and said: "The blacksmith is out. He is over at Greenford."

"I know," answered the other with silent laughter; "that is why I am calling on him."

"Norman," said the cleric, with his eye on a pebble in the road, "are you ever afraid of thunderbolts?"

"What do you mean?" asked the Colonel. "Is your hobby meteorology?"

"I mean," said Wilfred without looking up, "do you ever think that God might strike you in the street?"

"I beg your pardon," said the Colonel. "I see your hobby is folklore."

"I know your hobby is blasphemy," retorted the religious man, stung in the one live place of his nature. "But if you do not fear God you have good reason to fear man."

The elder raised his eyebrows politely. "Fear man?"

"Barnes, the blacksmith, is the biggest and strongest man for forty miles around," said the clergyman sternly. "I know you are no coward or weakling, but he could throw you over the wall."

This struck home, being true, and the lowering line by mouth and nostril darkened and deepened. For a moment he stood with the heavy sneer on his face. But in a moment Colonel Bohun had recovered his own cruel good humor and laughed, showing two doglike front teeth under his yellow mustache. "In that case, my dear Wilfred," he said quite carelessly, "it was wise for the last of the Bohuns to come out partially in armor."

And he took off the queer round hat covered with green, showing that it was lined within with steel. Wilfred recognized it, indeed, as a light Japanese or Chinese helmet, torn down from a trophy that hung in the old family hall.

"It was the first hat to hand, you know," explained his brother airily.

"The blacksmith is away at Greenford," said Wilfred quietly; "the time of his return is unsettled."

And with that he turned and went into the church with bowed head, crossing himself like one who wishes to be quit of an unclean spirit. He was anxious to forget such grossness in the cool twilight of his tall Gothic cloisters; but on that morning it was fated that his still round of religious exercises should be everywhere arrested by small shocks. As he entered the church, hitherto always empty at that hour, a kneeling figure rose hastily to its feet and came toward the full daylight of the doorway. When the curate saw it he stood still with surprise. For the early worshiper was none other than the village idiot, nephew of the blacksmith, one who neither would nor could care for the church, or for anything else. He was always called "Mad Joe," and seemed to have no other name. He was a dark, strong, slouching lad with a heavy white face, dark straight hair and a mouth always open. As he passed the priest his moon-calf countenance gave no hint of what he had been doing or thinking. He had never been known to pray before. What sort of prayers was he saying now? Extraordinary prayers, surely.

Wilfred Bohun stood rooted to the spot long enough to see the idiot go out into the sunshine, and even to see his dissolute brother hail him with a sort of avuncular jocularity. The last thing he saw was the Colonel throwing pennies at the open mouth of Joe, with the serious appearance of trying to hit it.

This ugly sunlight picture of the stupidity and cruelty of the earth sent the ascetic finally to his prayers for purification and new thoughts. He went up to a pew in the gallery which brought him under a colored window which he loved as it always quieted his spirit—a blue window with an angel carrying lilies. There he began to think less about the half-wit, with his livid face and mouth like a fish. He began to think less of his evil brother, pacing like a lean lion in his horrible hunger. He sank deeper and deeper into those cold and sweet colors of silver blossoms and sapphire sky.

In this place, half an hour afterward, he was found by Gibbs, the village cobbler, who had been sent for him in some haste. He got to his feet with promptitude, for he knew that no small matter would have brought Gibbs into such a place at all. The cobbler was, as in many villages, an atheist, and his appearance in church was a shade more extraordinary than Mad Joe's. It was a morning of theological enigmas.

"What is it?" asked Wilfred Bohun rather stiffly, but putting out a trembling hand for his hat.

The atheist spoke in a tone that, coming from him, was quite startlingly respectful and even, as it were, huskily sympathetic.

"You must excuse me, sir," he said in a hoarse whisper, "but we didn't think it right not to let you know at once. I'm afraid a rather dreadful thing has happened, sir; I'm afraid your brother——"

Wilfred clenched his frail hands. "What deviltry has he done now?" he cried in involuntary passion.

"Why, sir," said the cobbler, coughing, "I'm afraid he's done nothing and won't do anything. I'm afraid he's done for. You had really better come down, sir."

The curate followed the cobbler down a short winding stair which brought them out at an entrance rather higher than the street. Bohun saw the tragedy in one glance, flat underneath him like a plan. In the yard of the smithy were standing five or six men, mostly in black, one in an inspector's uniform. They included the doctor, the Presbyterian minister and the priest from the Roman Catholic chapel, to which the blacksmith's wife belonged. The latter was speaking to her, indeed, very rapidly, in an undertone, as she, a magnificent woman with red-gold hair, was sobbing blindly on a bench. Between these two groups, and just clear of the main heap of hammers, lay a man in evening dress, spread-eagled and flat on his face.

From the height above Wilfred could have sworn to every item of his costume and appearance down to the Bohun rings upon his fingers, but the skull was only a hideous splash, like a star of blackness and blood.

Wilfred Bohun gave the one glance and ran down the steps into the yard. The doctor, who was the family physician, saluted him, but he scarcely took any notice. He could only stammer out: "My brother is dead. What does it mean? What is this horrible mystery?" There was an unhappy silence, and then the cobbler, the most outspoken man present, answered: "Plenty of horror, sir," he said, "but not much mystery."

"What do you mean?" asked Wilfred with a white face.

"It's plain enough," answered Gibbs. "There is only one man for forty miles around that could have struck such a blow as that, and he's the man that had most reason to."

"We must not prejudge anything," put in the doctor, a tall, black-bearded man, rather nervously, "but it is competent for me to corroborate what Mr. Gibbs says about the nature of the blow, sir; it is an incredible blow. Mr. Gibbs says that only one man in this district could have done it. I should have said myself that nobody could have done it."

A shudder of superstition went through the slight figure of the curate. "I can hardly understand," he said.

"Mr. Bohun," said the doctor in a low voice, "metaphors literally fail me. It is inadequate to say that the skull was smashed to bits like an eggshell. Fragments of bone were driven into the body and the ground like bullets into a mud wall. It was the hand of a giant."

He was silent a moment, looking grimly through his glasses; then he added: "The thing has one advantage: that it clears most people of suspicion at one stroke. If you or I, or any normally-made man in the country, were accused of this crime, we should be acquitted as an infant would be acquitted of stealing the Nelson Column."

"That's what I say," repeated the cobbler obstinately. "There's only one man that could have done it and he's the man that would have done it. Where's Simeon Barnes, the blacksmith?"

"He's over at Greenford," faltered the curate weakly.

"More likely over in France," muttered the cobbler.

"No; he is in neither of those places," said a small and colorless voice, which came from the little Roman priest who had joined the group. "As a matter of fact, he is coming up the road at this moment."

The little priest was not an interesting man to look at, having stubbly brown hair and a round and stolid face. But if he had been as splendid as Apollo no one would have looked at him at that moment. Every one turned around and peered at the pathway which wound across the plain below, along which was, indeed, walking at his own huge stride and with a hammer on his shoulder, Simeon, the smith. He was a bony and gigantic man, with deep, dark, sinister eyes and a dark chinbeard. He was walking and talking quietly with two other men, and, though he was never specially cheerful, he seemed quite at his ease.

"And there's the hammer he did it with," cried the atheistic cobbler.

"No," said the inspector, a sensible-looking man with a sandy mustache, speaking for the first time. "There's the hammer he did it with, over there by the church wall. We have left it and the body exactly as they were."

All glanced around, and the short priest went across and looked down in silence at the tool where it lay. It was one of the smallest and the lightest of the hammers, and would not have caught the eye among the rest, but on the iron edge of it were blood and yellow hair.

After a silence the short priest spoke without looking up, and there was a new note in his dull voice. "Mr. Gibbs was hardly right," he said, "in saying that there is no mystery. There is at least the mystery of why so big a man should attempt so big a blow with so little a hammer."

"Oh, never mind that!" cried Gibbs in a fever. "What are we to do with Simeon Barnes?"

"Leave him alone," said the priest quietly. "He is coming here of himself. I know those two men with him. They are very good fellows from Greenford, and they have come over about the Presbyterian chapel."

Even as he spoke the tall smith swung around the corner of the church and strode into his own yard. Then he stood there quite still, and the hammer fell from his hand. The inspector, who had preserved impenetrable propriety, immediately went up to him.

"I won't ask you, Mr. Barnes," he said, "whether you know anything about what has happened here. You are not bound to say. I hope you don't know and that you will be able to prove it. But I must go through the form of arresting you in the King's name for the murder of Colonel Norman Bohun."

"You are not bound to say anything," said the cobbler, in officious excitement. "They've got to prove everything. They haven't proved yet that it is Colonel Bohun, with the head all smashed up like that."

"That won't wash," said the doctor aside to the priest. "That's out of the detective stories. I was the Colonel's medical man and I knew his body better than he did. He had very fine hands, but quite peculiar ones. The second and third fingers were the same in length. Oh, that's the Colonel right enough."

As he glanced at the corpse upon the ground the iron eyes of the motionless blacksmith followed them and rested there also.

"Is Colonel Bohun dead?" said the smith quite calmly. "Then he's damned."

"Don't say anything! Oh, don't say anything," cried the atheist cobbler, dancing about in an ecstasy of admiration of the English legal system. For no man is such a legalist as the good secularist.

The blacksmith turned on him, over his shoulder, the august face of a fanatic.

"It's well for you infidels to dodge like foxes because the world's law favors you," he said; "but God guards His own in His pocket, as you shall see this day."

Then he pointed to the Colonel and said: "When did this dog die in his sins?"

"Moderate your language," said the doctor.

"Moderate the Bible's language and I'll moderate mine. When did he die?"

"I saw him alive at six o'clock this morning," stammered Wilfred Bohun.

"God is good," said the smith. "Mr. Inspector, I have not the slightest objection to being arrested. It is you who may object to arresting me. I don't mind leaving the court without a stain on my character. You do mind, perhaps, leaving the court with a bad setback in your career."

The solid inspector for the first time looked at the blacksmith with a lively eye, as did everybody else except the short, strange priest, who was still looking down at the little hammer that had dealt the dreadful blow.

"There are two men standing outside this shop," went on the blacksmith with ponderous lucidity, "good tradesmen in Greenford whom you all know, who will swear that they saw me from before midnight till daybreak, and long after, in the committee room of our Revival Mission, which sits all night, we save souls so fast. In Greenford itself twenty people could swear to me for all that time. If I were a heathen, Mr. Inspector, I would let you walk on to your downfall. But as a Christian man I feel bound to give you your chance and ask you whether you will hear my alibi now or in court?"

The inspector seemed for the first time disturbed, and said: "I should be glad to clear you altogether now."

The smith walked out of his smithy with the same long and easy stride and returned with his two friends from Greenford, who were indeed friends of nearly every one present. Each of them said a few words, which no one even thought of disbelieving. When they had spoken, the innocence of Simeon stood up as solid as the great church above them.

One of those silences struck the group which are more strange and insufferable than any speech. Mainly, in order to make conversation, the curate said to the Catholic priest:

"You seem very much interested in that hammer, Father Brown."

"Yes, I am," said Father Brown. "Why is it such a small hammer?"

The doctor swung around on him.

"By George, that's true!" he cried. "Who would use a little hammer with ten larger hammers lying about?"

Then he lowered his voice in the curate's ear and said: "Only the kind of person that can't lift a large hammer. It is not a question of force or courage between the sexes. It's a question of lifting power in the shoulders. A bold woman could commit ten murders with a light hammer and never turn a hair. She could not kill a beetle with a heavy one."

Wilfred Bohun was staring at him with a sort of hypnotized horror, while Father Brown listened with his head a little on one side, really interested and attentive. The doctor went on with more hissing emphasis:

"Why do these idiots always assume that the only person who hates the wife's lover is the wife's husband? Nine times out of ten the person who most hates the wife's lover is the wife. Who knows what insolence or treachery he had shown her? Look there!" He made a momentary gesture toward the red-haired woman on the bench. She had lifted her head at last, and the tears were drying on her splendid face. But the eyes were fixed on the corpse with an electric glare that had in it something of idiocy.

The Reverend Wilfred Bohun made a limp gesture as if waving away all desire to know; but Father Brown, dusting off his sleeve some ashes blown from the furnace, spoke in his indifferent way.

"You are like so many doctors," he said; "your mental science is really suggestive. It is your physical science that is utterly impossible. I agree that the woman wants to kill the corespondent much more than the petitioner does. And I agree that a woman would always pick up a small hammer instead of a big one. But the difficulty is one of physical impossibility. No woman ever born could have smashed a man's skull out flat like that." Then he added reflectively, after a pause: "These people haven't grasped the whole of it. The man was actually wearing an iron helmet and the blow scattered it like broken glass. Look at that woman. Look at her arms."

Silence held them all up again, and then the doctor said rather sulkily: "Well, I may be wrong. There are objections to everything. But I stick to the main point: No man but an idiot would pick up that little hammer if he could use a big hammer."

With that the lean and quivering hands of Wilfred Bohun went up to his head and seemed to clutch his scanty hair. After an instant they dropped and he cried: "That was the word I wanted—you have said the word."

Then he continued, mastering his discomposure: "The words you said were, 'No man but an idiot would pick up that little hammer.' "

"Yes," said the doctor. "Well?"

"Well," said the curate, "no man but an idiot did."

The rest stared at him with eyes arrested and riveted, and he went on in a febrile and feminine agitation:

"I am a priest," he cried unsteadily, "and a priest should be no shedder of blood. I—I mean that he should bring no one to the gallows. And I

thank God that I see the criminal clearly now, because he is a criminal who cannot be brought to the gallows."

"You will not denounce him?" inquired the doctor.

"He would not be hanged if I did denounce him," answered Wilfred, with a wild but curiously-happy smile. "When I went into the church this morning I found a madman praying there—that poor Joe who has been wrong all his life. God knows what he prayed, but with such strange folk it is not incredible to suppose that their prayers are all upside down. Very likely a lunatic would pray before killing a man. When I last saw poor Joe he was with my brother. My brother was mocking him."

"By jove!" cried the doctor, "this is talking at last. But how do you explain ——"

The Reverend Wilfred was almost trembling with the excitement of his own glimpse of the truth. "Don't you see, don't you see," he cried feverishly, "that is the only theory that covers both the queer things, that answers both the riddles? The two riddles are the little hammer and the big blow. The smith might have struck the big blow, but would not have chosen the little hammer. His wife would have chosen the little hammer, but she could not have struck the big blow. But the madman might have done both. As for the little hammer, why, he was mad and might have picked up anything. And for the big blow—have you never heard, Doctor, that a maniac, in his paroxysm, may have the strength of ten men?"

The doctor drew a deep breath and then said: "I believe you've got it."

Father Brown had fixed his eyes on the speaker so long and steadily as to prove that his large, gray, oxlike eyes were not quite so insignificant as the rest of his face. When silence had fallen he said with marked respect: "Mr. Bohun, yours is the only theory yet propounded which holds water every way and is essentially unassailable. I think, therefore, that you deserve to be told, on my positive knowledge, that it is not the true one." And with that he walked away and stared again at the hammer.

"That fellow seems to know more than he ought to," whispered the doctor peevishly to Wilfred. "That priest is deucedly sly."

"No, no," said Bohun with a sort of mild fatigue. "It was the lunatic. It was the lunatic."

The group of the two clerics and the doctor had fallen away from the more official group containing the inspector and the man he had arrested. Now, however, that their own party had broken up they heard voices from the others. The priest looked up quietly and then looked down again, as he heard the blacksmith say in a loud voice:

"I hope I've convinced you, Mr. Inspector. I'm a strong man, as you say, but I couldn't have flung my hammer bang here from Greenford. My hammer hasn't got wings that it should come flying half a mile over fields."

The inspector laughed amicably, and said: "No, I think you can be considered out of it. But it's one of the rummiest coincidences I ever saw. I only ask you to give us all the assistance you can in finding a man as big and strong as yourself. By George, you might be useful if only to hold him! I suppose you yourself have no guess at the man."

"I may have a guess," said the pale smith, "but it is not at a man." Then, seeing the scared eyes turn toward his wife on the bench, he put his huge hand on her shoulder and said, "Nor a woman, either."

"What do you mean?" asked the inspector jocularly. "You don't think cows use hammers, do you?"

"I think no thing of flesh held that hammer," said the blacksmith in a stifled voice. "Mortally speaking, I think the man died alone."

Wilfred made a sudden forward movement and peered at him with burning eyes.

"Do you mean to say, Barnes," came the sharp voice of the cobbler, "that the hammer jumped up of itself and knocked the man down?"

"Oh, you gentlemen may stare and snigger," cried Simeon, "you clergymen who tell us on Sunday in what a stillness the Lord smote Sennacherib. I believe that One who walks invisible in every house defended the honor of mine, and laid the defiler dead before the door of it. I believe the force in that blow was just the force there is in earthquakes, and no force less."

Wilfred said, with a voice utterly indescribable:

"I told Norman myself to beware of the thunderbolt."

"That agent is outside my jurisdiction," said the inspector with a slight smile.

"You are not outside His," answered the smith. "See you to it." And turning his broad back he went into the house.

The shaken Wilfred was led away by Father Brown, who had an easy and friendly way with him. "Let us get out of this horrid place, Mr. Bohun," he said. "May I look inside your church? I hear it's one of the oldest in England. We take some interest, you know," he added with a comical grimace, "in old English churches."

Wilfred Bohun did not smile, for humor was never his strong point. But he nodded rather eagerly, being only too ready to explain the Gothic splendors to some one more likely to be sympathetic than the Presbyterian blacksmith or the atheist cobbler.

"By all means," he said; "let us go in at this side." And he led the way into the high side entrance at the top of the flight of steps. Father Brown was mounting the first step to follow him when he felt a hand on his shoulder, and turned to behold the dark, thin figure of the doctor, his face darker yet with suspicion.

"Sir," said the physician harshly, "you appear to know some secrets in this black business. May I ask if you are going to keep them to yourself?"

"Why, Doctor," answered the priest, "there is one very good reason why a man of my trade should keep things to himself when he is not sure of them, and that is that it is so constantly his duty to keep them to himself when he is sure of them. But if you think I have been discourteously reticent, I will go to the extreme limit of my custom. I will give you two large hints."

"Well, sir," said the doctor gloomily.

"First," said Father Brown quietly, "the thing is quite in your own province. It is a matter of physical science. The blacksmith is mistaken, not, perhaps, in saying that the blow was divine, but, certainly, in saying that it came by a miracle. It was no miracle, Doctor, except in so far as man is himself a miracle, with his strange and wicked and yet half-heroic heart. The force that smashed that skull was a force well-known to scientists— one of the most frequently debated of the laws of Nature."

The doctor, who was looking at him with frowning intentness, only said: "And the other hint?"

"The other hint is this," said the priest. "Do you remember the blacksmith—though he believes in miracles—talking scornfully of the impossible fairy tale that his hammer had wings and flew half a mile across country?"

"Yes," said the doctor; "I remember that."

"Well," added Father Brown with a broad smile, "that fairy tale was the nearest thing to the real truth that has been said today." And with that he turned his back and stumped up the steps after the curate.

The Reverend Wilfred, who had been waiting for him, pale and impatient, as if this little delay were the last straw for his nerves, led him immediately to his favorite corner of the church, that part of the gallery closest to the carved roof and lit by the wonderful window with the angel. The little Latin priest explored and admired everything exhaustively, talking cheerfully but in a low voice all the time. When, in the course of his investigation, he found the side exit and the winding stair down which Wilfred had rushed to find his brother dead, Father Brown ran not down but up with the agility of a monkey, and his clear voice came from an outer platform above.

"Come up here, Mr. Bohun," he called. "The air will do you good.

"Might be the map of the world, mightn't it?" said Father Brown.

"Yes," said Bohun very gravely, and nodded his head.

"I think there is something rather dangerous about standing on these high places, even to pray," said Father Brown. "Heights were made to be looked at, not to be looked from."

"Do you mean that one may fall over?" asked Wilfred.

"I mean that one's soul may fall, if one's body doesn't," said the other priest.

"I scarcely understand you," remarked Bohun indistinctly.

"Look at that blacksmith, for instance," went on Father Brown calmly. "A good man, but not a Christian—hard, imperious, unforgiving. Well, his Scotch religion was made up by men who prayed on hills and high crags and learned to look down on the world more than to look up at Heaven. Humility is the mother of giants. One sees great things from the valley: only small things from the peak."

"But he—he didn't do it," said Bohun tremulously.

"No," said the other in an odd voice; "we know he didn't do it."

After a moment he resumed, looking tranquilly out over the plain with his pale gray eyes: "I knew a man," he said, "who began by worshiping with others before the altar, but who grew fond of high and lonely places to pray from, corners or niches in the belfry or the spire. And once, in one of those dizzy places where the whole world seemed to turn under him like a wheel, his brain turned also, and he fancied he was God. So that, though he was a good man, he committed a great crime.

"He thought it was given to him to judge the world and strike down the sinner. He would never have had such a thought if he had been kneeling with other men upon a floor. But he saw all men walking about like insects. He saw one, especially, strutting just below him, insolent and evident by a bright green hat—a poisonous insect."

Rooks cawed around the corners of the belfry, but there was no other sound till Father Brown went on:

"This also tempted him: that he had in his hand one of the most awful engines of Nature; I mean gravitation—that mad and quickening rush by which all earth's creatures fly back to her heart when released. See, the inspector is strutting just below us in the smithy! If I were to toss a pebble over this parapet it would be something like a bullet by the time it struck him. If I were to drop a hammer—even a small hammer——"

Wilfred Bohun threw one leg over the parapet, and Father Brown had him in a minute by the collar.

"Not by that door," he said quite gently. "That door leads to hell."

Bohun staggered back against the wall and stared at him with frightened eyes

"How do you know all this?" he cried. "Are you a devil?"

"I am a man," answered Father Brown gravely, "and, therefore, have all devils in my heart. Listen to me," he said, after a short pause. "I know what you did; at least, I can guess the great part of it. When you left your brother you were racked with unrighteous rage to the extent even that you snatched up a small hammer, half inclined to kill him with his foulness on his mouth. Recoiling, you thrust it under your buttoned coat instead and rushed into the church. You prayed wildly, in many places, under the angel window, upon the platform above and on a higher platform still, from which you could see the Colonel's eastern hat like the back of a green beetle, crawling about. Then something snapped in your soul and you let God's thunderbolt fall."

Wilfred asked: "How did you know that his hat looked like a green beetle?"

"Oh, that?" said the other with the shadow of a smile. "That was common sense. But hear me further. I say I know all this, but no one else shall know it. The next step is for you. I shall take no more steps. I will seal this with the seal of confession. If you ask me why, there are many reasons, and only one that concerns you. I leave things to you because you have not yet gone very far wrong—as assassins go. You did not help to fix the crime on the smith when it was easy, or on his wife, when that was easy. You tried to fix it on the imbecile because you knew that he could not suffer. That was one of the gleams that it is my business to find in assassins. And now come down into the village, and go your own way, as free as the wind, for I have said my last word."

They went down the winding stairs and came out into the sunlight by the smithy. Wilfred Bohun carefully unlatched the wooden gate of the yard, and going up to the inspector said: "I wish to give myself up. I have killed my brother."

THE FIRST BIRDMAN

by J. W. Mitchell

SAMUEL PIERPONT LANGLEY is still the least understood man, and perhaps the most important one, in the history of aviation. An observatory scientist who specialized during most of his life in sunspots and solar radiation, he set out at the age of fifty-two to solve the secret of self-sustained flight, and succeeded. But when he died twenty years later, the world was still laughing at what it considered his ridiculous failure. The reasons for this are set forth with clarity and professional understanding in the following article.

The *Post* was playing no favorites in this piece; it had already paid full tribute to Alberto Santos-Dumont, the Wright brothers, Glenn H. Curtiss and other pioneer "birdmen." As early as 1900 it had reported that the British were using military balloons made of gold-beater's skin in the fighting in South Africa, and added, "Many lurid pictures have been drawn of airships flying over forts and cities and dropping high explosives. The idea is by no means an exaggeration." In 1914 it published a prophetic description of "The Coming Atlantic Air Flight," by Harry N. Atwood, and in the 1920's it was the forum for Brigadier General William (Billy) Mitchell's controversial pleas for a separate United States air force.

SEPTEMBER 17, 1910

IT has taken me, indeed, but a few years to pass through the period when the observer hears that his alleged observation was a mistake; the period when he is told that if it were true it would be useless, and the period when he is told that it is undoubtedly true, but that it has always been known.
—*S. P. Langley:* STORY OF EXPERIMENTS IN MECHANICAL FLIGHT.

IN THE present revival of interest in aeronautics, and in the general enthusiasm that attends the solution of the problem of mechanical flight, there is danger that the public, at least, will overlook the credit due to the one man who did more than any other to bring about the modern development. He was the late Samuel Pierpont Langley, Secretary of the Smithsonian Institution, who was unquestionably the first man to fly a heavier-than-air machine driven by its own power. This was on May 6, 1896.

It is true that Professor Langley never flew a man-carrying machine. There is likewise a report, which has been questioned in some quarters, of a man-carrying machine having been flown by Clement Ader, in France, in 1892. But there is no question that Professor Langley flew a thirty-pound steam-driven model on the date mentioned. At the first trial it flew half a mile and he made numerous flights after that up to almost a mile. It was the first time that a heavier-than-air machine had ever flown for even a small fraction of that distance, and Professor Langley regarded the problem as scientifically solved. He said, in a paper written at the time, that he had finished the work that seemed to be especially his, and that

for the commercial development of the machine the world in all probability would have to look to others.

He was not allowed to remain in peaceful and scientific retirement. The United States was then drifting, as the officials of the Government well knew, into the inevitable war with Spain. Mr. Roosevelt was Assistant Secretary of the Navy and he recognized the immense value of an aeroplane as an instrument of war. He stirred up the War Department and the Navy Department, as he was in the habit of stirring up things even then, and the joint Board of Ordnance and Fortifications applied to Professor Langley to know if he could build a flying machine. He replied that probably he could, and Congress appropriated fifty thousand dollars with which to do the work, the sum to be expended under the direction of the Board of Ordnance and Fortifications. Then commenced the work that ended in what was publicly heralded as failure and that resulted in the death of Professor Langley, due as much to the fun made of him in the public press as to anything else. It was unfortunate that most of the criticisms were founded on complete ignorance of the facts. But newspapermen are human and not given to taking anything very seriously. They had a long personal score to settle with Professor Langley, who had offended them because he did not know how to avoid doing so.

Some explanation of the misunderstanding is due to both sides. When it was learned that the United States was actually building a flying machine, of course the papers wanted the story. Professor Langley was not only a peculiar-minded man personally, but he was the possessor of a cast-iron New England conscience. He felt that he was working for the Government, and that, as he was guarding a military secret, the only way to guard it was to bar out the papers completely. The officers of the War and Navy Departments, many of whom knew all about the machine, said they knew nothing about the work; that it was entirely up to Professor Langley. This was an easy way of not answering questions and avoiding giving personal offence.

Never was there a military secret so well guarded. Professor Langley got to believe firmly that newspapermen were personal emissaries of the devil. He knew nothing about newspapers; in fact, that was not what he was paid for knowing. It got to be a standing joke in newspaper offices and bureaus in Washington to send a cub reporter down to the Smithsonian Institution to interview Professor Langley on his flying machine. Of course the reporter never got within hailing distance of the professor, and there was always another added to the needlessly long list of Professor Langley's newspaper enemies.

At this time if there had been a single man, who knew the newspaper business and who was also a personal friend of Langley, to do a little "jollying," there was not a newspaper in the country that would not have willingly refrained from printing anything about the maturing machine and from uttering any unfriendly criticism after the apparent failure to fly. But the buffer state was wanting. As the time approached for the trial of the big machine over the Potomac the newspapers, which had been denied access to the inner sanctum of the Smithsonian, were eager to send special boats to Widewater, Virginia, where the trials were to be held, in order to "get the story." There was one paper that kept a tugboat in commission for three weeks at an expense of one hundred and twenty-five dollars a day and got as the result two photographs and one story of a failure. There was barely a newspaper man in the fifty or more waiting for the flight who would not rather have written a story of failure than one of success. This may not have been a Christian attitude to take, but it was a very natural one.

When the trials were over the reporters wrote their stories and promptly forgot all about it. Newspapers that have to handle sensations from all over the world every day cannot afford to spend much thought on a single incident. If an editorial writer felt like it later he wrote a flippant editorial about the failure of the Langley flying machine and then forgot all about that too. But Professor Langley did not forget. It is said by his friends that he considered this light newspaper criticism deep-seated personal animosity.

The popular estimation of flying machines was shown at the time by the refusal of Congress to appropriate any more money for experiments. Whatever individual members may say to the contrary, Congress is very gun-shy when it comes to newspaper criticism. Congress was afraid of ridicule, and refused to make any further appropriation.

Unlimited money was offered Professor Langley from private sources to continue his work; in fact, he was urged to continue it. But his feelings were deeply hurt at the way his previous researches had been received, and he said that if the American people would not support the work that had been done primarily for them he would not continue it under private auspices. Of course any one is welcome to give his own verdict as to this course. It delayed the development of aviation in the world about six years. Possibly also it opened the way to the present tangled legal situation about flying machines. Professor Langley had done his work for the Government. He applied for no patents, but he took the precaution of presenting photographs of his work to the examiners in the Patent Office and he had them sign and date the negatives of various essential photographs. All this he intended to throw open to the world.

It seems tolerably certain that he had some system of balancing and guiding his machines that was different from anything now in use. There were no flexing wings as in the Wright and other modern machines, but there was a two-way tail—that is, a big tail with horizontal and vertical surfaces.

The secret of the balance was in this tail and so far it never has been disclosed. In one of the very few papers that he wrote about the machine Professor Langley tantalizingly came this near to explaining it: "There is not room nor occasion here to describe the automatic rudder and how it performs its functions. Suffice it to say it does perform them."

There is no question that it did perform them. There were flights of the model machines made from a quarter of a mile to a mile, and the machine would mount, circle in the air and alight where it was wanted without any guiding hand on board.

Professor Langley has been dead since February 27, 1906, and the notes of his pioneer experiments have since been in the hands of Charles Manley, of New York, who is to prepare them for publication. Mr. Manley was an expert engineer and was Professor Langley's closest confidant. Mr. Manley says that for lack of time the notes have never been given to the world. Those who are interested in aviation and who feel an interest in securing recognition for Professor Langley's work say that this delay is doing an injustice to the dead man, and that if the publication of his investigations is delayed much longer they will be interesting merely as ancient history.

Professor Langley at different times told something of his own story as to how he was drawn into his aerial investigations. He says that as a boy he can remember lying on his back in a New England pasture and watching the effortless flight of a hawk which sailed for half an hour without moving its wings, and whose progress along the "great overhead highway" was devoid of the obstacles that had to be surmounted by the boy in traveling to his place beneath the birds.

For many years the subject of mechanical flight was held in abeyance. There were other things that claimed the interest of the scientist. He explored the realms of astrophysics—almost invented the science, in fact—and extended the then known spectrum a third of its accepted length far into the realm of the ultraviolet rays. He was called to the manifold activities of the head of the Smithsonian Institution, but he found time there to work at the problem of mechanical flight and gradually solved it.

At that time it was as much as a man's scientific reputation was worth to let it be known that he seriously regarded the flying machine as a problem. The Patent Office had classed it with perpetual motion and demanded the presentation of a working model before they would consider a claim for a patent.

Man had wanted to fly ever since time was first recorded. Ancient myths dealt with the subject. There have been almost two hundred recorded machines tried since the time of Leonardo da Vinci, in 1500. Many of them were the work of serious men like Sir George Cayley, Stringfellow and Phillips, but none of them even approached success. The only machine driven by its own power that had ever sustained itself in the air for even a few seconds was the ingenious toy aeroplane of Penaud, driven by twisted rubber bands.

Yet Langley risked his scientific reputation by venturing into this maze of failure and charlatanry. He said himself that the spirit of investigation was reawakened in him by listening to Charles Lancaster at a meeting of the American Association for the Advancement of Science in 1886. Lancaster had spent five years in Florida studying soaring birds and had constructed some well-considered gliding models. He attempted to demonstrate them before the association, and because they would not work as he had said they would his statements on the whole were received with scant consideration.

Professor Langley, however, heard the address and decided to do some investigating himself. The world at that time knew absolutely nothing about aerodynamics. Newton's law for the increase of air resistance with the increase of the speed had stood for three hundred years, principally because nobody had ever thought to question it. Professor Langley said that just about the time he started active work a French mathematician had proved conclusively enough by the use of existing formulas that a barn-swallow, to reach the speed it is known to attain, must have more than the strength of a man. Professor Langley said he could see nothing to do but reject theories that led to such absurd conclusions, and do some original investigating.

He was at the time employed in the Allegheny Observatory. He went to a number of wealthy men to secure funds for his experiments, among them Andrew Carnegie. But Andrew said, in effect, "Hoot, mon; there's nothing in it." The reply of most of the others was to the same effect. It is rather interesting in this connection to reflect that Mr. Carnegie within a few months has offered a prize of twenty-five thousand dollars for the first pupil in his technical school at Pittsburgh who will build a flying machine that will fly.

There was one man among the Pittsburgh millionaires who, whatever he thought of the investigation, gave Professor Langley five thousand dollars with which to experiment. This was William Thaw, the father of Harry Thaw. One of Professor Langley's most important books, *The Internal Work of the Wind,* is dedicated to Thaw in acknowledgment of this aid.

One of the first pieces of apparatus that Professor Langley constructed at Allegheny was what he called the "whirling table." As a matter of fact, a great revolving derrick would be a more exact description. The arm of this derrick described a circle two hundred feet in circumference and was driven by a nicely governed steam engine up to a speed of seventy miles an hour. The objects to be tested were hung at the end of this arm and the measurement of their "lift" and "drift" was carefully recorded as they were towed through the air.

One of the simplest and most astonishing experiments was in the early stages of the work. A brass plate weighing just a pound was hung at the end of the rotating arm. Of course it pulled down just a pound against a spring balance. But, when the arm of the derrick was started and the speed increased, the weight of the plate decreased as it flew through the air. At a speed of seventy miles an hour it exerted a pull of less than one ounce. Thus, paradoxical as it seemed, it took less power to travel at high speed through the air than it did to travel slowly. It was in this way that Langley's law came to take the place of Newton's law.

It must be understood, however, that this does not apply practically to the construction of flying machines. The head resistance of the engine, the struts, the guy wires and the operator must all be taken into account, and though it is theoretically possible to drive two hundred pounds through the air with one horse-power, this applies merely to plane surfaces and not to complicated flying mechanism.

After six years of experiment Professor Langley commenced building his first power-driven model. He says that he knew absolutely nothing about steam engineering, but, after experiments with carbonic acid gas, compressed air, electricity and various other motive powers, he decided that as there was more known about steam than any other motive power it would be best to start with this. So, though already an old man, he started to study steam engineering with a view to building an engine.

There was literature in abundance on the subject, but he was aiming to build such an engine as had never been built before. All the problems were practically new and he set about solving them with the help only of a few trusted workmen in the Smithsonian. It was largely the fear of ridicule that made him keep his first work so concealed.

Professor Langley had a very peculiar bent. He was a scientist—none better in the higher ranks; but if there was need of doing anything in the mechanical field he could usually find a way of doing it, as witness his system of an air-blast to keep the stars visually steady in a telescope.

When the steam engine was finally installed in his aeroplane it was a queer combination; such

that any trained engineer would have said would not work. However, it did work. The chances are that it was the only sort of an installation that would have worked.

During the period of experiment after Professor Langley came to Washington he constructed thirty different models driven by springs and twisted rubber bands. Some of these were monoplanes, some biplanes, and some had spring wing-tips very closely approaching the flexing wings which are the essential features of the present Wright machine; in fact, Professor Langley made some models with wings that could be flexed so as to present different angles of incidence to the air, but this flexing was done before the model started its flight and, there being no passenger on board, could not of course be varied after the adjustment was once made.

Upon the whirling table, both in Allegheny and in Washington, Professor Langley experimented with all sorts and shapes of aeroplanes, and his conclusion was that mechanical flight was theoretically possible even with the engines then in use; but he said that the real difficulty lay in what might be termed "secondary problems," the chief of which was to make a machine which would automatically continue a rigorously horizontal flight and which would not be upset by the vagaries of the wind, just as a gyroscope torpedo is able to steer a straight course in spite of waves and contrary currents.

It was several years after he concluded that mechanical flight was possible before he undertook the extremely difficult work of making a power-driven model that would fly a much longer time than was possible with the twisted rubber bands used in his little machine. It was during the prosecution of this work that enough difficulties were encountered to have stopped almost any man. The first four models that were built all greatly exceeded their estimated weight, and none of them developed the power which their engines should have delivered. Every possible form of boiler was tried and finally at the fifth attempt, when, as Professor Langley said, weight had been reduced to the utmost limit and further reduction was still necessary, a boiler was constructed from a helical coil of very thin copper tubing and heat furnished from an adaptation of a plumber's gas torch. This engine and boiler worked at a pressure of one hundred and fifty pounds to the square inch and delivered about one and one-half horse-power to seven pounds of total weight.

It was at the end of many years of heartbreaking experiment and failure that this result was achieved. Work on the actual construction of the first machine was commenced in 1892, but it was not until 1896 that the first machine was flown. Four models were actually built before one was made that was theoretically light and powerful enough to fly.

With a sensitive man working in secret and a hostile press, eager to laugh at any supposed failure, it may be imagined that the years of suspense and discouragement were enough to sap almost any one's vitality.

The scene of the prospective launching was finally selected near Widewater, Virginia, a little place thirty miles below Washington, whence the return trip took the best part of a day. Here a small scow was secured and a house built on it, and the work that had been done in a well-protected shop in Washington had all to be done over under different atmospheric conditions that disarranged the apparatus and involved more harassing trials and failures than had been previously experienced.

Even after the machine had been built that was to be given a trial in free flight twenty trips were made between Washington and the experiment station before a successful launch was secured. These were not trips made on successive days either, but extended over a period of two years, with intervals of shopwork to repair some trifling but discouraging flaw that had unexpectedly developed—waits for favorable weather and other sorts of delays that could not possibly have been anticipated.

It was found when the first open-air trials were attempted that working out-of-doors was vastly different and more discouraging than working in a protected shop. Even in a light breeze the fragile apparatus could not be left alone for two seconds without being upset. There had to be a launching device made that would hold the model firmly till the instant of free flight and then would unquestionably and instantly release it.

Even when the model, which was thirteen feet across the wings, was launched it was found that the wings were distorted by their weight in the air out of all resemblance to their theoretically proper shape. It was necessary then to turn the machine on its back and dredge fine sand to the weight of the machine itself all over the wings, and then tighten up the guy wires and stays till the wings were the shape they should be when the machine was supported with its own weight in air.

Perhaps the account of the final triumph can best be given in Professor Langley's own words, which give an idea of the nerve-wrecking period of experiment through which he had passed and an unconsciously pathetic record of human achievement against odds. He says in part:

"I will spare an account of the numberless delays from continued accidents and from failures in attempted flights which prevented an entirely satisfactory one during nearly three years after a machine with the power to fly had been attained. It is true that the aerodrome maintained itself in the air many times, but some disaster had so often prevented a complete flight that the most persistent hope must at some time have yielded. On the sixth of May, 1896, I journeyed, perhaps for the twentieth time, to the distant river station and commenced the weary routine of another launch with very moderate expectations indeed; and when—on that, to me, memorable occasion —the signal was given and the aerodrome sprang into the air I watched from the shore with hardly a hope that the long series of accidents had come to a close. And yet it had, and for the first time the aerodrome swept through the air like a living thing, and as second after second passed on the face of the watch till a minute had gone by and it still flew on, and I heard the cheering of the few spectators, I felt that something had been accomplished at last; for never in any part of the world, or in any period, had any machine of man's construction sustained itself in the air for even half of this brief period. Still the aerodrome went on in a rising course till at the end of a minute and a half—for which time only it was provided with fuel and water—it had accomplished a little over half a mile. It then settled rather than fell into the river with a gentle descent. It was immediately taken out and flown again with equal success, and there was nothing to indicate that it might not have continued indefinitely except for the limit put upon it.

"And now, it may be asked, what has been done? This has been done: A flying machine, so long a type for ridicule, has really flown. It has demonstrated its practicability in the only satisfactory way—by really flying; and by doing this again and again under conditions that leave no doubt.

"There is no room here to enter on the consideration of the construction of larger machines or to offer reasons for believing that they will be built to remain for days in the air and reach speeds greater than any with which we are now familiar.

"Neither is there room to enter on a consideration of their commercial value or of those applications which probably will first come in the arts of war rather than in those of peace. But we can at least see that these may be such as to change the whole condition of warfare. When two opposing hosts will have their every movement known to each other, when no lines of fortifications will keep out the foe, and when the difficulties of defending a country against an attacking enemy in the air have grown, we may hope that this will hasten rather than retard the coming of the day when war shall cease."

This was the record of Professor Langley's final success after failures enough to have stopped any ordinary man. It was written at a time when the present achievements in mechanical flight were undreamed of, when Langley himself was known in his success to only a limited number of friends, and when the man-carrying flying machine was still a vision so little considered that the man who had made it possible was being driven to death with a broken heart over the fashion in which his pioneer work was received.

Just how little wealth and recognition Mr. Langley expected to win may be judged from the paragraph with which he closed his reference to that part of his experiments. He said:

"I have so far had a purely scientific interest in the result of these labors. Perhaps, if it could have been foreseen at the outset how much of labor there was to be, how much work and how much of life itself would be given to it, and how much care, I might have hesitated to enter upon it at all. And now reward must be looked for, if reward there be, in the knowledge that I have done the best I could in a difficult task with results which it is to be hoped will be useful to others. I have brought to a close the portion of the work which seemed to be specially mine—the demonstration of the practicability of mechanical flight; and for the next stage, which is the practical and commercial development of the idea, it is probable that the world will have to look to others. The world, indeed, will be supine if it does not realize that a new possibility has come to it and that the great universal highway overhead is soon to be opened."

It would have been well for Professor Langley's peace of mind, even for the popular conception of his scientific reputation, if he had stopped with demonstrating the practicability of mechanical flight. But he was drawn by the call of the Government into building a man-carrying machine. This was one of the most remarkable pieces of mechanical work that was ever executed.

The framework of the machine was built of French steel tubing two inches in diameter and almost as thin as writing-paper. This frame was of oval shape and at either end had big wings set at identical levels so that in reality it was a tandem monoplane. The propellers were set midway the length of the machine and revolved outside and on each side of the main framework. They made from one thousand to twelve hundred revolutions a minute. Inside the frame a very light bicycle seat supported the operator.

Every pulley, guy-wire and rib of the machine was hollowed out and reduced to the lowest possible weight. The total weight of the machine and engine was just eight hundred pounds and the supporting surface of its wings totaled ten hundred and forty square feet. When this is compared with the weight of from two to four pounds to the square foot of supporting surface carried by a modern aeroplane it will be seen that the machine was abundantly light to fly.

The most difficult as well as the most essential part of the machine was the motor. Professor Langley, in company with Mr. Manley, personally interviewed the foremost engine builders in Europe and America. He finally secured a contract with one of them to build an engine weighing not over ten pounds per horse-power. This contract, however, was never fulfilled, and almost a year was wasted in waiting for the engine which never came.

Professor Langley at that time had discarded steam and relied upon a gasoline motor. The one which eventually was built in the Smithsonian shops is rated by competent engineers to be the best gas engine which even yet has been produced. Much of the designing was due to Charles Manley, who also performed a very large part of the actual construction. Special carburetors were adopted after experiments had been made with dozens of different types, and the engine was connected with the propellers by a series of gears, dispensing with chains altogether and running absolutely without vibration.

The engine, which is now on exhibition in the National Museum, has five stationary cylinders arranged in the form of a five-pointed star. It is a marvel of light but durable construction, and delivers fifty-two horse-power for one hundred and fifty-five pounds of weight, including the radiators and batteries.

Those who are familiar with the construction of the best gasoline engines of the present day know that many of them are catalogued at three and four pounds to the horse-power and rated at from forty to fifty horse-power. Those who have attempted to get a light engine for aeronautic work know, however, that this weight is predicated on stripping the engine of radiators, batteries, cooling water and other essentials and that the actual horse-power, when it is put on a brake test, often falls from a rating of forty to a delivery of twenty.

The wings of the big machine were a marvel of light and efficient construction. In view of the modern construction of aeroplane wings, which is light and strong, but by no means delicate, it would seem as though they exceeded the limit of accuracy. The ribs were built on the plan of the quills in the wings of a Harpy eagle, this form of construction being the lightest and strongest among Nature's flying creatures. These quills were square in structure, tapered almost to a fishing-rod point at the small end. They were hollow and were put together with marine glue and braced with tiny wooden struts inside. Weight for weight they were as strong as Nature's model after which they were built.

The whole workmanship of the big machine is exquisite. For those who really enjoy fine machine work, such as nearly approaches mathematical-instrument work, it is a revelation. Every ounce of superfluous metal has been cut out. The machine carries less weight to the square foot of supporting surface and has more actual power than any machine that is flying today. It also has less head resistance, and the chances are that if it were entered in a world-speed contest against the fastest modern machines it would make a world's record.

It is the sort of machine that one can picture young millionaire sportsmen using a decade hence, not necessarily in the model but in the workmanship. It compares with the machines now flying about as a modern racing car would compare with the old automobile in which the Comte de Dion won the first Paris-Bordeaux automobile road race.

The engine of the big flyer is on exhibition in the National Museum, but the big machine has never been publicly shown. The officials of the Smithsonian say this is because of lack of room. The chances are that this reticence is due partly to a feeling of resentment over the scant recognition that has been given to Professor Langley's work.

While Doctor Cyrus Adler, one of Professor Langley's closest personal friends, was the librarian of the Smithsonian Institution, he was asked whether the persistent report that the big machine would be given another trial was true. He shook his head and said: "No; it has made history and it belongs to history. It will remain a relic."

Before trying his big machine Professor Langley made a final flight with a model driven by a gasoline engine. This model was just a quarter of the size of the man-carrying machine. It flew perfectly and the launching apparatus, which eventually wrecked the big machine, worked perfectly also.

When it came to the trial of the man-carrying machine both Mr. Manley and the officers of the Board of Ordnance and Fortifications, under whom the tests were to be made, distrusted the launching device. It was true that this device had worked well on numerous occasions, but they insisted that for such a test as was contemplated it would be better to try the machine on wheels over the ground. Mr. Manley was to operate the machine, and he insisted that if he was willing to take the risk it was nobody else's business. Professor Langley said, however, that he was not willing to risk the life of the operator over land, and he was firm in demanding that the trial be made over water. In view of what has been done in subsequent years by aeroplanes mounted on wheels it is almost certain a launch of this sort would have been a success. But Professor Langley sacrificed his own ambitions on the score of greater safety to the operator.

It was on October 7, 1903, that the first test of the big machine was made. Newspaper accounts are so recent as to render unnecessary a repetition of the details of this trial; but it is essential to say that when the first trial was made two little pieces of iron on the ways, each not more than half an inch in diameter, caught in the frame of the machine and as the launching ways fell, at the end of the run across the top of the houseboat, they dragged the machine down and prevented it from getting into the air. The second and last trial was made on December 8 of the same year, just below Washington. Money was exhausted and the season was so far advanced it was impossible to wait longer. Little was expected in this final trial, and it was made altogether under the most disadvantageous circumstances.

For a second time the launching ways failed to work and the machine was again thrown into the river, so that the series of trials closed without getting the aeroplane into the air and giving it a chance to prove whether or not it would fly.

It would seem, even at this late day, essential—in fairness to Professor Langley—to show that the alleged failure of the big machine was not a failure to fly, but was due entirely to a fault in the launching device and to the humane insistence of the builder, who would not risk the safety of the operator by a trial except over the water.

WORDS AND MUSIC

by Irvin S. Cobb

ONE NIGHT IN 1911 editor Lorimer invited Irvin S. Cobb to be his guest at a banquet of the American Publishers Association in New York. At the time Cobb was the star reporter and rewrite man of the New York *Evening World*, and had sold some short fiction and humor to the *Post* by mail. After the dinner, which Cobb remembered as "quite moist," he and Lorimer took a ride through Central Park in a horse-drawn hansom cab. The *Post*'s editor seemed wholly relaxed and was singing his favorite song on such occasions, "Glow, Little Glowworm, Glimmer, Glimmer." Suddenly he stopped singing and fixed his guest with an eye that glimmered business. "How about hooking up with the *Post* when your time's up at that treadmill down in Park Row?" he demanded. "I'd like it," said Cobb, and thus began an association which was highly profitable for both of them during the next dozen years.

Cobb was the perfect *Post* contributor—a veteran reporter who always thrilled at a big story, a phenomenally fast writer, a skilled craftsman of magazine fiction, and a big, flavorful personality whose wit never cut too deep. With all this he combined a streak of the grotesque and even morbid which, in such *Post* stories as "Blacker Than Sin" (November 20, 1915) foreshadowed the nightmare South of William Faulkner. "Words and Music" is the first of the long series he wrote on Judge Priest of Paducah, Kentucky.

OCTOBER 28, 1911

WHEN BRECK TANDY KILLED a man he made a number of mistakes. In the first place, he killed the most popular man in Forked Deer County—the county clerk, a man named Abner J. Rankin. In the second place, he killed him with no witnesses present, so that it stood his word—and he a newcomer and a stranger—against the mute, eloquent accusation of a riddled dead man. And in the third place, he sent north of the Ohio River for a lawyer to defend him.

On the first Monday in June—Court Monday —the town filled up early. Before the field larks were out of the grass the farmers were tying their teams to the gnawed hitch-racks along the square. By nine o'clock the swapping ring below the wagonyard was swimming in red dust and clamorous with the chaffer of the horse-traders. In front of a vacant store the Ladies' Aid Society of Zion Baptist Church had a canvas sign out, announcing that an elegant dinner would be served for twenty-five cents from twelve to one, also ice cream and cake all day for fifteen cents.

The narrow wooden sidewalks began to creak and churn under the tread of many feet. A long-haired medicine doctor emerged from his frock-coat like a locust coming out of its shell, pushed his high hat off his forehead and ranged a guitar, sundry bottles of a potent mixture, his tooth-pulling forceps and a trick-handkerchief upon the narrow shelf of his stand alongside the Drummers' Home Hotel. In front of the little dingy tent of the Half Man and Half Horse a yellow Negro sat on a split-bottom chair limbering up for a hard day. This yellow Negro was an artist. He played a common twenty-cent mouth organ, using his left hand to slide it back and forth across his spread lips. The other hand held a pair of polished beef bones, such as end men wield, and about the wrist was buckled a broad leather strap with three big sleigh-bells riveted loosely to the leather, so that he could clap the bones and shake the bells with the same motion. He was a whole orchestra in himself. He could play on his mouth organ almost any tune you wanted, and with his bones and his bells to help out he could creditably imitate a church organ, a fife-and-drum corps, or, indeed, a full brass band. He had his chair tilted back until his woolly head dented a draggled banner depicting in five faded primary colors the physical attractions of the Half Man and Half Horse—Marvel of the Century—and he tested his mouth organ with short, mellow, tentative blasts as he waited until the Marvel and the Marvel's manager finished a belated breakfast

125

within and the first ballyhoo could start. He was practicing the newest of the ragtime airs to get that far South. The name of it was "The Georgia Camp-Meeting."

The town marshal in his shirt sleeves, with a big silver shield pinned to the breast of his unbuttoned blue waistcoat and a hickory stick with a crook handle for added emblem of authority, stalked the town drunkard, fair game at all seasons and especially on Court Monday. The town gallant whirled back and forth the short hilly length of Main Street in his new side-bar buggy. A clustering group of Negroes made a thick, black blob, like hiving bees, in front of a Negro fish-house, from which came the smell and sounds of perch and channel cat frying on spitting-hot skillets. High up on the squat cupola of the courthouse a red-headed woodpecker clung, barred in crimson, white and blue-black, like a bit of living bunting, engaged in the hopeless task of trying to drill through the tin sheathing. The rolling rattle of his beak's tattoo came down sharply to the crowds below. Mourning doves called to one another in the trees round the red-brick courthouse, and at ten o'clock, when the sun was high and hot, the sheriff came out and, standing between two hollow white pillars, rapped upon one of them with a stick and called upon all witnesses and talesmen to come into court for the trial of John Breckinridge Tandy, charged with murder in the first degree, against the peace and dignity of the commonwealth of Tennessee and the statutes made and provided.

But this ceremonial by the sheriff was for form rather than effect, since the witnesses and the talesmen all sat in the circuit-court chamber along with as many of the population of Forked Deer County as could squeeze in there. Already the air of the crowded chamber was choky with heat and rancid with smell. Men were perched precariously in the ledges of the windows. More men were ranged in rows along the plastered walls, clunking their heels against the cracked wooden baseboards. The two front rows of benches were full of women. For this was to be the big case of the June term—a better show by long odds than the Half Man and Half Horse.

Inside the low railing that divided the room and on the side nearer the jury box were the forces of the defense. Under his skin the prisoner showed a sallow paleness born of his three months in the county jail. He was tall and dark and steady eyed, a young man well under thirty. He gave no heed to those who sat in packed rows behind him, wishing him evil. He kept his head turned front, only bending it sometimes to whisper with **one** of his lawyers or one of his witnesses. Fre-

quently, though, his hand went out in a protecting, reassuring way to touch his wife's brown hair or to rest a moment on her small shoulder. She was a plain, scared, shrinking little thing. The fingers of her thin hands were plaited desperately together in her lap. Already she was trembling. Once in a while she would raise her face, showing shallow brown eyes dilated with fright, and then sink her head again like a quail trying to hide. She looked pitiable and lonely.

The chief attorney for the defense was half turned from the small counsel table where he might study the faces of the crowd. He was from Middle Indiana, serving his second term in Congress. If his party held control of the state he would go to the Senate after the next election. He was an orator of parts and a pleader of almost a national reputation. He had manly grace and he was a fine, upstanding figure of a man, and before now he had wrung victories out of many difficult cases. But he chilled to his finger-nails with apprehensions of disaster as he glanced searchingly about the close-packed room.

Wherever he looked he saw no friendliness at all. He could feel the hostility of that crowd as though it had substance and body. It was a tangible thing; it was almost a physical thing. Why, you could almost put your hand out and touch it. It was everywhere there.

And it focused and was summed up in the person of Aunt Tilly Haslett, rearing on the very front bench with her husband, Uncle Fayette, half hidden behind her vast and overflowing bulk. Aunt Tilly made public opinion in Hyattsville. Indeed she was public opinion in that town. In her it had its up-comings and its out-flowings. She held herself bolt upright, filling out the front of her black bombazine basque until the buttons down its front strained at their buttonholes. With wide, deliberate strokes she fanned herself with a palm-leaf fan. The fan had an edging of black tape sewed round it—black tape signifying in that community age or mourning, or both. Her jaw was set like a steel latch, and her little gray eyes behind her steel-bowed specs were leveled with a baleful, condemning glare that included the strange lawyer, his client, his client's wife and all that was his client's.

Congressman Durham looked and knew that his presence was an affront to Aunt Tilly and all those who sat with her; that his somewhat vivid tie, his silken shirt, his low tan shoes, his new suit of gray flannels—a masterpiece of the best tailor in Indianapolis—were as insults, added up and piled on, to this suspendered, gingham-shirted constituency. Better than ever he realized now the stark hopelessness of the task to which his hands were set. And he dreaded what was coming almost as much for himself as for the man he was hired to defend. But he was a trained veteran of courtroom campaigns, and there was a jauntily assumed confidence in his bearing as he swung himself about and made a brisk show of conferring with the local attorney who was to aid him in the choosing of the jurors and the questioning of the witnesses.

But it was real confidence and real jauntiness that radiated from the other side of the inclosure, where the prosecutor sat with the assembled bar of Forked Deer County on his flanks, volunteers upon the favored side, lending to it the moral support of weight and numbers. Rankin, the dead man, having been a bachelor, State's Attorney Gilliam could bring no lorn widow and children to sit before the jurors' eyes and win added sympathy for his cause. Lacking these most valued assets of a murder trial he supplied their places with the sisters of the dead man—two sparse-built elderly women in heavy black, with sweltering thick veils down over their faces. When the proper time came he would have them raise these veils and show their woeful faces, but now they sat shrouded all in crape, fit figures of desolation and sorrow. He fussed about busily, fiddling the quill toothpick that hung perilously in the corner of his mouth and evening up the edges of a pile of law books with freckled calfskin covers. He was a lank, bony garfish of a man, with a white goatee aggressively protruding from his lower lip. He was a poor speaker but mighty as a cross-examiner, and he was serving his first term and was a candidate for another. He wore the official garbing of special and extraordinary occasions—long black coat and limp white waistcoat and gray striped trousers, a trifle short in the legs. He felt the importance of his place here almost visibly—his figure swelled and expanded out his clothes.

"Look yonder at Tom Gilliam," said Mr. Lukins, the grocer, in tones of whispered admiration to his next-elbow neighbor, "jest prunin' and honin' hisse'f to git at that there Tandy and his dude Yankee lawyer. If he don't chaw both of 'em up together I'll be dad-burned."

"You bet," whispered back his neighbor—it was Aunt Tilly's oldest son, Fayette, Junior—"it's like Maw says—time's come to teach them murderin' Kintuckians they can't be a-comin' down here a-killin' up people and not pay fur it. I reckon, Mr. Lukins," added Fayette, Junior, with a wriggle of pleased anticipation, "we shore are goin' to see some carryin's-on in this cote-house today."

Mr. Lukins' reply was lost to history because just then the judge entered—an elderly, kindly-looking man—from his chambers in the rear, with the circuit-court clerk right behind him bearing large leather-clad books and sheaves of foolscap paper. Their coming made a bustle. Aunt Tilly squared herself forward, scrooging Uncle Fayette yet farther into the eclipse of her shapeless figure. The prisoner raised his head and eyed his judge. His wife looked only at the interlaced, weaving fingers in her lap.

The formalities of the opening of a term of court were mighty soon over; there was everywhere manifest a haste to get at the big thing. The clerk called the case of the Commonwealth versus Tandy. Both sides were ready. Through the local lawyer, delegated for these smaller purposes, the accused man pleaded not guilty. The clerk spun the jury wheel, which was a painted wooden drum on a creaking wooden axle, and drew forth a slip of paper with the name of a talesman written upon it and read aloud:

"Isom W. Tolliver."

In an hour the jury was complete: two townsmen, a clerk and a telegraph operator, and ten men from the country—farmers mainly and one blacksmith and one horse-trader. Three of the panel who owned up frankly to a fixed bias had been let go by consent of both sides. Three more were sure they could give the defendant a fair trial, but those three the local lawyer had challenged peremptorily. The others were accepted as they came. The foreman was a brown-skinned, sparrowhawk-looking old man, with a smoldering brown eye. He had spare, knotted hands, like talons, and the right one was marred and twisted, with a sprayed bluish scar in the midst of the crippled knuckles like the mark of an old gunshot wound. Juror No. 4 was a stodgy old man, a small planter from the back part of the county, who fanned himself steadily with a brown-varnished straw hat. No. 7 was even older, a white-whiskered patriarch on crutches. The twelfth juryman was the oldest of the twelve—he looked to be almost seventy, but he went into the box after he had sworn that his sight and hearing and general health were good and that he still could do his ten hours a day at his blacksmith shop. This juryman chewed tobacco without pause. Twice after he took his seat at the back end of the double line he tried for a wooden cuspidor ten feet away. Both were creditable attempts, but he missed each time. Seeing the look of gathering distress in his eyes the sheriff brought the cuspidor nearer, and thereafter No. 12 was content, chewing steadily like some bearded, contemplative ruminant and listening attentively to the evidence, meanwhile scratching a very wiry head of whity-red hair with a thumbnail that through some injury had taken on the appearance of a very thick, very black Brazil nut. This scratching made a raspy, filing sound that after a while got on Congressman Durham's nerves.

It was late in the afternoon when the prosecution rested its case and court adjourned until the following morning. The state's attorney had not had so very much evidence to offer, really—the testimony of one who heard the single shot and ran in at Rankin's door to find Rankin upon the floor, about dead, with a pistol, unfired, in his hand and Tandy standing against the wall with a pistol, fired, in his; the constable to whom Tandy surrendered; the physician who examined the body; the persons who knew of the quarrel between Tandy and Rankin growing out of a land deal into which they had gone partners—not much, but enough for Gilliam's purposes. Once in the midst of examining a witness the state's attorney, seemingly by accident, let his look fall upon the two black-robed, silent figures at his side and, as though overcome by the sudden realization of a great grief, he faltered and stopped dead and sank down. It was an old trick, but well done, and a little humming murmur like a breeze coming through treetops swept the audience.

Durham was sick in his soul as he came away. In his mind there stood the picture of a little, scared woman's drawn, drenched face. She had started crying before the last juror was chosen and thereafter all day, at half-minute intervals, the big, hard sobs racked her. As Durham came down the steps he had almost to shove his way through a knot of natives outside the doors. They grudged him the path they made for him, and as he showed them his back he heard a snicker and some one said a thing that cut him where he was already bruised—in his egotism. But he gave no heed to the words. What was the use?

At the Drummers' Home Hotel a darky waiter sustained a profound shock when the imported lawyer declined the fried beefsteak with fried potatoes and also the fried ham and eggs. Mastering his surprise the waiter offered to try to get the Northern gentleman a fried pork chop and some fried June apples, but Durham only wanted a glass of milk for his supper. He drank it and smoked a cigar, and about dusk he went upstairs to his room. There he found assembled the forlorn rank and file of the defense, the local lawyer and three character witnesses—prominent citizens from Tandy's home town who were to testify to his good repute in the place where he was born and reared. These three would be the only witnesses, except Tandy himself, that Durham meant to call. One of them was a bustling little man named Felsburg, a clothing merchant, and one was Colonel Quigley, a banker and an ex-mayor, and the third was a Judge Priest, who sat on the circuit-court bench back in Kentucky. In contrast to his size, which was considerable, this Judge Priest had a voice that was high and whiny. He also had the trick, common to many men in politics in that part of the South, of being purposely ungrammatical at times.

This mannerism led a lot of people into thinking that the judge must be an uneducated man—until they heard him charging a jury or reading one of his rulings. The judge had other peculiarities. In conversation he nearly always called men younger than himself, son. He drank a little bit too much sometimes; and nobody had ever beaten him for any office he coveted. Durham didn't know what to make of the old judge—sometimes he seemed simple-minded to the point of childishness almost.

The others were gathered about a table by a lighted kerosene lamp, but the old judge sat at an open window with his low-quarter shoes off and his white-socked feet propped against the ledge. He was industriously stoking at a home-made corncob pipe. He pursed up his mouth, pulling at the long cane stem of his pipe with little audible sucks. From the rocky little street below the clatter of departing farm teams came up to him. The Indian medicine doctor was taking down his big white umbrella and packing up his regalia. The late canvas habitat of the Half Man and Half Horse had been struck and was gone, leaving only the pole-holes in the turf and a trodden space to show where it had stood. Court would go on all week, but Court Monday was over and for another month the town would doze along peacefully.

Durham slumped himself into a chair that screeched protestingly in all its infirm joints. The heart was gone clean out of him.

"I don't understand these people at all," he confessed. "We're beating against a stone wall with our bare hands."

"If it should be money now that you're needing, Meester Durham," spoke up Felsburg, "that boy Tandy's father was my very good friend when I first walked into that town with a peddling pack on my back, and if it should be money ——?"

"It isn't money, Mr. Felsburg," said Durham. "If I didn't get a cent for my services I'd still fight this case out to the end for the sake of that game boy and that poor little mite of a wife of his. It isn't money or the lack of it—it's the damned hate they've built up here against the man. Why, you could cut it off in chunks—the prejudice that there was in that courthouse today."

"Son," put in Judge Priest in his high, weedy voice, "I reckon maybe you're right. I've been projectin' around cotehouses a good many years, and I've taken notice that when a jury look at a prisoner all the time and never look at his women folks it's a monstrous bad sign. And that's the way it was all day today."

"The judge will be fair—he always is," said Hightower, the local lawyer, "and of course Gilliam is only doing his duty. Those jurors are as good solid men as you find in this county anywhere. But they can't help being prejudiced. Human nature's not strong enough to stand out against the feeling that's grown up round here against Tandy since he shot Ab Rankin."

"Son," said Judge Priest, still with his eyes on the darkening square below, "about how many of them jurors would you say are old soldiers?"

"Four or five that I know of," said Hightower —"and maybe more. It's hard to find a man over fifty years old in this section that didn't see active service in the Big War."

"Ah, hah," assented Judge Priest with a squeaky little grunt. "That foreman now—he looked like he might of seen some fightin'?"

"Four years of it," said Hightower. "He came out a captain in the First Tennessee Cavalry, you know."

"Ah, hah." The Judge sucked at his pipe.

"Herman," he wheezed back over his shoulder to Felsburg, "did you notice a tall sort of a saddle-colored darky playing a juice-harp in front of that there sideshow as we came along up? I reckon that nigger could play almost any tune you'd a mind to hear him play?"

At a time like this Durham was distinctly not interested in the versatilities of strange Negroes in this corner of the world. He kept silent, shrugging his shoulders petulantly.

"I wonder now is that nigger left town yet?" mused the old judge half to himself.

"I saw him just a while ago going down toward the depot," volunteered Hightower. "There's a train out of here for Memphis at 8:50. It's about twenty minutes of that now."

"Ah, hah, just about," assented the judge. When the judge said "Ah, hah!" like that it sounded like the striking of a fiddle-bow across a fiddle's tautened E-string.

"Well, boys," he went on, "we've all got to do the best we can for Breck Tandy, ain't we? Say, son"—this was aimed at Durham—"I'd like mightily for you to put me on the stand the last

one tomorrow. You wait until you're through with Herman and Colonel Quigley here, before you call me. And if I should seem to ramble somewhat in giving my testimony—why, son, you just let me ramble, will you? I know these people down here better maybe than you do—and if I should seem inclined to ramble, just let me go ahead and don't stop me, please?"

"Judge Priest," said Durham tartly, "if you think it could possibly do any good, ramble all you like."

"Much obliged," said the old judge, and he struggled into his low-quarter shoes and stood up, dusting the tobacco fluff off himself.

"Herman, have you got any loose change about you?"

Felsburg nodded and reached into his pocket. The judge made a discriminating selection of silver and bills from the handful that the merchant extended to him across the table.

"I'll take about ten dollars," he said. "I didn't come down here with more than enough to just about buy my railroad ticket and pay my bill at this here tavern, and I might want a sweetenin' dram or something."

He pouched his loan and crossed the room.

"Boys," he said, "I think I'll be knockin' round a little before I turn in. Herman, I may stop by your room a minute as I come back in. You boys better turn in early and git yourselves a good night's sleep. We are all liable to be purty tolerable busy tomorrow."

After he was outside he put his head back in the door and said to Durham:

"Remember, son, I may ramble."

Durham nodded shortly, being somewhat put out by the vagaries of a mind that could concern itself with trivial things on the eve of a crisis.

As the judge creaked ponderously along the hall and down the stairs those he had left behind heard him whistling a tune to himself, making false starts at the air and halting often to correct his meter. It was an unknown tune to them all, but to Felsburg, the oldest of the four, it brought a vague, unplaced memory.

The old judge was whistling when he reached the street. He stood there a minute until he had mastered the tune to his own satisfaction, and then, still whistling, he shuffled along the uneven board pavement, which after rippling up and down like a broken-backed snake dipped downward to a little railroad station at the foot of the street.

In the morning nearly half the town—the white half—came to the trial, and enough of the black half to put a dark hem, like a mourning border, across the back width of the courtroom. Except that Main Street now drowsed in the heat where yesterday it had buzzed, this day might have been the day before. Again the resolute woodpecker drove his bloodied head with unimpaired energy against the tin sheathing up above. It was his third summer for that same cupola and the tin was pocked with little dents for three feet up and down. The mourning doves still pitched their lamenting note back and forth across the courthouse yard; and in the dewberry patch at the bottom of Aunt Tilly Haslett's garden down by the creek the meadow larks strutted in buff and yellow, with crescent-shaped gorgets of black at their throats, like Old Continentals, sending their clear-piped warning of "Laziness g'wine kill you!" in at the open windows of the steamy, smelly courtroom.

The defense lost no time getting under headway. As his main witness Durham called the prisoner to testify in his own behalf. Tandy gave his version of the killing with a frankness and directness that would have carried conviction to auditors more even-minded in their sympathies. He had gone to Rankin's office in the hope of bringing on a peaceful settlement of their quarrel. Rankin had flared up; had cursed him and advanced on him, making threats. Both of them reached for their guns then. Rankin's was the first out, but he fired first—that was all there was to it. Gilliam shone at cross-examination; he went at Tandy savagely, taking hold like a snapping turtle and hanging on like one.

He made Tandy admit over and over again that he carried a pistol habitually. In a community where a third of the male adult population went armed this admission was nevertheless taken as plain evidence of a nature bloody-minded and desperate. It would have been just as bad for Tandy if he said he armed himself especially for his visit to Rankin—to these listeners that could have meant nothing else but a deliberate, murderous intention. Either way Gilliam had him, and he sweated in his eagerness to bring out the significance of the point. A sinister little murmuring sound, vibrant with menace, went purring from bench to bench when Tandy told about his pistol-carrying habit.

The cross-examination dragged along for hours. The recess for dinner interrupted it; then it went on again, Gilliam worrying at Tandy, goading at him, catching him up and twisting his words. Tandy would not be shaken, but twice under the manhandling he lost his temper and lashed back at Gilliam, which was precisely what Gilliam most desired. A flary, fiery man, prone to

violent outbursts—that was the inference he could draw from these blaze-ups.

It was getting on toward five o'clock before Gilliam finally let his bedeviled enemy quit the witness-stand and go back to his place between his wife and his lawyer. As for Durham, he had little more to offer. He called on Mr. Felsburg, and Mr. Felsburg gave Tandy a good name as man and boy in his home town. He called on Banker Quigley, who did the same thing in different words. For these character witnesses State's Attorney Gilliam had few questions. The case was as good as won now, he figured; he could taste already his victory over the famous lawyer from up North, and he was greedy to hurry it forward.

The hot round hub of a sun had wheeled low enough to dart its thin red spokes in through the westerly windows when Durham called his last witness. As Judge Priest settled himself solidly in the witness chair with the deliberation of age and the heft of flesh, the leveled rays caught him full and lit up his round pink face, with the short white-bleached beard below it and the bald white-bleached forehead above. Durham eyed him half doubtfully. He looked the picture of a scatter-witted old man, who would potter and philander round a long time before he ever came to the point of anything. So he appeared to the others there too. But what Durham did not sense was that the homely simplicity of the old man was of a piece with the picture of the courtroom, that he would seem to these watching, hostile people one of their own kind, and that they would give to him in all likelihood a sympathy and understanding that had been denied the clothing merchant and the broadclothed banker.

He wore a black alpaca coat that slanted upon him in deep, longitudinal folds, and the front skirts of it were twisted and pulled downward until they dangled in long, wrinkly black tails. His shapeless gray trousers were short for him and fitted his pudgy legs closely. Below them dangled a pair of stout ankles encased in white cotton socks and ending in low-quarter black shoes. His shirt was clean but wrinkled countlessly over his front. The gnawed and blackened end of a cane pipestem stood out of his breast pocket, rising like a frosted weed stalk.

He settled himself back in the capacious oak chair, balanced upon his knees a white straw hat with a string band round the crown and waited for the question.

"What is your name?" asked Durham.

"William Pitman Priest."

Even the voice somehow seemed to fit the setting. Its high nasal whine had a sort of whimsical appeal to it.

"When and where were you born?"

"In Calloway County, Kintucky, July 27, 1839."

"What is your profession or business?"

"I am an attorney-at-law."

"What position if any do you hold in your native state?"

"I am presidin' judge of the first judicial district of the state of Kentucky."

"And have you been so long?"

"For the past sixteen years."

"When were you admitted to the bar?"

"In 1860."

"And you have ever since been engaged, I take it, either in the practice of the law before the bar or in its administration from the bench?"

"Exceptin' for the four years from April, 1861, to June, 1865."

Up until now Durham had been sparring, trying to fathom the probable trend of the old judge's expected meanderings. But in the answer to the last question he thought he caught the cue and, though none save those two knew it, thereafter it was the witness who led and the questioner who followed his lead blindly.

"And where were you during those four years?"

"I was engaged, suh, in takin' part in the war."

"The War of the Rebellion?"

"No, suh," the old man corrected him gently but with firmness, "the War for the Southern Confederacy."

There was a least bit of a stir at this. Aunt Tilly's tape-edged palmleaf blade hovered a brief second in the wide regular arc of its sweep and the foreman of the jury involuntarily ducked his head, as if in affiance of an indubitable fact.

"Ahem!" said Durham, still feeling his way, although now he saw the path more clearly. "And on which side were you engaged?"

"I was a private soldier in the Southern army," the old judge answered him, and as he spoke he straightened up.

"Yes, suh," he repeated, "for four years I was a private soldier in the late Southern Confederacy. Part of the time I was down here in this very country," he went on as though he had just recalled that part of it. "Why, in the summer of '64 I was right here in this town. And until yistiddy I hadn't been back since."

He turned to the trial judge and spoke to him with a tone and manner half apologetic, half confidential.

"Your Honor," he said, "I am a judge myself, occupyin' in my home state a position very simi-

lar to the one which you fill here, and whilst I realize, none better, that this ain't all accordin' to the rules of evidence as laid down in the books, yet when I git to thinkin' about them old soldierin' times I find I am inclined to sort of reminiscence round a little. And I trust your Honor will pardon me if I should seem to ramble slightly?"

His tone was more than apologetic and more than confidential. It was winning. The judge upon the bench was a veteran himself. He looked toward the prosecutor.

"Has the state's attorney any objection to this line of testimony?" he asked, smiling a little.

Certainly Gilliam had no fear that this honest-appearing old man's wanderings could damage a case already as good as won. He smiled back indulgently and waved his arm with a gesture that was compounded of equal parts of toleration and patience, with a top-dressing of contempt. "I fail," said Gilliam, "to see wherein the military history and achievements of this worthy gentleman can possibly affect the issue of the homicide of Abner J. Rankin. But," he added magnanimously, "if the defense chooses to encumber the record with matters so trifling and irrelevant I surely will make no objection now or hereafter."

"The witness may proceed," said the judge.

"Well, really, your Honor, I didn't have so very much to say," confessed Judge Priest, "and I didn't expect there'd be any to-do made over it. What I was trying to git at was that comin' down here to testify in this case sort of brought back them old days to my mind. As I get along more in years"—he was looking toward the jurors now—"I find that I live more and more in the past."

As though he had put a question to them several of the jurors gravely inclined their heads. The busy cud of Juror No. 12 moved just a trifle slower in its travels from the right side of the jaw to the left and back again.

"Yes, suh," he said musingly, "I got up early this mornin' at the tavern where I'm a-stoppin' and took a walk through your thrivin' little city." This was rambling with a vengeance, thought the puzzled Durham. "I walked down here to a bridge over a little crick and back again. It reminded me mightily of that other time when I passed through this town—in '64—just about this season of the year—and it was hot early today just as it was that other time—and the dew was thick on the grass, the same as 'twas then."

He halted a moment.

"Of course your town didn't look the same this mornin' as it did that other mornin'. It seemed like to me there are twicet as many houses here now as there used to be—it's got to be quite a little city."

Mr. Lukins, the grocer, nodded silent approval of this utterance, Mr. Lukins having but newly completed and moved into a two-story brick store building with a tin cornice and an outside staircase.

"Yes, suh, your town has grown mightily, but"—and the whiny, humorous voice grew apologetic again—"but your roads are purty much the same as they were in '64—hilly in places—and kind of rocky."

Durham found himself sitting still, listening hard. Everybody else was listening too. Suddenly it struck Durham, almost like a blow, that this simple old man had somehow laid a kind of spell upon them all. The flattening sunrays made a kind of pink glow about the old judge's face, touching gently his bald head and his white whiskers. He droned on:

"I remember about those roads particularly well, because that time when I marched through here in '64 my feet was about out of my shoes and them flints cut 'em up some. Some of the boys, I recollect, left bloody prints in the dust behind 'em. But shucks—it wouldn't a-made no real difference if we'd wore the bottoms plum off our feet! We'd a-kept on goin'. We'd a-gone anywhere—or tried to—behind old Bedford Forrest."

Aunt Tilly's palmleaf halted in air and the twelfth juror's faithful quid froze in his cheek and stuck there like a small wen. Except for a general hunching forward of shoulders and heads there was no movement anywhere and no sound except the voice of the witness:

"Old Bedford Forrest hisself was leadin' us, and so naturally we just went along with him, shoes or no shoes. There was a regiment of Northern troops—Yankees—marchin' on this town that mornin', and it seemed the word had traveled ahead of 'em that they was aimin' to burn it down.

"Probably it warn't true. When we got to know them Yankees better afterward we found out that there really warn't no difference, to speak of, between the run of us and the run of them. Probably it warn't so at all. But in them days the people was prone to believe 'most anything—about Yankees—and the word was that they was comin' across country, a-burnin' and cuttin' and slashin', and the people here thought they was goin' to be burned out of house and home. So old Bedford Forrest he marched all night with a battalion of us—four companies—Kintuckians and Tennesseeans mostly, with a sprinklin' of boys from Mississippi and Arkansas—some of us ridin' and some walkin' afoot, like me—we didn't always

have horses enough to go round that last year. And somehow we got here before they did. It was a close race though between us—them a-comin' down from the North and us a-comin' up from the other way. We met 'em down there by that little crick just below where your present railroad depot is. There warn't no depot there then, but the crick looks just the same now as it did then—and the bridge too. I walked across it this mornin' to see. Yes, suh, right there was where we met 'em. And there was a right smart fight.

"Yes, suh, there was a right smart fight for about twenty minutes—or maybe twenty-five—and then we had breakfast."

He had been smiling gently as he went along. Now he broke into a throaty little chuckle.

"Yes, suh, it all come back to me this mornin'—every little bit of it—the breakfast and all. I didn't have much breakfast, though, as I recall—none of us did—probably just corn pone and crick water to wash it down with." And he wiped his mouth with the back of his hand as though the taste of the gritty cornmeal cakes was still there.

There was another little pause here; the witness seemed to be through. Durham's crisp question cut the silence like a gash with a knife.

"Judge Priest, do you know the defendant at the bar, and if so, how well do you know him?"

"I was just comin' to that," he answered with simplicity, "and I'm obliged to you for puttin' me back on the track. Oh, I know the defendant at the bar mighty well—as well as anybody on earth ever did know him, I reckon, unless 'twas his own maw and paw. I've known him, in fact, from the time he was born—and a gentler, better-disposed boy never grew up in our town. His nature seemed almost too sweet for a boy—more like a girl's—but as a grown man he was always manly, and honest, and fair—and not quarrelsome. Oh, yes, I know him. I knew his father and his mother before him. It's a funny thing too—comin' up this way—but I remember that his paw was marchin' right alongside of me the day we came through here in '64. He was wounded, his paw was, right at the edge of that little crick down yonder. He was wounded in the shoulder—and he never did entirely git over it."

Again he stopped dead short, and he lifted his hand and tugged at the lobe of his right ear absently. Simultaneously Mr. Felsburg, who was sitting close to a window beyond the jury box, was also seized with nervousness, for he jerked out a handkerchief and with it mopped his brow so vigorously that, to one standing outside, it might have seemed that the handkerchief was actually being waved about as a signal.

Instantly then there broke upon the pause that still endured a sudden burst of music, a rollickingly jingling air. It was only a twenty-cent mouth organ, three sleigh bells and a pair of the rib bones of a beef-cow being played all at once by a saddle-colored Negro man, but it sounded for all the world like a fife and drum corps:

> *If you want to have a good time,*
> *If you want to have a good time,*
> *If you want to ketch the devil—*
> *Jine the cavalree!*

To some who heard it now the tune was strange; these were the younger ones. But to those older men and those older women the first jubilant bars rolled back the years like a scroll.

The sound swelled and rippled and rose through the windows—the marching song of the Southern trooper—Forrest's men, and Morgan's, and Jeb Stuart's and Joe Wheeler's. It had in it the jingle of saber chains, the creak of sweaty saddle-girths, the nimble clunk of hurrying hoofs. It had in it the clanging memories of a cause and a time that would live with these people as long as they lived and their children lived and their children's children. It had in it the one sure call to the emotions and the sentiments of these people.

Strangely enough not one listener had come to the windows to look out. The interruption from without had seemed part and parcel of what went on within. None faced to the rear, every one faced to the front.

There was Mr. Lukins now. As Mr. Lukins got upon his feet he said to himself in a tone of feeling that he be dad-fetched. But immediately changing his mind he stated that he would preferably be dad-blamed, and as he moved toward the bar rail one overhearing him might have gathered from remarks let fall that Mr. Lukins was going somewhere with the intention of being extensively dad-burned. But for all these threats Mr. Lukins didn't go anywhere, except as near the railing as he could press.

Nearly everybody else was standing up too. The state's attorney was on his feet with the rest, seemingly for the purpose of making some protest.

Had any one looked they might have seen that the ember in the smoldering eye of the old foreman had blazed up to a brown fire; that Juror No. 4, with utter disregard for expense, was biting segments out of the brim of his new brown-varnished straw hat; that No. 7 had dropped his crutches on the floor, and that no one, not even their owner, had heard them fall; that all the jurors were half out of their chairs. But no one saw these things, for at this moment there rose up Aunt Tilly Haslett, a dominant figure, her huge wide back blocking the view of three or four immediately behind her.

Uncle Fayette laid a timid detaining hand upon her and seemed to be saying something protestingly.

"Turn loose of me, Fate Haslett!" she commanded. "Ain't you ashamed of yourse'f, to be tryin' to hold me back when you know how my only dear brother died a-followin' after Gineral Nathan Bedford Forrest. Turn loose of me!"

She flirted her great arm and Uncle Fayette spun flutteringly into the mass behind. The sheriff barred her way at the gate of the bar.

"Mizz Haslett," he implored, "please Mizz Haslett—you must keep order in the cote."

Aunt Tilly halted in her onward move, head up high and elbows out, and through her specs, blazing like burning-glasses, she fixed on him a look that instantly charred that unhappy official into a burning red ruin of his own self-importance.

"Keep it yourse'f, High Sheriff Washington Nash, Esquire," she bade him; "that's whut you git paid good money fur doin'. And git out of my way! I'm a-goin' in there to that pore little lonesome thing settin' there all by herself, and there ain't nobody goin' to hinder me neither!"

The sheriff shrunk aside; perhaps it would be better to say he evaporated aside. And public opinion, reorganized and made over but still incarnate in Aunt Tilly Haslett, swept past the rail and settled like a billowing black cloud into a chair that the local attorney for the defense vacated just in time to save himself the inconvenience of having it snatched bodily from under him.

"There, honey," said Aunt Tilly crooningly as she gathered the forlorn little figure of the prisoner's wife in her arms like a child and mothered her up to her ample bombazined bosom, "there now, honey, you jest cry on me."

Then Aunt Tilly looked up and her specs were all blurry and wet. But she waved her palmleaf fan as though it had been a baton of command.

"Now, Jedge," she said, addressing the bench, "and you other gentlemen—you kin go ahead now."

The state's attorney had meant evidently to make some sort of an objection, for he was upon his feet through all this scene. But he looked back before he spoke and what he saw kept him from speaking. I believe I stated earlier that he was a candidate for reëlection. So he settled back down in his chair and stretched out his legs and buried his chin in the top of his limp white waistcoat in an attitude that he had once seen in a picture entitled, "Napoleon Bonaparte at St. Helena."

"You may resume, Judge Priest," said the trial judge in a voice that was not entirely free from huskiness, although its owner had been clearing it steadily for some moments.

"Thank you kindly, suh, but I was about through anyhow," answered the witness with a bow, and for all his homeliness there was dignity and stateliness in it. "I merely wanted to say for the sake of completin' the record, so to speak, that on the occasion referred to them Yankees did not cross that bridge."

He got up somewhat stiffly, once more becoming a commonplace old man in a wrinkled black alpaca coat, and made his way back to his vacant place, now in the shadow of Aunt Tilly Haslett's form. As he passed along the front of the jury-box the foreman's crippled right hand came up in a sort of a clumsy salute, and the juror at the other end of the rear row—No. 12, the oldest juror—leaned forward as if to speak to him, but remembered where his present duty lay in time. The old judge kept on until he came to Durham's side, and he whispered to him:

"Son, they've quit lookin' at him and they're all a-lookin' at her. Son, rest your case."

Durham came out of a maze.

"Your Honor," he said as he rose, "the defense rests."

The jury were out only six minutes. Mr. Lukins insisted that it was only five minutes and a half, and added that he'd be dad-drotted if it was a second longer than that.

As the lately accused Tandy came out of the courthouse with his imported lawyer—Aunt Tilly bringing up the rear with his trembling, weeping, happy little wife—friendly hands were outstretched to clasp his and a whiskered old gentleman with a thumbnail like a Brazil nut grabbed at his arm.

"Whichaway did Billy Priest go?" he demanded—"little old Fightin' Billy—whar did he go to? Soon as he started in talkin' I placed him. Whar is he?"

Walking side by side, Tandy and Durham came down the steps into the soft June night, and Tandy took a long, deep breath into his lungs.

"Mr. Durham," he said, "I owe a great deal to you."

"How's that?" said Durham.

Just ahead of them, centered in a shaft of light from the window of the barroom of the Drummers' Home Hotel, stood Judge Priest. The old judge had been drinking. The pink of his face was a trifle more pronounced, the high whine in his voice a trifle weedier, as he counted one by one certain pieces of silver into the wide-open palm of a saddle-colored Negro.

"How's that?" said Durham.

"I say I owe everything in the world to you," repeated Tandy.

"No," said Durham, "what you owe me is the fee you agreed to pay me for defending you. There's the man you're looking for."

And he pointed to the old judge.

ALIBI IKE

by Ring W. Lardner

RINGGOLD WILMER LARDNER, better known as Ring W., made his *Post* debut March 7, 1914, with a story loaded down by its title, "A Busher's Letters Home . . . Incidents Following a Call to the Big Show, as Told in Some Letters of Jack Keefe, Pitcher, to His Friend, Al Blanchard, in Bedford, Indiana." This was the start of the "You know me, Al" baseball yarns which promptly became a national craze. It is said that Lorimer bought the first Busher Letters over the unanimous protest of his staff, who thought Lardner was a pretty good sports reporter for the Chicago *Tribune* but no great shakes at writing fiction. They were wrong and Lorimer was right. During the next few years Lardner wrote a number of *Post* stories which are still the best there are about baseball. He continued to write stories which were not only funny but devastating of various frauds and phonies until his death in 1931. One critic, surveying his whole work, has called him "the greatest and sincerest pessimist America has produced." But he was still keeping his pessimism under control when he wrote "Alibi Ike."

JULY 31, 1915

HIS RIGHT NAME was Frank X. Farrell, and I guess the X stood for "Excuse me." Because he never pulled a play, good or bad, on or off the field, without apologizin' for it.

"Alibi Ike" was the name Carey wished on him the first day he reported down South. O' course we all cut out the "Alibi" part of it right away for the fear he would overhear it and bust somebody. But we called him "Ike" right to his face and the rest of it was understood by everybody on the club except Ike himself.

He ast me one time, he says:

"What do you all call me Ike for? I ain't no Yid."

"Carey give you the name," I says. "It's his nickname for everybody he takes a likin' to."

"He mustn't have only a few friends then," says Ike. "I never heard him say 'Ike' to nobody else."

But I was goin' to tell you about Carey namin' him. We'd been workin' out two weeks and the pitchers was showin' somethin' when this bird joined us. His first day out he stood up there so good and took such a reef at the old pill that he had everyone lookin'. Then him and Carey was together in left field, catchin' fungoes, and it was after we was through for the day that Carey told me about him.

"What do you think of Alibi Ike?" ast Carey.

"Who's that?" I says.

"This here Farrell in the outfield," says Carey.

"He looks like he could hit," I says.

"Yes," says Carey, "but he can't hit near as good as he can apologize."

Then Carey went on to tell me what Ike had been pullin' out there. He'd dropped the first fly ball that was hit to him and told Carey his glove wasn't broke in good yet, and Carey says the glove could easy of been Kid Gleason's gran'-father. He made a whale of a catch out o' the next one and Carey says "Nice work!" or somethin' like that, but Ike says he could of caught the ball with his back turned only he slipped when he started after it and, besides that, the air currents fooled him.

"I thought you done well to get to the ball," says Carey.

"I ought to been settin' under it," says Ike.

"What did you hit last year?" Carey ast him.

"I had malaria most o' the season," says Ike. "I wound up with .356."

"Where would I have to go to get malaria?" says Carey, but Ike didn't wise up.

I and Carey and him set at the same table together for supper. It took him half an hour longer'n us to eat because he had to excuse himself every time he lifted his fork.

"Doctor told me I needed starch," he'd say, and then toss a shovelful o' potatoes into him. Or, "They ain't much meat on one o' these chops," he'd tell us, and grab another one. Or he'd say: "Nothin' like onions for a cold," and then he'd dip into the perfumery.

"Better try that apple sauce," says Carey. "It'll help your malaria."

"Whose malaria?" says Ike. He'd forgot already why he didn't only hit .356 last year.

I and Carey begin to lead him on.

"Whereabouts did you say your home was?" I ast him.

"I live with my folks," he says. "We live in Kansas City—not right down in the business part —outside a ways."

"How's that come?" says Carey. "I should think you'd get rooms in the post office."

But Ike was too busy curin' his cold to get that one.

"Are you married?" I ast him.

"No," he says. "I never run round much with girls, except to shows onct in a wile and parties and dances and roller skatin'."

"Never take 'em to the prize fights, eh?" says Carey.

"We don't have no real good bouts," says Ike. "Just bush stuff. And I never figured a boxin' match was a place for the ladies."

Well, after supper he pulled a cigar out and lit it. I was just goin' to ask him what he done it for, but he beat me to it.

"Kind o' rests a man to smoke after a good work-out," he says. "Kind o' settles a man's supper, too."

"Looks like a pretty good cigar," says Carey.

"Yes," says Ike. "A friend o' mine give it to me—a fella in Kansas City that runs a billiard room."

"Do you play billiards?" I ast him.

"I used to play a fair game," he says. "I'm all out o' practice now—can't hardly make a shot."

We coaxed him into a four-handed battle, him and Carey against Jack Mack and I. Say, he couldn't play billiards as good as Willie Hoppe; not quite. But to hear him tell it, he didn't make a good shot all evenin'. I'd leave him an awful-lookin' layout and he'd gather 'em up in one try and then run a couple o' hundred, and between every carom he'd say he'd put too much stuff on the ball, or the English didn't take, or the table wasn't true, or his stick was crooked, or somethin'. And all the time he had the balls actin' like they was Dutch soldiers and him Kaiser William. We started out to play fifty points, but we had to make it a thousand so as I and Jack and Carey could try the table.

The four of us set round the lobby a wile after we was through playin', and when it got along toward bedtime Carey whispered to me and says:

"Ike'd like to go to bed, but he can't think up no excuse."

Carey hadn't hardly finished whisperin' when Ike got up and pulled it.

"Well, good-night, boys," he says. "I ain't sleepy, but I got some gravel in my shoes and it's killin' my feet."

We knowed he hadn't never left the hotel since

we'd came in from the grounds and changed our clo'es. So Carey says:

"I should think they'd take them gravel pits out o' the billiard room."

But Ike was already on his way to the elevator, limpin'.

"He's got the world beat," says Carey to Jack and I. "I've knew lots o' guys that had an alibi for every mistake they made; I've heard pitchers say that the ball slipped when somebody cracked one off'n 'em; I've heard infielders complain of a sore arm after heavin' one into the stand, and I've saw outfielders tooken sick with a dizzy spell when they've misjudged a fly ball. But this baby can't even go to bed without apologizin', and I bet he excuses himself to the razor when he gets ready to shave."

"And at that," says Jack, "he's goin' to make us a good man."

"Yes," says Carey, "unless rheumatism keeps his battin' average down to .400."

Well, sir, Ike kept whalin' away at the ball all through the trip till everybody knowed he'd won a job. Cap had him in there regular the last few exhibition games and told the newspaper boys a week before the season opened that he was goin' to start him in Kane's place.

"You're there, kid," says Carey to Ike, the night Cap made the 'nnouncement. "They ain't many boys that wins a big league berth their third year out."

"I'd of been up here a year ago," says Ike, "only I was bent over all season with lumbago."

II

IT RAINED DOWN IN CINCINNATI one day and somebody organized a little game o' cards. They was shy two men to make six and ast I and Carey to play.

"I'm with you if you get Ike and make it seven-handed," says Carey.

So they got a hold of Ike and we went up to Smitty's room.

"I pretty near forgot how many you deal," says Ike. "It's been a long wile since I played."

I and Carey give each other the wink, and sure enough, he was just as ig'orant about poker as billiards. About the second hand, the pot was opened two or three ahead of him, and they was three in when it come his turn. It cost a buck, and he throwed in two.

"It's raised, boys," somebody says.

"Gosh, that's right, I did raise it," says Ike.

"Take out a buck if you didn't mean to tilt her," says Carey.

"No," says Ike, "I'll leave it go."

Well, it was raised back at him and then he

made another mistake and raised again. They was only three left in when the draw come. Smitty'd opened with a pair o' kings and he didn't help 'em. Ike stood pat. The guy that'd raised him back was flushin' and he didn't fill. So Smitty checked and Ike bet and didn't get no call. He tossed his hand away, but I grabbed it and give it a look. He had king, queen, jack and two tens. Alibi Ike he must have seen me peekin', for he leaned over and whispered to me.

"I overlooked my hand," he says. "I thought all the wile it was a straight."

"Yes," I says, "that's why you raised twice by mistake."

They was another pot that he come into with tens and fours. It was tilted a couple o' times and two o' the strong fellas drawed ahead of Ike. They each drawed one. So Ike throwed away his little pair and come out with four tens. And they was four treys against him. Carey'd looked at Ike's discards and then he says:

"This lucky bum busted two pair."

"No, no, I didn't," says Ike.

"Yes, yes, you did," says Carey, and showed us the two fours.

"What do you know about that?" says Ike. "I'd of swore one was a five spot."

Well, we hadn't had no pay day yet, and after a wile everybody except Ike was goin' shy. I could see him gettin' restless and I was wonderin' how he'd make the get-away. He tried two or three times. "I got to buy some collars before supper," he says.

"No hurry," says Smitty. "The stores here keeps open all night in April."

After a minute he opened up again.

"My uncle out in Nebraska ain't expected to live," he says. "I ought to send a telegram."

"Would that save him?" says Carey.

"No, it sure wouldn't," says Ike, "but I ought to leave my old man know where I'm at."

"When did you hear about your uncle?" says Carey.

"Just this mornin'," says Ike.

"Who told you?" ast Carey.

"I got a wire from my old man," says Ike.

"Well," says Carey, "your old man knows you're still here yet this afternoon if you was here this mornin'. Trains leavin' Cincinnati in the middle o' the day don't carry no ball clubs."

"Yes," says Ike, "that's true. But he don't know where I'm goin' to be next week."

"Ain't he got no schedule?" ast Carey.

"I sent him one openin' day," says Ike, "but it takes mail a long time to get to Idaho."

"I thought your old man lived in Kansas City," says Carey.

"He does when he's home," says Ike.

"But now," says Carey, "I s'pose he's went to Idaho so as he can be near your sick uncle in Nebraska."

"He's visitin' my other uncle in Idaho."

"Then how does he keep posted about your sick uncle?" ast Carey.

"He don't," says Ike. "He don't even know my other uncle's sick. That's why I ought to wire and tell him."

"Good night!" says Carey.

"What town in Idaho is your old man at?" I says.

Ike thought it over.

"No town at all," he says. "But he's near a town."

"Near what town?" I says.

"Yuma," says Ike.

Well, by this time he'd lost two or three pots and he was desperate. We was playin' just as fast as we could, because we seen we couldn't hold him much longer. But he was tryin' so hard to frame an escape that he couldn't pay no attention to the cards, and it looked like we'd get his whole pile away from him if we could make him stick.

The telephone saved him. The minute it begun to ring, five of us jumped for it. But Ike was there first.

"Yes," he says, answerin' it. "This is him. I'll come right down."

And he slammed up the receiver and beat it out o' the door without even sayin' good-by.

"Smitty'd ought to locked the door," says Carey.

"What did he win?" ast Carey.

We figured it up—sixty-odd bucks.

"And the next time we ask him to play," says Carey, "his fingers will be so stiff he can't hold the cards."

Well, we set round a wile talkin' it over, and pretty soon the telephone rung again. Smitty answered it. It was a friend of his'n from Hamilton and he wanted to know why Smitty didn't hurry down. He was the one that had called before and Ike had told him he was Smitty.

"Ike'd ought to split with Smitty's friend," says Carey.

"No," I says, "he'll need all he won. It costs money to buy collars and to send telegrams from Cincinnati to your old man in Texas and keep him posted on the health o' your uncle in Cedar Rapids, D. C."

III

AND YOU ought to heard him out there on that field! They wasn't a day when he didn't pull six or seven, and it didn't make no difference whether he was goin' good or bad. If he popped up in the pinch he should of made a base hit and the reason he didn't was so-and-so. And if he cracked one for three bases he ought to had a home run, only the ball wasn't lively, or the wind brought it back, or he tripped on a lump o' dirt, roundin' first base.

They was one afternoon in New York when he beat all records. Big Marquard was workin' against us and he was good.

In the first innin' Ike hit one clear over that right field stand, but it was a few feet foul. Then he got another foul and then the count come to two and two. Then Rube slipped one acrost on him and he was called out.

"What do you know about that!" he says afterward on the bench. "I lost count. I thought it was three and one, and I took a strike."

"You took a strike all right," says Carey. "Even the umps knowed it was a strike."

"Yes," says Ike, "but you can bet I wouldn't of took it if I'd knew it was the third one. The score board had it wrong."

"That score board ain't for you to look at," says Cap. "It's for you to hit that old pill against."

"Well," says Ike, "I could of hit that one over the score board if I'd knew it was the third."

"Was it a good ball?" I says.

"Well, no, it wasn't," says Ike. "It was inside."

"How far inside?" says Carey.

"Oh, two or three inches or half a foot," says Ike.

"I guess you wouldn't of threatened the score board with it then," says Cap.

"I'd of pulled it down the right foul line if I hadn't thought he'd call it a ball," says Ike.

Well, in New York's part o' the innin' Doyle cracked one and Ike run back a mile and a half and caught it with one hand. We was all sayin' what a whale of a play it was, but he had to apologize just the same as for gettin' struck out.

"That stand's so high," he says, "that a man don't never see a ball till it's right on top o' you."

"Didn't you see that one?" ast Cap.

"Not at first," says Ike; "not till it raised up above the roof o' the stand."

"Then why did you start back as soon as the ball was hit?" says Cap.

"I knowed by the sound that he'd got a good hold of it," says Ike.

"Yes," says Cap, "but how'd you know what direction to run in?"

"Doyle usually hits 'em that way, the way I run," says Ike.

"Why don't you play blindfolded?" says Carey.

"Might as well, with that big high stand to

bother a man," says Ike. "If I could of saw the ball all the time I'd of got it in my hip pocket."

Along in the fifth we was one run to the bad and Ike got on with one out. On the first ball throwed to Smitty, Ike went down. The ball was outside and Meyers throwed Ike out by ten feet.

You could see Ike's lips movin' all the way to the bench and when he got there he had his piece learned.

"Why didn't he swing?" he says.

"Why didn't you wait for his sign?" says Cap.

"He give me his sign," says Ike.

"What is his sign with you?" says Cap.

"Pickin' up some dirt with his right hand," says Ike.

"Well, I didn't see him do it," Cap says.

"He done it all right," says Ike.

Well, Smitty went out and they wasn't no more argument till they come in for the next innin'. Then Cap opened it up.

"You fellas better get your signs straight," he says.

"Do you mean me?" says Smitty.

"Yes," Cap says. "What's your sign with Ike?"

"Slidin' my left hand up to the end o' the bat and back," says Smitty.

"Do you hear that, Ike?" ast Cap.

"What of it?" says Ike.

"You says his sign was pickin' up dirt and he says it's slidin' his hand. Which is right?"

"I'm right," says Smitty. "But if you're arguin' about him goin' last innin', I didn't give him no sign."

"You pulled your cap down with your right hand, didn't you?" ast Ike.

"Well, s'pose I did," says Smitty. "That don't mean nothin'. I never told you to take that for a sign, did I?"

"I thought maybe you meant to tell me and forgot," says Ike.

They couldn't none of us answer that and they wouldn't of been no more said if Ike had of shut up. But wile we was settin' there Carey got on with two out and stole second clean.

"There!" says Ike. "That's what I was tryin' to do and I'd of got away with it if Smitty'd swang and bothered the Indian."

"Oh!" says Smitty. "You was tryin' to steal then, was you? I thought you claimed I give you the hit and run."

"I didn't claim no such a thing," says Ike. "I thought maybe you might of gave me a sign, but I was goin' anyway because I thought I had a good start."

Cap prob'ly would of hit him with a bat, only just about that time Doyle booted one on Hayes and Carey come acrost with the run that tied.

Well, we go into the ninth finally, one and one, and Marquard walks McDonald with nobody out.

"Lay it down," says Cap to Ike.

And Ike goes up there with orders to bunt and cracks the first ball into that right-field stand! It was fair this time, and we're two ahead, but I didn't think about that at the time. I was too busy watchin' Cap's face. First he turned pale and then he got red as fire and then he got blue and purple, and finally he just laid back and busted out laughin'. So we wasn't afraid to laugh ourselfs when we seen him doin' it, and when Ike come in everybody on the bench was in hysterics.

But instead o' takin' advantage, Ike had to try and excuse himself. His play was to shut up and he didn't know how to make it.

"Well," he says, "if I hadn't hit quite so quick at that one I bet it'd of cleared the center-field fence."

Cap stopped laughin'.

"It'll cost you plain fifty," he says.

"What for?" says Ike.

"When I say 'bunt' I mean 'bunt,'" says Cap.

"You didn't say 'bunt,'" says Ike.

"I says 'Lay it down,'" says Cap. "If that don't mean 'bunt,' what does it mean?"

"'Lay it down' means 'bunt' all right," says Ike, "but I understood you to say 'Lay on it.'"

"All right," says Cap, "and the little misunderstandin' will cost you fifty."

Ike didn't say nothin' for a few minutes. Then he had another bright idear.

"I was just kiddin' about misunderstandin' you," he says. "I knowed you wanted me to bunt."

"Well, then, why didn't you bunt?" ast Cap.

"I was goin' to on the next ball," says Ike. "But I thought if I took a good wallop I'd have 'em all fooled. So I walloped at the first one to fool 'em, and I didn't have no intention o' hittin' it."

"You tried to miss it, did you?" says Cap.

"Yes," says Ike.

"How'd you happen to hit it?" ast Cap.

"Well," Ike says, "I was lookin' for him to throw me a fast one and I was goin' to swing under it. But he come with a hook and I met it right square where I was swingin' to go under the fast one."

"Great!" says Cap. "Boys," he says, "Ike's learned how to hit Marquard's curve. Pretend a fast one's comin' and then try to miss it. It's a good thing to know and Ike'd ought to be willin' to pay for the lesson. So I'm goin' to make it a hundred instead o' fifty."

The game wound up 3 to 1. The fine didn't go, because Ike hit like a wild man all through that trip and we made pretty near a clean-up. The night we went to Philly I got him cornered in the car and I says to him:

"Forget them alibis for a wile and tell me somethin'. What'd you do that for, swing that time against Marquard when you was told to bunt?"

"I'll tell you," he says. "That ball he throwed me looked just like the one I struck out on in the first innin' and I wanted to show Cap what I could of done to that other one if I'd knew it was the third strike."

"But," I says, "the one you struck out on in the first innin' was a fast ball."

"So was the one I cracked in the ninth," says Ike.

IV

You've saw Cap's wife, o' course. Well, her sister's about twict as good-lookin' as her, and that's goin' some.

Cap took his missus down to St. Louis the second trip and the other one come down from St. Joe to visit her. Her name is Dolly, and some doll is right.

Well, Cap was goin' to take the two sisters to a show and he wanted a beau for Dolly. He left it to her and she picked Ike. He'd hit three on the nose that afternoon—off'n Sallee, too.

They fell for each other that first evenin'. Cap told us how it come off. She begin flatterin' Ike for the star game he'd played and o' course he begin excusin' himself for not doin' better. So she thought he was modest and it went strong with her. And she believed everything he said and that made her solid with him—that and her make-up. They was together every mornin' and evenin' for the five days we was there. In the afternoons Ike played the grandest ball you ever see, hittin' and runnin' the bases like a fool and catchin' everything that stayed in the park.

I told Cap, I says: "You'd ought to keep the doll with us and he'd make Cobb's figures look sick."

But Dolly had to go back to St. Joe and we come home for a long serious.

Well, for the next three weeks Ike had a letter to read every day and he'd set in the clubhouse readin' it till mornin' practice was half over. Cap didn't say nothin' to him, because he was goin' so good. But I and Carey wasted a lot of our time tryin' to get him to own up who the letters was from. Fine chanct!

"What are you readin'?" Carey'd say. "A bill?"

"No," Ike'd say, "not exactly a bill. It's a letter from a fella I used to go to school with."

"High school or college?" I'd ask him.

"College," he'd say.

"What college?" I'd say.

Then he'd stall a wile and then he'd say:

"I didn't go to the college myself, but my friend went there."

"How did it happen you didn't go?" Carey'd ask him.

"Well," he'd say, "they wasn't no colleges near where I lived."

"Didn't you live in Kansas City?" I'd say to him.

One time he'd say he did and another time he didn't. One time he says he lived in Michigan.

"Where at?" says Carey.

"Near Detroit," he says.

"Well," I says, "Detroit's near Ann Arbor and that's where they got the university."

"Yes," says Ike, "they got it there now, but they didn't have it there then."

"I come pretty near goin' to Syracuse," I says, "only they wasn't no railroads runnin' through there in them days."

"Where'd this friend o' yours go to college?" says Carey.

"I forget now," says Ike.

"Was it Carlisle?" ast Carey.

"No," says Ike, "his folks wasn't very well off."

"That's what barred me from Smith," I says.

"I was goin' to tackle Cornell's," says Carey, "but the doctor told me I'd have hay fever if I didn't stay up North."

"Your friend writes long letters," I says.

"Yes," says Ike; "he's tellin' me about a ball player."

"Where does he play?" ast Carey.

"Down in the Texas League—Fort Wayne," says Ike.

"It looks like a girl's writin'," Carey says.

"A girl wrote it," says Ike. "That's my friend's sister, writin' for him."

"Didn't they teach writin' at this here college where he went?" says Carey.

"Sure," Ike says, "they taught writin', but he got his hand cut off in a railroad wreck."

"How long ago?" I says.

"Right after he got out o' college," says Ike.

"Well," I says, "I should think he'd of learned to write with his left hand by this time."

"It's his left hand that was cut off," says Ike; "and he was left-handed."

"You get a letter every day," says Carey. "They're all the same writin'. Is he tellin' you about a different ball player every time he writes?"

"No," Ike says. "It's the same ball player. He just tells me what he does every day."

"From the size o' the letters, they don't play nothin' but double-headers down there," says Carey.

We figured that Ike spent most of his evenin's answerin' the letters from his "friend's sister," so we kept tryin' to date him up for shows and parties to see how he'd duck out of 'em. He was bugs over spaghetti, so we told him one day that they was goin' to be a big feed of it over to Joe's that night and he was invited,

"How long'll it last?" he says.

"Well," we says, "we're goin' right over there after the game and stay till they close up."

"I can't go," he says, "unless they leave me come home at eight bells."

"Nothin' doin'," says Carey. "Joe'd get sore."

"I can't go then," says Ike.

"Why not?" I ast him.

"Well," he says, "my landlady locks up the house at eight and I left my key home."

"You can come and stay with me," says Carey.

"No," he says, "I can't sleep in a strange bed."

"How do you get along when we're on the road?" says I.

"I don't never sleep the first night anywheres," he says. "After that I'm all right."

"You'll have time to chase home and get your key right after the game," I told him.

"The key ain't home," says Ike. "I lent it to one o' the other fellas and he's went out o' town and took it with him."

"Couldn't you borry another key off'n the land-lady?" Carey ast him.

"No," he says, "that's the only one they is."

Well, the day before we started East again, Ike come into the clubhouse all smiles.

"Your birthday?" I ast him.

"No," he says.

"What do you feel so good about?" I says.

"Got a letter from my old man," he says. "My uncle's goin' to get well."

"Is that the one in Nebraska?" says I.

"Not right in Nebraska," says Ike. "Near there."

But afterwards we got the right dope from Cap. Dolly'd blew in from Missouri and was goin' to make the trip with her sister.

V

WELL, I want to alibi Carey and I for what come off in Boston. If we'd of had any idear what we was doin', we'd never did it. They wasn't nobody outside o' maybe Ike and the dame that felt worse over it than I and Carey.

The first two days we didn't see nothin' of Ike and her except out to the park. The rest o' the time they was sight-seein' over to Cambridge and down to Revere and out to Brook-a-line and all the other places where the rubes go.

But when we come into the beanery after the third game Cap's wife called us over.

"If you want to see somethin' pretty," she says, "look at the third finger on Sis's left hand."

Well, o' course we knowed before we looked that it wasn't goin' to be no hangnail. Nobody was su'prised when Dolly blew into the dinin' room with it—a rock that Ike'd bought off'n Diamond Joe the first trip to New York. Only o' course it'd been set into a lady's-size ring instead o' the automobile tire he'd been wearin'.

Cap and his missus and Ike and Dolly ett supper together, only Ike didn't eat nothin', but just set there blushin' and spillin' things on the tablecloth. I heard him excusin' himself for not havin' no appetite. He says he couldn't never eat when he was clost to the ocean. He'd forgot about them sixty-five oysters he destroyed the first night o' the trip before.

He was goin' to take her to a show, so after supper he went upstairs to change his collar. She had to doll up, too, and o' course Ike was through long before her.

If you remember the hotel in Boston, they's a little parlor where the piano's at and then they's another little parlor openin' off o' that. Well, when Ike come down Smitty was playin' a few chords and I and Carey was harmonizin'. We seen Ike go up to the desk to leave his key and we called him in. He tried to duck away, but we wouldn't stand for it.

We ast him what he was all duded up for and he says he was goin' to the theayter.

"Goin' alone?" says Carey.

"No," he says, "a friend o' mine's goin' with me."

"What do you say if we go along?" says Carey.

"I ain't only got two tickets," he says.

"Well," says Carey, "we can go down there with you and buy our own seats; maybe we can all get together."

"No," says Ike. "They ain't no more seats. They're all sold out."

"We can buy some off'n the scalpers," says Carey.

"I wouldn't if I was you," says Ike. "They say the show's rotten."

"What are you goin' for, then?" I ast.

"I didn't hear about it bein' rotten till I got the tickets," he says.

"Well," I says, "if you don't want to go I'll buy the tickets from you."

"No," says Ike, "I wouldn't want to cheat you. I'm stung and I'll just have to stand for it."

"What are you goin' to do with the girl, leave her here at the hotel?" I says.

"What girl?" says Ike

"The girl you ett supper with," I says.

"Oh," he says, "we just happened to go into the dinin' room together, that's all. Cap wanted I should set down with 'em."

"I noticed," says Carey, "that she happened to be wearin' that rock you bought off'n Diamond Joe."

"Yes," says Ike. "I lent it to her for a wile."

"Did you lend her the new ring that goes with it?" I says.

"She had that already," says Ike. "She lost the set out of it."

"I wouldn't trust no strange girl with a rock o' mine," says Carey.

"Oh, I guess she's all right," Ike says. "Besides, I was tired o' the stone. When a girl asks you for somethin', what are you goin' to do?"

He started out toward the desk, but we flagged him.

"Wait a minute!" Carey says. "I got a bet with Sam here, and it's up to you to settle it."

"Well," says Ike, "make it snappy. My friend'll be here any minute."

"I bet," says Carey, "that you and that girl was engaged to be married."

"Nothin' to it," says Ike.

"Now look here," says Carey, "this is goin' to cost me real money if I lose. Cut out the alibi stuff and give it to us straight. Cap's wife just as good as told us you was roped."

Ike blushed like a kid.

"Well, boys," he says, "I may as well own up. You win, Carey."

"Yatta boy!" says Carey. "Congratulations!"

"You got a swell girl, Ike," I says.

"She's a peach," says Smitty.

"Well, I guess she's O. K.," says Ike. "I don't know much about girls."

"Didn't you never run round with 'em?" I says.

"Oh, yes, plenty of 'em," says Ike. "But I never seen none I'd fall for."

"That is, till you seen this one," says Carey.

"Well," says Ike, "this one's O. K., but I wasn't thinkin' about gettin' married yet a wile."

"Who done the askin', her?" says Carey.

"Oh, no," says Ike, "but sometimes a man don't know what he's gettin' into. Take a good-lookin' girl, and a man gen'ally almost always does about what she wants him to."

"They couldn't no girl lasso me unless I wanted to be lassoed," says Smitty.

"Oh, I don't know," says Ike. "When a fella gets to feelin' sorry for one of 'em it's all off."

Well, we let him go after shakin' hands all round. But he didn't take Dolly to no show that night. Some time wile we was talkin' she'd came into that other parlor and she'd stood there and beard us. I don't know how much she heard. But it was enough. Dolly and Cap's missus took the midnight train for New York. And from there Cap's wife sent her on her way back to Missouri.

She'd left the ring and a note for Ike with the clerk. But we didn't ask Ike if the note was from his friend in Fort Wayne, Texas.

VI

WHEN WE'D CAME TO BOSTON Ike was hittin' plain .397. When we got back home he'd fell off to pretty near nothin'. He hadn't drove one out o' the infield in any o' them other Eastern parks, and he didn't even give no excuse for it.

To show you how bad he was, he struck out three times in Brooklyn one day and never opened his trap when Cap ast him what was the matter. Before, if he'd whiffed oncet in a game he'd of wrote a book tellin' why.

Well, we dropped from first place to fifth in four weeks and we was still goin' down. I and Carey was about the only ones on the club that spoke to each other, and all as we did was remind ourself o' what a boner we'd pulled.

"It's goin' to beat us out o' the big money," says Carey.

"Yes," I says. "I don't want to knock my own ball club, but it looks like a one-man team, and when that one man's dauber's down we couldn't trim our whiskers."

"We ought to knew better," says Carey.

"Yes," I says, "but why should a man pull an alibi for bein' engaged to such a bearcat as she was?"

"He shouldn't," says Carey. "But I and you knowed he would or we'd never started talkin' to him about it. He wasn't no more ashamed o' the girl than I am of a regular base hit. But he just can't come clean on no subjec'."

Cap had the whole story, and I and Carey was as pop'lar with him as an umpire.

"What do you want me to do, Cap?" Carey'd say to him before goin' up to hit.

"Use your own judgment," Cap'd tell him. "We want to lose another game."

But finally, one night in Pittsburgh, Cap had a letter from his missus and he come to us with it.

"You fellas," he says, "is the ones that put us on the bum, and if you're sorry I think they's a chancet for you to make good. The old lady's out to St. Joe and she's been tryin' her hardest to fix things up. She's explained that Ike don't mean nothin' with his talk; I've wrote and explained that to Dolly, too. But the old lady says that Dolly says that she can't believe it. But Dolly's still stuck on this baby, and she's pinin' away

just the same as Ike. And the old lady says she thinks if you two fellas would write to the girl and explain how you was always kiddin' with Ike and leadin' him on, and how the ball club was all shot to pieces since Ike quit hittin', and how he acted like he was goin' to kill himself, and this and that, she'd fall for it and maybe soften down. Dolly, the old lady says, would believe you before she'd believe I and the old lady, because she thinks it's her we're sorry for, and not him."

Well, I and Carey was only too glad to try and see what we could do. But it wasn't no snap. We wrote about eight letters before we got one that looked good. Then we give it to the stenographer and had it wrote out on a typewriter and both of us signed it.

It was Carey's idear that made the letter good. He stuck in somethin' about the world's serious money that our wives wasn't goin' to spend unless she took pity on a "boy who was so shy and modest that he was afraid to come right out and say that he had asked such a beautiful and handsome girl to become his bride."

That's prob'ly what got her, or maybe she couldn't of held out much longer anyway. It was four days after we sent the letter that Cap heard from his missus again. We was in Cincinnati.

"We've win," he says to us. "The old lady says that Dolly says she'll give him another chancet. But the old lady says it won't do no good for Ike to write a letter. He'll have to go out there."

"Send him to-night," says Carey.

"I'll pay half his fare," I says.

"I'll pay the other half," says Carey.

"No," says Cap, "the club'll pay his expenses. I'll send him scoutin'."

"Are you goin' to send him to-night?"

"Sure," says Cap. "But I'm goin' to break the news to him right now. It's time we win a ball game."

So in the clubhouse, just before the game, Cap told him. And I certainly felt sorry for Rube Benton and Red Ames that afternoon! I and Carey was standin' in front o' the hotel that night when Ike come out with his suitcase.

"Sent home?" I says to him.

"No," he says, "I'm goin' scoutin'."

"Where to?" I says. "Fort Wayne?"

"No, not exactly," he says.

"Well," says Carey, "have a good time."

"I ain't lookin' for no good time," says Ike. "I says I was goin' scoutin'."

"Well, then," says Carey, "I hope you see somebody you like."

"And you better have a drink before you go," I says.

"Well," says Ike, "they claim it helps a cold."

CONSIDER THE LIZARD

by Eugene Manlove Rhodes

No WRITER OF Western stories ever brought such love and training to the job as Eugene Manlove Rhodes, the cowboy Conrad. Rhodes was born in a log house in Nebraska in 1869 and grew up along the cattle frontier in Kansas and New Mexico, where his soldier-father was Government agent to the Mescalero Apaches. He was a cowpuncher at thirteen and a military guide and scout during Geronimo's uprising at seventeen. After one year at the University of the Pacific he went back to New Mexico and homesteaded a vast ranch in the wild San Andres mountains, near the present White Sands proving grounds. His prowess as bronco-buster, poker player and rough-and-tumble fighter was equal to that of any man's in that expansive country. He also read books, which sometimes occasioned comment. One contemporary has told of finding him sitting on the head of a horse that had just tried to throw him, calmly reading from a pocket volume of Browning's poems.

After twenty years of herding cows Rhodes began writing stories, which were always based on men and incidents he had known at first hand. His work reached the *Post* in 1907 and stayed there until shortly before his death in 1934. At its best it preserved for all time the cattle kingdom's golden age of chivalry, when men were indeed men, but seldom felt called upon to raise their voices about it. The title of one of his *Post* serials, *Pasó por Aquí* (He Passed This Way) is engraved on his tombstone in a New Mexico mountain pass that was named for him.

JUNE 28, 1913

JOHNNY BUILT THE BREAKFAST. Todd unharnessed and watered the team from twenty-gallon casks slung amidships on the deep-sea wagon—the roadrunner—of Oasis. Serving out hobbles and corn, he filled a canteen, saturating the cloth cover, and hung it to cool, unstoppered. Last, he spread a tarp under the wagon and suggins thereupon, fore and aft, for skipper and crew. They had driven twenty-five miles since moonrise: their high purpose was to make a little six-hour nooning, dinner about three P. M., and a homestretch spurt to Oasis.

Hot biscuit, black coffee, bacon and reckless rabbit; then the shade of the wagon, coat and boots for heading. It will be pleasant to remember these things hereafter.

Seen from this point of view, the world had no limits. Between the wagonspokes it stretched away to a quivering heat-haze, where there was no more to see. In vain Todd assured himself that he had but to raise his head to see the far-off mountains. It did not help; he still felt like a very small Saint Simeon Stylites on a very large pillar drifting in empty space. Next, prompted by the blistering glare of the sun, came the reflection, new to Todd, that interstellar space must be perpetual sunlight. He said as much aloud.

"Huh? What's that?" said Johnny's drowsy voice.

Todd repeated his statement.

"Suppose it does—what you goin' to do about it, you little runt? Go to sleep!"

"Little? Come—I like that!" said Todd in tones exceedingly bitter, the inference being he did not like that. "I'm five-feet-six, half an inch taller than you, and I outweigh you twenty pounds."

"Fat," said the voice scornfully. "Piffly fat!"

Todd's eyes filled with tears. A lizard from nowhere appeared on the felly. His tail curled aquiver; he cocked an impudent eye at Todd, as who should say: "Huh! Fat little runt!" He winked; he thrust out a swift black tongue; his throat pulsed stormily. Tears gave way to a cherubic smile. Todd began a mental note of the visitor's color-scheme. Presto! The lizard blinked, whisked, frisked—and was gone. Todd vainly tried to eke out his notes by memories of all the lizards he had ever seen. He had a vague impression of gray or olive green, black bars. Oh, confound it!

"Johnny, what color is a lizard?"

"Idiot!"

"Yah! You can't tell! You don't know. That's

the trouble with you outdoor men. You don't use what few and elementary faculties you have. A trained and intelligent observer like myself can tell you more about your own country, after a week of it, than you have found out for yourself in a lifetime. But a lizard's markings are so strikingly beautiful, at once fantastic and orderly—man, dear man! Haven't you any idea what an ordinary lizard looks like?"

"Sure! Beautiful fleshmarks, at once fantastic and orderly, sort of—er—gray color and—and brown stripes, I reckon."

Todd groaned.

"Stripes? You great gipe! There's just one stripe —wavy dull brown stripe down his back. Then there's an elaborate double row of tessellated designs on each side, alternating in shape and color —first, a bright brown T, and then a red circle like a target, with a green bull's-eye. And every other T is upside down. Stripes! Sweet spirit hear my prayer!"

"What's a gipe?" said Johnny fearfully.

"You are. A guttural gipe—a gruesome, gibbering, guttural gipe!"

"Well, anyhow," said Johnny, after a crushed silence, "that's your specialty—fauna and floradoras. Things you know nothing about, your eyes ain't such a much. Cards, now. Ever notice what court cards look alike?"

Todd winced at this unkind speech. He was a field naturalist of some note and of an affectionate disposition, now field-naturally listing the smaller Southwestern mammalia for the Smithsonian and making yet other researches on the side. For the rest, in his own habitat Todd had been triumphant and undisputed champion rummy player: it grieved his proud spirit that New Mexicans, irrespective of age, sex or color, languidly and gently beat him at it. The game of Con Quien is native to the Southwest. It is easy to see how the name was corrupted to "Coon Can" in transplanting; but why it is pronounced "Rummy" is not known. It beats Cholmondeley.

"King o' diamonds has one eye, meat-ax, Vandyke, and reverse english on his curls," said Johnny Dines dreamily. "The other three are left-handed; they got swords and two eyes apiece, and they all part their beards in the middle. But the king of clubs, he had his trimmed lately on an election bet. King of hearts wears his Buffalo Bills curling to his neck on the left side and curling away from his neck on the right side; and his upper lip is shaved, and he's fixing to fetch somebody a wallop with his sticker. All the queens are packin' posies; and she of spades is twiddlin' hers, real flirty, and she's got a chair-leg for emergencies."

Todd raised to his elbow very cautiously. Johnny was stealthily fingering an old deck; his drawling persiflage was to gain time for research. Todd glared.

The able mariner continued his discourse:

"The Jack of hearts, he stole some tarts, and he's only got one eye and a battle-ax. The other three carry doodads and dingbats. Jack of spades, one eye and two entirely different suits of curls—gets 'em a-comin' and a-goin'. I'll fix yours that way this evenin' if you want. . . . Oh, well, just as you say! Spade cards all have their little coatees trimmed with spades, and the diamonds all wear diamonds; but the others ——"

Todd pounced upon his perfidious companion and shook him violently.

"Cheater! Sneak! Jackass! *Je vous accuse! Canaille!* Cutthroat! Scab! Demagogue! Mugwump! No principle—no sportsmanship—not even common decency!"

He clasped his left hand to the back of Johnny's neck just below the ears; he rubbed Johnny's chin firmly with finger and thumb—this exercise is known as the "suasion." If you have bristles under your skin get some discreet friend to try it on you.

"Ouch! Help! Yelp! Leggo!"

Johnny made a furious attempt to bump his assailant's head against the reach, and so broke loose from the suasion.

"Cheat, will you?"

"Oh, what's the matter with you, you fat swab? What you howling about? Didn't you swell up like a hoptoad just now—coming the high and mighty over me, and you lookin' at a lizard all the time?"

"It's a black lie!" hissed Todd. "I'm incapable of such an action. I wasn't looking at any lizard at all. I just made that up!"

II

FOR SHEER skillful engineering, New Mexican railroads know no rivals. Neglecting fractions, spurs and feeders, consider only the trunklines. Four of them were built from border to border without touching a town!

Ill-natured people speak of townsites and hogsties in this connection. They say—these malicious ones—that when many-millioned railroads came begging, as is the custom, for gifts of land and cash, those hardheaded and benighted Southwestern towns cordially declined, mentioning terms of barter and sale. Nor could any high-salaried press agent manufacture enthusiasm, charm he never so wisely. The New Mexican's mind was, and is sometimes to this day, a primitive affair. But, as it has never been misused as a storehouse for odds and ends of useless information, he uses this mind or thinker, such as it is, to do his thinking with; and resolutely prefers to do his thinking with his own mind rather than with any other mind soever —even a mind with all the latest new-fangled improvements.

So far from an offering of yards on a lordly dish, garnished with bonus and bonds, the railroads faced the astounding and insulting proposition that they should buy what they needed, just as you and I have to do.

Hence new townsites were hatched in an incubator, hand-raised, coddled and taught to gobble the unearned increment. New Mexico is a land of twin cities. Commonly one name serves for both towns, with a prefixed Old or New. When the old town was left too far afield there are two names—as in the case of Mesilla and Las Cruces.

Not one of these recalcitrant old cities got a station within her borders—and not one weakened. They had been wont to freight from Independence by ox team; their unit of distance was twenty-five miles, and a little jaunt to the station held no terrors for them. They were hardy old towns and they foraged for themselves a goodly share of the increment they had earned by a few centuries of hardship.

Also, in some instances, Old Town made annual visits of condolence in the matter of a few feet of Rio Grande water in New Town's first floor. In these pious pilgrimages Old Town sat on the bank, offering sympathy and advice. Results varied, but an enjoyable time was had.

Now you know why Oasis Station is one mile west of Oasis. It remains to be seen why the station agent's family firmly declined to live in the rooms above the depot—thoughtfully provided for their use and in fixing the agent's salary—but dwelt in Oasis proper: why even the section hands trudged a mile to work and back again.

After all, human nature is one of the most natural things possible. Oasis irresistibly brings to mind—if you have that kind of mind—Emerson's noble line of those lives which "advance the standard of humanity some furlongs farther into chaos." Physically, that is—pushing out garden, orchard and field, a league of brave defiance to the besieging desert. It is a convincing desert—no semi-arid nonsense about it. In reaction that same human nature has made Oasis a riotous bravado of shade.

The town was founded that year in which Paris began to speak patronizingly of the young man Bonaparte, who had shown some military ability at Toulon. Each generation of Oasis made sorties against the desert, with conquest of new fields: builded new streets, and lovingly lined those streets with cottonwoods. They arch and meet now, those old trees, home of a million mockingbirds to thrill the dawn with unimaginable sweetness. Literally the town cannot be seen from the outside. There are no towers and minarets and things. The houses are adobe, one story high and a block long—recumbent skyscrapers.

Strangers arriving by rail condemn this prodigality of shade trees as wasting the slender resources of water and soil; but those who come in from the desert find no fault with the arching cottonwoods.

Indeed, Oasis has all the drawbacks you mention and some you would never guess; civically speaking, it is "link'd with one virtue and a thousand crimes."

Yet—for that deep and cool and generous shade, and the brave tinkling of her hundred acequias—men in the world's showplaces think with a pang of that dim and far old town, and name her puny river with a kindling eye, as Naaman spake of Abana and Pharpar, rivers of Damascus.

Now you know why the night operator of Oasis curses the company from franchise to dividends, standing up or sitting down, walking or lying, sleeping or waking.

He is lonesome. His nearest neighbor is one mile away.

So much was needful. In addition it will do you no harm to know that a near-by mountain range about the size of Palestine makes the eastern horizon for Oasis—a range never lower than highest Lebanon, capped by a peak to peer Mont Blanc, overhanging Oasis; or that the visible West, desert and mountains beyond, is pretty much the size and shape of England. For these things are dominant, ever-present, unescapable —they draw out the minds of men; they teach a sense of proportion.

The westbound flyer is an aristocratic institution—excess fare; limited baggage; carrying only through passengers, through mail, through express. Running south through New Mexico, it is not immediately apparent where the westbound flyer gets the title. That is not even the name of the train. It is only what the name of the train is called. The name of the train, officially, is The Goldplate Limited—but the train really is Number One. Towns where it does not stop mention it, with rancor, as Flossy.

Flossy is due at Oasis at eight-fifteen P.M. It stops there to drop passengers from St. Louis or beyond, to take passengers for Los Angeles or beyond, and for derailment or collision—not otherwise.

Flossy paused rather snippily this particular eight-fifteen. Miss Carroll qualified, coming all the way from Covington to visit her brother, the Indian agent at Mescalero. That gentleman is waiting with a Government ambulance. In a moment he will whisk her away and you will see them no more. Delightful people, no doubt—important to us only because for them the Limited stopped at Oasis.

Yeardsley, the express messenger, yelled to the night operator and dropped a heavy box from his door—a stout and padlocked chest not unlike those in which valuable express is carried, but smaller, new and unpainted.

"Here you are, Oasis!—P. Crandall, La Golendrina Mining Company—Rush! Here's your waybill."

"First time we ever got express off the flyer!" said the night man. "Ugh! Heap heavy!"

"Thought I might as well dump it off, so long as we stopped here ——"

"All aboard!"

"—— instead of takin' it on to Mecca to come back on the local."

The messenger shouted back the last words as the train moved off. Turning into his car he noticed a man and a heavy gun. The man wore a new cap, a mask made of a new handkerchief, and a voluminous new slicker, which reached the floor. The gun was cocked and pointed accurately at the messenger's left eye.

"That's right!" said the man behind the gun. He referred to Yeardsley's hands, which were stretched up in search of an imaginary trapeze. A second man appeared, arrayed precisely like the first. He carried a sack. The long oilskins made a perfect disguise, completely hiding the form. Evidently they had climbed in at the farther door during that brief chat with the operator. Number Two passed swiftly through the door to the other half of the car, the baggage compartment.

"Goin' to rain, do you think?" said Yeardsley.

Number One smothered a laugh. Number Two returned escorting the baggage-wrangler. He secured Yeardsley's gun and took a long rope from the sack.

"Hands behind you!" said Number One.

The messenger's hands were bound quickly and securely.

"Now sit down," advised the spokesman.

"Say, there's no good doing this! Timelock on the safe, you know!" remonstrated the messenger as his feet were swiftly knotted to the chairlegs and a turn taken round his body.

"Yes; set for eight-thirty-seven—so you can check up contents with your relief between Mecca and El Paso. Don't worry—we'll tend to that. Goin' to back up in a minute. We'll jolly the passengers while we wait on your little old lock. A swell bunch like that ought to shell out a nice piece of money."

Meanwhile the baggageman was trussed up by Number Two's nimble fingers.

"Gag 'em?" queried that deft bandit, speaking for the first time.

"Shucks, no! What's the use? No one living along the track or in ten mile of it. Let 'em holler if they want to. It develops the lungs."

He turned to the captives. "Now, old hands, we hate to do you this way. Take it easy. The boys have got your pardner in the mailcar hog-tied the same way, if that'll make you feel any better."

He pulled the bellcord and the train slowed down. Before it stopped two other robbers—capped, masked and slickered—swung in at the side door.

From the sack-of-all-trades the chief took a set of climbing irons, a pair of pliers, and a pair of incredibly large shoes—all fire-new. Leaving these behind, he threw the sack over his shoulder. "We must leave you now—going to take up a little collection," he explained. They filed into the vestibule.

The affair passed off pleasantly. The train stopped and instantly backed up. Passengers remarked the presence of fishermen three—Wynken, Blynken and Nod—come to fish for the herring fish that live in this beautiful sea. To be sure, there were four fishermen instead of three. What of it? The Three Guardsmen were four. A single fisherman so far inland would have been noteworthy; at four the passengers assumed the attitude of those who say *La sus!*—especially as regards the hands. Trainmen, when met, were held under herd.

Wynken held attention in the first car, Blynken in the second, while Nod and his sack-bearing chief passed into the third and last. The train was backing at full speed.

"The congregation will now stand up!" announced the spokesman—"except the ladies, who will be getting their offerings ready. Hands up, please!"

While his brother-in-arms kept the assembly amused, Nod induced the porter to carry the famous sack; and into it dropped pocketbooks, watches, rings, and such trinkets. He did not indulge in any brilliant badinage. His chief was the entertainer: Nod's was a practical, sordid mind, wholly intent on fish. They passed into the middle car, taking the conductor and the porter with them.

By this time they had backed past the station. But financial operations were transacted much faster now, for there were two willing workers instead of one. Four miles north of Oasis, negotiations were satisfactorily concluded: the train stopped on a northward slope. A procession trooped back from the engine; the engineer and fireman, followed by a fifth outlaw in the regulation uniform—cap, yellow slicker, mask and gun. At his instigation the fireman undid the couplings between the Pullman and the baggage coach ahead. A bandit opened the vestibule door and dropped off, tripping back to the engine with Number Five. The other three stepped over to the platform of the baggage car, first uncoupling the bellcord.

"Well, so long, old sports!" said the cheerful chieftain to the train crew, still under herd. "Put out a flag! We'll send the expressman and his pals back to you afoot in a few minutes—don't shoot 'em when they come."

He took the sack of valuables and tipped the porter; he pulled the bellcord and the first half of the flyer, under the new management, slid away into the night.

It stopped something like half a mile south. One robber took the pliers and climbing-irons and departed, obviously to cut the telegraph wires —stepping, all shod as he was, into those mighty brogans. Another went to the mail car, cut loose the clerk and brought him back. The leader did the same kindly service to the baggageman and turned him over to his mate for guarding. Then he looked at the messenger's watch and laid it on the safe.

"Eight-thirty-five," he said, cutting the ropes. He picked up the watch and held it open in his hand. "At eight-thirty-seven I'll say, Go! Then you get to working the combination on that safe. If it's open at eight-thirty-eight you can hike along back to the Goldplate." He held the gun—cocked —in the other hand. "And if it isn't you won't! Go!"

The messenger twirled the knobs earnestly and opened the outer and inner doors. So at eight-thirty-eight he dropped out of the side door and the man on guard climbed in.

"Thanks! Be good to yourselves, gentlemen! Toddle along now!" said the leading man. "Got those wires cut? Hop on, then. All aboard!"

III

MECCA, the county seat, is fourteen miles south of Oasis, where the next little stream runs down from the mountains. Those miles are pure desert and no man lives between the two towns. Mecca cannot see the approach of southbound trains until they pass the cut through a low ridge, a mile north of town; just north of this ridge a thirty-mile spur leaves the main line to bring lumber from the mountains. Mecca is a railroad town— division point, machine shops and all that.

At eight-seventeen Oasis reported Number One by on time. At eight-twenty-five the train dispatcher sent orders through to a freight train at Malaga, forty miles north. At eight-thirty-five, or thereabout, the flyer's headlight should have flashed into sight; she was due at Mecca at eight-thirty-seven.

She did not come. The dispatcher called Oasis. There was no answer. For minutes he clicked out the imperative call: O S—O S—O S. He began to sweat, with visions of a wreck. He took down the receiver.

"Hello! Get me the Oasis depot—quick!"

He heard the sharp, decisive call for Oasis Central before he hung up. He called an assistant and set him to pounding the O S call. There was a bare chance that the operator was merely out of the depot. He looked at the clock and shuddered. On time fourteen miles away, the flyer was now fifteen minutes late! The telephone rang:

"Oasis says depot don't answer."

"Get me Lipton's saloon then. Tell her if any one's on the line to cut 'em off!" Sweat was rolling down his face. "Hello! Is this Lipton?"

"Lipton's not here and the barkeep don't speak English. This is Johnny Dines. Can I do anything for you?"

"Yes. This is the train dispatcher at Mecca. The flyer's not in yet. I can't get the Oasis depot. Please go down and see what's the matter with him. I'll have the wrecker out—— What's that?"

"Wait a minute! . . . Hold your wrecker! Your flyer's been held up! She just left here a-goin' south, hell-for-leather, carryin' the black flag! Hold the wire! Your operator's here—run all the way up. He'll report to you as soon as he gets his breath."

The dispatcher got his own breath. Train robbery was bad, but not like a wreck. He looked at the time. It was nine o'clock.

A special was slung together with a jerk. It pranced at the heart-breaking delay while the destined passengers were found and gathered up by phone and message—the sheriff, and Ben Cafferty, the railroad's special officer; the division superintendent; the Wells-Fargo agent; linemen for telegraph repairs; gangs of doctors and sectionmen for possible other repairs.

The special crept her way cautiously. On any mile of the single track they might smash into the piratical flyer, coming without lights or standing still without them—or a rail might be taken out to wreck inquiry and delay pursuit; but they did not meet her. They made Oasis about ten o'clock, finding there part of Number One's train crew, who had walked in, and the entire male population of Oasis.

Down from the north, while they questioned her trainmen, came the hysterical Pullmans of Flossy, pushed by a blasphemous freight train. Plainly, then, the black-flag half of the train had run down within a mile of Mecca and backed up on the High Line spur—perhaps had gone all the way to the lumber woods with her booty. And traffic was piling up from both ways!

The break in the telephone wire was found and mended a few poles away. A second special was ordered up the spur to capture the outlaw train; the sheriff called up men of Mecca to go with it as his representatives, and set himself to get the facts of the robbery from the victims.

The railroad straightened out its own tangles in its own way. North and south went linemen to mend the breaks, using the special and the peevish engine of the sidetracked freight. From the crowd the sheriff picked men for deputies to go with them—Bat Wilson, his ranch partner, and Petey Crandall, of the Golendrina. They reported all wires cut—through and local, railroad and commercial—at about the same distance on each side of town, and the same set of footprints at each break—the track of gigantic shoes; for the first impulse of the frontiersman is to "read sign."

"And there's something dead wrong about this thing, Bill," declared Bat Wilson; "for we could see the marks of climbin'-irons on both them two poles—but a man to fit them shoes could 'a' bit the wires in two without ever stretchin' hisself! Them was sure the largest brogans ever made in captivity!"

Meanwhile the investigators—sheriff, superintendent and detective—had elicited two new facts, upon which passengers and crew were at one: None of the robbers had been either notably tall or very short; also, since their hands had been ungloved, it was certain that not one of them was a Mexican. Upon this latter discovery the Mexicans of Oasis drew apart, somewhat ostentatiously, with expressions of pained and sniffy virtue.

"And now," said Sheriff Bill Hamilton to his coadjutors, "we'll go in and interview this night operator. Let's see—I want a lot of men to get out at daylight and ride sign on both sides of the track. Pete, you see to that. I'll have a bunch hike out from Mecca and Cadiz and ride the High Line. I guess the robbers went that route all right; but, so long as we're up here, we'll just take a look round. Bat, you come with me. You, too, Cornish—you come in and take notes and take notice. You're an educated man."

Then up spake Johnny Dines:

"I'll just declare myself in on this, sheriff, if you don't mind—me and my pardner. We'd like to hear Mr. Operator. We heard him once, briefly, and we'd like to hear it all."

Hamilton leveled his brows at this.

"Who do you represent, Johnny?"

Todd strutted out and patted his chest.

"We represent ourselves—and other innocent men here present, if any."

"I will ask you to notice," said Johnny grandly, "that all these Oassassins and Oassistants are under suspicion except my friend and myself, who are very short men of high character. Besides," he added sadly, "we didn't come in time—just got in tonight. That ain't all either. My pardner is a very intelligent man, he tells me."

The sheriff shrugged his shoulders, rather annoyed at the intrusion.

"Oh, very well! It isn't often there's any devilment afoot you're not mixed up in, Johnny—I suppose that you want to make the most of it."

The superintendent called in one of his young men to hold down the key, making eight in the party. They moved toward the depot door. The sheriff stopped and pointed:

"Whose rig is that? I'm going to take a look!"

It was a covered wagon, backed up to the freight platform at the farther end. Bat laughed.

"Good eye, Bill! It's yours. I brought down a couple of hindquarters of beef to ship to Mecca—was aimin' to load up some freight, but it hadn't come; so I unhitched and went back to town. Take a good look and maybe you'll find the money!"

As they went into the office the sheriff spoke to the superintendent: "You examine him, Mr. Jones—he's your man."

Mr. Jones delayed his operations while the party were finding seats. There were only three chairs in the room. Todd and Bat Wilson sat on a chest; Johnny and the detective climbed on the ticket counter; Bert Cornish opened the baggage room and dragged in a new flat-topped trunk. The superintendent eyed this performance askance. He privately disliked having so many present at the inquiry.

Cornish caught the glance and laughed frankly.

"It's my trunk, Mr. Jones. I just got in yesterday from a little *pasear* in Oklahoma. Have a seat with me, Mr. Sheriff?"

The superintendent began:

"Let me see—your name is Blinn, is it not—Fred Blinn? Well, Mr. Blinn, we wish to ask you some questions. How long have you worked here?"

"Two months."

"Has Number One ever stopped here before?"

"Not since I have been here."

"Mr. Blinn, did you know that Number One was to stop here tonight?"

"Certainly, sir. A message came for Mr. Carroll, at the Agency, saying his sister would arrive tonight."

"Did you tell any one?"

Blinn flushed with obvious resentment. He was a young man, good-looking, well-dressed, with big blue eyes and reddish hair.

"I telephoned the message to Mr. Carroll, at Mescalero—if you call that telling. Any one could have heard it who cared to rubber."

"Are you sure you spoke to no one else?"

Blinn reflected.

"Why, yes, sir—I spoke of it to Mr. Howe in a jocular way when he relieved me yesterday morning."

"And to no one else?"

"To no one else."

"Now, Mr. Blinn, you came on duty last night at six, I believe?"

"At six-thirty. Mr. Howe lights the switch-lamps at night and I bring them back in the morning."

"Isn't that irregular? Are you not supposed to have the care of the lamps?"

"Perhaps. It is an arrangement between ourselves. We get the work done." The tone was sullen and defiant.

"May I ask the reason for the change?"

"You may. It is for our own convenience. Mr. Howe hangs out the lamps, and also fills and cleans them for me—work which must be done in daytime. In return, I do some of his office work for him at night."

"Let that matter rest for the present. Now, Mr. Blinn, after you came on tonight did you see any men round or in the depot?"

"No, sir—not until Mr. Carroll and his man came, about eight. Oh, yes, I did too—Mr. Wilson, over there, shipped some beef about seven or a little after."

"Could there have been any men in or about the freight cars on the sidetrack?"

"Certainly, sir. There might have been a hundred. It is no part of my duties to look for burglars under the bed."

"Easy, Blinn—easy!" said Ben Cafferty. "Keep your shirt on! You're taking the wrong tack."

"How'd you like it yourself?" rejoined Blinn hotly. "Don't you suppose if I'd seen masked men hanging about I should have mentioned it before? What's the sense of baiting me like this? It gets me rattled and it don't catch you any train-robbers." He jumped up and snapped his fingers at Superintendent Jones. "Do you mean to insinuate that I've got an engine and two cars hid in my vest pocket? Because, if you do, I don't like it, job or no job—I'll tell you that right now!"

Cornish laughed.

"Mr. Sheriff, you called me in here. Am I supposed to keep my mouth shut or may I offer an observation?"

"Let's have it."

"Well, then—our redheaded friend is young and excitable; but the general bearing of his remarks strikes me as extremely judicious. Where we ought to be is up on the High Line, where the outlaws went. To hurry things up—if Mr. Jones will not be offended—I suggest that we allow Mr. Blinn to tell his story his own way, just so we'll get done quicker."

"All right!" said Jones grimly. "Young man, I am sorry if I hurt your feelings about that missing engine. Go ahead!"

"There's not much to tell. The young lady got off. The messenger threw off a box. I reported Number One to Mr. Davis, about eight-eighteen, having been delayed a little to take the check for the young lady's trunk."

"Did Carroll go to Mescalero or did he stop at the hotel?" asked Wilson.

Blinn glared at him rebelliously.

"How do I know? Suppose you find out! See here, Mr. Jones, I judge there'll be a big reward out for these outlaws. If you'll let me turn the office over to this new man you brought in I'll go look for 'em—if these gentlemen don't intend to."

"All in good time. We want to hear your story before we do anything else. Go on!"

The operator chafed at what he seemed to consider a useless harrying and delay.

"Well, I didn't hear the flyer backing up till she was right here. She didn't whistle. I ran out on the platform. She was going fast. I saw a man in the gangway keeping the engine men covered with a sixshooter. The fireman was throwing in coal and the firebox was open; so I could see plainly. The robber was masked and wrapped up in a long slicker. I ran back and tried to call up Mecca. I got no answer. I tried every wire I could use. I called for a long time—both Mr. Davis and the Mecca depot. Then I rang up Oasis on the telephone—and couldn't get them."

"What time was this?"

"I didn't notice at first. I was excited. When I

gave it up and went to the telephone it was eight-thirty."

Ben Cafferty nodded.

"The dispatcher got orders for Number Twenty-seven through to Malaga at eight-twenty-five. They must have left a man to cut the wires where they backed up. He would have had just about enough time. What next, Blinn?"

"Well, I called up Mecca again—maybe half a minute. Then I began calling to the north—Saragossa, Santa Rosa, Tucumcari. I thought we could get over the Central to the Santa Fe, and so down to El Paso and back up to Mecca. They didn't answer and I heard the train coming back again. I ran down to the north switch. I could see there wasn't any lighted cars behind; and, at first, I intended to wreck 'em. Then I weakened and let 'em go by. They were running close to a mile a minute. I thought the engineer and fireman were still aboard. If I had only known I could have put them in the ditch! Then I ran up town and gave the alarm—and that's all."

"Let's see that switchkey," said the sheriff curtly.

The baited operator almost flung the switch-key at the sheriff. "Think I'd swallowed it?" he sneered. But that taciturn officer showed the key to Cafferty, without retort, and when Cafferty nodded, he tossed it back.

"H'm! What about the express package that came in on the flyer? Did you bring it in?" asked Bat.

"You're sitting on it!" said Blinn wrathfully. "What did you think I'd do with it? Hang it on the semaphore?"

"Well, you didn't say," replied Bat weakly.

Todd moved and looked at the label attentively.

"Didn't say?" snapped Blinn. "When you brand a calf you turn it loose afterward, don't you? Shut up, you fellows! They're calling O. S."

So, like the snowy-haired Lieutenant-General Bangs, "they stopped to take the message down, and this is what they learned":

The missing half of the train had been found on the High Line spur, barely a quarter of a mile from the junction. The postal clerk was certain the mail had not been tampered with. The express safe was innocent of treasure—in it, piled in a neat and orderly array, five slickers, five masks, five caps; climbing-irons, pliers and a pair of enormous shoes. The whole was capped by a way-bill, on which was penciled the insulting legend: Exhibit A.

"Oh, you Captain Kidd!" murmured Todd.

"They're on the way for us now—be here any minute," said Jones. "We'll go down at once. Mr.

Blinn, you are exonerated from all blame or suspicion. So far as I can see you did everything any man could have done. If you wish to go along with us you may. Thompson, you will act as operator until further orders."

"You two mighty innocent people can come along if you want to," said Hamilton.

"Why, thankee, sheriff—I guess we'll go to bed," said Johnny. "Me and Todd, we been a-driving nights. We'll take a good sound sleep and tomorrow we'll wake up with our little heads all nice and clear. Then we'll stir round and find that money."

Once outside the door he took Todd firmly by the arm. "If you want to find out what color a lizard is," he said, "you've got to look close!"

IV

EAST AND WEST and south and north, the riders flashed in the morning sunlight, seeking for signs and finding none—save the derisive trail of a malicious giant, where the telegraph wires were cut. No fresh track of men afoot, on horseback or in wagons left the railroad along the scene of last night's adventure—except, of course, round the depot at Oasis, where the thoughtless—or thoughtful—had trampled everywhere. It was as if the wooden shoe had come down from the skies bearing homeward the fishermen three—Wynken and Blynken and Nod. And where, oh, where was all that money gone?

Wild reports were abroad concerning the amount of booty—beginning with any amount and going as far as you liked. The express company would give no figures of their loss, but they offered one thousand dollars apiece for the robbers. Rewards by railroad, county and state totaled as much more.

At Lipton's, the social center, Oasis talked it over. Entire familiarity with local conditions had been shown in this brilliant affair; it was plainly the work of local talent, and Oasis was uplifted accordingly. Every one knew every one else; no one man was missing and unaccounted for—much less five; they had unsuspected ability in town. It was as Johnny Dines had said—every American in Oasis was under a cloud. They showed the effect of this cruel suspicion in their own peculiar way.

To this gathering came Johnny and Todd, fresh from a combined dinner and breakfast and smiling sleepily.

"Hello, you train-robbers!" was Johnny's greeting. "Anything new?"

"Mecca claims all the credit to herself," grumbled Lipton. "To hear them tell it, they beat their way up from there on a freight train, went back to the junction on the head end of Number One, and walked on home, packing the sack of boodle. Mecca was always a hateful town!"

"Dern likely too!" said the town doctor indignantly. "That stroke of business was planned and pulled off by men right in this room likely."

"At least one man went down on the engine—probably two," objected Johnny. "How'd they get back?"

The doctor smiled knowingly and turned the subject.

A seedy man bustled in the doorway and elbowed the bar importantly.

"You know that little bill you got chalked up against me, Tobe? I'll be round and settle it in a few days—soon as things simmer down a little."

Two shabby and mournful seven-up players sat in the corner. "That team of horses, Sim," said one in a confidential undertone, "that you was pricin' the other day and that I offered you so cheap—I don't want to sell 'em now. I've changed my mind."

"Well," said Sim in the same guarded but plainly audible tone, "I've about concluded to get me an automobile anyway."

"What I don't see," said Todd dreamily, "is where you fellows got all those new slickers!"

"Them? I had 'em shipped——" Lipton corrected himself hastily: "I mean, neither does the sheriff. He's inquiring about it in every store within a hundred miles—that and the rest of the stuff. It was all new—everything."

"Dines," said Todd loftily, "we do not want to associate with these—er—people. I think we had better saddle up and ride out in the—er—uncontaminated air."

"Quite right, me deah fella!" drawled Johnny. "A wuffianly lot they are, to be shu-ah!"

"Hold on a minute!" said Lipton. He fished two new bandannas from under the bar and shook them open. Each one had two eyeholes snipped out. "Take these. Every man in town has got one. When the sheriff and his bunch get back we're going to give 'em the Chautauqua salute!"

The innocents found an uncontaminated spot on a high knoll just out of town and lay in the shade of their horses.

"Now, Mr. Trained Observer, let's have an exhibition of that superhuman sagacity of yours."

"You first, Johnny—you're better looking than I am. I've got my notebook. If you should happen to say anything sensible I'll jot it down."

"I am handsome!" admitted Johnny. "Such being the case, here goes! But I hardly know where

to begin. This whole design is so beautiful—at once so fantastic and so orderly! . . . A few general reflections first. There was at least one railroad man on the job; at least one man who knew how to follow a trail, and so didn't propose to leave any—some old-timer; at least one Easterner —no one out here ever saw a cap; and at least one man who had mighty good reason to know that it isn't safe to monkey with Uncle Sam—else why was it they didn't touch a thing in the mailcar? . . . Yet they hog-tied the postal clerk and put him off. Now what was that for? They didn't rob the mail. They could have left him in the car while they ran down to Mecca if that was all they did. . . . Consider the lizard! There was something they didn't want him to see—something besides cutting the wires and backing in over the High Line. Shucks, my head aches already!"

"Now we'll get down to cases. We'll begin with that message for Carroll. They knew the Flossy train was to stop. Any operator along the line might have known that. But we'll just play, for the present, that our man Blinn stood in on the deal."

"Let X equal Fred Blinn—for the present," agreed Todd. "There was certainly some one on the job who knew exactly where the trains were, or they wouldn't have dared to back round so recklessly. We'll nominate Blinn for the goat. Anyway, he overplayed his part the first thing, in my opinion. Too fiery, he was—hot-headed, injured innocence, and all that. And for an excitable man he showed wonderful presence of mind in the emergency—thinking right offhand of wiring round by the Sante Fe, and throwing the train in the ditch!"

"If he's innocent—and he may be—he did it just as he tells it," said Dines. "If he is one of the bunch he told it to account for the elapsed time. It was nine o'clock when he came to Lipton's. That's thirty minutes and more by his own account, since he saw 'em back by. That was while the gang was doing something—making a getaway and hiding the stuff right here in Oasis, I guess. Ten to one they stopped here. That the engine went down to the junction almost proves that they went to Mecca. Therefore, as they're such a cunning bunch, they didn't. Yet at least one went to drive the engine. Tut! Tut!" He scratched his head. "And the kings are all lefthanded! Now if they had all wanted to stay here they might have started the engine up, and jumped off. But they didn't. They turned the switch and backed up on the spur. They knew how to run an engine. But they took a big chance of a smashup if Mecca had got nervous and started a rescue train as soon as the flier didn't show up. There must have been some one mighty anxious to get to Mecca—and, if our guess about Blinn is correct, they had some reason for wanting to get there by nine o'clock. Now who was it that had to be in Mecca by nine o'clock, and why?"

"I can think of two persons, who—if they were in it—would have a mighty good reason for wanting to be there by nine o'clock," said Todd.

"Blest if I do!" said Johnny. "But that's the proper number—two—engineer and fireman. Who was it? I don't keep up with you."

"You wouldn't. I'll tell you after a while. One thing at a time. The train dispatcher says he used the wire at eight-twenty-five. Blinn says it wouldn't work at some time before eight-thirty. The Limited people said that when the train stopped the first time it backed up immediately; so if the wire was cut before eight-thirty, there must have been still another man—and another pair of big shoes to make those tracks. Do you think that likely?"

"No, I don't. That would mean one more man to split the money with—and no need of it if Blinn was standing in with them as we think. He could just play that he called up Mecca when the flier backed by—he didn't actually have to call. They could cut the wires south of town as they went down the last time."

"But we don't know that Blinn is guilty and we mustn't build entirely upon that. He may possibly be all right after all."

"Whoosh! Hooray! We've got him—by George! we've got him dead to rights!" Johnny sat up, his big, black eyes snapping. "I thought all the time that nobody could get up a lie that wouldn't show through to field naturalists used to counting the spots on lizards. Blinn said that he tried to call up Saragossa and the other towns to the north at eight-thirty—remember? And we know positively, by the evidence of the expressman and baggageman and the postal clerk, that the north wire was being cut at eight-thirty-seven! Blinn lied seven whole minutes!"

Todd made a correction in his notes.

"X is Fred Blinn," he said. "What next?"

"You're next. Do you want me to do all the heavy work? Get to grindin' and find those other men! Who was it you knew about, so wild and fierce, that had good reason to be in Mecca by nine o'clock?"

"There are just two men alive who—provided they were in this thing and knew when Blinn was set to give an alarm—knew positively that they would be looked for in Mecca immediately afterward; and they were the very people to know best how inadvisable it is to trifle with the United States Mail. They were the sheriff and the rail-road's special officer! And it is a ten-to-one shot that one of them—Cafferty—can drive an engine. But where's the money? And who were the other men?"

"The other men—why, they are the sheriff's posse! I am a man singularly free from vanity," said Johnny, "but I thought at the time 'twas a strange thing that Bill Hamilton should pick that bunch and leave me out—just as I thought it queer that he didn't notice what a break Blinn had made in not getting some capable person—like me—to size up the tracks before he gave the alarm and sent the whole blame town down there. You and me, we went down right off; but the sign was all mummuxed up before we got there—where they cut the telephone wire and where they hot-footed back to town."

"Maybe they didn't come back to town," suggested Todd. "Maybe they just stayed down there and oozed in with the crowd!"

"No, they didn't—they came uptown to set a good example marking out tracks. Bat Wilson and Petey Crandall are old-timers—they know what a telltale a footprint is if it's not queered. Whoever cut the telephone wire wouldn't wear those enormous shoes—'twould have been a give-away on Blinn. And they had to come up to town to hide the money too. No! By Heck! I see it all now—perfectly clear from start to finish! Bat smuggled them down in his wagon to begin with—so they couldn't be seen by any accident and wouldn't leave any tracks. The slickers——"

Todd broke in:

"I see! The new slickers, new masks, new caps, new climbers, new pliers, new Number Fourteen shoes—Bert Cornish brought them the day before in his new trunk—after Blinn had wired him when Miss Carroll was coming. On the same train he had the chest sent—that new chest—by express, on the off chance that the messenger would drop it off when the train stopped here. Why, it works out like the tabby end of a solitaire game! And the money—— Of course! Come along! It's all over but the shouting."

"Shooting, maybe!" suggested Johnny grimly. "But I guess we can surprise 'em. We will now send for Mr. Superintendent Jones. He's all right. See how he rambled round with his questions! But them others—they had the whole play rehearsed so fine they didn't waste a word. There's that switchkey! If the sheriff hadn't borrowed it to get in on the High Line with he would never have thought of asking if Blinn had it. Too smart! Come along!"

They shunned the town and rode to the solitude of the depot, where they held deep converse with Agent Howe. An hour later, in answer to their imperative summons, Superintendent Jones alighted from a northbound freight, accompanied by a Man Some Higher Up in express circles, who had hurried from El Paso to investigate.

"You claim you have a clew?" said Mr. Jones anxiously as they came to the office.

"Why, you might call it a clew—certainly," said Todd. "We've got the money anyhow!"

"What!"

"Yes—and we know the robbers; but we haven't got 'em yet. They're out of town. Here's a list of their names—but don't open it till we make good."

"Why, how on earth——"

"Exercise of pure reason," said Johnny. "We're very intelligent, Todd and me, for all we're so handsome. At that, I don't mind admitting that we lost a little sleep on it. The money—well, we took a little liberty, which we trust you'll excuse." He raised a saddle blanket, which was spread over a chest—the chest! He kicked the lid open, exposing currency in bundles; coin in stacks, sacks and packages; billbooks, watches and jewelry.

"We knew it was either in this box or in a certain trunk we knew of—but we felt a certain impatience to see it; so we didn't wait. One of us tolled Mr. Howe away and the other just naturally unlocked it with an ax. It was very rude—but we had to do it. We were getting palpitation of the heart."

"We busted the trunk too," said Todd. "No money in it or anything else that was in any way suspicious. Just a gentleman's wardrobe and not much of that. That doesn't make any odds—we had a clear case anyhow; but I'm sorry about breaking 'em open too," he added wistfully. "I wanted to send for a bunch of keys, take out the money, fill it up with junk, and let 'em take it home to divide. That would have been jolly!"

"Well—this is the most extraordinary circumstance!" gasped the expressman. "Will you explain how it happens that you made these discoveries rather than the officers?"

"Johnny will," said Todd. "I furnish the brains for this establishment, but Johnny is the orator. Look at your list."

The superintendent unfolded the paper. This is what he saw:

CAFFERTY, Railroad Detective
HAMILTON, Sheriff
CRANDALL ⎫
WILSON   ⎪
CORNISH ⎬ The Posse
BLINN   ⎭

"You see," said Johnny, "it might have been some time before that bunch found the culprits."

"I can't believe it possible!" said Jones.

"I'll tell you what then—you believe half of it and maybe this gentleman can believe the other half."

"For Heaven's sake, man, tell us what happened here and how you found it out!"

Johnny shook his head sagely.

"I'll buy," said Jones. "Tell us what happened."

V

"To MY notion," said Johnny, "Cornish must have planned the whole thing. If it was any other way he couldn't have been in it at all. He had to put something into the partnership—so he furnishes brains. Hamilton and Bat and Petey Crandall are old residenters—Bat is Hamilton's accomplice in the cow business. They've got plenty of brains, but they're the right-now kind of brains—not the day-after-tomorrow kind.

"Cornish's first idea was that if the sheriff and Detective Cafferty were in the play they might not arrest themselves. Or was that it? Was it the train-robbin' scheme that sent him corruptin' the officers, or knowing the officers that made him think of train-robbin'? Anyhow he got 'em. And Blinn—they had to have Blinn to make things come out even.

"They ciphered out every point. They knew the Flossy train dropped the diner at Saragossa after supper, to be picked up on the return trip. That left three coaches. They wanted to make out with just as few to divvy up with as they could have and be safe—so they wouldn't be obliged to shoot anybody. You want to give 'em credit for that. That made five men—one for the engine, one for manager of each coach, and one to pass the plate. There's where the sheriff takes in Bat and Petey, knowin' them to be reliable.

"I judge by this time the sheriff was kind of taking the lead. Anyhow him and Cafferty had seen too much of Uncle Sam's work from the inside—they wouldn't hear to takin' a thing from the mail car.

"Everybody knew that Miss Carroll was coming pretty soon. So Cornish he goes back to Oklahoma. Nobody notices that—he's always taking little trips. He buys all that new stuff and packs it in his trunk.

"Then he rigs up this chest and sends it, or maybe leaves it—we don't know whereall he's been—with some good responsible person in Kansas City, to be sent by express on this particular train when notified by telegraph. Anyway, the box came from Kansas City, as per label.

Cornish is mighty particular not to send it himself. He's got a long head. You want to go easy on these lads, Mr. Jones—they took a heap of pains to manage not to kill the express messenger. That was the idea for sending that chest—so they could hop on quietly while the messenger was dropping the chest out the door. Another thing—all they set out to do was to keep clear themselves; they didn't try to hang it on somebody else. That was decent of 'em. Mention that to the court, will you? No; you needn't. I'll do it myself."

"I'll not forget it either," said Jones.

"All set then! Miss Carroll tells her brother when she'll be here—night message of course; Blinn wires Cornish; Cornish wires his friend to send the box, and then comes back from Oklahoma, a day ahead of Miss Carroll, leaving his trunk in the depot.

"Last night, soon as Mr. Howe's gone, Bat Wilson brings the bunch down here, all cozy and out of sight in his covered wagon. No knowin' where he picked them up—different places, I reckon. Bat, he takes his team to the pastures and slips back. The beef and the freight was just a blind."

"The freight came today," said Howe.

"Yes," said Johnny admiringly. "They didn't miss many bets. Just one thing they overlooked—there never was yet a man so good but there was another one just a little better—except Ty Cobb.

"Well, they opened up little Bertie's trunk—in here—put on their masquerade duds, and got over beyond the freight cars on the far track before Lieutenant Carroll drove down with his little old ambulance.

"You know the rest—up to the time they coaxed the messenger to open the safe. While they were gone, Blinn opened up this box and dumped out what was in it—coal in little sacks packed tight—into the coalbin. They packed the swag in it, and they put back the sacks and enough coal to make it weigh about what it did before. There wasn't really any need of this. They could have put it in Cornish's trunk. I reckon that was Cornish's scheme, on the long chance that if anything went wrong Petey would be implicated and he wouldn't if nobody turned state's evidence. And I don't believe any of them fellows would do that—unless 'twas Cornish or Blinn.

"Yes, that was Bert Cornish. Just consider this: Blinn and Pete Crandall and Bat, they was all clamped down to this depot last night if things went wrong—Bat's wagon; the box for Pete's and Blinn's job. Hamilton and Ben Cafferty, they took their chance sloping with the train and maybe being seen when they walked the track from where they left it. They had to get home—for, of course, they was going to be called on right off to hunt down the perpetrators of this highhanded outrage. They had just nicely time to answer 'Present' to the rollcall. But Bertie —— He's certainly some slick crook!—he ain't takin' no chances. There ain't a thing on him right now but a moral certainty—that and him bein' on the sheriff's posse."

"That's the way it looks to me," said the expressman dryly, "unless the others implicate him —as, of course, they will."

"Do you think so?" said Todd anxiously. "Maybe we'd better slip a little loot in his trunk to save trouble?" This ingenious project was negatived.

"Well, but you've overlooked one thing!" said the expressman. "Didn't they have inside information as to what money was carried by express? It looks like it."

"Not at all," said Johnny. "Such information, to be of any value, would have to coincide with the date of Miss Carroll's arrival, which is entirely improbable. No, sir; they were sure of a pretty good thing from the passengers alone, and they just took a gambler's chance on the express. If they made a big haul from you, which I don't know ——"

"He can only count up to nineteen!" explained Todd.

"—— it just happened that way. That's all, I guess—only that they're all on the posse because they dassent trust each other! They aim to stick together till things quiet down, and then, in a day or two, take the box out to the mine and declare a dividend. You'd better put this stuff in the safe and watch the safe, I reckon. Don't you want to hire a good honest man to watch you?"

"You always want me to do all the work!" said Todd bitterly.

"But how are you going to capture your sheriff and his posse?" said Jones. "Won't it be dangerous?"

"Oh, them? Shucks! I don't know yet. I'll rig up some sort of deadfall, so we won't have to kill 'em. One good turn deserves another—and they sure was mighty thoughtful about the express messenger! Well, I guess we'll shack along uptown now. Hey! You silly ass! Where you going?"

The last words were addressed to Todd, who had walked out the front door, crossed the track, and was now heading out for the desert. Todd stopped and partly turned round.

"Me? I'm going to catch me a lizard. I want to see what they look like!"

VI

ABOVE the hitching rack flaunted a gay sign-board, riotous in color, enormous in lettering:

LUIZ TRUJILLO: TIENDA BARATA

The sonorous syllables merely bespeak a cheap store—in the Spanish idiom, Store Cheap—preceded by the owner's name. Suspended from this eye-filling announcement was a smaller board of modest black and white, lettered with the pungent pleasantry:

Why Go Elsewhere to Be Cheated?

Luiz Trujillo knew his Oasis. This was effective psychology—color, magnificence, mass and processional pomp for the gay and volatile Latin —two sides of many-sided truth, in one ironic glimpse, for the sober Saxon. An unfortunate phrase, this last: please substitute "the graver Saxon."

Columbus stood the egg on end and John Milton invented Satan. Other people have done these things better since, but the credit remains with the first discoverers. So with Mr. Trujillo's literary venture, which stirred up emulation.

Mr. Lipton's establishment was a quadrangle. The hotel was on one side of the big gateway, the saloon on the other; the inclosed square was a feed corral, with stables in the rear; and over the gateway was a high arch, bearing the ambiguous legend:

ENTERTAINMENT WITHIN FOR
MAN AND BEAST

Johnny Dines sat at his balanced ease on the beam of the hitching rack. He was in his shirt-sleeves; his hat was on the back of his head; his heels clicked idly together; he twisted the ends of his drooping mustache; by and large, he presented the picture of a man without a care—presumably with a vacant mind; and he trolled a stave of astonishing import:

> *Oh, the spring—the spring I sing!*
> *There's nothing like fried onions!*
> *Because the skies are almost overhead,*
> *Let us lean up against the seashore!*

The sheriff and his party turned the corner from Cadiz Road—six dusty but jaunty horse-men. As they rode slowly down the long street, their coming suddenly became a triumphal progress. The windows blossomed with laughing girls: serious-eyed men strolled from every house. It was a beautiful, clear day; but all those serious-eyed men wore slickers or carried them rolled in a neat bundle; and every man, as the sheriff passed, fluttered a red and ostentatiously slitted kerchief.

"Got 'em in jail, Bill?"

"Never touched us!"

"Bet they bought you off!"

"Find any clues?" demanded one, wearing climbers slung conspicuously from his neck.

"Say, sheriff, what'll you give me to turn state's evidence?"

"Sheriff, these pesky fellers ain't using you right," said Lipton soothingly. "They oughta be ashamed! You come in and wash up. You must be all tired out. Supper'll be ready in a jiffy. Must be five o'clock or after."

He pulled out a watch, looked at it, shook it, held it to his ear. Then, from various pockets on his round and goodly person, he produced, one after another, five more watches, all of which he gravely consulted. In this process he dropped a pair of pliers from a side pocket and forthwith set a foot upon them, shod in the mightiest shoe Oasis could furnish. The posse grinned sheepishly.

No—they were not heartless, these people; the king's horses and the king's men could not have drawn them to this cruelly mistimed mockery had they known what waited.

The seven picked men who knew bore no hand in the foolery. There had been no discussion of this point; it was part of the fitness of things that they should not. Johnny Dines felt a twinge of pity—almost wished that the luckless wretches might sense their danger and turn and flee; but he had a better thought as well—of trainmen and messengers slaughtered without mercy—and he hardened his heart.

The sheriff paused before Trujillo's and fixed Johnny with a quizzical eye.

"Caught your men yet, Dines?"

"Not yet."

Todd came from the hotel, carrying a camera.

"Wait half a sec, sheriff, before you go in! I'm going to write this thing up for the El Paso papers, and I'd like to get a photograph of your crowd, guns and all, just as you came in from the manhunt. Won't take but a minute! Oh, never mind the dust—it won't show. We can't get a good picture in the shade. Just ride over in that sunny place by Rosalio's, where we can have the adobe wall and the old house for a background."

The posse complied, nothing loth. Todd planted his tripod and proceeded to arrange his group.

"I want to take two exposures—in case one plate isn't good. Not too close together now— don't let the horses crowd! And don't try to line up—you're not soldiers! Sit naturally in the saddles. Blinn, you're too stiff. Cornish, your hat's down over your eyes—push it back a little! Hi! You other fellows—stand back! You're crowding in the picture. I'll take some of you, all in good time, when you get what's coming to you."

A crowd had followed, after the manner of humans. They stood back obediently; Johnny Dines and five others, all in shirt-sleeves, even jumped over into the garden and ducked behind the crumbling wall to make sure they were out of the way.

Todd dived under the camera cloth. He popped up his head again.

"That's pretty fair! When we're ready keep perfectly still till you hear the machine click the second time. But don't look at the camera. Hold your heads up like you would if you were out on the plains looking at something a long way off. There! That's good! Hold that!"

He made another dive and the camera clicked once—twice. Todd came up smiling.

"Now one more—a profile this time. Just turn your heads a little toward the garden wall."

The posse obeyed—and were annoyed to ob serve six shotguns rested on the garden wall— each man looking down the barrels of an indi vidual shotgun to a steady eye beyond.

"Look pleasant, please!" said Johnny Dines.

WHO'S WHO—AND WHY:
W. CHURCHILL

IN THE TWO items reprinted below the *Post*'s readers were given an early and somewhat satirical glimpse at two budding world statesmen. Both were probably written by Samuel G. Blythe, the *Post*'s longtime specialist in politics and world affairs. Blythe was never a hero worshipper, but he could write more gently on occasion. In 1923 his *Post* article, "A Calm Review of a Calm Man," helped ease the dying moments of the President about whom it was written. Mrs. Warren G. Harding was reading the piece to her husband in a San Francisco hotel room shortly after it was published. "That's good. Go on. Read some more," said Harding, and then a blood clot reached his brain.

Both Churchill and Franklin Roosevelt, incidentally, are on the *Post*'s long list of "big-name" authors. Churchill wrote an article about British army reform for the *Post* in 1900, and thirty years later he contributed a prophetic discussion of "The United States of Europe." Roosevelt's name was signed to a 1920 article called "Can the Vice-President Be Useful?" At the time he was running for the job on the Democratic ticket, but he was not given a chance to enact his own answer.

DECEMBER 7, 1912

WHEN IT COMES to a neat, factful, comprehensive description of a leading personage of England who once escaped from prison, I acknowledge the exceeding talent of the unknown Boer who wrote a paragraph about Winston Churchill, the biggest young man in England, now First Lord of the Admiralty, but at that time a war correspondent in South Africa.

Boers run largely to whiskers and assay but a trace of imagination to the pound. This particular Boer saw concretely. He said: "Englishman; twenty-five years old; indifferent build; walks a little bent forward; pale appearance; red-brownish hair; small mustache, barely perceptible; talks through his nose; cannot pronounce the letter S properly and does not know one word of Dutch."

I have watched Winston Churchill in action and in repose, and so have many others; but none of us is able to improve on that paragraph, albeit the red-brownish hair is thinner now than it was then, the mustache is gone, and the years have thickened the frame a bit. He still walks a little bent forward, still has the pallor and still fails when he tackles the letter S. He couldn't say "She sells seashells by the seashore" if he were promised ten new dreadnoughts from Parliament as a reward.

Not that that makes any difference. Very few people want to say "She sells seashells"; and the mere fact that the letter S, occurring now and again in the language, causes Churchill to fizz linguistically like a bottle of soda pop, doesn't detract from his ability as an orator, but rather adds to the piquancy of his speech. Moreover, when it comes to writing the letter S, and all other letters in combinations of words, there are very few persons indulging in that pastime at present who can convey their thought so clearly, so picturesquely, so effectively, as this same young man.

He is only thirty-eight now, and he is a member of the English Ministry, the biggest figure in English politics—bar Lloyd George—and bigger in many ways than that Welshman; and he has been the wonder of the empire since he was twenty-five. The only American to whom he can be compared is Roosevelt; and that comparison isn't especially apt, for Churchill writes far better than Roosevelt does, talks far better, and at thirty-eight has gone farther than Roosevelt had when he reached that age. Of course Churchill never can be king, and Roosevelt has been president; but Churchill will undoubtedly be a Prime Minister of England one of these days—and to be Prime Minister of England is no small shakes of a job!

They have points in common—both are impetuous, virile, enthusiastic, belligerent demagogues in the good sense of the word. Both take their careers as adventures. Both are crusaders. Both have had no hesitancy in shifting political obligations when the time seemed opportune. Both are, indeed, opportunists. Both are men of wide information and great and interesting experience. Both have been soldiers and both are born politicians. Both are tremendous workers.

Both are men of gentle birth, and both are held high in popular esteem, though each is basically of aristocratic tendencies and sympathies.

When Churchill was a youngster he was, speaking Americanwise, a fresh youngster. They used to make him run round the cricket grounds at school a set number of times for talking too much. When he was a subaltern with his regiment he suggested that Lord Kitchener—even then the great general—should be brought over and introduced to him, instead of going over to be introduced to Kitchener. When he came into public life his supporters called this quality charming impudence, and his enemies referred to it as insufferable insolence. Whatever it was, in his early days he had the grand manner. He was quite impressed with his own superiority. He considered himself a natural dominator. He never asked a man to do a thing, but told him to do it—not as if he wanted a favor, but as if he expected it as a right. In his early days in politics he took none of the stodgy political pretensions of the older statesmen seriously, but flouted them, laughed at them, was insolent, impudent, satirical, sarcastic, by turns. He would break a lance with any of them, and had no reverence for age, reputation or awe of convention and precedent. The son of Lord Randolph Churchill, himself an English statesman of much renown, he had a great name back of him, and he saw nothing but a future of adventure before him.

So he weighed in, essaying anything that came to hand and considering himself a knight in search of any hazard that might ensue. His quality of mind was, and is still, that boyish quality that sees a deed of high emprise in anything in which he may be engaged. He thinks in terms of the apotheosis. Let him take up a subject, and that subject immediately becomes the most important subject in the world. The fate of the nation is always impending with Churchill; the ship of state is always going on the rocks; the edge of the precipice is forever close at hand. His sunsets are always more beautiful, his sunrises more glorious, his dangers more vivid, his pleasures more pronounced, than those of any other. As he looks at it, the sunset is his personal perquisite, and the sun always rises for his especial benefit.

When he starts to set forth a proposition he sets it forth in the ultimate manner. Do this—else you perish! He detects the crack of doom when the noise may be only a peaceful Englishman opening an egg. Intrinsically a soldier, he thinks largely in terms of soldiering—Up, guards, and at them! His natural tendency is to boil over like a geyser. He is as ebullient as Old Faithful. In his early days, his friends say, his impudence

amounted to rudeness. He defied the whole universe and considered himself eminently capable of making it over to suit his large ideas.

It might be thought that, with attributes of this kind, Churchill would be an impressionist instead of a plodder; but though he is a man who takes impressions instantly, who flashes over a situation and comprehends it, he is in reality a most astonishing digger. He writes and rewrites his important speeches, polishing them for days before he delivers them. He rehearses them time after time, and his industry is monumental. He always has his subjects well in hand. When he speaks he allows himself no asides, such as those that come up to perplex Lloyd George. He has a good breadth of view, and the facility for preaching economy, for example, and at the same time proposing an unprecedented naval expenditure, weeping the while over the pathetic necessity for the outlay.

Like every great orator and every great politician, Churchill is an actor. His natural tendency is to exaggeration—that is, his mind, because of that boyish quality I have mentioned, tends to make every impression a great impression, and tends also to lead him to tricks of manner that are impressive, though artificial. When he sits down with an air of weariness he seems to be the weariest man in the world. When he puts his hand on his brow he presents a picture of a man thinking greater thoughts than any other ever has. When he declaims a peroration it is with the conviction that this is the final pronouncement on the subject, the acme of all the wisdom of all the universe—for he convinces himself that this is so.

Politics began as an adventure with him, and now it is a passion. He has changed in manner, not because he has really changed in nature but because he has thought it expedient to curb that gay spirit of turbulent dissent and assent, and apparently to be discreet. He wears solemn blacks, gives the air of heavy responsibility, checks his impulsiveness, talks infrequently. This isn't natural. It is artificial and done after thought, clearly mapped out and definitely decided upon as the proper course. Within, Churchill is the same flamboyant, crusading, eager, headlong person he always was—but he is a politician also, and that accounts for his present attitude.

He went into the army when he was twenty-one, and saw service in India, in Africa and elsewhere. He was a war correspondent, has been a lecturer, has written several books, all of them excellent, and one—his biography of his father, Lord Randolph Churchill—a work that has been held to be one of the best of English life stories.

What this young man will do in the next twenty

years is one of the fascinating problems of English politics. No one can predict, for Churchill isn't subject to predictions. The most favored opinion is that eventually he will be the leader of a party composed of Sir Edward Grey and the younger Tory Democrats against Lloyd George, leading the Radicals and Socialists. Churchill has worked the greater-navy game with good effect; and he goes on the theory that the English people want to be governed, not legislated for, and that the English hate all foreigners, especially the Germans—which is quite true. But he should have a kindly feeling for Americans, for, you see, his mother is an American and that likewise may account for many things—his quickness of mind, for example!

WHO'S WHO—AND WHY: ROOSEVELT II

JUNE 14, 1913

APPARENTLY IT IS quite impossible to keep Administration house without a Roosevelt, and this new Administration of ours prudently laid one in. Mr. Taft did not have a Roosevelt to his name—and look what happened to him!

Oh, yes, it is quite certain we must have an executive Roosevelt somewhere round the place. And isn't it a tribute to the versatility—to say nothing of the forehandedness—of that great family to find, no matter what the emergency may be, there is a Roosevelt for the job? No sooner comes along a Democratic Administration than gallantly steps forward a Democratic Roosevelt and offers himself generously for the duties entailed! A versatile family, as I have remarked.

Likely as not there is a Woman-Suffrage Roosevelt, a Socialist Roosevelt and a Prohibition Roosevelt concealed in the high grass awaiting the call and the opportunity. This present Roosevelt, who is keeping the record straight and preserving the precedent for Mr. Wilson, is by name Franklin D.; and at the present time he occupies the post once held by the illustrious Theodore—that is to say, he is assistant secretary of the navy. Theodore, as may be recalled, was assistant secretary of the navy just previously, prior to and before the war with Spain. That isn't so long ago, but there are many legends connected with Theodore's occupancy of the post. Indeed, as assistant secretary of the navy T. Roosevelt is the hero of many thrilling tales now embodied in the folklore of the nation.

There is this much about it though: He—Theodore—certainly set a mark as assistant secretary of the navy for all future assistants on the same job to shoot at; and it will be a long time before one of them hits it, so far as that goes. Still, we have hopes. Here, for example, is Franklin D. Roosevelt—he'll shed that middle D. before long—no Roosevelt should have more than one given name; albeit many standpat Republicans call Theodore an extra name beginning with D. However, here, as has been observed, is Franklin Roosevelt in the same chair from which that other Roosevelt emerged to become soldier, statesman, and whatever else your political beliefs compel you to dub him—ranging from best to among the worst. And think this over: Suppose we should have a war with Japan!

Hadn't considered that, had you? Slipped your memory entirely! Well, here it is, staring you in the face: Suppose we have war with Japan! Or suppose California secedes; or Hawaii joins Switzerland because the Democrats are going to put sugar on the free list; or suppose any old warscare you like—if you can't think up a warscare the general staffs of the army and navy will supply one for you; they keep a stock of them on hand to use when they want increased appropriations—but, suppose we have a war!

Should there be a war Franklin Roosevelt will simply resign as assistant secretary of the navy, simply organize a regiment, simply take command, and simply knock the spots off the invading foe. After that the world will be his. It is foreordained, prearranged—provided some one will kindly supply the war. Hey, boy, bring on a war! Fetch a war, I tell you, and be quick about it! Will that boy never come with that war?

So far as can be learned, this particular Roosevelt—he is a cousin or something—maybe a nephew; anyhow he is kin of T. R.—this particular Roosevelt early consecrated himself to public service. He had himself elected to the legislature in the state of New York, where he lives up-country and not far from the metropolis. He was and is a Democrat. It so fell out that the particular legislature to which Mr. Roosevelt had himself elected had in hand the task of selecting a successor to Chauncey M. Depew for United States senator to represent the Empire State with E. Root, in that distinguished and greatest deliberative—three cheers!—forum in the world! The Democrats were in the ascendancy and it had been decreed that William F. Sheehan was to replace Mr. Depew. The decree that was decreed was a fine, definite decree; but it wasn't inclusive. Though the decreer, by name Charles F. Murphy of Tammany Hall, so called, had earnestly striven to include all Democrats within the boundaries of his decree, he failed.

A little gathering of legislators, led by this same Franklin Roosevelt, refused to be decreed at by Mr. Murphy. As you might say, they decried his decree.

Stepping four paces to the front they announced in clarion tones that Charles F. Murphy might decree until he was purple as far down as his third chin for all they cared—and not a whit whitted they. In parliamentary language they didn't give a hoot how much he decreed or whom he decreed about. They told him—Mr. Murphy

—he couldn't press down William F. Sheehan on their independent brows; and the chief teller was this same Roosevelt. The consequence was that the person who is now sharing the honor of upholding the dignity of the Empire State in the Senate is by name O'Gorman—not Sheehan; and thus was the Democratic branch of the Roosevelt family exalted into fame.

He is a young man, this Democratic Roosevelt, and he seems to have a modicum at least of the family nerve and verve. He is taller north and south than his kinsman and not so tall east and west. He wears the family eyeglasses; but dentally he is quite inferior—that is to say, though he may have as many teeth as Theodore, he refrains from odontologic publicity. A clean-cut, good-looking, alert young fellow, his associates speak well of him; and his friends say he has ability and only needs a chance to demonstrate. He can demonstrate until further orders right where he is; for any young man who is assistant secretary of the navy has tons of demonstrating material close to his hand in the persons of those grizzled old seadogs who have grown grizzled while enduring the dangers of running the navy from their swivel chairs, and have fought nobly for years and years at every tea, reception, dinner and dance in the fashionable section of the Capital. If he can get a few of these grizzled old seadogs out on salt water he will be a Roosevelt indeed! That was more than his relative could do, notwithstanding his prowess.

ADVERTISING and *The Saturday Evening Post* grew up together and did a great deal toward helping each other along. The album of old *Post* ads in the following pages is frankly designed to put the reader in a nostalgic mood and provide a few chuckles besides. It gives only a small indication of the enormous role *Post* advertising has played in the upward march of the American way of life. For many a big business today an ad in the *Post* was the start on the highroad to success. Editor Lorimer stated the case neatly. "Advertising is to business what electricity is to the city—light and power," he said.

When Cyrus H. K. Curtis bought the *Post* in 1897 its advertising revenue, as already stated, did not exceed $7,000 a year. Since then American businessmen have poured more than $1,500,000,000 in advertising revenue into the *Post*, and the *Post* has given them back full value. In 1927, when the *Post* had its first fifty-million-dollar advertising year, Lorimer threw a big Christmas party for the staff and handed out twenty-dollar gold pieces on the dance floor. But the fifty-million-dollar figure looks small today; in 1953 the *Post* sold more than eighty million dollars worth of ads.

From the beginning of the Curtis regime the *Post* imposed one of the strictest advertising codes in the business; all liquor, medical, "immoral" or "extravagantly worded" ads were taboo. In the early nineteen hundreds the *Post* did run a few stock-selling ads from companies like U. S. Steel and even helped sell real estate. But that kind of advertising was banned before 1910. (The *Post* has had ads from labor unions too—see page 168.)

Some of the *Post*'s best ads were the ones it printed to promote itself (at right). The *Post*'s boy salesmen ranged the United States from Teddy Roosevelt's White House to the battleships of the Pacific fleet in the good old days. Many a budding statesman, author or millionaire got his start that way. In the early 1940's this method of selling magazines was abandoned, and the ponies and baseball gloves that once went out as prizes to enterprising sellers of copies of the *Post* are no longer available at the big building in downtown Philadelphia. That is too bad, but times do change, as the pages you are about to see give abundant proof.

DOLLARD & CO.,

TOUPEE.   WIG

1223
CHESTNUT ST.,
Philadelphia.
Premier Artistes

IN HAIR

Inventors of the CELEBRATED GOSSAMER VENTILATING WIG, ELASTIC BAND TOUPEES, and Manufacturers of Every Description of Ornamental Hair for Ladies and Gentlemen.

Instructions to enable Ladies and Gentlemen to measure their own heads with accuracy:

TOUPEES AND SCALPS, INCHES.

No. 1.   The round of the head.
No. 2.   From forehead back as far as bald.
No. 3.   Over forehead as far as required.
No. 4.   Over the crown of the head.

FOR WIGS, INCHES.

No. 1.   The round of the head.
No. 2.   From forehead over the head to neck,
     No. 2.
No. 3.   From ear to ear over the top.
No. 4.   From ear to ear round the forehead.

They have always ready for sale a splendid Stock of Gents' Wigs, Toupees, Ladies' Wigs Half Wigs, Frizettes, Braids, curls, etc., beautifully manufactured, and as cheap as any establishment in the Union. Letters from any part of the world will receive attention.

Dollard's Herbanium Extract for the Hair.

This preparation has been manufactured and sold at Dollard's for the past fifty years, and its merits are such that, while it has never yet been advertised, the demand for it keeps steadily increasing.

Also DOLLARD'S REGENERATIVE CREAM to be used in conjunction with the Herbanium when the Hair is naturally dry and needs an oil.

Mrs. Edmondson Gortor writes to Messrs. Dollard & Co., to send her a bottle of their Herbanium Extract for the Hair. Mrs. Gortor has tried in vain to obtain anything equal to it as a dressing for the hair in England.

    MRS. EDMONDSON GORTER,
       Oak Lodge Thorpe,
Nov. 29, '88.   Norwich, Norfolk, England,
    NAVY PAY OFFICE, PHILADELPHIA,

I have used "Dollard's Herbanium Extract of Vegetable Hair Wash," regularly for upwards of five years with great advantage. My hair, from rapidly thinning, was early restored, and has been kept by it in its wonted thickness and strength. It is the best wash I have ever used,

    A. W. RUSSELL, U. S. N.
To MRS. RICHARD DOLLARD,
      1223 Chestnut st., Phila.

I have frequently, during a number of years, used the "Dollard's Herbanium Extract," and I do not know of any which equals it as a pleasant, refreshing and healthful cleanser of the hair.

    Very respectfully,
      LEONARD MYERS,
Ex-Member of Congress, 5th District
Prepared only and for sale, wholesale and retail, and applied professionally by

DOLLARD & CO.,

1223 CHESTNUT STREET.

GENTLEMEN'S HAIR CUTTING AND SHAVING, LADIES' AND CHILDREN'S HAIR CUTTING. None but Practical Male and Female Artists Employed.

August 14, 1897

March 30, 1901

OTHER PEOPLE'S BRAINS

Can help you rise in the world. If you possess a fair education, why not utilize it by
Learning Proofreading?
We are the original instructors by mail.
Home Correspondence School, Philadn.

LEARN TO DRAW
By Mail, for Newspapers

Big money and publicity await you in positions when you learn. If you have a liking or natural talent for drawing send us your name and address and receive a free lesson circular with particulars.

New York School of Caricature
World Building, New York

December 14, 1901

As they Sometimes are.

"SAVE-THE-HORSE" Spavin Cure
Registered Trade Mark.

Don't Fire or Blister Your Horse! Write for booklet, also letters from business men and trainers on every kind of case. "Save-the-Horse" Permanently Cures Spavin, Ringbone (except low Ringbone), Curb, Thoroughpin, Splint, Shoe Boil, Wind Puff, Injured Tendons and all lameness without scar or loss of hair. Horse may work as usual.

$5.00 per bottle, with a written guarantee, as binding to protect you as the best legal talent could make it. Send for copy and booklet.
At Druggists and Dealers or Express paid.
TROY CHEMICAL CO., Binghamton, N. Y.

August 5, 1905

1897   STANDARD OF THE WORLD

Columbia
BICYCLES. $100 TO ALL ALIKE

One secret of Columbia superiority lies in the infinite care taken to bring all the features into harmonious relation. Well rounded and thoroughly adjusted in its smallest details it may be examined with minute scrutiny, with certainty of finding construction that is not equalled nor even approached. There is beauty and strength in every line. • • • • • •

189? Columbias, $75.
HARTFORD BICYCLES,
$60, $55, $50, $40.
POPE MFG. CO.,
Hartford, Conn.

Catalogue free from any dealer; by mail for one 2-c. stamp.

August 14, 1897

February 11, 1899

I LOVE YOU SO!

LATEST POPULAR SONG and CHORUS

Regular price is 50 cents, but we will send you a copy in COMPLETE SHEET FORM, together with our MUSICAL BULLETIN, CATALOGUE OF MUSIC and BARGAIN LISTS OF MUSIC, for 10 cents in stamps.
ADAMS MUSIC COMPANY, Department H, 64 Winfield Avenue, Jersey City, N. J.

162

Leave Chicago this evening on the

Golden State Limited

via the El Paso–Rock Island route and in less than three days you will arrive at Los Angeles.

An hour later you can be on the shores of the Pacific, listening to the roar of the surf, drinking in the wine-like air; the bluest of blue skies above you and the most charming landscapes in America all about you. This, mind you, at a time of year when the thermometer at home is 'way below zero and the newspapers are filled with details of the "greatest snow-storm in years."

Rock Island System

Cut out this ad. and mail it, with name and address, and beautifully illustrated book about California will be sent free. Tickets, berths and full information at this office.

Jno. Sebastian, P. T. M., Chicago, Ill.

January 17, 1903

" Mamma won't care! Water can't hurt her Corset!"

WARNER'S RUST-PROOF

February 24, 1900

ORNAMENTAL FENCES

Iron or Wire, built to your order.

The finest at lowest prices. Satisfaction guaranteed.

Enterprise
Foundry & Fence Co., 301 S. Senate, Indianapolis, Ind.

April 7, 1906

ON EVERYBODY'S TONGUE

Chiclets

REALLY DELIGHTFUL

THAT DAINTY MINT COVERED CANDY COATED CHEWING GUM
Send us 10c for sample packet. Frank H. Fleer & Company, Inc. Philadelphia

At All the Better kind of Stores
5 cents the Ounce
or in 10-cent and 25-cent Packets

April 7, 1906

March 30, 1901

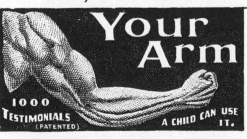

YES, 1 INCH IN 1 MONTH!

Your Arm

1000 TESTIMONIALS (PATENTED)

A CHILD CAN USE IT.

CAN BE ENLARGED 1 INCH and strengthened 50 PER CENT. In ONE MONTH by using the HERCULES GRADUATED GYMNASTIC CLUB and STRENGTH TESTER 5 Minutes each day. It will develop and strengthen the arms, shoulders, chest, back, waist and hips in less than one-quarter of the time required by any other method, with or *without* apparatus. It induces sound slumber, rids you of many aches and pains, writer's cramp, and aids digestion. Makes the brain active and the complexion clear. The club can be used by the weak man and the strongest athlete. For men, women and children. *Write for descriptive pamphlet and price list to*

THE HERCULES CLUB CO., Room 12, 16 South St., Boston, Mass.

Maule's Up-to-Date Collection of 10 New Sweet Peas

One packet of each of the above, 10 separate packets, New Large-Flowering Sweet Peas, for only **20 cts.**

Maule's Banner Collection for 1899

Is the Best Floral Offer of the Year. 70 cts. worth of Flower Seeds for only 15 cts.

Maule's Special Pansy Offer

One packet each of 6 Fancy Mammoth Flowering Pansies (regular retail value, 60 cts.) for only 25 cts.

One packet of each of the above 12 varieties of Flower Seeds, postpaid, for only **40 cts.**

Everything mentioned upon this page sent, postpaid, upon receipt of only **$2.00**

Maule's Collection of 6 Dazzling New Cannas

We will send, postpaid, to any address, one strong, blooming-size bulb of the above Cannas, each distinctly labeled,

For only **75 cts.**

Maule's Bouquet Collection of 6 New Dahlias

One good strong root of each of the 6 New Dahlias mentioned above, postpaid,

For only **$1.00**

My Large Illustrated Catalogue—FREE

To all readers of The Saturday Evening Post who apply for it. It contains everything worth having, old or new, in Vegetable or Flower Seeds, Flowering Plants, Bulbs, etc. Hundreds of illustrations; four colored plates. It gives up-to-date cultural directions, and offers cash prices to club agents. It is pronounced by all the brightest and best seed book of the year, and you need it before placing your order for 1899. Address

WM. HENRY MAULE, - 1711 Filbert Street, Philadelphia

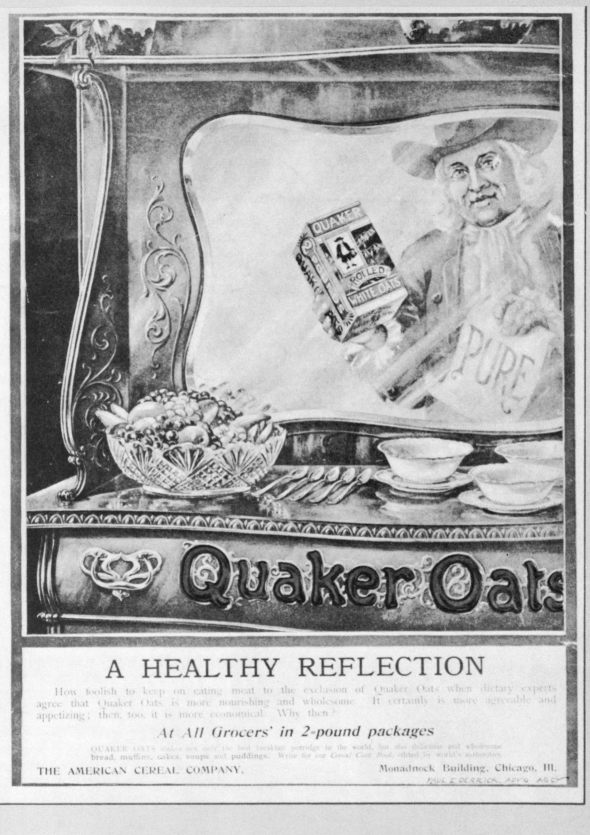

A HEALTHY REFLECTION

How foolish to keep on eating meat to the exclusion of Quaker Oats when dietary experts agree that Quaker Oats is more nourishing and wholesome. It certainly is more agreeable and appetizing; then, too, it is more economical. Why then?

At All Grocers' in 2=pound packages

QUAKER OATS makes not only the best breakfast porridge in the world, but also delicious and wholesome bread, muffins, cakes, soups and puddings. Write for our *Cereal Cook Book*, edited by world's authorities.

THE AMERICAN CEREAL COMPANY,   Monadnock Building, Chicago, Ill.

PAUL E. DERRICK, ADV'G AG'CY

Post's first full-page cover ad (left) ran March 4, 1899. The first cover
ad in two colors (above) appeared September 30, 1899.

Trade "Standard" Mark

Baths and Lavatories

are a revelation in modern bathroom equipment, not only in the added convenience and perfect sanitation they afford, but also in the extraordinarily long service their installation assures.

CAUTION.—Every genuine "Standard" fixture bears the "Standard" Green and Gold Guarantee Label. Without this label the piece is an inferior substitute and should be instantly rejected. The Green and Gold Label is the guarantee of all that the trade-mark, "Standard", on a fixture means.

Write for our beautifully illustrated 100-page book, "Modern Bathrooms"—the most complete and practical book ever issued on the bathroom subject. Enclose six cents postage and give name of your architect and plumber, if selected.

Address Standard Sanitary Mfg. Co., Dept. B, Pittsburgh, Pa., U.S.A.

Offices and Showrooms, New York: 35-37 West 31st Street. Pittsburgh: 949 Penn Avenue. St. Louis: 100-102 North Fourth Street. Louisville: 325-329 West Main Street. Philadelphia: 1128 Walnut Street. New Orleans: Corner Baronne and St. Joseph Streets. Cleveland: 648-652 Huron Road, S. E. Toronto, Canada: 59 Richmond Street, East. Montreal, Canada: 39 St. Sacrament St.

A BATH FOR 2 CENTS
Is Furnished by the

VICTOR INSTANTANEOUS WATER HEATER

Which occupies but little room; is ready for use night or day; furnishes hot water instantly for bathing, shaving, sickness, and all domestic purposes when hot water is required. Uses Gas or Gasoline. Ask your dealers for it, or send for free catalogue.

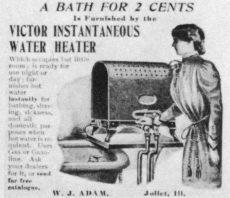

W. J. ADAM, Joliet, Ill.

YOU CAN HAVE HOT WATER

Instantly and when you want it, no limit to quantity, with an ACME Instantaneous Heater in your home. These are the only practical Heaters made. Having large cylindrical heating surface, no small tubes to clog from lime in water, and furnish 2 to 3 gallons of Hot Water a minute, not merely a small stream, that cools before there is sufficient water in the tub for a bath. The fuel, Gas or Gasoline, costs less than 2c. per bath. Ten styles. For information about them ask your plumber, or write for catalogue to

THE INSTANTANEOUS WATER HEATING CO.
Orleans Street, Chicago

June 30, 1900

March 30, 1901

Behold this vain infant of two!
He is certainly pleased with the view.
You'll forgive him—I hope—
For he's used Ivory Soap.
You would feel just the same. Try it, too.

For bath, toilet and fine laundry purposes; for the nursery; for shampooing; for everything and anything that necessitates the use of a better-than-ordinary soap, Ivory Soap is unequalled.

Ivory Soap . . . . It Floats.

Ivory soap ads have been runnning in the *Post* since 1902. This one appeared September 4, 1909.

September 19, 1908

April 7, 1906

March 8, 1902

April 7, 1906

ONLY a tailor can fit you? Don't be so sure! Go to your Kuppenheimer store and see the Fractional Sizes and special models— the Forward Model for the man who carries the head and shoulders forward — the In-Between sizes, the Stout and Hafstout. Conservative styles for business and professional men. $22.50 to $45. Write for our book "Styles for Men."

By
The House *of*
Kuppenheimer
Chicago

Copyright, 1917, The House of Kuppenheimer

October 6, 1917

March 13, 1920

March 7, 1914

November 14, 1914

September 29, 1906

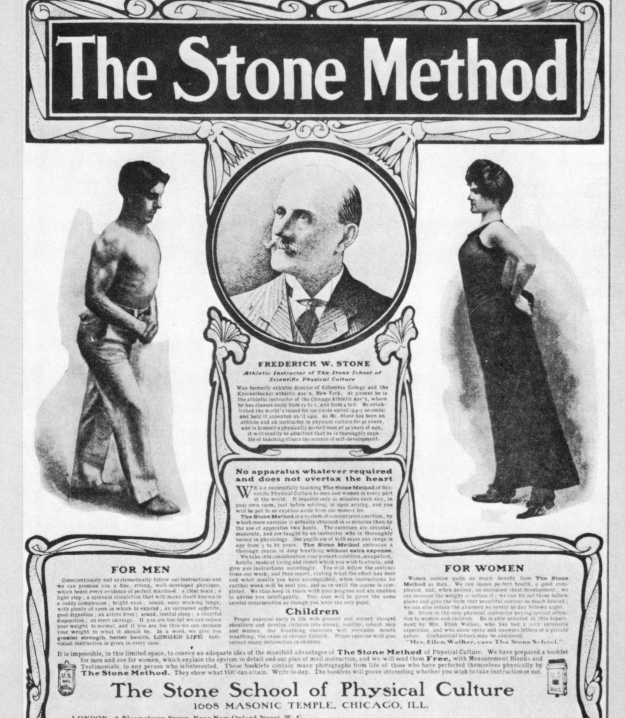

September 6, 1902

"NATIONAL"
Tailored Suits

Made-to-Measure $10 to $40 Express
New York Styles $10 to $40 Charges Prepaid

Fall Style Book and Samples FREE

"NATIONAL" Suits are made to the measure of our customers, all of whom send us their orders by mail. We have been making these perfect-fitting suits in this way for Twenty-One Years. And all of this Twenty-One Years of experience and knowledge and skill can go into the making of Your Suit this Fall.

You only need to write us today for your FREE copy of the "NATIONAL" Fall Style Book and Samples pictured below. You select your material from the samples we send you. You select your suit from the Style Book. We do all the rest and we take all the risk.

The "NATIONAL" Policy

Every "NATIONAL" Garment has the "NATIONAL" Guarantee Tag — our signed Guarantee — attached. This tag says that you may return any "NATIONAL" garment not satisfactory to you and we will refund your money and pay express charges both ways.

The "NATIONAL" prepays expressage and postage to all parts of the world.

"NATIONAL" Ready-Made Garments

Waists	Furs	Hosiery
Skirts	Dresses	Underwear
Cloth Coats	Sweaters	Misses' Suits and Coats
Fur Coats	Hats	Girls' Suits and Coats
Rain-Coats	Petticoats	Boys' Clothing

Why not learn all the desirable new fashions from Your Copy of the "NATIONAL" Style Book? Why not see the New Duchess and Gainsborough Hats, the New Dresses, which return this season to the pretty styles of the Twelfth Century, the New Long Coat Sweaters, the new "Silhette" Petticoat, something you have never seen before, and all the new ideas in Misses' and Girls' Suits, Dresses and Coats? It gives you so many new style lines, elegantly set much so you can get such complete information about what is going to be worn that it is the one indispensable fashion guide of the season.

This "NATIONAL" Style Book
Belongs to You—You Only
Need Write for It

The "NATIONAL" Fall Style Book pictured below is your property. Will you write for it? In writing for this Style Book be sure to state whether you wish samples for a Tailored Suit and state the colors you prefer. Samples are sent gladly, but only when asked for.

National Cloak & Suit Co.
Largest Ladies' Outfitting Establishment in the World
214 West 24th St., New York City
Mail Orders Only.　　No Agents or Branch Stores

September 4, 1909

If Your Feet Hurt—Your Health Suffers

"It fends with the foot"

If your foot hurts, every step is a strain on the whole body.

Do you know why they hurt?

The foot bends, but the sole of the shoe is stiff. At every step the ball of the foot bearing the entire weight of the body rubs against this sole.

This rub, rub, rub, makes the feet burn and ache. It keeps every nerve under constant tension.

The Red Cross Shoe is absolutely comfortable.

The sole, made of leather tanned by a special process, is flexible; it is of regular walking thickness yet so supple that it follows every movement of the foot. This leather is not used in any other shoe.

The heel, of the same bargain leather (with stitched top), takes the jar off the spine.

One woman writes: "My feet are very tender. I have been wearing Red Cross Shoes for ten days and do not hesitate to say they are the most comfortable shoes I have ever worn."

The Red Cross prevents the evils that come from wearing stiff soles, for it supports and protects the foot, yet it is delightfully light and cool.

With its perfect comfort the Red Cross has style. It is made in all lasts from "common sense" to the most fashionable.

Our booklet "Women Today" shows the importance of foot-comfort. Write for it.

Insist on seeing this trademark with the name Krohn, Fechheimer & Co. stamped on the sole. Imitations have neither the comfort, style nor wearing qualities of the genuine. Leading dealers have the Red Cross. If yours hasn't, order direct from us at Oxford, $3 and $3.50; High Shoes, $3, $4 and $5.

Krohn, Fechheimer & Company
629 Eggleston Ave., Cincinnati, O.

Three Favorite Flowers

SWEET PEAS
PERFECTED ROYAL SHOW PANSIES
NASTURTIUMS

I mail One Package of each of above for 6¢
ONLY SIX CENTS

How to Grow Flowers From Seeds

The Pioneer Seedswoman, MISS C. H. LIPPINCOTT, 319 S. 6th St., Minneapolis, Minn.

March 4, 1899

You can make either of these smart gowns yourself

They have all the style a dress could have, are correct in every detail and represent the style ideas of fashion experts. Yet you can duplicate them exactly by using

Ladies' Home Journal Patterns

These patterns ask nothing of you except that they be followed. The patented "Guide Chart" on each envelope is an accurate plan requiring no allowances or guess work. Most women need more dresses than they have. Ladies' Home Journal Patterns will enable them to have all they need on their present dress allowance and have every dress a stylish and becoming one.

Ask at the store you patronize for Ladies' Home Journal Patterns. If you cannot get them, write direct to us. These patterns are shown in The Ladies' Home Journal, the Criterion of Fashion, the Home Style Book and Children's Clothes.

Ladies' Home Journal Patterns
629 West 43rd St., New York
Owned and controlled by The Curtis Publishing Company

March 7, 1914

Miss Baird's Home School for Girls

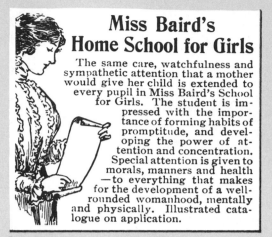

The same care, watchfulness and sympathetic attention that a mother would give her child is extended to every pupil in Miss Baird's School for Girls. The student is impressed with the importance of forming habits of promptitude, and developing the power of attention and concentration. Special attention is given to morals, manners and health —to everything that makes for the development of a well-rounded womanhood, mentally and physically. Illustrated catalogue on application.

June 30, 1900

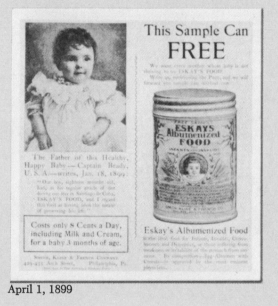

This Sample Can FREE

We want every mother whose baby is not doing to try ESKAY'S FOOD. Write us, mentioning the Post, and we will forward you sample free, delivery cost.

The Father of this Healthy, Happy Baby — Captain Brady, U. S. A.—writes, Jan. 18, 1899:

"Our boy, eighteen months old, had, in his regular attack of not doing our duty in Santiago de Cuba, ESKAY'S FOOD, and I regard this food as having taken the means of preserving his life."

Costs only 8 Cents a Day, including Milk and Cream, for a baby 3 months of age.

SMITH, KLINE & FRENCH COMPANY,
419-431 Arch Street, Philadelphia, Pa.

Eskay's Albumenized Food

Is the ideal food for Infants, Invalids, Convalescents and Dyspeptics, or those suffering from weakness or disability of the stomach from any cause. Its composition—Egg-Albumen with Cereals—is approved by the most eminent physicians.

April 1, 1899

THE NEW STYLE FIGURE

Can be obtained by wearing the

G-D Chicago Waist

Style No. 340.   Price One Dollar

Sizes 18 to 30 Waist Measure

This Corset Waist gives the effect of straight front; is elegantly made and finished, and in every way equal to any corset waist sold at higher prices. The materials are White, Drab or Fast Black Sateen, and every waist has our patented attachment for hose supporters.

Get it from your dealer, or if he cannot supply you send One Dollar to us, stating size and color desired.

Gage-Downs Co., 265 Fifth Ave., Chicago

March 30, 1901

"Bother about my complexion?—Oh! no. I really never give it a thought; Hinds Honey and Almond Cream keeps it clear and fresh.   My skin stays soft and smooth all summer long."

Every woman will find this dainty snow-white liquid a perfect protection against

SUNBURN

and all the skin troubles of hot weather.   Use Hinds Honey and Almond Cream every day and you may enjoy all sorts of Summer outdoor life without fear of the hot sun, wind or dust. It quickly relieves mosquito bites.

Our free sample is large enough to show you how delightfully refreshing it is,— how quickly it will cool and soothe parched, dry skin burned and roughened by exposure.

Drop us a postal for free sample bottle, or get the regular 50c size from your druggist.

Nothing you can use is so positive a protection against the torment of sunburn as Hinds Honey and Almond Cream—nothing could possibly be a more delightful toilet help.   It removes blemishes and eruptions, gives a youthful fairness and freshness to the complexion, even with women of advanced years.

We positively guarantee

Hinds Honey and Almond Cream

to contain no harmful ingredients—that it is not greasy or sticky—will not cause a growth of hair—will not injure or irritate the most delicate skin.

Mothers will find Hinds Honey and Almond Cream unequaled for babies' delicate skins—for many years it has been recognized as most effective for soothing and relieving Prickly Heat, Chafing, Rash and other skin troubles of infants.

Men who shave are the most enthusiastic about Hinds Honey and Almond Cream—nothing equals it for taking the smart out, stopping the irritation due to close shaving. It prevents dry skin.

Price 50 cents. Sold everywhere or mailed postpaid by us. Do not buy substitutes. There's nothing like Hinds Honey and Almond Cream.

A liberal trial bottle sent free

A. S. HINDS, 89 West Street, Portland, Maine

August 5, 1911

Any Open Type FORD Car for Summer

Summer Days For Automobile Riding

was a satisfactory condition a few years ago. Buyers expected to keep their cars in storage all winter. That was partly due to the inability of those cars to make good in snow, ice and slush, partly due to the fact that an automobile was regarded entirely as a pleasure vehicle for use on sunshiny days. That is a condition of the past. A good car is good 365 days in the year, and an owner wants his car as much in December as in June. Often he wants it more in December on account of the conditions under-foot. But he does not always want an open car and on the other hand objects to having to purchase a new car for the few months that a closed car is desirable.—A Ford buyer does not have to.

Buy a Ford Touring Car For $950.00

fully equipped, for instance, use it while the weather is suitable and then when the season changes and a Coupe, Landaulet, or Town Car is wanted, an hour's labor makes a closed car out of the other. The only expense is the nominal cost of the closed body. This Ford car which has cost you so little will answer every purpose which its $5,000.00 competitor serves. Fact is there are a great many buyers who have nerved themselves up to the ordeal of paying the high price who, learning of the Ford Model "T," investigated it, bought it, used it and are well pleased both with the car and the saving.

The Ford Car is the Only Low Priced

car manufactured. Get that? A price is only low when compared with values and prices of other makes. Because it is possible to obtain the Model "T" car at that price, any car now on the market, or in the embryonic or announcement stage, selling at any price, is not low priced. It might be designated medium priced in that Webster defines medium as having a middle position. The Ford is not a cheap car—there is small market for such and too many ready to supply it. But Ford can make a car more cheaply because he makes only the one car, makes an enormous quantity of that one car, and all his energy, ability and factory is devoted to making that one single solitary 4 cylinder, 20 h. p. wonder.

Specialization Makes Low Price

possible if the out-put can be made large enough. The entire Ford plant is devoted to building this one model, and 25,000 cars is the 12 months production. The manufacturer turning out a high-priced car, a so-called medium priced car and a cheap car, skimps somewhere—it's not on the high-priced end—and the production is limited to a few of each. We refer to actual production—not paper production. We are now delivering between 450 and 500 1910 Model "T" cars, every six days. While other manufacturers are planning their 1910 cars, we are producing. Every problem has been worked out and tested in service. This announcement deals in realities, not prospects. There are right now over 9,500 Model "T" cars on the streets and roads of this and other countries. The price was fixed after the car was finished—not while in the promoter's brain.

Ford Won the New York-Seattle Race

with a 1910 Model "T"—just exactly the car every Ford buyer gets. That was the hardest, toughest, most gruelling contest ever run. The lowest priced competitor sold for over five times the price of the Ford. The winner established a record for the trip, made the journey in 20 days and 52 minutes in open competition and averaged 230 miles per day. Not only did it win at the finish, but it was first at 27 out of 30 checking stations. It won in mud, in sand, on mountains and in valleys. It was a winner from start to finish and it beat the pick of American and foreign high priced and heavy cars. This same car is traveling back and has already added 4,000 miles to its previous total. When you get a Model "T" Ford, you secure a car that would, if called upon, duplicate this performance. The story of the Race will be sent upon request.

SPECIFICATIONS

MOTOR—4 cylinder, 4 cycle, vertical, 20 h. p., 3¾ in. bore, 4 in. stroke, cylinders cast in one block with water jackets and upper half of crank case integral, water jacketed cylinder head detachable.

CRANK CASE—Upper half integral with cylinder casting. Lower half pressed steel and extended to form lower housing for magneto and transmission.

COOLING—Thermo-syphon.

IGNITION—Ford magneto generator, low tension, a built-in integral part of engine.

TRANSMISSION—New design Ford spur planetary, bathed in oil, all gears from heat-treated Vanadium steel. Silent and easy in action.

LUBRICATION—Combination splash and gravity system—simple and sure.

CLUTCH—Multiple steel discs, operating in oil.

CONTROL—All forward speeds by foot pedal. Reverse by hand lever. Spark and throttle under steering wheel.

FINAL DRIVE—By cardon shaft with single universal joint to bevel drive gears in live rear axle. Ford three point system—patented in all countries.

FRONT AXLE—One piece drop forging in I-Beam section, specially treated, Vanadium steel.

BRAKES—2 sets; A Service brake on transmission; B Internal expanding brakes in rear hub drums.

TIRES—Pneumatic: front 30 x 3 in. rear 30 x 3 in. Twice the usual life in every set.

WHEEL BASE—100 in. tread 56 in. or 60 in. for Southern roads where ordered.

GASOLINE CAPACITY—10 gallons, 200 miles. Cylindrical gasoline tank directly on frame.

PRICE—Touring car $950.00. Tourabout $950.00. Roadster $900.00 complete with top, automatic brass windshield, gas lamps, generator and speedometer; for car equipped only with 3 oil lamps and horn deduct $75.00.

Coupe $1,050.00, Landaulet $1,100.00, Town car $1,200.00 equipped with 3 oil lamps and horn.

All prices F. O. B. Detroit.

BRANCHES IN
Boston, Mass.
Buffalo, N. Y.
Chicago, Ill.
Cleveland, O.
Denver, Col.
Detroit, Mich.
Kansas City, Mo.
New York, N. Y.
Philadelphia, Pa.
St. Louis, Mo.
Seattle, Wash.
Paris, France
London, England

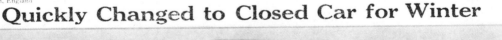

Ford Motor Company

Standard Manufacturers— A. M. C. M. A.

266 Piquette Avenue, Detroit, U. S. A.

Canadian trade supplied by

THE FORD MOTOR CO. OF CANADA, Ltd.

Walkerville, Ont.

Branch: Toronto, Ont.

Dealers in all principal towns and cities of the world

WRITE FOR CATALOG

Quickly Changed to Closed Car for Winter

The history of the auto industry is written in *Post* advertising.

The Earliest and the Latest Oldsmobile

The oldest Oldsmobile and the Oldsmobile "Autocrat" of to-day, present an interesting picture of automobile development in America. The Oldsmobile was not only one of the first practical motor cars in this country, but the famous little "curved dash runabout,"—which succeeded the antiquity shown above,—did more to popularize motoring than any other car of the time.

Year after year, the Oldsmobile has been more than a car that conformed to accepted standards; it has created new standards. Each year its most severe critics have been the engineers and designers of Olds Motor Works who have selected with almost unerring judgment those features which were destined to endure.

Changes, quite radical in early years, have become slighter and slighter, until at present only closest inspection reveals the difference between the "Autocrat" as improved to date and the "Autocrat" as first announced, the design of the power plant and the method of power transmission remaining practically unchanged.

The value to the owner of a car with this sort of history is twofold; first, many years of constant study insures the production of a car that has the *very latest improvements*; second, on account of the long experience of the makers, these *improvements are time-tried and not experimental*.

For example, the "Autocrat" and the "Limited" were the first seven-passenger cars to be regularly equipped with 38 and 42 inch tires, respectively. Exhaustive experiment has shown these sizes to be far superior in durability and riding qualities to the maximum of 36 inches used before.

The Oldsmobile was one of the first really quiet cars. Its long-stroke motor develops phenomenal pulling power, which is not dependent on fly-wheel speed and is quite free from vibration at any speed. These qualities, together with its stability of construction, make the car as a whole practically indestructible.

The "Autocrat"
four-cylinder—45 H. P.
38 inch tires—$3500

The "Limited"
six-cylinder—60 H. P.
42 inch tires—$5000

Touring, Roadster, Tourabout and Limousine Bodies

OLDS MOTOR WORKS   LANSING, MICH.

COPYRIGHT 1911, OLDS MOTOR WORKS

These appeared (left) September 4, 1909, (right) August 5, 1911.

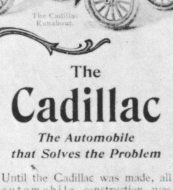

The
Cadillac
The Automobile
that Solves the Problem

Until the Cadillac was made, all automobile construction was more or less experimental. This machine is made on a new system developed from the experiences of all previous makers: the faults and weaknesses of the old methods have been avoided and a new ideal of motor travel developed that gives a perfect vehicle for comfort, speed, absolute safety, greatest durability, simplicity of operation, wide radius of travel, and reliability under all conditions of roads. You should not buy before examining this wonderful new machine. Price f. o. b. at factory, $750.

The new tonneau attachment, at an extra cost of $100, gives practically two motor vehicles in one, with a seating capacity of two or four, as required—a very graceful effect in either use. Write for new illustrated booklet.

CADILLAC AUTOMOBILE COMPANY
Detroit, Mich.

With detachable tonneau

One of the first car-hops in America appeared in this Coca-Cola ad, August 5, 1905.

January 17, 1903

April 7, 1906

February 7, 1903

April 11, 1903

October 6, 1917

January 17, 1903

April 7, 1906

March 7, 1914

This happy scene around a Christmas Victrola ran December 14, 1912.

All out-doors invites your Kodak.

Let Kodak keep a picture record of your every outing. There's a new pleasure in every phase of photography—pleasure in the taking, pleasure in the finishing, but most of all, pleasure in possessing pictures of the places and people that *you* are interested in.

KODAKS, $5.00 to $100.00.　　　　BROWNIES (*they work like Kodaks*), $1.00 to $12.00.

Catalogue free at the dealers or by mail.

EASTMAN KODAK COMPANY,

ROCHESTER, N. Y., *The Kodak City.*

Kodak is one of the *Post*'s oldest advertisers, beginning in 1899.
The Kodak girl above belongs to the date May 20, 1911.

"We smash 'em HARD"

One of the Yank Veterans

WHITE
OWL
Invincible
Shape
7c

OWL
Square-
end
6c

WHITE
OWL

"Did I bayonet my first Hun? Sure! How did it feel? It *doesn't* feel! There *he* is. There *you* are. One of you has got to go. I preferred to stay.

"So when sergeant says, 'Smash 'em, boys'—we do. And we go them one better like good old Yankee Doodle Yanks. For bullets and bayonets are the only kind of lingo that a Hun can *understand!*"

* * * *

The *dependable* Yank, whose photograph appears above, first met the *dependable* Owl Cigar while boosting that *dependable* investment—the Liberty Loan.

We didn't tell him about the $2,000,000 stock of leaf that is always aging for Owl and White Owl. Nor the over 100,000,000 Owls and White Owls sold last year. We just swapped him a White Owl for a smile. And it doesn't look like the smile came hard, does it?

Why don't you, too, try an Owl or White Owl—*today?*

DEALERS:
If your distributor does not sell these dependable cigars, write us.
GENERAL CIGAR CO., INC., 119 West 40th Street, New York City

TWO DEPENDABLE CIGARS

OWL 6c white OWL 7c

Branded for your

Banded protection

August 31, 1918

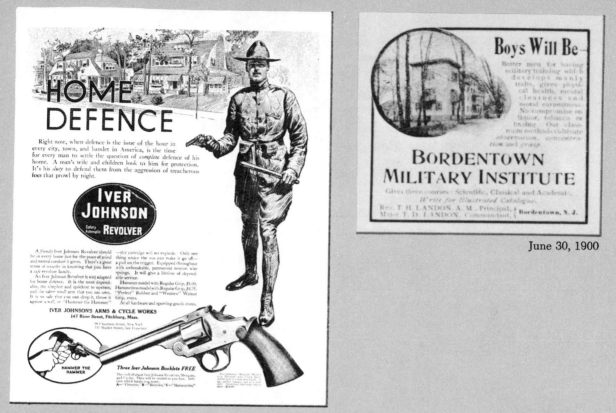

October 13, 1917

June 30, 1900

April 7, 1906

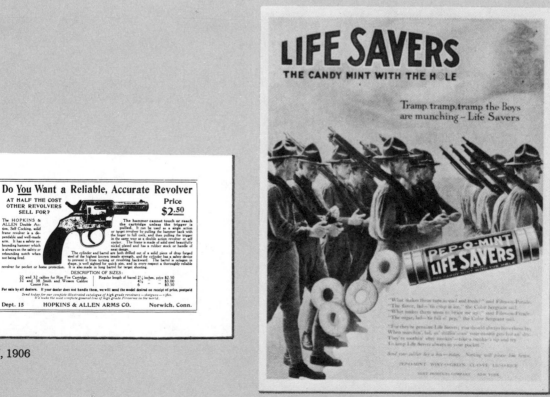

November 3, 1917

COOPER'S
BENNINGTON
Spring Needle Underwear-

ASTRIDE the wheel-horse of a plunging fieldpiece, guiding a tractor plow, or training a battleship's guns; three thousand feet o'erhead or knee deep in trench mud; bombing an outpost or buying supplies; wherever you find American manhood you will also find real appreciation for Cooper's-Bennington Spring Needle Underwear.

Cooper's-Bennington is made to meet men's needs. It fits in any posture. In field or factory, gun turret or counting-house; in the homeless wilderness, or the great city's wilderness of homes, Cooper's-Bennington is the first choice of men who demand utmost comfort, utmost service and reasonable price. It assures

True Fit for America's Finest

Cooper's Spring Needle Fabric gained for Cooper's-Bennington the name "three year underwear." The close Spring Needle stitch, drawn tight in the knitting, requires a full mile more of yarn than ordinary underwear, but gives a full year more of wear.

The closed crotch, the French neck, the flat unchafing seams, the shoulder insert, shaped legs, rib knit cuffs and ankles all add to the comfort, fit and wear service of the garment.

Dealers who buy and sell on a quality basis will gladly supply you with Cooper's-Bennington Underwear in sizes and styles and prices which will be found suitable to your needs.

BLACK CAT TEXTILES CO.
Kenosha and Sheboygan, Wisconsin
and Bennington, Vermont
Makers Also of Black Cat Reinforced Hosiery for All the Family

Trademark Protection

In times of value uncertainties like the present, careful buyers insist upon trademarked merchandise which, from years of past experience, they know to be of proven quality.

October 13, 1917

HOLEPROOF HOSIERY

When the Nation Called for Economy
New Thousands Turned to Holeproof

War-time economy in hosiery need not mean personal hardship.

It can bring you to better hose than you have known—unless you already wear Holeproof Hosiery. Millions of Holeproofs yearly, for over 16 years, have proved to outwear average hosiery, two to one.

With Americans learning to live efficiently, Holeproof is gaining thousands of new users.

Give boxes of Holeproof Hosiery at Christmas—thus make your giving serve in the national war on waste. Meanwhile, begin economy at home—have all your family wear these strong, fine textured hose.

That will save women hours of mending; it will reduce your hosiery purchases about one-half.

All will delight in months of perfect stockings—fine, shapely, shimmering, free from "runs" and holes.

Men's, 30c a pair and upward.
Women's, 40c and up.
Children's, 35c and up.

Any accommodating store can supply you with Holeproofs—Pure Thread Japanese Silk—Lusterized Lisle—Fine-spun Cotton—Artificial Silk.

Mail us your address for illustrated booklet of styles and prices. Write today.

HOLEPROOF HOSIERY COMPANY, Milwaukee, Wis.

Holeproof Hosiery Co. of Canada, Limited, London, Canada   Holeproof Hosiery Co., 10 Church Alley, Liverpool, England

December 1, 1917

183

This Self-Working Washer Cuts Out
Your Laundry Bills

November 18, 1905

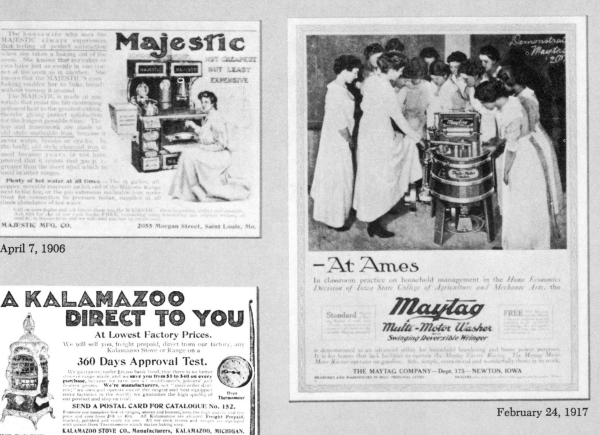

April 7, 1906

A KALAMAZOO
DIRECT TO YOU
At Lowest Factory Prices.

We will sell you, freight prepaid, direct from our factory, any Kalamazoo Stove or Range on a

360 Days Approval Test.

We guarantee, under $20,000 bank bond, that there is no better stove or range made, and we **save you from $5 to $40 on every purchase**, because we save you all middlemen's, jobbers' and dealers' profits. **We're manufacturers**, not "mail-order dealers;" we own and operate one of the largest and best equipped stove factories in the world; we guarantee the high quality of our product and ship on trial.

SEND A POSTAL CARD FOR CATALOGUE No. 152.

Examine our complete line of ranges, stoves and heaters, note the high quality, and low price and save from 20% to 40%. All Kalamazoos are shipped Freight Prepaid, blacked, polished and ready for use. All our cook stoves and ranges are equipped with patent Oven Thermometer which makes baking easy.

KALAMAZOO STOVE CO., Manufacturers, KALAMAZOO, MICHIGAN.

WE PAY THE FREIGHT

November 18, 1905

—At Ames

In classroom practice on household management in the Home Economics Division of Iowa State College of Agriculture and Mechanic Arts, the

Maytag
Multi-Motor Washer
Swinging Reversible Wringer

is demonstrated as an advanced utility for household laundering and home power purposes. It is for homes that lack facilities to operate the Maytag Electric Washer. The Maytag Multi-Motor Washer operates on gasoline. Safe, simple, economical and wonderfully itself in its work.

THE MAYTAG COMPANY—Dept. 175—NEWTON, IOWA

February 24, 1917

184

April 29, 1899

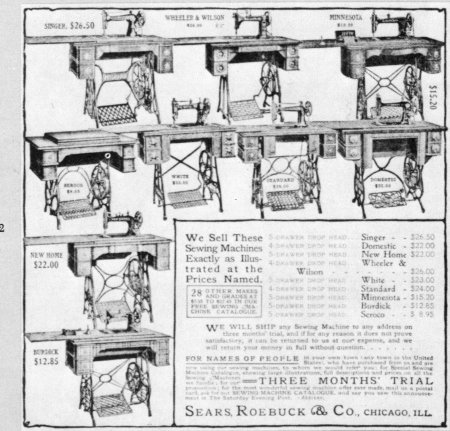

December 6, 1902

He wanted to make sure the Varnish was Valspar!

HE had seen our advertisements picturing a man pouring boiling water on a Valsparred table, so he decided to make the same test on his own newly varnished floor.

This little scene actually took place.

The family was very much startled—but they survived the shock.

And so did the floor, for it really was Valsparred.

Therefore, even the boiling water could not spot it white or harm it in the slightest.

That's why Valsparred floors are so desirable—to clean them you simply wash them with hot water—even hot soapy water.

Thus our friend thoroughly satisfied himself on two points—

First, that our advertising claims for Valspar are true, and

Second, that he got Valspar on his floor as ordered.

And so, this man, like many others who have tested Valspar, decided then and there to use nothing else when varnish was needed.

There are many places about the house where Valspar—the absolutely waterproof varnish—should be used. On woodwork and floors in bath rooms, kitchens, pantries and front halls; on porch ceilings, furniture, front doors or window sills;—where ordinary varnishes would spot from water, Valspar remains bright and new.

Valspar may be had from most good paint and varnish dealers. You will have where to buy it by the large posters in the dealers' windows.

VALENTINE'S VALSPAR
The Varnish That Won't Turn White

Special Offer

VALENTINE & COMPANY, 456 Fourth Ave., New York

March 11, 1916

Shade Won't Work

Because it isn't mounted on

THE IMPROVED HARTSHORN SHADE ROLLER

A perfect article. No tacks required. Notice name on roller when buying your shades.

June 30, 1900

The Improved Method of FINISHING FLOORS

Filling cracks with Grippin's Filler and Patent Applier.

old or new, for rugs or otherwise, with GRIPPIN'S WOOD CRACK and CREVICE FILLER and FINISHING SPECIALTIES, is very simple and economical, not requiring skilled labor though the highest degree of perfection is attained. We give full instructions for treating all surfaces. Write to-day for our descriptive matter to

GRIPPIN MFG. CO.
Dept. 4, Newark, New York

March 5, 1904

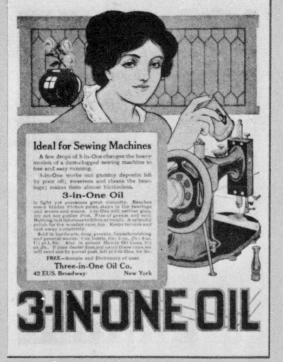

Ideal for Sewing Machines

A few drops of 3-in-One changes the heavy motion of a dust-clogged sewing machine to free and easy running.

3-in-One works out gummy deposits left by poor oil; sweetens and cleans the bearings; makes them almost frictionless.

3-in-One Oil

is light yet possesses great viscosity. Reaches every hidden friction point, stays in the bearings and wears and wears. 3-in-One will neither gum, dry out nor gather dust. Free of grease and acid. Nothing in it injurious to fabric or metals. A splendid polish for the wooden case, too. Keeps treadle and rust away completely.

Sold in hardware, drug, grocery, house-furnishing and general stores. 1-oz. bottle, 10c; 3-oz. 25c; 8-oz. (½ pt.), 50c. Also in patent Handy Oil Cans, 3½ oz. 25c. If your dealer does not carry these sizes we will send one by parcel post, full of 3-in-One, for 30c.

FREE—Sample and Dictionary of uses

Three-in-One Oil Co.
42 EUS. Broadway   New York

3-IN-ONE OIL

November 14, 1914

March 30, 1901

She: "It's Uncle John and Aunt Mary. Now what's to be done? The cook is out, you know."

He: "Oh! throw something together. Anything will do for Sunday night supper."

She: "'Anything will do!' Uncle John thinks more of his meals than he does of his money, and you know I can't cook!"

He: "Yes, I *do* know! But you have some of Libby's good things and that little book about preparing Libby's cooked and ready-to-serve foods."

She: "Oh! I never thought! You open a can of Melrose Paté. I'll cream it in the chafing dish, and there's one can of Chicken Loaf; we'll have that cold. With the Deviled Ham for sandwiches, we'll have a feast, and Uncle John will imagine himself at a banquet."

The many varieties of Libby's delicious food products in key-opening cans are always ready for emergencies if you have them on your pantry shelf. Ask your grocer for them. Send for the little book, "*How to Make Good Things to Eat*," mailed free. Libby, McNeill & Libby, Chicago,

The World's Greatest Caterers.

Parquet and Hardwood

Floors

Wax Floor Polish, etc.

J. DUNFEE & CO.

Cor. Franklin and Washington Sts.
CHICAGO

Send for Book of Designs

June 30, 1900

IN DAYS OF OLD
YE WITCHES BOLD
SWEPT COBWEBS
FROM THE SKY

BUT MODERN MAID
IS NOT AFRAID
SAPOLIO
TO TRY.

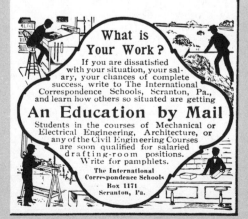

What is Your Work?

If you are dissatisfied with your situation, your salary, your chances of complete success, write to The International Correspondence Schools, Scranton, Pa., and learn how others so situated are getting

An Education by Mail

Students in the courses of Mechanical or Electrical Engineering, Architecture, or any of the Civil Engineering Courses are soon qualified for salaried drafting-room positions. Write for pamphlets.

The International
Correspondence Schools
Box 1171
Scranton, Pa.

March 4, 1899

February 11, 1899

September 4, 1909

February 15, 1908

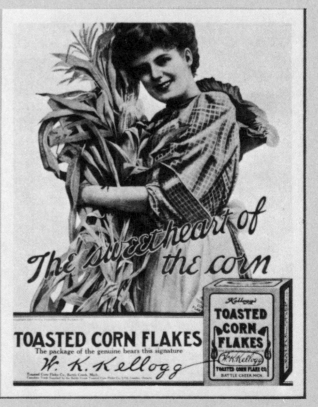

"NOW you must tell me true," she cried,
  When he declared his soul was raptured,
"For I must feel your love is tried,
  Before I yield my heart as captured."

"See! here above thy head I hold,
  'Nabisco' sweet, and all my treasure,
And you must tell me, lover bold,
  Which choice will give you keenest pleasure."

"Fair one," he cried, "here at thy feet,
  'Tis hard to choose 'twixt one and 'tother,
So just to prove my taste is sweet,
  I'll eat the one, and keep the other."

NABISCO SUGAR WAFERS

Enthralling in their subtle flavor, they tempt beyond resistance those who love life's sweetest joys.
The flavors are Lemon, Orange, Chocolate, Vanilla and Mint.

FESTINO — Another confection from the National Biscuit Company. Like an almond in appearance and flavor, with a shell that dissolves on your tongue and surprises you with a delicious kernel of cream.

NATIONAL BISCUIT COMPANY

October 1, 1904

189

November 28, 1914

Suppose we haven't made a million,
Let's be grateful this Thanksgivin'
For all those daily blessin's
That make our lives wuth livin'—
Thankful that we've got kind fren's—
No debts we cannot pay,
A lot o' health, enough o' wealth
An' three good meals a day.
I'm thankful I can stretch my legs
Befo' a cheerful fire,
An' smoke cool, mellow VELVET
In my sweet, old, seasoned briar.

Velvet Joe

IN THIS season of thankfulness for the fruits of earth, let us not forget the "blessed weed" that grows in the Blue Grass Country—Kentucky's *Burley de Luxe*, that in the form of VELVET, The Smoothest Smoking Tobacco, brings cheer and comfort to millions of men.

Many a Thanksgiving feast will be topped off with a sweet, old, seasoned pipe, full of cool, slow-burning VELVET whose aged-in-the-wood mellowness brings content.

May *your* Thanksgiving pipe be sweet with it.

10c Tins   5c Metal-Lined Bags
One Pound Glass Humidors

Liggett & Myers Tobacco Co.

VELVET TOBACCO

THE EDISON

PHONOGRAPH

The Acme of Realism.

"LOOKING FOR THE BAND."

Perfect Reproductions of Sound

Are obtained by using EDISON RECORDS and GENUINE EDISON PHONOGRAPHS

Nine Styles.   From $10.00 to $100.00
Catalogues Everywhere.   All Dealers

NONE GENUINE WITHOUT
Thomas A. Edison
THIS TRADE-MARK.

NATIONAL PHONOGRAPH CO., 135 Fifth Avenue, New York

February 9, 1901

$8,000 TO $10,000 Yearly.

IMPROVED RIDING GALLERY

HERSCHELL-SPILLMAN CO. NORTH TONAWANDA N.Y. U.S.A. CAN BE OPERATED BY STEAM OR ELECTRICITY.

This is not a large profit for owners of Merry-Go-Rounds.   It is a delightful, attractive, big paying, healthful business.   Just the thing for the man who can't stand indoor work or is not fit for heavy work.   Just the business for the man who has some money and wants to invest it to the best possible advantage.   We make the finest appearing and easiest running Merry-Go-Rounds manufactured.   They are simple in construction and require no mechanical knowledge to operate.   If you want to get into a money-making business, write today for catalogue and particulars.

HERSCHELL-SPILLMAN CO.
Park Amusement Outfitters

172 Sweeney Street   North Tonawanda, N. Y., U. S. A.

April 7, 1906

December 1, 1917

He Knows
Ralston
Breakfast Food
is good.

All the goodness
of Gluterean
Wheat makes

Ralston
Breakfast
Food

Famous with folks fond of fine living, who are
careful of their health.
That delicious flavor comes from the best
wheat Nature can produce. Ralston Breakfast
Food children are red cheeked and robust—
the embodiment of health.

Sample free for your grocer's name

There's variety in our Pure Food family to please
every palate: Ralston Health Oats, Ralston Hominy
Grits, Ralston Barley Food, Purina Pankake Flour and
Purina Health Flour which makes "Brain Bread." Ask
your baker for "Brain Bread" or bake it yourself, following Mrs. Rorer's recipes, which will be sent on
application.
Ralston-Purina Cereals are distinguished by Checker-
board packages.
See Special offer in March *TRUTH*.

PURINA MILLS,
"*Where Purity is Paramount*"

804 Gratiot Street,   **St. Louis, Mo.**

Why don't YOU drink
HIRES
Rootbeer?

"who-o?"

"You!"

HIRES Rootbeer is the ideal
spring tonic and home beverage. It
cleanses and cools the blood, revives
and refreshes the whole system—
fits you for the summer's heat.

To be had everywhere in carbonated
form or in packages. A package makes
five gallons—sent by mail for 25 cents.
Dealers, write for our big offer this year.

CHARLES E. HIRES COMPANY, Malvern, Pa.

March 30, 1901

March 30, 1901

If you want the truth, go to a child

JEPSON had a spectacular record as a salesman. They used to call him "Crash-'em-down" Jepson. And the bigger they were, the harder they fell.

Lately, though, Jepson felt himself slipping. He couldn't seem to land the big orders; and he was too proud to go after the little ones. He was discouraged and mystified. Finally, one evening, he got the real truth from his little boy. You can always depend on a child to be outspoken on subjects that older people avoid.

*   *   *

That's the insidious thing about halitosis (unpleasant breath). You, yourself, rarely know when you have it. And even your closest friends won't tell you.

Sometimes, of course, halitosis comes from some deep-seated organic disorder that requires professional advice. But usually—and fortunately—halitosis is only a local condition that yields to the regular use of Listerine as a mouth wash and gargle. It is an interesting thing that this well-known antiseptic, that has been in use for years for surgical dressings, possesses these unusual properties as a breath deodorant.

It halts food fermentation in the mouth and leaves the breath sweet, fresh and clean. *Not* by substituting some other odor but by really removing the old one. The Listerine odor itself quickly disappears. So the systematic use of Listerine puts you on the safe and polite side.

Your druggist will supply you with Listerine. He sells lots of it. It has dozens of different uses as a safe antiseptic and has been trusted as such for half a century. Read the interesting little booklet that comes with every bottle. *Lambert Pharmacal Company, Saint Louis, U. S. A.*

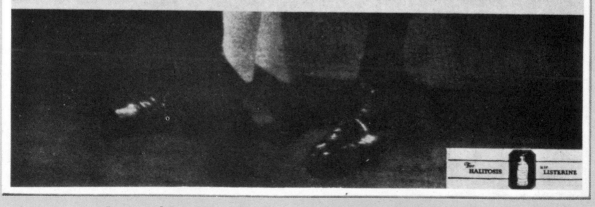

Listerine ad, January 12, 1924, began new era in intimate advertising.

A LITTLE TOWN CALLED
MONTIGNIES ST. CHRISTOPHE

by Irvin S. Cobb

IN THE FIRST week of August 1914 the *Post*'s Irvin Cobb was casting for bass in a lake in Quebec; ten days later he was bouncing via chartered taxicab into a spirited little fight between German and Belgian cavalry on the road from Brussels to Louvain. The Germans "captured" him and promptly turned him loose to write front-line dispatches for the *Post*. Cobb's frenzied dash from Canada to New York to London to Belgium and through the onrushing German army during the first days of World War I was a remarkable feat in itself. But his ability to smuggle uncensored reports across the Dutch border and get them to the *Post*'s Philadelphia office in time for publication a few weeks later was pretty close to a miracle. Articles like the following made Cobb a celebrity; after he returned to the United States in 1915, and after the operation which is described elsewhere, he went on a nation-wide lecture tour by popular demand.

OCTOBER 10, 1914

WE PASSED through it day before yesterday in the afternoon—this little Belgian town called Montignies St. Christophe —just twenty-four hours behind a dust-colored German column. I am going to try now to tell how it looked to us.

I am inclined to think I passed this way a year ago, or a little less, though I cannot be quite certain as to that. Traveling 'cross country, the country is likely to look different from the way it looked when you viewed it from the window of a railroad carriage.

Of this much, though, I am sure: If I did not pass through this little town of Montignies St. Christophe then, at least I passed through fifty like it—each a single line of gray houses strung, like beads on a cord, along a white, straight road, with fields behind and elms in front; each with its small, ugly church, its wine shop, its drinking trough, its priest in black, and its one lone gendarme in his preposterous housings of saber and belt and shoulder straps.

I rather imagine I tried to think up something funny to say about the shabby grandeur of the gendarme or the acid flavor of the cooking vinegar sold at the drinking place under the name of wine; for that time I was supposed to be writing humorous articles on European travel.

Something has happened to Montignies St. Christophe to lift it out of the dun, dull sameness that made it as one with so many other unimportant villages in this upper left-hand corner of the map of Europe. The war has come this way; and, coming so, has dealt it a side-slap.

We came to it just before dusk. All day we had been hurrying along, trying to catch up with the German army's rear guard; but the Germans moved faster than we did, even though they fought as they went. They had gone round the southern part of Belgium like coopers round a cask, hooping it with tight bands of steel. Belgium —or this part of it—was all barreled up now: chines, staves and bung; and the Germans were already across the line, beating down the sod of France with their hobbed marching boots.

Besides we had stopped often, for there was so much to see and to hear. There was the hour we spent at Merbes-le-Château, where the English had been; and the hour we spent at La Bussière, on the river Sambre, where a brisk fight had been fought two days earlier; but Merbes-le-Château is another story and so is La Bussière. Just after La Bussière we came to a tiny village named Neuville and halted here while the local Jack-of-all-trades mended for us an invalided tire on a bicycle.

As WE grouped in the narrow street before his shop, with a hiving swarm of curious villagers buzzing about us, an improvised ambulance, with a red cross painted on its side over the letters of a baker's sign, went up the steep hill at the head of the cobbled street. At that the women in the doorways of the tiny cottages twisted their gnarled red hands in their aprons, and whispered fearsomely among themselves, so that the sibilant sound of their voices ran up and down the line of houses in a long, quavering hiss.

The wagon, it seemed, was bringing in a wounded French soldier who had been found in the woods beyond the river. He was one of the last to be found alive, which was another way of saying that for two days and two nights he had been lying helpless in the thickets, his stomach empty and his wounds raw. On each of those two nights it had rained, and rained hard.

Just as we started on our way the big guns began booming somewhere ahead of us toward the southwest; so we turned in that direction. We had heard the guns distinctly in the early forenoon, and again, less distinctly, at about noontime. Thereafter, for a while, there had been a lull in the firing; but now it was constant—a steady, sustained boom-boom-boom, so far away that it fell on the eardrums as a gentle concussion; as a throb of air, rather than as a real sound.

For three days now we had been following that distant voice of the cannon, trying to catch up with it as it advanced, always southward, toward the French frontier. Therefore we flogged the belly of our tired horse with the lash of a long whip, and hurried along.

There were five of us, all Americans. The two who rode on bicycles pedaled ahead as outriders, and the remaining three followed on behind with the horse and the dogcart. We had bought the outfit that morning and we were to lose it that night. The horse was an aged mare, with high withers, and galls on her shoulders and fetlocks, unshorn, after the fashion for Belgian horses; and the dogcart was a venerable ruin, which creaked a great protest at every turn of the warped wheels on the axle. We had been able to buy the two—the mare and the cart—only because the German soldiers had not thought them worth the taking.

In this order, then, we proceeded. Pretty soon the mare grew so weary she could hardly lift her shaggy old legs; so, footsore as we were, we who rode dismounted and trudged on, taking turns at dragging her forward by the bit. I presume we went ahead thus for an hour or more, along an interminable straight road and past miles of the checkered light and dark green fields, which in harvest time make a great backgammon board of the whole country.

The road was empty of natives—empty, too, of German wagon trains; and these seemed to us curious things, because there had until then been hardly a minute of the day when we were not passing German soldiers or meeting Belgian refugees.

ALMOST WITHOUT WARNING we came on this little village called Montignies St. Christophe. A six-armed signboard at a crossroads told us its name —a rather impressive name ordinarily for a place of perhaps twenty houses, all told. But now tragedy had given it distinction; had painted that straggling frontier hamlet over with such colors that the picture of it is going to live in my memory as long as I do live.

At the upper end of the single street, like an outpost, stood an old château, the seat, no doubt, of the local gentry, with a small park of beeches and elms round it; and here, right at the park entrance, we had our first intimation that there had been a fight.

The gate stood ajar between its chipped stone pillars, and just inside the blue coat of a French cavalry officer, jaunty and new and much braided with gold lace on the collars and cuffs, hung from the limb of a small tree. Beneath the tree were a sheaf of straw in the shape of a bed and the ashes of a dead camp fire; and on the grass, plain to the eye, a plump, well-picked pullet, all ready for the pot or the pan.

Looking on past these things we saw much scattered dunnage: Frenchmen's knapsacks, flannel shirts, playing cards, fagots of firewood mixed together like jackstraws, canteens covered with slate-blue cloth and having queer little hornlike protuberances on their tops—which proved them to be French canteens—tumbled straw, odd shoes with their lacings undone, a toptilted service shelter of canvas; all the riffle of a camp that had been suddenly and violently disturbed.

As I think back it seems to me that not until that moment had it occurred to me to regard the cottages and shops beyond the clumped trees of the château grounds closely. We were desperately weary, to begin with, and our eyes, those past three days, had grown used to the signs of misery and waste and ruin, abundant and multiplying in the wake of the ironshod hard-pounding hoofs of the German conquerors.

Now, all of a sudden, I became aware that this town had been literally shot to bits. From our side —that is to say, from the north and likewise from the west—the Germans had shelled it. From the south, plainly, the French had answered. The village, in between, had caught the full force and fury of the contending fires. Probably the inhabitants had warning; probably they fled when the German skirmishers surprised that outpost of Frenchmen camping in the park.

One imagined them scurrying like rabbits across the fields and through the cabbage patches. But they had left their belongings behind, all their small petty gearings and garnishings, to be wrecked in the wrenching and rocking apart of their homes.

A railroad track emerged from the fields and ran along the one street. Shells had fallen on it and had exploded, ripping the steel rails from the crossties, so that they stood up all along in a jagged formation, like rows of snaggled teeth. Other shells, dropping in the road, had so wrought with the stone blocks that they were piled here in heaps, and there were depressed into caverns and crevasses four or five or six feet deep.

Every house in sight had been hit again and again and again. One house would have its whole front blown in, so that we could look right back to the rear walls and see the pans on the kitchen shelves. Another house would lack a roof to it, and the tidy tiles that had made the roof were now red and yellow rubbish, piled like broken shards outside a potter's door. The doors stood open, and the windows, with the windowpanes all gone and in some instances the sashes as well, leered emptily at us like eye-sockets without eyes.

So it went. Two of the houses had caught fire and the interiors were quite burned away. A sudden smell of burned things came from the still smoking ruins; but, the walls, being of thick stone, still stood.

Our poor tired old nag halted and sniffed and snorted. If she had had energy enough I reckon she would have shied about and run back the way she had come, for now, just ahead, lay two dead horses—a big gray and a roan—with their stark legs sticking out across the road. The gray was shot through and through in three places. The right fore hoof of the roan had been cut smack off, as smoothly as though done with an ax; and the stiffened leg had a curiously unfinished look about it, suggesting a natural malformation. Dead only a few hours, the carcasses had already begun to swell. The skin on their bellies was as tight as a drumhead.

We forced the quivering mare past the two dead horses. Beyond them the road was a litter. Knapsacks, coats, canteens, handkerchiefs, pots, pans, household utensils, bottles, jugs and caps were everywhere. The deep ditches on each side of the road were clogged with such things. The dropped caps and the abandoned knapsacks were always French caps and French knapsacks cast aside, no doubt, in the road for a quick flight after the mêlée.

The Germans had charged after shelling the town, and then the French had fallen back—or at least so we deduced from the looks of things. In the débris was no object that bespoke German workmanship or German ownership. This rather puzzled us until we learned that the Germans, as

tidy in this game of war as in the game of life, make it a hard-and-fast rule to gather up their own belongings after every engagement, great or small, leaving behind nothing that might serve to give the enemy an idea of their losses.

We went by the church. Its spire was gone; but, strange to say, a small flag—the Tricolor of France—still fluttered from a window where some one had stuck it. We went by the *taverne,* or wine shop, which had a sign over its door—a creature remotely resembling a blue lynx. And through the door we saw half a loaf of bread and several bottles on a table. We went by a rather pretentious house, with pear trees in front of it and a big barn alongside it; and right under the eaves of the barn I picked up the short jacket of a French trooper, so new and fresh from the workshop that the white cambric lining was hardly soiled. The figure 18 was on the collar; we decided that its wearer must have belonged to the Eighteenth Cavalry Regiment. Behind the barn we found a whole pile of new knapsacks—the flimsy play-soldier knapsacks of the French infantrymen, which are not half so heavy or a third so substantial as the heavy sacks of the Germans, which are all bound with straps and covered on the back side with undressed red bullock's hide.

Until now we had seen, in all the silent, ruined village, no human being. The place fairly ached with emptiness. Cats sat on the doorsteps or in the windows, and presently from a barn we heard imprisoned beasts lowing dismally; but there were no dogs. We had already remarked this fact —that in every desolated village cats were thick enough; but invariably the sharp-nosed, wolfish-looking Belgian dogs had disappeared along with their masters. And it was so in Montignies St. Christophe.

On a roadside barricade of stones, chinked with sods of turf—a breastwork the French probably had erected before the fight and which the Germans had kicked half down—I counted three cats, seated side by side.

It was just after we had gone by the barricade that, in a shed behind the riddled shell of a house, which was almost the last house of the town, one of our party saw an old, a very old woman, who peered out at us through a break in the wall. He called out to her in French, but she never answered—only continued to watch him from behind her shelter. He started toward her and she disappeared noiselessly, without having spoken a word. She was the only living person we saw in that town.

Just beyond the town, though, we met a wagon —a furniture dealer's wagon—from some larger community, which had been impressed by the

Belgian authorities, military or civil, for ambulance service. A jaded team of horses drew it, and white flags with red crosses in their centers drooped over the wheels, fore and aft. One man led the near horse by the bit and two other men walked behind the wagon. All three of them had Red Cross brassards on the sleeves of their coats.

The wagon had a hood on it, but was open at both ends. Overhauling it we saw that it contained two dead soldiers—French footsoldiers. The bodies rested side by side on the wagon bed. Their feet somehow were caught up on the wagon seat so that their stiff legs, in the baggy red pants, slanted upward, and the two dead men had the look of being about to glide backward and out of the wagon.

The blue-clad arms of one of them were twisted upward in a half-arc, encircling nothing; and as the wheels jolted over the rutted cobbles these two bent arms joggled and swayed drunkenly. The other's head was canted back so that, as we passed, we looked right into his face. It was a young face—we could tell that much, even through the mask of caked mud on the gray-white skin—and it might once have been a comely face. It was not comely now.

Peering into the wagon we saw that the second dead man's face had been partly shot or shorn away—the lower jaw was gone; so that it had become an abominable thing to look on. These two had been men the day before. Now they were carrion and would be treated as such; for as we looked back we saw the wagon turn off the high road into a field where the wild red poppies, like blobs of red blood, grew thick between rows of neglected sugar beets.

We stopped then, and watched. The wagon bumped through the beet patch to where, at the edge of a thicket, a trench had been dug. The diggers were two peasants in blouses, who stood alongside the ridge of raw upturned earth at the edge of the hole, in the attitude of figures in a painting by Millet. Their spades were driven upright into the mound of fresh earth. Behind them a frieze of poplars rose against the sky line.

We saw the bodies lifted out of the wagon. We saw them slide into the shallow grave, and saw the two diggers start at their task of filling in the hole.

Not until then, as I remember, did it occur to any one of us that we had not spoken to the men in charge of the wagon, or they to us.

There was one detached house, not badly battered, alongside the road at the lower edge of the field where the burial took place. It had a shield on its front wall bearing the Belgian arms and words to denote that it was a customs house. A glance at our map showed us that at this point the French boundary came up in a V-shaped point almost to the road. Had the gravediggers picked a spot fifty yards farther on for digging their trench, those two dead Frenchmen would have rested in the soil of their own country.

The sun was almost down by now, and its slanting rays came lengthwise through the elm-tree aisles along our route. Just as it disappeared we met a string of refugees—men, women, and children—all afoot and all bearing pitiably small bundles. They limped along silently in a straggling procession. None of them were weeping; none of them looked as though they had been weeping. During the past ten days I had seen thousands of such refugees, and I had yet to hear one of them cry out or complain or protest.

These persons who passed us now were like that. Their heavy peasant faces expressed dumb bewilderment—nothing else. They went on up the road into the gathering dusk as we went down, and almost at once the sound of their clinking tread died out behind us. Without knowing certainly, we nevertheless imagined they were the dwellers of Montignies St. Christophe going back to the wrecked shells that had been their homes.

An hour later we passed through the back lines of the German camp and entered the town of Beaumont, to find that the General Staff of a German army corps was quartered there for the night, and that the main force of the column, after sharp fighting, had already advanced well beyond the frontier. France was invaded.

IN ALSACE

by Edith Wharton

In 1915 the war in France seemed to have settled down to a thing of trenches, No Man's Land, indecisive bloodletting and endless watchful waiting. Edith Wharton, the author of *Ethan Frome* (1911) and other distinguished novels, was devoting all her time to relief and Red Cross work in Paris, which had been her home for years. To dramatize the need for more hospitals, the Red Cross asked her to visit the front and write about it for American magazines. From a cottage garden in Clermont-en-Argonne Mrs. Wharton watched the French troops recapture some strategic heights on the way to Verdun, then she went on and explored the trenches all the way down to Alsace. This was not her only *Post* appearance; several of her short stories, some of them based on war experiences, ran in the magazine between 1918 and 1932.

NOVEMBER 20, 1915

AUGUST 13TH, 1915.

MY TRIP to the east began by a dash toward the north. Near Rheims is a little town—hardly more than a village, but in English we have no intermediate terms such as *bourg* and *petit bourg*—where one of the new Red Cross sanitary motor units was to be seen in action. The inspection over, we climbed to a vineyard above the town and looked down at a river valley traversed by a double line of trees. The first line marked the canal, which is held by the French, who have gunboats on it. Behind this ran the highroad with the first-line French trenches, and just above, on the opposite slope, were the German lines. The soil being chalky, the German positions were clearly marked by two parallel white scorings across the brown hill front; and while we watched we heard desultory firing and saw, here and there along the ridge, the smoke-puff of an exploding shell. It was incredibly strange to stand there, among the vines humming with summer insects, and to look out over a peaceful country heavy with the coming vintage, knowing that the trees at our feet hid a line of gunboats that were crashing death into those two white scorings on the hill.

Rheims itself brings one nearer to the war by its look of deathlike desolation. The paralysis of the bombarded towns is one of the most tragic results of the invasion. One's soul revolts at this senseless disorganizing of innumerable useful activities. Compared with the towns of the north, Rheims is relatively unharmed; but for that very reason the arrest of life seems the more futile and cruel. The Cathedral Square was deserted, all the houses round it were closed. And there, before us, rose the cathedral—*a* cathedral, rather, for it was not the one we had always known. It was, in fact, not like any cathedral on earth. When the German bombardment began the west front was covered with scaffolding; the shells set it on fire, and the whole church was wrapped in flames.

Now the scaffolding is gone, and in the dull provincial square there stands a structure so strange and beautiful that one must search the Inferno or some tale of Eastern magic for words to picture the luminous, unearthly vision. The lower part of the front has been warmed to deep tints of umber and burnt sienna. This rich burnishing passes, higher up, through yellowish-pink and carmine to a sulphur whitening to ivory; and the recesses of the portals and the hollows behind the statues are lined with a black denser and more velvety than any effect of shadow to be obtained by sculptured relief. The interweaving of color over the whole blunted, bruised surface recalls the metallic tints, the peacock-and-pigeon iridescences, the incredible mingling of red, blue, umber and yellow of the rocks along the Gulf of Ægina. And the wonder of the impression is increased by the sense of its evanescence; the knowledge that this is the beauty of disease and death, that every one of the transfigured statues must crumble under the autumn rains, that every one of the pink or golden stones is already eaten away to the core, that the Cathedral of Rheims is glowing and dying before us like a sunset.

AUGUST 14TH.

A stone-and-brick château in a flat park with a stream running through it, pampas grass, geraniums, rustic bridges, winding paths; how bourgeois and sleepy it would all seem but for the sentinel challenging our motor at the gate!

Before the door a collie dozing in the sun and a group of staff officers waiting for luncheon. Indoors a room with handsome tapestries, some good furniture and a table spread with the usual military maps and aëroplane photographs. At luncheon, the general, the chiefs of the staff—a dozen in all—and an officer from the general headquarters. The usual atmosphere of *camaraderie,* confidence, good humor, and a kind of cheerful seriousness that I have come to regard as characteristic of the men immersed in the actual facts of the war. I set down this impression as typical of many such luncheon hours along the front.

AUGUST 15TH.

This morning we set out for reconquered Alsace. For reasons unexplained to the civilian this corner of old-new France has hitherto been inaccessible—even to highly placed French officials; and there was a special sense of excitement in taking the road that led to it.

We slipped through a valley or two, passed some placid villages with vine-covered gables, and noticed that most of the signs over the shops were German. We had crossed the old frontier unaware and were presently in the charming town of Massevaux. It was the Feast of the Assumption, and mass was just over when we reached the square before the church. The streets were full of holiday people, well-dressed, smiling, seemingly unconscious of the war. Down the church steps, guided by fond mammas, came little girls in white dresses, with white wreaths in their hair, and carrying, in baskets slung over their shoulders, woolly lambs or blue and white Virgins. Groups of cavalry officers stood chatting with civilians in their Sunday best, and through the windows of the Golden Eagle we saw active preparations for a crowded midday dinner. It was all as happy and parochial as a Hansi picture, and the fine old gabled houses and clean cobblestone streets made the traditional setting for an Alsatian holiday.

At the Golden Eagle we laid in a store of provisions and started out across the mountains in the direction of Thann. The Vosges, at this season, are in their short midsummer beauty, rustling with streams, dripping with showers, balmy with the smell of firs and bracken and of purple thyme on hot banks. We reached the top of a ridge, and, hiding the motor behind a skirt of trees, went out into the open to lunch on a sunny slope. Facing us across the valley was a tall, conical hill clothed with forest. That hill was Hartmannsweilerkopf, the center of a long contest in which the French have lately been victorious; and all about us stood other crests and ridges, from which German guns still look down on the valley of Thann.

Thann itself is at the valley head, in a neck between hills—a handsome old town with the air of prosperous stability so oddly characteristic of this tormented region. As we drove through the main street the pall of war sadness fell on us again, darkening the light and chilling the summer air. Thann is raked by the German lines, and its windows are mostly shuttered and its streets deserted. One or two houses in the cathedral square have been gutted, but the somewhat overpinnacled and overstatued cathedral which is the pride of Thann is almost untouched, and when we entered it vespers were being sung and a few people—mostly in black—knelt in the nave.

No greater contrast could be imagined to the happy feast-day scene we had left, a few miles off, at Massevaux; but Thann, in spite of its empty streets, is not a deserted city. A vigorous life beats in it, ready to break forth as soon as the German guns are silenced. The French administration, working on the best of terms with the population, is keeping up the civil activities of the town, as the canons of the Cathedral are continuing the rites of the Church. Many inhabitants still remain behind their closed shutters and dive down into their cellars when the shells begin to crash; and the schools, transferred to a neighboring village, number over two thousand pupils.

We walked through the town, visited a vast catacomb of a wine cellar fitted up partly as a hospital and partly as a shelter for the cellarless, and saw the lamentable remains of the industrial quarter along the river, which has been the special target of the German guns. Thann has been industrially ruined, all its mills are wrecked; but unlike the towns of the north it has had the good fortune to preserve its outline, its civic personality, a face that its children, when they come back, can recognize and take comfort in.

After our visit to the ruins a diversion was suggested by the amiable administrators of Thann, who had guided our sight-seeing. They were just off for a military tournament which a regiment of dragoons was giving that afternoon in a neighboring valley, and we were invited to go with them.

The scene of the entertainment was a meadow inclosed in an amphitheater of rocks, with grassy ledges projecting from the cliff like tiers of opera boxes. These points of vantage were partly occupied by interested spectators and partly by ruminating cattle; on the lowest slope the rank and fashion of the neighborhood were ranged on a semicircle of chairs, and below, in the meadow, a lively steeplechase was going on. The riding was extremely pretty, as French military riding always is. Few of the mounts were thoroughbreds—the greater number, in fact, being local cart horses barely broken to the saddle; but their agility and dash did the greater credit to their riders. The lancers, in particular, executed an effective musical ride about a central pennon, to the immense satisfaction of the fashionable public in the foreground and of the gallery on the rocks.

The audience was even more interesting than the artists. Chatting with the ladies in the front row were the general of division and his staff, groups of officers invited from the adjoining headquarters, and most of the civil and military administrators of the restored Département du Haut Rhin. All classes had turned out in honor of the fête, and everyone was in a holiday mood. The people among whom we sat were mostly Alsatian property owners, many of them industrials of Thann. Some had been driven from their homes, others had seen their mills destroyed, all had been living for a year on the perilous edge of war, under the menace of reprisals too hideous to picture; yet the humor prevailing was that of any group of merrymakers in a peaceful garrison town. I have seen nothing, in my wanderings along the front, more indicative of the good breeding of the French than the spirit of the ladies and gentlemen who sat chatting with the officers on that grassy slope of Alsace.

The display of *haute école* was to be followed by an exhibition of "transportation through the ages," headed by a Gaulish chariot driven by a trooper with a long horsehair mustache and a mistletoe wreath, and ending in a motor of which the engine had been taken out and replaced by a large, placid white horse. Unluckily a heavy rain began while this instructive number awaited its turn, and we had to leave before Vercingetorix had led his warriors into the ring.

AUGUST 16TH.

Up and up into the mountains! We started early, taking our way along a narrow, interminable valley that sloped up gradually toward the east. The road was encumbered with a stream of hooded supply-vans drawn by mules, for we were on the way to one of the main positions in the Vosges, and this train of provisions is kept up day and night. Finally we reached a mountain village under fir-clad slopes, with a cold stream rushing down from the hills. On one side of the road was a rustic inn; on the other, among the firs, a chalet occupied by the brigade headquarters. Everywhere about us swarmed the little *chasseurs alpins* in blue tam-o-shanters and leather gaiters. For a year we had been reading of these heroes of the hills, and here we were among them, looking into their thin, weather-beaten faces and meeting the twinkle of their friendly eyes. Very friendly they all were, and yet, for Frenchmen, inarticulate and shy. All over the world, no doubt, the mountain silences breed this kind of reserve, this shrinking from the glibness of the valleys. Yet one had fancied that French fluency must soar as high as Mont Blanc.

Mules were brought and we started on a long ride up the mountain. The way led first over open ledges with deep views into valleys blue with distance, then through miles of forest, first of beech and fir, and finally all of fir. Above the road the wooded slopes rose interminably, and here and there we came on tiers of mules, three or four hundred together, stabled under the trees, in stalls dug out of different levels of the slope. Near by were shelters for the men, and perhaps at the next bend a village of trappers' huts, as the officers call the log cabins they build in this region.

These colonies are always bustling with life—men busy cleaning their arms, hauling material for new cabins, washing or mending their clothes, or carrying down the mountain from the camp kitchen the two-handled pails full of steaming soup. The kitchen is always in the most protected quarter of the camp and generally at some distance in the rear. Other soldiers, their job over, are lolling about in groups, smoking, gossiping or writing home, the soldier's letter-pad propped on a patched blue knee, a scarred fist laboriously driving the fountain pen received in the hospital. Some are leaning over the shoulder of a pal who has just received a Paris paper, others chuckling together at the jokes of their own French journal—the Écho du Ravin, the Journal des Poilus or the Diable Bleu; little papers ground out in purplish script on foolscap and adorned with comic sketches and a wealth of local humor.

Higher up, under a fir belt, at the edge of a meadow, the officer who rode ahead signed to us to dismount and scramble after him. We plunged under the trees, into what seemed a denser thicket, and found it to be a thatch of branches woven to screen the muzzles of a battery. The big guns were all about us, crouched in these sylvan lairs like wild beasts waiting to spring; and near each gun hovered its attendant gunner, proud, possessive, important as a bridegroom with his bride.

We climbed and climbed again, reaching at last a sun-and-wind-burnt common which forms the top of one of the highest mountains in the region. The forest was left below us, and only a belt of dwarf firs ran along the edge of the great grassy shoulder. We dismounted, the mules were tethered among the trees, and our guide led us to an insignificant-looking stone in the grass. On one face of the stone was cut the letter F, on the other was a D; we stood on what, till a year ago, was the boundary line between republic and empire. Since then, in certain places, the line has been bent back a long way; but where we stood we were still under German guns, and we had to creep along in the shelter of the squat firs to reach the outlook on the edge of the plateau.

From there, under a sky of racing clouds, we saw outstretched below us the Promised Land of Alsace. On one horizon, far off in the plane, gleamed the roofs and spires of Colmar, on the other rose the purplish heights beyond the Rhine. Near by stood a ring of bare hills, those closest to us scarred by ridges of upheaved earth, as if giant moles had been zigzagging over them; and just under us, in a little green valley, lay the roofs of a peaceful village. The earth ridges and the peaceful village were still German; but the French positions went down the mountain almost to the valley's edge.

We stopped at a gap in the firs and walked to the brink of the plateau. Just under us lay a rock-rimmed lake. More zigzag earthworks surmounted it on all sides, and on the nearest shore was the branched roofing of another great mule shelter. We were looking down at the spot to which the night caravans of the *chasseurs alpins* descend to distribute supplies to the fighting line.

"Who goes there? Attention! You're in sight of the lines!" a voice called out from the firs, and our companion signed to us to move back.

We had been rather too conspicuously facing the German batteries on the opposite slope, and our presence might have drawn their fire on an artillery observation post installed near by. We retreated hurriedly and unpacked our luncheon basket on the more sheltered side of the ridge. As we sat there in the grass, swept by a great mountain breeze full of the scent of thyme and myrtle, while the flutter of birds, the hum of insects, the still and busy life of the hills went on all about us in the sunshine, the pressure of the encircling line of death grew more intolerably real. It is not in the mud of the trenches that one most feels the damnable insanity of war; it is where it lurks, like a mythical monster, in scenes to which the mind has always turned for rest.

We had not yet made the whole tour of the mountain top; and after luncheon we rode over to a point where a long, narrow yoke connects it with a spur projecting directly above the German lines. We left our mules in hiding and walked along the yoke, a mere knife edge of rock rimmed with dwarf vegetation. Suddenly we heard an explosion behind us—one of the batteries we had passed on the way up was giving tongue. The German lines roared back, and for twenty minutes the exchange of invective thundered on. The firing was almost incessant; it seemed as if a great arch of steel were being built up above us in the crystal air. And we could follow each curve of sound from its incipience to its final crash in the trenches.

There were four distinct phases: the sharp bang from the cannon, the long, furious howl overhead, the dispersed and spreading noise of the shell's explosion, and then the roll of its reverberation from cliff to cliff. This is what we heard as we crouched in the lee of the firs. What we saw when we looked out between them was only an occasional burst of white smoke and red flame from one hillside, and on the opposite one, a minute later, a brown geyser of dust.

Presently a deluge of rain descended on us, driving us back to our mules and down the nearest mountain trail through rivers of mud. It rained all the way—rained in such floods and cataracts that the very rocks of the mountain seemed to dissolve and turn into mud. As we slid down through it we met strings of *chasseurs alpins* coming up, splashed to the waist with wet red clay and leading pack mules so coated with it that they looked like studio models from which the sculptor has just pulled off the dripping sheet. Lower down we came on more trapper settlements, so saturated and reeking with wet that they gave us a glimpse of what the winter months on the front must be. No more cheerful polishing of firearms, hauling of fagots, chatting and smoking in sociable groups. Everybody had crept under the doubtful shelter of branches and tarpaulins; the whole army was back in its burrows.

AUGUST 17TH.

Sunshine again for our arrival at Belfort! The invincible city lies unpretentiously behind its green glacis and escutcheoned gates; but the guardian Lion under the Citadel—well, the Lion is figuratively as well as literally *à la hauteur.* With the sunset flush on him as he crouched aloft in his red lair below the fort, he might almost have claimed kin with his mighty prototypes of the Asurbanipal frieze. One wondered a little, seeing whose work he was; but probably it is easier for an artist to symbolize a heroic town than the abstract and elusive divinity who sheds light on the world from New York harbor.

From Belfort back into reconquered Alsace the road runs through a gentle landscape of fields and orchards. We were bound for Dannemarie, one of the towns of the plain, and a center of the new administration. It is the usual *gros bourg* of Alsace, with comfortable old houses in trellised gardens—dull, well-to-do, contented; not in the least the kind of setting demanded by the patriotism which has to be fed on pictures of little girls singing the Marseillaise in Alsatian headdresses and old men with operatic waistcoats tottering forward to kiss the flag. What we saw at Dannemarie was less conspicuous to the eye but much more nourishing to the imagination. The military and civil administrators had the kindness and patience to explain their work and show us something of its results; and the visit left one with the impression of a slow and quiet process of adaptation wisely planned and fruitfully carried out.

We did, in fact, hear the school girls of Dannemarie sing the Marseillaise—and the boys too—but, what was far more interesting, we saw them studying under the direction of the teachers who had always had them in charge, and found that everywhere it had been the aim of the French officials to let the routine of the village policy go on undisturbed.

The German signs remain over the shop fronts except where the shopkeepers have chosen to paint them out—as is happening more and more frequently. When a functionary has to be replaced he is chosen from the same town or the same district, and even the personnel of the civil and military administration is mainly composed of officers and civilians of Alsatian stock.

The heads of both these departments, who accompanied us on our rounds, could talk to the children and old people in German as well as in their local dialect; and as far as a passing observer could discern it seemed as though everything had been done to reduce to a minimum the sense of strangeness and friction which is inevitable in the transition from one rule to another. The interesting point was that this exercise of tact and tolerance seemed to proceed, not from any pressure of expediency but from a sympathetic understanding of the point of view of this people of the border. I heard in Dannemarie not a syllable of lyrical patriotism or postcard sentimentality, but only a kindly and impartial estimate of facts as they were and as they must be dealt with.

AUGUST 18TH.

To-day again we started early for the mountains. Our road ran more to the westward, through the heart of the Vosges and up to a fold of the hills near the borders of Lorraine. We stopped at a headquarters where a young officer of dragoons was to join us, and learned from him that we were to be allowed to visit some of the

first-line trenches which we had looked out on from a high-perched observation post, on our former visit to the Vosges. Violent fighting was going on in that particular region, and after a climb of an hour or two we had to leave the motor at a sheltered angle of the road and strike across the hills on foot. Our path lay through the forest, and every now and then we caught a glimpse of the highroad running below us in full view of the German batteries. Presently we reached a point where the road was screened by a thick growth of trees, behind which an observation post had been set up. We scrambled down and looked through the peephole. Just below us lay a valley with a village in its center, and to the left and right of the village were two hills, the one scored with French, the other with German trenches.

The village, at first sight, looked as normal as those through which we had been passing; but a closer inspection showed that its steeple was shattered and that some of its houses were unroofed. Part of it was held by German, part by French troops. The cemetery adjoining the church and quarry just under it belonged to the Germans, but a line of French trenches ran from the farther side of the church up to the French batteries on the right-hand hill. Parallel with this line, but starting from the other side of the village, was a hollow lane leading up to a single tree. This lane was a German trench, protected by the guns of the left-hand hill; and between the two lay fifty yards of ground.

All this was close under us; and closer still was a slope of open ground leading up to the village and traversed by a rough cart track. Along this track in the hot sunshine little French soldiers the size of tin toys were scrambling up with bags and loads of fagots, their antlike activity as orderly and untroubled as if the two armies had not lain trench to trench a few yards away. It was one of those strange and contradictory scenes of war that bring home to the bewildered looker-on the utter impossibility of picturing how the thing really happens.

While we stood watching we heard the sudden scream of a battery close above us. The crest of the hill we were climbing was alive with "seventy-fives," and the piercing noise seemed to burst out at our very backs. It was the most terrible war shriek I had heard—a kind of wolfish baying that called up an image of all the dogs of war simultaneously tugging at their leashes. There is a dreadful majesty in the sound of a distant cannonade; but these yelps and hisses roused only thoughts of horror. And there, on the opposite slope, the black and brown geysers were beginning to spout up from the German trenches; and from the batteries above them came the puff and roar of retaliation. Below us, along the cart track, the little French soldiers continued to scramble up peacefully to the dilapidated village; and presently a group of officers of dragoons, emerging from the wood, came down to welcome us to their headquarters.

We continued to climb through the forest, the cannonade still whistling overhead, till we reached the most elaborate trapper colony we had yet seen. Half underground, walled with logs and deeply roofed by sods tufted with ferns and moss, the cabins were scattered under the trees and connected with each other by paths bordered with white stones. Before the colonel's cabin the soldiers had made a banked-up flower bed sown with annuals; and farther up the slope stood a log chapel, a mere gable with a wooden altar under it, all tapestried with ivy and holly. Near by was the chaplain's subterranean dwelling. It was reached by a deep cutting with ivy-covered sides, and ivy and fir boughs masked the front. This sylvan retreat had just been completed, and the officers, the chaplain and the soldiers loitering near by were all equally eager to have it seen and hear it praised.

The commanding officer, having done the honors of the camp, led us about a quarter of a mile down the hillside to an open cutting which marked the beginning of the trenches. From the cutting we passed into a long, tortuous burrow walled and roofed with carefully fitted logs. The earth floor was covered by a sort of wooden lattice. The only light entering this tunnel was a faint ray from an occasional narrow slit screened by branches; and beside each of these peepholes hung a shield-shaped metal shutter to be used in case of emergency.

The passage wound down the hill, almost doubling on itself, in order to give a view of all the surrounding lines. Presently the roof became much higher, and we saw on one side a curtained niche about five feet above the floor. One of the officers pulled the curtain back, and there, on a narrow shelf, a gun between his knees, sat a dragoon, his eyes at a peephole. The curtain was hastily drawn again behind his motionless figure, lest the faint light at his back should betray him. We passed by several of these helmeted watchers, and now and then we came to a deeper recess in which a *mitrailleuse* squatted, its black nose thrust through a net of branches. Sometimes the roof of the tunnel was so low that we had to bend nearly double; and at intervals we came to heavy doors, made of logs and sheeted with iron, which shut off one section from another. It is hard to

guess the distance one covers in creeping through an unlit passage with different levels and countless turnings; but we must have descended the hillside for at least a mile before we came out into a half-ruined farmhouse.

This building, which had kept nothing but its outer walls and one or two partitions between the rooms, had been transformed into an observation post. In each of its corners a ladder led up to a little shelf on the level of what was once the second story, and on the shelf sat a dragoon at his peephole. Below, in the dilapidated rooms, the usual life of a camp was going on. Some of the soldiers were playing cards at a kitchen table, others mending their clothes or writing letters or chuckling together—not too loud—over a comic newspaper. It might have been a scene anywhere along the second-line trenches but for the lowered voices, the suddenness with which I was drawn back from a slit in the wall through which I had incautiously peered, and the presence of these helmeted watchers overhead.

We plunged underground again and began to descend through another darker and narrower tunnel. In the upper one there had been one or two roofless stretches where one could straighten one's back and breathe; but here we were in pitch blackness, and saved from breaking our necks only by the gleam of the pocket light which the young lieutenant who led the party shed on our path. As he whisked it up and down to warn us of sharp corners he remarked that at night even this faint glimmer was forbidden, and that it was a bad job going back and forth from the last outpost, till one had learned the turnings.

The last outpost was a half-ruined farmhouse like the other. A telephone connected it with headquarters, and more dumb dragoons sat motionless on their lofty shelves. The house was shut off from the tunnel by an armored door, and the orders were that in case of attack that door should be barred from within and the access to the tunnel defended to the death by the men in the outpost. We were on the extreme verge of the defenses, on a slope just above the village over which we had heard the artillery roaring a few hours earlier. The spot where we stood was raked on all sides by the enemy's lines, and the nearest trenches were only a few yards away. But of all this nothing was really perceptible or comprehensible to me. As far as my own observation went, we might have been a hundred miles from the valley we had looked down on, where the French soldiers were walking peacefully up the cart track in the sunshine. I only knew that we had come out of a black labyrinth into a gutted house among fruit trees, where soldiers were lounging and smoking, and people whispered as they do about a deathbed. Over a break in the walls I saw another gutted farmhouse close by in another orchard. It was an enemy outpost, and silent watchers in helmets of another shape sat there watching on the same high shelves. But all this was infinitely less real and terrible than the cannonade above the disputed village. The artillery had ceased and the air was full of summer murmurs. Close by, on a sheltered ledge, I saw a patch of vineyard with dewy cobwebs hanging to the vines. I could not understand where we were, or what it was all about, or why a shell from the enemy outpost did not suddenly annihilate us. And then, little by little, there came over me the sense of that mute reciprocal watching from trench to trench: the interlocked stare of innumerable pairs of eyes, stretching on, mile after mile, along the sleepless line from Dunkirk to Belfort.

My last vision of the French front, which I had traveled from end to end, was this picture of a shelled house where a few men, who sat smoking and playing cards in the sunshine, had orders to hold out to the death rather than let their fraction of that front be broken.

TURN ABOUT

by William Faulkner

THIS STORY OF American fliers and British torpedo-boat raiders in World War I was written and published long after the war was over. But it became a sensation immediately and was made into a Hollywood film, *Today We Live*. William Faulkner served with the Royal Canadian Air Force during the war and wrote a pair of war novels in the 1920's which were read with enthusiasm by associate editor Pete Martin of the *Post*. He wrote to ask if Faulkner didn't have some short stories for the *Post* and Faulkner sent in "Thrift," another wartime aviation story which appeared September 6, 1930. Thereafter the *Post* published sixteen more Faulkner stories, including "Lizards in Jamshyd's Courtyard" (1932), "Vendee" (1936), "The Bear" (1942) and "Shingles for the Lord" (1943).

MARCH 5, 1932

THE AMERICAN—the older one—wore no pink Bedfords. His breeches were of plain whipcord, like the tunic. And the tunic had no long London-cut skirts, so that below the Sam Browne the tail of it stuck straight out like a tunic of a military policeman beneath his holster belt. And he wore simple putties and the easy shoes of a man of middle age, instead of Savile Row boots, and the shoes and the putties did not match in shade, and the ordnance belt did not match either of them, and the pilot's wings on his breast were just wings. But the ribbon beneath them was a good ribbon, and the insigne on his shoulders were the twin bars of a captain. He was not tall. His face was thin, a little aquiline; the eyes intelligent and a little tired. He was past twenty-five; looking at him, one thought, not Phi Beta Kappa exactly, but Skull and Bones perhaps, or possibly a Rhodes scholarship.

One of the men who faced him probably could not see him at all. He was being held on his feet by an American military policeman. He was quite drunk, and in contrast with the heavy-jawed policeman who held him erect on his long, slim, boneless legs, he looked like a masquerading girl. He was possibly eighteen, tall, with a pink-and-white face and blue eyes, and a little dull gold mustache above a mouth like a girl's mouth. He wore a pea-coat, buttoned awry and stained with recent mud, and upon his blond head, at that unmistakable and rakish swagger which no other people can ever approach or imitate, the cap of a Royal Naval officer.

"What's this, corporal?" the American captain said. "What's the trouble? He's an Englishman. You'd better let their M.P.'s take care of him."

"I know he is," the policeman said. He spoke heavily, breathing heavily, in the voice of a man under physical strain; for all his girlish delicacy of limb, the English boy was heavier—or more helpless—than he looked. "Stand up!" the policeman said. "They're officers!"

The English boy made an effort then. He pulled himself together, focusing his eyes. He swayed, throwing his arm about the policeman's neck, and with the other hand he saluted, his hand flicking, fingers curled a little, to his right ear, already swaying again and catching himself again. "Cheerio, sir," he said. "Name's not Beatty, I hope."

"No," the captain said.

"Ah," the English boy said. "Hoped not. My mistake. No offense, what?"

"No offense," the captain said quietly. But he was looking at the policeman. The second American spoke. He was a lieutenant, also a pilot. But he was not twenty-five and he wore the pink breeches, the London boots, and his tunic might have been a British tunic save for the collar.

"It's one of those navy eggs," he said. "They pick them out of the gutters here all night long. You don't come to town often enough."

"Oh," the captain said. "I've heard about them. I remember now." He also remarked now that, though the street was a busy one—it was just outside a popular café—and there were many passers, soldier, civilian, women, yet none of them so much as paused, as though it were a familiar sight. He was looking at the policeman. "Can't you take him to his ship?"

"I thought of that before the captain did," the policeman said. "He says he can't go aboard his ship after dark because he puts the ship away at sundown."

"Puts it away?"

"Stand up, sailor!" the policeman said savagely,

jerking at his lax burden. "Maybe the captain can make sense out of it. Damned if I can. He says they keep the boat under the wharf. Run it under the wharf at night, and that they can't get it out again until the tide goes out tomorrow."

"Under the wharf? A boat? What is this?" He was now speaking to the lieutenant. "Do they operate some kind of aquatic motorcycles?"

"Something like that," the lieutenant said. "You've seen them—the boats. Launches, camouflaged and all. Dashing up and down the harbor. You've seen them. They do that all day and sleep in the gutters here all night."

"Oh," the captain said. "I thought those boats were ship commanders' launches. You mean to tell me they use officers just to —— "

"I don't know," the lieutenant said. "Maybe they use them to fetch hot water from one ship to another. Or buns. Or maybe to go back and forth fast when they forget napkins or something."

"Nonsense," the captain said. He looked at the English boy again.

"That's what they do," the lieutenant said. "Town's lousy with them all night long. Gutters full, and their M.P.'s carting them away in batches, like nursemaids in a park. Maybe the French give them the launches to get them out of the gutters during the day."

"Oh," the captain said, "I see." But it was clear that he didn't see, wasn't listening, didn't believe what he did hear. He looked at the English boy. "Well, you can't leave him here in that shape," he said.

Again the English boy tried to pull himself together. "Quite all right, 'sure you," he said glassily, his voice pleasant, cheerful almost, quite courteous. "Used to it. Confounded rough *pavé*, though. Should force French do something about it. Visiting lads jolly well deserve decent field to play on, what?"

"And he was jolly well using all of it too," the policeman said savagely. "He must think he's a one-man team, maybe."

At that moment a fifth man came up. He was a British military policeman. "Nah then," he said. "What's this? What's this?" Then he saw the Americans' shoulder bars. He saluted. At the sound of his voice the English boy turned, swaying, peering.

"Oh, hullo, Albert," he said.

"Nah then, Mr. Hope," the British policeman said. He said to the American policeman, over his shoulder: "What is it this time?"

"Likely nothing," the American said. "The way you guys run a war. But I'm a stranger here. Here. Take him."

"What is this, corporal?" the captain said. "What was he doing?"

"He won't call it nothing," the American policeman said, jerking his head at the British policeman. "He'll just call it a thrush or a robin or something. I turn into this street about three blocks back a while ago, and I find it blocked with a line of trucks going up from the docks, and the drivers all hollering ahead what the hell the trouble is. So I come on, and I find it is about three blocks of them, blocking the cross streets too; and I come on to the head of it where the trouble is, and I find about a dozen of the drivers out in front, holding a caucus or something in the middle of the street, and I come up and I say, 'What's going on here?' and they leave me through and I find this egg here laying —— "

"Yer talking about one of His Majesty's officers, my man," the British policeman said.

"Watch yourself, corporal," the captain said. "And you found this officer —— "

"He had done gone to bed in the middle of the street, with an empty basket for a pillow. Laying there with his hands under his head and his knees crossed, arguing with them about whether he ought to get up and move or not. He said that the trucks could turn back and go around by another street, but that he couldn't use any other street, because this street was his."

"His street?"

The English boy had listened, interested, pleasant. "Billet, you see," he said. "Must have order, even in war emergency. Billet by lot. This street mine; no poaching, eh? Next street Jamie Wutherspoon's. But trucks can go by that street because Jamie not using it yet. Not in bed yet. Insomnia. Knew so. Told them. Trucks go that way. See now?"

"Was that it, corporal?" the captain said.

"He told you. He wouldn't get up. He just laid there, arguing with them. He was telling one of them to go somewhere and bring back a copy of their articles of war —— "

"King's Regulations; yes," the captain said.

"—— and see if the book said whether he had the right of way, or the trucks. And then I got him up, and then the captain come along. And that's all. And with the captain's permission I'll now hand him over to His Majesty's wet nur—— "

"That'll do, corporal," the captain said. "You can go. I'll see to this." The policeman saluted and went on. The British policeman was now supporting the English boy. "Can't you take him home?" the captain said. "Where are their quarters?"

"I don't rightly know, sir, if they have quarters

or not. We—I usually see them about the pubs until daylight. They don't seem to use quarters."

"You mean, they really aren't off of ships?"

"Well, sir, they might be ships, in a manner of speaking. But a man would have to be a bit sleepier than him to sleep in one of them."

"I see," the captain said. He looked at the policeman. "What kind of boats are they?"

This time the policeman's voice was immediate, final and completely inflectionless. It was like a closed door. "I don't rightly know, sir."

"Oh," the captain said. "Quite. Well, he's in no shape to stay about pubs until daylight this time."

"Perhaps I can find him a bit of a pub with a back table, where he can sleep," the policeman said. But the captain was not listening. He was looking across the street, where the lights of another café fell across the pavement. The English boy yawned terrifically, like a child does, his mouth pink and frankly gaped as a child's.

The captain turned to the policeman:

"Would you mind stepping across there and asking for Captain Bogard's driver? I'll take care of Mr. Hope."

The policeman departed. The captain now supported the English boy, his hand beneath the other's arm. Again the boy yawned like a weary child. "Steady," the captain said. "The car will be here in a minute."

"Right," the English boy said through the yawn.

II

ONCE IN THE CAR, he went to sleep immediately with the peaceful suddenness of babies, sitting between the two Americans. But though the aerodrome was only thirty minutes away, he was awake when they arrived, apparently quite fresh, and asking for whisky. When they entered the mess he appeared quite sober, only blinking a little in the lighted room, in his raked cap and his awry-buttoned pea-jacket and a soiled silk muffler, embroidered with a club insignia which Bogard recognized to have come from a famous preparatory school, twisted about his throat.

"Ah," he said, his voice fresh, clear now, not blurred, quite cheerful, quite loud, so that the others in the room turned and looked at him. "Jolly. Whisky, what?" He went straight as a bird dog to the bar in the corner, the lieutenant following. Bogard had turned and gone on to the other end of the room, where five men sat about a card table.

"What's he admiral of?" one said.

"Of the whole Scotch navy, when I found him," Bogard said.

Another looked up. "Oh. I thought I'd seen him in town." He looked at the guest. "Maybe it's because he was on his feet that I didn't recognize him when he came in. You usually see them lying down in the gutter."

"Oh," the first said. He, too, looked around. "Is he one of those guys?"

"Sure. You've seen them. Sitting on the curb, you know, with a couple of limey M. P.'s hauling at their arms."

"Yes. I've seen them," the other said. They all looked at the English boy. He stood at the bar, talking, his voice loud, cheerful. "They all look like him too," the speaker said. "About seventeen or eighteen. They run those little boats that are always dashing in and out."

"Is that what they do?" a third said. "You mean, there's a male marine auxiliary to the Waacs? Good Lord, I sure made a mistake when I enlisted. But this war never was advertised right."

"I don't know," Bogard said. "I guess they do more than just ride around."

But they were not listening to him. They were looking at the guest. "They run by clock," the first said. "You can see the condition of one of them after sunset and almost tell what time it is. But what I don't see is, how a man that's in that shape at one o'clock every morning can even see a battleship the next day."

"Maybe when they have a message to send out to a ship," another said, "they just make duplicates and line the launches up and point them toward the ship and give each one a duplicate of the message and let them go. And the ones that miss the ship just cruise around the harbor until they hit a dock somewhere."

"It must be more than that," Bogard said.

He was about to say something else, but at that moment the guest turned from the bar and approached, carrying a glass. He walked steadily enough, but his color was high and his eyes were bright, and he was talking, loud, cheerful, as he came up.

"I say. Won't you chaps join ——" He ceased. He seemed to remark something; he was looking at their breasts. "Oh, I say. You fly. All of you. Oh, good gad! Find it jolly, eh?"

"Yes," somebody said. "Jolly."

"But dangerous, what?"

"A little faster than tennis," another said. The guest looked at him, bright, affable, intent.

Another said quickly, "Bogard says you command a vessel."

"Hardly a vessel. Thanks, though. And not command. Ronnie does that. Ranks me a bit. Age."

"Ronnie?"

"Yes. Nice. Good egg. Old, though. Stickler."

"Stickler?"

"Frightful. You'd not believe it. Whenever we sight smoke and I have the glass, he sheers away. Keeps the ship hull down all the while. No beaver then. Had me two down a fortnight yesterday."

The Americans glanced at one another. "No beaver?"

"We play it. With basket masts, you see. See a basket mast. Beaver! One up. The Ergenstrasse doesn't count any more, though."

The men about the table looked at one another. Bogard spoke. "I see. When you or Ronnie see a ship with basket masts, you get a beaver on the other. I see. What is the Ergenstrasse?"

"She's German. Interned. Tramp steamer. Foremast rigged so it looks something like a basket mast. Booms, cables, I dare say. I didn't think it looked very much like a basket mast, myself. But Ronnie said yes. Called it one day. Then one day they shifted her across the basin and I called her on Ronnie. So we decided to not count her any more. See now, eh?"

"Oh," the one who had made the tennis remark said, "I see. You and Ronnie run about in the launch, playing beaver. H'm'm. That's nice. Did you ever pl——"

"Jerry," Bogard said. The guest had not moved. He looked down at the speaker, still smiling, his eyes quite wide.

The speaker still looked at the guest. "Has yours and Ronnie's boat got a yellow stern?"

"A yellow stern?" the English boy said. He had quit smiling, but his face was still pleasant.

"I thought that maybe when the boats had two captains, they might paint the sterns yellow or something."

"Oh," the guest said. "Burt and Reeves aren't officers."

"Burt and Reeves," the other said, in a musing tone. "So they go too. Do they play beaver too?"

"Jerry," Bogard said. The other looked at him. Bogard jerked his head a little. "Come over here." The other rose. They went aside. "Lay off of him," Bogard said. "I mean it, now. He's just a kid. When you were that age, how much sense did you have? Just about enough to get to chapel on time."

"My country hadn't been at war going on four years, though," Jerry said. "Here we are, spending our money and getting shot at by the clock, and it's not even our fight, and these limeys that would have been goose-stepping twelve months now if it hadn't been ——"

"Shut it," Bogard said. "You sound like a Liberty Loan."

"—— taking it like it was a fair or something. 'Jolly.' " His voice was now falsetto, lilting. " 'But dangerous, what?' "

"Sh-h-h-h," Bogard said.

"I'd like to catch him and his Ronnie out in the harbor, just once. Any harbor. London's. I wouldn't want anything but a Jenny, either. Jenny? Hell, I'd take a bicycle and a pair of water wings! I'll show him some war."

"Well, you lay off him now. He'll be gone soon."

"What are you going to do with him?"

"I'm going to take him along this morning. Let him have Harper's place out front. He says he can handle a Lewis. Says they have one on the boat. Something he was telling me—about how he once shot out a channel-marker light at seven hundred yards."

"Well, that's your business. Maybe he can beat you."

"Beat me?"

"Playing beaver. And then you can take on Ronnie."

"I'll show him some war, anyway," Bogard said. He looked at the guest. "His people have been in it three years now, and he seems to take it like a sophomore in town for the big game." He looked at Jerry again. "But you lay off him now."

As they approached the table, the guest's voice was loud and cheerful: ". . . if he got the glasses first, he would go in close and look, but when I got them first, he'd sheer off where I couldn't see anything but the smoke. Frightful stickler. Frightful. But Ergenstrasse not counting any more. And if you make a mistake and call her, you lose two beaver from your score. If Ronnie were only to forget and call her we'd be even."

III

AT TWO O'CLOCK the English boy was still talking, his voice bright, innocent and cheerful. He was telling them how Switzerland had been spoiled by 1914, and instead of the vacation which his father had promised him for his sixteenth birthday, when that birthday came he and his tutor had had to do with Wales. But that he and the tutor had got pretty high and that he dared to say—with all due respect to any present who might have had the advantage of Switzerland, of course—that one could see probably as far from Wales as from Switzerland. "Perspire as much and breathe as hard, anyway," he added. And about him the Americans sat, a little hardbitten, a little sober, somewhat older, listening to him with a kind of cold astonishment. They had been getting up for some time now and going out and returning in flying clothes, carrying helmets and goggles. An orderly entered with a tray of coffee cups, and the guest realized that for some time now he had been hearing engines in the darkness outside.

At last Bogard rose. "Come along," he said. "We'll get your togs." When they emerged from the mess, the sound of the engines was quite loud —an idling thunder. In alignment along the invisible tarmac was a vague rank of short banks of flickering blue-green fire suspended apparently in mid-air. They crossed the aerodrome to Bogard's quarters, where the lieutenant, McGinnis, sat on a cot fastening his flying boots. Bogard reached down a Sidcott suit and threw it across the cot. "Put this on," he said.

"Will I need all this?" the guest said. "Shall we be gone that long?"

"Probably," Bogard said. "Better use it. Cold upstairs."

The guest picked up the suit. "I say," he said. "I say. Ronnie and I have a do ourselves, tomor —today. Do you think Ronnie won't mind if I am a bit late? Might not wait for me."

"We'll be back before teatime," McGinnis said. He seemed quite busy with his boot. "Promise you." The English boy looked at him.

"What time should you be back?" Bogard said.

"Oh, well," the English boy said, "I dare say it will be all right. They let Ronnie say when to go, anyway. He'll wait for me if I should be a bit late."

"He'll wait," Bogard said. "Get your suit on."

"Right," the other said. They helped him into the suit. "Never been up before," he said, chattily, pleasantly. "Dare say you can see farther than from mountains, eh?"

"See more, anyway," McGinnis said. "You'll like it."

"Oh, rather. If Ronnie only waits for me. Lark. But dangerous, isn't it?"

"Go on," McGinnis said. "You're kidding me."

"Shut your trap, Mac," Bogard said. "Come along. Want some more coffee?" He looked at the guest, but McGinnis answered:

"No. Got something better than coffee. Coffee makes such a confounded stain on the wings."

"On the wings?" the English boy said. "Why coffee on the wings?"

"Stow it, I said, Mac," Bogard said. "Come along."

They recrossed the aerodrome, approaching the muttering banks of flame. When they drew near, the guest began to discern the shape, the outlines, of the Handley-Page. It looked like a Pullman coach run upslanted aground into the skeleton of the first floor of an incomplete skyscraper. The guest looked at it quietly.

"It's larger than a cruiser," he said in his bright, interested voice. "I say, you know. This doesn't fly in one lump. You can't pull my leg. Seen them before. It comes in two parts: Captain Bogard and me in one; Mac and 'nother chap in other. What?"

"No," McGinnis said. Bogard had vanished. "It all goes up in one lump. Big lark, eh? Buzzard, what?"

"Buzzard?" the guest murmured. "Oh, I say. A cruiser. Flying. I say, now."

"And listen," McGinnis said. His hand came forth; something cold fumbled against the hand of the English boy—a bottle. "When you feel yourself getting sick, see? Take a pull at it."

"Oh, shall I get sick?"

"Sure. We all do. Part of flying. This will stop it. But if it doesn't. See?"

"What? Quite. What?"

"Not overside. Don't spew it overside."

"Not overside?"

"It'll blow back in Bogy's and my face. Can't see. Bingo. Finished. See?"

"Oh, quite. What shall I do with it?" Their voices were quiet, brief, grave as conspirators.

"Just duck your head and let her go."

"Oh, quite."

Bogard returned. "Show him how to get into the front pit, will you?" he said. McGinnis led the way through the trap. Forward, rising to the slant of the fuselage, the passage narrowed; a man would need to crawl.

"Crawl in there and keep going," McGinnis said.

"It looks like a dog kennel," the guest said.

"Doesn't it, though?" McGinnis agreed cheerfully. "Cut along with you." Stooping, he could hear the other scuttling forward. "You'll find a Lewis gun up there, like as not," he said into the tunnel.

The voice of the guest came back: "Found it."

"The gunnery sergeant will be along in a minute and show you if it is loaded."

"It's loaded," the guest said; almost on the heels of his words the gun fired, a brief staccato burst. There were shouts, the loudest from the ground beneath the nose of the aeroplane. "It's quite all right," the English boy's voice said. "I pointed it west before I let it off. Nothing back there but Marine office and your brigade headquarters. Ronnie and I always do this before we go anywhere. Sorry if I was too soon. Oh, by the way," he added, "my name's Claude. Don't think I mentioned it."

On the ground, Bogard and two other officers

stood. They had come up running. "Fired it west," one said. "How in hell does he know which way is west?"

"He's a sailor," the other said. "You forgot that."

"He seems to be a machine gunner too," Bogard said.

"Let's hope he doesn't forget that," the first said.

IV

NEVERTHELESS, Bogard kept an eye on the silhouetted head rising from the round gunpit in the nose ten feet ahead of him. "He did work that gun, though," he said to McGinnis beside him. "He even put the drum on himself, didn't he?"

"Yes," McGinnis said. "If he just doesn't forget and think that that gun is him and his tutor looking around from a Welsh alp."

"Maybe I should not have brought him," Bogard said. McGinnis didn't answer. Bogard jockeyed the wheel a little. Ahead, in the gunner's pit, the guest's head moved this way and that continuously, looking. "We'll get there and unload and haul air for home," Bogard said. "Maybe in the dark —— Confound it, it would be a shame for his country to be in this mess for four years and him not even to see a gun pointed in his direction."

"He'll see one tonight if he don't keep his head in," McGinnis said.

But the boy did not do that. Not even when they had reached the objective and McGinnis had crawled down to the bomb toggles. And even when the searchlights found them and Bogard signaled to the other machines and dived, the two engines snarling full speed into and through the bursting shells, he could see the boy's face in the searchlight's glare, leaned far overside, coming sharply out as a spotlighted face on a stage, with an expression upon it of childlike interest and delight. "But he's firing that Lewis," Bogard thought. "Straight too"; nosing the machine farther down, watching the pinpoint swing into the sights, his right hand lifted, waiting to drop into McGinnis' sight. He dropped his hand; above the noise of the engines he seemed to hear the click and whistle of the released bombs as the machine, freed of the weight, shot zooming in a long upward bounce that carried it for an instant out of the light. Then he was pretty busy for a time, coming into and through the shells again, shooting athwart another beam that caught and held long enough for him to see the English boy leaning far over the side, looking back and down past

the right wing, the undercarriage. "Maybe he's read about it somewhere," Bogard thought, turning, looking back to pick up the rest of the flight.

Then it was all over, the darkness cool and empty and peaceful and almost quiet, with only the steady sound of the engines. McGinnis climbed back into the office, and standing up in his seat, he fired the colored pistol this time and stood for a moment longer, looking backward toward where the searchlights still probed and sabered. He sat down again.

"O.K.," he said. "I counted all four of them. Let's haul air." Then he looked forward. "What's become of the King's Own? You didn't hang him onto a bomb release, did you?" Bogard looked. The forward pit was empty. It was in dim silhouette again now, against the stars, but there was nothing there now save the gun. "No," McGinnis said; "there he is. See? Leaning overside. Dammit, I told him not to spew it! There he comes back." The guest's head came into view again. But again it sank out of sight.

"He's coming back," Bogard said. "Stop him. Tell him we're going to have every squadron in the Hun Channel group on top of us in thirty minutes."

McGinnis swung himself down and stooped at the entrance to the passage. "Get back!" he shouted. The other was almost out; they squatted so, face to face like two dogs, shouting at one another above the noise of the still-unthrottled engines on either side of the fabric walls. The English boy's voice was thin and high.

"Bomb!" he shrieked.

"Yes," McGinnis shouted, "they were bombs! We gave them hell! Get back, I tell you! Have every Hun in France on us in ten minutes! Get back to your gun!"

Again the boy's voice came, high, faint above the noise: "Bomb! All right?"

"Yes! Yes! All right. Back to your gun, damn you!"

McGinnis climbed back into the office. "He went back. Want me to take her awhile?"

"All right," Bogard said. He passed McGinnis the wheel. "Ease her back some. I'd just as soon it was daylight when they come down on us."

"Right," McGinnis said. He moved the wheel suddenly. "What's the matter with that right wing?" he said. "Watch it. . . . See? I'm flying on the right aileron and a little rudder. Feel it."

Bogard took the wheel a moment. "I didn't notice that. Wire somewhere, I guess. I didn't think any of those shells were that close. Watch her, though."

"Right," McGinnis said. "And so you are going with him on his boat tomorrow—today."

"Yes. I promised him. Confound it, you can't hurt a kid, you know."

"Why don't you take Collier along, with his mandolin? Then you could sail around and sing."

"I promised him," Bogard said. "Get that wing up a little."

"Right," McGinnis said.

Thirty minutes later it was beginning to be dawn; the sky was gray. Presently McGinnis said: "Well, here they come. Look at them! They look like mosquitoes in September. I hope he don't get worked up now and think he's playing beaver. If he does he'll just be one down to Ronnie, provided the devil has a beard. . . . Want the wheel?"

<h3 style="text-align:center">V</h3>

AT EIGHT O'CLOCK the beach, the Channel, was beneath them. Throttled back, the machine drifted down as Bogard ruddered it gently into the Channel wind. His face was strained, a little tired.

McGinnis looked tired, too, and he needed a shave.

"What do you guess he is looking at now?" he said. For again the English boy was leaning over the right side of the cockpit, looking backward and downward past the right wing.

"I don't know," Bogard said. "Maybe bullet holes." He blasted the port engine. "Must have the riggers ——"

"He could see some closer than that," McGinnis said. "I'll swear I saw tracer going into his back at one time. Or maybe it's the ocean he's looking at. But he must have seen that when he came over from England." Then Bogard leveled off; the nose rose sharply, the sand, the curling tide edge fled alongside. Yet still the English boy hung far overside, looking backward and downward at something beneath the right wing, his face rapt, with utter and childlike interest. Until the machine was completely stopped he continued to do so. Then he ducked down, and in the abrupt silence of the engines they could hear him crawling in the passage. He emerged just as the two pilots climbed stiffly down from the office, his face bright, eager; his voice high, excited.

"Oh, I say! Oh, good gad! What a chap! What a judge of distance! If Ronnie could only have seen! Oh, good gad! Or maybe they aren't like ours—don't load themselves as soon as the air strikes them."

The Americans looked at him. "What don't what?" McGinnis said.

"The bomb. It was magnificent; I say, I shan't forget it. Oh, I say, you know! It was splendid!"

After a while McGinnis said, "The bomb?" in a fainting voice. Then the two pilots glared at each other; they said in unison: "That right

wing!" Then as one they clawed down through the trap and, with the guest at their heels, they ran around the machine and looked beneath the right wing. The bomb, suspended by its tail, hung straight down like a plumb bob beside the right wheel, its tip just touching the sand. And parallel with the wheel track was the long, delicate line in the sand where its ultimate tip had dragged. Behind them the English boy's voice was high, clear, childlike:

"Frightened, myself. Tried to tell you. But realized you knew your business better than I. Skill. Marvelous. Oh, I say, I shan't forget it."

<h3 style="text-align:center">VI</h3>

A MARINE with a bayoneted rifle passed Bogard onto the wharf and directed him to the boat. The wharf was empty, and he didn't even see the boat until he approached the edge of the wharf and looked directly down into it and upon the backs of two stooping men in greasy dungarees, who rose and glanced briefly at him and stooped again.

It was about thirty feet long and about three feet wide. It was painted with gray-green camouflage. It was quarter-decked forward, with two blunt, raked exhaust stacks. "Good Lord," Bogard thought, "if all that deck is engine ——" Just aft the deck was the control seat; he saw a big wheel, an instrument panel. Rising to a height of about a foot above the freeboard, and running from the stern forward to where the deck began, and continuing on across the after edge of the deck and thence back down the other gunwale to the stern, was a solid screen, also camouflaged, which inclosed the boat save for the width of the stern, which was open. Facing the steersman's seat like an eye was a hole in the screen about eight inches in diameter. And looking down into the long, narrow, still, vicious shape, he saw a machine gun swiveled at the stern, and he looked at the low screen—including which the whole vessel did not sit much more than a yard above water level—with its single empty forward-staring eye, and he thought quietly: "It's steel. It's made of steel." And his face was quite sober, quite thoughtful, and he drew his trench coat about him and buttoned it, as though he were getting cold.

He heard steps behind him and turned. But it was only an orderly from the aerodrome, accompanied by the marine with the rifle. The orderly was carrying a largish bundle wrapped in paper.

"From Lieutenant McGinnis, to the captain," the orderly said.

Bogard took the bundle. The orderly and the marine retreated. He opened the bundle. It contained some objects and a scrawled note. The objects were a new yellow silk sofa cushion and a Japanese parasol, obviously borrowed, and a comb and a few sheets of flimsy paper. The note said:

Couldn't find a camera anywhere and Collier wouldn't let me have his mandolin. But maybe Ronnie can play on the comb. MAC.

Bogard looked at the objects. But his face was still quite thoughtful, quite grave. He rewrapped the things and carried the bundle on up the wharf a way and dropped it quietly into the water.

As he returned toward the invisible boat he saw two men approaching. He recognized the boy at once—tall, slender, already talking, voluble, his head bent a little toward his shorter companion, who plodded along beside him, hands in pockets, smoking a pipe. The boy still wore the pea-coat beneath a flapping oilskin, but in place of the rakish and casual cap he now wore an infantryman's soiled Balaclava helmet, with, floating behind him as though upon the sound of his voice, a curtainlike piece of cloth almost as long as a burnous.

"Hullo, there!" he cried, still a hundred yards away.

But it was the second man that Bogard was watching, thinking to himself that he had never in his life seen a more curious figure. There was something stolid about the very shape of his hunched shoulders, his slightly downlooking face. He was a head shorter than the other. His face was ruddy, too, but its mold was of a profound gravity that was almost dour. It was the face of a man of twenty who has been for a year trying, even while asleep, to look twenty-one. He wore a high-necked sweater and dungaree slacks; above this a leather jacket; and above this a soiled naval officer's warmer that reached almost to his heels and which had one shoulder strap missing and not one remaining button at all. On his head was a plaid fore-and-aft deer stalker's cap, tied on by a narrow scarf brought across and down, hiding his ears, and then wrapped once about his throat and knotted with a hangman's noose beneath his left ear. It was unbelievably soiled, and with his hands elbow-deep in his pockets and his hunched shoulders and his bent head, he looked like someone's grandmother hung, say, for a witch. Clamped upside down between his teeth was a short brier pipe.

"Here he is!" the boy cried. "This is Ronnie. Captain Bogard."

"How are you?" Bogard said. He extended his hand. The other said no word, but his hand came forth, limp. It was quite cold, but it was hard, calloused. But he said no word; he just glanced briefly at Bogard and then away. But in that instant Bogard caught something in the look, something strange—a flicker; a kind of covert and curious respect, something like a boy of fifteen looking at a circus trapezist.

But he said no word. He ducked on; Bogard watched him drop from sight over the wharf edge as though he had jumped feet first into the sea. He remarked now that the engines in the invisible boat were running.

"We might get aboard too," the boy said. He started toward the boat, then he stopped. He touched Bogard's arm. "Yonder!" he hissed. "See?" His voice was thin with excitement.

"What?" Bogard also whispered; automatically he looked backward and upward, after old habit. The other was gripping his arm and pointing across the harbor.

"There! Over there. The Ergenstrasse. They have shifted her again." Across the harbor lay an ancient, rusting, sway-backed hulk. It was small and nondescript, and, remembering, Bogard saw that the foremast was a strange mess of cables and booms, resembling—allowing for a great deal of license or looseness of imagery—a basket mast. Beside him the boy was almost chortling. "Do you think that Ronnie noticed?" he hissed. "Do you?"

"I don't know," Bogard said.

"Oh, good gad! If he should glance up and call her before he notices, we'll be even. Oh, good gad! But come along." He went on; he was still chortling. "Careful," he said. "Frightful ladder."

He descended first, the two men in the boat rising and saluting. Ronnie had disappeared, save for his backside, which now filled a small hatch leading forward beneath the deck. Bogard descended gingerly.

"Good Lord," he said. "Do you have to climb up and down this every day?"

"Frightful, isn't it?" the other said, in his happy voice. "But you know yourself. Try to run a war with makeshifts, then wonder why it takes so long." The narrow hull slid and surged, even with Bogard's added weight. "Sits right on top, you see," the boy said. "Would float on a lawn, in a heavy dew. Goes right over them like a bit of paper."

"It does?" Bogard said.

"Oh, absolutely. That's why, you see." Bogard didn't see, but he was too busy letting himself gingerly down to a sitting posture. There were no thwarts; no seats save a long, thick, cylindrical ridge which ran along the bottom of the boat from the driver's seat to the stern. Ronnie had backed into sight. He now sat behind the wheel, bent over the instrument panel. But when he glanced back over his shoulder he did not speak. His face was merely interrogatory. Across his face there was now a long smudge of grease. The boy's face was empty, too, now.

"Right," he said. He looked forward, where one of the seamen had gone. "Ready forward?" he said.

"Aye, sir," the seaman said.

The other seaman was at the stern line. "Ready aft?"

"Aye, sir."

"Cast off." The boat sheered away, purring, a boiling of water under the stern. The boy looked down at Bogard. "Silly business. Do it shipshape, though. Can't tell when silly four-striper ——" His face changed again, immediate, solicitous. "I say. Will you be warm? I never thought to fetch ——"

"I'll be all right," Bogard said. But the other was already taking off his oilskin. "No, no," Bogard said. "I won't take it."

"You'll tell me if you get cold?"

"Yes. Sure." He was looking down at the cylinder on which he sat. It was a half cylinder— that is, like the hotwater tank to some Gargantuan stove, sliced down the middle and bolted, open side down, to the floor plates. It was twenty feet long and more than two feet thick. Its top rose as high as the gunwales and between it and the hull on either side was just room enough for a man to place his feet to walk.

"That's Muriel," the boy said.

"Muriel?"

"Yes. The one before that was Agatha. After my aunt. The first one Ronnie and I had was Alice in Wonderland. Ronnie and I were the White Rabbit. Jolly, eh?"

"Oh, you and Ronnie have had three, have you?"

"Oh, yes," the boy said. He leaned down. "He didn't notice," he whispered. His face was again bright, gleeful. "When we come back," he said. "You watch."

"Oh," Bogard said. "The Ergenstrasse." He looked astern, and then he thought: "Good Lord! We must be going—traveling." He looked out now, broadside, and saw the harbor line fleeing past, and he thought to himself that the boat was well-nigh moving at the speed at which the Handley-Page flew, left the ground. They were beginning to bound now, even in the sheltered water, from one wave crest to the next with a distinct shock. His hand still rested on the cylinder on which he sat. He looked down at it again, following it from where it seemed to emerge be-

neath Ronnie's seat, to where it beveled into the stern. "It's the air in here, I suppose," he said.

"The what?" the boy said.

"The air. Stored up in here. That makes the boat ride high."

"Oh, yes. I dare say. Very likely. I hadn't thought about it." He came forward, his burnous whipping in the wind, and sat down beside Bogard. Their heads were below the top of the screen.

Astern the harbor fled, diminishing, sinking into the sea. The boat had begun to lift now, swooping forward and down, shocking almost stationary for a moment, then lifting and swooping again; a gout of spray came aboard over the bows like a flung shovelful of shot. "I wish you'd take this coat," the boy said.

Bogard didn't answer. He looked around at the bright face. "We're outside, aren't we?" he said quietly.

"Yes. . . . Do take it, won't you?"

"Thanks, no. I'll be all right. We won't be long, anyway, I guess."

"No. We'll turn soon. It won't be so bad then."

"Yes. I'll be all right when we turn." Then they did turn. The motion became easier. That is, the boat didn't bang head-on, shuddering, into the swells. They came up beneath now, and the boat fled with increased speed, with a long, sickening, yawing motion, first to one side and then the other. But it fled on, and Bogard looked astern with that same soberness with which he had first looked down into the boat. "We're going east now," he said.

"With just a spot of north," the boy said. "Makes her ride a bit better, what?"

"Yes," Bogard said. Astern there was nothing now save empty sea and the delicate needlelike cant of the machine gun against the boiling and slewing wake, and the two seamen crouching quietly in the stern. "Yes. It's easier." Then he said: "How far do we go?"

The boy leaned closer. He moved closer. His voice was happy, confidential, proud, though lowered a little: "It's Ronnie's show. He thought of it. Not that I wouldn't have, in time. Gratitude and all that. But he's the older, you see. Thinks fast. Courtesy, *noblesse oblige*—all that. Thought of it soon as I told him this morning. I said, 'Oh, I say. I've been there. I've seen it'; and he said, 'Not flying'; and I said, 'Strewth'; and he said 'How far? No lying now'; and I said, 'Oh, far. Tremendous. Gone all night'; and he said, 'Flying all night. That must have been to Berlin'; and I said, 'I don't know. I dare say'; and he thought. I could see him thinking. Because he is the older, you see. More experience in courtesy, right thing. And he said, 'Berlin. No fun to that chap, dashing out and back with us.' And he thought and I waited, and I said, 'But we can't take him to Berlin. Too far. Don't know the way, either'; and he said—fast, like a shot—said, 'But there's Kiel'; and I knew ——"

"What?" Bogard said. Without moving, his whole body sprang. "Kiel? In this?"

"Absolutely. Ronnie thought of it. Smart, even if he is a stickler. Said at once, 'Zeebrugge no show at all for that chap. Must do best we can for him. Berlin,' Ronnie said. 'My gad! Berlin.' "

"Listen," Bogard said. He had turned now, facing the other, his face quite grave. "What is this boat for?"

"For?"

"What does it do?" Then, knowing beforehand the answer to his own question, he said, putting his hand on the cylinder: "What is this in here? A torpedo, isn't it?"

"I thought you knew," the boy said.

"No," Bogard said. "I didn't know." His voice seemed to reach him from a distance, dry, cricket-like: "How do you fire it?"

"Fire it?"

"How do you get it out of the boat? When that hatch was open a while ago I could see the engines. They were right in front of the end of this tube."

"Oh," the boy said. "You pull a gadget there and the torpedo drops out astern. As soon as the screw touches the water it begins to turn, and then the torpedo is ready, loaded. Then all you have to do is turn the boat quickly and the torpedo goes on."

"You mean ——" Bogard said. After a moment his voice obeyed him again. "You mean you aim the torpedo with the boat and release it and it starts moving, and you turn the boat out of the way and the torpedo passes through the same water that the boat just vacated?"

"Knew you'd catch on," the boy said. "Told Ronnie so. Airman. Tamer than yours, though. But can't be helped. Best we can do, just on water. But knew you'd catch on."

"Listen," Bogard said. His voice sounded to him quite calm. The boat fled on, yawing over the swells. He sat quite motionless. It seemed to him that he could hear himself talking to himself: "Go on. Ask him. Ask him what? Ask him how close to the ship do you have to be before you fire. . . . Listen," he said, in that calm voice. "Now, you tell Ronnie, you see. You just tell him—just say ——" He could feel his voice ratting off on him again, so he stopped it. He

sat quite motionless, waiting for it to come back; the boy leaning now, looking at his face. Again the boy's voice was solicitous:

"I say. You're not feeling well. These confounded shallow boats."

"It's not that," Bogard said. "I just —— Do your orders say Kiel?"

"Oh, no. They let Ronnie say. Just so we bring the boat back. This is for you. Gratitude. Ronnie's idea. Tame, after flying. But if you'd rather, eh?"

"Yes, some place closer. You see, I ——"

"Quite. I see. No vacations in wartime. I'll tell Ronnie." He went forward. Bogard did not move. The boat fled in long, slewing swoops. Bogard looked quietly astern, at the scudding sea, the sky.

"My God!" he thought. "Can you beat it? Can you beat it?"

The boy came back; Bogard turned to him a face the color of dirty paper. "All right now," the boy said. "Not Kiel. Nearer place, hunting probably just as good. Ronnie says he knows you will understand." He was tugging at his pocket. He brought out a bottle. "Here. Haven't forgot last night. Do the same for you. Good for the stomach, eh?"

Bogard drank, gulping—a big one. He extended the bottle, but the boy refused. "Never touch it on duty," he said. "Not like you chaps. Tame here."

The boat fled on. The sun was already down the west. But Bogard had lost all count of time, of distance. Ahead he could see white seas through the round eye opposite Ronnie's face, and Ronnie's hand on the wheel and the granite-like jut of his profiled jaw and the dead upside-down pipe. The boat fled on.

Then the boy leaned and touched his shoulder. He half rose. The boy was pointing. The sun was reddish; against it, outside them and about two miles away, a vessel—a trawler, it looked like—at anchor swung a tall mast.

"Lightship!" the boy shouted. "Theirs." Ahead Bogard could see a low, flat mole—the entrance to a harbor. "Channel!" the boy shouted. He swept his arm in both directions. "Mines!" His voice swept back on the wind. "Place filthy with them. All sides. Beneath us too. Lark, eh?"

VII

AGAINST THE MOLE a fair surf was beating. Running before the seas now, the boat seemed to leap from one roller to the next; in the intervals while the screw was in the air the engine seemed to be trying to tear itself out by the roots. But it did not slow; when it passed the end of the mole the boat seemed to be standing almost erect on its rudder, like a sailfish. The mole was a mile away. From the end of it little faint lights began to flicker like fireflies. The boy leaned. "Down," he said. "Machine guns. Might stop a stray."

"What do I do?" Bogard shouted. "What can I do?"

"Stout fellow! Give them hell, what? Knew you'd like it!"

Crouching, Bogard looked up at the boy, his face wild. "I can handle the machine gun!"

"No need," the boy shouted back. "Give them first innings. Sporting. Visitors, eh?" He was looking forward. "There she is. See?" They were in the harbor now, the basin opening before them. Anchored in the channel was a big freighter. Painted midships of the hull was a huge Argentine flag. "Must get back to stations!" the boy shouted down to him. Then at that moment Ronnie spoke for the first time. The boat was hurtling along now in smoother water. Its speed did not slacken and Ronnie did not turn his head when he spoke. He just swung his jutting jaw and the clamped cold pipe a little, and said from the side of his mouth a single word:

"Beaver."

The boy, stooped over what he had called his gadget, jerked up, his expression astonished and outraged. Bogard also looked forward and saw Ronnie's arm pointing to starboard. It was a light cruiser at anchor a mile away. She had basket masts, and as he looked a gun flashed from her after turret. "Oh, damn!" the boy cried. "Oh, you putt! Oh, confound you, Ronnie! Now I'm three down!" But he had already stooped again over his gadget, his face bright and empty and alert again; not sober; just calm, waiting. Again Bogard looked forward and felt the boat pivot on its rudder and head directly for the freighter at terrific speed, Ronnie now with one hand on the wheel and the other lifted and extended at the height of his head.

But it seemed to Bogard that the hand would never drop. He crouched, not sitting, watching with a kind of quiet horror the painted flag increase like a moving picture of a locomotive taken from between the rails. Again the gun crashed from the cruiser behind them, and the freighter fired point-blank at them from its poop. Bogard heard neither shot.

"Man, man!" he shouted. "For God's sake!"

Ronnie's hand dropped. Again the boat spun on its rudder. Bogard saw the bow rise, pivoting; he expected the hull to slam broadside on into the ship. But it didn't. It shot off on a long tangent. He was waiting for it to make a wide sweep,

heading seaward, putting the freighter astern, and he thought of the cruiser again. "Get a broadside, this time, once we clear the freighter," he thought. Then he remembered the freighter, the torpedo, and he looked back toward the freighter to watch the torpedo strike, and saw to his horror that the boat was now bearing down on the freighter again, in a skidding turn. Like a man in a dream, he watched himself rush down upon the ship and shoot past under her counter, still skidding, close enough to see the faces on her decks. "They missed and they are going to run down the torpedo and catch it and shoot it again," he thought idiotically.

So the boy had to touch his shoulder before he knew he was behind him. The boy's voice was quite calm: "Under Ronnie's seat there. A bit of a crank handle. If you'll just hand it to me ——"

He found the crank. He passed it back; he was thinking dreamily: "Mac would say they had a telephone on board." But he didn't look at once to see what the boy was doing with it, for in that still and peaceful horror he was watching Ronnie, the cold pipe rigid in his jaw, hurling the boat at top speed round and round the freighter, so near that he could see the rivets in the plates. Then he looked aft, his face wild, importunate, and he saw what the boy was doing with the crank. He had fitted it into what was obviously a small windlass low on one flank of the tube near the head. He glanced up and saw Bogard's face. "Didn't go that time!" he shouted cheerfully.

"Go?" Bogard shouted. "It didn't —— The torpedo ——"

The boy and one of the seamen were quite busy, stooping over the windlass and the tube. "No. Clumsy. Always happening. Should think clever chaps like engineers —— Happens, though. Draw her in and try her again."

"But the nose, the cap!" Bogard shouted. "It's still in the tube, isn't it? It's all right, isn't it?"

"Absolutely. But it's working now. Loaded. Screw's started turning. Get it back and drop it clear. If we should stop or slow up it would overtake us. Drive back into the tube. Bingo! What?"

Bogard was on his feet now, turned, braced to the terrific merry-go-round of the boat. High above them the freighter seemed to be spinning on her heel like a trick picture in the movies. "Let me have that winch!" he cried.

"Steady!" the boy said. "Mustn't draw her back too fast. Jam her into the head of the tube ourselves. Same bingo! Best let us. Every cobbler to his last, what?"

"Oh, quite," Bogard said. "Oh, absolutely." It was like someone else was using his mouth. He leaned, braced, his hands on the cold tube, beside the others. He was hot inside, but his outside was cold. He could feel all his flesh jerking with cold as he watched the blunt, grained hand of the seaman turning the windlass in short, easy, inch-long arcs, while at the head of the tube the boy bent, tapping the cylinder with a spanner, lightly, his head turned with listening, delicate and deliberate as a watchmaker. The boat rushed on in those furious, slewing turns. Bogard saw a long, drooping thread loop down from somebody's mouth, between his hands, and he found that the thread came from his own mouth.

He didn't hear the boy speak, nor notice when he stood up. He just felt the boat straighten out, flinging him to his knees beside the tube. The seaman had gone back to the stern and the boy stooped again over his gadget. Bogard knelt now, quite sick. He did not feel the boat when it swung again, nor hear the gun from the cruiser which had not dared to fire and the freighter which had not been able to fire, firing again. He did not feel anything at all when he saw the huge, painted flag directly ahead and increasing with locomotive speed, and Ronnie's lifted hand drop. But this time he knew that the torpedo was gone; in pivoting and spinning this time the whole boat seemed to leave the water; he saw the bow of the boat shoot skyward like the nose of a pursuit ship going into a wingover. Then his outraged stomach denied him. He saw neither the geyser nor heard the detonation as he sprawled over the tube. He felt only a hand grasp him by the slack of his coat, and the voice of one of the seamen: "Steady all, sir. I've got you."

VIII

A VOICE roused him, a hand. He was half sitting in the narrow starboard runway, half lying across the tube. He had been there for quite a while; quite a while ago he had felt someone spread a garment over him. But he had not raised his head. "I'm all right," he had said. "You keep it."

"Don't need it," the boy said. "Going home now."

"I'm sorry I ——" Bogard said.

"Quite. Confounded shallow boats. Turn any stomach until you get used to them. Ronnie and I both, at first. Each time. You wouldn't believe it. Believe human stomach hold so much. Here." It was the bottle. "Good drink. Take enormous one. Good for stomach."

Bogard drank. Soon he did feel better, warmer. When the hand touched him later, he found that he had been asleep.

It was the boy again. The pea-coat was too small for him; shrunken, perhaps. Below the cuffs his long, slender, girl's wrists were blue with cold.

Then Bogard realized what the garment was that had been laid over him. But before Bogard could speak, the boy leaned down, whispering; his face was gleeful: "He didn't notice!"

"What?"

"Ergenstrasse! He didn't notice that they had shifted her. Gad, I'd be just one down, then." He watched Bogard's face with bright, eager eyes. "Beaver, you know. I say. Feeling better, eh?"

"Yes," Bogard said, "I am."

"He didn't notice at all. Oh, gad! Oh, Jove!"

Bogard rose and sat on the tube. The entrance to the harbor was just ahead; the boat had slowed a little. It was just dusk. He said quietly: "Does this often happen?" The boy looked at him. Bogard touched the tube. "This. Failing to go out."

"Oh, yes. Why they put the windlass on them. That was later. Made first boat; whole thing blew up one day. So put on windlass."

"But it happens sometimes, even now? I mean, sometimes they blow up, even with the windlass?"

"Well, can't say, of course. Boats go out. Not come back. Possible. Not ever know, of course. Not heard of one captured yet, though. Possible. Not to us, though. Not yet."

"Yes," Bogard said. "Yes." They entered the harbor, the boat moving still fast, but throttled now and smooth, across the dusk-filled basin. Again the boy leaned down, his voice gleeful.

"Not a word, now!" he hissed. "Steady all!" He stood up; he raised his voice: "I say, Ronnie." Ronnie did not turn his head, but Bogard could tell that he was listening. "That Argentine ship was amusing, eh? In there. How do you suppose it got past us here? Might have stopped here as well. French would buy the wheat." He paused, diabolical—Machiavelli with the face of a strayed angel. "I say. How long has it been since we had a strange ship in here? Been months, eh?" Again he leaned, hissing. "Watch, now!" But Bogard could not see Ronnie's head move at all. "He's looking, though!" the boy whispered, breathed. And Ronnie was looking, though his head had not moved at all. Then there came into view, in silhouette against the dusk-filled sky, the vague, basketlike shape of the interned vessel's foremast. At once Ronnie's arm rose, pointing; again he spoke without turning his head, out of the side of his mouth, past the cold, clamped pipe, a single word:

"Beaver."

The boy moved like a released spring, like a heeled dog freed. "Oh, damn you!" he cried. "Oh, you putt! It's the Ergenstrasse! Oh, confound you! I'm just one down now!" He had stepped in one stride completely over Bogard, and he now leaned down over Ronnie. "What?" The boat was slowing in toward the wharf, the engine idle. "Aren't I, Ronnie? Just one down now?"

The boat drifted in; the seaman had again crawled forward onto the deck. Ronnie spoke for the third and last time. "Right," he said.

IX

"I WANT," Bogard said, "a case of Scotch. The best we've got. And fix it up good. It's to go to town. And I want a responsible man to deliver it." The responsible man came. "This is for a child," Bogard said, indicating the package. "You'll find him in the Street of the Twelve Hours, somewhere near the Café Twelve Hours. He'll be in the gutter. You'll know him. A child about six feet long. Any English M. P. will show him to you. If he is asleep, don't wake him. Just sit there and wait until he wakes up. Then give him this. Tell him it is from Captain Bogard."

X

ABOUT A MONTH LATER a copy of the *English Gazette* which had strayed onto an American aerodrome carried the following item in the casualty lists:

MISSING: Torpedo Boat XOOI. Ensigns R. Boyce Smith and L. C. W. Hope, R. N. R., Machinist's Mate Burt and Torpedo-man Reeves, Channel Fleet, Light Torpedo Division. Failed to return from coast patrol duty.

Shortly after that the American Air Service headquarters also issued a bulletin:

For extraordinary valor over and beyond the routine of duty, Captain H. S. Bogard, with his crew, composed of Second Lieutenant Darrel McGinnis and Aviation Gunners Watts and Harper, on a daylight raid and without scout protection, destroyed with bombs an ammunition depot several miles behind the enemy's lines. From here, beset by enemy aircraft in superior numbers, these men proceeded with what bombs remained to the enemy's corps headquarters at —— and partially demolished this château, and then returned safely without loss of a man.

And regarding which exploit, it might have added, had it failed and had Captain Bogard come out of it alive, he would have been immediately and thoroughly court-martialed.

Carrying his remaining two bombs, he had dived the Handley-Page at the château where the generals sat at lunch, until McGinnis, at the toggles below him, began to shout at him, before he ever signaled. He didn't signal until he could discern separately the slate tiles of the roof. Then his hand dropped and he zoomed, and he held the aeroplane so, in its wild snarl, his lips parted, his breath hissing, thinking: "God! God! If they were all there—all the generals, the admirals, the presidents and the kings—theirs, ours—all of them."

A VICTORY DANCE

by *Alfred Noyes*

THE BITTER DISILLUSIONMENT which followed World War I was summed up perfectly in Alfred Noyes' "A Victory Dance," to which the *Post* devoted an entire page in 1920. Later the poem was converted into a popular ballet in which fat profiteers whirled about the stage with their arms around laughing women, while the ghosts of dead soldiers tried wistfully to cut in—an idea suggested by M. L. Blumenthal's original illustrations in the *Post*. The author, who now lives on the Isle of Wight, presented the manuscript of "A Victory Dance" to the Library of Congress in 1940.

JUNE 19, 1920

The cymbals crash,
  And the dancers walk
With long silk stockings
  And arms of chalk,
Butterfly skirts,
  And white breasts bare,
And shadows of dead men
  Watching 'em there.

Shadows of dead men
  Stand by the wall,
Watching the fun
  Of the Victory Ball.
They do not reproach,
  Because they know,
If they're forgotten,
  It's better so.

Under the dancing
  Feet are the graves.
Dazzle and motley,
  In long bright waves,
Brushed by the palm fronds,
  Grapple and whirl
Ox-eyed matron
  And slim white girl.

Fat wet bodies
  Go waddling by,
Girded with satin,
  Though God knows why;
Gripped by satyrs
  In white and black,
With a fat wet hand
  On a fat wet back.

See, there is one child
  Fresh from school,
Learning the ropes
  As the old hands rule.

God, how that dead boy
  Gapes and grins
As the tom-toms bang
  And the shimmy begins!

"What did you think
  We should find," said a shade,
"When the last shot echoed
  And peace was made?"
"Christ," laughed the fleshless
  Jaws of his friend;
"I thought they'd be praying
  For worlds to mend;

"Making earth better,
  Or something silly,
Like whitewashing hell
  Or Picca-dam-dilly.
They've a sense of humor,
  These women of ours,
These exquisite lilies,
  These fresh young flowers!"

"Pish," said a statesman,
  Standing near,
"I'm glad they can busy
  Their thoughts elsewhere!
We mustn't reproach 'em.
  They're young, you see."
"Ah," said the dead men,
  "So were we!"

Victory! Victory!
  On with the dance!
Back to the jungle
  The new beasts prance!
God, how the dead men
  Grin by the wall,
Watching the fun
  Of the Victory Ball!

PERSHING AT THE FRONT

by Arthur Guiterman

No *Post* POEM except "A Victory Dance" has ever drawn so many requests for reprinting as Arthur Guiterman's "Pershing at the Front," which was written in quite a different spirit nine years after the war. The author was America's favorite craftsman of light verse for decades, but there was more than humor in many of his lines. When he died in 1943, the *Post* suggested that his epitaph might well be the following lines from his "Elegy in Any Churchyard"—

> We wrought in matter, dream and rime;
> And, like yourselves, who likewise doubt it,
> We lived and had a darned good time,
> For all our sighs and groans about it.

FEBRUARY 19, 1927

The General came in a new tin hat
To the shell-torn front where the war was at;
With a faithful Aide at his good right hand
He made his way toward No Man's Land,
And a tough Top Sergeant there they found,
And a Captain, too, to show them round.

Threading the ditch, their heads bent low,
Toward the lines of the watchful foe,
They came through the murk and the powder
    stench,
Till the Sergeant whispered, "Third-line trench!"
And the Captain whispered, "Third-line trench!"
And the Aide repeated, "Third-line trench!"
And Pershing answered—not in French—
"Yes, I see it. Third-line trench."

Again they marched with wary tread,
Following on where the Sergeant led,
Through the wet, and the muck as well,
Till they came to another parallel.
They halted there in the mud and drench,
And the Sergeant whispered, "Second-line
    trench!"
And the Captain whispered, "Second-line
    trench!"
And the Aide repeated, "Second-line trench!"
And Pershing nodded: "Second-line trench."

Yet on they went through mire like pitch,
Till they came to a fine and spacious ditch,
Well camouflaged from planes and Zeps,
Where soldiers stood on firing steps
And a Major sat on a wooden bench;
And the Sergeant whispered, "First-line trench!"
And the Captain whispered, "First-line trench!"
And the Aide repeated, "First-line trench!"
And Pershing whispered, "Yes. I see.
How far off is the enemy?"
And the faithful Aide he asked, asked he,
"How far off is the enemy?"
And the Captain breathed in a softer key,
"How far off is the enemy?"
The silence lay in heaps and piles
As the Sergeant whispered, "Just three miles."
And the Captain whispered, "Just three miles."
And the Aide repeated, "Just three miles."
"Just three miles!" the General swore,
"What in hell are we whispering for?"
And the faithful Aide the message bore,
"What in hell are we whispering for?"
And the Captain said in a gentle roar,
"What in hell are we whispering for?"
"Whispering for?" the echo rolled;
And the Sergeant whispered, "I have a cold."

"SPEAKING OF OPERATIONS—"

by *Irvin S. Cobb*

"SPEAKING OF OPERATIONS" is probably the most famous piece of straight humor that any magazine ever printed. In the piece itself Cobb did not say why he had to have the operation; that might have spoiled the effect. While following the German army in France in 1914 he had seen trainload after trainload of wounded arrive at the railroad yards in Maubeuge; the orderlies who carried them to a nearby hospital collapsed from fatigue, and Cobb and other war correspondents pitched in to help. While lifting the wounded Cobb suffered a minor hernia. The operation was performed in April 1915 and soon afterward editor Lorimer wrote the sufferer as follows: "Dear Cobb: When your wife's letter reached me today, saying that you were to be put on a diet, I had just finished dictating a note to Delmonico's, asking them to send you a case of Pol Roger, '98, two bottles of crusty old port, and to see that you were served every day with a double porterhouse covered with mushrooms. Of course, I shall have to cancel the order now and substitute White Rock and one of Mrs. Lorimer's dog biscuits. . . ."

NOVEMBER 6, 1915

NOW THAT the last belated bill for services professionally rendered has been properly paid and properly receipted; now that the memory of the event, like the mark of the stitches, has faded out from a vivid red to a becoming pink shade; now that I pass a display of adhesive tape in a drug-store window without flinching—I sit me down to write a little piece about a certain matter—a small thing, but mine own—to wit, That Operation.

For years I have noticed that persons who underwent pruning or remodeling at the hands of a duly qualified surgeon, and survived, liked to talk about it afterward. In the event of their not surviving I have no doubt they still liked to talk about it, but in a different locality. Of all the readily available topics for use, whether among friends or among strangers, an operation seems to be the handiest and the most dependable. It beats the weather, or Roosevelt, or Bryan, or when this war is going to end, if ever, if you are a man talking to other men; and it is more exciting even than the question of how Mrs. Vernon Castle will wear her hair this winter, if you are a woman talking to other women. Wherever two or more are gathered together it is reasonably certain that somebody will bring up an operation.

Until I passed through the experience myself, however, I never really realized what a precious conversational boon the subject is, and how great a part it plays in our intercourse with our fellow beings on this planet. To the teller it is enormously interesting, for he is not only the hero of the tale but the rest of the cast and the stage setting as well—the whole show, as they say; and if the listener has had a similar experience—and who is there among us in these days that has not taken a nap 'neath the shade of the old ether cone?—it acquires a doubled value.

"Speaking of operations ——" you say, just like that, even though nobody present has spoken of them; and then you are off, with your new acquaintance sitting on the edge of his chair, or hers as the case may be and so frequently is, with hands clutched in polite but painful restraint, gills working up and down with impatience, eyes brightened with desire, tongue hung in the middle, waiting for you to pause to catch your breath, so that he or she may break in with a few personal recollections along the same line. From a mere conversation it resolves itself into a symptom symposium, and a perfectly splendid time is had by all.

If an operation is such a good thing to talk about, why isn't it a good thing to write about too? That is what I wish to know. Besides, I need the money. Verily, one always needs the money when one has but recently escaped from the ministering clutches of the modern hospital. Therefore I write.

It all dates back to the fair, bright morning when I went to call on a prominent practitioner here in New York, whom I shall denominate as Doctor X. I had a pain. I had had it for days. It was not a dependable, locatable pain, such as a tummyache or a toothache is, which you can put your hand on; but an indefinite, unsettled, undecided kind of pain, which went wandering about from place to place inside of me like a strange ghost lost in Cudjo's Cave. I never knew

219

until then what the personal sensations of a haunted house are. If only the measly thing could have made up its mind to settle down somewhere and start housekeeping I think I should have been better satisfied. I never had such an uneasy tenant. Alongside of it a woman with the moving fever would be comparatively a fixed and stationary object.

Having always, therefore, enjoyed perfectly riotous and absolutely unbridled health, never feeling weak and distressed unless dinner happened to be ten or fifteen minutes late, I was green regarding physicians and the ways of physicians. But I knew Doctor X slightly, having met him last summer in one of his hours of ease in the grand stand at a ball game, when he was expressing a desire to cut the umpire's throat from ear to ear, free of charge; and I remembered his name, and remembered, too, that he had impressed me at the time as being a person of character and decision and scholarly attainments.

He wore whiskers. Somehow in my mind whiskers are ever associated with medical skill. I presume this is a heritage of my youth, though I believe others labor under the same impression. As I look back it seems to me that in childhood's days all the doctors in our town wore whiskers. I recall one old doctor down there in Kentucky who was practically lurking in ambush all the time. All he needed was a few decoys out in front of him and a pump gun to be a duck blind. He carried his calomel about with him in a fruit jar, and when there was a cutting job he stropped his scalpel on his bootleg.

You see, in those primitive times germs had not been invented yet, and so he did not have to take any steps to avoid them. Now we know that loose, luxuriant whiskers are insanitary, because they make such fine winter quarters for germs; so, though the doctors still wear whiskers, they do not wear them wild and waving. In the profession bosky whiskers are taboo; they must be landscaped. And since it is a recognized fact that germs abhor orderliness and straight lines, they now go elsewhere to reside, and the doctor may still retain his traditional aspect and yet be practically germproof. Doctor X was trimmed up in accordance with the ethics of the newer school. He had trellis whiskers. So I went to see him at his offices in a fashionable district, on an expensive side street.

Before reaching him I passed through the hands of a maid and a nurse, each of whom spoke to me in a low, sorrowful tone of voice, which seemed to indicate that there was very little hope. I reached an inner room where Doctor X was. He looked me over, while I described for him as best I could what seemed to be the matter with me, and asked me a number of intimate questions touching on the lives, works, characters and peculiarities of my ancestors; after which he made me stand up in front of him and take my coat off, and he punched me hither and yon with his forefinger. He also knocked repeatedly on my breastbone with his knuckles, and each time, on doing this, would apply his ear to my chest and listen intently for a spell, afterward shaking his head in a disappointed way. Apparently there was nobody at home. For quite a time he kept on knocking, but without getting any response.

He then took my temperature and fifteen dollars, and said it was an interesting case—not unusual exactly, but interesting—and that it called for an operation.

From the way my heart and other organs jumped inside of me at that statement I knew at once that, no matter what he may have thought, the premises were not unoccupied. Naturally I inquired how soon he meant to operate. Personally I trusted there was no hurry about it. I was perfectly willing to wait for several years if necessary. He smiled at my ignorance.

"I never operate," he said; "operating is entirely out of my line. I am a diagnostician."

He was too—I give him full credit for that. He was a good, keen, close diagnostician. How did he know I had only fifteen dollars on me? You did not have to tell this man what you had, or how much. He knew without being told.

I asked whether he was acquainted with Doctor Y—Y being a person whom I had met casually at a club to which I belong. Oh, yes, he said, he knew Doctor Y. Y was a clever man, X said— very, very clever; but Y specialized in the eyes, the ears, the nose and the throat. I gathered from what Doctor X said that any time Doctor Y ventured below the thorax he was out of bounds and liable to be penalized; and that if by any chance he strayed down as far as the lungs he would call for help and back out as rapidly as possible.

This was news to me. It would appear that these up-to-date practitioners just go ahead and divide you up and partition you out among themselves without saying anything to you about it. Your torso belongs to one man and your legs are the exclusive property of his brother practitioner down on the next block, and so on. You may belong to as many as half a dozen specialists, most of whom, very possibly, are total strangers to you, and yet never know a thing about it yourself.

It has rather the air of trespass—nay, more than that, it bears some of the aspects of unlawful entry—but I suppose it is legal. Certainly, judging by what I am able to learn, the system is being carried on generally. So it must be ethical. Anything doctors do in a mass is ethical. Almost anything they do singly and on individual responsibility is unethical. Being ethical among doctors is practically the same thing as being a Democrat in Texas or a Presbyterian in Scotland.

"Y will never do for you," said Doctor X, when I had rallied somewhat from the shock of these disclosures. "I would suggest that you go to Doctor Z, at such-and-such an address. You are exactly in Z's line. I'll let him know that you are coming and when, and I'll send him down my diagnosis."

So that same afternoon, the appointment having been made by telephone, I went, full of quavery emotions, to Doctor Z's place. As soon as I was inside his outer hallway I realized that I was nearing the presence of one highly distinguished in his profession. A pussy-footed male attendant, in a livery that made him look like a cross between a headwaiter and an undertaker's assistant, escorted me through an anteroom into a reception room, where a considerable number of well-dressed men and women were sitting about in strained attitudes, pretending to read magazines while they waited their turns, but in reality furtively watching one another.

I sat down in a vacant chair, holding fast to my hat and my umbrella. They were the only friends I had there and I was determined not to lose them without a struggle. On the wall were many colored charts showing various portions of the human anatomy and what ailed them. Directly in front of me was a very thrilling illustration, evidently copied from an oil painting, of a liver in a bad state of repair. I said to myself that if I had a liver like that one I should keep it hidden from the public eye—I would never permit it to sit for its portrait. Still, there is no accounting for tastes. I know a man who got his spleen back from the doctors and now keeps it in a bottle of alcohol on the what-not in the parlor, as one of his most treasured possessions, and sometimes shows it to visitors. He, however, is of a very saving disposition.

Presently a lady secretary, who sat behind a roll-top desk in a corner of the room, lifted a forefinger and silently beckoned me to her side. I moved over and sat down by her; she took down my name and my age and my weight and my height, and a number of other interesting facts that will come in very handy should anyone ever be moved to write a complete history of my early life. In common with Doctor X she shared one attribute—she manifested a deep curiosity regarding my forefathers—wanted to know all about them. I felt that this was carrying the thing too far. I felt like saying to her:

"Miss or madam, so far as I know there is nothing the matter with my ancestors of the second and third generations back, except that they are dead. I am not here to seek medical assistance for a grandparent who succumbed to disappointment that time when Samuel J. Tilden got counted out, or for a great-grandparent who entered into Eternal Rest very unexpectedly and in a manner entirely uncalled for as a result of being an innocent bystander in one of those feuds that were so popular in my native state immediately following the Mexican War. Leave my ancestors alone. There is no need of your shaking my family tree in the belief that a few overripe patients will fall out. I alone—I, me, myself—am the present candidate!"

However, I refrained from making this protest audibly. I judged she was only going according to the ritual; and as she had a printed card, with blanks in it ready to be filled out with details regarding the remote members of the family connection, I humored her along. When I could not remember something she wished to know concerning an ancestor I supplied her with thrilling details culled from the field of fancy. When the card was entirely filled up she sent me back to my old place to wait. I waited and waited, breeding fresh ailments all the time. I had started out with one symptom; now if I had one I had a million and a half. I could feel goose flesh sprouting out all over me. If I had been taller I might have had more, but not otherwise. Such is the power of the human imagination when the surroundings are favorable to its development.

Time passed; to me it appeared that nearly all the time there was passed and that we were getting along toward the shank-end of the Christian era mighty fast. I was afraid my turn would come next and afraid it would not. Perhaps you know this sensation. You get it at the dentist's, and when you are on the list of after-dinner speakers at a large banquet, and when you are waiting for the father of the Only Girl in the World to make up his mind whether he is willing to try to endure you as a son-in-law.

Then some more time passed. One by one my companions, obeying a command, passed out through the door at the back, vanishing out of my life forever. None of them returned. I was vaguely wondering whether Doctor Z buried his dead on the premises or had them removed by a secret passageway in the rear, when a young woman in a nurse's costume tapped me on the shoulder from behind.

As I jumped she hid a compassionate smile with her hand and told me that the doctor would see me now.

As I rose to follow her—still clinging with the drowning man's grip of desperation to my hat and my umbrella—I was astonished to note by a glance at the calendar on the wall that this was still the present date. I thought it would be Thursday of next week at the very least.

Doctor Z also wore whiskers, carefully pointed up by an expert hedge trimmer. He sat at his desk, surrounded by freewill offerings from grateful patients and by glass cases containing other things he had taken away from them when they were not in a condition to object. I had expected, after all the preliminary ceremonies and delays, that we should have a long séance together. Not so; not at all. The modern expert in surgery charges as much for remembering your name between visits as the family doctor used to expect for staying up all night with you, but he does not waste any time when you are in his presence.

I was about to find that out. And a little later on I was to find out a lot of other things; in fact, that whole week was of immense educational value to me.

I presume it was because he stood so high in his profession, and was almost constantly engaged in breaking into members of the first families, that Doctor Z did not appear to be the least bit excited over my having picked him out to look into me. In the most perfunctory manner he shook the hand that has shaken the hands of Jess Willard, George M. Cohan and Henry Ford, and bade me be seated in a chair which was drawn up in a strong light, where he might gaze directly at me as we conversed and so get the full values of the composition. But if I was a treat for him to look at he concealed his emotions very effectually.

From this point on everything passed off in a most businesslike manner. He reached into a filing cabinet and took out an exhibit, which I recognized as the same one his secretary had filled out in the early part of the century. So I was already in the card-index class. Then briefly he looked over the manifest that Doctor X had sent him. It may not have been a manifest—it may have been an invoice or a bill of lading. Anyhow, I was in the assignee's hands. I could only hope it would not eventually become necessary to call in a receiver. Then he spoke:

"Yes, yes-yes," he said; "yes-yes-yes! Operation required. Small matter—hum, hum! Let's see —this is Tuesday? Quite so. Do it Friday! Friday at—" he glanced toward a scribbled pad of engagement dates at his elbow—"Friday at seven A.M. No; make it seven-fifteen. Have important tumor case at seven. St. Germicide's Hospital. You know the place?—up on Umpty-umph Street. Go' day! Miss Whoziz, call next visitor."

And before I realized that practically the whole affair had been settled I was outside the consultation room in a small private hall, and the secretary was telling me further details would be conveyed to me by mail. I went home in a dazed state. For the first time I was beginning to learn something about an industry in which heretofore I had never been interested. Especially was I struck by the difference now revealed to me in the preliminary stages of the surgeons' business as compared with their fellow experts in the allied cutting trades—tailors, for instance, not to mention barbers. Every barber, you know, used to be a surgeon, only he spelled it chirurgeon. Since then the two professions have drifted far apart. Even a half-witted barber—the kind who always has the first chair as you come into the shop—can easily spend ten minutes of your time thinking of things he thinks you should have and mentioning them to you one by one, whereas any good, live surgeon knows what you have almost instantly.

As for the tailor—consider how wearisome are his methods when you parallel them alongside the tremendous advances in this direction made by the surgeon—how cumbersome and old-fashioned and tedious! Why, an experienced surgeon has you all apart in half the time the tailor takes up in deciding whether the vest shall fasten with five buttons or six. Our own domestic tailors are bad enough in this regard and the Old World tailors are even worse.

I remember a German tailor in Aix-la-Chapelle last year who undertook to build for me a suit suitable for visiting the battle lines informally. He was the most literary tailor I ever met anywhere. He would drape the material over my person and then take a piece of chalk and write quite a nice long piece on me. Then he would rub it out and write it all over again, but more fully. He kept this up at intervals of every other day until he had writer's cramp. After that he used pins. He would pin the seams together, uttering little soothing, clucking sounds in German whenever a pin went through the goods and into me. The German cluck is not so soothing as the cluck of the English-speaking peoples, I find.

At the end of two long and trying weeks, which wore both of us down noticeably, he had the job done. It was not an unqualified success. He regarded it as a suit of clothes, but I knew better: it was a set of slip covers, and if only I had been a two-seated runabout it would have proved a perfect fit, I am sure; but I am a single-seated design and it did not answer. I wore it to the war because I had nothing else to wear that would stamp me as a regular war correspondent, except of course, my wrist watch; but I shall not wear it to another war. War is terrible enough already; and, besides, I have parted with it. On my way home through Holland I gave that suit to a couple of poor Belgian refugees, and I presume they are still wearing it.

So far as I have been able to observe, the surgeons and the tailors of these times share but one common instinct: If you go to a new surgeon or to a new tailor he is morally certain, after looking you over, that the last surgeon you had, or the last tailor, did not do your cutting properly. There, however, is where the resemblance ends. The tailor, as I remarked in effect just now, wants an hour at least in which to decide how he may best cover up and disguise the irregularities of the human form; in much less time than that the surgeon has completely altered the form itself.

With the surgeon it is very much as it is with those learned men who write those large, impressive works of reference which should be permanently in every library, and which we are forever buying from an agent because we are so passionately addicted to weekly payments. If the thing he seeks does not appear in the contents proper he knows exactly where to look for it. "See appendix," says the historian to you in a footnote. "See appendix," says the surgeon to himself, the while humming a cheery refrain. And so he does.

Well, I went home. This was Tuesday and the operation was not to be performed until the coming Friday. By Wednesday I had calmed down considerably. By Thursday morning I was practically normal again as regards my nerves. You will understand that I was still in a state of blissful ignorance concerning the actual methods of the surgical profession as exemplified by its leading exponents of to-day. The knowledge I have touched on in the paragraphs immediately preceding was to come to me later.

Likewise Doctor Z's manner had deceived me. It could not be that he meant to carve me to any really noticeable extent—his attitude had been entirely too casual. At our house carving is a very serious matter. Any time I take the head of the table and start in to carve it is fitting to remove the women and children to a place of safety, and bystanders should get under the table. When we first started housekeeping and gave our first small dinner party we had a brace of ducks cooked in honor of the company, and, I, as host, undertook to carve them. I never knew until then that a duck was inclosed in a burglarproof case. Without the use of dynamite the Red Leary-O'Brien gang could not have broken into those ducks. I thought so then and I think so yet. Years have passed since then, but I may state that even now, when there are guests in for dinner, we do not have ducks. Unless somebody else is going to carve, we have liver.

I mention this fact in passing because it shows that I had learned to revere carving as one of the higher arts, and one not to be approached except in a spirit of due appreciation of the magnitude of the undertaking, and after proper consideration and thought and reflection, and all that sort of thing. If this were true as regards a mere duck, why not all the more so as regards the carving of a person of whom I am so very fond as I am of myself? Thus I reasoned. And finally, had not Doctor Z spoken of the coming operation as a small matter? Well, then?

Thursday at noon I received from Doctor Z's secretary a note stating that arrangements had been made for my admission into St. Germicide that same evening and that I was to spend the night there. This hardly seemed necessary. Still, the tone of the note seemed to indicate that the hospital authorities particularly wished to have me for an overnight guest; and as I reflected that probably the poor things had few enough bright spots in their busy lives, I decided I would humor them along and gladden the occasion with my presence from dinnertime on.

About eight o'clock I strolled in very jauntily. In my mind I had the whole program mapped out. I would stay at the hospital for, say, two days following the operation—or, at most, three. Then I must be up and away. I had a good deal of work to do and a number of people to see on important business, and I could not really afford to waste more than a week-end on the staff of St. Germicide's. After Monday they must look to their own devices for social entertainment. That was my idea. Now when I look back on it I laugh, but it is a hollow laugh and there is no real merriment in it.

Indeed, almost from the moment of my entrance little things began to come up that were calculated to have a depressing effect on one's spirits. Downstairs a serious-looking lady met me and entered in a book a number of salient facts regarding my personality which the previous investigators had somehow overlooked. There is a lot of bookkeeping about an operation. This detail attended to, a young man, dressed in white garments and wearing an expression that stamped him as one who had suffered a recent deep bereavement, came and relieved me of my hand bag and escorted me upstairs.

As we passed through the upper corridors I

had my first introduction to the hospital smell, which is a smell compounded of iodoform, ether, gruel, and something boiling. All hospitals have it, I understand. In time you get used to it, but you never really care for it. The young man let me into a small room tastefully decorated with four walls, a floor, a ceiling, a window sill and a window, a door and a doorsill, and a bed and a chair. He told me to go to bed. I did not want to go to bed—it was not my regular bedtime—but he made a point of it, and I judged it was according to regulations; so I undressed and put on my night clothes and crawled in. He left me, taking my other clothes and my shoes with him; but I was not allowed to get lonely.

A little later a ward surgeon appeared, to put a few inquiries of a pointed and personal nature. He particularly desired to know what my trouble was. I explained to him that I couldn't tell him—he would have to see Doctor X or Doctor Z; they probably knew, but were keeping it a secret between themselves.

The answer apparently satisfied him, because immediately after that he made me sign a paper in which I assumed all responsibility for what was to take place the next morning.

This did not seem exactly fair. As I pointed out to him, it was the surgeon's affair, not mine; and if the surgeon made a mistake the joke would be on him and not on me, because in that case I would not be here anyhow. But I signed, as requested, on the dotted line, and he departed. After that, at intervals, the chief house surgeon dropped in, without knocking, and the head nurse came, and an interne or so, and a ward nurse, and the special nurse who was to have direct charge of me. It dawned on me that I was not having any more privacy in that hospital than a goldfish.

About eleven o'clock an orderly came; and, without consulting my wishes in the matter, he undressed me until I could have passed almost anywhere for September Morn's father, and gave me a clean shave, twice over, on one of my most prominent plane surfaces. I must confess I enjoyed that part of it. So far as I am able to recall, it was the only shave I have ever had where the operator did not spray me with cheap perfumery afterward and then try to sell me a bottle of hair tonic. Having shaved me, the young man did me up amidships in a neat cloth parcel, took his kit under his arm and went away.

It occurred to me that, considering the trivial nature of the case, a good deal of fuss was being made over me by persons who could have no personal concern in the matter whatsoever. This thought recurred to me frequently as I lay there, all tied in a bundle like a week's washing. I did not feel quite so uppish as I had felt. Why was everybody picking on me?

Anon I slept, but dreamed fitfully. I dreamed that a whole flock of surgeons came to my bedside and charted me out in sections, like one of those diagram pictures you see of a beef in the Handy Compendium of Universal Knowledge, showing the various cuts and the butcher's pet name for each cut. Each man took his favorite joint and carried it away, and when they were all gone I was merely a recent site, full of reverberating echoes and nothing else. I have had happier dreams in my time; this was not the kind of dream I should have selected had the choice been left to me.

When I woke the young sun was shining in at the window, and an orderly—not the orderly who had shaved me, but another one—was there in my room and my nurse was waiting outside the door. The orderly dressed me in a quaint suit of pyjamas cut on the half shell and buttoning stylishly in the back, *princesse mode*. Then he rolled in a flat litter on wheels and stretched me on it, and covered me up with a white tablecloth, just as though I had been cold Sunday-night supper, and we started for the operating room at the top of the building; but before we started I lit a large black cigar, as Gen. U. S. Grant used to do when he went into battle. I wished by this to show how indifferent I was. Maybe he fooled somebody, but I do not believe I possess the same powers of simulation that Grant had. He must have been a very remarkable man—Grant must.

The orderly and the nurse trundled me out into the hall and loaded me into an elevator, which was to carry us up to the top of the hospital. Several other nurses were already in the elevator. As we came aboard one of them remarked that it was a fine day. A fine day for what? She did not finish the sentence. Everybody wore a serious look. Inside of myself I felt pretty serious too—serious enough for ten or twelve. I had meant to fling off several very bright, spontaneous quips on the way to the table. I thought them out in advance, but now, somehow, none of them seemed appropriate. Instinctively, as it were, I felt that humor was out of place here.

I never knew an elevator to progress from the third floor of a building to the ninth with such celerity as this one on which we were traveling progressed. Personally I was in no mood for haste. If there was anyone else in all that great hospital who was in a particular hurry to be operated on I was perfectly willing to wait. But alas, no! The mechanism of the elevator was in perfect order—entirely too perfect. No accident of any character whatsoever befell us en route, no dropping back into the basement with a low, grateful thud; no hitch; no delay of any kind. We were certainly out of luck that trip. The demon of a joyrider who operated the accursed device jerked a lever and up we soared at a distressingly high rate of speed. If I could have had my way about that youth he would have been arrested for speeding.

Now we were there! They rolled me into a large room, all white, with a rounded ceiling like the inside of an egg. Right away I knew what the feelings of a poor, lonely little yolk are when the spoon begins to chip the shell. If I had not been so busy feeling sorry for myself I think I might have developed quite an active sympathy for yolks.

My impression had been that this was to be in the nature of a private affair, without invitations. I was astonished to note that quite a crowd had assembled for the opening exercises. From his attire and general deportment I judged that Doctor Z was going to be the master of the revels, he being attired appropriately in a white domino, with rubber gloves and a fancy cap of crash toweling. There were present, also, my diagnostic friend, Doctor X, likewise in fancy-dress costume, and a surgeon I had never met. From what I could gather he was going over the course behind Doctor Z to replace the divots. And there was an interne in the background, playing caddy, as it were, and a head nurse, who was going to keep the score, and two other nurses, who were going to help her keep it. I only hoped that they would show no partiality, but be as fair to me as they were to Doctor Z, and that he would go round in par.

So they placed me right where my eyes might rest on a large wall cabinet full of very shiny-looking tools; and they took my cigar away from me and folded my hands on the wide bowknot of my sash. Then they put a cloth dingus over my face and a voice of authority told me to breathe. That advice, however, was superfluous and might just as well have been omitted, for such was my purpose anyhow. Ever since I can recall anything at all, breathing has been a regular habit with me. So I breathed. And, at that, a bottle of highly charged sarsaparilla exploded somewhere in the immediate vicinity and most of its contents went up my nose.

I started to tell them that somebody had been fooling with their ether and adulterating it, and that if they thought they could send me off to sleep with soda pop they were making the mistake of their lives, because it just naturally could not be done; but for some reason or other I decided to put off speaking about the matter for a few minutes. I breathed again—again—agai——

I was going away from there. I was in a large gas balloon, soaring up into the clouds. How pleasant! . . . No, by Jove! I was not in a balloon—I myself was the balloon, which was not quite so pleasant. Besides, Doctor Z was going along as a passenger; and as we traveled up and up he kept jabbing me with the ferrule of a large umbrella which he had brought along with him in case of rain. He jabbed me harder and harder. I remonstrated with him. I told him I was a bit tender in that locality and the ferrule of his umbrella was sharp. He would not listen. He kept on jabbing me. . . .

Something broke! We started back down to earth. We fell faster and faster. We fell nine miles, and after that I began to get used to it. Then I saw the earth beneath and it was rising up to meet us. A town was below—a town that grew larger and larger as we neared it. I could make out the bonded indebtedness, and the Carnegie Library, and the moving-picture palaces, and the new dancing parlor, and other principal points of interest. At the rate we were falling we were certainly going to make an awful splatter in that town when we hit. I was sorry for the street-cleaning department.

We fell another half mile or so. A spire was sticking up into the sky directly beneath us, like a spear, to impale us. By a supreme effort I twisted out of the way of that spire, only to strike squarely on top of the roof of a greenhouse back of the parsonage, next door. We crashed through it with a perfectly terrific clatter of breaking glass and landed in a bed of white flowers, all soft and downy like feathers.

And then Doctor Z stood up and combed the débris out of his whiskers and remarked that, taking it by and large, it had been one of the pleasantest little outings he had enjoyed in the entire course of his practice. He said that as a patient I was fair, but as a balloon I was immense. He asked me whether I had seen anything of his umbrella and began looking round for it. I tried to help him look, but I was too tired to exert myself much. I told him I believed I would take a little nap.

I opened a dizzy eye part way. So this was heaven—this white expanse that swung and swam before my languid gaze? No, it could not be—it did not smell like heaven. It smelled like a hospital. It was a hospital. It was my hospital. My nurse was bending over me and I caught a faint whiff of the starch in the front of her crisp blue blouse. She was two-headed for the moment, but that was a mere detail. She settled a pillow under my head and told me to lie quiet.

I meant to lie quiet; I did not have to be told. I wanted to lie quiet and hurt. I was hurty from head to toe and back again, and crosswise and cater-cornered. I hurt diagonally and lengthwise and on the bias. I had a taste in my mouth like a bird-and-animal store. And empty! It seemed to me those doctors had not left anything inside of me except the acoustics. Well, there was a mite of consolation there. If the overhauling had been as thorough as I had reason to believe it was from my present sensations, I need never fear catching anything again so long as I lived, except possibly dandruff.

I waved the nurse away. I craved solitude. I desired only to lie there in that bed and hurt—which I did.

I had said beforehand I meant to stay in St. Germicide's for two or three days only. It is when I look back on that resolution I emit the hollow laugh elsewhere referred to. For exactly four weeks I was flat on my back. I know now how excessively wearied a man can get of his own back, how tired of it, how bored with it! And after that another two weeks elapsed before my legs became the same dependable pair of legs I had known in the past.

I did not want to eat at first, and when I did begin to want to they would not let me. If I felt real peckish they let me suck a little glass thermometer, but there is not much nourishment really in thermometers. And for entertainment, to wile the dragging hours away, I could count the cracks in the ceiling and read my temperature chart, which was a good deal like Red Ames' batting average for the past season—ranging from ninety-nine to one hundred and four.

I shall never forget my first real meal! There was quite a good deal of talk about it beforehand. My nurse kept telling me that on the next day the doctor had promised I might have something to eat. I could hardly wait. I had visions of a tenderloin steak smothered in fried onions, and some French-fried potatoes, and a tall table-limit stack of wheat cakes, and a few other incidental comfits and kickshaws. I could hardly wait for that meal.

The next day came and she brought it to me, and I partook thereof. It was the white of an egg. For dessert I licked a stamp; but this I did clandestinely and by stealth, without saying anything about it to her. I was not supposed to have any sweets.

A little later on, seeing that I had not suffered

an attack of indigestion from this debauch, they gave me junket. In the dictionary I have looked up the definitions of junket. I quote:

JUNKET, v. I. t. To entertain by feasting; regale. II. i. To give or take part in an entertainment or excursion; feast in company; picnic; revel.

JUNKET, n. A merry feast or excursion; picnic.

When the author of a dictionary tries to be frivolous he only succeeds in making himself appear foolish. In a hospital, junket is a custard that by some subtle process has been denuded of those ingredients which make a custard fascinating and exciting. It tastes as though the eggs, which form its underlying basis, had been laid in a fit of pique by a hen that was severely upset at the time. Hereafter when the junket is passed round somebody else may have my share. I'll stick to the mince pie à la mode. And the first cigar of my convalescence—ah, that, too, abides as a vivid memory! Dropping in one morning to replace the wrappings Doctor Z said I might smoke in moderation. So the nurse brought me a cigar, and I lit it and took one deep puff; but only one. I laid it aside. I said to the nurse:

"A mistake has been made here. I do not want a cooking cigar, you understand. I desire a cigar for personal use. This one is full of herbs and simples, I think. It suggests a boiled New England dinner, and not a very good one at that. Let us try again."

She brought another cigar. It was not satisfactory either. Then she showed me the box—an orthodox box containing cigars of a recognized and previously dependable brand. I could only conclude that a root-and-herb doctor had bought an interest in the business and was introducing his own pet notions into the formula.

But came a day—as the fancy writers say when they wish to convey the impression that a day has come, but hate to do it in a commonplace manner—came a day when my cigar tasted as a cigar should taste and food had the proper relish to it; and my appetite came back again and found the old place not so greatly changed after all.

And then shortly thereafter came another day, when I, all replete with expensive stitches, might drape the customary habiliments of civilization about my attenuated frame and go forth to mingle with my fellow beings. I have been mingling pretty steadily ever since, for now I have something to talk about—a topic good for any company; congenial, an absorbing topic. I can spot a brother member a block away. I hasten up to him and give the grand hailing sign of the order. He opens his mouth to speak, but I beat him to it.

"Speaking of operations ——" I say. And then I'm off. Believe me, it's the life!

SCATTERGOOD BAINES—INVADER

—— by Clarence Budington Kelland ——

THE AUTHOR OF this story ranks second only to Mary Roberts Rinehart as the *Post*'s most enduring author. He was born in 1881, educated as a lawyer, chose newspaper work in Detroit instead, and won a reputation as author of the "Mark Tidd" stories and editor of the *American Boy* before selling his first *Post* story in 1916. He still comes up with a serial or two every year, and he has probably made more money writing than anyone else alive. "Scattergood Baines," he writes, "came into being in 1915 while I was in Vermont inefficiently helping my brother-in-law to manufacture clothespins. There was no human original, but rather he expressed my notion of what a true Vermonter was like." The first Scattergood story was the one which follows. Two more ran in the *Post* and then editor Lorimer made one of his rare mistakes. He asked Kelland to drop the character. Instead, Kelland took him to the *American Magazine,* where he thrived for one hundred more stories and one full-length novel before winding up his fabulous career.

JUNE 30, 1917

THE ENTRANCE of Scattergood Baines into Coldriver Valley and the manner of his first taking root in its soil are legendary. This much is clear even past disputing in the post office at mail time, or evenings in the grocery—he walked in, perspiring profusely, for he was very fat.

It is asserted that he walked the full twenty-four miles from the railroad, subsisting on the country, as it were, and sagged down on the porch of Locker's grocery just before sundown. It is not implied that he walked all of the twenty-four miles in that single day. Huge bodies move deliberately.

He sagged down on Locker's porch, and it is reported the corner of the porch sagged with him. George Peddie has it from his grandfather, who was an eyewitness, that Scattergood did not so much as turn his head to look at the assembled manhood of the vicinity, but with infinite pains and audible grunts succeeded in bringing first one foot, then the other, within reach of his hands, and removed his shoes. Following this he sighed with a great contentment and twiddled his bare toes openly and flagrantly in the eyes of all Coldriver.

He is said then to have uttered the first words to fall from his mouth in the town where were to lie his life's unfoldings and fulfillments. They were significant—in the light of subsequent activities.

"One of them railroads runnin' up here," said he to the mountain just across the road from him, "would have spared me close to a dozen blisters."

Conversation had expired on Scattergood's arrival, and the group on the porch converted itself into an audience. It was an audience that got its money's worth. Not for an instant did the attention of a single member of it stray away from this godsend come to furnish them with their first real topic of conversation since Crazy French stole a box of Paris green, mistaking it for a new sort of pancake flour.

Scattergood arose ponderously and limped out into the middle of the dusty road. From this vantage point he slowly and conscientiously studied the village.

"Uh-huh," he said. " 'Twouldn't pay to do all that walkin' just for a visit. Calc'late I'll have to settle."

He walked directly back to the absorbed group of leading citizens, his shoes dangling one in each hand, and addressed them genially.

"Your town," said he, "is growin'. Its population jest increased by me."

"Sizable growth," said Old Man Penny dryly, letting his eye rove over Scattergood's bulk.

"My line," said Scattergood, "is anythin' needful. Outside of a railroad, what you figger you need most?"

Nobody answered.

"Is it a grocery store?" asked Scattergood.

Locker stiffened in his chair.

"Me and Sam Kettleman calc'lates to sell all the groceries this town needs," he said.

"How about dry goods?" said Scattergood.

Old Man Penny and Wade Lumley stirred to life at this.

"Lumley and me takes care of the dry goods," said the old man.

"Uh-huh. How about a clothin' store?"

"We got all the clothin' stores there's room for," said Lafe Atwell. "I run it."

"Kind of got the business of this town sewed up, hain't you?" Scattergood asked admiringly. "Wouldn't look with favor on any more stores?"

"We calc'late to keep what business we got," said Old Man Penny. "A outsider would have a hard time makin' a go of it here."

"Quite likely," said Scattergood. "Still, you never can tell. Let some feller come in here with a gen'ral store, sellin' for cash—and cuttin' prices, eh? How would an outsider git along if he done that? Up-to-date store. Fresh goods. Low prices. Eh? Calc'late some of you fellers would have to discharge a clerk."

"You hain't got money enough to start a store," Old Man Penny squawked. "Why, you hain't even got a satchel. You come walkin' in like a tramp."

"There's tramps—and tramps," said Scattergood placidly.

He reached far down into a trousers pocket and tugged to the light of day a roll that his fingers could not encircle. He looked at it fondly, tossed it up in the air a couple of times and caught it, and then held it between thumb and forefinger until the eyes of his audience had assured themselves that the outside bill was yellow and its denomination twenty dollars. The audience gulped.

"Meals to the tavern perty good?" Coldriver's new citizen asked.

"Say!" demanded Locker. "Be you really thinkin' about startin' a cash store here?"

"Neighbor," said Scattergood, "never give a valuable information without gittin' somethin' for it. How much money would a complete and careful account of my intentions be worth to you?"

Locker snorted.

"Bet that wad of bills is a dummy with a counterfeit twenty outside of it," he said.

Scattergood smiled tantalizingly. Locker had not, fortunately for Scattergood, the least idea how close to the truth he had been. On one point only had he been mistaken. The twenty outside was not counterfeit. However, except for three fives, four twos and ninety cents in silver, it represented Scattergood's total cash capital.

"I'm goin'," said Scattergood, "to order me two suppers. Two! From bean soup to apple pie. It's my birthday. Twenty-six to-day, and I always eat two suppers on my birthdays. Glad you leadin' citizens see fit to give me such a hearty wel-

come to your town. Right kind and generous of you!"

He turned and ambled down the road toward the tavern, planting his bare feet with evident pleasure in the deepest of the warm sand and flirting up little clouds of it behind him. The audience saw him seat himself on the tavern steps and pull on his shoes. They were too far to hear him say speculatively to himself:

"I never heard tell of a man gittin' a start in life jest that way—but that hain't any reason it can't be done. I'm going to do this town good, and this valley. Hain't no more'n fair them leadin' citizens should give me what help they feel they kin."

Scattergood ate with ease and pleasure two complete suppers—to the openly expressed admiration of Emma, the waitress. Very shortly afterward he retired to his room, where, not trusting to the sturdiness of the bed slats provided, he dragged mattress and bedding to the floor, and was soon emitting snores that Landlord Coombs assured his wife was the beat of anybody ever slept in the house, not countin' that travelin' man from Boston.

Next morning Scattergood was about early, padding slowly up and down the crossed streets which made up the village. He was studying the ground for immediate strategic purposes, just as he had been studying the valley on his long trudge up from the railroad for purposes related to distant campaigns. Though Scattergood's arrival in Coldriver may have seemed impromptu, as his adoption of the town for a permanent location seemed abrupt, not to say impulsive, neither really was so. Scattergood rarely acted without reason or before reflection.

True, he had but a moment's glimpse of Coldriver before he decided to move there, but the glimpse showed him the location was the one he had been searching for. Scattergood's specialty —his hobby—was valleys. Valleys down which splashed and roared sizable streams, whose mountain sides were covered with timber, and whose flats were comfortable farms—such valleys interested him with an especial interest. But the valley he had been looking for was one with but a single possible outlet. He wanted a valley whose timber and produce and products could not go climbing off across the hills, over a number of easy roads, to market. His valley must be hemmed in. The only way to market must lie down the valley, with the river. And the river that flowed down his valley must be swift, with sufficient volume all twelve months of the year to turn possible mill wheels. As yet he thought only of the direct application of power. He had not dreamed yet of great turbine generators that should transport thousands of horsepower, written in terms of electricity, hundreds of miles across country, there to light cities and turn the wheels of huge manufactories.

Coldriver Valley was that valley! He felt it as soon as he turned into it; certainty increased as he progressed between those gigantic walls, black with tall, straight, beautiful spruce. So when he sat shoeless, resting his blistered feet, on Locker's porch, he was ready to make his decision. The mere making of it was a negligible detail.

So Scattergood Baines found his valley. He entered it consciously as an invader, determined to conquer. Pitiful as were the resources of Cortez as he adventured against the power of Montezuma, or of Pizarro as he clambered over the Andes, they were gigantic compared with Scattergood's. He was starting to make his conquest backed by one twenty, three fives, four twos and ninety cents in silver. It was obvious to him the country to be conquered must supply the sinews of war for its own conquest.

Every village has its ramshackle, disused store building. Coldriver had one, especially well located and not so ramshackle as it might have been. It was big; its front was crossed by a broad porch; its show windows were not show windows at all, but were put there solely to give light. Coldriver did not know there was such a thing as inviting patronage by skillful display.

"Sonny," said Scattergood to a boy digging worms in the shade of the building, "who owns this here ruin?"

"Old Tom Plummer," said the boy, and was even able to disclose where Old Tom was to be found. Scattergood found him feeding a dozen White Orpingtons.

"Best layers a man can keep," said Scattergood sincerely. "Man's got to have brains to even raise chickens."

"I git more eggs to the hen than anybody else in town," said Old Tom. "But nobody listens to me."

"Own a store buildin' downtown, don't you?"

"Calc'late to."

"If you was to git a chance to rent it, how much would it be a month?"

"Repairs or no repairs?"

"No repairs."

"Twenty dollars."

"G'mornin'," said Scattergood, and turned away.

"What's your hurry, mister?"

"Can't bear to stay near a man that mentions so much money in a breath," said Scattergood with his most ingratiating grin.

"How much could you stay and hear?"

"Not over ten."

"Huh! Seein' the buildin's in poor shape I'll call it fifteen."

"Twelve-fifty's as far's I'll go—on a five-year lease," said Scattergood. It will be seen he fully intended to become permanent.

"What you figger on usin' it fur?"

"Maybe a opry house, maybe a dime museum, maybe a carpenter shop, and maybe somethin' else. I hain't mentionin' jest what, but it's law-abidin' and respectable."

"Five-year lease, eh? Twelve-fifty."

"Two months' rent in advance," said Scattergood.

"Squire Hastings'll draw the papers," said Old Tom, heading for the gate.

Scattergood followed, and in half an hour was the lessee of a store building, bound to pay rent for five years, with more than half his capital vanished—with no stock of goods or wherewith to procure one, with not even a day's experience in any sort of merchandising to his credit.

His next step was to buy ten yards of white cloth, a small paintbrush and a can of paint. Ostentatiously he borrowed a stepladder and stretched the cloth across the front of his store, from post to post. Then, equally ostentatiously, he mounted the stepladder and began to paint the sign.

He was not unskilled in the business of lettering. The sign, when completed, read:

CASH AND CUT PRICES IS MY MOTTO

Having completed this, he bought a pail, a mop and a broom, and proceeded to a thorough house-cleaning of his premises.

Old Man Penny and Locker and the rest of the merchants were far from oblivious to Scattergood's movements. No sooner had his sign appeared than every merchant in town—except Junkin, the druggist, who sold wall paper and farm machinery as side lines—went into executive session in the back room of Locker's store.

"He means business," said Locker.

"Leased that store for five year," said Old Man Penny.

"Cash and Cut Prices," quoted Atwell, "and you fellers know our folks would pass by their own brothers to save a penny. He'll force us to cut too."

"Me—I won't do it," asserted Kettleman.

"Then you'll eat your stock," growled Locker.

"Fellers," said Atwell, "if this man gits started it's goin' to cost all of us money. He'll draw some trade, even if he don't cut prices. Safe to figger he'll git a sixth of it. And a sixth of the business in this region is a perty fair livin'. If he goes slashin' right and left nobody kin tell how much trade he'll draw."

"We should 'a' leased that store between us. Then nobody could 'a' come in."

"But we didn't. And it's goin' to cost us money. If he puts in clothing it'll cost me five hundred dollars a year in profits anyhow, maybe more. And you other fellers clost to as much."

"But we can't do nothin'."

"We can buy him off," said Atwell.

The meeting at that moment became noisy. Epithets were applied with freedom to Scattergood, and even to Atwell, for these were not men who loved to part with their money. However, Atwell showed them the economy of it. It was for them either to suffer one sharp pang now or to endure a greater dragging misery. They went in a body to call upon Scattergood.

"Howdy, neighbors," Scattergood said genially.

"We're the merchants of this town," said Old Man Penny shortly.

"So I judged," said Scattergood.

"There's merchants enough here," the old man roared on. "Too many. We don't want any more. We don't want you should start up any business here."

"You're too late. It's started. I've leased these premises."

"But you hain't no stock in."

"I calc'late on havin' one shortly," said Scattergood with a twinkle in his eye the meaning of which was kindly concealed from the five.

"What'll you take not to order any stock?" said Atwell abruptly.

"Figger on buyin' me off, eh? Now, neighbors, I've been lookin' for a place like this, and I calc'late on stayin'. I'm goin' to become all-fired permanent here."

"Give you a hundred dollars," said Old Man Penny.

"Apiece?" asked Scattergood, and laughed jovially. "It's my busy day, neighbors. Better call in again."

"What's your figger to pull out now—'fore you're started?"

"Hain't got no figger, but if I had I calc'late it would be about a thousand dollars."

"Give you two hundred," said Old Man Penny. Scattergood picked up his mop.

"If you fellers really mean business, talk business. I've figgered my profits in this store, countin' in low prices, wouldn't be a cent under a couple of thousand the first year. And you know

it. That's what you're fussin' round here for. Now fish, or git to bait cuttin'."

"Five hundred dollars," said Atwell, and Old Man Penny moaned.

"Tell you what I'll do," said Scattergood. "You men git back here inside of an hour with seven hundred and fifty cash, and lay it in my hand, and I'll agree not to sell groceries, dry goods, notions, millinery or men's or women's clothes in this town for a term of twenty years."

They drew off and scolded each other and glowered at Scattergood, but came to scratch.

"It's jest like robbery," said Old Man Penny tremulously.

"Keep your money," retorted Scattergood. "I'm satisfied the way things is at present."

Within the hour they were back with seven hundred and fifty dollars in bills, a lawyer and an agreement, which Scattergood read with minute attention. It bound him not to sell, barter, trade, exchange, deal in or in any way to derive a profit from the handling of groceries, dry goods, notions, millinery, clothing and gents' furnishings. It contained no hidden pitfalls, and Scattergood was satisfied. He signed his name and thrust the roll of bills into his pocket. Then he picked up his mop and went to work as hard as ever.

"Say," Old Man Penny said, "what you goin' ahead for? You jest agreed not to."

"There wasn't nothin' said about moppin'," grinned Scattergood; "and there wasn't nothin' said about hardware and harness and farm implements neither. If you don't believe me, jest read the agreement. What I'm doin', neighbors, is git this place cleaned out to put in the finest cash, cut-price, up-to-date hardware store in the state. And thank you, neighbors. You've done right kindly by a stranger."

II

To THIS POINT the history of Scattergood Baines has been for the most part legendary; now we begin to encounter him in the public records, for deeds, mortgages and the like begin to appear with his name upon them. His history becomes authentic.

Seven hundred and fifty dollars is not much when put into hardware, but Scattergood had no intention of putting even that into a stock of goods. He had a notion that the right kind of man, with five hundred dollars, could get credit for twice that amount, and as for farm machinery he could sell by catalogue or on commission. His suspicion was proved to be fact. But it was not in Scattergood to sit idle while he waited for his stock to arrive. Coldriver doubtless thought him idle, but he was studying the locality and the river with the eye of a commander who knew this was to be his battlefield. What Scattergood wanted now was to place himself astride Coldriver Valley somewhere below the village so that he could control the upper reaches of the stream. It was not difficult to find such a location. It lay three miles below town at the juncture of the North and South branches of Coldriver. The juncture was a big marshy, untillable flat from which hills rose abruptly. From the easterly end of the flat the augmented river squeezed in a roaring rapids through a sort of bottle neck.

Scattergood stood on the hillside and looked upon this with satisfied eye.

"A dam across that bottle neck," he said to himself, "will flood that flat. Reg'lar reservoy. Mill pond. Git a twenty-foot fall here easy, maybe more. Calc'late that'll run about any mill folks'll want to build. And"—he scratched his head as a sort of congratulation to it for its efficiency—"I can't study out how anybody's agoin' to git logs past here without dickerin' with the man who owns the dam."

Plenty of water twelve months a year to give free power; a flat made to order for reservoir or log pond; a complete and effective blockade of both branches of the river which came down from the country richly timbered. It was one of the spots Scattergood had dreamed of.

Scattergood knew perfectly well he could not stop a log from passing his dam. Nor could he shut off the stream. Any dam he built must have a sluice which could be opened for the passage of timber, and all timber was entitled to "natural water." But, as he well knew, natural water was not always enough. A dam at this point would raise the level on the bars of the flat so that logs would not jam, and a log which used the high water caused by the dam must pay for it. What Scattergood had in mind was a dam and boom company. It was his project to improve the river, to boom backwaters, to dynamite ledges, to make the river passable to logs in spring and fall. It was his idea that such a company, in addition to demanding pay for the use of improvements, could contract with lumbermen up the river to drive their logs. And a mill at this point! Scattergood fairly licked his lips as he thought of the millions upon millions of feet of spruce to be sawed into lumber.

The firm foundation that Scattergood's strategy rested upon was that lumbering had not really started in the valley. The valley had not opened up, but lay undeveloped, waiting to be stirred to life. Scattergood's strength lay in that he could see ahead of to-day and was patient to wait for the developments that to-morrow must bring. To-day his foresight could get for him what would be impossible to-morrow. If he stepped softly he could obtain a charter from the state to develop that river, which, when lumbering interests became actually engaged, would be fought by them to the last penny. And he felt in his bones that day would not long be delayed.

The land Scattergood required was owned by three individuals. All of it was worthless—except to a man of vision; so, treading lightly, Scattergood went about acquiring what he needed. His method was not direct approach. He went to the owners of that land with proffers to sell, not to buy. To Landers, who owned the marsh on both shores of the river, he tried to sell the newest development in mowing machines, and his manner of doing so was to hitch to the newly arrived machine, haul it to Landers' meadow, where the owner was haying, drag it through the gate and unhitch.

"Here," he said, "try this here machine. Won't cost you nothin' to try it, and I'm curious to see if it works as good as they say."

Landers was willing. It worked better. Landers regarded the machine longingly and spoke of price. Scattergood disclosed it. "Hain't got it, and can't afford it," said Landers.

"Might afford a swap?"

"Might. What you got in mind?"

"Say," said Scattergood, changing the subject, "ever try drainin' that marsh in the fork? Looks like it could be done. Might make a good medder."

Landers laughed.

"If you want to try," he chuckled, "I'll trade it to you for this here mowin' machine."

"Hum-m-m," grunted Scattergood, and higgled and argued, but ended by accepting a deed for the land and turning over the machine to Landers. Scattergood himself had sixty days to pay for it. It cost him something like half a dollar an acre, and Landers considered he had robbed the hardware merchant of a machine.

One side of the bottle neck Scattergood took in exchange for a kitchen stove and a double harness; the third parcel of land came to him for a keg of nails, five gallons of paint, sundry kitchen utensils and twelve dollars and fifty cents in money. And when Coldriver heard of the deals it chuckled derisively and regarded its hardware merchant with pitying scorn.

Then Scattergood left a youth in charge of his store and went softly to the state capital. In after years his skill in handling legislatures was often remarked upon with displeasure. His young manhood held prophecy of this future ability, for he came home acquainted with nine-tenths of the legislators, laughed at by half of them as a harmless oddity, and with a state charter for his river company in his pocket. When folks heard of that charter they held their sides and roared.

Scattergood returned to selling hardware, and waited. He had an idea he would hear something stirring on his trail before long, and he fancied he could guess who and what that something would be. He judged he would hear from two gentlemen named Crane and Keith. Crane owned some twenty thousand acres of timber along the North Branch; Keith owned slightly lesser limits along the South Branch. Both gentlemen were lumbering and operating mills in another state; their Coldriver holdings they had acquired and, as the saying is, forgotten, until the time should come when they would desire to move into Coldriver Valley.

Now these holdings were recalled sharply to memory, and both owners took train to Coldriver. Scattergood had not worried about it. He had simply gone along selling hardware in his own way—and selling a good deal of it. His store had a new front; his stock was augmented. It was his business to sell goods, and he sold them.

For instance, Lem Jones stopped and hitched his team before the store one chilly day. His horses he covered with old burlap, lacking blankets. While Lem was buying groceries, Scattergood selected two excellent blankets, carried them out and put them on the horses. Then he went back into the store to attend to other matters. Presently Lem came in.

"Where'd them blankets come from?" he asked.

"Hosses looked a mite chilly." said Scattergood without interest, "so I covered 'em."

" 'Bleeged," said Lem. Then, awkwardly: "I calc'late I need a pair of blankets, but I can't afford 'em this year. Wife's been sick ——"

"Sure," said Scattergood. "I know. If you want them blankets take 'em along. Pay me when you kin. Jest give me a sort of note for a memorandum."

So Scattergood marketed his blankets, taking in exchange a perfectly good interest-bearing note. Also, he made a friend, for Lem could not be convinced but that Scattergood had done him a notable favor.

Scattergood now had money in the bank. No longer did he have to stretch his credit for stock. He was established—and all in less than a year.

Hardware, it seemed, had been a commodity much needed in that locality, yet no one had handled it in sufficient stock because of the twenty-four-mile haul. That had been too costly. It cost Scattergood just as much, but his customers paid for it. The difference between him and the other merchants was that he sold goods while they allowed folks to buy.

So, wisely, he kept on buiiding up in a small way while waiting for bigger things to develop. And as he waited he studied the valley until he could recite every inch of it, and he studied the future until he knew what the future would require of that valley. He knew it before the future knew it and before the valley knew it, and was laying his plans to be ready with pails to catch the sap when others, taken by surprise, would be running wildly about seeking for buckets.

Then Crane and Keith arrived in Coldriver. That day marked Scattergood's emergence from the ranks of country merchants, though he retained his hardware store to the last. That day marked distinctly Scattergood's launching on a greater body of water. For forty years he sailed it with varying success, meeting failures sometimes, scoring victories, but interesting, characteristic in every phase—a genius in his way and a man who never took the commonplace course when the unusual was open to him.

III

"I SUPPOSE YOU'VE LOOKED this man Baines up," said Crane to Keith when they met in the Coldriver Tavern.

"I know how much he weighs and how many teeth he's had filled," Keith replied.

"He ought not to be so difficult to handle. He hasn't capital enough to put this company of his through, and his business experience doesn't amount to much."

"For monkeying with our buzz saw," said Keith, "we ought to let him lose a couple of fingers."

"How's this for an idea, then?" Crane said, and for fifteen minutes he outlined his theory of how best to eliminate Scattergood Baines from being an obstruction to the free flowage of their schemes for Coldriver Valley.

"It's got others by the hundred," agreed Keith. "This jayhawker'll welcome it with tears of joy."

Whereupon they went gladly on their way to Scattergood's store, not as enemies, but as business men who recognized his abilities, and preferred to have him with them from the start, that they might profit by his canniness and energy, rather than to array themselves against him in an effort to take away from him what he had obtained.

Only by the exercise of notable will power could Crane keep his face straight as he shook hands with ungainly Scattergood, and saw with his own eyes what a perfect bumpkin he had to deal with.

"I suppose you thought we fellows would be sore," he said genially.

"Dunno's I thought about you at all," said Scattergood. "I was thinkin' mainly about me."

"Well, we're not. You caught us napping, of course. We should have grabbed off that dam location long ago, but we weren't expecting anybody to stray in with his eyes open—like yourself. Of course your property and charter aren't worth a great deal till we start lumbering."

"Not to anybody but me," said Scattergood.

"Well, we expect to begin operations in a year or so. We'll build a mill on the railroad, and drive our logs down the river."

"Givin' my company the drivin' contracts?"

"Looks like we'd have to—if you get in your dam and improvements. But that'll take money. We've looked you up, of course, and we know you haven't it—nor any backing. That's why we've come to see you."

"To be sure," said Scattergood. "Goin' to drive way to the railroad, eh? How if there was a mill right at my dam? Shorten your drive twenty mile, wouldn't it, eh?"

"Yes," said Keith, laughing at Scattergood's ignorance; "but how about transportation from your mill to the railroad? We can't drive cut lumber."

"Course not," said Scattergood; "but this valley's goin' to open up. It's startin'. There's only one way to open a valley, and that's to run a railroad up it. Narrow gauge 'ud do here. Carry mostly lumber, but passengers too."

"Thinking of building one?" asked Crane, almost laughing in Scattergood's face.

"Thinkin' don't cost nobody nuthin'," said Scattergood. "Ever take a look at that charter of mine?"

"No."

"I'll let you read it over a bit. Maybe you'll git a idea from it."

He extracted the parchment from his sate and spread it before them.

"Kind of look careful along toward the end—in the tail feathers of it, so to speak," he advised.

They did so, and Crane looked up at the fat hardware man with eyes that were not quite so contemptuous.

"By George," he said, "this thing's a charter for a railroad down the valley too."

"Uh-huh," said Scattergood. "Dunno's the boys quite see what it was all about, but they calc'lated to please me, so they put it through jest as it stood. Mighty nice fellers up to the legislature."

"Pretty far in the future," said Keith, "and mighty expensive."

"Maybe not so far," said Scattergood; "and I could make a darn good start narrow-gaugin' it with a hundred thousand."

"Which you've got handy for use," said Crane.

"There is that much money," said Scattergood, "and if there is, why, it kin be got."

"Let's get back to the river now," said Keith. "If we're going to start lumbering in a year, say, we've got to have the river in shape. Take quite some time to get it cleared and dammed and boomed."

"Six months," said Scattergood.

"Cost a right smart pile."

"The work I'm figgerin' on would come to about thirty-odd thousand."

"Which you haven't got."

"Somebody has," said Scattergood.

"We have," said Crane. "That's why we came to you—and with a proposition. You've grabbed this thing off, but you can't hog it, because you haven't the money to put it through. Our offer is this: You put in your locations and your charter against our money. We'll finance it. Your enterprise entitles you to control. We won't dispute that. You can have fifty-one per cent of the stock for what you've contributed. We take the rest for financing. We're known and can get money."

"How you figger to work it?"

"We'll bond for forty thousand dollars. Keith and I can place the bonds. That'll give us money to go ahead."

Scattergood reached down and took off a huge shoe. Usually he thought more accurately when his feet were unconfined.

"That means we'd sort of mortgage the whole thing, eh?"

"That's the idea."

"And if we didn't pay interest on the bonds, why, the fellers that had 'em could foreclose?"

"But we needn't worry about that."

"Not," said Scattergood, "if you fellers sign a contract with the Dam and Boom Company to give them the exclusive job of drivin' all your timber at, say, sixty cents a thousand feet of logs. And if you'd stick a clause in that contract that you'd begin cuttin' within twelve months from date."

"Sure we'd do that," said Keith. "To our advantage as much as to yours."

"To be sure," said Scattergood.

"It's a deal, then?"

"Far's I'm concerned," said Scattergood, slipping his foot inside his shoe, "it is."

That afternoon, the papers having been signed and the deal consummated, Scattergood sat cogitating.

"I've been done," he said to himself solemnly, "accordin' to them fellers' notion. They come and seen me, and done me. They planned out how they'd do it, and I didn't never suspect a thing. Uh-huh. Seems like I was fortunate, just gittin' a start in life like I be. Bonds, says they. Uh-huh. They'll place 'em, and place 'em handy. First int'rest day there won't be no int'rest, and them bonds'll be foreclosed—and where'll I be? Mighty ingenious fellers, Crane and Keith. And I up and walked right into it like a fly into a molasses barrel. Them fellers," he said even more somberly, "come here calc'latin' to cheat me out of my river—me bein' jest a fat man without no brains."

Crane and Keith had left Scattergood the executive head of the new Dam and Boom Company, and had confided to him the task of building the dam and improving the river. He approached it sadly.

"Might as well save what I kin out of the wreck," he said to himself, and quietly manufactured a dummy contracting company to whom he let the entire job for a lump sum of thirty-eight thousand seven hundred dollars. The dummy contractor was Scattergood Baines.

The dam was completed, booms and cribbing placed, ledges blasted out well within the six months' period set for those operations. Every thirty days Scattergood, in the name of the dummy contractor, was paid eighty per cent of his estimates, and at the completion of the work he received the remainder of the whole sum.

"I wouldn't 'a' done it to them boys," he said as he surveyed a deposit of upward of seven thousand dollars, his profit on the transaction, "if it hadn't 'a' been they organized to cheat me out of my river. I calc'late in the circumstances, though, I'm most entitled to what I kin salvage out of the wreck."

Now the Coldriver Dam and Boom Company, Scattergood Baines president and manager, was ready for business, which was to take the logs of Messrs. Crane and Keith and drive them down the river at the rate of sixty cents per thousand feet. It was ready and eager, and so expressed itself in quaintly worded communications from

Baines to those gentlemen. But no logs appeared to be driven.

"Jest like I said," Scattergood told himself, and, the day being hot and the road dusty, he removed his shoes and rested his sweltering bulk in the shade to consider it.

"It's a nice river," he said audibly. "I hate to git done out of it."

After long delays Crane and Keith made pretense of building camps and starting to log. But one difficulty after another descended on their operations. In the spring, when each of them should have had several millions of feet of spruce ready to roll into the water, not a log was on rollways. Not a man was in the camps, for, owing to reasons not to be comprehended by the public, the woodsmen of both operators had struck simultaneously and left the woods.

Presently the first interest day arrived, with not even a hope of being able to meet the required payment at a future date. Bondholders—dummies just as Scattergood's contractor was a dummy—met. Their deliberations were brief. Foreclose with all promptitude was their word, and foreclose they did. With the result that legal notices were published to the effect that on the sixteenth day of June the dam, boom, cribbing, improvements, charter, contracts and property of whatsoever nature belonging to the Coldriver Dam and Boom Company were to be sold at public auction on the steps of the county courthouse. Scattergood had lost his river.

IV

"TERMS OF THE SALE are cash with the bid," said Crane to Keith. "I saw to that."

"Good! Wasn't necessary, I guess. There hasn't been even a wriggle out of Baines."

"Won't be. We'll have to send somebody up to bid it in. It's just taking money out of one pocket to put it into the other, but we've got to go through the motions."

"Anyhow, let's get credit for grabbing a bargain," said Keith. "Bid her in cheap. No use taking a big wad of money out of circulation even for a few days."

"Ten thousand'll be enough. Say ten thousand six hundred, just to make it sound better. Have to have two bidders there."

"Sure," agreed Keith. "I guess this'll teach our fat dreamer of dreams not to get in the way of the cars."

Scattergood's stock had gone down in Coldriver. True, his hardware store was thriving. In the two years his stock had increased from what his seven hundred and fifty dollars, with credit added, would buy to an inventory of better than five thousand dollars, free of debt. It is true also that, with the long winter coming on, he had looked about for a chance to keep his small surplus at work for him, and his eyes had fallen upon the item of firewood. In Coldriver were a matter of sixty houses and a hotel, all of which derived their heat from hardwood chunks and cooked their meals on ranges fired with sixteen-inch split wood. The houses were mostly of that large, comfortable country variety which could not be kept warm with one fire. Scattergood figured they would burn on an average fifteen cords of wood.

Now stove wood, to be really useful, must have seasoned a year. It is not pleasant to build fires with green wood. Appreciating this, Scattergood ambled about the countryside and bought up every available stick of wood at prices of the day —and under, for he was a good buyer. He secured a matter of a thousand cords—and then waited hopefully.

It was a small transaction, promising no great profits, but Scattergood Baines was never, even when a rich man, one to scorn a small deal. Within sixty days he turned over his corner in wood, realizing a profit of something over four hundred dollars—this is merely to illustrate how Scattergood's capital grew.

On June sixteenth Scattergood drove to the county seat. He now owned a horse and a buggy, the seat of which he more than comfortably filled. In the county seat Scattergood was not unknown, for various county officers had been helped to their places by his growing influence in his town—notably the sheriff.

There was little interest in the sale, and what interest there was Scattergood caused by his unexpected appearance. Nobody had imagined he would be present. Now that he was there nobody could imagine why. He did not enlighten them, though he was delighted to sit in the sun on the courthouse steps, waiting for the hour of the sale, and to chat. He loved to chat, especially if he could get off his shoes and wriggle his toes in the sunshine. And so he sat, bare of foot, when the sheriff appeared and made his announcement of the approaching sale. Scattergood chatted on, apparently not interested.

"All the dams, booms, cribbings, improvements and property of the Coldriver Dam and Boom Company ——" the sheriff read.

"Includin' the contracts and charter," amended Scattergood.

"Including the contracts and charter," agreed the sheriff, and Scattergood continued his chat.

Bidding began. It was not brisk or exciting. Five thousand was the first offer, from a young man appertaining to Crane. Keith's young man raised him five hundred. Back and forth they tossed it, carrying on the pretense, until Keith's young man reached the sum of ten thousand six hundred dollars. A silence followed.

"Ten thousand six hundred I'm offered," said the sheriff loudly, and repeated it. He had been a licensed auctioneer in his day. "Do I hear seven hundred? Seven hundred—six-fifty"—a portentous pause—"going at ten thousand six hundred, once. Going at ten thousand six hundred, twice ——"

"Ten thousand seven hundred," said Scattergood casually.

Crane's young man looked at Keith's young man in a panic. They had on them only the sum they had bid. Cash with bid were the terms of sale. Scattergood, out of the corner of his eye, saw them rush together and confer frenziedly. His eye glinted.

"Ten thousand eight hundred," Crane's youth bid desperately.

"Cash with bid is terms of sale," said Scattergood. "I object to listenin' to that bid without the young man perduces."

He smiled at the sheriff.

"Mr. Baines is right," said the sheriff. "Protect your bid with the cash or I cannot receive it."

"Make him protect his bid," shouted Crane's young man.

"Certain," said Scattergood, approaching the sheriff and drawing a huge roll of bills from his sagging trousers pocket. "Calc'late you'll find her there, Mr. Sheriff, and some besides. Make your change and gimme back the rest."

"I'm waitin' on you, young feller," said the sheriff, eying the young men. "Ten thousand seven hundred I hear. Going at ten thousand seven hundred, once—twice—three times. Sold to Mr. Baines for ten thousand seven hundred dollars."

So ends the first epoch of Scattergood Baines' career in Coldriver Valley. Here he emerges as a personage. From this point his fame began to spread, and legend grew. Had he not, in two brief years, after arriving with less than fifty dollars as a total capital, acquired a profitable hardware store—donated in the beginning by competitors? Had he not now, for the most part with money wrenched from Crane and Keith by his dummy contracting, been enabled to bid in for ten thousand seven hundred dollars a new property worth nearly three times that much? He was a man into whose band wagon all were eager to clamber.

But Scattergood did not change. He went back to his hardware store and waited—waited for Crane and Keith to start their inevitable logging operations. For in his safe reposed ironclad contracts with those gentlemen, covering the future for a decade, compelling them to pay him sixty cents for every thousand feet of timber that floated down his river. It was a good two years' work. He could well afford to wait.

Scattergood sat on the porch of his store in the sunniest spot, twiddling his bare toes.

"The way to make money," he said to the mountain opposite, "is to let smarter folks 'n you be make it for you—like I done."

BEYOND THE BRIDGE

by Joseph Hergesheimer

ABOUT THE SAME time that editor Lorimer discovered Ring Lardner and Irvin S. Cobb, he also discovered Joseph Hergesheimer. This pudgy, owlish, introspective Philadelphian was the son of a violin-playing scientist and the grandson of a well-to-do typefounder. He had spent his whole inheritance in one lazy year in Venice, where he lolled in a private gondola and rolled his own cigarettes. Then he came home and wrote diligently for fourteen years before selling his first book in 1914 and his first *Post* short story in 1915. *Java Head* was a popular *Post* serial in 1918 and *Balisand* in 1924. Hergesheimer became moderately rich again and carried on a friendly rivalry with Lorimer in collecting American antiques. But Lorimer's biographer, John Tebbel, tells us that the editor never fully enjoyed his friend's fiction, although he respected it, and printed a great deal of it. One reason for his uneasiness may be seen in the following story. For Lorimer success was always a great and satisfying adventure, but Hergesheimer had looked at its darker side.

DECEMBER 11, 1920

HE WAS past fifty-four when John Harden Rawle first discovered the extraordinary relief of a complete, if temporary, mental and spiritual freedom, and it was the result of a most unlikely and trivial set of circumstances. It began really at the dinner Ella and he gave their daughter, Ashley, on her return from the long motor trip that was the honeymoon of Henry Plank and herself. It was a very noisy dinner—the cocktails, since prohibition, seemed to have multiplied potency with their cost; and the Gibbons, Mary and Edward, undoubtedly raised the roof, but then they usually did. It was the performance of James Ross, the senior member of Rawle's law firm, that made the party notable.

He imitated several well-known comedians of the knockabout variety at the table and unsuccessfully kissed Mary Gibbon in the hall. Mary was rowdy, but at heart sound, and a lawyer with a large family—absent in Maine—couldn't kiss her seriously. Ordinarily she would have managed Ross with privacy and dispatch. Now, however, inspired by orange blossoms, she broke into loud merriment and the announcement, in the manner of a train dispatcher, of what had happened.

Altogether the dinner was most unfortunate, the worse for Rawle because he had had a persistent headache all day. He steadily wished that midnight would come and his guests depart, but the evening dragged on interminably. It was close and still, at the end of August; and on the lawn James Ross and Henry were playing croquet at a dollar a wicket. The moonlight was bright, and in the shadows smoothly burning candles were fastened to the hoops.

Gibbon was smoking sullenly on the terrace, and a little distance away the women were seated in wicker chairs—Ashley and her mother, Mary and Katherine Barker. Katherine's magnificent emeralds occasionally and mysteriously glittered, and Ashley's engagement ring hinted at its frosty, prismatic perfection. Henry Plank was rich, very rich indeed; and, Rawle knew, Ella considered their daughter's marriage to him the chief success of their lives. For not only was Plank's income large; he was on every count eligible—by birth and inclination good form. The croquet over, the younger man, nine wickets ahead, triumphantly collected as many dollars and extended himself on the grass at Ashley's feet. Ross found a place by John Rawle.

"I'll have to go down to Northeast Harbor tomorrow," the former reminded Rawle; "and Arnold won't be fit for town before October, so you will have to keep an eye on things; but there isn't much on the calendar. See that young Stokes, with his mother in Italy, doesn't get too far into his next quarterly; and if, in Hitchcock's opinion, the Geltner will is a forgery, call Marks. We simply won't let ourselves in for any action, with all the criminals on the jury."

Rawle nodded silently. There had been no need for Ross' repetition. He knew the other was leaving for Maine to-morrow; that Arnold, their third partner, was sick in the country; and that they, Ross, Arnold & Rawle, practically never departed from an orphans' court practice. It suddenly occurred to him that a good half—no, three-quarters—of all that was said was equally purposeless —silly! He could hear the low murmur of feminine voices, and then Ashley's clear, high, decided tones. She was talking about the motor trip.

"The most we did was three hundred and seventy miles; then another day three hundred and twenty. The banging about was frightful, and hurt my head. When we got in at night I simply collapsed on a bed. No, not much, but there wasn't a lot to see—just country. Yes, one—with a flivver. The man was rather hurt, but it was his fault. I hate flivvers anyhow, the way they toot about and turn in at such unexpected places. We stayed with the Sawyers at Pittsburgh and Henry played golf. They called it golf, but—my dear! Lambert Sawyer was worse than Henry. Jane is ridiculously grown up, and has rows with the family continually; while we were there it was about wearing her stockings turned down from her knees. Lambert got six barrels of whisky and two of gin."

"How much did he pay?" Ross cut in.

"He didn't say," Ashley replied.

"I found a half barrel of bourbon for twenty-eight dollars a gallon," Ross continued. "But it's the devil to buy good gin. I suppose you're well supplied, Plank."

"Fairly," Rawle's son-in-law admitted; "seventy-five cases of Pol Roger and enough Rutherford. I don't like rye."

Rawle's supply, he reflected, was low. It was a tremendous nuisance to buy whisky and gin. He didn't specially care for drinking; and now all the necessary secrecy and evolutions with his car in retrospect annoyed him. He wondered why he took so much trouble. The ceaseless talk about liquor, too, fretted him. It was as tiresome as its effects—as, for example, the conduct of the Gibbons to-night. He happened to know that cocktails disagreed with Ross. The latter's doctor had warned him against taking them; yet Ross continued, and let himself in additionally for such exhibitions as he just made of himself.

The night was, Rawle discovered, beautiful. His clipped lawn was alternately flooded with moonlight and sharply black with the shadows of trees. The low façade of his house was clearly revealed in every copied English detail. The dining room was lighted, and he could see Henderson moving about, putting away the silver and china. Above, in his room, the maid would be turning back his bed. Suddenly he viewed all this—his place and profession, his success—as a whole, as a concrete actuality, and it surprised him. As a boy he had had plenty, gone to a good school and

university. He had been, to some extent, used to things. But this house, impressive if small; the well-tended lawn and orderly trees; the discrete garage and expensive car and chauffeur; his wife in an elaborate dinner dress; Ashley married to Henry Plank—it all now amazed him.

It surprised him, seen so solidly, for the ridiculous reason that he couldn't connect it with himself. It appeared foreign to him, to have been wished on him while asleep. Very admirable, however. He was, the opinion ran, to be envied— he was envied. Past fifty-four—the years had gone like a shot. Ella rose and moved by him into the house, joined by Henry and Katherine Barker and Ross—bound, Rawle knew, for the bridge table. A detached view of his wife, handsome and stout, deepened his sensation of amazement. She was positively like a stranger. He had married, twenty-seven years before, a slender girl with a mass of shining hair and an unconquerable determination to get the best life had to offer; and in a second, it seemed to him in his peculiar mood, she had been transformed into a middle-aged woman with gray hair and a strand of pearls on her prominent and tightly confined breast.

II

GIBBON REMAINED stubbornly silent, his cigar glowing energetically, and Mary wandered off alone over the sod. The owls that inhabited a willow tree began an exchange of low gurgling cries, and the August burden of locusts hummed like a vibrant metallic string. There was the sound of shaken cocktails within, raised voices and then the avaricious stillness of bridge. Rawle was glad that he had been left alone, and his thoughts turned to Charles, his son and younger child, who had been killed in action at Bazoches. Charles, he reflected, had been tragically unlucky—a sensitive boy, hating all discord, already promising in an absorbed devotion to the composition of music, who had accepted an arbitrary duty without enthusiasm or illusions.

Rawle wished vainly that he had seen more of Charles. He had nothing with which to reproach himself. He had been a fair parent, at once firm enough and generous; but he had never taken the trips with his son they had projected. Nothing had interfered, only for countless small reasons they had fallen through. A nice, difficult boy, who had exasperated his mother because of his indifference to what she held as principally important. His hair, for instance—it was never brushed in the sleek precision of Henry Plank's. Henry answered Ella's every requirement. Rawle's thoughts turned from Charles to himself. This introspection was unusual, and had been brought about perhaps by his headache. The pain was gone, but it had left a dull, palpable soreness.

The seemingly interminable evening, he realized, was drawing to an end; and a few minutes before twelve he went in. The bridge was just over, and Katherine was paying her debt to Henry Plank with a twenty-dollar bill and some silver. Henry's luck at games, he recalled, was phenomenal.

"You'll have to take Katherine home," Ella told him. "Henry's car is in the shop, and it's plain the Barkers are not sending for her. I don't know where Emery is."

Rawle was not displeased at this. He was glad that the chauffeur couldn't be found. The drive, he told himself, through the serene night was just what he needed before sleep. It would clear his head of the fumes of gin, and the lingering oppression. Turning his long car from the drive to the highway, he told Katherine Barker, with an unavoidable implication, that it would be a welcome relief to motor without an accompanying gabble of strained voices.

Without even replying, and with crossed knees beside him, she gazed coldly and indifferently before her. Rawle forgot her at once. Ordinarily he detested fast driving, but to-night, with an empty, hard road and a growing sense of—of dissatisfaction, of query, he sped in an increasing, smooth, lunging momentum. The eleven-odd miles to the Barkers' were dropped behind in almost as few minutes. He left his companion at the porte-cochère of the large, indistinct bulk of her dwelling and moved away with an added satisfaction at being alone. All desire for speed had left him, and he drove abstractedly, with the humming of the motor almost inaudible.

He had no wish, no need to reach home soon; and at a crossroads bore to the left instead of directly back. The night was marvelous. On both sides there were wide, sweeping lawns, ornamental gates and lodges or blank expanses of wall. It was a select countryside of broad estates, imposing houses and meadows filled with expensive cattle; a region of millionaires. Rawle wasn't that; he was far short of it. His place, comparatively, was small—a couple of acres; but its situation, from Ella's view, was unexcelled.

He turned again, for no other reason than the unfamiliarity of the road, and found it rougher than the way he had left. Rawle mounted a hill and slipped into the valley beyond. Trees met above him; the gloom was hardly broken by stray silver patches and glimmers. He kept on and on, indifferent to distance or the lapse of time. The night had grown cold. There was a faint tang of autumn mold in the air and the vapors were being swept from his head.

He didn't now know just where he was. Crowning a short, steep ascent was a covered wooden bridge, an old-fashioned, echoing bridge, of which but few remained, and he hesitated between crossing it or returning. In the end he went on. Loose boards creaked under the wheels of his heavy car. The walls inclosing him were broken at intervals by openings, framed glimpses of a stream and over-hanging foliage. Beyond, he saw, the character of the country was utterly changed. The estates were gone, and in their place smaller farm succeeded to farm. The meadows were no less smooth, but the trees grew naturally, unfashioned by landscape architects. Massive stone Tudor houses, French spires, were replaced by farmhouses, withdrawn behind pines. The walls of the barnyards shone with a startling blanched whitewash. On his left the trees gathered, thickening into a wood; and where at home he had been conscious of the locusts as a remote vibration, here the volume of their sound reached an uproar. The locusts and the katydids were clamorous.

On the right were open fields, brilliantly colorless under the moon, at once strange and commonplace, at the far edge black with shadow. White cows slept in the hollows, where he could perfectly trace the course of streams with sodded banks. Above the sky was a clear, frigid vault, vaguely green, in which the moon was as sharp and pale as ice. Rawle was caught, held immobile in the spell of the night. He shut the power off, switched out the lights and sat bathed in the negative radiance, the shrilling silence, the chilling release from the heat of living, of the hour.

It was then exactly that he discovered the possibility of, at the least, a momentary freedom. Suddenly the moon, the locusts, the open tranquillity, invaded and saturated him; they blotted out past and future, and for an instant he was wholly at peace. He sat relaxed, his hands before him, with his face, stamped with mental toil and touched by sorrow, turned slightly up to meet a flooding purity too bright for stars. It lasted perhaps for ten breaths, perhaps for twenty, and then was broken by an alien, familiar thought, a memory of his immanent being. All that he had been poured back into his brain, and he made a subconscious gesture toward his cigarette case. At this, however, he was aware of a deep resentment, an anger that his quiet had been disturbed. It seemed to him that for the first time in life he had been at rest, freed from innumerable contentions and irritating pressures.

III

TURNING HIS GAZE resolutely to the fields and illusive slumbering cows, to a serenity which, lacking the realism of day, was steeped in an appearance of timeless repose, Rawle was again submerged in the vast, total calm. It seemed to him that a quality deeply buried in his heart, and long suppressed, stirred and breathed and took life within him. Another John Rawle asserted himself, vivified by keen drafts of the cool darkness. What he saw about him grew familiar, natural. He distinguished between the scent of aromatic grasses and the harsher goldenrod. The voices of the woods became separately and audibly clear. His own individual and febrile personality, however, he lost in an absorbing unity with the land.

Returning at last, not now unwillingly, to his accustomed consciousness, he wondered if his emotion hadn't been very much like the blind acceptances of boyhood. As well as he could remember that remote period, his sensations had been identical—a participation in a natural existence, an appropriate world. How far he had come from that! He understood, too, the formula of his present so short escape. Any idea, any thought, was inexplicably connected with the myriad others which spent his brain, and which, since maturity, had bound him in a tightening net.

If his gaze rested on the darkened bulk of the automobile, instantly it built up in his mind the entire shadowy edifice of his obligations—his house, Ella's clothes, the chauffeur, Henry and Ashley pounding at insane speed through the country. These things claimed and invaded him, choking that other and different quietude within; and they were all absolutely unimportant to him. Essentially he regarded them with a profound unconcern. All his life, he almost shouted aloud —all his life he had been concerned with precisely such ridiculous nullities.

A fundamental excitement possessed him at this realization. It grew and amplified into the knowledge that through his best years he had been victimized by a tyrannical uselessness; he had submitted himself in a slavery to values without the slightest meaning for him. He had uncritically accepted the standards he found ready, waiting for him. It had begun in college, with the select fraternity into which he had gained admission; it had followed him through the law school and into his practice, his living afterward. A rigid type of clothes, a certain formula of slang, the correct girls and women and dinners—he had given everything to their upholding. Ella, even young and bright haired, had focused all this in a sharp attention on social appearances. It might be said that their lives were dedicated to the preservation of accents.

Not vulgarly, though, for basically their accents were right enough. They hadn't imitated anything, but merely upheld the conventions of rank in America. Rawle considered the location of his house, typical of what filled his mind. It was south of the railroad, in the proper section, and he had paid thirty thousand dollars for the ground. A quarter of a mile away, north of the tracks, he could have procured the same space, land just as high and good, for ten—no, eight thousand. Ever since his admittance to the bar he had toiled for precisely the same ends.

Well, he'd been bamboozled! He had been tricked, defrauded, not so much because of what he had done but in what, consequently, he had ignored. Of course, he could blame no one but himself; he had been blind, no better than a sheep. Rawle paused in his thought, lost in amazement at the spectacle of all the men he knew who were giving their lives for nothing, for worthless and absurd privileges, artificial habits. He saw plainly how the net had closed about him. He saw this, but it was relatively unimportant. What occupied him was the attempted realization of what he had lost.

The moments of his contact, his harmony, with the night, the sky and the ground, had filled him with the easiest possible sense of a kinship, a part in anonymous Nature. He had been tranquil, unbothered, breathing as simply and easily as the earth. He had been a man, an animal, and not a ridiculous sham social being. He had been aware, in addition, of a beauty, a splendor, before denied him. A sharp envy of the remote, dark farmhouses invaded him. Rawle wanted above everything to be sleeping, exhausted with physical labor, in one of their bare rooms, and wake up with the dawn to a long day in the fields and orchards and barns.

It seemed to him, in his newly discovered being, that work with the soil was more admirable than wrangling over the properties of the dead in the orphans' court. He hadn't been born in the country. So far as he knew, there were no farmers among his immediate ancestry. No, it was only a desire to merge himself into an existence with roots in the ground. He had an overpowering hunger for reality, a hatred of what, home, awaited him.

Yet a perceptible weariness crept over him. His eyes blurred, and he switched on the blinding lights of the automobile, started it into life. Rumbling over the wooden bridge, he had a last glimpse of the broad stream moving without a sound in its bath of moonlight, under the foliage of its trees. Back in a familiar setting, it seemed to him as though, for a little, he had found another and infinitely preferable world. The bridge became a symbol, magical, and already he wondered when he would return. It might be to-morrow night; but no—he was going with Ella to the Barkers' for dinner. The next night, too, he had an annoying engagement. All the nights he could think of were filled with maddening commitments.

He couldn't, of course, take Ella. She would call him absurd, and, anyhow, he didn't want her. What in the name of heaven, on such an occasion, would they talk about? Ella would never be still. And in spite of the fact that, except for bridge, she talked incessantly, he was unable to recall a thing of importance she had said to him for years! He could not remember when she had spoken to him with warmth or enthusiasm, or when he had hurried to her with an irrepressible need for communication.

She lived within her circle of duties and pleasures, while—wholly insulated from her—he was inclosed in his obligations. Rawle had been able to talk to Charles, but Ashley was foreign to him —she was a replica of her mother. Of course, neither woman knew the slightest detail about his profession nor took the smallest interest in it. They recognized that it was the occupation of a gentleman, and that he brought them not inconsiderable sums of money for their clothes, for clubs and cars and parties and trips, but that was absolutely all. Four-fifths of his life was a closed and uninteresting book to Ella, and he had inevitably come to regard her course with no more than a perfunctory politeness. They had nothing in common but the pretenses he so hotly resented.

IV

THE FOLLOWING MORNING, however, unexpectedly she had a very great deal to say to him, to everybody. Sometime in the night burglars had entered the house and carried away an expensive burden of silver. Henderson, it developed, had carelessly neglected to close the safe concealed in the pantry wall, and Ella incontinently demanded his arrest. The man was calm and not to be shaken in his apologetic admission, and finally Rawle was relieved by the necessity to accept his assurances. But Ella continued loudly in her denunciations and conviction of confederates.

Looking over the breakfast table at the silver coffee service, the plate and candles on a buffet, Rawle said, "I can't see what's missing."

"Nothing that we use," his wife returned impatiently. "A good deal of it was wedding presents, and the rest silver that I put away because it is so impossible to clean."

He thought, "Nine hundred dollars of silver that we didn't use—that was in reality useless."

This fact occupied his mind: Nine hundred dollars spent practically for nothing. It was surprisingly in keeping, supplementary, with his last night's mood. He counted, for amusement, the purposeless things on the breakfast table. The glass dish that held his cut peaches stood on a plate that was removed with the other; a finger bowl followed, again on a plate with an expensive scrap of lace; the coffee had been transferred, in the kitchen, from the pot to the silver urn before him, brought in on a heavy silver platter; the maid passed him a spoon resting on a folded napkin.

Outside it had been touched, held, by two or three pairs of hands; it had been washed and dried, moved from sink to table and brought into the dining room by Henderson. What utter nonsense! What waste! The girl, in a silly cap, had been summoned from the pantry to hand Ella a rack of toast easily within all their reaches. Henderson, disturbed by the robbery, was moving impotently about with a dusting cloth in the hall. Heaven knew what the cook and upstairs girl, the chauffeur and gardener, were doing—probably eating broiled lambs' kidneys and bacon in an imitation of the upper slavishness here.

It was no better at his office, for hardly had he finished with the mail when young Stokes entered informally to explain exactly why he had bought another car.

"You already had a practically new one," Rawle remonstrated.

"You see," the youth told him, "this was such an unusual opportunity that I'd have been an idiot to let it go by. This is the car that won at Dayton. It can beat ninety-five, and no trouble. I just happened to meet the man who owned it at the Racquet Club. He's Totten, the squash player, and he said he'd have to let it go at once for as low as seven thousand. Now, I ask you! The old car's a pleasant little one for hacking about, but in this I can go to the coast, to the moon, anywhere, and simply no one can touch me."

"You'll find the law will touch you," Rawle commented, "if it's what I expect—one of those things all pipes like a calliope. You will get arrested simply standing by a curb." The boy turned sullen. "It's my money, isn't it?"

"It is," the other replied crisply, "and you will be surprised to learn that, suddenly, I don't care what you do with it; that is, so you kill no one but yourself. If you said you'd buy this atrocity, buy it you must. After all, your word should mean something."

When he had gone, Rawle, sitting idly at his impressive mahogany desk, wondered if a criminal practice weren't better, more real, than this select juggling of estates. Hitchcock appeared and said that undoubtedly the so-called Geltner will was a forgery. This necessitated the summoning of Marks, who, in his turn, thought that Mrs. Creath and her son could be forced to compromise. Their position was very strong. Mrs. Creath, a woman of questionable antecedents, had appeared in the Geltner house coincidental with old Geltner's last illness, nursed him with a show of affectionate tears, and after his death produced an informal will in which his family was entirely ignored for dear Agnes' faithfulness.

Leaving the city late in the afternoon with the prospect of the Barkers before him, Rawle was inundated by a weariness, a sense of futility, that almost reached nausea. Even his studs, which he forced with difficulty through the starch of his shirt, exasperated him. His neck, short and rather thick, was utterly unfit for the stiff collar he bound about it. Returning from the Barkers', Ella was enraged at him for having signaled for a no trump after two passes.

The truth was that he had been thinking of the moonlighted country, the serenity and quiet beyond the bridge. He was visualizing the barns with their white walls, the peaceful farmhouses. He found that even sitting with Ella he could banish his objective world, sink for an instant into his newly found secret release. During dinner at home he put casually some of his speculations into words.

"Isn't it foolish, Ella, not to have more or less anything on one plate? Wouldn't that be simpler? And we don't want Henderson fussing about. Why can't we give each other things? It seems to me that nearly all we do and pay for is needless. I was looking about my room before I came down, and it's littered with expensive truck; that cigarette holder with emeralds Ashley gave me— I like a cigarette better without it—and the gold case—two or three hundred dollars. There's a lot of such stuff, far too much. The clothes, too—a press full—trousers for this and knickerbockers for that, morning coats to wear in the afternoon, business coats and coats named after some cursed footling duke. Thank heaven Prince Alberts went! And the shoes! Think how much easier it would be to have one stout pair, or at most two, and some easy carpet slippers. Splendid!

"If this is so of me, I should think you'd welcome a relief from all you go through. You see, we're no longer young; and you must be tired of lacing yourself into a bottle shape and having your hair crimped and wearing hats that can't be comfortable. You're heavy now, too, and those satin slippers I see you in with the pinched toes— how about them?"

Ella Rawle gazed at him in a long astonishment. Finally she said coldly: "I haven't any idea, none at all, of what you are talking about. You might easily be trying to insult me. And please don't say such things before the servants. They'll think you are mad."

She studied him in a fleet perplexity, obviously altogether at a loss to comprehend his intention. It had been a mistake to speak to her—they had nothing except habit in common. His thoughts, what he had experienced, were for himself alone. Life was a solitary affair.

V

WHATEVER HIS RELATIONSHIP with Ella might have been—was once—candor compelled the realization that nothing of it remained except the shell of custom, or—at very most—convenience —for her. The emotion which at one time had held them together in a common identity and bond had vanished, leaving no trace of its generosity of warmth. More shortly, he didn't love Ella and she had no love for him. After the maturity of their children and Charles' death and Ashley's marriage, even the semblance of a household had dissolved. Ella's life was very full; she was very satisfied. The bridge through the afternoon and evening, the women's lunches, her particular charities with their intellectual coloring, the orchestra, a score of preoccupations that slipped his mind absorbed her entirely, while he had had the office.

Rawle wondered, sitting in his room at night, what effect it would have had on their mutual life if Ella had known at least something about his practice? Would this, he continued, have given them a different, more durable, base for the future? It seemed to him now that two lives so completely apart as theirs must come to a severance. Not necessarily with wrangling or promiscuity, but exactly in the way that had overtaken them. But this wasn't the heart of his roused curiosity, his stirred sensibilities; and dismissing the subject of his marriage he thought again of the betrayal and waste of his energies and limited time.

He wasn't merely becoming, at this late date, humane; he wasn't suddenly filled with love for the world and a desire to do good. He was concerned with no one but himself; but his sharpened penetration showed him a whole society struggling, often heroically, for nothing at all. He couldn't say when the preposterous game of pretense had begun, but now it included his apprehended world. A great relentless battle, in which women were generals, waged for the foolish, the incredible end of moving from north to south across a railroad track. The money spent, flung away, in this was astounding—for automobiles, Georgian façades, pearls, laces, the ornamental shows and hypocrisies. Either they were provided by idle capital stored up by a restless power and energy and dissipated with lax hands; they represented the utmost labor, the last pennies of men driven by the tyranny of the hollowness they served; or, as in his own case, they had been bought without thought, indifferently.

It wasn't the loss of money that disturbed him; for money, he saw, had no reality. It was only the symbol of toil and brains and luck—or dishonesty. So much money said no more than that so much human energy had been successfully directed to a given end. The money was nothing but drops of blood, the ravelings of nerves, the breaking of tissues.

It was all this assumption of social elegance and superiority that was to blame. A fatal flaw in ninety-nine hearts in a hundred, the last but one in a million. How soon America had lost the freedom, the magnificence, promised by its stupendous spaciousness! How it had spoiled its inheritance! On the mantel in the hall Ella had arranged some old pewter plates, in the past the implements of a sheer practical necessity; but she had bought them, at a nonsensical price, as ornaments. Lost in thought, he found himself mechanically clamping trees in his shoes, and with a gesture of anger he threw them clattering across the floor.

His mood changed from its initial indignation —temper—to a more philosophical amusement, for he recognized that nothing could be done; the few words with Ella had proved that. Never before had there been so highly developed the pleasure in luxury, the determination to live in the silk. No one would take any interest in the simplicity that had breathed on him beyond the bridge. He was back there again, alone, with the lights of his car turned off, parked on the grassy margin of the road. There was no moon, but the sky had been burning with northern lights, and there was a lingering afterglow.

In place of the moon's cold radiance there was a veiling of dusk and a dim haze over the streams; the cows, moving slowly, seemed magnified; the green was so deep that it was often blue. Autumn was perceptible. There was a trace of burning leaves in the air and an aroma, at once faint and sharp, of apples. This was the most delicious odor he had ever known; it was familiar to him— as though, long away, he was again, at last, returning to his own land—but he couldn't remember any apple orchards in his youth. The sense of an inner simple being again possessed him.

This innate consciousness was stronger, younger, than his actual years. Only the soil, the shrilling locusts and katydids, the woods, black with night, brought it out. Old age here, he recognized, was wholly other than age in cities, the lapsing of the men he knew. Here it came to trees and men alike, a slow losing of sap, a stiffening of arms and branches, and then winter. He recalled the South, the hotels filled with men spent, broken, in middle age; gaunt men with their desires still turned to the markets of the world. Rawle thought of the sanitariums for the revivifying of strained and jaded energies.

The simplicity within him spread till it held him in its grip. He half opened the door of the automobile in the impulse to walk across the rough wet grass—to be free. He almost wanted to take off his clothes, his silk and buckskin and gold and flannels, and run up over the hill into the gloom, feel the chill of the night against his naked body. It would be remarkable, that sensation. His desires mounted and mounted. He was choked by the intensity of his longing, his passionate hunger to be a part of his surroundings. God only knew how sick he was of the other, how he resented and detested it! He could hardly support the thought of going back again into the lies and noise and empty futility.

It was too late to begin over there. If this had only happened to him thirty years ago, how different his life would have been! Well, it hadn't. He was fortunate to have had a glimpse of peace, of a natural fate. Then, too, he could come back to it very often, cross the bridge, flood himself with the beauty. A new idea occurred to him; and, returning, he dwelt upon it with an increasing absorption. It might be called a vacation—why not? Other men went to Canada, fishing, or shot quail in South Carolina, railbirds in Georgia. What he was considering was far more reasonable, less expensive. Indeed, it would cost nothing; it could be made to pay for itself. When Ross got back and Arnold recovered ——

But he didn't wait for that. On a late September morning of thrilling beauty, moved by an uncontrollable impulse, he telephoned Henderson that he would not be home for a day or two, and arbitrarily closing the office deserted the city.

VI

THE STATION at which he left the suburban train, as near as he could calculate to the bridge, proved to be seven miles distant. He could inquire his direction only generally, and when he arrived at the region of his desire it was past midday. He continued walking, however, for he wanted to penetrate beyond any possibility of contact with his other world. Rawle grew tired. The backs of his legs burned with fatigue, but he took a certain pleasure in forcing his muscles to an unaccustomed and painful task. He came at last to a farm, characteristic of its setting and purpose, and followed the long informal lane that led down and then up to the buildings.

The barn stood at his right, built in the long past of gray stone, with a high, solid wall about the yard, into which at a prolonged calling irregularly black-and-white cows were crowding. Beyond he could see the farmer's house, long and low, with a shallow pent on its length and wide chimneys against the gables. There was an iron fence across the face, and within it still some bright flowers—dahlias and small copper-colored chrysanthemums among a tangle of greenery. Farther away, covering the southern slope of a hill, was a large, aged apple orchard, silver and amber and green.

A young man was calling the cows, a youth with a stolid face and large, scarred hands; probably, Rawle decided, a laborer; but he saw the farmer immediately after. The latter, his own age, was thin and stooped, in suspenders and bareheaded. He saluted Rawle and listened silently as the other clearly explained his purpose there.

"I've never spent a night in the country, the real country," he proceeded, "and I'd be glad if I could stay that long with you. There's no reason why you should accept me, and I suppose there are farms where they take boarders, but I don't want that. It's not what I mean. I'm not trying either to force myself on you with an absurd sum of money. I'd like to pay for the trouble, or even work, if there had been time."

Rawle was, the farmer told him, a character; and he asked him if, maybe, he had been a boy on a farm. Rawle smiled.

"No," he acknowledged, "I am afraid that I wasn't. It would be very pretty to think of me as a successful man turning back, for a night, from the world to his memories. Unfortunately that would be far from the truth. I am, I suppose, about as successful as you, and a lawyer."

He was, with practically no hesitation, accepted at his own valuation, and Homer Ganges, introducing himself, led Rawle up to the house.

"I'm not going to excuse the supper," Ganges declared, "because it's good enough for any man; and I'll not let you pay me. We don't do things like that. Perhaps I'll find out something about lawing and beat you anyhow."

He conducted him into a darkened and musty best room, where there was a cabinet filled with countless trifles, a fine, severe mahogany secretary, some ornate chairs with a vicious red varnish and green plush seats, an enlarged photograph framed in deep gold on an easel, and a table with an onyx top.

"I wouldn't ask a horsefly to stay in here," Ganges proclaimed, "but the women will think you were badly treated if I take you right out back. I guess my wife will ease up on you."

Mrs. Ganges, appearing after an audible confusion, both in the direction of the kitchen and above Rawle's head, still bore the flush of her surprise. She was a stout woman, amazingly large, really, and considerably younger than her husband. She was, as well, handsome for all her bigness. Her face, while sleepy in expression, had a high, clear color, and—except her teeth—her features were good.

"I am right glad you stopped with us," she said directly. "It'll give Mr. Ganges someone to talk to, and he's a great hand for talking. He sets right at the men after supper. But, law, it doesn't take him an hour to find out what they know! I told him he ought to have been a scholar instead of a farmer."

There was an additional commotion at the door, and two children, both girls, entered shyly.

"They're mine," Mrs. Ganges told Rawle. "I'm his third wife." She laughed without constraint. "He's dreadful hard on them—but not really; I was only having a joke. There are Arch and Francis by the first, and none by the second. Arch went for a sailor and was killed in the North Sea, and Francis is still in a hospital for gas poisoning. It comes down right hard on us at harvest. The men you hire are just nothing."

"My son, Charles," Rawle said, "was killed at Bazoches."

Nothing further was necessary. The third Mrs. Ganges almost propelled him into the kitchen, a large, pleasant room, where the table for supper was spread with a red-fringed cloth. The farm hand Rawle had seen at the barn, and who proved to be all but inarticulate, was joined by a grizzled individual who gave out the ingrained odors of the earth, and supper began. It was, as Ganges had promised, good enough for any man. The table's situation, hardly removed from the stove, made it possible for Mrs. Ganges and a slight, pallid girl helping her to bring the bubbling ham, the hot soda biscuits and boiled potatoes directly from the fire to the big plates. The coffee, in deep cups, corded with cream, burned Rawle's mouth.

Afterward, smoking on the contracted porch by the kitchen, he discovered that Ganges wanted nothing more from him than an audience for a torrent of speculations about the politics and future of the country. The farmer was a compendium of all the alarms, the theories and dreams that had swept the country for the last three decades. He had been vaguely influenced by socialism, particularly as it touched the country districts; he had a scattered knowledge of the problems of rents and labor; he had considered the single tax; and he was fundamentally opposed to capital. At the same time he had an instinctive skeptical attitude toward life, an absence of formless Utopian hopes and impractical planning, which gave his discourse a balanced, intelligent tone.

The night deepened before Rawle. The west faded, the stars came out and the scents grew stronger. The metallic chorus of insects had perceptibly lessened, but frogs croaked in a marsh, the owls kept up their crying, and there was a distant, somnolent iteration of whippoorwills. His spirit was folded in an unutterable tranquillity. He woke once in the night. There was a creaking in the old oak floors, the light, scampering feet of mice in the walls. Not a breath of air stirred the cold without. Ganges had said that there would be frost; frost lying white on the grass in the early morning, on the rough rails of the fences, immaculately pure.

VII

IT WAS LATE in the following afternoon when he reached home, and as he went on up to his room Ella called to him from the library: "Where can you have been? James Ross telephoned from town yesterday and twice this morning. No one seems to have had the slightest knowledge of your plans—most disconcerting."

He paused on the steps, considering a reply; then, convinced of its uselessness, he mounted without speech. Whatever Ross wanted was unimportant. Of all the possibilities of their practice, Rawle couldn't think of a case which might demand immediacy, which was in reality pressing. It was all a pretense, a playing at living, a making up for the sterility, the emptiness of existence by a solemn game. He wondered a little at the change which had come over him, for which apparently there had been such a slight cause—only a breath of summer peace, a drift of moonlight. A strange, potent influence had touched him, like that glimpse of Diana which made men forever dissatisfied with all the circumstances of their worldly being and loves.

Such a thing had, indeed, happened to him, he suddenly realized, the silvery magic not of a slim huntress, but of the truth. He had had, in that radiant night at the end of August, a fleet vision that had made the rest of life dull and tawdry and vain. It had separated him from all his former engagements and ties, alienated him from his own blood. Rawle was amazed at the strength, the persistence of that illumination. It was exactly as though, abruptly, he had been given sight in a world of the blind. Dinner passed in a dream. He was aware of his wife—he caught the hard, brilliant flashes from her rings—and he made adequate responses to her remarks; but essentially he was filled with uneasiness, with the desire to get away from all the sham, the hypocrisy of his home and lose himself beyond the bridge.

Nevertheless, his thoughts returned later to Ella and the problem of his old obligations. It had been a long while, he repeated, since they had exchanged any but perfunctory sentences or needs. Yes, their lives had grown utterly apart, no longer connected by a saving trace of common sympathy. He was, for Ella, nothing but a source of income, while for him she was even less. The servants kept the house in order, servants prepared his meals, arranged his room. When, last year, he had been sick with influenza, servants had tended, nursed him. What good was Ella to him or he to Ella? She didn't even need the money he made for her, since she had an annuity of seven thousand nine hundred dollars, safe during her life. The additional thousands he added all, all went for pure craven nonsense.

Rawle was standing at his window. The night was crisp, clear, when a tyrannical nostalgia seized him, an absolute necessity to go out into the dark, the open, and there find a release from his choking sense of waste. He might conceivably escape from the tragic botch of his life; and, though it was too late for him to begin again, he could, for a day or two, regain his freedom, his lost superiority. In place of that he forced himself into a troubled slumber, and the next day silently met the exasperation of James Ross.

"You should have seen Judge Nichols," Ross proceeded—"had a caveat filed. Now there's the devil to pay, not only in this, but in everything that touches the Brownells. You may be sure Clara Brownell will take it out of our wives."

Rawle said, without thinking, "What rot!"

Ross almost glared at him.

"Positively, John," he declared. "I don't know what's the matter with you. I've never seen you so—so strange. Well, we will put that behind us. I'm having lunch with Arnold at the club, and you'd better join us."

"Thank you, no," he replied.

He hated all such clubs, Rawle told himself, alone in the office—strongholds of artificial, vicious distinction. An air of smugness hung like a curtain at their doors. In the outer office a stenographer was eating a lunch brought with her. How sensible that was—decent food carefully prepared at home; and he amused himself at the thought of Ella's face should he demand such a lunch put up. Leaving the city by train, he had swift prospects of countryside, the gray green of orchards and smoke curling from farmhouse chimneys. He recalled the Ganges kitchen, and the desire to return there rose in him. Soon it would be time for apple picking. The Ganges' made apple butter.

Henry Plank and Ashley came in for dinner. The latter, at the table, gazed frowning at her father.

"Why don't you go up to Northeast?" she suggested. "The Ross cottage is still open and they'd be glad to have you there. You seem tired, to me, and you've got a lot older looking lately."

Rawle shook his head negatively; that wasn't what he wanted. A wave of contentment swept over him. Soon, he felt, he would be back again where, rather than any other place in the world, he wished to be. The vision of truth, like a flicker of moonlight, hung before him. Seen through it, his family were no more than gesticulating shadows; their words were as empty, as sharp and brittle as the fall of broken glass.

The Gibbons came in, the eternal bridge was taken up, to be temporarily halted by an acrimonious disagreement about the propriety of a one-club bid for no trumps. Ella's face got quite red, and her breast, sheathed in a complexity of expensive materials, heaved; Mary Gibbon whispered sharply to her husband; and Ashley coldly said that she thought such discussions were excessively common. When the Gibbons had gone, Ella, recalling Mary's doubtful conduct, decided against having her again to dinner. Ashley supported her mother with rumors of Mary Gibbon's rashness, while Henry Plank maintained an indifference from the eminence of his great wealth.

Rawle, in spite of a heroic effort, could think of nothing to say to his son-in-law beyond a query after the health of his automobiles.

"I sold the limousine in New York," he returned. "Got seventy-two hundred for it; and bought an English car—a small convertible four-passenger with a gray body. You must insist, if you want a gray car, on an undercoat of white lead—only way to prevent its going bad. I spent all of twenty thousand dollars before I learned that—have a passion for the color."

Plank's complacency was unendurable. Rawle asked, "Did you ever have a passion for anything else?"

His son-in-law, surprised, stared at him without answering.

It was plain that he found John Rawle indecently queer. From the bottom of the lawn a frog croaked faintly; the stars made shining paths in the sky.

VIII

However, on a ladder in the leafy depths of an apple tree, an Albemarle pippin, Rawle forgot all the meaningless circumstances and shapes of his past. The half-bushel can, suspended about his neck by a strap, was more than half full of golden apples; and dragged by its increasing weight he had to be careful of his footing and balance. The morning was very cool. There had been a heavy frost, and already the sun had lost something of its heat. There was a stir beyond, where, invisible to him, another picker was at work; while from the direction of the barn came the stuttering sound of the gasoline engine running the machinery that sorted the apples into four sizes.

He had been back with the Ganges' for three days, not a boarder now, but working, a farm hand. His shirt was open at the throat and his legs covered by overalls of worn and stained blue denim. Below he could see an old felt hat resting where it had fallen from his head. He must get it when he descended with the canful of apples. On the ground, he replaced his ladder, and then climbed its airy, swaying length. He was insuperably tired and miraculously happy. His submerged self was wholly at ease, in unrestrained evidence. Never before had he watched an entire day wheel from dark to dark, from sunrise to dusk!

The morning had been born in a cold, clear, rosy glow, a widening of light and then the pale stream of sunlight. At noon the shadows gathered under the trees, and at dusk they crept out toward the east and merged and floated up to the pure green sky. His back and legs ached and burned with fatigue. In bed he was sick with weariness, unable to sleep, and a species of waking stupor settled over him. He thought he was young, beginning life, striding out into it; but all the while there was a heavy burden on his shoulders, weighing him down, holding him back. It must be thrown off.

The next day was a long agonized effort, but after that the difficult task of apple picking grew easier. Soothed by its automatic, ever-repeated motions, he lived in a waking somnolence like the realization of a heavenly dream. For the first time he had a feeling of earning money, of getting useful money in return for a useful, an indispensable act. He had a supreme right to the food he consumed, turning it back at once into his necessary activity. At every face he was in contact with life. His feet were planted in the earth identically in the manner of the trees and grasses, his head was among the fragrant boughs and fruit.

There, among the leaves, he discovered an unsuspected world—the crimson-winged flash of a scarlet tanager, the burnished, purple-black sheen and scolding voices of crows, woodpeckers with red heads clinging vertically to the trunks, the discarded, amber-colored shells of the locusts, now stilled, that had so moved him with their high shrilling. Rawle's senses were ravished by the scents of autumn liberated in the searing frost. He came to like the rich ammoniac odor of the barn, the dry, dusty smell of the hay in the loft, the flat, warm breath of fresh milk. He grew familiar with the diversity of the surrounding life —the harsh, dry guinea hens, the angry geese, the ducks like important Chinamen, the excitable, gregarious chickens, apoplectic turkeys and insensate, aërial pigeons. The dogs, the half-bred collie and the nondescript dog, rough and strong, with all the imaginable virtues, he had as his own. He knew the characteristics of various cows, the farm horses and the bull in the lower field. Rawle understood, as well, the personalities of the flivver truck, the tractor and the engine of general purpose. He discovered a particular facility with the last. For an unexplained reason it balked, choked with everyone but him.

A feeling of deep subconscious fellowship with the other laborers, with Homer Ganges and Valma, his wife, permeated Rawle. Each was interrelated to the other, and the whole formed a recognizable and common humanity. It was extraordinary to know men severed from their clothes, from a thousand prejudices and artificialities! As individuals he would not have been strongly drawn to them; but together, absorbing him, he had a warm satisfaction in their actuality. They were men. He talked but little to them, or rather they were constrained in their conversation with him; but in the evening by the barn he sat and listened to their rustic speculations, their superstitious and husky oaths. Rawle learned the sign of the moon under which to plant Lima beans from the laborer of indeterminate age with a head like an earth-browned skull ornamented with a ragged mustache and pale blue, suspicious eyes. All his speech was combative, an arrogance of tone, a surety of statement, covering a doubting, obscured spirit.

He, the laborer, had, it developed, a brother who was a painter of houses, a man who at one time had been in a position to be defrauded of a lot of money.

"Sure he was," the narrator asserted, looking about in preparation for skepticism. "I painted for him myself on a job at Lakewood."

He had worked at Lakewood and a hundred other places—a wandering, solitary, unhappy being, slowly drawing closer to the earth that would, in the not distant future, envelop him. He had, it was plain, consumed a vast amount of cheap and destructive drink. There clung to him reminiscences of the gutter, of nights in small jails, together with the evidence of prodigious interrupted toils.

Where once Rawle would have passed him without notice, now he was aware of the human flame burning within the wrecked body. Removing, together, a stump from the corner of a field, they sat on the grassy slope by a fence; and the smoke from Rawle's pipe joined the bitter smoke from the other's blackened clay bowl. John Harden Rawle was unshaven; his arms, on which the sleeves of a draggled shirt were torn, were dark with the mold of rotten wood; his trousers were secured by a harness strap and his shoes caked with dried mud. His companion was no less dilapidated in appearance. Dirt and sweat! Rawle reflected that until now he had been too clean—a lay figure in starch and polished shoes. He had been in the habit of importing his dressing for tan leather from England. His derby hats had come from Vienna, the silk hats and stiff straws from Bond Street. Silk hats! He laughed, and the man beside him turned belligerently.

The latter rose on legs at once insecure and serviceable, tapping out his pipe on a knuckle as gnarled as an old hickory knot.

"She ought to come soon," he said shortly of the stump. "If I had a stick of giant powder I'd heave her up. Well, I don't care. The work's too hard here anyhow. I'll be getting along tomorrow."

Rawle suddenly wondered what Ella, what Ashley and Henry were doing; how things were in the orphans' court. They had no idea of where he was.

IX

HE CONSIDERED THIS, returning home. He had been absent practically three weeks, and the apple crop had been harvested. Rawle had gone, this latter time, in the familiar, obscured manner. All at once he had had to leave the accumulation of trivialities in the office for reality. His inner self had driven him away from the scene of his ludicrous pretending. But his duty to Ella—he tried to remind himself of this, but the effort was a failure. Essentially his acts were of no moment to her; she depended on him for nothing. Rawle might have lied to her, made up an imaginary necessity. That, however, was no part of his present state. The truth, and not lies, possessed him.

The potency of truth, even of the brief glimpse come to him, as it were, on a ray of moonlight, astounded him. At the merest realization that he, an individual, was alive, with deep individual needs and possibilities, that he was something more than a member, a slave, of a ridiculous, purposeless social tyranny, his entire known world had been blasted into fragments. Perhaps some day truth would descend on life. A great deal must be destroyed—a new beginning necessary—but with an inconsequential loss. Old fellows like him would be swept into oblivion. He had had only a glimmer; and, like Moses gazing at the far Promised Land, he projected himself wistfully toward a life he could never know.

Ella, to his surprise, said very little; she was reserved with him, preoccupied in air; and when later he referred to the office she told him that there was no need at present for his going into town.

"James Ross sent word it was unnecessary," she said, standing at the door to his room. "George Arnold is back and there is very little to be done."

Already, lost in thought, he had forgotten her. The moon was bright and created outside spaces of illusive, swimming radiance. The following day was cold, with a high wind that swept troops of leaves from the maples, spreading them in uneasy sheets of gold over the ground. Rawle came into the house late in the afternoon and found, laid on the bed, his dinner jacket and formal linen. Henry Plank and Ashley, his wife told him, were expected with a friend. Ella was even more abstracted than yesterday. She seemed positively nervous, and avoided meeting his gaze. Henry, too, when he arrived, was unnatural. His friend, whose name, Rawle learned, was Simmons, was a big man, with a strongly marked, smooth face. He was not unlike an actor. His voice was resonant, self-confident, his manner dramatic.

"I understand, Mr. Rawle," he said at the table, "that you have been away—a small private excursion."

Rawle studied him, touched by the edge of an instinctive resentment.

"Yes," he replied shortly, and then he realized that he had made no explanation of his absence. There was no reason for concealing where he had been. He had wanted to avoid argument, dissent; but, curiously, Ella hadn't asked him a question. He announced, "I have been picking apples."

The reception of his statement was ridiculously out of keeping with its commonplace, homely truth. Ella started to speak and then averted her head. Ashley dropped a spoon, Henry gazed at him in a dumb questioning. Only Mr. Simmons was unmoved.

"Exactly," he echoed—"picking apples. This, I believe, is the appropriate season. Very interesting."

His voice bore a query—it might have been sympathetic, understanding.

"More than interesting," John Rawle cried—"absorbing, fascinating. You have no idea of the sense of reality it brings! An apple is a fact—it can't be denied—and it must be picked; very carefully, too; not torn away from the stem." He turned to Ella. "You must have wondered about me, wondered and not worried. That would have made a difference. Well, I was living. I can't make it any clearer. For the first time in my life I was alive, I was useful, doing something actual. I was worth four dollars a day."

"That doesn't seem monumental," Simmons once more annoyingly interrupted in his self-important air. "I should have thought the law paid you very much better."

"More money, yes," Rawle replied, "and yet not nearly enough for what it had in return. I was a lay figure for litigation, a fence for rotting money. You may not know that it rots, but it does. It rots and spoils in dead accumulations, and corrupts everyone who touches it. For money's life," he developed his conviction—"or rather it's the sign of life. A dollar is the record of so much accomplished, not perhaps by you, but by someone, some effort in the past. And the other men's efforts, payment, are no good to you or me. We must create, by our faithfulness and labor, our own money; not spend it, but add—add.

"Don't you see, can't you see that the sum of our gold, our real gold, is the sum of ourselves, of each man alone? Picking apples at four dollars a day is creating four dollars a day; but subtracting four thousand from a dead man's energy, fattening on it like worms, is only a dissipation. But even that isn't the most important thing. When we do work, create something, we fling away all our ability and strength and time. We change it into worthless nonsense; we change ourselves into objects that would be funny if they were not fatal.

"Everything for nothing! We don't breathe, we

never live, we are never, for a healthy moment, animals. The slaves of plates and hours and ambitious women! We pay out all that we are and get less than nothing in return—the privilege of living with critical strangers, of supporting a thousand absurdities in which we've no interest. And it's getting worse—the waste and pretense and extravagance. The lies are growing thicker every day. Nine-tenths, ninety-nine one-hundredths of what I spend is for lies. Those pearl studs are lies, and my shirt's a lie, and my waistcoat—a scrap of stuff that cost sixty dollars—is a bigger lie than the rest. They are lies, because they're not worth what I pay for them, what I do to get them—all sham. A suit of clothes isn't worth more than ten dollars of any man's spirit and strength and days—thrown away for nothing."

Suddenly, in an overwhelming sense of impotence, he realized the vanity of so much talk. His wife's face was stony, his daughter only impatient. For a moment, swept away by his vision of honesty, of truth, he had deserted the only possibility of release for him—the quiet insistence on preserving what, so late, he had discovered for himself. The dining room, the winking candles and show of silver, the elaboration of the women, their hair twisted into artificial shapes, oppressed him beyond endurance. Outside he could see the windy spaces of the moon, and he rose abruptly, in the need for a gulp of cold, pure stillness.

Henry Plank's friend, Simmons, rose with him.

"Don't go!" Simmons said. "You have been very interesting."

Rawle looked at him in a wave of temper.

"What the devil!" he exclaimed—"what the devil ——"

His daughter rushed from the room.

"Matthews," Simmons called; and, half turning, Rawle saw a man enter with capable shoulders and ready hands. Instantly, with a numbed heart, he understood the significance round him.

"Be quiet, Mr. Rawle," Simmons continued, approaching him. "We want to fix it so you can pick all the apples you like."

"Your precautions are unnecessary," John Harden Rawle told them. "We can dispense with Matthews. I made the mistake of thinking it was my world that was crazy."

Within him was an utter thankfulness for what, before he died, he had had—a flame of adoration for the beauty of sheer life.

TUTT AND MR. TUTT—
IN WITNESS WHEREOF

by Arthur Train

ON JUNE 7, 1919, a long, lean Yankee lawyer who smoked poisonous cheroots and fought his hardest battles for the clients who paid him least made his first appearance in the *Post*'s pages. Twenty-five years and eighty-three "Tutt and Mr. Tutt" stories later, he reached the end of his recorded career. During that time Ephraim Tutt, Esq., was undoubtedly the best-known lawyer in America; *Who's Who* wrote to ask for his biography, and his words were quoted in courtrooms all the way up to the Supreme Court in Washington. Thousands of his admirers simply refused to believe that he did not exist; when author Train wrote a *Post* article to prove it (February 26, 1944) one indignant reader replied, "The fact is, Mr. Tutt invented Train." There was some substance to this claim. Train had some of the same characteristics as Mr. Tutt, thought like him, and to some extent lived like him. He was an assistant district attorney of New York from 1901 to 1908 and remained an active lawyer until 1923. As early as 1905 he began writing stories and articles for the *Post* and continued to do so until just before his death in 1945. Nor did he confine himself to the adventures of Mr. Tutt. In 1914 he wrote a remarkable *Post* serial (*The Man Who Rocked the Earth*) which predicted that World War I would end through the explosion of an atomic bomb. He was one war too soon with that idea.

MAY 7, 1921

WHAT I WANT is a lawyer who can deliver the goods; I don't care what it costs. Can I talk business with you?" The grim-visaged woman sitting opposite Mr. Ephraim Tutt, the senior partner in the celebrated firm of Tutt & Tutt, attorneys and counselors at law, looked across the desk at him significantly.

"I don't know why not," replied the lawyer affably. "Business is what I'm looking for; what every lawyer is after, I guess!"

"Well"—she hesitated, striving to penetrate the sphinxlike mask of his wizened old face, which had defied lawyers and judges and poker players alike for half a century—"you drew Cabel's will, and you're the executor named in it. I know that much, because he's told me so. Now, it's this way: Cabel wants to make some changes in that will of his, but, besides being old and feeble, he's crotchety and cantankerous and suspicious of almost everybody. But he'll listen to you. You're his executor and the proper one to do it anyway."

"Well," hazarded Mr. Tutt blandly, "as I said before, why not?"

"So naturally I've come to you. Besides, I've heard quite a lot about your firm; and I guess you and I can get along pretty well together."

"I'm sure we can," smiled the attorney. "I always strive to please."

"What's more, I'll see that your fee is promptly paid—with maybe a little besides!" she concluded meaningly.

Mr. Tutt searched her face.

"Am I to understand then that you—and not Mr. Baldwin—are my client?" he inquired pointedly.

Mrs. Alfreda Baldwin smiled to herself. She wasn't going to let the old fox catch her—put her in a position where maybe she would have to pay his bill.

"Not at all!" she retorted. "It is my husband who wants his will changed. He's your client—not me. All I say is that you don't need to worry about getting paid. Anyhow, I don't see what difference it makes which of us is your client."

Mr. Tutt fumbled in a long box upon his desk and selected a cigar resembling in shape and general appearance what a coiffeur would refer to as "a rat."

"Do you mind if I smoke?" he inquired ceremoniously. "Answering your question—it might make a lot of difference which of two persons happened to be one's client."

250

"How do you mean?" she demanded. "Of course I don't mind if you smoke."

Mr. Tutt carefully ignited the attenuated stogy which he had excavated from its stratified brethren.

"A lawyer has to be faithful to his retainer—even if sometimes he doesn't get it," he announced, exhaling a poisonous cloud of greenish-gray smoke. "It is the duty of the attorney to be loyal to the interests of the person who employs him and to carry out his wishes to the best of his ability, just as it is the duty of the client to compensate him for his services.

"Now, if those interests conflict with those of any other person ——"

"Oh, I understand all that!" she interrupted. "That doesn't enter into it here. Mr. Baldwin is your client. I am only his agent—his messenger, if you choose. He will pay your bill. But, as it happens, our interests and wishes are identical."

Mr. Tutt nodded behind his smoke screen.

"That's all right, then!"

She returned his glance fixedly. He had not put anything over on her and he had, she opined, absorbed her hint about the "little besides" and all the rest of it.

"I don't want to have Mr. Baldwin disturbed any more than is absolutely necessary," she continued. "We both thought that I could tell you what he wanted to do with his money and that you could draw up a codicil here in your office and bring it up to the house for him to sign. That's the simplest, easiest way, isn't it? A codicil?"

"Quite so!" agreed Mr. Tutt. "I can easily do that if you really know what changes he wants to make in the disposition of his property. But there's no use preparing a codicil and having it engrossed only to find you've got to do it all over again."

"You won't have to do that in this case. I know—that is, Mr. Baldwin knows—exactly what he wants to do. I've been over it with him most carefully. It's all written down right here."

She produced from a black bead bag several sheets of folded note paper covered closely with handwriting. Mr. Tutt drew toward him a yellow pad, regretfully laid down his stogy and took up a pencil. Mrs. Baldwin put on a pair of heavy spectacles, which intensified her already hawkish appearance, and settled back in her chair.

"First, he wants to bequeath outright ten thousand dollars each to the Museum of Art, the Museum of Natural History, the Children's Aid Society, the Charity Organization Society, St. Luke's Hospital and Columbia University."

"That makes sixty thousand dollars," commented Mr. Tutt, jotting down the names. "What next?"

"Then he wants to leave thirty thousand dollars to Alvin H. Spearman, of Englewood, New Jersey."

"Who is he?" asked the lawyer, his pencil poised.

"An old friend of his," she answered. "And thirty thousand dollars to his wife, Rowena Howell Spearman."

"That makes another sixty thousand dollars," said Mr. Tutt.

"Twenty thousand each to Alfred Spearman, the son of Alvin Spearman; Esther S. Bowman, of Trenton; Anna S. Rawson, of Scranton; and Josephine S. Briggs, of New York City."

"Now you've got one hundred and forty thousand."

Mrs. Baldwin eyed him a trifle suspiciously.

"What's that?" she snapped.

"In personal legacies, I mean," he explained quickly. "He's disposed of two hundred thousand in all."

Mrs. Baldwin checked off something on the sheet of note paper in her lap.

"Then he wants to leave ten thousand each to the following: Almina Bostwick, of Jersey City; Georgina H. Hibbard, of Flatbush, Long Island; Isabel F. Hawkins, of Flushing, Long Island; Mary P. Daly, of Riverdale, New York; Edith L. Mills, of Yonkers, New York; and Althea W. Rose, of Ringwood, New Jersey."

"Sixty more," scored Mr. Tutt. "Makes two hundred and sixty thousand dollars. Then what?"

"Twenty-five thousand to The Nurses' Benefit Club."

"What's that?"

"A charitable corporation," she answered shortly. "Then fifteen thousand each to his physicians, Dr. Samuel Woodman and Dr. Richard Aspinall."

"I have it," said the lawyer.

"Then there are a few smaller legacies: Five thousand dollars to Bridget Mulcahy, the cook; five thousand to Patrick Moynahan, the butler; five thousand to Pierre Larue, the valet; and five thousand to Agnes Roony, the parlor maid. He believes in being liberal with servants."

"So I see!" observed Mr. Tutt. "And with the medical profession as well!"

"Oh, he's very fond of both Doctor Woodman and Doctor Aspinall!" she assured him. "They have been lifelong friends!"

"Anything more?"

"Only his legacy to me—two hundred and fifty thousand—and, of course, I'm also to be the residuary legatee," said Mrs. Baldwin, folding up her notes. "You'll continue as executor. How soon can you have the codicil ready?"

"By to-morrow afternoon," he replied. "It's quite simple."

"Then bring it up to-morrow evening so that Mr. Baldwin can sign it," she directed. "About nine o'clock, say?"

"As you like," he agreed. "If that will be more convenient for your husband than to have him come here."

"Oh, he couldn't possibly come here!" she asserted. "He's sick in bed!"

Mrs. Baldwin arose and pulled down her black jacket, which had a tendency to ride upward upon her ample figure; and Mr. Tutt arose also. There was something about her—which inspired in him more than dislike, he could not say exactly what, whether it was the beetling nose, the compressed lips, the expansive, tightly corseted bosom, the flabby brown skin beneath her chin, which merged into the pendulous cheeks—like an old mastiff he decided. A full-rigger! How could any man in his senses have married her? And the thought quite naturally suggested that perhaps the man hadn't been.

II

"WHERE DID YOU GET little Eva?" chirped Tutt, peering at his partner over his goggles through the door after the lady's departure. "I was quite worried at first over leaving you alone with her!"

Mr. Tutt's long wrinkled face wreathed itself in an expansive grin.

"Isn't she terrible!" he ejaculated.

"Some crocodile!" asserted the lesser Tutt. "I can see now what the fellow meant when he said that the female of the species is more deadly than the male! What kind friend passed her on to us?"

"Nobody—she came herself," replied the senior partner. "I think she must like my looks!"

"B-r-r-rh!" shivered Tutt, shielding his face with his hands. "I hope she won't take a fancy to me!"

"You're safe!" laughed his partner. "Mrs. Georgie Allison has rendered you immune to the attractions of the opposite sex for all time."

"Who told you about that?" queried Tutt rather peevishly.

"Never mind! Never mind!" returned the old lawyer airily. "You can't keep all your little peccadillos concealed from the public eye."

"I know! Miss Wiggin must have told on me!" growled Tutt. "Well, reverting to the subject we were discussing, what was the Lady Gorgon's name?"

"Mrs. Cabel Baldwin."

"Wife of the old fellow that married his trained nurse?"

Mr. Tutt gave a fervid start of surprise.

"What!" he ejaculated. "Really?"

"Don't you recall the case? 'Nurse Spearman' —and all that? It was in the papers," Tutt reminded him. "He got out of bed when he had the pneumonia or something and beat it over to Jersey and married her before a J. P. without telling even his own daughter. That was about three years ago. He was seventy-two; she was forty-seven. He'd be over seventy-five now, and she'd be fifty."

"She would! She is!" assented Mr. Tutt. "Or stronger!"

"There was a grand row about it!" said Tutt. "But nobody could do anything. The Constitution guarantees to every man the inalienable right to marry his trained nurse. But she was such an old chisel face that it seemed as though she must have chloroformed him first. She'd been married before, too; twice, I mean!"

"So that's it!" remarked Mr. Tutt. "Did you say there was a daughter?"

"I have an idea there was, but if I remember correctly she was away at college or somewhere. I don't recall all the details. But look out for her! What did she want?"

"To have us draw a codicil to her husband's will."

"Oho!" piped Tutt. "And does little birdie get the big fat worm?"

"She gets half of it; the other half of the worm goes to various individuals and charities."

"That's funny!" commented the junior Tutt, pursing his lips. "If she was after the kale why should she let anybody else have a rake-off?"

Mr. Tutt took a turn up and down his office, then he amputated another stogy, lit the remains, leaned back in his swivel chair, crossed his Congress boots upon his desk and folded his hands behind his head.

"That's the artistic way to do it," said he. "Don't you remember the Blodgett case? Blodgett was ninety-one and dead at the top; he'd had senile dementia for fifteen years. A woman got hold of him—only that time it was a young one— and induced him to make a will in her favor. All she had to do was to take him out to concerts and ride him round the park in a victoria. Well, when he died it was discovered that he'd left her the greater part of his fortune; a couple of millions; but—and here was the clever part of it— he'd apparently divided another million between Harvard, Yale and Princeton, with the result that, although the heirs at law and next of kin contested the probate, they found three of the most influential universities in the country lined up against them, with all their counsel, naturally including the leaders of the bar, alongside Little Bright Eyes—who succeeded in probating the will, got her two millions and bought a foreign prince and a château on Lake Geneva with them."

"Pretty good!" nodded Tutt. "And is that the game our old battle-ax is trying to pull?"

"Here's the horoscope. Read it for yourself," answered Mr. Tutt, pushing the yellow pad toward his partner with his foot. "You'll note that the very first thing she did was to square a few of our more select public institutions—like the Museum of Art and St. Luke's Hospital."

"Holy crickets!" mused Tutt. "I wonder if she could be the same girl—tired of living on Lake Geneva with her prince—and looking for further adventures!"

"No," declared his partner. "You couldn't give this one away with a bonus of two million dollars."

"Aha! What's this?" suddenly cried Tutt, scanning the prospectus of Mr. Baldwin's proposed benefactions. "Here's another little joker! Twenty thousand dollars to the domestics and thirty to the doctors! She's got all the witnesses signed, sealed and delivered! He could be a raving maniac and there'd be nobody to prove it. No doctor—that is, no bug doctor—is going to admit that any patient of his can have senile dementia who has sense enough to leave him fifteen thousand dollars! We ought to take Alfreda into partnership!"

"But you haven't covered it all yet!" said Mr. Tutt. "I'll wager that if we looked into it we'd find she's not only given herself a quarter of a million and the residuary, but in order to prevent any possible slip-up she's salted a quarter million around where she can get hold of it afterward if she misses out on her own legacy. She's left her father and mother thirty thousand each, and the four little Spearmans eighty more; to say nothing of half a dozen of her intimate female friends and a nursing society of which she probably controls the board of directors."

"Rather a speedy client!" affirmed Tutt.

Mr. Tutt shook his head.

"She's not our client."

"Who is, then?"

"Her husband."

"It's all the same thing," affirmed the lesser Tutt. "You can soak her a thousand or fifteen hundred just for drawing a codicil like that! And think of the fight we'll have on our hands when the old boy dies! Makes no difference to us which

way the cat jumps. If she gets him to execute your codicil we'll have to defend it against the heirs on the ground of mental incapacity; and if he won't execute it we'll be attacking all his prior wills in her behalf on the same ground. Coming and going! Both ends against the mid. It'll take six months in court—after we finally get there! Why, it's worth thirty thousand dollars to us!"

"Do you really think so, now?" murmured his partner. "Thirty thousand dollars is a lot of money—a powerful lot of money!"

The morality—or rather the immorality—of lawyers has been the subject of jest since the days when the bare fact that a man could read and write rendered him immune to punishment for crime. "Benefit of clergy" was felt to be a joke; and so was the law. The pun that made "lawyer" and "liar" indistinguishable dates doubtless from considerably before the days of Falstaff. Not only, as Bumble said, was the law "a ass, a idiot," but lawyers were natural-born pettifoggers, crooks, thieves, tricksters and rascals. An honest lawyer? There was no such animal!

We have no desire at the present writing to enter into a general defense of the conduct of our brethren of the bar, but merely take occasion to point out that in many instances the lawyer is really no more deserving of censure than the layman, the product of whose skill is subsequently used by another for an unlawful or immoral purpose. Shall no more whips be manufactured because some ruffians use them upon their wives? Or chisels, lest burglars avail themselves of them in their unholy business? Shall the cobbler cease from cobbling for fear that someone may hurl his shoe after a blushing bride? Tut-tut! There is nothing under the sun that cannot be made subject to the devil's ingenuity. We have even heard of two murders committed within a single month by means of oyster shells. Yet, shall we be forbidden oysters?

The reader has already grasped our analogue. Shall there be no cakes and ale because a custard pie can be used as an instrument of assault? And, similarly, because a will, deed, bond or other paper writing may, perhaps, be used eventually to perpetrate a fraud, is that any reason why an innocent attorney should not draw it up? He may suspect that old Hardscrabble intends to cheat the Widow Perkins, or that the rifles for which he has drawn the bill of sale to Mr. Jones are intended for Mr. Villa; but the very law by which the attorney earns his livelihood requires him to give the benefit of the doubt to an accused and presume him innocent until the contrary is proved. Why, then, should he not give that same doubt to Uncle Jonas Hardscrabble, to Mr. Jones —and to himself?

Thus, shall a lawyer refuse to draw a will because his client might—if he were made the subject of prolonged study by a faculty of alienists— be shown to be without testamentary capacity? Shall he take the bread out of his children's mouths because the fruit of his professional labors may, in the hands of another, be used to work an injustice? Must every attorney maintain a hospital, an observation ward in connection with his office? Nay! Such a thought is nonsense! It is no part of a lawyer's business to act as a spy upon his client or anticipate and expose his contemplated iniquities.

Had Tutt & Tutt refused to draw the codicil to Mr. Baldwin's will Alfreda would simply have given the job to some other firm. They knew well that a will is like any article of merchandise purveyed in market overt; for instance—a bologna. If the buyer is planning to administer the bologna to an infant of tender years—or days—it may, it is true, thereby become an instrument of infanticide; and in like case if a will or a codicil is about to be offered for signature to an imbecile it may become a link in a chain of fraud; but why gratuitously visit upon either the will or the bologna a foul suspicion which may in fact be entirely unwarranted?

Let us admit at once—whether or not the reader be convinced by this reasoning, which we contend is as sound as most legal argument and equally edifying—let us admit freely, frankly and without reserve that it did not occur to Tutt or even to Mr. Tutt to decline to draw the codicil proposed by Mrs. Baldwin. It was a perfectly good legal job for anybody. It would take Mr. Tutt, with his stereotyped regular office form before him, twenty minutes—no more, probably— to dictate it to Miss Sondheim, who would thereupon pound it out on the typewriter; then Mr. Tutt would correct and possibly revise it; and Scraggs, the inebriated scrivener in the wire cage in the outer office, would have a perfect time writing it all out in a beautiful Spencerian hand on glossy imitation parchment; after which Miss Wiggin, the chief clerk, Willie, the office boy, and Miss Sondheim would deck it out like a newborn babe in dainty blue ribbons, tie a beautiful red seal around its neck, roll it up tenderly in tissue paper and put it to sleep in the top drawer of a desk until it was time for somebody to unwrap it, spread it out upon the counterpane of the death chamber and, pointing to the final paragraph, beginning with the fateful words "In witness whereof," place the pen in the shaking hand of the testator and say: "Well, Mr. Smith, you

understand, of course, that this is your will? Yes, I said, 'Your will.' Will. W-i-l-l—WILL! Yes! Sign here!"

And Tutt & Tutt would thereupon receive in due course from the executors a check for a thousand dollars, of which about nine hundred and ninety-three would be net. Why should Mr. Tutt have refused this choice titbit of humdrum practice—particularly as will drawing was one of the best things that he did? Can he properly be censured for so doing? Yet, quite naturally, what might be called the internal evidence of possible fraud contained in the codicil itself excited his interest. Certainly every step had been taken to render the instrument, if executed, impregnable to attack. However, there was no particular reason why it should be assumed that the scheme had not emanated from the mind of the old gentleman himself. Many a testator provides his legatees with a doughty legal champion by leaving a fat legacy to some eleemosynary institution which will lose it if the will is denied probate. But in this instance, it is true, there were other indications that Mrs. Baldwin was engaged in feathering her nest in an expert manner and safely anchoring said nest against the assaults of outraged kin and next of kin.

Now, Mr. Tutt practiced law largely for the fun of it, for he really didn't need the money, and he scented in the visit of Mrs. Alfreda Baldwin a plot almost as exciting as a detective story. And that was why he sent for Mr. Bonnie Doon, that wise and finished specimen of young-gentleman-about-town who made himself generally useful to Tutt & Tutt, and instructed him to ascertain by whatever means were at his disposal all he could about the past career of Mrs. Cabel Baldwin, née Alfreda Spearman, daughter of Alvin Spearman, Esquire, of Englewood, New Jersey.

III

"TELL OSCAR I want him here at nine o'clock without the car," said Mrs. Baldwin from her desk in the library to the girl sitting listlessly by the center table with her hands in her lap. "Don't send the message, either. Speak to him yourself. And tell the other servants they can have the evening out."

The girl arose silently. She was languid, pale, harassed, with dark circles under her eyes, but she bore herself with dignity.

"Why don't you answer when you're spoken to?" snapped the older woman. "One would think you—and not I—was the mistress of this house!"

"I haven't any such delusion," answered the girl tonelessly. "I will take your message. You know very well I'd not stay here another day except for my father."

"You know well enough where your bread is buttered!" shot back her stepmother with a sneer. "You are dependent upon me for everything you have in this world. And you had better mind your p's and q's."

"Shall I tell Oscar what you want him for?" asked the girl.

"Ha!" replied the other. "You want to find out, do you? Well, it's none of your business!"

The girl shrugged her shoulders and walked slowly towards the door.

"And then come back here!" ordered Mrs. Baldwin. "I don't want you hanging round your father. He can't stand your whining and crying!"

The girl controlled herself with difficulty, and once in the privacy of the hall outside the library burst into tears. She had been living under the same strain ever since the previous spring, upon her graduation from college, where her father had sent her at the death of her mother four years before that. She had gone away from home, leaving him a melancholy but apparently well old man. A year later she had received a sudden telegram from him announcing his marriage in Jersey City to an unknown woman who, it turned out, had been acting as his nurse during a sudden attack of pneumonia, followed by heart trouble.

She had been startled, shocked, crushed, not only by her father's forgetfulness of her mother in so short a time but by the notoriety that had followed the old man's escapade and the state of mental and physical deterioration in which she found him on her return. From being a handsome, vigorous, upstanding old gentleman he had shriveled away into a bent, tottering, querulous invalid afraid of his own shadow, at times; when they were alone, responding to her caresses with something of his former affection, but in general furtive, suspicious, cowering before this strange, ugly woman who had in some sinister way secured mastery over him—fearful in her presence to call his soul his own. There seemed to be something hypnotic about the ex-nurse's influence, for the mere sound of her voice was enough to set his shrunken old limbs trembling. And if she heard him up and moving about in his room when she was downstairs she had only to call up through the well, and he would obediently clamber back into bed again.

So Lydia Baldwin found herself half servant, half prisoner in her father's house. She would, as she had said, have fled out into the world and earned her own living had it not been for the possibility that she might be of some service to him. She saw her father getting weaker and

weaker, but was not allowed to minister to him save under the direction and supervision of her jailer. Everybody employed in the establishment —in fact everybody who came there—was on her stepmother's pay roll. Even the doctors were persons of the latter's own choosing, with whom she had had some mysterious association in the past. Surrounded by spies, without money, Lydia Baldwin was treated as a hostage, all her movements watched and reported upon.

At rare intervals her father would awake as from a nightmare and, once a month, perhaps, would have a day when he seemed almost like himself again and would even make feeble jokes about his condition. These exceptional phases occurred without premonition and were immediately followed by states of depression in which he believed his end to be near and during which he insisted upon the constant presence of his wife, upon whom he then seemed utterly dependent. At such times Lydia suffered torture, since she could not even render her father the solace of her affection. Then, and only then, was she really tempted to accept Henry Holborn's offer of marriage and escape from the domestic hell in which she lived. For, although Henry was only twenty-five—she was twenty-three—he was earning a good salary in an architect's office, and his abilities were recognized as such as to entitle him to view the future with confidence. That she would remain penniless Lydia had no doubt. Her stepmother would never permit her father to leave her anything; and although he had once told her shortly after her mother's death that she would one day be a rich woman, since his second marriage he had never referred to the subject.

IV

IT WAS PRECISELY nine o'clock when Mr. Tutt mounted the front stoop of the Baldwin mansion and rang the bell. Mrs. Baldwin opened the door herself.

"Good evening," she said affably, extending a muscular hand, with a smile as convincing as that of a hyena. "Glad you're so prompt!"

Over her shoulder the old lawyer could see the drooping figure of a young girl standing disconsolately at the head of the stairs leading to the next floor. As he took off his coat and hat she turned away and retreated into the shadow.

"Lydia, come down here!" called up Mrs. Baldwin. "I don't want you bothering your father. Come and meet Mr. Tutt!"

The girl obediently emerged once more and, resting her hand upon the rail of the staircase, came wearily down. Descending thus, with the half light falling upon her pale face against the background of shadow, she reminded him of a Burne-Jones figure standing at evening beside some lily-covered pool. Mr. Tutt's parched old soul yearned to her like a withered tree whose leaves thirst for a cool breeze after a sultry day.

"Hurry up!" ordered Mrs. Baldwin. "Don't keep us waiting all the evening."

The girl lifted her chin proudly and as she did so caught the tender gleam in the old man's eyes. There was no mistaking that look of pity, almost of affection with which he was regarding her. She smiled faintly.

"This is my stepdaughter, Lydia," said Mrs. Baldwin.

Mr. Tutt moved a step forward, took the girl's hand and bent over it as she still stood upon the stairs above him. Then, still holding it in his, he led her down the remaining steps. Something— we do not know what it is that leaps from heart to heart on such occasions—passed between them. Neither spoke. Yet each said to the other, "I am your friend!"

"I want you to sit here in the front parlor, Lydia," said Mrs. Baldwin, "and when I call to you, send up Oscar to your father's bedroom. If anybody should ring the front doorbell, you answer it. The servants are out."

"Very well," answered Lydia coldly.

"Now," continued Mrs. Baldwin, "if you are all ready we'll go upstairs." She lowered her voice to a whisper, so that Lydia, who had gone into the drawing-room, might not hear. "Have you got the codicil all ready?"

Mr. Tutt nodded and followed her up to the next landing. The woman turned the knob of the door nearest the head of the stairs and pushed it open with a suggestion of stealth. Certain people cannot move without giving the impression of trying to stalk some prey. Usually it is a man trying to stalk a woman. This time it was a woman trying to stalk a man.

In a large high-ceiled room, dimly lighted by only a green-shaded reading lamp, an old man lay propped up in bed. The face was gaunt, the eyes lusterless, the mouth drooping. Both arms were extended across the sheet in front of him, motionless and parallel.

"Here is somebody to see you, grandpa!" said Mrs. Baldwin as if she were speaking to a child who must be at one and the same time cajoled and warned to be good.

The old man in the bed licked his lips and a hardly perceptible quiver passed over his features.

"This is the lawyer," announced his wife. "Mr. Tutt. You know him."

A puzzled look—of recollection, almost of recognition—flickered in the senile eyes, followed by one of dread fused with cunning.

"Yes," he replied thickly in a half whisper, "I know him."

"He has drawn up the codicil for you to sign." She might as well have added the words "like a good little boy."

Mr. Baldwin made no reply. He appeared for the moment to have forgotten that they were there.

"Cabel!" said Mrs. Baldwin in a metallic tone, stepping towards the bed. "Cabel—pay attention!"

The old man shrank back as if he had been slapped in the face.

"I'm listening," he protested feebly, blinking.

"Sit down, won't you?" directed the wife. "He's a little dopey to-night. But he's all right. You take that chair by the bed."

Mr. Tutt did as he was told. What was the truth behind this rather grisly tableau? What was the old man's real condition? Was he of sound and disposing mind and memory?

Mrs. Baldwin stepped to the foot of the bed, facing her husband.

"Now, Cabel, listen to me!" she repeated, articulating with meticulous distinctness. "You're going to make a codicil to your will—understand?"

The old man peered craftily at her out of the shadowy caverns of his eyes.

"My will," he muttered slyly. "I've made my will."

"But you're going to make a codicil to it. You want to!" she said, focusing her eyes upon him. "Grandpa wants to make a codicil to his will— all nice and fresh!"

"A codicil," mumbled Mr. Baldwin, as if to himself. "Yes—yes! That is so. I want a codicil. Where is it?"

"The lawyer has it—right there!" she said. "Here is the pen. Put the paper there in front of him."

"But I must read it over to him first," declared Mr. Tutt. "I must be sure it contains his wishes."

"It isn't necessary!" she answered quickly. "I've been all over it with him a dozen times. You see how hard it is to get him to concentrate! I was a week finding out what he wanted. The sooner it is done the better!"

"But it is necessary that I should read it to him!" protested the lawyer. "It would be most irregular if I did not! Mr. Baldwin, I am about to read over to you the provisions of the codicil which I have drawn according to what I understand to be your wishes. Will you kindly give me your attention?"

Mr. Baldwin turned and stared vacantly at Mr. Tutt.

"I've made my will," he repeated.

"This is a codicil."

"Oh, yes. A codicil."

Mr. Baldwin nodded once or twice as if now entirely conversant with what was going on.

"Shall I read it to you?" inquired Mr. Tutt a little impatiently.

"Yes—read it to me," said Mr. Baldwin.

Mr. Tutt held the carefully engrossed document beneath the lamp and began:

" 'In the name of God, amen! I, Cabel Baldwin, being of sound mind and memory, do hereby make, publish and declare this as and for a codicil to my last will and testament ——' "

Suddenly the old gentleman began to whimper.

"I want my milk!" he whined. "I want my hot milk! Where is it?"

Mrs. Baldwin uttered an exclamation of annoyance.

"Can't you wait a minute?" she cried angrily. "It will only take a moment."

"I want my milk! I can't do anything without my milk!" he moaned pettishly.

"Well, well! I'll get it for you!" she exclaimed. "I'll be right back."

She was gone about five minutes, at the end of which she returned with a glass of warm milk, which she put to the old gentleman's lips.

"Have you read him the will?" she asked out of the corner of her mouth.

"No," answered Mr. Tutt. "I waited for you to come back. 'In the name of God, amen! I, Cabel Baldwin, being of sound mind and memory, do hereby make, publish and declare this as and for a codicil to my last will and testament, which I otherwise confirm in all respects not inconsistent herewith:

" 'First: I give and bequeath out of my personal estate ten thousand dollars each to the Metropolitan Museum of Art ——' "

Slowly, distinctly, carefully, Mr. Tutt proceeded to read through the document. It was impossible to tell whether Mr. Baldwin heard him or not.

"Do you understand what I have been reading to you?" asked Mr. Tutt at the end of the performance.

"Yes; it is a codicil to my will," assented Mr. Baldwin. "The codicil you have drawn for me to sign."

"Now," said the wife eagerly, "I will have the chauffeur come up and we can witness it." She hurried to the door. "Lydia! Send up Oscar!"

Almost immediately there was a sound of footsteps, and a heavily built man in livery entered.

"This is the other witness," explained Mrs. Baldwin to Mr. Tutt. "Oscar Boynton, our chauffeur."

Mr. Tutt arose and spread open the last page of the instrument upon the bedclothes in the old man's lap.

"This is the codicil to his last will and testament, which Mr. Baldwin desires you to witness," he stated. "He will sign first, and after him Mrs. Baldwin and yourself. You must both sign in his presence and in the presence of each other. Mr. Baldwin, do you understand this to be a codicil to your will? And do you wish these witnesses to attest it by signing their names?"

"Yes—yes," murmured the old man in the bed.

"Then," said Mr. Tutt, "write your name in the blank space at the foot of the paragraph beginning 'In witness whereof.' "

He held out the fountain pen supplied by the wife. But Mr. Baldwin did not seem to see it.

Mr. Tutt placed it gently in the fragile blue-veined right hand.

"Here!" he directed. "Below the words 'In witness whereof.' "

Mr. Baldwin's fingers closed over the pen. He appeared to be making a heroic effort to bring his mind to bear upon what was expected of him. Helplessly, like a child, he looked from the pen to Mr. Tutt and back again.

"Write!" ordered his wife icily.

"Write!" repeated the old man. "Yes, write!"

Dropping his chin towards the paper, he pressed down the pen and painfully began tracing the word "Cab——"

Mrs. Baldwin watched him hungrily. The strain was too much for her.

"Here!" she cried, going round beside him and, taking the trembling fingers firmly in her own, "I'll help you!" And she guided the pen along the paper until below the inscription "In witness whereof" appeared in straggling characters the signature of Cabel Baldwin.

Mr. Tutt blotted the name and removed the codicil to a table, where Mrs. Baldwin and Boynton each signed it as a witness. Then he folded it and placed it again in the envelope from which he had removed it. Mr. Baldwin had fallen back on his pillow and closed his eyes, exhausted.

"What shall I do with the codicil," asked Mr. Tutt; "put it in my safe?"

"No," returned Mrs. Baldwin tartly. "You can leave it here. I'll attend to it."

V

CONTRARY TO his wife's expectations, Mr. Baldwin did not die for a long time, but when at last he did, on that same day Lydia Baldwin left the house forever, and within the week after her father's funeral was married to Henry Holborn before a justice of the peace. It was on the afternoon of Lydia's marriage that the Widow Baldwin appeared at the offices of Tutt & Tutt and asked for the senior partner. He received her in silence, standing.

"Well," she greeted him, looking more vulture-like than ever in her weeds, "I guess it's time to start probating the will and codicil. Is there anything particular I have to do?"

Mr. Tutt did not invite her to sit down. Coldly he replied: "Mrs. Baldwin, I cannot undertake any business for you."

"What's the matter?" she demanded acidly. "Isn't my money as good as anybody else's?"

He shook his shaggy head.

"No," he returned shortly, "it isn't. A lawyer has some choice in the matter of clients, and I want no business of yours."

"That's pretty good!" she cried, flushing. "You were ready enough to act as my attorney the last time I called on you and asked you to draw the codicil. What's the matter? Are you scared of anything? Don't go back on me now!" she begged, changing her attack. "You can charge me what you like!"

"You may recall," answered Mr. Tutt sternly, "that on that occasion I specifically inquired for whom I was acting, and that you replied categorically that I represented your husband and not you. I drew a codicil and superintended its execution by my client at his request. I was paid for it. That ended the matter. I shall, of course, proceed at once to offer for probate the will in my possession, in which I am named as executor. In so doing I represent your husband's estate and not you. If you are legally entitled to anything, you will get it in due course."

She stared at him, open-mouthed.

"Get anything! Why, I get everything!"

"Do you?" tossed off Mr. Tutt coolly.

"You drew the codicil yourself! Unless you fooled me by substituting another paper!"

The old lawyer grunted savagely.

"Be assured, I did not."

"What's the hitch, then?"

"If you want to know, Mrs. Baldwin, I will have nothing to do with you."

Mrs. Baldwin seemed to swell until her dimensions threatened to prevent her exit.

"Well, I never!" she exploded. "I never heard of such treatment!" She paused, swallowed and lost color. "If you've tricked me—put anything over—I'll ——" She dropped her shoulders limply, turning momentarily sick with apprehension. "Is there ——" she gasped.

"Simply to relieve your anxiety," said Mr. Tutt coldly, "I will say that the codicil executed—or partly executed—in your husband's bedchamber isn't worth the paper it is written on."

"Nonsense!" she cried, losing all control of herself. "I know what's the matter! You've got cold feet! You're afraid to go on with it! You're scared they'll show Cabel had senile dementia or something—wasn't legally fit to make a codicil. Well, you might as well stick! Be hung for a sheep as well as a lamb. It would look fine, wouldn't it, for Ephraim Tutt to admit in court that he allowed a senile old man to execute a codicil when he didn't know what he was doing? Why, it would ruin you forever! All right, coward! There are plenty of lawyers who've got courage as well as brains. Some day when I've got half a million in the bank you'll wish you had your share!"

Mr. Tutt gave a low chuckle. Reaching over to the cigar box he selected the usual stogy and lighted it with deliberation.

"I remember you don't mind smoking," he remarked reminiscently, "or I shouldn't venture." Then as he exhaled a voluminous cloud of sulphurous vapor he added: "As I was saying, that document will never be probated. The only instrument of your husband's that is of any value is the one I drew six months after you married him, in which he leaves practically everything to his daughter, Lydia."

VI

When Surrogate Sampson entered the great court room of the Hall of Records at half after ten the following Friday morning, he found it more than ordinarily crowded. Indeed, it seemed to him as if he had never before seen so many noted counsel sitting together in the leather arm-chairs at the long mahogany table whose marvelous patina had been polished by generations of distinguished legal elbows. The surrogate liked to see his court filled with the leaders of the bar, for it gave him a sense of importance and stirred his pride.

"Good morning, Mr. Philbrick!" he murmured genially as he bestowed his gown on the judicial chair. "Ah, Mr. Goodwin! And Mr. Lowenthal! What is the occasion of this illustrious gathering?"

Mr. Philbrick, Mr. Lowenthal and the rest of the constellation of juridical luminaries simpered and bowed in unison, and Surrogate Sampson, who did not expect any answer to his interrogation, since it had been purely hortatory, blew his nose with one hand, picked up the calendar with the other and cleared his throat.

"Matter of Baldwin?" he called out briskly.

Simultaneously the company of the elect before him arose and with military precision presented arms. So did several other rows immediately behind them; a cohort of office boys, clerks, assistants and junior counsel, carrying bags, books, parcels and bundles of papers, closed in behind in a compact body.

"Er—if Your Honor please!" began Mr. Philbrick, in his capacity of chief of staff, in an ingratiating voice, "this is the contested probate of the codicil to the last will and testament, offered coincidently, of the late Cabel Baldwin, a distinguished resident of this city, under which he gives a large percentage of his property to various public institutions, of which I represent one."

"Who appears in opposition?" inquired the surrogate over his spectacles. "I may as well get this straight from the beginning. There are so many of you!"

For a moment there was no response; then out from behind the jury box sauntered Mr. Ephraim Tutt.

"I appear for Mrs. Henry Holborn, who was Lydia Baldwin, the sole heir and next of kin," said he quietly. "The daughter and only child of the deceased, who is also the chief beneficiary under the will."

"Ah, Mr. Tutt," commented Surrogate Sampson, "I suppose you have duly filed your objections?"

"Oh, certainly!" answered the lawyer, and there was something ominous in his manner. "I drew the original will for Mr. Baldwin and am the executor named in it. I have offered it for probate—and so far as I know there is no objection to it. Indeed, there can't very well be any, since unless the will stands the codicil which these distinguished gentlemen are offering—and to which I object—falls too."

"Quite so!" nodded the judge. "Let me see the will."

Immediately a clerk handed a paper to Mr. Philbrick, who in turn passed it to an attendant, who gave it to an officer, who duly delivered it to His Honor, while the throng round the table parted to allow Mr. Tutt to approach the dais.

"Well," remarked His Honor curtly, after glancing through it, "the will seems simple enough. The testator revokes all previous wills and after a provision in lieu of dower to his wife devises a large quantity of realty described specifically by metes and bounds to his only daughter, Lydia, whom he thereafter makes the residuary legatee of all his property, both real and personal.

"He names you as executor. The usual affidavits are before me, made by the attesting witnesses. Is there any reason, gentlemen, why I should not receive this will for probate?"

He looked along the table. Obviously in the nature of things there could be no opposition, for the reception of the codicil depended upon the acceptance of the will.

"I'll receive it for probate, then," announced the surrogate. "Now we come to the codicil. Who offers it?"

"I do," answered Mr. Philbrick, "at the request of the chief beneficiary and sole residuary legatee, the widow."

"Is she in court?"

Mr. Philbrick waved towards a figure behind him.

"Yes, Your Honor."

"Please step forward, madam. Perhaps it will be more comfortable if you sit here beside me in the witness chair." He bowed courteously.

Mrs. Baldwin, aggressive as ever in her habiliments of mourning, yet with a worried look superimposed upon her features, drawn into the semblance of grief, took the seat indicated.

"Are you the widow of Cabel Baldwin, deceased?"

"Yes, I am," she replied aggressively.

"You offer for probate a codicil to his will?"

"Yes, I do."

"Let me see it, please."

Mr. Philbrick promptly handed up the document.

"H'm!" exclaimed His Honor. "This is a rather lengthy instrument. I'll not bother to go through it now." And he leaned back and began polishing his glasses, in anticipation of an interesting morning. "What are the grounds of your objections to my admitting it to probate, Mr. Tutt?"

"Simply that the proposed paper is not sufficiently attested under our statutes," stated the lawyer solemnly.

The surrogate turned to the last page of the codicil which lay on the desk before him.

"There seem to be two witnesses," he remarked —"all the law requires."

"But one of them is the lady beside you, who under this codicil is made chief beneficiary and sole residuary legatee. As an interested party she cannot qualify—unless, to be sure, she is prepared to waive her legacy, which alone amounts to a quarter of a million dollars," declared Mr. Tutt quietly.

Mrs. Baldwin had grown white. Defiantly she watched the surrogate as he now perused the codicil in its entirety.

"That seems to be so," he said with a puzzled air. "Mr. Tutt's point is perfectly well taken.

There are only two witnesses to this propounded codicil, and one of those witnesses is undoubtedly as interested party; in fact could hardly be more interested. Madam, do you understand the situation? Under the law you can't qualify as a witness to prove the codicil unless you renounce your legacy; and if you don't qualify I shall have to reject the codicil, having only one witness, as insufficiently attested. Extraordinary!" he added to himself.

There was a murmur of interest throughout the rows and a closer crowding together of the group of counsel before the dais. Mrs. Baldwin sucked in her cheeks.

Mr. Philbrick smiled conciliatingly in the direction of the bench.

"That is, of course, true," said he. "But we—that is, Mrs. Baldwin—has arranged after consulting with counsel to waive her legacy and qualify as a witness."

"Is that correct, madam?" queried the surrogate, peering at her over his spectacles. "Are you willing to forfeit your legacy of two hundred and fifty thousand dollars as well as your residuary interest under this codicil if I admit it to probate?"

"If that's the law I guess I've got to!" she snapped viciously. "But I've been tricked—hoodwinked! All the same, the rest will get their money!"

The surrogate gazed bewilderedly at the cluster of attorneys. Then he turned to Mr. Tutt.

"Under these circumstances is there any reason why I should not admit the codicil after the witness has signed a written waiver and given her testimony? That meets your objection, doesn't it? Have you anything further?"

"Only this," replied the lawyer, and the court room became as quiet as a country churchyard at midnight. "Two years ago, at the request of Mr. Baldwin, I drew the will which you have just admitted to probate and in which, as you have observed, after a provision for his widow in lieu of dower, he left all his property to his only daughter, my present client. She is here. Please stand up, Mrs. Holborn."

There was a rustle on the lower seat of the jury box to the right as Lydia arose, pale as a ghost in her black dress. With her stood up a tall young man, as if to protect her from the stares of the spectators. The woman in the witness chair shot in their direction a single venomous shaft.

"Thank you," went on Mr. Tutt. "That will do. If Your Honor will refer to the instrument you will see that in it Mr. Baldwin describes himself as 'of the city of Fall River, in the state of Massachusetts.' That was his permanent legal residence,

his domicile. He had been in business there all his life, had lived, voted and paid his personal taxes there.

"He was merely taking a vacation and spending the winter in New York City when his wife died."

"He was previously married to another lady?" asked the surrogate.

"Oh, yes; for fifteen years," said Mr. Tutt. "Now all his property—both real and personal—with the exception of a comparatively trifling sum in a Fifth Avenue bank where he kept a checking account—is situated in Massachusetts, the place of his domicile. And his estate consists almost entirely of various parcels of land and office buildings in Fall River, which he specifically bequeathed to his daughter, Lydia, in the will drawn by me, which has three witnesses as required by Massachusetts law. The schedules, which I have prepared, show that his personal estate amounts to less than fifteen thousand dollars."

There was a buzz of consternation from the lawyers about Mr. Philbrick, whose owl-like countenance wore an expression of dismay and wrath.

"Now," continued Mr. Tutt amiably, "even if this good lady with the laudable object of sacrificing the quarter million and her interest in the residuary, which this codicil purports to give her, in order that these charitable institutions, represented by my friend Philbrick and his associates, and her manifold relatives and friends named in the codicil as legatees may secure what is given to them—even if, I say, she renounces her legacy and qualifies as a witness, and, in consequence, Your Honor is enabled to admit the codicil to probate, there will be nothing out of which to pay the legacies given under it, for"—and he could not help a chuckle—"the testator has expressly directed in each instance that the legacy shall be paid out of his personal estate. And there isn't any."

A wave of astonishment swept across the benches.

"But," began Mr. Philbrick pompously, "they—the realty is more than sufficient to pay them all; and under the principles governing equitable conversion ——"

"Oh, no!" contradicted the surrogate briskly. "Even if the codicil is probated it will not affect the real estate devised to the daughter under the will, if for no other reason than, as Mr. Tutt says, the laws of Massachusetts require three witnesses for a devise of realty—and the codicil has only two."

The woman in the witness chair swayed.

"I've been robbed—cheated!" she cried savagely, gritting her teeth.

"Please be quiet, madam," rebuked the surrogate. "We must have no scenes here."

"Anyhow," she declared, glaring at him, "as widow I'll take my third under the Massachusetts law! I'll get that much anyway!"

"That is for the courts of Massachusetts to decide!" returned the surrogate with asperity.

"That question won't bother them much," interjected Mr. Tutt carelessly. "For the woman sitting in that chair beside Your Honor is not the legal widow of Cabel Baldwin. She has a husband living—a railroad brakeman from whom she has never been legally divorced. I have here affidavits showing that he was never served in the divorce proceedings brought by her and upon which she must rely to establish the validity of her subsequent marriages. I say 'marriages,' for this is not her only matrimonial experience. She was wedded to two others of her patients who later died; and, I may add, she inherited property from both."

The ex-nurse had half started from her seat. Mr. Philbrick had turned a bright pink.

"If this is so ——" he began faintly.

"It's a lie!" cried the woman in a shrill voice. "An absolute lie! I am Cabel Baldwin's widow—and I'll prove it! I don't care what that old crook says!"

"Be quiet, madam!" shouted the surrogate angrily, banging with his gavel. "I will adjourn this matter for one week." Then he paused as he gathered the papers together. "One more question, gentlemen," said he. "I should like to know who drew the codicil that is here offered for probate."

"I did," affirmed Mr. Tutt boldly.

There was a hiatus during which the only noise audible was the sudden hysterical intake of the relict Baldwin upon the witness chair.

"You did!" returned the surrogate. "And you now appear in opposition to it—contest the legality of your own work? That is a most astounding proceeding!"

"Exactly," answered Mr. Tutt, entirely unmoved. "I drew the codicil which this woman is now seeking to probate, and I superintended its execution."

"Knowing that she could take nothing under it?" persisted the judge.

"Knowing that she wouldn't get one cent!"

Surrogate Sampson leaned back and removed his spectacles with an expression of blank amazement.

"Did you do this with the approval and consent of the testator?" he asked curiously.

Mr. Tutt smiled inscrutably.

"What passed between my client and myself at the time he executed this codicil," he replied, picking up his stovepipe hat, "is a privileged communication made in the course of my professional employment, which the law does not permit me to reveal!"

TACT

by Thomas Beer

THOMAS BEER WROTE about one hundred and twenty-five short stories for the *Post;* his novel, *Sandoval*, was serialized there in 1923 and his biography of Mark Hanna in 1929. For a decade or more Beer averaged $35,000 a year from his *Post* writing alone. Yet critics have not regarded him as a popular writer and, in a sense, he wasn't; his complicated prose pleased a large minority of *Post* readers but probably not a majority. Fastidious, scholarly and extremely shy, Beer lived with his mother and brother in an old-fashioned house in Yonkers and often wrote in his pajamas, lying flat on his stomach in bed. He created more *Post* "series" characters than any other writer: Lupus van Eck, Ailanthus Westland, Stukely Kent, the Toobey family. But his most famous invention was Ma Egg, who saw her huge son Adam through many adventures, including the strange romance described below. Beer's last *Post* story was in 1936; he died in 1940.

JULY 1, 1922

YOU MAKE ME SICK," said Mrs. Egg. She spoke with force. Her three daughters murmured, "Why, mamma!" A squirrel ran up the trunk of an apple tree that shaded the veranda; a farm hand turned from weeding the mint bed by the garage. Mrs. Egg didn't care. Her chins shook fiercely. She ate a wafer, emptied her glass of iced tea and spread her little hands with their buried rings on the table.

"You make me sick, girls," she said. "Dammy's been home out of the Navy precisely seven weeks an' two days, an' a hour hasn't passed but what one of you've been phonin' me from town about what he has or ain't done unbecomin' to a boy that's engaged to Edith Sims! I don't know why you girls expect a boy that was champion heavyweight wrestler of the Atlantic Fleet an' stands six foot four and a half inches in his bare feet to get all thrilled over bein' engaged. A person that was four years in the Navy an' went as far as Japan has pretty naturally been in love before, and ——"

"Mamma!"

Mrs. Egg ate another sugar wafer and continued relentlessly in her soft drawl "——ain't likely to get all worked up over bein' engaged to a sixteen-year-old girl who can't cook any better than a Cuban on his own say-so. As for those spiced guavas he sent home from Cuba in March," she mused, "I thought they were fierce. As for his takin' Edith Sims out drivin' in his overalls and a shirt, Adam John Egg is the best-lookin' person in this family and you know it. You three girls are the sent'mentalest women in the state of Ohio and I don't know how your husbands stand it. My gee! D'you expect Dammy to chase this girl around heavin' roses at her like a fool in a movie?" She panted and peered into the iced-tea pitcher. Emotion made her thirsty. Mrs. Egg aimed an affable bawl at the kitchen door and called, "Benjamina! I'd be awful obliged if you'd make up some more iced tea, please. Dammy'll be through pickin' peaches soon and he's usually thirsty about four o'clock."

Her new cook nodded and came down the long veranda. The daughters stared civilly at this red-haired girl, taller than their tall selves. Benjamina lifted the vacant pitcher and carried it silently away. Her slim height vanished into the kitchen and the oldest daughter whispered, "Mercy, mamma, she's almost as tall as Dammy!"

"She's just six feet," said Mrs. Egg with deliberate clarity meant to reach Benjamina; "but extremely graceful, I think. My gee! It's perfectly embarrassin' to ask a girl as refined as that to clear the table or dust. She went through high school in Cleveland and can read all the French in the cookbook exactly as if it made sense. It's a pleasure to have such a person in the house."

The second daughter leaned forward and said, "Mamma, that's another thing! I do think it's pretty—untactful of Dammy to take this girl's brother around in the car and introduce him to Edith Sims and her folks as if ——"

"I think it was extremely sensible," Mrs. Egg puffed. "Hamish is a very int'restin' boy, and has picked up milkin' remarkably when he's only been here a week, and Dammy's taught him to sem'phore, or whatever that wiggling-your-arms thing is called. And he appreciates Dammy a lot." The plate of sugar wafers was stripped to bare crumbs. Mrs. Egg turned her flushed face and addressed the unseen: "Benjamina, you might bring some more cookies when the tea's ready, and some of those cup cakes you made this mornin'. Dammy ate five of them at lunch."

Benjamina answered "Yes, Mrs. Egg" in her slow fashion.

"Mamma," said the youngest daughter, "it's all right for you to say that Dammy is absolutely perfect, but the Simses are the most refined people in town, and it does look disgraceful for Dammy not to dress up a little when he goes there, and he's got all those beautiful tailor-made clothes from New York."

Mrs. Egg patiently drawled, "Fern, that's an awful uninterestin' remark. Dammy looks exactly like a seal in a aquarium when he's dressed up, his things fit so smooth; but a boy that was four years in the Navy and helps milk a hundred and twenty-seven cows twice a day, besides mendin' all the machinery on the place, is *not* called upon to dress up evenings to go see a girl he's known all his life. He's twenty-one years and nine weeks old, an' capable of managin' his own concerns. . . . Thank you, Benjamina," she told the red-haired girl as the fresh pitcher clinked on the table and the cup cakes gleamed in yellow charm beside it. "I do hate to trouble you."

Benjamina smiled nicely and withdrew. Mrs. Egg ate one of the cup cakes and thought it admirable. She broke out, "My gee! There's another thing! You girls keep actin' as if Dammy wasn't as smart as he should be! On the other hand, he drove up to Cleveland and looked at the list of persons willin' to work in the country and didn't waste time askin' the agency questions, but went round to Benjamina's flat and ate some choc'late cake. Then he loaded her and Hamish into the car and brought 'em down, all between six in the mornin' and twelve at night. I've had eight days of rest an' comfort for a result. . . . My gee! Your papa's the second biggest dairyman in this state, but that don't keep me in intell'gent cooks!"

The three young matrons sighed. Mrs. Egg considered them for a moment over her glass, and sniffed, "Mercy! This has been a pleasant afternoon!"

"Mamma," said the first-born, "you can't very well deny that Dammy's awful careless for an engaged man. He ought to've got a ring for Edith Sims when he was home at Christmas and the engagement came off. And ———"

Mrs. Egg lost patience. She exclaimed, "Golden Jerusalem! Dammy got engaged at Judge Randolph's party the night before he went back to Brooklyn to his ship! My gee! I never heard such idiotic nonsense! You girls act as if Edith Sims—whose ears are much too big even if she does dress her hair low—was too good for Adam Egg! She's a nice child, an' her folks are nice and all the rest of it! . . . Dammy," she panted as the marvel appeared, "here's your sisters!"

Adam came up the long veranda with a clothes basket of peaches on his right shoulder. He nodded his black head to his sisters and put the basket noiselessly down. Then he blew smoke from both nostrils of his bronze, small nose and rubbed its bridge with the cigarette. He seldom spoke. Mrs. Egg swiftly filled a glass with iced tea and Adam began to absorb this pensively. His sisters cooed and his mother somewhat forgave them. They had sense enough to adore Adam, anyhow. In hours of resolute criticism Mrs. Egg sometimes admitted that Adam's nose was too short. He was otherwise beyond praise. His naked dark shoulders rippled and convulsed as he stooped to gather three cup cakes. A stained undershirt hid some of his terrific chest and his canvas trousers hung beltless on his narrow hips. Mrs. Egg secretly hoped that he would change these garments before he went to call on his betrothed. The three cup cakes departed through his scarlet, wide mouth into his insatiable system of muscles, and Adam lit his next cigarette. Smoke surged in a tide about his immovable big eyes. He looked at the road beyond the apple trees, then swung and made swift, enigmatic gestures with his awesome arms to young Hamish Saunders, loitering by the garage. The valuable Hamish responded with more flappings of his lesser arms and trotted down the grass. The letter carrier approached the delivery box at the gates of the monstrous farm.

"What did you sem'phore to Hamish, lamb?" Mrs. Egg asked.

Adam said "Mail" and sat down on the floor.

He fixed a black stare on the pitcher and Mrs. Egg filled his glass. Muscles rose in ovals and ropes under the hairless polish of his arm as he took the frail tumbler. His hard throat stirred fleetly and his short feet wriggled in moccasins of some soiled, soft leather, indicating satisfaction. Mrs. Egg sighed. Benjamina made tea perfectly. She must tactfully tell the girl that Adam liked it. No female could hear that fact without a thrill.

"Package for you," said young Hamish, bounding up the steps. He gave Adam a stamped square box, announced "I signed for it," and retired shyly from the guests to read a post card. He was a burly lad of sixteen, in a shabby darned jersey and some outgrown breeches of Adam's. Mrs. Egg approved of him; he appreciated Adam.

The marvel tore the box to pieces with his lean fingers and extracted a flat case of velvet. Two rings glittered in its satin lining. Adam contemplated the diamond of the engagement ring and the band of gold set with tiny brilliants which would forever nail Edith Sims to his perfections. His sisters squealed happily. Mrs. Egg thought how many pounds of Egg's A1 Butter were here consumed in vainglory and sighed gently.

She drawled, "My gee, Dammy! Nobody can poss'bly say you ain't got good taste in jewelry, anyhow," and shot a stare of fierce pride at her daughters. They rose. She knew that the arrival of these gauds would be known in Ilium forthwith. She said "Well, good evenin', girls," and accepted their kisses affably.

Adam paid no attention to the going of the oldest daughter's motor car; he was staring at the rings, and the blank brown of his forehead was disturbed by some superb and majestic fancy current under the dense smoothness of his jet hair. Hamish Saunders came shyly to peep at the gems and stooped his curly red head. The boy had large gray eyes, like those of his sister, and her hawk nose, which Mrs. Egg thought patrician.

She said, "Hamish, you ain't had any tea yet, lamb. Dammy's left some. Benjamina puts in exactly sugar enough, an' I never heard of mint in iced tea before. It's awful interestin'."

Hamish soberly drank some tea and asked Adam, "Want the motor bike, Mr. Egg?"

Adam nodded. The boy went leaping down the flagged walk to the garage and busily led Adam's red motorcycle back to the veranda steps. Then he gazed with reverence at Adam's shoulders, felt his right biceps and sadly walked off toward the barns. The herd of the Egg Dairy Company was an agitation of twinkling horns and multicolored hides in the white-fenced yard. The ten hired men were sponging their hands at the model washstand by the colossal water tower's engine house. Mrs. Egg ate the last cup cake and looked off at the town of Ilium, spread in a lizard of trees at the top of a long slope. The motor containing her female offspring was sliding into the main street. The daughters would stop at the Sims house to tell the refined Edith that her engagement ring had come.

Mrs. Egg pursed her lips courageously and said, "Dammy, you might change your duds, dear, before you take Edith her sol'taire. It's a kind of a formal occasion, sort of."

The giant pronounced lazily the one syllable "Bunk," and turned his face toward his mother. Then he said, "You've got awful pretty hands, mamma."

"Mercy, Dammy," Mrs. Egg panted, flushing.

Her prodigiousness shook in the special chair of oak under the blow of this compliment. She tittered, "Well, your papa—I do hope it ain't so hot in Chicago—used to say so before I got stout."

Adam blew a snake of smoke from his left nostril and surprised her with a whole sentence. He drawled, "Was a oiler on the Nevada that sung a song about pale hands, pink tipped like some kind of a flower, mamma."

"My gee," said Mrs. Egg, "I know that song! A person sang it at the Presbyterian supper in 1910 when the oysters were bad, and some people thought it wasn't correct for a church party, bein' a pretty passionate kind of song. It was awful popular for a while after that . . . Benjamina would know, her papa havin' kept a music store. I'll ask her. Help me up, lamb."

Adam arose and took his mother kindly out of her chair with one motion. Mrs. Egg passed voluminously over the sill into the kitchen and addressed her superior cook, beaming at the girl.

"There's a sent'mental kind of song that Dammy's interested in which is about some gump lovin' a woman's pale hands beside the shallow Marne or some such place."

Benjamina brushed back her blazing hair with both slender hands and looked at the rosy nails.

She said, "Pale Hands. I think —— No, it's the Kashmir love song. It used to be sung a great deal."

Adam said "Thanks" in the doorway.

Then he turned, jamming the jewel case into his pocket, and lounged down the steps. His shoulders gleamed like oiled wood. He picked a handful of peaches from the basket, which would have burdened two mortals, and split one in his terrible fingers. He ate a peach absently and threw the red stone at a roaming chicken, infamously busy in the nasturtiums. Mrs. Egg leaned on the side of the door. A slight nervousness made her reach for the radishes which Benjamina was cleaning. Radishes always stimulated Mrs. Egg. She ate two and hoped that Edith Sims wouldn't happen to look at Adam's back. The undershirt revealed both shoulder blades and most of the sentiment "Damn Kaiser Bill" tattooed in pink across Adam. It seemed indecorous at the moment of betrothal, and Mrs. Egg winced.

Then she wondered. Adam took another peach and pressed it in a cupped hand. Its blood welled over his shoulder and smeared the rear of the shirt brilliantly. He scrubbed it thoroughly into the back of his cropped hair and massaged his flat abdomen with a second fruit. After some study he kicked his feet out of the moccasins and doubled down in his fluid manner to rub his insteps with black grease from the valves of the waiting motorcycle. Then he signaled his contentment with these acts by a prolonged exhalation of smoke from his mouth, gave his mother an inscrutable glance as he tucked the cast moccasins into the fork of the apple tree and fled down the driveway with a coughing of his machine's engine, barefoot, unspeakably soiled and magnificently shimmering with peach blood.

"My gee!" said Mrs. Egg.

Benjamina looked up from the radishes and asked "What did you say?" gravely.

So Mrs. Egg meditated, eating a radish, on the simple pleasure of talking to the admirable girl about this spectacle. Adam had favored Benjamina with some notice in these ten days, and his approval of her cooking was silently manifest. He had even eaten some veal goulash, a dish which he usually declined. The girl was a lady, anyhow. Mrs. Egg exploded.

"Benjamina, Dammy's up to somethin'! His sisters keep tellin' me he ain't tactful, either! My gee! He simply washed himself in peach juice and went off to give Edith Sims her engagement ring! And left his moc'sins in the apple tree where he always used to put his cigarettes when his papa didn't think he was old enough to smoke. But heaven knows, I can't see that anything ever hurt Dammy! He's always been the neatest boy that ever lived, and had all his clothes made when he was in the Navy. It's perfectly true that he ain't dressed respectable once since he got home. Mercy, the other day he went in to see Edith in a half a khaki shirt that he'd been usin' to clean the garage floor with!"

Benjamina pared a radish with a flutter of her white fingers and asked, "How long have they been engaged, Mrs. Egg?"

"He had ten days' liberty at Christmas and was home. It perfectly upset me, because Dammy hadn't ever paid any attention to the child. They got engaged at a dance Judge Randolph gave. It was extremely sudden," Mrs. Egg pondered, "although the Simses are very refined folks and Edith's a nice girl. . . . A boy who was four years in the Navy naturally ought to know when he's in love or not. But men do fall in love in the most accidental manner, Benjamina! They don't seem to have any intentions of it. My gee! A man who takes to runnin' after a girl for her money is within my comprehensions, or because she's good-lookin'. But what most men marry most women for is beyond me. I'm forty-six years of age," she said, "but I still get surprised at things. I think I'll lie down. . . . Do you man'cure your nails, or are they as pink as that all the time?"

"They're naturally pink," Benjamina smiled.

"They're awful pretty," Mrs. Egg yawned, pausing in her advance to the door of the living room. Then it seemed guileful to increase this praise. She added "Dammy was sayin' so," and strolled into the living room, where twenty-five photographs of Adam reposed on shelves and tables.

She closed the door and stopped to eat a peppermint from the glass urn beside the phonograph's cabinet. Excitements worked in her. She brushed a fly from the picture of Adam in wrestling tights and sank on a vast couch. The leather cushions hissed, breathing out air under her descent. She closed her eyes and brooded. . . . If Adam wanted to annoy Edith Sims, he had chosen a means cleverly. The girl was elaborate as to dress and rather haughty about clothes. She had praised the attire of Judge Randolph's second son before Adam pointedly on Sunday at tea in the veranda. Perturbations and guesses clattered in Mrs. Egg's mind. Then a real clatter in the kitchen roused her.

"I milked three cows," said Hamish Saunders to his sister in a loud and complacent voice.

Benjamina said less loudly but with vigor, "Hamish, you got a post card! I saw you reading it! I told you not to write anyone where we'd gone to. Now ———"

Mrs. Egg knew that the boy was wiggling. He said, "Oh, I wrote Tick Matthews. He won't tell Cousin Joe, Benjy."

"He'll tell his mother and she'll tell everyone in the building! I didn't want anyone to know where we'd gone to!"

Mrs. Egg sat up. In a little, the lad spoke with a sound of male determination. He spoke airily. His hands must be jammed into his pockets. He said, "Now Cousin Joe ain't going to come runnin' down here after us, Benjy. You've gone off, so that ought to sort of show him you ain't going to marry him. I was asking Adam if there's any law that a person's guardian can make 'em live with him if they don't want to ———"

"You told him!"

"I did not!"

The girl said, "Don't talk so loud, Hamish! Mrs. Egg's taking a nap upstairs. You told him!"

"I didn't tell him a thing! I said there was a guy I knew that had run off from his guardian and ———"

Benjamina burst into queer, vexed laughter. She said, "You might as well have told him! The day he came to the flat he asked who else lived there besides us. Cousin Joe's pipes were all over the place. It ———"

"Look here! There's a judge in this town, and Mrs. Egg or Adam would tell him we're not children or imbeciles or nothin'! If Cousin Joe came down here lookin' for us ——" Presently he said with misery on each syllable, "Don't cry, Benjy. . . . But nothin'll happen. . . . Anyhow, you'll be twenty-one in October and the court'll give you our income, 'stead of payin' it to Cousin Joe. . . . Bet you a dollar it's more than he says it is!" He whistled seven notes of a bugle call and then whimpered, "Quit cryin', Benjy!"

"F-finish these radishes," Benjamina commanded; "I want to go brush my hair."

There was the light sound of her rubber soles on the back stairs. Mrs. Egg lay down again, wishing that the urn of peppermints was within reach. In the kitchen Hamish said "Aw, hell!" and the chair by the table creaked as he slumped into it. He would pare radishes very badly in that mood, Mrs. Egg thought.

She now thought of Benjamina with admiration. Adam had seen the girl's name on a list of women willing to take service in the country, at a Cleveland agency. He had gone to interview Benjamina, Mrs. Egg gathered, because a cook on the U. S. S. *Nevada* had been named Saunders and the word looked auspicious. Accident, said Mrs. Egg to herself, was the dominant principle of life. She was much interested. Benjamina had taken proper steps to get away from an unpleasant guardian and should be shielded from any consequences. Certainly a girl who could cook to satisfy Adam wasn't to be given back to some nameless male in Cleveland, in a flat. Mrs. Egg abhorred flats. A man who would coop two children in a flat deserved no pity or consideration. And Adam required gallons of peach butter for winter use. Mrs. Egg arose, stalked openly into the kitchen and addressed Hamish as an equal. She said, "Bub, you're an awful tactful boy, and have sense. Dammy said so himself. Honesty is my policy, an' I may as well say that I could hear all you were talkin' with Benjamina right now. . . . Who is this Cousin Joe you've run off from?"

Hamish cut a radish in two and wretchedly stammered, "H-he's dad's cousin. He's a louse!"

Mrs. Egg drawled, "My gee! That's a awful good description of your relation! Now, I haven't any intention to lose Benjamina when she's the best cook I ever had, an' you're not as bad at milkin' as you might be. If this person comes down here or makes any fuss I'll see to it that he don't get anywheres. So if Benjamina gets frightened you tell her that I'm goin' to look after this."

"Yes'm," said Hamish.

He looked at Mrs. Egg with an amazed awe that was soothing. She beamed and strolled out of the kitchen. Descending the steps one by one, she came to the level walk of the dooryard and marched along it toward the barns. Egg was taking a holiday with his sister, married to a dyspeptic clergyman in Chicago, and it was her duty to aid Adam by surveying the cows. She entered the barnyard and rounded the corner of the cows' palace into a group of farm hands bent above a trotting of dice on the clay. Adam looked up from this sport and said " 'Lo, mamma," cheerfully.

"My gee," Mrs. Egg faltered, regarding a pile of silver before his knees, "I never saw you win a cent at any game before, Dammy!"

The giant grinned, cast the dice and raked three dollars toward him. His eyes were black lights. He announced "This is my lucky day, mamma!" and all the worshipful youths chuckled as he stood up. He walked over a Swede's stooped back and dragged Mrs. Egg away from her husband's hirelings. Then he lit a cigarette and consumed half its length in an appalling suction. The smoke jetted from his nostrils in a flood. He patted Mrs. Egg's upper chin with a thumb and said, "She gave me the air, mamma!"

"What?"

"She told me to fly my kite! She's off me! She's goin' to marry Jim Randolph. It's all flooie. . . . I'd like a tub of champagne an' five fried hens for supper! Mamma," said Adam, "I ain't engaged to that girl any more!" Therewith he took all the silver from his pocket and sent it whirling in a gay, chiming shower up the roof of the cow barn. His teeth flashed between his parted lips and dimples invaded his brown cheeks. He swung his arms restlessly and his mother thought that he would break into a dance. Adam reflected, "It's hell what happens by accident, mamma. Was a bowl of punch in the lib'ry at that dance of Judge Randolph's Christmastime that'd knock the teeth out of a wildcat. Had six cups. Saw this girl's hand hangin' over the banisters when I was headin' for the front door. I kissed it. Mamma, there ain't any way of tellin' a nice girl that you don't mean anything when you kiss her. They don't understand it."

A devastating admiration of her child made Mrs. Egg's heart cavort. His manners were sublime. He lit another cigarette and stated, "Well, that's all of that." Then, wearied with much speech, he was still.

"Mercy, Dammy! This is an awful relief! Your sisters have been holdin' forth about Edith Sims bein' much more refined than God all afternoon. I was gettin' kind of scared of her. . . . What's that phonograph plate, lamb?"

Adam didn't answer, but ripped the envelope

from the grained disk, and Mrs. Egg saw, on the advertising, "Kashmiri Song." But her thoughts had sunk to a profound and cooling peace; there would be no more Edith Sims. She drawled, "Edith's pretty awful sedate, Dammy. I don't think she'd have the sand to run off from—a person she didn't like, or make her own livin'."

The giant flung up his arms and made certain gestures. Hamish Saunders came hurtling from the house for orders. Adam said, "Go get me some clothes, kid—white. And shoes 'n a cake of soap. Then come swimmin'. Put this plate with the rest. Hustle!" He ground his nose with a fist, staring after the boy, then said, "Nice kid, mamma."

"Mercy, yes, Dammy! Dammy, it's pretty ridiculous to have Benjamina and the boy eat in the kitchen, and it takes tact to keep a nice girl like that contented. I think they'd better take their meals with us, sweetheart."

He nodded and strode off among the regular files of apple and pear trees toward the aimless riverlet that watered the farm. Mrs. Egg felt hunger stir in her bulk. She plucked an apple leaf and chewed, marching up the walk, its fragrant pulp. Benjamina was soberly chopping the chickens for dinner into convenient bits.

Mrs. Egg applauded her performance, saying, "We'd better have 'em fried, I think. Dammy prefers it. And when you've got time you might go get one of those very big green bottles of pear cider down in the cellar, honey. It's awful explosive stuff and Hamish hadn't better drink any. And lay the table for four, because it's pretty lonely for Dammy eatin' with me steadily. . . . Edith Sims busted their engagement this afternoon, by the way, though it isn't at all important."

"Isn't it?"

Mrs. Egg refreshed herself with a bit of cracker from the table and drawled, "Not a bit, deary. I've never heard of anybody's heart breakin' under the age of thirty over a busted engagement. Dammy's pretty much relieved, though too polite to say so, and Edith'll marry Judge Randolph's second boy, who's a very nice kid and has curly hair, although his teeth stick out some. So it don't seem to matter except to my daughters, who'll want Dammy to go into full mourning and die of sorrow. They're tearful girls, but nice. Let me show you how Dammy likes tomatoes fried when they're done with the chicken."

"Mrs. Egg," said Benjamina, "you're—a remarkable person." The slim, pale fingers twisted themselves against her dull blue frock into the likeness of a frightened white moth. She went on, "You—you never get excited."

"My gee! I haven't any patience with excitement, Benjamina. Things either go right or they go wrong. In either case, it's no good foamin' at the mouth and tryin' to kick the roof off. I'm like Dammy. I prefer to be calm," said Mrs. Egg. "As for scatterin' rays of sunshine like a Sunday-school hymn, most people don't thank anyone to do so—nor me, when I have indigestion."

"I—I feel much calmer since I've been here," Benjamina said. "It was so hot in the flat in Cleveland, and noisy. And it's very kind of you to ask Hamish and me to eat with you and Mr. Egg."

Her hands had become steadfast. She smiled a little.

"It'll be much more sociable, honey," Mrs. Egg reflected. "Even if Dammy don't talk, he likes company, havin' been in the Navy where he had lots. . . . Where's the biscuit flour? There's time to make some before supper."

The kitchen dimmed and Benjamina's tall body dulled into a restful shadow. She moved without noise and her pleasant voice was low. Mrs. Egg devised biscuits in comfort and smelled Adam's cigarettes in the living room. Hamish came to stimulate the making of this meal by getting his large feet in the way, and Mrs. Egg was scolding him tranquilly when the phonograph loosed a series of lazy notes. Then it sang, fervidly, of pale hands that it had loved beside some strange name.

"It's that Kashmir business," said Mrs. Egg. "Open the door, bub, so's we can hear."

The music swelled as the door opened and a circle of smoke died in the kitchen. Mrs. Egg saw Adam as a white pillar in the gloom. The machine sobbed "Where are you now? Where are you now?" with an oily sadness.

"Real touching," Mrs. Egg mentioned.

A crashing of the orchestra intervened. Then the voice cried, "Pale hands, pink tipped, like lotus flowers that ——" The words jumbled into sounds. Mrs. Egg hungrily yawned. The tenor wailed, "I would have rather felt you on my throat, crushing out life, than waving me farewell!" and the girl stirred beside the doorway, her hands in motion. The song expired with a thin noise of violins. Adam stopped the plate. An inexplicable silence filled the house, as if this stale old melody had wakened something that listened. Then Adam lit a cigarette.

"Supper near ready, mamma?"

"Pretty near, lamb," said Mrs. Egg.

Supper was pleasant. Hamish talked buoyantly of cows. He was impressed by their stupidity and their artless qualities. Benjamina gazed at the four candles with gray eyes and smiled at nothing. Adam ate fourteen hot biscuits and three mounds of an ice cream that held fresh raspberries. He stared at the ceiling gravely, and his white shirt tightened as he breathed out the first smoke above a cup of coffee.

Then he said, "We'll go to the movies. Get your hat, Miss Saunders."

"But the dishes aren't washed!" Benjamina exclaimed.

"The kid and I'll wash 'em," Adam vouchsafed.

Mrs. Egg yawned, "Go ahead, Benjamina," and watched the girl's hands flutter as she left the green dining room.

Adam blew a ring of smoke, which drooped, dissolving about a candle. He reached across the table for the coffeepot and filled his cup, then looked at Hamish.

"What's she scared of, kid?"

"Cousin Joe," said Hamish presently. "He's—our guardian—wants to marry her. Y'see, we have some money from dad's store. Cousin Joe's a lawyer and the bank pays him the money."

"Lived with him in Cleveland?"

Hamish groaned, "You saw where we lived! Benjy couldn't keep the place lookin' decent. He knocked his pipe out wherever he sat. But Benjy'll be twenty-one in October and the bank'll pay her the money."

"An' this Joe's a sour plum?"

"Well," said Hamish, with the manner of last justice, "he can sing pretty well."

Mrs. Egg was thinking of bed at ten o'clock when the telephone rang and the anguished voice of her youngest daughter came pouring from Ilium:

"Mamma! Dammy's got that girl in a box at the movies!"

"I'm glad," said Mrs. Egg, "that they're sitting in a box. My gee! It's hot as I ever felt it for this time of year, Fern! Benjamina's such a large person that she ——"

"Oh, mamma! And it's all over town that Edith Sims is going to marry ——"

"I can't pretend that I'm either surprised or sorry, Fern. As for Dammy marryin' a girl he would have had to stoop over a yard to kiss after breakfast, it never seemed a just kind of arrangement to me, although I didn't want to criticize her. The Simses are nice folks—awful refined. Mercy, but don't Dammy look well in white pants?"

"Mamma! You simply haven't any heart!"

"I'll be forty-seven in December, Fern," said Mrs. Egg. "Good night."

She drowsily ascended to her cool bedroom, where a vacuum flask of iced lemonade stood with a package of oatmeal crackers on the bed-side table. In the dark she lay listening to the obliging wind that now moved in the ten acres of orchard, and sometimes she chuckled, nibbling a cracker. Finally she slept, and was wakened by Adam's voice.

"Was it a nice picture, Dammy?"

"Fair. Where's that law dictionary dad got last year, mamma?"

"It's in the pantry, under the paraffin for the preserves, sweetheart."

"Thanks," said Adam, and his feet went softly away.

Mrs. Egg resumed her slumbers composedly, and woke on the first clash of milk pails in the barnyard. Day was clear. Adam could get in the rest of the peaches and paint the garage roof without discomfort. She ate a cracker, dressing, and went down the back stairs to find Benjamina grinding coffee in a white, fresh gown that showed gentle color in her cheeks.

"Mercy," said Mrs. Egg, "but you're up real early!"

"I don't think it can be very healthy for Mr. Egg and Hamish to wait so long for breakfast," the girl said.

"The men's cook down at the bunk house always has coffee for Dammy. It's a sad time that Dammy can't get himself a meal around here, honey. But it's nice to have breakfast early. I think he's hungriest in the mornin'."

"Isn't he always hungry?"

"Always," Mrs. Egg assured her happily, beginning to pare chilled peaches; "and he likes your oatmeal, I notice. Bein' Scotch by descent, you understand the stuff. You've been here ten days, and it's remarkable how you've learned what Dammy likes. If he was talkative it wouldn't take so much intelligence. A very good way is to watch his toes. If they move he likes what he's eatin'. My gee! It was easy to tell when he was little and went barefooted. He's too tactful to complain about anything."

"He said, driving down from Cleveland, that he hated talking much," Benjamina murmured.

Adam's black head showed above his blue milking shirt in the barnyard. Mrs. Egg watched the tall girl's gray eyes quicken as she gazed down the wet grass. Morning mist fairly smoked from the turf and the boles of apple trees were moist. Hamish was lugging pails to the dairy valiantly.

"The high school here," said Mrs. Egg, "is very good for the size of the town, and Hamish will be perfectly comfortable in winters. You mustn't be alarmed by my husband when he comes back from Chicago. It's a nervous habit he has of winkin' his left eye. It don't mean a thing. I'm tryin' to get hold of some girl that's reasonably intell'gent to do waitin' on table and dusting, which is not good for your hands."

"It's very nice here," Benjamina said, still looking at the barnyard.

Mrs. Egg decided that she was a beautiful creature. Her color improved breath by breath, and her face had the look of a goddess on a coin. The vast woman ate a peach and inspected this virgin hopefully. Then the pale hands shot to Benjamina's throat and she whirled from the window. Hamish tumbled through the door, his shoes smeared with milk and his mouth dragged into a gash of fright.

He gulped, "It's Cousin Joe! He's gettin' out of a buggy at the gate!"

"Gracious!" said Mrs. Egg.

She rose and walked into the veranda, smoothing her hair. The man limping up from the white gates was tall and his shoulders seemed broad. He leaned on a cane. He wore a straw hat made of rough rings of straw. Mrs. Egg greatly disliked him at once, and went down the steps slowly, sideways. Adam was lounging up from the barnyard and some farm hands followed him in a clump of tanned faces. The light made their eyes flash. The woman sighed. There might be a deal of angry talk before she got rid of the lame person in black. He advanced and she awaited him under the apple tree below the steps. When he approached she saw that his hair was dull brown and sleek as he took off his hat.

"Mrs. Egg?"

"I am," said Mrs. Egg.

The man smoothly bowed. He was less than six feet tall, but burly and not pale. His mouth smiled charmingly. He glanced at Adam, smoking on the steps, and twirled the cane in his hand. He said, "My name's Hume. I'm an attorney. I'm the guardian of Benjamina and Hamish Saunders, my cousin's children. They're here, I understand?"

"I understand," Mrs. Egg drawled, "that you ain't much of a guardian, and they're better off here."

Adam's voice came over her shoulder, "They're goin' to stay here."

Cold sweat rose in Mrs. Egg's clenched hands. She turned and saw Adam's nostrils rigid, yellow on his bronze face. She said, "Go in to breakfast, Dammy. I'm talkin' to this person."

Adam might lose his temper. He must go away. She looked at him for a moment, and the farm hands made new shadows on the turf, approaching curiously. Then Adam turned and walked into the kitchen.

"We're wasting time," the man observed, always smoothly. "Benjy's my ward and she's going back to Cleveland with me."

"I don't see as that follows, precisely," Mrs. Egg panted.

"The nearest justice would."

"Then you'd better get the nearest justice to say it," said Mrs. Egg, "because Benjamina's perfectly well off here. As for sendin' her back to Cleveland for you to make love at in a flat—my gee!"

She felt herself impolitic and tactless in saying this, but rage had mounted. Her chins were shaking. The man's clothes smelled of pipe smoke. His collar wasn't clean. He was a dog. The kitchen door slammed. She dreaded that Adam might lose his temper and thrash this fellow. The man looked over her head.

"Here," said Adam, "get out the way, mamma, please! Let's settle this! Come ahead, Benj'mina. He can't hurt you." He was leading the girl down the steps by a hand. Smoke welled from his nostrils and his eyes had partly shut. He brought the white girl to face her cousin and said, "Now! My name's Adam Egg. Benjamina's married to me. Show him your rings, kid."

The farm hands gasped and an Irish lad whooped. Adam undid his brown fingers from the pale hand. The big diamond and the circlet of little stones blazed below the rosy nails. Mrs. Egg put her palm on her mouth and a scream was a pain in her throat. She hadn't seen Adam married! He threw away the cigarette by a red motion of his tongue and drawled, "Go back in the house, kid!"

The man clamped a hand on his cane and said, "Without my permission!"

"She's twenty," Adam grunted, his shoulders tremulous under the thin blue shirt, "so what you goin' to do?"

Then nothing happened. Benjamina walked up the steps and stood with an arm about Hamish at the top. A farm hand lit a pipe. Mrs. Egg's heart beat horribly with the pain of having missed Adam's wedding. The man's face was getting green. He was odious, completely. He said, "Their property stays in my control!"

"To hell with their property!"

Nothing happened. The man stood poking his cane into the turf and turning the thick end among grass blades. Hamish came down one step. Then the man backed and whirled up his cane.

Mrs. Egg shrieked "Dammy!" and bruised her lip with her teeth.

The heavy cane seemed to balance a long while against the sun. Adam stood. The thing fell across his right shoulder and broke with a cracking sound. The blue shirt tore and Benjamina screamed. Adam's whole length shook and his lips were gray for a second. He slung out both hands and caught the fellow's throat. He said, "Now! You've 'saulted me with a dangerous weapon, see? Now, get out of here! Here's your witnesses! You hit me! All I've got to do is walk you in to a judge and you'll get a year, see? That's law! Get out of this! I could kill you," he drawled, "an' I will if you ain't out the gates in one minute!"

His shoulders heaved. The shirt split down his back. The man went spinning in a queer rotation along the grass, like some collapsing toy. Adam stood with his hands raised, watching. The figure stumbled twice. Then it lurched toward the white gates in a full run, and the farm hands yelled. Adam dropped his hands and ripped the shirt from his shoulder. A band of scarlet had risen on the bronze of his chest. He said thickly, "Damn if he ain't a husky! Hey, Hamish, get me some iodine, will you?"

Benjamina ran down the steps and dragged the rings from her fingers. She babbled, "Oh! Oh, Adam! What did you let him strike you for? I'm so sorry!" She thrust the rings into one of his palms and cried, "You shouldn't have let him hit you! He's so strong!"

"What was I goin' to say if he said to show any weddin' certificate? If he hit me it was assault, an' I could get rid of him."

Mrs. Egg wailed, "Then you ain't married, Dammy?"

"No."

Adam leaned on the apple tree and stared at Benjamina, turning the rings in his hand. After a moment the girl flushed and walked away into the orchard of rustling boughs. A morning wind made the giant's torn shirt flap. He sent his eyes to the gaping hired men and drawled "What about those cows?"

Feet thudded off on the grass. Hamish came bounding down the steps with a bottle of iodine and a handkerchief.

"My gee, Dammy," said Mrs. Egg, grasping the bottle, "if your sisters have the nerve to say you're tactless after this I'll —— Sit down, lamb! Oh, Dammy, how can you think as fast as that?"

Adam lit a cigarette and blew smoke through his nostrils. His face was again blank and undisturbed. He asked "Peaches for breakfast?" absently.

"Anything you want, lamb! Benjamina has oatmeal ready."

He clicked the rings in his hand and his feet wriggled in the moccasins. Then he said "Mamma," strangely.

"Yes, Dammy."

"Mamma, I've put Miss Saunders in a hell of a position, sayin' we're married."

"That's so, Dammy. It'll be all over town in no time."

Adam arose from the grass and examined his mother for a whole minute. His nostrils shook somewhat. He took the engagement ring from one palm and handed it to Hamish, ordering, "Kid, you go take that to your sister and tell her it's with my compliments. I hate talkin'."

The boy's red hair went flashing under the trees. Mrs. Egg watched him halt by his sister, who was wiping her eyes beside a trunk. They conferred. Soon Hamish turned about and began to make swift signs with his arms.

Adam said, "Good enough. . . . I guess I'll call her Ben." He lit his next cigarette and walked up to the steps.

Mrs. Egg screamed, "Dammy! Ain't you goin' to go kiss her?"

Adam's eyes opened on his mother in alarm.

He said, "I'm thirsty, mamma. And I've got to get a fresh shirt. Couldn't kiss anybody in this one. It wouldn't be polite."

Then he waved his cigarette to his new love and slammed the kitchen door behind him.

BABYLON REVISITED

by F. Scott Fitzgerald

THE JAZZ AGE may be said to have arrived in the *Post* on page ninety-nine of the issue for May 29, 1920, when a girl named Ardita "took a carved jade case from her pocket, extracted a cigarette and lit it with a conscious coolness, though she knew her hand was trembling a bit." This occurred in a story by F. Scott Fitzgerald called "The Offshore Pirate" and broke a long-standing *Post* taboo against heroines who smoked in public. In other Fitzgerald-*Post* stories of the early 20's young Americans drank large amounts of wood alcohol and champagne, called each other flappers, and wound up all-night dancing parties by running off to get married, just as many of their living contemporaries were doing. Fitzgerald himself was having a wonderful time; when he sold his first story to the *Post* for $400 in 1920 he got roaring drunk and flooded his hotel by leaving on the tap in his bathroom. In a 1924 *Post* article called "How to Live on $36,000 a Year," he told of much larger earnings but confessed he was spending more than he made. The payoff came quickly; Fitzgerald's personal tragedy is more than hinted at in the following story. He continued to write *Post* stories until 1937, three years before his death.

FEBRUARY 21, 1931

AND WHERE'S MR. CAMPBELL?" Charlie asked.

"Gone to Switzerland. Mr. Campbell's a pretty sick man, Mr. Wales."

"I'm sorry to hear that. And George Hardt?" Charlie inquired.

"Back in America, gone to work."

"And where is the snow bird?"

"He was in here last week. Anyway, his friend, Mr. Schaeffer, is in Paris."

Two familiar names from the long list of a year and a half ago. Charlie scribbled an address in his notebook and tore out the page.

"If you see Mr. Schaeffer, give him this," he said. "It's my brother-in-law's address. I haven't settled on a hotel yet."

He was not really disappointed to find Paris was so empty. But the stillness in the bar was strange, almost portentous.

It was not an American bar any more—he felt polite in it, and not as if he owned it. It had gone back into France. He had felt the stillness from the moment he got out of the taxi and saw the doorman, usually in a frenzy of activity at this hour, gossiping with a *chasseur* by the servants' entrance.

Passing through the corridor, he heard only a single, bored voice in the once-clamorous women's room. When he turned into the bar he traveled the twenty feet of green carpet with his eyes fixed straight ahead by old habit; and then, with his foot firmly on the rail, he turned and surveyed the room, encountering only a single pair of eyes that fluttered up from a newspaper in the corner. Charlie asked for the head barman, Paul, who in the latter days of the bull market had come to work in his own custom-built car—disembarking, however, with due nicety at the nearest corner. But Paul was at his country house today and Alix was giving him his information.

"No, no more. I'm going slow these days."

Alix congratulated him: "Hope you stick to it, Mr. Wales. You were going pretty strong a couple of years ago."

"I'll stick to it all right," Charlie assured him. "I've stuck to it for over a year and a half now."

"How do you find conditions in America?"

"I haven't been to America for months. I'm in business in Prague, representing a couple of concerns there. They don't know about me down there." He smiled faintly. "Remember the night of George Hardt's bachelor dinner here? . . . By the way, what's become of Claude Fessenden?"

Alix lowered his voice confidentially: "He's in Paris, but he doesn't come here any more. Paul doesn't allow it. He ran up a bill of thirty thousand francs, charging all his drinks and his lunches, and usually his dinner, for more than a year. And when Paul finally told him he had to pay, he gave him a bad check."

Alix pressed his lips together and shook his head.

"I don't understand it, such a dandy fellow. Now he's all bloated up ——" He made a plump apple of his hands.

A thin world, resting on a common weakness, shredded away now like tissue paper. Turning, Charlie saw a group of effeminate young men installing themselves in a corner.

"Nothing affects them," he thought. "Stocks rise and fall, people loaf or work, but they go on forever." The place oppressed him. He called for the dice and shook with Alix for the drink.

"Here for long, Mr. Wales?"

"I'm here for four or five days to see my little girl."

"Oh-h! You have a little girl?"

Outside, the fire-red, gas-blue, ghost-green signs shone smokily through the tranquil rain. It was late afternoon and the streets were in movement; the *bistros* gleamed. At the corner of the Boulevard des Capucines he took a taxi. The Place de la Concorde moved by in pink majesty; they crossed the logical Seine, and Charlie felt the sudden provincial quality of the left bank.

"I spoiled this city for myself," he thought. "I didn't realize it, but the days came along one after another, and then two years were gone, and everything was gone, and I was gone."

He was thirty-five, a handsome man, with the Irish mobility of his face sobered by a deep wrinkle between his eyes. As he rang his brother-in-law's bell in the Rue Palatine, the wrinkle deepened till it pulled down his brows; he felt a cramping sensation in his belly. From behind the maid who opened the door darted a lovely little girl of nine who shrieked "Daddy!" and flew up, struggling like a fish, into his arms. She pulled his head around by one ear and set her cheek against his.

"My old pie," he said.

"Oh, daddy, daddy, daddy, daddy, dads, dads, dads!"

She drew him into the salon, where the family waited, a boy and girl his daughter's age, his sister-in-law and her husband. He greeted Marion with his voice pitched carefully to avoid either feigned enthusiasm or dislike, but her response was more frankly tepid, and she minimized her expression of unshakable distrust by directing her regard toward his child. The two men clasped hands in a friendly way and Lincoln Peters rested his for a moment on Charlie's shoulder.

The room was warm and comfortably American. The three children moved intimately about, playing through the yellow oblongs that led to other rooms; the cheer of six o'clock spoke in the eager smacks of the fire and the sounds of French activity in the kitchen. But Charlie did not relax; his heart sat up rigidly in his body and he drew confidence from his daughter, who from time to time came close to him, holding in her arms the doll he had brought.

"Really extremely well," he declared in answer to Lincoln's question. "There's a lot of business there that isn't moving at all, but we're doing even better than ever. In fact, damn well. I'm bringing my sister over from America next month to keep house for me. In fact, my income is bigger than it was when I had money. You see, the Czechs ———"

His boasting was for a specific purpose; but after a moment, seeing a faint restiveness in Lincoln's eye, he changed the subject:

"Those are fine children of yours, well brought up, good manners."

"We think Honoria's a great little girl too."

Marion Peters came back into the little salon. She was a tall woman with worried eyes, who had once possessed a fresh American loveliness. Charlie had never been sensitive to it and was always surprised when people spoke of how pretty she had been. From the first there had been an instinctive antipathy between them.

"Well, how do you find Honoria?" she asked.

"Wonderful. I was astonished how much she's grown in ten months. All the children are looking well."

"We haven't had a doctor for a year. How do you like being back in Paris?"

"It seems very funny to see so few Americans around."

"I'm delighted," Marion said vehemently. "Now at least you can go into a store without their assuming you're a millionaire. We've suffered like everybody, but on the whole it's a good deal pleasanter."

"But it was nice while it lasted," Charlie said. "We were a sort of royalty, almost infallible, with a sort of magic around us. In the bar this afternoon"—he stumbled, seeing his mistake—"there wasn't a man I knew."

She looked at him keenly. "I should think you'd have had enough of bars."

"I only stayed a minute. I take one drink every afternoon, and no more."

"Don't you want a cocktail before dinner?" Lincoln asked.

"I take only one drink every afternoon, and I've had that."

"I hope you keep to it," said Marion.

Her dislike was evident in the coldness with which she spoke, but Charlie only smiled; he had larger plans. Her very aggressiveness gave him an advantage, and he knew enough to wait. He wanted them to initiate the discussion of what they knew had brought him to Paris.

Honoria was to spend the following afternoon with him. At dinner he couldn't decide whether she was most like him or her mother. Fortunate if she didn't combine the traits of both that had brought them to disaster. A great wave of protectiveness went over him. He thought he knew what to do for her. He believed in character; he wanted to jump back a whole generation and trust in character again as the eternally valuable element. Everything wore out now. Parents expected genius, or at least brilliance, and both the forcing of children and the fear of forcing them, the fear of warping natural abilities, were poor substitutes for that long, careful watchfulness, that checking and balancing and reckoning of accounts, the end of which was that there should be no slipping below a certain level of duty and integrity.

That was what the elders had been unable to teach plausibly since the break between the generations ten or twelve years ago.

He left soon after dinner, but not to go home. He was curious to see Paris by night with clearer and more judicious eyes. He bought a *strapontin* for the Casino and watched Josephine Baker go through her chocolate arabesques.

After an hour he left and strolled toward Montmartre, up the Rue Pigalle into the Place Blanche. The rain had stopped and there were a few people in evening clothes disembarking from taxis in front of cabarets, and *cocottes* prowling singly or in pairs, and many Negroes. He passed a lighted door from which issued music, and stopped with the sense of familiarity; it was Bricktop's, where he had parted with so many hours and so much money. A few doors farther on he found another ancient rendezvous and incautiously put his head inside. Immediately an eager orchestra burst into sound, a pair of professional dancers leaped to their feet and a maître d'hôtel swooped toward him, crying, "Crowd just arriving, sir!" But he withdrew quickly.

"You have to be damn drunk," he thought.

Zelli's was closed, the bleak and sinister cheap hotels surrounding it were dark; up in the Rue Blanche there was more light and a local, colloquial French crowd. The Poet's Cave had disappeared, but the two great mouths of the Café of Heaven and the Café of Hell still yawned— even devoured, as he watched, the meager contents of a tourist bus—a German, a Japanese, and an American couple who glanced at him with frightened eyes.

So much for the effort and ingenuity of Montmartre. All the catering to vice and waste was on an utterly childish scale, and he suddenly realized the meaning of the word "dissipate"—to dissipate into thin air; to make nothing out of something. In the little hours of the night every move from place to place was an enormous human jump, an increase of paying for the privilege of slower and slower motion.

He remembered thousand-franc notes given to an orchestra for playing a single number, hundred-franc notes tossed to a doorman for calling a cab.

But it hadn't been given for nothing.

It had been given, even the most wildly squandered sum, as an offering to destiny that he might not remember the things most worth remembering, the things that now he would always remember—his child taken from his control, his wife escaped to a grave in Vermont.

In the glare of a *brasserie* a woman spoke to him. He bought her some eggs and coffee, and then, eluding her encouraging stare, gave her a twenty-franc note and took a taxi to his hotel.

II

HE WOKE upon a fine fall day—football weather. The depression of yesterday was gone and he liked the people on the streets. At noon he sat opposite Honoria at the Grand Vatel, the only restaurant he could think of not reminiscent of champagne dinners and long luncheons that began at two and ended in a blurred and vague twilight.

"Now, how about vegetables? Oughtn't you to have some vegetables?"

"Well, yes."

"Here's *épinards* and *choux-fleur* and carrots and haricots."

"I'd like *choux-fleurs*."

"Wouldn't you like to have two vegetables?"

"I usually only have one at lunch."

The waiter was pretending to be inordinately fond of children. "*Qu'elle est mignonne la petite? Elle parle exactement comme une française.*"

"How about dessert? Shall we wait and see?"

The waiter disappeared. Honoria looked at him expectantly.

"What are we going to do?"

"First we're going to that toy store in the Rue St. Honoré and buy you anything you like. And then we're going to the vaudeville at the Empire."

She hesitated. "I like it about the vaudeville, but not the toy store."

"Why not?"

"Well, you brought me this doll." She had it with her. "And I've got lots of things. And we're not rich any more, are we?"

"We never were. But today you are to have anything you want."

"All right," she agreed resignedly.

He had always been fond of her, but when there had been her mother and a French nurse he had been inclined to be strict; now he extended himself, reached out for a new tolerance; he must be both parents to her and not shut any of her out of communication.

"I want to get to know you," he said gravely. "First let me introduce myself. My name is Charles J. Wales, of Prague."

"Oh, daddy!" her voice cracked with laughter.

"And who are you, please?" he persisted, and she accepted a rôle immediately: "Honoria Wales, Rue Palatine, Paris."

"Married or single?"

"No, not married. Single."

He indicated the doll. "But I see you have a child, madame."

Unwilling to disinherit it, she took it to her heart and thought quickly: "Yes, I've been married, but I'm not married now. My husband is dead."

He went on quickly, "And the child's name?"

"Simone. That's after my best friend at school."

"I'm very pleased that you're doing so well at school."

"I'm third this month," she boasted. "Elsie"— that was her cousin—"is only about eighteenth, and Richard is about at the bottom."

"You like Richard and Elsie, don't you?"

"Oh, yes. I like Richard quite well and I like her all right."

Cautiously and casually he asked: "And Aunt Marion and Uncle Lincoln—which do you like best?"

"Oh, Uncle Lincoln, I guess."

He was increasingly aware of her presence. As they came in, a murmur of "What an adorable child" followed them, and now the people at the next table bent all their silences upon her, staring as if she were something no more conscious than a flower.

"Why don't I live with you?" she asked suddenly. "Because mamma's dead?"

"You must stay here and learn more French. It would have been hard for daddy to take care of you so well."

"I don't really need much taking care of any more. I do everything for myself."

Going out of the restaurant, a man and a woman unexpectedly hailed him!

"Well, the old Wales!"

"Hello there, Lorraine. . . . Dunc."

Sudden ghosts out of the past: Duncan Schaeffer, a friend from college. Lorraine Quarrles, a lovely, pale blonde of thirty; one of a crowd who had helped them make months into days in the lavish times of two years ago.

"My husband couldn't come this year," she said, in answer to his question. "We're poor as hell. So he gave me two hundred a month and told me I could do my worst on that. . . . This your little girl?"

"What about sitting down?" Duncan asked.

"Can't do it." He was glad for an excuse.

As always, he felt Lorraine's passionate, provocative attraction, but his own rhythm was different now.

"Well, how about dinner?" she asked.

"I'm not free. Give me your address and let me call you."

"Charlie, I believe you're sober," she said judicially. "I honestly believe he's sober, Dunc. Pinch him and see if he's sober."

Charlie indicated Honoria with his head. They both laughed.

"What's your address?" said Duncan skeptically.

He hesitated, unwilling to give the name of his hotel.

"I'm not settled yet. I'd better call you. We're going to see the vaudeville at the Empire."

"There! That's what I want to do," Lorraine said. "I want to see some clowns and acrobats and jugglers. That's just what we'll do, Dunc."

"We've got to do an errand first," said Charlie. "Perhaps we'll see you there."

"All right, you snob. . . . Good-by, beautiful little girl."

"Good-by." Honoria bobbed politely.

Somehow, an unpleasant encounter, Charlie thought. They liked him because he was functioning, because he was serious; they wanted to see him, because he was stronger than they were now, because they wanted to draw a certain sustenance from his strength.

At the Empire, Honoria proudly refused to sit upon her father's folded coat. She was already an individual with a code of her own, and Charlie was more and more absorbed by the desire of putting a little of himself into her before she crystallized utterly. It was hopeless to try to know her in so short a time.

Between the acts they came upon Duncan and Lorraine in the lobby where the band was playing.

"Have a drink?"

"All right, but not up at the bar. We'll take a table."

"The perfect father."

Listening abstractedly to Lorraine, Charlie watched Honoria's eyes leave them all, and he followed them wistfully about the room, wondering what they saw. He met them and she smiled.

"I liked that lemonade," she said.

What had she said? What had he expected? Going home in a taxi afterward, he pulled her over until her head rested against his chest.

"Darling, do you ever think about your mother?"

"Yes, sometimes," she answered vaguely.

"I don't want you to forget her. Have you got a picture of her?"

"Yes, I think so. Anyhow, Aunt Marion has. Why don't you want me to forget her?"

"She loved you very much."

"I loved her too."

They were silent for a moment.

"Daddy, I want to come and live with you," she said suddenly.

His heart leaped; he had wanted it to come like this.

"Aren't you perfectly happy?"

"Yes, but I love you better than anybody. And you love me better than anybody, don't you, now that mummy's dead?"

"Of course I do. But you won't always like me best, honey. You'll grow up and meet somebody your own age and go marry him and forget you ever had a daddy."

"Yes, that's true," she agreed tranquilly.

He didn't go in. He was coming back at nine o'clock and he wanted to keep himself fresh and new for the thing he must say then.

"When you're safe inside, just show yourself in that window."

"All right. Good-by, dads, dads, dads, dads."

He waited in the dark street until she appeared, all warm and glowing, in the window above and kissed her fingers out into the night.

III

THEY WERE WAITING. Marion sat behind empty coffee cups in a dignified black dinner dress that just faintly suggested mourning. Lincoln was walking up and down with the animation of one who had already been talking. They were as anxious as he was to get into the question. He opened it almost immediately:

"I suppose you know what I want to see you about—why I really came to Paris."

Marion fiddled with the glass grapes on her necklace and frowned.

"I'm awfully anxious to have a home," he continued. "And I'm awfully anxious to have Honoria in it. I appreciate your taking in Honoria for her mother's sake, but things have changed now" —he hesitated and then continued strongly—

"changed radically with me, and I want to ask you to reconsider the matter. It would be silly for me to deny that about two years ago I was acting badly ——"

Marion looked up at him with hard eyes.

"—— but all that's over. As I told you, I haven't had more than a drink a day for over a year, and I take that drink deliberately, so that the idea of alcohol won't get too big in my imagination. You see the idea?"

"No," said Marion succinctly.

"It's a sort of stunt I set myself. It keeps the matter in proportion."

"I get you," said Lincoln. "You don't want to admit it's got any attraction for you."

"Something like that. Sometimes I forget and don't take it. But I try to take it. Anyhow, I couldn't afford to drink in my position. The people I represent are more than satisfied with what I've done, and I'm bringing my sister over from Burlington to keep house for me, and I want awfully to have Honoria too. You know that even when her mother and I weren't getting along well I never let anything that happened touch Honoria. I know she's fond of me and I know I'm able to take care of her and—well, there you are. How do you feel about it?"

He knew that now he would have to take a beating. It would last an hour or two hours, and it would be difficult, but if he modulated his inevitable resentment to the chastened attitude of the reformed sinner, he might win his point in the end. "Keep your temper," he told himself. "You don't want to be justified. You want Honoria."

Lincoln spoke first: "We've been talking it over ever since we got your letter last month. We're happy to have Honoria here. She's a dear little thing, and we're glad to be able to help her, but of course that isn't the question ——"

Marion interrupted suddenly. "How long are you going to stay sober, Charlie?" she asked.

"Permanently, I hope."

"How can anybody count on that?"

"You know I never did drink heavily until I gave up business and came over here with nothing to do. Then Helen and I began to run around with ——"

"Please leave Helen out of it. I can't bear to hear you talk about her like that."

He stared at her grimly; he had never been certain how fond of each other the sisters were in life.

"My drinking only lasted about a year and a half—from the time we came over until I—collapsed."

"It was time enough."

"It was time enough," he agreed.

"My duty is entirely to Helen," she said. "I try to think what she would have wanted me to do. Frankly, from the night you did that terrible thing you haven't really existed for me. I can't help that. She was my sister."

"Yes."

"When she was dying she asked me to look out for Honoria. If you hadn't been in a sanitarium then, it might have helped matters."

He had no answer.

"I'll never in my life be able to forget the morning when Helen knocked at my door, soaked to the skin and shivering, and said you'd locked her out."

Charlie gripped the sides of the chair. This was more difficult than he expected; he wanted to launch out into a long expostulation and explanation, but he only said: "The night I locked her out ——" and she interrupted, "I don't feel up to going over that again."

After a moment's silence Lincoln said: "We're getting off the subject. You want Marion to set aside her legal guardianship and give you Honoria. I think the main point for her is whether she has confidence in you or not."

"I don't blame Marion," Charlie said slowly, "but I think she can have entire confidence in me. I had a good record up to three years ago. Of course, it's within human possibilities I might go wrong any time. But if we wait much longer I'll lose Honoria's childhood and my chance for a home. I'll simply lose her, don't you see?"

"Yes, I see," said Lincoln.

"Why didn't you think of all this before?" Marion asked.

"I suppose I did, from time to time, but Helen and I were getting along badly. When I consented to the guardianship, I was flat on my back in a sanitarium and the market had cleaned me out of every sou. I knew I'd acted badly, and I thought if it would bring any peace to Helen, I'd agree to anything. But now it's different. I'm well, I'm functioning, I'm behaving damn well, so far as ——"

"Please don't swear at me," Marion said.

He looked at her, startled. With each remark the force of her dislike became more and more apparent. She had built up all her fear of life into one wall and faced it toward him. This trivial reproof was possibly the result of some trouble with the cook several hours before. Charlie became increasingly alarmed at leaving Honoria in this atmosphere of hostility against himself; sooner or later it would come out, in a word here, a shake of the head there, and some of that dis-

trust would be irrevocably implanted in Honoria. But he pulled his temper down out of his face and shut it up inside him; he had won a point, for Lincoln realized the absurdity of Marion's remark and asked her lightly since when she had objected to the word "damn."

"Another thing," Charlie said: "I'm able to give her certain advantages now. I'm going to take a French governess to Prague with me. I've got a lease on a new apartment ——"

He stopped, realizing that he was blundering. They couldn't be expected to accept with equanimity the fact that his income was again twice as large as their own.

"I suppose you can give her more luxuries than we can," said Marion. "When you were throwing away money we were living along watching every ten francs. . . . I suppose you'll start doing it again."

"Oh, no," he said. "I've learned. I worked hard for ten years, you know—until I got lucky in the market, like so many people. Terribly lucky. It didn't seem any use working any more, so I quit. It won't happen again."

There was a long silence. All of them felt their nerves straining, and for the first time in a year Charlie wanted a drink. He was sure now that Lincoln Peters wanted him to have his child.

Marion shuddered suddenly; part of her saw that Charlie's feet were planted on the earth now, and her own maternal feeling recognized the naturalness of his desire; but she had lived for a long time with a prejudice—a prejudice founded on a curious disbelief in her sister's happiness, and which, in the shock of one terrible night, had turned to hatred for him. It had all happened at a point in her life where the discouragement of ill-health and adverse circumstances made it necessary for her to believe in tangible villainy and a tangible villain.

"I can't help what I think!" she cried out suddenly. "How much you were responsible for Helen's death, I don't know. It's something you'll have to square with your own conscience."

An electric current of agony surged through him; for a moment he was almost on his feet, an unuttered sound echoing in his throat. He hung on to himself for a moment, another moment.

"Hold on there," said Lincoln uncomfortably. "I never thought you were responsible for that."

"Helen died of heart trouble," Charlie said dully.

"Yes, heart trouble." Marion spoke as if the phrase had another meaning for her.

Then, in the flatness that followed her outburst, she saw him plainly and she knew he had somehow arrived at control over the situation. Glancing at her husband, she found no help from him, and as abruptly as if it were a matter of no importance, she threw up the sponge.

"Do what you like!" she cried, springing up from her chair. "She's your child. I'm not the person to stand in your way. I think if it were my child I'd rather see her ——" She managed to check herself. "You two decide it. I can't stand this. I'm sick. I'm going to bed."

She hurried from the room; after a moment Lincoln said:

"This has been a hard day for her. You know how strongly she feels ——" His voice was almost apologetic: "When a woman gets an idea in her head."

"Of course."

"It's going to be all right. I think she sees now that you—can provide for the child, and so we can't very well stand in your way or Honoria's way."

"Thank you, Lincoln."

"I'd better go along and see how she is."

"I'm going."

He was still trembling when he reached the street, but a walk down the Rue Bonaparte to the quais set him up, and as he crossed the Seine, dotted with many cold moons, he felt exultant. But back in his room he couldn't sleep. The image of Helen haunted him. Helen whom he had loved so until they had senselessly begun to abuse each other's love and tear it into shreds. On that terrible February night that Marion remembered so vividly, a slow quarrel that had gone on for hours. There was a scene at the Florida, and then he attempted to take her home, and then Helen kissed Ted Wilder at a table, and what she had hysterically said. Charlie's departure and, on his arrival home, his turning the key in the lock in wild anger. How could he know she would arrive an hour later alone, that there would be a snowstorm in which she wandered about in slippers for an hour, too confused to find a taxi? Then the aftermath, her escaping pneumonia by a miracle, and all the attendant horror. They were "reconciled," but that was the beginning of the end, and Marion, who had seen with her own eyes and who imagined it to be one of many scenes from her sister's martyrdom, never forgot.

Going over it again brought Helen nearer, and in the white, soft light that steals upon half sleep near morning he found himself talking to her again. She said that he was perfectly right about Honoria and that she wanted Honoria to be with him. She said she was glad he was being good and doing better. She said a lot of other things—very friendly things—but she was in a swing in a white dress, and swinging faster and faster all the time, so that at the end he could not hear clearly all that she said.

IV

HE WOKE UP feeling happy. The door of the world was open again. He made plans, vistas, futures for Honoria and himself, but suddenly he grew sad, remembering all the plans he and Helen had made. She had not planned to die. The present was the thing—work to do and someone to love. But not to love too much, for Charlie had read in D. H. Lawrence about the injury that a father can do to a daughter or a mother to a son by attaching them too closely. Afterward, out in the world, the child would seek in the marriage partner the same blind, unselfish tenderness and, failing in all human probability to find it, develop a grudge against love and life.

It was another bright, crisp day. He called Lincoln Peters at the bank where he worked and asked if he could count on taking Honoria when he left for Prague. Lincoln agreed that there was no reason for delay. One thing—the legal guardianship. Marion wanted to retain that a while longer. She was upset by the whole matter, and it would oil things if she felt that the situation was still in her control for another year. Charlie agreed, wanting only the tangible, visible child.

Then the question of a governess. Charlie sat in a gloomy agency and talked to a buxom Breton peasant whom he knew he couldn't endure. There were others whom he could see tomorrow.

He lunched with Lincoln Peters at the Griffon, trying to keep down his exultation.

"There's nothing quite like your own child," Lincoln said. "But you understand how Marion feels too."

"She's forgotten how hard I worked for seven years there," Charlie said. "She just remembers one night."

"There's another thing." Lincoln hesitated. "While you and Helen were tearing around Europe throwing money away, we were just getting along. I didn't touch any of the prosperity because I never got ahead enough to carry anything but my insurance. I think Marion felt there was some kind of injustice in it—you not even working and getting richer and richer."

"It went just as quick as it came," said Charlie.

"A lot did. And a lot of it stayed in the hands of *chasseurs* and saxophone players and maîtres d'hôtel—well, the big party's over now. I just said that to explain Marion's feeling about those crazy years. If you drop in about six o'clock tonight before Marion's too tired, we'll settle the details on the spot."

Back at his hotel, Charlie took from his pocket a *pneumatique* that Lincoln had given him at luncheon. It had been redirected by Paul from the hotel bar.

Dear Charlie: You were so strange when we saw you the other day that I wondered if I did something to offend you. If so, I'm not conscious of it. In fact, I have thought about you too much for the past year, and it's always been in the back of my mind that I might see you if I came over here. We did have such good times that crazy spring, like the night you and I stole the butcher's tricycle, and the time we tried to call on the president and you had the old derby and the wire cane. Everybody seems so old lately, but I don't feel old a bit. Couldn't we get together sometime today for old time's sake? I've got a vile hang-over for the moment, but will be feeling better this afternoon and will look for you about five at the bar.
Always devotedly,
LORRAINE.

His first feeling was one of awe that he had actually, in his mature years, stolen a tricycle and pedaled Lorraine all over the Étoile between the small hours and dawn. In retrospect it was a nightmare. Locking out Helen didn't fit in with any other act of his life, but the tricycle incident did—it was one of many. How many weeks or months of dissipation to arrive at that condition of utter irresponsibility?

He tried to picture how Lorraine had appeared to him then—very attractive; so much so that Helen had been jealous. Yesterday, in the restaurant, she had seemed trite, blurred, worn away. He emphatically did not want to see her, and he was glad no one knew at what hotel he was staying. It was a relief to think of Honoria, to think of Sundays spent with her and of saying good morning to her and of knowing she was there in his house at night, breathing quietly in the darkness.

At five he took a taxi and bought presents for all the Peters'—a piquant cloth doll, a box of Roman soldiers, flowers for Marion, big linen handkerchiefs for Lincoln.

He saw, when he arrived in the apartment, that Marion had accepted the inevitable. She greeted him now as though he were a recalcitrant member of the family, rather than a menacing outsider. Honoria had been told she was going, and Charlie was glad to see that her tact was sufficient to conceal her excessive happiness. Only on his lap did she whisper her delight and the question "When?" before she slipped away.

He and Marion were alone for a minute in the room, and on an impulse he spoke out boldly:

"Family quarrels are bitter things. They don't go according to my rules. They're not like aches or wounds; they're more like splits in the skin that won't heal because there's not enough material. I wish you and I could be on better terms."

"Some things are hard to forget," she answered. "It's a question of confidence. If you behave yourself in the future I won't have any criticism." There was no answer to this, and presently she asked, "When do you propose to take her?"

"As soon as I can get a governess. I hoped the day after tomorrow."

"That's impossible. I've got to get her things in shape. Not before Saturday."

He yielded. Coming back into the room, Lincoln offered him a drink.

"I'll take my daily whisky," he said.

It was warm here, it was a home, people together by a fire. The children felt very safe and important; the mother and father were serious, watchful. They had things to do for the children more important than his visit here. A spoonful of medicine was, after all, more important than the strained relations between Marion and himself. They were not dull people, but they were very much in the grip of life and circumstances, and their gestures as they turned in a cramped space lacked largeness and grace. He wondered if he couldn't do something to get Lincoln out of that rut at the bank.

There was a long peal at the doorbell; the maid crossed the room and went down the corridor. The door opened upon another long ring, and then voices, and the three in the salon looked up expectantly; Richard moved to bring the corridor within his range of vision, and Marion rose. Then the maid came along the corridor, closely followed by the voices, which developed under the light into Duncan Schaeffer and Lorraine Quarrles.

They were gay, they were hilarious, they were roaring with laughter. For a moment Charlie was astounded; then he realized they had got the address he had left at the bar.

"Ah-h-h!" Duncan wagged his finger roguishly at Charlie. "Ah-h-h!"

They both slid down into another cascade of laughter. Anxious and at a loss, Charlie shook hands with them quickly and presented them to Lincoln and Marion. Marion nodded, scarcely speaking. She had drawn back a step toward the fire; her little girl stood beside her, and Marion put an arm about her shoulder.

With growing annoyance at the intrusion, Charlie waited for them to explain themselves. After some concentration Duncan said:

"We came to take you to dinner. Lorraine and I insist that all this shi-shi, cagy business got to stop."

Charlie came closer to them, as if to force them backward down the corridor.

"Sorry, but I can't. Tell me where you'll be and we'll call you in half an hour."

This made no impression. Lorraine sat down suddenly on the side of a chair, and focusing her eyes on Richard, cried, "Oh, what a nice little boy! Come here, little boy." Richard glanced at his mother, but did not move. With a perceptible shrug of her shoulders, Lorraine turned back to Charlie:

"Come on out to dinner. Be yourself, Charlie. Come on."

"How about a little drink?" said Duncan to the room at large.

Lincoln Peters had been somewhat uneasily occupying himself by swinging Honoria from side to side with her feet off the ground.

"I'm sorry, but there isn't a thing in the house," he said. "We just this minute emptied the only bottle."

"All the more reason coming to dinner," Lorraine assured Charlie.

"I can't," said Charlie almost sharply. "You two go have dinner and I'll phone you."

"Oh, you will, will you?" Her voice became suddenly unpleasant. "All right, we'll go along. But I remember, when you used to hammer on my door, I used to be enough of a good sport to give you a drink. Come on, Dunc."

Still in slow motion, with blurred, angry faces, with uncertain feet, they retired along the corridor.

"Good night," Charlie said.

"Good night!" responded Lorraine emphatically.

When he went back into the salon Marion had not moved, only now her son was standing in the circle of her other arm. Lincoln was still swinging Honoria back and forth like a pendulum from side to side.

"What an outrage!" Charlie broke out. "What an absolute outrage!"

Neither of them answered. Charlie dropped into an armchair, picked up his drink, set it down again and said:

"People I haven't seen for two years having the colossal nerve ——"

He broke off. Marion had made the sound "Oh!" in one swift, furious breath, turned her body from him with a jerk and left the room.

Lincoln set down Honoria carefully.

"You children go in and start your soup," he said, and when they obeyed, he said to Charlie:

"Marion's not well and she can't stand shocks. That kind of people make her really physically sick."

"I didn't tell them to come here. They wormed this address out of Paul at the bar. They deliberately ——"

"Well, it's too bad. It doesn't help matters. Excuse me a minute."

Left alone, Charlie sat tense in his chair. In the next room he could hear the children eating, talking in monosyllables, already oblivious of the scene among their elders. He heard a murmur of conversation from a farther room and then the ticking bell of a phone picked up, and in a panic he moved to the other side of the room and out of earshot.

In a minute Lincoln came back. "Look here, Charlie. I think we'd better call off dinner for tonight. Marion's in bad shape."

"Is she angry with me?"

"Sort of," he said, almost roughly. "She's not strong and ——"

"You mean she's changed her mind about Honoria."

"She's pretty bitter right now. I don't know. You phone me at the bank tomorrow."

"I wish you'd explain to her I never dreamed these people would come here. I'm just as sore as you are."

"I couldn't explain anything to her now."

Charlie got up. He took his coat and hat and started down the corridor. Then he opened the door of the dining room and said in a strange voice, "Good night, children."

Honoria rose and ran around the table to hug him.

"Good night, sweetheart," he said vaguely, and then trying to make his voice more tender, trying to conciliate something, "Good night, dear children."

V

CHARLIE went directly to the bar with the furious idea of finding Lorraine and Duncan, but they were not there, and he realized that in any case there was nothing he could do. He had not touched his drink at the Peters', and now he ordered a whisky-and-soda. Paul came over to say hello.

"It's a great change," he said sadly. "We do about half the business we did. So many fellows I hear about back in the States lost everything, maybe not in the first crash, but then in the second, and now when everything keeps going down. Your friend George Hardt lost every cent, I hear. Are you back in the States?"

"No, I'm in business in Prague."

"I heard that you lost a lot in the crash."

"I did," and he added grimly, "but I lost everything I wanted in the boom."

"Selling short."

"Something like that."

Again the memory of those days swept over him like a nightmare—the people they had met traveling; then people who couldn't add a row of figures or speak a coherent sentence. The little man Helen had consented to dance with at the ship's party, who had insulted her ten feet from the table; the human mosaic of pearls who sat behind them at the Russian ballet and, when the curtain rose on a scene, remarked to her companion: "Luffly; just luffly. Zomebody ought to baint a bicture of it." Men who locked their wives out in the snow, because the snow of twenty-nine wasn't real snow. If you didn't want it to be snow, you just paid some money.

He went to the phone and called the Peters' apartment; Lincoln himself answered.

"I called up because, as you can imagine, this thing is on my mind. Has Marion said anything definite?"

"Marion's sick," Lincoln answered shortly. "I know this thing isn't altogether your fault, but I can't have her go to pieces about this. I'm afraid we'll have to let it slide for six months; I can't take the chance of working her up to this state again."

"I see."

"I'm sorry, Charlie."

He went back to his table. His whisky glass was empty, but he shook his head when Alix looked at it questioningly. There wasn't much he could do now except send Honoria some things; he would send her a lot of things tomorrow. He thought rather angrily that that was just money— he had given so many people money.

"No, no more," he said to another waiter. "What do I owe you?"

He would come back some day; they couldn't make him pay forever. But he wanted his child, and nothing was much good now, beside that fact. He wasn't young any more, with a lot of nice thoughts and dreams to have by himself. He was absolutely sure Helen wouldn't have wanted him to be so alone.

FLORIDA LOAFING

by Kenneth Roberts

KENNETH LEWIS ROBERTS began his *Saturday Evening Post* career with a short story ("Good Will and Almond Shells," Dec. 22, 1917) and emerged from it as one of America's best-selling historical novelists (*Arundel*, 1930). But in between he was best known as the *Post*'s roving reporter on the U.S. and European postwar fronts. Author Roberts has written more than two hundred *Post* articles, and he has rarely hesitated to take sides on topics that stirred him. He has crusaded against women's knickerbockers and unlimited immigration, and reported favorably on the rise of Mussolini and the collecting of antiques. The following is one of several articles he wrote documenting the great Florida land boom of the twenties.

MAY 17, 1924

CHAPTER I

Of the retired business men who cheat—of the peculiar attitude of Floridians anent their climate—and of the distinguishing nature between a stump and a Florida conch

ANY INVESTIGATION OF FLORIDA for the purpose of discovering what the idle rich or near-rich and the retired business men are doing, and how much they spend in doing it, is apt to be severely handicapped by the discovery that the rich refuse to stay idle and the business men refuse to stay retired.

There is a great deal of cheating in Florida on the part of people who some years ago solemnly announced to their relatives and friends in Iowa, Pennsylvania, New York, Connecticut or some similar Northern state that discountenances loafing among its residents that they were going to Florida for the purpose of taking life easy and doing nothing with the utmost enthusiasm and persistence amid the soothing, flutelike notes of the filliloo birds, the restful fragrance of the orange blossoms and the bland and brow-cooling breezes from the Gulf Stream.

One gets wind of a man who came to Florida not many months in the past with a trick kidney or a touch of the gambler's rot to live on an income of $3000 or $4000 a year; but when one runs him down to find out how he does it, one is more than likely to discover that he is in the act of developing a subdivision in the middle of a piece of waste land that nobody but the blue herons would look at as far back as three years ago, that he has entirely forgotten about his kidney and that he is in a fair way to make $1,000,000.

A large part of this cheating is evidently due to the justly celebrated Florida climate, which is without question the most wonderful climate in the world. It has only one failing; and it holds this failing in common with the California climate, which is without question the other most wonderful climate in the world—except for certain parts of Arizona, Texas, Louisiana, Mississippi and a few other Southern and Western states, where climates are also the most wonderful in the world, except when they are too hot or too chilly.

The one great failing of the Florida—and California—climate is its occasional unwillingness to show off before strangers in the way that the old residents wish it to show off. And by an old resident of Florida one means a person who has lived there more than thirty days.

When an old Florida resident talks about climate he has in mind a temperature that will permit one to run around in the sun without feeling at all hot, and at the same time to ride around hatless and coatless in an automobile without feeling at all chilly. Since this is a difficult combination to get, the Floridian—like the Californian—spends a great deal of valuable time explaining to strangers that he doesn't know what to make of this weather; that he can't remember when there has been any weather like this; that a person might come down here every year for a thousand years without finding it as hot as this—or as cold as this, or as dry as this, or as rainy as this, or as windy as this.

That is the great failing of the Florida climate. If the old residents would only stop talking about it, more than 90 per cent of the visiting climate hounds would soon wake up to the fact that a Florida winter is just about like a Maine August —fairly warm at times, fairly cool at times, and occasionally fairly rotten, but on the whole a very excellent spell of weather.

Florida is badly in need of a conspiracy of silence on the part of her old residents on the subject of weather—at least until southbound travelers have learned that they have bought tickets for Florida and not for heaven.

The Florida climate, however, appears to have a striking effect on many persons who take up their residence in the state. Persons who are born in the state are usually immune to the climate, as may be seen from the sluggish actions of the Florida cracker, or conch—the latter word being pronounced conk.

The Florida conch is an individual who lives in the waste spaces of the state, eking out a lazy and contented existence by languidly catching an occasional fish or moodily plucking a few limes ever and anon and sending them to market. It is well known in Florida that when one is traveling through the flat expanses of the southern part of the state and sees in the distance an object that may be a stump or a conch, one may possibly discover what it is by stopping and watching the object patiently. If, at the end of several hours, the object has moved at all, it is probably a stump.

THE LAND FEVER

The Northerner who comes to Florida, on the other hand, is more favorably affected by the climate, if all of the so-called old residents of the state are to be credited. These people make the flat statement that every person who comes to Florida adds ten years to his life. Some old residents, indeed, make such strong claims concerning the life-giving qualities of the Florida climate that if their claims are true, many Floridians now living will probably have to be knocked on the head with clubs in order to insure their demise on Judgment Day.

CHAPTER II

Of the relentless booming of the Florida real-estate boom—of methods of arousing the cupidity of newspaper readers—and of the mystification of Floridians at certain aspects of the boom

It is certain that there are many hale and hearty gentlemen swinging mean mashies on Florida golf links who entered the state for the purpose of dying not so many years ago; so it is not at all unlikely that the climate is responsible for the unretiring natures of the retired business men who have retired to the activities of Florida.

Tremendous numbers of persons who are supposed to be living on their incomes in Florida and enjoying a life of ease, free from the carking cares of business, are dealing in real estate with as much energy as though they were only two jumps ahead of the sheriff. This may be due to the fact that all Southern Florida, like all Southern California, is in the relentless and racking throes of a real-estate boom that is booming as persistently as the bass drum in a band that is playing *The Stars and Stripes Forever.*

Due to this boom, everybody in Southern Florida has just bought a piece of real estate, or has just sold a piece of real estate, or is on the verge of buying or selling a piece of real estate.

The St. Petersburg, West Palm Beach, Miami and Orlando newspapers are as full of real-estate advertisements—full-page, half-page, quarter-page, and even smaller outbursts—as a tin of English bloaters is full of smell.

Anyone who reads the real-estate advertisements in these papers for two or three days in succession becomes thoroughly convinced that failure on his part to buy a lot or two in Blinkavista Estates or Sharkfin Gables or Hollobello Fruitlands, or any of the other 57,000 subdivisions that exist in Southern Florida, is as criminally careless as would be the using of $1000 bills in place of a Cape Cod lighter in an open fire.

The cupidity of the newspaper readers is further aroused by auctioneers' advertisements which speak highly of their power to enrich everybody. One auctioneer, confidently addressing "all readers who wish to make money," urged them to read the following letter to him, which he published in full with names and addresses:

Dear Mr. ——: You will be surprised in getting this I am sure, but my husband told me to write as he thought it wouldn't be fair not to.

We bought 5 lots from you 2 years ago. We

are people of moderate means and it strained us a little, but you said it was a good buy. We paid $2300 for them, we sold them last week for $11,000 and thank you very much for insisting on us taking 4 other lots, as the profit on those lots will enable us to complete our home. With best wishes, Mrs. ——.

Few persons have the stubbornness to refuse to inhale this bait with a low moan of excitement, and to call eagerly for more.

In the winter the Floridians occupy themselves almost entirely in selling to visitors from the North. In the summer, when the tourist tide has receded, the Floridians sell their real estate to one another just to keep their hands in. The women as well as the men participate in this orgy of real-estate dealing; and thousands of Florida couples have bitter daily fights because he didn't grab a corner lot for $3000, or because she sold a lot for a profit of $250 when any half-wit should have known that she could have made $1000 if she'd only hung on for another two weeks.

Large amounts of raucous laughter are directed at this great Florida real-estate boom. Floridians almost die laughing at it themselves. A Floridian buys a piece of land somewhere for $750, and suddenly wakes up to the fact that he has been cruelly stuck. Controlling his anger as best he can, he hides in a doorway until a gullible Northerner comes along. Then, springing out on the Northerner, he tells him all the old ones about the climate, speaks touchingly of the delight of owning a little place where you can have an orange and a grapefruit tree in the back yard, and sells him the same piece of property for $2200. Then, keeping his face straight with difficulty, he waits until the Northerner is out of earshot, whereupon he laughs himself sick to think that anybody could be so foolish.

All this is perfectly all right; but in a few months' time the gullible Northerner turns around and sells his $2200 lot for $4500, at which point the Floridian ceases his reminiscent chuckling, scratches his head in a meditative manner, and asks blankly, "Well, what do you know about that?"

The real-estate boom in Southern Florida has now been under way for several years, during which time nearly everyone who has had the slightest idea what he was buying has profited when he bought in or in the vicinity of established cities and resorts like Palm Beach, West Palm Beach, Miami, Miami Beach, Orlando or St. Petersburg.

CHAPTER III

Of the possible continuation of the boom—of the understandable gullibility of Floridians—and of certain exciting incidents in the exchange of Florida real estate

A distinguished northern statistician and dopester has figured out that Florida's development has only started. He claims that whereas the state has a population of only a million at the present time, it will have a population of about twenty-five million in another twenty years. If he is correct—and only a foolhardy man would dare to scoff at his prediction in the light of the many unexpected things that have happened in Florida in the last few years—then the demand for Florida real estate and Florida houses will increase instead of diminish, and the so-called boom will boom merrily onward and upward indefinitely.

Nowadays a Floridian will believe almost anything that he is told concerning real-estate development and the possibilities in it. He hasn't always been so gullible. In 1913 a large real-estate advertisement of an auction sale of water-front land at Miami Beach was run in a Miami paper by the real-estate firm that was conducting the sale.

The advertising writer spread himself on the advertisement and told what were regarded as a number of whoppers. Among other things, he said that hundreds of thousands of dollars would be spent on completing improvements at Miami Beach. Since that time $21,000,000 has been spent in improvement work at Miami Beach.

The lots that were sold at this auction went for $500 and $600 apiece. The auctioneer who did the selling was upset over the affair, as he well knew the lots weren't worth anything like $500 apiece. He talked about it to his friends at considerable length, and remarked several times that he thought he'd give up auctioneering and go into some more refined pursuit, like burglary, in which he would only hold up the people that could afford to be held up. Three or four years later this same auctioneer returned to Miami Beach and paid $6000 for one of the lots that he had sold for $500. A fair valuation of each one of those lots today would be from $25,000 to $40,000.

In 1900 an elderly gentleman purchased two corner lots in Miami for $1700. When his son heard of this criminal expenditure of money, he galloped into court, had the deeds canceled and had his father placed in a sanitarium as incompetent. This same bit of land is now appraised at $300,000.

In 1920 a prominent New York lawyer paid $80,000 for a house and an ocean-front lot at Palm Beach. People thought that his willingness to disgorge this stupendous sum indicated he had been affected by overwork and was becoming a trifle balmy in the upper story, as the saying goes. This year he refused $240,000 for the same house and lot.

In 1919 a wealthy tobacco merchant was offered a choice bit of real estate in St. Petersburg for $30,000. He refused to take it because the price looked to him as though he was regarded as being sufficiently ripe to fall from the bough and burst with a pulpy thud on the ground beneath. Since the offer was made to him, a portion of the same bit of property was sold as a hotel site for $160,000, another portion was divided into six building lots that sold for $10,000 apiece, and still another portion was divided into eight building lots that sold for $15,000 apiece.

In 1922, when one happened into Miami, he found a plethoric subdivision in the first throes of being sold to the public. It was partly sand and partly palmetto scrub, and it was six miles from Miami. Brass bands lured the credulous investor to the auto busses that plied between the city and this embryo suburb; and when the busses were getting ready to start and all the brass bands were rendering three or four popular tunes at one and the same time, the uproar was similar to that which occurs when a football team returns to the dear old college town after knocking the daylight out of the Big Blue team—or the Big Red team or the Big Green team or the Big Yellow team, as the case may be—for the first time in seven years.

Good conservative residents of Miami shook their heads soberly over the brass bands and the hullabaloo and did considerable viewing with alarm. Two years ago the average price of a lot in this waste of sand and palmetto scrub was $700. Today the average price of a lot in the same subdivision is $2500, and the cheapest lot that one can buy is $1600. The palmetto scrub and the jungle have vanished, and in their places are lawns, palm trees, macadamized roads; sidewalks and electric lights and excellent golf links; big, airy shops, fine schools, an outdoor swimming pool and hundreds of attractive Spanish-type stucco houses.

The Miami people who at first viewed the development with alarm as being located in an inaccessible and unattractive spot are building houses in it and moving their families out to live in them. The company that is developing the subdivision now runs nineteen auto busses to it from every part of Florida, and gives prospective buyers free transportation, food and lodging during two and three day trips. Nobody would be surprised if this company ran auto busses to its subdivision from the Grand Cañon and Los Angeles.

CHAPTER IV

Of the evils of Florida real-estate promotions—of the fuddlement of Northern tourists by the good old ballyhoo—and of the misconceptions concerning the income needed to enjoy Florida life

The great danger of relating these glittering stories of sudden riches that have been acquired in Florida real estate lies in the fact that persons with small capital in many parts of the North, without any knowledge whatever of Florida conditions, may pick up the idea that they can rush to Florida, drop all their money into the first thing offered to them and meet with nothing but success. Many persons, lured by talk of quick returns and large crops, have sunk all their savings into Florida farmlands or real-estate projects that were insufficiently developed. Sometimes this land has been under water. Sometimes it has been shrouded in palmetto scrub and jungle, which is about as easy to clear—for an inexperienced agriculturist without resources—as for a Filipino to clear a twenty-acre polar tract of snow and ice with a bolo.

When this happens—and it has happened frequently—the man who has been fleeced can't live on his land, for it is too much of a jungle to yield a living. He has to leave it and hunt for a job, and jobs are hard to walk into in Florida. He can't resell his land, because persons who are familiar with it won't buy it. Usually there's little for him to do except curse Florida and go home.

And too frequently Florida real-estate projects have been promotions instead of developments—

promotions engineered by non-Floridians for the purpose of hooking the fuddled tourist, who seems to pack his sense of proportion away in moth balls with his heavy flannels and his old brown suit when he leaves the North. Thus deprived of his sense of proportion, the cold-eyed, stern-jawed Northerner who wouldn't think of paying $6000 for a lot six blocks from the city hall in his home town will listen open-mouthed to the jazz and the ballyhoo of the Florida land promoters and fairly break his neck to pay $6000 for a lot six miles from the city hall in a Florida city. If the lot happens to be in a promotion instead of in a development, and if he has bought it as a speculation instead of as an investment, he has an excellent chance of regretting his bargain if the real-estate boom ends or even hesitates.

Unfortunately, there were ten promotions for every development during the early days of the Great Growth. The promoter took his money and got out. The buyer, in some cases, made money; but his purchase was a pure speculation, as dangerous as any speculative purchase in the stock market.

The tales of great increases in Florida land values are set down here in order to show one of the chief reasons for the optimism in regard to real estate that exists on every side in Florida, and for the consequent inability of the retired business man to stay retired.

There is great difference of opinion in Florida as to the amount of income that a person should have in order to retire from the bleakness of Northern winters and live in lazy abandon amid the oranges and grapefruit, the sand spurs and the coconut trees, the idle rich and the apologists for the climate, the real-estate enthusiasts and the perfect-thirty-four bathing girls and the Spanish bungalows and all the other delights that Florida holds out to weary dwellers in the slush belt.

It is popularly thought in Northern circles that the person who owns a winter home in Florida, or who rents a house or an apartment in any Florida resort, must of necessity have horny spots on the thumb and forefinger of his right hand from clipping the coupons from his towering stack of bonds.

Fortunately for the Florida real-estate dealers, this idea is as erroneous as the belief that all residents of Paris, France, are immoral. The idea is probably due to the fact that the representatives from Florida, who are heavily advertised in the rotogravure sections of the Sunday papers from January until March each year, are largely members of the Part-Your-Name-On-The-Side Club, whose heaviest and most protracted cerebration is devoted to originating ways in which to spend the money that somebody else made for them.

The rotogravure sections do not advertise the Smiths of St. Petersburg or the Browns of Orlando or the Joneses of Sarasota or the Greens of Bradentown or the Whites of New Smyrna or the Blacks of Titusville or the Grays of Fort Pierce or the Guffs of Delray or the Blanks of Fort Lauderdale or all the other thousands of good folk in the scores of palm-bowered Florida towns, each one of which has its full quota of hibiscus, bougainvillea, subdivisions, vine-clad bungalows, balmy breezes, boosters and people who tell all strangers that they never had any climate like this before.

None the less, the Smiths and the Browns and the Joneses and the Greens and the Guffs and the Blanks are Florida, just as they are all the rest of the United States; and the B. Hoister Ogles and the H. Pierpont Brindles merely provide the publicity value, which is one of the essential features of present-day life.

Even Palm Beach, whose very name is synonymous with wealth, and the odor of whose residents' twenty-dollar-an-ounce perfumery can be detected eleven miles at sea when the wind is right, has many unobstreperous, intelligent and highly desirable winter residents whose income is less than $10,000 a year—and $10,000 a year, according to the popular conception of Palm Beach, isn't enough to permit one to wager property on a single game of polo, let alone living on such a beastly sum for any length of time.

CHAPTER V

Of a fly in the ointment—of Floridians' claims concerning fuel, overcoats and heavy underwear— of Florida house-costs—and of the comforts of life in Florida

The general consensus of opinion among Florida bankers, architects, climate fiends, real-estate agents, retired business men and newspaper editors and reporters seems to be that an income of $2500 or $3000 a year, after the recipient of the income has invested in a house and lot, is sufficient to allow any man and his wife to live simply but well in any Florida resort, to keep an automobile, to join a golf club and to rub elbows with perfect *aplomb* and *savoir-faire* with the J. Dashit Whortleberrys and the S. Oakum Van Grypers.

The fly in the ointment, so far as this particular statement goes, lies in the fact that so many of the Floridians who insist that a $2500 income is plenty if one wishes to live in Florida are spending considerably more than that on their own living expenses.

Whenever one expresses some doubt as to whether a person can really have all the advantages of the best resorts on $2500 a year, the Floridians become indignant.

"Of course he can!" they declare, with a trace of peevishness in their voices. "Of course he can! It's much cheaper to live in Florida in winter than to live in the North. Why, a person doesn't have to buy any fuel, and he doesn't have to have a winter overcoat or heavy underclothes! Why, look at all he saves by living in Florida!"

One idea that one gathers from Florida enthusiasts is that the bulk of Northern incomes during the winter months is spent on fuel, overcoats and heavy underwear. In fact, if a stranger to the United States were to drop into Miami, St. Petersburg, West Palm Beach or any other flourishing Florida community and ask a few questions about Northern winters, he would soon get the impression that every Northerner divided his days equally between buying fuel, buying overcoats, eating, sleeping, buying heavy underwear and shivering.

One can get a sort of Gregorian chant effect out of Florida travel by stopping any casual passer-by and asking the question, "Why is it cheaper to live in Florida than in the North?" And then quickly adding, "You don't have to buy any fuel." His words will synchronize with the passer-by's reply, which will be exactly the same.

As a matter of fact, living expenses in Florida are just about what they are in the North. One doesn't need winter overcoats and heavy suits, but one makes up for it by buying more light clothes. Food costs are about what they are in the North, because so many foodstuffs have to be freighted to Florida, and the consumer must pay the freight. Rents are about as high as Northern rents.

Initial costs, however, are lower. Owing to the fact that the houses have no cellars and don't have to be built with an eye to the frost-laden blasts of winter, one can build for $8000 or $10,-000 or $12,000 a home that is equal in comfort and beauty to a house that would cost $18,000 or $20,000 or more in the North.

It costs as much to live in Florida as in the North; but in return for the expenditure, Florida offers far more in comforts, luxuries and contentment than does the North; and anybody who cares to regard that statement as an overenthusiastic boost for Florida is entitled so to regard it until his regarding muscles atrophy from overuse.

Necessarily, there are people all over the world who live on the exact amount of money which is theirs to spend. Since Florida is no exception to the general rule, and since there are many in Florida with small incomes, there are many there who live on much less than the $2500 or $3000 a year so frequently specified by Floridians as the income necessary for comfort.

CHAPTER VI

Of various northerners who live in Florida on moderate sums—of staggering rents—and of the indecent speed with which Florida homes materialize

In one flourishing city on the West Coast of Florida, for example, there is a retired New York fireman whose only income consists of a monthly pension of $93. On this he spends half the year in Florida, paying $300 rent for his home. He and his wife do all the cooking; they contribute to the church and take in an occasional movie; they say that they live well and have plenty to eat and can get along in Florida much more cheaply than they can in New York; and they have bought a piece of land on which they intend to build in the near future.

In the same city there is a man from Hartford, Connecticut, with a wife and an eighteen-year-old son. They pay $300 a year for a three-room kitchenette apartment, and the wife makes all her own clothes. Their total yearly income is $1000 and they are entirely happy.

A mother, with her son and daughter, lives in this city, and pays $500 rent for a small bungalow and an accompanying garage. They have no maid, but they have an automobile that gets them there and gets them back; and whenever the growing son and daughter raid the ice chest they always find enough in it to assuage the hunger that is ever gnawing at the vitals of all growing girls and boys. This family's income is $3000 a year.

A man from Oklahoma City who lives in one of Miami's most flourishing subdivisions figured up his living costs for me, after announcing impressively that the person who lives in Southern Florida doesn't have to buy any fuel, can wear summer clothes forever and can throw away his overcoat. And it may be mentioned in passing that there is no Florida law to force a man to throw away his overcoat, and that if he ever intends to ride in an automobile at night or on Florida's occasional chilly days, he might as well retain it unless he wishes to develop such violent shivers as to crack all the enamel off his teeth.

However, this man owns an eight-room house on a lot that is 80 feet by 100 feet. He has a big car, plays golf almost daily—his membership in the golf club costs $65 a year—and lives well on a total expenditure of $5000 a year, which, he claims, is a smaller expenditure than he would have to make if he still lived in Oklahoma City.

After a moment of reflection, he then added that anyone ought to be able to live well in any part of Florida for $3500 a year.

There is no call, however, for the weary Northerner who has accumulated a capital of $50,000 to rush to Florida with his family, harboring the theory that he will be able to rent a charming

Spanish villa for five or six or seven hundred dollars a season. Even in Palm Beach it is possible to build one of the popular Spanish-type homes for $10,000 or $12,000 and to buy a centrally located lot on which to build it for $4000 or $5000; but the rent that one has to pay for such a house is in the neighborhood of $2500 for a five months' season.

Building sites, however, are plentiful and Florida contractors have so developed the business of building a house that it seems more like a natural force than a human operation. The feverish speed with which a mushroom emerges from nothing and reaches maturity is almost being rivaled by the indecent rapidity with which Florida houses attain their growth. A Florida house builder runs some cement out on the ground to serve as a foundation, slams up a framework to which he nails black paper with a chicken-wire attachment, slaps two or three layers of cement on the chicken wire, and thus apparently obtains a full-grown and highly successful residence in the time that a Northern contractor or builder occupies in getting the blue prints unrolled.

CHAPTER VII

Of the Florida secret of getting something for nothing—of the raving of Florida financial enthusiasts—and of Florida land investment in general

A Floridian can tell anyone exactly what to do with a capital of $50,000 in order to conserve one's income nearly intact, get a house for nothing and place himself in a position to double his money in no time at all—and in perfect safety.

"The Northerner," explains the Floridian, "comes down here with his $50,000 invested in high-class bonds that yield him somewhere around 5 or 5.5 per cent. That gives him something like $2500 or $2800 a year, doesn't it? All right. Well, that's a foolish yield. He proposes to live in Florida, where he can be happy for the rest of his life; so the first thing he ought to do is to sell all his bonds and get his $50,000 in cash. Having done so, he sets aside $10,000 for the purchase of a house and lot. For that amount he can get a nice lot and a pretty little house. That's all right, isn't it? All right. He sets aside another $10,000 for real-estate investment; and with that $10,000, if he has any sense at all, he'll make an income of another $5000 or $10,000 a year. Huh? Sure he will! Why, Florida is crowded with people who need houses right now; and tens of thousands more residents are pouring into the state every winter! They must have places to live, mustn't they? Now mustn't they, hey? Well, all right then.

And any fool can make money by buying land and selling it to the people that need it. Can't he? Huh? All right! Why, Florida is the world's greatest sure thing! It's the only frontier state left. Anybody who buys land in Florida for years to come will make money just like finding it! In a few years they'll be pouring in by the millions to revel in our sunshine and our balmy breezes; to mingle with the birds and the fish and the flowers; to bow down before the shrine of ——" blah-wah, wah-hoo-wah, blah, blah, blah, and so on until he is jolted back to earth and told to get on with his story.

"Well," says the Floridian, when he has wiped the perspiration from his brow and the foam from his lips and pulled himself together again—"well, that leaves him $30,000, doesn't it? All right! He takes the $30,000 and puts it into well-selected first mortgages, which are the best mortgages anywhere in the world and pay 8 per cent all over Florida. Eight per cent on $30,000 is $2400; so you see he'd have just about the same amount of money that he came here with, and he'd also have his house and his lot, and another $10,000 invested in sure-fire real estate that will make money for him just as certainly as there are fish in the

Gulf Stream; and when he makes his first turn-over he can build himself a better house on a nicer piece of land, and then he can sell his first house and lot at a profit and then ——" blah, blah, wahblahwah, blah blah; and one has to use force to get him quieted down so that he stands silent and shaking all over and doesn't attempt to force his ravings on anyone.

Large numbers of Northerners who have come to Florida to retire have done exactly what this Floridian outlined. The 8 per cent first mortgage is universal throughout Florida. Florida banks are permitted to invest their funds in them. There are many of these 8 per cent mortgages, of course, that are not properly secured, just as there are some 6 per cent mortgages in other states whose safety is somewhat dubious. But with the exercise of a little care one can obtain a return of 8 per cent on his capital with the same amount of safety that he can get by investing in good bonds.

And so far as can be discerned with the naked eye, the Floridians are right concerning the generous profits to be made from land investment. The demand for land and living quarters on the part of newcomers of moderate means is equaled only by the similar demand in Los Angeles, California; and the population of the city of Los Angeles alone is as large as, if not slightly larger than, that of the entire state of Florida.

In the past the state of Florida has been somewhat in the position of a large bottle with a diminutive neck. The roads to Florida from the North have been bad and railway accommodations have been more restricted than they should have been. Consequently, people haven't poured into the state as rapidly as they might have—a fault that bids fair to be remedied soon.

As the people pour in and the natural resources of the state begin to be developed the Floridian who fails to profit from the state's growth should have his head examined for osseous formations.

CHAPTER VIII

Of the respective advantages of the east and west coasts—and of Miami's pity for localities that can't raise certain trees

There is great argument among Floridians and among outlanders as well over the advantages of the West Coast of Florida as compared with the East Coast, and of the East Coast as compared with the West Coast. It has been my experience—if prospective travelers to Florida wish an unbiased opinion—that when I am on the East Coast I greatly prefer it to the West Coast; and when I am on the West Coast I find it much preferable to the East Coast.

What with the fishing and the hunting and the perfect roads and the loafing on dazzling beaches in the hot sun and the wallowing around in milk-warm water and the amiable and hospitable people that one encounters everywhere, one can be happy in any Florida resort; and as soon as one is happy he prefers the place in which he is to the place in which he is not.

There are features to every Florida resort that endear it to its residents above all other towns or cities or resorts. Some people like the hurry and bustle of a Southern city and the added conveniences that may be had in its suburbs. Some people are so attached to a particular sort of tree that their deepest sympathy goes out to the community or district that cannot—because of climatic handicaps—grow it.

"Why," said a resident of Miami to me, almost with tears in his eyes, "I came back from California a little while ago, and I almost froze to death out there; and let me tell you, sir, I pity those people. Yes, sir, I pity 'em! Why, sir, they can't raise coconut trees out there!"

Other people like the glamour of the smart shops and the widely press-agented names of Palm Beach's idle rich; while still others crave the simplicity and restfulness of unspoiled country. One never knows what part of Florida he will like the best until he has traveled through most of the state; and when he has done that, he usually has a craving to invest in each town that he has visited.

CHAPTER IX

Of some superiorities of Florida to the French and Italian Rivieras—of the mild and beneficent East Coast country—of the whiskered telegraph wires of New Smyrna—and of the pleasant bass and baseball infested road from New Smyrna to Tampa

There are worse trips than a run up the Florida coast in January or February, through the tree-bowered stucco houses of Miami's suburbs that were waste land two years ago, and along the wide avenues of Miami Beach to the endless stretch of white sand stretching up to Palm

Beach and beyond. This land along the beaches is cleared and marked off to streets and avenues. Two years or three years ago it sold by the acre. Today it sells by the front foot, and the people who bought it by the acre have tripled and quadrupled their investment.

There is more to fill the eye in a journey along the French or the Italian Riviera; but neither the French nor the Italian Riviera can offer nearly so much sunshine or warmth or dependability or comfort as can the coast of Florida.

North of Palm Beach and West Palm Beach one runs through the orange groves that border the banks of Indian River—which looks more like a turquoise-colored inland sea than a river—and a dozen pleasant towns. In between the towns there are incipient real-estate promotions—an ornamental gateway standing alone in the glaring white sand and the rank green of the palmetto scrub; or an endless expanse of scrub pine, and slightly askew amid it a post bearing a board marked BROADWAY.

At one spot a complete town is laid out with corner posts and street signs, but not a house has risen on it. A signboard optimistically announces that it is Olympia, the New Town, and maybe it is. Maybe another two years will see a far-flung community there, with hotels, churches, schools and handsome stucco dwellings, just as the past two years has witnessed a similar development in the middle of the flat land between Miami and Palm Beach.

Along this road to the North one encounters deserted asparagus plantations, shielded from the sun by acres of rotting laths, like endless chicken coops for communities of giants. Everywhere there are ringneck plover, screaming nervously to one another and leaping into or swooping down from the cloudless sky. White herons flap from roadside pools, orange trees disseminate a pleasing odor and the hot sun scorches the back of the neck. Truly a mild and beneficent country!

At New Smyrna, where all the trees and even some of the telegraph wires have sprouted long and benevolent-looking whiskers of gray moss, one is able to bear off to the westward and start across the state. It is along this road that one begins to catch glimpses of a new sort of Florida— a Florida of rolling land instead of the flat waste that surrounds the southern resorts, and of pleasant lakes by the sides of which excited fishermen with popping eyes tell you of innumerable and voracious black bass whose sole object in life seems to be the inhaling of fishing tackle.

It is also along this road that one finds the training camps of many of the big-league baseball teams—a fact which tends to confirm the raucous claims of the residents of St. Petersburg and Orlando that the climate in this neck of the woods is the veritable and only *ne plus ultra* of climates. Here and in this vicinity gambol the Cleveland Indians, the Boston Braves, the Brooklyn Dodgers, the Washington Senators, the Cincinnati Reds, the Chicago Cubs, the St. Louis Cardinals, the New York Giants, the Philadelphia Nationals and the Indianapolis American Association team. Next year the New York Yankees and the Philadelphia Americans are scheduled to join the happy throng—unless deterred by the unpleasant spring of 1924, although the Floridians explained to everyone that they didn't know what to make of that weather; that they couldn't remember when there had been any weather like that; that a person might come down every year for a thousand years without finding anything like it; that blah-blah-blah-blah, and so on.

Big-league baseball teams are not exactly newborn babes in credulity and what not, and eleven of them wouldn't camp along the New Smyrna-St. Petersburg road unless there was more to the climate than the hot air of the natives.

CHAPTER X

Of Orlando and its twenty-two lakes and its prettiest girls in the world—of its superior orange groves and its kind-hearted residents—and of the universal desire of all visitors to Orlando

Orlando is a flourishing city of 17,000 population, a city of beautiful homes and wonderful outlook, for it is built around twenty-two fresh-water lakes—so many evidently that it has always been able to see itself perfectly mirrored and thus avoid the ills of so many cities; such ills as graft and filth and gimcrack building and eagerness to snatch for individual enrichment the things that belong to all men.

Everywhere through Orlando and in the suburbs there are orange groves and tree-shaded streets. Orlando people say that Orlando girls are the prettiest girls in the world. I am no judge of the standing of the different American cities in this matter; but the young women that were pointed out to me by Orlando residents in support of their contention appeared to have all the necessary qualifications.

The Orlando people are passionately addicted to whisking strangers around the city and explaining all about it—all about the lakes and the four new bank buildings that were built during 1923, and the two new ten-story buildings; and how all four of the ten-story buildings in town were built entirely by local capital without a cent of outside help; and how land in the business section of Orlando is worth $2600 a front foot; and how the city is crowded with visitors, in spite of the two new hotels; and how nobody knows how the visitors are going to be taken care of; and how Orlando will have a population of 30,000 by 1930; and all the time one is being introduced to a new lake, or one's guides are busy raising their hats to bevies of the girls who are reputed to be the prettiest girls in the world, until one is quite dizzy and cannot possibly keep his mind on all the statistics. It is certain, however, that if this were not a prohibition country, there would be many deaths from drowning in Orlando; for if a drunken man were to start back in horror at finding himself wabbling on the brink of one of the twenty-two Orlando lakes, he would be almost certain to fall into one of the twenty-one others.

The country around Orlando is excellent orange country, and land is comparatively cheap. Orange-grove land, with the trees in prime bearing condition and yielding from two to three hundred boxes of fruit to the acre, fruit that usually brings $1.50 a box but that only brought a dollar a box in 1924, can be bought for $1000 an acre. And the Orlando people, who are a very kind-hearted lot, cannot refrain from throwing in the information that in California the same sort of land with the same sort of trees would cost $5000 an acre, and have to be irrigated. Florida sand is remarkably fertile and needs no irrigation.

From a recent advertisement of an established Orlando real-estate firm one reads: "Eighteen acres—10 acres in big bearing orange trees. Good home—electric light and water. Big crop of trees. Price, $17,500." And another: "Twenty acres in city limits of Orlando—about 900 bearing orange and grapefruit trees. Price, $17,500." Some persons prefer this sort of thing for $17,500, while others prefer to pay the same money for a smaller acreage at Palm Beach, within hearing distance of the dulcet screams of the distinguished society leader, Mrs. J. Custon Frimp, as she enters the water each morning, or the lady-like profanity of the lovely movie star, Miss April Sunshine, as she bawls out her husband, Mr. Milton Fishback, on the dance floor at the Coconut Grove.

There is a fine hospital in Orlando, and a splendid library, and spacious schools by the lakesides with 3500 pupils in them. Practically every resident owns his own home, and most of the residents live in Orlando during the summer as well as during the winter months; and altogether it is the sort of town that one would like to live in, what with its excellent country club and its prettiest girls in the world and its balmy climate and the masses of flowers that rim its lakes and what not. So you say to your guide, "I wouldn't mind having a little place here—just a simple ——"

Then the guide interrupts.

"Yes, yes," says he soothingly. "I know exactly what you want. Everyone wants exactly the same thing. All you want is a little place here—just a simple little place on a lake; one that's simple enough to take care of yourself, and with a few orange and grapefruit trees on it. That's what you want. That's what everyone wants, and he always does his wanting in exactly the same language. Well, it's easy enough; why doesn't everyone do it? We've all done it, and we're the happiest people in the world."

CHAPTER XI

Of St. Pete, where the sun does its most enthusiastic shining—of the loud roars emitted by Doctor Van Bibber concerning the climate of St. Pete—of the deft wallops delivered by the St. Peters—and of the plethora of green benches and slipper-slappers and pelicans and what-not

On leaving the happy people and pretty girls of Orlando with a slight sensation of envy, one passes through many more orange groves; and eventually, after touching the large and bustling city of Tampa, circles around onto a pleasant peninsula, with Tampa Bay on one side and the Gulf of Mexico on the other, and comes to the city of St. Petersburg, sometimes known as the Sunshine City because the sun appears to do more shining there than in most parts of the world. There is a large and enterprising daily paper in St. Petersburg which undertakes to give everybody a free copy on the day when no sun shines within the city's purlieus, and in the last thirteen years this enterprising paper has given away seventy-two editions. This, translated into the argot of the day, means that the sun fails to shine in St. Petersburg—familiarly known as St. Pete, by the way, to all its residents—only about five days out of each year, on the average.

The residents of St. Pete are the greatest climate fiends in the world. They are not content with saying that the St. Pete climate is remarkable or unusual. They unequivocally state that the climate of the peninsula on which the city is built—Pinellas Peninsula—is the absolute cream of the 18,000,000 brands of climate known to exist in the world.

In proof of their contention they produce an essay written in 1885 by Dr. W. C. Van Bibber, of Baltimore, for the Journal of the American Medical Association; and since St. Petersburg in 1885 was nothing but a large and undeveloped tract of farmland, Doctor Van Bibber cannot be suspected of being on the pay roll of the chamber of commerce or anything like that.

At any rate, what Doctor Van Bibber says about the climate of Pinellas Peninsula—which means St. Petersburg—is a great plenty. He nonchalantly disposes of most of the other health resorts in the world with an airy wave of his hand.

"We have all heard," writes Doctor Van Bibber enthusiastically, "of Pau, Pisa, Mentone, Monaco, Cannes and other European resorts, and may be familiar with what has been said concerning the banks of the Nile, or Mexico, and Southern and Lower California; but none of these, it may be said without fear of contradiction, can compare with Florida as a peninsula climate, or as a land having peculiar attractions as a winter residence."

Incidentally, it may be said without fear of contradiction that Doctor Van Bibber didn't know much about the disposition of the residents of California if he thought that they weren't going to rush to the front with a wholesale and categorical denial of any and all remarks tending to imply that the California climate is inferior to anything, anywhere.

However, he then goes on to argue that since the winds of Pinellas Peninsula are warmed by the Gulf on one hand and tempered by Tampa Bay on the other, and generally cooled, heated and aërated by the peninsula's location, to say nothing of the water being changed every day by the obliging tide so that its temperature will remain constant, its temperature is sufficiently potent to cure almost everything except decapitation and electrocution.

Armed with this talk about the climate and a certain energy which may come from the climate or from youth, the residents of St. Pete are always on the warpath to gain converts and put in a deft wallop for their fair city. They tell you it is the world's greatest opportunity for investment. They say the town is only where Miami was six years before all the Miamians began to make fortunes. They point to their $6,000,000 worth of fine new hotels, freshly opened in 1923 and 1924; and then they take you over to the chamber of commerce and let you see the lodging bureau digging up private rooms in the residences of St. Petersburg's first families because of the mob of tourists who cannot be happy unless they linger indefinitely in St. Pete—and who cannot be accommodated except in the homes of residents.

Subdivisions are being sold up and down the coast. A huge bridge—the longest bridge in the world—is rising to join Tampa and St. Petersburg, cut thirty-three miles from the present distance between the cities and open up an entirely new real-estate world. All the St. Peters are crazy on the subject of real estate. Real-estate dealers lurk behind pillars in the hotels, leap out at newcomers and urge them to accept unrivalled opportunities to become wealthy. One of the great fundamental truths about St. Pete, unless somebody is lying, is that everybody buys and sells and never loses.

St. Petersburg is a friendly city. Its streets are lined with green benches, on which a goodly percentage of the population sits and talks to itself about its real-estate deals and Northern illnesses. Anyone who sits down on one of the benches will, within two minutes, be certain to find someone from New York, Pennsylvania, Iowa, Massachusetts or Indiana to whom he can tell all his troubles.

In the center of things is Williams Park, named for the founder of the city. Here the band plays. Here the slipper-slappers or horseshoe pitchers exercise themselves with their mules' oxfords. Here rings out the low cry of "That's a good shoe!" as someone wraps the implement around the pin. Here galleries of 300 and 400 persons sit tensely through hair-raising games of roque between the world's greatest exponents of the game, while a keen-eyed roque reporter for the morning paper takes down every move for the edification of the city's roque fans. Here the checker, chess and domino tables, always filled with eager players, emit a hushed clicking and clacking as the contestants settle their ancient grudges. Politicians publish advertisements in the papers, wildly advocating more green benches, horseshoe pitches and roque courts. It is a great place for tourists.

There is a municipal pier, from which large numbers of the 600 or 700 varieties of fish that infest the Gulf can be caught; and when one's interest flags in other matters he can wander out to the end of the pier and watch the pelicans lighting beside the fishermen with sprawling legs and a horrified appearance, and begging with an air of tense suspicion for a bit of bait.

Out along the beaches and up the bayous there are beautiful and expensive homes. Land can be bought close to the water for $10,000 a lot, from which the prices sink to $1500 or $1800 in less-desirable locations. As at Palm Beach and Miami, pretty little stucco houses can be built for $8000 or $10,000 or $12,000, though one of the St. Petersburg subdivisions insists on a minimum of $15,000 for every house built on it.

CHAPTER XII

Of the passionate talk of those who love St. Pete—of the eastern architect who was cured of a broken back—of his remarks concerning the joyous life of St. Pete workmen—of his theory concerning Florida as the only remaining frontier state—of his hellish life in Boston—and of Florida, the earthly heaven

Those who love St. Pete—and all its residents do, and seemingly with good reason—talk one's ear to a ragged shred if given half a chance. Like the boosters for Miami and West Palm Beach, they insist that an income ranging between $2500 and $3000, or a capital of $50,000, is sufficient to enable any man to live well in St. Petersburg. This is probably exaggerated. It will enable him to live well according to the ideas of some people, but it is doubtful whether this would be living well according to the lights of the man who has saved $50,000.

A well-known Eastern architect, a man of culture and refinement and a collector of rare books, came to me to say a few good words for St. Petersburg. A few years before, he had fallen from a building which was being made from his plans and had broken his back. The doctors gave him up, as the saying goes, and said he could live only a few weeks. One of them told his wife that his life might be prolonged a few weeks if he were taken to St. Petersburg. She took him to St. Petersburg.

Eight weeks after arriving in St. Petersburg he was able to walk out on the golf links and handle a golf club one-handed. Today he is one of St. Petersburg's leading citizens. He is also able to get around the links under ninety—still playing one-handed. He says that he owes his life to St. Petersburg and that he is naturally enthusiastic about the place. It might be remarked in passing that about 25,000 St. Petersburgers talk as though they owed their lives to it.

"Look here," said this Eastern architect, gesticulating wildly in the general direction of a wall-less public school whose pupils, evidently accustomed to the ravings of their fellow townsmen, cast not a look in our direction—"look here! The children and the workmen down here take no account of holidays, because every day is a holiday. All the workmen finish their work at four o'clock, and there's scarcely a day in the year that they can't step out on the pier or walk a few yards down the shore and get some of the best fishing in the world. Up North people make laborious preparations for Labor Day or Decoration Day or the Fourth of July, and then it rains. Down here all the stores close on Thursday afternoons. The people can walk a block and fish or walk a couple of blocks in the other direction and play golf. A man can make his plans to go anywhere he wants to and know that the weather won't interfere with him. It's always going to be a good day. What's Labor Day or any other holiday in his young life?

"If he wants to he can go out and dig up Indian relics, though there's no telling whether they have been planted by Indians or some development company. Some of the development companies would have found Tutenkhamun's tomb in St. Petersburg if they had known the publicity value of it.

"People don't eat much meat down here. Think of the difference between, say, a bricklayer in the North and a bricklayer down here. Up North he works seven or eight months a year. His savings are negligible and in the winter he must walk from job to job to get work, plugging through cold and slush and snow. He has to provide for his wife and children and feed them well on meat to keep them warm. Down here the bricklayer doesn't need fuel.

"When work is slack he can have stone crabs, clams, fish and vegetables for nothing.

"The head plasterer who worked on my house was always singing. Look at that house, by the way. It's a fine house. It looks like $20,000 at least, and it lives the same way. It cost $8000. Well, this head plasterer was always singing and I asked him about it. He had good reason. He spent seventeen years in Cincinnati and never saved a penny. He's been in St. Petersburg for seven years and he's salted away $17,000. Why shouldn't he sing?

"A thirty-one-year-old plumber came to our bank last week to borrow $7000. He wanted it to make his final payment on $230,000 worth of property that he owned free and clear. There's a young doctor down here. He came out of the Army and went back to his home town to discover that a lot of cheap young nonfighters had stolen his practice. He came to St. Pete, and the bank advanced him $35,000 on his name. He built a hospital and made $50,000 last year. The banker who loaned him the money peddled pie on the streets of St. Petersburg twenty-five years ago.

"It's a pioneer state—the only frontier state left in America. It's at the beginning of its growth, and we want men—anybody that's right, anybody who'll work. If he hasn't any money we'll show him how to get it. If he's got it we'll take it away from him and give it to someone who hasn't. We don't have foreign cliques down here. Our laborers are Negroes, and the whites don't work with them.

"There are hundreds—thousands—of retired businessmen and farmers living here who haven't a cent more than $3000 a year. Think what life holds for them by comparison with a man with the same income in the North! Why, we not only have no state income tax in Florida but the legislature has passed a law that we shall never have one. Think of it! No state income tax! And we have other advantages too.

"There's a man from Boston here, for example, who has exactly $3000 a year. He owns a little house near Boston which he rents for enough to pay the taxes and the upkeep. He has a second-hand automobile that cost him $800 or $900. He comes here from Boston over the road every October and rents a little apartment for $350 a year. For his pleasures he and his wife belong to the New England Society, which meets every week; and for his sport he takes up roque, for which one needs to purchase only a mallet and a ball. A Chautauqua ticket gives him a course of lectures. When real-estate companies hold auction sales at distant beaches he takes advantage of the free ride. The ocean is free and the fishing is wonderful. If he wants to meet people he only needs to run over to the chamber of commerce, where he can find a score of substantial citizens of Northern states anxious to breathe their life histories into his shell-like ear. He stays here until mid-June, and then cruises back to New York and stays with his married daughter for a month. He putters around his own home for a couple of weeks, visits friends in Maine and on Cape Cod for a few weeks more—and then it's time to oil up the old bus and take the road back to St. Pete again. Think of the pleasure he gets out of life!

"Life used to be hell for me in Boston. We had a butler, a cook, an upstairs maid, a second maid, a gardener and a chauffeur to bother with all the time. If we had a cook the maid was gone; if we had a chauffeur the cook was gone. It was fuss, fuss, fuss, all day long. Down here we have one girl—a cook. She comes at seven in the morning and goes at seven in the evening. She does the laundry. We pay her twelve dollars a week. It's like heaven.

"There are people here who spend $20,000, $25,000, $50,000 a year. Most of the people live simply and reasonably. Will you tell me why Northerners who can quit their Northern jobs and come down here with $3000 or $5000 or $8000 a year don't do it?"

Since his question permitted no satisfactory reply, it went unanswered.

293

THREE POEMS

by Edna St. Vincent Millay

IN THE 1920's most college students could repeat the lines

> My candle burns at both ends;
> It will not last the night;
> But ah, my foes, and oh, my friends—
> It gives a lovely light.

The author was a copper-haired charmer from Vassar who lived in Greenwich Village and won the Pulitzer Prize for poetry in 1922. "We were very, very poor and very, very merry," she wrote of those days. In the mid-20's she moved to a farmhouse in Columbia County and lived there in seclusion until her death in 1950, occasionally publishing a slender volume of carefully wrought verse. The *Post* printed a number of her individual poems during those years, including the posthumous "Thanksgiving . . . 1950" (November 25, 1950). "The Buck in the Snow," which is reprinted below, became the title piece of one of her books after it appeared in the *Post*.

JUNE 16, 1928

MIST IN THE VALLEY

These hills, to hurt me more
That am hurt already enough,
Having let the sea behind,
Having turned suddenly and left the shore
That I had loved beyond all words, even a song's
  words, to convey,

And built me a house on upland acres,
Sweet with the pinxter, bright and rough
With the rusty blackbird long before the winter's
  done,
But smelling never of bayberry hot in the sun,
Nor ever loud with the pounding of the long white
  breakers. . . .

These hills, beneath the October moon,
Sit in the valley white with mist,
Like islands in a quiet bay,

Jut out from shore into the mist,
Wooded with poplar dark as pine,
Like points of land into a quiet bay.

(Just in that way
The harbor met the bay)

Stricken too sore for tears,
I stand, remembering the islands and the sea's
  lost sound. . . .
Life at its best no longer than the sand-peep's cry,
And I two years, two years
Tilling an upland ground!

SONG

Gone, gone again is summer the lovely.
  She that knew not where to hide

Is gone again like a jeweled fish from the hand,
  Is lost on every side.

Mute, mute, I make my way to the garden,
  Thither where she last was seen;
The heavy foot of the frost is on the flags there,
  Where her light step has been.

Gone, gone again is summer the lovely,
  Gone again on every side,
Lost again like a shining fish from the hand
  Into the shadowy tide.

THE BUCK IN THE SNOW

White sky, over the hemlocks bowed with snow,
Saw you not at the beginning of evening the
  antlered buck and his doe
Standing in the apple orchard? I saw them. I saw
  them suddenly go,
Tails up, with long leaps lovely and slow,
Over the stone wall into the wood of hemlocks
  bowed with snow.

Now lies he here, his wild blood scalding the
  snow.

How strange a thing is death, bringing to his
  knees, bringing to his antlers
The buck in the snow.
How strange a thing, a mile away by now, it
  may be,
Under the heavy hemlocks, that as the moments
  pass,
Shift their loads a little, letting fall a feather of
  snow—
Life, looking out attentive from the eyes of the
  doe.

THE TERRIBLE SHYNESS
OF ORVIE STONE

by Booth Tarkington

BOOTH TARKINGTON BEGAN writing best-sellers in 1899, the year Lorimer became editor of the *Post*. But he waited until 1907 to write his first *Post* serial, and he wrote most of his Penrod stories for other magazines. (One of them, "Talleyrand Penrod," ran in the *Post* June 21, 1913.) Around 1928 Tarkington began to be a *Post* regular; his popularity was so great that even during the lean depression years he could still get $5,000 for his Little Orvie stories and $50,000 for such serials as *Presenting Lily Mars* (1932). Partially blinded by cataracts, he continued to dictate *Post* stories—mostly about the adventures of Mr. Rumbin, the art dealer—until 1945, the year before his death.

JUNE 24, 1933

ON A WARM and bright Saturday morning in May, Master Orvard Stone, a large-headed, partly toothless little boy not yet eight years old, was being dressed in his best by Corbena, the indulgent colored woman more usually familiar to his sight against a background of kitchen. The fact that Corbena was dressing him emphasized in his mind the brilliant unusualness of the day, the wedding anniversary of his grandfather and grandmother, though Orvard, naturally, felt no interest whatever in his grandparents' part in the celebration and was preoccupied with imaginings about himself and also with a few predominant physical sensations. Sometimes while he was being dressed, one of his legs desired to make twisting movements, impulses he encouraged; sometimes an arm or shoulder moved with a like urgency for self-expression, and at other times he itched here or there, and consequently scratched himself, to the detriment of Corbena.

She spoke to him with warmth, loudly, yet not unreasonably. "Listen me! You the squirmishest little boy in the United States, Orvie Stone! How many times I been told you, you got to stand still? Tooken me half an hour to git them little white shorties and white socks and shirt waist and one them little shiny leather shoes on you, and how'm I ever goin' git that other shoe and necktie and little blue jacket on you in time you can start to you' grammaw and grampaw's big party wif you' papa and mamma? You take and cut out all 'iss twis'in' and slidin' and scratchin' and half settin' down and 'en stretchin' up, and wiggle-footin' and turtle-headin'! Listen me! I rather undertaking put socks and pants on seven squirrels right fresh out the wild wood!"

Orvard's father, in white trousers, brown shoes, a soft-collared shirt, and with his hair wet, appeared in the open doorway. "Orvie!" he said sternly. "If you don't stand still and let Corbena get you ready in time, your mother and I won't take you to the anniversary at all, and then you'll miss meeting your dear little Cousin Marie that you've never seen and's come all the way from Kansas City with her papa and mamma for your grandfather's and grandmother's wedding anniversary. If you're not ready you'll have to spend the whole day here with Corbena, because the party begins this morning and won't be over until this evening. All your nice little cousins will be having a jolly day in Grandpa's big yard; but you'll have to stay here in the house all alone with Corbena! What do you suppose your mamma and I will have to say when all the uncles and aunts and cousins ask where our little boy is? We'll have to tell them he wouldn't stand still long enough to be dressed, so we had to leave him at home! That would be very mortifying to your mother and me. You don't want to mortify your mamma and papa, do you?"

Orvie made no reply. Instead, he put the knuckle of his right thumb into the unobstructed front section of his mouth and looked with apparent earnestness at a high-colored wall-paper bird he hated because of its oppressive repetitions.

"Answer me!" his father said, with increasing severity. "Do you want to mortify your mamma and papa? Orvie, take that thumb out of your mouth and answer me! Do you wish your mamma and papa to have to feel mortified about their little boy?"

Orvie didn't care a continental whether or not his mamma and papa would have to feel mortified about their little boy. He was so indifferent upon the point, indeed, that his father's voice was principally an ineloquent sound in the ears. Moreover, Mr. Stone's threat to feel mortified lost weight because of a vacancy in the son's vocabulary, the word "mortified" as yet having no place therein, no matter how often heard. In addition, Orvie could not have accepted calamity as possible to his parents, because they were grown people, all-powerful and therefore impervious. He continued to look at the oppressive bird and somewhat to enjoy the presence of the knuckle of his thumb in his mouth.

"Take that thumb out of your mouth!" his father said again. "If you're not ready in time, you don't go with us, and that's all there is to it. My goodness!" Then he disappeared from the doorway, but could still be heard speaking. "I can't do a thing with him, Clara—not a thing! My goodness!"

Orvie was glad his father had gone away from the doorway and thus had stopped looking at him. What his father said only bored him; but Orvie felt actively uncomfortable if people looked at him. He couldn't bear to look at people when they were looking at him, and when he thought people were going to look at him he always hurriedly did whatever he could to avoid being aware of their regard.

He didn't so much mind children's looking at him, if he knew them well, because they seldom looked at him for more than an instant at a time; but grown people kept their eyes fixed on him intolerably, and it made his insides feel queer.

"You heard whut you' papa say!" Corbena warned him. "How I goin' git 'iss little shoe on you, lessen you unscrunch you' foot? Listen me! Turn 'em toes up straight. Keep 'at foot scrunch' and you ain't goin' to no grampaw-grammaw weddin' party!"

From the next room, voices were audible in discussion of Orvard; he heard them uninterestedly. "My goodness!" his father said. "I can't even get him to take that eternal thumb out of his mouth! It's a perfectly horrible habit at his age. At his age he ought to know better. I declare it's disgusting!"

"It's his shyness," Orvie's mother said. "It's his terrible shyness, Frank."

"Shyness! It's time he got over it. Other children don't behave that way at his age."

"I know they don't," Mrs. Stone admitted. "I believe Orvie's the shyest child I ever knew, Frank. Miss Peters spoke of it to me again the other day—about its effect on him at school. She says she thinks he's as bright as any child she has **and** probably knows the answers to questions;

but in the schoolroom he's simply too shy to speak. In spite of everything she does, she can hardly get him to open his mouth, and when he does he usually just mutters something and keeps turned half away from her. Here at home, if he happens to be in the room when callers come in, or even some of the neighbors that he knows well, why, if I make him stay, he positively goes and stands behind the door or gets under a table or behind the sofa or even under a chair. Really, it's embarrassing; but I've simply given up, Frank. I've said everything on earth to him that I could; but you absolutely can't reason it out of him."

"No; I've tried that enough, myself, goodness knows!"

Mrs. Stone's voice became more plaintive. "Well, after all, you can't punish a child, simply for being abnormally shy. I suppose I'll have the same kind of time with him at your father's today that I usually do when I take him to any kind of a party. If it's indoors and he can find a staircase, he's usually under it, and if it's outdoors you have to look for him in the bushes! Maybe he'll behave a little better today, though, because the children will all be his relatives."

"He'd better!" Mr. Stone said darkly. "I don't intend to be mortified about him, especially before George and Emma, who've never seen him. Their little girl, Marie, is a perfectly wonderful, lovely little child, and when I went out to Father's last night to see George and Emma, they said she'd been the pet of everybody all the way on the train; you could tell they were just bursting with pride over her, and when you see her, Clara, you won't wonder why—really, she's just a little darling!"

"Well, of course, little girls are different," Mrs. Stone said. "I don't think they're so apt to suffer from shyness as boys are, Frank."

"Suffer!" Mr. Stone repeated with a vehement grimness. "Never mind! If I find Orvie hiding around in the bushes in Father's yard today, with his thumb in his mouth, I'll take measures to get some of this idiotic shyness out of him. My goodness!"

In the next room, little Orvard took his thumb out of his mouth, looked at it affably, and put it back again.

Thus to overhear his parents discussing him was no novelty to Orvard; frequently he was in the same room with them when they talked about him to each other, and he was often present when either or both of them talked about him to other people. He was used to it, even hardened to it; in particular, he was impenetrably incased in indifference when the subject was, as it seemed perpetually to be, his shyness. He didn't know what his shyness was, though he understood it to be somehow connected with his inward disturbances when people looked at him, and he knew, in a bored way, that his parents were determined to annoy him about it. What he deduced from the conversation of his father and mother, as they completed their dressing, was that when he and they arrived at his grandfather's, it would be wiser to keep out of the shrubbery.

Therefore, a little later, when young Mr. and Mrs. Stone and their son had driven out to old Mr. and Mrs. Stone's place at the end of Walnut Street, Orvie quitted his parents as inconspicuously and hurriedly as possible as soon as they entered the gate; then, avoiding the lilac and mock orange and hydrangea bushes, he immediately went behind a tree.

It was a large, old, gray beech tree, and the thickness and solidity of its intervention between himself and the public gave him a feeling of comfort. Moreover, it stood near the remoter border of the broad, old-fashioned, shady yard and at a reassuring distance from the big brick house. Orvie supposed the grown people would presently all go into the house, and he hoped that this incarceration would cause his parents to forget him, as it sometimes did; but the continuing sound of adult voices numerously engaging in laughter and lively talk disappointed him, and justifiably he began to fear that this all-day party was going to be outdoors.

Placing the knuckle of his thumb in its customary niche, he leaned back against the beech tree, and, wobbling here and there with different parts of his person, and at times scratching a shoulder blade against an imperfection of the bark that soothed him through his jacket, shirt waist and slight inner garment, he remained for half an hour in his chosen arboreal but really fragile seclusion. Then the approach of gay voices alarmed him, and he foresaw the possible necessity of a dash to another tree; but, before risking so sharp a peril of exposure, he decided to study the danger with one eye.

This eye, therefore, together with a corner of his forehead and some adjacent brown hair, was projected from the sheltering circumference of the beech tree and qualmishly surveyed the jovial and rather noisy scene before it. Uncles, aunts, great-uncles, great-aunts, cousins of all degrees and ages, were everywhere upon the lawn, chatting, laughing, moving, shifting, breaking up merry groups only to form merrier others. In the shade of the tall walnut tree near the house, Orvie's grandfather and grandmother sat in two easy-chairs on a ceremonial rug, and here most of the great-uncles and great-aunts and elderly cousins seemed to cluster. Little danger threatened from that quarter; but there was another unpleasantly different group, a group in motion not thirty feet from the beech tree, and, perceiving the direction of this movement, the surveying eye had a tendency to protrude. The group consisted of Orvie's mother and an astounding little girl about eight years old, and nine or ten more customary little girls and boys, Orvie's first and second and even third cousins.

In the one flashing instant of perception before he swiftly withdrew the reconnoitering eye, Orvie was startled by the visibility of the astounding little girl as a concentration of heavenly pinkness and goldness. She had upon him the effect of a Fra Angelico painting first glimpsed by a susceptible lover of art, and, as a seemingly ancient memory quivered dimly within him, he realized that her name beautifully was Marie. Nevertheless, she horrified him.

"Now, children," he heard his mother saying loudly, "all spread out and look for little Orvie. He must come and meet his darling little Cousin Marie and his dear Uncle George and Aunt Emma that he's never seen. We'll make a little game of it; we'll look in all the bushes and behind all the trees."

But Mrs. Stone had no more than uttered the frightful word "trees" when there rose upon the air a gloating screech from young throats. Orvie risked his all upon a dash for another tree, and lost. "There he goes!" screamed his hateful little cousins Bennie, Georgie, Paulie, Ernie, Malvern, Sadie, Josie, Henrietta, Pauline and Babe. "I'll get him!" every one of these shrieked cruelly, already in pursuit; but it was Orvie's mother who got him.

As she reached him he put his body upon the ground, hunched up, with his face turned dumbly away. Stooping, she took him under his arms, so not to disarrange his broad white collar and other neck gear, and lifted him. Orvie shut his eyes and imparted such laxity to his legs as would make it impossible to set him properly upon his feet, and he continued this simple defense until his mother said to him privately, "Shame on you!" in a whisper the fierceness of which he dared not disregard. His legs resumed their powers; he opened one eye as a compromise and found himself confronting not only a cluster of contemporary cousins but, so closely that she stood almost touching him, the startling pinkness and goldness —in a word, that mystic ineffability—already recognized by him as composing the being of his new little cousin, Marie.

His mother's voice came from above him, speaking dreadfully, commanding him to do the unthinkable. "Shame on you, Orvie! This is your dear little Cousin Marie all the way from Kansas City, and you must come and meet her papa and mamma, your dear Uncle George and Aunt Emma. First, kiss dear little Marie and then we'll go see dear Uncle George and Aunt Emma. Orvie, kiss your precious little cousin!"

Thus, in a provoked tone of false good-fellowship, his terrifying mother asked of him the impossible. Uttering faint sounds of horror, Orvie sought to depart through his mother's skirt; but it proved impenetrable, and Mrs. Stone used compulsion. "Nonsense!" she said, and, placing her right hand behind his head and her left hand behind little Marie's head, appallingly pushed Orvie's face against little Marie's face somewhat brusquely.

Orvie's open mouth had the sensation of encountering with a rubbing motion several noses and cheeks and some hair. His own nose, flattened, was dazed with a momentary suffocation, yet smelled fabric, soap and hair. When the stupefying contact was concluded, he had, in fact, a hair in his mouth, which worked feebly to eject it.

"There!" his mother said. "That's nice. Now we'll go and see dear Uncle George and Aunt Emma."

She seized him irresistibly by his right wrist and dragged him across the grass. Orvie would have sat down, like a pup resisting a leash; in fact, attempting this mode of opposition, he made a rapid series of squatting motions, but was jerked along too swiftly to complete the purpose of any of them. Mrs. Stone thus energetically hauled him to the group about his grandfather and grandmother, where, not relaxing her hold upon him, she placed him before two tall grown-up people, complete strangers to him, and said, "This is our little Orvie. Kiss your dear Uncle George and Aunt Emma, Orvie."

Still powerfully constrained by the wrist, Orvie felt with repugnance a moist part of his Aunt Emma's face against his cheek, and then his Uncle George's smoky mustache repulsively tickling his nose. "Pfoo!" Orvie said indistinctly, in protest, but stood helpless, still trying to work a golden hair out of his mouth.

"That's nice," his mother said, and released him among all his little cousins; for they had closely attended upon his heels. "Don't let him run away again, children," she said benignly, as she turned away. "Don't let him hide behind any more trees or anywhere."

The grown-up people, again bent upon their own concerns, immediately seemed remote. Orvie found himself spiritually alone, a solitary, serious figure surrounded by malignantly humorous kinsfolk of his own age. His little Cousin Bennie kicked him from behind and his little Cousin Malvern, a copyist, did the same.

"That'll teach you!" little Bennie said.

"So'll that!" said Malvern.

Then little Bennie and Malvern and Georgie and Paulie and Ernie and Sadie and Josie and Henrietta and Pauline and Babe, hideously thrusting forward their faces at him, screeched goadingly in his ears, "Yi, yi, yi, yi, yi, Orvie! Yi, yi, yi, yi, yi!"

In the midst of them, Orvie again found himself confronting the exquisite pink-and-gold child, Marie. The others continued their taunting clamor; but Marie stood silent, dreamily looking at Orvie's perturbed mouth. She affected him strangely. Sunshine flashed from her hair; her pink dress had hypnotic white polka dots all over it, and she put a pink forefinger upon her pink chin in a mysterious way that made him tremble. Suddenly, for the first time in his life, he was in love. In his eyes Marie became a wavering, rosily gilded glamour; he still had her hair in his mouth, and, staring at her, continued to alter the shape of his face in the effort to get rid of it.

The alterations interested Marie. Hemmed in by yipping cousins, who pressed upon them and sometimes kicked Orvard or poked his sides with fists or stiffened fingers, the two stood looking at each other's chins. The dramatic tenderness that is part of love seemed to emanate from one to the other and to vibrate between them; and thus for a few moments, amid all the yi-yi-ing, these two found each other.

Then the spell was broken. There were adult calls for the little Marie, and Aunt Emma pushed through the vociferating circle and took the lovely child by the hand. "Hush, children," Aunt Emma said. "Hush! Your little Cousin Marie is going to recite a poem her dear papa wrote for the wedding anniversary. Your little Cousin Marie is quite celebrated for the way she recites and sings and dances, and you must all be very quiet now while she declaims this poem to dear Grandpa and Grandma. Come, Marie, darling."

Aunt Emma took Marie away from Orvard; he stood where he was and watched the golden hair and white-dotted pink dress as they receded. All the grown people, and children, too, now formed a large circle about the two chairs where sat the beaming grandfather and grandmother, and, in the center of the circle, facing the chairs, the bright figure of little Marie was alone, but nowise disturbed by this conspicuousness. She smiled with a charming complacency, curtsied, and, in a voice as clear and sweet as silver bells, recited:

"Dear Grandpa and Grandma, on this happy day,
The children bring garlands and round your
*   knees play.*
For full forty years of loving accord
With good deeds and kindness your memories
*   are stored.*

"Your sons and your daughters,
Your grandchildren all,
Your nephews and nieces,
Your sisters and brothers
Who survive, and still others
Gladly come at your call.

"So happiness reigns on this wedding day bright,
In your oldest descendants and in each little
*   mite,*
Like your little Marie, and by that I mean me,
For I came all the way from far Kansas City
To bring you my love and recite you this ditty."

She curtsied again, to a response of vehement handclapping and outcries of delighted appreciation. Her grandparents laughed and glowed upon her with pleasure; aunts, uncles and other adult relatives beamed upon her, exclaiming, "Exquisite child!" "Like a lovely little fairy in a glade!" "Perfectly enchanting!" "What talent!" "Really, she's as good as anything on the professional stage!" "They ought to take her straight to Hollywood!"

Little Marie ran modestly to her mother, but, as the applause continued insistently, she came forward again, curtsied again and recited again. Her triumph was so emphatic, indeed, that she recited four times. She recited Little Orphant Annie, two passages from Hiawatha, and Wynken, Blynken and Nod. Then, as the applause was still exuberant, her happy and blushing mother announced that instead of reciting any more just now, little Marie would sing Don't Cry, Little Girl, Don't Cry. Little Marie sang Don't Cry, Little Girl, Don't Cry with so great an effect of pathos that several aunts and uncles sniffled flatteringly, her grandfather touched his eyes, and, when the song was finished, the applause was greater than ever. Her Uncle Henry, the fattest uncle present, lifted her upon his shoulder, and she sat there, kissing her little hands sweetly in acknowledgment of huzzas and waving handkerchiefs.

Then Uncle Henry set her down and she returned to the group of her contemporaries, who, in their own way, made evident their admiration of her. Little Cousin Josie took one of her hands and held it; little Pauline held the other, and little Sadie, standing behind Marie, poked among the golden curls with a forefinger. Little Bennie cried, "Look, Marie! Want to see me jump?" and so did little Malvern. Little Ernie said, "No, look at me, Marie! Look how I jump!" and all of them, except one, made much of her. The older people glanced down caressingly upon these manifestations, murmuring, "Sweet!" and it became clear that little Marie was the heroine and bright jewel of Grandpa and Grandma's wedding anniversary.

In this loving, happy, big family she was the adored of all adorers—with one exception. Master Orvard Stone stood at a little distance behind his child cousins; he had, of course, his thumb in his mouth, but he was slowly twisting both feet and one hip, and a curious new mood had begun to dominate his being. A change was taking place within Orvard; his feelings toward little Marie had altered and already he no longer loved her.

Her exhibitionism had touched, roused, and even stung, something deep, deep inside of him—something at first inarticulate; but it was in agitation and boiled toward expression. The change effervesced, increasing within him rapidly. He began to be conscious of dislike—dislike for little Marie—and so profound and swift was the alteration of him that although he was unnoticed and at liberty, he did not even sidle toward a tree or a bush; he no longer had any desire to hide himself.

On the contrary, all at once, he wished to display himself. He was seized by an importunate desire to do something sparkling and magnificent that would make everybody look at him and clap their hands as loudly for him as they had for little Marie; and then, imagining this accomplished, he had a slight, bitter pleasure in picturing himself as maltreating little Marie, possibly kicking her and yelling, "Yi, yi!" spitefully in her face. For now he hated little Marie like poison and wished to make everybody look not at her but at himself continuously.

He said nothing, did nothing; but all the while, within him, his new mood became more turbulent, pressing for action. A piano sounded the Washington Post March indoors; he permitted himself to be lined up with the other children behind Grandpa and Grandma, and marched into the house to receive sustenance. Little Marie sat at Grandpa and Grandma's table, between them, throughout the merry luncheon; Orvie, in another room with the other children, could see her through an open doorway, and every time he looked at her he muttered, "Haw poot!" to himself.

After lunch, everybody marched outdoors again, Grandpa and Grandma returned to their chairs on the rug and kept little Marie with them; and then, presently, neighbors and friends began to come in with congratulations. A little later there was an agreeable flutter and commotion, as the governor of the state and his wife arrived.

Orvie saw Aunt Emma take little Marie into the house mysteriously; then a wooden door was brought forth from the cellar and laid upon the grass before Grandpa and Grandma and the Governor and the Governor's wife, while a large circle was formed by all the guests about this nucleus. Cousin Frank and Cousin Rupert, grown-up men who had come from college for the celebration, stood near the door on the grass and began to play banjos. Then Aunt Emma returned with little Marie, and this hated child now wore little silver slippers, little silver trunks, a little silver brassière, and, upon her golden curls, a silver cap with a silver feather.

At the sight, Orvie could not restrain himself. He said, "Haw poot! Haw poot! Haw poot!" audibly, and was reproved by an adult voice near by. "Shame! Hush! Be quiet! Darling little Marie's going to do a tap dance for Grandpa and Grandma and the Governor."

Little Marie stepped upon the door and did the tap dance to an accompaniment of banjos and irrepressible bursts of applause, loudest when she made the clattering of her little silver shoes upon the door noisiest and most rapid. The sight of the intensely vibrant little silver figure and the sound of the applause were almost intolerable for Orvie. He looked about him upon the ground naïvely considering the possibility of throwing some sort of missile at little Marie; but instinct rather than experience warned him that such a course would be inadvisable. He could no longer restrain himself, however, when, as an encore to the tap dance, little Marie gave utterance to a Blues croon, with the banjos plunking haltingly to assist her. The large circle of grown-up people and children listened in a rapturous hush, intent upon the infantile silver voice that wailed above the plunkings, "She done stole my man away!"

Orvie withdrew to a point sheltered from observation, a corner beyond a bay window of the house and invisible from the circle. There he lifted up his voice with all his might, squawking and bawling as loudly as he could, "Haw poot! Yay, yay, yay, yay, yay! Yi, yi, yi, yi! Lo, lo, lo, lo! Boo, boo, haw poot! Hoy, hoy, loy, loy! Yay ——"

His fat Uncle Henry detached himself from the circle and came seeking the desecrator, calling out, "Stop that! Who's doing that? Who's making that disgusting noise?" He caught sight of Orvie and approached him appallingly. "Stop that instantly, Orvie! Shame on you! I thought you were always such a nice quiet little boy. 'S matter with you? My goodness! Don't you know little Marie's singing? What do you mean, making that uproar? Stop that! Shame on you!"

Orvie wished to say, "Haw poot!" as scornful repartee; but Uncle Henry's fat face was too malevolently contorted. Alarmed, Orvie went hurriedly in silence round the corner of the house, where he was out of sight of everybody. Here, after waiting some moments, while the silver crooning still complained, "She done stole my man away," he again lifted up his voice to its utmost.

"Baw! Baw! Baw! Yi, yi, yi! Hoo, hoo, hoo! Haw! Yi! Boo! Ack, yack, kack! Ya-a-a-ay!"

Then, before anyone could come to admonish him, he moodily passed through the open front doorway of the house and ascended the stairs to the second floor.

He had no conscious motive for going upstairs. That is to say, he ascended without knowing why he did so; but his action had a cause that he did not stop to analyze. One day his father had taken him to an amusement park, and Orvie had seen a man climb to a tiny platform high, high in the air at the top of a spindly tower, poise there, waving to the multitude of upturned faces far, far below him, and then dive all the long way down into a little, insignificant tank of water, out of which he instantly emerged, undamaged and triumphant, to receive salvo on salvo of applause. Nothing had ever made a more decisive impression upon Orvie; hundreds and hundreds of times since he had thought of the figure glittering high in the sky, with everybody looking up at it, and then sliding swiftly and gracefully down through the air to spurt himself through a little liquid and thence lightly out upon the ground, amazing the world. Often as he fell asleep in bed, Orvie had fancied himself to be that wondrous diving man who was now vaguely and fragmentarily in the back of his mind as he ascended his grandfather's stairway. What moved Orvie up that stairway was a dumb urge to place himself upon a height where he would have to be looked up at. He could not recite, he could not sing, he could not tap dance, and, if he bellowed, grown people with murderously contorted faces came harshly to stop him; but heights perhaps were open to him. Probably the seat of his impulses at first dimly contemplated some sort of exhibition performed upon Grandpa and Grandma's roof.

When he reached the top of the stairs, however, he decided to look down upon the fête from the roof of Grandpa and Grandma's side veranda. Therefore he went through a room, climbed across the sill of an open window and stood upon this roof, which was a tin one, protected by a white balustrade with a rail as high as Orvie's chest. He went to the rail and gazed down upon the pleasant scene beneath him.

On the grass, almost straight below him, had been placed a table covered with white damask, and upon this were large, round layer cakes and plates of many intricate kinds of little cakes, and even candies; furthermore, there were plates of sandwiches and baskets of fruit, and all these were the adjuncts of a great glass bowl wherein floated, in a garnet liquid, cubes of ice, slices of orange and lemon, various berries. Looking almost directly down upon these regalements from a position some fourteen feet above them, Orvie was not permitted by his unprecedented emotional condition to feel the interest in them that he would have felt had he been his average self. His glance lingered not for an instant, even upon the candies, though as yet no one was near the refreshment table, which had recently been placed beside the veranda; and he could easily have retraced his steps, hurried quietly downstairs and outdoors for a safely unobserved free raid upon sweets of which he would otherwise obtain later no more than a watched little boy's so-called proper share. No, so radical was the disturbance within little Orvie that he did not then give one thought to the delectable table. His whole being concentrated upon what was taking place beyond, on the lawn.

The company still stood in a great circle—a quiet one now, for little Marie's Blues crooning was finished. She sat upon Grandpa's knee, while the Governor, standing alone at a little distance before Grandpa and Grandma, was talking noisily and moving one of his arms in a peculiar way, often pushing his hand out toward Grandpa and Grandma as if he wanted everybody to notice it. Nobody else was saying anything; all eyes were upon the Governor, the baldness of whose head, odiously visible from above, produced in Orvie's nervous system the same sensation of annoyance that had been the first symptom of his dislike for little Marie.

All at once the Governor began to talk tremendously; he made slow motions with both arms, eliciting strong handclapping from the circle, and little Orvie's annoyance with him, developing swiftly, became a kind of hatred. Little Orvie hated little Marie by far and far the more; but he hated the Governor too.

Looking down poisonously, he saw that little Marie, on Grandpa's knee, was chewing gum self-contentedly and conceitedly swinging a tap-dancing silver foot to and fro, so perfectly at ease and accustomed she was to seats of honor. Near by stood little Orvie's mother, listening to the Governor, but at times glancing at little Marie and smiling tenderly.

Orvie called down to his mother loudly, "Mamma! Mamma, look at me up here! Look at me, Mamma! Look! Watch me, Mamma!" With that, he began to run up and down the roof, within the railing, stamping his feet on the tin as hard as he could and shouting, "Look, Mamma! Look at me up here, Mamma! Mamma! Watch me, Mamma!"

People, looking up angrily, shouted, "Stop that noise!" and "Be quiet!" The Governor stood silent and waited while little Orvie's father came beneath the veranda and called up huskily, but in a tone of almost incredible viciousness, "Hush! Stop that! Orvie, how dare you? What on earth's got into you? Do you want everybody to think you're an idiot? When the Governor's making a speech to Grandpa and Grandma—shame on you! Come down from there this instant! This instant!"

Orvie retired a few steps toward the wall of the house, where he was out of view. Mr. Stone, red, returned to his place in the circle; the Governor resumed his speech and finished it to emotional applause. When Orvie morosely returned to the railing and looked down again, the circle was once more quiet—and little Marie in her slight silver bedeckings was out in the center again, reciting again. Orvie removed his thumb, let his mouth remain open, and, though not aware that he was doing anything difficult, swallowed consecutively without closing his lips.

Little Marie received another ovation from untiring relatives; the Governor kissed her, and once more the sickening fat Uncle Henry lifted her to his fat shoulder and bore her aloft, where she rode, kissing her little hands. The Governor gave Grandma his arm and they led the way to the refreshment table just below Orvie. Uncle Henry began to gallop and prance as he moved in that direction with little Marie joyously riding him.

The upper surface of the rail of the balcony was flat and about three inches wide. Impelled by hatreds and by stinging and unbearable ambitions more powerful than himself, little Orvie climbed upon this rail and somewhat totteringly stood erect upon it. No one observed him immediately; even in the minds of his parents he had again become so inconsequent a factor in the pleasures of the day that his presence on the roof of the veranda had been forgotten. Almost straight below him, Grandma was filling the first goblet of harmlessly garnet punch for the Governor, and undoubtedly the large glass punch bowl suggested something or became a symbol in the imagination of little Orvie.

Neither he nor anyone else understood this matter afterward; but, at the moment when he contrived to poise himself erect upon the rail, the punch bowl was to him the symbol or at least the suggestion of a tank of liquid far, far beneath a glittering figure upon a little platform high in the air.

"Look at me, Mamma!" little Orvie bawled startlingly, standing upon the rail. "Look, Mamma! Look at me, everybody! Hay, everybody! Look, Grandpa and Grandma! Look at me, everybody! Yi-i-i-i-i! Hurrah for me!"

With that, and with all upturned eyes indeed looking at him, but no opened mouth yet able to become vocal, he squatted himself somewhat, to enhance his spring, and jumped forth from the rail magnificently into the airy void.

A falling body descends a fraction over sixteen feet in the first second of its fall; consequently, a person has no time for reflection during a drop of something less than sixteen feet, and of course the circumstances prevent a reconsideration of the project—nevertheless, there is a period of poignant emotion, however brief. Little Orvie's feeling was not regret precisely but an intensified sensation of the kind an impulsive person sometimes has when he feels that he has perhaps overstepped or gone a shade too far.

The conclusion of his descent was complex. The impact was first, in a partially sitting position, upon the punch bowl. He caromed, upsetting the punch bowl, the table and his grandmother; but not the Governor, whose clothes, however, became mainly garnet. Little Orvie's grandmother sustained a bent rib, a thorough wetness, discolorations and an unsettling nervous shock. Little Orvie himself suffered no injury whatever, except the ruin of his clothes and being locked up in his grandfather's bathroom, unclad, for three hours before being taken home, put to bed and exhorted tragically and tediously. In fact, he became so bored with the passionate question, "What if you'd killed your dear Grandma dead?" that he finally went to sleep while it was being put to him.

The great and lasting effect upon little Orvie of the part he took in Grandpa's and Grandma's wedding anniversary may be understood if we think for a moment of the effect upon the Duke of Wellington of the part he took in the Battle of Waterloo. Not at all an egoist, the Duke of Wellington after that battle naturally comprehended his immense position, and, knowing that everybody everywhere knew who he was, he felt more authoritative. Two weeks after Grandpa and Grandma's wedding anniversary, Orvie's mother happened to meet Miss Peters, his teacher, upon the street, and asked her if she didn't feel that little Orvie was beginning to get the better of his shyness.

Miss Peters stared protuberantly. "Shy!" she exclaimed. "Shy! Oh, dear me! I remember there was a time once when I used to think little Orvie was shy. Oh, good heavens!"

TUGBOAT ANNIE

by Norman Reilly Raine

As ALL HER admirers know, Tugboat Annie is as tough and amphibious as a female hippo, but underneath her oilskins she has a wily brain and a heart as big as a bailing bucket. She first burst upon *Post* readers in the following story, and has been delighting a large army of them ever since. The author who created her is an adventurous Canadian who worked as a reporter in various United States cities, fought with the Canadian and British air forces in World War I, and now lives in Hollywood, where he writes scenarios and sometimes accompanies members of the Los Angeles homicide squad on special assignments. He is also the man behind the *Post*'s Mr. Gallup series.

JULY 11, 1931

I'M FIRED? Who says I'm fired?" Tugboat Annie Brennan leaned across the desk of the president of the Deep-Sea Towing and Salvage Company, and thrust her formidable jowls into his red, embarrassed face. She repeated, with husky emphasis: "Who says so?"

"Now, Annie! Please ——"

"Don't you 'Now, Annie' me, Alec Severn! And answer my question!"

"Why ——" Mr. Severn coughed, and mopped his perspiring brow. "Well—hrrmph! It's Mr. Conroy. The business needs money, and he's putting it in—a lot of it. Enough to buy that new tugboat we want so badly. He's an absolute godsend. But he's got ideas—about women, I mean."

"Huh! What man hasn't? And what is these fool ideas?"

"Well, he—he thinks that managing a towing and salvage company is a man's job. He has the notion that women lack the—well, intelligence was the word he used—to handle the active side of the business. Says men won't do their maximum of efficient work under a woman chief. They resent her."

Tugboat Annie snorted, "I'd like to see any o' the boys on the Narcissus resent me. I'd heave 'em ——"

"I know—I know! But Mr. Conroy doesn't understand. You and I belong to the old school, Annie, and our ways don't seem to fit these days somehow. Mr. Conroy, now, he's modern. He's efficient and understands modern business methods." He hesitated and lowered his voice: "Tell you the truth, Annie, I don't just fancy the man. There's something about him—cold. If there was any other way of getting the money I'd see him in —— I mean, I wouldn't have him! But there isn't. And he thinks that —— Wait a minute. Here he comes up the stairs. He can tell you himself—thank the Lord!" he concluded.

Tugboat Annie drew herself up and glared, first out the window, to the crowded shipping of the harbor and the busy wharves, and then at the office door. She was large-framed, solidly built, with rugged, almost masculine features, and shrewd, quick, blue eyes, and her movements had an elephantine energy that galvanized everyone with whom she came in contact. When she passed through a room, dust and odd bits of paper danced in her wake. And when she stood, as now, with beetling brows and sturdy legs apart, the feather in her antiquated bonnet nodding raffish defiance, she looked not unlike a blowzy but exceedingly combative bulldog.

The door opened and Severn held his breath. Mr. Conroy entered, a business man from his crisp, graying hair, precisely parted, to his efficiently polished English oxfords. Mr. Conroy liked to convey the impression of a micrometrically functioning, hard-glazed piece of steel mechanism; and his impersonation was highly successful.

"Morning, Severn," he said crisply; but Tugboat Annie heaved herself forward.

"Say!" she demanded. "Are you the lallapaloosa that says I'm fired?"

Mr. Conroy drew back, hastily adjusting his glasses. "Why, I'm afraid I don't understand."

"Neither do I. Neither does Alec. So who does?"

Severn said, placatingly, "This is Mrs. Brennan, Mr. Conroy. You remember we discussed her ——"

"Tugboat Annie Brennan! That's what the water front calls me. And I didn't get the name pushin' toy boats around the bathtub, either! Now, what you firin' me for?"

Severn interposed again: "You see, Conroy, Mrs. Brennan's husband, Terry, was senior captain of the company for a good many years. He was a good tugboat man, but ——"

"Terry was a drunken sot. But he was the best husband a woman ever had, Lord rest his soul! And in between his rasslin' bouts with old John ——"

"John?" said Conroy, with raised eyebrows.

"Barleycorn!" said Tugboat Annie briefly. "In between bouts I ran his job for him. A year ago he died o' ——"

"Syncope," Severn hastily interpolated.

"Water poisonin'!" Tugboat Annie corrected grimly. "Drank a glass o' water, thinkin' it was gin, and his stomach couldn't stand the shock. Alec let me stay in his place, and I done a good job of it too. Ain't I, Alec?"

"Yes, you have, Annie," Severn assented. "Mrs. Brennan knows her work and this coast, Conroy, as few men do. She's been at it for twenty years or more, and I've full confidence in her. Don't you think ——"

During the recital Conroy's thin lips had tightened to an obdurate line.

"The opinion I expressed to you yesterday, Severn, has not altered. It has been strengthened. To be quite frank, Mrs.—er—Brennan does not impress me. She is too—shall we say, informal? I propose, if I enter this company, to make it the strongest on the seaboard, and the position of senior captain will be one of responsibility, dignity. No doubt she knows something about the work. But she is a woman, and—in this business particularly—that is not a good thing."

Tugboat Annie choked, was ready with a stormy interruption, but Conroy held up a peremptory hand.

"Her influence, in what essentially is a man's sphere, is bound to have undesirable results. I think I can see it, even now, in small things. The names of your present vessels, for instance."

"I named them tugs! What's the matter with 'em?" Annie demanded furiously.

Conroy shrugged. "Tugs connote strength; rude but efficient power. And instead of calling them appropriate names, such as, say, Trojan, Titan, Atlas, Hercules, they are called"—he smiled acridly—"Daffodil, Asphodel, Pansy and Narcissus."

"What of it? Can't a person like posies?"

"May I remind you that I am not deaf?"

"Mebbe you're not, but you're awful dumb! Here I've give twenty years of my life to the company, and you come along and I'm throwed out like an old sweat rag. Didn't it ever occur to you, Mr. Conman, or whatever your name is, that loyalty and hard work's worth something to business, as well as a lot o' fancy names? Huh?

... Oh, well! What's the good o' spinnin' me jaw? When do I go, Alec?"

Conroy said magnanimously: "I have no objection to your carrying on until we get a man to fill the place, Mrs. Brennan."

"You have no objection, ye cold-blooded haddock! What have you got to say about it? You ain't even in the company yet. I'll take my sailin' orders from Alec here, if he ain't lost his tongue."

"Go back to the Narcissus, Annie," said Severn unhappily. "I'll let you know. I'm sorry ——"

Conroy moved apprehensively aside as Tugboat Annie barged toward him, but she passed without a word and went down the stairs to the bright, dust-hazed sunlight of the busy waterfront street. Trucks rumbled and bumped over the pavement, motor traffic roared past, a long line of box cars was shunted by, and from the harbor beyond the sheds came a sonorous chorus of whistles—tugs, liners and deep-water tramps. Blind and deaf to it all, her hat feather bobbing deliriously, she fussed through the traffic and was nearly run down by a three-horse dray. She looked up at the grinning driver and stopped, inclined for battle.

"Don't ye know the rules o' the road, ye cockeyed baboon?" she roared.

Crossing the railroad tracks, she got one shoe half full of gravel, which did not improve her temper. She limped painfully out on the long, dingy wharf alongside which were berthed the tugs of the Deep-Sea Towing and Salvage Company, and, part way, stopped to remove the gravel from her shoe. She shook the shoe irascibly, and it flew from her grasp and disappeared with a splash into the dock. Tugboat Annie watched it sink, her lips moving wordlessly, then limped on her stockinged foot, great toe protruding, the length of the wharf.

The Narcissus, biggest of the fleet, was moored at the end; and when she saw the familiar, powerful snub bow with its great collision mat of woven hemp, bleached by hard service in sun and rain and salt water, the glass-inclosed pilot house, the heavy towing bitts on the fantail, and the grimy red and white and black of the house, she forgot for a moment that it was no longer her home.

"Ain't she the dirty old tramp?" she muttered pridefully to herself. "Got to get a new sta'board fender, though."

She stepped heavily from the stringpiece to the narrow deck, and crossed through, over the engine-room grating, to the port side. A gangling man in stained dungarees, with a prominent Adam's apple, a stubble of beard and amiable, washed-out eyes, was seated on the pilot-house steps, his neglected paint pot beside him, while he sucked on a cigarette. He looked up at her approach, flung the butt hastily over the side and commenced furiously to slap paint on the house. Tugboat Annie bellowed at him:

"Shiftless, you been poundin' your ear all mornin' while I been ashore? Ye have, ye lazy numskull! Look at that house! Hardly a dab on it! Come here!"

With an uncertain grin, Shiftless approached, an elbow raised to protect his ear. "Aw, now, Annie ——" he protested.

She gave him a hearty cuff. "You been drinkin' some o' Rosinski's snake blood again, too, ye worthless hound! You lemme sniff that stuff on ye again and I'll skin ye alive. D'ye hear?"

"Yes, Annie."

"Don't forget it! Where's Sam—in the engine room?"

"Yes'm."

"Go below, then, and tell him I want a complete list of engine-room stores by six o'clock tonight. And stop in the galley and tell Pinto I want a list o' grub on hand from him." She noticed his startled stare. "What's the matter—you paralyzed? . . . Well, go on, then! Move!"

She watched, grimly, as he dropped his brush and ran. "They won't say I didn't turn the old hooker over to 'em shipshape," she grunted. "Frozen-faced old sculpin!"

She went into her cabin and flung her bonnet, with its agitated feather, on the settee. Then she commenced to change, her gaze roving around the familiar, cluttered room that had been her only home for so many years. Her glance rested finally, after purposely avoiding it, upon a large tinted chromo of the late Captain Brennan, in a plush-and-gold oval frame. The departed's face was round and beefily good-natured, with a half grin under the large, black, bartender's mustache, a lock of glossy hair plastered down his forehead, and the humorous, dark eyes of Erin.

Tugboat Annie stood motionless, regarding it. "You certainly was a soak, Terry," she muttered huskily, "but —— Oh, go on, you big louse! What are ye starin' at?" She turned the picture to the wall and rubbed her nose hard with her knuckles. "Sentimental old fool I'm growin' to be! Where the devil'd I put me other shoe?"

They were at supper—the small ship's company of the Narcissus, with Pinto, the cook—when the telephone on the wharf rang sharply. It was for Tugboat Annie. She lumbered out onto the quay, her capacious mouth full of steak and potatoes, and with a slice of bread and butter in her fist.

"Hello," she said, gulping hastily. "Wha'—what's that? . . . A ship ashore? Where? . . . All right, Alec. I'll take the Pansy along, too, huh? . . . What's that? Conroy coming? . . . No—no! I wasn't swearin'—just swallerin' me supper. Tell him to shake a leg, then. If he shakes it hard enough mebbe it'll break. Wants to l'arn something about the work, huh? Hmmph! . . . All right, Alec. Same to you, wi' knobs on it, you old gafoozeler!"

She waddled hastily back to the Narcissus, cramming her face with bread and butter as she went, and burst into the tiny saloon.

"Git below, Sam, and you, too, Shiftless. One of you other boys stand by to cast off. And somebody tell Pinto to keep the supper warm."

"What's all the excitement, Annie?" asked Sam, a slow-speaking, slow-moving mountain of mechanical competency.

"There's a ship—the Barracuda—beached and on fire in Juan de Fuca Strait, near Neah Bay. You know her—the one that runs to California and Mexican ports, with old Skinflint Crabtree in command. Look alive, now! The Puget Sound Towing Company'll be sending a tug; so will the Secoma Salvage crowd; so it'll be a race. Oh, cuss it!" She stopped suddenly. "We've got to wait for a passenger. Feller called Conroy, who's goin' to be Severn's partner in the company. Well, go on, all of you; don't stand there goggle-eyed! Alec can have a partner if he wants, I guess!"

She went to the pilot house and looked out the door. Conroy was proceeding sedately along the wharf. Tugboat Annie bawled:

"Get a move on, queer feller! A person'd think ye was walkin' on fly paper!"

He came to the rail, jumped down. "What's the hurry?" he inquired crisply. "Don't you know that haste breeds inefficiency?"

"So does a litter o' feathered pigs! . . . All right, Henry; cast off!"

Tugboat Annie spun the wheel over. The engine-room signal jingled and the Narcissus drew away from the wharf and piled up a big bow wave as she headed up Puget Sound. The fresh breeze of the afternoon had dropped, and the night was calm and almost sultry; and as darkness came and Secoma fell astern, the lights of the towns scattered along the sound danced with jeweled brilliance over the water that spread like a sheet of rippling orchid silk to the far, island-dotted shore. Two hundred yards astern, the riding lights of the Pansy glowed, ruby and emerald and topaz, in the velvet dusk.

For a time Tugboat Annie steered in silence, with Conroy standing on deck outside the pilot house. Suddenly she addressed him:

"You had your supper yet?"

"No"—testily.

"Ain't that just too bad?" Tugboat Annie gave her attention to her steering. Then she shook herself in a burst of exasperation and ripped out: "Darn me, anyway! . . . I never give meself no peace! Go on along to the cabin, then! The boys'll be finishin' their supper presently, and I'll have Pinto set a place for ye."

Conroy eyed her coldly. "You mean I'm to eat with the crew?"

"Why not?" Tugboat Annie snapped. "It won't poison 'em, mebbe."

"I'll have mine alone," Conroy said firmly. "I'm practically a member of the firm now, you know. Mr. Severn and I came to an agreement this afternoon."

"That was clever of Alec," Tugboat Annie grunted.

"What was?"

"Comin' to an agreement wi' you" She put her head out the door. "Pinto! Pinto!"

A voice hailed back, "Yaas, ma'am?"

"Set a place for the queer feller in the cabin. If he don't come for it, he don't eat."

"Yaas, ma'am!"

Conroy was no fool. He went aft to his meal.

The night passed, and at daybreak Tugboat Annie was again at the wheel, relieving the yawning mate. The Narcissus was forging steadily through the wind-ruffled blueness of Juan de Fuca Strait, with the snowy peaks of the Olympic Peninsula far off to port, making a glory of the morning sky. The Pansy was a mile astern; and to starboard, one slightly ahead, the other abeam, were the big wrecking tugs of the rival companies. Conroy, who had been forced to sleep on the pilot-house settee, was also up and about, stretching his limbs after an uncomfortable night.

He stood on the sloping forward deck of the Narcissus, drinking in the sharp, salt-laden air, when Tugboat Annie hailed him.

"Ye came aboard to l'arn things, didn't ye, mister?"

"To observe things, Mrs. Brennan."

"Aye? Well, there's Lesson No. 1 in the tugboat business, or any other kind o' business."

"What is that?"

"Not to let your competitors beat ye to a job," she elaborated. "See them tugs over there? One's the Firefly and the other's the General Mason, both belongin' to rival companies. And see that point o' land ahead? That's Cape Flattery. That's where the Barracuda's piled up. Look at them tugs pushin' the water away. Whoops! Go along and tell Sam to make her give everything she's got!"

Caught against his will in the current of rivalry, Conroy obeyed. Black smoke poured from the Narcissus' funnel crown, and there was a slight access of speed. But the competing tugs also cracked on their ultimate ounce of pressure and the positions of the three remained unchanged. The nearest tug—the Firefly—edged close, and a red-whiskered giant in her pilot house leaned out.

"Hey there, Annie!" he bawled. "What'll ye give me to go home?"

"Hello, Red!" Tugboat Annie boomed. "I'll tell your wife where I seen ye night afore last, if ye don't. Go on now; beat it, afore that face o' yours turns me breakfast!"

Red Whiskers chortled delightedly. They exchanged further rough persiflage, in which Tugboat Annie more than held her own, and he sheered away.

They surged around the point almost abreast, and their quarry lay before them; a big five-thousand-ton steamer, with rusty, red-lead-patched hull, dun-colored houses and an orange funnel. She was lying with a slight list to starboard, her forefoot on a shelving rock and her stern afloat in deep water. Some distance off her stern the flooding tide boiled and receded over the hidden reefs through which she had made her course the previous day. A pale streamer of smoke still spiraled upward in the quiet air from one of the forward holds. Simultaneously the racing tugs whistled, and figures waved in response from the stranded vessel's deck.

Tugboat Annie signaled the engine room and the Narcissus threaded skillfully through the reefs and came to rest in the clear water almost under the vessel's stern, with the words on her counter —Barracuda, San Pedro—looming above. A short distance off, the other tugs rounded to, rolling lazily in the long swell.

There was confused shouting on the Barracuda's deck, and a seaman ran aft and leaned over the poop rail. He addressed the Narcissus: "Captain Crabtree says, will you come abreast o' the gangway? There's clear water there."

Tugboat Annie looked faintly puzzled. Then she set her massive jaw, and calling Henry to the wheel, walked casually along the port side to the fantail, inspecting the stranded tramp's position. She halted and looked over the side for a moment, as though gauging the depth of water and the position of the rocks under the steamer's stern; then returned to the pilot house. The Narcissus sloshed around and nosed into line with the other two, abreast of the partly lowered gangway.

A thin, walnut-faced man with prim lips and a small nose, slightly drooping at the end, stood in the waist at the head of the gangway. His calculating eyes surveyed the three tugs, waiting on the other side of the reef like dogs about to scramble for a bone, with the Pansy coming rapidly up astern. He raised a megaphone and shouted, with a slightly nasal twang:

"This is just a towing job, boys, for we'll float off at high tide, or kedge off; and we can proceed ourselves in a pinch. But we've a list, and water in No. 1 Hold, and our steering gear's jammed through runnin' in here among the rocks. So I'd ruther be towed in. Now, what's your price to Secoma?"

Conroy turned impatiently to Tugboat Annie. "Get a bid in quick."

Tugboat Annie croaked: "Quit your brayin' and shut up! I'll handle this!"

"By the way," resumed the Barracuda's master, "you boats all belong to the same company?"

"Yes!" shouted the red-whiskered one.

"No!" replied the master of the General Mason. Tugboat Annie did not speak.

"The 'no's' have it," shouted Captain Crabtree with a sly grin. "So ye'll have to bid for it."

Red Whiskers exchanged a few lurid compliments with his rival, and it was a minute or two before they got back to business.

"Come on, boys! We haven't got all week!" the Barracuda's master reminded them. "What's your price?"

"Six hundred dollars, includin' haulin' you off the rocks!" bellowed Red.

"Five hundred and fifty!" countered the General Mason.

"Why the deuce don't you say something?" Conroy demanded angrily of Tugboat Annie.

"Will you close your jaw, horseface?" Annie demanded. She stuck her massive head, adorned with a disreputable felt hat of the late Captain Brennan, out of the door and stared up at the master of the Barracuda.

"What about you?" he called. "You goin' to quote me foolish prices too?"

"What's your cargo?" she bellowed.

Captain Crabtree appeared to hesitate. He said reluctantly: "Fish oils, turpentine, paint ——"

"—— alcohol, glycerin and tar paper!" she finished for him. "From San Francisco, for Secoma. I know the stuff you generally carry." She left the pilot house and lumbered out on deck.

The master of the Barracuda registered astonishment, "Sa-ay, you're a woman!"

"They ain't no law against that!" Tugboat Annie shot back. "What did ye think I was—a giraffe?"

"But it's kind of unusual ——"

"So's elephant's eggs! . . . Come on, Crabtree; get down to business! A ship on fire and an inflammable cargo—my price is eight hundred dollars!"

"So's mine!" the competing captains amended hastily.

"You're a bunch o' pirates!" Crabtree yelled wrathfully. "The usual price is about three hundred dollars. Ye'll have to bring that bid down."

"You're a skinflint," Tugboat Annie informed him, "but I'm bringin' it down. Seven hundred and fifty."

"Seven twenty-five!" shouted the General Mason.

"Seven hundred!" Red countered.

"Six hundred and seventy-five!"

"Six hundred and fifty!" Tugboat Annie bawled. "I got two tugs—that little Pansy there, and this one. Two tugs to haul ye off and into Secoma for only six-fifty! And I'll stand ye a gallon o' beer when we git in!"

"Six hundred flat!" howled the General Mason's skipper. "Cuss you, Annie! You tryin' to ruin the job?"

For half an hour the battle raged. The General Mason dropped out at five hundred, and her disgruntled master stood off and listened. "You're a fool, Red," he volunteered bitterly, "lettin' Annie suck ye into this! Can't you see she's gone off her nut?"

But the Firefly's master was of tougher metal, and the price was hammered down to three hundred and fifty dollars. And there, face and whiskers flaming, and streaming with sweat, he stuck.

"That's my final word, and not a cent less. It ain't worth it." He was dancing with disappointed chagrin. "I wouldn't have run the price that far down, Annie, only ye got me so mad ——"

"Take a runnin' jump over the side afore ye catch afire, Red!" she counseled. She looked up at Crabtree, hugely enjoying himself at the head of his vessel's gangway.

"You're sure the fire's under? And what other damage is there beyond the jammed steerin' gear and water in the hold?"

"That's all, missus. Come on; beat the captain's bid! It'll be a bargain for you at three hundred."

Tugboat Annie seemed perplexed, unsure of herself. Her brow was corrugated, her large mouth set in a grim line. She rubbed her nose with her knuckles, then turned abruptly to Conroy.

"Well, fish ears, what would you say?"

Conroy had lost his cool self-possession. He was white with temper.

"Say? I'd say you're the world's colossal ass.

woman! You heard what those two captains said, didn't you? You get yourself in a jam, then have to have a man to solve your problem for you. That's woman's business efficiency! If you take that job on now, I stay out of the company!"

Tugboat Annie looked up at the grinning master of the Barracuda. "Three hundred it is, captain!" she said promptly. "We'll stand by to take your line and drag you off."

But Captain Crabtree shook his head. "Oh, no. You're doing the towing, so we'll use your line. And if our steerin' gear's repaired before we get in, I won't need your small tug; so I want a deduction of 30 per cent per land mile off the towin' price from the point of repair to Secoma."

"You see? You're properly hooked!" Conroy snarled. "Probably there's nothing much wrong with his steering gear. He'll have it fixed by the time you get under way, and with 30 per cent off, you'll have to tow him to Secoma for two hundred and ten dollars! Hah! Woman's clear brain! Woman's business intuition!"

"Let's get going!" Captain Crabtree hailed. "What do you say, there, missus?"

The Firefly surged past, close to the Narcissus' bulwark, with only the lift of a sea between, and her bewhiskered master called across:

"Tell him to go to hell, Annie! I sure would hate to see you stuck like this. We'll all go home and leave him there to rot!"

"You go play parchisi wi' your grandma, Red. I know what I'm doing!" But Tugboat Annie's rugged face was grim as she again turned to the Barracuda. "There's weather comin' up; so when we get ye off and it comes on to blow, use your own power to ease the strain off the towline."

"What? Use my own coal when I'm paying you to tow me? Ha-ha-ha! Not a chance!"

"All right, Captain Shylock!" Tugboat Annie shouted in a sudden rage. "Have it all your own way!"

The wind was blowing along the strait. With the flood tide and the terrific hauling strength of the Narcissus and the Pansy, the Barracuda slowly was snaked off the rock shelf, through the reef, and into deep water beyond. She was down by the head, with the water in the forward hold, but not seriously so. It was nearing dark, with an overcast sky, and sudden squalls spattered the deck with rain. The Narcissus took up the pull of the heavy hawser; the Pansy, with a line aboard, did her bit; and the Barracuda began slowly to forge ahead.

Tugboat Annie stood at the wheel with a huge bean sandwich in one fist and a blue-granite mug of steaming coffee near by, dividing her time between eating, steering and watching speculatively the head of Conroy, who stood on the forward deck, his hostile face turned toward the stormy waters of the strait ahead. She hailed him:

"Foul-weather Jack's abroad, so if ye like fresh air ye'll get plenty before the night's out."

He rounded on her, his eyes hard as flint through his glasses, his clothes wrinkled and spattered with salt spray. But before he could deliver the spiteful comment that rose to his lips, one of the deck hands appeared in the pilot house.

He said, "Annie, Sam sent me to tell you that Shiftless is drunk as a fiddler's dog. He can't go on watch."

"What's that?" Tugboat Annie roared. "Here! Take the wheel. . . . Look out, ye clumsy ox! . . . There now. Keep her as she is."

She lumbered hastily aft and disappeared down the engine-room housing. For a few minutes there was the sound of a minor hurricane below, dominated by her vigorous bellow. She reappeared, breathless and disheveled, followed by the oil-grimed figure of Sam, the engineer.

"That'll l'arn him, eh?" she threw over her shoulder. The big man grinned.

Conroy turned on her.

"Another sample of feminine muddle-headedness, eh, Mrs. Brennan?" he snapped sarcastically. "No extra fireman. Do you know what you're going to do now?"

"Yes," she wheezed, "I know. It's one problem you're going to answer for me."

"Don't be humorous," he told her shortly, but the expression on her face, heavy and lowering, like an angry mastiff, was anything but that. She balanced easily on the heaving deck and spoke, her voice strident over the rising wind:

"Mebbe you'll think it's funny! But I've something to say to you. The other day ye had me fired, ye cold-blooded squid! Why? Because I was a woman! Then ye came aboard here to snoop; get something on me to feed your mean little ideas about women who do a man's job for a livin', huh? Wanted to see how a fool woman did things. Well, you're goin' to find out. I was kind o' hopin' that mebbe ye'd forget yourself and get a little human, but I see it ain't in ye. But ye've the outward carcass of a man, and I'm goin' to put it to work."

"What do you mean?" Alarmed, Conroy stepped back before her menacing advance.

"Mean?" she erupted. "I'm goin' to let ye practice some of that efficiency you're always gassin' about. A bent tool is better than none—so get ye below to the stokehold. You're goin' to spell the other fireman and help keep the steam pressure up till we git in. It'll mebbe sweat some of the conceit out of ye; and even if it don't, ye'll have something to remember Tugboat Annie by!"

Conroy felt the wind in his hot face, looked out at the driving whitecaps overside.

"Don't be ridiculous! I'm practically part owner ——"

"You're part owner of a coal scoop from now on. . . . Sam ——"

The big engineer brought his hulking frame into the foreground and jerked his thumb.

"That way," he growled.

Conroy clung to the rail, half crying with humiliation, but Sam grasped him from behind with sinewy hands and frog-marched him along the narrow deck. They disappeared into the housing. There was a clatter, a couple of sharp smacks, and a cry abruptly silenced.

"And that," mused Tugboat Annie in her cabin sometime later, to the appreciative chromo of the late Captain Brennan, "was that!"

Shortly after dark, with a half gale blowing, and the seas, white-crested and angry, catapulting past the rail, the lights of a moving vessel, yawing and dipping, came swiftly up from astern and swung as close to the Narcissus as safety would permit. It was the Pansy. Her master megaphoned across:

"The Barracuda's got her steering gear repaired and Crabtree cut us adrift. That's something off his towing bill."

"The dirty old curmudgeon," Tugboat Annie growled. She shouted back: "All right! Don't worry! Just stand by in case we need you!"

Shortly after midnight the towline parted with a crack, and the Narcissus lurched away on the crest of a sea. She picked up the Barracuda's lights, but in a darkness intensified by driving rain squalls, and battered by wildly mounting seas, it was impossible to get another line aboard, and an anxious vigil ensued which lasted until daybreak. Dawn spread over a green and tumbling waste, and the Barracuda, drifting with wind and current, and with the seas spouting up her rusty side, was rounded up. It was nearly noon, however, before Tugboat Annie's superb seamanship was effective and a line again was taken on board.

Red-eyed with lack of sleep, but indomitable, she stood at the wheel as the slow, heartbreaking voyage was resumed, gauging each charging comber, easing off, bringing up the head, inching down the coast that was almost obscured by driving spindrift. Conroy, who had come off watch, stood in the lee of the house, dividing his attention between cruelly blistered palms and the smoking combers that thundered up from astern, swooped under the fantail and roared away into the maelstrom ahead. He was quiet now, outwardly subdued, but he had watched with angry concentration the battle to pick up the drifting Barracuda, and he promised himself his full innings when and if the voyage was done. Once he ventured near the wheelhouse, like a scorched moth which cannot resist the flame.

"What if the Barracuda breaks adrift again and piles up on the beach?" he said in surly tones.

Tugboat Annie did not turn her head. "If that happens, queer feller," she rasped, "you'd better say your prayers, if ye know any, for I'll go after her. I'm goin' to get that vessel to port if I have to chase her ashore and put wheels under her. Now get away from the pilot house before I forget I'm a lady."

The gale had blown itself out by dark, and although the seas still were menacing, Tugboat Annie's expert knowledge of Puget Sound waters enabled her to take the leeward of every available point of land. The sky had cleared and the light-spangled hills of Secoma blazed like a heavenly galaxy ahead. Slowly they moved up the harbor to a vacant berth and the Barracuda was made fast.

Tugboat Annie, coming from the pilot house to the deck, encountered Conroy as he emerged from the engine room.

"I'm going ashore now ——" he began, but Tugboat Annie's rough croak interrupted him:

"And who cares? I hope ye've l'arned something of a woman's ways on a deep-water tug. Good night and bad luck!"

She turned in to her bunk as she was. But at nine o'clock the next morning, with her feathered shore-going bonnet perched defiantly on her tousled head, she sat in her cabin awaiting the arrival of Alec Severn and Captain Crabtree. Severn arrived first. His red face was depressed and unhappy.

"Hello, Annie," he said tonelessly.

"Hello, Alec. What are you looking so glum about?" she rumbled. "It'd give a body the belly-ache to look at ye."

For a moment he did not answer. Then he looked up and met her bovine gaze.

"I fought your battle for you with Conroy all the rest of that day, Annie. And I told him, finally, that rather than let you go I'd see him and his money some other place. Then he came around a bit, for he's really keen about taking over the company. And he's got a reputation ——"

"Hmmph! What kind? There's several, ye know!"

"It's the right business kind, it happens. Finally I persuaded him to go out with the Narcissus that night and see for himself how efficiently you really could handle a difficult job. . . . Well, no use going into the horrible mess you made of it. He telephoned me last night after you got in."

"He would," Tugboat Annie rasped, but Severn continued without heeding her:

"The job was worth five hundred dollars at the least, considering we had two tugs and had to pull him off the rocks and all. But you let your stubborn dislike of Conroy override the interests of the company, and you got well hooked by the Barracuda's master as a result. What got into you, Annie? You never let me down before!"

"It must be the tie ye're wearin', Alec," said Tugboat Annie. "It's kind of a bilious color. Is Sweet Forget-Me-Not comin' along here this mornin'?"

"Yes, he's due any time now—him and the master of the Barracuda."

The two men arrived together—Conroy again the cold, immaculate machine, and Captain Crabtree looking, in his shore-going clothes, like an apple that had hung too long on the tree. Conroy bowed stiffly to Severn, ignoring Tugboat Annie.

"Had your lemon juice this morning?" she asked solicitously.

Severn motioned her to silence. He came abruptly to the point:

"Don't you think, Captain Crabtree, that in consideration of what the Narcissus pulled you through last night, it only would be fair if you paid the full towing fee of three hundred dollars, as originally agreed?"

"No, I don't," said Captain Crabtree with a grin.

"But you might have lost your ship."

" 'Might' is a chancy word, sir. And an agreement's an agreement. I can't afford to be kindhearted. With the 30 per cent reduction which became effective when we repaired our steering-gear breakdown, I figger I owe you two hundred and forty dollars."

"No, ye don't," grunted Tugboat Annie.

"Don't what?"

"Ye don't owe us one cent on the agreement we made."

Captain Crabtree stared at her with gratified surprise. "Well, that's very nice. You haven't took leave of your senses, though, have you, missus?"

"I leave that to shipmasters o' vessels in distress," Tugboat Annie replied.

Severn interfered, his face pink with vexation.

"Now, look here, Annie; you keep out of this. You've done damage enough."

"Sure. I forgot!" Tugboat Annie rumbled. "It's the men that's the smart ones! You, and Crabtree, and Frog-Face there! I'm just a dumb tugboat skipper. Is that it? All right! Now you hold your jaws, all of ye, till I tell ye something. Crabtree, here, took me for a sucker yesterday. Well, I was! I let 'em beat me at every turn—steerin'-gear business and all!" She snorted contemptuously. "Why, I'd have towed him home for nothin', knowin' what I did! See? He knows already what I'm gettin' at, the wizened little rascal!" She pointed a horny, accusing finger at Captain Crabtree, who twisted his head in his over-large collar and looked remarkably uncomfortable.

"What do you mean?"

"I'll make it plain enough. I tumbled to his game the minute he told his man to order the tugs abreast of the gangway, where he had to talk with a megaphone, instead of over the Barracuda's poop, where it would ha' been much easier. There was something around the stern of his ship he wanted to hide. . . . That right, Crabtree?"

The shipmaster essayed a nonchalant smile. It was not successful. Tugboat Annie continued:

"I had a good look for meself, found out what I wanted, and moved up alongside the others. The bidding was most interesting, though our passenger didn't seem to enjoy it overmuch. Crabtree could make all the stipulations he liked, after he'd answered one question I'd put him. Remember it, captain? You bet your Sunday tights ye do! I asked him if his vessel had sustained any damage beyond the fire, water in the hold and jammed steering gear. He said no, as there's witnesses to prove; and on that basis we entered into an agreement which covered towage alone. But the book says —— Wait a minute ——"

Tugboat Annie went to a shelf and took down a dog-eared manual of maritime law, wet her thumb lavishly and turned over to the required page.

"Ah! Here it is, as plain as the cast in yon queer feller's eye." She read:

"Where a towage service is entered into on the assumption that the tow is in a seaworthy condition, and she conceals from the tug any material fact which would tend, if known, to increase the amount of remuneration agreed upon, the tug is not prevented by the fact of prior agreement from claiming further reward; for in such case the towage may cease to be towage and become, in effect, salvage."

"Well," said Conroy sharply, "what are you getting at?"

"Just this, Mr. Great Thinker—that because he concealed from me the fact that the Barracuda had stripped her propeller in among the rocks, our towing agreement didn't mean a thing, and we've got an unbeatable claim for salvage. If I'd left him piled up on the rocks, the Barracuda would have been pounded to pieces in the gale. But bein' just a stupid, mutton-hearted female, I yanked her home. So instead of a lousy towin' fee of two hundred and forty dollars, we'll get a salvage award of about a third the value of the ship and cargo." Tugboat Annie halted and blew her nose with an elephantine flourish. "And now, if ye can see clear to lend me sixty cents till pay day, Alec, I'd like to go ashore and telegraph me daughter."

Captain Crabtree was on his feet, shouting profane defiance, but Tugboat Annie soon reduced his bluster.

"Go outside before ye explode, ye nasty little feller!" she trumpeted. "And as for denials, ye can save 'em up for the marine surveyor. Now, go on; get out o' here afore I fetch ye a kick in the rear!"

The chastened and badly frightened Captain Crabtree having hastily departed, Tugboat Annie stood with rugged, flushed face at the head of her bunk, her eyes resting on the hand-tinted features of the late Captain Brennan in their plush-and-gold oval frame. She was queerly silent for a time, and so were the two men before her. Then she puffed her lips, blew a vast, irritable breath, and addressed Severn:

"Well, Alec! What about that sixty cents?"

"What are you going to say to your daughter, Annie?"

"Her home's in Vancouver. I'm goin' to ask her if she's got room for her ma, since there's no room for me here."

Severn's florid face went deeper red than usual with embarrassment. He said, "You'll do nothing of the kind, Annie. Your place is here, and I'm not letting you go on anybody's terms. Maybe I can't find the right words to tell you ——"

"Perhaps I can," said Conroy, rising briskly. "Mrs. Brennan, I'm sorry. I apologize for misjudging you. You're clever—and you've taught me something about women. And, Severn, I'd like very much to put through our agreement of the other day and buy an interest in the company. As for Mrs. Brennan, I'd be proud and delighted ——"

Severn looked up swiftly and met Tugboat Annie's eyes, and an almost imperceptible signal was exchanged. Tugboat Annie favored the departed Terry with a wink. Then she faced Conroy with booming voice:

"So ye discovered that a woman could be clever, did ye, Columbus? And ye'd like to buy into the company, now it'll be well off without your dirty money? Hmmph! I've no doubt! And ye're sorry—and ye'd be proud and delighted! Well, if ye ain't glued to that chair, I'll be proud and delighted if ye'll take yourself and your sorrow and drop 'em both in the dock. It'll be hard on the fishes, but they can stomach ye a sight easier than I can. And the sooner ye do it, the better!"

As Conroy moved toward the door she pulled off her dilapidated, shore-going bonnet and flung it on the settee. She grinned at Severn. "I feel more like meself now," she puffed, and her small, roving eyes once more met the framed, ingratiating smirk of the late Captain Brennan.

"What's that ye said, ye wicked man?" she asked huskily; and to ears and eyes that understood his kind of language, the smiling defunct made adequate reply.

ROOM TO BREATHE IN

by Dorothy Thompson

IN THE SPRING of 1933 most Americans were worrying more about when the banks would reopen than about the odd little man with a mustache who had just become Chancellor of Germany. But Dorothy Thompson, who was on the spot, felt differently. Her reports to the *Post* contained a clear warning that Hitler's shout for more *Lebensraum* was not as funny as it sounded in the newsreels. Miss Thompson, as Jack Alexander has written in a *Post* profile, "is perhaps the only person in the United States who makes a career out of stewing publicly about the state of the world." She has been doing this in a useful way ever since she was a streetcorner orator for the Woman Suffrage party, back in 1914. When she wrote the following article she was married to another *Post* writer, Sinclair Lewis. They were divorced in 1942.

JUNE 24, 1933

RECENTLY TWO BOOKS appeared by English authors, one from the pen of the eminent British mathematician and sociologist, Bertrand Russell, and the other by the novelist descendant of one of England's most distinguished scientists, Mr. Aldous Huxley. Lord Russell's book was an essay, and he called it *The Scientific Outlook*. Mr. Huxley's book was a Utopian novel, and he took his title from Shakespeare, and called it *Brave New World!* Both books were ironical pictures of a future society when the chance and accident, the working of free economic competition, the chaotic political life produced by parliamentary government and parties, free biological choice, the catch-as-catch-can of modern liberal democracy should be replaced by a truly scientific form of government.

In that future state, as foreseen both by Bertrand Russell and by Aldous Huxley, "every little boy or girl that's born into this world alive" will not be "either a little Liberal or else a little Conservative" as Gilbert and Sullivan had it, but will be conditioned by methods of psychological suggestion. Social classes will be formed not by the competitive methods of individual striving but by eugenic selection. The drawers of water and hewers of stone, without whom even a new scientific society cannot exist, will be bred from the working classes and they will have it impressed upon them from birth by gentle radio messages which work while they sleep, that it is eminently desirable to be a member of the hewers-of-stone class. But the nobility will also be eugenically bred—in Mr. Huxley's *Brave New World,* in bottles—and will be decanted as rulers of the Alpha class, and conditioned to a sense of *noblesse oblige* by subtle suggestion. This new world is to be totally unsentimental, completely organized; there will be no illness, no suffering, no unhappy love, no psychological complexes, no unemployment, no hunger or poverty; all the world will be as efficient as a Diesel engine, and all life as determined as death.

Reading these books, we shudder at the horror of the world portrayed, and laugh, because, obviously, these are only the Pucklike dreams of imaginative men. How resigned we are to our chaotic world as we lay down these books. It is dreadful to be hungry, to be humiliated, to be frustrated, as many of us are, in this sad old world. Obviously, our social system is atrociously organized. But who would not rather tramp the road unsure where he will lay his head at night, than live in the handsomest, most hygienic, most comfortable prison?

Then the disturbing afterthought comes: Perhaps we do not think like this because there is any ultimate truth in our conception of life. Do we not think as we do, merely because the idea of freedom has been suggested to us from childhood? Is not a lion born in a zoo as happy, and infinitely healthier and better cared for, than one roaming the jungle, a prey to hostile forces of nature? Are we not all silly romantics?

Artists have a kind of prophetic sight. I have just come back from Germany—the Germany of Adolf Hitler and National Socialism—I have watched with unbelieving eyes the developments of the first ten or twelve weeks of the German revolution. And as I read the German newspapers, following the decrees of the new dictatorship, I have a strange apprehension that I am reading Aldous Huxley's book come true. Is this, perhaps, the Brave New World?

312

Revolutions create phrases in which an epoch, a world outlook, a form of life, are expressed. Liberty, equality, fraternity—the conception of the French Revolution—is embodied in our own Constitution, in the Declaration of Independence, in the Gettysburg address. "The dictatorship of the proletariat," "The permanent revolution"—the two phrases sum up Russia under the Soviets. "The total state"—and we think immediately of Mussolini and Fascist Italy.

The German revolution is not altogether original. It has taken the concept of the permanent revolution from Trotsky; Joseph Goebbels, the Minister of Propaganda, has publicly explained that revolution is not the final achievement of a condition but the continuous achieving of it through history. The idea of the total state has been taken over from Mussolini. But the German revolution is better expressed in its own word. All students of contemporary world affairs must learn it. The word is *Gleichschaltung. Gleichschaltung* means "bringing into line." It means "conformity." It means, quite simply, "making everything alike."

Whoever has followed the German press since the revolution on the fifth of March has seen this word over and over again. *"Gleichschaltung* of the provincial governments." *"Gleichschaltung* of the civil servants." . . . *"Gleichschaltung* of the professions." . . . *"Gleichschaltung* of the schools, of the universities." . . . *"Gleichschaltung,"* finally, of every individual human being. "Brains and fists," wrote Joseph Goebbels, fiery Minister of Propaganda, in a call to the people on April twenty-eighth, "must make an unbreakable alliance. The peasant behind the plow, the worker in his study, the physician at the sickbed, the engineer at his drawing board, all must realize that the nation and its future are above everything, and that each man in his place is judged by his service to the fatherland, and thus to the general good."

There are to be no minorities of opinion in the new Germany and no division of loyalties.

KEEPING GERMANY'S KULTUR UNTARNISHED

IF ONE THINKS for a moment, one realizes that this conception is as severe an attack on the principles of the modern *bourgeois* democracy as is Communism. The nations into which we all were born, and in which some of us still live, had no such theory. They leave room for all sorts of loyalties. No one dreams of telling the scientist, investigating the atom, that his findings must be in the interest of France, the United States or Great Britain. It is recognized that devotion to scientific truth involves a quite different set of loyalties from those concerned with patriotic feel-

ings. The command to "render therefore unto Cæsar the things which are Cæsar's, and unto God the things that are God's" implies a liberty of conscience in many matters besides those entirely religious. No scientist will accept the right of any state to dictate what is truth above the findings of science itself. If the earth moves around the sun and not the sun around the earth, the scientist will not reverse the order to please the powers even though he burn for it.

But Germany goes further, and demands, in effect, that her people accept the theory that the world moves around Germany, and no voice dare raise itself in protest. The new German state is ushered in with a set of principles with which every manifestation of life must be brought into conformity, and no moral or intellectual doubts are allowed. It tells the world, for instance, that it is anxious to remain at peace, is truly peace loving, and does not desire anything more than equality with other nations; but if any German citizen should rise in a public place tomorrow and express the belief that the best means of achieving this condition of international peace would be, in his humble opinion, to bring up children in the belief that other civilizations are perhaps as good as his own, that Germany was also partly responsible for the last war, and that general militarization weakens the chances of maintaining peace, he would be clapped into prison for high treason.

The new German state, with which everything must be brought into conformity, rests upon a scientific thesis which is, to say the least, highly questionable. This scientific thesis is the intellectual justification of the campaign against the Jews. The theory, of which a Frenchman, Gobineau, and an expatriate Englishman, Houston Stewart Chamberlain, were the chief modern exponents, is that mental and spiritual values and tendencies inhere in the human chromosome and are physically transmitted. Certain races have, therefore, certain incorrigible characteristics. The maintenance of a culture rests upon the maintenance of a pure race. Mixed races lose their vitality and produce weak cultures which fall before stronger, pure cultures and races.

This is a scientific theory, and in a free society would be judged according to scientific principles —that is, according to whether historical evidence and biological experiment support the thesis. In Germany it is today a dogma, and no scientist dare dispute it. If a German college professor, tomorrow, were to advance the theory that man has a social, as well as a racial inheritance, and that it is this social inheritance which determines his mind form; that social forms can change races;

that actually racial characteristics have changed profoundly under changed social conditions—that the Jews, for instance, were, in the time of Josephus, a warlike race, disliked for their extreme pugnacity and much desired as mercenary soldiers—if he were to suggest that, perhaps, it is not true that the purest races produce the most vital cultures—for it is a question whether the culture of the Scandinavian countries, racially probably the purest in Europe, is more vital than the cultures of such mixed races as make up the United States, England, France, and—alas, for Mr. Hitler—Germany—that professor would lose his job. He would prove that he has not been "*Gleichgeschaltet*," not brought into conformity —is guilty, in fact, of the heinous crime of thinking for himself.

The new Germany does not want people who think for themselves, because people who think for themselves build minorities and invariably spoil the pattern. The National Socialist conception of the state is of a perfectly functioning machine, where each person takes his place as efficiently as a cog, and the whole moves when the leader pushes the button.

The first thing to be brought into line was the provincial governments. Germany was, until yesterday, a federation of largely autonomous states held together by a common language, a common community of economic interest vis-à-vis the outside world, and a common patriotism. The characteristics of the Bavarian differed greatly from those of the Prussian, as his landscape and religion differ. The Rhinelander, the citizens of the Free Hanseatic cities, while affirming their common German origins, were proud of their local history and characteristics. This particularism of the Reich had unquestionable disadvantages from the viewpoint of national efficiency, and the existence of numerous fiscal policies was particularly wasteful, as Parker Gilbert often pointed out when he was commissioner for the Dawes Plan in Berlin. Its exponents claimed for it cultural advantages, and it certainly gave to German life a large measure of its variousness and charm. It was abolished overnight by *force majeur,* and Hitler and his followers rejoice that not even Bismarck made such an achievement. A dry reply might be that perhaps Bismarck did not wish to do so.

The "making of everything alike" is, of necessity, a gradual process, but the National Socialists must be congratulated on having made extreme progress in a few weeks. Having conquered all the political positions, they immediately passed to the conquest of the economic and cultural positions, unquestionably envisaging the goal when the whole economic and social life will be made over in a National Socialist sense.

The professions and trades were switched into line immediately. The various professional groups in Germany are thoroughly organized. There are chambers of commerce and chambers of smaller employers—handworkers, such as bakers, butchers, and so on—trades unions, societies of lawyers, of physicians, both economic and professional, teachers' organizations, student bodies, peasant societies. There is no branch of German life which has not its free societies, until now independent of the state. Technically, these remain independent, but actually, by the process of making everything alike, they become instruments of the state, and, in any case, leave no room for the building of minorities. The procedure was simple. Such organizations all have executive committees. A National Socialist commissar dissolved them and demanded their reorganization according to the "leader principle," which from now on is to be the basis of "true German democracy."

It is, therefore, well to become acquainted with this leader principle. Do you think, perhaps, that it means that each society elects its leader, and then renders him obedience? Such was the leader principle of the old Germanic tribes—selection from the mass; complete responsibility when selected. But the leader principle of new Germany is something quite different. It consists in one leader getting himself elected—by methods which I have dealt with in a preceding article—and then appointing all the lesser leaders. Not I, as a member of the group, decide who shall be my leader, but the decision is made from outside and from above. Thus, slowly, every economic, professional and cultural organization is being reformed with a National Socialist at the head, or with someone thoroughly in sympathy with National Socialism.

For many years Europe has celebrated Labor Day, May first. Germany used this occasion to bring the trades unions and their affiliated organizations, coöperatives and banks into line. At a stroke, all trade-union houses were occupied by S. A. troops and commissars, and the German working classes were informed by newspaper, radio and a great mass demonstration that National Socialism had "freed them from Marxism and restored them to the bosom of the fatherland." There was no protest; there was no apparently universal joy that the bonds which had fettered the working classes for generations were suddenly broken.

But is there not something sinister, something strange, in this universal acceptance of a new order? What, after all, was Marxism, from which the working classes have been freed? It was an intellectual theory, summarized in the belief that the means of production should belong to the people and not be operated for the profit of individuals. Mr. Hitler opposes to this the theory that "common use must take precedence over individual use." Does this mean approximately the same thing, or does it mean something else? Is it possible that the several millions of German workers who have clung to a brief in state ownership of the means of production over a period of many years, and have tried to achieve it by gradual political methods, have all suddenly changed their minds, from one day to the next? And where have the German workers been all the time, while they fought Germany's war, while they put through the passive resistance in the Rhineland, if not in the bosom of the fatherland?

These are counter-revolutionary questions. The wave rolls forward, bringing everyone into line. Teachers are wanted for the new Spartan state. Out with everyone who believes in "humanitarianism." Whipping is reintroduced into the schools; dueling is restored in the universities, not to the position it had before the war, when it was tolerated but not legalized, but to the position it enjoyed centuries ago, and at venerable Heidelberg the students can boast that a duel was attended by the rector and municipal authorities for the first time in 500 years! German children must learn how to stand punishment; the new order is for those who can command and who can obey. Most modern education, to be sure, is based on a quite different principle—on the theory that he survives best who learns to coöperate. But this is un-German. Sport is brought into line. The ideal is no longer tennis, football, and other childish pastimes, but *Wehrsport*—military sport—long tramps in silence with a heavy pack, and military drill. "Hooray," cries little Hans, aged twelve, "in two years I can learn in my school how to handle a rifle." The schoolbooks are brought into line. The traitorous republic, along with most western nations, has tried to teach children an objective view of history; not all German wars have been holy wars; not all German diplomacy has been successful. This must stop! Siegfried Kauverau, the head of the Society for Decisive School Reform, which has been working with an educational committee of the League of Nations, is put into jail on a charge of high treason. The leader, Mr. Hitler, says: "The first object of education must be a sound body. Then, in a second instance, comes the education of the mentality. But here, again, character is more important than intellect. Our people must be given every suggestive power that lies in self-confidence. The youngest child

must be brought up in the belief that he is unquestionably superior to others. In his own body, he must feel that his people are unconquerable."

At the great industries the process of Bringing Into Line hesitates a moment. Not, to be sure, before the Federation of German Industries, whose secretary, Geheimrat Kastl, is relieved of office immediately. Not, to be sure, before the Langnam Verein—the federation for representing united industrial interest in the Rhineland and Westphalia. In this mighty industrial organization a National Socialist is put in for every specialized department—for coal, iron, and so on. Not before the film industry, where the Jews are expelled and National Socialists put in charge. But before the vast chemical trust, the I. G. Farben Industrie, the process of *Gleichschaltung* pauses. But only two months have passed and it is certainly too early to predict that the National Socialist state will not eventually cut into the capitalistic system as it is at present constituted as ruthlessly as it has already cut into the labor organizations. But the National Socialist economic theory is not Communism; it certainly does not favor the organization of industry in the interest of the proletariat, or, indeed, of any social class. It wishes here, also, to introduce the leader principle, and the statements of its leaders envisage a kind of planned economy in the interest of the highly militarized state, a sort of war-time economy such as was introduced into every country during the Great War.

Nor does the process of achieving conformity stop with the churches. At the portals of the Roman Catholic Church, it makes a halt. Catholic Christianity is older than Germany, and it is difficult to bring the Pope into line.

The Weimar Constitution, which created the German republic, separated church and state in Prussia, and the churches became incorporated religious societies, recognized as such in law. The various provincial Protestant churches, thus independent of the state, united in 1922 in the German Evangelical Church Alliance. Now, since the Reich reform has made a united Germany, the twenty-eight separate provincial churches are in the air. Obviously, a new "German" church must be created. Whether this will be an independent church or whether it will again be a state church is not yet clear. If the Nazis win here, as they have everywhere else, the Protestant church in Germany will become an instrument of the state. In Mecklenburg, the National Socialists even put a National Socialist commissar into the High Church Council. Leading National Socialist Protestant religious leaders are working to bring about a German interpretation of the New Testament. It is the contention of Herr Kube, the leader of the Nazi movement inside the church for Prussia, that Germans require a version of Christianity peculiar to themselves and that the church should be an organ for anti-Semitic nationalism. The more radical of the leaders would like to expel from the church all Protestants marrying members of an alien race, and particularly wish to free the church of any pacifistic taint. Therefore, a creed has been proposed which says: "God has made me a German. Germanism is the gift of God. God wishes that I should fight for my Germanism. Military service is no violation of the Christian conscience. Towards a state which furthers the powers of darkness, the believer has the right of revolution."

And the Jews?

The Jews, alone, are not to be brought into line. That is to say, only those Jews are to be treated as other Germans whose fathers fell in the war or who themselves saw service in the front-line trenches. These Jews, even, are to be citizens of the second class, because their children will be discriminated against in educational matters, and they will never under any circumstances be allowed to hold positions of real leadership in the new German state. All the rest are to be treated as guests, as aliens with restricted rights. They may not hold public office, nor sit on the executive bodies of important public or semipublic societies. Only a limited number of them may practice law, and a limited number practice medicine. On principle, they may not teach in Aryan schools, and only by special permission may they be members of the staffs of newspapers. It is preferred that they neither act, dance nor sing on the German stage, to say nothing of directing German theaters. It is not believed, in principle, that it is possible to bring the Jews into line. They are described in National Socialist speeches and literature as a disturbing, decomposing element. They are feared as being international, pacifist and, above all, critical. They are to be tolerated, but in an inferior position, as long as they behave themselves. But if anything goes wrong, they may expect to bear the brunt of the blame, as once, on April first, they have already had to do.

Germany has failed in one attempt to bring things into line. She has not brought world opinion into line. Not all the speeches of Hitler and Goebbels, of Goering and Von Papen, have wrung applause from the world for the German revolution. The greatest and most ingenious department of the Nazi state is the Department of Propaganda, but as far as outside countries are concerned, it is a frost. Germany united within by force and a new enthusiasm faces a world united in greatly disliking the turn German events have taken.

But this fact makes no appreciable impression on National Socialist mentality. It makes no more impression than world opposition made upon Communist Russia. The Nazis have offered the German people a vision; the German people in overwhelming numbers believe that this vision will become a reality; they believe that the nation has arisen, and that a new day has dawned.

Try to envisage the National Socialist state when it has approximated perfection.

There will be a German nation of Aryan blood. If any Jews are left, their position will be similar to the one they held in Germany in the eighteenth century; they will be petty traders, sequestered in ghettos. What law does not do, public opinion will, for every school child will be brought up to realize the profound difference between Jew and German. When the one-day boycott of the Jews was made on April first, the official Nazi organ, Voelkische Beobachter, rejoiced that "from this day on, every school child knows who is and who is not a Jew." No German woman will marry a Jew; no German a Jewess.

This German nation of Aryan blood will be led by leaders. The leaders will ultimately be bred for the purpose, if Walter Darré, the head of the Nazi Bauernbund, has his way. He advocates that breeding stations be established and eugenic laws determine what women must marry and bear children, what women may marry but produce no children, and what women may neither marry nor breed.

Education will be completely regulated. Children of all citizens and even of all resident aliens may learn to read and write, but the number of students admitted to higher education will be strictly limited.

Not everyone who wants to study will be allowed to. Only a certain number of physicians, lawyers, teachers, scientists, artists, technicians, engineers, will be produced, and the state will decide which young people shall have opportunities. All the rest will be good soldiers and workers. In any event, only a tiny per cent—based upon their numerical ratio to the population—may be Jews.

The political system will be a religious dogma, and all heretics will be confined in prisons or concentration camps, the latter built by "voluntary labor units."

There will be no unemployment. Eventually all people who cannot find work in normal economic life will be recruited into a huge army which will drain swamps, build roads for National Socialists and prisons for any dissenters who may be left over, and will be fed, clothed and freed from responsibility, and paid a pittance per day, and may at any moment be drafted into the military army.

The apotheosis of the state will be the soldier, and every citizen will be a member of the army, for the ideal of the Hitler government is "a nation in arms." All military virtues will be glorified. All education will emphasize that war, not peace, is man's normal state, and that fighting is man's only hope against degeneration.

All art will be propaganda. No books will make men's hearts restless with yearning for some other world; no plays or poems will lift the individual out of his Germanness into humanity. Whenever one twiddles the dial of a radio, some voice, as clear, as persuasive, as masterly as the voice of Dr. Joseph Goebbels, will tell the worker over and over again that National Socialism has freed him from his chains; will tell the small *bourgeois* that National Socialism has elevated him to glory; will tell every listener that since he has placed his whole fate in the hands of his leader, he lives in the best of all possible worlds.

Most men will wear uniforms, the badge of their membership in that secret, mystic community of blood brothers, the German state. Women will, by preference, wear kitchen aprons and will stay at home and take care of the children, which they will gladly bear in large numbers for Germany. They will not hold political opinions—but then, neither will anyone else.

Everyone will be kept healthy by the state, but the weaklings will be allowed to perish.

All science will be in the hands of the state, and all scientific discoveries bent to the service of the state.

The nation will be virtuous. Women will not smoke or drink. Men will do so in moderation. Manifestations of wealth will be frowned on; all the brave show of opulence will be abolished. Thrift, economy, simple living—these will be the nation's ideals.

Nobody will long for any other kind of life, because nobody will get reports of any other kind of life, except as they come through a strictly censored press. And if a war comes, it is blessed to die for one's country—one has learned that from babyhood.

And lest there be heretics, a careful, secret-police system will be constantly on the watch. While the voices of leaders on the radio repeat over and over again that everything is quiet, and happy, and well in Germany, the police, subject

to no authority other than their own, will remove any dissenters to this chorus and put them gently into protective arrest, where they remain without trial as long as they live.

Everything will be in the service of the state—even love.

Does this seem an exaggerated picture? I do not think it is. Hitler advocates marriage according to a eugenic system based on the theory that mixed races lose their vitality, and Walter Darré actually has proposals for categorizing German women as potential mothers. The new government has already introduced a numerus-clausus law, not only for Jews but for all Germans. From now on, not everyone can have a higher education in Germany who wants one. The number of the educated will be limited and the selection in the hands of state authorities. The political credo is already a dogma to which all must subscribe or pay the penalty of imprisonment; the new state will be frankly military; Doctor Goebbels has already decreed that no art can exist for itself or in the service of supernatural ideals; restaurants already display signs: German Women Do Not Smoke, and night clubs are being broken up. Already the censorship keeps from Germans any hint of what the outside world thinks about their revolution; already a whole people is being hypnotized into the belief—without a single definite proof that it is so—that on March 21, 1933, the day of the State Act in Potsdam, Germany entered into a new period of grandeur.

As for the police: On the twenty-eighth of April the following small announcement appeared from the Wolff Bureau, the official German news agency, announcing the creation of a German G. P. U.:

The Prussian Minister-President Goering has divorced the political police from the Berlin Police Præsidium, and has made it an independent organ. The secret state police department, thus created, whose activities are governed by a law of April 26, 1933, stands directly under the Minister of the Interior and has the duty of seeking out and fighting all political tendencies dangerous to the state. In this duty the rest of the police are subservient to the secret police, which also enjoys special executive powers. Its authority reaches over the entire state territory.

Oh, Brave New World!

But perhaps there is a joker in all this. Long ago, a state existed which was not unlike Mr. Huxley's Utopia. When Doctor Goebbels was asked by foreign correspondents what the ideal of the New Germany was, he answered: "Our model is Sparta." But Sparta did not, as history records, prove to be a very strong state. And perhaps, like Sparta, Hitler's Germany will not prove itself the toughest of organisms, but one of the brittlest, cracking before cultures where the strain is better distributed, where the spirit is more adventurous and ingenious.

How did all this come about in Germany?

Largely because so-called civilized people did not believe it could.

The man who calls himself civilized, whose actions and habits of thought are based upon carefully cultivated differentiations, especially as to loyalties, and upon fostered inhibitions, stands skeptical and helpless before demonstrations of a mass mentality. Because in normal times he has a large directing part in the forces which form public opinion, he is susceptible to the error that his own tastes and prejudices are universally ingrained. In time of war, to be sure, he sees quite vividly that this is not so, but even then he regards lapses from his own standards as abnormal. Civilized people in and out of Germany dismissed Adolf Hitler lightly, because he did not in any sense fulfill their æsthetic ambitions as to a leader. This article is by way of being a confession. I judged in the same manner. I looked at Mr. Hitler, and thought: "Considerable psychic powers." It is interesting that he comes from Braunau, a fantastic little Austrian village where half the population attend spiritist seances, and from where come the two most famous European mediums, Willy and Rudi Schneider. "Not well bred; no real, inner self-reliance; carries himself badly; doesn't know what to do with his hands; thinks confusedly; talks nonsense." The twenty-five points of the National Socialist program seemed, to me, nonsense, because I judged them from an intellectual standpoint, asking whether the thesis which they presented was true. It would have been far more to the point to ask whether the thesis was one which would be likely to appeal to vast masses of Germans, and whether it might not furnish them with a new mythology. The thesis might be utter nonsense from an intellectual and rational viewpoint, and still overcome a whole world. There are plenty of instances in history of widespread popular mania.

Viewed intellectually, the proposal to create, in the midst of modern Europe, a "folk state" seems preposterous. Since when has the modern state been a herd of blood brothers? Not since the emergence of the first urban civilization, which precisely consisted in collecting people of different races and different mentalities and merging them together into a community of interest, and with this step came the dawn of modern culture. If Hitler's thesis is true, the entire North American experiment is doomed to failure.

And Hitler's biology! The simple eugenics of the kennel or the stud, applicable to humans also, no doubt, if you are sure for what qualities you wish to breed—for swiftness of limb or length of nose. But how breed a Goethe, or a Shakespeare, or a Copernicus?

And the economic program. Capitalism is to be maintained, but interest is to be destroyed. The great industrial monopolies represent a truly German tendency, but the department stores do not, and must be annihilated. Where is the line in this program? Where the theory? Is there any beyond the assumption that the chemical trust and the steel trust are in the hands of powerful Germans and most of the department stores are in the hands of Jews?

All these questions are intellectual, and all of Germany's intellectuals have been against Mr. Hitler. They said: "He cannot come to power in a country which has much wiser men." They said: "If he does come to power, he won't carry out this absurd program."

But civilized people were wrong. They thought that the complex of prejudices, standards and ideals accumulated at the cost of great sacrifice over a period of some hundreds of years was really greatly cherished by all men. Civilized people did not see that this culture is, actually, to the vast masses no treasure at all, but a burden, which can be borne only under exceptionally favorable circumstances. Beyond that point—if, for instance, by reason of economic malfunctioning vast masses of people are, for years, hungry and idle, then the will grows to look upon civilization as a restraining, impeding force, and to identify revolt against it with freedom.

The shortsightedness of the world in imposing upon Germany so severe a peace that the nation felt itself humiliated, impoverished and delivered over to the enemy; the succession of slights and insults, all exaggerated inside Germany by German leaders for the purpose of keeping public opinion mobilized; the succession of catastrophes—the loss of the war, which shook the faith of the people in the one thing in which they implicitly believed—their incomparable military machine—the inflation, which proletarianized the middle classes and turned them into revolutionary material; the depression, which resulted in six millions of idle, half fed, utterly discouraged unemployed—these have added to the burden which civilization itself imposed: The burden of suppressing the aggressive instincts; of responsibility of thinking for oneself and making judgments; the burden of conforming to a complex law; the burden of educating one's children and trying to get on in the world; the burden of making adjustments to uncomfortable changes, particularly of men to emancipated women, with their right to divorce and their economic independence; the burden of tolerating and being agreeable to people unlike oneself, with other habits, tendencies and faces.

Added to all these burdens, in Germany, was the complexity of a tortuous political system, worked out, with the best will in the world, in the hope of achieving genuine democracy, but resulting in a tangle of political parties and programs, in governments which were perpetually based upon difficult compromise. The public mind became sick with effort; there arose a vast hatred against the complexities of life; civilization was costing too much; the burden was agonizing.

Hitler succeeded for one reason: He knew a great deal better than civilized people do, what the German masses want. Certainly more than the intellectuals, who have lost their touch with the masses. Freedom—freedom for intellectual and artistic expression; freedom of choice and opportunity; freedom which means room to breathe in—is life itself to some—Shakespeare, listing the manifestations of his times which made him long for "restful death," named "art made tongue-tied by authority"—but to most people, freedom is, perhaps, never obtained nor even desired.

I remember some years ago meeting a young Fascist who asked me what I thought of his country's government. "I don't like it much," I confessed. "There is such a suppression of liberty." "Liberty!" cried this compatriot of Garibaldi. "Whatever can you do with liberty?"

"Breathe it," I might have answered, but I could not have said, "Eat it." Hitler knew per-

fectly well that millions would be willing to exchange liberty for bread, and probably it is easier to feed a working army than to restore an army of individuals to normal economic life.

Germany has gone back to a simpler culture. If, on the one hand, the organization of the mass is to be ever so much more thoroughgoing and inescapable than before, the demands upon individual responsibility are to be much lighter. If the Communist revolution represents a movement of the masses toward greater opportunities, the National Socialist revolution is just as much a mass movement, but toward less responsibility. In tomorrow's Germany, there is to be a lower standard of living for everyone, but there is also to be less risk.

And, above all, the National Socialist revolution has caught into itself the young Germany, who for years have been growing up, with no future, unemployed, idle, in a world which did not want them. Hitler has said: "We want you!" Hitler has said: "This country is yours!" He has appealed to the heroic instinct. He has asked youth, not for something easy but for sacrifice. He has reintegrated youth, if not into a society— well, into a herd. The point is that when society fails to absorb men, they will turn to a herd. The profound influence of Hitler was expressed in a speech which he made to the S. A. troops, which ended with the phrase: "As long as I live, you belong to me and I belong to you."

The German masses have revolted against the complexities, difficulties and duties of modern civilization. In a profound sense, the National Socialist revolution is defeatist. And it is a terrific challenge to the *bourgeois* world, to that era which reached its height at the end of the nineteenth century, and is perhaps truly in decline. For the credo of that era was that mankind can and must lift himself to ever higher reaches of individual development.

EVERYBODY OUT

by George S. Brooks

GEORGE S. BROOKS has been needling the professional patriots ever since he got out of the army following World War I. In the 1920's he and another newspaperman collaborated on a satirical Broadway play, *Spread Eagle*, which caused one organization to begin an underground investigation of the authors' loyalty. In the course of this Brooks received a letter asking him to donate $25 toward the cause of investigating himself. He wrote back that he could supply all the information needed: he was born in upstate New York in 1895, of old New England stock, and through nine American generations there had never been a Red in his family tree. Since then he has been elected Mayor of Groton, New York, while his onetime collaborationist, Walter B. Lister, is managing editor of the highly respectable *Evening Bulletin* of Philadelphia.

DECEMBER 29, 1934

GOVERNOR JOHN Z. SHERMAN, EXECUTIVE MANSION.

DEAR JACK: After two days of taking testimony, we have uncovered the facts about the so called Red Riot at State University.

In a political sense, the whole affair is packed with more dynamite than a Chicago pineapple. In fact, if our findings ever leak out, the State University campus is going to explode in your face and ours.

The joint committee from the legislature, Chairman Jansson dissenting, has asked me to forward you this summary and to inquire what is your pleasure.

I can be reached by phone tomorrow morning, here at the College Inn. Between eight and nine o'clock, I'll be in my room. After nine o'clock, have me paged in the tap room.

Listen, Jack. Pay no attention to Senator Jansson. He has no more diplomacy than a three-year-old bull. You know that we can't line up college kids and shoot them, just because they waved a red flag. Senator Jansson is a fool, and the worst thing you have to contend with in politics is a fool in your own party.

I am nervous as a mouse in a revolving door, and I won't feel better until I hear from you.

Yours,
SETON O'BRIEN,
Special Deputy Attorney General.

P. S.: The first witness is a student here and a great-grandson of the Hon. Horatio Chadwick, Civil War governor of this state. Young Chadwick has a pleasing personality. He is not the type of boy commonly associated with subversive, revolutionary and seditious activities.

Moreover, keep in mind that his father is A. L. Chadwick, of Salmon Falls, party leader of Salmon County, which you carried both times. [By 4653 votes in 1932 and by 7359 in 1934, official figures.]

P. P. S.: Burn this. Burn everything.

SUMMARY OF TESTIMONY

Donald T. Chadwick, aged 21, sworn.

ABOUT EIGHT O'CLOCK last Saturday morning, as I was crossing the Circle near the Administration Buildings, I found that I was being followed by several members of the Gamma fraternity.

I heard them yelling to certain students to stop me. . . .

Yes, I was carrying something. . . .

It was a red flag. . . .

I dare say that was the reason they were chasing me. Yes, sir. . . .

No, senator. I do not call myself a Communist, anarchist or Socialist. I am a Lambda. . . .

That's a college fraternity. . . .

I wouldn't venture to express an opinion. There are a great many Lambdas in some eighty colleges all over the country. I have no way of knowing what they believe. . . .

Well, Senator Jansson, I see you are an Elk. Could you tell me in a word what Elks believe? Or the purpose of the organization? . . .

No, sir. The Lambdas are not against the Government. . . .

Some of our members have had trouble with the police, the provost and the dean at one time or another, but we don't boast of it. . . .

If we are against anything, we are against the Gammas on account of their dirty politics. The Gammas stooped to very low practices when next year's football captain was chosen. A man from my fraternity was supposed to be elected. We had a working agreement with the Delts, Taus and neutrals to that effect. The Gammas went behind our backs, corrupted the Taus and two neutrals, and put in their man. . . .

But it is pertinent. That's why I was carrying the red flag across the Circle. Yes, sir. . . .

Just as the Gammas overtook me, I yelled, "All Lambdas out." Several members of my fraternity hurried to my assistance. . . .

When the four Gammas who were trying to take the red flag from me saw that they were outnumbered, one of them yelled, "All Gammas out." . . .

We Lambdas were fighting to keep the flag. The Gammas were trying to wrest it from us. . . .

It wasn't a big red flag. No, sir. I should say it was a convenient size. . . .

Well, on ordinary occasions, we Lambdas can be identified by our scholarship, gentlemanly behavior and the large jeweled pins we wear upon our vests. . . .

The reason I am not wearing my pin this afternoon is that a young lady is wearing it. . . .

No, senator. She is not a Lambda. She couldn't be. It's against our by-laws. She's a Chi. . . .

Not Chow, senator. Chi—C-h-i. . . .

The Chis are a sorority. That's the female of fraternity. . . . Why, a henhouse where the coeds live. . . .

Pardon me, senator. I am not trying to joke. I am very serious-minded. . . .

Very well. The stenographer has my address, in case you wish to recall me for further questioning.

Donald T. Chadwick, first witness, excused.
William G. Parker, aged 23, sworn.

LAST SATURDAY MORNING, about eight o'clock, I was eating my breakfast. . . .

Nothing else. Just eating. I was late. I didn't even have time to talk. . . .

As I sat in the dining room, I heard the front door bang. Someone had run out of the house. So I immediately went to the front window to see who it was. . . .

No, sir. I did not anticipate any trouble. . . .

My reason for getting up from the table was because I am chapter president of the Gamma fraternity. We charge fifteen cents for breakfast in the Gamma dining room. But you can get a breakfast for ten cents over in the university cafeteria. I wanted to see what brother in Gamma was such a darn cheap chiseler as to save a nickel by eating at the cafeteria. I intended to censure him publicly at the next chapter meeting. That's why I went to the window when the door banged.

To my surprise, I saw a sneak thief running across our front lawn. . . .

Yes, senator. I did recognize the sneak thief. It was Donald Chadwick, a Lambda.

He had stolen our red flag from above our fireplace mantel. I saw it in his hand. . . .

No. It wasn't a burglary. Not exactly. Our front door is never bolted. Locks are not necessary in a Gamma fraternity house. . . .

Of course, the brothers keep their good shirts and ties and dress clothes locked up. But the house is always open. . . .

Personally, I don't believe any member of the Lambda fraternity would have sufficient moral courage to commit a burglary. Sneak-thieving is more in their line.

The Lambdas are notorious upon the campus. They have done more than any other group to corrupt class elections. Why, not two months ago the Lambdas made a deal that would have disgraced a state politician.

I beg your pardon, senator. That just slipped out. I meant to say, that would have disgraced a New York State politician.

The Lambdas double-crossed us and elected the president of the senior class, the president of the Student Association and put three of their men on the Honor Committee. Why, the very idea of a Lambda upon the Honor Committee is humorous. . . .

Yes, of course I admit that Don Chadwick took the red flag from the mantel in our fraternity house. I am accusing him of taking it. . . .

That flag was one of our most cherished possessions. . . . No. It hasn't been a part of our ritual. We've only had the flag a short time. But that doesn't prevent its being very dear to us. . . .

Well, it's not the flag so much. It's the sentiment. It's the principle of the thing. . . .

But I'm trying to tell you what it's all about. . . .

I called to the three fellows at the breakfast table to follow me and I chased Chadwick, who was running toward the Circle. I'm a track man, a quarter-miler and anchor man on the varsity relay team. So, naturally, I overtook Chadwick very quickly near the Founder's statue. I knocked him down and was about to recover our red flag, when several Lambdas ran up. . . .

They had already knocked me down and thrown snow in my face when my fraternity brothers came to my assistance. After that, I lost my temper and I don't know what happened. . . .

Well, I don't care to say how the red flag came into our possession. . . .

All right, then. I refuse to answer on the

grounds that it might incriminate or degrade me. . . .

I refuse to answer that question on the same grounds. As president of the local chapter of a secret society, I cannot violate my oath and reveal the nature of our ritual, our constitution and our by-laws.

William G. Parker, second witness, was excused, although warned not to leave the immediate vicinity.

NOTE: *Attention of the governor:*

Parker, the second witness, is the eldest son of Herman Parker, head of the Breeders' Association and the State Grange. Though inclined to be hot-headed, most of the committee members feel that the young man is sound at heart, although mistaken in some of his radical tendencies. The father, Herman Parker, is very influential with farmers and dairymen all over the state.

Cadet Captain Bert Gailey, aged 22, sworn.

I AM ranking student officer of the State University Reserve Officers Training Corps.

On Saturday morning last, about 8:05 o'clock, as I came out of the university cafeteria, I saw a group of students engaged in a brawl near the base of the Founder's statue. They seemed to be fighting for possession of a Communist flag. . . .

Yes, senator. A red flag. It was about so long and about so wide. . . . Yes, sir. So, by so. . . .

I did recognize many of the men engaged in the rioting. Later, when by myself, I wrote down a list of those whom I recognized. . . . Yes, sir. I have the list of names. Here it is.

NOTE: *The list of names of rioters prepared by Cadet Captain Gailey was offered in evidence, marked for identification and received as Exhibit A.*

My first thought, when I saw the red flag, was to protect the national colors, which were flying from the tall flagstaff in front of the Administration Hall. . . .

I called Sergeant George K. Pitt and Corporal Peter Washburn from the cafeteria to assist me. We hurried around the Circle. We avoided the rioters and were not observed by them. We proceeded to the flagpole, hauled down the United States colors, folded them and returned them to the flag locker in the office of the Superintendent of Janitors. I took the key to the flag locker, so that none of the rioters could get possession of it. . . .

Yes, Senator Jansson. It certainly was very stupid of the Superintendent of Janitors to report that the United States flag was hauled down and destroyed during the riot. Had he looked in his locker, he would have found it just where it

belonged, folded carefully with the blue union on top. . . .

Thank you, sir. I was only doing my duty. The first duty of a cadet officer is to assume authority in case of emergency. . . .

Having saved the flag, I watched the progress of the rioting. The number of those engaged was increasing. As men arrived for eight-o'clock classes, they threw themselves into the brawl. There were cries of "Freshmen out!" "Sophs out!" About seventy-five freshmen on their way to a personal-hygiene lecture charged in mass, yelling, "Everybody out!" . . .

In an effort to restore order, I directed Sergeant Pitt and Corporal Washburn to help me drag the fire hose from the wall cabinet in the lobby of the Administration Building. Sergeant Pitt and I held the muzzle of the hose pointed toward the rioters while Corporal Washburn turned the valve which released the water pressure. Instantly the automatic fire alarm sounded, adding to the clamor and confusion. . . .

Well, senator, no sooner had the stream of water hit the rioters than they ceased fighting for the flag and attacked us. They wrested the hose from our hands. We attempted to escape back through the Administration Building, but found the doors locked in our faces by the frightened stenographers in the general offices. So there was nothing left for us to do except retreat across the Circle. As we went, the rioters turned the hose upon us, knocking us down several times before we were out of range. . . .

When I returned from my dormitory room, wearing dry clothes, the city police were looking at the red flag flying from the flagpole before the Administration Building. The water had been shut off by the city firemen, but the entire Circle was a mass of slushy snow and ice. The rioters had escaped. I approached the nearest policeman with the intention of telling him how I had preserved the national colors. "Officer," said I, "I hauled down the flag ——"

But my words enraged him. He had received a bloody nose and a black eye shortly before. "The hell you did," he replied, at the same time bringing down his billy upon my head. When I regained consciousness, I was in a cell at police headquarters. I learned I was charged with disorderly conduct, public intoxication, desecration of the national emblem, conspiracy to cause a riot, assault, battery, interfering with a police officer in the performance of his duty, resisting arrest, being a fugitive from justice and residing in this country illegally. . . .

No one would listen to my explanations, even when I was arraigned Monday morning. So I asked for an adjournment of one week to engage an attorney, to communicate with my family and to secure a copy of my birth certificate to prove my citizenship. My mother came here from home and posted $1000 cash bail in order to secure my release.

Cadet Captain Gailey, third witness, was excused with the thanks of the investigating committee for his patriotic conduct under the most trying circumstances.

G. W. Haynes, aged 19, sworn.

No, I DID not see the start of the so-called Red Riot. . . .

When it began, I was in Professor Kennedy's lecture room in the Science Building. Professor Kennedy had not come in yet. No, sir. I was at his desk, looking through his class book to see if I was due to be called on for an oral quiz. . . .

I'd been at the Freshman dance the night before and I wasn't prepared. I thought that, if I was due, it would be smarter to tell Professor Kennedy I wasn't prepared before the class began. If I wasn't due, I needn't say anything about it. . . .

About that time, I heard some noise in the Circle. I heard a yell, "All Lambdas out!" Yes, sir.

Therefore, I left the lecture room and ran downstairs. . . .

No, sir. I'm not a Lambda. I'm not a Gamma. I'm pledged Sigma. In a fight between the Lambdas and the Gammas, I would be absolutely neutral. Surely. I was free to assist either side. . . .

No, I did not assault Professor Kennedy upon the stairs. Absolutely not. . . .

Unfortunately, in leaving the lecture room, I collided with Professor Kennedy at the top of the stairs and he fell to the first landing. . . .

Why, senator, I'd be a sucker to sock Professor Kennedy. I wouldn't bite the hand that marks my quiz papers. Not on your life. . . .

When I reached the Circle, I saw some fellows trying to turn the fire hose on some other guys. The water knocked several of them down. I saw Don Chadwick get knocked down. He was carrying a red flag. So I went to his assistance. . . .

Well, because he had the flag and because I like him. "Listen, Don," I said, "if we put the flag on the big flagpole, it wouldn't get wet."

He thought that was a very good idea. So we went over to the big flagpole in front of the Administration Building, tied Don's flag to the lanyard, knotted the lanyard and raised the red flag. Then we cut off the other lanyard, so it couldn't be hauled down without the use of the firemen's extension ladder.

About that time, I observed police and firemen coming into the Circle and I left.

Oh, nuts, senator. . . . Yes, I said "nuts." It did not injure the peace of the people of this state and their dignity. The people of this state aren't out of bed at eight A.M. on Saturday mornings. . . .

Go ahead and prosecute. Go ahead and indict me. Do anything you want. . . . Yes, I've talked it over with my attorney. . . . Why, my father is my attorney. You ought to know him. He's Supreme Court Justice George Haynes.

G. W. Haynes, fourth witness, excused.

Patrick Timothy O'Connor, aged 22, sworn.

YES, I have engaged in very important campus activities. I'm right tackle on the varsity football team. I play a little ice hockey, throw the hammer and put the shot on the track team, and catch for the baseball team. . . .

No, I didn't see any red flag Saturday morning. I just didn't notice it. I never knew it was there, until I read about it afterward. . . .

There was a fight, wasn't there? . . .

No, I'm not a revolutionary. Yeah, I hit a cop. I wouldn't wonder if I hit two cops. My knuckles are still tender. . . .

When I first noticed them, they were getting out of the patrol wagon. I asked them what course they were taking, and the first one made a pass at me. . . .

That's right. He called me a damned Communist and made a pass at me. Uniform or no uniform, no one can make a pass at me and get away with it. Besides, I knew that cop who insulted me. He's a left-hander. Yeah, an Orangeman. His people came from Belfast. . . .

They took me to headquarters, but didn't hold me. The chief of police saw they'd made a mistake. He knows my old man.

Patrick Timothy O'Connor, fifth witness, excused.

Louis A. Spears, aged 21, sworn.

THE RED FLAG in question belonged to us. It was stolen from our fraternity house. . . . That's right. The Gamma house. . . .

Why, Brother Parker brought it home from the Freshman hop the night before it was stolen. . . .

I don't know why the Freshmen had a red flag at their dance. I never heard of a red flag at a senior ball or a junior prom. . . .

It was about two A.M. when Brother Parker brought it into the living room. I was sitting on a steam radiator. I was trying to get a warm. . . .

Brother Parker hung the red flag over the mantel. . . .

No, I made no protest. . . . No, I didn't ask him where he got it or what it meant. . . .

"That does me a lot of good," was all he said when he put the red flag in its place. . . .

I didn't say anything. If it made him feel good, I was for it. . . .

He didn't ask me to take any oath to any political creed or anything like that. He just said he felt good and he was going to bed. . . .

There wasn't any other conversation, except that he asked me if the fire in the furnace had gone out. I said I thought it had. He said our Freshmen were damn lazy, because they didn't build better fires. . . .

Yes, sir. Those were his last words. . . .

I'm not for anything. I'm not against anything. I have too much to think about, as it is. . . .

Free love would be all right, if you could find any. . . .

No, I wouldn't care to live in Russia. I don't like that sour cream they put in their cabbage soup.

Louis A. Spears, sixth witness, excused.

Paul Henry, aged 18, sworn.

YES, SIR. I was chairman of the frosh hop committee last Friday night. . . .

There was no red flag inside the gymnasium. No, sir. Absolutely not. No red flags and no stick in the punch. Those gin bottles out back have been there ever since the alumni smoker. . . .

Have I got to tell? . . .

Well, I did see a red flag outside the gym.

Parker stole it out of the back seat of Don Chadwick's old car. . . .

Have I got to tell that too? . . .

Well, I saw Chadwick put it in there a little while before Parker stole it. . . .

I'll probably get into trouble for telling you this. Josephine Kent gave it to Chadwick. Don put it in his car and Parker stole it from there. . . .

Josephine Kent, who is a coed, came out from the gym to her car. It's a nice new closed car. Don Chadwick was with her. . . .

She took out a parcel and handed it to Don. He unwrapped it and looked at the red flag. . . .

Then he kissed her. . . .

Then she kissed back. . . . .

I saw this, because I was sitting in a parked car right beside Josephine Kent's. . . . Well, I'd come out there from the dance floor, because I don't like to be jostled publicly. . . .

No, sir. I was not alone. . . .

Don and Josephine didn't notice me, because they did not suspect anybody would be sitting in that particular car. It belongs to the head of the Department of Household Science. She was one of our chaperons. She asked me to put her car keys in my pocket because she didn't have a pocket. Since she'd loaned me the keys, I knew she wouldn't mind if I borrowed the use of her sedan for a little while, to rest in. . . .

Can I go now? . . .

As I said, Don took the flag over to his car, which is an open job, and put it in the back, where Parker stole it. Josephine got in her coupé and started the motor. . . . Why, so her heater would work, of course. She and Don sat in there quite a while. . . .

Catching up on their loving. . . .

We couldn't see much, because the windows of Josephine's car frosted over after the heater got going. . . .

I wouldn't know about red propaganda. I'm only a Freshman. But did you ever see Josephine Kent? . . .

What's that? Would I join the Communists if Josephine asked me to? You mean, if she went to work on me the way she did on Chadwick? . . .

Boy! I'd join anything. I'd join the church. And so would you, senator. So would you.

Paul Henry, seventh witness, was dismissed with a warning that, since he appeared to be young and impressionable, he had better choose his associates with caution and seek the advice of a mature person.

Josephine Kent, spinster, aged 20, sworn.

I DO NOT KNOW the purpose of this investigation. . . .

Yes, that is a fur coat I'm wearing. I don't know what it cost. It's matched mink and fairly expensive. . . . Yes, senator. A present from my father for passing off my conditions in math. . . . I'm glad you like it. Is this what the investigation is about? The kind of fur coat I wear? . . . Sorry. I was just asking. . . .

I think I came from a good home, although the south wing doesn't heat well in very cold weather. . . .

Oh, yes. In a moral sense, I am sure you would call it a good home. We save all the old magazines for the Salvation Army truck. . . .

I never heard my father say which political party he is identified with. It's my impression he can't afford to be a member of any party. For business reasons, you understand. He sells certain supplies to the state. . . .

Oh, gasoline and lubricating oils and road oil and roofing materials. . . .

The Kent Corporation. . . . Yes, senator. I

have heard him mention your name. Something about the competitive bidding in the state purchasing agent's office, wasn't it? He said he expected you'd want your ———

Yes, of course, we must keep to the point. . . .

No, I don't vote as a member of any party. I don't vote at all. I was under the impression that I couldn't vote until I'm twenty-one. . . .

Thank you, senator. I'm glad that I look older. . . .

That's stupid of me. I'll take off the glasses and be my age. I just wear them for close work. You were saying? . . .

A red flag? . . .

Yes, I recall that red flag. At least, I recall a red flag. . . .

You see, I spent a few days in New York, and I picked up that flag as a present for a very dear friend of mine. . . .

I wanted to bring him something different, something he didn't have. You know how it is. You give a man a tie and perhaps he won't like it. Or a neck scarf. They must have dozens of neck scarfs. But I was certain he did not have a red flag. . . .

Yes, I did exact a promise from him at the same time when I gave him the flag. I'd prefer not to discuss that. . . .

I'm not just sure where I got the flag. That is, I'm not sure of the street and number. I know I'd recognize the place if I saw it again. . . .

It might have been near Union Square. I really couldn't say. . . .

A policeman questioned me about it, almost on the spot. I thought I was caught. But I smiled him off. That's why I couldn't get the rest of Don's engagement present. The officer was right there and I know I looked guilty. . . .

I admit it, senator. I had a consciousness of guilt. . . .

Of course the sign was important. . . . Yes, it explained the meaning of the flag. The whole significance. . . .

Are you trying to kid me, or what? The sign said what it naturally would say: DANGER. MEN AT WORK.

Josephine Kent, eighth and final witness, excused.

DEAR JACK: Senator Jansson is still mad and won't agree to anything. But I'm telling you that if this ever leaks out that the legislature appropriated and we spent $7500 on this investigation, you'll be out of the executive mansion. Jansson and I and the rest of us will all be working for the FERA for $24.10 a week.

Yours hastily,
SETON.

WILDFIRE

by Elsie Singmaster

ELSIE SINGMASTER GREW up among the Pennsylvania Germans, near Allentown, and has been writing stories about them since 1909. "She does not caricature or satirize," one critic has noted, "but treats her people with sympathy and deep understanding." A small, squarely built woman with bright black eyes, she now lives in Gettysburg and works in an attic studio overlooking Seminary Ridge. "Wildfire" is a story of the age-old struggle between superstition and education which still goes on in parts of Pennsylvania.

MARCH 30, 1935

MRS. KALKBRENNER rose at six o'clock, put on her clothing in the dark, took her shoes in her hand and went softly down the back stairs into the kitchen, her broad body almost filling the narrow space. She went silently—the stairs were padded with thick rag carpet—and she went carefully—her neighbor, Mrs. Lentz, who was only a little larger, had pitched head-first down a similar stairway and had to be dragged out by four strong men. Mrs. Kalkbrenner's daughter Helen, a graduate of the Teachers' College and herself a teacher, used the front stairs; Mrs. Kalkbrenner never did.

The kitchen was very cold, but to Mrs. Kalkbrenner it was not uncomfortable; in fact, the icy linoleum felt pleasant enough through her thick stockings. She snapped on the electric light, put on her shoes, donned a brown gingham allover, shook the grate of the stove, opened the lower door, adjusted the chimney draft for a quick fire, descended to the cellar and treated the furnace in the same fashion, returned and stepped into the outkitchen, whose walls were not brick, but boards. Here stood another stove, in which a fire was laid, but not lighted. She applied a match, and instantly paper and wood flamed, and now the room filled with the odor of burning kerosene in which a stick or two had been soaked. She replaced the lid, pulled over the fire box a boiler filled with water, glanced at the tubs, in one of which clothes were soaking, said, "So!" and went back to the kitchen.

From this stove issued promising murmurs and cracklings. Mrs. Kalkbrenner opened the solid door of a tall wooden cupboard painted gray and built like a secretary, in two parts. On the lower shelf of the upper section stood plates and cups and saucers; on the second, cans of coffee, oatmeal, rice, raisins, spices and other commodities. She took down the can of coffee and reached into the cupboard in the lower section for the pot.

Then, suddenly, she cocked her head; in the front room upstairs Helen was moving about. She crossed the kitchen and, taking from the wall a little mirror, moved with it under the electric bulb. Her eyes were brown, and so was her smoothly parted hair; her cheeks were full and round. She did not look at her eyes or at the parting of her hair; she looked at a red spot beside her nose. The skin was slightly raised and purplish red. She touched it with the tip of her finger—a space the size of a half dollar was hard.

She hung the mirror back on its nail, measured coffee and water into the pot, added the shell of an egg, and cooked two strips of bacon. Usually she ate four strips and two eggs, but this morning her good appetite failed her. When, fifteen minutes later, Helen came down the front steps and back into the kitchen, she called through the closed door from the outkitchen:

"I ate already. You cook you two eggs."

Helen was like her mother in being short and round-faced, but she was slender and her color was very bright. A slight frown was becoming habitual; she grieved for her father, who had died six months ago; she worried over the closing of the bank where the family funds were deposited, and the two cuts in her salary. She was constantly worried and irritated by her mother.

"What's the use of getting up to wash in the middle of the night?" she demanded, soundlessly, of the closed door. She was inaccurate—dawn was brightening the window.

In the outkitchen, Mrs. Kalkbrenner spoke also. She was enveloped in steam; it was that, she thought, which made her a little lightheaded.

"Whatever happens, one must wash and iron," she declared. "One thing I know—it's no boil. No boil would lay me so out."

Helen ate her breakfast; then she washed the dishes which her mother had left and her own; then she entered the steam-filled outkitchen. Mrs.

Kalkbrenner was rubbing on the board clothes which were not soiled. The rising sun shone through the window, gilding drops of condensed vapor.

"Don't hang the clothes outside," begged Helen.

"I always hang outside if it don't rain."

"Why, mother, what have you on your face?"

"*Ach*, just such a little outbreaking."

"It's almost zero, mother."

"I guess I have a coat and gloves and a head shawl and gums," Mrs. Kalkbrenner bent over her tub. "Let me be!" said every stroke. "Let me be!"

Helen did not close the door behind her, and Mrs. Kalkbrenner left it open. She heard Helen moving about upstairs making the two beds. She came down into the sitting room and packed fifty examination papers into her brief case. Then she put on her hat and coat before the mirror in the hatrack and pulled on her goloshes. She called good-by and went out the front door. Mrs. Kalkbrenner stepped quickly into the kitchen and through the hall into the parlor; there she peered through the curtains in the bay window, watching Helen until she turned a distant corner. Suddenly she sobbed.

Returning to her washtubs, she rubbed several garments for the second time. She rinsed, she blued, she wrung. Finally she put on her coat, her head shawl, her thick cotton gloves and her overshoes, and, opening the door, carried the basket down the icy boardwalk. The air stung her nostrils and stiffened her face.

"It's the cold," she thought. "Not that the spot gets bigger."

By eleven o'clock the clothes were frozen into a condition sufficiently dry, and she brought them in and folded them for ironing.

"If it gave something to lie on, I'd lay me a little down," she thought. Instead she slept heavily in the kitchen rocking-chair. When she woke, she tried in vain to eat. The hard space on her cheek was larger; as she placed the ironing board, she avoided looking into the mirror.

All afternoon she hoped that Annie Getzendaner would come in. Annie was a smart little woman who belonged to her church and was her best friend. But Annie did not appear. She finished ironing, put the clothes away, cleaned the ashes from the outkitchen stove, and put coal on the kitchen stove. Not until then did she look into the mirror. At what she saw she cried out, "*Gott im Himmel!*"

She went slowly upstairs, carrying a pitcher of hot water. She undressed, bathed, put on her warm nightgown and got into bed. Then she got out and opened the heavy lower drawer of her old-fashioned bureau and lifted the white cloth which covered its contents. A stranger might have thought that a dead woman lay there. Mrs. Kalkbrenner was not frightened; these were merely the underclothes, shoes and stockings for her burial. Petticoats, underbody and shoes were arranged as they would some day be on Mrs. Kalkbrenner; on top lay a pair of stockings and a folded chemise. All the undergarments were made by hand and trimmed with crocheted lace.

She pressed her palm down on the chemise. Inside lay a soft cylinder—five ten-dollar bills in a roll; her precious treasure, saved toward her coffin. Having satisfied herself that it was there, she got back into bed and drew the covers to her chin. Her face was swelling so that soon her head would be a perfect sphere. The hard space was much larger, the ghastly red was deeper and greater in area.

"Surely, Annie will come," she thought. "Surely, she'll come soon and she'll fetch her."

By "her" Mrs. Kalkbrenner did not mean Helen; she meant the powwower, Mrs. Mary Haller, a widow, famous far and wide, who could exorcise the evil spirit which had inflamed and hardened her skin and set her head throbbing and her body burning. Mrs. Haller lived at the opposite side of the city, in a three-story brick house which she had earned by exorcising evil spirits. Three times three times she laid her hand on sore joints or on a hard spot in one's side, and three times three she pronounced magic words. Her magic was not evil, it was good; each formula concluded with the names of the Trinity. Doctors hated her, some educated people laughed at her, but with her fine house filled with gifts and a bankbook filled with entries, she did not need to care what anyone thought or said. She dared ask no money, but money she received, sometimes in large amounts, and money she naturally preferred to bowls, chop plates and glass pitchers with red or yellow or green tumblers to match; even to radios and self-playing pianos, which were the gifts of fools. It was true that she had not cured the chloasma, popularly called "liver spots," which darkened large brown areas on Annie Getzendaner's little face, but she was treating her, and Annie expected a cure.

"I'll pay her good money," thought Mrs. Kalkbrenner. "Ten dollars from what I saved toward my burial." She began to mutter, "Annie! Annie!"

II

MRS. KALKBRENNER lay unpillowed on her bed. On Monday, returning from school at half past four, chilled through in spite of her youth and her warm clothing and her quick step, Helen had heard her mother muttering. Now it was Friday morning, and Mrs. Kalkbrenner's cheeks and chin were so swollen that she could not rest her head on the thinnest pillow. In narrow spaces between cloths soaked with a solution prescribed by Doctor Zinzer showed her skin, here fiery red, here purple. She was constantly drowsy and in pain; in the afternoons her temperature climbed as high as 105.

Like her mother's temperature, thought Helen, mounted Doctor Zinzer's bill and the deduction from her salary for a substitute. She could not pay a trained nurse; thus far she had nursed her mother night and day. Friends and neighbors brought food, but erysipelas was contagious and as long as she could manage alone, she would accept no further help.

In the daytime, Mrs. Kalkbrenner moaned; in the evening she muttered or called, "Annie! Annie!" as though Annie might be downstairs. Annie, Helen explained, was in Reading, nursing a sick brother. Mrs. Kalkbrenner seemed to understand, but in a moment she was calling again.

Now, well-nigh exhausted by the changing of her sheets, she drank milk through a tube. She heard Helen set a chair back against the wall and pull down the shade, and she opened one eye far enough to see Helen gathering bedding in her arms.

"You boil it good?" she asked faintly.

Even with bedding in her arms, Helen went down the front stairs. Her mother heard steps from the hall carpet on the linoleum, then she heard a thud, which she did not interpret as the falling of a human body, worn by labor and lack of sleep.

Helen had been able to let herself down to her knees; then she lay at full length. In another moment the outer door opened and a woman entered, short and thin, with a pointed nose. Her face appeared to be peeling off a summer's deep tan, brown skin and natural skin now queerly divided in area. "Good heavens, girl!" she cried, so loudly that the sound penetrated Mrs. Kalkbrenner's dull ears. "I just this minute heard about your mom."

The voice was lowered; Mrs. Kalkbrenner tried to call, but excitement paralyzed her throat. There was the click of china, the smell of coffee.

"No breakfast!" cried Annie. "Do you think you're made of iron?"

Again Mrs. Kalkbrenner tried to call. Tears scalded her eyelids. She heard quick steps climbing the stairs, crossing the matting.

Annie stood beside her bed. "My God, Sabina! I could 'a' come sooner home!"

"I thought it was all up," whispered Mrs. Kalkbrenner.

Annie bent over the bed. "Wouldn't she fetch her?"

"I didn't say anything. It would be no use."

Annie continued to bend over the bed; she was protected against contagion and other evils. "I'll get her here," she promised.

The tears dried on Mrs. Kalkbrenner's hot cheeks. Annie and Helen talked in the kitchen, but she did not try to listen; she was too heavy, too hot, too confused. "Annie!" she began to mutter, "Annie!"

Helen came into the room with a basin in her hand. Unable to endure the whole of her mother's almost obliterated countenance, she removed and replaced the cloths one at a time.

"Mother," she said, "Annie's coming this evening to stay all night."

"So?"

"She wants me to go to the third story to sleep."

Mrs. Kalkbrenner was slow about answering. Thus a prisoner, dulled by incarceration, disease and despair, might struggle to understand plans for her release. She tried to recapture the gleam of hope which she had seen, and failed. "Annie!" she called. "Annie!"

III

It was Monday night at eleven o'clock, and, her head still unpillowed, her face still swollen almost out of human semblance, Mrs. Kalkbrenner lay in bed. Round the electric bulb had been wrapped a piece of red calico, and in the dim light Annie Getzendaner, bent so that she seemed to sew with her nose, was sewing patchwork. There was no sound in the house and to this back room came no sound from the street. In the third story, Helen slept for the third night, a sleep like death.

Mrs. Kalkbrenner opened one eye. She was still confused, but she began to organize her scattering thoughts. She was in pain, there was something very much the matter with her face, she was very sick. She studied the figure under the red light; it was not Mrs. Lentz; she would be afraid to come. It was not Helen. It was brown little Annie Getzendaner! Mrs. Kalkbrenner's heart threatened to leap from her side. She was sick, perhaps dying. Doctor Zinzer could not help her, though he came daily, but Annie could bring help.

"I have the wildfire, like my mom once had," she thought. "Annie said she'd sure fetch her." She tried to speak, but her lips were stiff. She reached out and tapped the head of the bed. Instantly Annie laid down her sewing. "Will you fetch her?" murmured Mrs. Kalkbrenner.

Annie bent close. "Listen, Sabina," she whispered earnestly. "She's been twice here and tonight she'll come for the last time. You're getting better."

Mrs. Kalkbrenner turned her head a half inch and rolled her aching eyes toward the next room.

"Helen sleeps in the third story. The doctor gives her something. In the mornings I must call her, she sleeps so heavy. Soon the powwower will come, Sabina. *Ach,* she's here, Sabina!"

Annie tiptoed into the hall and down the back steps. Only intently listening ears could have heard the clicking latch of the outer kitchen door, the muttered words, the slight scraping of the iron shovel in the coal bucket, the careful steps on the back stairs. Sabina heard them all; through a narrow slit between her eyelids she watched the door. Her eyelids fluttered; she seemed to be sinking to unfathomable depths.

Mrs. Haller entered the door and crossed the room. She was tall; to Mrs. Kalkbrenner she looked gigantic. She had not taken off her coat or hat; she carried the kitchen shovel, on which was a little heap of faintly glowing coals. She placed herself on one side of the bed and Annie stood opposite. She spoke in Pennsylvania German in a deep grumble:

"Wildfire, I banish you; depart, wildfire, in the name of Father, Son and Holy Ghost."

She handed the shovel across the bed to Annie, who brought it back round the foot, and returned to her place to receive it again and once again.

Mrs. Kalkbrenner lost all sense of time and space. When she woke, Annie was sewing patchwork under the red light. She tapped on the bed and Annie bent over her.

"Couldn't you lay once a little down in Helen's room?"

"I guess I could. I'll first get your milk."

Mrs. Kalkbrenner sucked the milk through a tube. "It tastes good," she murmured. "I'm better."

"To be sure, you are!" said Annie.

IV

"I NEVER HEARD that it could come right back," said Mrs. Kalkbrenner tremulously.

She sat in the kitchen rocking-chair; Annie Getzendaner stood before the stove, carefully turning slices of breaded veal. The skin of Mrs. Kalkbrenner's round face had a yellow cast; when she bathed, shreds of skin peeled off. Nowhere was it purplish red or hot and hard to the touch. Round the waist of her dark blue calico dress was tied a white apron; she wore a becoming white collar, her hair was evenly parted and smoothly brushed. She had lost fifteen pounds, but had recovered at least five.

This was the first time in seven weeks that she had been up all day. It was true that she had not come downstairs till ten o'clock, and that Annie had come in to get dinner and look after the fires, but far as it was from her normal living, it was vastly better than lying in bed all the twenty-four hours, her flesh burning, the threat of death hanging over her.

On the window sill lay a letter addressed to Helen, left by the postman after she had gone. In the corner was printed, ARTHUR M. ZINZER, M.D.; inside was a single half sheet of paper containing a little printing and a few words and numerals. Mrs. Kalkbrenner knew what it was; she had addressed the writer in her own mind. "I didn't tell you to come," said she. No doubt Annie's sharp eyes had seen it.

Annie turned from the stove. "I knew a woman who was well a week, then it took her again. She had it first on the outside; when it came back it went through her nose in her throat and choked her. I heard of another; with her it went backwards through her hair and at the neck it struck inwards and upwards to the brain. She, too, trusted foolishly in doctors."

The possibility of a return of the erysipelas was terrifying; for the moment Mrs. Kalkbrenner could not contemplate so great a disaster. "It's still cold, if February is almost through," she remarked feebly.

Annie lifted the breaded veal to a platter and the boiled potatoes one by one into their dish.

"It's too cold for you to go and pay her," she said. "I can pay her for you."

Mrs. Kalkbrenner walked unsteadily to the table. She ate veal and potatoes and slaw and warm apple pie.

When they had finished, Annie washed the dishes and put on her hat and coat.

"I'd pay her soon," she advised. "It's a good deal over a month since she was here."

"This evening I'll have it for you," promised Mrs. Kalkbrenner. Agonized, she saw herself unfolding her chemise and extracting one of the ten-dollar bills. "What should I give her?"

"You must decide," said Annie. "She was three times here in the middle of the night in zero weather, and this isn't weak like doctor's medicine."

The day was dull, and when the door closed, it seemed as though twilight were at hand, though it was only one o'clock. Mrs. Kalkbrenner rested her head against the back of the chair; then she went slowly into the front hall and up the front steps, helping herself with both hands on the banister. She knelt on shaky knees and pulled open the heavy drawer. There lay her burial clothes, there her folded chemise. Once, Annie told her, they thought she would die in the night. What would be more natural than for Helen to see that her burial clothes were ready and what more sensible than to use her money when there was need?

She pressed her palm on the soft fabric—there was the little roll. Trembling, she lay down on the bed. At four o'clock she crept down to the kitchen, feeling chilled and terrified.

Helen came in at half-past four, running in on the boardwalk at the side of the house. She had gained none of the ten pounds she had lost and the furrows on her forehead were deepened.

"How are you, mother?" she asked anxiously, her eye instantly upon the window sill.

"So, so."

Slowly Helen took off her coat and hat, and walked into the hall and hung them on the rack. When she came back she sat down by the window and opened the envelope and took out the half sheet. She looked at it and tears came into her eyes. She looked at her mother; Mrs. Kalkbrenner's head rested against the back of her chair and her eyes were closed.

Helen put supper on the table, moving briskly, not with the natural energy of youth, but with the nervousness of exhaustion. Her cheeks were flushed; surreptitiously she wiped away tears.

"I'll get you to bed, mother; then I must run out for a few minutes. Is Annie coming back?"

Mrs. Kalkbrenner held her hand under her chin, her thumb on one side, her fingers on the other, both pressing her throat. She had the look of one choking herself. At this moment she discovered hard glands which had been in her neck since she was born.

"Yes, she is." She rose and walked swiftly toward the hall door, hers the energy of terror. Her throat felt hot and hard.

"Shall I help you, mother?"

"No."

"I'll put the key out for Annie."

Mrs. Kalkbrenner turned on the light in her room and pressed her face close to the mirror. It might be that the darkness was only the shadow of her chin, but the hard lumps were there; they were substance and not shadow. When Annie came, she lay on the bed in all her clothes with the blanket pulled over her.

"In the lower drawer, Annie, in the folded shimmy, is money."

Annie opened the heavy drawer and gathered out the little roll as a bird hooks a worm.

"Will it take all?" gasped Mrs. Kalkbrenner.

Annie counted the bills. Every patient she brought to Mrs. Haller made the cure of her liver spots more certain. "If it's the best you can do, it's all right," she said. "One of the legislatures from Harrisburg had the wildfire and he sent a grand car for her. Five hundred dollars he paid her."

"Feel here," said Mrs. Kalkbrenner.

Annie pressed Mrs. Kalkbrenner's glands. "That's nothing. By tomorrow, now that she's paid, those spots will be soft."

The latch of the kitchen door clicked and Helen came up the steps. She still wore her hat and coat; she was too happy to bear her relief alone.

"I went to see Doctor Zinzer. His bill was only fifty dollars. He was here twenty-five different days and sometimes he was here twice. I had to tell him that my salary for last month went to my substitute and to ask him to wait. He said he would. I hated to do it; he has heavy expenses. He said you made a good recovery, mother."

Mrs. Kalkbrenner glanced at Annie and Annie looked back. "She could have saved her fifty dollars," said both glances. They did not like to be hard on Helen, but she had made the foolish debt, no one else. Mrs. Kalkbrenner leaned out of bed so that she could see the lower drawer—it was safely closed.

"Yes," said Annie, "she sure did—after she got started."

LIGHTNING NEVER STRIKES TWICE

by Mary Roberts Rinehart

MARY ROBERTS RINEHART holds the all-time endurance record among *Post* authors: her first *Post* serial was "The Borrowed House," in 1909; her latest, "The Frightened Wife," was published just last year. Both were mystery stories, but murder is only one of Mrs. Rinehart's specialties. As a *Post* reporter in World War I she scored an impressive beat with her exclusive interviews with the King and Queen of the Belgians. Her "Tish" and "Sub-deb" stories were landmarks of *Post* light fiction; Letitia Carberry, the indomitable spinster of the Tish series, began her career by hunting for some lost false teeth in 1910 and ended with a visit to the coronation of George VI in 1936. In the 1920's Mrs. Rinehart even tried her hand at the "new realism" of Sinclair Lewis and Ernest Hemingway. "It was not one of my real successes," she wrote in her interesting autobiography, *My Story*. "I had to realize that my readers wanted romance or crime from me, not stark reality." But there is a good deal of reality, along with sly humor, in the following story of a wife who discovered that divorce was not such a disaster after all.

JUNE 6, 1936

CAMILLA ROSSITER WAS IN the early forties when the lightning struck her. Later on she was to wonder whether a better simile would not have been going over Niagara Falls in a barrel, but perhaps this was a mistake. One has some volition about a barrel, or at least some time to worry while it drifts along before it drops; and in her case she had had neither. So far as she could tell, everything was as usual, and then—if you like the barrel idea—suddenly she was dropping through space, and no way to stop and get out and go somewhere.

It was the unexpectedness which hurt. It had always seemed such a satisfactory marriage. At dinner parties, when someone would state that there was no such thing nowadays, someone else was sure to say, "Well, look at Camilla and Jay Rossiter." That always ended the discussion, so it could go back to Roosevelt and taxes, as usual.

Camilla herself had always thought she was a happy woman, and that things would go on as they were until the end of time. She was a simple woman, so she took that for granted. Not Jay, of course. She never took Jay for granted. Indeed, she had developed quite a pucker between the eyes from keeping him contented and watching to see if everything was all right. However, all women did that, she thought, and Jay was very much of a man. Everybody said that, too, and Camilla always remembered with a thrill the time the housemaid turned out to be a thief, and, when

discovered, locked herself in the attic with the flat silver and Camilla's wrist watch in a suitcase.

Jay was superb then. He got a hatchet from the cellar and threatened to break down the door if it wasn't unlocked at once, and when the girl came out he held her firmly until the police came. Camilla was filled with admiration for him that day, although she was just a trifle sorry for the girl, who turned out to have a sick mother, and a sweetheart who had planned the job for her. But Jay got her five years, and everybody in the courthouse was very deferential to him. This did not surprise Camilla, naturally. It was simply Jay having things the way he wanted them, as usual, and being looked up to by the community, also as usual.

She had never really got over her surprise that he had married her. He knew so many things, such as the law and how to keep the score at baseball games and what the figures meant on the financial page. She herself always felt small and unintelligent beside him, and she always blushed when they played bridge and she had to count the rule of eleven—Jay insisted on the rule of eleven—when she had to count it on her fingers.

"Any eight-year-old child could do better than that," he would say, coming home in the car.

She took it all meekly, and there were, of course, other times that made up for it. Sometimes when she was dressed for a dinner and went to see Jay give the final touches to his white tie—after throwing two or three on the floor—he would turn around in his shirt sleeves and give her a complacent glance of approval.

"You're looking very pretty, my dear," he would say, if the tie had finally tied properly. "I've got a very pretty wife." And he would look at her not only with approval but with a faint surprise, as though he had just remembered her.

She was still pretty in an anxious sort of way at forty-two, and when the lightning struck. She had never cut her hair, because Jay hated short-haired women, and in the evenings she wore a good bit of pale blue, because he liked it. She loathed it herself. It made her feel obliterated, so to speak. But she wore it, although other women were wearing strong colors that year.

"How quaint, Camilla!" they would say, and she would shiver inside.

But she was pretty and appealing, and on the way home, if they had not played cards and Jay reached over and took her hand, she would wonder what other women saw in the men they had selected, and would look like anything but a woman with a married daughter and Jay, Junior, at college.

It had never occurred to her that she was submerged, as J. J.—short for Jay, Junior—put it later. It seemed quite natural to her that Jay's clothes took most of her closet space as well as the closet-like space he called his dressing room, and to order only the food he liked.

"We might have onion soup," she would say to the cook in the morning. "Mr. Rossiter likes it." Or: "Do have the roast very rare. Mr. Rossiter said the last one was overdone." And that night she would dutifully eat her onion soup, although it gave her indigestion, or play with the rare meat which sickened her, and Jay would sit back at the end of the meal and light a cigarette and glance comfortably at her across the candles.

"Very nice dinner, my dear," he would say, his handsome square-jawed face relaxed and contented. Then he would look around the dining room, at its well-polished silver on the sideboard, at the shining old mahogany, at the low flowers on the table—he liked them low, so he could see Camilla when he talked to her—and last of all at Camilla. And she would know what was in his mind—that this fastidious living, these flowers and candles, the neat waitress in her black and white, and perhaps even Camilla herself, were the proof to him that he was a man in a world of men, and successful beyond most of them. When the dinner had been particularly Jay-ish, he would put his arm around her as they went out.

"Pretty good little housekeeper, aren't you?" he would say.

"I aim to please," she would answer demurely, and feel very happy although rather undernourished.

It had never occurred to her that between the hours of nine A.M. and six P.M.—except, of course, on Sunday—she knew nothing about him at all. As to his being Jay-ish, it was Jay, Junior, who had coined it. To J. J. his father was Jay-ish when he came home after a good game of golf, or had won a case, or descended the stairs in his evening clothes, very impeccable, and stood erect in the hall while Gertrude put him into his overcoat and handed him his hat and gloves. Long afterward Camilla remembered the first time she had heard the word.

"Jay-ish?" she said. "Why, J. J., what on earth do you mean?"

"Complacent," he said, grinning at her. "Good looking. Prosperous. Smug. Center of the world. That sort of thing."

"That's unkind, J. J. He is a good father to you, and you know it."

"Sure he is," said J. J. "I forgot that. Good looking, good lawyer, good husband, good father. Mother, doesn't it pall on you?"

"Never," said Camilla firmly. "And if this is what you learn at college ——"

There were actually tears in her eyes, and J. J. saw that he was tearing down something she had built up over quite a number of years, and kissed her.

"After all," he said cheerfully, "he's Jay-ish twenty-four hours a day, but you've only got it evenings and Sundays. It's a break for you."

"You talk as though you hadn't any proper feeling for him."

"Good Lord, mother! Of course I have. It's only—well, I'm fond of you in my own way"—he grinned at her—"and I'd like to see you being something more than the accompaniment while he sings."

"That's nonsense," said Camilla firmly. "He knows more than I do. If I defer to that ——"

"Oh, hell," said J. J. "You know a lot he never heard of. Let's stop this. Who started it anyhow?"

She put that conversation out of her mind. Life was a fixed and definite thing. When one day she found a few gray hairs in the mass which Jay had refused to let her cut, she accepted them as she accepted the fact that the clothes nowadays went on over the head, so that one dressed and then had to do one's hair, which was always awkward, and sometimes almost impossible when that hair was long. But Jay did not like them. He came in one night when she was brushing her hair under the hard light of her dressing table and stood staring down at them.

"Don't tell me you're getting gray, Camilla."

"We're not children any more, Jay-dear."

He stood behind her for a moment, looking first at her and then at himself in the mirror. His face was rather like the face she had seen when he stood outside Mary's door with the hatchet, or like whoever it was—Camilla was vague on history—who had commanded the waves to stand still, or the tide to come in, or something. Then he bent down and examined his own head, which showed no gray at all.

"We're certainly not old," he said stiffly, and straightened himself, as though—instead of the tide or waves, or whatever it was—it was time itself he was defying. Something about his attitude and his voice roused what little spirit he had left her, and perhaps she was a trifle malicious when she said in her soft voice:

"It's queer that you haven't any. You are eight years older."

"Seven and a half," he said shortly, and turned and went out of the room.

There was a change in him after that. Nothing you could put a finger on. Camilla, having accepted her graying hair, which was rather beautifying than otherwise, forgot all about it. But Jay began to play more golf than usual, and one day he sent home a scale and had it installed in his bathroom. After that she could hear him moving the weights in the mornings after his bath, and one day he ordered no fattening foods at dinner, and she and the cook went almost frantic trying to feed him well without butter or sugar or starch. Camilla almost starved during that period, and quite often the look he cast around the dining room after dinner was more nearly a glare. But he did lose weight, and if Camilla lost it, too, he did not notice.

"Down to a hundred and seventy-five," he said one day. "I'll bet I could wear the clothes I was married in."

Camilla's wedding dress would have hung on her, but she said nothing, and some time later she heard him rummaging about. When he came down, he had on his ancient morning coat—he still had it; he kept all his old clothes—and by letting out all his breath he could button it.

"Perfect fit," he said. "Another couple of months and I'll be back to my weight in college."

He was so boyish about it that she smiled, although another couple of months of the diet and she would have to stand twice to make a shadow. He did look younger, however, although that did not worry her. He was faithful to her. She knew that, although it was a long time since, unless she coughed, he had really known that she was in the next bed.

"It's a dirty game," he would say. "This thing of giving your wife a diamond bracelet out of remorse as a peace offering! Besides ———"

"What, Jay?"

"Well, a man's a fool to let himself in for that sort of trouble. I see enough of it in my business."

Not a sign of the lightning then. A clear sky and the sun by day, and the stars by night. Onion soup—not fattening—and rare roast beef and raw wild ducks that turned Camilla's stomach in the shooting season. Jay eating an apple every night before he went to bed and taking a liver pill Wednesdays and Saturdays. New clothes to fit his new figure and still nothing to give to the Thrift Shop. An occasional check to Milla, who was going to have a baby, but a slight sense of grievance at her, as though by so doing she had played him an unfriendly trick. Otherwise no clouds in the sky, save for now and then a week end out of town on business, and a Monday morning grouch as a result.

If the week ends gradually increased, she did not notice it. When he was about, she catered to him, and when he was away she thought of him. There were one or two mental pictures of him that she particularly cherished. One of them, of course, was the day they were married in her father's garden. They had built an altar there, and, what with the rector in full canonicals and the assistant rector and the women's dresses and the garden flowers, the scene had been most impressive. Only, in the very middle of things, a bee had tried to settle on Jay's handsome nose, and he had to slap at it. Over and over, it came back, and at the end he looked faintly dazed; as though he had hardly known he was being married at all. And another was the time they were riding together, and his horse had thrown him in the middle of a creek. He had merely sat there, looking surprised, and he had been furious when she laughed. He had never ridden since.

There were one or two others. She did not know why she remembered them, but probably it was because they reduced him to the level of common humanity.

There were other memories, of course; very sacred ones, such as the evening after Milla's wedding, and something he had said then. J. J. had gone back to school, and the house was fairly orderly once more. The caterer's men had taken away the gilt chairs for the reception, the furniture was in place again, and except for the odor of the flowers—which smelled like a funeral—it might have been any evening. She had taken off her blue taffeta dress and put on something loose, and was slipping her feet into low-heeled slippers when Jay came into the room.

"Well, that's over, thank God," he said. "I've been looking at the presents. She got a lot, didn't she?"

"More than she can use."

"Well, after all, why not?" he demanded. "We've given enough. And we count in the community. Why fool ourselves about that? If a man does his best, it's bound to tell in the end."

J. J. would have called that Jay-ish, she thought. Nothing about her. Nothing about Milla and her joyous youth. But she dismissed that as *lèse-majesté*, and he surprised her then by putting an arm around her.

"Just you and me now, my dear," he said. "We'll have to stick pretty close, won't we?"

And she had turned her face up to him as a sunflower—or almost any other flower, or vegetable, too, for that matter—to the sun, and her eyes had filled with tears.

"I've been so frightfully happy with you, Jay," she said huskily. "I was sitting here, thinking about our own wedding. Do you remember? And the bee?"

He looked bewildered.

"What bee?" he said. "What's a bee got to do with it?"

II

IT WAS a year after Milla's marriage that he told her one night that he would like the divorce. Just like that. Just the way he would ask for a clean handkerchief. "D'you mind getting me a handkerchief, Camilla?" It would have been easier, possibly, if he had shouted, as he did when the studs were not in his dress shirt or the car was late. But not at all. He stood very calmly on the rug in front of the library fire, and looked exactly the way he used to look when J. J.'s school report was bad.

"You and I must talk this over, J. J. If you think I'm going to pay good money for your education and let you throw it away ——"

It was rather like lightning, and he stood like Jove, or whoever it was, pitching his thunderbolt. For there had been no preliminaries at all. They had been out to dinner and, so far as she could remember, he had eaten a normal meal and afterward had played a normal game of bridge. In the car, coming home, he had been rather quiet; but then, he often was quiet unless he was telling her, without rancor, where she had thrown away a game here or there.

Actually, she had thought he looked more than usually handsome that night; and sitting back in her corner of the car, she had glanced now and then at his fine profile. The only thing unusual she had noticed was that he had said nothing about her dress, which was new and, of course, pale blue.

"What? Another blue dress?" Milla had said when she saw it. "Why in the world don't you let me go with you when you get your clothes? Blue again, for heaven's sake!"

"Your father likes it, Milla."

Milla, however, had gone rather silent after that.

So, leaning back in the car, she thought of Milla. She had her baby now, a little thing with tremendous lungs, but very sweet for all that. Camilla did not feel like a grandmother, but there it was, and Jay had said that they would have to stick pretty close. Well, they were doing it. She felt warm and happy, but she knew better than to put that feeling into words, so she slipped her hand into his and he held it for a moment. Then he let it go, and the next moment he was looking at the back of the chauffeur's head—only a dark silhouette ahead of them—and saying:

"Why on earth don't you tell Smith he needs a haircut?"

There was no way of knowing then that Smith needed a haircut, but that was like Jay. He would see something and take note of it, and then bring it out when nobody expected it. Which was precisely what happened when they reached the house. He turned into the library and stood there while she slipped off her evening coat in the hall, and she was surprised to hear him say, through the open door:

"Do you mind coming in for a few minutes, Camilla?"

"I'd better heat your milk first."

A glass of hot milk at night had been a part of his diet, and he still kept it up. But he did not want it, it appeared.

"Hot milk?" he said, with an edge to his voice. "I tell you I have something important to say, and you babble about hot milk."

From his voice, one would have gathered that Camilla's habit was to babble, but she was accustomed to things of that sort.

"In a second," she said, and stood for just about that instant of time in front of the hall mirror, smoothing her hair. What she saw was really very nice, and certainly slim enough, in all conscience, and she felt pretty and almost young when she turned away and went in. And Jay looked at her with eyes that never saw her at all, and said:

"Camilla, I don't want to hurt you, but I'd better say this and get it over."

"Say what, Jay?"

"I want a divorce."

Just like that. No preamble. No explanation. A clean surgical cut and then it was all over. Or was it? For she was merely looking bewildered.

"Are you joking?" she asked uncertainly.

"Do I look as though I am joking?"

She looked at him then. In the firelight he appeared much as usual—as though what he wanted was not a divorce at all, but his clothes sent to the cleaner's. His voice was odd, however, so she took a long breath and said:

"I see. You want a divorce. But what for? I don't ——"

"What does any man want a divorce for?" he said impatiently. Then it dawned on her.

"You're not telling me you want to marry again? At your age! I don't believe it."

"I'm not Methuselah!"

Her chief feeling was one of intense amazement. Perhaps she would suffer later. She supposed women did suffer over things like this. She even supposed that Jay had expected her to faint —which she had never done—or to go into hysteria. All she did, however, was to sit down and try to stop the queer feeling that her brain was whirling inside her skull.

"Then there is another woman?" she managed to say.

"What do you think I'm telling you?"

"And—you're in love with her?"

"Do we need to go into that?"

She did not speak at once. She sat in her chair, looking up at Jay on the hearthrug and trying to see him as the chief figure of some great passion, a man capable of tragedy and pain, ready to cast the world away for love. All she saw, however, was Jay, who wore holes in the heels of his socks and took a liver pill on Wednesdays and Saturdays and liked his breakfast eggs turned.

The first words she said were apparently inconsequential:

"I suppose it's Milla's baby."

"Don't be an idiot. What has Milla's baby to do with it?"

"It made you a grandfather."

"It didn't make me senile. Look here, Camilla; if this is the way you are going to treat a serious thing, a vital thing ——"

"Oh, don't orate, Jay," she said wearily. "If you want a divorce, you'll get it. You always get what you want."

He looked as if a pet canary had turned and bitten him.

"I had hoped you'd be reasonable about this thing, Camilla. After all, you're a sensible woman. As to getting what I want, you've always had what you wanted, haven't you?"

She got up. Her long blue dress trailed about her and hid her shaking knees.

"I've always had what you wanted me to have. There's a difference," she said carefully. "I suppose you have it all worked out, so why discuss it? And I suppose we'll do the conventional thing too. You'll sleep in your dressing room tonight, and tomorrow you'll go to the club. I'm rather inexperienced in such matters, but that's usual, isn't it?"

He stared at her. This was not the Camilla he knew at all. She was letting him go lightly, easily, without a struggle. It hurt his pride, and it demanded assuagement.

"It isn't," he said, "as though I really meant anything to you. I haven't meant anything to you for years."

And to her eternal credit, she used what amounted to her last breath to move to the door, and pausing there, to throw a barb instead of a sop.

"I wouldn't say that, Jay," she said gently. "You've supported me."

Then she went out of the room, leaving him staring after her as though he had never seen her before.

He was still astounded when, having put out the lights, he went upstairs that night. He was loaded with words, things he had meant to say to her. Kindly things, of course, such as still being fond of her and intending to see that she was well provided for. Even an explanation or two, such as the immorality of two people living together after they had grown apart, and also just how she had lost him, and so on. He liked things clean-cut and in the open. He had the exact amount of her alimony fixed in his mind as he climbed the staircase.

Unluckily, Camilla had shut her door and locked it, and was inside along with all his pajamas and his dressing gown. He stalked into his dressing-room, so-called, and surveyed it with distaste, but at last he went to the mirror and surveyed himself. What he saw was a man going through hell for the sake of his first real love; a tired man, but certainly not Methuselah; a man worn with the struggle of supporting a wife who did not appreciate him and two children who simply used him as a source of signed checks.

Then very carefully he took out his wallet and extracted from it the picture of a youngish woman on a horse. She held what was apparently a cocktail glass in her hand, and there was the tail of a hound in the immediate foreground.

He refused to get out his glasses to see it properly, but he knew it by heart anyhow. Dear Mae. Darling, gay, high-spirited Mae. All that money, and unspoiled. A child of Nature and the open fields.

As a sudden afterthought, he remembered his riding boots, which he had not used for years, and looked about for them. But they, too, like his pajamas, were in Camilla's room, and Camilla had locked her door and gone into the silence. Reluctantly he put away the picture, and crawling into the bed, which was too short for him, prepared to sleep in his skin; an outraged figure which grew cold toward morning and practically forgot the great passion in a severe attack of gooseflesh. He had no idea where the blankets were kept, but at daylight he wandered stealthily along the hall, searching for the closet, and it was Gertrude who, coming down early with a toothache, caught a glimpse of him there and fled with a squeal.

That settled it; and when, having ascertained that the hall was clear again, he crept back to his dressing room, he merely took a hot bath to warm himself, and, having dressed and shaved, proceeded to pack what he could find. True, most of the things he wanted were in Camilla's room, but she had apparently had a warm and comfortable night and was still sleeping.

Before going, however, he left a note for her. It began without preamble:

I am going to the country for a couple of weeks and shall need the usual things. Please send suitcase to club.   J. R.

P. S.: Also my riding boots.

Camilla was apparently still sleeping when he left, and Gertrude failed to appear. The cook served his breakfast and had forgotten to turn his eggs, and he left his home for the last time like almost anything but a great lover. Nor were things better at the club. His room looked exactly like all the other rooms, and when he had time— it was still early—to realize that he had taken his first step toward his life's real happiness, he found it extremely hard to think about it at all. The situation was not improved by the discovery that he wore one black and one blue sock and had no others with him, and, all in all, the only passion observable in the Jay Rossiter who stalked into his law office at 8:30 that morning and found his secretary sitting on his desk chewing gum was one of pure fury.

He sent out for a pair of socks and looked over his mail. Then he got a long-distance number in the hunting country in Virginia, feeling quite sure

that the operator at his switchboard was listening in, and held a brief conversation with a lady obviously just roused from sleep.

"Is that you, Mae?" he said with dignity.

"Darling! But what an hour! I've just gone to bed."

"Sorry," he said stiffly. "I just called to say that it's all right. I'll take the night train."

"Darling! I can't believe it. Was it terrible?"

"Not at all," he said. "Some details still to be arranged, but that's all."

The telephone operator took off her earphones and looked at the office boy.

"I win," she said briefly. "She's got him."

"Holy mackerel!" said the office boy, and reluctantly produced a quarter from his pocket.

III

BACK AT THE HOUSE, Camilla lay, still stunned, in her bed. She had a feeling that her world had suddenly shot her off into space and that she was whirling there alone. She had not slept all night, and when she heard Jay slam out of the house, she got up and looked at herself in the mirror, as though she had to reorient herself among the world of the living. What she saw was not comforting—a woman who had lost her girlishness overnight, and whose swollen eyes looked out from a blotched and certainly fortyish face.

She crawled back into her bed. On the next one lay Jay's pajamas, and she wondered briefly how he had slept without them. On a chair was his silk dressing gown, and beneath it his slippers. It seemed incredible that he was not inside them, shouting to know what had happened to the hot water, or why the devil the laundress couldn't learn to do his shirts. And she wished now that she knew something about the other woman, so that she could have something to hate.

That was the most cruel thing of all. She had nobody to hate. She could form no mental picture at all. She could not see Jay with his arms around anything but empty space.

She ran over all the women she knew. Jay had shown no interest in any of them, so far as she knew. Most of them bored him almost to violence.

"Lot of empty-headed fools," he would say. "All they want is a man to support them, clothes and dancing and night clubs. Exhibitionists, too, showing as much of their bodies as they dare. Indecent exposure, that's what it is."

No, it would be none of them. It would be some brilliant woman, a woman with brains who would further his ambitions. She herself had not been clever. All she had done was to try to make him comfortable. It was, however, very difficult to visualize a woman's brains. She remembered a picture in her schoolbooks long ago, showing a head with queer convolutions inside it, but, outside of that, all she could remember was the calves' brains at the butcher's shop, and Jay had never allowed them in the house.

She cried now and then, but she was too stunned for many tears. She felt weak, as though she had had a long illness, and when Milla called up the next morning to report on the baby, she could hardly lift the telephone. The baby, it appeared, was fine and had gained six ounces. For just a moment she hated the baby, because of what it had done to her.

"That's fine. Your father's gone away, Milla."

"On a trip? Well, take a good rest, darling," said Milla, and hung up.

She lay back resenting that. Why did both J. J. and Milla think that life had been difficult with their father? As though she needed a rest. As though he was not the very pattern of her life. She could have lost a leg, she thought grimly, and missed it less.

The house was very still, as though there had been a death in it. Did the servants suspect, she wondered? Were they shut in the pantry now, whispering together? She lay back, her long hair loose on the pillow, and wondered how she was to get Jay out of the house. All those clothes of his, she thought wearily. His desk and the papers in it. His golf clubs and his pipes and the humidor for his cigars. Even his bed. His bed would have to go.

It seemed terrible, now that she had lain in her own for twenty years and tried to shut out the sound of his eating his nightly apple. Even with a hand over an ear and the other ear buried, she could hear it crunching. It seemed silly, too, for her to have resented his refusal to let her read in bed. What did that matter? What did anything matter but that he was gone?

It was only later, when the full significance of his note dawned on her, that she began rebuilding the woman in the case from this new angle. Boots. She rode. She was a big angular woman who rode horses and played good golf. Jay would ride, and that would keep his stomach down. But Jay hated horses. What strange things love did to a man! And with the thought of Jay being in love with another woman the tears came, and she began to cry again.

Afterward she thought she had wept for weeks. Milla came and sat in the dark room, going now and then for a fresh handkerchief for her and telling her not to be so silly.

"After all, mother," she said, "it isn't as though you were old, you know. Why don't you get yourself a boy friend and step out a little?"

"How can you talk like that, Milla?"

Milla moved impatiently.

"You make me sick, both of you," she said in her brisk young voice. "You're incurable sentimentalists, both you and father. Father gallivanting around with a love affair at his age, and you mourning like a sick dove! If you could see yourselves! You're like a picture of the 90's."

Camilla passed that over for what was the real question in her mind, so real that she sometimes felt that it was burning a hole there.

"But who is it, Milla? Who is it?"

Milla, however, was as much in the dark as she was. "He's been mighty secretive about it, whoever she is," she said. "Of course, he always was secretive."

"Not with me."

Milla laughed.

"Most of all with you, darling."

It wasn't that Milla was not sorry for her, she knew, but, like all her generation, Milla was a realist. You made your life with a man or you didn't. In case you didn't, you merely began all over again; with another man, if possible. It didn't bother you to see his shaving brush—which Jay had forgotten—or the chair he always sat in, or his empty bed. You simply got rid of them and went out and got a new permanent or a new hat or a new husband, and started again.

J. J., however, was different. He came home, when Milla sent for him, in a white heat of anger, and confronted his mother, pale with indignation.

"The old fool!" he said. "The old fool! After the way you've submerged yourself all your life for him!" He was proud of that word, for all his fury. "Who is this woman, anyhow?"

"I don't know."

"Well, I'll know, and darned quick. Mind you, I don't want him back. He can go, and be damned to him. But he's got to look after you. I'll make him pay through the nose, if it's the last thing I do on earth."

"I don't want his money, J. J."

"Well, you're going to get it anyhow."

She felt less lost with J. J. around the house, slamming doors and sitting across the table from her at meals. She fed him roast beef medium and no onion soup whatever, and when she mended his socks, it was comforting to find that he wore them out at the toes instead of the heels. She wondered dully sometimes whether, after all, it was really Jay she missed, or merely a man about the house.

He was out a good bit, however, and one day he disappeared and was gone for twenty-four hours. Then one evening he came home and, standing tall and indignant in front of her, told her that he had got what he called the dope.

"She's a widow," he said. "He's been settling her estate for her, and there's a lot of it to settle. I gather she fell hard for him the minute she saw him, and she's done most of the courting. Her name's Barker, if that interests you, and her first name is Mae. Get that, mother. M-a-e."

She sat very still, trying to see Jay calling another woman "Mae." Dearest Mae. Mae darling. My own Mae. It was too bad that she knew the very words he would use. They were all in his old letters to her upstairs. It was too bad that she should know exactly how he would put a strong well-cared-for finger under this Mae's chin and tilt her face for a kiss. It was too bad that he still had no secrets whatever from her. But J. J. was still talking. The Barker woman had a house in Newport and a place in Virginia where she hunted. She was there now, having a house party.

"You know, mother. Ride all day and drink all night. And in the morning they ring a bell and everybody goes back to the room where he belongs."

"Please, J. J."

Anyhow, it appeared that his father was there now and—still according to J. J.—it would do no harm if he fell off a horse at a fence and broke his neck. She looked up incredulously.

"He is hunting? Are you sure?"

"Saw him myself," he said, grinning. "Hid in the corner of a field, trying to look like a rabbit, and he darned near went over me. If ever I saw a man scared when he took that jump ——"

"But he did take it," she said, not without pride.

"Sure he took it. He had to. The horse did, and he had to go along."

That indeed was J. J.'s idea of the whole situation. Mae apparently was taking the fences and Jay was going along. It did not sound like him, but then men do queer things when they set out to prove to themselves that they are as young as ever they were. J. J., however, held out no hope. Mae had money and, in his vernacular, was pretty glamorous into the bargain. She had Jay in a bag, and the thing to do was to forget the whole mess and begin again.

She thought that over later on. Begin again! How did one begin again? She tried to see a strange man in the house, a sort of hypothetical husband, but she shivered at the thought. It had taken her twenty-odd years to know Jay, and then it turned out that she had never known him at all. Twenty-odd years of onion soup and rare beef and watching Jay at bridge when she played

a hand. He had a way of leaning back and glancing around the room when she made a misplay, as though his very eyes could not endure the torture to which she was subjecting him. As to a strange man eating an apple in the other bed, or later on snoring loudly ——

She felt a fresh pang of homesickness at that. So many nights she had known that he was there, safely beside her, because only a completely deaf woman could have doubted it for a second.

One thing she could do, and, after that talk with J. J., she did it at once. She got Jay out of the house. She packed innumerable trunks and suitcases with those old garments of his and sent them to his club. Then, with the first real closet room she had had since her marriage, she sat down and simply waited for the next step.

She had, however, a faintly malicious feeling when she learned that Milla was going to have another baby. Let Jay ride all he wanted and jump fences if he could. He was more and more a grandfather. . . .

Jay was indeed jumping fences at that time. Mae had no use for men who didn't hunt, so, every day when he turned in his horse, he prayed that it would die in the night.

It never did, however, so he would follow the field, letting the brute go where it wanted; and on coming in, he would put his stiff bones in a long hot bath and take ten grains of aspirin, and dress the part of the great lover for the evening, with arms and legs so stiff that he could hardly get into his trousers.

Not that great lovers were in any real demand in Mae's establishment, he discovered. There was no time. Either one was risking sudden death outside or one was drinking in a crowd, or eating the same way, or playing bridge for high stakes until God knows when. But Mae was a great girl. She was a wonder, and after marriage she would settle down. She was easy to get along with too. She did not seem to mind if, in the middle of telling her what a great girl she was, he suddenly yawned.

"Poor old darling!" she would say. "Go on up and take a nap."

"Nonsense! I don't want a nap."

Now and then they went into the ballroom and danced. Jay had been a good dancer, but now his knees were always stiff and—while he preferred standing up to sitting down—he sat out quite a few dances. Mae would drag him out, however, and for a few minutes, as he held her, he would see himself as young and gay and deeply in love. It never occurred to him that in some ways Mae was merely a younger edition of

Camilla, plus a faint odor of the stables and an ability to stay up all night and be fresh as paint the next morning; and that what he was actually doing was setting the clock back ten years. Or the calendar, or what have you.

Mae was loving enough, of course, when she had to be, but there were always people around, or servants. One fell over servants in every corner, and, like the house party, they seemed never to go to bed. And she was proud of him. She never got over being proud of him.

"Let me look at you, darling. You're so wonderful to look at. I wish these people would go, and leave us alone."

They would go, of course, but it always turned out that there were others coming. The beds never really got a chance to cool off. It was hardly decent, he sometimes thought. And after the first week, he actually got to dreading her knock on his door in the early morning, when he had just settled down and his bed had stopped taking fences.

"Get up, darling. It's a perfect morning for a ride."

He would get up, hurrying as fast as his stiffened muscles would let him, and after a while it would be fine to be riding beside Mae on some country trail, knowing how much she loved him and how well she understood him. Not that she always did what he wanted. One day he told her he would like to see her in a pale blue evening dress, and she said that was the only time he had shown his age.

It was about that time that he began to feel slightly bilious, and to take bicarbonate of soda at odd moments. But he stayed—stayed until, his law partner having made the arrangements, Camilla had started for Reno. Then he went back to town, to his dreary room at the club and a Turkish bath or two to get the alcohol out of his system.

Camilla was still on the train while he lay in the hot room—a Camilla cheered on by J. J. and Milla, but a Camilla who felt as though life had ended at forty-two and had a faint hope that the train would fall off a trestle.

"Good-by, mother. And don't be silly."

"Good-by, darlings. I'm all right. I'm perfectly all right."

Nothing happened to the train, however; and after she grew accustomed to it, Reno was not so bad. Was quite gay, indeed. Most of the people she met were excited and pleased about being free again and starting life all over. Of course, they had not been married to Jay, but still, there it was. They seemed to have no idea of everything being over. Quite a lot of them intended to remarry at once, which made her shiver. But quite a lot of them liked her, and even admired her looks and her clothes.

She was surprised, too, to find that they thought her bridge was very good; and she learned to knit. She would sit in the lobby of the hotel in the evenings, knitting an afghan for the new baby, and watch the gaiety going on around her. But she did not join in it. She still felt too much like an extracted tooth, and there were nights in her room upstairs when the very silence wakened her out of a sound sleep, as though Jay had stopped snoring and might be dead. She would find herself sitting up and listening, with her heart pounding.

Otherwise she supposed everything was as well as might be. She had some money of her own, and Jay was ready to pay substantial alimony. But she had nothing to think of and very little to hope for. One day, on impulse, she walked into a beauty shop and had her hair cut off and a permanent wave put in. Then she went utterly berserk and had a facial and bought some rouge and a lipstick. She had never used rouge before, and the very pallid lipstick of the Jay days had always been hidden among her handkerchiefs.

That night she made up her face—very delicately, of course—and hardly knew herself in her mirror. Her eyes, however, were still rather like those of a dead fish, and when she looked at her hands, the left one looked almost naked without her wedding ring. The finger had shrunk under it, as happens in such cases, and she herself felt shrunken.

One day a very nice man named Browning asked her if she would take a drive and have dinner somewhere. She went, but she felt, somehow, that it was highly improper. He was very quiet, however, and she ended by enjoying it. She slept that night, too, what with the fresh air and having eaten more because there was someone across the table. She had always hated eating alone.

After that they often drove, and one day he asked her if she thought that two halves could ever make a whole again. It was some time before she understood what he meant. Then she colored and said "No," very firmly.

He eyed her.

"It's as bad as that, is it?" he said. "What a rotten married life you must have had!"

"Not at all. I was perfectly happy until ——"

She cried then, and he drew her head down on his shoulder and patted her. That, however, reminded her of Jay when they were first married, and did not help a great deal; and Mr. Browning, whose first name was Ted, had a queer look in his ugly, kind face when he let her go.

"The human heart is a damned nuisance, isn't it?" he said, and hummed softly to himself on the way back.

She went home soon after that. The proceedings had taken only a few minutes, and on the way back in the train she tried to realize that she was free again. She did not feel any more free, however, than an amputated leg, and when Milla met her at the station and admired her hair and her clothes and made a quite unusual fuss over her, she felt a little sick at her stomach. At the house, her room looked empty and bare without Jay's bed, and she found herself staring at the place where it had stood. Like running a tongue into the place where a tooth has just gone, she thought drearily.

"Now, please, mother!" said Milla. "Stop looking like that. Just remember that you're free, white and forty, and better looking than you've ever been."

"Forty-two," said Camilla with her devastating honesty. "All right, darling. I'll try to forget and start again, although just what I am to start ——"

"Start living," said Milla. "You never have lived, have you?"

All of which was well enough, save that Jay would not let himself be forgotten just then. The wedding had been announced, and that very day there was a news picture of Mae in an ermine coat entering the Metropolitan, and a piece of an overcoat beside her which presumably was Jay. But Mae still had no reality to Camilla, and as time went on she remained merely a newspaper picture surrounded, according to the press, by orchids, horses, butlers, footmen, limousines and people. Hundreds of people. Thousands of people. After her simple fashion, Camilla sometimes wondered just when Jay was doing his courting. Which was not unlike what Jay himself was thinking at the time.

It was during that interval that Camilla developed a sort of psychosis. This was that people had only liked her because of Jay, and that now nobody cared about her. As a result, there was a long blank when she went nowhere and saw nobody, and when she slipped bleakly into the comfortable ways of lonely women. She no longer had to get up for breakfast with Jay, so she had a tray in bed and the morning paper. Jay had always read it at the table before, and, as often as not, had carried it downtown with him also. And she avoided every contact with the past. When Milla's new baby came, she stayed in the hospital until it was over, and then had a nurse telephone Jay. He came up, but she was gone before he arrived, so that was all right.

It was a day or two later that Milla said, quite suddenly:

"Father looks dreadful. He's jaunty. Good Lord, how jaunty! It would make you sick! But he looks dreadful!"

Camilla felt as though a hand had clutched at her heart.

"What do you mean, dreadful? Not sick, Milla?"

"Sick of her. Sick of the whole mess, if you ask me. He's too old," she said, with the brutal callousness of youth. "He gets up early in the morning and rides in the park with her; he works all day at the office; and I'd like to bet he hasn't been in bed at a respectable hour for six months. It's written all over him. He can't sit still. He can hardly sit at all, for that matter. If ever a man hated the thought of a horse, he's it."

"He must like her." She tried to make her voice casual.

But Milla was not even sure of that. She had gathered a surprising amount of information about Mae. How she hated being alone and had a party or went somewhere every night. How she had a book with sketches of her clothes, so she could look at it and decide what to wear. How she had a secretary to seat her dinners, and a sunken bath tub, and even how her bed was on a dais and had peach-colored curtains falling from a gilt crown on the wall.

"I'd love to see him in it," she said vindictively. "What do you bet he wants them baby blue?"

Camilla was scandalized.

"No matter what he has done," she said primly, "he is still your father."

"That's your fault, not mine, mother dear," said Milla wickedly.

The last thing she heard Milla say as she left was that Mae had a mean temper, and, glory, how she would like to see the first real fight. But Camilla went home very anxious. She wanted Jay to be happy. She had never really felt bitter about him; all she had had was a sense of failure, that she had not held him. Now she was anxious. She went into the house, where the front door never slammed now when he came home in a bad humor and where nobody shouted because there was a button off a shirt, and, stopping in front of the hall mirror, inspected herself.

Just so had she stopped that night when he had called her into the library and told her that he wanted a divorce. She had wanted to get his hot milk, but he had not given her a chance. He had not even broken the thing to her gently.

She had gone in, in that sickening pale blue dress, and he had dismissed her. Like a servant.

Suddenly she was angry—angry and affronted. She threw up her head, and, walking into the library, picked up the first cigarette of her life and deliberately lighted it. It nearly choked her, but it was at last a gesture of defiance for Jay— as definite as though she had put her thumb to her nose at him.

IV

JAY was to be married in a week or two, when one day she met him face to face in a downtown hotel. Ted Browning had come to town and asked her to lunch with him, and—still carrying the flag—she bought herself a new hat and tucked an orchid or two in her furs and went to meet him. She looked very pretty and surprisingly young that day. Not because she was meeting Ted, but because the whole thing really was rather like going over Niagara Falls in a barrel. Nothing could stop it now. And all at once Jay was in front of her, holding out his hand and saying:

"Aren't you going to speak to me, Camilla?"

She was so shaken that she trembled. Part of it was shock, of course, as though the barrel had hit a rock. All the memories that lay between them, for one thing—the big ones and the little ones—the onion soup, and the day Milla was born and he'd wanted a boy, and the fuss when the roof leaked, and the time J. J. was almost drowned and they'd had to roll him over the bottom of a boat. But the rest was sheer surprise, for what she remembered about him—and she remembered plenty—had little to do with this dapper individual who looked all his age, and more, and who was staring down at her as though she was somehow strange to him.

"I'm sorry. I didn't see you."

He had her hand now and was holding on to it. A sort of desperate clutch, she thought, although he was smiling and there was a fresh carnation in his buttonhole.

"You're looking wonderful," he said, eying her. "I don't know when I've seen you looking so well."

"Thanks. I'm splendid."

But there was a curious look on his face; and suddenly she realized what it was. He had thought of her all this time as wan and grieving for him, and now, seeing her as she was, he was shocked and astounded. She smiled again, conscious of her new hat, her short hair, her general air of smartness and well-being. Smiled and released her hand.

"I've got to go," she said cheerfully. "I'm lunching with a man, if I can find him."

"A man?" he said sharply. "What man?"

"Good gracious," she thought, "he's being Jay-ish again. I'm glad the children aren't here." She was quite calm on the surface, however, and she looked him straight in the eyes.

"That," she said pleasantly, "I should regard as strictly my own affair."

She had the feeling, as she went on, that he had not moved, but was staring after her as she went briskly along on knees that still were shaking wildly under her.

Ted Browning proposed to her again that day, offering her his simple heart, his sturdy body and his rather considerable worldly goods. But the meeting with Jay had confused her.

"I'll be good to you, my dear. You know that."

"Yes, I know that."

"It's no, anyhow? Is that it?"

"I'm afraid so, Ted. You see, I can't get over feeling married to someone else."

Because that was the final effect of that meeting on her. She still felt married to Jay. She lay in her bed that night with her book and realized that he had brought an upsurge of memories with him. She did not love him any more, but the chains were still there. And he had not looked happy that day. She was quite confident that he was neglecting his liver, for one thing.

She could not sleep, and after a time she went downstairs to the kitchen and heated herself a glass of milk. The kitchen was brilliantly clean and tidy, and she sat there thoughtfully sipping. After all, why should she worry about him? It was his liver now.

She yawned and went upstairs to her bed.

It was two days later that she returned from a bridge party to find Gertrude all of a twitter in the hall and gesturing wildly toward the library.

"He's in there, ma'am."

"Who's in there?"

"Mr. Rossiter."

She turned to the hall mirror and automatically straightened her hat. Gertrude was watching her, and so she took out her vanity case and powdered her nose also.

"Has he been here long?" she asked.

"About half an hour, ma'am."

Well, let him wait. Let him stew in his own juice, as J. J. would have said. Why should she hurry for him? He had let her wait long enough. All those months —— And what did he want? What could he want of her now? He had killed her. Was it true that men always came back to the scene of a crime?

Nevertheless, she was brightly casual when she opened the door and went in. He had no imagination, she thought, or he would not have been standing, just as he had stood that night long ago, in front of the fireplace. In the dim light it might have been the same scene they were re-enacting, only now ——

"Well, Jay!" she said. "How nice of you to come."

He did not offer to shake hands. He merely stood there, jauntily dressed and with a flower in his lapel, and seeming to be puzzled.

"I hardly seem to know you, Camilla," he said finally. "You've changed somehow."

"I've cut my hair. Maybe that's it," she offered.

"You're not like yourself."

"No? Well, that may be for the better."

He frowned.

"Look here," he said. "Do you have to be flippant? I came here for a serious talk, and I'm damned if you don't seem to think it's funny."

A serious talk. He had said something like that before. She smiled.

"Funny? Oh, no, Jay. There was never anything funny about you."

And that, she suddenly realized, was the truth for once. There was nothing funny about him. He had no humor. He had never thrown back his head and really laughed in all his life.

"I'm sorry," she said, more soberly. "Do sit down. Would you like a highball?"

"No," he said, with sudden violence. "I don't want a highball. I never want anything to drink again. I never want to see a horse again either. Or people. Or parties. Or night clubs."

"I thought you looked bilious," she said companionably. "You always show it in the whites of your eyes. Well, maybe when it's all over and you can settle down ——"

"I'm telling you it is over."

She was too stunned for speech. She sat there looking up at him, and she saw that he was still the same Jay; only now he wanted pity and comforting instead of onion soup and his eggs turned. But she knew, too, that there was nothing left in her of either pity or comfort.

"You mean that you are not marrying her?" she managed at last.

"That's what I said."

"I'm sorry, Jay."

"There's nothing to be sorry about," he said. "It is a mutual arrangement. She is a very fine woman," [Of course! He would never admit a mistake.] "but she's considerably younger than I am, and she likes gaiety. I'd rather not discuss that part of it."

She felt a cold chill going down her spine, and the backs of her knees felt suddenly hollow.

"Then what did you come to discuss, Jay?"

He looked more like his old self then—a trifle condescending, but reasonable. He had always said he was a reasonable man. He cleared his throat.

"After all, Camilla, we know each other. We like the same things." She lifted her eyebrows at that, but he did not see it. "And I've never forgotten you. I—I've often thought of you. Of course, you've had the children, but still ——"

"But still I'm lonely? Is that it? Jay, are you proposing to come back to me?"

"I thought we might at least discuss it," he said stiffly. "After all, you're a sensible woman, and in a sense this is my home. I'm uncomfortable at the club, and the food's bad. Besides, we lived together happily for a good many years. If we can see eye to eye in this —— You were a good wife to me, Camilla. Don't think I don't appreciate it."

To his amazement, she looked horrified. Suddenly she knew what this would mean. Her dearly bought peace, her small comforts, even Ted Browning—whether she married him or not—and against all that, this Jay in front of her, still incredibly Jay-ish, still a good citizen, still handsome, if slightly shopworn, and now offering to take her back after—well, after dropping her over the falls.

She leaned over and took a cigarette.

"And what sort of a husband do you think you have been to me, Jay?" she said quietly.

He did not answer. He was staring at the cigarette in her hand.

"Since when did you take to that?" he demanded.

It was her turn not to reply. She sat back in her chair and looked at him. So this was Jay, back again. And she did not love him. She did not even like him. He was pompous and arrogant and incredibly naïve. Suddenly she found herself laughing out of sheer relief.

"Oh, Jay, Jay!" she said. "And to think that I once thought I was in love with you!"

He was staggered. For almost the first time in his life he had nothing to say. She got up and moved over to him.

"Listen," she said. "I don't want to hurt you, but you can't throw me away and keep me too. I thought I missed you, but I don't, Jay. I'm very happy without you. Happier than I ever was with you."

"I don't believe it."

"It's true, believe it or not. You know, Jay, lightning doesn't strike twice in the same place."

He eyed her suspiciously.

"What's that got to do with it?"

"You blasted me once. You'll never do it again."

"What sort of talk is that?" he said furiously.

"You don't look blasted. You never looked better in your life." He took a step toward her. "Camilla, are you thinking of marrying another man?"

"Well, yes and no," she said reflectively. "I can marry again if I want to. I may, someday. But that has nothing to do with you, Jay. I just simply don't want you back."

He stood staring at her as though he could not believe his own eyes, and then, to her surprise, there crept in from the hall the delicate and familiar aroma of onion soup. It reached him, she knew, for she saw him lift his head and give a wild and haunted look around the familiar room. Then he turned on his heel and went out.

She was entirely calm and rather interested, and she went to the window to see the last of him. She had expected the front door to slam, but it did not; and what she saw as he left the house was a man, still handsome but past middle age, who moved stiffly, as though his muscles hurt him, and who gave every indication of being a gentleman on his way to a bad club dinner and a dreary club bedroom. Not only for that night but for all the nights to come.

She viewed him with complete detachment, as though the very closing of the car door had shut away both him and her memories. Then she made a little gesture, as though she was drawing her house comfortably about her. Like a barrel. A soft, well-padded barrel.

Gertrude was waiting in the hall, and she turned and spoke to her.

"What on earth is cook doing with onion soup?" she asked. "She knows I can't eat it."

"I'm sorry, ma'am. It isn't soup. We were having a bit of liver and onions in the kitchen."

Well, that was life too. The shadow for the substance, or whatever it was. It was enough that Jay had thought it was onion soup and had had to leave it behind, just as she had left a lot of things a long time ago.

She went into the library and picked up the evening paper. The front page said that the marriage was off, and there was quite a lot about it. On another, however, there was a belated picture of Jay taking a fence in Virginia, with a look of agony on his face and every possibility that he would never hit the saddle again.

She looked at it, quite unmoved. It was nothing to her whether he hit the saddle again or not. He was nothing to her. She was sorry, but she could feel nothing about him whatever. She could not even hate him. It seemed rather pathetic, she thought, that he had not left her anything even to hate. He was gone, and he had not left anything.

But he had, at that. There was something on the floor, and she saw that it was the flower from his lapel. She looked at it for some time. Then she got up and carefully dropped it into the ashes of the fireplace.

THE DEVIL
AND DANIEL WEBSTER
by Stephen Vincent Benét

STEPHEN VINCENT BENÉT came to the *Post* by way of its rural cousin, *The Country Gentleman*, which began publishing his short stories in 1926. His first *Post* appearance was "A Life at Angelo's," May 2, 1931; his last was "Freedom from Fear," published with a painting by Norman Rockwell on March 13, 1943, which, by a strange coincidence, was the day that Benét died. In between these dates the *Post* printed some of his finest stories, which are surely among the finest any American has written. "The Devil and Daniel Webster" has long since become a classic. The *Post* also ran "The Curfew Tolls" (1935), "Johnny Pye and the Fool Killer" (1937), "Doc Mellhorn and the Pearly Gates" (1938), "The Bishop's Beggar" (1942), and nearly a dozen more.

OCTOBER 24, 1936

IT'S A STORY they tell in the border country, where Massachusetts joins Vermont and New Hampshire.

Yes, Dan'l Webster's dead—or, at least, they buried him. But every time there's a thunderstorm around Marshfield, they say you can hear his rolling voice in the hollows of the sky. And they say that if you go to his grave and speak loud and clear, "Dan'l Webster—Dan'l Webster!" the ground'll begin to shiver and the trees begin to shake. And after a while you'll hear a deep voice saying, "Neighbor, how stands the Union?" Then you better answer the Union stands as she stood, rock-bottomed and copper-sheathed, one and indivisible, or he's liable to rear right out of the ground. At least, that's what I was told when I was a youngster.

You see, for a while, he was the biggest man in the country. He never got to be President, but he was the biggest man. There were thousands that trusted in him right next to God Almighty, and they told stories about him and all the things that belonged to him that were like the stories of patriarchs and such. They said, when he stood up to speak, stars and stripes came right out in the sky, and once he spoke against a river and made it sink into the ground. They said, when he walked the woods with his fishing rod, Killall, the trout would jump out of the streams right into his pockets, for they knew it was no use putting up a fight against him; and, when he argued a case, he could turn on the harps of the blessed and the shaking of the earth underground. That was the kind of man he was, and his big farm up at Marshfield was suitable to him. The chickens he raised were all white meat down through the drumsticks, the cows were tended like children, and the big ram he called Goliath had horns with a curl like a morning-glory vine and could butt through an iron door. But Dan'l wasn't one of your gentlemen farmers; he knew all the ways of the land, and he'd be up by candlelight to see that the chores got done. A man with a mouth like a mastiff, a brow like a mountain and eyes like burning anthracite—that was Dan'l Webster in his prime. And the biggest case he argued never got written down in the books, for he argued it against the devil, nip and tuck and no holds barred. And this is the way I used to hear it told.

There was a man named Jabez Stone, lived at Cross Corners, New Hampshire. He wasn't a bad man to start with, but he was an unlucky man. If he planted corn, he got borers; if he planted potatoes, he got blight. He had good-enough land, but it didn't prosper him; he had a decent wife and children, but the more children he had, the less there was to feed them. If stones cropped up in his neighbor's field, boulders boiled up in his; if he had a horse with the spavins, he'd trade it for one with the staggers and give something extra. There's some folks bound to be like that, apparently. But one day Jabez Stone got sick of the whole business.

He'd been plowing that morning and he'd just broke the plowshare on a rock that he could have sworn hadn't been there yesterday. And, as he stood looking at the plowshare, the off horse began to cough—that ropy kind of cough that means sickness and horse doctors. There were two children down with the measles, his wife was ailing, and he had a whitlow on his thumb. It was about the last straw for Jabez Stone. "I vow," he

said, and he looked around him kind of desperate
—"I vow it's enough to make a man want to sell
his soul to the devil! And I would, too, for two
cents!"

Then he felt a kind of queerness come over
him at having said what he'd said; though, naturally, being a New Hampshireman, he wouldn't
take it back. But, all the same, when it got to be
evening, and, as far as he could see, no notice had
been taken, he felt relieved in his mind, for he
was a religious man. But notice is always taken,
sooner or later, just like the Good Book says.
And, sure enough, next day, about suppertime, a
soft-spoken, dark-dressed stranger drove up in a
handsome buggy and asked for Jabez Stone.

Well, Jabez told his family it was a lawyer,
come to see him about a legacy. But he knew who
it was. He didn't like the looks of the stranger,
nor the way he smiled with his teeth. They were
white teeth, and plentiful—some say they were
filed to a point, but I wouldn't vouch for that.
And he didn't like it when the dog took one look
at the stranger and ran away howling, with his
tail between his legs. But having passed his word,
more or less, he stuck to it, and they went out behind the barn and made their bargain. Jabez
Stone had to prick his finger to sign, and the
stranger lent him a silver pin. The wound healed
clean, but it left a little white scar.

After that, all of a sudden, things began to
pick up and prosper for Jabez Stone. His cows
got fat and his horses sleek, his crops were the
envy of the neighborhood, and lightning might
strike all over the valley, but it wouldn't strike
his barn. Pretty soon, he was one of the prosperous people of the county; they asked him to stand
for selectman, and he stood for it; there began to
be talk of running him for state senate. All in all,
you might say the Stone family was as happy and
contented as cats in a dairy. And so they were,
except for Jabez Stone.

He'd been contented enough, the first few
years. It's a great thing when bad luck turns; it
drives most other things out of your head. True,
every now and then, especially in rainy weather,
the little white scar on his finger would give him
a twinge. And once a year, punctual as clock-
work, the stranger with the handsome buggy
would come driving by. But the sixth year, the
stranger lighted, and, after that, his peace was
over for Jabez Stone.

The stranger came up through the lower field,
switching his boots with a cane—they were handsome black boots, but Jabez Stone never liked
the look of them, particularly the toes. And, after
he'd passed the time of day, he said, "Well, Mr.
Stone, you're a hummer! It's a very pretty property you've got here, Mr. Stone."

"Well, some might favor it and others might
not," said Jabez Stone, for he was a New Hampshireman.

"Oh, no need to decry your industry!" said the
stranger, very easy, showing his teeth in a smile.
"After all, we know what's been done, and it's
been according to contract and specifications. So
when—ahem—the mortgage falls due next year,
you shouldn't have any regrets."

"Speaking of that mortgage, mister," said
Jabez Stone, and he looked around for help to
the earth and the sky, "I'm beginning to have
one or two doubts about it."

"Doubts?" said the stranger, not quite so pleasantly.

"Why, yes," said Jabez Stone. "This being the
U. S. A. and me always having been a religious
man." He cleared his throat and got bolder. "Yes,
sir," he said, "I'm beginning to have considerable
doubts as to that mortgage holding in court."

"There's courts and courts," said the stranger,
clicking his teeth. "Still, we might as well have a
look at the original document." And he hauled
out a big black pocketbook, full of papers. "Sher-
win, Slater, Stevens, Stone," he muttered. "I,
Jabez Stone, for a term of seven years —— Oh,
it's quite in order, I think."

But Jabez Stone wasn't listening, for he saw
something else flutter out of the black pocketbook. It was something that looked like a moth,
but it wasn't a moth. And as Jabez Stone stared
at it, it seemed to speak to him in a small sort of
piping voice, terrible small and thin, but terrible
human. "Neighbor Stone!" it squeaked. "Neighbor Stone! Help me! For God's sake, help me!"

But before Jabez Stone could stir hand or foot,
the stranger whipped out a big bandanna handkerchief, caught the creature in it, just like a butterfly, and started tying up the ends of the bandanna.

"Sorry for the interruption," he said. "As I
was saying ——"

But Jabez Stone was shaking all over like a
scared horse.

"That's Miser Stevens' voice!" he said, in a
croak. "And you've got him in your handkerchief!"

The stranger looked a little embarrassed.

"Yes, I really should have transferred him to
the collecting box," he said with a simper, "but
there were some rather unusual specimens there
and I didn't want them crowded. Well, well, these
little contretemps will occur."

"I don't know what you mean by contertan,"
said Jabez Stone, "but that was Miser Stevens'
voice! And he ain't dead! You can't tell me he is!
He was just as spry and mean as a woodchuck,
Tuesday!"

"In the midst of life ——" said the stranger, kind of pious. "Listen!" Then a bell began to toll in the valley and Jabez Stone listened, with the sweat running down his face. For he knew it was tolled for Miser Stevens and that he was dead.

"These long-standing accounts," said the stranger with a sigh; "one really hates to close them. But business is business."

He still had the bandanna in his hand, and Jabez Stone felt sick as he saw the cloth struggle and flutter.

"Are they all as small as that?" he asked hoarsely.

"Small?" said the stranger. "Oh, I see what you mean. Why, they vary." He measured Jabez Stone with his eyes, and his teeth showed. "Don't worry, Mr. Stone," he said. "You'll go with a very good grade. I wouldn't trust you outside the collecting box. Now, a man like Dan'l Webster, of course—well, we'd have to build a special box for him, and even at that, I imagine the wing spread would astonish you. He'd certainly be a prize. I wish we could see our way clear to him. But, in your case, as I was saying ——"

"Put that handkerchief away!" said Jabez Stone, and he began to beg and to pray. But the best he could get at the end was a three years' extension, with conditions.

But till you make a bargain like that, you've got no idea of how fast four years can run. By the last months of those years, Jabez Stone's known all over the state and there's talk of running him for governor—and it's dust and ashes in his mouth. For every day, when he gets up, he thinks, "There's one more night gone," and every night when he lies down, he thinks of the black pocketbook and the soul of Miser Stevens, and it makes him sick at heart. Till, finally, he can't bear it any longer, and, in the last days of the last year, he hitches up his horse and drives off to seek Dan'l Webster. For Dan'l was born in New Hampshire, only a few miles from Cross Corners, and it's well known that he has a particular soft spot for old neighbors.

It was early in the morning when he got to Marshfield, but Dan'l was up already, talking Latin to the farm hands and wrestling with the ram, Goliath, and trying out a new trotter and working up speeches to make against John C. Calhoun. But when he heard a New Hampshireman had come to see him, he dropped everything else he was doing, for that was Dan'l's way. He gave Jabez Stone a breakfast that five men couldn't eat, went into the living history of every man and woman in Cross Corners, and finally asked him how he could serve him.

Jabez Stone allowed that it was a kind of mortgage case.

"Well, I haven't pleaded a mortgage case in a long time, and I don't generally plead now, except before the Supreme Court," said Dan'l, "but if I can, I'll help you."

"Then I've got hope for the first time in ten years," said Jabez Stone, and told him the details.

Dan'l walked up and down as he listened, hands behind his back, now and then asking a question, now and then plunging his eyes at the floor, as if they'd bore through it like gimlets. When Jabez Stone had finished, Dan'l puffed out his cheeks and blew. Then he turned to Jabez Stone and a smile broke over his face like the sunrise over Monadnock.

"You've certainly given yourself the devil's own row to hoe, Neighbor Stone," he said, "but I'll take your case."

"You'll take it?" said Jabez Stone, hardly daring to believe.

"Yes," said Dan'l Webster. "I've got about seventy-five other things to do and the Missouri Compromise to straighten out, but I'll take your case. For if two New Hampshiremen aren't a match for the devil, we might as well give the country back to the Indians."

Then he shook Jabez Stone by the hand and said, "Did you come down here in a hurry?"

"Well, I admit I made time," said Jabez Stone.

"You'll go back faster," said Dan'l Webster, and he told 'em to hitch up Constitution and Constellation to the carriage. They were matched grays with one white forefoot, and they stepped like greased lightning.

Well, I won't describe how excited and pleased the whole Stone family was to have the great Dan'l Webster for a guest, when they finally got there. Jabez Stone had lost his hat on the way, blown off when they overtook a wind, but he didn't take much account of that. But after supper he sent the family off to bed, for he had most particular business with Mr. Webster. Mrs. Stone wanted them to sit in the front parlor, but Dan'l Webster knew front parlors and said he preferred the kitchen. So it was there they sat, waiting for the stranger, with a jug on the table between them and a bright fire on the hearth—the stranger being scheduled to show up on the stroke of midnight, according to specification.

Well, most men wouldn't have asked for better company than Dan'l Webster and a jug. But with every tick of the clock Jabez Stone got sadder and sadder. His eyes roved round, and though he sampled the jug you could see he couldn't taste it. Finally, on the stroke of 11:30 he reached over and grabbed Dan'l Webster by the arm.

"Mr. Webster, Mr. Webster!" he said, and his voice was shaking with fear and a desperate courage. "For God's sake, Mr. Webster, harness your horses and get away from this place while you can!"

"You've brought me a long way, neighbor, to tell me you don't like my company," said Dan'l Webster, quite peaceable, pulling at the jug.

"Miserable wretch that I am!" groaned Jabez Stone. "I've brought you a devilish way, and now I see my folly. Let him take me if he wills. I don't hanker after it, I must say, but I can stand it. But you're the Union's stay and New Hampshire's pride! He mustn't get you, Mr. Webster! He mustn't get you!"

Dan'l Webster looked at the distracted man, all gray and shaking in the firelight, and laid a hand on his shoulder.

"I'm obliged to you, Neighbor Stone," he said gently. "It's kindly thought of. But there's a jug on the table and a case in hand. And I never left a jug or a case half finished in my life."

And just at that moment there was a sharp rap on the door.

"Ah," said Dan'l Webster, very coolly, "I thought your clock was a trifle slow, Neighbor Stone." He stepped to the door and opened it. "Come in!" he said.

The stranger came in—very dark and tall he looked in the firelight. He was carrying a box under his arm—a black, japanned box with little air holes in the lid. At the sight of the box, Jabez Stone gave a low cry and shrank into a corner of the room.

"Mr. Webster, I presume," said the stranger, very polite, but with his eyes glowing like a fox's deep in the woods.

"Attorney of record for Jabez Stone," said Dan'l Webster, but his eyes were glowing too. "Might I ask your name?"

"I've gone by a good many," said the stranger carelessly. "Perhaps Scratch will do for the evening. I'm often called that in these regions."

Then he sat down at the table and poured himself a drink from the jug. The liquor was cold in the jug, but it came steaming into the glass.

"And now," said the stranger, smiling and showing his teeth, "I shall call upon you, as a law-abiding citizen, to assist me in taking possession of my property."

Well, with that the argument began—and it went hot and heavy. At first, Jabez Stone had a flicker of hope, but when he saw Dan'l Webster being forced back at point after point, he just sat scrunched in his corner, with his eyes on that japanned box. For there wasn't any doubt as to the deed or the signature—that was the worst of it. Dan'l Webster twisted and turned and thumped his fist on the table, but he couldn't get away from that. He offered to compromise the case; the stranger wouldn't hear of it. He pointed out

the property had increased in value, and state senators ought to be worth more; the stranger stuck to the letter of the law. He was a great lawyer, Dan'l Webster, but we know who's the King of Lawyers, as the Good Book tells us, and it seemed as if, for the first time, Dan'l Webster had met his match.

Finally, the stranger yawned a little. "Your spirited efforts on behalf of your client do you credit, Mr. Webster," he said, "but if you have no more arguments to adduce, I'm rather pressed for time ——" and Jabez Stone shuddered.

Dan'l Webster's brow looked dark as a thundercloud.

"Pressed or not, you shall not have this man!" he thundered. "Mr. Stone is an American citizen, and no American citizen may be forced into the service of a foreign prince. We fought England for that in '12 and we'll fight all hell for it again!"

"Foreign?" said the stranger. "And who calls me a foreigner?"

"Well, I never yet heard of the dev—of your claiming American citizenship," said Dan'l Webster with surprise.

"And who with better right?" said the stranger, with one of his terrible smiles. "When the first wrong was done to the first Indian, I was there. When the first slaver put out for the Congo, I stood on her deck. Am I not in your books and stories and beliefs, from the first settlements on? Am I not spoken of, still, in every church in New England? 'Tis true the North claims me for a Southerner and the South for a Northerner, but I am neither. I am merely an honest American like yourself—and of the best descent—for, to tell the truth, Mr. Webster, though I don't like to boast of it, my name is older in this country than yours."

"Aha!" said Dan'l Webster, with the veins standing out in his forehead. "Then I stand on the Constitution! I demand a trial for my client!"

"The case is hardly one for an ordinary court," said the stranger, his eyes flickering. "And, indeed, the lateness of the hour ——"

"Let it be any court you choose, so it is an American judge and an American jury!" said Dan'l Webster in his pride. "Let it be the quick or the dead; I'll abide the issue!"

"You have said it," said the stranger, and pointed his finger at the door. And with that, and all of a sudden, there was a rushing of wind outside and a noise of footsteps. They came, clear and distinct, through the night. And yet, they were not like the footsteps of living men.

"In God's name, who comes by so late?" cried Jabez Stone, in an ague of fear.

"The jury Mr. Webster demands," said the stranger, sipping at his boiling glass. "You must pardon the rough appearance of one or two; they will have come a long way."

And with that the fire burned blue and the door blew open and twelve men entered, one by one.

If Jabez Stone had been sick with terror before, he was blind with terror now. For there was Walter Butler, the loyalist, who spread fire and horror through the Mohawk Valley in the times of the Revolution; and there was Simon Girty, the renegade, who saw white men burned at the stake and whooped with the Indians to see them burn. His eyes were green, like a catamount's, and the stains on his hunting shirt did not come from the blood of the deer. King Philip was there, wild and proud as he had been in life, with the great gash in his head that gave him his death wound, and cruel Governor Dale, who broke men on the wheel. There was Morton of Merry Mount, who so vexed the Plymouth Colony, with his flushed, loose, handsome face and his hate of the godly. There was Teach, the bloody pirate, with his black beard curling on his breast. The Reverend John Smeet, with his strangler's hands and his Geneva gown, walked as daintily as he had to the gallows. The red print of the rope was still around his neck, but he carried a perfumed handkerchief in one hand. One and all, they came into the room with the fires of hell still upon them, and the stranger named their names and their deeds as they came, till the tale of twelve was told. Yet the stranger had told the truth—they had all played a part in America.

"Are you satisfied with the jury, Mr. Webster?" said the stranger mockingly, when they had taken their places.

The sweat stood upon Dan'l Webster's brow, but his voice was clear.

"Quite satisfied," he said. "Though I miss General Arnold from the company."

"Benedict Arnold is engaged upon other business," said the stranger, with a glower. "Ah, you asked for a justice, I believe."

He pointed his finger once more, and a tall man, soberly clad in Puritan garb, with the burning gaze of the fanatic, stalked into the room and took his judge's place.

"Justice Hathorne is a jurist of experience," said the stranger. "He presided at certain witch trials once held in Salem. There were others who repented of the business later, but not he."

"Repent of such notable wonders and undertakings?" said the stern old justice. "Nay, hang them—hang them all!" And he muttered to himself in a way that struck ice into the soul of Jabez Stone.

Then the trial began, and, as you might expect,

it didn't look anyways good for the defense. And Jabez Stone didn't make much of a witness in his own behalf. He took one look at Simon Girty and screeched, and they had to put him back in his corner in a kind of swoon.

It didn't halt the trial, though; the trial went on, as trials do. Dan'l Webster had faced some hard juries and hanging judges in his time, but this was the hardest he'd ever faced, and he knew it. They sat there with a kind of glitter in their eyes, and the stranger's smooth voice went on and on. Every time he'd raise an objection, it'd be "Objection sustained," but whenever Dan'l objected, it'd be "Objection denied." Well, you couldn't expect fair play from a fellow like this Mr. Scratch.

It got to Dan'l in the end, and he began to heat, like iron in the forge. When he got up to speak he was going to flay that stranger with every trick known to the law, and the judge and jury too. He didn't care if it was contempt of court or what would happen to him for it. He didn't care any more what happened to Jabez Stone. He just got madder and madder, thinking of what he'd say. And yet, curiously enough, the more he thought about it, the less he was able to arrange his speech in his mind.

Till, finally, it was time for him to get up on his feet, and he did so, all ready to bust out with lightnings and denunciations. But before he started he looked over the judge and jury for a moment, such being his custom. And he noticed the glitter in their eyes was twice as strong as before, and they all leaned forward. Like hounds just before they get the fox, they looked, and the blue mist of evil in the room thickened as he watched them. Then he saw what he'd been about to do, and he wiped his forehead, as a man might who's just escaped falling into a pit in the dark.

For it was him they'd come for, not only Jabez Stone. He read it in the glitter of their eyes and in the way the stranger hid his mouth with one hand. And if he fought them with their own weapons, he'd fall into their power; he knew that, though he couldn't have told you how. It was his own anger and horror that burned in their eyes; and he'd have to wipe that out or the case was lost. He stood there for a moment, his black eyes burning like anthracite. And then he began to speak.

He started off in a low voice, though you could hear every word. They say he could call on the harps of the blessed when he chose. And this was just as simple and easy as a man could talk. But he didn't start out by condemning or reviling. He was talking about the things that make a country a country, and a man a man.

And he began with the simple things that everybody's known and felt—the freshness of a fine morning when you're young, and the taste of food when you're hungry, and the new day that's every day when you're a child. He took them up and he turned them in his hands. They were good things for any man. But without freedom, they sickened. And when he talked of those enslaved, and the sorrows of slavery, his voice got like a big bell. He talked of the early days of America and the men who had made those days. It wasn't a spread-eagle speech, but he made you see it. He admitted all the wrong that had ever been done. But he showed how, out of the wrong and the right, the suffering and the starvations, something new had come. And everybody had played a part in it, even the traitors.

Then he turned to Jabez Stone and showed him as he was—an ordinary man who'd had hard luck and wanted to change it. And, because he'd wanted to change it, now he was going to be punished for all eternity. And yet there was good in Jabez Stone, and he showed that good. He was hard and mean, in some ways, but he was a man. There was sadness in being a man, but it was a proud thing too. And he showed what the pride of it was till you couldn't help feeling it. Yes, even in hell, if a man was a man, you'd know it. And he wasn't pleading for any one person any more, though his voice rang like an organ. He was telling the story and the failures and the endless journey of mankind. They got tricked and trapped and bamboozled, but it was a great journey. And no demon that was ever foaled could know the inwardness of it—it took a man to do that.

The fire began to die on the hearth and the wind before morning to blow. The light was getting gray in the room when Dan'l Webster finished. And his words came back at the end to New Hampshire ground, and the one spot of land that each man loves and clings to. He painted a picture of that, and to each one of that jury he spoke of things long forgotten. For his voice could search the heart, and that was his gift and his strength. And to one, his voice was like the forest and its secrecy, and to another like the sea and the storms of the sea; and one heard the cry of his lost nation in it, and another saw a little harmless scene he hadn't remembered for years. But each saw something. And when Dan'l Webster finished he didn't know whether or not he'd saved Jabez Stone. But he knew he'd done a miracle. For the glitter was gone from the eyes of judge and jury, and, for the moment, they were men again, and knew they were men.

"The defense rests," said Dan'l Webster, and stood there like a mountain. His ears were still ringing with his speech, and he didn't hear anything else till he heard Judge Hathorne say, "The jury will retire to consider its verdict."

Walter Butler rose in his place and his face had a dark, gay pride on it.

"The jury has considered its verdict," he said, and looked the stranger full in the eye. "We find for the defendant, Jabez Stone."

With that, the smile left the stranger's face, but Walter Butler did not flinch.

"Perhaps 'tis not strictly in accordance with the evidence," he said, "but even the damned may salute the eloquence of Mr. Webster."

With that, the long crow of a rooster split the gray morning sky, and judge and jury were gone from the room like a puff of smoke and as if they had never been there. The stranger turned to Dan'l Webster, smiling wryly.

"Major Butler was always a bold man," he said. "I had not thought him quite so bold. Nevertheless, my congratulations, as between two gentlemen."

"I'll have that paper first, if you please," said Dan'l Webster, and he took it and tore it into four pieces. It was queerly warm to the touch. "And now," he said, "I'll have you!" and his hand came down like a bear trap on the stranger's arm. For he knew that once you bested anybody like Mr. Scratch in fair fight, his power on you was gone. And he could see that Mr. Scratch knew it too.

The stranger twisted and wriggled, but he couldn't get out of that grip. "Come, come, Mr. Webster," he said, smiling palely. "This sort of thing is ridic—ouch!—is ridiculous. If you're worried about the costs of the case, naturally, I'd be glad to pay ——"

"And so you shall!" said Dan'l Webster, shaking him till his teeth rattled. "For you'll sit right down at that table and draw up a document, promising never to bother Jabez Stone nor his heirs or assigns nor any other New Hampshireman till doomsday! For any hades we want to raise in this state, we can raise ourselves, without assistance from strangers."

"Ouch!" said the stranger. "Ouch! Well, they never did run very big to the barrel, but—ouch! —I agree!"

So he sat down and drew up the document. But Dan'l Webster kept his hand on his coat collar all the time.

"And, now, may I go?" said the stranger, quite humble, when Dan'l'd seen the document's in proper and legal form.

"Go?" said Dan'l, giving him another shake. "I'm still trying to figure out what I'll do with you. For you've settled the costs of the case, but you haven't settled with me. I think I'll take you back to Marshfield," he said, kind of reflective. "I've got a ram there named Goliath that can butt through an iron door. I'd kind of like to turn you loose in his field and see what he'd do."

Well, with that the stranger began to beg and to plead. And he begged and he pled so humble that finally Dan'l, who was naturally kindhearted, agreed to let him go. The stranger seemed terrible grateful for that and said, just to show they were friends, he'd tell Dan'l's fortune before leaving. So Dan'l agreed to that, though he didn't take much stock in fortune-tellers ordinarily. But, naturally, the stranger was a little different.

Well, he pried and he peered at the lines in Dan'l's hands. And he told him one thing and another that was quite remarkable. But they were all in the past.

"Yes, all that's true, and it happened," said Dan'l Webster. "But what's to come in the future?"

The stranger grinned, kind of happily, and shook his head.

"The future's not as you think it," he said. "It's dark. You have a great ambition, Mr. Webster."

"I have," said Dan'l firmly, for everybody knew he wanted to be President.

"It seems almost within your grasp," said the stranger, "but you will not attain it. Lesser men will be made President and you will be passed over."

"And, if I am, I'll still be Daniel Webster," said Dan'l. "Say on."

"You have two strong sons," said the stranger, shaking his head. "You look to found a line. But each will die in war and neither reach greatness."

"Live or die, they are still my sons," said Dan'l Webster. "Say on."

"You have made great speeches," said the stranger. "You will make more."

"Ah," said Dan'l Webster.

"But the last great speech you make will turn many of your own against you," said the stranger. "They will call you Ichabod; they will call you by other names. Even in New England, some will say you have turned your coat and sold your country, and their voices will be loud against you till you die."

"So it is an honest speech, it does not matter what men say," said Dan'l Webster. Then he looked at the stranger and their glances locked.

"One question," he said. "I have fought for the Union all my life. Will I see that fight won against those who would tear it apart?"

"Not while you live," said the stranger, grimly, "but it will be won. And after you are dead, there are thousands who will fight for your cause, because of words that you spoke."

"Why, then, you long-barreled, slab-sided, lantern-jawed, fortune-telling note shaver!" said Dan'l Webster, with a great roar of laughter, "be off with you to your own place before I put my mark on you! For, by the thirteen original colonies, I'd go to the Pit itself to save the Union!"

And with that he drew back his foot for a kick that would have stunned a horse. It was only the tip of his shoe that caught the stranger, but he went flying out of the door with his collecting box under his arm.

"And now," said Dan'l Webster, seeing Jabez Stone beginning to rouse from his swoon, "let's see what's left in the jug, for it's dry work talking all night. I hope there's pie for breakfast, Neighbor Stone."

But they say that whenever the devil comes near Marshfield, even now, he gives it a wide berth. And he hasn't been seen in the state of New Hampshire from that day to this. I'm not talking about Massachusetts or Vermont.

MONEY

by Gertrude Stein

ONE OF GEORGE HORACE LORIMER'S last editorial acts at the *Post* was to buy this short article by a writer who was celebrated for her non-objective prose. According to John Tebbel's biography, the rest of the staff was solidly opposed to the purchase but Lorimer, as always, prevailed. "Why did you buy that stuff, Boss?" one of the editors asked him later. Lorimer seemed genuinely surprised. "Because," he said, "it amused me."

JUNE 13, 1936

EVERYBODY now just has to make up their mind. Is money money or isn't money money. Everybody who earns it and spends it every day in order to live knows that money is money, anybody who votes it to be gathered in as taxes knows money is not money. That is what makes everybody go crazy.

Once upon a time there was a king and he was called Louis the fifteenth. He spent money as they are spending it now. He just spent it and spent it and one day somebody dared say something to the king about it. Oh, he said, after me the deluge, it would last out his time, and so what was the difference. When this king had begun his reign he was known as Louis the Well-beloved, when he died, nobody even stayed around to close his eyes.

But all the trouble really comes from this question is money money. Everybody who lives on it every day knows that money is money but the people who vote money, presidents and congress, do not think about money that way when they vote it. I remember when my nephew was a little boy he was out walking somewhere and he saw a lot of horses; he came home and he said, oh papa, I have just seen a million horses. A million, said his father, well anyway, said my nephew, I saw three. That came to be what we all used to say when anybody used numbers that they could not count well anyway a million or three. That is the whole point. When you earn money and spend money every day anybody can know the difference between a million and three. But when you vote money away there really is not any difference between a million and three. And so everybody has to make up their mind is money money for everybody or is it not.

That is what everybody has to think about a lot or everybody is going to be awfully unhappy, because the time does come when the money voted comes suddenly to be money just like the money everybody earns every day and spends every day to live and when that time comes it makes everybody very unhappy. I do wish everybody would make up their mind about money being money.

It is awfully hard for anybody to think money is money when there is more of it than they can count. That is why there ought to be some kind of system that money should not be voted right away. When you spend money that you earn every day you naturally think several times before you spend more than you have, and you mostly do not. Now if there was some arrangement made that when one lot voted to spend money, that they would have to wait a long time, and another lot have to vote, before they vote again to have that money, in short, if there was any way to make a government handle money the way a father of a family has to handle money if there only was. The natural feeling of a father of a family is that when anybody asks him for money he says no. Any father of a family, any member of a family, knows all about that.

So until everybody who votes public money remembers how he feels as a father of a family, when he says no, when anybody in the family wants money, until that time comes, there is going to be a lot of trouble and some years later everybody is going to be very unhappy.

In Russia they tried to decide that money was not money, but now slowly and surely they are coming back to know that money is money.

Whether you like it or whether you do not money is money and that is all there is about it. Everybody knows it. When they earn it and spend what they earn they know it they really know that money is money and when they vote it they do not know it as money.

That is the trouble with everybody, it is awfully hard to really know what you know.

When you earn it and spend it you do know the

difference between three dollars and a million dollars, but when you say it and vote it, it all sounds the same.

Of course it does, it would to anybody, and that is the reason they vote it and keep on voting it.

So, now please, everybody, everybody everybody, please, is money money, and if it is, it ought to be the same whether it is what a father of a family earns and spends or a government, if it isn't sooner or later there is disaster.

HUNDRED-TONGUED CHARLEY, THE GREAT SILENT ORATOR

by Alva Johnston

ALVA JOHNSTON WAS a fabulous figure among newspapermen before he began writing for the *Post* in 1934. Many of them thought he was the best city-room reporter in the United States. A lanky, loose-jointed man with eyes that darted and scowled or peered off innocently into space, Johnston has been described by old friends as looking like a hard-bitten coyote, or a fugitive embezzler. His neatest trick was taking notes in his pocket with a small pad and pencil, without being noticed by the person he was talking to. For the *Post* he specialized in personalities, but a Johnston piece always took in plenty of territory. The article which follows, for instance, began as a profile of Charley Michelson, the Democratic ghost writer, and became a revealing portrait of the New Deal's whole political machine. Johnston died November 23, 1950, at the age of sixty-two.

MAY 30, 1936

CHARLES MICHELSON, the press agent of the Democratic National Committee, has been the miracle man of oratory in this country in the past seven years. He has split himself into two parts and delivered two different speeches at the same moment, one in the Senate and one in the House of Representatives. He has made speeches at the same moment in widely separated sections of the United States. He often talks with a Southern accent, but he has used the down-East nasal twang, the flat pronunciation of the Middle West and the language of the prairies, the Rockies and the Pacific Coast. He is generally clean-shaven, but sometimes twirls a mustache or wags a beard. He has frequently taken the form of John N. Garner. He appears in the guise of Sen. Pat Harrison and Sen. Joe Robinson. Now and then he is Postmaster General Farley. All together, he has been more than a hundred senators, representatives, Cabinet secretaries and other Democratic chieftains. He has even been Gen. Hugh S. Johnson.

"The wise Ulysses," wrote General Johnson, after leaving the NRA, "who kept my erring feet on the path when he could reach me was Charley Michelson. As long as I was where Charley could edit my speeches or manage NRA publicity, I never made any very bad blunders. He is the only man who ever wrote any part of a speech for me, and the part he wrote was the best part."

General Hugh Johnson is a born rhetorician, full of pride in his oratory. When General Johnson loaned his body and lungs to be used for a speech by Charley Michelson, it was a case of one great old master acknowledging a greater one. No wonder that lesser orators of Congress and the New Deal have begged for the privilege of having Michelson's words put into their mouths. Charley is a Walt Disney. He creates animated cartoons, but his Donald Ducks and Mickey Mice and Three Little Pigs squeak and quack on the floors of the Senate and House.

The Democrats have recognized the merits of Charley Michelson, but the Republicans have made a sort of god of him—a malignant deity, it is true. Some of them credit him with "smearing Hoover," with "obscuring his achievements," and with defeating him in 1932. They think that, except for Michelson, the Republicans would be in power today and the country would be in clover. This impression is strengthened by the current belief that press agents run the universe. Most people think, for example, that British propagandists got us into the World War. We were not influenced in the least by Germany's violation of Belgian neutrality, by Germany's sinking of our ships, by her effort to induce Mexico to make war on us or by the danger that a German victory would make this country Germany's next victim; on the contrary, the United States was tricked into the war by limey press agents. Anybody who studies the feeble inventions and general incompetence of the British propagandists during the war will be greatly taken aback; he may even go to the extent of imagining that this country was moved by mighty events rather than by the imbecilities of cockney ballyhoo artists. If he wants to be orthodox, however, he must assume that this nation is always led by the nose by publicity men. The best evidence of this is that the publicity men confess it. They write books telling how they did it. Almost any press agent will tell you how he made nations jump through hoops.

The fame of Michelson is partly based on the superstition that press-agentry is the chief motive force in the world today. The gullible element, which formerly laid all untoward phenomena on witches and evil spirits, now attributes them to the black magic of publicity men. This tends to give a legendary or mythological character to the very real achievements of Michelson. It is probable that the depression, rather than Michelson, beat Hoover in 1932. It is unlikely that Michelson could have made headway against Coolidge in 1924 or against Hoover in 1928. This is not, however, to belittle Michelson. He is the one press agent who has made good.

The awe in which Michelson is held by Republicans is almost comic. Regarding the very name of Michelson as magic, they have hired a cousin of his as a publicity man for the Republican National Committee. They are trying to fight one Michelson with another. They have gone out and hired a relative of Charley Michelson by the name of Peter Michelson. It would make an interesting show in Washington if Peter could develop a troupe of Republican dummies and puppets to equal Charley's Democratic robots and televoxes. A considerable part of Congress could go on the road as Charley & Pete Michelson's Greatest Deliberative Body in the World.

Michelson would in all probability still be an obscure, hard-working journalist, except for John J. Raskob. Raskob ran the Democratic national campaign in 1928, and his pride was deeply hurt by his ignominious defeat. He had played an important part in the growth of General Motors; he was not willing to admit that a great industrialist like himself could be baffled at the simple game of politics. "I have never been connected with an enterprise that was a failure, and I am not going to this time," he said. The Democratic Party in 1928 was shattered and spirit-broken. Raskob was full of confidence; he began to organize for victory, and to pay for the organization out of his own pocket. The idea of starting a publicity campaign three years ahead of the national campaign was a novelty; it was the application of long-headed business principles to politics. Jouett Shouse, Raskob's right-hand man, picked Michelson to handle the publicity. Raskob paid Michelson $20,800 a year. That was smart in itself. That figure commands respect. In the past,

the publicity chief of a national party was lucky to get half that much. A big salary arbitrarily and automatically increases a man's importance in politics. People will listen attentively to a $20,-800-a-year man when they will yawn at a $12,-000-a-year man.

Michelson was not the first choice for the post. It was offered first to another man, who declined. Charley was considered one of the ablest newspapermen in Washington, but he was sixty years old and was not then suspected of being the greatest silent orator in America. There is a historic controversy as to who developed the technique of using the mouths of statesmen to bombard the country with a press agent's copy. It is claimed that Jouett Shouse, seeing that statements in his name or that of the National Democratic Committee commanded little attention, ordered that they should be sponsored by big Democrats in and out of Congress. Others give the credit to Michelson. In any case, the system worked. Editors who would have said, "Throw away that tripe," if it came in the form of canned headquarters publicity, featured it when it was delivered by a big name.

Michelson had a magnificent equipment for this work. As a journalist he had an intimate knowledge of the politics of the country for forty years. He has the memory of an elephant, and an almost supernaturally exact recollection of the missteps and the skeletons in the closet in the careers of public men. He is a master of insinuation and innuendo. With a few innocent sentences he can leave an indelible impression that a certain man is an arrogant pickpocket. He has a fine satirical quirk and perfect judgment as to what will catch the attention of the public. He had the advantage of being trained by William Randolph Hearst for thirty years in literary skill and political ethics.

Michelson took his post late in 1928. In 1929 he began to assault the Republicans with a hundred jawbones. He frequently changed the records in his eminent phonographs, but the leading theme was that President Hoover was in a conspiracy with big interests to fix the tariff so that it would rob the poor and enrich the industrial giants. From the very first, the Michelson speeches hurt.

It was a long time before the Republicans discovered what was happening.

By painful experience they learned to identify the Michelson style. If, for example, a senator delivered a dull and lifeless anti-Hoover speech, it was probably the senator's own. If the Hoover Administration was picking splinters out of its skin for a week afterward, it was a Michelson speech. Any one of scores of persons might have delivered the wallop, but if it caused great agony it was Michelson's. The Hoover Administration developed a discriminating sense of pain, like that of Hudibras, of whom it was written:

Some have been beaten till they know
What wood a cudgel's of by th' blow;
Some kick'd until they can feel whether
A shoe be Spanish or neat's leather.

After this sort of thing had been going on for more than a year, Michelson was "exposed." His method of "smearing Hoover" by using the bellows and vocal cords of eminent but inarticulate Democrats was described in Scribner's by Frank R. Kent. Rep. Will R. Wood, chairman of the Republican Congressional Campaign Committee, described Michelson's silent but incessant oratory as "unparalleled in the history of the United States." Rep. John Q. Tilson, Republican leader in Congress, said there was "no parallel in American history" for Charley's campaign against Hoover through a battalion of mouthpieces. All this did not hurt Charley's feelings or his prestige. It was like abusing St. George for smearing the dragon or berating David for smearing Goliath. Charley's reply was to describe himself as a humble little fellow and to ask why the onslaught was not directed at the big names which were attached to his statements. Before these complaints against him, Michelson had started to issue a weekly letter to the press, entitled Dispelling the Fog. Few newspapers had used it.

After his "exposure" there was a great demand for his column, and several hundred newspapers printed it. Charley's utterances began to command attention for their own sake; his name became more important than that of his average dummy.

Charley had one great advantage over the various Republican press agents who competed with him. Charley had a free hand. Many Democrats gave him carte blanche to issue any statement he wanted to under their names. Others seized the speeches he wrote for them and delivered them on a no-questions-asked basis. Michelson did not have to waste time conferring about commas. On the other hand, the work of the Republican press agents had to run a gantlet of jittery Republican leaders. At one time a piece of Republican publicity had to have seven O.K.'s before it could be issued. If it was considered at all important, it had to have President Hoover's sanction. Whatever good points Hoover may have had, he lacked smartness about publicity. He was a fussy editor, and would toil over an ordinary press release as if it were a last will and testament or an inscription for a public building. Of course, Michelson's reputation for judgment and common sense helped to win him a free hand. It is not always safe policy to give carte blanche to a publicity man. The Republicans tried it in Washington, and one of the first results was a Republican press release arraigning the New Deal for not spending enough money.

Michelson is also distinguished for the ability to wait. He would not, for example, permit his organization to exploit in any way the "Hoover books"—nonsense volumes which, on the basis of no evidence whatever, represented Hoover as an exploiter and despoiler of coolies and an occasional trader in slaves. The authors and publishers of the books thought they could sell them to Democratic headquarters by the tens of thousands. "I have no way of checking these books, and I won't touch them," said Michelson. Pressure was brought to bear on him by Democratic politicians. Michelson winked and said, "Wait." A duel of silences developed at this time, with Michelson on one side and James A. West, the Republican press agent, on the other. Pressure was put on West to cause him to issue a statement alleging that the National Democratic press bureau was secretly promoting the Hoover books. West refused, insisting that it would advertise the books by making such charges. Finally, a big Republican politician overruled West and made the charge. Michelson, through his human megaphones, bellowed denials. The books became the center of a controversy. Previously neglected, they became best sellers. Michelson had both the moral glow of righteousness and the practical satisfaction of seeing a Democratic objective accomplished by Republicans.

Many political experts think that Charley "hung the depression on Hoover." They feel that, except for Hundred-tongued Charley, the people might have attributed the crash and panic to world-wide causes and not to any one man. It is firmly believed that Michelson and his parrots elected a Democratic Congress in 1930 by convincing the people that Hoover and the Smoot-Hawley tariff had ruined the country.

The high tariff killed prosperity, according to Charley. The New Deal was inferentially pledged, by the campaigns of 1930 and 1932, to lower the tariff and make everybody well-to-do. Except for a few changes, effected mainly by Secretary Hull's treaties, however, the Smoot-Hawley tariff is still betraying the country. If Charley was right about the high tariff ruining us in 1930, it is still ruining us in 1936. Other Hoover iniquities that Charley pointed out have not been wholly corrected by the New Deal. Charley set all his tongues a-wagging against the "Hoover commissions"; the New Deal has created about ten times as many commissions, usually calling them "administrations." Charley blatted with every larynx at his command against Hoover bureaucracy and against Hoover extravagance.

When Roosevelt came into power Charley's mission changed. It became more important to avert bad publicity than to create good publicity. Charley distinguished himself in the second phase of his career fully as much as in the first. He is, if anything, even better at parrying blows than delivering them. He has done remarkable work in smearing the would-be smearers of Roosevelt. His campaign against the American Liberty League was in his best manner. Through a leak somewhere in the American Liberty League headquarters, Charley got advance information that the League's committee of lawyers was about to issue a statement denouncing certain New Deal legislation as unconstitutional. Before the lawyers had completed their statement attacking the New Deal, Michelson had completed two statements attacking the lawyers. He assailed them for incompetence on the grounds that they had poor batting averages in their own litigations before the Supreme Court. In another statement he attacked the lawyers for being corporation lawyers and gave lists of corporations which each represented. Both of Michelson's statements were effective, though somewhat disingenuous. He gave the batting average of Liberty League lawyers who had fared ill before the Supreme Court, suppressed the records of those who had been highly successful. In attacking the lawyers for being corporation lawyers, he did not mention the fact that practically all lawyers, except the representatives of cutpurses and second-story workers, are corporation lawyers; that even President Roosevelt's old firm is a firm of corporation lawyers.

The best bull's-eye that Charley scored on the Liberty League was scored against Al Smith. When Charley heard that Smith was going to attack the New Deal, he had his research workers look up every speech that Al had delivered since 1924. He knew that any man who has made a great many speeches over a period of twelve years has said many things that can later be used against him. He found many real or apparent contradictions between what Smith had said on earlier occasions and what he said before the Liberty League. The most telling point against Smith was taken from an obscure item in the *New York Times*. This quoted Al as having said that in a great public emergency the thing to do was to put the Constitution on the shelf. Before the Liberty League, Smith was the great defender of the Constitution, but before a small religious gathering several years ago, he had said, "Put the Constitution on the shelf." This was more extreme than President Roosevelt's horse-and-buggy statement. It became the keystone of Michelson's anti-Smith radio speech. Senator Joseph T. Robinson read the speech haltingly, as if he had not seen the text before the radio hour. The text, for example, referred to Al as "the unhappy warrior"; Robinson misread it as "the happy warrior." The text said that the New Deal had added two billions to "the purchasing power of the farmer"; Robinson misread it as saying that the New Deal had added two billions to the "purchasing price of the farmer."

Charley's attack on the Liberty League was, in the military phrase, a combination of the strategical defensive and tactical offensive. That is his general policy—to defend the New Deal by onslaughts on its adversaries. He had to mark time during the early part of the year. It was his business to smear the leading candidates for the Republican nomination, but it was difficult to pick the right one to smear. Charley seldom wastes ammunition on an ill-timed attack. The hope was cherished of smearing Landon with oil, since he had been connected with the oil industry; also to smear him with Hearst. It was a curious situation. Here was Charley, his patient back covered with Hearst saddle boils for three decades. Here was President Roosevelt, his withers still wrung with the Hearst yoke, which he carried in 1932; in the pre-convention campaign of 1932, in fact, Roosevelt, through Big Jim Farley, sought a private interview with Hearst in order to prove that Roosevelt and Hearst saw eye to eye on important issues. The whole situation called for care, and at least up to early in April, Michelson had not unlimbered his guns against Landon.

Charley has been invaluable to the New Deal in another respect—that of stopping boomerang publicity. General Hugh Johnson referred to Michelson as the wise Ulysses who prevented mistakes. Charley intervened more than once to prevent New Dealers from making unnecessary enemies. During the palmy days of the NRA some of the NRA boys wanted to announce that Henry Ford was to be indicted. Ford's case had been referred to the Department of Justice. Michelson was afraid of making a martyr of Ford, whose standards were higher than the NRA. Other fire-breathing young New Dealers wanted to announce that other big industrialists were about to be indicted. Charley said, "No." He was afraid that there would be a reaction, a general cry of "persecution." Except for Michelson, the New Deal would have incurred vastly greater odium from the NRA than it did. Government prosecution has chimed in with New Deal propaganda, but not enough to make itself ridiculous. The Government may or may not have a case against Pierre S. Du Pont and John J. Raskob under the income-tax law, but the Government's sensational attack on them just before the American Liberty League dinner was an obvious case of timing. Another fairly obvious bit of timing took place when Roosevelt turned back the air mail to the civilian flyers. With a heroic gesture the President had snatched the air mail from the civilian companies and turned it over to the Army. Fraud and corruption were charged, but never proved. The whole thing is still mysterious, and the motive seems to have been political. The Army failed to carry the air mail satisfactorily. Ten Army flyers were killed in the attempt. It was clear that Roosevelt had acted rashly as well as mysteriously. Each new death of an Army flyer was politically dangerous to him. He had to withdraw from his position to avoid further personal responsibility for loss of life. On March 10, 1934, he announced the return of the air mail to the civilians. This was an ignominious retreat. It was covered, however, by the Department of Justice, which announced on the same day that it was going after Mellon and other big fellows on income-tax charges. On one side of the front page, the *New York Times* had a headline saying, MELLON, WALKER, T. S. LAMONT FACE ACTION ON TAXES. It had a headline on the other side of the page telling of the President's retreat on air mail. This may have been coincidence, but it looks like smothering bad publicity with good publicity.

Before 1932 Michelson was linked with the Raskob-Shouse-Smith faction. On that account, he was slightly under a cloud when the New Deal moved into Washington. It was thought at first that he would not be needed. Louis Howe, the President's right-hand man, was pre-eminent as a political publicity man. Roosevelt himself was considered a master of political publicity. Louis Howe's ill health during the last two years of his life prevented him from exercising his talents. Michelson's craft and sagacity gradually won recognition. He began to sit in at the White House press conferences. He was away at the time of the horse-and-buggy interview, or he might have prevented that, the worst of Roosevelt's blunders. In recent months Charley has continued his mass production of speeches, but his most important work has been more subtle. His greatest usefulness is in advising the Administration what to ignore. Old experience has given him a prophetic power to estimate the developments which look big and menacing today, but are forgotten by next week if left alone. The journeyman press agent wants to reply to everything; Michelson won't reply to an attack unless he is convinced that it ought to be met. Even then his reply may be a delicate bit of showmanship which nobody recognizes as a reply.

Last summer a small holy war was started against President Roosevelt from many pulpits. It was a hot summer in Washington, and the President was working hard. He, like millions of his fellow countrymen, took occasional outings on Sunday. Pulpit criticism resulted. Generally speaking, the country has very little sympathy with complaints of this kind, but an epidemic of clerical attacks is dangerous. The thing was recognized as a menace when the Associated Press began to carry paragraphs on the subject. On July fourteenth of last year one such paragraph contained a criticism made by the Rev. Dr. I. M. Hargett at a camp meeting at Des Plaines, Illinois. On August eighteenth another AP paragraph contained the comment of the Rev. Dr. Norman V. Peale, at Syracuse, New York. There were scores of similar utterances, but few got national publicity. The situation had to be met. A mediocre press agent might have sought to publish the President's score of church attendance and prove that he outstripped Benjamin Harrison or Rutherford B. Hayes. Nothing of that kind happened. What did happen was that the President made a quiet visit to his home at Hyde Park, New York. He went with his family to services at the village church. He was photographed standing in the church door with the pastor. He spent the afternoon at a meeting of the church vestry, of which he is a member. He was represented as very keen and eager about the church's budget. The *New York Times* quoted friends as saying that the President "considers the business affairs of the church one of his serious responsibilities."

The vestry meeting occurred on September sixteenth. Seven days later, the President sent a personal letter to all the clergymen in the nation. It was a very flattering letter. It informed the clergymen of their vast knowledge of conditions, and asked them to "tell me where you feel our Government can better serve our people." There is only one thing about all this which does not seem to bear the earmarks of Charley Michelson—the letter was plagiarized bodily from a letter which Governor La Follette had sent at an earlier date to the clergymen of Wisconsin. This seemed to taint the whole gesture slightly with insincerity.

Michelson does not make mistakes like that. What use has been made of the replies of the clergymen has not been made public at this writing. It apparently failed to inspire the clergy with affection for the New Deal, as the *Literary Digest* poll made in January of this year indicated that 70 per cent of the clergy are anti-New-Dealers.

Michelson is difficult to scare. The word "boondoggling" alarmed some New Dealers, but Charley pretended to adopt it as an asset. He traced the word to Daniel Boone and said that it was a fine, red-blooded, old, backwoods Americanism. He coined the word "boomdoggling" when Republicans first started having boomlets. Shortly after Michelson embraced "boondoggling," President Roosevelt suggested that the word would probably become "enshrined" in the hearts of the American people. To show his pretended contempt for the Republican criticism of waste and extravagance, Charley invented the word "squanderlust" and announced that he was making a gift of it to the Republican National Committee. A further demonstration that he had no fear of charges of extravagance was his well-known wisecrack at the President's press conference. The President said that there was no news, except that Charley Michelson needed a haircut. "Well," said Charley, "somebody in this Administration has got to economize." The word coinage that Charley is proudest of is "DuPontifical." He applied that to his old employer, Jouett Shouse. Shouse is not a bad orator, but is a little pontifical and is also a close ally of the Du Ponts, so Charley hit him off on both points in one adjective.

Charley is rarely caught in an error that can be proved against him, but this has happened. While defending Roosevelt from the charge of disregarding the Constitution, he asserted that Hoover had signed several laws which the Supreme Court had nullified. This was false. Hoover had signed no laws which the Supreme Court had declared unconstitutional. Certain laws signed by his predecessors had been thrown out by the Supreme Court during Hoover's term in office. Harold Ickes, Secretary of the Interior, was the unfortunate loud-speaker who trumpeted Charley's error to the land. Ickes was cornered by Hoover and forced to retract. Charley, too, retracted—after his fashion. He wrote a Dispelling the Fog column abusing Hoover for having been so ungallant and unchivalrous as to have passed the blame for these unconstitutional laws on to his predecessors. Charley claimed to be particularly grieved by the fact that Hoover had "pinned the blue ribbon" for unconstitutionality on Coolidge.

Charley's biggest day consisted in three long speeches delivered by three of his cardboard orators—one in the United States Senate, one on a national hookup, and one at a banquet. The only audience that hears Charley deliver speeches in his own person is his secretary, Bill Janson. Charley's method is unusual. He does not dictate speeches to a stenographer. Bill Janson takes them down on a typewriter. As an ancient newspaper veteran, Charley likes the rattle of the machine. He thinks and speaks exactly as fast as Janson pounds the keys. The moment Charley finishes talking, the manuscript is completed. This avoids the delay of having a stenographer translate his notes. The saving of time is important, as many of Charley's orations are rattled off to meet some urgent crisis in Congress.

There was a streak of genius in the Michelson family. The late Prof. A. A. Michelson, a brother of Charley, was a Nobel Prize winner for physics and one of the greatest of American scientists. He was called "prince of experimenters"; Einstein based his theory of relativity on an experiment by Michelson which proved that ether did not exist. The great divergence in the career of the two brothers can be traced to the family history. A. A. Michelson, seventeen years the senior of Charley, was born in Prussia. In A. A.'s early years the family migrated to the United States and settled in San Francisco. After some years in the real-estate business, the father moved to Virginia City, Nevada, and opened a store in that rich silver-mining camp. The older brother, reared in San Francisco, had a wide choice of careers, and he selected science. Charley, reared in a Wild Western town, got a totally different view of life in his early years. He absorbed the local prejudice against scholarship. He regarded colleges as factories for turning out sissies.

Because his parents insisted on educating him, he ran away from home at the age of thirteen years. The Nevada mining town had become too sedate for him, and he went to Arizona to find a more red-blooded atmosphere. In Arizona, Charley was a miner, sheepherder and pilot of a forty-ox team. His earliest burst of prosperity came after he had ushered 1000 sheep for a couple of hundred miles. He was fired for making a suggestion to the head sheepman and was sent to the paymaster for his money. He was paid $172 more than he was entitled to.

"You've paid me too much," said Charley.

"Teaching me my business, are you?" said the paymaster. "Get out!"

The paymaster had made a mistake. The payment was based on the number of sheep in the original herd. One hundred and seventy-two lambs had been born en route and erroneously counted in favor of Michelson. When the error was discovered, a search was made for the youngster, but he was far away.

During his stay in Arizona, Charley wrote letters home. His brother-in-law, owner of the Virginia City *Chronicle,* admired Charley's style and offered him a job as a reporter, which Charley accepted. That was in the late 80's. An offer of seven dollars a week tempted him to San Francisco, where he worked on the *Post.* He left this to join the San Francisco *Examiner* after William Randolph Hearst started there on his journalistic career.

For years Charley covered the big train and stagecoach robberies, the noble crimes and the roaring politics of California. He got a severe lesson in accuracy in connection with the celebrated Skeleton of Kilgore Hill. The wife of the man who lived on Kilgore Hill in Northern California had disappeared. A little later a skeleton was found on the hill. Charley rushed from San Francisco to Kilgore Hill and scooped the world on the story. He unearthed a series of skeletons and discovered that not only the wife but also a series of farm hands had disappeared. Charley made the most of the sensational multiple-murder case until the wife and the entire series of farm hands turned up alive. They said they had quit Kilgore Hill because they could not stand the old farmer's cantankerousness. In the meantime beads and arrowheads were found in the graves, and the skeletons were identified as those of Indians. The farmer had a clear million-dollar libel suit, but settled for $200.

Michelson rose in the Hearst service until he became assistant Sunday editor of the San Francisco *Examiner.* Mortally offended when another man was promoted over his head, he resigned and went to work on the San Francisco *Call.* He was assigned to get an interview with Collis P. Huntington, the railroad builder, but failed repeatedly. Finally, by a characteristic stroke, Michelson got a gigantic interview with the old rail king. Steeping himself in the history of the Southern Pacific and Union Pacific by reading the Congressional Record and other documents, Michelson developed a theory that the two roads owed huge sums to the United States Government. He wrote a long questionnaire in the most insulting language he could command, and he was already a connoisseur of the language of insult. He sent the questionnaire to Huntington. It shocked the old fellow out of his shell. He wrote replies at great length to each question. In California journalism the pursuit of an interview with Huntington was something like the quest of the Holy Grail.

Charley was made. Hearst, who had gone to New York to found the *Journal,* sent for him at once. Hearst at the time was planning to present his fellow countrymen with a little war, and he assigned Charley to aid in this enterprise.

It was in 1895 that Charley first went to Cuba. He got through the Spanish lines and got the story of a massacre near Guantanamo. On his return to Havana he was thrown into Morro Castle, charged with violating military regulations, assaulting the Civil Guard and offering an insult to the uniform of the King of Spain. The "insult" was an old charge revived. Charley had stayed the arm of a Spanish policeman who was taking a chop with a sword at a drunken American who was entering a theater with an umbrella, in violation of an army regulation against entering a theater with an umbrella. Michelson was released after ten days in Morro Castle.

Michelson was now one of Hearst's greatest favorites. When the war actually broke out, Hearst was so anxious to have Charley cover everything that he actually covered nothing except one small scrimmage in Puerto Rico. Hearst kept changing his mind about where the big naval battle and the big land battle were to be fought, and he kept starting Charley in this direction and that, and then recalling him.

After the war Michelson became a Hearst star in New York and Chicago, covering the glorious murders and scandals of the period. Discovering that Charley's pen was full of vitriol, Hearst made him an editorial writer and then managing editor. Charley seared and skinned people for Hearst until 1913. He then began writing scenarios for Essanay. He turned out movies almost as fast as he later turned out speeches. He refused, however, to follow the movies to California. Instead, he went to Washington, sat down at his old vitriol-stained desk and started skinning people alive again for the jolly old publisher of San Simeon. Finally he deserted his old chief and became Washington correspondent of the New York *World.* Late in 1929 he was lured away from the *World* by the Raskob gold. For seven years now he has been writing typical Hearst editorials for Democratic statesmen to recite over the radio and in the halls of Congress. He will probably keep on doing this to the end of his life.

In Charley's early days in California the most glamorous of the bandits was Black Bart. He was so good at his trade that he threatened to ruin the Wells-Fargo Express Company. The Wells-Fargo directors finally solved the problem by pensioning off Black Bart, on condition that he would stay off the highways. The Republican Party might find a moral in this.

DYGARTSBUSH

by *Walter D. Edmonds*

WALTER DUMAUX EDMONDS was born in 1903 at Boonville, New York, in the region north of the Mohawk River, and has lived there ever since, with intervals in New York City and Cambridge, Massachusetts. His first upstate novel, *Rome Haul*, appeared in the *Atlantic Monthly* in 1929. Since 1932 he has written many short stories for the *Post*. His knowledge of the border warfare of the Revolution is great, but his instinctive understanding of the people who did the fighting is even more impressive. "Dygartsbush" is one of a series of *Post* stories which were inspired by short passages in Jeptha Simms' famous book, *The Frontiersmen of New York*. "I wrote them," says Mr. Edmonds, "immediately after finishing *Drums Along the Mohawk*, with almost no reference to sources because I was still so saturated with the background of the novel."

MAY 15, 1937

JOHN BORST was the first settler to come into Dygartsbush after the war. He came alone in the early fall of 1784, on foot, carrying a rifle, an ax, a brush scythe, a pair of blankets and a sack of corn meal. He found the different lots hard to recognize, for there was no sign left of the houses. Only the charred butt logs remained, surrounding a layer of dead coals that the rain had long since beaten into the earth. The fields had gone to brush; the piece where he had had his corn was covered with a scrub of berry vines, rough grass, yarrow and steeplebush. Young poplars had begun to come in along the edge. But near the center of it he found a stunted, slender little group of tiny cornstalks, tasseled out, with ears that looked like buds.

Whenever the work of clearing brush seemed everlasting, he would go over and look at that corn and think how good his first crop, seven years ago, had looked. It was good land, with a southerly slope and water near by. That was why he had come back to it. Other people were pushing westward; many of them Yankees from New England who had seen something of the country during the war or heard tell of it from returning soldiers. But John Borst thought it would be many years after their farms became productive before they would find a market for their crops. The war had taught him to prefer the things he knew and remembered.

After he found that his wife had been taken captive to the Indians' towns, he had joined the army. They had given him a fifty-dollar bounty and a uniform.

As soon as his enlistment ended, he volunteered from his militia class for the Levies and was assigned the land bounty of two hundred acres. This he had left with Mr. Paris, of Stone Arabia, who was now with the legislature in New York City, to sell for him on a commission basis.

If he were lucky enough to sell, he would become comparatively rich; but John Borst was a methodical man who did not believe in waiting for good luck. When he had his land readied again, and his house rebuilt, it would be time enough to think of buying stock and household goods.

He needed next to nothing now. He lived on his corn meal and pigeons he knocked off a roosting tree at dusk each evening. All his daylight hours he spent in the field, cutting down the brush and arranging it for burning. He slept in a small lean-to he had set up the first day in. And it was at nights, as he lay in his blankets and watched the fire dying, that he felt lonely. He had had no inclination to remarry, though he knew of several men whose women had been carried off by the Indians who had taken new wives in the past year.

One of the Devendorf girls, living in Fort Plain, he thought would marry him if he asked her. She had been pretty plain about it too. She wasn't a bad girl either, and he had thought seriously whether he would not be wise to take her. But that would have meant building a cabin, first off, for her to live in; and, now that he was back on the land, he knew he would have begrudged the time spent raising one and the money necessary to hire help, since there were no neighbors to come to a raising bee. Besides, he had never got over his feeling that Delia would come back. He felt it more strongly here in Dygartsbush than he had in the past seven years.

At nights he would remember her in their one

month of married life—cooking his supper for him when he came in; the way she knelt in front of the fire and handled the pans and dishes; sitting beside him fixing his clothes after the meal; getting ready for bed when he had stepped outside the last thing. He would come in to find her in her nightdress, combing her brown hair before the hearth, and the light of the red coals showed him the shadow of her body. She had been a long-bodied girl with fine square shoulders; she stood straight, even after a day of helping him in the corn piece. He did not think that the Devendorf girl would work the way Delia had and seem happy and gay in the labor.

He worked alone all through September. In October, when the dry winds began to parch the ground, he burned his land. Then, when he was ready to return to Fort Plain, three men turned up in Dygartsbush.

When he first sighted them, he went over to the edge of the burning for his rifle. There had been cases, during the past two years, of settlers who had gone back to their farms being murdered by Indians or renegades. But the men shouted to him that they were friends, and as they came nearer, he saw that one of them was Honus Kelly.

With Kelly were two New Englanders, named Hartley and Phelps, who came to look over the land. Honus explained that he had decided to sell his lot and that he had the selling of the Dygarts' also. As both these touched on John Borst's land, John spent a day with them, running the boundaries. Hartley and Phelps liked the country and suggested to John that the four of them raise three cabins, so that they could move in, in the spring.

John had not figured on building his cabin that fall, but the men had horses to skid the logs and it seemed like a good chance to get his house built without using cash. He spent half that night deciding that he would build his new house exactly on the site of the old one. When Honus Kelly asked him why, he replied that in 1776 it had seemed to him the best site, and he had found no reason to change his mind now. Kelly laughed and said it was just Dutch stubbornness, and Hartley said he thought it would make uneasy living; there might be ghosts around. "Nobody got killed here," John explained.

In the back of his mind, however, was the thought of how it would seem to Delia when she came back. With the cabin raised, the place would look to her the way it had the day he had brought her in the first time. "My, it's a nice house; it's a nice place, John. I think it's beautiful." He remembered her words, her fresh deep voice. That

was the first time she had not sounded shy. All the way in she had been shy with him, so that he had wondered whether he had been too strong with her. He was a big, powerful, heavy man, and, like most slow-moving men, he did not realize his full strength.

They built the three cabins in the next three weeks, cutting and skidding the logs with the New Englanders' horses; and then John helped them burn their land with the brush standing; and then they left to file their deeds and return to New England for their families. They would come back, they said, as soon as the roads were passable.

"Ain't you coming out with us, John?" Honus asked him.

John said no. He would stay and do finishing work on his cabin and maybe fell some timber, over in the hardwood lot. He would want to put in wheat next fall. The price of wheat was bound to go up with the influx of new settlers.

Honus did not laugh at him. "You're right," he said. Then he added, "They're going to have a treaty with the Indians this month. They're going to ask for all prisoners to get sent back."

"That's good," John said. He stood stubbing his toes in the dirt, as if to settle his feet.

"Delia ought to be back next summer," Honus said understandingly. "They wouldn't kill a girl like her. They liked her." He turned to the two New Englanders. "I'd probably have my hair hanging on an Indian post right now if it wasn't for John's wife. She helped me get away after they took us. They killed every other man but me and my brother and John here. Delia's a fine girl; she'll make a good neighbor for your families."

John flushed. Phelps, the older of the two, said it would be fine for his wife to have a woman neighbor. Especially for his mother-in-law, who didn't like the idea of their coming. He would tell his mother-in-law about Mrs. Borst.

"Tell her she's pretty," said Honus. "One of the prettiest women I ever saw."

John did not flush again. It was a fact, not flattery. The younger man, Hartley, looked round the clearing as if he were trying to imagine what an Indian raid was like. "Must 've been pretty bad," he said.

Honus said, "It was bad enough." And they left.

It seemed lonelier to John the day after they left. He had got to like them. They didn't seem like Yankees, especially. It would be good to have neighbors, he thought. Delia would like it. She used to say she liked people round, not that she liked to gad a lot, but just to hear and see them every week or so.

The rainy weather set in and he hunted him a deer and then spent time in his new cabin, chinking the walls. The men had had some paper, which he used in his window, and the inside of the cabin he fixed up with shelves like the old one; but these were made of split logs, like the benches. He would have to buy boards for a table, or buy a table secondhand.

He went out when the snow came, and worked at what he could find around Fort Plain, and then trapped a little. In the spring he had thirty dollars left of his bounty money and thirty-five dollars from trapping, over and above the cost of the traps. He bought a mare for thirty-five dollars, a heifer in calf for twelve, and three hogs for four dollars, at a bargain. With what was left he bought his corn seed, a log chain and a plow, and hired a man to help him drive in his stock.

It was a bare beginning, but he considered himself well off. He was starting his planting when the Phelpses came in: Phelps, his wife, one child, and Mrs. Cutts, his mother-in-law, a thin-faced woman with a dry way of speaking. John Borst got to like her pretty well.

The Hartleys came later, hardly in time to plant, and John Borst thought he would not make so good a neighbor. He said he was late because he did not like slush-traveling; he wanted to have warm weather to settle. He got John and Phelps to lend him a hand with his first field.

Mrs. Hartley was a frightened-acting girl, who seemed to take a fancy to John. She was always running over to the Borst place to be neighborly, offering to mend his things. Once she took some home with her when she found he was out. He went over next day to get them back and thank her, and, looking round her cabin, he thought privately that if Mrs. Hartley put her mind to it she would find so much work to do to catch up her own work she would not have time to take on his. She made him take back a loaf of bread, and when he got home he found that it was soggy in the middle.

But he had to admit that the sight of even Mrs. Hartley, who was a pretty-looking girl, for all her sloppy ways, made him lonely. Next day, though he could have put off the trip for another week, he went out to Fort Plain for flour and stopped in to see Honus Kelly. He asked Honus whether any women had been brought in from the Indian towns.

Honus thought quite a few had. "They most of them get left at Fort Stanwix." He seemed to understand how John felt. "Anyway, when Delia shows up she'll most probably come through here. I'll tell her you're back at Dygartsbush."

"Thanks," said John. He fumbled round for a minute. "Do you think there's any chance of her coming back?"

"Sure I do. I told you before, the Indian that took her treated her real good. Pete told you that too." Honus didn't feel it was his business to tell John the old Indian planned to make a squaw of her.

"Yes, you told me that." John Borst looked out the window. "I wonder if it would do any good if I went out looking for her. They say it's safe enough traveling in the Indian country."

"You'd probably never find her that way. She might turn up just after you left here and then you both would have much more time waiting."

"I guess that's right." Honus had told him that before too. Honus knew a lot about the Indian country. A man wouldn't have any chance out there finding out about a particular white woman. He said good-by to Honus and went over to the store to do his trading. He bought himself some flour and a bag of salt and some salt beef. He didn't know quite how it was, but when he happened to see a new bolt of dress goods, he decided to buy some. Later, he decided it was because the brown striping reminded him of the color of her hair. He told the storekeeper's wife he wanted enough for a tall girl, about so high, and he held his hand level with his cheekbones.

He started back about two hours before sunset, though he knew that he would have to go slow the last part of the way, as the mare was still unfamiliar with the trail. It was after dark when he reached the outskirts of Dygartsbush, and he could see, off on his left, the light from the Hartleys' cabin, a single small square glow, appearing and disappearing among the trees with the mare's progress. He had a glimpse of Mrs. Hartley crossing the lighted space. She had her hair down her back, as though she were preparing for the night. The sight brought him a sense of intimacy, from which he himself was excluded. He had no companionship but the sound of the mare's hoofs, the smell of sweat, and the motion of her walk between his legs.

He did not see any light from Phelps', but he heard the child crying. The thin sound was muffled. John knew that the child and the grandmother slept in the loft. By the time he reached his own clearing the sound of crying had died away, and he was alone with the mare under a dark sky. He rode heavily, leaning his hands on her withers, paying no attention to the trail; and he was entirely unprepared when the mare threw up her head and stopped short, snorting.

She nearly unseated him and, as it was, his cheek struck painfully against her head. He started to kick her sides, jerking her head angrily, when she moved forward again of her own accord, but with her head still raised and ears pointed. Looking up himself he saw, at the far end of the clearing, a light in his own window.

It made a dim orange pattern through the paper panes. He could see no shadow of any person moving in the house, but a spark, jumping from the chimney mouth, caught his eye, and he guessed someone had freshened a fire on the hearth.

He stopped the mare and dismounted and got his rifle ready in his hand. Honus had told him that there were still a few Tories and Indians who had lived along the valley, who were trying to get back. Down in Fort Plain they had an organization to deal with them.

He knew how far the light reached when the door was opened. Before he came into the area he let the mare have her head and slapped her flank. She stepped ahead quickly, passing the door to go round to the shed. John lay down in the grass, with his rifle pointed.

The door opened, shedding its light over the mare, but there was no ambush from the field. A whippoorwill had started singing, but John did not hear it. A woman was standing in the door, looking out with large eyes at the mare. The beast stopped again, snorting uneasily, then moved on. The woman cupped her hands on each side of her face, to act as blinders from the light, and stepped past the mare. He could see her plain now. She wore Indian clothes, moccasins and skirt and a loose overdress. He could tell by her height who she was.

He got up slowly, a little uncertain in his arms and legs, walked over to her and leaned on his rifle and looked into her face to make sure.

But he knew anyway. She stood erect, looking back at him, her hands hanging at her sides. He did not think she had changed, except for her Indian clothes and the way she wore her hair in two braids over her breast. He saw her lips part to say, "I'm back, John," but her voice was the barest whisper. He shifted a little so that her face, turning with him, came into the light, showing him again, after seven years, the curve of her cheek and the tenderness of her mouth. Then he saw that her eyes were wet. Neither of them heard the whippoorwill still calling in the young corn.

II

AT TIMES, John Borst had the feeling that he and Delia had taken up their lives exactly where they were the night the Indians raided Dygartsbush. That night also, he had been coming home from Fort Plain with flour, almost at the same time. But then he had been afoot instead of riding his own mare.

That night might have been a dream—the burning cabins and the firing, and the rain. He had come into Hawyer's clearing just in time to see the Indians reach that place. He could tell by the fires that the Indians had surrounded every house. He had seen Hawyer shot in his door and Mrs. Hawyer hauled out of the house. The Indian had her by the hair and was dragging her, the way a man might lug along a stubborn dog to put it out for the night. Then they had spotted John, half a dozen of them, and he had set out to run for the fort.

He told Delia about it the day after her return —they had not done any talking that first night. He told her how he had got fifteen men to come back with him and they had found every house in ashes. They had picked up the tracks at the end of his lot, followed them for half a dozen miles. Then they had come back and buried the dead. That task had taken them the rest of the day. They had had to camp the night just off Hawyer's clearing, and it was sheer luck that John had waked to hear the crying of a little girl. He said if he had not heard it then Mrs. Dygart's daughters would probably have wandered off and got lost in the woods. When he found them they were walking away from the ashes of the Dygart house, because the seven-year-old one did not think it was theirs. She was hauling the little one along, trying to find their house. When they heard him coming they just crouched down, still as rabbits. Now, he said, they were with their mother who had been brought back by General Sullivan's army.

Delia had been crouching in front of the fire, like an Indian squaw, and while he talked she had suddenly got down on her knees, the way she used to do. It gave him a vaguely uneasy feeling to see the slow pink rising in her cheeks, as though she had corrected herself in a mistake. Now she lifted her face and her eyes regarded him with their old searching level glance.

"Did you think I was dead, John?"

He thought a while. "No. I didn't think so. But I thought I probably wouldn't ever see you again. I joined the army. There wasn't anything left for me here, and I didn't get back to Tryon County for more'n a year. Then I found out that Caty Breen had got back. She came back married to a man that had got himself exchanged. I don't remember his name. She's living up in Kingsland now."

Delia said, "I'm glad. She was so scared. They took her off from the rest of us, two Indians did." She turned her attention back to her cooking.

"Where was that?" he asked.

"Near the head of a river. I don't know what one. We went on to the Genesee, the rest of us, except for Peter Kelly and the Mitchel girl."

"They got back five years ago," John told her. "They ran away. Honus told me about it. He told me Pete hadn't heard anything of you."

"Honus was good to me, John."

"He told me how you helped him get away."

"What else did he tell you?"

John looked at her. "Why, I don't know. Just about how he got away. He kept telling me, too, he didn't think the Indians would hurt you any. He said the one that took you thought a lot of you. He had a comic name, High Grass, I think Honus said."

"Yes, High Grass. Gasotena."

She drew her breath slowly, and became quite still. He had noticed that about her in the one day she had been home—the way she fell into a stillness. Not silence, for she always answered him at once if he said anything. He did not know how to describe it to himself, but he supposed it was because she felt some kind of strangeness getting back to white people. Maybe, he thought, she felt strange with him. Seven years was a long time to be away from a man; maybe a woman got to feeling different about things.

He said, "It must be queer, coming back to me after so long. Must seem like taking up with a man without getting married, almost." He tried to say it in a light, joking kind of way.

But she whirled suddenly, lifting her face and looking closely into his. "What makes you say that?" He saw her lips tremble and become still.

"I didn't mean to make you jump. I thought, maybe, I'd seem like almost a strange man. Like, maybe, there was things you'd disremembered about me. Things, maybe you didn't like so well."

He could see her throat fill and empty.

"Did you think that last night?"

He felt himself coloring. "No."

"Are there things about me?"

"No," he said. "God, no." There was visible pain in her eyes. He was a fool, he thought. "Look out, Delia. That fat's catching fire."

She turned back to the cooking quickly and silently, and he looked down on her back. It always seemed to him the most homely thing in the world for a man to sit watching his wife bend to cook his dinner. She had done up her hair in braids wound round her head, but she still wore her Indian clothing. It was good to work in, she said. They couldn't afford to throw away good clothes. Now she was still again for a long time, and he thought she had gone off into one of her spells until she began to speak.

Then her voice was throaty and pitched low, and she seemed to have difficulty with her words. It was hard to hear her. One of the hogs had wandered up to the shed door and was oinking to himself and rubbing his hide against the door-jamb. Her words came through the sound of the pig and the dead June heat.

She said: "I used to wonder if you'd got caught. But they never brought in your scalp. I got to believe you were alive, John. Then after I'd been in the Indian town for a while I began to think I'd have to stay there all my life. We knew the army was coming. I thought it might come near, but it never did come near. Then, after a long time, it seemed as if I didn't have anything to hope for. I wasn't bad off like some other prisoners. The Indians were good to me, but it wasn't like white people being good to you. I didn't mind the work, John. Work helped, somehow, but no work you did was for yourself. No house belongs to any one person among the Indians. Their gardens are for the whole house, all the people in it. The squaws didn't ever plant flowers by their houses. I used to think about the little dark red pinks I planted just outside the door and wonder if they ever blowed."

Listening to her in a kind of fascination John heard himself say, "I don't know, Delia," but she went on quietly.

"I guess the fire scorched them to death. I looked for them when I came back, but it was getting near dark then, so I couldn't tell. I looked this morning, but there weren't any. Indians don't plant flowers, though they like picking wild ones. The children would pick wild ones and carry them round till they were dead and throw them away. I put some in water once to show them, but they never caught on. Sometimes I used to think maybe you had come back and was tending the pinks for me. But I knew that was silly, that you couldn't come back till the war was over." She drew a long breath. "I used to wonder and wonder about you, what you were doing, and who you were with, John. Did you wonder about me?"

"Yes."

"When they told me about the treaty and said I could go home, I was afraid, John. I thought, it's seven years and you haven't heard from me. I thought maybe you'd found another woman and married her."

"I saw plenty," he said. "I never had the urge to marry."

"I didn't know that. I wouldn't have blamed you, though. But I had to come back to find out. Ganowauges brought me. He knew the southern way better, and he said he'd bring me as far as Fort Plain. Most went to Fort Stanwix, I think.

I asked him if we could come through here and he said we could do it. We got here just about dark, John. We came in the same way Gasotena took me away. We came out of the woods and we both smelled hoed land. Then I looked and saw the house, just the way it was, right in the same place. I was so frightened I could scarcely move. Ganowauges pointed to it and told me to go. I asked him if he would wait. I thought then I would go back with him if there was a woman in it. He acted kind of nervy and said he'd rather wait in the woods. I went to the house, John. I had to see what she looked like."

"She wasn't there, was she?"

Delia glanced at him in a startled way, saw his eyes, and tried to smile.

"No. First I thought maybe you'd taken her to Fort Plain with you. Then I went inside and I saw you'd been living alone."

"How did you know that?"

She smiled this time, to herself.

"I knew it was you too. I could tell because of the way the tooth twig was laid against the sack of gunpowder. You always laid it standing up so the brush end would dry out. It was so much the same. I just sat down and cried. I didn't want to light the light because I wanted to get my crying done before you came. I forgot all about Ganowauges. I never even thanked him. John, did you build the house right here on purpose?"

He said, "Yes."

He saw her eyelids trembling, and got up and went out to wash. When he came in again she seemed peaceful. She had laid out their food on the board table. He said, "It's not so well fixed. But I'll get a glass sash before winter and a chest of drawers for you to keep your clothes in. I've got a little money left."

She drew a deep breath, looking round.

"It's all ours. John, I don't care if we're poor. It's no matter to me. All I want to do is work for you, and for you to be happy, and have you care for me the way you used to. I'm older than I was. I guess I show it. But I'm healthy and strong, still." Her voice trailed off.

He said, "You look all right." He felt strangely troubled. He could not tell why. He tried to talk about something else. "I'll have to take you over to the neighbors. They're Yankee people. But I like the Phelpses. I like Mrs. Cutts too. She's kind of like the way Mrs. Staats was, but she's sensible."

"Which one is she?"

"Mrs. Phelps' mother. She's elderly. Hartleys are always borrowing. You'll have to watch out for them. They mean all right. They're just shiftless." He got up. "Guess I'll begin mowing grass over in the swale this afternoon. We got to have hay for the mare and cow, next winter."

"We didn't have a cow and horse before, did we? It makes it seem more like a farm, even if we haven't got a glass window. When's the cow due?"

"They thought in September. I think maybe August. I had a chance to get her cheap," he explained. "I meant to get a window first."

"I'd rather have the cow. I used to make butter fine."

John went out, leaving her looking happy, he thought. More the way she used to be. He took his scythe and went toward the swale; but as soon as he entered the woods he made a circuit and picked up Delia's tracks. He found the Indian's plain enough. The Indian had been like a fox nosing the clearing. After Delia went toward the house, he had moved along the edge of the woods until he was opposite the door. There, in crushed ferns, John found the imprint of the Indian's body. He must have lain there for quite a while. Probably he had been there when John came home. John stood still, thinking what a plain mark he must have made. He didn't like the thought of it, even though the Indian hadn't done anything.

Delia came to the door with the bucket she had been washing the dishes in and threw away the water with a swinging motion, making a sparkle of drops through the sunlight. Then she stood for a moment, resting her weight on one hip, and staring after the way John had gone. He thought he had never seen her look so pretty as she did in her Indian dress. Just why, he wasn't sure. He thought maybe it was the strangeness of it—as if she was something he didn't really have a right to. After a moment she let her head bend, and then she turned and put up her arm against the jamb of the door and rested her forehead on it. She might have been crying.

Suddenly it came to John that he was spying on his wife. His face reddened, even though he knew himself alone and unobserved; and he went back through the edge of the woods, cut across to the swale, and set down the point of the scythe snath in the grass.

He began whetting the scythe. The high sound of the stone against the blade, the heat of the sun on the back of his neck, the waves of warm air shimmering above the grass, and the whine of a hot-weather bird all seemed to go together. He mowed with a full sweep. He prided himself on being a four-acre mower; but that afternoon he could not put his heart into the mowing. The image of his wife leaning her head against the doorjamb kept coming before his eyes to trouble him.

III

SHE BECAME suddenly shy of the idea of calling on the neighbors and, after twice mentioning it, John let her alone. But next day, meeting Phelps, who had come over to mow his half of the swale, John thought it only polite to mention Delia's return. Phelps thought it was almost miraculous. He shook John's hand and vowed he would tell his womenfolk that evening. John explained that Delia felt shy about meeting people. She had no decent clothes yet. Just the Indian things she had come home with. Phelps said he understood, and they mowed all day without taking up the subject again.

But Mrs. Cutts was a curious woman, and made a point of passing through Borst's clearing on her way home from the berry patch on Dygart's knoll. With no warning, Delia had no decent chance of getting out of her way and, when Mrs. Cutts asked if she could come in, smiled hesitantly and stood aside from the door.

"It's a good thing for John you've come back, Mrs. Borst," said the old woman, sitting down. "My, the sun's hot. But I got some dandy strawberries. I'll leave you some. I've got a real likin' for John." Her keen old eyes examined Delia frankly. "Phelps—I always called him Phelps; he used to be my hired man—Phelps said you was shy about your clothes. Land sakes! If I was a part as pretty in them I wouldn't be living with my son-in-law."

She smiled as Delia flushed.

"You ain't very talkative, are you?" she asked, after a moment.

Delia got even pinker. "It's hard to be with people again—white people, I mean."

"It must have been hard," said Mrs. Cutts. "Did they burn everything you had?"

Delia nodded. "But I don't seem to mind it now. Not what happened to our place. We were lucky that way."

"Yes. John told me he was away. He said every other man but one and a boy got killed."

"That was the bad part, wondering what had happened to John." She walked over to the window. "I don't like to think about it, Mrs. Cutts."

"No wonder. Indians must be awful people. I expect they made a kind of slave out of you. They do that with their own women, I've heard tell."

"Squaws don't think they're slaves. So they didn't treat me bad by their lights. You see, I got adopted into a house."

Mrs. Cutts studied her shrewdly.

"You mean you was just like one of them?"

Delia nodded.

"I guess that's why you feel uneasy with white women. Listen, Mrs. Borst," she said, after a moment. "I don't know what happened to you out there. I don't want to know unless you want to tell me. I'm no gadder, if you want to. But I like John. You won't make him happy if you keep troubling yourself about what happened. It wasn't your fault, was it?" Delia shook her head. "You're healthy and pretty-looking, and you're still young. There's a long time ahead of you. It's not so easy for a woman to begin over as it is for a man—I don't know why. But you can do it if you want to."

Delia swung round on the old woman, who now had stooped to pick up her berries. "Give me a dish, dearie, and I'll fill it from my pail."

But Delia made no move to. She stared at Mrs. Cutts with painful intensity. "What do you think happened to me, Mrs. Cutts?"

"I don't know. It's not my business and I'm not asking. Don't you worry. My tongue's my own, and I keep it where it belongs." She gave Delia a hearty smile. "Now, where's a dish?"

Mrs. Cutts heaped the dish with the fresh berries and went out of the door. She was a dozen yards down the path before Delia thought of thanking her.

She ran after the old woman, who, by then, had her shawl over her head and was stumping along like a vigorous witch. Delia moved so quietly in her Indian moccasins that she startled Mrs. Cutts.

"I meant to thank you for the berries. They're lovely."

"You're real welcome to them," said Mrs. Cutts. "When you feel ready to, come over and see us. Bring John or come alone."

"Thank you. I'll walk along a way with you. It's time I went and told John to come to dinner."

"That's neighborly."

Mrs. Cutts did not speak. She thought maybe the girl would unload her trouble. She knew she had one, and the only way to get her to tell it was by keeping quiet.

But Delia walked also in silence. She was a good head taller than Mrs. Cutts. Glancing sidewise, the old woman could see the thoughtfulness in her face. "Think of an Indian with that," she thought to herself, studying the round of the chin, the straight nose and reserved eyes, and the large mouth. They parted at the fork of the path without having said another word. Mrs. Cutts wasn't planning to say anything, but at the last moment she unexpectedly made up her mind.

"Delia Borst," she said, "just remember that there's some things a man is a lot happier for not knowing. It may be hard on you, but it's true."

"The man might find out sometime. Then what would he think?"

"I'd let him take his chance of it."

Delia looked over the top of Mrs. Cutts' shawl.

"But I love John," she said.

IV

SHE MADE UP her mind to tell him that night. When he came in from the swale half an hour after her, he could tell that something was on her mind.

She had been helping him all afternoon, raking his mowing of the day before into haycocks. She seemed to take pleasure in the work, and they kept at it all afternoon in companionable silence. But she didn't say anything until she had given him his cornbread and broth, and then she came at it roundabout.

"Mrs. Cutts stopped in this morning, John. We had a talk."

"She's a neighborly woman," he said. "Though she's kind of short-spoken."

Delia got the dish of berries. "She left these for us. I didn't like her at first, but, after a while, I thought she was nice."

"She tell you about the way she broke her wrist?" Delia shook her head. "She will. She likes to talk about her troubles, but she don't let them hinder her from doing what she wants."

"She didn't mention it. We got talking about what men think."

"Did you?"

"She said it was better for a man not to be told everything by his wife."

John said, "I guess that depends on the wife."

"That's what I said." She finished her berries and sat still, leaning slightly toward him over the table. She had the look of taking hold of herself with both hands. They were folded on the table edge, so that when she leaned against them they fitted the cleft in her breasts. Her hands could feel the beating of her heart.

"You look worried," John said suddenly.

But she did not notice him. Her eyes seemed lost in the darkness gathering beyond the open door. There was a fringe of balsams beyond the swale and their tips were like small arrowheads in the line of pale light still showing under a west-moving bank of clouds.

They had not lit the dip. Their only light was from the fire. An exploratory June bug buzzed through the door, flipped on one wing tip between them, and hit the stone back of the fireplace. Delia shivered and turned her eyes to her husband's.

"John, I've been home most of a week, and you've never asked me what happened to me in Onondarha."

"Where was that?"

"That's the name of the town I lived in. You see, you never even asked me that."

John Borst also had become quiet. His big hands, which had been resting on the table, he put into his lap. She could imagine them holding his knees. His heavy face with its slow-moving eyes stared back at her. She drew her breath slowly, thinking how kind it looked. She had never heard his voice sound the way it did when he spoke to her.

"I didn't ask you because I figured you would tell me what you wanted I should know. What's all right with you is all right with me. I've wondered what happened to you sometimes. I got crazy about it sometimes. But, now you're back, I don't want you to tell me what you don't want to."

She was surprised and touched. "Mrs. Cutts almost said the same thing, John. Do you know what I said? I said I loved you too much. Maybe it's bad to love someone too much."

"Maybe," he said. It sounded stupid. He could see her trembling. The lift of her chin toward him was a hurtful thing to see; the complete quiet of her struggle with herself.

"I've got to tell you, John. You can send me away then if you want."

"I won't never send you away."

She put out her hand quickly as though to stop his lips, then let it fall to the table between them. "I won't take that for a promise," she said. "You've got to listen. I can't bear you loving me unless you know. High Grass, the Indian that took me, got me adopted into his house. The women dressed me up and showed me how to make a cake and told me to give it to the old woman of the house. I didn't know what they said; I hadn't learned Indian then. You believe that?"

His voice sounded heavy. "Yes, I believe it."

"I didn't know I was getting married. I wanted to please them. I wanted to stay alive, so I could come back to you. I didn't know till night, when he came into my place. I didn't know it was his place till then. There were thirty people in that house all round me, John."

He didn't say anything. He didn't look at her. Her voice became more urgent.

"I couldn't do anything. Anything, John. I couldn't. I didn't think I could live."

"You did, though."

"Yes, I did." She sounded suddenly calmer. "After a year, I had a baby, John. He was the only thing I loved. I didn't love him, either. Every time I saw him I thought of you. I thought how you'd hate me."

"I don't hate you."

Her lips stayed parted. She licked them suddenly with her tongue, but even then she could not speak. After a while John got up. He turned to look out of the door.

"Where's the baby?"

"He died."

"You didn't leave him, did you?"

"No, John."

"That would have been a bad thing. Did you have any more children?"

"No." She whispered, leaning forward over the table. "I couldn't have come back, leaving a child, could I? And I couldn't come back with one. I thought, when he died, it was like providence telling me I could come back. I knew I had to tell you, but when I got here, I couldn't, John. Honestly, I'm sorry."

He didn't notice her.

"This High Grass," he said. "What's he doing?"

"He went off on a war party. He didn't come back. They told me he got killed."

"My God," he said. "I can't do nothing."

He turned through the door abruptly, leaving her at the table. She sat alone for a long time. She could hear him walking round, but she could not move. She waited like a prisoner until at last he came in. He said, "Ain't you done the dishes?" But she only shook her head and watched him. "Come on," he said, "I'll help you."

She rose slowly, reaching for the dishes blindly. "Do you want me to stay?"

He turned on her, his voice heavy with sarcasm.

"Where in hell could you go to this time of night?"

V

AN OUTSIDER would have seen nothing unusual in their relations. Delia herself sometimes almost persuaded herself that John was putting what she had told him from his mind. But, in a day or so, she would catch him watching her; and at such times something in his eyes made her feel whipped and humiliated. She accepted the feeling as part of the payment she would have to make for what had happened to her—that she had known all along she would have to make. A good woman, she thought, a Christian saint, would have died first. But Delia hadn't wanted to die; she had wanted to get back to John; now she must take the future with patience.

It was hard to be patient, living with John. Times were when she wanted to cry out, "Stop looking at me that way. I'd rather you'd whip me,

if you wanted. I didn't do anything bad." While they were working together in the field, it was more like old times; or hauling the hay up to the sheds in small loads on a sledge. The rick built slowly, but when it was high, John sometimes grinned, pitching the hay up to her.

In the evenings was the time their reserve came between them. It arrived with the intimate darkness. She felt that he thought of her as just a useful body, something one accepted as one accepted the weather. But her resentment was less against him—she remembered how he had waited seven years for her and built the cabin where she expected it to be—than against the providence that had played tricks with her. It got so she prayed that it might be reversed, for even just one day.

One way he had changed was in laying down the law about their neighbors. He kept after her until she had made a dress from the calico he had brought. She could hardly bear to touch it, thinking of the impulse that had made him buy it at the very time of her return, and of what her return had resulted in. But he said he didn't want the neighbors to think he wasn't proud to show her off.

They made the visits one Sunday, she in the calico that felt like a cold rag touching her limply, he with his coat brushed. They went first to the Hartley house; to get the worst part over quick, John said. Delia disliked them both. The man eyed her with open and curious admiration. The woman, in the one moment they had to be alone, asked, "Tell me, Mrs. Borst, are Indian men the same as other men?"

"Why should I know?" Delia asked frigidly.

Mrs. Hartley whinnied softly. "With the shape you've got. Oh, my! Listen, I'd like to see you dressed in squaw's clothes. Phelps said you come back in them. Would you show them to me?"

They were a strange couple to find in Dygartsbush, Delia thought; but she found the Phelpses nice simple people.

John was pleased the way the Phelpses took to Delia and she to them. He wouldn't feel easy about leaving Delia alone when he went down to Fort Plain, if she didn't have a place she could go to. Mrs. Cutts had said they'd be glad to have Delia visit them the next time he went down. The old woman had seen, with one look, that there was something between the Borsts; she guessed what had happened. She took John aside as they were leaving and said, "John, I want to tell you I think she's one of the best sort of women. You can see she's honest." Then she added, "When a person's young he or she's likely to set a lot of store in notions that don't amount to much when they get older." She gave his shoulder a sharp pat and sent him after his wife before he could think of a reply.

He walked silently and morosely until he and Delia were near home. Then he asked, "Did you tell Mrs. Cutts anything about you and that Indian?"

As she turned her head to answer he could see that she was close to tears. "No. I didn't think anybody but you had any right to know."

"I think she must have guessed about you then," he said gloomily.

Thank God, he thought, Mrs. Cutts wasn't a talkative woman. She was smart, though, and she had probably guessed it. He couldn't hold it against Delia. He watched her getting their Sunday supper, and then got down his rifle to oil it. He would have to go down to Fort Plain again soon and he thought he might as well go that week. Anything to get out of the house. He glanced up, to surprise her covertly studying him from the hearth. She turned her head at once, paling slightly. She made him think of an abused dog when she did that, and he felt a senseless and irrational burst of anger.

"What do you always want to be staring at me for?"

"I didn't mean to be staring at you. I didn't want to make you mad."

"I get sick of it."

She watched the fire. Then, "You hate me, don't you, John?"

"No. I don't hate you. But I can't stand that way you look." He got up suddenly to replace the gun. "Don't start talking that way either."

"I can't talk at all, can I?" She turned on her knees to face him. "John, what sense is there in us living together like this?"

"Stop it. I'm going out. When you've got the supper ready I'll come in. I'm going to look at the heifer."

It was a feeble excuse. He felt ashamed. The heifer wasn't due for a couple of weeks yet. He tramped down to the shed and looked her over. He stayed there, fussing aimlessly about nothing, until he heard Delia's tentative call. When he entered the house, she was sitting on her side of the table, and he felt an impulse to say something that would make her feel better.

"I guess I'll go down to Fort Plain tomorrow," he said. "I've got to get flour, and I might as well go sooner as later. Maybe I'll hear something about my bounty land."

Neither of them believed he would hear.

"I'm sorry I talked that way," he said.

The corners of her mouth quivered.

"I know it's hard for you, John. It's hard for me. When you talk like that and look that way you make me feel like something dirty."

He relapsed sullenly into silence.

VI

THOUGH it was raining, he started next morning, letting the mare take her time, so that they reached Fort Plain toward noon. He did his trading before dinnertime, finding that the price of salt beef had risen like everything else. Flour was pretty near prohibitive, as far as he was concerned. Then he went round to Honus Kelly's to visit and ask whether there had been any news from Mr. Paris about his bounty land. Honus had gone out earlier that morning, he was told; no, no word had come for him from Mr. Paris. He might find Honus down at the tavern.

John didn't like to ask Honus' hired girl to give him food, and she didn't offer him any, so he went down to the tavern in a gloomy state of mind. Nobody was in the place except the landlord and a couple of women in the kitchen. The landlord came into the tap and said he could give John some cold pork. John asked for some, and ordered a glass of strap.

The landlord said, "Quite some rain, ain't it?"

John said it was.

"I been looking in my almanac." The landlord fished out a worn book from under the bar, flipped the pages to August with a licked thumb, and said, "Look what the bug-tit wrote down about the weather." John looked at the column of Various Phenomena for August, but the landlord read out the words, "Very hot. Hot and dry. Then he says Cooler winds. Way down at the bottom he's put in Wandering thun. showers. I paid two and a half shilling for this book. Why, hell, I could 've wrote down that kind of stuff myself. And look at it rain and no thun.—that's what he calls thunder—neither."

John said it didn't look very good to him and asked for Honus Kelly.

"He come in this morning," the tavern keeper said casually. "He got Walrath, Pierce and the two Devendorfs, and they went off after an Indian that was in here."

John said, "That's too bad. I wanted to see him. Who was the Indian?"

A stout, red-cheeked woman brought in a plate of sliced fresh ham, bread, a cold roast potato with a slice of raw onion leaning against it. The landlord leaned over it as if to smell the onion. They looked desultory, like any two men in a taproom on a rainy afternoon. An investigating fly buzzed over from the window and the landlord slapped him down with the glass rag. Through the open door the sound of the eaves' drip from the low stoop continued steadily.

"Why, he acted all right when he come in here. Said he was heading south, and asked about the settlements. I said there was some people living in Dygartsbush." The landlord looked up. "Why, that's where you're settled, ain't it? I forgot. You don't come down much."

John left off eating. His big face leaned intently toward the tavern keeper's. "What was the matter with him?"

The tavern keeper poured himself a drink.

"Makes my stomach turn to think of it. He got a couple of rums inside and commenced acting big. I told him to behave himself. I said we killed fresh Indians round here, but he just slammed his hand-ax down on the bar and said he'd kill me if I didn't behave myself, the lousy old skunk! I didn't dast move out of the tap, and there wasn't anybody else to send for Honus. So I just waited, and pretty soon he got nervy and said he'd had enough, and I told him what he owed me. Then you know what he did? He hauled out a kind of funny-looking purse and I looked at it and said it was funny-looking, and he held it out for me to look at. Mister, it was the skin off a human hand. Looked to me like a woman's, honest-to-God."

The tavern keeper looked into John's flushed face.

"Makes you feel ugly, don't it? He paid me in British money too. I knowed then he was a genuine bad one. But I didn't tell him English money was worth twice York money. I made him pay straight, yes, sir. He paid me and went right through that door, putting that purse back in his coat pocket, and he clumb the fence and went into the woods. I tell you, I went right after Honus."

"How long was it before Honus got after him?"

" 'Bout an hour and a half. Honus has got the boys organized pretty well. I figure he'll pick him up before too long a time."

John spoke slowly, half to himself. "It's hard tracking in a rain like this one."

"Ain't it the truth? I hadn't thought of it. Still, Honus is good. Ain't any of these Indians has got away from him yet. The boys tell me about it, because they know I keep quiet. Tie 'em to trees, they say; don't hurt 'em at all. Only they use the neck-and-limb method."

The landlord had to laugh. Then he met John's eye and stopped short. "No offense, you know, mister."

John ignored him. "What did the Indian look like?"

"Why," he said, "looked like any Indian. He had on an old hat and a coat, he'd probably stole.

Looked pretty old—he'd let his hair grow, and there was some white in it. But he was fat. I knew there was something about him. He had the biggest stomach you ever saw."

"Did he say what his name was?"

"Said he was Christian Indian. Christian boy, he said. Bet he was sixty years old. Called himself Joe Conjocky. Ever hear of him?"

John pulled out his purse. "What do I owe you?"

"You've hardly et."

John picked up his rifle and started. But he stopped in the doorway, and the tavern keeper thought his face was strangely set.

"Hey, you! Did you tell Honus how that Indian asked about Dygartsbush?"

"Why, no. Come to think of it, I guess I didn't."

"You fool!"

John went out. He didn't run, but his big legs took him swiftly along the muddy road to the barn. He saddled his mare, packed on his flour and beef and salt, re-primed his rifle, and led her out of the barn. It was still raining.

The wind was southwest, bringing the rain against their faces, and the mare flickered the first drops from her ears. He swung up on her and headed her home. He had a sick feeling in his insides: twenty miles; a wet trail; and the Indian had started at about ten o'clock. John figured it would be past one, now. Even if he pushed the mare hard enough to founder her, he could not expect to reach his cabin before suppertime. Delia would be coming back from Phelps' long before that. He felt a sudden blaze of anger against the tavern keeper. If the fool had only had the sense to tell Honus, Honus would have headed straight for Dygartsbush when the tracking got slow. But Honus wouldn't hurry. He'd follow his usual plan of getting up with the Indian about dark and taking him by his campfire. That was safe and easy, Honus said; and it saved a man the bother of lighting a fire for himself. The one sign of intelligence the fool tavern keeper had shown was to recognize the Indian as a bad one. He couldn't help it, though, after seeing that purse.

John wasn't an imaginative man, but he could guess how it had happened. A woman alone in her cabin, maybe with a child, you couldn't tell, and her man away for the day, hunting, or gone in to a settlement. The Indian, mousing into the clearing, quite openly, to beg some food, and finding out she was alone. Sitting himself down in the cabin. The woman scared half to death getting his dinner. Him eating and watching her get more and more scared and cleaning his plate. Watching her clean up, waiting till she made a move to slip out.

The mare came to the first ford and nearly lost her footing. John jerked her up and kicked her across. The creek had risen since morning. The rapids were frothy and beginning to show mud. The rain fell into the gorge without much wind, but John could see the trees swaying on the rim of the rock walls. The scud of cloud in the narrow belt of sky seemed to take the gorge in one jump.

The mare was a willing brute, but she had always been a fool about her feet. John settled himself grimly to ride her. He managed to keep her trotting a good part of the time, sitting well forward and squinting his eyes to look into the rain.

He had told Delia to stay at Phelps' till he came home, but she wouldn't. She would start out in time to get home well before him. She said it was what a woman ought to do. A man ought not to come home from a long trip to have to wait for his food. She'd be there now, fixing the fire.

He seemed to see her kneeling in front of the fireplace, blowing the fire, pink-cheeked. And he could see the fat figure of the Indian trotting along through the woods for the clearing. Even a fat Indian could cover the ground; he'd have plenty of time to get there before dark. Delia wouldn't hear him. She wouldn't see anything either, not even his face in the window, because the panes were made of paper. She'd only hear the door squeak on its wood hinges; and even then she'd think it was John.

"God help her," John said, and the mare pricked her ears and he gave her a cut. He knew then that what had happened to Delia in the Indian country made no difference to him. It was what might happen to her before he could get home.

The ride became a nightmare for him. There was a lot of stony footing in the upper part of the creek section through which the mare had to take all the time she needed. It was nearly dark in the gorge. The wet sky in the narrow opening was just a color overhead, without light. He got off and walked at the mare's head, and they came to the turn by the beech tree and climbed the steep ascent to the flat land, side by side. The mare was blowing heavily.

John counted fifty to let her blow herself out, but she spent most of the time shaking herself. He swung onto her again and started her off at a trot.

On the high flats the woods thinned and, now and then, he got a canter out of her. They had more light, also, and in the west the clouds showed signs of breaking and he saw the sun

once, nearly down, in a slit over the woods. Night came, however, when he was still three miles from home.

He thought he had made a mistake when he saw the light off the trail. For a minute it seemed to him that the mare must have done a lot better than he realized and that he had already reached Hartley's. Then he knew that the light was too close to the earth to come from Hartley's window. Someone was camping off the trail.

He cursed himself for not realizing it sooner, and brought the mare up hard and tied her to a tree. To be sure, he picked out the priming of his rifle for the second time and re-primed. Then he slid into the underbrush and began working his way up to the fire.

He had not gone fifty yards before he saw that there were five men sitting round the fire and he recognized Honus Kelly's black beard. They were hunched close to the flames, with their backs to a brush lean-to they had set up, eating bologna and bread.

John got to his feet and started for them, shouting Kelly's name. He saw them stop laughing and pick up their guns and roll out of the firelight, like a comical set of surprised hogs. When he got into the firelight he couldn't see any more of them than the muzzles of their guns.

"John Borst," roared Kelly, rising up. "What are you doing here?"

"Where'd that Indian get to?" John asked.

"Oh, the Indian. How'd you know about him?"

"I've been down to Fort Plain. I heard about him in the tavern. The fool said he didn't tell you the Indian was asking about my place."

Honus let out a laugh. The others, who had resumed their places, left off picking the leaves from their bread to grin too.

"You didn't think he'd get away from us now, did you?" asked Honus. "The Indian's all right. He's just a piece above us."

He sat down, pointing his thumb over his shoulder. Looking upward, John saw moccasined legs hanging beside the bole of a maple. The fat body was like a flour sack, three parts full, inside the old coat.

Honus Kelly, watching John's face, said, "Sit down. You'd better."

But John shook his head. He could hardly speak for a minute. He was surprised because he still wanted to get home. But he tried to be polite.

He said at last, "You boys better come back with me. It's only a short piece, and you can have a dry bed on the floor."

"No, thanks," said Honus. "We got a good place here." He saw that John was anxious to get on, so he rose to his feet and put his hand on John's shoulder and walked back with him toward the mare. "Delia and you won't be wanting a bunch like ourselves cluttering your place tonight," he said. Then he swore. "If Frank had told me about it, I'd have sent a couple of boys straight up to you. We had a time tracking him. It's been lucky all round."

John shook hands with him.

"You don't need to thank me," said Honus. "I always wanted to get even with that Indian. Don't you remember him? He used to hang out west of the settlement. Him and me had trouble over my trap line once or twice."

He watched while John mounted. Then he caught hold of the bridle to say, "We'll bury the rat. It's near the trail." He looked up, his eyes showing white over his beard. "You won't tell Delia?"

John shook his head.

"Best not," agreed Honus. "Well, good luck." He slapped the mare's quarter and let her go.

VII

IT HAD stopped raining, but drops were still shaking off the leaves. There were no stars. The woods smelled of the rain, fresh and green. The air was light and felt clear when he breathed it, and the mare moved more perkily between his thighs. When she came into their clearing, John saw a light in the cabin window. He saw it with a quick uplifting of his heart, and he was glad now that Delia was pig-headed about being home before him. He remembered how it used to be before her return, coming home alone, and fumbling his way in the dark.

He rode by to put the mare in the shed and carried the load round to the door. It squeaked on its hinges as he pushed it open. Delia was kneeling by the fire, blowing it, her face flushed. She swung round easily. He had a quick recollection of the image he had made of the Indian entering. But her face wasn't afraid. It was only apologetic.

"I thought you weren't coming home, John. I let the fire go down. Then I heard the mare."

Her eyes were large and heavy from her effort to keep awake. He warmed himself before the sputtering fire, watching her struggle to get back her faculties. Suddenly she straightened up. "You're wet. You're hungry."

"I got delayed," he said. She went to the saddlebags, rummaging for food, and he said awkwardly, "I wanted to get some sausage, but beef was so dear I didn't have money left for it."

"Oh, John," she said, "I don't care." She started to heat water.

"There's a little tea, though, and half a dozen loaves of sugar."

"White sugar?"

"Yes. You'd better have tea with me."

"I don't need it."

He felt embarrassed and shy. He didn't know how to tell her what he wanted to. He couldn't say, "I thought there was an Indian going to bust in on you and I got scared. But Honus hanged him, so it's all right." That wouldn't explain it to her at all. She was looking at him, too, in a queer, breathless, tentative way.

"You always used to like tea," he said. "You remember the first tea we had."

Her gaze was level, but her color had faded. Her voice became slow and her lips worked stiffly.

"You said, 'Will you have some tea?'"

John for a moment became articulate.

"No, I didn't say that."

"You did." The look in her face was suddenly pitiful.

But he shook his head at her.

"I said, 'Will you have tea with me, Mrs. Borst?'"

She flushed brilliantly.

"Oh, yes, John. And I said, 'I'd love to, Mr. Borst.'"

He needn't have worried about her understanding. It all passed between them, plain in their eyes. She didn't ask anything more.

PULL, PULL TOGETHER

by J. P. Marquand

WRITING ABOUT himself for the *Post* in 1939, John P. Marquand observed that he had traveled extensively in England, France, Italy, Germany, Japan and China, and had also visited Manchukuo, the Mesopotamian desert, California, Baghdad, Singapore and Minneapolis. "You might think that these experiences would have given me a rich and varied background," he added, "but they have only left me more confused than when I started, and still unable to decide what anything is all about." Marquand has always maintained that he does not understand things, a claim which readers of *The Late George Apley* (serialized in the *Post* in 1936) and *Wickford Point* (ditto in 1939) must regard as exaggerated. It is certain that he fully understands the job of writing salable fiction. From 1921 to 1940 he was one of the *Post*'s most dependable producers, writing stories and serials about everything from Harvard Square to Mr. Moto, who earned him a small fortune. "Pull, Pull Together" is a splendid example of the best Marquand technique: utter confusion, shrewdly observed, and neatly pinned down on paper.

JULY 24, 1937

I T TOOK almost a quarter of a century for me to learn that the generations of boyhood move with a fixed similarity. It is amazing, but I swear it is true that when we cease to be boys we are followed by others who exactly represent our type. In any school today our juvenile past is being re-enacted. I used to think that a maladjusted boy like my friend, Diapers Chadwick, was unique, and that there was no one quite so objectionably superior as my old companion, Buzzo Harrison. Not until my own son went to school did I realize vaguely that there must always be a Buzzo Harrison. Not until I took my son to see the school for the first time did Buzzo Harrison walk from the past and mingle himself with the present, and the intervening years had not affected our relationship. When I met Buzzo Harrison again face to face, experience made no difference, nor superficial manners. He was one thing and I was another, as definitely as we had been when we had gone to school together in the years when old Doctor Murchison was headmaster.

Julius Caesar wrote his memoirs in the third person, and so did Gertrude Stein, and there are many obvious advantages in third-person narration, if one is clever enough to achieve the form. If I had the ability I should like to put this in the third person, but somehow it does not go. It does not, although I felt at the time completely detached from myself and uncommonly able to observe my own physical and mental deficiencies. It was a day of reckoning, in a way, which every father of a son must face when he leads his son from home to meet what the educators call "the broader challenge."

When my son pulled at my sleeve, I was sufficiently involved with myself to have forgotten that I had a son who could pull it.

"Hey," he said, "is that it?" There was a reticence between my son and me for which I had, and still have, considerable respect. The names connected with paternity are, when one considers them, embarrassingly banal for daily use between two rational human beings. Pops, daddy, dad and papa are terms inadequate for a serious situation or even for a friendly relationship.

"Hey," my son had said again, "I asked you, is that the place?"

"Yes," I answered in sonorous, pontifical tones that surprised me, "that's the school, Jim."

As I guided our low-priced motor vehicle along a narrow road darkened by midsummer shade, I seemed to be making another speech. Perhaps I as good as made it, although I did not say it.

"Yes, my dear little fellow," I was saying, "this is the old school where your father went and for which you were entered when you were in the hospital babies' room. It is undoubtedly the best institution of its kind in America. You can see what it has done for me and what it has meant to me. I am giving you to it, because you are my son. I hope that it will turn you into a man of whom I can be proud. I hope that you will make the best of the advantages which it offers in culture and in the building of character."

Yes, I had all the illusion of making some such

speech. I declare that I had that sanctimonious desire as soon as I saw the white steeple of the chapel and the brick buildings and the goal posts of the football field. I felt an unbalancing, ridiculous surge of sentiment, a tenderness that made my throat smart, although it was meretricious and I knew that it was. I hoped, more poignantly than I any longer thought that I was capable of hoping, that he would do well in that beautifully monastic place, that he would fit in happily with his kind.

The feeling that I experienced was partially vicarious, and I was two people, myself and my own son. I could tell what he was thinking, because I had thought his own thoughts once. I was old and yet not old. I was cynical and yet not cynical.

"Hey," my son said again, "it's big, isn't it? I never thought it would be so big."

"Yes," I said, "it's a large school, Jim, larger than when I was here, but it looks very much the same."

Upon my word, it had not changed materially. There was the same smell of fresh-cut grass, the same shimmer of the sun on the slate roofs. The elm trees, the curve of the drive were just the same.

"Hey," my son said again, "we're going to see the headmaster, aren't we?"

"What?" I said.

"We're going to see the headmaster, aren't we?"

"Yes," I said. "Whom did you think we were going to see?" And I realized—it seemed incongruous, but it was true—that he was referring to Buzzo Harrison. Buzzo and I had been contemporaries at the school. Buzzo and I had been to Plattsburg. Buzzo and I had been to war. My son was plucking at my sleeve.

"Hey," he said, "if we're going to see the headmaster, you better straighten your tie."

"What?" I said.

"You'd better straighten your tie, if you're going in to see the headmaster."

"Straighten yourself," I said, "and get that red hair out of your eyes." It occurred to me that it was not my colored hair but his mother's, and I could not feel responsible for it. I gave my tie a decisive wrench, not because I was going to see Buzzo Harrison but because I was going to see the head of an august institution. I was about to enter the office of the headmaster, not for reprimand, but because I was to introduce my son. Why? Because it was the school.

The building which housed the administrative offices and the rooms of the sixth form appeared no older than it had been. The rhododendron

bushes by the wide Georgian doorway were heavier, but that was all. A gardener was working by the flower beds near the doorstep—an old man, but he was not old Mike, who used to work on the grounds.

"Come on," I said to my son, "and remember to call him 'sir.' Maybe you'll call me 'sir' before you're through."

I opened the door and we walked into the hall with its brown battleship linoleum. The hall was cool, and remote from the midsummer heat, and its smell was just the same, an indelible compound of soap and humanity peculiar to a school. The pictures in the hallway had not changed. The huge photograph, in its brown frame, of the Roman Forum was there opposite the Acropolis of Athens, and there, sure enough, were the Discus Thrower and the Colleoni Horseman from Venice. I took off my hat while the boy stood looking toward the staircase and at the wooden chairs by the fireplace where there had never been a fire. I knew exactly the way he felt. I had the same sensation in the pit of my stomach that he had, although there was nothing awe-inspiring about that hallway. I knew well enough that it was rather ugly, quite devoid of imagination. That was an attribute of the school; there was no more imagination to it than the cold water of a gymnasium. Yet I took off my hat.

"Take off your hat," I said to my son. "Do you think you're in a synagogue?"

My remark had been unintentional and I was sorry for it, since I had no intention of humiliating him, and he was humiliated. I had reproved him in the presence of company. A woman was coming out of the school office, gray-haired, but not matronly, with brown-paper cuffs pinned over the sleeves of her shirtwaist. She might have been Miss Fewkes, who used to be there. There was the same glint to her glasses, the same decisive lines from the pointed nose to the corner of the mouth, but she was not Miss Fewkes.

"Will you sit down, please?" she said. "Doctor Harrison will see you in a few minutes."

I sat on one of the wooden chairs.

"You may look at that picture of the Roman Forum," I said to my son. "Maybe we'll go there some day. And don't snuffle. Blow your nose if you want to. Haven't you got a handkerchief?"

I had said the wrong thing again. I knew as soon as I had spoken, but I had been thinking of something else. Buzzo would be called "Doctor," of course. The headmaster of the school was always "Doctor." I sat there trying to remember that I must have sat in that same chair a dozen times before, and it produced the old mental malaise, the same uneasy suspense of waiting. My son was pulling at my sleeve again and his voice had dropped to a whisper.

"Hey," he said, "who else lives in here?"

"The headmaster's family," I said, and, although I had not intended it, my own voice sank low, as muted as though we were in some religious edifice. "And the sixth form lives on the second and third floors."

"Hey," my son said again, "give me a break, will you? Don't correct me when we go inside."

"I won't have to correct you any more," I told him, "not when you go here."

I had never thought of the situation in exactly that light before, but I could see that it was the true angle. I was giving the boy to the school, delegating my erratic authority to something which was more powerful than myself. Once the autumn term began, there would be no further need to mold him; he would come home as I had come home once, alive with ideas and enthusiasms which I might never share. He would come home and stare with the superiority of a stranger upon the vagaries of a parent's disordered life— nothing at home would be quite right. No old friends would be quite suitable, because they were not the school. The school—it was a strong place, mercilessly strong; its stamp stayed on many of its pupils to the grave. Some it kept perennially young, if infantile were not a better word; others it made cynics, but its stamp was on them all.

A door at the end of the hall opened. My chair legs scraped on the brown linoleum as I rose. Roger ["Buzzo"] Harrison was coming toward us. I hadn't seen the doctor for quite a while, and I envied him as I examined him with the calculating glance of middle age. It is interesting to grow up and to examine one's contemporaries, to observe how faces and waistlines sag, how hair disappears, how often eyes are veiled by disillusion. We all of us know too much when we get older. There is no longer that possibility of promise just around the corner, no longer the fascinating outside chance of hidden talent. For once in our lives we are exactly what we are.

I looked at Buzzo enviously, but I did not call him "Buzzo."

"How do you do, Roger," I said. "I brought James for you to look at."

Admittedly, I regarded Buzzo with envy. He had on rubber-heeled shoes, gray slacks and a brown Harris tweed coat. He was imposing in spite of his informality, and he still had the build and the easy walk of an athlete. His yellow hair was a bit thin, but his face was clear and confident, an angular, reliable, pinkish face with whimsical wrinkles about the eyes and forehead. I could imagine that his life was ordered enough so

he did not show his age—frugal meals, plenty of outdoor exercise, a rest at Christmas and Easter, and three months off in the summer. In spite of my intention not to be impressed, he was impressive. Moreover, he understood his job. He knew how to speak to a boy without condescension and with an understanding which any boy would like.

"Hello, Harold," he said. "It's grand to see you. . . . How do you do, James?"

He didn't say, "Well, well, so this is James, is it?" and his manner was not susceptible of such an implication.

"Let's go inside," he said. "Miss Thurston, will you please get me the Hendricks papers from the file? Come on, Harold; come on, James." His rubber heels padded resiliently on the linoleum as he walked behind us. I drew in my breath and smiled mechanically when we were in the headmaster's study. I had not been in that room for twenty-odd years, but if I had left it an hour before, it could not have been more familiar. There are a few scenes like that in life, a few shapes and sensations, which, thank heaven, do not change. I had perspired freely there once upon a time. Once upon a time I had been obliged to stand there fighting to keep my knees from smiting together, when the old doctor had sat behind the desk—the time we threw eggs at a boy whose name I now forget, behind the old gymnasium. Buzzo was in it, too, but Buzzo got away. I could hear the doctor's voice again, sonorous but bristling with righteous contempt.

"Filthy," he was saying, "vile and filthy, Hendricks, and besides, the act of a coward." He must have known that all boys were pitiless, savage brutes, given the proper occasion. In conclusion he had added: "The school is like a boat. You're not pulling your weight in it, and everyone in this school must pull together."

Then there was the time when I had broken bounds instead of walking off twenty-five demerits on the cinder track. Mr. Saunderson, the Latin master, had found me in Rooney's Pool Parlor downtown, near the railroad station, and I had been ushered into the same room where my son and I sat now, to face the possibilities of expulsion and disgrace. One thing alone had saved me—I had not smoked a cigarette. Mr. Saunderson had vouched that there had been no tobacco on my breath.

That was a long while ago, but I could still feel the tingling in my spine as the icy fingers of fear had gripped me. The dark clerical woodwork was still upon the walls, giving a conscientious imitation of a cloistered English study. It was a room for Tom Brown's Schooldays without the patina of age. The tooled backs of the classics in calf and sheep were just as the doctor had left them upon the shelves, his material legacy to the school. The same prints were above those shelves and there was the same huge flat Georgian desk. The carpet and the painting of the old doctor appeared to be the only furnishings that were new. The doctor looked down from his frame above the mantelpiece. He was what the portrait painter might call a speaking likeness; in no sense a work of art from the modern standpoint, but amazingly, grimly accurate. He was in his surplice, just as he had stood for so many years in chapel, angular, ruddy-faced and sure, as sure as a benevolent dictator. His gray-blue eyes looked calmly from the canvas straight toward the desk where we three were seated, and the old doctor's lips were slightly curved, half humorously, half imperiously. He still inspired in one a mingling of love and fear and of reluctant admiration which one feels for a man who has devoted a life for a cause. His cause had been the school.

"A good picture of the old man, isn't it?" Buzzo said.

"Yes," I answered, "excellent."

Buzzo tapped a leather box upon the desk.

"Have a cigarette?" he asked, and then he smiled. "That's one of the new ideas," he said. . . . "Make yourself at home, Harold, while James and I talk. I wonder if James knows enough to get into the second form."

"He ought to," I said, "he's old enough. Aren't you smoking?"

"No, thanks." Buzzo shook his head with a nonsmoker's inevitable implication of rebuke. "He's old enough, but you know the system here. We're still particular, Harold. We still keep up the standards. . . . You look well set up, James, for a boy your age. You play football, I suppose?"

"Yes, sir," my son said.

"That's right," said Buzzo. "Your father did, you know—and now let's get down to Latin."

It was my son who sat there answering, but it might have been myself, and it might have been the old doctor who was speaking, for I was experiencing that sensation one hears of, but believes so seldom. I was living in my son.

I was living my own past in his present. He was speaking, but I was speaking in him, answering those questions. I was trying again to conform as he was, with that anguished wish of the very young, to a life which he did not understand. I was going out again to face the world as he was, but with a solitary difference. I knew from experience he had yet to meet that the school was not the world. That knowledge was growing stronger, as I sat there in the study, until it made a fantastic combination of illusion and disillusion which moved before my mind in shifting patterns like the fragments of colored glass we have looked at as children in an ingenious Christmas toy. I was part of the pattern and Buzzo Harrison's voice was part of it. We were saying our lines for the benefit of my son. I could almost hear the monitor calling the old school roll as Buzzo sat there speaking.

"Hallet, Hammond, Harrison, Hendricks."

It was the same in the college lecture hall. The refrain had not changed much in the military training camps. Roll calls, monotonous and musical, had made us what we were, and now my son's name was going on the rolls. It was odd to think that those roll calls advanced us toward the world, bound us together always, and yet, at the same time, kept us out of it.

"Well," Buzzo was saying, "I think that's all. We can try James in the second form. It will be a challenge to him, but I think—I hope—that James may meet that challenge."

The elements in life which cause one to reach a decision are always beyond the realms of rational explanation, since there is not much apparent reason behind any human action. We get and we rationalize such action carefully afterward, but that is all. I had come there to enter my son in the school, glad that I had the privilege. I had been complacently pleased to see the Georgian buildings again and the lake and the wooded Connecticut hills beyond the football field. I had been proud that he was going to such an institution. It must have been the study and Buzzo's voice that made me see the school not as I wished it. All at once, at any rate, the school appeared as unbalanced and as divorced from fact as all the secondary education in America, no longer with individual merits, but a piece of all the fads and eccentricities and of all the pious apings of Westminster and of Rugby; and I knew too much about Buzzo in the bargain.

Buzzo was holding out a printed form.

"You sign here, Harold," he said, "and here's the customary list of equipment—linen, blankets and clothing. I needn't tell you how glad we all are here to welcome another Hendricks into the school. There's always a place for old boys' sons."

I reached for the pen he was holding toward me when an impulse made me stop.

"Wait," I said. "Jim, you run outside and look at the buildings. I want to speak to Doctor Harrison."

We forget that we possessed a well-developed intellect and fresh intuition when we were young. Thus it surprised me to see my son hesitate, just as aware as Buzzo was that something was not right.

"Go ahead, Jim," I said, "don't stand there looking at me. Walk out. I won't be long." We watched him walk across the study to the door and perhaps we both remembered that it was a long journey for self-conscious boyhood before the door was reached. When it closed, everything seemed more natural. Buzzo and I were like ourselves, or as nearly like ourselves as was possible in our different positions.

"What is it, old man?" said Buzzo. "Anything on your mind?"

"Yes," I said, "I've got a hell of a lot on my mind." As soon as I spoke I realized that the unholy expletive was partially out of place, and probably Buzzo realized it also.

"Get it off your chest, Hal," Buzzo said, with an unpleasant twinkle in his eye, which indicated his understanding that I was eccentric, and a card. "Nothing you say will hurt me, Hal. You've always said enough to me." His tone intimated righteously that he was a success and that I was not, that he would always be right and that I invariably would be wrong.

"Why don't you sign the paper, Hal?" Buzzo asked. "We've been saving the place since the boy was born."

"Because I've been taking a look at you," I said. "I came up here for that. I thought this place might be different with you running it, but you've turned into a stuffed shirt, Buzzo." I paused, enjoying the effect of this colloquialism, and decided grimly to emphasize my thought. "You think you're a broad-minded man of the world," I added, "when actually you're not even stuffed symmetrically. You're lopsided."

Buzzo Harrison stroked his upper lip.

"You haven't mastered your inferiority complex, Hal," he said. "I suppose you've wanted to say that to someone in this room for half your life. Frankly, there must be something else."

"I want to give my boy a chance, that's all," I said. "I'd like him to see what the school means before he gets in it. It's taken me many years to find out. I don't believe you ever have. I thought you were going to make this place different. I've heard you say what you were going to do."

Buzzo sighed. Buzzo was always good-natured, almost insensitively calm, always a splendid fellow.

"Get it off your chest, Hal," he said. "I like to hear you bellyache. What's the matter with the school?"

Now that I was faced with the question, it was hard to attack it logically. There was so much wrong with the school that it was difficult to know where to begin; and, besides, there was so much that was wrong with the world that the illness of the world mingled itself inextricably with scholastic errors. It was not reassuring to realize that Buzzo was probably right, that I had sought through the years for an opportunity to say what I thought and that I had never really met the opportunity except in some corner of a club. As I sat there examining Buzzo I was conscious that I was laying my own failures to the school, and the realization in itself added to my own annoyance.

Buzzo sat with his elbows on the desk, wearing a patient half-smile. All his personality radiated the tolerance of one who knew that he was right. It was the universal expression of every headmaster, according to my experience, and it made me decide to attack Buzzo first. He was concrete, not a nebulous idea.

"Buzzo," I said, "I wish you'd wipe that smile off. I'll tell you what's the matter with the school. It's what is wrong with most secondary schools. It's the headmaster."

The healthy tan on Buzzo's face assumed a deeper tint.

"We all make mistakes, of course," Buzzo said. "We can only do our best."

"It isn't your fault," I admitted. "Every one of you is made into an absolute monarch; every one of you has a chance to build up a world; every one of you has some catch-penny theory. You don't have to worry about your bread and butter as long as you have a suitable sales talk, Buzzo."

"Go ahead, Hal," said Buzzo. "What are some of our theories?"

"Some of you have projects," I said. "Some of you make the boys build gardens and make their own beds. Some of you have theories of self-government or military discipline or religion. You all are trying to remake the world, and when the boys go out, they find that the real thing is not your world. You don't know anything about life, because you're removed from life."

"That isn't so," said Buzzo. "I imagine I know as much about life as you—possibly rather more." He was almost like a human being when he said it.

"You don't," I said. "You've always lived on theories, ever since you were at school."

"So have you," said Buzzo. "You always were a sorehead."

"And you were always a big success," I said. "There's always one at school."

"I wish you'd shut up," said Buzzo. "Our crowd's done pretty well. You're only voicing the parents' stock complaint that school doesn't fit anyone for life. As a matter of fact, it does. Look at our own form."

"Well, what about them?" I said. Buzzo leaned forward comfortably on his elbows.

"There's you," he said, "there's me, and even little Rouse. He was an ace in the war."

"Go on," I said. I had not thought of Pinky Rouse for the last ten years, and now the faces of them all were coming back, young, eternally young, until their shadows seemed to fill the room.

"And Tom Meecher's giving us a swimming pool," Buzzo said, "and Bruce is in the diplomatic service, and all the rest of them are honest citizens. What's more, they have a stamp on them. You'd know them anywhere."

"You certainly would," I said.

Buzzo smiled, and he was almost lively because he was not trying to argue any longer. Our talk had fallen into nothing but silent reminiscence.

"Anyway," said Buzzo, "we had a mighty good time here, and we learned to behave ourselves. That's something, isn't it?"

"Did we?" I said.

"I did," said Buzzo. "Maybe you didn't. You're not behaving now."

I did not answer, for I was faced with the everlasting futility of argument, and I was thinking of his previous remark. It was true that we had all had a good time, a better time than most of us had had since.

"I don't suppose it occurs to you," I said at length, "that the world has changed considerably since we were here. This school and all others like it were meant for a Victorian civilization. I don't suppose it occurs to you that boys don't have security any more. I wonder if you give it any serious thought."

"Yes," said Buzzo, "I think about it sometimes. The only thing that we can do is to teach the boys how to behave."

"There are different types of behavior," I said, "suited for different circumstances. It doesn't help boys to teach them to behave like county squires. There aren't any counties where there are squires, not in America, unless they exist in your own imagination."

Buzzo moved impatiently.

"I wish you'd shut up, Hal," he said. "You don't know what our problems are. Are you going to send your boy here, or aren't you?"

"Not until I tell him what it's all about," I said.

"Go ahead and tell him," Buzzo said. "If you know yourself. I don't, but I'll be here all morning. Show him around the school."

"I'll tell him about you," I said.

"Go ahead," said Buzzo, "tell him about me."

It was not gratifying to realize that the conversation had brought me nowhere. No conversation with Buzzo ever had. I had not even been able to put my deep-rooted objections in a logical form fit to be presented to any rational being, although I could feel those objections surge inside me, moving through my mind in a series of disconnected phrases. I felt it all too keenly for adequate exposition. I had that intense wish of every parent that my son might have an easier time, that he might be different from myself, and better.

"You don't know what you want," Buzzo had told me once. "What's more, you never will."

But did anyone ever really know what he wanted, and, if so, did he want it, if he had it? I tried to consider my contemporaries. We were all of us a bewildered, disillusioned lot, whom the world had imbued with a tolerance which was close to surrender, a tolerance which made us immune to surprise. We had all started with illusions once, the illusions that had been fostered in us by the school.

The school stood in the hot sun in a neat architectural pattern of Georgian brick, the result of a New York architect's unimaginative conception of what a school should be, given a free hand and no particular financial restriction. Its buildings were symmetrically grouped on rising ground with the football fields and tennis courts behind, remote from the Connecticut village in the hollow, remote from the weary undulations of the distant hills, impressive in the perfection of their solitude—the library, the dining hall, the gymnasium, the recitation building connected with the dining hall by a covered walk. The gray roofs shimmered in the sun and there was the sad metallic hum of cicadas in the trees. Generations of cicadas had sung above that place, and when they died, autumn brought the voices of boys to take up the chorus. Now the loneliness of the school was solemn, but the solitude itself was full of life. The ghosts of boyhood were about the place, thousands of them; my own and Buzzo Harrison's were there; but my son was not a ghost. He was standing looking at a marble tablet across the lawn, the only being there in possession of a future.

When I saw the boy with his hands in his pockets, trying, although he was unconscious of my presence, to imitate my own bad posture, I realized that he was a fairly accurate replica of what I had once been. Life in that odd place must have repeated itself with hardly a deviation since I had attended the school.

The day had been just the same when my father

had brought me there. There had been the same sun, the same smell of fresh-cut grass, the same humming of the insects in the still bright air. The actual space of time since I had first set eyes upon the school appeared to have shrunk almost to a day. It was the morning when my father and I had descended from the hack which had carried us from the station. I recollected how my father had paused to look about him, stroking his mustache.

"Very nice," I heard him say as though it were only yesterday; "very nice."

I remembered how he had paused when he observed that we were not by ourselves. Another father with his son was walking across the lawn and the two were talking heatedly. Their words must have caused my father to alter, in a measure, certain preconceived ideas about the school, for they indicated, even to me, that the other man was not entirely of our walk of life. His dress indicated the same. His pepper-and-salt suit was almost shabby and his accent had all the crudity of an outlander's from the Middle West.

"I don't like it, Buzzo," he was saying. "I don't see how you're going to get along back home if you come to this place. I guess you'd better stay at home."

That was how I first saw Buzzo Harrison, a gawky, towheaded boy in a plaid cap which was not at all the style. Buzzo was embarrassed for his parent and I could feel a superior sympathy for his embarrassment. I was pleased that my own father, in spite of his many obvious crudities, was a more desirable and generally accepted model. At least my father was adequately turned out. I could share my parent's astonishment when the stranger walked up to him with the boy lagging behind.

"Hello," the stranger said. "I guess we're in the same boat."

"In the same boat?" my father inquired.

"I guess you're entering your boy here," the stranger said, "just the same as I am. I've just stepped outside to cool off for a minute. My name's Harrison and this is Buzzo."

My father was courteous, if his answer did imply surprise at the abruptness of the introduction.

"My name is Hendricks," he said, "and this is Harold."

"Well, I'm pleased to meet you," Mr. Harrison said. "I don't come East often and this is new to me. Are all the schools like this?"

"I don't quite understand you," my father answered, "but I should say most of them are on a similar pattern. I think this one is rather better.

Doctor Murchison had a very fine reputation. He's an Oxford man. He's very familiar with English public schools."

Mr. Harrison's voice, never well modulated, grew louder.

"Well, that's just it," he said; "that's why this place don't seem American. . . . Buzzo, you run along with this boy. I want to talk."

Buzzo Harrison and I walked away in an uncomfortable silence. I knew that he was ashamed, but it was not up to me to relieve him of his embarrassment, and I did nothing to set him at his ease. We glanced at each other sideways, furtively, once or twice.

"Where do you live?" Buzzo asked.

"New York," I said.

"I guess they treat the new fellers rough here, when they're outsiders," Buzzo said.

"Yes," I said, "I guess they do."

"Well," said Buzzo, "I don't care."

There had been nothing illuminating in the conversation, since boys of twelve are inarticulate with strangers. When Buzzo stood before me then in all his crudity, I could understand that I had something he wanted, which was mine by right of birth. Well, Buzzo had got what he wanted. Little did he realize then that he would be the "all-around" boy who made the best of his opportunities in studies and athletics, the boy who had his name for three years on the Griscom Cup, a triumphant outcome of Doctor Murchison's social experiment.

Doctor Murchison explained it himself when I was led into the study.

"Hal," my father had whispered, "take off your hat."

Doctor Murchison was a large florid man whose complexion shouted of cold showers and outdoor sports.

"I just met a Mr. Harrison outside," my father said.

"Oh, yes," said Doctor Murchison. "Oh, yes, Harrison. It's an idea of mine. I want all sorts of boys here—the leavening of the loaf. I want"—he paused and cleared his throat—"to make this more than a school. I want it to go down as an institution. I want to give the boys a stamp and a philosophy."

I was not listening carefully as the doctor continued. The snatches of words that I recall were the same which he often repeated afterward, and there was no doubt that he had done what he had wanted. Old Murchison had made the school and he had made Buzzo Harrison. When one stopped to consider, the whole school was as much his own creation as a picture was its artist's or a symphony its composer's. The boy in the school, when he was finished, reflected Murchison's ideas of what a gentleman should be—in the main, sound ideas, presenting only one possible objection. Beyond the school bounds there were not many Murchison gentlemen, or many Murchisons either.

It was all so confusing that one did not know exactly what to think, but at any rate Murchison was a man. He may have been a snob, actuated by a narrow-minded philosophy, but he had kept his faith and had maintained his allegiance to his own beliefs. He had died in the solid conviction that he was right. There was a right and there was a wrong, and he always knew that he was right. His attitude was right and mine was wrong. I could hear him speaking to me in the study, not an unusual occurrence, since he had me on the carpet there several times a year.

"Hendricks," he was saying, "I don't know what to say to you." He had a fine voice, the fear-inspiring voice of a leader. I have often wondered since how that headmaster's manner may have worked with his contemporaries, but it was impressive to a boy. He was apt to begin with a preface that he did not know what to say. It made one feel that one was a difficult, a well-nigh hopeless case, but actually he always knew exactly what to say.

"Hendricks," he said, "I don't know what to say to you. Your marks are above the average. There is nothing specifically wrong in your conduct sheet, and yet, what's the matter with you, Hendricks? I have pondered the question and I ask you—what's the matter?"

"I don't know, sir," I said.

"You're wrong," said Doctor Murchison; "you're absolutely wrong. You do know and I know too. It's your attitude, Hendricks. It's an attitude of disbelief that will cost you dearly all your life. You're not pulling your weight in the boat, Hendricks. Answer me, are you pulling your weight, or aren't you?"

"I don't know, sir," I said.

"Oh, yes, you do," he answered; "you do know very well. The school is like a boat. Every one of us has an oar to pull, a big oar or a little oar, depending on our strength. If one of us doesn't pull, if one of us shirks, the whole boat knows it. Why don't you pull your weight, boy?"

"I don't know, sir," I answered.

"Well, I know," he said; "I know very well. It's because you don't understand the type we want here, Hendricks. You don't understand the all-around boy who will be the all-around man. It's strange you do not understand, when an all-around boy sits right beside you in the school, eats beside you, sleeps beside you, plays beside you. I'm speaking of Harrison, Hendricks. I want you to be like him."

It was the first time I revolted against that overpowering presence, and the last, I suppose, but for once I stood for my own individuality in the doctor's presence.

"I don't want to be like Harrison, sir," I said.

"You don't want to be?" he repeated. "Why don't you want to be? Hendricks, tell me why."

"I don't know, sir," I answered, "but I don't want to be like Harrison."

The doctor placed a heavy hand upon my shoulder. I had to brace myself to support his weight. There were a good many things which I might have said, but I did not say them.

"I know what you're thinking," the doctor said, "and it's a narrow, unkindly thought. You're thinking that Harrison has not had your advantages. Remember what he has done with what he has, and he'll do more than that, mark you. He'll do more. You should be ashamed of yourself, Hendricks, very much ashamed."

I was not ashamed, although I did not tell him so, and it was not what I was thinking, not at all. Buzzo was a sedulous goody-goody. I was thinking in my bitterness that he was a teacher's pet. Yet beside all that, he had that social capacity entirely beyond most of us, of doing the right thing always. Buzzo had adjusted himself, as the psychiatrists now put it, perfectly and completely to his environment.

I sometimes wonder if adjustment is altogether desirable. Surely it has its stultifying side, and yet we maladjusted are always struggling to adjust. I was glad that I was not like Buzzo Harrison; I was pleased that I had never tried to be.

I thought of him as I had seen him a few minutes before, a continued miracle of adjustment, still sure of himself in changing time. I did not want him to teach my son. Old Murchison I should not have minded, but I did not want Buzzo to teach him.

I wanted to give my son a chance, but I did not like what I was going to say. The boy was standing, looking at the tablet, when I approached him. He turned and pulled at my coat sleeve.

"Hey," he said, "what's the tablet for? Your name's on it."

"Boys who fought in the war," I said. "Listen, I want to talk to you."

"Hey," he said, "where's the sixth-form room?"

"Over there," I said.

"Where do the new kids live?"

"Over there," I said.

"Well," he said, "what will they let me take to school, and when are we going to eat?"

"Wait," I said, "I want to tell you something."

"Can't you tell me when we're eating?" my son answered. "I'm hungry."

"No," I said, "I want to tell you now. I wanted you to see the school, but I don't want you to go here, Jim."

"What?" he said.

"I told you I don't want you to go. You'll have to earn your living some day, and when you do, you'll have to forget nearly everything you'd learned here. And then, there's the new headmaster. Don't argue with me, Jim."

I felt him pulling at my sleeve and I saw the agony in his face. One forgets so easily that life is hard when one is young.

"I don't know what you're talking about," I heard him say. "You went here, didn't you? You've always said I was going. I've told everyone I was going."

"Listen," I said, "don't yell. I want you to listen to me." But I knew already he would not listen.

I took him by the shoulders. It was hard to hold him when he tried to wriggle away. "You don't know about this, but I do," I told him. "Everything here is make-believe. Everyone who teaches you will try to be different from what he really is. Now, I know Doctor Harrison. I know him very well, better than I know you, probably, and I don't think—frankly, I don't think he'll help you much."

I was impressed by the logic of my son's answer as much as by its desperation.

"What difference does it make?" he asked. "You said he was trying to be different from what he is, didn't you? You promised me I could come here."

When I returned to the headmaster's office, Buzzo Harrison was writing a letter, leaning over the broad desk intently, careful not to look up from his labor. His self-conscious effort at scholarly concentration was not wasted upon me. Over the mantel behind Buzzo's tweed coat was the ruddy-faced portrait of old Murchison. It was exactly what I had said to my son; it was all make-believe. The school was an artificial fabrication, but then, perhaps the same was true of all human experience.

"May I break in upon your train of thought for a moment," I inquired, "even at the risk of its being a vulgar intrusion?"

"Why, Hal," said Buzzo, "there's always time for you."

"You're worse than you ever were," I said,

"but I want to wish you good luck, Buzzo. You always know how to get along. You win, I lose. I've been talking to the boy for half an hour, but he wants to come here just the same. Give me the paper, I'll sign it."

Buzzo smiled cordially. "Of course, he would want to come," he said. "He's a chip off the old block, Hal, and you really want him to, and you know it. You and I, we understand the school. And boys understand it better than we do."

"What do you mean by that?" I asked.

"Boys are conventional," Buzzo said, "the most conventional beings in the world. Truthfully, Hal, as man to man, I can sympathize with many of your objections. You and I both are rebels at heart. You think that certain aspects of our system are hidebound, and they are perhaps, but it isn't my fault. It's the boys'. They repeat themselves through all the school generations. The types don't change. Replicas of you and me and all the rest of us are always coming here. It's the boys who make the school. It's the boys who do everything you don't like. I don't. The boys ran old Murchison and now they run me. I should hesitate to tell that to most of the parents, but it's so."

I did not try to answer him, because I knew it probably was a pose and perhaps it did not matter. It was reassuring, however, to feel that education could not hurt boys much, that they might get along in spite of it.

"Well," I said, "you probably won't hurt them much."

"That's exactly what I was trying to say," said Buzzo. "I can't hurt them. I can't make an impression on you because you know too much about me, Hal, but I make a thundering good impression on everybody else, and that's about all I can do. That's about all any of us can do."

"Well," I said, "there's one thing you never did. Did you ever hear Murchison say that the school was like a boat?"

"It is like a boat," Buzzo said. "We each have to pull our weight in it."

I made a helpless gesture, because it was impossible for our minds to meet.

"It won't do any good to lecture me," I said. "I know all about you. Why, right here in this room I was told that if I couldn't be more like you, I needn't stay in school."

For some reason, he was impressed, undeniably impressed. "What?" said Buzzo. "You were told to be more like me? Who told you that?"

"The old man," I said, "in the picture right behind you. You always were a big success."

"You never told me that," Buzzo said. "I wish

you had, because it's interesting."

"Why?" I asked.

"Because it's ironical," Buzzo said. "You can't begin to believe what an ironical place the school world is, Hal, until you try to run it. I may as well tell you something. It may make you feel better. The old man had me in here too."

"Only to pat you on the back," I said.

"No," said Buzzo, "it wasn't that. It is surprising in view of what you've said. He wanted me to be more like you, but there wasn't really any need to tell me. I'd been trying ever since I first saw you. Do you remember when? As a matter of fact, I've always tried to be like you."

THE CHILD BY TIGER

by *Thomas Wolfe*

WHEN THOMAS WOLFE sold this story to the *Post,* he rubbed his big hands together and announced gleefully that he was going to sell a lot more. But he had only one year to go before his untimely death at thirty-eight, and he did not sell the *Post* another story. One which the *Post* rejected was bought later by the *Yale Review,* which paid $100 for it, and Wolfe used the money for what he called his "*Yale Review* overcoat." Wolfe was not a magazine writer anyway; he wrote gigantic novels which his editors toiled over endlessly to cut up into chunks that could be squeezed between book covers. "The Child by Tiger" was a small chip from such a novel and appeared later as a chapter in *The Web and the Rock* (1939). Like everything else Wolfe wrote, it was based on an episode in his own life.

SEPTEMBER 11, 1937

> Tiger, tiger, burning bright
> In the forests of the night,
> What immortal hand or eye
> Could frame thy fearful symmetry?

ONE DAY after school, twenty-five years ago, several of us were playing with a football in the yard at Randy Shepperton's. Randy was calling signals and handling the ball. Nebraska Crane was kicking it. Augustus Potterham was too clumsy to run or kick or pass, so we put him at center, where all he'd have to do would be to pass the ball back to Randy when he got the signal.

It was late in October and there was a smell of smoke, of leaves, of burning in the air. Nebraska had just kicked to us. It was a good kick, too—a high, soaring punt that spiraled out above my head, behind me. I ran back and tried to get it, but it was far and away "over the goal line"— that is to say, out in the street. It hit the street and bounded back and forth with that peculiarly erratic bounce a football has.

The ball rolled away from me down toward the corner. I was running out to get it when Dick Prosser, Shepperton's new Negro man, came along, gathered it up neatly in his great black paw and tossed it to me. He turned in then, and came on down the alleyway, greeting us as he did. He called all of us "Mister" except Randy, and Randy was always "Cap'n"—"Cap'n Shepperton." This formal address—"Mr." Crane, "Mr." Potterham, "Mr." Spangler, "Cap'n" Shepperton —pleased us immensely, gave us a feeling of mature importance and authority.

"Cap'n Shepperton" was splendid! It had a delightful military association, particularly when Dick Prosser said it. Dick had served a long enlistment in the United States Army. He had been a member of a regiment of crack Negro troops upon the Texas border, and the stamp of the military man was evident in everything he did. It was a joy, for example, just to watch him split up kindling. He did it with a power, a kind of military power, that was astounding. Every stick he cut seemed to be exactly the same length and shape as every other one. He had all of them neatly stacked against the walls of the Shepperton basement with such regimented faultlessness that it almost seemed a pity to disturb their symmetry for the use for which they were intended.

It was the same with everything else he did. His little whitewashed basement room was as spotless as a barracks room. The bare board floor was always cleanly swept, a plain bare table and a plain straight chair were stationed exactly in the center of the room. On the table there was always just one object: an old Bible almost worn out by constant use, for Dick was a deeply religious man. There was a little cast-iron stove and a little wooden box with a few lumps of coal and a neat stack of kindling in it. And against the wall, to the left, there was an iron cot, always precisely made and covered cleanly with a coarse gray blanket.

The Sheppertons were delighted with him. He had come there looking for work just a month or two before, and modestly presented his qualifications. He had, he said, only recently received his discharge from the Army and was eager to get employment, at no matter what wage. He could cook, he could tend the furnace, he knew how to drive a car—in fact, it seemed to us boys that there was very little that Dick Prosser could not do. He could certainly shoot. He gave a modest demonstration of his prowess one afternoon, with Randy's .22, that left us gasping. He just lifted that little rifle in his powerful black hands as if it were a toy, without seeming to take aim, pointed it toward a strip of tin on which we had crudely marked out some bull's-eye circles, and he simply peppered the center of the bull's-eye, putting twelve holes through a space one inch square, so fast we could not even count the shots.

He knew how to box too. I think he had been a regimental champion. At any rate, he was as cunning and crafty as a cat. He never boxed with us, of course, but Randy had two sets of gloves, and Dick used to coach us while we sparred. There was something amazingly tender and watchful about him. He taught us many things—how to lead, to hook, to counter and to block—but he was careful to see that we did not hurt each other.

He knew about football, too, and today he paused, a powerful, respectable-looking Negro man of thirty years or more, and watched us for a moment as we played.

Randy took the ball and went up to him. "How do you hold it, Dick?" he said. "Is this right?"

Dick watched him attentively as he gripped the ball, and held it back above his shoulder. The Negro nodded approvingly and said, "That's right, Cap'n Shepperton. You've got it. Only," he said gently, and now took the ball in his own powerful hand, "when you gits a littie oldah yo' handses gits biggah and you gits a bettah grip."

His own great hand, in fact, seemed to hold the ball as easily as if it were an apple. And, holding it so a moment, he brought it back, aimed over his outstretched left hand as if he were pointing a gun, and rifled it in a beautiful, whizzing spiral thirty yards or more to Gus. He then showed us how to kick, how to get the ball off of the toe in such a way that it would rise and spiral cleanly. He knew how to do this too. He must have got off kicks there, in the yard at Shepperton's, that traveled fifty yards.

He showed us how to make a fire, how to pile the kindling so that the flames shot up cone-wise, cleanly, without smoke or waste. He showed us how to strike a match with the thumbnail of one hand and keep and hold the flame in the strongest wind. He showed us how to lift a weight, how to tote a burden on our shoulders in the easiest way. There was nothing that he did not know. We were all so proud of him. Mr. Shepperton himself de-clared that Dick was the best man he'd ever had, the smartest darky that he'd ever known.

And yet? He went too softly, at too swift a pace. He was there upon you sometimes like a cat. Looking before us, sometimes, seeing nothing but the world before us, suddenly we felt a shadow at our backs and, looking up, would find that Dick was there. And there was something moving in the night. We never saw him come or go. Sometimes we would waken, startled, and feel that we had heard a board creak, the soft clicking of a latch, a shadow passing swiftly. All was still.

"Young white fokes, oh, young white gent'-mun,"—his soft voice ending in a moan, a kind of rhythm in his hips—"oh, young white fokes, Ise tellin' *you*"—that soft low moan again—"you gotta love each othah like a brothah." He was deeply religious and went to church three times a week. He read his Bible every night. It was the only object on his square board table.

Sometimes Dick would come out of his little basement room, and his eyes would be red, as if he had been weeping. We would know, then, that he had been reading his Bible. There would be times when he would almost moan when he talked to us, a kind of hymnal chant that came from some deep and fathomless intoxication of the spirit, and that transported him. For us, it was a troubling and bewildering experience. We tried to laugh it off and make jokes about it. But there was something in it so dark and strange and full of a feeling that we could not fathom that our jokes were hollow, and the trouble in our minds and in our hearts remained.

Sometimes on these occasions his speech would be made up of some weird jargon of Biblical phrases, of which he seemed to have hundreds, and which he wove together in this strange pattern of his emotion in a sequence that was meaningless to us, but to which he himself had the coherent clue. "Oh, young white fokes," he would begin, moaning gently, "de dry bones in de valley. I tell you, white fokes, de day is comin' when He's comin' on dis earth again to sit in judgment. He'll put de sheep upon de right hand and de goats upon de left. Oh, white fokes, white fokes, de Armageddon day's a-comin', white fokes, an' de dry bones in de valley."

Or again, we could hear him singing as he went about his work, in his deep rich voice, so full of warmth and strength, so full of Africa, singing hymns that were not only of his own race but familiar to us all. I don't know where he learned them. Perhaps they were remembered from his Army days. Perhaps he had learned them in the service of former masters. He drove the Shepper-tons to church on Sunday morning, and would wait for them throughout the morning service. He would come up to the side door of the church while the service was going on, neatly dressed in his good dark suit, holding his chauffeur's hat respectfully in his hand, and stand there humbly and listen during the course of the entire sermon.

And then, when the hymns were sung and the great rich sound would swell and roll out into the quiet air of Sunday, Dick would stand and listen, and sometimes he would join in quietly in the song. A number of these favorite Presbyterian hymns we heard him singing many times in a low rich voice as he went about his work around the house. He would sing Who Follows in His Train? or Alexander's Glory Song, or Rock of Ages, or Onward, Christian Soldiers!

And yet? Well, nothing happened—there was just "a flying hint from here and there," and the sense of something passing in the night. Turning into the square one day as Dick was driving Mr. Shepperton to town, Lon Everett skidded murderously around the corner, sideswiped Dick and took the fender off. The Negro was out of the car like a cat and got his master out. Shepperton was unhurt. Lon Everett climbed out and reeled across the street, drunk as a sot at three o'clock. He swung viciously, clumsily, at the Negro, smashed him in the face. Blood trickled from the flat black nostrils and from the thick liver-colored lips. Dick did not move. But suddenly the whites of his eyes were shot with red, his bleeding lips bared for a moment over the white ivory of his teeth. Lon smashed at him again. The Negro took it full in the face again; his hands twitched slightly, but he did not move. They collared the drunken sot and hauled him off and locked him up. Dick stood there for a moment, then he wiped his face and turned to see what damage had been done the car. No more now, but there were those who saw it who remembered later how the eyes went red.

Another thing: the Sheppertons had a cook named Pansy Harris. She was a comely Negro wench, young, plump, black as the ace of spades, a good-hearted girl with a deep dimple in her cheeks and faultless teeth, bared in a most engaging smile. No one ever saw Dick speak to her. No one ever saw her glance at him, or him at her, and yet that smilingly good-natured wench became as mournful-silent and as silent-sullen as midnight pitch. She went about her work as mournfully as if she were going to a funeral. The gloom deepened all about her. She answered sullenly now when spoken to.

One night toward Christmas she announced that she was leaving. In response to all entreaties, all efforts to find the reason for her sudden and unreasonable decision, she had no answer except a sullen repetition of the assertion that she had to leave. Repeated questionings did finally wring from her a sullen statement that her husband needed her at home. More than this she would not say, and even this excuse was highly suspect, because her husband was a Pullman porter, only home two days a week and well accustomed to do himself such housekeeping tasks as she might do for him.

The Sheppertons were fond of her. They tried again to find the reason for her leaving. Was she dissatisfied? "No'm"—an implacable monosyllable, mournful, unrevealing as the night. Had she been offered a better job elsewhere? "No'm"—as untelling as before. If they offered her more wages, would she stay with them? "No'm," again and again, sullen and unyielding, until finally the exasperated mistress threw her hands up in a gesture of defeat and said, "All right then, Pansy. Have it your own way, if that's the way you feel. Only for heaven's sake don't leave us in the lurch until we get another cook."

This, at length, with obvious reluctance, the girl agreed to. Then, putting on her hat and coat and taking the paper bag of "leavings" she was allowed to take home with her at night, she went out the kitchen door and made her sullen and morose departure.

This was on Saturday night, a little after eight o'clock. That afternoon Randy and I had been fooling around the basement and, seeing that Dick's door was slightly ajar, we looked in to see if he was there. The little room was empty, swept and spotless, as it had always been.

But we did not notice that! We saw it! At the same moment, our breaths caught sharply in a gasp of startled wonderment. Randy was the first to speak. "Look!" he whispered. "Do you see it?"

See it! My eyes were glued upon it. Squarely across the bare board table, blue-dull, deadly in its murderous efficiency, lay a modern repeating rifle. Beside it was a box containing one hundred rounds of ammunition, and behind it, squarely in the center, face downward on the table, was the familiar cover of Dick's worn old Bible.

Then he was on us like a cat. He was there like a great dark shadow before we knew it. We turned, terrified. He was there above us, his thick lips bared above his gums, his eyes gone small and red as rodents'.

"Dick!" Randy gasped, and moistened his dry lips. "Dick!" he fairly cried now.

It was all over like a flash. Dick's mouth closed. We could see the whites of his eyes again. He smiled and said softly, affably, "Yes, suh, Cap'n

Shepperton. Yes, suh! You gent'mun lookin' at my rifle?" he said, and moved into the room.

I gulped and nodded my head and couldn't say a word, and Randy whispered, "Yes." And both of us still stared at him, with an expression of appalled and fascinated interest.

Dick shook his head and chuckled. "Can't do without my rifle, white fokes. No, suh!" he shook his head good-naturedly again. "Ole Dick, he's—he's—he's an ole Ahmy man, you know. If they take his rifle away from him, why, that's jest lak takin' candy from a little baby. Yes, suh!" he chuckled, and picked the weapon up affectionately. "Ole Dick felt Christmas comin' on—he-he—I reckon he must have felt it in his bones"—he chuckled—"so I been savin' up my money. I just thought I'd hide this heah and keep it as a big supprise fo' the young white fokes untwil Christmas morning. Then I was gonna take the young white fokes out and show 'em how to shoot."

We had begun to breathe more easily now and, almost as if we had been under the spell of the Pied Piper of Hamelin, we had followed him, step by step, into the room.

"Yes, suh," Dick chuckled, "I was just fixin' to hide this gun away twill Christmas Day, but Cap'n Shepperton—hee!" He chuckled heartily and slapped his thigh. "You can't fool ole Cap'n Shepperton. He just must've smelled this ole gun right out. He comes right in and sees it befo' I has a chance to tu'n around. . . . Now, white fokes"—Dick's voice fell to a tone of low and winning confidence—"now that you's found out, I'll tell you what I'll do. If you'll just keep it a supprise from the other white fokes twill Christmas Day, I'll take all you gent'mun out and let you shoot it. Now, cose," he went on quietly, with a shade of resignation, "if you want to tell on me, you can, but"—here his voice fell again, with just the faintest, yet most eloquent shade of sorrowful regret—"ole Dick was looking fahwad to this; hopin' to give all the white fokes a supprise Christmas Day."

We promised earnestly that we would keep his secret as if it were our own. We fairly whispered our solemn vow. We tiptoed away out of the little basement room as if we were afraid our very footsteps might betray the partner of our confidence.

This was four o'clock on Saturday afternoon. Already, there was a somber moaning of the wind, gray storm clouds sweeping over. The threat of snow was in the air.

Snow fell that night. It came howling down across the hills. It swept in on us from the Smokies. By seven o'clock the air was blind with sweeping snow, the earth was carpeted, the streets were numb. The storm howled on, around houses warm with crackling fires and shaded light. All life seemed to have withdrawn into thrilling isolation. A horse went by upon the streets with muffled hoofs. Storm shook the houses. The world was numb. I went to sleep upon this mystery, lying in the darkness, listening to that exultancy of storm, to that dumb wonder, that enormous and attentive quietness of snow, with something dark and jubilant in my soul I could not utter.

A little after one o'clock that morning I was awakened by the ringing of a bell. It was the fire bell of the city hall, and it was beating an alarm—a hard fast stroke that I had never heard before. Bronze with peril, clangorous through the snow-numbed silence of the air, it had a quality of instancy and menace I had never known before. I leaped up and ran to the window to look for the telltale glow against the sky. But almost before I looked, those deadly strokes beat in upon my brain the message that this was no alarm for fire. It was a savage clangorous alarm to the whole town, a brazen tongue to warn mankind against the menace of some peril, secret, dark, unknown, greater than fire or flood could ever be.

I got instantly, in the most overwhelming and electric way, the sense that the whole town had come to life. All up and down the street the houses were beginning to light up. Next door, the Shepperton house was ablaze with light from top to bottom. Even as I looked, Mr. Shepperton, wearing an overcoat over his pajamas, ran down the snow-covered steps and padded out across the snow-covered walk toward the street.

People were beginning to run out of doors. I heard excited shouts and questions everywhere. I saw Nebraska Crane come pounding down the middle of the street. I knew that he was coming for me and Randy. As he ran by Shepperton's, he put his fingers to his mouth and whistled piercingly. It was a signal we all knew.

I was all ready by the time he came running down the alley toward our cottage. He hammered at the door; I was already there.

"Come on!" he said, panting with excitement, his black eyes burning with an intensity I'd never seen before. "Come on!" he cried. We were halfway out across the yard by now. "It's that nigger. He's gone crazy and is running wild."

"Wh-wh-what nigger?" I gasped, pounding at his heels.

Even before he spoke, I had the answer. Mr. Crane had already come out of his house, buttoning his heavy policeman's overcoat as he came. He had paused to speak for a moment to Mr. Shepperton, and I heard Shepperton say quickly, in a low voice, "Which way did he go?"

Then I heard somebody cry, "It's that nigger of Shepperton's!"

Mr. Shepperton turned and went quickly back across his yard toward the house. His wife and two girls stood huddled in the open doorway, white, trembling, holding themselves together, their arms thrust into the wide sleeves of their kimonos.

The telephone in Shepperton's house was ringing like mad, but no one was paying any attention to it. I heard Mrs. Shepperton say quickly, as he ran up the steps, "Is it Dick?" He nodded and passed her brusquely, going toward the phone.

At this moment, Nebraska whistled piercingly again upon his fingers and Randy Shepperton ran past his mother and down the steps. She called sharply to him. He paid no attention to her. When he came up, I saw that his fine thin face was white as a sheet. He looked at me and whispered, "It's—it's Dick!" And in a moment, "They say he's killed four people."

"With——" I couldn't finish.

Randy nodded dumbly, and we both stared there for a minute, aware now of the murderous significance of the secret we had kept, with a sudden sense of guilt and fear, as if somehow the crime lay on our shoulders.

Across the street a window banged up in the parlor of Suggs' house, and Old Man Suggs appeared in the window, clad only in his nightgown, his brutal old face inflamed with excitement, his shock of silvery white hair awry, his powerful shoulders, and his thick hands gripping his crutches.

"He's coming this way!" he bawled to the world in general. "They say he lit out across the square! He's heading out in this direction!"

Mr. Crane paused to yell back impatiently over his shoulder, "No, he went down South Dean Street! He's heading for Wilton and the river! I've already heard from headquarters!"

Automobiles were beginning to roar and sputter all along the street. Across the street I could hear Mr. Potterham sweating over his. He would whirl the crank a dozen times or more; the engine would catch for a moment, cough and sputter, and then die again. Gus ran out-of-doors with a kettle of boiling water and began to pour it feverishly down the radiator spout.

Mr. Shepperton was already dressed. We saw him run down the back steps toward the carriage house. All three of us, Randy, Nebraska and myself, streaked down the alleyway to help him. We got the old wooden doors open. He went in and cranked the car. It was a new one, and started up at once. Mr. Shepperton backed out into the snowy drive. We all clambered up on the running

board. He spoke absently, saying, "You boys stay here. . . . Randy, your mother's calling you," but we all tumbled in and he didn't say a word.

He came backing down the alleyway at top speed. We turned into the street and picked up Mr. Crane at the corner. We lit out for town, going at top speed. Cars were coming out of alleys everywhere. We could hear people shouting questions and replies at one another. I heard one man shout, "He's killed six men!"

I don't think it took us over five minutes to reach the square, but when we got there, it seemed as if the whole town was there ahead of us. Mr. Shepperton pulled the car up and parked in front of the city hall. Mr. Crane leaped out and went pounding away across the square without another word to us.

From every corner, every street that led into the square, people were streaking in. One could see the dark figures of running men across the white carpet of the square. They were all rushing in to one focal point.

The southwest corner of the square where South Dean Street came into it was like a dog fight. Those running figures streaking toward that dense crowd gathered there made me think of nothing else so much as a fight between two boys upon the playgrounds of the school at recess time. The way the crowd was swarming in was just the same.

But then I *heard* a difference. From that crowd came a low and growing mutter, an ugly and insistent growl, of a tone and quality I had never heard before. But I knew instantly what it meant. There was no mistaking the blood note in that foggy growl. And we looked at one another with the same question in the eyes of all.

Only Nebraska's coal-black eyes were shining now with a savage sparkle even they had never had before. "Come on," he said in a low tone, exultantly. "They mean business this time, sure. Let's go." And he darted away toward the dense and sinister darkness of the crowd.

Even as we followed him we heard coming toward us now, growing, swelling at every instant, one of the most savagely mournful and terrifying sounds that night can know. It was the baying of the hounds as they came up upon the leash from Niggertown. Full-throated, howling deep, the savagery of blood was in it, and the savagery of man's guilty doom was in it too.

They came up swiftly, fairly baying at our heels as we sped across the snow-white darkness of the square. As we got up to the crowd, we saw that it had gathered at the corner where my uncle's hardware store stood. Cash Eager had not yet arrived, but, facing the crowd which pressed in on them so close and menacing that they were almost flattened out against the glass, three or four men were standing with arms stretched out in a kind of chain, as if trying to protect with the last resistance of their strength and eloquence the sanctity of private property.

Will Hendershot was mayor at that time, and he was standing there, arm to arm with Hugh McNair. I could see Hugh, taller by half a foot than anyone around him, his long gaunt figure, the gaunt passion of his face, even the attitude of his outstretched bony arms, strangely, movingly Lincolnesque, his one good eye blazing in the cold glare of the corner lamp with a kind of cold inspired Scotch passion.

"Wait a minute! You men wait a minute!" he cried. His words cut out above the clamor of the mob like an electric spark. "You'll gain nothing, you'll help nothing if you do this thing!"

They tried to drown him out with an angry and derisive roar. He shot his big fist up into the air and shouted at them, blazed at them with that cold single eye, until they had to hear. "Listen to me!" he cried. "This is no time for mob law! This is no case for lynch law! This is a time for law and order! Wait till the sheriff swears you in! Wait until Cash Eager comes! Wait ———"

He got no farther. "Wait, hell!" cried someone. "We've waited long enough! We're going to get that nigger!"

The mob took up the cry. The whole crowd was writhing angrily now, like a tormented snake. Suddenly there was a flurry in the crowd, a scattering. Somebody yelled a warning at Hugh McNair. He ducked quickly, just in time. A brick whizzed past him, smashing the plate-glass window into fragments.

And instantly a bloody roar went up. The crowd surged forward, kicked the fragments of jagged glass away. In a moment the whole mob was storming into the dark store. Cash Eager got there just too late. He arrived in time to take out his keys and open the front doors, but as he grimly remarked, it was like closing the barn doors after the horse had been stolen.

The mob was in and helped themselves to every rifle they could find. They smashed open cartridge boxes and filled their pockets with the loose cartridges. Within ten minutes they had looted the store of every rifle, every cartridge in the stock. The whole place looked as if a hurricane had hit it. The mob was streaming out into the street, was already gathering round the dogs a hundred feet or so away, who were picking up the scent at that point, the place where Dick had halted last before he had turned and headed south, downhill along South Dean Street toward the river.

The hounds were scampering about, tugging at the leash, moaning softly with their noses pointed to the snow, their long ears flattened down. But in that light and in that snow it almost seemed no hounds were needed to follow Dick. Straight as a string right down the center of the sheeted car tracks, the Negro's footsteps led away until they vanished downhill in the darkness.

But now, although the snow had stopped, the wind was swirling through the street and making drifts and eddies in the snow. The footprints were fading rapidly. Soon they would be gone.

The dogs were given their head. They went straining on softly, sniffing at the snow; behind them the dark masses of the mob closed in and followed. We stood there watching while they went. We saw them go on down the street and vanish. But from below, over the snow-numbed stillness of the air, the vast low mutter of the mob came back to us.

Men were clustered now in groups. Cash Eager stood before his shattered window, ruefully surveying the ruin. Other men were gathered around the big telephone pole at the corner, pointing out two bullet holes that had been drilled cleanly through it.

And swiftly, like a flash, running from group to group, like a powder train of fire, the full detail of that bloody chronicle of night was pieced together.

This was what had happened. Somewhere between nine and ten o'clock that night, Dick Prosser had gone to Pansy Harris' shack in Niggertown. Some said he had been drinking when he went there. At any rate, the police had later found the remnants of a gallon jug of raw corn whisky in the room. What happened, what passed between them, was never known. And, besides, no one was greatly interested. It was a crazy nigger with "another nigger's woman."

Shortly after ten o'clock that night, the woman's husband appeared upon the scene. The fight did not start then. According to the woman, the real trouble did not come until an hour or more after his return.

The men drank together. Each was in an ugly temper. Shortly before midnight, they got into a fight. Harris slashed at Dick with a razor. In a second they were locked together, rolling about and fighting like two madmen on the floor. Pansy Harris went screaming out-of-doors and across the street into a dingy little grocery store.

A riot call was telephoned at once to police headquarters on the public square. The news came in that a crazy nigger had broken loose on Gulley Street in Niggertown, and to send help at once. Pansy Harris ran back across the street toward her little shack.

As she got there, her husband, with blood streaming from his face, staggered out into the street, with his hands held up protectively behind his head in a gesture of instinctive terror. At the same moment, Dick Prosser appeared in the doorway of the shack, deliberately took aim with his rifle and shot the fleeing Negro squarely through the back of the head. Harris dropped forward on his face into the snow. He was dead before he hit the ground. A huge dark stain of blood-soaked snow widened out around him. Dick Prosser seized the terrified Negress by the arm, hurled her into the shack, bolted the door, pulled down the shades, blew out the lamp and waited.

A few minutes later, two policemen arrived from town. They were a young constable named Willis, and John Grady, a lieutenant of police. The policemen took one look at the bloody figure in the snow, questioned the frightened keeper of the grocery store and, after consulting briefly, produced their weapons and walked out into the street.

Young Willis stepped softly down on to the snow-covered porch of the shack, flattened himself against the wall between the window and the door, and waited. Grady went around to the side and flashed his light through the window, which, on this side, was shadeless. Grady said in a loud tone: "Come out of there!"

Dick's answer was to shoot him cleanly through the wrist. At the same moment Willis kicked the door in and, without waiting, started in with pointed revolver. Dick shot him just above the eyes. The policeman fell forward on his face.

Grady came running out around the house, rushed into the grocery store, pulled the receiver of the old-fashioned telephone off the hook, rang frantically for headquarters and yelled out across the wire that a crazy nigger had killed Sam Willis and a Negro man, and to send help.

At this moment Dick stepped out across the porch into the street, aimed swiftly through the dirty window of the little store and shot John Grady as he stood there at the phone. Grady fell dead with a bullet that entered just below his left temple and went out on the other side.

Dick, now moving in a long, unhurried stride that covered the ground with catlike speed, turned up the long snow-covered slope of Gulley Street and began his march toward town. He moved right up the center of the street, shooting cleanly from left to right as he went. Halfway up the hill, the second-story window of a two-story Negro tenement flew open. An old Negro man stuck out his ancient head of cotton wool. Dick swiveled and shot casually from his hip. The shot tore the top of the old Negro's head off.

By the time Dick reached the head of Gulley Street, they knew he was coming. He moved steadily along, leaving his big tread cleanly in the middle of the sheeted street, shifting a little as he walked, swinging his gun crosswise before him. This was the Negro Broadway of the town, but where those poolrooms, barbershops, drugstores and fried-fish places had been loud with dusky life ten minutes before, they were now silent as the ruins of Egypt. The word was flaming through the town that a crazy nigger was on the way. No one showed his head.

Dick moved on steadily, always in the middle of the street, reached the end of Gulley Street and turned into South Dean—turned right, uphill, in the middle of the car tracks, and started toward the square. As he passed the lunchroom on the left, he took a swift shot through the window at the counter man. The fellow ducked behind the counter. The bullet crashed into the wall above his head.

Meanwhile, at police headquarters, the sergeant had sent John Chapman out across the square to head Dick off. Mr. Chapman was perhaps the best-liked man upon the force. He was a pleasant florid-faced man of forty-five, with curling brown mustaches, congenial and good-humored, devoted to his family, courageous, but perhaps too kindly and too gentle for a good policemen.

John Chapman heard the shots and ran. He came up to the corner by Eager's hardware store just as Dick's last shot went crashing through the lunchroom window. Mr. Chapman took up his post there at the corner behind the telephone post that stood there at that time. Mr. Chapman, from his vantage point behind this post, took out his revolver and shot directly at Dick Prosser as he came up the street.

By this time Dick was not more than thirty yards away. He dropped quietly upon one knee and aimed. Mr. Chapman shot again and missed. Dick fired. The high-velocity bullet bored through the post a little to one side. It grazed the shoulder of John Chapman's uniform and knocked a chip out of the monument sixty yards or more behind him in the center of the square.

Mr. Chapman fired again and missed. And Dick, still coolly poised upon his knee, as calm and steady as if he were engaging in a rifle practice, fired again, drilled squarely through the center of the post and shot John Chapman through the heart. Then Dick rose, pivoted like a soldier in his tracks and started down the street, straight as a string, right out of town.

This was the story as we got it, pieced together like a train of fire among the excited groups of men that clustered there in trampled snow before the shattered glass of Eager's store.

But now, save for these groups of talking men, the town again was silent. Far off in the direction of the river, we could hear the mournful baying of the hounds. There was nothing more to see or do. Cash Eager stooped, picked up some fragments of the shattered glass and threw them in the window. A policeman was left on guard, and presently all five of us—Mr. Shepperton, Cash Eager and we three boys—walked back across the square and got into the car and drove home again.

But there was no more sleep, I think, for anyone that night. Black Dick had murdered sleep. Toward daybreak, snow began to fall again. The snow continued through the morning. It was piled deep in gusting drifts by noon. All footprints were obliterated; the town waited, eager, tense, wondering if the man could get away.

They did not capture him that day, but they were on his trail. From time to time throughout the day, news would drift back to us. Dick had turned east along the river and gone out for some miles along the Fairchilds road. There, a mile or two from Fairchilds, he crossed the river at the Rocky Shallows.

Shortly after daybreak, a farmer from the Fairchilds section had seen him cross a field. They picked the trail up there again and followed it across the field and through a wood. He had come out on the other side and got down into the Cane Creek section, and there, for several hours, they lost him. Dick had gone right down into the icy water of the creek, and walked upstream a mile or so. They brought the dogs down to the creek, to where he broke the trail, took them over to the other side and scented up and down.

Toward five o'clock that afternoon they picked the trail up on the other side, a mile or more upstream. From that point on, they began to close in on him. The dogs followed him across the fields, across the Lester road, into a wood. One arm of the posse swept around the wood to head him off. They knew they had him. Dick, freezing, hungry and unsheltered, was hiding in that wood. They knew he couldn't get away. The posse ringed the wood and waited until morning.

At 7:30 the next morning he made a break for it. He got through the line without being seen, crossed the Lester road and headed back across the field in the direction of Cane Creek. And there they caught him. They saw him plunging through the snowdrift of a field. A cry went up. The posse started after him.

Part of the posse were on horseback. The men rode in across the field. Dick halted at the edge of the wood, dropped deliberately upon one knee and for some minutes held them off with rapid fire. At two hundred yards he dropped Doc Lavender, a deputy, with a bullet through the throat.

The posse came in slowly, in an encircling, flankwise movement. Dick got two more of them as they closed in, and then, as deliberately as a trained soldier retreating in good order, still firing as he went, he fell back through the wood. At the other side he turned and ran down through a sloping field that bordered on Cane Creek. At the creek edge, he turned again, knelt once more in the snow and aimed.

It was Dick's last shot. He didn't miss. The bullet struck Wayne Foraker, a deputy, dead center in the forehead and killed him in his saddle. Then the posse saw the Negro aim again, and nothing happened. Dick snapped the breech open savagely, then hurled the gun away. A cheer went up. The posse came charging forward. Dick turned, stumblingly, and ran the few remaining yards that separated him from the cold and rock-bright waters of the creek.

And here he did a curious thing—a thing that no one ever wholly understood. It was thought that he would make one final break for freedom, that he would wade the creek and try to get away before they got to him. Instead, he sat down calmly on the bank and, as quietly as if he were seated on his cot in an Army barracks, he unlaced his shoes, took them off, placed them together neatly at his side, and then stood up like a soldier, erect, in his bare bleeding feet, and faced the mob.

The men on horseback reached him first. They rode up around him and discharged their guns into him. He fell forward in the snow, riddled with bullets. The men dismounted, turned him over on his back, and all the other men came in and riddled him. They took his lifeless body, put a rope around his neck and hung him to a tree. Then the mob exhausted all their ammunition on the riddled carcass.

By nine o'clock that morning the news had reached the town. Around eleven o'clock, the mob came back along the river road. A good crowd had gone out to meet it at the Wilton Bottoms. The sheriff rode ahead. Dick's body had been thrown like a sack and tied across the saddle of the horse of one of the deputies he had killed.

It was in this way, bullet-riddled, shot to pieces, open to the vengeful and the morbid gaze of all, that Dick came back to town. The mob came back right to its starting point in South Dean Street. They halted there before an undertaking parlor, not twenty yards away from where Dick knelt to kill John Chapman. They took that ghastly mutilated thing and hung it in the window of the undertaker's place, for every woman, man and child in town to see.

And it was so we saw him last. We said we wouldn't look. But in the end we went. And I think it has always been the same with people. They protest. They shudder. And they say they will not go. But in the end they always have their look.

At length we went. We saw it, tried wretchedly to make ourselves believe that once this thing had spoken to us gently, had been partner to our confidence, object of our affection and respect. And we were sick with nausea and fear, for something had come into our lives we could not understand.

We looked and whitened to the lips, and craned our necks and looked away, and brought unwilling, fascinated eyes back to the horror once again, and craned and turned again, and shuffled in the slush uneasily, but could not go. And we looked up at the leaden reek of day, the dreary vapor of the sky, and, bleakly, at these forms and faces all around us—the people come to gape and stare, the poolroom loafers, the town toughs, the mongrel conquerors of earth—and yet, familiar to our lives and to the body of our whole experience, all known to our landscape, all living men.

And something had come into life—into our lives—that we had never known about before. It was a kind of shadow, a poisonous blackness filled with bewildered loathing. The snow would go, we knew; the reeking vapors of the sky would clear away. The leaf, the blade, the bud, the bird, then April, would come back again, and all of this would be as it had ever been. The homely light of day would shine again familiarly. And all of this would vanish as an evil dream. And yet not wholly so. For we would still remember the old dark doubt and loathing of our kind, of something hateful and unspeakable in the souls of men. We knew that we should not forget.

Beside us, a man was telling the story of his own heroic accomplishments to a little group of fascinated listeners. I turned and looked at him. It was Ben Pounders, of the ferret face, the fur-tive and uneasy eye, Ben Pounders of the mongrel mouth, the wiry muscles of the jaw, Ben Pounders, the collector of usurious lendings to the blacks, the nigger hunter. And now Ben Pounders boasted of another triumph. He was the proud possessor of another scalp.

"I was the first one to git in a shot," he said. "You see that hole there?" He pointed with a dirty finger. "That big hole right above the eye?" They turned and goggled with a drugged and feeding stare.

"That's mine," the hero said, turned briefly to the side and spat tobacco juice into the slush. "That's where I got him. Hell, after that he didn't know what hit him. He was dead before he hit the ground. We all shot him full of holes then. We sure did fill him full of lead. Why, hell, yes," he declared, with a decisive movement of his head, "we counted up to two hundred and eighty-seven. We must have put three hundred holes in him."

And Nebraska, fearless, blunt, outspoken, as he always was, turned abruptly, put two fingers to his lips and spat between them, widely and contemptuously.

"Yeah—*we!*" he grunted. "*We* killed a big one! We—we killed a b'ar, we did! . . . Come on, boys," he said gruffly. "Let's be on our way!"

And, fearless and unshaken, untouched by any terror or any doubt, he moved away. And two white-faced, nauseated boys went with him.

A day or two went by before anyone could go into Dick's room again. I went in with Randy and his father. The little room was spotless, bare and tidy as it had always been. But even the very austerity of that little room now seemed terribly alive with the presence of its black tenant. It was Dick's room. We all knew that. And somehow we all knew that no one else could ever live there again.

Mr. Shepperton went over to the table, picked up Dick's old Bible that still lay there, open and face downward, held it up to the light and looked at it, at the place that Dick had marked when he last read in it. And in a moment, without speaking to us, he began to read in a quiet voice:

"The Lord is my shepherd; I shall not want.
"2. He maketh me to lie down in green pastures: He leadeth me beside the still waters.
"3. He restoreth my soul: He leadeth me in the paths of righteousness for His name's sake.
"4. Yea, though I walk through the valley of the shadow of death, I will fear no evil: for Thou art with me ——"

Then Mr. Shepperton closed the book and put it down upon the table, the place where Dick had left it. And we went out the door, he locked it, and we went back into that room no more forever.

The years passed, and all of us were given unto time. We went our ways. But often they would turn and come again, these faces and these voices of the past, and burn there in my memory again, upon the muted and immortal geography of time.

And all would come again—the shout of the young voices, the hard thud of the kicked ball, and Dick moving, moving steadily, Dick moving, moving silently, a storm-white world and silence, and something moving, moving in the night. Then I would hear the furious bell, the crowd a-clamor and the baying of the dogs, and feel the shadow coming that would never disappear. Then I would see again the little room that we would see no more, the table and the book. And the pastoral holiness of that old psalm came back to me and my heart would wonder with perplexity and doubt.

For I had heard another song since then, and one that Dick, I know, had never heard, and one perhaps he might not have understood, but one whose phrases and whose imagery it seemed to me would suit him better:

What the hammer? What the chain?
In what furnace was thy brain?
What the anvil? What dread grasp
Dare its deadly terrors clasp?

When the stars threw down their spears,
And water'd heaven with their tears,
Did He smile His work to see?
Did He who made the lamb make thee?

"*What* the hammer? *What* the chain?" No one ever knew. It was a mystery and a wonder. There were a dozen stories, a hundred clues and rumors; all came to nothing in the end. Some said that Dick had come from Texas, others that his home had been in Georgia. Some said that it was true that he had been enlisted in the Army, but that he had killed a man while there and served a term at Leavenworth. Some said he had served in the Army and had received an honorable discharge, but had later killed a man and had served a term in a state prison in Louisiana. Others said that he had been an Army man, but that he had gone crazy, that he had served a period in an asylum when it was found that he was insane, that he had escaped from this asylum, that he had escaped from prison, that he was a fugitive from justice at the time he came to us.

But all these stories came to nothing. Nothing was ever proved. Men debated and discussed these things a thousand times—who and what he had come from—and all of it came to nothing. No one knew the answer. But I think that I have found the answer. I think I know from where he came.

He came from darkness. He came out of the heart of darkness, from the dark heart of the secret and undiscovered South. He came by night, just as he passed by night. He was night's child and partner, a token of the other side of man's dark soul, a symbol of those things that pass by darkness and that still remain, a symbol of man's evil innocence, and the token of his mystery, a projection of his own unfathomed quality, a friend, a brother and a mortal enemy, an unknown demon, two worlds together—a tiger and a child.

THE HUNTING OF THE HAGGIS

by Guy Gilpatric

On page ninety-four of the *Post* for January 4, 1930, the engineer of the *Inchcliffe Castle* reached under his bunk and drew forth a bottle labelled "Dew of Kirkintilloch." He drank a dainty tumblerful and then launched into a solo rendition of "Cock o' the North" on his bagpipe. It was the victory wail of Mr. Glencannon, a sound that became like sweet music to a vast number of *Post* readers. From 1930 to 1950 at least fifty Glencannon stories ran in the *Post*, but the demand for more was unceasing. "We publish all the Glencannon stories we can get," the *Post* pleaded publicly in 1938. "We don't publish more because Mr. Gilpatric doesn't write 'em."

The author was a native New Yorker who was a daring aviator at sixteen and vice-president of a Manhattan advertising agency at thirty. Then he quit business to live, write, hunt octopuses and practice fencing on the French Riviera at Antibes. In 1938 he published *The Compleat Goggler*, a book about goggle-fishing. World War II brought him back to California where, on June 7, 1950, he and his wife died together in a needless tragedy brought on by her fear of cancer.

JANUARY 14, 1939

CAPTAIN BALL smiled paternally as he watched his officers take their places at the supper table, but the smile was a trifle tremulous at the edges. In his throat—he kerhuffed, unresultfully—he could feel the same lump that was always there when he came down the lane to Kozey Kottage after a long voyage and saw Missus B. standing in the doorway beneath the mail-order trumpet vine, which they loved just as much as though it hadn't turned out to be a peculiarly repulsive sort of warty climbing squash. *Ten years,* Captain Ball was thinking. *Yes, tomorrow'll make the tenth Christmas this very same crowd of us has been together in the Inchcliffe Castle. M'm—well, all of us is older now than we was then, but particularly me. Yes, most damned particularly me.* He reminded himself that this was only because he'd had a head start of years on the rest of them, but there was scant consolation in the thought.

The steward brought in a covered dish and placed it on the table before him. "Ker-hem!" Captain Ball recalled himself brusquely. "Good evening, gentlemen, good evening!" He shook the crumbs and fragments of the noontime curry from his napkin. "Well, I spose we might as well learn the worst!" With the air of a coroner lifting a coffin lid at an overdue exhumation, he uncovered the dish and peered within. "Bwah!" he recoiled. "Curry! Again!" He sat back shuddering, and from the depths of his considerable paunch came murmurs and complaints, like the voices of a rebellious mob heard dimly in the distance. For some seconds he and the company hearkened to this ventriloquial *tour de force*; then, when the tumult and the shouting died, "Well, there you are, and I won't say 'pardon me'!" Captain Ball spread his hands. "You heard it, gentlemen, you heard my innermost sentiments, and I'm not ashamed to state I stand behind my stomach exactly one hundred per cent!"

"Bravvio!" applauded Mr. Glencannon, the chief engineer. "Yere spirit o' solidarity does ye proud, sir—e'en though I suspect ye're feeling as hollow as the rest o' us." He dragged the dish toward him, spooned out a heaping portion of curried rice and codfish, and fell to stowing it away in the hatchlike orifice beneath his walrus mustache.

"Hollow?" repeated Captain Ball. "Indeed, Mr. Glencannon, my stomach's as hollow as a cargo of bass drums! But my heart—ah, my heart is full to overflowing, both with joy and with sadness!" He paused lamely and smiled that same tremulous smile. "Maybe you'll say I'm a sentimental old fool, gentlemen, but, you see, I was just now figuring that this is the eve of our tenth Christmas together. Well, here we ought to be gloating over the bang-up dinner we ought to be having tomorrow and singing carols about good cheer and yew logs and what not and et cetera and so on—instead of which—ker-huff—where are we? Well"—he turned to the mate—"literally, of course, I spose such sticklers for accuracy as you, Mr. Montgomery, would say we was right here in Aden harbor, anchored in five fathoms

393

and a little over, and the chart would back you up. But what I really mean to say is—er—er—well, here it is the tenth anniversary of our happy family, as it were, but instead of looking forward to a fine old feed to celebrate it, our very constitutions is roaring riot and rebellion!"

"Yus!" agreed Mr. Montgomery, sourly. "And orl on account of the curry. Curry, curry, curry, day in, day out, and the narsty stuff is only a sort of low-grade dandruff they comb out of 'orses anyway! Welp, I wish a very curry Christmas to the rest of yer! Myself, I'll eat my dinner ashore tomorrer or my name's not Chauncey Montgomery!"

"Eh? Ah, now, see here! You don't really mean that, do you?" demanded Captain Ball in dismay. "Oh, come, come, Mr. Montgomery; surely you wouldn't, you couldn't, break up our regular Christmas family party on our tenth anniversary, will you? Maybe I'm silly, maybe I'm superstitious, but it—it's so unusual for the same old crowd to stick together so long in one ship and always get along so free from friction!"

"Per'aps," grunted Mr. Montgomery. "Orl I know is that I've got barnacles on my stomach from the fodder, and blisters on my soul from the friction." He glanced sidewise at Mr. Glencannon, who, from the shelter of his napkin, thumbed his nose in return. "No, captain, I've choked down all the curry and the hinsults I can stand! I'm going ashore tonight, I'm going to arsk Shapiro, the ship chandler, for the name of the least worst 'otel in Aden, and then I'm going to order a dinner for myself for tomorrer. I know I won't get turkey, I 'ope I won't get potomaine poisoning, but damned if I'll get curry!"

"No, no, of course you won't!" sighed Captain Ball. "I spose it was really pretty selfish of me to try to dissuade you. But—ha-ha!—there's no fool like an old fool, eh? H'm'm. Ten years!" He essayed a forkful of the curry, but either it or the lump in his throat choked him, so he gave it up. "Well, let's change the subject and talk about something pleasant! Turkey, you said?" The sounds from within him soared to the wild crescendo of hunger marchers chanting the International, then died on a gurgle of utter despair. "Ah, turkey! All roasted to a nice, rich tobacco-juice brown, with its abdomen stuffed with chestnuts and sausages and thyme and bread crumbs, like Missus B. always stuffs hers at home—though damme if I can ever remember whether the accent is on the 'ab' or the 'do.' She also makes a lovely, thick gravy out of the giblets."

"Lawks, 'ow delicious! The thought of it fair makes my teeth water!" declared Mr. Montgomery. "If we could only 'ave turkey with giblet gravy tomorrer, even watching Mr. Glencannon eat it couldn't spoil my happetite! But look"—he pointed through the open doorway toward the black rock mountains which reared above the lights on Steamer Point—"look! Why, blyme, yer'd find gold coins in the streets o' Glasgow before yer'd find a turkey in Aden!"

"A-weel," said Mr. Glencannon, "oot o' respect for the captain's vurra evident distress at yere decision, I'll owerlook for the moment the crude pairsonal slurs ye've just noo cast at me. And noturally, I willna attempt to dispute the fact that the turkey is a vurra noble and palatable bird. But all the talk o' stoomachs has reminded me that for great ceremoonial occasions—birthdays, bonquets, brawls and e'en such sacred, sentimental gatherings as Captain Ball was plonning for tomorrow—there's another dish fully as deleecious as the turkey. I refair, o' coorse to the haggis. Noo, look ye, Muster Montgomery; I'll give ye a chonce to be decent for once in yere life, e'en though it sprains ye! If I guarontee to cook up a nice, ploomp haggis for our little party, will ye no' accede to the captain's cherished wishes and eat yere Christmas meal with him and the rest o' us?"

"M'm, well, that depends," said Mr. Montgomery, loftily. "Just wot the 'ell's a 'aggis?"

Mr. Glencannon gazed at him in astonishment mingled with pity. "The haggis," he explained with a spacious gesture, "the haggis, Muster Mate, is the fruit o' a romonce o' lang, lang ago, involving the humble pudding and the lordly sossage. It is the culinary triumph o' Scotland, which is to say, o' the entire world! Oh, surely, my puir fellow, e'en in all yere pewling ignorance, ye dinna mean to say ye've ne'er thrilled to the deathless lines o' Robert Burns in his Address to a Haggis? Er—

> "Great chieftain o' the pudding race,
> Aboon them a' ye tak your place!
> His knife see rustic Labour dight
> And cut ye up wi' ready sleight,
> Trenching your gushing entrails bright
>   Lik' any ditch.
> And then, Oh what a glorious sight,
>   Warm-reekin', rich!"

"H'mph, it sounds ruddy nausyeating to me," said Mr. Montgomery. "Besides, leaving out the silly tuppenny poetry, you've only 'arf answered the question I arsked yer in the first place—to wit, wot the 'ell's a 'aggis?"

"Yes, yes, tell him!" urged Captain Ball, eagerly. "Explain him the full modus operanda of how you prepare this—er—delicious Highland titbit, Mr. Glencannon!"

Mr. Glencannon squinted a fishy eye at the gnats which swarmed around the polished brass lamp above the table. "Weel, making the haggis is rideeculously sumple," he declared. "Ye merely need a certain amoont o' oatmeal, some onions, and a five-gallon bucket. Er"—he turned to the second engineer—"what else wud ye say was needed for a haggis, Muster MacQuayle?"

"Pepper," said Mr. MacQuayle. "Ye must have plenty of pepper. Losh, I can see my auld Aunty Meg in Killiecrankie making a haggis the noo!"

"Oatmeal, onions and pepper—is that orl there is to it?" sneered Mr. Montgomery.

"Weel, proctically," said Mr. Glencannon, placidly filling his pipe, "though in enumerating the ingredients, ye left oot the five-gallon bucket. But once ye've got those four succulent essentials ready at hond, yere haggis is as guid as made. All that remains to do, then, is slaughter an ox, cut his hoofs off, skin him, rip his insides oot and ——"

"Not an ox—a sheep!" Mr. MacQuayle objected. "Ye commence by chopping his head off. My Aunty Meg in Killiecrankie always did the job with an auld claymore whuch belanged to my great-grandfather, Piper Jaimie McTooth, o' Stronachlachar. He went oot to India with the Argyll and Dumbartons in 1857 and won a bronze medal for getting shot in half at Lucknow. Aunty Meg cud fetch a sheep's head off with that auld claymore in one lick—squirp!— till the rheumatism cromped her style. After that, she'd sneak up on him through the heather and bosh him ower the head with a rock. While the sheep would be laying there groggy, she'd sit hersel' astroddle o' him with a cross-cut saw and ——"

Mr. Glencannon frowned and raised a hand for silence. "Pairdon me, Muster MacQuayle," he said, "ox! Ye hong up yere ox and ye let his bluid drain into the five-gallon bucket. His stoomach, his liver, his heart and all his heavier machinery ye put carefully to one side where the collies canna snotch them. His other, or auxiliary, mechanism is vurra useful to mak' glue oot of, so ye mustna throw any o' it awa'. Ah, losh, gentlemen"—Mr. Glencannon smacked his lips—"as ye can readily judge for yersels, the haggis is a vurritable feast for the gods!"

Mr. Montgomery shook his fists toward heaven. "But now, see 'ere!" he fumed. "Never mind the collies and the glue—it's the 'aggis, the 'aggis I want to know about!"

"Haw, listen to him, captain!" chuckled Mr. Glencannon. "His eagerness betrays his oppetite, and I dinna blame him! Oh, he'll be here with us tomorrow with a fork in each hond, mark my wurrds!" He struck a match, applied it to his pipe and puffed thoughtfully before continuing. "Ye tak' the heart o' yere ox ——"

"Sheep," said Mr. MacQuayle.

"Ox! Great swith, Muster MacQuayle, if ——"

"Oh, my eye!" snapped Mr. Montgomery. "Get a'ead with it, can't yer?"

"Aye, glodly, if ye'll only stop interrupting! Ye tak' all the parts ye dinna plon to use for glue except the stoomach. Ye hash them up. Ye mix them with yere oatmeal, yere onions and yere pepper. Then ye throw the whole business into the five-gallon bucket, sloshing it aroond with a broom hondle or a guid, stoot walking stick until it gives off a scupping sound, lik' when ye wade through the ooze in the bottom o' a dry dock. At this point, if ye care to, ye can add a sprig o' pursely and a few leaves o' rosemary, gently crushed betwixt the finger and the thumb, although discriminating haggis eaters o' the auld school maintain that this detrocts from the soobtile and deelicate flavor o' the whole."

"Ugh! Me, I'd add some disinfectant an 'eave the 'ole mess overboard!" declared Mr. Montgomery. "Yus, gorblyme, and I'd 'eave the bucket arfter it!"

Mr. Glencannon raised his eyebrows. "Muster Montgomery," he said, "pairmit me to obsairve that I think ye're vurra uncouth."

"Yes, shush, shush—softly, Mister Mate," Captain Ball admonished, pacifically. "So far, the haggis is raw, don't you see? . . . But—ker-hem— I mean to say, how do you cook it, Mr. Glencannon?"

"Ye cook it to a turn, sir," said the engineer. "For that, incidentally, ye must use a fire. But feerst ye pick up the ox's stoomach in yere left hond, grosping it firmly aroond the waistline, as in the auld-fashioned Viennese waltz. Then, with yere richt, ye stoof it full o' the stoof ye fish oot o' the five-gallon bucket. . . . Do ye check wi' me, Muster MacQuayle?"

"Dom, no, by no means!" blurted Mr. MacQuayle. "Ye dinna stoof the stoofing into an ox's stoomach at all; ye stoof it into a sheep's liver! My auld Aunty Meg in Killiecrankie ——"

"Foosh to yere auld Aunty Meg in Killiecrankie!" Mr. Glencannon banged on the table and stamped on Mr. Montgomery's foot. "Come, mon, come; dinna let us bicker and quibble ower details! Instead, let us combine our talents in making a haggis for the captain's Christmas party and a treat for Muster Montgomery wuch I doot he'll have the guid taste to appreciate!"

"Now, never you mind about my taste!" said Mr. Montgomery, tartly. "I don't think either of you two Scotch cannibals 'ave got the foggiest notion of 'ow to make yer 'orrid 'aggis, and I wouldn't eat it anyway. Besides that, where'll you get the ox, the sheep or wotever else you need to make it with? The only animals I've seen in Aden is camels, and I could 'ardly see them for the ticks."

"Ticks dinna matter, but camels willna sairve," said Mr. MacQuayle, sullenly. "To mak' a proper haggis, ye must have a shee ——"

"Oh, blosh and fuddlesticks!" shouted Mr. Glencannon, springing to his feet. "I'm at the end o' my patience! . . . Captain Ball, sir!" He turned to the shipmaster. "Here and noo I give ye my solemn promise to provide a Christmas dinner worthy o' our tenth anniversurra under your commond, and in spicht o' heel, I'll do it!" With a farewell snort at Mr. Montgomery, he stalked from the room, went over the side to the dinghy and rowed away into the night.

When the sound of the oars had died away in the distance, "Welp!" the mate leered sardonically. "That settles that—wotever it was! Now I'll just nip back to my room, put on a fresh suit o' whites, 'ail a bumboat and go ashore myself. . . . Sure you wouldn't like to 'ave a proper 'otel meal with me tomorrer, Captain Ball and the rest o' yer? Er"—he squirmed—"I mean, I don't suppose it could cost you more than about five bob apiece."

For a moment there was silence; then Captain Ball spoke for the crowd in a voice that quavered more than a little. "Why, no," he said, "no, thank you! I fancy we'd all rather eat together, here on the ship, like we've done for the past nine years, and—and as I was hoping you would, too, Mr. Montgomery! Tradition, sentiment, superstition —see what I mean? Damned silly of me, what? But—uh—well, anyway, m' boy, I really do hope you'll enjoy your Christmas dinner."

II

As Mr. Montgomery had remarked, Aden and its environs are anything but pastoral; lowing herds, bleating flocks and all else bucolic and edible are there as scarce as in the more arid purlieus of Hades. Instead of heading for this sterile shore, Mr. Glencannon rowed down the inner harbor toward the oil-bunkering berths, where, near the terminal buoy of the pipe line, a great gray vessel lay pale in the moonlight. She was the refrigerator ship Northern Princess, on her regular run from Majunga, Madagascar, to Marseille with frozen meat. The still air around her throbbed to the muffled, monotonous pulsation of pumps, some of them handling the fuel oil, others driving through her complex metal arteries the chemicals which proofed her cargo against

even such withering heat as there was that night in Aden.

"Losh!" murmured Mr. Glencannon, resting on his oars and measuring her bulk. "She's carrying enough dead oxen to mak' a haggis the size o' the Rock o' Gibraltar! Noo, if only Wee Wully Anstruther is still her engineer ——"

From somewhere aft came thuds, shouted oaths and peals of ribald laughter. A bottle whizzed through the moonlight and plunged into the water like a three-inch shell.

"Haw!" chuckled Mr. Glencannon, "Wee Wully Anstruther's still in her beyant the shadow o' a doot! I only hope he's not in one o' his tontrums, because I forgot to bring my bross knuckles."

He made fast the dinghy to the platform of the ladder, ascended to the deck and strode aft toward the sounds of disturbance. In the open doorway of the engineer's saloon he halted, amazed at the strange rite in progress within. Around the table at the center of the smoke-filled room stood a number of lumpy, ruddy-faced gentlemen, as well as a number of others slightly less lumpy and ruddy, but obviously equally tough. Mr. Glencannon identified the former as butchers and refrigeration engineers and the rest as the engine-room staff of the Northern Princess. All were shouting advice and encouragement to a diminutive four-striped officer who, blindfolded and with his hands bound behind him, was kneeling on the table apparently endeavoring to drown himself in a dish of consommé.

"He looks lik' Wee Wully," muttered Mr. Glencannon. "He is Wee Wully. But what in the world is he doing?"

Moving closer, he perceived that the diminutive one was lapping up the consommé with the thirst of the worn hart that panteth after the water brooks. At length, strangling but triumphant, he straightened up, a silver coin between his teeth.

"Four minutes, thirteen seconds!" announced somebody.

Amidst hoarse cheers, bonds and blindfold were stripped from the hero and he was assisted to the floor. Swaying slightly, he acknowledged the plaudits of the multitude and wrung out his sodden necktie.

"Anstruther!" exclaimed Mr. Glencannon, hurrying forward and shaking his hand. "How are ye, Wee Wulliam, how are ye?"

The little man blinked up at him uncertainly; then, "Colin Colcollin!" he proclaimed, raspingly. "Merry Chrishmash, Crolin, Mrerry Chrishmash! . . . Come, fill up the plate again, ladsh, and let my auld friend Grencrarron have a gro at it!"

"Oh, thonk ye, Wully; ye're really too kind!"

Mr. Glencannon demurred. "I'd dearly love to tak' part in yere innocent little game, especially as I obsairve that the prize is a half crown. But to tell ye the honest truth, Wully, I sumply canna drink clear soup."

"Who osked ye to drink clear soup?" demanded Mr. Anstruther, truculently. "Who osked ye to drink thick soup? Who osked ye to drink green-turtle soup, pink-turtle soup, purtle-turtle soup or mocking-turtle soup? Thash no' soup in yon plate, ye gowk; it's whushky!"

"Eh?" Mr. Glencannon vaulted to the table, knelt before the dish and sniffed a magical aroma. "Why, it's Duggan's Dew o' Kirkintilloch!" he cried. "Come, blindfold me, gentlemen! Tie my honds! . . . There, noo! Ready, timekeeper? Go!"

He found the pastime distinctly to his taste, especially as his walrus mustache, acting like a sponge, augmented his natural prowess. So rapidly did he lower the level of the plate's contents that Mr. Anstruther, fearing for his own record, approached on tiptoe and restored it from a fresh bottle. Sensing despite his blindfold that he was the victim of sharp practice, Mr. Glencannon redoubled his efforts, emptied the plate and retrieved the half crown in the phenomenal time of four minutes flat.

The plaudits which acclaimed his exploit were perfunctory, and in them he sensed a vaguely hostile note. Moreover, his teeth were so firmly embedded in the half crown that he suspected it was lead.

"Dom!" rasped Mr. Anstruther, making a wry face. "Why, ye've qualified for the finals with yere vurra feerst try! But then, Glencannon, ye auld snake, ye always were a dangerous mon at parlor games and parties!"

"True," admitted Mr. Glencannon, disengaging the coin from his lower incisors and tossing it through the porthole. "As a matter o' fact," he raised his voice to make himself heard above the considerable din—"as a matter o' fact, Wully, it's precisely because o' a party that I've come aboord to consult ye. Ye see, I've promised to mak' a Christmas haggis."

"A haggis?" repeated Mr. Anstruther. "Ye mean a guid, auld, steaming, peppery, juicy, Heeland haggis? Weel, weel, weel, let's drink a drink to it! The only trooble is, where are ye going to get the billy goat's blodder?"

"A-weel," said Mr. Glencannon, "if I hoppened to want a billy goat's blodder, one o' the feerst places I'd look for it wud be in the neighborhood o' a billy goat. But why shud I want it?"

"Because, dom it, ye canna mix it, stoof it, cook it, have it or eat it withoot it!" asserted Mr. Anstruther. "I can't, eh? Who says I can't?" He

arose, bit a crescent-shaped fragment out of the visor of his cap and sat down again. "Yes, yes, precisely! I've followed ye to a *T*, so noo ye can follow me to a whusky."

"Glodly!" said Mr. Glencannon. "However, Wully, I fear we dinna quite understond each other. I cudna use a billy goat's blodder, because I dinna want to mak' a futball, a bagpipe or a hot-water bottle. What I told ye I wanted to mak' was a haggis."

"A haggis?" Mr. Anstruther repeated again. "Ye mean a guid, auld, steaming, peppery, juicy, Heeland haggis? Weel, weel, weel, let's drink a drink to it! The only trooble is—er—er —— Trooble? Ho! If it's trooble ye're looking for, ye ugly brute, ye've only to ——"

"Noo, wait, Wee Wulliam!" Mr. Glencannon restrained him. "You and I are auld friends and ye're *Bura Misteri Sahib* o' the Northern Princess, the whuch is a vurritable Noah's Ark full o' frozen cattle. Weel, I was thinking that if ye cud see yere way clear to lending me the loan o' a nice, tender dead ox oot o' yere cargo, I ——"

Mr. Anstruther yawned, removed his trousers, pulled them over his head as though they were a nightshirt, thrust his arms through the legs and buttoned the fly snugly around his neck. Then he stared down at his bare, gnarled knees. "Why, look!" he bawled. "Look! There's somebody aroond here, there's some skulking thief aroond here, that has stole the vurra troosies off my breech!" He lurched forward and leveled an accusing finger at Mr. Glencannon. "There he is, lads!" he shouted. "Let's heave the scoondrel owerboord!"

With a menacing growl they made for him. Mr. Glencannon snatched up a full whisky bottle from the sideboard and, wielding it clubwise, fought his way to the door. He fled along the deck toward the ladder, the pack at his heels, but so hotly were they pressing him when he reached it that he dared not attempt to descend to his dinghy. Through alleyways, up and down companions, round and about the ship they sped, the decks drumming to their foot-falls and the night made hideous with the sounds of hue and cry.

Turning a corner and momentarily out of sight of his pursuers, Mr. Glencannon slid halfway down a steep iron ladder and fell the remainder of the distance. Thanks to his presence of mind in clutching the bottle to his breast, there were only personal casualties. He found himself in a narrow, dimly lit passage at one end of which was a door marked KEEP OUT; THIS MEANS YOU! "Aye, but it doesna mean me!" he gasped, turning the knob. It was not, as he had surmised, a collision door, for despite its considerable thickness it was surprisingly light in weight. He stepped over the high sill, slammed the portal after him, and was in Stygian darkness. Instantly, miraculously, the sounds of pursuit were stilled; in fact, as he stood there straining his eyes and ears, he felt that the blackness was palpable, that it was packed in around him under pressure and that it shut him off from all the world. Here, at last, was sanctuary!

He lit his pocket flash. Its beam licked an ebonite panel upon which were various switches and instruments and a brass plate, engraved HANDLING CHAMBER, No. 3 HOLD. " 'Let there be licht!' " he quoted, closing several switches at once. Suddenly dazzled, he saw that he was in a spacious, white-enameled room. There were banks of pipes on the bulkheads, and from the deckhead above, chain hoists hung on curving steel tracks. The tracks ran from doors in the port and starboard sides of the vessel, converging amidships at the entrance to the hold.

"H'm, weel, it's all vurra tronquil and commendably saniturra," he remarked. "I'll mak' mysel' comfortable till yon murderers get tired o' sairching for me, and then I'll sneak oot. Whoosheroo, it's a job to mak' a haggis!" He sat with his back against the pipes and broached his bottle. The silence was broken by a liquid, gurgling sound. This was natural enough in the circumstances, but when he had recorked the bottle, the gurgling continued.

"Strange!" he mused. "Uncanny! Weel, they're peculiar craft, these great floating ice chests! Noo, evidently this so-called Hondling Chamber is insulated, so that frozen meat can be unloaded through it withoot opening the hatches and raising the temperature in the hold proper. They sumply open yon door amidships, hook their oxen on the chain hoists and drog them ower to the door on whichever side they hoppen to be discharging from. I wonder—noo, I wonder—if a mon cud steal an ox oot o' here single-honded? O' coorse, if Wee Wully Anstruther and his butchers and his bondits shud catch him at it—brhh!"

The very thought made his blood run cold, so he fortified himself with a few thermal units from the bottle. Feeling no reaction, he consumed a few more. As he did so, the neck of the bottle rattled dismally against his teeth, and vice versa. "Why, guid losh, mon, yere hond is treembling lik' a leaf! Ye're—ye're treembling all ower! Can it be ye're in for a bout o' fever?" He felt a dull ache across his shoulder blades and another farther down. "Spinal meningitis!" he gasped, endeavoring to rise. "But, heavens! I canna stand up! Paralysis! Help!" he bawled. "Anstruther! Somebody! Help!"

He realized with a surge of horror that no voice, no human sound, could penetrate those insulated walls.

"Aloss!" he moaned. "They'll unload my puir cadaver at Marseels with the rest o' the meat! Christmas Eve—ah, what a nicht to die!"

Resignedly, he bowed his head and buried his face in his hands. Soon he was conscious of a painful constriction in his armpits and across the chest. His first diagnosis was pleurisy; then he discovered that he was leaning foward into the slack of his jacket like a papoose in a blanket, and that the back and shoulders, crusted with hoarfrost, were firmly frozen to the pipes.

"Ah, come!" he growled, his breath turning to steam in the icy air. "What silly horseplay is this?" He undid the buttons and squirmed out of the garment, which hung rigid as a knightly panoply on the wall. "Ho, I see it all, noo! Anstruther has turned on the freezing system—that explains the gurgling! He intends to freeze me to death alive!" With difficulty he unstuck his jacket from the brine pipes, stamped upon it until it regained some measure of flexibility, and donned it. Skidding across the frosty floor, he made for the instrument panel. A dial, marked FAHRENHEIT TEMPERATURE, HANDLING CHAMBER, registered 26 degrees. Even as he scanned it, the needle dropped to 24, then to 22, and so continued downward. "Och, horrors!" croaked Mr. Glencannon, holding his bottle to the light, gauging its contents and taking a mammoth sowp of them. "If I'm no' rescued soon, I'll have to put mysel' on half rations! Where are the Soviet ice-breakers? Where are the Yonkee planes? Where are the Alaskan dog teams, the Canadian Quintriplets and the doughty Odmiral Byrd? Am I to be obondoned here to freeze?"

Very cautiously he unlatched the door by which he had entered and pressed his ear to the crack. "Noo, two o' ye wait richt here," he heard Mr. Anstruther's rasping voice. "If he comes down this way, clout him ower the head and ——"

Mr. Glencannon let the latch click back into place. He crossed to the door of the hold and swung it open. From the shadowy spaces beyond came a gust like the polar breath of Antarctica.

"Ah, foosh!" he cringed, fumblingly uncorking the bottle. "Grim death confronts me where'er I turn! I'd better drink up this whusky before it freezes solid, for my teeth are chottering so I cudna hope to chew it!"

He was about to close the door when he discerned within the hold a level expanse of beef carcasses so vast that its limits were lost in the gloom. It was the top layer of the cargo; the legs of the beasts, hewn off to stumps in precise conformity to market specifications, jutted up in ranks as orderly and rigid as the Grenadier Guards on parade. Here, dead, frozen and far from their lush native pastures, was a whole Malagasy herd! Here was meat to feed a multitude! Here, to a quester after haggis, was El Dorado!

For a moment, Mr. Glencannon stood gnawing at the frozen fringe of his mustache and expelling the brittle fragments. Then he dragged the fall of one of the chain hoists into the hold, fixed the hook in the nearest carcass and hoisted it clear. Pulling, hauling and butting it with his shoulders, he slid it along the overhead conveyor rail to the starboard side. He swung open the insulating panel which covered the loading door in the hull and unscrewed the dozen iron dogs which secured the clamps.

"Noo, then!" he panted. "All I've got to do is open it, let my ox doon into the water and climb doon the chain mysel'. It'll be a short swim forward to the dinghy; I'll row it back, tak' my ox in tow and return in triumph to the Inchcliffe Castle. But I'd best turn oot the lichts, lest Anstruther and his thugs shud spot me."

One by one he flipped the switches; the lights went out and simultaneously the liquid gurgling ceased. "Shish-shish!" he simpered, blushing in the darkness. "Weel, wud ye believe it? It must have been I, mysel', that turned on all the winter weather in the feerst place!"

Slowly, soundlessly, he swung back the hull door and stood gratefully in the flood of tropic air which wafted through the opening. But though the heat was as a benison to his body, it had a strange effect upon his brain.

"Whoa!" He swayed dizzily. "Hold hard, Glencannon, hold hard! Ye've had only a little ower a bottle and a half o' whusky, but anybody'd think ye'd had a drap too much!"

Not without difficulty he slung the carcass clear of the side and lowered it until the slack in the chain indicated that it was afloat. It lay on its back with its stump legs in the air. He clambered down the chain and, still grasping it, stood on the buoyant beef while he took stock of the situation. He could see his dinghy bobbing at the ladder foot with Wee Willy Anstruther drowsing in the stern of it. Due to the manner in which he was wearing his trousers, Mr. Anstruther had a sinister, hunchbacked look about him. Even more sinister, however, was the twelve-inch Stillson wrench which lay ready to his hand on the thwart.

"Ho, deary me!" groaned Mr. Glencannon. "What's to be done the noo?" He moved a trifle aft along the beef and sat down to lower its metacenter and increase its stability. This brought its neck out of water like a clipper's bow, but caused the after portion to float almost awash. To avoid wetting his feet, Mr. Glencannon stepped down into the vent in the belly as though it were a cockpit and seated himself in the stern sheets. "Haw, vurra snoog," he murmured, conning the little craft with an appreciative eye. "Vurra tidy and vurra shipshape. If only it had a bit more sheer and another strake o' freeboard, it wud be the most sea-worthy ox in all the Gulf o' Aden. What more cud an auld sailor osk?" He squinted across the harbor and distinguished the lights of the Inchcliffe Castle. "Foosh to the dinghy, they'll bring it back when they've sobered up. I'll novigate hame in my ain' haggis!" He unhooked the chain hoist and, paddling with his hands, made off into the night.

"Ah, but it's grond to be at sea again." He sniffed the breezes gratefully. "Although come to think o' it, I havena been ashore since we left Mombasa." He raised his voice in a rollicking blue-water chantey. He was putting his whole soul into the chorus of "yo heave ho's!" when he realized that his lingual mechanism was actually giving off the words and music of a sentimental ballad that he recalled as Sweet Mary of Argyll.

Weel, weel, let it have its ain way, he thought, tolerantly. *After all, Sweet Mary is a beautiful auld song. Listen.* But he listened vainly, for now, despite himself, he was reciting Burns' Address to a Haggis.

"Ah, swith!" he growled, when the poem ended. " 'Tis all vurra oggravating! I suspect there must have been a certain amoont o' alcohol in Wee Wully's whusky!"

Whether or not the suspicion was justified, he found it increasingly difficult to hold to his course or even to remember where the course lay. From time to time he paused in his splashing to take a star sight, but the stars were swooping and dipping in the celestial vault, playing tag with the lights on shore and generally behaving in a scandalous manner.

"Peerplexing!" he said, lifting his hands out of the water and raising them smartly on high in the Toss Oars position prescribed in the Royal Navy. "I almost wish I had Montgomery aboord to novigate this craft for me. But, no, on second thocht, no! Though I'm forced to associate with him on the Inchcliffe Castle, domned if I'd tolerate him on my ain private yacht! But where, oh, where is the Inchcliffe Castle?" He strained his eyes into the night and descried Djebel Ishan and its brood of lesser peaks looming black against the sky. His view of them was somewhat obstructed by a row of tree trunks rising out of the water in the near foreground. "Tut, tut!" he objected. "There's no forest in the middle o' Aden harbor, and therefore I doot if I see one. There's some sort of a swundle, here, or pairhops it's a mirage. But"—he reached out and touched the nearest trunk—"but no; it's solid!"

There was a soft swish, a gleam of phosphorescence on the starboard beam. Something struck his frail craft amidships, causing it to tremble from brisket to rump. The sea gushed onto his lap through a gaping puncture just below the water line.

"Torpedoed!" he cried. "We're holed in the tenderloin! All honds abandon ship!"

He scrambled to his feet. The beef rolled gunwales-under. To prevent it capsizing, Mr. Glencannon threw his arms around the tree trunk. There was a second shock, a ripping, rending sound and lo, the carcass was dragged from under him by an eight-foot shark! Clinging to the tree with everything but his eyelashes, he saw the great fish tearing at the meat, saw it joined by another and another, and watched in horror as they churned the water to foam a scant yard beneath his wincing coattails.

"Quick!" he urged himself. "Get higher, mon, get higher! Pull yersel' up onto a limb!"

He groped overhead and grasped a heavy, square-hewn timber. He realized, then, that he was not on a tree at all, but on one of the supporting piles of a wharf. He hoisted himself to the moon-bathed planking and sank down in a state of collapse.

"Whurra!" he panted. " 'Tis a sorra, thonkless tosk to mak' a haggis! Why, noo that I come to think o' it, e'en yon ox had all o' his machinery removed and so was useless anyway! If it wasna for my promise to guid auld Captain Ball and my loathing for that snipe o' a Montgomery, I'd say foosh to the whole domned party! But noo, let's see, let's see!"

III

MESSRS. Raoul and Cyril Shapiro (Shapiro Brothers, Ltd., Shipping Suppliers to H. M. Navy, Contractors to Leading Mail, Passenger and Freight S. S. Lines, General Chandlers, Furnishers and Direct Importers of Fresh Provisions. Shapiros' Prices Please and Shapiros' Service Satisfies) were just about to close up the office in their premises on the Aden Crescent when they were visited by Mr. Montgomery.

"Good evening, gempmen," said the mate. "I'm orff the Inchcliffe Castle, that C. & C. ship that's laying out there by the Fairway buoy. You'll remember us, of course; our steward got drunk and bought a 'undredweight of curry powder off yer on the voyage out. That's why I've just stopped in to arsk yer if yer could direct me to a 'arfway decent 'otel in this 'ere town where a chap could eat 'is Christmas dinner tomorrer without choking on it."

"Well," said Mr. Raoul Shapiro, "if I may express myself candidly, sir—although, for obvious reasons, I must beg of you not to quote me—the hotels of Aden are uniformly of a distinctly inferior order."

"They are, indeed, lousy," agreed Mr. Cyril Shapiro. "But, why, sir, if I may venture to ask, are you thinking of eating your Christmas repast in Aden when such a magnificent meal will be served aboard your own ship?"

"Eh?" said Mr. Montgomery. "Magnificent meal? On the ruddy Inchcliffe Castle? 'Ere, now, don't make me weep!"

"Yes, yes, on the Inchcliffe Castle," affirmed the other, referring to a ledger on the table. "The gentleman, our valued client, said he was giving a party for his colleagues and insisted on everything being of the very best. Er—two tinned Gold Seal Royal Banquet Roasting Turkeys, three tinned The Chef of Windsor Castle's Own Recipe Plum Puddings, five tins of Extra Selected Imported French Asparagus, four boxes of The London Jockey Club's Private Brand Havana Cigars, three cases of—er—yes, pepper, four cases of Duggan's Dew of Kirkintilloch Whisky——"

"Duggan's Dew? Four cases? Lawks!" gasped Mr. Montgomery. "Why, it must 'ave been the chief hengineer! And you say he bought all that stuff for—for the party 'e's giving tomorrer? Think of it! Well, I always did say 'e was a decent sort, bless 'is dear old soul!"

"Yes, quite," said Mr. Shapiro. "He came in here a trifle—er—under the weather, if I may say so, sir. Gave us to understand that he was looking for an ox's—er—stomach. But when he saw the vast assortment of fancy high-grade delicacies on our shelves, he favored us with his most valued order."

"Turkey! Sparrowgrass! Plum pudding!" Mr. Montgomery was rolling his eyes. "Of course I know 'e can afford it, but orl the same, I must say it's right down jolly noble of 'im! Wot a meal! Wot a Christmas! And—yus, wot a pal!"

When he had gone, "Phooey!" said Mr. Raoul Shapiro. "Am I glad to hear what he said about that Scotchman being able to afford it? After all, you know, he only signed a personal chit for it, so I was worrying maybe we was stuck. What was his name again?"

Mr. Cyril Shapiro consulted the sprawling signature in the chit book. "Chauncey Montgomery," he read.

POEMS

by Ogden Nash

OGDEN NASH HAS been writing his own special brand of poetry for the *Post* since 1932. The two examples reprinted below were published fairly close together, but reflect quite different views on a subject of wide interest.

WINNING IS MORE FUN THAN LOSING

JANUARY 11, 1936

Hi there, you, smiling like a pussy cat, pussy cat,
    that has eaten the canary, canary, where have
    you been?
Well, I haven't been to London to see the queen,
And I haven't been to the Rainbow Room, and I
    haven't been to Tony's,
But I've been out picking the ponies,
And may I remark as an obiter dictum,
That I pictum.
This was the day for which I have waited long,
Because, like an occupant of a certain well-adver-
    tised bed, I couldn't go wrong,
This is the day the horses treated me royal,
They ran according to Hoyal, and I was Hoyal.
In the words of Carroll, the horses were frabjous,
    and, in the words of Lear, they were runcible,
And for a pleasing improvement in my financial
    condition, they are respuncible.
Oh, what a noble piece of work is a horse!
How like an angel, how like sunlight or water
    power or some other beneficent natural force!
How nobly they prance, like a captain who has
    been promoted to be a major!
How beautiful they look when they are all be-
    hind except the one that is intrusted with your
    wager!

Horses are also tactful, because they make you
    think you are very clever,
Because they make the money for you, and you
    feel that you earned it yourself, through your
    own shrewdness and endeavor.
Goodness, it must be wonderful to be a horse,
And to feel the thrill of power that comes from
    knowing that, according to whether you run
    fast or slow, a lot of people are going to be over-
    whelmed with bliss or remorse,
And yet horses are the soul of modesty,
Though you would think that, the way they con-
    trol human destiny, they would strut and swag-
    ger like gods in the Iliad or the Odesty.
Oh, sometimes even the best of us are mistaken,
And then it behooves us to admit it when to our
    error we awaken,
And up until this afternoon I thought that all
    horses were good for was their skin, so that
    sports writers could refer to the horsehide when
    they got tired of referring to the pellet or the
    bulb or the apple,
But now I see that horses are man's best friends,
    and I say that as long as they act as they did
    today, I don't care whether they are chestnut or
    dapple.

HARK! HARK! THE PARI-MUTUELS BARK!

JUNE 6, 1936

Willow waley and woe and sorrow,
The horses are coming to town tomorrow.
Chestnut and bay and black and gray
Sport and cavort and snort and neigh.
The horses, the horses are on the way!
The horses are coming to town tomorrow,
And some must beg and others borrow.
The horses are coming and how I dread it,
Here come the horses, there goes my credit.
The horses are coming, enter the horses,

Exit the remnant of my resources.
This is the end of me, never a doubt of it,
And the horses don't even get anything out of it.
They don't get money or love or fun,
Why in the world must the horses run?
Or if they must, by all that's holy,
Why must some of them run so slowly?
I tell you, the country's crying need
Is horses that run at an equal speed
And a stone-dead heat on every track

And everyone getting their money back.
Willow waley and woe and sorrow,
The horses are coming to town tomorrow.
Every horse with a personal grudge
Against this modestly hopeful judge,
Holding its life as cheap as a song,
If its death in the stretch should prove me wrong.
Well, listen, horses, I know you hate me,
But do not think to intimidate me,

Or drive from the track, by deed or threat,
The man who has never cashed a bet.
Some day I'll hold a winning ticket,
And swagger up to the teller's wicket,
And take my money and catch a boat
To the land of the horse-meat table d'hôte.
Oh, I'll sit in Paris till Doomsday breaks,
Chewing over my old mistakes.

MY FATHER WAS THE MOST WRETCHEDLY UNHAPPY MAN I EVER KNEW

by Gene A. Howe

ATCHISON AND EMPORIA are only about 100 miles apart, in the eastern part of Kansas. But miles could not measure the distance between Edgar Watson Howe and William Allen White, the two most famous country editors of their time. Ed Howe was a rebellious pessimist who hated women and churches, terrorized his own family and brooded darkly over the eternal failings of man. White was a constructive optimist who labored cheerfully for all good causes and could always see victory ahead. About the only things the two men had in common were that both ran widely quoted newspapers and both wrote often for the *Post*.

Ed Howe died in 1937. Four years later the *Post* ran the following article about him by the man who knew him best, his son Gene. Jack Alexander, a *Post* associate editor who knows a good deal about profile-writing, thinks this is the most unusual one that any magazine has published in the last twenty years. The author had intended to print it in instalments in his own newspaper, the Amarillo *News-Globe*. But while he was on a vacation trip, his staff, on their own responsibility, sent it to the *Post*. Gene Howe died, by his own hand, June 24, 1952.

OCTOBER 25, 1941

ALTHOUGH MY FATHER and I were very close in his later years, I still cannot throw off the terror with which he filled me when I was a youth. I was scared to death of him as a child and as a young man. He was Ed Howe, the sage of Potato Hill, the philosopher of common sense, who lived at Atchison, Kansas, and published The Atchison Globe for thirty-six years. He died at the age of eighty-four. The Atchison Globe has been in our family now for sixty-six years; he presented me with the controlling interest in it thirty years ago.

Probably it is ill becoming his son, one to whom he has been more than generous, to say that in my opinion he made but little of his opportunities and possibilities; but I believe that for every yard of success he hewed out for himself so painfully he should have made miles. I know of no one endowed as he was who accomplished so little. He should have been almost another Will Rogers. I am convinced he had the soundest, rarest sense of humor of any man of his time. He was a master of English, a pioneer in literary style, and he had a great wealth of fire and force and enthusiasm.

As a conversationalist I have never known his equal. He should have been one of the country's most brilliant speakers, as he was so witty and alert. But he never tried to adjust or adapt himself to the public mind, or to edit or check himself with the help of others. He was always breasting the stream, scaling the bleakest, most rugged mountains, when, at least occasionally, he should have been coasting down the valleys as others less gifted have done. His path to fame—and no inconsiderable amount of fame came to his doorstep—was strewn with hard work, disappointment, humiliation, discouragement and heartbreaks. He was the most wretchedly unhappy person I have ever known.

Why? Because my father was a reformer, a fanatical reformer by nature. The call to save mankind was in him so strong that it was irresistible. It was a tide of fate that held him helpless. He had that unswerving determination, that zeal that knows no turning aside, of the man who must rescue the world. He was evangelical in his fervor, and strange as it may seem, the rock wall he could never budge or dent, and which caused him so much unhappiness, was religion itself.

My father was half English and half Pennsylvania Dutch, as nearly as we could learn. The

403

Howes were a deeply religious family. One of our forefathers was a chaplain in Cromwell's army. We were Methodists from far back.

Father's father was a circuit rider over in the hills of North Missouri. He was stern and unforgiving and exacting. His children were brought up by the rod, and with puritanical rigidity they observed the Sabbath and attended church and Sunday school.

They lived at Bethany, Missouri. A circus came to town, and father and his brother, Uncle Jim, were forbidden to attend because circuses were in league with the devil. Grandfather Howe rode about the countryside on horseback, with my father behind him, from one church to another, preaching night after night. He often preached five and six hours without stopping, and when father, who had to occupy the front pew, would fall asleep, he was given a severe whipping that night.

Here permit me to say that nearly all of this family history has been written by father himself and has been published. I am not giving away any family secrets.

Father received a shock from which he never recovered when his father ran away from home and abandoned my grandmother and a handful of small children. Before this, father had observed that Grandfather Howe had been entirely too friendly with women members of his flock whom he invited to his home of nights; and when he ran away, it was with one of these women.

Father was about fourteen years of age when this devastating, tragic disaster overtook the family, and the result was an unreasoning, unrelenting hatred of religion that embittered his entire life. Something early in life also must have influenced his attitude toward women, as from young manhood he waged his crusade against religion and women.

Grandfather Howe was the publisher of a weekly newspaper at Bethany, Missouri, as well as a circuit rider, and father learned the printing trade in that office. After the family crash he left home to work over the country as a tramp printer. He became a journeyman, and for one summer worked for Brigham Young in Salt Lake City.

Father was between twenty-one and twenty-two when he and his brother Jim started The Atchison Globe. It was nothing more than a handbill, as the two brothers did all the writing, reporting and typesetting themselves. But the Globe was so sparkling and newsy, and so crisply edited, that two competitive newspapers passed out of the picture within a few years.

Once father obtained control of the field in Atchison, which was a prosperous town of about 13,000, he began his attacks on religion and the churches. He is the only editor of a daily newspaper in the United States who blasted and ridiculed religion year in and year out, and survived the opposition he created.

Atchison had churches of all denominations, and the religious groups were as strong and as well organized as in most any Texas city today. New papers were started. The Globe was boycotted by advertisers and subscribers, and there was civic warfare that disrupted the citizenship.

But father never backed up an inch. There were periods when he would subside, but he never retracted or apologized, and when he had accumulated fresh energy and hopes he would resume the combat.

Some of those who knew my father regarded him as a natural fighter. They believed that he attacked religion because of the sheer joy of battle; that he had chosen the biggest, most powerful opponent in sight because he wanted a fight worthy of his mettle. Even though they didn't agree with him, they admired his courage, and he was described far and wide as one who could give and take, and who reveled in combat.

But little did they know him. No person could have been more sensitive. He cringed at every blow that was struck back. Tirades from subscribers, cancellations of advertising contracts and subscriptions, threats and fist fights, editorials in church papers and rebuffs in many forms tore into his heart. They brought about terrific mental depressions and he suffered excruciating torture of the mind.

In such a mood, he would lower his head and tear into his newspaper work. Day and night he worked, tramping the streets and the countryside seeking out items and information from people in all walks of life. He knew most everyone within miles of Atchison, and he wrote about people and their neighbors. He was the greatest reporter in America; he was so regarded by many leading newspapermen. The Globe vibrated with his sparkle and humor, and it became the most quoted daily in the United States. Opposition could not stand against it; Atchison people simply could not resist reading his paper.

When father was working so hard at newspaper work to dull the aches in his heart, he wrote little about religion, but as the indignation subsided because of his silence, his spirits would revive. He would begin to react to the favorable attention he was attracting because of the excellence of his newspaper, and he would enter a period of exhilaration. He was happy and cheerful and walking on air with his head in the clouds.

His exuberance would begin to overflow and

his ambitions soar. The spirit of the crusader would reassert itself and he'd begin planning a new attack.

"It's me and not my ideas," I have heard him say many times. "I haven't been able to make people understand; I must make everything so plain, so simple that they will see the truth."

And he would plunge in again and the world wouldn't understand him. His blasts would be hurled back and his very soul would be crushed again.

It is because his suffering and humiliation were so intense that I say he was the unhappiest man I have ever known. I'd say he was depressed 80 per cent of the time.

There are those in Atchison and elsewhere who will think I am not writing the truth, but his wretchedness is hardly believable. I have lived in the same house with him for six weeks at a stretch without his speaking to me. I was his own son, the person I believe he thought more of than anyone in the world; yet he went for weeks and weeks without saying a word to me, outside of an occasional order such as asking me to go down to the grocery store for a cigar. I have tiptoed into the house at night, past his bedroom, and heard him swearing to himself as he tossed about the bed, unable to sleep. I have stopped and listened and heard him continue thus for minutes.

At these times, when he awakened me in the morning, I would feel the bed shake and would see him staring at me, his face dark and forbidding. He would see that I was awake and would turn on his heel and go down to breakfast. He would usually finish his breakfast before I had mine, and then he would walk downtown to the office. Occasionally, if I ate fast, I would walk with him and the two of us would arrive at work without a word having been spoken.

At his work he had to be civil to those he met. He had to obtain news from them and to solicit business. He did this hurriedly, feverishly driving himself and the others in the office. But at home he relaxed his politeness and never spoke to anyone except when necessary.

He wasn't mad at me; he simply was in such a terrible mental state that he didn't want to talk to anyone. I sensed the situation and kept away from him.

And then would come one of his periods of exaltation. I do not know what else to call it. His joy of living would embrace everyone close to him. Happy days were back, life was grand and wonderful. He would come into my bedroom in the morning and awaken me by jumping into bed with me. He'd take me swimming out at Deer Creek. The two of us would drive out there to-

gether and we'd swim in a swimming hole. He'd take me down to the office evenings and teach me how to set type; he wanted me to be a "swift," as he was rated when he worked on Brigham Young's newspapers. He was lavish, rather than generous with me, at these times.

But these respites were brief, and soon he would be back tossing in his bed of nights and cursing to himself; and I would be tiptoeing around when I had to be near him.

My father called himself a materialist. He insisted that sentimentalism and emotionalism and Socialism were menaces to progress and better living, and that religion was the embodiment of the three of these. But he wasn't merely a materialist or an agnostic; he was an atheist, as I understand the word. He didn't believe in any supreme being or hereafter or anything. He believed that when we die we are dead; that when the human body and mind stop, the story is over. So many have inquired as to whether father weakened in his last illness. He didn't in the slightest.

His last years were occupied largely by his eagerness to enlighten the people to their danger. He was writing a book called Final Conclusions, and told me again and again how he intended to make it so "simple, so plain, that everyone could know the truth." It was not more than a third completed at his death.

I came across something recently in his later writings which may afford some idea of how he groped to put across his philosophy, and how he wounded others. I do not believe there ever lived a writer who could hurt as he did; who was so blunt and direct, and who could lacerate so deeply. I know he did not realize this himself.

I quote from him as follows:

"Let me say here, I shall not urge my opinions impudently; I shall print them modestly, as the opinions of one man who has thought a good deal, who knows people intimately and who honestly desires their good; if I ever consciously write anything that harms humanity, I hope my hand may be withered. I do not believe there is any such power, but I invoke it if I may be mistaken.

"But I do not believe there is an educated, intelligent man on the face of the earth who actually believes in religion. To me, the most wonderful thing in civilization is religion. That people should have advanced so marvelously in everything else, as they have done, and carried along with them a doctrine they know to be untrue, is a fact I have marveled at all my life. Never have I known a sincere religious man or woman.

"I shall write more of this subject in the future, but modestly, I hope, for I have little respect for the fanatic, whatever his opinions. But it seems to me that it is a great human question, worthy of your attention and mine. If religion is true, let's accept it; if it isn't true, we are not just to ourselves to continue to teach it halfheartedly, but with apologies. People often say, 'If we give up religion, what will take its place?' We don't need anything to take its place, if it isn't true."

He printed articles equally brutal and frank and much more bitter when he published The Atchison Globe. He did not seem to know that his onslaughts against religion were a millstone around his neck, that he was creating for himself handicaps that had wrecked every other editor who had bucked them.

The other weakness in his philosophy was women. I lived with him for years, and yet I was unable to understand his ideas about women. He couldn't make even me understand, and I tried my best. He expended a tremendous amount of his energy trying to convince men that they were being led to ruin and demoralization by their womenfolks. The development of man was such that men and women had become enemies, he believed; women had become spoiled and extravagant and so impossible that the very foundations of our civilization were threatened. He actually talked of a countrywide revolt of the men against the women, and believed it might be brought about. This is the truth if I ever told it.

He believed literally, and I am not exaggerating in the slightest, that a girl should have but one engagement and one marriage. A young girl who had a puppy-love affair with a man should not marry another man if the first engagement was broken. What should become of them and just what place they should occupy in our scheme of things he never stated. Understand, the question of chastity was not involved in this. A girl "pawed over" was lost if not married by the young man who did the pawing.

Father was being constantly shocked and confused by friends who married widows. "I cannot understand it; he must be crazy," I've heard him remark again and again. I honestly believe that if he had had the power he would have enacted laws forbidding such. And he always blamed the woman.

In every community there are serious, agonizing, boy-and-girl affairs where the girls get into trouble. Father was always helping some boy who had skipped town; always taking the "man's side," as he said. "The boy couldn't help it; it's up to the girls to protect themselves," he'd say. "Holding off the men is women's oldest profession. It's their instinct and their raising; and it pays them the biggest dividends."

When a boy married a girl he believed that she should become his property, his abject slave; that as his wife she was entitled only to the necessities and the reasonable comforts of life, and that she should not want anything beyond this. If her husband chose to provide her with anything more, all well and good, but for her to demand anything additional, no matter how much money the husband might have, was unpardonable.

I can show you his written belief to the effect that when a husband has degenerated to the point where he helped his wife on with her coat before putting on his own, he had become henpecked, and that for his own good he should leave his wife.

And he wasn't joking when he wrote this.

My father could not tolerate any form of criticism from a woman, and the older he became the more acute was his oversensitiveness.

I well remember an Atchison woman of whom he was particularly fond. They were long, intimate friends. They met on the street one day. It was a cold winter afternoon and he was wearing a sweater under his coat. She remarked, carelessly and lightly, that she didn't like the sweater; that he didn't look well in it. Father never spoke to her again. She had insulted him; she had transgressed his rights. So many of his friendships, scores of them, were shattered by remarks of even less consequence.

My boyhood was a nightmare. My mother never spoke a harsh or unkind word to anyone. She was a sentimental woman, quite religious when young, but most conscientious and hardworking. Five children were born to mother and father. Bessie and Ned, the first born, died when about five or six years of age, within a few hours of each other, of what was then known as black diphtheria. Jim was the oldest; Mateel, now Mrs. Dwight Farnham, the novelist, was the second, and I was the youngest of the remaining children.

My first recollections are of the terrific rages of father, and how all of us were frightened of him. I can remember approaching him in the evenings or mornings timidly, furtively, as a rabbit ventures from the weeds into the open road in the evening, to find out whether he was in one of his black moods or was in good humor.

Father was upbraiding mother most of the time. She was often crying openly or trying to hide tears from the children, and he was spending more and more of his time away from home. When she was not outright displeasing him or arousing his wrath, she was "getting on his nerves." No spirited woman could have lived with him as his wife; his demands were so exacting, his whims so impossible to anticipate.

I can remember mother taking me to Sunday

school, and father's anger at this and how it increased. She was a Methodist and she insisted I be brought up in church. She never gave in on this. I think I was baptized as a youngster, but I am not certain. My brother, Jim, when sixteen or seventeen years of age, had an ambition to be a doctor and asked father to send him away to college. Father had a brainstorm over this; Jim was to be a newspaperman and any suggestion otherwise was an insult. Father had whipped Jim, and Jim had defied him; and this breach between them was continued through their lives. Mateel was asking for things, mother was asking for things for us children, and Jim had insisted in asking to be educated as a doctor.

I sensed when very young that father would boil over when asked for anything, and I learned my lesson, or lost my courage, early, for I never asked him for anything in my life. This attracted him to me and I became his favorite. I was never close to my mother; my father took me in charge and I became weaned away from her. I never knew her well; I couldn't have been more than ten or twelve years of age when father and I moved into a cottage in the yard at home. Mother and Jim and Mateel stayed in the big house; father, who wasn't speaking to mother, and I lived in the small house.

This was a town sensation, naturally, and my life for a few years was bewildering. Neighbor women, some of them, accused me of abandoning the others by living with father. Mother herself was hurt and tearful. The big house, where I visited every day, of course, was a place of sorrow and despair. Father was having his terrific black moods. Other children were repeating terrible tales to me on my father which weren't true, and the newspaper was being boycotted, and father was being threatened. A divorce followed after a year or two, and mother left home, never to return, taking the two other children with her. Father and I moved back into the big house. But I wasn't there long; I got drunk publicly on my first drink of whisky and father sent me out West to shift for myself. He had been tossed out into the world; it would be good for me, he said.

He wasn't particularly angry at me, as I recall, but thought a little hustling for myself might save me from being a bum and a drunkard.

My sister, Mateel, was a very strong-minded young girl, and quickly clashed with father when she reached the "asking age."

After my mother and my father were divorced, my sister came home to visit father once or twice a year, and she never left the house at the conclusion of these visits with father saying good-by to her. Always they had violent rows because she

had asked for something other girls asked of their fathers without the slightest hesitancy.

When she left home to be married, she was crying so loud that I heard her sobs in the kitchen. Father had refused to kiss her good-by, to wish her luck and happiness. And it was all because he had wanted to phrase her wedding invitations and she had insisted that they follow the approved form of that time. The invitation in itself was not important, but his daughter had dared to question his judgment!

All of my early life I was afraid of ministers. I was brought up to avoid them as I would the plague; to believe that all stanch church members were a strange sort of people you couldn't trust.

I have never identified myself with any church. My womenfolks belong and I contribute to their church and other churches regularly. I'm ashamed that I haven't been to church more than I have. I go occasionally. The world needs more churches and more religious people; the breakdown of religion in other parts of the world hasn't helped civilization. Ministers and church people generally, wherever I have been, have been most considerate of me.

One of my closest friends and advisers is Dr. R. Thomsen, of the Central Presbyterian Church in Amarillo. I have made few important moves since I have been in Texas without consulting him.

Atchison people, church people and all, began to accept father as he was. They ignored his tirades against religion; they laughed, perhaps, at some of his other ideas; and they took satisfaction in his success as the most famous small-town editor in the United States, as the nation's best-known paragrapher, and as the writer who, single-handed, made The Atchison Globe the most frequently quoted newspaper in the land. They gave him loving cups and presents, to which the public contributed, and he was honored with local and state dinners. Everywhere Atchison was known as "Ed Howe's town." I do not believe that any community was ever more thoroughly dominated by one man. He was respected by all and loved by many in his later years.

He retired from The Atchison Globe when he was fifty-seven. H. L. Mencken wrote a book on father's style and philosophy. A family heirloom is an old marked copy of The Boston Globe. The editor sent it to father. The one issue contained fifty-eight paragraphs clipped from The Atchison Globe.

How he could write paragraphs! Here are a few of them:

A woman is as old as she looks before breakfast. . . . The difference between a good woman and a bad one is that a bad woman raises hell with a good many men, while a good woman raises hell with only one. . . . Some girls have the married-woman whine. . . . If you see something that no one else sees, or hear sounds that no others hear, that is what it means to go crazy. . . . Somehow, when we see a woman who has been married and divorced a number of times, we are reminded of the man who was always failing in business. . . . Families with babies and without babies are sorry for each other. . . . You can throw most men off their feet by crowding them. . . . About the wisest thing in the world is a country boy who has been boarding in town three or four months, studying law. . . . What people say behind your back is your standing in the community in which you live. . . . Make a woman mad and she is no more polite than a man.

When cheerful and happy, he was such a grand character, such a wonderful person, and the most entertaining companion I have ever known. He was so generous with me, at intervals.

I remember a high spot of my youth when I was about twelve years of age. He said I was engaged in too much duck hunting; he said he realized how much I enjoyed it, but he believed it was having a bad influence on me. So he offered me $500 cash to stop. And I took it. That was a fortune to me in those days.

It wasn't two weeks later until he saw me standing on a corner overlooking the Missouri River. A norther was blowing and ducks in great droves were streaming down the river. I was standing there big-eyed, looking at them and bleeding inside.

Father slipped up on me before I knew it.

"How are you feeling?" he asked.

I gulped out that I was feeling all right.

"No, you're not," he said, as he laughed out loud. "You want to go hunting, don't you?"

"Yes," I replied.

"Well," he said, "go on up home and get your dog and gun and drive down to Sugar Lake, and don't be in a hurry coming home."

I got to keep the $500, and I kept on with my hunting.

My father was happier after his retirement than when he was publisher of the Globe.

Ed Howe's Monthly, as he called his publication, never did catch on as he had hoped. The price was but twenty-five cents a year, but the subscription list never numbered more than a few thousand.

In Ed Howe's Monthly he said exactly what he pleased, sparing no one. But he always had done this in The Atchison Globe. He rallied to the cause of business and cracked down on politicians and the have-nots and the liberals. He editorialized unceasingly, and constant criticism is not popular. His subscribers grew fewer.

His fanaticism cropped out in his defense of business. When the Teapot Dome scandal broke, he rallied to the support of Harry Sinclair. Money was the measuring rod of success, he wrote. The man who made a million dollars was ten times smarter, ten times a harder worker, ten times more fair and just, than the man who made but $100,000. Honesty was the best, the only policy, he said; success was easier than failure. A man who could not find work, he insisted, could not do good work when he found it.

The humor and information and news that he had crammed into the Globe was missing; his scoldings, his protests, his indignation did not sell the monthly, and he finally abandoned it.

My father's last crusade, before he began work on his Final Conclusions, was for more politeness and better manners. What articles he did write for publications were pleas for people to be more considerate, more polite, and to work harder and attend to business more strictly. He was lonesome for company and invited many to his home. He studied good manners and was the perfect host.

But he never could throw off those spells of despondency, and only those who lived with him knew of his continuing unhappiness and disappointment.

It should be explained that father considered himself a plain man, a man of the people. Plain People was the name of one of his books—his autobiography. While he admired outstanding giants of business, he shared this appreciation with all men who made a good living.

The prosperous farmer, the expert mechanic, the foreman risen from the ranks, the promising young railroad superintendent, the fast typesetter, the crack reporter—any and all men who worked and improved themselves and made for themselves an increasingly comfortable livelihood were his gods. He had innumerable warm friends among the farmers and skilled workingmen; he knew them and wrote of them. But he persisted in his belief that the more money a man had the more certain it was that he had worked harder and longer and had been more fair and more honest.

Yes, I'm still afraid of my father. I always will be. But probably I needed this discipline. I owe much, so very much, to him, and we were close to each other in his last years. I had no affection for him when I lived with him as a child; all I knew was I was so terribly frightened that I didn't know my soul or my mind was my own. I always felt like I was treading on explosives; I never was anything but completely intimidated.

But after he gave me The Atchison Globe and later, when I came to Texas, he became more tolerant of me than of any other person. We took trips together. I got so I could express my own opinions somewhat, though cautiously. I told him of attending church occasionally, and most anything I did was all right. He offered, at one time, to hand over to me a substantial part of his life's savings in an enterprise in which I was interested, but I told him frankly I didn't care to have the responsibility. He never invested money with me because I didn't want it, and he understood it perfectly. I even had the courage to tell him that I had voted for Roosevelt, Franklin D., and, complete conservative that he was, he predicted that the historians would record that the dark ages for the United States began with Hoover's defeat. He said my voting for Roosevelt the second time was the most foolish, damnable thing I had ever done, and that I would live to realize it.

I can say for my father that I do not believe he ever wrote a dishonest word in his life, that he believed implicitly and wholly in every public or personal article he ever penned. Maybe it is well that he did as he did do. Maybe if he had restrained and suppressed what he thought the world should know, the hypocrisy practiced by most of us would have dimmed or quenched the flames that burned so fiercely in him and which made him such an extraordinary person. He punished others, he punished himself, but he never retreated. He dedicated his life, mistakenly I know, trying to be helpful to his fellow men.

If I have offended any of his old-time friends, I'm sorry. All I can say is that if I have deviated from the truth as regards my father, as I saw him, I hope that "my hand be withered."

THE ATOM GIVES UP

by William L. Laurence

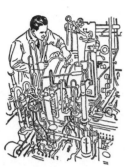

FIVE YEARS BEFORE the big explosion at Hiroshima the *Post* printed this dramatic account of the discoveries that made it possible. The article also told how Nazi scientists were frantically trying to make use of atomic power for war. Further than that the author did not go, although he knew as much as anyone about the possibilities of an atomic bomb. As science reporter for *The New York Times* he was the only newsman present at the world's first atomic explosion in New Mexico, and he flew with the mission which dropped the second military bomb on Nagasaki in August, 1945. The only time he ever ran into trouble was when he took a copy of his 1940 *Post* article with him to Oak Ridge, where he was helping prepare the first Government press releases on the atomic bomb. A guard took the magazine away from him, stamped it SECRET, and locked it in a safe while he was there.

William Leonard Laurence (original name "Siew") was born in Lithuania in 1888, attended Harvard and the University of Besançon, fought with the A.E.F. in World War I, and worked four years for the New York *World* before joining the *Times* in 1930. He has won two Pulitzer Prizes and has translated stories of Maxim Gorki and Leonid Andreyev from the Russian.

SEPTEMBER 7, 1940

ON SUNDAY, May fifth, on the eve of one of the greatest upheavals in man's history, the world learned about the discovery of a new source of power, millions of times greater than anything known on earth. A newly extracted natural substance, present in relative abundance in many parts of the world, but very difficult to isolate, had been found capable of liberating energy at such an unbelievable rate that one pound of it was the equivalent of 5,000,000 pounds of coal or 3,000,000 pounds of gasoline. In explosive power one pound of the new substance would be equal to 15,000 tons of TNT. Only one chief obstacle remained—to find a method for isolating the substance in large quantities, and scientists were hopeful that such a method would not be long in developing.

The name of the new substance, a veritable Prometheus bringing to man a new form of Olympic fire, is uranium 235, or U-235 for short. It is a rare form of uranium, each 140 pounds of uranium containing one pound of U-235. It differs from uranium in its atomic weight, ordinary uranium being 238 times as heavy as hydrogen (the lightest of the ninety-two elements), whereas U-235 weighs 235 times as much as hydrogen. Hence the name. Even the existence of U-235 was not known until 1935, when it was discovered by means of a highly ingenious "atomic microscope" by Prof. Arthur J. Dempster, at the physics laboratory of the University of Chicago. There

was not the slightest reason at the time to expect anything unusual from this newly found relative of the royal uranium family of elements.

The complete story behind the story of this astonishing development, that may turn out later to be "the greatest story in the world," has until now remained largely untold. The story had its beginning about a year and a half ago, in Berlin, with experiments on uranium conducted by Dr. Lise Meitner and Prof. Otto Hahn, a scientific team that had worked together for twenty years. Like many an explorer before them, among whom Columbus is the best known example, they were seeking a new route between two known points, and came instead upon a miraculous new continent of matter, as rich and wonderful in its way as the Americas proved to be many years after their discovery. And, like Columbus, these modern discoverers of a new continent of vast resources did not themselves realize the nature and extent of their discovery. This was to be determined by later explorers, largely in America.

Meitner and Hahn had set out to repeat a famous experiment carried out by Prof. Enrico Fermi, Nobel Prize winning physicist, who left Fascist Italy to continue his work at Columbia University. Professor Fermi had discovered a strange game of "atomic golf," in which atomic balls, known as neutrons (fundamental, electrically neutral building blocks of the universe), could be made to score "holes in one" with much

410

greater frequency if they were made to travel with slow speed, the "hole" in this case being the nucleus, or core, of the atom.

The purpose of this game is to liberate part of the enormous energy locked up in the nucleus of the atom. In playing this game, using uranium as the "atomic golf course," Professor Fermi observed strange Alice-Through-the-Looking-Glass phenomena that did not seem possible. It appeared that in the course of this game new elements had been created heavier than the heaviest found in nature, elements beyond uranium, heavyweight of the natural components of the physical universe.

Meitner and Hahn devised a highly delicate "atomic microscope" that enabled them to "see" what was happening chemically on the "atomic golf course" more clearly than could be done before, then proceeded to fire slow-speed neutrons à la Fermi at the uranium nucleus. And the result surprised and startled them so much that they believed some serious error had been made. They repeated the experiment, only to observe once again what they had seen in the first place— an "atomic ghost" that had no business being there. Instead of an element resembling uranium they observed an element totally different, having an atomic weight only little more than half the weight of uranium. The "atomic ghost" was seen to materialize itself, and lo, here, out of nowhere, appeared the element used in the taking of X-ray pictures of internal organs—barium.

Barium! How the deuce did it get there? Where could it have come from? There definitely was not a trace of barium present when the experiment was started, and yet here it was. It was like placing a duck's egg in an incubator and suddenly seeing it hatch out into a chicken.

Before a solution could be found to this scientific mystery of the first magnitude, Hitler's racial decrees brought Doctor Meitner's career in Germany to an end. It had been discovered that Doctor Meitner, a scion of a family that had lived in Germany for many generations, was not "Aryan." She was forced to leave her native land to seek a haven where she could resume her life's work.

Lise Meitner was on the train bound for Stockholm, sadly looking out of the window at the Berlin where she had spent her life devotedly in the pursuit of knowledge. That was a closed chapter. She was sixty years old, unmarried, and a woman without a country. She was going to a strange land, where she would try to resume her work, her unfinished strange experiment, barium.

She could not get barium out of her mind. Could it have been an impurity? Doctor Hahn was the most careful of chemists. He had been meticulously careful to exclude any possibility of the uranium being contaminated with barium, and yet, in spite of the most careful precautions, the barium appeared, like Hamlet's ghost on the ramparts. Where could the barium have come from? Nothing ever comes from nothing, and there had been no barium there to start with.

Lise Meitner's thoughts wandered far afield and kept coming back to barium. Suddenly, what seemed at first an idle thought, to be dismissed as daydreaming, flashed into her mind. Barium has about half the atomic weight of uranium. Could it be possible that the bombardment of the uranium with the slow-speed neutron bullets split the uranium atoms in two nearly equal halves, one of which was the mysterious ghost of barium that appeared in the experiments?

She attributed the thought as most likely being due to the strain she had been under during the past few days. It was too fantastic to be true. For nothing like it had ever happened before in the hundreds of thousands, if not millions, of atom-smashing experiments in leading scientific institutions all over the world, during the past twenty years. Not even the most powerful atom-smashing machines in America, largest of their kind anywhere in the world, had ever succeeded in chipping off more than a small bit of an atom. Even an elementary student of physics knew that there was not enough power available anywhere on earth to split an atom in halves, particularly the heaviest of all the elements.

She began jotting down figures on paper. Every well-informed layman knows by this time that the material universe is made up of ninety-two fundamental elements, beginning with hydrogen, the lightest, at No. 1, and ending with uranium at ninety-two. What makes the elements differ from one another is the number of positively charged electrical particles, known as protons, in their nucleus, or core. Thus hydrogen has only one positive electrical particle in its nucleus. Helium has two. Carbon has six, nitrogen seven, oxygen eight, and so forth. If helium were to be split in halves, each half would be not helium but hydrogen. If oxygen were to lose one positive particle (proton) it would no longer be oxygen but nitrogen. Mercury contains eighty positive particles in its nucleus and gold has seventy-nine; hence if one of these could be knocked out of the mercury nucleus it would be transmuted into gold. Similarly, uranium contains ninety-two, barium fifty-six, and krypton thirty-six positive particles respectively, in their central core. Hence, if uranium could be split by some process into two uneven pieces, of fifty-six and thirty-six units

411

each, the broken parts would be, respectively, barium and krypton.

Having scribbled the figures 56 and 36 on her notebook, Lise Meitner began doing a little more involved calculation. It takes tremendous energy to hold the unit particles in the central core of the atoms together. This is known as the "binding energy" of the atom. If an atom were to be broken in halves a certain portion of this binding energy would be released, and, in the case of a heavy atom, the amount of such binding energy that would be released should be of tremendous proportions. How much? she wondered. With expert mathematics she quickly arrived at the result and then went over her figures to make sure. . . . Yes, she was right. If a uranium atom of ninety-two positive particles were to be split into two parts, one of which consisted of 56 (barium) and the other of 36 (krypton) particles, the amount of atomic binding energy released would be the hitherto-undreamed-of figure of the order of 200,-000,000 electron volts per atom, an energy 5,-000,000 times greater than that released in the burning of coal.

The figures before her overwhelmed her. She was experiencing sensations that must have been akin to those of Columbus when he first sighted land, without knowing exactly what the land was. Was it the East Indies? A mirage? A new continent of untold wealth? If her figures were right, and they could well be checked, she and Doctor Hahn had accidentally stumbled upon one of the greatest discoveries of the age. They had come upon the trail of what might lead to the shores of the Promised Land of Atomic Energy.

When Lise Meitner arrived in Stockholm she did two things that started off a set of events as dramatic as any in the history of man's endless quest for new means of mastery over his material environment. First, she prepared a report of the results of her strange experiment for a scientific journal, so that scientists in other parts of the world, both inside and outside Germany, might take up the quest for an answer to the puzzle. Second, she telegraphed the gist of her findings to a scientist friend in Copenhagen, Dr. R. Frisch.

It so happens that Doctor Frisch is the son-in-law of Prof. Niels Bohr, of Copenhagen, Denmark, one of the world's most famous pioneers in the investigation of the atom. Professor Bohr was at that time—it was January, 1939—in America, carrying on investigations with his colleague, Einstein, at the Institute for Advanced Study, Princeton, New Jersey, and also with his other Nobel Prize winning colleague, Fermi, at Columbia. Doctor Frisch did two things. He at once cabled the news from Doctor Meitner to Doctor Bohr in America, and he set to work repeating the Hahn-Meitner experiment in Doctor Bohr's physics laboratories at the University of Copenhagen.

The news reached Doctor Bohr on or about Tuesday, January 24, 1939. He lost no time in communicating the startling developments to Doctor Fermi. These two master minds in modern science began making some calculations of their own. Without knowing the full details of Doctor Meitner's figures, they soon arrived independently at the same conclusions. Sure enough, if the uranium atom could be split into two pieces, the parts would fly apart like gigantic atomic cannon balls, the greatest ever produced in any laboratory, each fragment traveling with an energy close to 100,000,000 electron volts, or a total of 200,000,000 electron volts of energy, by far the greatest ever liberated anywhere.

If their calculations were right then the "atomic thermometer" of Columbia's giant atom-smasher should register the fact. They called together a conference of the Columbia atom-smashers, headed by Prof. J. R. Dunning, under the general supervision of Dean George B. Pegram. For a day and a night they labored, preparing, testing, checking, observing. Then, on Wednesday, January twenty-fifth, their labors were finished—a tired group of scientists were anxiously standing around the "atomic thermometer." One of them pressed a button. Yes, the uranium atom was definitely being split. Little David was cracking nature's Goliath in two and forcing him to give up an enormous amount of his strength.

It so happened that on Friday following the experiments there was to be held at George Washington University, Washington, D. C., a conference on theoretical physics in which Doctor Bohr, Doctor Fermi, and a select group of leading American physicists were scheduled for informal discussions on the latest developments in their probings inside the atom.

There was nothing to indicate that anything out of the ordinary was about to take place when Doctor Bohr rose to speak that afternoon of January 27, 1939, in one of the lecture rooms at George Washington University. It took some minutes before the import of what he was saying, in low, even tones, had impressed itself on their critical minds. Had anyone other than the great Bohr, or another of his stature, uttered the words they were hearing it is doubtful if they would have taken them seriously.

Suddenly there was a commotion and the room became nearly empty. Calm young scientists, leaders in their field, never observed to show undue excitement about anything, were seen rushing to the nearest telephones. One or two science reporters present sensed there was something momentous in the air, but the young physicists were too busy to talk to them. Excitedly they got their colleagues in their laboratories on the telephone. Bohr has just reported something tremendous. Sounds fantastic, unbelievable, but they must get hold at once of a sample of uranium and repeat the experiment Doctor Bohr had just told them about. Columbia had already done it, but they must not lose time to do it on their own.

In almost no time the giant atom-smashers at the Carnegie Institution of Washington, Johns Hopkins University, and a number of other leading scientific institutions, were engaged in a blitzkrieg against the uranium atom, hurling against it billions upon billions of atomic projectiles in the form of slowed-up neutrons. There was no sleep that night in January for any of these scientists in the laboratories of various parts of America, and they kept working on through the morning and into the afternoon.

Finally, late Saturday afternoon, the news came through to the group of physicists at the Washington conference. It was true. The barium came as a result of the uranium atom having been split in two unequal pieces, releasing in the process a quantity of atomic binding energy 5,000,000 times the energy of burning coal.

Then came word from Doctor Frisch by cable to Doctor Bohr that he had achieved the same results a few days ahead of the Americans.

No sooner was the great barium mystery solved than another, equally baffling, presented itself. When the uranium is split in two parts a number of high-speed atomic bullets, in the form of neutrons, should be released in the process from the atom's core. If these neutrons were to be slowed down (slow neutrons are the most accurate) they should start a cyclic action in the manner of a string of firecrackers, one split atom automatically setting off another, which, in turn, would set off a third, and so on, in rapid succession, resulting in a terrific explosion.

When no such explosion was observed, and no chain reaction in the manner of "cosmic firecrackers," the scientists set to wondering. There must be something that extinguishes the cosmic fire. What could that something be?

Doctor Bohr, in collaboration with Dr. J. A. Wheeler, of Princeton, was the first with a theoretical explanation for the problem. Ordinary uranium, it had been found by Doctor Dempster in 1935, consisted of a mixture of three types of the substance differing in their atomic weight, the largest part consisting of atomic weight 238, while the two other types had atomic weights of

235 and 234, respectively. It had also been determined that the ratio of the uranium 238 to uranium 235 was 1 to 139—that is, in every 140 pounds of ordinary uranium there is one pound of pure uranium 235 (U-235), scattered so finely that the job of separation had up till then been regarded as impossible. Uranium 234 is much the rarest of the three, existing in a ratio of 1 to 17,000 of ordinary uranium.

It was the U-235, Doctor Bohr and Doctor Wheeler concluded on the basis of theoretical reasoning, that was starting the atomic fires going. The U-238 was the element that was quenching the fires. If only a sample of the U-235 could be obtained in pure form! But no such sample was available, and until that could be done the world could not know for certain.

Quietly, and it may be imagined feverishly, another scientific race was set going in our leading scientific laboratories. The industrial research laboratories of the General Electric Company, fully realizing what was at stake, joined in the race with improved apparatus. And the race gained impetus by reports that kept trickling out of Germany, through a grapevine in which exiles from German laboratories played a significant part.

Shortly after Lise Meitner was exiled from Germany, Doctor Hahn published a preliminary report on the experiment in a German scientific journal in which he confined himself to the facts, without interpreting them. Since the spectacular corroboration of the experiment, and its full significance, has been published in America not a word has come out officially from German laboratories. But in spite of the strict censorship, and the thick veil of secrecy, reports began trickling through, all fitting together the scattered parts of a jigsaw puzzle. By direct order of Hitler, according to the reports, some 200 of Germany's greatest scientists were concentrating all their joint energies on the solution of the one problem—U-235.

The problem of separating twins of the same element so close to each other in weight was a formidable one and required a considerable amount of experimental ingenuity for its solution. Credit for being the first in the field with a tiny sample of the precious substance goes to Dr. Alfred O. Nier, twenty-seven-year-old physicist of the University of Minnesota. Shortly thereafter another, slightly larger, sample was isolated at the General Electric research laboratories at Schenectady, New York, by Dr. K. H. Kingdon and Dr. H. C. Pollock. Both samples were rushed to Columbia University and submitted to tests, and both provided experimental proof that Doctor Bohr and Doctor Wheeler were right in their theoretical predictions that it was the U-235 that had been split in two and released the greatest amounts of atomic energy ever to be observed.

These first microscopic bits of U-235 may, therefore, well be regarded in the not-too-distant future as the very cornerstone of a new civilization. Fifty years from now, when the present war may be but a memory, the generation then living may look upon this discovery as one of the turning points in human history. Certain it is that it will be regarded as one of the great discoveries in modern science.

But nature has a way of tantalizing man by placing before him a luscious morsel and then interposing seemingly insuperable obstacles between him and the desired object. No sooner was the discovery made of the tremendous power-potentialities of U-235 than it was realized that nature had locked it up so tightly with ordinary uranium that it was, to all intents and purposes, impossible to separate it in pure form in large quantities. The methods used for separating the first tiny samples at the University of Minnesota and the General Electric Company yielded the substance at the rate of one millionths of a gram every ten days, working twenty-four hours a day. At this rate it would take 26,445 years to produce one gram, and 11,995,074 years to extract one pound. It was, therefore, at once realized that the principal problem to be solved before atomic power could become a reality was to devise a method, or methods, that would make possible the extraction of U-235 in practical quantities.

The prize at the end of the rainbow was in itself great enough to start a friendly scientific race among America's leading university and industrial laboratories. But this friendly race, usual among scientists as among the rest of mankind, assumed an ominous aspect as the tentacles of the swastika cast a shadow on the tranquil walls of our laboratories. For here again it was realized that, with all their superior equipment and ingenuity, the American scientists, because of the very limited funds available for research, were at a considerable disadvantage in working against scientists of totalitarian Germany, who had practically unlimited resources at their disposal. What if the Germans succeeded in attaining their goal? A few hundred pounds of U-235, even in a concentration of only 10 to 50 per cent purity, according to calculations, would place in German hands potentially the most powerful fuel ever dreamed of.

It is the prevailing opinion among American scientists that, in spite of the enormously greater resources at the disposal of the German laboratories, they could not possibly solve the problem in less than ten years, and probably much longer. Yet developments in science move so fast these days that no one is willing to make definite predictions as to what might, or might not, be done in the near future.

Even now there are signs on the horizon promising considerably improved methods for the separation of U-235 in larger quantities. A number of new methods are being quietly developed in American laboratories, and one of them in particular, known as the "thermal-diffusion method," taking advantage of differences in temperature to separate lighter particles from their heavier components, is being thoroughly investigated as the most promising for the present.

The development of this method furnishes another fine example of the fact that progress in modern science is the result of contributions by many scientists in many lands. The method was originally developed in Germany for other purposes a few years ago. Later it was improved upon in America. More recently, Prof. W. H. Furry, of Harvard, Prof. Lars Onsager, of Yale, and others, worked out by mathematics a theory for employing the method with greater efficiency. Taking advantage of all these contributions, Prof. Wilhelm Krasny-Ergen, of the University of Stockholm, Sweden, designed an apparatus last summer which, he believed, would increase the yield of U-235 more than 12,500 times over present methods, provided certain chemical compounds of uranium could be produced.

Unfortunately, the invasion of Norway brought Doctor Krasny-Ergen's work to a stop before he had even completed his apparatus, so that for the present it still remains a purely theoretical calculation, and with no one willing to swear that the theory behind the calculations is watertight. All that scientists are willing to say now is that "it appears probable that it will work," but that "there may be several years of concentrated work needed before success is reached." Even then, when U-235 is obtained, they add, "there is the very serious problem of shielding the operators from the U-235's radiation." The screens may have to be so bulky as to prohibit the use of the material as a lightweight power source.

Moreover, practical scientists point out, even if the Krasny-Ergen method did work, a method that increases the rate of yield by 12,500 times would still be very slow, requiring some 350,000 days (960 years) for the isolation of one pound.

However, still speaking theoretically, this would be true only for one unit of the apparatus.

If the apparatus should be found to work, and scientists believe that it probably would, the problem would become largely an economic one. If it would take 350,000 days for one unit to produce one pound, then 1000 units would produce a pound in 350 days, and 100,000 such units, easy and cheap to make, would yield one pound of U-235 every three and a half days.

In a country like Germany, with its totalitarian economy, the cost of any undertaking is a very minor consideration when the government decrees that it is vital for the national economy, and, if the reports are correct, the Nazi government has so decreed.

One pound of pure U-235 would have the explosive power of 15,000 tons of TNT, or 300 carloads of fifty tons each. But such a substance would not likely be wasted on explosives. A five-pound lump of only 10 to 50 per cent purity would be sufficient to drive ocean liners and submarines back and forth across the seven seas without refueling for months. And the technique that would be required for its utilization would be even more simple than the burning of coal or oil, according to present theories based on small-scale experiments.

Just as coal needs a fire to release its energy, the U-235 would need only water. All that would be needed to start it would be to place it in water. The water would first be turned into steam and the steam would run powerful turbines.

When all the water had been used up the process would automatically stop, until more water was supplied to start it again. A constant supply of cold water, well regulated, would keep the process going on for months, or even years, depending on the quantity of the U-235 present.

The basis for these theoretical considerations rests on the discovery by Professor Fermi that neutrons when slowed down, by being made to go through water, become thousands of times more accurate in hitting bull's-eyes square into the hearts of atoms. Fast neutrons have tremendous speed, but no control. They pass right through, or by, atoms without hurting them. Neutrons slowed down to low speeds, the lower the better, gain in control what they lose in speed. They go straight for the heart of the atom, and once they enter it they have not enough energy to get out. In the case of the U-235 atom, because of its bulk and inherent instability, the slow neutron, on entering, splits it in half. The splitting, it is believed, automatically releases other neutrons, which, slowed down in turn, will split more U-235 atoms, starting a firecracker action in a process that would be both automatic and self-regulating.

The neutrons have a weight very close to that of hydrogen. Since two thirds of the atoms of water consist of hydrogen, the neutrons, on being made to pass through water, strike the equal weights of the hydrogen atoms, and in doing so yield up most of their energy, so that they are slowed down to speeds corresponding to energies of one fortieth of an electron volt (an electron volt is a very small fraction of an erg, or unit of work).

On being slowed down the neutron is said to become "tuned" to the central core of the atom, so that it heads straight for it. To use a golf analogy, the slow neutron behaves as though a golf ball were magnetized and aimed at a hole containing a powerful magnet. Even the poorest of golfers could, under such circumstances, make holes in one.

To start the fires of atomic energy burning in U-235 it would not be necessary, according to theory, to provide neutrons from an outside source. What are known as "free" neutrons are present everywhere in the universe. Cosmic rays that keep entering the atmosphere from the outside at all times during day and night, and minute amounts of radium present in the air, continually collide with the oxygen and nitrogen atoms in the atmosphere with such force that fast neutrons are liberated. When a piece of U-235 will be placed in water, these fast neutrons would therefore be slowed down and start the automatic release of atomic energy, as long as there was water at the proper cool room temperature. Hot water, or steam, would not slow the neutrons down sufficiently to be effective.

Tremendous as the release of atomic energy from U-235 is, it must be realized that it constitutes only a very small fraction, less than one tenth of 1 per cent, of the total power contained in the U-235 atom if its mass could be completely utilized as energy. Each unit of atomic weight has an equivalent in energy of a billion electron volts, so that U-235, having 235 such units, contains the enormous energy of 235,000,000,000 electron volts, or 1175 times greater than the 200,000,000 electron-volt energy yielded by the splitting of the U-235 atom. In other words, if all the mass of one pound of U-235 could be converted into energy it would yield the equivalent in power of 5,875,000,000 pounds of coal. Stated in other terms, one pound of U-235 contains a total energy of 10,000,000,000 kilowatt hours of electricity, of which only less than one tenth of 1 per cent, or 10,000,000 kilowatt hours, could be utilized by the splitting of the U-235 atoms with slow neutrons.

Not even in the stars and sun is the entire mass

of atoms converted into energy. It has been calculated that one thirtieth of a gram of water (there are 453.59 grams per pound), converted into pure energy, would yield enough heat to turn 1000 tons of water into steam. In one whole gram of water there is a sufficient store of energy to raise a load of 1,000,000 tons to the top of a mountain six miles high. A breath of air would operate a powerful airplane continuously for a year; a handful of snow would heat a large apartment house for a year; the pasteboard in a small railroad ticket would run a heavy passenger train several times around the globe; a cup of water would supply the power of a great generating station of 100,000-kilowatt capacity for a year.

Writing in the General Electric Review for June, 1940, Doctor Kingdon sums up the general attitude of the research worker in the field as follows:

While it seems unlikely that this energy source will displace our present means of getting power, it cannot be denied that such a source should have important applications, as it is estimated that several million times as much power could be obtained from U-235 as from an equal weight of coal. These applications will involve problems of proper control of the power, and protection against the tremendous neutron and X-ray radiations which will accompany it. It may be that the use of these radiations in therapy will be one of the most important applications. But detailed discussion of these questions is premature until further progress has been made in the separation of large quantities of U-235.

Indeed, it would be just as premature to discuss in detail the possible applications and potentialities for the future of U-235 as a new source of power as it would have been to discuss the potentialities of the electromagnetic (radio) wave when it was first produced by Hertz, or of the steam engine, dynamo, internal-combustion engine or airplane, when they were first invented. For the next few years, at least, operators of coal mines and oil wells, and distributors of power need not lose sleep over U-235.

Nevertheless, it would be lacking in farsightedness for our industrialists not to watch with keen interest the developments in this field, and it would be downright shortsighted not to aid the pioneer scientists in this highly important research so that America may be in the lead when the time comes for the practical application of this tremendous new potential source of power. It would be tragic indeed, if America were to lose the lead it is now believed to have in this field because its scientists, as the result of lack of funds, could not keep up in the race with their totalitarian rivals. A few thousands of dollars invested for research now may be worth hundreds of millions in the future.

Fortunately, the indications are that some of our leading industrialists and public-utility leaders are already taking a keen interest in the matter. This is shown by the fact that at a round-table discussion in April to "explore the public utilities outlook" for the immediate future, under the auspices of the Savings Bank Journal, attended by more than thirty industrial and political authorities in the field, U-235 was one of the topics discussed, and, according to an editorial comment in the Savings Bank Journal for May, 1940, "aroused great interest and speculation."

CITY IN PRISON

by Joseph Alsop

JOSEPH ALSOP, LIKE the late Justice Oliver Wendell Holmes, believes in taking a personal part in the actions and passions of his time. That is why the news of Pearl Harbor found him already at war, collecting planes and equipment at Hong Kong for Brigadier General Claire Chennault's Flying Tigers. He was seized and interned by the Japanese, who probably would have shot him if they had known what he was up to. His account of that experience ran in two instalments in the *Post*; in the following version it has been somewhat condensed, with the author's consent.

Reporter Alsop was born in Connecticut in 1910, attended Groton and Harvard, went to work for the New York *Herald Tribune* in 1936 and began writing a Washington column with Robert Kintner a year later. Since 1945 his usual writing partner has been his brother Stewart, who was in the O.S.S. during World War II, parachuted into France on D-Day and fought with the Maquis. Singly, jointly and in combination with others the Alsops have written for the *Post* on a wide range of subjects, from the hospital treatment which removed sixty-five pounds from brother Joe's frame in the late 1930's to the making of the first hydrogen bomb in the early 1950's.

JANUARY 9 & 16, 1943

IT WAS a warm winter morning, lit by a pale sunlight that grimly illuminated the wounds of the city, when the Japanese ordered all British, Dutch and American nationals in Hong Kong to report at the Murray Parade Ground with such personal effects as they could carry. Along with nearly 3500 others—men, women and children, old and young, sick and healthy—I began that day the experience of internment.

It endured for me until the Americans were exchanged six months later, and still endures for the 3000-odd British and Dutch who remain behind the barbed wire in Stanley Camp. It was a singular experience, different from military internment— we were all civilians or pretended civilians—and perhaps more interesting, for we were the bits and pieces of a complete, highly organized peacetime society which had been blown sky high and come down together again at haphazard. And for this very reason it was a most curious commentary on people and their relations to one another and to their surroundings, and seems worth writing about even now in America, where the war is so incredibly distant despite the gaps in families and the uniforms in the streets, where respectable people who began scrabbling in garbage cans would be hastily bundled off to the psychiatrists.

The society I speak of was the former ruling caste of the British crown colony of Hong Kong. I was, of course, an interloper, only there at all because the Pan American shuttle clipper had brought me to Hong Kong the night before Pearl Harbor, on my way back from a mission to Manila for Gen. C. L. Chennault and the American Volunteer Group. Being an island, the place was a trap and I could not return to my post on General Chennault's staff.

They wanted no last-minute volunteers. So, while the days of fighting passed with dreadful swiftness, I picked up wounded until the surrender came on Christmas Day. That afternoon, before the first files of Japanese troops—little, animal-looking men—marched into the deathly still center of the city, I burned my passport and papers and obtained from the American consulate officials roosting gloomily in their big office a new "certificate of identification" as a newspaperman. So, barring the accidents of investigation, since I was not in uniform, I was ready for what was to come.

Between the surrender on Christmas Day and the Japanese order that settled our fate, there was more than a week of suspense—of crowding together, day after day, in the odd places where the abrupt end of fighting had left us; of anxious discussion of Japanese intentions, and of occasional sallies into the streets to buy food and supplies from the Chinese hawkers, who soon swarmed everywhere with the miscellaneous loot of the city in little boxes and baskets. The Hong Kong garrison was interned at once, but civilians and ostensible civilians were let alone.

417

Everyone tried vaguely to prepare for an unforeseeable future. My efforts, which turned out better than the average, were the purchase of a small canned-food reserve and the manufacture of emergency bedding out of a borrowed blackout curtain and two chair cushions from the American Club. I spent most of this limbo time at the club, where several scores of people were sleeping on the floor each night and carrying on a strange caricature of the normal club life by day. But on the night before internment I removed to the Gloucester again, to stay with the local A.P. correspondent, Vaughn Meisling, who had, with great generosity and courage, offered to support my self-identification as a newspaperman.

We had an odd night of it. Besides me, Meisling was also giving shelter to Bill O'Neill, the Reuters' correspondent, and a tough, violent little man who was half crazed because his wife was one of the three volunteer nurses raped and bayoneted by the Japanese on the day of the surrender. At eight P.M. a Chinese friend tipped us off that the notice ordering us to report for internment was being printed by the South China Morning Post press. As the hotel food was uneatable and we had more canned stuff than we could carry, we all gorged ourselves on corned mutton and dill pickles and Vaughn's last bottle of whisky, much in the manner of savages consuming their stores to keep them from the enemy. After the meal, I slipped down the corridor to ask an acquaintance's beautiful Portuguese girl friend to sew some sapphires I had bought in Burma into the collar of my coat. She took a long time, for she was a careful, convent-trained seamstress, and she had to work by candlelight. Three lumps of bright blue sapphire matrix were too big to be hidden. I gave them to her, and she gave me a piece of soap, and we said good-by and wished each other luck. Then I went back to Vaughn's room and packed, and we all tried to get some sleep.

Next morning the Queens Road, the broad street which runs past the Murray Parade Ground, was filled with English and Americans of all sorts, alone and in groups, all lugging suitcases and bundles. Huge crowds of Chinese, unaccustomed to seeing the city's privileged caste carrying anything heavier than the morning newspaper, looked on from the sidewalks in pleased astonishment. The parade ground, a big, square, railed-in space at the heart of the city, next to the barracks, was filled with more people, all milling about aimlessly, or sitting limply on little heaps of battered-looking luggage. Shortly before noon a detachment of Japanese gendarmes and interpreters drove up, and after a good many misunderstandings everyone was lined up in a column of fours. After a short inspection, the 200 people at the head of the column were marched off by a couple of gendarmes. The column moved forward, and the inspection and marching off were repeated several times, until my section of the column was reached. We fell to the lot of a squat captain of *gendarmerie* with a face like a dog and an unshakable belief that any command in Japanese, if only shouted loudly, would be understood by all. He had a way of kicking people in the stomach if they did not grasp his wishes soon enough, but, luckily, he generally gestured when he bellowed. We moved off docilely behind him, between the walls of Chinese spectators, down Queens Road into the poorer district of the city.

After trudging a mile and a half, we turned abruptly into a narrow alley and were halted before the grilled door of an ancient, dilapidated and very dirty building. Painted on the peeling plaster was an announcement in Chinese that it was the Stag Hotel, offering comfortable rooms at cheap rates. In reality, it was a Chinese brothel of the third class.

In response to the gendarme captain's hammerings and bellowings, the grille was opened by the brothel proprietor, an evil-looking, pale green Chinese with bad teeth, and we all marched in. What we found was a brusque eye-opener to those who had been cherishing delusions about their lot as captives of the Japanese—as had most of the smug relics of Chamberlain's England, corroded with complacency and corrupted by easy profits, who were numerous in Hong Kong. They still inclined to the belief that outrages had only to be reported to the nearest policeman.

The Stag must, I think, have been built as a private house by a rich early China trader. The original rooms were very large, and there were still traces of good workmanship here and there. But now the rooms had been partitioned off into innumerable little cells, and the partitions, which were of chicken wire after the first eight feet, had been put in without regard to light or ventilation.

For furniture the cells had only large, very hard Chinese beds, a broken-down chair or so and a grimy washstand. Each cell which had once housed a single Chinese prostitute was now marked in chalk on the door as accommodation for a minimum of three and commonly four or five people.

But there was no time to complain. We all scrambled for rooms, while the gendarme captain and his staff tramped up and down the corridors, hustling the elderly and bewildered, and constantly making the queer barking sounds habitual in irritated Japanese. The brothel proprietor and his seedy runners stood about in obvious enjoyment of our discomfiture. They resented us, since our arrival had deprived them of their customary means of livelihood.

On paper the ensuing seventeen days look pretty macabre. There were about 140 of us in the Stag—seven other brothels held the balance of the civilian internees in Hong Kong. There was no heat, no light, no bedding except what the internees had brought or the prostitutes left behind. There were only three toilets in the entire establishment, and all three worked only intermittently. It was bitterly cold a good part of the time, with the damp, penetrating chilliness which Hong Kong in winter shares with Boston.

The effect of the cold was vastly increased by the shortage of food. The Japanese occasionally delivered a little rice and the scrag end of an animal, but the deliveries were made to the brothel proprietor, and, except in the last few days, the cooking was in the hands of the brothel runners. They were naturally anxious to find in us the profits we had cost them. They took a heavy squeeze. As a result, we lived on what we had brought in, what we could buy at staggering prices from the brothel runners, and an official issue of two cups of rice and two cups of gruel daily. Most people had little more than the official issue. Nor could one forget the facts of life in the Stag by plunging into happy pastimes. Except for a borrowed Bible and Vaughn's pocket edition of Dante, I could find no reading matter, and although I had cards, one began to freeze at the extremities after a couple of rubbers of bridge. Finally, there was nowhere to exercise except on the roof, the dry-rotted beams of which cracked audibly all day long under the feet of groups of people seeking air and release from the confinement of their cells.

The groups in some of the cells were downright fantastic. In one, a tired-looking Anglo-Portuguese father from Macao, a brisk Scots mother, and six children, the youngest under a year, all sheltered together. In another, the bed nightly contained a luxury-loving Hong Kong merchant; an aging but grandiloquent Jewish gunman soldier of fortune; a peevish young blonde; the blonde's poisonous child, and the child's plump nurse, whose battle cry, "Tommy, stop picking your nose; it's dirty," continued to resound until dawn. We used to speculate on whether the nurse talked in her sleep or stayed awake all night. Because we had a very small cell, Vaughn and I had only one roommate, but even he had his drawbacks.

I had bedding of my own and minded rats far less than too much company, so I slept on the floor. Vaughn and our roommate used the bed. As Vaughn is six-foot-four, neat-minded, and far from fond of people at close quarters, it would never have been easy for him to share his couch. Fortunately, our roommate claimed Irish Free State citizenship and was exempted from internment after the first fortnight.

On our seventeenth morning in the brothel, the expectation of transfer to a permanent internment camp was fulfilled. We were herded out into the alley, formed up in a column of fours again, and trudged off between the usual Chinese crowds, who now looked somewhat more sympathetic. Our destination was a pier on the water front, but when we reached it the entrance was closed and we waited endlessly in the street. The audience there, particularly big, was being policed by more gendarmes, and, like most Chinese crowds, they were not very promptly responsive to policing. We understood the changed expressions on the Chinese faces when a cretinous-looking gendarme suddenly dragged into the open an inoffensive Chinese who had evidently failed to understand a shouted order. After giving the man two shattering blows across the shoulders with a heavy bamboo carrying pole, the gendarme tried to make him kneel for a formal beating. The Chinese, crazed by fear and pain, attempted to wriggle away. At that, the gendarme, who was plainly enjoying putting on a show for the waiting procession of British and Americans, gave way to a sort of frenzy, bringing the carrying pole crashing down on his victim's head and shoulders until he fell to the ground.

By this time a second gendarme, strangely armed with a steel golf club, had hurried up to help. Although the Chinese had fainted, they continued to beat him for five minutes, sometimes striking him across the face, and sometimes pounding him in the stomach and groin with the butt ends of their weapons. At last the Chinese gave a convulsive shudder, which could mean only one thing. Then the two gendarmes walked back to their stations, smiling proudly, leaving the broken body where it lay. All this had happened in a terrible silence, broken only by the grunts of the gendarmes and the moans of the Chinese.

After our suitcases and bundles had been searched for weapons, a big old harbor boat took us around Hong Kong Island to Stanley Peninsula. Stanley Peninsula, which was to be our home until our release, is a narrow, hilly, infertile neck of land running out to a bigger hill on which stands Stanley Fort. It had been the scene of the hardest fighting during the war, and it was at Stanley on the day of the surrender that the VAD's had been raped and bayoneted, forty unarmed prisoners bayoneted, and all the wounded bayoneted in their beds in St. Stephen's College and the Maryknoll Mission Field Hospital. The Hong Kong jail lay at the end of the neck, and we were housed in the warders' quarters and administrative establishment of the jail and the school building and masters' houses of St. Stephen's College. The entire camp area, a rough square one could walk around in half an hour, was surrounded by barbed wire, to which coolies were still adding the last strands when we arrived.

Many of the buildings had been badly battered during the fighting. The first tasks of the camp clean-up squads were to bury the dead that still lay on the hills and to incinerate the blood-stained mattresses of the wounded from St. Stephen's College. The corpses of the bayoneted nurses, wounded and prisoners had already been burned by the Japanese, but the big field-hospital rooms, dirty, disordered and blood-bespattered, told their story only too clearly. Yet the camp was not too bad at first glance. The buildings, of the styleless stucco-and-tile sort which is modern official architecture in the Far East, were solidly constructed, and most of their plumbing had survived the bombardment. The space for exercise was considerable, which prevented the Black-Hole-of-Calcutta feeling of the brothels, and the situation was even rather pretty. Although our little neck of land was bleak enough, it lay between two fine bays across which one looked to high, bluish-green hills rising abruptly out of the water.

Billeting was the first great problem. It was done at haphazard, on the principle of first come, first served, except that large blocks had been set aside for special groups. The American bachelors' quarters were in the former warders' club.

I was assigned to this building, where shellfire had scattered furniture, plaster, glass, bad prints illustrating Dickens, warders' bar books and score books for billiards, darts and skittles in a fantastic confusion of souvenirs of war and peace.

Meisling and I were again fortunate. Warned by experience, we seized the smallest room we could find—a bedchamber the size of a jail cell, about ten feet by seven—and because of its smallness were permitted to occupy it alone. But although it would have needed a shoehorn to get another man in with us, we enjoyed what stood for luxury in Stanley. The overcrowding was appalling. I remember one medium-sized room in the British married quarters which was shared by a businessman, his spoiled but ornamental wife and two young children; a youthful Hong Kong civil servant, his wife and three babies—all suffering from impetigo contagiosus—and three unmarried girls. Nor was this room in any way remarkable.

The first three or four days were wholly given over to the effort to make the new quarters livable. There was hardly an object in the entire camp area which a normal community would not instantly have condemned to the junk pile. But old lumber, broken furniture, rusty nails, shell-torn curtains, blankets discarded by the prisoners in the jail, tin cans, clothes and food caches left behind by the troops on the hills, convicts' uniforms, warders' cast-off boots—all these were things of price, for which men, women and children scrounged all day while friends or relatives guarded their rooms and their luggage.

It was an object lesson in the mutability of human values to see the paunchy taipan of a great merchant house returning from the day's search with two thirds of a chair, an old pair of boots and a dead soldier's mackintosh, with the pride of a man bringing home treasure-trove. The incinerated mattresses of the bayoneted wounded were the only things wasted in Stanley, and even of these one or two were snatched from the bonfire, cleaned a little, and put to use. No doubt it was not pleasant to sleep on the half-washed-out bloodstains, but for an unknowing child it was better than sleeping on the floor, which a great many people had to do.

At first the Japanese authorities had little to do with us. A small detachment of gendarmes occupied the Hong Kong jail, which was within the camp limits, but not used as quarters for internees. Our regular guards, however, were either renegade Sikhs from the Hong Kong police and military garrison, or Wang Ching-wei troops. The official supervisor of the camp was a certain Cheng, a Chinese Wang Ching-wei supporter to whom the *gendarmerie* chieftains had sold us as a sort of concession. The Japanese made themselves responsible for maintaining the camp guard and delivering our rations to Cheng to be issued. The main authority within the camp was entirely in Cheng's hands, while our internal affairs were managed by our community councils.

Cheng, a flabby, tubercular, grossly avaricious man, was assisted by a number of other Chinese Quislings of the same type. His object was to make hay while the sun shone, and besides taking bribes for special favors from the richer internees, Cheng and his gang chiseled on the rations, keeping back a portion of them and selling it on the rocketing Hong Kong food market. What the

Japanese actually delivered was little enough—chiefly second-grade rice, with a tiny quantity of dead buffalo or half-putrid fish, and a few heads of wilted and flavorless Chinese cabbage. What we got after Cheng had taken his cut was close to nothing at all. During the first three months of internment the daily ration was not more than two small bowls of rice and two small cups of a sort of thin gruel made with the meat and vegetables. The doctors in the camp checked the ration daily, and their carefully computed figures showed that each internee was getting about 1000 calories of food per day. Even if the food had been all health-giving meats and vegetables, instead of soggy, second-grade rice, wetted with gruel, the quantity would have insured ultimate starvation.

Under the circumstances, food obsessed us all nearly to the point of insanity. Some individuals did, in fact, go temporarily mad. There was, for instance, the faded, carefully genteel woman whose husband's beriberi was so severe that the camp council set aside for him the kidneys of the ration buffaloes. The woman had always been a model wife, yet after a couple of months it was found that the kidneys which were issued to her to take to the camp hospital were not reaching her husband. She was eating them, raw, in her room.

There was also the eminent Hong Kong barrister who used to spend a part of every day near the door of the British communal kitchen, for the pleasure of hissing, "Thieves, you're all thieves," when the cooks came out to take the air. And it was not only by the behavior of individuals that one was often reminded of the terrible passage in Scott's South Pole diary about the last ghastly days of the fated expedition. In that time, when the food was almost exhausted, the great explorer and his companions would divide and redivide the morsel of pemmican for the evening meal until all agreed that the division was exactly even. The pieces were then distributed by blind lot, yet the diary records that every man was unshakably convinced that he had somehow been cheated by his friends. The same psychology was common throughout the internment camp.

Once, I recall, the Japanese surprisingly issued a duck egg each to all the internees. In the British married quarters excitement ran so high, and differences over how to cook the duck eggs became so angry, that a public meeting was held. Even after prolonged debate, no agreement could be reached. The final result was a compromise, under which the fried-egg bitter-enders signed up for fried eggs, while the others took their eggs in chow fan, a Chinese dish of fried rice, garnished with bits of eggs and scraps of meat and vegetables. When the morrow came, the cooks put a few microscopic scrapings of meat bones and slivers of greenstuff into the chow fan, in order to carry out the recipe. The sight of these extras in the dishes of their neighbors so enraged a party of the fried eggers that their leader, the perfectly sound-minded mother of a large family, physically assaulted the chairman of the kitchen committee, beating him about the head with an umbrella.

In the American community there was the great garbage-pail scandal. This occurred when three guardians of the public morality—a businessman of some importance, the wife of a distinguished teacher and a female missionary—one day peered into the communal garbage pail to check up on possible wastefulness by the communal cooks. They found a number of fish heads. The fish heads were no more meaty than the heads and tails people leave on their plates when served with whole trout or sole, yet they were extracted from the garbage pail with cries of triumph and accusation. By scraping off the slivers of meat, boiling the bones to make a sort of infusion, and adding the results to rice, the fish heads were then transformed into the semblance of a fish pilau, and the pilau, which would not have made a meal for a three-year-old child, was exhibited all over the camp.

It was whispered that the cooks were patrons of the camp *bordello,* where three Eurasian women sold their favors for things to eat, and that if the wicked scheme had not been frustrated, the Eurasian women would have crept up at dead of night to find their reward among the garbage. In the end, feeling ran so high that another public meeting was held. Charges were so freely hurled about that, although they obtained a vote of confidence, the cooks later resigned.

By the end of the third month, the diet of 1000 calories a day was telling visibly on the camp's health. The first cases of beriberi had already occurred, and everyone had lost many pounds with unhealthy speed. Because the camp had previously been a battlefield, hard clean-up work had been necessary at first. But during the third month persons doing severe physical labor on the camp fatigue squads began to be taken ill, and the clean-up program had to be reduced to the absolute minimum requisite to maintain sanitary conditions. The British and American communities in Hong Kong had once been rather plethoric and overfed, but now there were gaunt faces everywhere in the camp, and it was plain that unless the diet was soon improved very serious consequences would rapidly ensue.

The story of how the camp was temporarily saved from this danger is a stirring one, for the job was risky, and our savior was a pretty, gentle, delicate woman, with white hair and a still young face. She had, it happened, been born in Japan and educated with Japanese children of the highest caste—the sons and daughters of the ancient Japanese families closest to the throne, from whom the empresses, princesses and court officials are chosen. Now, there are at least five quite different versions of the Japanese language, each with its special caste implications, and the highest and most rarefied of these is the court language, which very few Japanese beyond the confines of the court can speak, but which our fellow internee had learned to speak fluently and beautifully. It made it more difficult for her to be understood by the Japanese in Hong Kong, for she was roughly in the position of someone addressing a denizen of lower Brooklyn in the accents of Henry James; but it conferred on her an unusual position. The respect of the Japanese for their hierarchy is such that she trailed through her syllables, as it were, clouds of the godhead. Where they would do nothing for others, even the most brutal gendarme always tried to oblige her. And she used her gift wholly for the benefit of the community at large.

I well remember one afternoon when I went to see her. Two beriberi cases in the camp hospital were threatened with death. In the hospital, the limited drug supplies did not include the specific for beriberi in its advanced, acute form. This drug was known to be in the dispensary inside the prison, and my friend had tried and failed to get the gendarme captain in charge to release some of it. Then, knowing the Japanese fondness for children, and although the gendarme was an unpredictable brute, she had sent her completely charming eight-year-old son into the jail to see what he could do. He spoke the same Japanese as his mother, but this seemed a slight protection, and we waited anxiously for an hour in the gathering dusk, until the little boy returned from the jail, happily talking of the cakes the gendarme had given him, and with his pockets stuffed with the needed drug. He had perfectly remembered its name—which I have now forgotten. When he asked for it prettily and politely "for my uncle, who is sick," the gendarme had taken him to the dispensary and given him as much as he could conveniently carry away.

When the food situation became acutely dangerous, my friend and Lawrence Neilson, chairman of the British community, laid out a bold plan. She went to the gendarme officers in the camp, told them as politely as possible that the condition was unbearable and that the supervisor, Cheng, was stealing our official rations; warned them that Japan would lose face if many of us died of hunger, and asked that Neilson be allowed to present the case to the higher authorities. Partly because the appeal was well made, and perhaps partly because Cheng had not been giving them their share of the boodle, the gendarmes agreed to help after several carefully secret talks.

The lieutenant commanding the guard was party to the arrangement, and permitted Neilson to slip out of the camp one evening to visit a big villa near by, where the high gendarme officers enjoyed the luxuries of old Hong Kong life. With the aid of an interpreter he explained the situation to them, and immediately discovered that all previous appeals, forwarded through Cheng, had been suppressed at the source. In the interval since the establishment of the camp at Stanley, a new Hong Kong military government had been set up, and the officers who had sold Cheng his concession had lost power. Accordingly, the gendarmes took a favorable view. Yamashita, a former barber at a Hong Kong hotel, was quietly sent into the camp as Cheng's assistant, to verify the complaints. And in a few days Cheng was abruptly removed and Yamashita promoted to be supervisor.

Yamashita was a fairly decent little fellow, immensely self-important, but reasonably well-intentioned. He wished to improve conditions, and he was backed by the handsome, civilized chief of the Hong Kong military government's foreign-affairs section, Colonel Oda, who now shared control over us with the *gendarmerie*. The obstacle to reform was the gendarme high command. When Oda and Yamashita pressed for reforms, the gendarmes objected that we were getting Japanese army rations—an argument often heard, in which the only flaw is that while the Japanese soldier gets approximately the same food, he receives infinitely more of it, and a far higher proportion of meat, fish and vegetables. In the end, all Oda and Yamashita succeeded in doing was to obtain permission for friends of internees in Hong Kong to send them packages, and to arrange for the issue of a considerable quantity of weevily flour every day.

The flour brought the energy content of the diet up to the barely adequate figure of about 2000 calories a day, and those who were fortunate in getting regular packages of extras were soon healthy again. But in order to feed their people and their army, the Japanese had stripped the godowns of the city of every ounce of foodstuffs. Food prices, even in town, were enormous, and by the time the Americans left, the scarcity was so great that enterprising butchers were murdering their wares in dark alleys and police were patrolling the markets to prevent the sale of human flesh.

Consequently, not many people in the camp had Chinese friends rich enough to send packages regularly. And while the addition of the flour had improved the diet's energy content, it had not made our food in the slightest degree more healthy. Vitamin-deficiency diseases became rife —which was hardly surprising, considering that the average meat issue was five ounces per week per person, including buffalo bones. At the end of the first six months, when the Americans were exchanged, more than 15 per cent of the camp had either beriberi or pellagra in an early stage. The hospital supplies of drugs by which serious disability and death were being prevented had already run so low that the doctors were watering the injections of vitamin B to make them last and keep everyone's courage up. The vitamin-deficiency diseases were certain to spread and grow more acute in their effects by a predictable geometric progression.

During the first six months in Stanley, the black market was the most striking and the most superficially important result of the general starvation. Because we were all civilians or pretended civilians who had had a considerable period between the surrender and the internment to prepare for the worst, almost everyone entered the camp with small sums of money, and a few favored people had very large sums indeed. Although the Japanese methodically looted the city and took any visible valuables, like wrist watches and jewels, from the people who were foolish enough to wear them, they never subjected the internees to a systematic search. Consequently, the camp had, in the aggregate, a considerable capital to spend.

Where there is money, goods will somehow appear for sale. A completely inadequate supply of goods was brought out to the camp at intervals and sold at an official canteen, but as a twelve-ounce tin of jam every month or so was as much as an individual could expect to obtain from the canteen, the main job of supply was done by the black market. This was strictly forbidden by the Japanese, but nevertheless flourished like the green bay tree.

Importations were made through three main sources—the Chinese guards, the Chinese camp superintendents, and a group of internees of the lowest type who had formed connections with the gendarmes and acted for them in acquiring the gold watches, U. S. currency and other portable valuables of which the Japanese in Hong Kong could never get enough. Besides these main sources, there were accidental and occasional sources, as when a number of British police broke into a government warehouse full of army stores which was within the camp area. Some of them were caught and badly knocked about by the Japanese, but the others made a big haul. They sold their surplus for thousands of dollars, but their prices were comparatively low, and the camp feasted on cheap jam, margarine and bully beef for a couple of weeks.

Each of the regular sources of supply operated on a different principle. The internee fences for the Japanese were the suppliers of the desperately hungry. Calculating, brutal men, they made no bones about charging all that the traffic would bear. The most important of them lived together in the former Indian warders' quarters, in a small dark room which presented as disagreeable a scene of human meanness and degradation as you would find in Swift. I went there once, when things were bad with me, to barter a piece of gold jewelry for a little oatmeal. The chief of the firm, a beefy young deserter from the Hong Kong volunteers who spoke good Chinese and had made the firm's connection with a Chinese-speaking gendarme, was lying on the bed, half wrestling with, half making love to a couple of young girls. His accomplices were watching over two primus stoves—in themselves above rubies and burning kerosene like liquid gold—on which bubbled and sputtered an evening meal such as not more than five or six people in the camp had tasted for three months. I produced my trinket, and one of the accomplices went to a huge box in a dark corner of the room to get out the oatmeal I wanted. The girls exclaimed loudly over the box's richly furnished interior. Then the younger and plumper, whose eyes had kept returning to the primus stoves even while she was making the grossest advances to the bully on the bed, whiningly suggested that she and her friend be allowed to bring their rice to the room and share supper. "It'll be good fun, like last time," she said. At that, she and her companion were rudely pushed away. When they whined more pleadingly, "Ah, come on, Bob; it'll be real fun," the bully's accomplices each seized one of them and hustled them, now sobbing with hunger and shame, out of the room.

In truth, there was something corrupting about this trade in the basic necessities of life, in whatever form it took. The least disagreeable aspect of it was the importation of more reasonably priced food and tobacco by the Wang Ching-wei guards. They were polite, shifty little men in baggy uniforms, and their natural talent for smuggling was such that even the Japanese decree making smuggling a capital offense hampered them not at all. I can remember seeing one of them slip into our house in the late evening, open his tunic, pull his trouser ends out of his boots, and although he had looked quite normal when he entered, shower down 152 packages of Chinese cigarettes. Tobacco was the single luxury most internees could not learn to do wholly without, but all subjected themselves to stringent disciplines. For example, I, who had been in the habit of smoking between fifty and sixty special cigarettes a day, cut myself down to eight, which I rolled from toilet paper and a well-named Chinese tobacco called Eight Agricultural Smells.

Yet even the poor man's black market run by the guards produced its crop of grisly episodes. There was, for instance, the British police sergeant's shrewd Chinese wife, who made the earliest deal with two of the Chinese guards, and for a time possessed a tobacco monopoly in the camp. Starting with a pair of gold earrings, she doubled her capital daily in the clump of shrubbery where she crouched under a bush all afternoon with her stock in trade in false pockets of her coat. She was well on the way to making a substantial fortune when two other policemen's wives broke the monopoly by obtaining supplies from coolies working on the camp's barbed-wire circuit fence. In her greed, she informed against the coolies, and the Japanese promptly beheaded three of them. In punishment, her husband was formally beaten by his fellow policemen, while she was taken to a quiet place by the women of the police block married quarters, gagged, whipped and subjected to such merciless and successful hair-pulling that she showed the marks for some time thereafter. No more informations were laid, and as the beheading of a few friends woud never stop a Chinese from smuggling, the tobacco monopoly was not restored.

Hunger, the complete lack of privacy and the absence of steady occupation darkly colored the community life and brought out the worst in many people in Stanley. One found oneself engaged in a perpetual struggle not to yield to petty and mean impulses, and I think few persons who were there would claim to have won the fight all the time.

The lack of privacy was nearly as bad as the inadequate food. Except by sitting on a hillside for an hour, no one could hope to escape from incessant, intimate contact with others. In the larger rooms, where families and single persons were mixed at haphazard, the most fantastic neuroses flourished. Old friends quarreled irremediably because one could not bear the other's habit of clearing his throat. Roommates whose mattresses perforce touched at night refused to speak all day. Men and women who were leaders of the community in the outer world wildly and publicly accused each other of petty pilfering. The most generous and sane developed the habit of mouth watching, as we used to call the envious glances everyone cast at the food of others. In the two daily ration line-ups every eye followed each plate as it was brought away from the rice bowl, as eyes follow the ball in tennis matches.

As for daily occupations, it can be imagined how difficult they were to find in a crowded, barren area, dotted with thickly packed buildings and cut off from the outer world by guards and barbed wire. Love and sports, the two most easily available pastimes, demanded too much energy to be widely popular in a semistarving community. The more enterprising and unscrupulous became black-market traders, and besides the Eurasian *bordello,* there were several other business establishments in the camp, where wooden clogs were made for the shoeless, clothes washed and repaired for the richer internees, and tin cans transformed into eating utensils or cook pots for the shiftless. There was a store of books in the camp, and politics also offered an outlet, but the majority, after they had cleaned themselves and their rooms, done their best to find more food and done their camp chores, seemed not to care to exert themselves. The days passed in petty tasks, petty gossip and the exchange of rumors, which seemed, sometimes, to be the main industry in Stanley. The rumors were of all kinds, some about internal camp affairs, some about the Japanese plans for us, and most about the course of the war.

The Japanese printed, largely for our benefit, an English-language Hong Kong daily; there was supposed to be a concealed radio somewhere in the camp, and occasional people taken into Hong Kong for special medical treatment brought back news from the city. The Japanese paper was grossly untruthful. If there was a radio, the people who ran it garbled the news to protect themselves. And most of the visitors to town were hopelessly incompetent reporters. Consequently, most of the stuff so eagerly passed about and canvassed in the camp was a farrago of exaggeration and pure fiction. Yet, although this was several times proved when a sensible person got permission for a Hong Kong visit, the camp could not resist living in the rumor-filled dream world it made for itself.

It is true, moreover, that while the camp brought out the worst in people, it also brought out the best. The relief-organization official who carried in 2000 vitamin B tablets, enough to give preventive doses for two months to all beriberi patients, and himself consumed them in secret, terrified, solitary handfuls, was balanced by the woman who worked herself into a physical breakdown, and thence into beriberi, in the effort to keep the young children in the camp well and healthy. The people who slavered over the Japanese and the Chinese Quislings to secure privileges were equally balanced by my friend of the beautiful court Japanese, whose opportunities were far greater, yet who never lost her dignity or sought to benefit herself alone. And so it went.

For myself, I could never quite forget my bad luck in missing the great AVG show, after spending the most interested and excited months of my life watching and working under General Chennault while he and our pilots prepared for it. Yet I cannot altogether regret the Stanley experience. I lost some twenty-five pounds, which I could well spare, but by careful management of my small resources I kept myself and the one or two others for whom I felt responsible in reasonably good health until we left. I had a complete rest from work, which I had wanted for five years, and I had time to think through many problems which, had I been wise, I should have thought through before. I learned a great deal about the nature of human society, and of the men and women who compose it. And I avoided the more serious ill effects of the internment by keeping fairly busy.

To anyone who has the bad luck to be interned, my advice is: Carry in everything you can. Avoid medicated toilet paper, because it is useless for rolling cigarettes. And keep as busy as may be. I kept busy in two ways—by laying plans to escape, which came to nothing because the Japanese had stopped the bolt holes before I found suitable companions; and by studying the Chinese classics. Very fortunately, a young Chinese master of St.

Stephen's College, one of the prisoners bayoneted by the Japanese on the day of the surrender, had left an exceedingly fine Chinese library in his house within the camp area. With the help of Dr. Charlotte Gower, the brilliant professor of anthropology at Ling Nan University, I got through, in the original, most of Confucius and Mencius, selections from several other ancient philosophers, a few of the Odes, and the musical and constitutional sections of the Book of Rites.

The reading itself was immensely rewarding, for old Chinese is like a very elegant, very complicated puzzle, and the Chinese classics have as much wisdom as the Greek, and, to Western eyes brought up on the Greeks, more freshness and novelty. And to be able to read classical Chinese is a quite useless but unusual accomplishment which, for reasons I find it difficult to explain, fills me with inordinate pride.

But it is very different for me and the other Americans, and for the people we left behind in the internment camp. I have nothing, now, to remind me of those months, beyond my useless accomplishment, a little added knowledge of the world, and friendships, with Charlotte Gower, Stephen Balfour and one or two others, which will, I hope, prove enduring. Those who were left behind at Stanley, and those who are in other Japanese internment camps all over the Far East, are still living the same life that now seems a mere bad dream to me. They are still eating the same food and living in the same crowded rooms. And they are still coming daily nearer to the moment when the cumulative effects of undernourishment will be expressed in disease and death.

[ED. NOTE: *The above has been condensed from two articles.*]

HOW THE BRITISH SANK THE
SCHARNHORST

by C. S. Forester

When Prime Minister Churchill and President Roosevelt were meeting at sea to frame the Atlantic Charter, Churchill's bedside reading was *Captain Hornblower, R.N.* "I find Hornblower admirable," he told the man who had lent him the book. Many of Cecil Scott Forester's stories about the fabulous Hornblower have appeared in the *Post,* but during the war he was tapped to write special articles about the Royal Navy. His story of the sinking of the *Scharnhorst* has been called the best piece of naval reporting to come out of World War II.

MARCH 25, 1944

In those almost forgotten days when there were pleasure cruises, we used to see posters advertising trips to The Land of the Midnight Sun. Of course, those were summer cruises; if any steamship company had been so foolish as to try to induce people to go to North Cape in winter, they would have had to advertise "The Land of the Midday Night." On December twenty-sixth in those latitudes, seventy-five degrees north, the sun never comes above the horizon, and it is poor compensation to know it is circling not far below the horizon.

In ordinary weather it is never pitch dark. At noon it is a pale gray, and from noon it darkens imperceptibly until at midnight everything is dark gray. On a fair proportion of days and nights the green-and-yellow streamers of the aurora borealis give a fitful and erratic illumination. But there are just as many nights when the wind blows down from the Pole, tearing the tormented sea into lumpy mountains and engulfing the world in flurries of snow, so that the black sky gives no light and one cannot, literally, see one's hand before one's face.

Those are the times when it is not well to be a lookout, shivering in ten thicknesses of wool inside a sheepskin coat. The depth charges freeze to the decks; the breeches of the guns are covered with ice—unless precautions are taken—so that the breech-blocks cannot be opened; the lubrication of the ammunition hoists freezes solid. No ship can fight a battle in those wintry waters without special accessories for keeping the weapons clear of ice and for keeping life in the officers and men wedged, so that they can hardly move, in the exposed gunnery-control stations.

It is through these waters that the life line runs to Russia. The heavy convoys, laden with all the innumerable materials of war from the mines and factories of the world, make their way to Murmansk round the most northerly point of Norway. The farther north they keep, the longer is the journey they must make, at a time when even hours are important; the stormier are the seas they meet, and the greater are their chances of encountering ice. The farther south they keep, the quicker they make their run—and the more exposed they are to German attacks launched from Norway, above the surface of the sea, on the surface of the sea and below the surface of the sea.

Attacks by airplane and by submarine, in present technical conditions, however, can only harass the convoys and not stop them. There is only one thing that could stop them, in fact, and that is superior sea power. If Germany had a fleet more powerful than that of the United Nations, not a convoy would move on the high seas, not a single ship, save for occasional furtive blockade runners. But Germany does not have a superior fleet; she has a very inferior one. If the inferior fleet fights, it is destroyed. If it stays at home, it yields free use of the sea to the enemy, and might as well never have been built.

Between the two horns of this dilemma the weaker naval powers have always tried to find a profitable middle course. If the weaker power has a secure base within striking distance of the trade routes, the presence of its fleet there imposes certain troublesome precautions on the stronger power. It offers the threat of sallying out at a moment of its own selection, so that every convoy moved by the superior power must be guarded by a force greater than the whole fleet of the inferior power, and that necessarily involves strain and potential loss—the strain of staying at sea and of replacing the oil fuel consumed, and the losses from submarines and from the hazards of the sea.

But the threat must always be a real one. The weaker fleet must come out sometimes or it will find itself simply ignored. Moreover, mutinies breed readily in stagnant fleets, especially when the best of the men are steadily drained away for the submarine service. And even in a guarded base things can happen, as when the British midget submarines crept in and torpedoed the Tirpitz.

It was this loss which must have roused the Nazi government to desperation. The Russian offensive was rolling along unchecked. Something must be done at all costs to check the flow of supplies to her, before something should happen to the Scharnhorst as well. The Tirpitz was a wreck, only kept afloat by the constant attention of a salvage ship; the Gneisenau was in even worse condition at Gdynia. The Spee and the Bismarck had been sunk. Of Germany's twenty-six destroyers, eleven were at the other end of Europe, waiting to bring in a blockade runner from the east. The Nazis could not foresee that in less than a week they would be foiled in their object and three of them sent to the bottom, and the blockade runner along with them. The straggling remainder of Germany's navy was in the Baltic, for the possibility of the loss of the command of that sea to the Russian navy was something too horrible to contemplate.

Maybe the Nazis knew about the presence of that convoy to the north of North Cape. Maybe a U-boat had sighted it and had radioed information of its position and course. Maybe some unguarded word spoken in a British port may have told a Nazi spy what he wanted to know. Maybe the Scharnhorst was sent out into the Arctic night on the mere chance of striking against something. At any rate, out she went from her Norwegian fiord, wearing at her masthead the flag—a black cross and two black balls on a white ground—of Rear Admiral Bey, commanding German destroyers.

For the purposes of a raid she had all the desirable qualities. Designed for a speed of twenty-nine knots, she was faster—or so, at least, the Nazis hoped—than any British battleship. With nine 11-inch guns she was more powerful than any British cruiser; with her displacement of 26,000 tons she carried sufficient armor and was sufficiently compartmented to be able to receive a number of hard knocks without being crippled. And her enormous secondary armament of twelve 5.9-inch guns and fourteen 4.1's would insure that if she once got into a convoy she would sink ships faster than a fox killing chickens in a henroost.

At her high speed she could cover the whole distance in darkness, leaving her Norwegian fiord at the end of twilight one day and arriving in the area through which a convoy would be likely to pass at the beginning of twilight the next, so that she could be firing shells into helpless merchantmen before any British plane or submarine could detect her absence or catch a glimpse of her on passage. For closely associated reasons she had no destroyer escort; destroyers are running short in the Nazi navy; to give orders for destroyers to join her would give an additional chance for the Intelligence of the United Nations to get wind of the scheme; and, above all, a German ship steaming by herself on the high seas has the supreme advantage of the certainty that anything she sights is an enemy—she can open fire instantly, without having to wait for challenge and recognition.

She left on the afternoon of Christmas Day, and such was her good fortune or so accurate was her information that at precisely the right time, just when the gloomy northern sea was beginning to be faintly illumined and the dark gray of the sky was being replaced by something the merest trifle brighter, she made her contact with the convoy. There was any amount of shipping there, anything up to half a million tons. It was possible for her, in the next hour, to do as much damage as the whole U-boat navy could achieve in six months. In an hour she could put back the hands of the clock of war by four weeks.

At 9:30 in the morning of the day after Christmas, the British convoy was heading east some 150 miles to the northward of North Cape. It was guarded against submarine attack by a ring of corvettes and destroyers, small craft, twenty of which together would hardly equal the Scharnhorst in size. That was the antisubmarine protection; to guard against attack by surface vessels, Admiral Burnett had three cruisers, Belfast, Norfolk and Sheffield. The southeast was the most dangerous quarter, from which attack was most likely to come, so that it was to the southeast of the convoy that Burnett had stationed his squadron, and it was from the southeast that Bey arrived.

It could not be called bad luck that the Scharnhorst's first contact was made with the escort instead of with the helpless merchant ships. She could expect nothing else, for the British cruisers and destroyers covering the convoy must be disposed in a manner to guard against any possible attack. It might be considered possible for her, with all the advantage of surprise, to crash

427

through the screen and plunge in among the unarmed ships which were her real objective. It would be dangerous, for there is great danger in approaching too close to an enemy who is still in a condition to launch torpedoes. Bey had hardly more than seconds in which to make up his mind whether he should make the attempt. The Scharnhorst and the British escort sighted each other at six miles. A thousand yards short of that distance, decisive torpedo range begins, and battleship and escort hurtling together would close the range by 1000 yards in less than a minute.

Aboard the British ships, the unsleeping eye which all United Nations ships carry—the eye that can see in the dark, can see through the Arctic night, through fog or snowstorm—had been watching over their safety. It had given the first alarm, and now was reporting to bridge and to gunnery-control tower just where this intruder, this almost certain enemy, was to be found and whither she was headed. The guns were training round in accordance with its observations, and the gunnery officers in their control towers were eying the "gun-ready" lamps and awaiting the moment to open fire.

It was as if the shepherd's dogs, guarding the flock, had scented the approach of the wolf, and had rushed forward to put themselves between the wolf and the flock, baying the warning which the masthead signal lamps sent through the twilight to the commodore of the convoy. Ponderously, in obedience to the commodore's orders, the convoy turned itself about—not an easy thing to do with heavy columns of unhandy merchant ships—while the Norfolk, the Sheffield and the Belfast went dashing forward to meet the enemy.

In a broadside or in a given interval of time, the Scharnhorst could fire rather more than the weight of shells that could be fired by the three cruisers all put together. It would be a fortunate light cruiser that could sustain a hit from one of the 11-inch shells of the Scharnhorst and live through it. The armor that the Scharnhorst carried over her vitals could be relied upon to keep out the cruisers' shells at all but the closest range. Mathematically, the approaching conflict was to the last degree unfair.

Yet in war at sea mathematics plays, even in these days of machinery, only a minor part. There are the discipline and training of the crews to be taken into account, the experience and resolution of the captains, and, above all, there is chance—the chance that will take a ship unscathed through a hail of salvos, the chance that will direct a shell to the one point where it will rend a ship in two, the chance that will direct a desperate torpedo to its mark.

The three cruisers flung themselves upon the Scharnhorst. Twenty-six thousand tons tearing through a rough sea at thirty knots displace a prodigious amount of water. Even though in that gloomy twilight—9:30 A.M., and very little light creeping round the curve of the earth as yet—the glittering white bow wave flung up by the Scharnhorst could be seen even when her gray upper works were invisible. A gun was fired in the British squadron and a star shell traced a lovely curve of white light through the twilight before it burst fairly over the battle cruiser, lighting up her and the sea for a mile around her more brightly than any winter noontime in those latitudes. It hung in the sky like the Star of Bethlehem at another Christmas-tide as its parachute sustained it in the air seemingly without falling at all, and, as it hung, the cruisers' guns opened fire on the target.

The shells went screaming on their mission—long range for 6-inch, only medium range for 11-inch—and the spotting officer of the Norfolk, staring through his glasses, saw, just at that very second when the Norfolk's shells should land, a vivid green flash from the Scharnhorst's black hull. The Norfolk carried 8-inch guns—the other cruisers only 6-inch—and there was a chance—although not a very big one—that the Scharnhorst might be badly hurt.

The Scharnhorst spun about so rapidly that the next salvo fell harmlessly into the sea where she would have been had she maintained her course, and dashed out of the illuminated circle. When ships are six miles apart and traveling at a combined speed of sixty miles an hour touch is broken as quickly as it can be made. She vanished into the twilight.

Bey is dead now. We do not know, and very likely we never shall know, what were the motives that induced him to turn away. It is just possible that he was deterred by the sight of the three British cruisers flinging themselves upon him like a trio of wildcats—possible but hardly probable. It is not likely that a man could rise to admiral's rank in the Nazi navy if he were of the stuff that flinches. The hit that the Norfolk scored may have caused enough damage to force him to turn, but it takes time—several seconds, if not more—for details of damage to be ascertained and reported to the bridge, and it seems certain that the Scharnhorst turned away the moment she was hit.

Most likely, Bey was acting on a plan he had devised long beforehand. It was the convoy he was after. He did not want to fight ships of war and risk damage to his precious battleship unless circumstances compelled him to do so. If he stayed and fought it out with the three cruisers, there was a chance that the Scharnhorst might be hit and crippled; in another two minutes there would be eighteen torpedoes launched from the cruisers' decks and hurtling toward him, and any one of those might slow him up enough to incapacitate him. He thought the odds were not profitable in terms of the stake, and he withdrew.

He knew now where were the main defenses of the convoy, and he could guess with some accuracy where the merchant ships themselves were to be found. He could circle away, losing himself in the gloom, and then, turning back, he could make a fresh stab which ought to slip past the British guard.

Admiral Burnett was in command of the British cruiser force, with his flag flying on the Belfast. A sailor of vast experience, this was by no means the first convoy which he had escorted to Murmansk. But now he was presented with no mere problem of navigation or seamanship. No rule of thumb could be of the least assistance to him in this present situation. What he had to do was to guess what Bey would do next. Anybody could be quite certain that Bey's one aim was to get in among the merchant ships, but to guess where and when he would make his attack was something that was far more difficult to foresee.

A thirty-knot battleship tearing through the gloom could sweep in an hour all round the convoy at a distance which would make her safe from detection, even by the instruments which the British ships carried. It would take the Scharnhorst no more than five minutes to come in over the horizon within range of the merchant vessels and no more than five minutes after that, as has already been said, to wipe out a month's efforts by all the factories in the world. So there was no margin whatever for miscalculation on the part of the British; Burnett had to put himself in the path of the Scharnhorst's next attack, and that attack might come from north or east or west or south.

If it should come from the east when Burnett was in the west, the British cruisers might as well be in the Pacific for any protection they could give to the merchant ships. It was not a question of having to guess which of two possible courses Bey would adopt; it was a question of guessing which of some sixteen courses. Burnett had to guess within a very few degrees on what bearing Bey would reappear over the horizon, and he had to have his cruisers there. It was strictly his problem—a one-man decision. The staff at the Admiralty, reading off the scrappy wireless intercepts, might be able to offer him advice, but they could not relieve him of the responsibility. He

had a purely intellectual problem to solve as he stood on the crowded and exposed bridge, with the spray flying aft as the Belfast tore at top speed over the heaving sea.

He solved it. It was 9:30, the beginning of the winter day, when the Scharnhorst made her first contact with the cruisers from the southeast. At 12:30—high noon—the Scharnhorst reappeared from the northeast, to find Burnett and his cruisers right in her path. It was an extraordinary achievement on Burnett's part, seeing that the Scharnhorst could have appeared anywhere along the circumference of a circle of at least 100 miles; her speed, well over twice that of the convoy, gave her, of course, complete liberty of action. What Bey thought of this extraordinary apparition of three indomitable cruisers right in his path when by all the laws of chance they should have been twenty miles away can be guessed from his actions. There was a sudden flurry of salvos, during which a single shell landed and burst on the Norfolk's stern, and then Bey turned and ran for home.

It was dangerous for him to stay out longer. Three hours had elapsed since the British had first become aware that the Scharnhorst was out. It would take another hour or two, at least, of maneuvers if he were to make another attempt to strike at the convoy without fighting his way through, and the arguments against fighting his way through were as cogent now as they had been three hours earlier. He did not wish to risk being cut off from his base, and if he headed for home now, he had just sufficient time to reach his protecting fiord before next morning's daylight. He could not doubt that three hours ago, the moment Burnett first sighted him, hurried messages had been broadcast to the British Admiralty and to the main British fleet; nor could he doubt that the British were at this moment straining every nerve to send ships and aircraft to guard their precious convoy and to attack a ship as valuable as the Scharnhorst.

As a matter of fact, there was far more risk than he knew. One hundred and fifty miles to the southwest of him, and steaming fast to cut him off, was a force which could make scrap iron of his ship. This was the Duke of York with her attendant cruiser, the Jamaica, and her screen of four destroyers. From her masthead flew the St. George's cross of a full admiral—no less a person than Sir Bruce Fraser, commander in chief of the Home Fleet. Nobody outside a few favored persons knows how many times the patient Royal Navy had set that trap, how many times a battleship force had plodded along from England to Russia on a course parallel to, but well away from, that of the convoy, in the hope of intercepting any Nazi force sent out from Norway. Probably it had been done over and over again, and this was the first time that patience and resolution were to be rewarded.

Fraser, in the Duke of York, was about 200 miles away from the convoy when, at 9:30, came Burnett's first message of the appearance of the Scharnhorst. There would have been nothing gained, and the risk of much being lost, if he had been any nearer. The wary and elusive enemy had an advantage in speed of several knots. Fraser had to be sure of being able to interpose between the Scharnhorst and her base; any mere pursuit was doomed to failure before it started.

Not that there was any certainty about cutting the enemy off from his base. The sea is wide and the Arctic night can be intense. Unless Fraser was able to place himself squarely across the Scharnhorst's path, there was every chance that she would slip past him. Hence during that Sunday morning while Burnett was wondering where the Scharnhorst would reappear, Fraser was having to decide upon his own course of action. He sent his men to action stations, and at increased speed he and his cruiser and destroyers headed toward the strategical center of gravity—the nearest point of a straight line between the Scharnhorst's last known position and the German base.

In the British battleship, as in every other ship, the only men who moved from their posts during that day were those sent down to the galleys to fetch their comrades' dinners. It was a Sunday dinner—soup, pork chops and baked potatoes—and this the men ate at their posts, squatting on the heaving decks, jammed closely in turrets and shell rooms or swaying about in the gunnery-control towers 100 feet above the surface of the sea.

Dinner had hardly been eaten in these uncomfortable circumstances when the next flash of news came from Burnett; the Scharnhorst had made her second appearance, and Fraser now knew her exact position again. She was still 150 miles away, Fraser was nearer to her base than she was, but it was certain that contact would only be made—if it was made at all—in three or four hours' time, long after twilight had ceased.

It was time for Burnett to distinguish himself again. The Scharnhorst, after scoring her hit on the Norfolk, had headed south through the twilight. Burnett swung his ships to starboard in pursuit. It was of the utmost importance that Fraser should be kept informed of the Scharnhorst's course and position, so that he could place himself to meet her as she came down from the north. Burnett had to keep in touch with the Scharn-

horst, but to keep in touch with a ship that mounts nine 11-inch guns is more easily asked than done. Those 11-inch guns were capable of hitting a target clean over the horizon, farther than the eye could see, and it needed only one of those salvos, landing square, to smash any one of the frail cruisers into a sinking wreck.

During that anxious afternoon the listeners at the Admiralty took in message after message which told them of how Burnett was maintaining contact, and on their charts they could prick off the Scharnhorst's position as she came nearer to the safety of the Norwegian coast. They knew that somewhere in that neighborhood was the commander in chief, steering steadily eastward in grim wireless silence. So far, he had done nothing to reveal his position, for he knew perfectly well that a score of stations in Norway and Germany were eagerly taking in every message that passed over the ether, even if they were unable to decipher them. One whisper from the Duke of York's radio and the direction-finding stations would locate it instantly, and the transmitting stations would flash the news to the Scharnhorst of the presence of another British force—strength unknown, but obviously to be avoided—to the southward of him. But the Germans did not know Fraser was at sea; Bey did not know; and although Burnett and the Admiralty knew he was at sea, they did not know where he was. They could only hope.

Then all doubts were suddenly resolved in one glorious moment. The Duke of York broke her wireless silence, and the message which the Admiralty listeners took in was an order from Fraser to Burnett to "illuminate the enemy with star shell." Then they knew that Fraser's calculated position was very close to the position which Burnett was reporting for the Scharnhorst. The Duke of York's navigating officers had done a neat professional job. Counting every turn of their ship's propellers, making allowance for current and wind, they had fixed their own position accurately on the chart. At the same time they had deduced from Burnett's reports what was the Scharnhorst's course and what would be her present position. Burnett's navigators had been equally brilliant, for they could only report the Scharnhorst's position with reference to their own calculated position. It should be remembered that at Jutland in World War I, over distances not nearly so great, Jellicoe and Beatty miscalculated their relative positions with a total error of seven miles and serious results to Jellicoe's deployment. An error of seven miles in the present circumstances would give the Scharnhorst every chance of dashing by unharmed.

It was 4:30, quite dark, when Fraser broke wireless silence and the warning gong sounded in the Duke of York. The Scharnhorst was on his port bow, and the Belfast was eight miles astern of the Scharnhorst. Before the Scharnhorst's wireless telegraphists, having heard the Duke of York signaling, could have communicated to Bey on the bridge the appalling news of an enemy close ahead, the fifth act of the tragedy—played throughout in the dark, like Macbeth—had begun. A streak of white fire shot from one of the Belfast's guns and soared against the black sky, eight miles in twenty seconds. The shell burst high up, with a faint report unnoticeable in the blustery night, and then the tremendous white flare blazed out, sinking slowly under its supporting parachute and lighting up the scene over a two-mile radius.

Right in the center of that blaze of white light was the Scharnhorst, and the lookouts and spotters and gunnery officers in Fraser's force saw her upper works brightly lit, standing out boldly against the horizon. The rating at the director sight trained his instrument upon her; the 14-inch guns moved their thousands of tons of dead weight round in obedience to its dictation, and when the gunnery officer said "Open fire," five 14-inch guns roared out with the incredibly loud din of their kind and sent three and a half tons of shells—three and a half tons of hot steel and high explosive—at their mark. For a score of seconds the shells rumbled through the air; one of the destroyers in the Duke of York's screen under the arch of their trajectory heard them pass overhead like maddened express trains.

Then they landed, flinging up their 200-foot splashes under the unearthly illumination of the star shell. So closely had the range been estimated that this first salvo was registered as a "straddle," with some shells falling this side of the mark and some the other. And the next salvo, following less than half a minute later, recorded a hit. At least one shell, of three quarters of a ton weight, had struck home on the Scharnhorst, so that there were Germans on board who were killed without even knowing of the sudden dramatic appearance of a British battleship on the Scharnhorst's starboard bow.

Chance dictated that she should be struck without being disabled. Half a minute elapsed between the moment when the Duke of York was illuminated by the blaze of fire from her gun muzzles and the moment when the Scharnhorst staggered under the titanic blow of the striking shell; that half minute was long enough for Bey to grasp the implications of those gun flashes on the horizon and to give the order which spun the Scharnhorst's wheel hard aport and sent her wildly seeking safety in the eastward darkness.

The Scharnhorst sped eastward with every revolution her engineers could wring from her turbines, and after her came the British ships. There was still hope, for Bey knew he had an advantage of several knots in speed over any British battleship. In two hours' flight he could be out of range, and in darkness and at those colossal speeds there was nothing fantastic in hoping that his ship would avoid fatal injury for that time—to say nothing of the fact that his own fire might disable his enemy first. He turned his stern square to his pursuer, thereby at the same time presenting the smallest possible target and making the best use of his difference of speed, and he trained aft those of his guns that would bear, fired a star shell, and began a methodical return fire upon the Duke of York.

His hope of hitting the Duke of York on her water line or in her engines, and thereby slowing her down, came to nothing, but one of his shells scored a hit which might have proved equally important. Fragments struck the mast, and one of them cut away the wireless aerial. By that stroke the commander in chief of the Home Fleet was sundered from communication with the rest of the world and was rendered unable either to coordinate the action of the four cruisers and the four destroyers under his command or to report his position and progress. Had the Duke of York remained unable to give orders to the destroyers, the Scharnhorst might possibly have survived. But Lt. H. R. J. Bates effected a temporary repair in the quickest possible way. He climbed the mast —in the dark, with the wind whipping round him and the ship lurching fantastically over the waves —and he held the ends of the aerial together for the orders to pass. Eleven-inch shells were being fired at the ship while he did so, and the splashes from near misses rose to his level.

The Scharnhorst survived the broadsides of the Duke of York for more than an hour, and although she was hit and hit again, she was not wounded sufficiently to make any immediate difference to her speed. The time interval had been long enough for her to increase her distance from the Duke of York by at least five miles, and before half past six she was out of range, battered, on fire, but safe from the Duke of York for the moment. But hardly had the exasperated gunnery officer in the Duke of York given the word to cease fire when a new blaze of gunfire lit the horizon far ahead where the Scharnhorst had last been seen. She was having to defend herself against new enemies.

The four destroyers of the Duke of York's

screen, Savage, Saumarez, Scorpion and Stord— the last a vessel of the Norwegian navy—found themselves, when the action began between the two battleships, ahead of the Duke of York and astern of the Scharnhorst. Their superiority of speed enabled them to head-reach upon the Scharnhorst even while the Scharnhorst was drawing away from the Duke of York. The Savage and Saumarez overhauled her on the starboard side, the Scorpion and Stord on her port side. In that hour and a half they were able to sweep right round her and then dash in, two on either bow— torpedo attacks, to be effective, must be launched from ahead of the target.

The attacks were made in the nick of time, just as the Scharnhorst escaped from the battle-ship's guns. The Scharnhorst saw them and opened fire with all the innumerable guns of her secondary battery, but destroyers charging in at forty knots from opposite sides are hard to stop. Moreover, she had been hard hit by half a dozen heavy shells, with the almost certain result of damage to her guns and system of communications.

It seems that at this very moment her speed suddenly fell to twenty knots as the result of injuries inflicted on her by the Duke of York's guns; at a guess, a condenser had been damaged and a boiler eventually put out of action by the entrance of salt water. From a spectacular point of view, her defense was dramatic enough. She was one vast glow from the orange-red flames of her guns, and from this central nucleus radiated the innumerable streaks of tracer shells— tracers that she was firing at the destroyers and tracers which every ship arriving in range fired back at her.

Yet her fire was singularly ineffective. Only the Saumarez was hit, and although the damage to the destroyer's upper works resulted in regrettable casualties, her fighting value was not greatly impaired. The destroyers pressed home their attack to the uttermost limit. They did not loose their torpedoes at the 10,000-yard range which is the torpedo's maximum, nor at the 6000 yards which experience has sometimes shown to be the nearest a destroyer can hope to approach a well-defended capital ship. They pressed in to 2000 yards and less, launched their torpedoes, and then, with their wheels hard over, sheered away from the doomed battleship.

Several of the torpedoes—how many there is no means of knowing—struck home, but the battle flared up with even greater violence. One singular advantage which the German navy has always possessed was clearly demonstrated at this crisis. As the weaker naval power, she has never

had to design her ships for ability to keep the sea for long periods of time; swift and sudden blows were all she expected of them, with the result that habitability is not considered a necessity. They can lie in harbor with their crews on shore in barracks most of the time, so that they can be compartmented in a fashion impossible to British or American ships. The Scharnhorst survived these several underwater blows and maintained a tremendous volume of fire, comparatively ill-directed but impressive.

With the Scharnhorst falling off in speed, the Duke of York came up in range again, and the 14-inch guns began to smash her to pieces. At the same time every British ship closed in and opened fire. The Duke of York's attendant cruiser, Jamaica, which had been firing intermittently during the whole easterly run, drew up on one side of her to use her 6-inch guns at point-blank range. Burnett and his three cruisers pressed in on the other, and the wretched ship, unable any longer to keep her fires under control, blazed out in a sudden volcano of flame even while she maintained her return fire, dropping several shells close to the Duke of York.

Nor were these her only assailants, for there now arrived on the scene four more destroyers, part of the convoy escort, who, having made sure that no other enemy was likely to attack their charges, came dashing down with proper military instinct to where the battle was taking place. There was danger of effort being wasted by all this concentration of force. It is impossible for gunfire to be properly directed when several ships are firing on one target in unco-ordinated fashion. In the pitch darkness no fewer than eight destroyers, four cruisers and a battleship were tearing about at their highest speed round the Scharnhorst. Torpedoes were being launched and guns were being fired by eager captains anxious to be in at the kill. British fighting blood was aflame. Hotheads might be carried away by their own enthusiasm, and it was time for the master hand to take control again. The signal sent out by the commander in chief can be given in its entirety because, owing to the urgency of the occasion, it was in plain English, so publication gives the Nazis no chance of breaking the British code.

The message was perfectly calm and methodical, betraying no sign of the excitement of the moment. "Clear the area of the target," it said, "except for those ships with torpedoes and one destroyer with searchlight." It was like the bugles blowing for the death at a bullfight. The arena was cleared as the ships obeyed orders and sheered away. One destroyer trained her search-lights on the wreck—long, long pencils of intense white light reaching for miles through the darkness—and the Jamaica came in like a matador for the kill. She swung round and a salvo of torpedoes leaped from her deck and began their fifty-mile-an-hour run toward the target. At that very moment a great billow of smoke eddied out from the Scharnhorst's sides and hid her, but the Jamaica put her helm over and sent another salvo of torpedoes hurrying after the first.

With the tremendous explosions when they hit the mark, the smoke cleared away, and the Scharnhorst was revealed for the last time, on her side, with her bottom exposed, and yet with the flames of her ammunition fires still spouting from her. Then the smoke closed round her again and she went to the bottom, while the British cruisers raced in to try to pick up survivors. There is on record the comment made by one of the British sailors who went into that smoke, but it is not well to repeat it. More than 1000 men had burnt in those flames.

It is hard to criticize the Nazi tactics or the Nazi strategy. The Scharnhorst came out and was destroyed, yet if she had stayed at home the naval historian of the future would have condemned the Nazi High Command for her inactivity. She refused to face Burnett's wildcat attack at the opening of the day, although we know now that nothing worse could have happened to her than actually did happen, and she hardly could have inflicted less damage than she actually did inflict. If she had fought Burnett she might have been disabled and sent to the bottom, leaving us to comment that a more cautious commander would have withdrawn, as soon as he was discovered, and got clean away.

Yet in the months to come, the Nazi sailor who is ordered out will remember the Spee and the Bismarck and the Scharnhorst, and will go with a reluctance that will not increase his efficiency. And the Japanese, on the other side of the world, must have heard of the loss of the Scharnhorst with dismay, for it meant that at least one more British battleship was freed to make the voyage east and add to the pressure of seapower that will slowly constrict Japan to her death.

THE IMMORTAL HARPY

by Hobert Douglas Skidmore

NO SHORT STORY of World War II made a deeper impression on the *Post*'s editors than this haunting tale of an American bomber crew who refused to be shot down. The author was born April 11, 1909, at Webster Springs, West Virginia, and attended the University of Michigan, where he and his twin brother Hubert both won Avery Hopwood Awards for creative writing. When the war came he was working for Twentieth Century-Fox; he enlisted and served as a combat correspondent with the Air Force in the Pacific area. He has lived and written in New York City, Elmira, New Orleans, Yucatan, Vancouver, San Francisco and the San Juan Islands.

JULY 8, 1944

THE runway spun beneath the Harpy and she pulled up from it like a thing that must leave the earth. She ate the air and blew it back across her body. The runway held its drab color up to her fuselage, then fell away, colorless and spent. The propellers ate on, sucking in the air, and she was free and air-borne.

They passed over the predawn dimness of the hangar and saw the fellows waving to them. Inside the Harpy, there was a slow, grinding noise as the landing gear retracted. Her pilot, Capt. Jerry Lawler, let her ride, gaining height. The ridge dropped from sight beneath them, and nothing lay ahead but the Pacific and the clouds that came down and seemed to melt into it.

Jerry looked across at his copilot, Watts, and grinned, winking. It was an expression of mutual knowledge, a recognition of each other and what must be shared.

"I'll hold her up for a while," Watts suggested.

"Okay, I'll go back and beat the breeze," Jerry said.

"Good deal," Watts grinned, and a moment later he had the ship in his hands alone for the first time.

"At-a-girl, take her easy," he mumbled. Already he felt a trembling begin at his spine and move toward his shoulders. It moved down his arms, and he clenched his hands furiously, forcing the feeling to stop. Now, slicing through illimitable space, the feeling quieted in his arms, and for a moment the Harpy, like a proud horse, seemed to accept his mastery of her. She rode free and easy, racing down the sky. He had come to her with no family, but she together with Jerry, and the rest of her brood, was his family now.

In his high, transparent plastic roost, Sgt. Walter Kazmierczak, gunner, saw light coming over the rim of the world. The same light that had hours earlier covered his home, his girl, his place of life. He thought of the moving sun rays as being the light that had come down Walnut Street in Elmira, New York. *It had gone around the world to find Ginnie,* he thought, *and I wish to heaven I was there with her.* But he wasn't there. He was here on the Harpy, with those who served her. With Pon and Chief and Mike Sheren and the others wakened before the light by Jerry, who had called, "Get out of your sacks. I got something you guys'll be glad to hear. This is our big day. We hit them late this afternoon. Tomorrow morning, the marines and the infantry land."

The Harpy was pulling a little heavy, but she was hauling a terrific load. Her gas weighed on her, waiting to feed her, and the huge bombs in her racks made her stomach heavy. But she was on her way, and she seemed to know it. The Harpy wouldn't have it any other way, her radioman, Sgt. Mike Sheren, told himself, not any more than he would. The unstopping roar of the Harpy's engines became a thing so familiar you didn't hear them, he decided. Then, after your thoughts had been away from her, oh, thousands of miles distant, and you laid off remembering other things and let your mind come back to her, you were conscious of their roar again.

Mike had been on missions before. He had gone to Munda and down to Rendova and to Tarawa and to scores of little atolls left burning and popping like magnesium dropped into the Pacific. After one such mission he remembered buying a half dozen native handkerchiefs at a native store. He had printed "Mrs. Ida Sheren" in large, crooked letters, adding the street and town. *Mom's going to be surprised,* he thought, as he carried the package to the mail window. Afterward, he had looked at three P-40's running along the rim of the mountain, riding the air currents.

That's where he wanted to be, he knew—up there in the sky where things became clear and apparent. It was then that he felt that he stood at the beginning of a passageway which led to some kind of a world, somehow known, but unseen. He had noticed that there was a strong camaraderie among the infantry—a physical thing, something that came from hand-to-hand combat, from seeing men die on the ground beside you. It wasn't like that with him, Mike knew. The old Harpy carried her full crew, but it was only a handful of men; men who fought and lived inside the Harpy's warm fuselage. There was something that happened up here where he was, in the quiet, silent places where death waited, but he could not be sure what it was. He knew only the limitless ranges that fanned upward from the earth, and they had given him a curious feeling of expectancy.

Sometimes, on leave, when he felt that way, he said, "Let's get stinkin'," and Pon—Tech. Sgt. Chester Poniatowski—would say, "You ain't just whistling, bud. Let's." But when the time came for the pouring of the musty, slightly bitter beer down their gullets, Pon would be on the ground in front of the Harpy or under her, looking up at her belly. They seemed to be standing guard over each other—Pon and the Harpy; even when they weren't on the ground any more, but were drumming above it, it seemed that way.

The Harpy was box-shaped and unappealing while she was inert, but once she felt the air against her wings, she seemed to change. She was graceful and proud, and flew with assurance, for she had been to battle before, and she went to it calmly again. There was something about the Harpy up here in the element she had been born to live in that made her more than a battling old bag of bolts. The Harpy had a spirit about her that could not be assailed even by death. Pon loved her and sensed the immense power that rested within her. He liked to go back and forth inside the ship, touching her and taking care of her.

Even with all the others locked with him in flight above the Pacific, he felt alone with her; the others shut out and away from his communion with the Harpy. He felt alone with her the way he used to be alone with his car in a garage full of people. Below him, the water danced in the plane's movements. As the air hit the Harpy, the whitecaps rose and fell. *This is the best life in the world,* he told himself. There was no feeling like it. He wondered proudly what those doubters, who had always seemed amazed that he had been able to make the old jalopy run, would think now, if they could see the Harpy with the miles slipping through under her stomach, across her fuselage and into the unposted spaces behind them.

Standing on her catwalk, he let his eyes take inventory of the way the neat wires ran down her inner walls, the thousands of mechanical parts of her, her guns, the slick bomb racks. He knew that it was silly, but often when he was alone with her he sensed that she was grateful to him. It was something he imagined, he knew, but he had worked with engines all his life and he knew how they reacted—an engine was a thing you could depend on. If you were faithful to them, they would be faithful to you and would run forever. The Harpy hit a shallow bump and bobbed a little beneath him, and he thought, *If we treat her right, she'll stay up here, clean and switchin' her tail at death after we're gone.*

The hours went easily. All the crew checked the instruments of their particular function and looked occasionally at the restless blue surface beneath them. They felt a sense of freedom, being away from the earth and the things it held, and yet, more strongly than at any other time, they felt a part of a group.

By afternoon, Pon, like most of the others, had removed his shirt and trousers, and in his shorts he rode the Harpy down to the left of the dropping sun. Idly, he let his gaze rest on the coppery back of Sgt. "Chief" Washington, the Harpy's armament man. Only "coppery" wasn't quite the right description, Pon thought. Chief's skin, that rippled over long muscles, seemed to be made of thick cream and the cream diluted the dusty reddish hue. His cap was turned sideways on his black hair, and the long, square-brim visor stuck up above his right ear like a feather worn by one of his ancestors.

Then out of a tumbling mountain of cloud two P-40's came in, one at a time, and roared down the sky to meet the Harpy, like workmen gathering along the road. Those on the Harpy watched them, knowing they had a date together down over the horizon, and that it was going to be an important one.

Where they were there were no markers for time or space, but they met as easily as if they had traveled this way a thousand times. His people had the same gift, Chief thought. A waste of land, hard shadowed under a molten sun, rolled into infinity with the heat wavering up from it, and strangers to it were lost and their bones were bleached white by that sun because they could not read it and it was a place foreign to them. Yet to those who were at home in the vast, brown, crawling hills, there were signposts innumerable pointing the way.

The hours passed with only the roar of the Harpy's engines to mark their going. Jerry Lawler, back at the controls, called to the Harpy's crew over the intercom, telling them to settle down. The ship was pulling easier, now that the greedy engines had drained some of her weight of gas from her. She moved steadily, not lagging or impatient, and the sureness and calmness of her journey spilled out from her and into his arms and hands, up through his body.

In the Harpy's tail, Norry—Sgt. Frank Norris —idly rolled the .50-calibers back and forth, aiming indistinctly at the sky in mock battle. When he dreamed, he dreamed about being again at school, and about the graduation dance and the way Edith had looked in her first formal—the broad, pretty stripes that ran around the full skirt of her dress, the clean, suddenly mature look of her face. He had taken her home at midnight, and they had said good night very quietly and seriously. The things they had said to each other seemed to have new value then.

Not that he had much time for dreaming. The need for knowing the Harpy in all her moods, of doing a job for her, and doing it as naturally as breathing, possessed all of them on trips along the ship's catwalk. He looked at Lt. George Kristenson bent over the navigator's table. Krist kept his hair cut short, hardly an inch long, for he hated to have it falling over his face. No navigator in the Pacific could bring a ship down on a pin-point atoll with the cool assurance that Krist had. When he said coolly, "You can take her down now," Norry and the others knew that it was as sure as driving down from the ramp of a towering bridge; the runway would be there. When he marked the spreading terror of a hurricane, his voice became emotional, and he sounded like the voice of the storm itself. Jerry called him "Old Elements," though he was only twenty-two.

The names of winds held poetry for Krist: monsoons, squalls and typhoons, tropical hurricanes and all the storms of the temperate zones. They fascinated him just as the texture and the feel of each piece of his .50-caliber fascinated Johnny Curtin. Johnny knew every inch of her. But though he had more than two hundred combat hours as a waist gunner, he was still uncertain as to what it was that caused him to be here on the Heartless Harpy. Life had been on the sweet side: a good job, plenty of money and women, and if the boss got too cranky, he could tell him to go blow it. And then one afternoon the radio music had stopped, and into the quiet, sunny peacefulness a voice had come, clear and sharp. Hitler was marching his men through the shadow of the Eiffel Tower. *I'll join up tomorrow,* he told himself, and even yet he didn't know why.

The sun came in through the huge bubble of the nose turret and made a brave nimbus of Bombardier Lt. Frank Story's mustache. There was a shine to the day that reminded him of the mornings when he and Elsa hurried down Fifth Avenue in time to see the morning light come down through the stained-glass windows of the cathedral. He and Elsa always walked from the church exalted and proud of being alive. Looking down, he watched the backward-moving, foamy white-caps, wondering if Elsa still went to the cathedral. He wanted to think that she did and that she was happy. It was the only vow they had made to each other. They had said, "Keep yourself happy. Keep yourself happy, now, of all times." He was happy, now, knowing their target, its installations, its fighter protection, just as the others of the Harpy's family did. Only their happiness was serious and thoughtful, for they knew the enemy would give it up only when he no longer existed. But the target had to be blasted out. It stood as protection to one of the arteries to the heart of the enemy, and when men talked of it they were grave and their voices were quiet.

The Harpy was flying the No. 1 position. Behind her, two Liberators rode smoothly above the soft carpet of clouds. Mike watched them in their easy flight. Even in his heavy suit, his body felt light and free, and there was only the strong determination in his mind to remain alert. He passed his eyes around and around the uncharted spaces. He remembered the days he had gone on past the people shoving and hurrying along the streets, and for all of them he felt a quiet pity. There was no way of telling them how a man felt when his vision buried itself in the milky distance. He and the others knew a solitary communion here that made all the other things that filled a man's life trivial and transient. Often, riding through the great shafts of light that broke upward through the sky, he felt as if he had glimpsed some part of another world, a place luminously beautiful. It had taken all fear out of him, and on a morning like this he felt that he knew what to expect when the inevitable arrived.

Beneath him, Krist bent over his charts. He knew that if a line had been drawn across the skies, he could show that they were not a yard off their course. He checked his charts again, but they had ridden these skies for so many endless hours and days that he knew the figures, the latitudes and longitudes, the stars and planets, as if they were markers on some insubstantial highway.

He snapped the intercom. "We should be there in thirty-two minutes," he said.

"Okay, Elements," Jerry answered. . . . "Keep your eyes open, fellows. They'll be coming up soon."

Krist returned to his charts. It made little difference to him what happened outside the ship. That was not his job. He was to guide her there and guide her back. Almost irritably, he shoved his charts aside and placed a sheet of white paper before him. He thought he'd scribble a note, but he couldn't think of anyone to whom he wanted to write. It had been like this all his life, he knew. The things that made other people happy or miserable seemed always to leave him unmoved. As a child, he remembered, he had watched the other children playing, and wanting tearfully to join them, but he had no capacity for laughter and play. He often wondered if death would disturb him, but after deliberate consideration he could not tell himself that it would.

Down in the nose, Story decided it would be safe to finish a chapter before he laid his book aside. It was a frightening plot, and he read quickly, wanting to trap the murderer before the fighters came in on them. He checked the two .30-calibers again, glanced at his bomb sight and then returned to the mystery novel.

Chief's brown eyes moved across the far distances, glanced upward and then looked down to the side. Nothing coming yet. There was a curious lightness about him, similar to fever, but he knew he wasn't ill. It was only the awful weariness, the fatigue that ached in bones and settled stiffly in muscles.

"Lower the turret, Walt," Jerry called over the intercom.

"Right. Going down," Walt answered. A moment later, he slipped into it and began checking his guns, his ammunition, his range mechanism, his gun sight, switches, buttons and pedals. It worked as fluently as a ball twisting and turning in water. He remembered the day the mechanisms hadn't worked and the resentment that he had felt. In the days and nights that followed, he had learned that the war isn't an individual; it isn't one mechanism. It is the total of all men and their willingness to die for the things they believe. He had become a part of it now, he knew, and it was larger than any emotion he had known he could feel.

"Comin' in at five o'clock!" Norry shouted. "Four of them! Five o'clock! Three Zekes and a Rufe!"

The words, sharp and loud, ran through the intercom system, jarring the men as if their own nerves had been touched. It would be a long run. It was at least twenty minutes in to the target, and they would have the fighters on them all the way.

Walt swung his turret around and down, so he faced as if he were falling from some high precipice. As he started to turn, a Jap fighter and another and another broke through the clouds directly beneath them, climbing as if they had been fired from some gigantic gun. "Three at six o'clock! Comin' up at six o'clock!"

"Send them around here!" Chief shouted back, laughing.

The men tensed, waiting. The Harpy rode on her course, oblivious of the planes that attacked from below and to the rear, where they hoped to be protected by the upright rudders.

Walt held his fire, and then, as the spurts of fire began to break from the fighters' wings, he opened up. His guns rattled and the tracers went to the left and ahead of the lead ship. Slowly, he moved back on it, but as his fire closed, the fighter flipped over on its wing and drove off to the left. "Comin' over at eight! Get her, Johnny!" he shouted, and pulled his fire back on the other ships.

They separated, one driving downward beneath the clouds, and the other making a wide turn to the right and pulling in just ahead of the fighters that drove in from the rear.

Norry let them have a burst. John swung his guns across and back, but they did not peel off.

It was then that the first bullet ripped up through the Harpy, tearing a small hole in the floor near Pon's foot. He heard the sound of the bullet rattling through the fuselage, and swore quietly. He wanted Jerry to roll slowly to the right, so he could get a shot at the plane which had sent the first bullet into the Harpy.

Now the two other belly-turret gunners opened up in the ships behind them, and the planes rolled away, headed for the protection of the cloud bank.

"Comin' in at two!" Chief yelled. "Three of them! Two o'clock!"

He caught the closer one in his sight and held it there. He waited, tense and ready, and then he let his fire go, raising it a little, pulling it down again, catching the fighter dead center. Suddenly, flames leaped up from it, but it did not falter or change its course. He gave it another burst, and now suddenly, flaming and smoking, it seemed to be on them.

"My God, there's a war goin' on out here!" Story shouted, and grabbed the gun beside him, giving the second plane a long burst. It peeled off to the left.

But it didn't seem to make any difference; it was too late now. The flaming ship did not seem more than fifty feet away.

In the cockpit, Jerry and Watts suddenly threw all their weight on the controls. They acted together, without speaking, and the giant Harpy flipped up her right wing as she turned her nose to the left.

Involuntarily, Walt flung his arms over his eyes as the ship passed beside him. He could see the pilot shoving hard to get himself free of the ship. He could see the straps of the parachute, even the dials that showed through the puffs of smoke.

The third fighter saw his chance and made for it. In turning to avoid the flaming ship, the Harpy exposed her belly. He turned on her and opened all his guns. Walt saw the tracers as if they were lines running from his eyes. He shoved his foot down, swung his guns and his turret. He couldn't miss now, for the thing was almost on top of him. It was running a seam of holes down the Harpy's stomach. He gave the Zero everything he had, and held it on the plane until suddenly it seemed to explode in the air. What had been a plane was wreckage and bundles of flame falling down through the skies toward the ocean below.

Pon did not know he had been hurt until the Harpy righted herself, and he threw his weight back on his right foot. It crumpled beneath him, and then he felt the warm fluid draining into his soft leather boot. There was only the warmness, though, and no pain, so he raised his eyes and looked along the bottom of the Harpy. A series of holes, evenly spaced and whistling with the air that tore through them, ran up toward the bomb-bay doors.

Thank God, he thought, *they missed the auxiliary gas tanks.*

"Take her down," Krist said quietly. "Target three minutes ahead. Take her down."

"Get ready for anything!" Jerry called. He waited a moment to see if the Harpy responded. Her giant nose slowly lowered, and she rode down easily and surely. "They're going to throw all they've got at us!"

Only Norry did not hear him. He had ripped the phones from his ears and was trying to force his hands inside his flying suit. Something had ricocheted against the side of the Harpy. It had come down through his left shoulder, and now his fingers found the fragment. It was lying inside his shirt, halfway between his shoulder bone and his heart. He pulled it out and looked at it, though

his fingers were already freezing from the cold air. He let the shrapnel rest in his hands, holding his body backward from the handles of his guns, and he smiled slightly. The rest he had wanted was coming now. It was slipping up his legs and arms and gathering in his stomach. He thought that the next time he wrote home he'd tell mom and dad how the rest had come, and then he decided to let his head fall forward, so he could sleep easier. But as he moved, the Harpy dropped her nose downward, her giant tail pointed upward in the sky, and he looked into the clear whiteness above. It seemed that he could touch it, if only he didn't want to rest so badly. It seemed that he could reach out and touch everything that was in the heavens, only he wanted to rest.

As the Harpy came down through the clouds, the target lay ahead and to the north. Story looked quickly along the palms which fringed the beach, remembering the photographs he had studied so often. That was the ammunition dump ahead, where the low sheds huddled beneath the palms. That was where he was going to lay them. There was an immense dark cloud above the enemy base. It would make fine cover to head into as soon as they dumped the eggs. He moved his eyes back and across, wondering what had happened to the formation which had gone in ahead of them. And then he saw what it was. The dark cloud was ack-ack smoke. It was so heavy it looked as if you could walk on it. "They're sure sending it up," he said softly. The whispered words ran back through the intercom, back through the Harpy, and ended in Norry's insensible ears.

Watts reached over and grabbed Jerry by the arm pointing down and to the right with his free hand. They were doing better than a hundred and fifty, and Jerry leaned forward, looking out toward the sea. The lagoon seemed to rush toward him. But his eyes caught and held. The enemy was moving in innumerable reinforcements for the attack. They were unloading men and equipment.

"Look at those ducks!" he yelled. "Look at them!"

In the belly turret, Walt swung his gun around to five o'clock. He had to see the ships. They were unloading crack troops, men trained to fight on the atolls, indoctrinated with a love of death. They would be waiting tomorrow to attack the American marines and infantrymen as they piled out of the landing barges and raced across the reef and up the beach. He knew what would happen to the men as the doors of the LCI's dropped down. The men would have to hit the water running. They would hit shoulder deep, trying to hold their rifles above their heads. The treacherous, uneven coral would make progress slow and unsteady, holding the men like slowly trudging targets.

In those awful moments, the hundreds of enemy soldiers, fresh and fanatic, would open up on them. Unable to move back, with a rain of fire rippling the water before them, the men would be trapped. They would die there, fixed by the water.

"Let's get them, Jerry!" Story shouted. "Let me pick them off!"

For a moment, Jerry hesitated. All his training, his knowledge, the long months of his flying, told him that he had to stick to the planned attack. The objectives must be hit. That was the only way it worked.

"Stick to your targets!" he ordered.

"They'll wipe them out tomorrow, Jerry! There are thousands of them!"

Jerry looked down and he knew he could not keep the realization away for long. The water below him held victory or failure. All the weeks of raids, of planning and training, would be lost. The stroke that would break the enemy's lines in the South Pacific would be turned back, snapped and buried in the blue water. Even the Harpy seemed to see her destined glory, but he righted in his seat and pulled her back on her course.

"Comin' in at one o'clock!" Mike yelled. "Like a bat out of hell, at one o'clock!"

Suddenly, the intercom was shrieking wildly. Chief and Mike and Johnny all saw them. Three of them were coming down as if they were rushing at the peaked end of lightning. Mike held his fire until they closed to eight hundred and then he gave them a long burst.

There was nothing to do but wait, John knew. If they peeled off on his side, he would get a crack at them. It was less than the shaving of a second, but he waited impatiently. His eye was ringed by the familiar sight, the stubby grips in his hands, his thumbs extended and ready. This was the one moment in which he felt no urge to be elsewhere. He felt as if suddenly a picture of himself had been brought into focus; this was him.

The Zekes screamed, pulling up. Mike gave them another burst. It was so close he could see the slugs hit the cowling as if he were throwing stones against it.

"Coming over, Pon!" he yelled.

Pon hobbled a little to the rear of his slot, swung his gun, and as the smoking ship pulled up beyond the Harpy, stalling in her climb, he let his fire go. The Zeke seemed to hang there for a moment as if the bullets had pinned it to the sky. Then it slid down and spilled over into a flaming descent.

Mike never saw the two others. Abruptly, the Harpy leaped sidewise, fell downward. It seemed to have been struck by a tremendous hammer. He heard the shattering rip of metal, the rain-spattering sound of the small shrapnel, and as he hit the floor by the radio cabinet, the Harpy caught heavily in the air. He could feel the jarring halt. As he straightened, Krist tumbled onto the same spot where he had fallen. He just lay there clutching his chest with one hand and ripping the oxygen mask from his face with the other. Mike straightened him out, shoved the mask back on his face and jumped up to his gun again.

Krist could feel the oxygen running along his nose and down into his lungs. It was a pleasant and cooling sensation, but he dismissed it as temporary. He wished he had his glasses on. Perhaps he could see better, he thought, but he dismissed that too. It wasn't important. It was the terrible storm going on outside that was important. He wanted to get to his feet, grab up his charts and see where he had made his mistake. Somewhere he had miscalculated, he told himself.

He brought his hands up, placing them on the floor at either side of his head, thinking he could push himself to his feet. He felt a deep revulsion growing in his stunned entrails. It swept upward, as if he would disgorge everything inside himself, but the nauseous wave passed into his head, clarifying it, and in that moment he felt a great release. Recognition grew slowly in his mind, and it left his tattered body trembling. *I hate them,* he said silently. *I hate them. I have always hated them. I have hated them as long as I can remember, and it has made me fight.* There had been this hatred in him, and it had kept him bent incessantly over his charts. The Harpy had never once been off her course. He had taken her to the enemy and brought her back, and he had never failed.

The Harpy was still rocking violently. It seemed to Mike that it took him forever to get his intercom working again. And all the time he was working with it, he kept repeating, *No, not yet not yet.*

Story bent slowly over his bomb sight. The ack-ack was coming up so thick that the trees and shacks were becoming indistinct. *I'll put it right in their lap,* he thought. He began yelling for Jerry to pull her over.

Walt pulled his turret up. The stuff was spraying around him like hail hurled upward. He wanted to get his face up. *This might be it. It has to come sometime, and this might be it,* he kept telling himself, *but I don't want to get it in the face. I don't want it in the face.*

Pon swung his waist gun around. The fighters were gone. They were taking cover down toward five o'clock. He swung his gun forward, and then he saw it. The outside engine was on fire.

"Jerry! Number Four's on fire! It's on fire!" he yelled.

Jerry opened the extinguisher and, at the same time, he turned the Harpy over to Story. "She's yours, Story!"

A moment later, Pon yelled, "She's out! She's out!" he repeated softly, and the words held a quiet terror. The engine was dead.

John threw the mask from his face. They were getting down now. An eager, violent anger shook him, as if it had been long awaited. His anger did not spring from the terrible fire that exploded upward, the horrible cracking of the air. It was something deeper and stronger and more impersonal. Looking downward, it seemed that the roads of Ohio should be running there. All his life he had known the open, wide roads and searched them. He had smelled their tar and cement and sand and clay, the white schoolhouses and the whiter churches. He had asked for rides and given them. There was no freedom in the world like the freedom of America and her roads. It seemed that it would be drowned beneath him, and he screamed in bitter challenge. He screamed again and again, as if, when eternity quieted all things, the sound of his outraged voice would still be heard.

Jerry waited. He was helplessly overcome by a desire to strike something with all his might. He knew he was cool. He knew everything that was happening. He had to make the decision in a moment. In just one second more it had to be made. *We can't warn the convoy,* he thought. *It's too late. They don't keep up contact. They can't. They'd give themselves away. Tomorrow morning they are coming in, and they will be slaughtered. They'll be drained of blood in the beguiling water. They should be climbing the beach, crossing the island, clearing it, grasping victory quickly. But they won't. Not if the Harpy returns home.*

"Story, save half of them!" he called sharply. "We'll get those boats!"

He leaned forward, his nerves as alert as if they were held on the blade of a shining scalpel. He felt no need to hurry, to force the ship. She was moving to her goal.

Story leaned forward, his fingers cool and flex-

ible. He adjusted the sight as carefully as a musician adjusts his instrument. The Harpy pulled heavily. Her dead engine weighed on her wing. *Come on, girlie,* he begged. *Come on, Harpy.*

They were racing up the edge of the beach now. The fire was bursting below him as if he held his face in the mouth of a volcano. They were just a little to the left. He moved her slowly, his head cocked as a violinist listens to his tuning.

"Bomb bays open!"

Now, come along, girlie; come along to the Darktown Strutters' Ball. The rhythm was wonderful in his mind and fingers, marking the time as the earth rushed beneath them, rushed backward, drawing the target into his sight.

"Bombs away!"

Jerry and Watts grabbed the Harpy. The ships were anchored about three miles down the reef, and along every inch of the lagoon ack-ack shoved upward.

"Norry! . . . John! Keep your eyes open!"

"Right!" John shouted, and waited for Norry's voice. It did not come.

"Norry, Norry!" he called, and then he slipped his intercom loose and flung himself back through the ship. It smelled hot, like a radiator without water in it, and oily. He put his hand against the side next to the life raft, and the jagged holes gouged his fingers.

Ahead of him, he saw Norry slumped in his seat. He crawled to him, calling, "Norry, Norry, did they get you?" and then his voice trailed off. Norry sat there, quietly erect, a piece of enemy shrapnel in his hand. John lifted him out of the turret and carried him deeper into the ship.

Krist was the only one who could handle Norry's gun now. John hurried forward. The air rushed up through the open bomb bays, tearing at his clothing, and below him, on either side of the narrow catwalk, he saw the land moving dimly beneath the dark erupting smoke. Blood was running down Krist's face and across the front of his dislodged mask.

Krist opened his eyes slightly, as if he had never opened them wider. "John, drive them into the water. Blow them up," he whispered hoarsely, and his eyes closed.

John raised himself slowly, looking down at Krist. There was something unstrained and happy in the face. The whole face was gentle and sensitive now.

Turning, he started the trip back across the bomb bay. He walked almost slowly. That was it. He had almost known it all the time. He had known it since that afternoon on the road in Ohio. They had forgotten what America meant, and those who became alert quickest, fought quickest, sacrificed readily. It was as simple and right and inevitable as that, he realized.

Pon grabbed him as he walked by, shaking him. "Take the tail!" Pon shouted. "I'll handle these!" He nodded at the two waist guns, and then shouted into the intercom, "Jerry, Norry is gone! Norry is out!"

Jerry did not answer. He was pushing with all his weight and all his might at some terrible burning thing that caught in his stomach. He forced his weight down on his feet until his body shoved itself against the safety straps, and then suddenly the release came and he fell back. It felt good and clean, as if he had been plunged into cool water. The air rushing through the splintered plastic felt wonderful, only it was smoky. They were going out over the water. *I must be tired,* he thought. *Sleepy.* It was smoky and cool, like an autumn night, like the one when he had met Betts, and he was sleepy, deeply and gratefully sleepy, for the release was coming now.

Watts did not have time to more than glance at him. The target was out in front; two heavy barriers, crowded and threatening. They alone held meaning, and the Harpy descended on them as if she barely needed his guidance.

"Story, Jerry is out," he said quietly. "We're going down low. Lay them on the decks."

"Take the big one first," Story said. "Then we'll cross the stern on the other one."

In the belly turret, it seemed to Walt that the ships were flinging themselves upward from the water. Hundreds of men, small but growing larger, scrambled about.

"I've got her!" Story shouted.

Watts let her ride.

Pon turned his gun downward, starting a spray toward the deck. Men dropped from the debarking net, leaped from the decks, flinging their equipment wildly.

Walt saw the two bombs free themselves and then spin downward. He watched them even in the moment when they struck the deck and the deep port side. Then the whole ship exploded, and then exploded again and again. *Ammunition,* he thought, as the Harpy lunged forward, rocked by the tremendous concussion.

Watts pulled on the Harpy. She banked awkwardly, pulled around and headed for the other ship. They were down now, not more than eight hundred feet from the water.

Mike waited in the top turret, looking into the exploded skies. The formation behind them was just coming in. According to plan, the Harpy should be far down over the lagoon, but as she neared the second ship, Mike could look ahead and see the thousand-pounders heading downward for the gun emplacements. He glanced up at the Liberators again. It seemed that they were tremendously high and that the Harpy would never get up there again. He did not think there was any power in the world that could lift her back into the heavens.

Chief stared ahead at the superstructure of the boat. He wondered if they would clear it. It didn't matter much any longer. He did not think he could summon the strength to lift his head from the base of the gun, anyway. As the light came down on his brown face, Chief recalled the fires he had built as a child, the cool canyons, the mesquite and pine nuts, the places he had seen in America. Rich and sturdy and endlessly giving, this America had always been. But now, thinking of America, his face held compassion and love, quiet nobility and unknown strength. All these were deep in the lines of his face, but they were brushed across by a quiet serenity and peace.

He rested his head, thinking of the wonderful years in which his people had known their country, the seasons which had passed, the autumns and springs they had known, the fierce winters and the last end of summer which had taken their name. The Creator had said there was a season for everything. "A time to love, and a time to hate; a time of war, and a time of peace." In all history of man's growth these words had been true. And now his time was here, Chief knew—the time of war.

"Here we go!" Story shouted, and he shoved all the bombs free. He couldn't miss, he knew. It was like dropping rocks off a bridge. He turned to grab the .30-calibers beside him, but as he got to his knees, the whole world seemed to shatter before him. Everything broke with a brilliant, crystal clarity, cracking into new shapes, as intricate and beautiful as hoarfrost, and he just sat down easily and smiled. *It's not so bad,* he kept telling himself. *It's not so bad, only the wind comes in so strongly. If there just wasn't the wind to take my breath away. Or perhaps it wasn't the wind.*

As he touched his body, he knew there was no place the spattering shrapnel hadn't cut its way.

"Whatever they give you to do, I want you to be happy, remembering."

The light came back, the glorious luminous light in the shrine in the cathedral that always remained after the red and blues and greens had become harsh and dissolved in the brash morning. The luminous light remained always.

Watts tried to anticipate the explosion. He tried to bank the Harpy a little, so she wouldn't catch it full force against her wings. He was afraid they'd snap off. But just as he banked, it hit her, driving her downward and forward.

Walt felt the concussion, saw the black cloud of smoke surround him, and out of it the leaping dull-red flames with the brilliant orange tongues. They encircled him, and for a moment he thought the turret would melt. He flung his arm across his face, felt the force of the blow throw him about the turret, and then he was grasping for something to steady himself. The turret was turned downward, and he faced directly toward the water. It was only about a hundred feet below him and they were losing altitude rapidly. The whitecaps were rushing up toward him. He watched them come up. It seemed that he could almost touch them.

Watts felt the sweat all over his body. It was cold, as if he sat with his body clamped in wet towels. *We should be hitting any second,* he told himself, and he kept yanking and pulling. He kept hoping the Harpy would find enough air to hold onto and pull herself up from the surface of the ocean.

"No, Harpy, no!" Pon shouted. None of them who could still move made any effort to leave the ship. Pon would not. He had never pictured the Harpy's end, but he knew it wasn't here. It wasn't in a whirling, exploded bay where the debris still rained down from the skies.

She held. She held as if her very wing tips were caught on the edge of some unseen support. Watts flung himself forward, working with the engine. Suddenly, the No. 4 caught. The right wing pulled down a little, leveled, and they roared forward into the billowing black smoke. She was riding now. Watts could feel her under his hands. She had taken on life. He turned as sharply as he dared with the speed they had, and started back out across the exploded ships. He had to get out to sea and get some speed. It was the only hope.

Looking down, Walt saw the larger of the two Nip ships slowly tumble on its side and roll over as if it had become unbalanced. Equipment and men were thrown free into the air and downward onto the burning water. The other ship sat quiet and fat, like a child's bath toy, only the flames roared upward for better than a hundred feet. The infantry and marines and all the others could come in now. The resistance was broken. The winds of America could blow westward as they had in Kula Gulf and Kahili and Munda and Midway, Guadalcanal and Makin and Tarawa. The season of war would soon be gone, and there would be the season of peace.

Slowly and purposefully, the Harpy gained altitude. She was climbing toward some secret place. Mike jumped down to look at Krist, and it

was in that moment the fighters came down from above. Two of them came out of the billowing smoke clouds, and only John saw them. He grabbed his gun and began to fire. He was unused to the tail turret, and he knew he was going wild. His hands were steady and his guns were spitting cartridges with the neat rapidity of a sewing machine, but he knew it was coming. The Zekes crossed just above the Harpy and their fire left an $\times$ seamed across her fuselage. Mike ripped into the one going off to his left and held his fire on her until something heavier than a hammer struck his arm and knocked it away from the gun.

He took the handkerchief he always wore around his neck and stuffed it down the sleeve of his suit. He could feel the warm blood down there, but it wasn't hurting him much. It was then, as he turned back to his gun, that he saw Jerry slumped sidewise in his seat. He crawled up beside him and felt his forehead. It was warm, he thought, but he couldn't be sure. Everything was warm, the fume-filled air was sticky with oily, smoky heat. Unsnapping the belt, he lifted Jerry easily and carried him back beside Krist. He laid him on the platform and turned back to Watts. It was then he saw the fighter coming in at two o'clock, straight ahead of them, and its whole wing edge seemed to be ablaze with firing guns.

Watts opened his eyes a little and looked up. "Take it! Take it, Mike. I ——"

Mike saw that one of the bullets had ripped along the edge of Watts' head, and blood was pouring down around his ear. Mike fell into the pilot's seat. His hands and legs stopped stiffly, helplessly. He looked at the things he thought must be done, but he was helpless to move. The Harpy was riding into a cloud bank that rested above the ocean's surface. She was climbing quickly, and before he realized it, the cloud flooded in around them, blotting out the disaster they had left, obstructing everything that lay ahead. Mike started to reach for the throttles, but paused again.

Just then, something moved beside him, and he turned to see Pon. Mike did not know how he had been warned, but there he stood, straight and thin, his face whiter than Mike had ever seen it. But it wasn't fear that made it white, nor anger, nor any emotion that Mike had ever known. It was white as if it had always been that way, and it was calm.

Without speaking, Pon lifted Watts gently from the copilot's seat and placed him back of them on the flight deck. Unhurried, as if now more than ever in their lives there was no need to hurry, no cause to be concerned with time. It was curious how dreamlike were the movements of men when they were timeless. Mike stared at him. It seemed as if he had never known him before. And yet he was not sure. There was some curious recognition in his face. Pon reached for the controls. It was then that Mike noticed how thin his hands were and how he held them, the fingers partially bent in a sort of repose.

It seemed a long while that they rode through the dark, rain-filled cloud. The fuselage of the Harpy hummed with the rain, but it no longer held terror for them. It was a soothing, gentle and unending sound, and beneath Pon's hands, the Harpy seemed to take on new spirit. From some unmeasurable source, she drew strength. She sang as if time and space were unlimited to her. New and untried air pushed up against her wings, and when the cloud fell away, she was high in the sky.

Mike leaned back, his eyes closed against the wind that poured through the shattered pane. This was what he had always dreamed of—this quiet riding in the valley of the sky.

A sweet serenity spread over him, and he felt a completeness within himself, and yet this was part of a continuity, he knew. This was the end for which the beginning had been made; this was the beginning for which the end had been promised.

The sun had fallen away over the horizon, far down across the earth. It flung a shaft of light upward. The vaulted space between the dark cloud and shaft was golden, and colored all the heavens about it. The shaft rose upward into infinite space, passing through the deep and distant blue, and into that shaft the Harpy climbed easily, moving unhindered, like some great homing bird.

The sound of her motors sang through the heavens, clear and loud and endless. They sang through the sunset and into the darkness. Long after midnight, and in the midnights to follow, her ground crew, lying on the mat with their eyes in the starry distance, believed they heard the sound of the Harpy's singing. But they did not speak of it, for all men who ride on the wings of the heavens listen for the Harpy, knowing her spirit was infinite.

SOLID CITIZEN

by Pete Martin

ONE DAY IN 1944 associate editor Pete Martin was riding The Lark from San Francisco to Los Angeles on *Post* business, just as he says in the article below. A man in the club car began talking to him and Martin began taking mental notes, interrupting occasionally to dash into the men's room and put them down on paper. The result was a definitive self-portrait of that thorough-going heel: the homefront chiseler of World War II.

Editor Martin was born in Charlottesville, Virginia, in 1901, and christened William Thornton, a name which got shortened to Pedro and then to Pete while he was a track and football star in high school and a track star at the University of Pennsylvania, class of 1924. At Penn he was also editor of the *Punch Bowl*. After leaving school, he served for a time as art editor of *College Humor* and then, in 1925, went to work for the *Post*. He has done just about every kind of editorial work on the latter publication. He has judged manuscripts, edited copy, written short stories, articles and serials, and for a number of years he was art editor of the *Post*. In recent years he has been devoting most of his time to the writing of articles about the entertainment world—including collaboration with Bing Crosby and Bob Hope on their full-length autobiographies.

MAY 6, 1944

WE WERE on The Lark, the overnight streamliner between San Francisco and Los Angeles, due in the land of the platinum nutburger stand at dawn. In the lounge car a few feet away, General Vandegrift was nibbling at a plate of food. In addition to the general, there were Navy stripes and Army uniforms and a sprinkling of citizens shaved a rosy pink and wearing executive responsibility as easily as their custom-tailored, double-breasted suits. We were being shot through the hard white sunshine southward.

A waiter in a mess jacket brought us the news that there had been "a slight derailment" down the line. Not a wreck, but a "derailment." This was California, where words were important and gaudy. A Navy captain due to inspect a new ship at ten o'clock worried about the fact that he would be lucky to make it by four. But the man seated solidly next to me was unperturbed. He took out a cigar, looked at it calmly and held a flame to its tip. We had been discussing the rigors of travel in a day of overburdened transportation systems and railroads straining every coupling to do a staggering job. There was, he said, "nothing to it." All you had to do was to learn a few angles.

"When I was in New York, I was in a terrible jam trying to get West again," the solid man remembered. "Somebody suggested that I see a girl named Jones who was supposed to have know-how and be able to pull space out of a hat when Joe Public just couldn't get it. I took my troubles to her and she went to work. In half an hour she had my space from Chicago west nailed down. It took her a little longer to get me set from New York to Chicago. I suppose she had connections with other Miss Joneses around the country or a Mr. Jones or two—somebody smart enough to take advantage of the well-known law of supply and demand. Maybe they built up a pool of space reservations to draw on the moment they were put on sale. I wouldn't know about that. I slipped her twenty bucks. It was worth it. She told me that some weeks she made as much as a hundred and fifty dollars that way. Another useful thing to know is about the bell captains in some of the hotels who buy up reservations in advance and peddle them through bellhops. They got to make something out of it, but you can't kick if you're getting a break." The solid man set great store by sportsmanship.

He had the travel-food situation figured too. "On a lot of these trains out here, they serve only two meals a day," he said. "You get breakfast and dinner, and that's all. For dinner, you choose between feathers and fins."

I admitted that I had already encountered the fish-and-chicken limitations.

444

The solid man's eyes beamed reminiscently. "On my last trip," he confided, "I sent for the dining-car steward to come to my compartment. I told him my wife and I had our mouths all set for a good dinner, and what was he going to do about it? Then I slipped him a five-dollar bill, all folded up. He went outside for a minute to look at it. When he came back, he said, 'I'll send the waiter—the one I call my upstairs boy—in here to see you. We've got a roast in the icebox, and I think I can slice off a couple of nice tender steaks for you.' I ate so much I almost foundered."

Thinking about food made the solid man remember the OPA. He was very tolerant about it. "Someday after it's gone the way of the NRA, we'll be laughing at it," he said. "For that matter, it's already a laugh. I've got a friend who's interested in one of the small distilleries. He sells carloads of case goods to his customers at whatever the law of supply and demand brings, regardless of the ceiling. It's a cash transaction. The purchasers come in with packages of bills wrapped up like a loaf of bread. The banks are apt to keep a record of thousand-dollar bills, so the bills in those packages are one-hundred-dollar ones. My friend is convinced that before anybody gets around to checking up on him the war will be over, the ceilings will be discontinued." The solid one chuckled in admiration of his friend's brilliance.

We stopped to let a freight train pass. It was made up of boxcars, tank cars of oil, and flats with war goods crated or covered with canvas.

When it had rattled by, the solid man resumed his task of educating me. "I ran into another friend the other day who said he'd like to have me up to his house for dinner, only he'd used up all of his meat points. I just looked at him. 'Don't you know any butchers who like Scotch?' I asked. He said he knew one whose tongue was hanging out. 'Take some of that Scotch you've got hived up in your cellar,' I told him, 'and wave it in front of that butcher's nose. You were smart enough to lay in a lot of canned goods before they were rationed. And I didn't think I'd have to give *you* any hints.' He got the idea right away. We went to his house for a case, and I waited for him outside the meat shop. When he came out, he had bundles of roasts and steaks and chops and bacon and a lot of other stuff. We lugged it into his house and tucked it away in his quick-freeze unit. His wife's face was a sight. 'We won't be able to have anybody in for dinner,' she complained. 'If we give them a roast like that, they'll know we didn't have enough points to buy it honestly.' Then I stepped into the picture. 'Look,' I said, 'wise up, Mary. You won't lose

any friends. They'll be begging for invitations. Besides, maybe they know a few little tricks themselves.'

"People can be very foolish," the solid man said seriously. "I know people who have given up trying to get hold of a bottle of cheer in a locality where liquor is unrationed because the salesmen in the stores tell them it's all gone. All you've got to do is scurry around a little, and you can find some guy on a third-floor-back someplace who was smart enough to see the shortage coming and stock up. He might make you buy a case of light wines along with your Scotch, and you'll have to pay two or three times what the wine is worth, but a man deserves some reward for being foresighted. And technically I don't regard paying a premium like that as the beginning of another wave of bootlegging. And even if it is, why should I hold back and do without my highball? What could one man do to stop it?

"Then I've got a good friend, a banker who lives about four miles from the nearest suburban station and only had enough gas to drive to the station twice a week. So you know what that dope was doing?" The solid one's voice became the voice of a man discussing a particularly distressing mental case. "He was walking four miles each way. He asked me how I managed to avoid tramping the road as he was doing, and I told him. I'd been giving a garageman I knew two or three gas tickets and a five-dollar bill, and he'd been filling my tank up all the way and I didn't ask questions about the change.

"It's like a fellow I know in the dress business who goes to New York to buy dresses for a chain of women's-clothing shops. I met him one day, and he was looking low in his mind. He explained his despondency by saying that the dresses he had been buying wholesale at four dollars and seventy-five cents a dress, to be sold at six ninety-eight by his shops, couldn't be had any more. The wholesale OPA price was fixed at four seventy-five, and the manufacturer said he simply wouldn't sell at that price, since, if he did, he'd lose nine cents a dress. According to him, they cost him four dollars and eighty-four cents to make. The next time I saw that buyer, happiness stuck out all over him. 'We worked out a way,' he told me. 'I found a guy in that dress company who couldn't count higher than ten. He sends me the dresses, and bills me for twelve dresses, in each box he sends, at four seventy-five a dress, but when I open the boxes there are only ten dresses in each box. That's oke with me. Now, if I can only work out some way to still make my old profit on them when I put a price tag on them in my window, everything will be jake.' "

The solid man chuckled. "He'll work out a way somehow," he said. "He's no sucker. But I got away from that story about the banker. He saw the light. No more hoofing for him now."

We were pulling into Glendale. The porter was gathering the luggage and stacking it in the vestibules at the ends of the sleeping cars. A man and his wife walked between the rows of shoes on each side of the narrow corridor. In front of them went a bright-haired boy.

For the first time, the solid man next to me seemed unsure of himself. "We've got a hell of a juvenile-delinquency problem back home," he said. "Kids in their early teens are running hog wild. They've no respect for other people's rights. They've got no decency or ethics." He paused, puffed his cigar; then he put his finger squarely on the core of the problem. "The trouble is they've no respect for their elders," he announced. "I just can't understand it."

THE LAST NIGHT

by Storm Jameson

WHEN THIS ANGRY and prophetic story was published in the *Post*, the liberation of Czechoslovakia was still two years away. But when it came it followed very much the pattern envisioned by the author, at least so far as the Germans were concerned. Margaret Storm Jameson is a blonde, bicycle-pedaling Yorkshirewoman who has been writing novels, mostly about ships and shipmasters, since 1919. "Toward struggling strength she has deep and warm sympathy," an English critic has observed. "For weakness she has no pity at all."

JANUARY 30, 1943

WHEN I WAS A CHILD I lived on our farm in Ruge, in East Prussia. The farmhouse had been built by my great-great-grandfather in the dip in the ground between two birch woods. The lake was beyond the nearer wood. In front of the house, the plain—its fields, woods, other lakes, the river—was all day long in full light, even when the shadow of the birches covered the house.

My grandfather, my mother—his daughter-in-law—and I lived in the house with the house servants. The others slept in the low building that formed one side of the courtyard. Slept, I say, because for a long time I supposed that even their children were outside at work always. And this —at least when I was a child—was nearly true. Then my father died, in 1926, of the effects of his war wounds—he was a volunteer in the first war against England—and under the gentler rule of my grandfather there was more gaiety. The truth is that in our family a severe Reichel is always followed by a sensitive and less effective one; my grandfather would never, as did my father, have risked buying land in the bad years, or driven his laborers to their limit to make the risk good. As for me, his son, I am neither hard, nor assured, nor sound. All the same, I am a Reichel, and when I look in the glass I see any Reichel—the sunken eyes, face hollowed under strong cheekbones, long mouth.

My mother and my grandfather are the same sort. I grew up between them like the grass between two birches—a little too fine. Not that they were soft with me. But there was a sympathy between us which made a closed family circle, and what is closed from the world never masters it. I had on my bed table a photograph of my father in his lieutenant's uniform. Since I was so young when he died, this photograph was my father. I cannot call up any other image of him. If now and then I think I remember a living man, the memory easily escapes and fades, shrinks, into the dry image on paper. Once I questioned my grandfather about his son. What was he like? Was he very brave, a hero?

After a minute my grandfather said quietly, "He was a farmer, turned good soldier."

When I was four years old a stallion broke loose from the groom leading it. I was in the path of its brute flight, my leg was fractured in three places, and for all the Berlin surgeon my grandfather fetched, I was lamed. I drag one foot—the right—as I walk. It was because of this that I lived quietly at home; I was not able to serve the Leader except by preparing to manage the farm well, grow more food and, in time, marry and have children. I learned to ride. In spite of all, I became something of a jockey and believed I understood horses. It grieved me, when I was older, to know that my grandfather had had the stallion shot. My father would not have done it.

I was barely sixteen when England attacked Germany for the second time—this time through Poland. Because I could not look forward to being a soldier, I did what I could to live a life worthy of the war. I slept outside. In winter a piece of my skin froze to the rug I was using as a pillow and tore off when I moved. The pain heartened me.

After four years, the miracle. I was called up. When the order came, I was alone in the house. I knelt in front of the photograph and thanked the Leader for his mercy to me, his poor lame one. "You will see," I told him, "that I am not a weakling." I heard my mother in her room and went down.

In my happiness I had expected her to show pride, and I was disappointed when she said, staring at me, "I thought you would be left to us."

With my grandfather, she was all the love, all the gentleness, all the warmth of my life; and I saw, at the time, only a door opening and myself running through it into the world. I was not more selfish than other children. It is even right that children turn their backs on a mother, a grandfather. You can see in other countries—in France, for example—how love of the past destroys a people. Looking at my mother when she lit the lamp, I saw for the first time the lines, scored downward, on her fine skin.

All my grandfather said was, "It will be summer before you are trained."

I began to be afraid that during the weeks or months of training some officer would say, "This lame fellow is no good." A week after I reached Berlin I was in a train going east. I had been given a uniform, taught how to use a submachine gun, and had shown that I can use a rifle. I saw nothing of Berlin and had no chance to see how much of it the barbarians have destroyed.

In the train I realized what I owed to living at Ruge. The other young men in the carriage were all, like me, what our machine-gun instructor called "defective parts." One of us was almost blind, another had lost two fingers of his left hand, a third coughed until we all wearied of him. But where I was strong and perfectly healthy, nothing wrong except my dragging foot, these others were under-fed, sickly, frightened. I became a little friendly with the half-blind boy. My body was light and bursting with joy—the same feeling precisely as the cherry trees at Ruge gave me each spring. Afterward I only felt hungry, like the others. We had been given four biscuits, dry and quite tasteless, and the journey to Prague took ten hours. Before we crossed into the protectorate a corporal drew the blinds in the carriages and we were ordered not to touch them.

The others were kept in Prague. Only I was handed over to a sergeant, to get into another train and go farther east.

Sergeant Renner was middle-aged, clumsy, big. In the last war he had been wounded in the stomach, and that made him unfit for drill. But he knew how to rule men. He had many prejudices, but he was kind as well as arbitrary. When the train started, "What's your name?" he said.

"Johann Reichel."

"H'm'm." He gave me a sharp glance from small bloodshot eyes. "When an officer asks you, answer, 'Reichel, Johann.' Have you had any food?"

"Four biscuits since yesterday."

Lumbering from his corner, he fetched a canvas bag from the corridor, and among blankets and some ragged undergarments he found a parcel of cheese and bread. He divided it, giving me a half share.

At dawn the train stopped. We got out, Renner shaking himself like a bear, I numb with cold. There were fields, a stream and, hanging over the village, hills covered in trees. There was a guard on the single platform, two men with machine guns. Renner spoke to them in his offhand way, and we left the station and plunged into air like fine glass, the sky clear and gray, along a narrow road beside the stream to the village. It was the same air as in Ruge.

I walked beside Renner, who said nothing. We walked the length of the village between fast-shut houses to a big house at the far end, nearest the hills.

Renner took me into a room where there were men on guard before a second door. It opened, an officer in the uniform of the SS came through the room, and at once Renner, like the others, became rigid. I copied them.

A voice from the inner room said, "Sergeant Renner? Come in."

When Renner beckoned me, I stood in the doorway and saluted. I had to walk the length of the room to the desk at the far end. The colonel watched me come. Too tired to feel any fear, I looked at him; he was broad-shouldered, his face broad, with pale lips flattened against it, and gray eyes boring into my skull and emptying it of its few thoughts. There was neither kindness nor severity in the face. It was a landscape rather than a face, and I do not pretend to know what lived there.

"So they're sending me cripples now," he said without seeming interested. "Name?"

"Reichel, Karl Johann."

"What can you do?"

"I can ride and look after horses."

"Excellent," he said in the same voice. "Can you write a legible hand? Can you add?"

"Yes, sir."

He took a couple of papers from the pile on his desk. "Copy this. Check the figures from the second sheet."

Renner stepped forward and pointed me to a table against the wall. I sat down and began, my hands wooden with cold, to copy a long list of items: "twenty pigs, eight kegs butter——" I had no idea what it meant, and only later knew that I was listing the month's supplies sent from this district to Berlin, where they were bitterly needed in our war with England. I copied for two hours, then Renner took the papers from me, checked them, and sent me to find my own way to the mess.

After swallowing some hot soup I went outside to see what sort of place I was stationed in. It was a large farm, built round a courtyard. Standing in the yard, I could hear the stream and stare up at the hills—dark green of firs and the thin young green of oaks, scarcely a veil yet, it was too early in the year. You could not say that it was like Ruge, but one northern farm is never unlike another—the same smell of wet earth, herbs, stables. A sentry outside the stables let me look in at three fine horses, only fit for riding. They must, I knew, belong to the colonel and the SS lieutenant I had seen.

"Where does the colonel ride?" I asked. I had a crazy vision of myself being called on to attend him as groom.

"He doesn't any longer," the man said.

I went away and leaned against the gate leading from the yard into a rough orchard. At one side of the orchard were barns, and after a minute I saw that the nearer barn was lived in. A woman came to the door and poured out a little water on the ground. I heard a girl's voice. And suddenly I was sleepy. I stumbled to the house and slept until a corporal woke me for duty.

On the second evening I had a chance to speak to Renner. He was mending a shirt; he liked using his hands. "Who lives in the barn?" I said.

He gave me one of his sharp glances; his face was so big and worn that to discover in it an arched delicate nose, the nose of an aristocrat, was a shock.

"Palivec," he said calmly.

"Who ——"

He interrupted me, "Palivec was the mayor of the village. He's a farmer. He used to live in this house. To keep him more or less under his eye, Colonel Werder put him and his family in the barn when we took the house." He paused, biting an end of the thread with discolored teeth. "For a Czech, he's not a bad chap at all."

I had been two, nearly three days in the protectorate, and I had not yet seen a Czech, except for the glimpse of a woman in the door of the barn. The evening before, when I wanted to go out and look at the village, I had been told it was forbidden to go alone.

"They're brutes, aren't they?" I said.

When he answered, something in Sergeant Renner's offhand voice made me feel small. He looked over my head. "There's not much difference in human beings."

To cover up my feeling of humiliation, I said, "How many of them pig it in that barn?"

"I shouldn't think they pigged it," he said dryly. "They seem very decent. There's Palivec himself, his wife, his son, his son's wife, his married daughter and her husband. And another daughter, a good deal younger than the others." He looked at me again. "If you're thinking of calling on them ——" His little joke made him laugh in a chuckling way that shook his loose, heavy body.

I learned that our task was to guard the railway. It was the main east-to-west line, carrying men and supplies to the defensive zone in the east. There had been so many accidents at this place— the hills were ideally useful to Czech brigands— that two years ago Colonel Werder had been sent to stop them. In the last few months, every soldier under forty had been taken from him. Their places were filled by older men and "defective parts." One young officer of the picked SS troops was left—the lieutenant.

This officer reminded me at sight of a schoolmaster in the Ruge school, a young man we children hated for his sarcasm. He never spoke to us except sneeringly, and when he punished he treated the culprit to ten minutes of biting irony first. Lieutenant Vogt spoke little, and was arrogant rather than sarcastic, but he had much the same type of face—smooth, with fine narrow features, colorless lips, light hair. It was he and not the colonel who gave the villages their first lesson in correct behavior. The colonel had gone home on leave, and the first night he was away a patrol brought into the farm two Czechs they had picked up near the railway, long past the hour when the villagers were forbidden to leave their houses. The men said they were from another village, but they would not give their names. The lieutenant and four of his men questioned them all night in the anteroom to the colonel's room. In the morning the Czechs were dead, or rather, one dead and the other dying, and the lieutenant exposed them on a sort of cross, back to back, in the street outside the farm.

The soldier who told me about it did not like severities of this sort; he approved of severity, but he thought it ought to take the form of shooting or hanging. There were other similar stories about Lieutenant Vogt. He had seized any chance, when the colonel was absent, to impress his own idea of discipline on the village. Now that all the SS men, except himself, had gone to the front, he was less ambitious and worse-tempered, and his orderly had a bad time with him. I noticed, one day when he ordered me to come with him to the station, that any villager we met in the street turned into the nearest house to avoid passing him. We others were only ignored.

I had no temptation to break any of the rules against fraternizing with Czechs. The atmosphere in the village was stifling with dislike. It was as though each of us Germans walked about in a cloud formed of his own breath. If I spoke to a villager during a requisition of straw or food, perhaps he answered, if it was a man, without glancing at me. The women looked you in the face, but with a sort of surprise and distaste which was not pleasant. I knew why Vogt struck one of them suddenly across the mouth when she was handing over her pillows. Yet I wished he hadn't.

One morning when I went into the courtyard I saw that the cherry trees in the orchard were coming into blossom. As I leaned on the gate, Palivec came out of his barn and came toward me. His women took a long way round to the village, but he was used to coming through the farm. I watched him coming for a moment, trying to think whom he reminded me of. He was a tall man, his head narrow, yet because of the big forehead and high cheekbones, it looked strong. When he was almost at the gate I stepped back and swung it open. I did it involuntarily. He halted; he must have supposed I was coming through into the orchard.

Still holding the gate open, I said, "Good morning."

Palivec did not reply. After another moment he came on, passing me in the gateway.

"The sun is bringing on your trees," I said.

He looked away from me as he answered, "Last year I was able to supply you with five hundred kilos."

He was walking through the gate as he said it, and he neither slowed nor quickened his long stride.

"Wait," I said. He stood still.

I was confused. I knew that if anyone heard me I should have trouble in explaining what I was about. In fact, I could not have given myself an explanation—unless it was the likeness to someone I knew at home which was worrying me. Who was it? To cover up my insanity, I said the first thing that came into my head.

"It's almost spring."

Palivec did not turn his head toward me. In a calm voice he said, "May I get on with my work?"

As he walked off, I shut the gate and went on staring at the cherry trees to give my face time to cool. Why had I spoken to a lout of a Czech?

My work for the colonel was exacting but not difficult. A never-dry stream of forms flowed out from Berlin to every local headquarters in the protectorate, and I suppose into all the conquered countries. We made lists on demand of every conceivable thing, down to the chairs and cups in the village houses; lists of the things we had sent home; the things we expected to be able to send; reports on the crops; reports on every incident, trivial or not. I was writing and copying ten and twelve hours a day.

The colonel treated me, always, exactly as on the first day. He did not speak to or look at me as if I were a person; simply I was his writing hand. His glance, when he gave an order, passed over my face like an acid that obliterated my features. I thought he was not dissatisfied with me, but nothing he said—he said nothing, simply gave orders—gave me the right to think it. As for me, I admired him more than I could have admired anyone in the world, except the Leader. Naturally, I guarded myself from letting a sign of my worship—it was that—show in my face or voice. His calm energy was remarkable. If, as happened sometimes, he worked through the night, neither his face nor his manner was fatigued. He carried, I think, the map of the country in his head. Now and then he had to advise headquarters in Prague on some military operation. Then, to see his mind at work, a tiger able to think, was a fearful joy. I used to wonder why he was not in a more glorious place, and not a general.

Catching Sergeant Renner alone one day, I asked him.

"There's such a thing as being too intelligent," he said in his casual way. "I don't really know. I did hear that he was too clever with some field marshal on one occasion, but I know nothing about it. Take my advice, and ask fewer questions."

Disregarding this—I was no longer afraid of Renner, though I had respected him all the more since one of the soldiers talked to me about his war record—I said, "How did he succeed in stopping the accidents on this railway?"

For a moment, Renner did not speak. His face wore that look of patience strangely mixed with pride which had struck me before. I think he was a well-educated man, though I never saw him reading. He was silent so long that I grew nervous.

At last he growled, "There's no reason why you shouldn't know. What he did was quite simple. He called a meeting of the villagers and told them that if there was an accident he wouldn't waste time looking for brigands, he would simply shoot, at once, every man of twenty to twenty-nine years of age in the village. And if there was a second accident, he would shoot the thirties to thirty-nines, and so forth. The mayor—I mean Palivec—told him, very courageously, I thought, that none of the accidents had been the work of men living in the village, and that it was a brutal plan. Colonel Werder's answer was that he knew the brigands didn't live in the village, but they got help and information from villagers. Palivec tried to argue, and the colonel said, 'Hold your tongue. If I have to shoot, you're responsible.' Yes, the accident was three months later. They derailed a troop train very competently, killing two men. Oh, and holding up other trains, of course. The colonel did what he'd said; the men were rounded up—I dare say some got away into the hills—there were thirty-one here in the yard. The colonel came and looked them over and said, 'I'm not going to waste the men's time swilling the yard. Take them to the other side of the orchard and shoot them there; do the ground good.' And so they were shot, with a machine gun, in Palivec's orchard."

Renner unclasped his hands and began to rub the palm of one round his scalp—it was one of his gestures.

"It was effective. There hasn't been an accident in this district since."

He had told the story dryly and calmly, but I was trembling with excitement.

"My God, he's a great man!" I cried.

Renner cocked one eye at me. "Who?"

"The colonel, of course. It was a magnificent thing to do."

"How old are you?" Renner said.

"Twenty," I said. "Why?"

"Nothing, nothing," he mumbled.

He yawned, went to his blanket and lay down. He used to lie on his back, awake, hands folded on his chest. He said he'd lost the habit of sleeping.

Next day, when I was off duty for an hour in the afternoon, I went through the orchard and stood at the spot where I supposed the thirty-one had been killed. Were they buried here?

I looked round. The grass was the same everywhere and I thought how little difference it makes to the earth that men live a little and then die. And then—no doubt the spring was disordering my mind slightly—I thought: *But the young men may have had something to say, when they found themselves lying next to the roots of trees.*

I had nearly reached the gate into the courtyard when Palivec's younger daughter came out of their barn. I knew she was the unmarried one; she was a girl. I knew her name. Renner, who must —why?—have taken the trouble to find out a good deal about the Palivec family, dropped it in our talk. Marja. She was sturdy, very fair-skinned, with blue eyes and light hair—yellow. The devil, or the spring, prompted me to speak to her.

"Your orchard is very fine."

If she had said, "No finer for your being in it," or made any such insolent remark, or if she had curled her lip, I should have felt I had scored over her. She walked past me as though she had not heard me, as if I weren't even there. I felt myself crimson.

Later in the afternoon the colonel sent me, with one of the older men, to fetch a parcel from the station. I was glad to be out in the sun, and I

began to feel better. That is perhaps why—although I had been vaguely conscious of something changed in the village—it was not until we were coming back that I realized what it was. The Czechs we passed looked at us.

I was so astonished that I seized my companion's arm. "Did you see that?" I said.

He shook my hand off—he was a surly old boy. "What?"

"They look at us."

"Well, why shouldn't they?" he grumbled.

I looked at him. Yes, he felt it, too, but he was not going to talk about it to a "defective part." When the next Czech passed us, I was ready for him. I stared back. The look in his eyes was like all the others, a mixture of hate and— yes—curiosity. It was this last that startled me.

"I shan't be sorry to leave this place," I blurted.

My companion laughed in the jeering way these old soldiers laughed at us recruits. "When d'you expect to leave?" he said.

"After we win the war," I said. I was irritated.

In a different voice—soft, almost kind—he said, "We shan't win the war."

Old fool, I said to myself. It jumped into my mind that he was making fun of me. I shrugged my shoulders and said nothing.

Sergeant Renner and I slept in a little room together above the colonel's, so that he could rouse us at any hour by banging his stick on the ceiling. In the middle of that night we were wakened by one of the men on duty. There had been an accident to the night train.

I sat at my table in the colonel's room, copying from Renner's scrawled list the names of the villagers who had been arrested during the night. They were shut in the big cellar, twenty-nine of them—the men from thirty to thirty-five. The colonel's first order had been "thirty to thirty-nine." Then, for some reason, he changed it.

He and Lieutenant Vogt were discussing it at his desk. They had the habit of talking freely in my presence, since neither of them regarded me as a living or thinking object.

"Why not take the rest?" Vogt said.

The colonel spoke in a drawling voice, as if Vogt bored him. I think certainly he didn't like him and his SS jerkiness.

"Because, now it's started again, it will go on, and we shall need hostages. Suppose we shoot too many men, the few left will feel indifferent."

I went on writing. I had just copied the name Jírko. Jírko, Vincenc. I moved my finger down Renner's list—it was easy to lose one's place among Czech names. Something turned quickly in my stomach. Next on the list came: Palivec, Jan. Palivec's son.

Lieutenant Vogt was saying, "We could still shoot the wives."

"If it should be necessary," the colonel said, in the voice he used to close a conversation.

Vogt went out.

At this moment I realized that I detested the SS lieutenant as fervently as I admired Colonel Werder. Was it the contrast between the colonel's god-like calm and Vogt's quick, violent voice? No, Vogt was hateful in himself: he was smooth and impudent, he bullied his servant mercilessly, he treated Sergeant Renner with a rudeness which Renner withstood by an extraordinary air of detachment.

I glanced, without moving my eyelids, at the colonel. His eyes were fixed, staring, as though whatever he was thinking about were a long way in the past or the future. Could he, I wondered, dissolve past and future events simply by looking at them? My heart ached with love—yes, love. If he had said to me, "Reichel, take my revolver and blow your brains out," I should only have felt happiness.

One of the guards came in. "Sir, the Czech, Palivec, is outside. He is asking permission to speak to you."

The colonel's face never showed a feeling, yet I imagined that he had expected Palivec.

"Send him in."

Seeing them together, I saw that they were of an age. They were perhaps in the middle fifties—like, I thought, Renner. I realized, in the same instant, another thing: whatever Colonel Werder thought about Palivec—whether, I mean, he despised him as a savage or mistrusted him as a Czech—he did not dislike him. You cannot be anyone's slave, as I had made myself the colonel's, without learning to read them by signs not perceptible to others.

The colonel told Palivec to sit down. Palivec hesitated. Not, I saw, because he was surprised or diffident, but because he had no mind to sit with a German.

"I ask you to sit," the colonel repeated softly. His little finger tapped lightly, briskly.

Palivec took a chair facing the colonel across the desk.

"I know why you've come," my colonel said. "You know that I'm going to shoot your men who are in the cellar under this room; you know it's a waste of time to argue about it. You've come to do something even more childish. You're going to ask me to let them off and shoot you."

Palivec's eyebrows twitched. "No," he said, in a dry voice.

"I'm wrong?" The colonel was staring in his face.

"Yes, you're wrong," Palivec said. "I'm a Czech, not a sentimental Prussian. I know the value of a soldier. An experienced soldier." He spoke good German, with the same abrupt precision as Sergeant Renner when he was talking in his natural, not his military, voice.

"A year ago, six months ago, you wouldn't, if you were speaking to me, have called yourself a soldier, experienced or otherwise." The colonel's voice was as dry as Palivec's.

Palivec looked at him. "Six months ago, though I knew Germany had lost the war—and you knew it—you would have laughed at me if I had said so. You won't give yourself the trouble of laughing today. I know, and you know I know, that your troops are being withdrawn from my country, back into Germany. Not only from this country they're going back, but from every country in Europe. Here, so far, they haven't been molested. I don't know anything about other occupied countries."

"You must want me to laugh," the colonel said calmly. "How does even an experienced Czech—what is it you call them?—legionary?—guerrilla?—molest a German division?"

Palivec was looking down at his hands. "Not all your outposts equal a division," he said slowly. "This is an outpost."

I was listening and pretending to write. My wrists felt weak. I had not taken in the sense of what Palivec said when he was speaking, and what stupefied me now was that the colonel accepted his statement.

"Well," my colonel said.

Palivec leaned forward. "I give you my word," he said, as coldly as if he expected his word to be taken, "no soul in the village was involved in last night's accident. No one here expected it."

"What has that to do with it?"

"What good will it do you," Palivec said, "to murder a few innocent Czechs, adding them to the others, innocent or not so innocent, you've killed since 1938? When you know as well as I do—better, I dare say, than I do—that you're at the end of your time here."

Colonel Werder interrupted, "Near the end, not at the end."

"As you like," Palivec said indifferently.

"You don't convince me. And I'm sure you didn't expect me to be alarmed." After a minute, the colonel added, "You haven't mentioned that among the men in the cellar under us is your son."

"My son-in-law, Vincenc Jírko, as well," Palivec said quietly. "I don't come to ask for their lives, more than for the lives of the others."

"Why did you come?"

"Not even to bargain with you," Palivec said. "The safety of your outpost for our men's lives. I thought it just possible you would listen to reason, when reason is mercy."

There was a silence. To my profound amazement, I noticed the colonel's little finger tapping, tapping. He lifted his head to look at Palivec, and shook it.

"No, my friend," he said. "You do your duty and I'll do mine." He smiled—yes, smiled. "You know that I've no other reason for living, except to do what I was trained to do."

He pushed his chair back. Palivec got up. He stood for a moment, as if reflecting, and again I was plagued by his likeness to someone I must have seen somewhere. It eluded me again. He turned and went out without looking at my colonel, who watched him without a change in his face.

An hour or so later I was in the courtyard when four of the Czechs were fetched out of the cellar. Renner, who was there, handed out spades as though they were walking sticks. With a guard of eight of our men, carrying rifles, they were marched, not into the orchard, but into a field at the far side, away from the barn. It came over me that they were going to dig the graves for all of them, and I realized, in the same moment, with horror, that I did not want to see the shooting. The mere thought turned me up.

I may have shown it. Renner came over to me; he had a handful of papers, those eternal lists. "I want a fair copy of these before twelve," he said roughly. "Get on with them."

Shut in the colonel's room, I heard the rest of the Czechs singing in their cellar, then Renner's voice, then their footsteps on the cellar steps, then silence. Then, after about ten minutes, the clatter of a machine gun. I felt a sickening wrench in my body.

In the evening I ventured into the courtyard. There was a light cold wind, such as often came at that hour, after the warmth of the April sun. In the last day or two the cherry trees had lost their brightness and turned ragged, but against the wall of the barn there was a plum tree coming into flower. I stood in the yard looking at it. You can understand that I felt disinclined to go into the orchard.

The door of the barn opened and the three Czech women came out. There was the mother, Palivec's small gray-haired wife, and the two wives. Without lifting their eyes to the farm, they went toward the field. I had no wish to see them, but I stood there. Then other women began coming. They came along the way the Palivec women took when they wanted to go to the village—one alone, then two together, then one. None wept. They went past with perfectly dry eyes.

Suddenly one of them—the only one who did it—turned and looked at me as she passed the gate. I felt cold. Cold came to me from the Czech woman.

A fortnight or so later, I was sitting at my table waiting for orders. Lieutenant Vogt came into the room, and the colonel told him that armed bodies of Czechs had murdered all the men at two of our posts in a part of the country nearer the frontier.

"Where are they getting arms?" said Vogt.

The colonel lifted his eyebrows. "What do you think? Did you really suppose that either we or the police had unearthed every rifle and machine gun hidden in cellars and caves?"

He spoke to me without turning his head. "Get out. I don't want you just now."

I went out and looked for Renner. He was in our room, at his favorite trick of mending some garment or other.

"Is this an outpost?" I asked him.

"I shouldn't call it an outpost," he said. "I should call it a cover post. As long as troops and supplies are being brought back along the railway, we stay here and try to prevent accidents. See?"

I went over to the window. From it you saw the valley, the stream, the church no larger than a farmhouse, the houses marching from it one way to the hills and another to the stream and the road leading to Prague.

"And when shall we be brought back?" I had my back to Renner. He was a time answering, and I turned round. He looked at me—his big unkempt head tilted back, eyes half shut—with indifference and kindness.

"Never," he said softly. "We shall never get home."

I revolted against his words. "Why do you say such things?" I cried.

"I thought you asked me," he said in his casual way.

I was hurt and angry. We were in danger, and he sat there fiddling with a patch on one of his two shirts.

"Isn't there anything we can do?" I said.

"What do you mean?" he said with a slight smile. "My poor Reichel, a great many men as young as you have been certain they wouldn't be killed. The only thing to do is not to tell oneself any lies." He gave me a friendly, sly look. "I shan't say this to any of the others."

He couldn't have found words better designed to steady me. I began to feel another sort of confidence—not so much in myself as in the company. With officers like the colonel and Sergeant Renner, what could go wrong with us? I remembered that it was more than a fortnight since I had written home, and I got out my note-book and began: "My dear little mother ——" There I stuck; my head felt positively leathery. Could I tell her I might never see her and Ruge again, or about the shooting? I struggled with a sentence or two, and gave up.

Renner had watched me absently. When I put the paper away, he said, "In your reports—I mean, in the colonel's reports—have you come across a fellow called Míloš the Soldier? A Czech, of course."

"No."

Renner looked away. "He must have written his own report about it," he muttered.

"Well, who is this Míloš?" I asked.

"I don't know," Renner said. "It seems there's a fellow calling himself Míloš the Soldier—not just Míloš—a sort of leader inside the country. Not one of those fellows who have been fighting and cursing outside. He's very clever. So clever that though it's known he exists, and is probably at the bottom of a good deal of the mischief these Czech devils make, no one has run him to earth." He yawned. "I thought you might have seen something. I must say I admire a chap who risks his life that way."

I avoided going through the village. There is something worse than being ignored—that is, being loathed. When I could not get out of my turn of duty at the station, I walked past the Czech houses, feeling that any moment a door would open and a woman stand there and look at me as the woman looked on the day of the shooting. The more I tried to stiffen myself— after all, what are Czechs?—the more sore and humiliated I felt. Also I was afraid. It is shameful, but true. For the first time since I came, the thought that we were only a handful of German soldiers set down at bay in the middle of a hostile country weighed on me. Not simply the people and their village, but the trees, the river, the hills, were enemies.

I still went into the orchard. *Dead Czechs can't do any harm,* I thought. But to show you the state of mind I was in now, the afternoon when I fell there, my instant panicky thought was of a hand stretching up through the grass to grasp my ankle. I got up quickly, and collapsed again, cursing. I had wrenched my sound ankle, and now, with both of them gone, I was lamer than any cripple. I looked at it. It had swelled, and the pain, when I tried to walk, made me set my teeth. Helping myself from tree to tree, I walked back. When I had to pass the barn there were no more trees, and I moved as painfully as a crushed snail, praying to God that no one came out.

It was the girl who came out. Marja. From the corner of my eye I saw that she started forward, then drew back. *Yes, yes,* I thought, *it's a lame man, but it's a German.* I dragged on. Suddenly I felt giddy, and stumbled. I stopped. She had watched all this, that Marja, without moving.

I was startled when she spoke. Such a clear voice!

"Have you always been lame?"

"Not like this," I muttered.

"But you are lame?"

"My right foot."

"Are there many lame German soldiers?"

This mockery was spoken in a cool, almost friendly voice. I did not answer. I should have gone on—I felt better—but I longed for her voice, her girl's voice, to say a few more words in precise simple German, like a well-brought-up German child. I felt the sun on the back of my head, and there was a light scent of lilacs. I could not see the tree and turned my head to look for it.

"Where are your lilacs?" I asked.

"Behind the barn."

She turned away as soon as she had said it, back into the barn, and the door shut. The sun, which had been a German sun for a second, turned Czech again, like the cherry trees, the lilacs I couldn't see, the air, the dry ground under my feet. I got back to the house and had my ankle bandaged. One of the men found a stick for me to hobble about with, and so I got on. At night I was glad to lie down.

I don't know how long I had been asleep when it started. There were first shouts I heard in my sleep, then Sergeant Renner's foot in my side rousing me, then the shots.

Renner grumbled, "The light's gone! Damn it, why haven't I my torch?"

I was feeling in the dark for my tunic, the only garment I took off at night now. I found it and my stick and rifle, and stumbled out on the stairs.

The darkness was full of confused noise and shots. I could hear a man screaming outside, and suddenly the lights came on, on the landing and in the anteroom. I was on the lowest stair now and I dropped my stick and began to fire off my rifle at two men. I don't think I hit either before I felt the blow from a fist on the side of my head. It echoed in my head in a blackness.

I found I was on the floor of the colonel's room. I sat up. No one took notice of me. There were about a dozen of our men—nine of the old soldiers and the rest "defective parts"—legs and hands bound; Lieutenant Vogt roped to a chair;

the colonel leaning against the desk, his hand gripping his left arm; a trickle of blood came through his fingers. And there, close to me, lying on the floor with his knees in his stomach, my poor Renner. In spite of the war and the shootings, he was the first dead man I had seen in my life. He was not horrible, he was only pitiful and majestic with his big forehead and arched nose. Beside him lay a dead Czech with a hurt angry face, young, almost a child.

Czechs, Czechs with rifles—one with a machine gun—were between us and the door. The anteroom was filled with them. By now I knew many of the villagers by sight. These men were not from the village, except for one big gaunt man we called "the Englishman," because he had lived in America and spoke their dog's language.

Palivec came in. He looked at our dozen soldiers and said, "Take them into the stable and hang them. Don't waste ammunition on them."

One of the Czechs pulled me to my feet. Palivec noticed me then for the first time. "Have you your first aid?" he asked me.

When I tried to answer, my tongue was too thick and heavy for me to move it, but I took out the little roll of lint and the stuff like cotton waste they said was really wood or glass.

"Bandage your officer," he said.

I ripped the colonel's sleeve with his own pocketknife and did what I could with a gash from which blood had oozed.

"Are you in pain?" Palivec asked him.

"No," my colonel said. "A little." He was as controlled as usual. "How many people have you here?"

"Fifteen hundred."

"You thought it would take that many, did you?"

Palivec almost smiled. Then he turned to Vogt, sitting bound to his chair. His face turned a graystone color, his eyes moved a very little in their pits—I thought of a snake I had seen at Ruge, ready to kill. Even his voice had altered.

"You," he said. "You wretched murderer. Do you remember making a cross of Karel and Petr? Do you remember ——"

There were a number of other things he invited the SS lieutenant to remember. Some of them I would rather not remember myself. But Vogt gave no sign of hearing what Palivec said. I dare say Palivec noticed this.

He paused and said, "It wouldn't be any use our torturing you; nothing we could bring ourselves to do would be enough. You will be beheaded."

And that is what they did. They untied the lieutenant and made him kneel across a stool in the doorway to the anteroom, and two of the Czechs held him while "the Englishman" tried to detach the bayonet from his rifle. It did not come off, and another Czech handed over his. *O God,* I prayed, *let me die now.* I looked at the colonel. He was calm. He kept his eyes steadily on the doorway. They were wide open and seemed paler than ever. He had spoken to Vogt when they were loosing him from his chair, and Vogt only said, "Yes." He said nothing else, until, when the knife was working on his neck, he screamed and went on for an endless minute.

My sight went. I fell and fell, into blackness and confused noise.

I came back into a light that seemed very vacant and cold. After a moment I realized that it was the early morning coming into the room through a window that was swinging open. I turned my head. There were two, only two people in the room, the colonel and Palivec. They had taken away Lieutenant Vogt and Sergeant Renner and the Czech boy. Palivec and my colonel were sitting down, facing each other, as on that other day, across the desk. How long, I wondered dully, had they been facing each other? From the quiet way they talked, it might have been a long time, hundreds of years. The colonel was speaking.

". . . nor have you solved anything, my friend. And what you are beginning again, no one knows. You, least of all."

"We have not had our orders for the future," Palivec said. He lifted one of his long hands. "Not yet. Where does the end of terror and torment lead—the end of German protection? I don't know of any precise road, but to something that you have no idea of, you a German. Acceptance of freedom, love for the usual, the humble, the weak. Why do you smile?"

"I don't understand you."

"How could you?" Palivec said softly. "Our grandchildren may understand each other; you've seen to it that I have no sons to understand yours, if you have a son. The blood between you and all other peoples in Europe is too wide a flood for you to hear what I'm saying."

My colonel's shoulders jerked. He looked across the room and said in his driest voice, "I'm dying for sleep. That's not your intention, is it?"

Palivec pushed his chair back. He stood up. "Do you know who I am?"

"I began to suspect it yesterday."

"Only yesterday?" I thought Palivec sounded a little vexed.

"If I'd suspected sooner, you wouldn't be talking to me today. I was going to arrest you today and get rid of you, in order to make sure."

"It wouldn't have made any difference," Palivec said slowly. He began to walk toward the door. "You understand," he said over his shoulder, "I couldn't spare you even if I wanted to, and I don't know that I do. But you put too many of us to bed in my orchard."

"I did what I had to," the colonel said dryly. "There's only one way to keep order."

Palivec stood still. "Why were you keeping it in my country? You weren't invited."

"Don't let's begin again," the colonel said, smiling.

"Why? Don't you want to know what I'm going to do to you?"

"Do it."

Palivec had his hand on the door. He pulled it open, and at once four Czechs, who must have been waiting there like proper sentries, came in. Palivec jerked his head.

"Take Colonel Werder into the orchard. Shoot him."

The colonel stood up. It came over me that it was my turn next. I struggled to sit up, but I was dizzy and fell back against the wall. I felt nothing except the most terrible longing for him to speak to me. One word—one single encouraging word. Then I shouldn't be afraid.

"My colonel!" I cried.

He was stepping past me; his eyes passed over my face, wiping it out. He was completely indifferent. I might not have been there.

I watched him go out. Now I was alone. I shut my eyes. The darkness that filled my mind was nothing so pleasant and kind as unconsciousness; it was the darkness all over Europe, the dark of the night when Germans are killed. We had gone into every country, we had covered Europe like a flood; now, when we were going back, the outposts everywhere, men like us, left without reinforcement, stranded without help miles from Germany, were lost. The people would rise in all the countries, to kill us Germans as we went back or stood. Dark it was; dark everywhere.

I held my eyes open and saw Palivec standing by the desk. Perhaps I imagined the trace of regret on his face; if it was there, it was the merest trace. I heard rifle shots. Palivec lifted his head. The light was strengthening. It must have been nearly sunrise.

Then—I had not heard her coming—Palivec's wife came into the doorway. She stood there with that look of patience and deep tiredness in her face.

"Can we begin cleaning the house now?" she asked her husband.

"Yes," Palivec said absently.

He turned his head, and seemed for the first time to recognize me. He came and bent over me, and now I knew who it was he was like. If my father had lived into his fifties, he would have had the same face, narrow, the eyes sunk behind big cheekbones, the long mouth. It was not a close likeness, but it was very clear.

"Can you walk?" he said.

I tried again, without success, to get up. Palivec stooped and picked me up easily.

I can't say that I hoped anything in this moment, but certainly I resigned myself.

He carried me across the yard to the barn, and dropped me on a bed—his own, I think.

"Anna," he called. His daughter came in quickly—you could see that he was used to being obeyed. "Look at this boy's leg."

I must have stayed there a week—longer. My ankle was bathed. I was fed—always in this room. Usually, Anna brought me my soup and bread, but once it was Palivec's wife, who looked at me gravely and said something in Czech which did not sound harsh. There seemed always people coming and going in the courtyard, and once when I had the curiosity to look out I saw it full of Czechs with machine guns—they seemed to be camping there. Marja I never saw. I heard her laugh once. It must have been her laugh.

I don't think I troubled much about my future. One evening Palivec came in. I stood up.

"Can you walk?" he said briskly. "Good. You'll leave tomorrow."

He went out before I could ask a question. I was still standing against the little window when the door opened again. There was Marja. She came a step or two into the room.

"Where am I to go?" I said.

"Wherever you came from," she said in her light voice.

"Home?"

"I suppose so."

My mind cleared suddenly. "Why haven't I been shot or hanged?"

There must have been a sarcastic note in my voice, though God knows I had no right to use it with her. A hot color came into her face.

"We're sending you home for you to remember that, belonging to the people you do, it would have been better if you had not been born," she said softly. She turned to go.

"Don't go," I exclaimed.

The door shut on her. I saw her again next morning when I was leaving. When I looked at her, she turned her head aside.

I was wearing clothes Palivec had fetched me that morning. I think they were his son's. "You'll be safer on the road in these than in a German uniform," he said indifferently. "You're not in much danger from Germans; mighty few of them are walking along the roads, and they're not in a mood to shoot. When Czechs stop you, show them this paper." He gave me a piece of paper with a few lines written in Czech.

How long was I tramping on the road toward Prague? Weeks? Days? I didn't count and I don't remember. I showed my paper in villages. The man or woman who read it looked at me, some with distaste, some inquisitively, one or two even with kindness. They let me sleep in outhouses and gave me food, and once a cup of wine. And then one morning when I was walking—it had rained and the air smelled of it and the wet grass—a lorry filled with Czechs drew up in front of me, and one of them beckoned. I handed up my paper. It passed from hand to hand, while heads poked over the edge of the lorry to look at me, and finally an officer of sorts sang out in sharp German, "Get in. We'll take you to Prague."

I climbed in, awkwardly because of my foot. Two of them helped me, but when I was in, and the lorry started, they took no more notice of me. Toward evening we came to Prague. There was a castle, I remember, and crowds in the streets, women walking with bundles in their arms as if they had so much to do they could not walk slowly. And at a corner three or four children in khaki jackets singing in their language. They waved at the lorry, and the soldiers shouted.

We stopped outside a barracks. The officer spoke to me. "Wait. You don't belong here."

"May I have my paper back?" I asked.

He gave it me, with a quick smile. After a few minutes, two soldiers came and hustled me along between them to a building in another street, and into a large room where there were hundreds of my countrymen, waiting, like me, to be sent home. One of them could translate my safe-conduct for me.

The bearer is to be spared because he is a cripple; he is to be pitied because he is a German. Signed, MÍLOŠ THE SOLDIER.

I sat down in the large room among the others. I was trying to think of Ruge, to see it as it must look now in spring. *Shall I ever*, I thought, *be happy again?*

A FEW KIND WORDS FOR UNCLE SAM

by Bernard M. Baruch

BERNARD BARUCH IS the only *Post* author who was ever able to repeat on titles. In 1930 he wrote a *Post* article called "A Few Kind Words for Uncle Sam," which described the American effort in World War I from the inside viewpoint of a top administrator. Eighteen years later he used the same title for the valuable summing up of American activities in World War II and after, which is reprinted below. The repetition was no accident; if anyone knows the right words to say for Uncle Sam it is Mr. Baruch, who has been the friend and adviser of seven Presidents, and author of the original United States plan for outlawing atomic warfare.

JUNE 12, 1948

SHORTLY after we entered World War I, President Wilson invited me to a White House discussion of a critical oil shortage which threatened to disrupt our military plans. One official proposed we seize the Mexican oil fields at Tampico. Squadrons of marines had already been alerted. The President had only to give the word for them to push off.

President Wilson hardly waited for the finish of the argument. When aroused, he would speak in firm, measured tones, which left no doubt what was in his mind.

"What you are asking me to do is exactly what we protested against when committed by Germany," he reprimanded. "You say this oil in Mexico is necessary for us. That is what the Germans said when they invaded Belgium, 'it was necessary' to get to France. Gentlemen," he concluded, "you will have to fight the war with what oil you have."

This incident, in which the President of the United States refused to bend to the totalitarian dictum that "necessity knows no law," has never been related publicly before, to my recollection. It flashed into my memory recently while I was thinking of how widely and unjustly this country has come to be besplattered as a "money grabber" and "imperialist," concerned only with profit-getting and national aggrandizement.

Contrasting their own devastation and misery with our untouched cities and prosperity, many Europeans feel the United States somehow profited while engaged in the recent war, and greatly since. Some go so far as to regard our generous postwar aid as an obligation we owe to "balance the burdens" others suffered. Exploiting these resentments, Soviet propagandists have been belittling what we did to defeat Hitler and Japan, and besmearing our motives in the peacemaking as seeking a "new war in lust for profits from the blood of millions."

I have favored assisting Europe and the rest of the world to help themselves. For Europeans or others to adopt a posture of reliance upon us, in the mistaken illusion that the war has enriched America, is to invite a tragic future disillusionment which could readily wreck any hopes of the free nations holding together. It may help avert future embitterments of "Uncle Shylock" to set forth now just what America's contribution to the war and peace-making has been.

That record, never brought together before, is presented here not to detract from what others did—the Chinese, who resisted longest of all; the Russians, who lost the most lives and whose villages were rubbled under the conqueror's heel; the English, who braved Hitler's bombings alone for so long; or of others who joined against the common enemy. These facts are marshaled in hopes of inspiring a better appreciation of both the spirit and the magnitude of our endeavor, in which we hazarded everything with no impulse of reward, other than to gain peace for all.

It is a record for which no American need feel anything but pride. It is particularly worth examining now, when everything this country symbolizes is under assault by enemies, abroad and at home, who would destroy our faith in ourselves. The role thrust upon us by today's peace-waging is remarkably like the one we performed so magnificently during the recent war. Once again, demands beyond our resources tug at us from all over the world—Western Europe, China, Turkey, Greece, Korea, South America. We again face the necessity of developing that global leadership and decisiveness of internal unity—this time in peaceful equivalents—which enabled us to achieve global victory in the war. Knowing what we did before, and therefore can do again, may hearten and comfort this greatest stronghold of righteous power left in the world.

Probably the one caricature of America circulated most persistently abroad is that of Uncle Sam as a walking fistful of dollars using his wealth to buy other peoples as "cannon fodder" to do his fighting.

In actual fact, more than one half of all munitions produced by all the Allies were stamped "made in America." Our war expenditures of $330,000,000,000, through the fiscal year of 1946, exceeded those of Great Britain and Soviet Russia combined. However, this astonishing outpouring of production and dollars came in addition to bearing our full share of fighting.

Although the United States was forced into the war twenty-seven months later, American military casualties exceeded those of the entire British Empire in both dead and wounded. Of the ninety divisions which stormed through Western Europe sixty-one were American. The initial landing waves of all but a few of the beachhead assaults on the many Pacific islands were American, aided by gallant, yet small, Australian, New Zealand and Filipino forces, and by China's dogged, holding attrition. The World Almanac totals the casualties for England, Australia, Canada, New Zealand, South Africa and the colonies, together at 353,652 military dead, 475,070 wounded, 90,844 missing and 60,595 civilians killed, or 980,161 casualties in all. American dead numbered more than 400,000 and there were nearly 670,000 wounded. Our toll of dead would have been higher but for the remarkable care given the wounded.

Doing both—producing the implements of war and using them on fighting fronts across two oceans—was a deliberate choice. Let me stress that. Early in 1943 what Washington correspondents like to term a "revolt" developed in Congress, with a fairly strong group demanding a reduction in the size of the Army, then projected at 10,800,000 men. Some Government statisticians undertook to prove it would be impossible to draft the 4,400,000 additional men needed and still leave enough workers to produce all the ships, guns and airplanes scheduled.

President Roosevelt named a special "war mobilization committee" to review the problem. No announcement was made of the committee's creation. James F. Byrnes, then serving as "assistant President," was its chairman. The other members were Admiral William D. Leahy, Roosevelt's Chief of Staff, Harry Hopkins, Samuel I. Rosenman, the President's Counsel, and myself, the only member without official position.

Broadly, the decision before us was which should get preference, our fighting or our production? To cut the Army would have meant fewer men in uniform, more in overalls. The committee decided that the armed forces had to be given all the manpower needed to carry through the military offensives pledged our Allies. If anything was to be held back, it would be production.

Most of the committee felt we could do both, and so it worked out. With 14,000,000 men and women mobilized, we still produced 60 per cent of all Allied munitions. When the committee made its recommendation, President Roosevelt agreed, remarking, "We'll take everything that is necessary to carry out the fighting program."

That was the spirit which governed our total conduct of the war. If American cities escaped destruction, it was because of geographical good luck in being so distant from the lanes of bomb fight. We did not keep, for our own protection, weapons which could have been employed on fighting fronts. To the contrary, we deliberately exposed our defenses—not without protests from some Americans—so that everything possible could be shipped overseas. To Britain alone, more than 45,000 antiaircraft guns were sent.

The wartime aid contributed to our Allies soared to $50,000,000,000, from which $10,000,-000,000 should be deducted for reverse Lend-Lease and other settlements. For a nation which, according to its detractors, is motivated by selfish ends, we were remarkably insensible to opportunities for exacting materialistic gains as the price of this astronomical assistance. Perhaps it would have been wiser had we done so, as some who believe we were taken for Uncle Sap today contend. Instead, we drove no bargains, not even when the British and Russian plights seemed most despairing. Literally opening our Treasury, we pooled all our resources without limit, thought of repayment or haggling for postwar advantage.

To meet the Allies' needs, America's industrial capacity was vastly expanded. Some may point to that as a "war gain." Any idea that the war swelled America's net physical wealth evaporates if one compares our wartime imports and exports. Into the United States after Pearl Harbor were brought 106,000,000 tons of cargo of every type; shipped out were 268,000,000 tons. The difference is one measure of the physical resources expended as part of our war contribution. The 5,800,000,000 barrels of oil pumped from the American earth would keep all the automobiles in the country running for twelve years.

For what went abroad, we were paid virtually nothing, the bulk going to American forces or as gifts to Allies. For what we imported, we paid dollars, which represent claims upon our future production still to be made good. Our public debt jumped five times. In 1939, taxes took as tribute one of thirteen dollars of our national income; today they exact one of every four dollars Americans earn. Still, the American people have continued their giving into the war's aftermath with additional loans and gifts, so far, of $21,000,000,000—not including our contribution to the World Bank and Monetary Fund—in UNRRA grants, the British loan, surplus-property credits and, most recently, the European Recovery Program. To Europe alone, last year, individual Americans sent more than 23,000,000 parcels through the mails and CARE, plus an estimated $120,000,000 in remittances to relatives and friends, and another $250,000,000 of relief in cash and goods through private organizations.

One could search vainly mankind's whole history for comparable generosity. Yet, to some critics abroad and apologists at home, this is the record of a nation scheming to "exploit" and "enslave the world"!

Applying the principle of complete good faith to the Soviets always was a thorny problem. With the British, military operations were fully coordinated through the Joint Chiefs of Staff. A side light will illustrate how intimate this cooperation was. President Roosevelt and Prime Minister Winston Churchill were frequently in direct cable and telephone communication, the President often neglecting to inform the American Chiefs of Staff. The Joint Chiefs of Staff, though, had arranged for each to show the other all military messages. In several instances our top military people learned what President Roosevelt was thinking from the British!

The Soviets insisted on conducting all operations on their own. They afforded us no access to their activities, although Roosevelt and Stalin did communicate directly. Stalin's cables followed what Roosevelt once described as "the darnedest" pattern. There would be one, two, three messages of fatherly commendation; then "a blisterer." At first, Roosevelt would telephone Churchill and the two would compose a reply to these "blisterers." That didn't prove satisfactory and Roosevelt hit upon a new stratagem. "I save up the good cables until a bad one comes along," he explained, "then I acknowledge the good and bad ones together."

Roosevelt strove constantly to prevent suspicion from interfering with the prosecution of the war. "We must treat Russia as an equal and give her our full confidence," he often remarked. Only with difficulty was he able to convince Churchill this was the course to follow. The President asked me to "speak to Winston about his attitude towards the Russians." This I did, in Roosevelt's presence, shortly after the Quebec conference.

"The Russians are killing more Germans than the rest of us put together," I started out. "We should be glad of it and help them all we can. As long as they go along with us a hundred per cent we should go along with them a hundred per cent."

Roosevelt nodded his approval.

"But what will happen when Germany is beaten?" demanded Churchill. "What are we going to do about Russia afterwards?"

"We have to win the war first. In the meantime let us be guided by their actions," was my reply. "When the war is over, Russia will be sorely devastated. We must impress upon the Soviets the importance of a just peace or no assistance for Russia's reconstruction can be forthcoming from the American people. Whether we will be able to come to an understanding with Russia, no one can know now," I ended. "Let us give them no grounds for suspicion, keeping all our promises, while insisting they fulfill their pledges meticulously."

This episode is related solely to show the complete good faith we sought with the Soviets. It is beyond the scope of this article to determine what caused the present impasse or to weigh the wisdom of what was done or not done at Teheran, Yalta and Potsdam. To do so, one would have to consider the strategic situation at the time of these Big Three meetings, the choice of actions open to us, the commitments the American people could be counted on to support, what might have happened had all Russian demands been refused, whether any agreements which might have been reached would have been kept.

Whatever suspicions may have crept through the Kremlin corridors were of Russian imaginings. The last time I saw President Roosevelt was about three weeks before his death. He had asked me to fly to London to see Churchill, and I had come to Washington for final instructions before leaving. Admiral Leahy joined us and he and the President talked of a surrender "feeler" from Marshal Kesselring, then commanding the German forces in Italy.

Informed of the surrender bid, Stalin had cabled back, virtually accusing the President of attempting to negotiate a separate peace with Germany and insisting that Soviet officials be present at the "first contact" with any Germans or negotiations be broken off. Roosevelt was plainly hurt. He was not one to whimper or make excuses when things went wrong. His disappointment was evident, as he explained how carefully we had tried to avoid any action which might be construed as seeking a separate peace. He did not object to the Soviets taking part in surrender negotiations, but didn't want to delay until Russian officials could be brought to the Italian front. If Hitler's Gestapo got wind that Kesselring was trying to surrender his army, Roosevelt feared Kesselring would be shifted and the fighting in Italy needlessly prolonged.

The President and Admiral Leahy were still discussing what reply should be sent Stalin when I left. While in England, I learned Kesselring's "surrender" had fallen through; also that Roosevelt had cabled Stalin, expressing sharp resentment over any implications we might not be keeping our agreements. At almost the same time Roosevelt assured Churchill he intended that the Soviets should live up to their part of all agreements. So much for the spirit with which we dealt with our Allies.

Two thirds of our Lend-Lease aid went to the United Kingdom, about a fourth—$11,000,000,-000—to the Soviet Union. Such sums speak their own importance. Still, since the Soviet Government has chosen to dismiss this assistance as "incidental," these additional facts might be brought forth.

Our aid was concentrated upon filling Russia's most critical needs, like night-fighter airplanes which the Soviets could not produce, or aviation gasoline, in which Russian output was woefully deficient. The 1981 locomotives and 3,786,000 tires we shipped the U.S.S.R. were more locomotives and tires than the Soviets produced in any full prewar year. Soviet truck production before the war ran around 200,000 units a year. We sent the Soviet Union 375,000 trucks. Being vastly superior to those made in Russia, these trucks probably equaled two years' normal Russian output.

Without American trucks, tires and locomotives and such items as 52,000 jeeps, 35,000 motorcycles, 415,000 telephone sets, 15,000,000 pairs of soldiers' boots and 4,000,000 tons of food, the Red Army never could have achieved the superior mobility which was one of its principal military advantages over the Germans. Being able to shift their troops more rapidly, the Soviets could choose Germany's weakest salients for their attacks.

Out of her own resources, Russia could not have supplied the 22,000,000 men the Red Army is estimated to have mobilized. Workers and peasants would have had to be kept back on factories and farms. Russian munitions production would have been curtailed to fill the gaps we plugged. Nor should it be forgotten that we stimulated Russia's own productivity through nearly $500,000,-000 of American machine tools and another $2,-500,000,000 of industrial materials, like armor plate, aluminum, copper and zinc.

Soviet military operations profited from American and British bombing of German industry and lines of communication. Our unceasing pressure upon the Japanese after the Battle of Midway was certainly a powerful restraint against the Japs attacking Russia and forcing her to fight on two fronts.

"Who won the war?" is a futile speculation. In as much as the Soviets have taken to boasting they beat Hitler virtually singlehanded, it must be said that without the United States, the German Army would not have been driven from Russia's soil.

Russia not being a maritime nation, it is doubtful whether Soviet leaders ever really appreciated the difficulties we had to hurdle. I recall General Marshall's account of the second-front discussion at Teheran. Why did amphibious operations require such enormous preparations, Marshal Stalin wanted to know.

"The Red Army has had to cross many rivers," Stalin pointed out. "What is so difficult about crossing a body of water?"

Marshal Voroshilov added, "When we come to a river, we send several small parties across to feel out the enemy. Then we throw our full force at the weakest points. Why can't you do that?"

"That's the last thing to do in an amphibious landing!" General Marshall exclaimed. "When it comes to ground operations, I will sit and listen at your feet, for you have defeated the greatest ground army in the world. But of amphibious operations you know nothing. When you land amphibiously, you must hit with everything. A failure on a river crossing is a reverse. A failure in an amphibious operation would be a catastrophe. All our operations are conducted at the end of a steamship line," General Marshall went on. "Everything must be planned six months ahead of time."

That summed up the difference in the kinds of war we and the Russians were fighting. The Red Army had rivers to cross; we had oceans to cross. It does not lessen our appreciation of the incomparable courage and stamina of the Russian people in defense of their homeland to say they fought with one foot on home base. Our offensives had to leap two distant oceans. Nine days after General Eisenhower landed in Normandy, more than 3000 miles from the United

States, General MacArthur was assaulting the Marianas, 6000 miles from home.

That we could undertake two such operations, at opposite ends of the world, at the same time has never ceased being a source of marvel to me. No other nation in the world could have done it. Of all the belligerents, only the United States really fought a global war. While Russia and Britain, as well as Germany and Japan, participated on a few fronts at most, there was not a battlefield or staging area which did not see American food, weapons and, in most cases, American men. The tentacles of our communications stretched more than 56,000 miles.

If we are to win a global peace, we must recapture the three elements which enabled us to win the global war.

First, there was our production. One afternoon Harry Hopkins showed me a map which pinheaded the numerous outposts and battle fronts where American soldiers were stationed or which we were supplying. Using a school-teacher's pointer, he skipped from the Arctic to the desert, from mountains to jungles.

When Hopkins was through, I remarked, "Let me add one point. All those pins on that map depend on one thing—America's production. Each of those pins is a commitment. The bank that must make them all good is America's production, with its millions of branches in farms and factories."

In every field we set new production records. With fewer farmers, our output of food was lifted one third. Off the assembly lines of our "arsenal of democracy" during the five war years rolled nearly 300,000 airplanes, more than 15,000,000 rifles and carbines, 319,000 pieces of field artillery, 41,000,000,000 rounds of ammunition, 4,-200,000 tons of artillery shells, 86,000 tanks, 64,500 landing craft, 52,000,000 tons of merchant shipping—three ships a day—quadrupling our own merchant fleet. The Navy grew from 1,900,000 tons to 13,800,000 tons, greater than all the other fleets of the world combined.

How all the more remarkable those figures look when stacked against what we had when the war began! In 1940, for example, the Army's total air force was under 3000 airplanes. It is my belief that if America produced for peace as it did for war, all-out, without strikes or stoppages, inside of two years the foundations of economic stability in the world could be established.

The second ingredient of global victory was the fact that we had a global strategy—something still missing from the peace-waging. In addition to equipping our own armed forces, we supplied food or munitions to forty-three different nations.

At no time was there enough for everyone. Still, we managed to divide our not-enough so that our most distant Allies were heartened to continue in the struggle until America's own military machine was built up to score the decisive knockouts.

This global vision never fogged. In the blackest days immediately after Pearl Harbor, Roosevelt insisted something be sent to Australia, even if only a trickle. Later, Herbert Vere Evatt recalled, "Nothing heartened us so much in those dark days as that trickle of supplies which came to us through the long, Jap-infested sea and which told us we were not forgotten."

Whatever is written about Franklin Roosevelt, one tribute all historians will have to pay him and his aides, like General Marshall, Admiral Ernest King, General "Hap" Arnold and others—they saw the struggle in its global dimensions and developed the necessary world-embracing strategy.

For the "cold-war" attrition with the Soviets, the essence of any global strategy, I believe, lies in pacing ourselves. It will do no good to sprint like mad for a year or two when the race is a marathon. We must learn to distinguish between those areas where we can achieve a quick decision and "holding actions," where our plans must be shaped to a long, grueling contest. Let us remember the moral of the tortoise and the hare and be sure it is we who break the tape at the finish, so peace will be the pay-off.

Too many commitments we have taken on tend to weaken us. The strategic concepts and economic policies must be developed to turn many of these into sources of strength. Peace cannot be attained by dispersing or even sharing America's strength. We and our Allies must grow stronger together, mobilizing not only America's resources but those of free peoples everywhere. Otherwise, the democracies will waste the advantage of strength they now hold.

The third factor which made possible our wartime global adventure was what Woodrow Wilson described as "the highest form of efficiency . . . the spontaneous co-operation of a free people."

Twice in my lifetime I have seen the American nation transform itself from a peaceful, war-hating people into the most terrible instrumentality for destruction the world has ever seen and, even more swiftly, revert to its easygoing, anti-militaristic "normalcy." It is not accidental that Americans behave in this fashion; that we avoid war as long as possible, accepting it only as a last alternative; then, once in the struggle, fight with the fury of one possessed; and, the shooting over, scuttle and run back home.

The mainspring behind these actions is the American passion for freedom—that and the fact that war is the complete opposite of our normal ways, as night unto day. For 100 years, students of Marxism have parroted the libel that the capitalistic system is driven to war by its very nature, in its hunger for markets and profits. The truth is that modern warfare has developed so that no economic system is more conducive to peace than one based on private initiative, where a multitude of individuals pursue their happiness and profit, independent of the state.

What is the essence of modern warfare? Its indispensable requirement is dictatorship, with the government controlling every feature of economic activity. Communism and Fascism both have molded themselves to fit this totalitarian image of war. Both are systems of perpetual wartime mobilization. Both put guns above butter, the state's exactions for war ahead of improving the living standards of the people.

Before a modern capitalistic nation can go to war, it literally must turn itself inside out. Only great provocations justify such a transformation. This explains why America's strength has the quality of a storm, which, before it bursts, must gather unity from darkened, threatening skies. Only the clouding of great dangers will cause us to accept the restraints on our freedom which mobilization entails.

Even when we do, the spur remains our determination to preserve our system. We fight to banish the danger which forced us to band together, so we can go back to our normally free, individualistic habits. Often, Americans are accused of not knowing for what we fight. Yet, ours has been a consistent—though perhaps inadequate—war aim. We fight not to implant ourselves on foreign shores, but to come home; not to remain warlike, but to return to warhating; not to impose our will upon others, but so we can continue governing ourselves as we wish.

Considering this behavior, faithfully followed through two wars and their aftermaths, it is strange to have America accused of being "imperialistic." Such charges can spring only from malice or a failure to understand the American system. It is worth noting that the propaganda of "imperialistic grabbing" spread against us is always couched in the future tense. It is what we allegedly are going to do for which we are smeared, not what we have done. From neither the first nor the second world war did we take anything from some other people for our own enrichment.

The few islands in the Pacific under our control serve as part of a system of defense on which the security of all freedom-loving people rests. Economically, these islands are liabilities.

In his final report as Chief of Staff, Gen. Dwight D. Eisenhower wrote of the American proposal on atomic energy, "In truth, it demands nothing of others which the United States is not willing to give to the others, and it would give to all our knowledge of the application of atomic energy."

That can be repeated as a generalization about our conduct through the war and peacemaking—we have asked nothing we were not willing to give to others—namely, peace.

[ED. NOTE—*A cut of six paragraphs has been made at the end of this article.*]

VERMONT PRAISE

by *Robert P. Tristram Coffin*

"I AM A New Englander by birth, by bringing up, by spirit," says Robert Peter Tristram Coffin, and his poetry proves it. For more than thirty years this descendant of Nantucket whalers has been expressing the New England tradition in poems, many of which have appeared first in the *Post*. Since 1922 he has been professor of English at Bowdoin College in Brunswick, Maine, and he has read and lectured about poetry in every part of America.

APRIL 6, 1946

The young new preacher had an edge
   Like a well-whet knife;
His eyes were full of stars as he
   Spoke of eternal life.

He liked this little town in white,
   The steady, sober people;
He loved this church that might be his,
   With mountains by its steeple.

He gave his listeners all he had,
   Voice and brain and heart;
His sermon warmed him so he felt
   The teardrops burn and smart.

He finished, and the hush was deep
   In the little place.
A gray-haired deacon rose with calm
   Vermont upon his face.

He came forward, put his hard
   Hand on the preacher's arm.
"Young man," said he, "you didn't do
   That text you took no harm."

The young man's face was like the sun,
   The church was his, he knew;
He knew rapture when he heard it—
   He was a Vermonter too.

IS THERE A LIFE AFTER FORTY?

by Robert M. Yoder

"I WAS BORN in Gibson City, Illinois, on August 18, 1907, which my father said was a bad year all around," writes Robert M. Yoder. "I attended the University of Illinois and its law school and was educated covering night police for a newspaper in Decatur, Illinois. During some of the finest days in Chicago's boisterous history I worked in the Chicago bureau of the Associated Press, then moved to the Chicago *Daily News*, which is the paper I talk about when I am in my cups. In 1942 I presented myself in Washington in a blue Navy suit, ready for anything. They sat me down in front of a typewriter. My grandchildren will shake their heads in disbelief when I tell them I was an assistant to the special assistant to the assistant chief of naval operations."

En route to Chicago after the war reporter Yoder stopped over in Philadelphia to write articles for the *Post* and has been doing so ever since. "Is There a Life After Forty?" is based on bitter personal experience.

NOVEMBER 15, 1947

FOR SOME REASON or another, and all of them good, the age of forty is approached with dread and is a birthday in bold-face type. Men and women are glad to reach twenty-one, men at least like reaching thirty, nobody minds being thirty-eight and nobody minds being forty-two. But forty hangs in the mind like one of the big turning points, and not for good, either. Forty sounds like a turning point the way the fire was a turning point for Chicago or like a "Road Closed" sign on an auto trip. That is how you think of forty before you get there.

Well, the other day I reached that Jumping-Off-Place and am now in position to report how forty looks from the other side. I can report that it looks exactly as advertised. Before reaching forty you are likely to think of that birthday as one of life's major division points. Upon reaching forty you are convinced that forty not only is a division point on Life's Journey—why don't they fix that roadbed?—but probably is where the narrow gauge starts.

At forty you realize that it is no coincidence that entire books have been written to persuade people that this is not The End. You begin to understand why Prof. Walter Pitkin's famous *Life Begins at Forty* was a best seller; a book entitled *Drowning Can be Fun* would have the same sort of appeal, or one entitled *There's Money in Being Poor*. To reach forty not only gives you pause, but makes you wonder if you can start up again; it is a damned disturbing sensation. Because so many look upon this experience with fear and suspicion, I have kept notes on the experience. If you are one of the thousands to whom this will happen shortly, this report from The Great Beyond will not make you any happier about it. But if we can't grow old graciously, we can at least go down beefing.

To begin with, it is impossible to suppress the feeling that your Blue Book rating takes a bad tumble at forty. It is all too clearly the start of middle age, which is a raw deal to hand a broth of a boy like you and me. The actual event, however, is relatively quiet. (A quiet start for a long, quiet period, sonny.) One day you are thirty, and then, with little or nothing to account for the difference, you are forty. It does not bring general collapse; that idea is overdramatic. You don't wake up on your fortieth birthday with a film on the eyes and a gnarled cane by your bedside. You wake up feeling strange, but no stranger than you felt at thirty-nine. The main difference is emotional; the feeling is about what a race horse must feel when first he sees the dray wagon.

But as a matter of fact, people who are forty in the 1940's long since quit expecting to feel good. We were twenty in the '20's, and the '20's ended in a sensational collapse; we were thirty in the 1930's, which were years when the whole world went into a stall; and we are forty in a decade when a global war ended in a time of quiet frenzy. Fate's favorite patsies, that's us. God knows we've been in tune with our times. Here is the world going to pot, and look who's following suit. At forty you can look back a long way and see how you got here, although it's too late to do anything much about it. Still, if we have flopped, we're as appropriate to the twentieth century as a bride to a honeymoon.

One of the perquisites of being forty is a special note that creeps into doctors' voices, except that "creeps" isn't the word for it; it creeps into their voices like a yell creeps up on a cheerleader. All through your thirties they treat you with concern. You are pretty run down for thirty-five, they will say, or mighty decrepit for thirty-eight. But once you tell them you have passed the Great Boundary they grow kindly. The tone they use then, after examining the animate remains, is that of mechanics talking about a fine old 1920 Chalmers: the old wreck certainly sounds good, considering the model; though it must be hard to get acetylene for the lights. Their manner says clearly that all medical science can hope to do at this stage is to keep the battered old relic on the road; if you can walk to and from the doctor's office and play a little solitaire, they plainly regard it as a victory. No doctor will let you out of his office without volunteering the remark that, of course, at forty you can't do all the things you could do at twenty.

If you could, you could wrap the good doctor's stethoscope around his neck and throw him under the X-ray table, but you get this little truism in spite of all evidence of its truth. Most of the things they think you can't do are things you wouldn't have done at twenty-nine for three dollars an hour; the rest of the things you can't do at forty are things you didn't have money enough to do at twenty, anyway.

Forty is the real Awkward Age; you are old enough to realize that you would look silly doing things you are still young enough to wish you could do. One thing you realize is that you need no longer fear arousing mad passion on the part of young girls; you may safely be as attractive as you like, kid. Forty is when young girls who are your natural playmates get to acting a little strange. They start calling you "mister" in very much the same tone they would use for Lionel Barrymore, and they treat you in a curious way which, it dawns on you, is disinterest in its purest form. They regard you as one with the trees, the hills, and the Gettysburg battlefield. Now you are an interesting example of the game in mother's day, and that's all. They ought to tremble when they see a roué like you, but instead they yawn. The way to look at this development is to say that it keeps you out of a lot of trouble that you'd sure like to be into. Look at it this way: forty is a kind of vaccination against a lot of things, most of which you'd like to catch a heavy case of.

They say you have to be a little more careful of your health, guarding against exertion, which I'll be glad to do. You can't stay out all night any more, even on nights when it would take a Federal subpoena to get you out of the house. You have to go easy on drinking, which is made easier by the fact that by this time you begin measuring the party against the probable hangover, and you would rather not feel like that in the morning than get drunk on bonded bourbon with an all-star cast. People our age didn't survive prohibition gin and spiked beer just to get drunk with any casuals who are standing around a bar.

At forty you clearly aren't twice as smart as you were at twenty, and it is certainly more like two thirds of being sixty than it is like being four times ten. I avoid the possibility that forty is half of being eighty, which would suggest that forty is the adolescence of old age. That probably is true, but at forty you learn to skirt a lot of things that probably are true. There are clear-cut differences, however, between being forty and, say, twenty. They are differences largely of attitude.

At twenty you would climb a sixty-foot tree to get a leaf some girl said was pretty. At forty you'd mark her down as leaf-nutty and Nature-happy, and buy her a single ticket to the nearest arboretum.

At twenty, if a friend got thrown into jail for espousing some cause, you would organize mass meetings and demand to be thrown into jail with him. At thirty you would demand action by the Supreme Court. At forty you would telephone the precinct captain or the judge's sweetie and get action faster.

At twenty, if a girl gives you a long, direct look and smiles, you look into the next weighing-machine mirror to see why you are so attractive. At forty you look to see who's behind you or what's unbuttoned.

At thirty you notice you are putting on a little weight, which is a public calamity, like having the Discus Thrower get flabby or Venus develop a double chin. So you play handball two nights a week, cut down desserts and alcohol, and sweat off four pounds by strenuous exertion. At forty you take another drink, order pie à la mode and make a note to get pleated trousers.

At twenty, if nine P.M. finds you at home, you are sore. At forty, if the phone rings after seven, you wish whoever is coming to drink up your last bottle could pick a night when you didn't want to listen to the radio.

At twenty you welcome a chance to dive off a bridge, rescue a drowning man and be a Page One hero. At forty, if you did not get drowned trying, you would clip the man twice—once to rescue him and once for ruining your good suit.

At twenty you would be indignant if somebody

else got a mule trip into the Andes to do business with a wild tribe of white Indians. At forty you would locate their American branch in Rockefeller Center or the factory in Hohokus where they buy their quaint native handcraft; if you wanted to see their picturesque countryside, you would wait for a Technicolor travelogue at the neighborhood theater. You still have an occasional impulse to slap a mounted policeman on the horse or be the willing victim of a beautiful lady spy, but you are in no danger of running away to join the circus, and if the Foreign Legion wants you, they'll have to make striking changes in their program.

At twenty you will drive ninety miles an hour for 200 miles through a snowstorm to see one particular girl. At forty you would phone any girl who's home, invite her to come over by cab, and resent it if you miss the eleven-o'clock news broadcast.

At twenty you'd stand all night in line to ride in the first atomic-powered rocket plane. At forty you wouldn't stand in line to ride a magic carpet through Shangri-La on a pass; in fact, you wouldn't stand in line for anything except a place to sit down.

At twenty you'd work nights for a week to avoid missing a party. At forty you wouldn't stay out after midnight for anything up to and including one of the orgies of Imperial Rome, and even there you would have heard the stories. If the party is likely to involve dancing, you regard it with the same enthusiasm as if it involved an opportunity for ditch digging. On the dance floor you feel you ought to get taxi rates, say one dollar to pull your flag and fifty cents a yard anywhere in the city.

At twenty you will change ties six times to get one that looks smart with your new suit, and if the well-dressed man is wearing an ankle-length overcoat of green gunny sacking, you'll have one the minute you can raise the money. It would attract universal attention and cause serious distress if your studs were last year's model. At forty you would go to a White House reception in borrowed pants, wearing paper clips for cuff links, and any suit is in style that will still button.

At twenty you would sit in a hailstorm to see North Carolina Mining and Cowkeeping play Upper Nebraska for possession of the prized Wooden Turtle and the championship of the Soybean Belt. At forty you may get so fired with excitement as to say, "I'd like to see that game . . . in the newsreels," but you wouldn't go out into the traffic to see them play for the possession of North Carolina.

It seems to come down to this: Forty has its advantages, which you could put in your eye. It isn't the twilight of life. but it isn't youth's bright morning, either. There is a little gray in that handsome head of hair I was only yesterday soaking with pomade to get a smooth pompadour, and the dimples are longer now. A lot of my friends are looking pretty chunky and settled; they look like respectable citizens; they are pillars of the community who only yesterday were its chief worries. Once you thought that by this age you would be on top of the world and from forty or forty-five on you would be coasting. At forty you realize you are not coasting, but just skidding. Forty is the age by which you expected to be clipping coupons, and *at* which you find yourself trimming cuffs. About all I can say for it is that forty is no worse than thirty-nine, and probably not much better than forty-one. If anything begins at forty, I haven't noticed it.

NOTE ON DANGER B

by Gerald Kersh

ONE NIGHT IN 1947 a commentator told his radio listeners that a jet plane had crashed in Montana with a baby at the controls; a secret report on the matter, he said, was being suppressed by the Government. The report was wholly imaginary and had already been read by some twenty million people as a short story in the *Post*. But it was such a convincing simulation of fact that many people thought it had happened. Thousands of letters poured into the *Post* demanding further details.

Author Gerald Kersh has long specialized in this kind of fiction. In "The Monster" (February 21, 1948) he described a Japanese wrestler who was blown two centuries backward through time and halfway around the world by the atomic bombing of Hiroshima. In "The Mysterious Smile of Mona Lisa" (June 28, 1948) he suggested that the lady kept her mouth closed because she had bad teeth—an idea that was picked up several years later and sent out as a news story from Rome. Kersh is a 45-year-old Englishman who was a professional wrestler, among other things, before he turned author in 1935. His first book was withdrawn, he says, because of "several libel suits." His hobby is "wandering aimlessly about town" when in London.

APRIL 5, 1947

DOCTOR SANT SAYS that he and Captain Mayo exceeded 1000 miles an hour in the jet-propelled F.S.2 on April 11, 1945. The fact has yet to be confirmed.

Danger A was established as a real danger in October, 1946. Sober scientists have not yet fully acknowledged the existence of what Doctor Sant calls Danger B.

The suppressed pages of the Sant Report are curiously interesting, however. They bring back into memory one of the most remarkable theories ever put forward by an established mathematician. The mathematician was Berliner, who died in 1910. The work to which Doctor Sant refers is formidably entitled: LIVING CELLS AND THEIR RELATION TO TIME; WITH A NOTE ON TIME SO FAR AS TIME IS UNITED WITH VELOCITY AND SPACE. It was written by Berliner, revised and indexed by Wasserman in 1911, and published by Frischauer in 1912, in Vienna. Only 350 copies of this book were printed. It is extremely rare. There is a copy in the library of the British Museum, and another in the Bodleian Library. I know of no others.

GERALD KERSH.

After two years of departmental wirepulling and patient waiting, I have been granted permission to publish the suppressed pages of the Sant Report, which the War Department filed away as "Secret" in April, 1945. This is the document of which General Branch said, "It surely must be the most astounding thing of its kind that ever has been or ever will be written."

By "of its kind," General Branch meant "of the official kind, written by a responsible scientist in the proper language, and formally handed in to the proper authorities."

For the report was written by Doctor Sant. It deals with the first flight of the jet-propelled F.S.2, and with two of the dangers that threaten the flier who wants to cover too many miles a minute. He refers to them as Danger A and Danger B. Nobody had thought of them until Doctor Sant wrote that brief, brusque and utterly sensational report. The possibility of Danger A may have occurred to one or two of the more imaginative scientists. But no scientist could ever have considered or even dreamed of the possibility of Danger B. The War Department kept it quiet, because at that time the fact was not established, and seemed, indeed, unverifiable.

But now it appears that some crumbs of evidence scraped out of the smoldering wreckage of a machine that crashed in Montana have given the experts cause to think again.

Danger A has to be overcome when the flier catches up with sound and touches 700 miles an hour. Then your hurtling metal machine crushes the vague atmosphere into something hard—much as a manufacturing chemist's press squeezes fine, loose amorphous powder into an aspirin tablet. In effect, you put up a brick wall of compressed air and smash yourself in knocking it down. And so a shower of scorched and twisted metal comes back to earth.

This was to be tragically demonstrated by just such a catastrophe over England, in October, 1946. Doctor Sant had seen the possibility of such mishaps as long ago as 1934, when he had already evolved a sound theory of jet propulsion and had even made a blueprint of a workable jet-propelled machine which he called F.S.1. The letters F.S. stood for Flying Spade simply because the outlines of Sant's machine, in 1934, were reminiscent of the ace of spades. These outlines were modified by 1945; by which time—having been lucky and adroit enough to get moral, financial, technical and official support—he was building F.S.2, in which he and Captain Mayo made a test flight.

F.S.2 looked like the head of a harpoon; it had an appearance of keenness and complete efficiency. A fabulously wealthy motorcar manufacturer whose name I may not mention financed the experiment, with the approval of the War Department, and so F.S.2 was put together secretly somewhere in Nevada. It was finished before the end of March, 1945—the necessities of war had mothered inventions which made this possible.

F.S.2 took off on its first serious flight on April 11, 1945. This happened to be Doctor Sant's fifty-second birthday—a fact difficult to believe. In spite of his white hair, Doctor Sant looks like a well-preserved athlete on the right side of forty; an athlete of the agile, slender kind —a runner and a jumper. Yet he boasts that he has not taken a stroke of exercise in thirty-five years. He attributes his vigor and his youthful appearance to the fact that he never drank alcohol, never smoked cigarettes and never got married, but lived only for his work. "I gave myself completely to work," he says. "That is as good a way as any of staying young. Friends, enemies, wives and children—they just weren't for me. They'd have torn me to bits like four wild horses. Life hasn't marked me up, because I haven't had time to live it. I've just worked all the time. Although," he adds, laughing, "work can mark you up a bit, too"—and he points to his nose, which is very badly broken. He did not get this injury in any romantic way; in 1943 he was hit by a piece of flying steel when something exploded in his laboratory. "Still, it doesn't cut half as deep or hurt half as much as a sad man's wrinkle," says Doctor Sant.

Captain Mayo was born in Pasadena in August, 1919. He is one of those flying prodigies peculiar to our time, for whom the whirling earth is too slow and boggy. He could take a car to pieces and put it together again before he was fifteen

years old. Above all things he loves speed—speed for speed's sake. He resents the tyranny of the law of gravity; he wants to get away from everything that clutches man's feet. Therefore he, too, is still unmarried. In his business it is better to be a bachelor. The perils of mad speed in the upper air are fantastically incalculable—as Doctor Sant's nightmarish report clearly indicates.

I should say, in passing, that Doctor Sant overcame Danger A by a bold—almost a foolhardy— application of what he called the gun-and-candle principle. This principle is as old as the hills. Fire a soft wax candle from a smooth-bore gun, and the power behind it will send that candle right through an oak plank. Similarly, a fine needle embedded in a cork and struck smartly with a hammer will pierce a tough bronze penny—a needle that would snap if you tried to push it through a fold of canvas. Furthermore, Sant did not attempt to achieve his highest speed until F.S.2 was up on the lower curve of the stratosphere, thus eliminating some of the danger of air resistance.

Sant and Mayo took off on April 11, 1945, at nine o'clock in the morning. They were back on the airfield about fifty-five minutes later. Something had gone wrong with their speed indicator. This instrument was designed to record speed up to 1000 miles an hour. It was broken. Doctor Sant says that it broke when F.S.2 reached the speed of 1250 miles an hour or thereabout. I state the figures exactly as they are recorded in the report. They are questionable, because the indicator stopped working. In certain quarters there is no doubt at all that Sant and Mayo on that occasion traveled faster than any human beings had ever traveled before.

Doctor Sant was proud and, for him, excited.

Captain Mayo was ashamed; he had blacked out, or become momentarily unconscious, as they turned to come back. He wanted a cup of coffee. But, to everybody's astonishment, the first thing that Doctor Sant said when he set foot on the ground was, "Has somebody got a mirror?"

Somebody had a mirror. He looked at his reflection; explored his broken nose with anxious fingers; said, "Ha!" and went to his office, shouting "Berliner! Berliner! Berliner!"

He stayed there for three hours, reading a book and making notes on a little blue scribbling block.

That evening Doctor Sant wrote his report. The War Department cut out every reference to Danger B.

But now, after two years, the ban is lifted, and I may give you the substance of what Doctor

Sant wrote. In the original document, Doctor Sant quoted certain figures and formulas which it is at present pointless to print. The formulas, particularly, contribute nothing to the story as it may be understood by the man in the street, for whom this is written. Doctor Sant's figures take us into the higher mathematics—into the esoteric mathematics that made headlines when Einstein first made news.

Anyone who understands the theory of Berliner—and only five men in the world can make head or tail of this theory—may work out for himself exactly what Doctor Sant was driving at.

But any schoolboy may grasp the broader aspects of the suppressed part of his report, dated April 11, 1945, handed in on the morning of April twelfth.

Doctor Sant said:

... I am aware that the failure of the indicator discredits my claim to having traveled at over 1000 miles an hour. Nevertheless, having tested every instrument with the utmost care, I am convinced that the indicator broke down because of the excessive strain imposed upon it by the speed achieved by F.S.2. I cannot support this claim, yet I am satisfied that Captain Mayo and I, on this occasion, broke every existing speed record. Similarly, there is no way in which I can confirm Danger B, which I believe to be a real danger.

For the sake of investigators in the near future, who will take up F.S.3 and F.S.4, I believe that it is my duty to relate events as I experienced them.

I had overcome Danger A, and—according to the indicator—had touched 875 miles an hour. The coughing and roaring of the jet had died away, and there was a peculiar quiet. If it had not been for the flickering of the indicator needles and the vibration of F.S.2, it would have been easy for me to convince myself that we had stopped moving and were hanging perfectly still in space. But the indicator told me that we were traveling at 875 miles an hour, then 900, and finally, 1000 miles an hour.

As the needle touched the last mark on the dial and agitated itself as if it were trying to push away beyond, I felt an extraordinary sense of lightness. I can make this sensation clear only by saying that I felt suddenly younger. I asked Captain Mayo how he was feeling, and he replied, "I feel as if this is just a dream."

I did not look around at that time. F.S.2 is designed so that it may be dually controlled. I, sitting in front, kept my eyes ahead. But a second or two later my eyes filled with tears, as though I had been struck on the nose. Indeed, my nose at that same moment began to throb and ache.

It had throbbed and ached in a similar way shortly after the septum had been removed in the operation that followed the explosion in my laboratory in 1943.

The throbbing and the ache brought this very vividly back into my recollection. Two or three seconds later, instead of this throbbing, I was aware of a strange shocked numbness, which, even as I became aware of it, went away.

Something compelled me to loosen my mask for a moment and feel my face. First of all, I touched my nose. It was no longer broken.

It occurred to me, naturally, that this was an illusion such as one may be occasionally subject to at certain heights and under certain pressures.

I spoke to Captain Mayo and asked whether he was all right. He said, "Well, I guess I am." His voice sounded uneasy, and I asked him if he was sure that he was all right.

Captain Mayo did not answer, and so I turned my head and saw him touching himself uneasily and looking at his hands in a bewildered way.

"Too much oxygen? Too little?" I asked.

Captain Mayo replied, "I just feel a bit strange."

I said, "We've touched a thousand miles an hour."

"How did we ever get to do that?" he asked, and his voice was different. All the authority was gone out of it. Then he uttered a sharp cry and said, "My arm! My arm!"

I looked and saw that his left forearm was dangling. It would have been hanging vertically downwards but for the support of the layers of sleeve that enclosed it.

Even as I looked, Captain Mayo's arm straightened out with a jerk, and at that his whole manner changed. He squared himself, and said, "This is it, Bill! Let them have it!"

And then I remembered that these were the words Captain Mayo is reported as having said when he was flying in France in 1942 and, his arm smashed by flak, took a Marauder into a suicidal dive from which he emerged alive and unhurt—except for his shattered arm.

I felt remarkably light and cheerful. In an indefinable way I felt different. I began to remember things which had faded out of my memory long before—things trivial in themselves, yet somehow important at that moment.

The needle of the indicator had gone limp; yet I am sure that we were moving at 1000 miles an hour at least. Only the vibration of F.S.2 indicated to me that we were moving. But the speed indicator being dead, I had a strange and unreasonable sense of having gone out of this world. Strange, illogical anxieties crept into my mind. I said to myself, *Tomorrow, at about eleven o'clock, I must see what has happened to Led-better's castings.* And then I remembered that Ledbetter was in Canada and that he had not made a casting for me since 1938, when my hair was still black. I was unable to resist the impulse to peel my glove away from my cuff.

There was a reason for this. In the summer of 1938, a week before Ledbetter had finished my castings, I was rather severely bitten in the right wrist by a schnauzer dog belonging to my sister. This bite had worried me then; I had feared infection and disablement at a certain operative moment.

There was no disablement and no infection. The marks of the dog's teeth have faded, so that now they are scarcely visible. But as I looked I saw four half-healed lacerations in the skin of my wrist grow angry and inflamed, and then, in a split second, change so that they became bleeding red wounds and then, in a flash, disappear. And I observed, also, that the hair on my wrist, which, since 1937, has been gray, was black.

I felt my nose. When I took off with Captain Mayo, it was smashed flat and boneless, as it is at present. Yet under my fingers then, it was hard and straight as it had been before it was broken. I uncovered my face and looked at my reflection in the glass-covered dial of one of the instruments in front, and I saw that my face was different. I have been clean-shaven since 1936, and gray-haired since 1938. The shiny glass reflected my face, strangely young. The nose was unbroken, and under it I saw a short black mustache.

I have not had a mustache since late in the autumn of 1936, when I shaved clean at the request of a young lady whom I have since all but forgotten. As I looked at this incredible reflection of myself, I found myself wondering what this young lady was doing, and reproaching myself because on her account my mind was so easily taken away from the work upon which I had been so keenly concentrating. It was as if I had slipped back nine years in time. I did not like that.

And still we might have been motionless in the sky.

It is fortunate for Mayo and for me that I turned just then to say, "Tell me, how do I look?"

Captain Mayo was apparently unwell. He is, as the records show, about twenty-six years old, six feet tall, and one hundred and seventy-two pounds in weight. When I turned, just then, I saw him as a boy of about sixteen, ludicrously little, in a heap of heavy, complicated garments that were slipping away from him as he became smaller, line by line.

His mask had slipped. His eyes were closed and his mouth was open. He was saying, "Mother! Mother!"

I reached back to shake him. As I did so, one of his gloves slipped off, uncovering the hand of a little boy.

It is fortunate that I turned when I did. Another fifteen minutes might have put an end to everything. I knew in those few seconds that what Berliner had dreamed was basically true, concerning man in relation to time and velocity. Traveling at a certain speed, presumably in a given direction—I hesitate to specify or to say that it is necessary to specify direction—a man touches one of the grooves along which time travels.

Berliner maintains that time passes man, and not that man is swept along by time. In common with certain others, I used to laugh at this. Now I have modified my opinion.

In only a few minutes, at that speed, Captain Mayo and I were back ten years in time.

I am thankful that this occurred to me. If the principle of F.S.1 and F.S.2 had not been clear in my mind eleven years ago, we must have crashed. In a few minutes more I believe that we should have gone back to the period when F.S.2 was nothing but a theory. I believe that I should have found myself in that machine like a child in a nightmare isolated at a great height. And then there would have been a sickening sensation of falling, falling, falling! And behind me under those heavy clothes there would have been a baby crying.

Already there was a certain dreamy wooliness in my head. I was experiencing something I had experienced somewhere between sleeping and waking many years before. I knew exactly in what machine I was flying. But I no longer knew what made it what it was. It seemed to me that I was rushing back, faster and faster, toward the eleven-year-old deadline behind which I should be lost forever. The memory of the Christmas of 1934 was very vivid in my mind.

We were traveling faster and faster. My only hope was in a quick turn. Then, it seemed that I was in F.S.1. Even that was fading. Nevertheless, I managed to turn. I saw my face getting older. I felt the impact that broke my nose, and then the familiar ache and throb that resulted. Looking behind me, I saw Captain Mayo stirring uneasily. He had filled his clothes. In a minute or two he became conscious. He told me that he had a blackout, as it is called, on the turn.

I maintain that Berliner touched a certain aspect of the truth. In maintaining this and committing these notes to writing, I realize that I may be discrediting myself, and inviting suspicion of my other conclusions. Nevertheless, the danger which I call Danger B deserves investigation.

Doctor Sant's F.S.2 is regarded as vastly important. Apart from that which makes it fly, there is an automatic air-compression device and a "forward brake"—as they call it. Work is going forward on F.S.3. Hahningen's lined duralumin will make practical Sant's early dream of the double nose. Fowler's indicator will be foolproof, pressure-proof and altitude-proof. Weather permitting, F.S.3 should be tested in May, 1947.

That F.S.3 will almost certainly break every known record is unimportant, as I see it. The War Department believes in Doctor Sant. So do I. Doctor Sant believes in the improbable: so did Galileo, Marconi, Watt, Leonardo da Vinci and the Brothers Wright. And so do I.

It is pretty well established that Doctor Sant never committed himself without reason. I cannot understand what Berliner wrote any more than a journalist of the eighteenth century could understand what Newton wrote, but I have faith in Sant—like the War Department.

The Sant Report may indicate that when it is safe to travel fast enough, we may have conquered death—that is to say, the ordinary physical and emotional wear and tear of life and time. It is indicated that if we move fast enough, we can catch up with past years.

I put this baldly because it is necessary to convey the straight idea. Fine writing, imaginative writing—must come later.

I have the report of the Montana crash. Ted Oxen took off alone in a certain jet-propelled plane which crashed in Montana. Out of the scorched and twisted wreckage the authorities picked certain remains of a human being. This human being must have been a child nine or ten years old, according to the analysis of the carbonized fat. It remains to be worked out.

THE MURDERER

by Joel Townsley Rogers

JOEL TOWNSLEY ROGERS was born November 22, 1896, in Sedalia, Missouri, graduated from Harvard, *cum laude*, in 1917, and spent two years in the Navy's aviation branch during and after World War I. As soon as he was discharged, he wrote his first short story, which was rejected by *Snappy Stories*. He then sold it to *Harper's* for $100. "So," he adds, "I was sunk and lost and damned. I was a writer." He turned out "The Murderer" in three days; it has since been reprinted in a half dozen foreign countries, and dramatized on radio and TV. It is one of the most unusual mystery stories the *Post* ever ran.

NOVEMBER 23, 1946

JOHN BANTREAGH backed away from her a step on caving knees, with his gaze still on her. She looked so helpless, and somehow innocent, lying here on the meadow grass in the gray, still dawn, in front of his farm-truck wheels. In her white dress with its big red polka dots and red patent-leather belt, and her white shoes with their red heels. With her red mouth and light-brown curly hair, and her hazel eyes open.

Looking at him, it seemed like, out of dream-filled sleep, a little blankly. As she did sometimes in the early mornings, while he dressed quietly to go out and do the chores, with eyes wide open, though not yet all awake. But, of course, she wasn't. There was an opaqueness on her lenses, there was a cold dew on her face, and she was dead.

One wheel had gone over her throat and the other over her sheer-clad ankles. Her legs had hardly been hurt at all, he thought; the ground was soft, and they had just been pressed down into the mire and grass roots. Only her throat had been broken—the trachea, the larynx and pharynx, or whatever else there was in people's throats that made them live and breathe. That made them talk too. Her eyes were on him, with that look they had. But she would never say who had done it.

John Bantreagh felt as if his own throat had been crushed, as he tried to pull his gaze away, with his knees caving. As if a heavy wheel had rolled onto it, and—not like with her—had not backed away. He looked around him slowly with his reddened gaze. He had a feeling that other eyes were watching him, if not hers. But it was a lonely meadow, on a lonely road. Just dark pine woods around, and the dirt road two or three hundred yards away, beyond the tumble-down snake fence that bordered it.

His truck motor had died. He must start it and back down across the meadow to the road again. Get on back home before anyone was stirring. Let her be found by someone else. It would be hours, way off here—it might be even days. That would be too much to endure, knowing she was here. This evening, if no one had found her before then, he might suggest, just offhandedly, looking along here, as if it were something that had occurred to him without any reason. There was just so much a man could stand.

The air had lightened from dark silver to pearl. It was not full light yet, but it was no longer night. He had never known a moment so quiet and still. Across the meadow grass he could see the tracks of his truck coming in at a diagonal from the road, through the break in the fence, where the weeds were crushed down that grew in the shallow roadside ditch and along the field side of the fence. Two parallel lines, with only moderate waves in them, coming directly to where his truck stood now with its front tires almost touching her. Smooth-worn front tires, but cleated rear tires, which had left their tracks of broad, deep, transverse ridges. They were a pair he had ordered from the mail-order catalogue, and had cost a lot of money. He had got them from the freight office only yesterday morning, along with the things for Mollie and the kids, and the rest of the order; and had put them on when he got back home, with her and the kids watching him.

Just yesterday forenoon. Mollie had been rinsing out some things on the back-porch bench beside the pump, with her wrists buried in the washbasin, and soapy water splashing on the ground off the porch edge. She had paused to brush back her tendrils of damp hair with the inside of her elbow, squeezing out a handful of sand-colored fabric.

"You're proud of those tires, aren't you, John?"

"Sure am!" he told her as he knelt on the gravel

473

unwrapping one of them. "I'll bet nobody else has anything like them in the whole county. Eight-ply, tractor tread, guaranteed for fifty thousand miles. Could have got a good-enough tire for six-fifty less apiece, maybe. But it's smart to get something that lasts, as I can see it."

"I reckon you're pretty smart, John."

"Sure am, honey. I got you."

"How long do you figure I'm guaranteed for?"

"Till death do us part," he had replied, grinning.

She had laid the sand-colored fabric down on the bench and had squeezed out a handful of something black—her dark blue blouse, it must be, that looked black because it was wet. She didn't have any black things. She didn't seem altogether pleased. The tires had cost a lot of money. Maybe she was thinking of the nice things it could have bought.

"What are you washing out, honey?" he had asked her.

"Just my rayon stockings and some old things."

"Maybe someday you'll have a pair of nylons, so you won't have to take such care of those rayons. I saw Lilybelle wearing a pair the other day. I wouldn't know, but she said they were. I guess every woman likes them."

"Does Lilybelle have nylon underwear too?"

She liked to tease him at times about Lilybelle. It was just a joke. She wasn't really jealous of Lilybelle. She hadn't any reason to be that he knew of.

"She didn't say, honey," he told her.

She had said something else then, brushing back her hair again, but he hadn't heard, having begun to pry one of the old bare-tread shoes off a rim with a mallet and tire iron. The kids had been jumping around and yelling, and she might have been reprimanding them. Vaguely, in the back of his mind, he wondered who would take care of the kids now. It was the first time he had thought of it.

His knees caved and caved. He had heard of men's knees doing that, but it didn't seem natural. He couldn't control them, though. He stiffened them, and they jerked down again as if they were only water. He planted a hand on the mudguard of his truck, taking a dragging step back toward the seat. He must start his engine and back down to the road again and go on home. Now.

There was no sound of distant barn-yard roosters. It must be a good mile at least, maybe two or five, to the nearest house. If there was any wildlife in the woods around the meadow—fox, bobcat or possum—it was keeping very still.

A car was coming along the road already, though. A sedan with some early driver at the wheel. It slowed its bumping progress as it approached the break in the fence. It came to a momentary halt. The driver had seen his truck and him in the meadow, John Bantreagh thought, standing motionless. Maybe he could see the white of her dress in front of his wheels, though the truck might hide that from the road.

The car turned and came in, anyway. It drove slowly along the broad, deep, cleated tracks of his truck, approaching. That it should take the same course was perhaps inevitable, or at least expectable. Every field, however smooth, has its own hidden soft spots, waves and hummocks, and one car will tend to follow the same path across it as another, unless deliberately held to a different course. Particularly when a previous car has already made ruts at the grass roots. The driver of the approaching sedan probably didn't realize that he was flattening out those cleated and distinctive treads beneath the impress of whatever nondescript tire treads he might have himself. Perhaps he didn't notice them. Or if he did, he considered their preservation of no importance.

It wasn't important, of course, thought John Bantreagh. His truck was here, and he was here. He rested the palm of his left hand on the mudguard. His eyes burned red and sleepless. His throat was dry. His right hand hung down at his side with something in it. His truck crank, he realized. He didn't know how long he had had it in his hand. He had been quite unaware of it. He hadn't the strength now to place it back on the truck floor where he usually kept it. Not even to open his hand and let it drop into the grass.

The driver of the sedan stopped with his bumper nudging the back of the truck. He opened the door and got out. He was a big young fellow with a bronzed, square-jawed face and alert and steady gray eyes. He wore a black tropical suit, unbuttoned on an expanse of soft white shirt, black-necktied, and a black slouch hat. He overtopped John Bantreagh by four inches. His lithe, light-stepping frame had the massed weight of two hundred pounds. He was a dozen years younger than John Bantreagh—perhaps he was twenty-five. He looked fresh and well slept and newly bathed, competent and cool.

He pushed back his hat on his crisp black curls. He wore a nickeled badge, pinned to a red suspender strap over his white shirt. There was a polished walnut gun butt extruding from a black holster on his right hip, and a pair of handcuffs hanging beside it from his belt.

He gave a brief, alert glance at John Bantreagh's stained, red-eyed face and thin, shaking form. He stood looking down at the woman's body lying supine in front of the truck wheels, with his fists planted on his hips and his pectoral muscles expanded.

"What happened?" he said. "Run over?"

John Bantreagh swallowed. "Yes."

"It looks pretty much like it was deliberate," the big young fellow said quietly.

He squatted beside her, looking, not touching. With steady, alert eyes. With his alert and sleep-refreshed brain behind them.

"Name's Clade," he said. "Roy Clade, deppity, from over in Boomerburg. I was due at the courthouse this morning on a car-stealing case, and just happened to take the back road, first time in a year. Never thought I'd run into anything like this."

"No," John Bantreagh swallowed. "I reckon nobody would."

"Yep, she was murdered," the young deputy said quietly. "No two ways about it. Blood on the back of her head, matted with her hair. She was hit with a tire iron or something, and then laid on the ground when she was out cold, and the front wheels run up onto her. Know who she is?"

"Yes," John Bantreagh swallowed. "Her name's —her name was Mollie Bantreagh—Mrs. John Bantreagh—from over outside of Jeffersonville. Funny name, sounds like 'pantry,' " he said tonelessly—as he always did, to forestall banal remarks about it. "I don't know where it came from. Some say it's an aristocratic name in Scotland, but I don't know. She's—she was my wife."

"Your wife!" The young deputy shot up a quick, keen look at him. "You mean you were her husband?"

"Yes," John Bantreagh said. "That's right." He could not stop the wobbling of his knees. The dryness stuck in his throat. He rubbed his Adam's apple with his left hand to relieve the pressure on it.

"Tough!" said the young deputy, in a voice of proper sympathetic pitch. "Your wife! Gee! I thought you were just some stranger driving by. I'm not a married man myself. But your wife— she must have meant an awful lot to you. I'll bet this has hit you terribly."

"Yes," said John Bantreagh, feeling his throat. "We had our little disagreements at times, like everybody. I reckon the neighbors know. She always liked nice things a lot."

"All married people have their little battles, I expect," said the young deputy awkwardly. "It'd be kind of funny if they didn't. Gee, your wife, though! Kids, I suppose, too?"

"Three," said John Bantreagh. "Three. Two boys and a girl."

"And no one to look after them now, I reckon.

Tough!" the young deputy said again, with an effort at feeling. "It sure is an awful break for you, Mr. Bantreagh. Who could have done a thing like this, anyway?"

"I ——" said John Bantreagh, swallowing, "I thought maybe I could get Lilybelle to look after them for a spell. She's not very fond of kids, I don't think, but she might do it for me."

"Who's Lilybelle?"

"Lilybelle Turner, lives next place down the road," said John Bantreagh, rubbing his throat. "She's only a kid herself, just nineteen, and not seeming hardly that old, with her dark curls and blue eyes. All she can think of is having a good time and loving. Mollie—Mollie used to pretend to be kind of jealous of her, just joking. But she's a woman, anyway, and I reckon I can get her to pitch in and help with the kids, if the neighbors don't talk."

"There's always another woman, isn't there?" remarked the young deputy absently. "I mean there's always one to pitch in and help with the kids, I reckon, unless a man lives at the North Pole, when his wife goes."

But he hadn't been paying much attention to the problem, his manner indicated. He had pulled out a silver pencil and a brownish paper-bound notebook from his inner jacket pocket. He opened the notebook on his knee and unscrewed the pencil. John Bantreagh watched with dull, bloodshot eyes what he was writing.

"Mollie Bantreagh, Mrs. John Bantreagh, res. nr. Jeff'ville. Struck on back of head by tire iron or other instr'm'nt & run onto by car's front wheels. Body found by husband ——"

He looked up with sharp alertness at John Bantreagh, with his pencil halted. John Bantreagh swayed. He leaned back against his truck with his crank hanging from his hand. It was coming now—the question.

"What time did you find her, Mr. Bantreagh?"

John Bantreagh let his breath seep out. He stiffened his knees. It was bound to come. But this wasn't it yet.

"I haven't got a watch," he said tonelessly. "It was just getting kind of silver light. Maybe ten minutes ago. Maybe half an hour or three quarters—I don't know. It kind of knocked me out."

"I'll put it as four forty-five," said the young deputy sympathetically. "The exact time, I reckon, doesn't make any particular difference.

" 'Found by husband at four forty-five,' " he recited as he wrote. " 'Joined by Deputy Clade at five-oh-three and scene observed. No footprints. No tire tread discernible on body; smudge on nylon stockings indication possible print had been wiped off by hand. Possible tire tracks on field obliterated by husband's car and Deputy Clade's. Implement with which struck removed by killer. No other objects apparent on scene to indicate identity.' I guess that's the story, Mr. Bantreagh."

He put away his book and pencil. He pushed his hat off the back of his head and set it on levelly again, with his frowning gaze a moment on her staring eyes.

John Bantreagh swallowed. "They're nylons?" he said.

"What? Her stockings? Oh, sure. All the women've got to have them. What did you think they were?"

"I thought they were rayons," said John Bantreagh. "The pair I got for her last Christmas. I thought they were just rayons all the time. But then tonight I figured they were nylons."

"Oh, sure," the young deputy repeated mechanically. "All the women've got to have them."

He pushed his hat on the back of his head again and stood up, taking his eyes from her.

"Who could have done it?" he repeated quietly, with his fists planted on his hips, looking down at John Bantreagh's pallid face and bloodshot eyes with his keen, alert gaze, with his fresh, keen brain behind it. "Who do you suppose could have done it, Mr. Bantreagh? I mean," he explained with frowning brow, "she couldn't have been murdered for her jewels and money, because I don't reckon she had any—more than just her wedding ring that she's still got on, and maybe a couple of nickels in her coin purse on her belt or something like that. It couldn't have been just a maniac, because how could he have got her out to a lonely place like this to murder her, without her putting up some sort of a fight and screaming?

"It was some man she knew, who wanted to get rid of her. Because he was crazy about some beautiful little kid who was a few years younger than she was, maybe; and she knew about it, and was always nagging him, and stood in his way. And so he got her to ride out here with him, and he cracked her on the head with this tire iron or something that he had laid on the seat beside him handy, probably while he was making love to her, and then hauled her out and laid her down in front of his car, and ran his wheels up on her and crushed the life out of her. Figuring to drop her body in the ditch beside the road back near where she lived, like she had been struck by a hit-and-run while walking home.

"Only, after he had done it," the young deputy said, frowning at John Bantreagh, "he could see it wouldn't pass. The way her throat had been crushed would be only like she had been lying unconscious on the ground when she had been run over, just the way it had been done. There would be meadow mud and grass stains, maybe, on her dress. And maybe ten or a hundred other things that he couldn't think of at the moment, but that wouldn't let it pass. So it was murder," he said quietly, "and nothing else. And there was nothing for him to do but just leave her here, and go on home and go to sleep, like nothing had happened, waiting till somebody else happened to find her. Figuring that it wouldn't be for some hours yet, at least. And maybe days, because it was such a lonely road. Though hoping, too, that it wouldn't be too long.

"And so, as I figure it, Mr. Bantreagh, he got up quietly from where he was kneeling beside her, when he was sure that she was dead, and backed away from her, to get into his car again, that he had rolled back off her, and back it down across the meadow to the road again. Figuring that, if he had left any tire tracks, a few hours more might dim them out. Or that maybe somebody else had tires like his, or that maybe when somebody else would come along, they would roll over them with their own tracks before they had noticed them."

The young deputy pushed his hat off the back of his head and set it on again.

"Now, there's just one thing that I've got to ask you, Mr. Bantreagh."

A faint dawn breath across the dewed meadow stirred a drape of his crisp, freshly pressed black jacket as he stood looking down at John Bantreagh. It stirred the ends of the black knit four-in-hand upon his expanse of white shirt above his flat, quiet-breathing diaphragm. The skin upon his hard, young, fresh-shaven face was shiny and tight, and a little muscle rippled at the corner of his mouth, though John Bantreagh's eyes did not lift that high.

His knees—John Bantreagh's—caved, and he stiffened them. He leaned back against the windshield post of his truck, thrusting his heels against the ground. His bloodshot eyes swam, out of focus. He fingered his throat with his left hand, glancing involuntarily down. There was a deep scratch or cut across the back of his right hand, he saw, that was gripped about the crank handle. He didn't remember when he had got it, but it was still oozing. Some of the blood must have seeped stickily around onto his clenched palm, helping to glue it to the iron.

Now! he thought. What form the question would take, he didn't know. But it must come. The throat muscles of the big young deputy were still moving beneath his broad, smooth-shaven chin. He had paused only for a moment.

"Just one question, Mr. Bantreagh," he repeated. "It may seem kind of cold and brutal of me to ask it, at a time like this," he added, a little awkwardly. "But if I didn't, someone else would, anyway. And they still will, I reckon, and keep on asking it until they've found out whatever there is to know. You understand, a law officer's got his job to do, and it's just impersonal. What I mean is, Mr. Bantreagh, was there anybody that she had been going around with that you ever heard about? A boy friend that she had, I mean—someone that she had been two-timing you with? Of course," he added, "she might have been stepping out and you not have known anything about it. That happens too. But there must have been someone, just on the face of it, because he would have been the only man in the world who would have had any cause to have done it, as sure as hell. Did she ever drop any hint to you about him, Mr. Bantreagh, as to who he was? I don't mean to seem cold and brutal at a time like this."

John Bantreagh swallowed. "I know you've got to ask your questions," he said, pulling at the loose skin of his throat. "That's all right. Yes, I reckon there was"—he swallowed—"someone. She used to go down to the village two or three times a week after supper; it's only a couple of miles away. She'd tell me she was going to the free library to read magazines and books. She was always a great hand for reading. I couldn't drive her in the truck, because somebody had to stay home with the kids. I'd be asleep by the time she got home. But it seems she didn't really go to the free library at all. This fellow would pick her up on the road, and they'd go riding in his car. I only learned about it last night."

He swallowed again. He rubbed his forehead with his left hand. There was some small thing he was trying to remember. But there was much more that he wanted to forget.

"I woke up," he said tonelessly, "with one of the kids crying. He was cold, and wanted a blanket on him. Mollie always looked to their covers when she came home or got up in the night herself. But she hadn't got home yet. By the looks of the moonlight out on the yard, it looked kind of late. I held the alarm clock to the window, and it was one o'clock. I lit the lamp and put on my pants and shoes, and went out to the road in front and looked down it, but didn't see her coming. There was something white on the front porch of the Turner house a quarter mile down, but that was all.

"So I went back in and covered the kids up better, tucking them in. They sure looked cute in their new pajamas, and I wished she was there to see them. I'd got pajamas for them with my tire order that had come in the morning, pink and white stripes for the boys, and the baby's blue with white ducks on them. She hadn't seen them in them yet; she'd gone out right after supper, before I'd got them to bed. That made me think"—John Bantreagh swallowed—"of the nylons. Her birthday was tomorrow—today. Twenty-nine. And I had ordered her a pair of nylons. I figured she would like them. She had never had any.

"I had left them out in the truck in back, under the seat, to get and give her in the morning. But I thought it might be kind of nice to put them in her bottom drawer for her, where she kept her things, and kind of say something to her in the morning, joking like, that I had heard a mouse in her drawer last night, maybe it was making a nest. And she would hurry to open it and pull out all her things, and would find them at the bottom, and it would surprise her.

"So I brought them in in their envelope," said John Bantreagh tonelessly, "and opened her drawer and took out some of her things on top, the balls of socks that she generally wears, and her blouses and skirts that she had made, and a couple of starched house dresses. She kept her rayons in the drawer, I knew. But she was wearing them, I thought. I didn't know she had any other stockings." He swallowed. "But there were lots of stockings there, hid away at the bottom. A dozen pairs of them. They were the same color as her rayons, but they were smooth and slick. They had the feel of the nylons I had bought her now. And there were underthings—pink things, silk and nylon things, things with lace on them. There was even a set of black lace, step-ins and bras. They were what she had been wringing out, or others like them, when I'd been putting on my new tires that forenoon, in a little squeezed-up handful before my eyes. I don't know what there is about black lace things. They're not what a woman gets for herself. They make it seem more awful, somehow.

"I was kind of upwrought." John Bantreagh swallowed. "There was a pint out in the kitchen cupboard that her sister's husband had given me last summer when they visited, only I'm not much of a drinking man. But I got it down and took some now. I thought I'd better go and find her. I put on a shirt and coat, and put the matches up on the kitchen shelf where the kids couldn't reach them, and put out the lamp. I went out to crank the truck. I had just picked up the crank, when I looked around, and thought I saw her on the back porch behind me, among the moonlight and the vines. Only it wasn't her. It wasn't anything. It was just the moonlight moving."

John Bantreagh pulled at his throat. "I cranked

the truck then," he went on, swallowing, "and got in it, and went down the road towards the village. On the Turner porch steps, just off the road, there was something white sitting. It was Lilybelle, sitting in the moonlight in her nightdress with her arms about her knees. 'Hello, Mr. Bantreagh!' she called out to me, kind of low. 'Where are you going at this time of night? What's happened to Mrs. Bantreagh?'

"I stopped." John Bantreagh swallowed. "I didn't want any gossip started. 'What do you mean, what's happened to her?' I said.

" 'I woke up and came out on the steps a little while ago,' she said. 'The moonlight was so pretty. And I looked up the road, and thought I saw somebody going into your house, like she had just got home.'

" 'No,' I told her. 'It must have been me. Mollie's been home since ten o'clock.' Not wanting to start any gossip.

" 'I love the moonlight,' Lilybelle said. 'It's so quiet and so mysterious. I saw a lamp lit in your house, and then put out again. I heard your back screen door slam, and thought I heard you say something like, "What have you been doing, Mollie?" kind of sharp and mad. Then I could hear you cranking your car. I wondered if maybe she wasn't feeling well, and you were going for the doctor.'

" 'No,' I told her. 'I guess for a minute I thought maybe she had come out on the back porch behind me. But it wasn't her. It was just the vines moving in the moonlight. I just thought I'd take a ride to set my new tires right.'

"Then"—John Bantreagh swallowed—"I don't know why, but she looked so kind of pretty, with her dark curls and her big eyes, and the moonlight silver on her nightdress and her bare feet, and I had the nylons on the seat beside me, that I'd brought back out to the truck again, without knowing it; and I said to her, 'Would you like a pair of nylons, Lilybelle?' And she got up and came out to the truck, and stood up on the running board beside me and opened them.

" 'My!' she said. 'You sure know your way around, Mr. Bantreagh! What is it a bribe for? Have you murdered Mrs. Bantreagh, and you want me to keep it quiet?' "

John Bantreagh swallowed.

"Laughing," he said. "Just joking. She didn't have an idea that she was dead, of course. And she looked in the back of my truck, where I've got those old burlaps, and she said to me, 'Why, you did! You have! And you've got her body in there now, Mr. Bantreagh!'

" 'That's right,' I told her. 'No sense in trying to fool you. I hit her over the head with my truck crank because she'd been nagging me about you, Lilybelle. Now the deck's all clear for you and me. What'll it be—Niagara Falls?'

"Wanting to just take it along in stride with her." John Bantreagh swallowed. "Just joking, like a fellow does with a girl when she's pretty."

The young deputy, competent and cool, looked at him with alert and steady eyes, as gray as the dawn.

"For Pete's sake," he said, "is that all, Mr. Bantreagh? I thought you might know something about this fellow she had been stepping out with. But you don't even know for sure that there was anybody. She might have bought her stockings and lingerie stuff herself, with some grocery money that she had held out on you. Here she is dead. Somebody killed her. But all you can tell about is how you covered up your kids, and the new pajamas they were wearing, and thinking for a minute you saw her on the back porch when you were starting to crank your truck, only it was just the vine leaves and moonlight, and then some kidding conversation you had with this Lilybelle babe back and forth, to keep her from starting any gossip. But how is that telling anything about who killed her?" He shook his head with an exhalation of his flat diaphragm. "If it wasn't that it's murder, I could almost laugh," he said. "Maybe she didn't have any boy friend. Maybe nobody killed her."

"Oh, yes, she did," said John Bantreagh tonelessly. "Oh, yes, he killed her. I drove on into the village after leaving Lilybelle. Everything was all dark and shut up, except the Waldorf All-nite lunch wagon on the square across from the free library. I went in there, and the counterman was behind the counter, and a truck driver or somebody eating a piece of pie. I asked what time the free library had closed tonight. And the counterman said it had closed at five o'clock; it wasn't ever open at night.

"I said to him," he said tiredly, "had he seen a lady in a white dress with big red polka dots on it, and white shoes with her heels, with light-brown wavy hair and hazel eyes, and plucked eyebrows and a red mouth, about twenty-nine? And he said there was a lady like that who sometimes came in between eleven and midnight and got sandwiches or things like that, and took them out to her boy friend in their car, but she hadn't been in tonight. It was almost two o'clock now, he said, and so she probably wouldn't be in now.

"Then" — John Bantreagh swallowed — "the truck driver spoke up, and asked me if she lived upon Jaybird Road, and if she hung around the Swamp Run culvert bridge in the evenings, about half a mile out of town. I said yes, I reckoned she lived somewhere up that way. He said that he had seen her half a dozen times when he was going along Jaybird Road, sitting on the abutment of the culvert bridge in the evenings, like she was waiting for someone. And he had given her his horn and the high sign, only he was generally in a hurry, and there were babes like her along every road, and he could have all of them he wanted. But one time last month, he said, he had come coasting toward the culvert bridge with his engine off—there's a grade down before it, and he was a little low on gas—and he saw her sitting there, not knowing anyone was near. She was stretching out her nylon legs and tightening up her garters to some black lace things she had on. And she had looked up just as his truck rolled to her, and had smiled at him.

"It had driven him kind of wild," said John Bantreagh tiredly. "He had stopped his truck and jumped out to grab her. Just then he had looked around, and there was a car that was stopping at the side of the road, just off the culvert bridge, about twenty feet away in the shadows under the trees. There was some man in it, looking at him. He had let go of her and had jumped back into his truck again and driven off.

" 'What are you looking for her for?' he said to me. 'Are you trying to make her yourself? Brother, if I was you, I wouldn't! I'm big and plenty tough myself, and I'm not scared of anything. But there was something about that guy. . . . Your wife?' he said—I guess I must have said something—'If she was my wife, with those black lace things and that smile she had, I'd kill her!'

"So I knew." John Bantreagh swallowed. "But I had known when I found those nylons and things. I reckon I had kind of known all along, if I had thought about it. I drove around looking for her," he said tonelessly. "Along every road I came to. It was just breaking dawn when I came along the back road here. I saw something white off in the meadow, and I drove in through the break in the fence and found her. It kind of knocked me out."

The breath of dawn air across the silvered grass stirred the ends of the young deputy's black knit tie upon his expanse of snow-white shirt. He stood motionless with fists on hips. There was nothing else stirring about his hard, towering figure or about the world. Only John Bantreagh's knees, which caved and caved.

No, his knees weren't caving any more. It was just a lingering of ceased sensation, that they still were.

"Who was he?" the calm, alert voice of Deputy Roy Clade came to him. "I guess this counter-

man and this truck driver wouldn't know. But what did he look like? Did they say?"

"They didn't get a look at him," said John Bantreagh tiredly. "When she had come into the Waldorf, he had always stayed in his car across the street, with his lights out in the blackness under the trees around the square. The truck-driving fellow didn't see what he looked like either. He just got scared and jumped in his truck and drove away."

"Cagey," commented Roy Clade. "He was taking care that nobody saw him with her, if he ever had to get rid of her like he did. Maybe he knew from his experience that these married ones are hard to ditch. What kind of a car did he have, did they say?"

"They didn't know the make," said John Bantreagh tiredly. "It was just a black sedan."

"Nine cars out of ten ——" said Roy Clade, "nine out of ten are black sedans. I've got one myself. There's nothing in that, unless they got his license number. And they wouldn't have, if he was that cagey. He would have had his plates mudded over."

"No, they didn't get his license number," said John Bantreagh tiredly. "Nobody ever did, I reckon, that saw her with him. He was cagey, like you say."

The big young deputy shook his head. He sighed, with a quiet heaving of his diaphragm beneath his shirt.

"It's not any good, I'm afraid, Mr. Bantreagh," he said. "Nobody knows who he is, where he lives, what he looks like, the number of his car license or anything. Just this counterman and this truck driver who knew that she had been stepping out with some man that had a car, and maybe two or three more people here or around who may have seen her getting into it with him from a distance when it was getting dark, or getting out of it below the place next to yours when he brought her home. He was awful cagey. He did it, all right, I reckon. But he'll get away with it, as sometimes happens. I'm awfully sorry, Mr. Bantreagh, but I'm afraid the police have been left with nothing to go on at all."

John Bantreagh rubbed his forehead. So much —so much to forget. That he would try to forget. That he must keep from the kids forever. So much to forget, even of bright and tender things, of when he had been younger and she had been so very young, no older than Lilybelle, and all the world had been pink-colored and full of joy. He had known that he could never give her all she wanted. It hadn't been her fault that it had come to this. It had been his. If he had only been a little smarter. Though it could not be mended now. So much to forget, of shame and grief and failure. But some small, trivial thing to remember. And now he had remembered it.

"Nothing to go on, except what she told me," he said.

"What she told you?" said Deputy Roy Clade thinly. "I thought you said that she had never told you anything. That you never knew a thing about it or had the least suspicion until last night."

He stood motionless. His eyes were gray as the dawn. John Bantreagh lifted his blurred bloodshot gaze and met Roy Clade's gray eyes.

"What she told me after I had found her," said John Bantreagh. "Just before she died."

"You mean ——" said Roy Clade, with the muscles moving on his face. "You mean," he said, with his eyes as gray as dawn, "that she was still alive? You mean that she told you? Why, you're crazy, you damn apple-knocking liar! She's been dead since one o'clock!"

His right fist jerked from his hip. He jerked it upward against his shoulder, with a contorted look upon his face and his mouth opening in a scream.

John Bantreagh had got his pendent right arm in motion. He had swung it, stepping in on knees swift and wiry, no longer caving, cracking the truck crank across the bones of Roy Clade's thick, strong wrist as the young deputy's fist left his hip. With his wrist against his shoulder, Roy Clade screamed.

John Bantreagh snapped his left hand forward, grabbed the gun out of its holster, dropped his crank, side-stepping. He had the gun in his right hand now, and the hammer back.

"Both hands out from your shoulders!" he said, "no use to yell at me and damn me! Heel! You know what this is. You know how it shoots. Heel, and swing your arms slowly back behind you till I have got your handcuffs on!

"Maybe she didn't tell me," he said, with a dry gasp in his throat. "But you did! Here I was beside her body, with blood on my hand, with the crank that might have been the thing that knocked her out, with my truck tracks leading right up to her, and no other tracks but them upon the field! Here I was, her husband, the first man in the world to be suspicioned, even if there was nothing to show that I had ever been around here at all! Here I was, that had drunk whisky tonight, that had given a pair of nylons to Lilybelle after she was dead! That had told Lilybelle I had killed her and had her body in my truck! That had gone in and talked to the counterman and the truck driver kind of wild, and maybe said that I would kill her when I found her—I don't know. A man gets to talking wild when he thinks

of his wife and those black lace things, and his man's pride.

"Here I was, with everything saying it was me! Why, my best friends would have thought sure I'd done it! They would have figured some reason why—Lilybelle, or some argument we'd had about the kids, or about some fellow that she'd been stepping out with—wouldn't make any difference who. They would all have said that I had done it. At the least you might have asked me if I had. But you knew I hadn't done it. Only the man who had killed her himself, in all this world, would know that! No need to swear at me. Hold your hands behind you! You know what this is against your back.

"It took me a long time to figure out," said John Bantreagh tiredly. "I was knocked out. Just like a dummy. But I told you what her name was, and you pretended never to have heard it before. I didn't tell you how to spell it, though—I didn't think that you might write it down. Everybody who just hears it thinks it's spelled t-r-y, like 'pantry.' I always have a lot of trouble getting it spelled right. Thought sometimes of changing it myself. But you spelled it right without being told, when you wrote it down in your notebook. I've been trying to think how you knew, ever since you did.

"And other things you didn't think of, I reckon! You've got that tire iron in your car's tool kit or in your garage at home—you must still have it, you've mentioned it so often. And even if you've washed it with soap and water or kerosene, there will still be blood in the pores of the iron, that will show in some of these machines that they have these days, I reckon that you know. There will be blood on your car cushions. Maybe on the shirt and suit you wore last night.

"And you went home and slept," John Bantreagh said, "while I was out looking on every road for her all night! And got up, and took a bath, and shaved and rubbed yourself with sweet-smelling shaving lotion, and put on a clean white shirt and your crisp black suit and your black knit tie, and came on back here to park just inside the woods edge off the road, to wait for her to be discovered. Only I was already here when you came.

"There'll be the blood! There's her name, that you knew how to spell. And somewhere—yes, somewhere, when they get to looking, no matter how careful and cagey you have tried to be—there will be someone that has seen you and her together, when they go looking into it, and can tie you up in an iron way.

"Get into the back of your car! No need to blaspheme me. Kneel on the floor! I'm going to have to put some of my truck lashings around you. You're powerful, and your brain is fresh and new slept and smart. But I don't think you're going to get away. I'll try to get you to the doctor as quick as I can. I'm sorry that I had to hit so hard. I'm sorry that there'll be bumps.

"Kneel on the floor, and pray!" John Bantreagh said. "I wouldn't have ever known who you were. Nobody would have ever known about you, with nothing to start them looking into you. They would have put it on me, her husband, caught with her, caught red-handed, caught with motive, and I'd have got twenty years or life. And what would have happened to the kids is more than I can bear to think. The fear of it made my knees cave. It made me so blind that I could hardly see. If you had asked me whether I had done it, I would have fallen dead away. But it won't be that way. You told me."

He looked—John Bantreagh—at that still form lying in front of his truck wheels, with her staring eyes. "Perhaps," he said, "she helped."

THE COLONEL SAVED THE DAY

by Harold H. Martin

THE *Post*'s HAROLD MARTIN was in Okinawa on a global tour of United States defense bases when the Korean fighting broke out in June 1950. He went on the first carrier raid over Pyongyang and the first bomber raid over Wonsan and then joined the ground fighters. "I kept hearing that the hottest fighting man on the front was a young sprout named John Michaelis with a regiment called the Wolfhounds," he writes. "I got with him and stayed with him long enough to know that this report was not exaggerated."

Martin is the only *Post* associate editor who lives in Atlanta, Georgia, but that is only his base. Tall, dark and restless, he spends much of his time circulating freely about the world in search of *Post* stories. He was born in 1910 in the Georgia Piedmont cotton country and did his first creative writing in a high school essay on the pitching of Walter Johnson. Later on he was a construction worker, magazine salesman and manager of a "semi-burlesque" theater with thirty beautiful girls. But mostly he was a newspaperman, and he still writes a column for his old paper, the Atlanta *Constitution*. The Marine Corps put him to work as a combat correspondent in World War II, and a humorous piece he did called "The Fat Lady of Okinawa" (December 29, 1945) won the heart of editor Ben Hibbs, who hired him as soon as possible.

SEPTEMBER 9, 1950

WITH THE 27TH REGIMENT IN KOREA.

ON a hill above the Naktong River the dusty trucks rolled to a stop and the weary men got down. For five days the Wolfhound Regiment had been in battle in the mountains to the west. Behind them, 300 of their number had been killed or wounded or captured. But they had fought with magnificent courage and their morale was high. They had endured mortar fire, which is the great terror of all soldiers, and with inadequate weapons they had fought against tanks whose size made their own tanks look like C-ration cans. They had been many times surrounded and each time they had fought their way out of the trap, leaving mounds and rows of little men in shabby yellow-green uniforms strewing the rice paddies and the red clay slopes of the hills. They had been forced to retreat, but each time they withdrew they came back not in a rout but as a fighting unit still intact. And they had brought with them their wounded and their dead and their vehicles and their guns, which not all units had been able to do in this strange, encircling guerrilla war.

They were a green regiment when they went into the line. For only four days had they worked together as a regimental combat team; riflemen, artillery and tanks training together. Their officers were new and all their seasoned noncoms had been pulled out to beef up the elements of the 24th Division that had gone into action before them. But this raw, untrained command, which was not a regiment at all but a peacetime economy force of two instead of three battalions, was battle-hardened now, and the word had spread that of all the regiments in the line, the 27th under Lt. Col. John Michaelis best knew how to fight this war in which American troops, steeped in the doctrine of attack under the protection of overwhelming fire-power, found themselves, instead, fighting and falling back in a dogged holding action that swapped men and war machinery for days of precious time until the power finally could arrive.

And so, on the banks of the Naktong, where the troops stripped from their bodies the uniforms that were caked with the dried slime of the rice paddies and swam in the green clear water or sprawled on the ground asleep, too tired to wash or eat, I finally found John Michaelis, ex-paratroop regimental commander, ex-aide to Eisenhower, twice-wounded soldier of the last World War, to ask him how it was that his raw troops had fought so well.

I found him in his command post, which once had been the physics and the biology lab of a Korean high school. There is something about a

482

paratrooper that never leaves him until he dies—an insouciance, a swagger, a cocky confidence—and these attributes Michaelis possessed in full degree. He was a slim man, lean and wiry, with a cold blue eye and a voice that snapped, and though his short-cut hair was iron gray, his face was smooth and full and unlined and he looked even younger than his thirty-seven years.

He was by birth and training a professional soldier. Born in the Presidio, the son of an Army officer killed in the first World War, he had gone to West Point and upon his graduation there, in 1936, had served a tour of duty with Vinegar Joe Stilwell's 7th Division in the Philippines. When the first parachute battalions were formed, he had volunteered, and when the 502nd Parachute Infantry Regiment jumped in Normandy, he was its executive officer, taking over command on the ground when the regiment's CO was injured in the jump. He had jumped in Holland, where a ricocheting shell, glancing from a tank, had torn his belly open and, when he had recovered from this wound, he jumped again in the closing days of the battle for Bastogne, and again had been wounded. He had finished his combat career as chief of staff of the 101st Airborne Division and, after the war was over, he had served as aide to Eisenhower until Eisenhower had retired.

When the war in Korea broke out he was in the G-3 Section of the 8th Army at Yokohama. Old battles were just a memory, old wounds had healed and more important than past wars was the fact that after thirteen years of marriage, he at last had become the father of a son.

"I remember sitting there one afternoon," he grinned, "thinking how lucky I was in this fat desk job. I had seen enough of war to last me a lifetime. I was thinking of getting me a little flag to put on my desk and a little sign saying: 'Go get 'em, boys. We are all behind you.' The next morning I was on a plane bound for Taejon. Three days later, at the docks in Pusan, I took command of the regiment."

He shook his head. "It was a pretty depressing assignment. I was new. My executive officer was new. Some of the officers—only a few—were seeing green grasshoppers on their shoulders at the very thought of going to war. These had to be weeded out and sent back to desk jobs. The troops were green. Most of them had only eight months' service behind them. They came in with their duffel bags loaded down. The officers carried foot lockers. As a paratrooper, I learned that you have to travel and fight lightly loaded if you are going to fight at all. We had to have a general shakedown. We had all kinds of special-services gear—violins, banjos—God knows what

all. There must have been eight carloads of junk shaken out of the regiment before we started north. But when we started out, we traveled like a fighting soldier ought to travel. Each man had his weapon, his ammunition, his blanket, shelter half, mess gear, razor, soap and towel and an extra pair of socks. That was all, and that was enough."

His voice trailed off and his eyelids drooped, and I realized that I had been keeping from his bed on the floor a man who had had but little sleep for five days and nights.

"Talk again tomorrow," he mumbled, struggling out of his blouse. "Lots of things to tell you."

In the morning he was fresh and rested.

"I don't want to sound bitter," he said, "but there are a few hard things I want to say. And I hope that you can print them. As all the world knows by now, we have taken a heavy beating over here in the first weeks of the war. The big reason was that we had *too few troops* in here to fight the masses we have had to fight. The Red drive from the north was like a flood on the Mississippi. Every time we plugged one hole in the levee, the flood broke through somewhere else and we had to run to try to stop it there. There's no use complaining about that, for that's the chronic state of the American Army in Peacetime—too few men to fight if they have to fight.

"But we made one other error that was worse than that. In peacetime training, we've gone in for too damn much falderal. We've put too much stress on Information and Education and not enough stress on rifle marksmanship and scouting and patrolling and the organization of a defense position. These kids of mine have all the guts in the world and I can count on them to fight. But when they started out, they couldn't shoot. They didn't know their weapons. They have not had enough training in plain, old-fashioned musketry. They'd spent a lot of time listening to lectures on the difference between communism and Americanism and not enough time crawling on their bellies on maneuvers with live ammunition singing over them. They'd been nursed and coddled, told to drive safely, to buy War Bonds, to give to the Red Cross, to avoid VD, to write home to mother—when somebody ought to have been telling them how to clear a machine gun when it jams."

Outside in the compound, the troops were standing around the jeeps and trucks, cleaning their weapons. Suddenly there was the deep gruff bark of a .45 and a cry of "Medics! Medics here!"

The colonel put his head in his hands. "My God!" he said. "The fourth wild shot today!"

An officer put his head in the door. "He's dead, sir," he said to the colonel. "Cleaning his forty-five and shot himself in the head."

"See what I mean?" said the colonel. "They still don't know how to handle their weapons without blowing their own brains out. They've had to learn in combat, in a matter of days, the basic things they should have known before they ever faced an enemy and some of them don't learn fast enough.

"The commanders as well as the men have had to learn things fast in this war over here," the colonel said. "We've learned, for instance, that a roadbound army can't fight a defensive war against a guerrilla enemy that moves on foot through the hills at night—and the U.S. Army is so damn roadbound that the soldiers have almost lost the use of their legs. Send out a patrol on a scouting mission and they load up in a three-quarter-ton truck and start riding down the highway. I've seen the time I'd have gladly swapped every truck in my supply train for a good pack-mule outfit.

"We've had to learn some new tactical doctrine too. The book is still sound, but we've had to twist it around a little. We've had to make our tactics flexible. The classic deployment of a regiment is to place two battalions on the line with a battalion in reserve. And this is good deployment when your flanks are protected. But in this war we have often had to fight with nothing on our flanks but the hills, and the hills were crawling with enemy. So we had to work out something else. In the first place, we had but two battalions to deploy. So we placed them on a narrow front, no wider than could be covered by a company, and we strung them out in depth. And the Reds would strike head on, and we would let them have it, and then they would draw off and circle and begin probing at our flanks, and the outposts we had stationed on the hills would bring them under fire; for one thing we learned, and learned quick, was that you've got to own all the peaks and ridge lines that look down into your position. And when they would strike us on the flanks, they would run into heavy fire again, and as they probed farther and farther back along the line, the force that had held the point would fall back through the holding forces and take up positions to the rear. It was a process similar to a snake progressing backward by turning itself inside out, but it worked. For nearly a week we fought them this way in the mountains east of the Kum, and in all that time we gave up only a little less than three miles.

"But no matter how hard you fight and how much blood you draw from the enemy, there comes a time when you've got to decide whether or not you can stand against the forces attacking you any longer. You have to know when the moment comes—and here only instinct or intuition can help you—beyond which you cannot stay and fight without losing your artillery and your communications vehicles and all your transport. You can nearly always get the men out with their rifles, but it takes time and planning to turn a regiment around and head it away from the enemy. So you fight on until you have bought the last hour of time that you can afford to buy without letting yourself be destroyed as a fighting force. And then you high-tail it down the road and find a good defensive spot and send out your outposts to the hilltops and set up your narrow defense in depth and wait for them to come on again. It is not always possible to time this withdrawal right, of course, for a commander in the field makes his decisions under great pressure, ofttimes when the fire that is falling around him makes his entrails twist in his belly like ropes of ice. And when you stay and fight too long, they come in upon you in masses you can't stop. And that is why you read of units coming out of battle leaving all their equipment behind, and why you read of American soldiers being shot at by gooks carrying American guns and wearing American uniforms, and of captured Reds who were carrying American medical supplies. So far we've been lucky."

The field phone in its leather case tinkled.

The colonel answered, and I could tell from the look on his face that the news was not to his liking.

"Right, sir" was all he said before he hung up.

He turned to me with a funny smile. "You are a very lucky fellow," he said. "If you care to come along, you may witness what well may be the last stand of the Americans in Korea. While we were trying to plug the ratholes up here, they have broken through to the south. And we are moving south, almost to the sea."

It was midmorning. That night at midnight, in the railroad station at a little town called Chung-ni, Michaelis got his orders. While cow-bells tinkled in the dark, and white figures moved through the shadows outside, Maj. Gen. John H. Church, commanding officer of the valiant 24th Division, shattered and broken by its piece-meal commitment in the early days of the war, spread out a map upon a table. The general was old and his voice was tired.

"They are coming through here, and here," he said, pointing, while Michaelis and Col. Ned Moore, commanding the forces holding in the hills above the Nam River, followed his pointing finger. "They can come through anywhere along a hundred and twenty-five mile front, reaching from the sea to way up here. And all I've got to stop them with right now is what's left of your two regiments, Ned, and Michaelis' Twenty-seventh. The strongest threat seems to be on the northern flank, and I want you to hold, Ned, until Michaelis can get into position behind you, and then I want you to pull out and go north. The south along the coast looks all right, right now. The best intelligence we've got says they've got no strong forces down there. But we don't know. We just don't know. Right now Ned's forces hold this road junction here. So long as we hold that, we've got them blocked to the south."

The general left, and Moore went back to his command post in the hills, and Michaelis rolled in a blanket and slept in a drizzle of rain beneath a tree while behind him the trucks of his regiment toiled toward him through the dark. They came up at dawn and Michaelis led them on into the hills until we came to the rear of Moore's position and found the place, on high ground overlooking a great green valley, where we would take our stand.

And then the message came from Moore, and Michaelis looked suddenly old and worn and tired. In the night the Reds had struck with strong forces. The road junction had not been held. The road to the south was open.

The map told the story. From the Red-held town of Chinju the Reds could pour east to Masan unopposed, and from Masan on to Pusan it was only forty miles. Pusan was the port where the marines were coming in, and the 2nd Division, and all the help from home. It had to be held or we would be driven into the sea.

So, knowing that if he was right, there would be promotion and glory for him, and if he was wrong, he would face a court-martial for disobedience of orders, Michaelis made his decision. He turned his column around on the narrow mountain roads and hurled it, as fast as the trucks could roll, far to the south through Masan, and then westward to the little mud-walled town of Chindong-ni. And here, with the sea on his left hand and the mountains on his right, his regiment went into position across the road on which the Reds would come.

But there were no Reds. Patrols probing far to the west found no enemy forces on the move—only a great tide of refugees trudging east with their bundles and their burdened carts. But from his mountain position, where he had stayed when Michaelis moved south, Ned Moore reported heavy enemy pressure, and to the north, where Moore would have moved under the original plan, patrolling planes saw signs of enemy movement.

All these things added up to a bitter answer for John Michaelis.

"I gambled and lost," he said to his officers. "I brought you to the wrong place." He looked out the window. " 'Direct disobedience of orders,' the charge will read," he said. "And whatever they do to me, I'll deserve."

And then, all of a sudden, his face lit up and all the old paratrooper cockiness and confidence came back to him, and he laughed. "Hell," he said, "there's one thing I can do. I can attack. So the road is empty, is it? Then we'll drive along that road until we find them. We'll pull a little surprise on our good gook friends. I'll ask Moore to time his counterattack with our own push, and we'll take that road junction back. Then we'll push on to the high ground overlooking Chinju, and if they are coming, let them come. For every step they drive us back from there, we'll make them pay with dead men."

And so that night, with his decision made and his orders issued, John Michaelis slept a deep and contented sleep on the floor of the schoolhouse at Chindong-ni and in the early morning Lt. Col. Gilbert Check, a mild-looking little man holding his first combat command, led his battalion combat team up the road toward Chinju, looking for a fight.

But in the hills a mile away from the command post where Michaelis slept, Red soldiers watched Check's column pass, and when it had gone by they swarmed down from the slopes and set up machine guns and mortars along the road. The thing that every commander dreads had happened. Michaelis' force was split. The attack force was cut off from the regiment. The snap decision that had brought Michaelis boiling south in a thirty-six-hour march had not been wrong. The decision to commit a battalion deep into enemy territory had been. This was the route along which a heavy Red push was moving. Amid that swarm of refugees the patrols had noted, had moved the vanguard of the Red attack.

Among the panting columns that lined the roadsides had been Red soldiers by the score, disguised in the wide-brimmed hat and the torn white coat and trousers of the Korean farmer. In the huge packs of woven rice straw they bore on their backs had been mortars and machine guns, broken down, and ammunition. And singly and in twos and threes they had left the road and pushed off across the rice fields to the hills, and there, in assembly points where many antlike streams converged, they had changed their farmers' garb for uniforms. And now their guns controlled the road. Easy Company of the second battalion, which had guarded the jump-off line during the night, was cut off beyond the roadblock. A platoon of engineers, going out to repair a side road so patrols could pass, had been ambushed and cut to pieces. No traffic now could move on the road along which must flow Check's resupply—the gasoline for his tanks, ammunition for his guns, plasma and morphine for his wounded, food for his men.

"I overcommitted myself," Michaelis said. "I used damn bad judgment." All day he threw what force he had against the roadblock. He sent in his combat engineers and they fought for five hours without being able to blast the Reds from their nests. Troops of the Korean police went in, brave little brown men in ragged uniforms, winding up through the rice fields in files, and they came back one by one, panting and grimed with mud, and bleeding from ghastly wounds. Tanks went up and came under fire, and the guns of one wouldn't shoot and the other threw a track. And all through the day nothing could move up on the road.

Then, late in the afternoon, far up the road rose a cloud of dust and a crackle of rifle fire, and the sound of Red guns rose to a roar, and out of the dust a jeep came plunging. The first word had arrived from the cut-off battalion. Capt. Don Hickman, of Salt Lake City, and his sergeant, McHugh, and Bill Bradley, his driver, had run the blockade.

Back in the command post, Hickman told how the force had moved out in the morning, and for the first few miles there was never the sign of an enemy, until they had come upon a platoon asleep by the side of the road and had killed them all. They had gone on then for about ten miles more, and were going into a deep pass with high slopes on each side, when suddenly the column came under heavy fire. The tank in front was hit by a shell that drilled through the armor and wounded or killed every man inside, and the tank in the rear was hit and its crew wounded. Which left the column blocked there on the road with the fire pouring down on them, and there was nothing to do but leave the road and fight up into the hillsides to get at the guns which were pounding them.

"It was the artillery that saved us," Hickman said. "The artillery and the spotter planes. I never saw such fire as those gunners laid on. They cleared out the draws where the planes saw the gooks swarming in to get at us, and they tore the mountainsides to bits. I never saw artillery shoot so close to its own men. Then Bish's mortars got going—he had been wounded, shot in the shoul-

der or chest somewhere, when he lay in the ditch firing his grease gun—and by the time the mortars had worked them over for a while, there wasn't a sound from the hillside. We went up there and looked, and there were about two hundred and fifty of them dead. And we got some prisoners, but when we tried to send them back, we couldn't get through because they had cut us off from the rear. So I came back here to see about breaking that block some way, for we've got to get our wounded out. Old Bish told me that he thought he was liable to lose his arm if he didn't get help soon."

There was a sound at the door. A massive blond man, his face a dusty mask and his eyes glazed with pain, shambled like a wounded bear across the room. In his left hand he held a .45-caliber pistol. His right arm dangled limply at his side beneath the bloodstained bandage that swathed his shoulder. Second Lieutenant Bertram Bishop, of the heavy-mortar platoon, had come home. Slowly he lowered his great bulk into a chair.

"What the hell were you doing up there, Bishop?" the colonel said harshly.

"Had to go," Bishop said. "Best . . . platoon leader killed last week. Other one . . . too sick . . . to fight. Been shot . . . three times before," he said, his words coming jerkily. "Once in the chest at Salerno. But nothing ever hurt . . . me . . . as much as . . . this. I want to tell you . . . about the wounded. Truck load of them ahead of . . . my jeep. We ran into . . . fire on road. I turned . . . back. They went . . . on into it. I found a little road . . . over the mountains. It was . . . a . . . rough ——" His voice trailed off and his head sagged.

"Get him a shot of dope and put him in a truck for the evac hospital at Masan," the colonel said gently.

"The best mortar man in the Army," the colonel said when Bishop had gone. And then: "Nearly a thousand men," he said softly, and it seemed he was talking to himself. "And every man's life precious to him and to all who loved him. And every man's life my responsibility. I've been a damn fool. I've sent Check into a trap. And now, somehow, I've got to get him out again.

"Write this down, Hickman." He suddenly spoke briskly. Hickman reached for my notebook as Michaelis dictated: " 'To Check: Withdraw to Regimental C.P. immediately. Lead with tanks, if possible. Road under fire. Expedite move.' Give that to radio to pass on to the plane. They can drop the message to Check. Now get Artillery on the phone. Tell Gus Terry to get Check on the radio as soon as he comes in range and keep track of his position as he comes back down the road. Tell him to lay his 155's along that road ahead of the column and blast it until hell won't have it. We'll lead them in here down a lane of fire. Get those messages off, Don, and let me know the minute we get a roger from Check."

Hickman left.

The colonel looked at his watch. "Half an hour to get them turned around," he said. "Two hours on the road. Nothing now we can do but wait."

After a while the guns began to boom, meaning that Terry's artillerymen had made radio contact with the approaching column and were walking their fire in front of it down the road.

"Eight miles out, sir," the radioman called through the window.

Half an hour later Check walked in. He was gaunt and tired and he still looked more like a schoolteacher than a fighting man, but there was a great pride in him.

"We were pushing on toward the high ground when the message came," he said. "We turned around and came back fast as we could. We found a couple of men in the rifle companies—kids who had driven bulldozers—and put them on the tanks whose drivers had been wounded. They fooled around for about five minutes checking the buttons and levers, then we got going. We piled men all over the vehicles. It was a fire-fight all the way—harassing fire from the rear. Once we hit a hole in the road and had to stop until it was filled. The kids in the back kept yelling to hurry it up, they were under fire. We had some wounded, and once we stopped the whole column until a medic could give a wounded man an injection of plasma. It might have been a fool thing to do, but—well, we had some good men killed today, and I didn't want to lose any more. And now," he said, rising, "I think I'll get some sleep."

When Check had gone, we sat alone in the darkness, and finally the colonel said, "Well, is it a story? You know how it works now—how a man has to make a decision, not knowing whether it's right or wrong. You've seen how something that looks wrong at first, proves to be right—like coming down here against orders. And you've seen how a decision that looks right proves to be dead wrong—like sending that column up there without knowing for sure what it would face. And then you've seen how a bunch of men with skill and brains and guts, like Check and Hickman and Terry and Bishop and those kids who drove the tanks, can turn a wrong decision into a right one. But is it a story?"

And I told him honestly I didn't know, and he went to bed and I went out and stood in the dark night for a while. The big guns that were only 100 yards away were firing again now, on targets deep in the hills, and the blast of their firing shook the glass from the windows. But the sleeping men in blankets on the ground did not stir. And in between the roar of the howitzers, the night was quiet except for the calling of some sort of bird on the slopes of the hill above the command post, and all was dark except for one strange white light that glowed for a moment above the draw that led down from the hill to the bivouac. And I remembered how the colonel had said that when they were gathering for a night attack you could hear the sound of cuckoos calling around the camp, and that they fired green flares to show where resistance would be light and red flares to show where it would be strong. But this was no flare I had seen, and I didn't know what the call of a cuckoo sounded like, and anyway, up the draw and along the hillsides, eighty tough little Korean police were guarding the approaches to the camp.

So I went back and went to bed, and woke in the bright of the morning and slipped out quietly, for the colonel was still asleep, to the room down the hall where breakfast was being served. There were flowers on the table, and after breakfast we sat there for a while—Marguerite Higgins, the *Herald Tribune* correspondent, and a half-dozen officers and I—pouring coffee from the big tin pitcher, and talking. Somebody facing the window mentioned that up on the hill he had seen a little man with a rifle moving on the hillside, but nobody paid much attention, for there had been a great flap the morning before when somebody saw a file of Koreans trotting along, carrying rifles, headed for the camp. Everybody had scrambled for his gun, but, fortunately, somebody had yelled in time, "For God's sake, don't shoot! It's just the South Korean sentries coming in for chow!"

So Higgins and I wandered into the room where the G-2 Section had set up shop, to listen while the Japanese interpreter questioned a prisoner. He stood there blindfolded, a spiky-haired fellow named Kim Chan Ock. He smelled like an animal, though in the shabby kit they found on him were vials of perfume and scented soaps, raided probably from stores in the towns through which he had passed, along with the pitiful gear a soldier of any nation carries—the pictures and the letters and the little personal things. He had not been a talkative type. He was a farmer's son from the northern hills, he had said, and of low rank in the army, and he did not know the size of his forces, nor what their plans might be.

And I was feeling somehow a sort of pity for

the half-naked little man, swaying there blind-folded, when a rifle cracked on the hillside, and then another, and the crash of many rifles firing together, and threading through them came the deep clatter of a machine gun, and there was the whine of bullets through the room and splinters flying and all of us were on the floor, flat, but not flat enough, for the bullets were singing through the walls and through the windows above our heads. Except that passing bullets do not sing, but make a sharp, cracking sound, like the crack-ing of a whip. And for a while I lay there with my arms wrapped around my head, wishing I'd never left my helmet far down the hall where I had slept. And then I looked up, and there, almost within reach, was Kim Chan Ock, the prisoner. He was on his hands and knees, tearing the tight bandage from his eyes, and he pulled it down, and his eyes above it were big with terror. I mo-tioned him down, but even as I gestured he lunged forward on his face and lay there jerking, and a stream of blood began creeping from beneath him and spreading over the floor. And I lay there watching him as his head jerked a moment in quick spasmodic movements, and then he was still.

Then somebody yelled, "Let's go!" and we went through the big open windows in great, froglike dives. The bullets were coming through the room from both directions now, for the build-ing was only one room wide, and the soldiers be-neath the trucks could fire through the windows at the Koreans on the hill, and the fire from the hill was pouring through the building down into the compound where the trucks were parked.

It was a fine leap, and it carried me into a bed of cannas, where I landed on top of the Jap in-terpreter, a thin man who crunched into the soft earth when hit and swore fervently in fluent English. Then I rolled from the canna bed down to the flat ground of the parade ground, behind a little wall of rock. The fire from the Koreans on the hillsides could not reach here, and the fire from the parade ground was slackening, for Michaelis and his executive officer, Colonel Farthing, and the company commanders were booting the men from beneath the trucks who were firing wildly in the general direction of the enemy. Squad leaders were bellowing for their men, and now the compound was nearly empty, for the men were moving around the school build-ing and up the hill toward where the Korean machine guns were. First it was only the riflemen, ducking and bobbing and weaving up the hill, firing as they went. And then the mortars were going, and the .50 calibers, and the recoilless 75's, and then the artillerymen horsed the 105's around

to lay white phosphorus in the gulches where Lt. Carter Clarke, of the reconnaissance platoon, had spotted Koreans massing for a charge. And then the big guns, the 155's, lowered to their flattest trajectory, found targets and began to fire, and Lt. Kenneth George—"two damn wars and me not twenty-three"—roared by, riding a tank that he was guiding to a slope where he could bring its firepower on the enemy's flank. And finally the first hopeful word, coming from Captain Top-per from the hill, where he was raking the front of the enemy with .50-caliber fire, reporting that they were streaming from the hill overlooking the camp to a deep ravine, where they were tearing off their uniforms and putting on their white peas-ant garb again.

All these things were written down in the play-by-play of the battle I tried to keep as I sat there beside the wall. But the things that shine bright-est in memory were not written down. . . . Blood dropping on my leg, and a tall man carrying his shattered left arm cradled in his right hand po-litely saying "Excuse me" as he passed. . . . The phone ringing in the empty command post at the height of the battle, and stout Colonel Farthing crawling in the window to explain to General Kean that he was finding it a little difficult to hear what the general was saying because there was a little noise going on outside. . . . "The Fighting Parson," Able Company's Capt. Logan Weston, walking by to the aid station with a bullet wound in his leg, returning to his troops and coming back half an hour later with another wound in his arm. . . . The nameless soldier run-ning across the compound with a wounded com-rade on his back. . . . The white-faced kid stricken by terror, coming up out of the rice fields to crouch by the wheel of a truck, looking around him, wild-eyed. . . . The look of surprise on the face of the bandaged corporal fingering the blue hole in the big muscle of his shoulder and saying, "Hell. Here's one the medics missed." . . . The artillerymen from the big guns, rushing out to wipe out two machine guns the Koreans had brought in on the flank toward the sea to sweep us with crossfire. . . . Higgins, coming up from the aid station where she had been at work, ask-ing if the fight would be over in time for her to make her deadline with a cable from Masan. . . .

And Lieutenant Colonel Michaelis, with his eyes dancing and the first smile on his face that I had seen in the days we had been together, com-ing up to shout happily above the tumult of the firing, "The guns are making the decisions now!"

Slowly, as the hours passed, the firing died. When it was over, five Americans lay dead and forty were wounded. But on the hills and in the hollows around the command post—some of them almost close enough to touch—lay the bodies of 600 North Korean soldiers.

And whatever doubts John Michaelis might have had of the snap decisions that brought his command here to this fierce fire fight that held the southern road, they were not shared by those above him. In orders the next day, Lt. Col. Gilbert Check was awarded the Silver Star for conspicuous gallantry in action. And John H. Michaelis, by his "consistent display of initiative, gallantry and qualities of leadership which have distinguished him as a combat commander," had earned his colonel's eagles on the battlefield.

OLD IRONPUSS

by Arthur Gordon

ARTHUR GORDON got the idea for the following story from talking with Korean casualties in the Veterans' Hospital at Bay Pines, Florida, a few miles from his home in Clearwater, early in 1951. "I knew a little about the tensions and hatreds of an Army hospital ward," he says, "because of an ill-advised parachute jump which landed me in one of them in England, just before D-Day in 1944." Prior to that he was born in Savannah in 1912, was graduated from Yale, attended Oxford as a Rhodes Scholar, and was managing editor of *Good Housekeeping* when Pearl Harbor came along. He spent three years in the Eighth Air Force and wrote a book about its work, *Target: Germany*, with Richard Thruelsen, a *Post* editor. After that he edited *Cosmopolitan* for three years and wrote a novel, *Reprisal*, which was a Literary Guild selection. He is now a free-lance writer, shuttling back and forth between Florida and Long Island, with his wife, Pamela, and their three little girls.

MAY 12, 1951

CORKY NIXON is doing fine now as editorial writer on a Midwestern paper. He walks nicely with only a cane, and a pretty girl is said to be in love with him, and happiness is hanging there in front of him like a ripe peach. Soon he will reach out and pick it, and all will be well with Corky Nixon.

But this happened months ago, when things were not too good with Corky or any of the other inmates of Ward 7.

If a poll had been conducted among the patients of that particular military hospital—a poll to determine the relative popularity of the nurses —any one of several gay young things might have won it. But for last place there would have been no contest whatever. It would have gone to Old Ironpuss, hands down.

Her real name was Johansen, but people seldom used it. Her nickname, bestowed long ago by some forgotten genius, fitted her to perfection. She was a tall, gray-haired, rawboned woman with a face that looked as if it had been hacked in a hurry out of a block of oak. She had a pair of cold green eyes that showed no warmth, no sympathy, no concern for the welfare—or lack of it —of fellow human beings. Her voice matched her face: harsh, rasping, sardonic. When she walked through the wards, her spine might have been a ramrod, and if she heard the subdued hisses that sometimes followed her, she gave no sign.

She was efficient; no one denied that. In thirty years she had never been known to make a mistake. And she was a merciless disciplinarian; younger nurses under her jurisdiction were terri-

fied of her. Casualties back from Korea who thought their recent heroism entitled them to exemption from hospital regulations sometimes got a rude shock. If Old Ironpuss happened to be on duty, they were likely to find their normal privileges drastically reduced. In vain they protested to Colonel Gleason, the white-haired senior medical officer. The colonel was a fine surgeon, and a soft-spoken man. But he always upheld Old Ironpuss.

"Hell," said Corky Nixon disgustedly, "I think he's scared of her himself."

He was sitting in his wheel chair in Ward 7 hanging ornaments on a Christmas tree that had been set up between the rows of beds. Ward 7 was not the most cheerful place in the hospital; its patients were mostly frostbite cases—amputees, that is—and a couple of fliers who had been badly burned. But the Red Cross had brought in the Christmas tree, and Corky was decorating it. For one thing, he still had all ten fingers. For another, there was supposed to be a competition among the various wards with a prize for the best-looking tree, and Corky was not going to let theirs just stand there naked and ashamed.

He was a good boy, this Corky Nixon, with more resiliency of heart and mind than most. Frostbite was not his trouble; a land mine somewhere north of Seoul had done a neater job, taking off both legs just below the knee. For a while he had been in the black throes of despair that always come once the physical pain has died down. But he had fought his way back, partially at least, and if the ward had a leader, he was it. He had a portable typewriter set up on a table by his bed. He drummed a lot of his rage and bitterness out through the typewriter keys . . . and threw away most of what he wrote.

While he worked on the tree, the others watched him somberly. Most of the beds in the ward were empty; it was Christmas Eve, and Colonel Gleason had been lenient about letting some of the boys go home. Carefully, tenderly, their friends and relatives had come and wheeled them away. Counting Corky, there were only six left. Seven, if you included Hancock, the new arrival, in the little room off the ward reserved for patients on the critical list. Hancock had just come in that day.

Corky could have been a Christmas guest in a dozen private homes, but he had refused all invitations. He wanted to stay with the boys who couldn't leave the ward. Cramer, one of the fliers, couldn't leave because he was still a mass of bandages, unable to move hand or foot. Friedheim was there because he had shown a tendency to hemorrhage. Armstrong, the other flier, was still in the process of having his face rebuilt; his head was enveloped in gauze, except for three slits, two for his eyes, one for his mouth. Chudnowski was there because he was incredibly clumsy on his crutches. He had already had two bad falls; Colonel Gleason would not let him leave the ward. Finally there was Danforth, the red-headed Vermonter who had stopped a bullet on night patrol and played dead for twenty-four hours until his buddies went out and found him in the snow. Before he passed out, he had had the good sense to shove his hands inside his parka. They were still trying to save one of his feet.

Of all the patients in the ward, Danforth was the most bitter and the sharpest-tongued. Armstrong had a sense of humor and liked to tease Chudnowski, who had none. There were moments when Friedheim could joke about his tragedy in a grisly sort of way ("Look, ma, no hands!"); and Cramer, who was in constant pain, did not complain about it much.

But Danforth was always sounding off in his hard-edged New England fashion, and at this particular moment his target was Old Ironpuss. "I mean it," he was saying. "If Gleason won't do something about her, I'll send my own complaint through channels. I remember when they first brought me in here, feeling like hell, not caring whether I lived or died. What do I see, first thing? Old Ironpuss, standing right beside my bed."

"The face that sank a thousand ships," murmured Corky, hanging another silver globe on the tree.

"And what does she say to me?" Danforth demanded. " 'I understand you're a difficult patient. We have no time for difficult patients here. I'd advise you to bear that in mind!' " Danforth looked around, his face red and furious. "To me! She said that to me, lying there with a gook slug through my chest and a couple of frozen feet."

"You ain't kiddin'," said Chudnowski fervently. Only that afternoon Old Ironpuss had relieved him of a pint of bourbon left by some well-meaning visitor, and the memory lingered.

"I've seen some crazy things in my time," Danforth went on, "but letting an old barracuda like that come into contact with battle casualties is the worst. You take that guy in there, now"—he jerked his head in the direction of the room where Hancock was lying—"maybe he'll live, maybe not. It's touch and go, anyway. Now you'd think they'd get the best damn-looking nurse in Christendom, wouldn't you? Have her sit by him day and night. Hold his hand . . . if he's still got a hand. Stroke his forehead, anyway. Make him feel there's something to live for. But do they do it? Hell, no! They give him Old Ironpuss. It's enough to finish the guy off!"

"Aw, pipe down," muttered Friedheim. He and Danforth did not admire each other. "You talk too damn much."

"Hancock has Miss Baxter part of the time," Armstrong said through his mask. "She's not so bad."

Danforth's sharp face registered contempt. "Baxter? She's so scared of Old Ironpuss she doesn't know what she's doing! You make a little extra noise in here and you'll see. In she'll come, squeaking like a mouse: 'Boys, boys, please!' Baxter, hah!" Danforth gave a final snort of disgust and flung himself back against his pillows.

Corky finished the tree, wheeled himself over to the wall and switched on the colored lights. He sat there staring at his handiwork. It should have been cheerful, but it was not. He knew why, and he knew the others felt it too. The tinsel, the shining globes, the steadfast star on top—all these things reminded them of other Christmases when they had run, strong, laughing, eager, through their carefree worlds. Now there was only Ward 7, and the contrast was almost too painful to bear.

At about eight o'clock Miss Baxter came into the ward, looking flustered and upset. She said something in a whisper to Corky, and he let her wheel his chair through the swinging doors to the nurses' alcove just outside the ward. There he listened to her tale of woe, nodding sympathetically.

"And he won't take his medication," Miss Baxter said, almost wringing her hands, "and he won't eat, and he won't even answer me when I speak to him. I'm going off duty in a minute, and I'll have to report ——"

"All right," Corky said. "I'll see what I can do. But he probably won't talk to me, either. I know pretty much how he feels." He spun himself around. "Open the door for me, will you?"

Miss Baxter opened the door to the room where Hancock was lying, and Corky rolled his wheel chair in. Hancock was fully conscious; his eyes were open. But he was staring straight at the ceiling and his mouth was a thin gray line.

Corky said, not hoping for anything, "How's it going, fella?"

Hancock's eyes remained blank, indifferent. He said nothing.

Corky eased his wheel chair a little closer. "Look," he said, "I know how it is. It's tough. You think you don't want to live, that you'd be better off dead. But it's just a phase you go through. You'll come out of it."

Still Hancock said nothing, and Corky knew how it was with him: all the pain and misery and fear and bitterness screwed down so tight that it was almost like feeling nothing. When you got to that point, you wanted no part of anything or anybody; you just wanted to be left alone.

"Look," said Corky again, trying a different tack, "this nurse of yours is a nice kid. Why don't you give her a break? Swallow your pills or whatever the medicine is. She'll get in trouble if you stay frozen up like this. They'll blame her. I've seen it happen. Her boss is an old ——"

He stopped abruptly because the door opened and Old Ironpuss came in. She didn't say a word for perhaps half a minute. She stood there, gaunt and grim, ignoring Corky, staring straight at the man in the bed. Finally she spoke, and her voice had never sounded more harsh, more grating, "Miss Baxter tells me you're being as difficult as possible. I'm not surprised; you look like the self-centered type. You think you're a martyr, don't you? A noble sacrifice on the altar of freedom! Well, kindly remember you're still subject to military discipline, also that we have no use for cry-babies around here. Think it over . . . if you're not too saturated with self-pity to think at all!"

She swung around, her starched skirt rustling. She stalked out.

Corky sat there rigid, hands gripping the arms of his chair. He thought he had known anger, but he had never known anything like the blast of rage—blind murderous hatred—that roared through him now. To speak like that to a man half dead, a man maimed in the service of his country, a man who had given everything except his life so that this nation could remain serene, untouched, free —— He clenched his teeth.

Gleason would hear about this! Not later, when tempers had cooled, when excuses might be made! Now!

He whirled his chair toward the door and stopped. Hancock had turned his head. The blankness had gone out of his eyes. Something smoldered there, something that looked like a spark of the fury Corky was feeling.

"Tell her," said a hoarse voice from the blankets, "to take her damn pills and do you-know-what with them!"

It was a message Corky would have delivered with pleasure, but Old Ironpuss was not in the nurses' alcove to receive it. She was not visible anywhere. Corky swore and hurtled down the long corridors faster than was safe in a top-heavy wheel chair. He knew Colonel Gleason always worked late; he might still be in his office.

He was. The colonel looked weary. He had operated all afternoon; one of his patients had died on the table. Not his fault, but ——

He listened now to Corky's tirade; then he got up from his desk and went over to the window. Sleet tapped with frigid fingers against the pane.

"Dammit, colonel," Corky cried, forgetting propriety in his rage, "it was inhuman! The woman is a monster, or a sadist, or something! I don't see how you can let things like that go on!"

"What was Hancock's reaction?" the colonel asked, not turning around.

"Why, the natural one, of course! He told me to tell her to take her pills and ——"

"Do you realize," the colonel said slowly, "that those are the first words Hancock has spoken in five days?" He turned and eased himself down on the window sill. His face was gray with fatigue. "You're an intelligent guy, Nixon. Why don't you use your head? What's the most dangerous state for a patient to be in? I'll tell you; it's apathy. It's that frozen denial of all feeling, of all emotions because they're too painful to be borne. It's the most dangerous attitude of all . . . because it's only one step from death."

He came back to his desk and sat down. "We face it constantly here. You should know; you had a touch of it yourself. We have to get the patient out of it somehow. We've tried kindness; it doesn't work. We've tried sympathy; that doesn't work, either. Because under that frozen crust the predominant emotion of all you guys is rage. Anger. Resentment. You've been hurt; you've been maimed, and you're furious. With good reason, God knows."

He put his elbows on the desk. His hands—his fine surgeon's hands—massaged his face wearily. "We have to get through that crust, Nixon. Before it hardens, before it solidifies. So we reach for the emotion that's nearest the surface. I just told you what it was. Anger. If we can strike a spark of that—just one spark—the life process is regenerated. Now do you begin to see?"

Corky Nixon swallowed hard. "You mean . . . Old Ironpuss ———"

"In a hospital," the colonel went on, "there are tremendous emotional forces at work. Illness means pain, and pain means anger, and anger means hatred. So we have our lightning rod, that's all. Very few people know it. I shouldn't tell you, really, but—well, sometimes I think Old Ironpuss deserves a break." His eyes rested on the blanket that covered Corky's knees. "You've got your troubles, I know. And you've got your share of guts. But I doubt whether you could deliberately make yourself hated for thirty years, deliberately forgo the popularity and respect that could be yours." He paused, then added softly, "I know I couldn't."

Sitting there, facing the colonel, Corky felt his great rage shrivel down to a small cinder. He thought of that gaunt, lonely figure passing through the ward, with the sibilant hisses echoing behind her. He thought of a lot of things. He said, at last, "I'm sorry I bothered you, colonel."

"That's all right," the colonel said. "I'm glad you did. Go on back to the ward. Encourage the boys to hate Old Ironpuss. That's what she's there for." He stood up. "And another thing: this complaint of yours is an act of defiance. That's good. Get the others to defy her occasionally. We need a spirit of defiance around here." He opened the door. He smiled his tired smile. "And a Merry Christmas to you, Corky."

The gleaming corridors were dim and quiet. The rubber-shod wheels of Corky's chair made no sound. Outside Ward 7 Old Ironpuss was sitting at the desk in the nurses' alcove. Her stiff white figure was in shadow, but light from the desk lamp bounced off the blotter onto her formidable face.

She said to Corky in her acid voice, "Have you permission to be out of the ward?"

"I was talking to Colonel Gleason," Corky told her.

He wheeled himself forward, butted his way through the swinging doors. The ward was very quiet. From the radio, turned low, came the heartbreaking melody of "White Christmas." Armstrong lay flat on his back, staring through his slits at the ceiling. Chudnowski was picking lint out of the blanket. Danforth was playing solitaire, his face tight and expressionless. Friedheim was propped against his pillows, bandaged stumps crossed on his chest. In the center of the polished aisle the lights on the little Christmas tree glowed steadily.

Corky stopped his wheel chair at the foot of Cramer's bed. "Hey, fellers!" he said. "Old Ironpuss is on duty! Let's do something to annoy her!"

A quiver of interest seemed to agitate the lifeless air. Danforth looked up from his cards. Friedheim's eyes lost some of their deadness. Chudnowski stopped picking lint, and Armstrong came up on one elbow. "What, for instance?"

Corky whirled himself over to the radio and snapped it off. "You know how she hates noise? Well, I know some words to a Christmas carol that you won't find in any of the books. You all know the tune, though. Let's see how loud we can sing it!" He spun himself over to the table where his typewriter stood. "I'll write it out—make a carbon for each of you guys. . . . Charley, grab your crutches and swipe five bedpans from the shelf down there. And five spoons."

Chudnowski's forehead was furrowed. "Bedpans? Cripes, what for?"

"To bang on, of course. The more noise the better. Old Ironpuss'll have a spasm, but she won't dare do anything. Not on Christmas Eve!" Corky twirled the paper and carbons into his typewriter. "Wait'll you read this. It's called 'Good King Wence the Louse.' The first verse is kind of mild, but by the time you get to the end it's really rough." His fingers flew; the typewriter sputtered like a machine gun.

Once he glanced over his shoulder. Chudnowski was hopping down the aisle from bed to bed, not bothering to use his crutches. Armstrong was sitting up; under the bandages his mouth was stretched in a wide grin.

"Hey, stupid," said Friedheim to Danforth, "tie a spoon on my foot, will ya? If it'll annoy Old Ironpuss, I can kick the bottom out of a bedpan!"

"A spoon's too small," said Danforth. "Hold still; I'll fix you up with this elegant object." He brandished a small enamel container. "But what'll I use for string?"

"Use the sash of your bathrobe," Corky advised him. He ripped the papers out of his machine and wheeled himself rapidly from bed to bed, distributing the carbons. At Cramer's side he paused. "You gonna sing, Doc?"

"Hell, yes," said the bundle in the bandages. "Get Charley to hold it where I can read it. I'll drown you all out."

"That's the boy!" Corky wheeled himself back into the aisle, took the spoon and bedpan that Chudnowski handed him, and gazed sternly at his choir. Every eye was on him, bright with anticipation. Gone was the thin veil of melancholy, the gray film of self-pity. They were fired with a single unholy ambition: to annoy Old Ironpuss.

"Ready?" said Corky. He raised his spoon like a conductor's baton. "Let's go!"

Outside, in the nurses' alcove, Old Ironpuss raised her head sharply as the horrid clangor arose. She sat rigid for a moment, listening, then she stood up quickly and walked to the swinging doors that led into the ward.

But she did not go in. Through the square glass windows she saw the fantastic sight, and she heard the equally fantastic words, swelling into a full-throated roar of defiance—defiance of the worst the world could offer in terms of pain, of suffering, of death.

> *"Good King Wence the Louse looked out*
> *On the Feast of Stephen!*
> *Someone poked him in the snout,*
> *Made it all uneven!"*

Louder and louder the wild chorus swelled, Friedheim kicking his bedpan, Chudnowski thumping with his crutch and holding the carbon so that Cramer could see, Danforth shouting in a shrill, joyous voice, Cramer's clear tenor holding the melody true, Armstrong bouncing in his bed and beating his bedpan with such force that the spoon was bent and crumpled.

> *"Brightly shone the stars he saw,*
> *For the blow was cru-el.*
> *Then a damsel came in sight,*
> *Riding on a m-u-u-el!"*

On and on, more and more ribald, waves of vitality crashing out of the void where by rights there should have been none, flooding Ward 7, flooding the whole universe, the hoarse unconquerable battle cry of the human spirit.

Old Ironpuss stood there in the lonely corridor, and while she hesitated a thought came from somewhere like an arrow and pierced her heart: *God rest you merry, gentlemen; let nothing you dismay.*

Standing there, unable to play her part any longer, Old Ironpuss turned her granite face to the wall. And wept.

A BALLAD OF ANTHOLOGISTS

by *Phyllis McGinley*

PHYLLIS MCGINLEY HAS been contributing verses to the *Post* since 1936 and she has yet to write a dull one. The following sample was chosen for this volume as a special favor to Messrs. Simon and Schuster, who have had considerable experience with sedulous anthologists.

DECEMBER 20, 1941

An urchin at his father's knee
    Sat scribbling on his slate,
And "Dearest father," quavered he,
"When I grow up I long to be
    A writer, rich and great."
That parent gently laid his hand
    Upon the curly head,
And in a voice of deep command
    He sorrowfully said:

"Oh, shun, lad, the life of an author.
    It's nothing but worry and waste.
Avoid that utensil,
The laboring pencil,
    And pick up the scissors and paste.
For authors wear hand-me-down suits, lad;

    "Their cuffs, they are frayed at the wrist.
But castles and riches
And custom-made britches
    Belong to the anthologist,
My boy,
    Await on the anthologist."

"Now, father dear," the youth replied,
    "Mere wealth, I am above it.
It is the reputation wide,
The playwright's pomp, the poet's pride,
    That eagerly I covet."
Then wrath lit up his elder's face,
    And in an accent burning
He shouted, "From your mind erase
    Such vain creative yearning!

"You'd better compile a collection
    Of words that another has wrote.
It's the shears and the glue
Which will compensate you
    And fashion a person of note.
For poets have common companions.
    Their fame is a wraith in the mist.
But the critics all quarrel
To garland with laurel
    The brow of the anthologist,
My son,
    The brow of the anthologist."

Years passed. To heed, that urchin failed,
    What his papa had hinted.
Not thinking what the act entailed,
To magazines his lines he mailed
    And often got them printed.
But when reviewers passed him by
    For books he'd helped adorn,
"I wish I'd listened," he would sigh,
    "When father used to warn:

" 'Oh, shun, lad, the life of an author.
    It's a road unrewarding and vile.
For the miracle's wrought
With a mucilage pot
    And a feasible reference file.
Forever that Ode on the Urn, sir,
    Has headed the publishers' list.
But the name isn't Keats
On the royalty sheets
    That go out to the anthologist,
My lad,
    The sedulous anthologist.' "

THE ORDEAL OF JUDGE MEDINA

by Jack Alexander

ONE DAY IN 1941 a man in Toronto telephoned Jack Alexander at his home in New York. "I can't stop drinking and I'm going to kill myself," he announced. "What do you advise me to do?" Alexander, who had never heard of the man before, advised him to take it easy and call the cops. Nothing further was heard of this so perhaps the *Post* may have helped prevent a suicide. At any rate Alexander's pioneer piece on "Alcoholics Anonymous," which came out on the same day he got the phone call, has since brought him more than 6,000 letters, most of them asking for personal advice.

Associate editor Alexander was born in St. Louis in 1903, worked on the *Star* and *Post-Dispatch* in that city, the New York *Daily News* and the *New Yorker* before joining the *Post* staff in 1942. He has no superior in the fine art of profile-writing, which he defines as mostly amateur psychiatry. In "The Ordeal of Judge Medina" he has provided some psychological background for one of the important events of our time.

AUGUST 12, 1950

WHEN A LAWYER, in accepting a $15,000-a-year judgeship, happily bids farewell to a practice worth $100,000 a year, certain inferences are warranted. He is seeking a new challenge to his talents, or he has an acutely developed sense of public service, or he wants badly to be a judge. All these motives were present, in indeterminable proportions, when Harold Raymond Medina mounted the Federal bench in New York City as a district judge in July, 1947, an appointee of President Truman's. Not particularly worried about his motives at the time, Judge Medina at fifty-nine entered ea erly upon his new career. He hoped that it would be carried on, as the careers of 180-odd district judges throughout the country were, in comparative, though useful, obscurity.

As one of the nation's most skillful courtroom pleaders, he had amassed more money than he needed. He had homes in Manhattan and at Westhampton, Long Island, and he enjoyed the gratifying respect of his fellow members of the bar. An energetic and emotional man, he was passionately devoted to sailing, golf, billiards, music and the study of Latin, and he had a love affair of long standing with his alma mater, Princeton University, especially with the class of 1909, of which he was, and is, an active and dedicated member. His two sons, following in his footsteps, had become successful lawyers and had married attractive girls, and there were grandchildren with whom Medina wanted to get better acquainted.

The new work proved to be more than agreeably challenging, but by the time two years were up the obscurity had washed off under unforeseen and dramatic circumstances. This came about in 1949 as a result of a nine-month trial at which Medina presided. One of the longest and most turbulent trials in American criminal-court history, it ended with the conviction of eleven members of the Communist Party's national board. The charge, brought under the Smith Act, was that of conspiring to teach and advocate the overthrow of the United States Government by force and violence. When it was all over, Medina was nationally famous and seemed well on his way to becoming a figure in modern American folklore. Somehow, during the ordeal of the long trial, his deportment had aroused the sympathy and admiration of the citizenry. Under merciless badgering, baiting, shouting and whipsawing by defense counsel, he had scarcely raised his voice above a conversational pitch; and after the jury's verdict had been recorded, he had said quietly, "Now I turn to some unfinished business," and forthwith sentenced six of the counsel for contempt of court.

While the trial was in progress, Medina's daily mail consisted mostly of letters and telegrams from communists and communist sympathizers. Some were merely scurrilous, but a substantial number of the letters were so threatening that he was under guard as long as the trial lasted. One faithful, and anonymous, hater each day sent him a copy of the *Daily Worker*. The communist paper's running account of the evil capitalist trial was ringed in pencil, and on the margin of the front page, scrawled in red, was an insulting greeting. A typical one was "Hello, Harold, you old S.O.B."

Medina felt fine when the trial was over, thanks to a shrewdly calculated and sternly adhered to program of exercise, diet and sleep. The strain of the trial and of the threats had caused Mrs. Medina to lose thirteen pounds; the judge had lost only two. He got a puzzled sort of amusement out of suggestions from callers who urged him seriously to consider himself a candidate for governor of New York, for United States senator and for the presidency itself. Then the congratulatory letters, mostly from ordinary citizens, began to flood in, and within a week about 50,000 of them lay in stacks around his chambers. Some were signed by whole families, with an "X" awkwardly marked beside the name of each preschool child.

Medina, whose drooping mustache and thick, highly arched eyebrows give him a look of perpetual surprise—such as might be worn by an entomologist on discovering a new and revolutionary bug—was genuinely surprised by this phenomenon. As it was plainly impossible to answer all the letters, he took refuge in selective method, deciding to answer only those writers to whom a reply might mean a great deal—whole families, young people, very old people and friends whom he hadn't seen in years. These added up to about 2500 letters. For a fortnight, dictating to three stenographers in relays, he chipped away at the stacks; then, suddenly, the accumulated stresses of the trial caught up with him and he felt fatigued to the bone.

To restore himself physically, he took three months off and made trips to Bermuda and to the West Coast with his wife.

Other phenomena sprang up wherever he went. On the way to Bermuda he found running about in his head an unflattering chant whose metrical values fascinated him and caused him to recite it aloud to himself at odd moments, noting in its short terminal line a resemblance to the technique of the Latin poet Horace, of whose works he is a scholar. Communist pickets had shouted the chant at him as he left the Federal Courthouse on Foley Square after each trial day. It went:

> *Judge Medina is a s—o—b!*
> *Judge Medina is a s—o—b!*
> *How do you spell Ma-deen-a?*
> *R-A-T!*

One morning in Bermuda he picked up a newspaper at breakfast and found that he couldn't read it; the front page didn't seem to make sense. He put it aside and tried a novel, with no better luck. As golf had always had a relaxing effect on him, he went to the nearest links and played eighteen holes. When he returned, he was able to read both the newspaper and the novel, but only for short periods. He was suffering from an inability to concentrate, and it lasted for a week or so, gradually disappearing.

While in Bermuda he made another odd discovery. In writing post cards to his friends, he found himself running on in the message space at what seemed to be almost letter length. Wondering why this was, he stuck one of the cards in his pocket and later on compared the handwriting on it with a sample of his handwriting of a year before; it was just half its former size. During the long trial, which left a court record of more than 5,000,000 words, Medina, a highly methodical man, had kept his own record of the relevant testimony and of the 761 exhibits.

He kept it in a loose-leaf notebook, so wrapping up the essential points of the evidence, in 100 pages neatly penned on both sides of the paper, that he was able to straighten out counsel when a dispute arose as to what had been said weeks earlier. In condensing the trial into handy form, with cross references to the exhibits, Medina had unconsciously condensed his handwriting. The chirography of the private trial record and of Medina's present-day handwriting is tiny and exact, and as legible as an engraved wedding invitation.

Everywhere Medina went, strangers recognized him from newspaper photographs, and smiled or waved. Many came up and greeted him. After the trial, he went uptown for a medical checkup, and, on being pronounced exhausted but physically sound, took a bus downtown. Passengers in nearby seats smiled and chatted with him, and an exuberant matron, in passing down the aisle toward the exit, twittered, stopped long enough to give him an affectionate hug and got off the bus, still twittering. Some of the people who greeted him during his vacation travels annoyed him mildly because they were obviously trying to impress him with their importance in their own communities, going on at great length in this vein. Most of the greeters, though, struck him as sincere, and some—usually the less articulate ones —deeply moved him.

As he was crossing Madison Avenue at 75th Street on last New Year's Day, a coal truck came to a sudden stop. The driver leaned out of his cab, waved and said, "Happy New Year, Judge Medina!" As he was making a plane connection at Love Field, Dallas, a bulky man in open-throated shirt and baggy slacks shook his hand and said, "Judge, I don't want to introduce myself. I just want to say, 'Nice going.' " "Thank you, thank you very much," Medina replied, and hurried to catch his plane, swallowing a lump as he went. The greeting that aroused his emotions most, and was therefore the most memorable to him, took place as he was strolling in San Francisco. A young man dressed in work clothes and carrying a lunch box jumped off a cable car, ran up to him and, for just an instant, looked him in the eye and squeezed his arm. Then, without having uttered a word, he sprinted up the hill and caught his cable car again.

When Medina got back to New York, he tried to analyze his experiences. After some thought, he told a friend, "There seem to be millions of people filled with a love of country they don't quite know how to express. They just happened to pick on me, whom they saw as a nice fellow with a fair sense of humor, as a handy and current symbol. They seemed to feel that I had done something that was peculiarly American. I don't quite understand what it was, but there was no baloney about it. It makes you feel pretty humble, caught up in some great force you don't understand. I was mystified and bewildered by it all. It's really very curious."

Whenever Medina is bewildered, the bewildering element is some manifestation of unpredictable human nature. He manages to solve all his other problems by method and persistence, a combination he constantly urges young people to adopt. "Method is useless without persistence," he is fond of saying, "but the combination pays off on the long pull, and I am a guy who always figures things for the long pull."

The effectiveness of the combination was strikingly illustrated by his handling of the communists' trial. The son of a Spanish father, Medina was well aware that his impatient, explosive temperament might well be triggered off by needling and nagging lawyers, blowing the proceedings into a mistrial or causing him to make reversible errors. In effect, for nine long months he acted a wholly unfamiliar role—that of a judicial cucumber—with a consistency that the Barrymore family might have envied. This was done by imposing a gallingly strict discipline upon his natural inclinations and desires. He paid heavily for this extended run; despite the long post-trial vacation, he has never regained the energy he had at the trial's start, and he is now obliged to protect himself carefully from fatigue.

About a decade ago, Medina applied his method-and-persistence formula to a tent-caterpillar blight which was ruining the trees around Westhampton, including his own. On consulting specialized books, he learned that the only hope of success lay in collecting and destroying the caterpillars' egg clusters in fall and spring. To do this on an area basis, he needed a lot of collectors, and he set about recruiting the students at nearby Westhampton Beach High School. This took some doing, as there had been talk that tent caterpillars could infect human beings in some mysterious way. Medina countered this canard in an appearance he made at the high-school auditorium, in which he picked a caterpillar from a jar he had brought along and publicly swallowed it. A girl who came in after this performance stood up and expressed skepticism that it had happened. Medina convinced her by swallowing another.

That got the crusade under way. Each Saturday afternoon during the egg-cluster season, Medina held shop in his library cottage, which sits back from the main house on his fifty-five-acre estate. The children brought to his desk bags of the egg clusters they had collected during the week and he solemnly paid for them at a rate which varied, according to what he called "market conditions," from three to four clusters for a cent. To make the game more attractive, Medina paid off in shiny new coinage, and in a notebook kept a meticulous record of the clusters received and paid for. It was common for him to disburse thirty or forty dollars on a busy Saturday.

At first, skepticism was strong. A rumor got around that Medina was reselling the clusters elsewhere at a profit. He heard of this and thereafter burned the clusters in his library fireplace before the eyes of the collectors.

"It's funny," he says now quizzically, "but some of those youngsters didn't believe I was working *pro bono publico.*"

As a precaution against getting gypped himself, he examined the clusters with a magnifying glass; if the eggs had holes in them, they were last year's eggs. and there was no payment for these. Medina joined personally in the crusade. On week ends he drove about in a station wagon, and his neighbors got accustomed to seeing him in their back yards industriously removing clusters with a pruning pole. By 1947, with the aid of one exceptionally cold spring, the blight had been conquered

Earlier, he had applied method and persistence to golf, with outstanding results over the long pull. "I was not a natural golfer," he states in recounting his struggles. "Shot well over a hundred at first, and it took me ten years to break eighty." He took lessons regularly, and periodically had movies taken of his form, which he studied diligently for mistakes. On his grounds he constructed a duplicate of the thirteenth green of the Westhampton Beach Country Club, with a mowed strip three feet wide leading 250 yards back to a tee. During week ends he shunned the country club and practiced, using a small barrel of second-hand balls.

"I would stand on the tee and drive fifty balls," he once said with relish in telling of his efforts to improve his game. "Then I would move a few yards ahead and hit fifty brassie shots; a little farther along, fifty spoon shots. Then, moving ahead a bit at a time, fifty midirons and fifty mashies. By this time I would come to a hedge which blocked the green, and here I would pitch fifty balls to the green; putt them all out, go back and pick up what balls I could find, and start all over again. This went on for years."

A document attesting the startling result of his application to the mysteries of golf hangs in his chambers at the Federal Courthouse. It is a Westhampton Beach Country Club score card, on which is recorded his best score, a 38-33—71, two strokes below par, which he made on August 29, 1935.

"In golf, as in everything else I do, I am a perfectionist," he will say in a matter-of-fact way when showing the card to a visitor. "It sounds crazy, but that is what I try to be just the same."

A few months after becoming a judge, Medina noticed that his physical energy was beginning to decline. Foreseeing that in perhaps six or seven years golf would be a bit strenuous for him, he cast about for a less demanding sport to switch to at the appointed time. He chose billiards. The finesse it required appealed strongly to him. He began taking lessons on Wednesday mornings at the University Club from Leonard Howison, a noted billiard instructor. After the first lesson, Howison warned him that he would have to achieve perfection in the basic strokes before thinking of playing in competition. "The way you hit the ball now," he said, "you drive it into the next county."

Medina, exulting inwardly over having met a teacher of his own cast, gathered his forces for an attack on the tricky game. He had a billiard table installed in his library at Westhampton, and practiced his lessons on week ends. And he started making detailed entries in a big notebook captioned BILLIARDS, NOTES ON LESSONS BY HOWISON. The entries were illustrated by carefully drawn diagrams.

Medina's billard lessons were suspended during the communists' trial. He resumed them as soon as he could, and went to work on his billard diary where he had left off. He is still sticking to funda-

mentals and doesn't expect to be a good player until 1955.

Although always willing to learn, Medina has emphatic opinions about most subjects. One of these is the current state of prelegal education. He feels that in subjecting the prelegal student to law, economics and the like, the colleges are in error. He is all for strong doses of the humanities, especially Latin. The chore of translating difficult authors like Tacitus and Suetonius into exact English, he holds, develops traits of perseverance, industry and attention to small details, and stimulates the creative imagination.

In discussing this subject, Medina directly relates his long dalliance with Latin to the winning of one of his most successful cases as a lawyer. A businessman, who had recently insured his life for $375,000, was found dead of potassium-cyanide poisoning one morning in the bathroom of his apartment. The police listed the case as a suicide, and the insurance companies (there were three involved) refused to pay off.

The widow came to Medina with her claim. She was a Frenchwoman and at the time of her husband's death had been visiting in France, showing off her first child to its grandparents. Her case looked hopeless, but Medina decided, on the basis of a few details of her story, that it was worth a gamble.

There was no suicide note. The man's body was found nude—suicides rarely bother to remove their clothing, even night clothing. He had an odd hobby of making invisible inks, using the bathroom as his laboratory. The manufacture of his special inks involved the use of potassium cyanide; as a rather feeble gesture toward protecting others from getting poisoned, he let his wife and close friends know that the drinking glass he used for making the inks was the one on the left side of the medicine cabinet. He was also an arthritic, and was often awakened at night by acute pains which he relieved by taking a pill and soaking in a hot tub. Often his seizures were so severe that he had to be assisted to the tub, and for this reason his wife, on going abroad, had arranged for a male friend of theirs to live in the apartment during her absence.

Medina, employing his creative imagination, postulated a theory of accidental death, and set about seeing if it would stand up. First he spent a couple of weeks reading about poisons in the library of the Academy of Medicine, just to familiarize himself with the field. Then, with the aid of a New York University chemist, he proved that the amount of cyanide left in an unrinsed invisible-ink-experiment glass, even though dried, was a lethal dose. Comparing this residue with the amount listed in the autopsy report, he found them to be identical.

This coincidence plainly had the insurance companies' lawyers worried when the chemist testified at the trial. They looked even more worried when Medina, using his new-found wisdom about poisons, held a learned colloquy with the witness on a touchy question: Would the distinctively almondlike smell of cyanide necessarily warn a quick gulper? The answer was no; the smell would take a little time to rise.

Having thus anticipated a major defense point and demolished it, Medina put the roommate on the stand. The roommate testified that he heard the victim get up in the middle of the night and go to the bathroom; that when he heard water running into the tub he assumed it was for the usual hot bath, and went back to sleep. He said that when he went to the bathroom in the morning and found his host stretched out stiff, the water was still running—indicating that the victim had never succeeded in getting into the tub.

This was the climax of Medina's masterpiece of constructive confusion. A recess was called, and the defense lawyers huddled. They reviewed the evidence, and recalled that Medina, in his opening, had told the jury that he expected to prove that someone—the victim, his roommate or the maid—could have inadvertently shifted the bathroom glasses, and that the victim, in taking a pellet for his arthritic pains, could easily have drunk water from the wrong glass. The case never got to the jury and the question of suicide or accident remained unresolved. The defense was glad to settle the claim for a quarter of a million dollars.

Though respected by his fellow lawyers, Medina, while in active practice, was not especially well liked. His urbanity is a product of his later years. In the courtroom, he was aggressive, sarcastic and, some thought, overbearing. But when the judgeship he now holds was vacant, and Medina was one of twenty candidates discussed for the vacancy, the bar associations worked en masse for his appointment to it. This caused one veteran lawyer to recall, perhaps irrelevantly, a remark of Benjamin Franklin's at the Convention of 1787 when a question arose over whether Supreme Court justices should be chosen by the national legislature or the President. Franklin jokingly suggested that the United States adopt the old Scottish system "in which the nomination proceeded from the lawyers, who always selected the ablest of the profession, in order to get rid of him and share his practice among themselves."

Much of Medina's aggressiveness as a lawyer may be traced without an undue strain upon psychology to the social repercussions of the Spanish-American War upon his native Brooklyn. The war broke out while he was in public school and thereafter, because his father had come from Mexico, he was constantly taunted with the epithet "greaser." The upshot of this was that young Medina fought his way to and from school, and fought during the play periods. Being combative by nature, he battled with some joy, but afterward stewed a good deal over his failure to win the acceptance of his fellow pupils. His father, the late Joaquin Medina, a descendant of the early Spanish settlers of Yucatán, had stayed on in the States after graduation from a New Jersey prep school to which he had been sent by his parents, who owned a hemp plantation. The elder Medina had married Elizabeth Fash, a member of a pioneer Brooklyn Dutch family, and had built up a fairly prosperous importing business.

The importing business is still in existence under its original name, J. A. Medina Company. Judge Medina lists himself as a vice-president and director of the firm, and it is operated by his younger brother, Richard.

Harold was a mischievous boy, and somehow or other was always getting into trouble. The family summered regularly at a Westhampton Beach hotel, and when Harold was ten he got into a social jam that ended the family's vacations at that resort. Still striving for acceptance, he climbed a windmill and some big trees, and once balanced himself precariously on the hotel roof. The parents of the other children forbade them to play with young Medina and he became an outcast. In reminiscing about the impact of this experience, Medina said not long ago, "A good many years passed during which I felt, although I never spoke of it to anyone, that there was probably something wrong with me, and the makings of a pretty healthy inferiority complex were built up."

He was graduated from public school second in his class. The elder Medina tried to get him into one of the better prep schools, but failed—because, Medina believes, of his father's foreign origin—and he was sent to a military academy in New York State, where he led his classes and played fullback.

In the fall of 1905, at seventeen, Medina entered Princeton. He had a rough time of it on that beautiful campus. He was one of the most lippy of freshmen, always ready for an argument or a tussle, and he was unmercifully hazed. More than ever eager to attract friends and be thought well of, he tried his hand at all sorts of things, with indifferent success. No one called him "greaser," but the war with Spain had not been wholly forgotten. And he was in love. During his prematriculation summer he had become engaged while vacationing in Connecticut, and he fretted over the years that remained before he could afford to marry. The girl was Ethel Forde Hillyer, of East Orange, New Jersey, the daughter of an antiques appraiser for the United States Customs Bureau and a sister of Robert Hillyer, who was to become a well-known poet and professor of English.

Through tutoring backward students and reporting campus news for a Newark paper, Medina earned enough to buy his fiancée a $300 engagement ring. He studied hard, and won places on the fencing and water-polo teams, but generated few friendships. Largely through being noisy, he managed to irritate the men he admired most. To relieve his boredom and frustration, he allowed himself to be recruited to give sermons in non-denominational chapels which studded the surrounding farmlands. Someone supplied him with a horse and buggy, and on Sunday afternoons he doggedly made the rounds of the chapels, offering an impromptu prayer and then reading a chapter from a book of sermons.

Medina had a way with languages, and on being graduated from Princeton in 1909, with highest honors in French and a Phi Beta Kappa key, he played for a while with the idea of becoming a language teacher. He rejected it on learning what teachers' incomes were like—"I was awfully anxious to succeed and get along, and any time an honest dollar was involved I always said yes." Since early childhood, for a reason he cannot now remember, he had wanted to be a lawyer, so he moved in the fall to the Columbia University Law School, where for the first time he got on a firm footing. Nobody at Columbia held the war with Spain against him personally, and he reveled in the stimulating company of his gabby, argumentative law-school classmates. In his second year, through some financial aid from his father, he was able to marry Miss Hillyer. He got his degree in 1912, winning the Ordronneaux Prize for the best scholastic record in his class. By now Medina was a happy young man. He had finally won the acceptance of his peers and was confident that he had unusual talents.

With gusto and a firm faith in the future, he joined the downtown firm of Davies, Auerbach and Cornell, as a law clerk at eight dollars a week. The Medinas moved into a forty-dollar-a-month house in East Orange, and Medina commuted to Manhattan. Inside a few years, the couple, through extraordinary exertions by the future judge, were able to move to Riverside Drive. The law firm had discovered in its law clerk a youngster with brilliance, an amazing grasp of the law and a genius for simplifying abstruse problems through the application of method—thereby becoming the first to confirm Medina's estimate of himself. In 1915, Medina joined the faculty of Columbia Law at the invitation of Dean Harlan F. Stone, who was later to become Chief Justice of the United States.

Noting sagely that promotion on a law faculty fed on, among other things, the compilation of books, Medina began compiling one, and ultimately had ten law volumes to his credit. Meanwhile, when just a year out of Columbia, he had inaugurated another project which grew into a notable one-man institution. It was a private "cram" course for senior law students on the questions they could expect to encounter in taking the New York State bar examinations.

A strong believer in Justice Holmes' famous remark that to live is to function, Medina was soon functioning about fifteen hours a day and getting very little sleep. He got to Columbia an hour early in order to prepare for a nine-o'clock lecture. From 10:30 until late afternoon he was downtown practicing law. At 5:30 he began a two-hour cram lecture to the anxious bar candidates. After an 8:30 dinner, he put in several hours preparing for the next day's Columbia and cram-course lectures. He enjoyed this onerous schedule, despite the fact that in ten years of it his weight dropped from 170 to 135 pounds.

The cram course, which ran for six days a week over a period of five weeks in various rented auditoriums, cost the listeners thirty-five dollars a head. When Medina gave it up, after a twenty-nine-year run, he had indoctrinated around 40,000 candidates for admission to the bar. The candidates came to regard the lectures as a type of insurance against failing the State Board tests.

Through his Herculean exertions Medina was also getting an unusually broad postgraduate course in law himself. In 1918 he formed a law firm of his own, taking into partnership Eugene A. Sherpick, whom he had taught at Columbia. Sherpick's calm, scholarly approach to the law acted as a balance to Medina's brilliance and enthusiasm, and the firm of Medina and Sherpick was successful from the start.

Medina's specialty was arguing appeals, which is the blue-stocking side of law practice. He also tried civil cases, and on one occasion pounded the rail of the jury box so hard that he broke some bones in his hand. In the meantime, he was active on bar-association committees working for legal reforms, among them the banning of microphones, sound movies and still-picture cameras from New York courtrooms.

Outside the legal profession and the select circle of large corporate clients, Medina was almost unknown until the Bank of the United States collapsed early in the depression, and the bank's officers were indicted for misapplication of funds. One of the minor officers was a young law graduate named Herbert Singer, whose father was chairman of the board. Medina's defense of young Singer was his first large criminal case, and he took it because he felt that his client had been a mere errand boy in the bank, that he knew nothing about the complicated monkey business that had been going on at the higher levels, and that he was a victim of the public hue and cry over the collapse.

The jury which heard the case convicted both of the Singers and Bernard K. Marcus, the bank's president, but in the Court of Appeals at Albany, Medina won a reversal for Herbert Singer. Young Singer, a promising lawyer, who had been disbarred because of the conviction, won reinstatement and is now practicing law again in New York, and doing well.

The Herbert Singer victory, which is the one he is most proud of, marked a turning point in Medina's career. He continued to argue appeals, but devoted the bulk of his time, from choice, to criminal and civil jury trials. During the next fourteen years he tried thirteen more jury cases without losing one. The case he treasures most as a professional performance was one upon which he spent a total of a year's time without getting a fee, thereby missing out on about $100,000 in normal income.

It was that of Anthony Cramer, a naturalized German, who was indicted for treason early in World War II after having had some contacts with some of the four Nazi saboteurs who had been landed on Long Island from a U-boat. Feeling against Cramer was naturally running high. Chief District Judge John C. Knox, eager to preserve the American tradition of full justice for penniless defendants, asked Medina to undertake Cramer's defense. It was a distinctly unpopular assignment, but Medina accepted it. During the next three years he found additional reason for being surprised at human nature; many friends of long standing stopped speaking to him; their wives were especially bitter. And one day during the trial, as Medina was walking up the aisle to the counsel table, a male spectator leaned out and spat in his face.

Cramer, who had had a prewar acquaintance with one of the thwarted saboteurs, had kept some of the man's money in his own safe-deposit box; and on one occasion he had been seen drinking beer in a Long Island taproom with two of the Nazis. That, in essence, was the Government's case against Cramer. Despite its thinness and Medina's best efforts as an advocate, it was enough to convict Cramer and to cause the Circuit Court of Appeals to uphold the jury's verdict. Cramer's appeal then went before the Supreme Court of the United States. It was the first treason case ever to reach this tribunal. In preparing his argument, Medina spent a week of days and evenings in the Supreme Court library, rereading historic treason cases, and pouring over debates in the Convention of 1787, colonial diaries and related materials.

Things looked black for Cramer. After a secret wartime trial by a military commission, two of the Long Island saboteurs had already been electrocuted—along with four others who had been landed in Florida—and the other two had gone to prison, one for thirty years, the other for life. Cramer's own sentence was for forty-five years.

The courtroom was packed for the hearing. From the lonely lectern from which lawyers address the nine robed justices, and without recourse to books or notes, Medina argued for several hours, citing what he considered errors made by the trial judge and hoping for an order for a new trial, at best. Toward the end of his address, he went briefly into a discussion of what constituted an "overt act" as described in the Constitution.

Later on, the court asked him to make another appearance and enlarge upon his discussion of overt acts. He began informally by saying, "It has been four months since my earlier argument, but we'll pretend I was here just a couple of days ago, so I'll pick up where I left off." For almost a whole day's session, and again speaking off the cuff, he reviewed the history of British treason-case rulings and then covered American cases going back as far as the indictment of Aaron Burr in 1807, and the War of 1812. The outcome of his two appearances was a reversal of the Cramer jury's verdict, on the ground that Cramer's activities did not add up to an overt act. Cramer thereupon pleaded guilty to a lesser charge, trading with the enemy, and was sentenced to serve six years in prison.

Besides losing out on a year's income, Medina was out of pocket $800 more for hotel, traveling and stenographic expenses, but he was elated over his triumph as an advocate and over the exact pigeonholing of Cramer's crime which his efforts had wrought. Medina, a quietly elegant dresser, has a strong instinct for neatness; he keeps his clothes exactly arranged in his closet and sees that his shirts, ties and other items of haberdashery are arrayed in precise places in his chiffonier. In this trait he takes after his mother, an extremely conscientious housekeeper who, when her husband sat down for an after-dinner cigar, was accustomed to spread newspapers around his easy chair to protect the rug from stray ashes.

Only one aspect of the Cramer case distressed Medina. After he had returned to New York, following his first Supreme Court argument, an admiring friend telephoned and asked him for a transcript of it. Medina knew that oral arguments in the Supreme Court were not generally recorded, but he recalled that, as he had been speaking, a man near him had been making notes in a stenographer's notebook. He took an evening train to Washington and next day succeeded in locating the man with the notebook. The man turned out to be a stenographer from the Department of Justice, assigned to the hearing solely to record the utterances of the Government's attorney, the Solicitor General. When Medina was speaking, which was most of the time, the stenographer had merely doodled. He showed the doodles to Medina, who was crestfallen. "The greatest argument I ever made," he said gloomily, "and now it's lost, gone down the drain."

As happens to many lawyers, Medina, as he progressed through middle age, conceived a strong desire to wind up his career on the bench. He took the usual tack of telling lawyer friends about it, in the hope of fixing his availability in the minds of bar-association committees. Nothing happened. He then went to the extreme of confiding his ambition to the then chief judge of New York's Court of Appeals at Albany, and was advised to seek the support of some politician, as the higher state judicial jobs are elective. Medina, who, though a registered Democrat, abhors politics, couldn't bring himself to ask a favor of a Tammany district leader, and let the matter drop. He was astounded when he was proposed for his present judgeship, but recovered his poise quickly. When a bar-association committee asked him if he wanted to be a Federal district judge, he replied, "Certainly. I've wanted to be a judge for years. I see no point in beating about the bush." It was the bar associations, not the politicians, who persuaded President Truman that Medina ought to get the post.

The trial of the eleven communist Politburo members began a year and a half after Medina had become a judge, before he had had time to get his feet wet. He got the assignment from Chief Judge Knox partly because of his varied knowledge of the law and partly because of his physical vigor; Medina has always been an exercise fiend. At the time, the Government expected the trial to consume two or three months, and it didn't want a repetition of the 1944 mass sedition trial in Washington; in that case, after being harried by twenty defense lawyers for about seven and a half months, the judge dropped dead and the defendants were never tried again.

Medina had the tragic Washington fiasco in mind when the communists' trial began, and after three weeks of squabbling and insulting bickering by the defense lawyers, he concluded that they were out either to shorten his life or break him down mentally. To thwart these designs, he subjected himself to a daily regimen that revolutionized his private life during the nine months the trial actually lasted, and transformed him into something of a hermit. Normally a gregarious man, Medina was addicted to the theater, the opera and past-midnight discussions with his friends. He gave up all of these, and a custom of dining out twice a week.

His diet was carefully planned; he took his usual breakfast—a large glass of orange juice, hot cereal with thick cream, a poached egg on toast smothered in butter, and coffee. For lunch, which he ate alone in his chambers, he stuck to a medium-rare lamb chop and spinach, and took a half-hour nap before returning to the courtroom. In the evening he allowed himself two very dry Martinis. Dinner consisted of some easily digested meat, with salad and vegetables. Before retiring at 9:30, he took a sleeping pill prescribed by his doctor. He got up at 6:30 in the morning, and at 8:30 was in his chambers, where he boned up on the record of the previous day until court began at 10:30. After daily adjournment at 4:30, he walked to a health club in the nearby Woolworth Building and went through a rigorous set of exercises for a man in his early sixties. These exertions were followed by six minutes in the dry-hot room, then a hot shower, a cold shower and a body massage.

Throughout the trial, Medina wore a brace to keep in place two vertebrae which tended to get out of alignment, a souvenir of a freshman-football experience at Princeton in which someone jumped on his back after he had been tackled. The brace skinned his hips during the hot weather, but he didn't dare to discard it.

Fridays were invariably the worst days of the week for the judge. On that day he adjourned court for the day at one o'clock, and the defense lawyers did their worst to make him squirm. It was on a hot Friday in August that Medina, unable to restore order, abruptly sprinted for his chambers and lay down on a couch, feeling certain that he was dying of extreme fatigue, but fifteen minutes of rest enabled him to return to the battle. It was on another Friday that the defendants and their lawyers, during an especially acrimonious discussion, got up and marched toward the bench, all shouting at once. Deputy marshals were summoned from other courtrooms to avert a riot, but by the time they arrived Medina had quieted the clamor.

Because of the threats which Medina received, two city detectives traveled with him between his apartment and the courthouse, and spent the night in the apartment lobby, one sleeping while the other stood guard. On Friday afternoons, when Medina went to Westhampton for the week end, a pair of FBI special agents rode with him. From the Nassau County line his car was escorted by a state-police car which saw him safely to Westhampton and returned on Monday morning to pick him up. The FBI agents stayed with him through Saturday and Sunday, taking turns sleeping in the living room. As long as the trial lasted, Medina saw none of his friends and, except for Mrs. Medina, very little of his family.

There were a few breaks in the dull routine, though, most of them inspired by sentimental feelings. Medina took his six grandchildren to the circus at Madison Square Garden, and had to borrow a big carton from a concessionaire to carry home the toys, candy and favors he bought them. His only rounds of golf were in defense of a handicap cup he had won the year before, and he defended it successfully, his fellow club members carefully refraining from mentioning the trial. On several week ends he made pilgrimages to Princeton with other Class of '09 members and sat up late in the Nassau Tavern drinking and discussing the old days. Princeton, which had once given him the cold shoulder, had finally come around to returning his devotion. He had been made chairman of the advisory council of the modern-language department's Romance section, and his own class had elected him to its presidency for a five-year term, an honor which he rates as the finest that ever came his way.

Medina took his class presidency conscientiously. In spare moments after sessions of the trial, he worked for hours at designing a new blazer for the class's fortieth reunion, and won adoption of it. The blazer, as it ultimately emerged after many designs had landed in the wastebasket, was a white one with piping in the Princeton colors and an '09 patch on the left side. "I worried more about that damned blazer than I did about the trial," he says, "but it made '09

stand out at the reunion. If I do say so myself, it is a very snappy blazer."

The trial failed to interfere with an annual visit Medina had been making to a Brooklyn cemetery. At the grave of a classmate named Joshua C. Brush he laid a wreath bearing a floral design which spelled simply " '09," just as he had done every year on the anniversary of Brush's death. Brush, who died in 1942, was a New Jersey manufacturer. He had been a popular man on the Princeton campus and one of the few students with whom Medina had been able to strike up a friendship. In the years after class graduation, Brush had helped many of his more unlucky classmates with loans, and had labored to keep the class together.

As Brush's successor in this task, Medina misses no detail. Each morning on arriving at his chambers—and the big trial didn't cause him to forget—Medina consults the class records and dashes off a greeting, in the name of '09, to any of the 230-odd class members who happen to have a birthday coming up. His Christmas card for 1949 suggested that "on Christmas Night, wherever you may be at 7 o'clock, fill your glass and drink a toast to the Best Old Class of All." On the cover of the card was a photograph of the Medinas setting an example with a shaker of Martinis. Medina took some kidding for proposing the toast, but he estimates with satisfaction that more than half of the class members have accepted the idea, and predicts that the custom will spread.

Medina's personal regimen for the duration of the trial isolated him almost totally from his friends, his sons, his daughters-in-law and his grandchildren. During the week, he had plenty to do, but the Westhampton week ends dragged a bit. On Sundays, he would occasionally attend services at St. Mark's Episcopal Church, of which he is a vestryman. He would read Dickens for a while. Characteristically, this adventure was thorough and methodical. He started it off by reading a biography of Dickens. On reaching a mention of one of the novels, he would set the biography aside long enough to read the novel, then return to the biography until another novel was mentioned.

A slow, painstaking reader, he would read each novel from cover to cover, including frontispiece, preface and introduction. "In this way," he explained a few weeks ago, "you get a unity of the author and his works. It is much better than just taking the novels as you find them, without a chronological structure of reference. Right now I'm applying the same method to Sir Walter Scott."

From his Dickens reading, Medina moved on

to puttering around his private green, practicing chip shots, or to his library, where he tried out billiard shots he'd nearly forgotten. Then, after a few hours of sailing or of solitary fishing in Great South Bay, he would return to the house and entertain his FBI bodyguards with a demonstration of his proficiency with a yo-yo top, in which art he considers himself, and is, a virtuoso. Then he would try to liven up the dead atmosphere by blowing an assortment of New Year's Eve horns and operating a collection of mechanical noisemakers which he always keeps handy. Discouraged when this hideous performance won no more than educated smiles from the G-men, he would have dinner with them and Mrs. Medina and, after kneeling to say his evening prayers, which he never misses, retire early.

Thus the winter passed, and the spring, and the summer, until one day in mid-October, after all the evidence was in, Medina swung about in his big red-leather chair to deliver his charge. With the Politburo members and their now-quiet attorneys listening, and the nation watching from a distance, he began, "Ladies and gentlemen of the jury, you now approach the performance of one of the most sacred duties of citizenship, the meting out of justice. Just after you were sworn in as jurors I took occasion to make a few remarks which I shall now repeat in somewhat different form, as the thoughts I then expressed are peculiarly applicable to the period of your deliberations in order to reach a just and true verdict.

"I then told you to be patient and said that there are few qualities in life so important. I said that if you once get yourself in the frame of mind where you know that you have a task ahead and it has to be done carefully and it has to be done just right and you know that it will be wrong to let little things disturb you, then there comes a certain calm and peace of mind which are of the essence in the administration of justice.

"When you get yourself in that frame of mind you find not only that the task ahead becomes much easier, but, in addition, that the quality of your work in the administration of justice is of the quality that it should be. Justice does not flourish amidst emotional excitement and stress. . . ."

By that time Harold Medina had qualified for the first time in his life as an expert on patience.

DEATH ON M-24

by *John Bartlow Martin*

JOHN BARTLOW MARTIN has one of the most inquiring minds in America; his articles in the *Post* and other magazines have given a new importance to the word "reporting." His research methods are awe-inspiring. For "The Sheltons: America's Bloodiest Gang" (March 18, 1950) he compiled a pasteup outline one hundred and thirty feet long and reduced it to a rough draft of three hundred and three typewritten pages, which had to be trimmed down to forty-four pages before it ran in the *Post*. Reporter Martin was born in 1915 at Hamilton, Ohio, was graduated from DePauw University in 1937, and worked for the Indianapolis *Times*, covering City Hall, courthouse and other beats. He has free-lanced since 1938, except for two years in the army, and lives near Chicago. For the *Post* he has written a number of serious studies of crime and prison life, as well as articles on the Illinois Legislature and the Abraham Lincoln country. "Death on M-24" is more than the story of a gruesome automobile accident; it is a clinical examination of the worst single cause of property waste and human bloodshed in the United States today.

APRIL 5, 1952

A T 3:25 A.M. on November 10, 1951, Lt. Ted Gunn, of the sheriff's police, was cruising near Oxford, Michigan, when he received a radio call to investigate a bad accident ten miles to the south on M-24. M-24 runs north from Detroit over rolling, hilly country, two lanes of concrete twenty-two feet wide. The night was clear, the pavement dry. Lieutenant Gunn drove fast through the town of Lake Orion and about five miles beyond, topping a hill, saw, in the narrow valley below, the wreck. It had happened on a short flat straightaway between two hills, the steeper one called Bald Mountain. An ambulance arrived. Gunn, a brusque, stocky man, recalls, "We knew it was a bad one all right."

Two cars had hit head on. Then a third had plowed into the wreckage.

The concrete was strewn with auto parts and spattered with oil and glass and blood. A boy in his teens lay moaning in the middle of the road, a girl sat sobbing nearby. Other bodies were partly visible in the wreckage.

One of the cars had been driven by a young couple, Mr. and Mrs. Murray J. Moore. It stood on the shoulder of the road. It was a light 1946 two-door sedan. Where once had been the motor and hood now was nothing but a senseless snarl of tubing and wires and bent steel. It was just junk. Inside, Mrs. Moore, a young woman in a polo coat, lay with her mouth open and her face smashed into the glove compartment. The driver, her husband, had been thrown backward so that

his head and hands were in the rear seat. They both were dead.

The second car, a light 1941 four-door sedan, had contained five teen-agers. It stood in the center of the road. It apparently had spun part way around after the collision. The whole front end was squeezed accordion-fashion so that only about two feet separated the headlight from the place where the windshield once had been. In the front seat were three dead teen-agers. The driver, a boy, was jammed sideways against the dashboard. A girl lay partly out of the car, one leg folded oddly inside the car, the other leg out; she was wearing blue jeans and white ankle socks and one of her shoes had come off; her head was face down on the pavement, her hair spread out on the concrete. Lying partly under her was another boy, his head crushed flat.

The boy on the pavement was barely alive. The ambulance sped away with him. But he died at the hospital entrance.

Lieutenant Gunn radioed for more help. He gave an onlooker some red warning flares to set out. A second ambulance carried off the injured girl. Both her legs were fractured, bones sticking through the flesh. The officers could not extricate the Moores' bodies from their car; they towed it away with the bodies in it. They easily removed the girl's body from the teen-agers' car and pried the two boys' bodies free. In the front seat of the teen-agers' car, on a raised hump on the floor board that had covered the transmission, stood a bottle half full of beer, incredibly upright.

Recently the millionth American was killed in auto accidents—more Americans than have been killed in all of America's wars. So commonplace are auto accidents that nobody pays much heed to them any more—nobody, that is, except the orphaned children, the bereaved parents of the victims. Can nothing be done? Let us study this accident which killed six people and made orphans of eleven. What caused it? What were its effects? Could it have been prevented? Who were the people involved?

Murray J. Moore was a six-foot, two-hundred-pound, black-haired Irishman, thirty-six years old. He had a heavy, round face. Born in Toronto, he had lived most of his life in Royal Oak, one of the string of towns that runs north from Detroit to Pontiac. When he was twenty he married a high-school senior of seventeen, Mary Moss. Moore was a Catholic and Mary became one. She was a small, attractive girl, long-jawed, dark-haired, slender. She finished high school the following spring, 1936, and that September she bore their first child, Gerard, called Gerry. She bore another child every year or every two years thereafter until she died.

The Moores always had a hard time—too many children, not enough room, not enough money. Moore had a succession of jobs—taxi driver, painter, factory worker several times. They never could afford a big-enough house. Late in the war, Moore was drafted. He got out of the Army after seven months. But the owner of their rented house wanted it for himself, so the Moores had to move. They bought a house "on contract." But Moore fell ill and lost his job. They lost their home. For several months they were on relief. Then Moore found a $100-a-week job. But he couldn't find a place to live. He couldn't buy a house—he had no cash for a down payment. And nobody wanted to rent him one—he had eleven children. Finally in the summer of 1950 he rented a cottage at Cedar Island Lake.

That summer the oldest boy, Gerry, caddied at a golf course, giving his earnings to his parents to help them out. Gerry was not quite fourteen. Capt. Frank J. Van Atta, who interviewed him a year later after the accident, said, "There is a man." Gerry is a nice-looking, straightforward, sensible boy, well-spoken, well-mannered, with dark curly hair and fair skin. He often says, "I look just like my dad." Gerry worshiped his father. They went hunting and fishing together. "He was always just like a brother to me," Gerry says. "If anything ever went wrong, he always used to tell me about it. Like if he'd go to the races and lose money,

he'd tell me instead of telling my mother. She'd find out anyway. She didn't care, though. She didn't care about anything, long as she was with him. I'm glad they're still together now"—in death, that is. "Because one couldn't of lived without the other, I don't think."

The Moores never had taken a vacation; the sojourn at the lake was to be one. But when fall came they could find no other house. Winter came. They tried to keep warm with a bottled-gas cookstove. In February their car broke down. Unable to commute to work, Moore stayed in town. The youngest child, baby Dennis Michael, got sick. "He cried so," Gerry remembers. "He could hardly move. I went to the store and telephoned my dad. He told us how to fix him—keep him warm, feed him warm milk. My dad could always tell us what to do. But he didn't know how bad the baby was. He said he'd come home the next day. But the next morning a woman called the sheriff, and the sheriff came and took the baby to the hospital." The baby died of pneumonia. "I remember afterwards my dad told me that when my baby brother died my dad was watching and he was wishing God would let him crawl into the little bed and die for him. He said he'd do that for any of us. I know he would too. My mother, the same way."

They never went back to the cottage. "We couldn't," Gerry says. But they could find nowhere else to live. So they put the seven youngest children in an American Legion orphanage and put the eldest three in the Juvenile Home—a temporary arrangement to enable both Mr. and Mrs. Moore to work and save money for a down payment on a house.

House-hunting one week end, the Moores drove up to the farm town of Leonard, twenty-five miles north of Pontiac, taking Gerry with them. They saw a fine old rambling house surrounded by a big, shady yard. "It looked so big and nice," Gerry remembers. "We didn't think we could possibly get it with the down payment we had. But dad said he'd go see the real-estate man. Mother and I waited in the car and laughed at dad, trying to get that house."

He got it, though. And he got the best job he'd ever had. And, feeling that his luck had changed, he went to the races, won $100 and bought the newest car he'd ever had. They got the older children out of the Juvenile Home, and on October first moved into the house at Leonard. That same night their twelfth child was born to Mrs. Moore. Three weeks later the other children came home. The house cost $9000; they paid $700 down and were making payments of seventy-five dollars a month.

A week before the accident, Moore got a job nearer home. On November ninth he prepared dinner—"our favorite meal," Gerry recalls, "fish and chips"—then Gerry got out the cards to play canasta with his parents, as he often did, but they told him they were going out with some friends. They said they'd be home about one o'clock. But they were killed instead.

The driver of the car that hit theirs was Raymond Smith. He was a short, chunky, muscular young man of nineteen, with brawny shoulders and dark, bushy hair. His father, a small worried-looking man, raised him. Mr. Smith was born in rural Missouri. He moved around the Midwest, following construction. He and his wife were divorced in 1938, when Raymond was six, the middle child of three. A housebuilder, Mr. Smith arranged his working hours to suit the children's needs. He says, in his mild, flat monotone, "I used to take them with me to work. They would play around the car while I was working. Then I'd take them home at night, get their supper, cook and wash and iron, get their clothes ready for the next morning." He moved around a good deal, always taking care to have a house, not an apartment, "for the kids." Six years ago Mr. Smith bought his present small house in Clawson, a town adjoining Royal Oak and not far from Pontiac.

Mr. Smith did everything he could for the children.

"Raymond liked music, so I bought him a slide trombone. I bought him a set of drums too. He liked them better'n anything." As Raymond grew up it wasn't easy to keep track of where he was and what he was doing.

Raymond didn't like school. He quit after one semester of high school, in 1950, when he was seventeen. Already he had been working part time in filling stations. He was more interested in cars than in school. His father taught him to drive. "He was all the time messin' around with cars," his father says. Raymond bought his own car soon after leaving school. Then, quickly, he bought four others, all old. "He was a good driver," his father says. "Oh, he'd act crazy and get wild at times, cut up like boys do, but he always had the car under control. Yes, I thought Raymond was a pretty good driver. Of course," he adds, almost shyly, "I'm his dad."

The police, however, have a different view. They gave Raymond tickets, they recall, for having a noisy muffler and for failing to stop at a red traffic signal. Repeatedly they "lectured" Raymond about fast or reckless driving. One policeman recalls, "You couldn't tell Raymond Smith anything." Another: "We weren't surprised at the accident."

Clawson, a town of 6500, grew up on swampy flatland during the war boom. It is a working-man's town, small houses and muddy streets straggling out to the countryside. The business section is just the intersection of two roads. Evenings the teen-agers gather at the Dairy Bar or at the poolroom next door. There is no place else for them to go except the movie or the roller rink. The teen-agers grow up with cars; their fathers work in auto factories. Early on a recent evening a policeman cruising the streets of Clawson said, "It's quiet now. Wait till after midnight, she'll start to boom. The kids park with their girl friends, they do a little neckin', get a little beer in 'em. Then look out." A while back he chased a fourteen-year-old at seventy-five miles per hour. "Our kids aren't any worse than any other place, I guess. Most of them will co-operate with you. But some ——" He gestured. "I blame the parents. When you try to talk to the kids, the parents come rushing in and tell you to let them alone. Or else they don't know where they are and don't care. And some of them are headed for serious trouble."

Over at the Dairy Bar—a small place with a popcorn machine at the front and a juke box at the rear—six kids at the counter were talking about automobiles in esoteric hot-rod jargon. The juke box was playing noisily and two girls with frizzy hair were beating time with their feet, car keys in front of them on the counter. A fat boy was telling a story—telling it loudly, so all around could hear—a story about how a traffic light turned red as he approached at ninety miles an hour, how his car skidded "when I hit the brakes," how he stepped on the gas and ran the light at seventy, whereupon a witness called the cops. "The fiend," said a skinny lad. They finished their milk shakes and hamburgers, and the fat boy said, "Let's go shoot a few," and they moved toward the poolhall, pausing to watch as the two girls got into their father's car and roared away, sending gravel flying.

Raymond Smith was one of the boys who, while in high school, had hung out at the Dairy Bar and the poolroom. After quitting school he worked. He met a girl of twenty-two who worked for a biscuit company and they became engaged to be married. This pleased his father. "She was an awful nice girl," he has said. Raymond quit hanging around uptown. Mr. Smith felt that Raymond was growing up. "It seemed like in the last year or two he had just jumped from boyhood to manhood. I felt better about Raymond than I had for quite a while."

On November 9, 1951, Raymond came home from work about five P.M. His father asked him if he was going out. Raymond said he wasn't. Mr. Smith went to a movie. He came back about eleven P.M. Raymond was there, and so were Dick Burgess and Frank Swift. Frank Swift was seventeen and Dick Burgess sixteen. "They were playing the radio and having a good time," Mr. Smith recalls. "I cut up with them a little bit, then I went out in the kitchen and started writing some letters. About twelve o'clock Raymond said, 'Dad, I wish you'd move your car so I can get mine out.' So I did—I thought he was probably going to take the other boys home. They left then. That was the last time I saw them." All three boys were killed a few hours later.

The other teen-agers in the accident also lived in Clawson.

Dick Burgess was a big, black-haired, nice-looking kid. He lived with his mother and father on a shady street in a well-kept house on a small lot planted with evergreens. His father, a thin, erect, white-haired man, has been a truck mechanic for thirty-one years and has owned this home for sixteen years. Dick was a quiet boy. "Him and his mother was awful close," his father says. "If he wanted anything from me, he'd say, 'Mom, you ask dad for me.'" Dick's chief interest was in sports. "That guy played football, basketball, baseball, got letters in all of them," his father says. "I never made the boys work while they were going to school, didn't want it to interfere with their sports, because sports keeps them interested in school."

But Dick quit school anyway in 1951, shortly after he became sixteen. After that he did nothing. He spent many evenings at home watching television. When he did go out, there was no certain hour he had to be in, "long as we knew where he was."

Dick's closest friend was Frank Swift, a tall, shy, lanky boy with whom he played basketball. Dick's father recalls, "I'd get up in the morning and come into the living room, and there'd be the two of them; Frank'd be sprawled out with his legs up in the air, and I'd rave around—you know how you rave, none of the kids working but I'm working. And Frank'd unwind his legs and say, 'I guess I better go.' Then I'd say, 'Oh, stick around,' and pretty soon we'd all be laughing. I think Frank was over here more than he was at home."

The reason was that Frank didn't get along with his stepfather. Frank's mother and father had separated two months before he was born. Frank had seven sisters. "He was my only boy," his mother says. She is a sweet-faced, gray-haired, gentle, motherly countrywoman. Except during the depression, when she "took in washings and baked bread to help out," she never worked, always stayed at home and took care of her children. Her second husband died. She married a third time, in 1943, to her present husband, a welder.

Frank quit school about the time Dick Burgess did. He wanted to work. A relative hired him as a helper on his delivery truck. Frank never got in any trouble. "My kids knew they wouldn't get any sympathy from me if they were wrong," his mother says. A policeman recalls, "Frank was a nice boy, a good kid." Nearly everybody liked him.

On November ninth Frank had a date with a girl, but she washed her hair after work and it didn't dry, and her mother wouldn't let her go out. This is probably all that saved her life. On the other hand, Frank might not have been killed if he'd been with her. So Frank went uptown alone. There he met Dick Burgess and Raymond Smith. About midnight they went to the Dairy Bar. There they found two girls, Jeanette Palmer and Patsy Harwell. They asked the girls to go for a ride.

Now Jeanette Palmer is the only one who survived the ride. She is a tall, pretty girl, red-haired, full-lipped, freckled, with a slender throat and long hands and big eyes and a small voice, sixteen years old at that time. Both of her parents have worked most of her life, her father in factories, her mother in restaurants or taverns. They never had much money. They live in a tiny house on the muddy outskirts of Clawson. She quit school last June when she was sixteen, in eighth grade. Last summer she kept house for her parents. Evenings she went uptown. She was supposed to be in at 11:30 or midnight, "but you can't chain 'em up, you know," as her father says. She liked movies, any movies. She dated Dick Burgess a good deal. She liked to dance and went to a barn dance nearly every Saturday night, usually with a girl friend.

Her closest girl friend was Patsy Harwell. Patsy often stayed overnight with her. Patsy was the same age as Jeanette, a chubby, sweet-faced girl who wore glasses. Mrs. Harwell tried to raise Patsy carefully. "I've always driven the children where they want to go. I used to take Patsy and Jeanette swimming, take them to the show, take them to dances." When Patsy went alone to school dances, she had to be home at 10:30 or 11:00 P.M. Patsy didn't have any boy friends. She reproved boys who swore. Once she left a party early because the boys there were drinking. Patsy regularly attended a branch of the Pentecostal Church, though her parents do not. Mrs. Harwell's only big disappointment was that Patsy quit school in ninth grade last fall. She wanted to work so she could buy her own clothes. She worked in the Dairy Bar.

Patsy worked on November ninth and met Jeanette about seven P.M. They spent the evening helping Jeanette's sister and her sister's husband move into their new home; then, about 10:30 P.M., went to the Dairy Bar. Presently in came Raymond Smith, Dick Burgess and Frank Swift. At first the girls said they didn't want to go for a ride, but finally they agreed to. Raymond had bought the car that day. On the floor of the back seat was a beer case containing several bottles of beer—just how many never has been established. Another boy was with them, but they drove him home, which probably saved his life. Patsy moved to the front seat between Raymond, who was driving, and Frank Swift. Jeanette sat in back with Dick Burgess. "And we started ridin'," Jeanette says. "Just ridin' around." It must have been about one A.M.

Mr. and Mrs. Moore, having left their eleven children at home in the big house in Leonard, had met their friends, Mr. and Mrs. Carl Eddington, in a night club at Lake Orion. It was "too quiet," so they drove down to a night club in Pontiac. "They had a floor show, a nice crowd, drinks, dancing," Mrs. Eddington recalls. The Moores, she said, were very happy about their new house, their new car and Mr. Moore's new job. After leaving the night club they ate hamburgers and drank coffee at a nearby diner. They went out to their separate cars. The Eddingtons turned off at their street and the Moores drove on alone, heading north on M-24, going home. It was then about three o'clock in the morning.

The teen-agers had spent the last two hours just riding aimlessly, probably in the lake region near Lake Orion. Jeanette doesn't remember clearly where they went. Once Raymond tried to pass another car and, Jeanette recalls, "every time he tried the other guy acted smart, he speeded up or turned into the middle, so finally Raymond got mad and just took off and went around the other guy, then kind of cut him off, ran him off the road."

A policeman stopped them, but he didn't see the beer and, after talking to Raymond, he let them go. They stopped at a filling station to have the brake fluid replenished. Raymond and Frank took a bottle of beer apiece into the filling station and drank it there. Then they headed home, south on M-24. At Dick's suggestion, they heaved the

beer case into the ditch. The Moores were now coming north on M-24, only four or five miles down the road.

Raymond was "mad," Jeanette recalls. He was mad because the cop had stopped him. And now Frank Swift wanted to drive. Raymond was willing. But Patsy Harwell objected. She was sitting between them, and if Frank, who was young and shy, drove, Raymond Smith, who was older and angry, would take Frank's place beside Patsy. "Patsy didn't want to be with Raymond," Jeanette recalls. "So Raymond drove himself. After that he was just mad."

Evidently there was some talk about the way Raymond was driving, because Jeanette recalls that Dick Burgess reassured her and Patsy—"he just does that sometimes to try and show off."

They topped a hill and started down onto a flat, approaching Bald Mountain. The Moores' car came over Bald Mountain and started down. "Mr. Moore had bright lights on," Jeanette recalls. "Raymond kept flicking his lights on and off." Moore did not dim his lights. This enraged Raymond. Raymond purposely headed straight at the Moore car, Jeanette says. "He said he was going to hit that so-and-so."

Moore tried to dodge. He steered off onto the shoulder. He couldn't get off far enough—a row of guard posts trapped him. Jeanette recalls, "Raymond said he was going to fix him for not dimming his lights. I yelled for him to get back on his own side of the road. We all yelled at him. I guess he told us to shut up and then we hit ——" At the last instant, apparently, Raymond tried to turn out, but it was too late.

"When I woke up," Jeanette remembers, "I was kind of on the road, but my legs were still in the car. Dick was laying on them. I pulled my legs out. Dick kind of rolled out, too, then. I started yelling that my legs were broken. I yelled for Dick to help me. He just moaned."

A car stopped. The driver, Mallyn Hagemeister, went to the nearest farmhouse and called the police. He returned. Another car came over the hill. Hagemeister "flashed his light at him," Jeanette recalls, but he didn't stop. Jeanette dragged herself out of the way and the other car smashed into the teen-agers' car. The police arrived.

Mr. and Mrs. Moore, Raymond Smith, Frank Swift and Patsy Harwell all were dead of fractured skulls and necks and crushed chests, and Dick Burgess died soon of the same injuries. Dick evidently had been alive on the pavement before the third car plowed into the wreckage. So had Patsy, says Jeanette. Jeanette remembers trying to drag Patsy out of the way of the third car. It is possible that Jeanette is mistaken—Dick and

Patsy were dressed almost alike. The driver of the third car, James Sabisch, said Hagemeister's lights had blinded him. The official investigation placed no blame on him.

The police never learned where the boys bought the beer. Nor did they ever identify the policeman who stopped the teen-agers shortly before the accident. That the policeman allowed them to drive on is good evidence that they were sober. It seems likely that had Raymond Smith survived he could have been charged with manslaughter.

Raymond Smith's behavior is by no means unusual. Everybody knows the driver who is "going to teach that guy a lesson." Everybody knows the "show-off" driver. And everybody knows a dozen other varieties of homicidal driver. What can be done about them?

Raising the driver's licensing age would do no good—aggressiveness is not restricted to youngsters. Nor would tightening up the examination for drivers' licenses—an examiner is no psychiatrist. Nevertheless, Raymond Smith should not have been driving. He had given fair warning that he was a dangerous driver. The police were "not surprised" that he had a fatal wreck. They had stopped him several times—indeed, that very night. Instead of letting him off with a lecture, they could have charged him with reckless driving and a judge could have revoked his license.

However, we cannot blame the police for not doing so. Public opinion would not have supported them. People regard wild driving lightly. They say that revoking even a boy's license is a serious matter, that revoking an adult's may deprive him of his livelihood. This is true. But licensing a dangerous driver may deprive some innocent person of his life.

The problem is not simple. In spite of the courts, probably, some fools will always drive. Is there no way to protect other motorists from them? Well, perhaps automobiles themselves could be made safer. Recently Hugh De Haven, of the Cornell Medical College, pointed out that we pack dishes and other fragile goods very carefully for shipment, but we ship ourselves in automobiles unprotected. The human head, he said, weighs about as much as a ten-pound sledge hammer and when it strikes a solid object such as a dashboard at forty or fifty miles an hour, crushing injuries to the skull and brain are inevitable. Safety belts and harnesses and crash helmets might minimize damage. But, he said, people don't want to be encumbered with them. He therefore suggested to the Society of Automotive Engineers that they redesign auto interiors to reduce or eliminate solid and sharp points of contact.

Could not the manufacturers build a heavier steel shield around the passengers, pad it and round its corners, and provide safety harnesses for people willing to use them? And could they not explore other technical possibilities? Any single manufacturer might object that such engineering would not be competitive. But if it were required of all manufacturers, this objection would vanish. Perhaps if laws cannot control drivers they should control automobiles.

What of the parents of the teen-agers killed in this wreck? Mr. Burgess recalls, "The sheriff called me at 8:15 A.M., told me there'd been a bad accident. I said, 'The kid's gone, isn't he?' They said he was, that I should come up and identify him and get the body. That is the hardest thing I ever did, going up to the hospital and identifying my boy." Mr. Burgess is bitter because all the blame was placed upon the teen-agers. He considers the official investigation of the third car's role inadequate.

Frank Swift's mother was hurt by the publicity the teen-agers' drinking received. "People got the impression that all they did was carousing around. Frank was a good kid, I don't care what they say." After Frank's death, her husband criticized Frank, and she left him.

Mrs. Harwell says, "As long as she had to go, I hope she was killed instantly. The undertaker told us she was." Mrs. Harwell has wanted to visit the other parents and the Moore children, but has not felt able to do so.

Recently Jeanette sent ten dollars to Mrs. Harwell, asking her to buy flowers for Patsy's grave. "When I get able to walk real good, I want to go around and put flowers on the rest of the graves." She is learning to walk with crutches. Recently she met the Burgesses and visited them for a few days.

Mr. Smith, the driver's father, said recently, "My honest opinion is that Raymond got hold of that stuff, that beer, and drank it and just went crazy. Raymond was a good boy; everybody liked him." Like the other parents, Mr. Smith calls the accident "a terrible thing," and he feels very sorry for the eleven Moore orphans.

How have they fared? Moore left no estate. The children were widely publicized and good-hearted people sent them cash and merchandise worth nearly $20,000. Several people offered to adopt some of the children, and three offered to take them all. But the children did not want to be separated nor did they wish to move from the house their parents had bought for them. Probate Judge Arthur E. Moore appointed two of their uncles guardians. Mrs. Moore's mother and father are keeping house for the children, but they are elderly and the arrangement is only temporary.

Sometimes Gerry, though only fifteen, seems like a father to the other children. Recently, sitting in his living room, he was called upon within a few minutes' time to chase one of the children off a dollhouse roof, to arbitrate a dispute between two others over a stuffed dog, and to stop a fight; and he did it all without taking his eyes off the television screen, absently, as a father might, sitting on a sofa to which the littler kids came for redress of wrongs. Gerry intends to finish high school—"it would be my dad's wish, I know." He hopes to work next summer and buy a car—the kind of car his father always wanted, but never had. He intends to visit Mr. and Mrs. Eddington: "I want to see if my mom and dad had a good time that night."

THE SECRET INGREDIENT

by Paul Gallico

PAUL GALLICO IS a graduate of the New York *Daily News* who has written more than fifty stories and articles for the *Post* since 1931. Though he has complained in print that *Post* editors are not demonstrative—"They simply don't believe in coddling writers"—he has long been a favorite of both editors and readers. "The Secret Ingredient," a short story, is the result of his extensive researches into the art of French cooking.

JULY 5, 1952

NEXT TIME you are touring the château country of France and visit the string of airy castles cresting the hilltops along the placid Loire from Blois to Tours, you surely will drop down from the towered and mullioned keep of the Château Loiret, just below Chaumont, to eat a meal and drink the wine at the famous Auberge Château Loiret at the foot of the castle.

There you will unquestionably partake of that superb and unrivaled specialty of the house, *Poularde Surprise Treize Minets* and find your palate enthralled by the indefinable flavor imparted to the fowl by the mysterious ingredient which is the particular secret of Monsieur Armand Bonneval, host and chef of the *auberge*. And like so many, many others before you, you will attempt without success to identify the famous component X which to this day has defied the most educated taste buds of all France.

You also will encounter Monsieur Bonneval, stocky, red-faced with short-cut, upstanding, pepper-and-salt hair, youthful-looking because of the energy and kindliness in his face, and Madame Bonneval, a woman of large heart and girth, who, as always in France, will be seated behind the desk in charge of the cash box and the accounts.

And, either perched on the desk next to Madame Bonneval or twining at the feet of her husband as he appears at the dining-room door to check on the effect of his cooking, you will probably observe a small black-and-white cat—not a particularly beautiful specimen, owing to the fact that she is somewhat cross-eyed, but nevertheless the beloved pet and pride and joy of monsieur and madame, your hosts.

As a matter of fact, the famous and succulent recipe is in a way associated with her, Minette being her name. But *"Minet"* in France is also the generic nickname for cats, just as we call them "puss," and thus a literal translation of the by-now-world-renowned dish of *Poularde Surprise Treiz Minets,* might be "Chicken-surprise-in-the-style-of-thirteen-cats."

However, when it comes to inquiring of M. Bonneval how this epicure's delight was named or what it is that makes his *poularde* more tasty, stimulating and unforgettable than any other in the world, and what unknown ingredient is the key to this miraculous gastronomic blend, you will, I know, run up against a stone wall.

Guarded blueprints for airplanes, battleships and submarines are traded on an international bourse, diplomatic confidences are whispered over cocktails, the secrets of the atom bomb have been freely bandied about; but up to this moment, not one single person in the whole world outside of Monsieur and Madame Bonneval has been privy to the secret of the recipe for this famous delicacy.

Permit me then:

In the days prior to the events I am about to narrate, Armand Bonneval, former assistant chef of the Café de Paris, honorably retired, *Cordon Bleu* member of the Club de Cent, and now sole owner and proprietor of the Auberge Château Loiret, was consumed with a burning ambition.

In the Guide Michelin for 1951, that tourist's and gourmet's bible, which is the automobile traveler's survey of France, the *auberge* was designated by three crossed spoons and forks, denoting a "very comfortable restaurant." This was not at all bad, particularly for a restaurant in a village as small as Loiret, where the usual indication was one crossed spoon and fork or none at all. But it did not satisfy the artistic and creative soul of Monsieur Bonneval. In his day he had been a great cook. In his old age he longed for the tangible recognition of his genius. A higher rating would likewise make a considerable financial difference to himself and madame, his partner through forty years of unremitting toil.

The size and location of his *auberge* precluded his receiving the four or five crossed utensils reserved for the big, de-luxe restaurants of Paris, Lyon, Vichy and Cannes. However, the famous Guide Michelin annual has further signs to distinguish the superior cuisines it had tested and listed in villages and towns throughout France—namely, one, two or three stars added to the spoons and forks.

Three stars, denoting one of the best tables in the nation, and worthy of a special journey of many miles, were as beyond the reach and hopes of M. Bonneval as the stars that spangled the firmament above the Loire Valley at night. There were but seven of these awarded in all France.

Nor was there any better chance of achieving two stars, indicating an ". . . excellent cuisine: worth a detour," of which there were but fifty-one examples in all the thousands of restaurants, *auberges,* hotels and *bistros* throughout the land.

But Monsieur Bonneval did yearn most mightily with his honest heart and Frenchman's pride to be awarded the addition of the single star which would announce to traveler and native alike that he set *"une bonne table dans la localité"* and that the visitor to his board would be rewarded with something special.

If his winning of the three crossed spoons and forks had already made him an important man in the district, the star would elevate him to the status of distinguished citizen. If now they just managed to make both ends meet, the added star would enable them to amass a competency toward their final days. Alas, there was nothing specific that Monsieur Bonneval could do to achieve this ambition, for the matter was not in his hands.

As he would explain sadly to Madame Bonneval, when sitting quietly in their apartment above the *auberge* after hours, with his beloved Minette purring in his lap, there were literally hundreds of thousands of eating places throughout France that had to be covered; the inspectors, or official tasters, of the Guide Michelin were only so many; they had but one stomach apiece which would hold only so many cubic centimeters. Worked out mathematically, it might be years before one again appeared to sample the fare at the Auberge Loiret, and perhaps never again in their lifetime.

But it even by some chance one should appear, there was no opportunity for Monsieur Bonneval to prepare the kind of specialty that would be likely to bowl over the taster, for the simple reason that the Guide Michelin conducted its tests and listings with scrupulous integrity and fairness. One never knew when the inspector was in one's midst. He came and went in the guise of an ordinary tourist. The Grand Lottery in Paris was not handled with more honesty and care.

"Ah, if one could but know in advance sometime," he would groan, filled with ambition and desire. "Who knows but with the star I would be able to take you to Italy on that little trip we planned so long ago."

And Madame Bonneval would comfort him, "Never mind, Armand. I am sure you will receive your star somehow, because you deserve it. And besides, it would not be fair if you should know in advance."

One summer afternoon a letter arrived for Monsieur Bonneval that caused him to stare as though he could not believe his eyes, and then call loudly for madame to come and read it to him again, to make sure he had not been deceived. Madame did so, with her circle of additional chins quivering a little. It was short and to the point.

My dear Bonneval: I doubt whether you would remember me, but many years ago you had the occasion to do me a good turn when I was hungry and on my uppers, and I have never forgotten your kindness.

It so happens that I now find myself in a position to return the favor. Through my connections with the Guide Michelin, upon which I will not elaborate, I am advised that on Friday, the thirteenth of July, an inspector will be passing through Loiret-sur-Loire, and has been instructed to dine at the *auberge* to check on the quality of your meals. I know that your genius will find the best way to make use of this information. Wishing you the very best of luck, I am an old friend who must sign himself

"XYZ"

There it was—the bolt out of the clearest of skies. Not only was the longed-for visit to take place but Monsieur Bonneval was actually to have notice in advance and time to prepare one of his more superb specialties, such as duck stuffed with chopped truffles, liver paste and *champignons* with orange sauce or his own version of *coq au vin.*

"I will be famous! We will grow rich!" declared Monsieur Bonneval, feasting his eyes again on the page of the wonderful letter. But then he cried in alarm, "Great heavens! The letter is dated July eighth, but it has been delayed in transit. Friday the thirteenth, when the inspector is to come, is this very day."

It was true. The calendar on the wall displayed a large red "13." Suddenly the affair assumed an urgency that was not dispelled by the exclamation of Madame Bonneval, who had glanced out of the window, "And that must be he, arriving this very minute!"

A large and glittery car had poked its expensive snout alongside the *auberge* and discharged one who could only have spent the major portion of his existence sampling the finest foods and wines, for he was as fat as a prize pig stuffed for exhibition. He carried the Guide Michelin in his hand, and entered the front door with a combined expression of truculence and expectancy.

At once he became identified in Bonneval's mind as "Monsieur Michelin Taster," friend, enemy, instrument upon which he would play his gastronomic symphony, critic and bearer of the laurel wreath, or rather star, that would eventually be bestowed upon him.

However, one thing was patent. There was not a moment to lose. Already flustered by the unexpected imminence of his trial, Monsieur Bonneval rushed off to the kitchen, crying to madame as he made his exit, "I shall prepare him *le Homard dans la Lune!*" Which was not at all what he had meant either to say or to cook.

"Lobster in the Moon" was the last thing in the world he would have dreamed of making for such an important test, knowing full well that with lobster it can be this way or that way, whereas your ducks, chickens and *gigots* are always safe.

For the recipe is a tricky one, calling for one large lobster, *bien vivant*—in other words, a brisk and lively fellow—to be extracted, cut up, seasoned with salt and pepper, and sautéed in oil and butter, after which the oil is withdrawn and a tablespoon of finely chopped shallots or chives and a whisper of garlic is added. To give this mixture a little authority, a glass of cognac and another of white wine are now introduced, after which three tomatoes are broken into small bits with a half tablespoonful of chopped parsley and a shot of cayenne pepper, and the whole thing is cooked for twenty minutes in a casserole at a steady heat. The lobster is then removed and stuffed into the "Moon," a hollowed-out, crisp brioche. Now comes the delicate moment. The sauce is thickened with a little cream laced with a shot of brandy and the whole thing poured over the hot, crispy, lobster-filled pastry.

A man wants to be in complete command of himself to bring off a dish like that, particularly when it meant as much as it did to Monsieur Bonneval. That he was not, was evidenced when he almost bumped into Minette, the black-and-white cat, as he charged into the kitchen, bellowing loudly for Celeste, the kitchen maid, and Brazon, the man of all work, her lover.

This served only to unnerve him further, for it so happened that Minette had been so fortunate not long before as to encounter a gentleman friend in the park of the château who had been able to overlook the unhappy tendencies of her eyes to cross, and she was now imminently about

to be blessed with the fruits of this genuine affection, and a fair packet of them, too, if one could judge from her size.

Nor was it exactly a happy moment in the life of Celeste, who, a few weeks ago, had been seized with the idea of marrying Brazon, and of course had demanded an increase in pay to support this bizarre notion—a request which Monsieur Bonneval, backed by madame, had quite sensibly refused, since one did not say yes to such ideas the first time. As a result, Celeste was red-eyed and snuffly a good deal of the time, and not quite herself.

This was a pity, for she was to Monsieur Bonneval what the deft instrument nurse is to the great surgeon. With paring knife and chopping bowl, a veteran of a hundred routines, she had stood at his side ready to supply in an instant what the master needed in the line of utensils, saucepans, casseroles, chopped onions, shaved carrots, bouquets of herbs, and so on.

So there was already a considerable disaster building up in Monsieur Bonneval's kitchen, let alone its being Friday the thirteenth.

The lobster, when produced from the cold room, not only did not answer to the description of a brisk and lively fellow but, on the contrary, was practically in a state of rigor mortis. Cutting him up, hence, was no longer a culinary gesture, but an autopsy. It was Fate giving Monsieur Bonneval one more chance to evade what it had in store for him. Had he been in his right senses he would have dumped the crustacean corpse into the ashcan and started on something else.

But his mind was imprisoned by that inflexibility and rigidity that, in the face of a crisis, sometimes affects the best of cooks and housekeepers. Monsieur Bonneval was bent on making Lobster in the Moon, and so he rushed onward headlong to his doom.

Almost at once there commenced such a catalogue of kitchen catastrophes as can be appreciated only by the housewife or chef who has battled the extraordinary breed of gremlins that sometimes arrive to interfere, obstruct and frustrate when there is a truly important dinner to be got onto the table.

While Celeste reversed her instruction and scraped a *soupçon* of shallot into a tablespoon of chopped garlic, instead of vice versa, Brazon announced that there appeared to have been a change in the wind, affecting the draft of the huge iron stove, plus a blockade of some sort, and he could seem to put no heat in it, and Odette, the waitress, affected by the mounting tension, upset the soup into the lap of the fat man identified in the mind of Bonneval as Monsieur Michelin

Taster. This fetched a bellow of rage from the dining room, matched only by the sound emerging from the kitchen when Monsieur Bonneval discovered that Celeste, ruminating on the inhumanity of man, had taken his sautéeing pan, which for eighteen years had known no other cleansing than with salt and a piece of bread, and washed it with kitchen soap and water.

Disaster followed upon disaster. The stove, stuffed with newspapers, straw, kindling and coke, emitted clouds of acrid smoke, one whiff of which was sufficient to affect the delicate flavors planned by Monsieur Bonneval. The cream pitcher upset in the icebox, inundating everything therein, and at the critical moment it developed that Brazon had misplaced the key to the wine cellar.

Monsieur Bonneval moved as one in the grip of a hideous nightmare. Matters went from bad to worse as a tin of fat caught fire, the handle of his best frying pan broke and the lamp upset. Celeste and Brazon went completely haywire, the latter breaking the egg beater and short-circuiting the refrigerator, while the former achieved a new high in destructive confusion by putting salt in the egg whites in place of sugar, and cutting up, on the board reserved for crushing garlic, the almonds destined for the famous *soufflé à la curorange*.

Through all this, red-faced, sweating, the glare as of a wild animal filling his heretofore gentle eyes, struggling to retain his temper and his sanity in the face of trials that would have disjointed a saint, Monsieur Bonneval stolidly attempted to fight his way through the morass of calamities that was engulfing him.

It was a losing battle. Friday the thirteenth was not through with him yet. For just as he was stirring the delicate *sauce vanille* intended to go with the *soufflé* which was browning in the oven, Madame Bonneval, unnerved by the sounds of panic from backstage, abandoned her post next to the cash box and invaded the kitchen. Her faith in her husband's culinary powers shaken for the first time, she committed the unpardonable crime of opening the oven door to see how the confection was coming along, just as Brazon unlatched the back entrance, permitting a swirl of cool air to tear through the kitchen and smite the *soufflé* where it would hurt the most.

Purple with outrage, Monsieur Bonneval made a lunge to swing shut the oven door. It was at this precise moment that poor Minette chose to make one of her sagging promenades across the kitchen floor just in time to trip and unbalance Monsieur Bonneval and send the *sauce vanille* splashing onto the top of the range, where it made a most dreadful smell.

Something snapped inside Monsieur Bonneval. Flesh and blood could endure no more. Tortured beyond human endurance, he hauled back his right foot and applied it to the rear end of Minette, who happened to be aimed toward the back door at the moment.

With a terrible scream of outraged indignation, the loaded Minette took off like a blimp released from its moorings, and soaring majestically up into the night, vanished from sight.

Now Monsieur Bonneval turned upon the humans. *"Vache!"* he shouted at his wife. *"Animal!"* he bawled at Celeste. *"Crétin!"* he nominated Odette, the waitress. *"Cochon!"* he dubbed Brazon.

The reactions were immediate. Brazon resigned; Odette vanished; Celeste threw her apron over her head and had hysterics; while Madame Bonneval swept from the kitchen, went upstairs and locked herself in her room. Bonneval himself carried in the *soufflé* and placed it before Monsieur Michelin Taster, where it gave a soft sigh and collapsed flatter than an old-fashioned opera hat.

The fat man took one nibble at the edge of the thing and then let out a roar that shook the dining room.

"Criminal! Assassin! Poisoner!" he shouted. "You call yourself a chef! The lobster tastes of soap, the coffee of kerosene and your *soufflé* is flavored with garlic! Three spoons and forks they have given you, eh?" and at this point he waved the red-covered volume of the Guide Michelin under Monsieur Bonneval's appalled nose. "Well, when I am finished with you, you will no longer be able to swindle innocent travelers! Faker!"

And with this he tore the napkin from his collar and stalked from the room. When, a few moments later, the car thundered away from the *auberge,* it carried with it, in addition to the indignant fat man, the hopes, ambitions and large pieces of the broken heart of Monsieur Bonneval.

Monsieur Bonneval was of the breed that wastes no time crying over spilt cream, but faces manfully up to the blows of life and recovers quickly therefrom. But he needed the aid and companionship of his wife. Pocketing his badly damaged pride, he hurried to the door of madame's locked room, from which emerged sounds of grief, and spoke through the keyhole:

"Come now, my dear, it is all over. Nothing more can happen. I am punished for my sins. The inspector has departed to make his report, and we shall be poor again. But as long as I have you, I shall not lack the courage to make a start again—somewhere in a place where we are not known, perhaps. Come, old friend, we have been through much together. Do not take a little incident so to heart."

From within, Madame Bonneval cried, "Little incident! You called me a cow!"

Obviously a special effort was required. Monsieur Bonneval now addressed the door as follows: "Dear wife, I was wrong to let petty trifles exasperate me into forgetting myself. But look. Even in my anger against Fate, how careful I was in my choice of animals. For is not the cow the sweetest, the gentlest, the kindest and the most beautiful in all the kingdom? Does she not, with lavish generosity and warm heart, play mother with her milk to all mankind? Is not her glance melting, her disposition notable and her character beyond reproach? Does not her soft and expressive face invite caresses?" He ceased when he heard the key turning slowly in the lock.

Thereafter he went downstairs, soothed the waitress, apologized to Brazon and cured Celeste's hysterics with a promise of a raise in salary should the *auberge* not be forced to close.

Notwithstanding the peace declared within his domain, the heart of Monsieur Bonneval was as heavy as a stone, for Minette had not returned. His conscience was as black as the night because of the kick he had bestowed upon her, and particularly in the light of her delicate condition. He would rather have cut off his right arm than perpetrate an indignity, much less an injury, upon his little friend. He had called and called, but there had been no sign of her.

She had every right to be angry with him—if she was still alive. How, then, to persuade her of his love for her, and his terrible contrition? The hour was past eleven.

He had been calling her since ten. Suddenly an idea smote him. Minette was mad about chicken. He would tempt her with her favorite food.

Purpose now gripped Monsieur Bonneval, and he said to himself, *Little Minette, I shall cook you a Poularde Surprise Royale all for your very own. For you I will cook this as I have never cooked before, for I am very ashamed of having lost my temper and kicked you from the rear.*

He set to work at once, and everything seemed to work like magic, as though Friday the thirteenth had expended its malignancy, and Fate was no longer interested in harassing Monsieur Bonneval. The stove functioned like a charm, Brazon was as sharp as a razor and Celeste was her old, cool, efficient self, anticipating his every wish. Objects not only behaved themselves but positively co-operated, seeming to leap into his hand when he had need of them.

With a series of deft movements he boned the chicken and then stuffed it with goose-liver patty,

truffles and a stew of giblets and kidneys made in meat stock and laced with a jigger of port wine.

Poor Minette, he thought as he added the ruby-red liquid, *after what she has been through she will be in need of a little stimulant.*

Working now with supreme concentration and passion, the recipe burned into his memory the way a conductor knows every note of a great symphony without the score, he set about making a sauce for the bird, using the bones of the pullet, onions, carrots, leeks, celery and a bouquet, which he fortified with a half bottle of Bollinger '43. *One gives champagne to expectant mothers,* he said to himself as the yellow wine frothed into the brown gravy.

Exquisite odors began to fill the kitchen. It was art for love's sake, and like all true artists and lovers, he became inspired and began to improvise as he went along, making a daring and radical experiment with here an herb, there a spice, a bit of smoked fat, a glass of very old cognac. *For if she is a little drunk she will become mellow and forgive me the more readily,* he reasoned.

And then it was, as he ransacked his closet of herbs and spices, looking still further to delight the heart and appetite of Minette, that he found and added an ingredient that never before had been a part of *Poularde Surprise Royale* or any other dish.

When the bird was cooked to a turn, he performed some final rites, garnishing it with truffles and *pâté de foie gras,* poured the magnificent sauce over it, partitioned it, and putting one half onto a plate, went out into the night with this savory harbinger of everything good and perfect that man has learned to do with food.

"Minette! Minette!" he called, placing himself upwind, so that the evening breeze from the Loire would carry the fragrance to every corner of the courtyard where the missing Minette might be lurking. And still there came no answer.

Some time later, painfully and heartbroken and still bearing the dish, he returned to the kitchen, where, at the late hour just before midnight, he found an unaccustomed activity sparked by Madame Bonneval. Coffee was on the fire, a *soufflé* was in the process of being mixed by Brazon, and the other half of the *Poularde Surprise Royale* was missing.

"Ah, there you are," madame greeted him. "What a fortunate thing you decided to cook a *poularde.* Only fifteen minutes ago there arrived a traveler, a poor fellow whose car had broken down. He was starving, and begged for a bit of something cold left over. You can imagine how agreeably surprised he was when I was able to set before him your specialty. He is drinking a bottle of the '47 Loiret Suchez with it."

Monsieur Bonneval stared at his wife, aghast. "But, *maman!* It is impossible. I cooked this for poor little Minette, whom I kicked so bru——"

He did not finish, for the door leading from the dining room opened violently, admitting an excited bespectacled little man with a soup-strainer mustache and wearing a seedy suit, but whose eyes and expression nevertheless appeared to command authority.

He paused for a moment *en tableau*, looking from one to another in the kitchen. Then he rushed to Monsieur Bonneval, threw his arms about him and kissed him violently on both cheeks.

"It is you!" he cried. "You are the magician who has prepared this delectable, this fabulous, this supreme dish! Chef! Genius! Master! I salute you! Not in thirty-five years have I eaten such a *Poularde Surprise Royale*. And at midnight. A veritable palace of gastronomy, a Sorbonne of cookery. Well, you shall have your reward. A star —no, no, what am I saying?—two stars!" And here he paused, and his look changed slightly to one of cunning. "Three stars if you will tell me the secret ingredient in the *poularde,* the only one I was not able to recognize."

Monsieur Bonneval could only gape at him. Could it have been then that the other, that fat one, was not Monsieur Michelin Taster? "I do not—understand," he stammered.

"But it is simple, dear master," the man replied. "Know then that I am Fernand Dumaire, inspector for the Guide Michelin. I was on my way here to test your cookery when that villain of a vehicle ceased to function. And then, to arrive at midnight and at once to find set before me this masterpiece! Of two stars you are certain, but as a little deal between us, I will risk the third in exchange for your secret ingredient!"

Sweat suddenly beaded the brow of Monsieur Bonneval. "The — secret — ingredient?" he repeated.

"But of course. Naturally, I recognized the chervil and the delicate touch of burnet. It took courage to use the basil, and the idea of applying the marjoram to offset the tarragon was capital, while the amount of thyme and sage was perfectly balanced. I should judge the Oporto in the sauce was a trifle more *sec* than is usual—probably a '39—and the champagne, of course, was Bollinger '43, as anyone with half a palate would notice. But one flavor baffles and escapes me, and I, Fernand Dumaire, must know what it is. For you have changed, improved and glorified *Poularde Sur-*

prise Royale. It has become a new creation and you shall have the honor of naming it. But first tell me the ingredient that has baffled me, in exchange for the third star. Is it a bargain?"

There was a moment of silence. Then Monsieur Bonneval said slowly, "I cannot tell you, monsieur. I shall be content with the two stars you so generously promised me."

Madame Bonneval stared at her husband as though he were out of his mind, but the chief taster again fell on his neck and kissed him. "You are right, my friend, and noble and honest. A great chef must never reveal his secrets. I tempted you and you resisted. Well, two stars and five spoons and forks will distinguish you so that the world will beat a path to your kitchen."

At this moment there was an interruption. There came a sweet little call from the outer darkness, and Minette loped into the room, a thin and shapely Minette, though now more cross-eyed with love than ever. She deposited a newborn kitten in the box that had been made ready at the side of the stove. She retired. She came back with another kitten, and another and another. Thirteen times she departed and returned as they watched and counted, fascinated, and the tears of joy flowed from the eyes of Monsieur Bonneval.

When the last one had been deposited and Minette commenced nursing, Monsieur Bonneval declared with deep feeling, "You said, monsieur, that I might name my *poularde*. Very well. I name it *Poularde Surprise Treize Minets*."

At this moment Brazon produced the *soufflé curorange* prepared from the recipe of Monsieur Bonneval, a dream, a vision, high, potent, sturdy, uncollapsible, a beige cloud, with the interior construction apparently of reinforced steel. They joined around the table, and with a Moët and Chandon '37 they toasted the two stars of Monsieur Bonneval and the *Poularde Surprise Treize Minets*.

So then, the next time you tour in France and drop in at the Auberge Loiret to partake of Monsieur Bonneval's delectable "chicken à la thirteen kittens," do not, I beg of you, let on that I have given away his secret ingredient and the reason why he could not reveal it even for the honor and accolade of the third star.

It was simple, but a trifle unusual. As you have already suspected, for love of Minette he had seasoned the *poularde* liberally with that herb beloved of all felines, the strongly scented leaves of *Nepeta cataria,* a plant better known to one and all as catnip.

I GREW UP WITH EISENHOWER

—— *by R. G. Tonkin, as told to Charles Ramsdell* ——

R. GUY TONKIN was born at Hope, Kansas, in 1891, and moved seven years later to nearby Abilene, where he was a schoolboy chum of Dwight D. Eisenhower. He has since been a civil engineer, farmer, wildcat oil prospector, and writer for oil and gas publications, and now lives in San Antonio, Texas. Charles Ramsdell is a former newspaperman (San Antonio *Express*) whose free-lance writings range from an article on Texas in the *Encyclopaedia Britannica* to translations of Spanish historical documents in the national archives of Mexico. He contributes often to magazines, and has written a book on the Mexican state of Michoacan. In the following article these able collaborators have preserved for history a fresh and authentic account of the boyhood years of the thirty-third President of the United States.

MAY 3, 1952

[ED. NOTE — TWENTY-TWO PARAGRAPHS HAVE BEEN CUT FROM THE LEAD OF THIS ARTICLE.]

THE EXPRESSION that I best remember on the face of the boy Dwight Eisenhower in Abilene, Kansas, was not the grin that has become world famous, but a grimace of intense determination.

I can see him now, tall for his age—about nine or ten—with a mop of curly blondish hair flopping about on his forehead, as he grimaced through the strenuous motions of a game that we used to play on the school ground at recess, known as "shinny." It was patterned after the game of ice hockey, with the addition of the more homicidal gambits of football and polo. All rules were "ground rules." That is, they were made up on the spot, and then ignored.

Dwight was always in the big middle of this dangerous game, where the going was roughest. We started the game with a tin can, which soon became a battered wad of tin with sharp corners. We used clubs of all kinds and shapes. The deadliest were made from a wild shrub called ironwood. Part of the root was left on the shank, forming the head, and a husky boy with a heavy ironwood club could drive a beat-up can a couple of hundred feet with bullet-like speed. Casualties were numerous, and sometimes serious. Fortunately, the Eisenhower home was just across the street, and Dwight's mother, with her ever-ready bandages of clean rags and the old reliable bottle of turpentine, would patch us up. So our wounds seldom came to the notice of the teachers or principal.

Unluckily for us, however, our elders set over us a new principal, named McCormick, who was not only vigilant but humane. Noting the sinister aspect of the ragged can, this despot decreed that from them on we must play with wooden blocks instead. We hacked out, with our pocketknives, blocks of willow, oak and hickory.

To our great joy, the game was, for a while, made dangerous again when a brawny young fellow, Garcel Tolliver, whose folks owned a blacksmith shop, came up with a really formidable club, adapted from a buggy shaft. It was tops! He could drive the block from one end of the playing field clear across the goal line almost at will. Our only recourse was to guard him. This task, because it required alertness, was assigned to Dwight. But one day, as so often happened, Dwight stayed at home to work. The buggy shaft lofted the block mightily, and it struck a boy named Clifford square in the mouth, knocking out four or five front teeth. That ended our shinny.

Dwight was always first choice when sides were chosen up for either baseball or shinny, because he was dependable and played hard and well. His fierce enjoyment of games was whetted, no doubt, by the long hours of work he had to put in—nearly all his off-school hours. He helped his mother with the housework and the Monday-morning laundry, washed dishes, fed the rabbits, the chickens and the horses, cleaned the stable, weeded the garden, cut the kindling and brought in the coal.

On Saturdays he worked at the Belle Springs Creamery, where his father was chief engineer. The farmers would bring their milk and cream to the dock in buggies, buckboards and wagons. Dwight, as a boy of ten or eleven, had to swing

519

the five- or ten-gallon cans full of milk. After the milk was sampled, then dumped into a large vat, he had to steam the empty can thoroughly, to sterilize it, before returning it to the dock. This job was the first he had outside of the home, and it was a demanding one for a boy of his age. He inverted the can over a pipe sticking up out of a table, and opened a steam valve, sending the steam into the can with a roar. If the valve was opened too wide, the can would be blown off. This never happened while Dwight was on duty.

The condensing coils for the ice-making part of the plant were located on the roof, and now and then these had to be scaled off—another job that Dwight worked at after school and on Saturdays. As he grew bigger and stronger, still harder jobs were found to take up his time during vacation periods and after—even before—school hours. All these tasks he accepted as a matter of course. He never complained.

When he became husky enough to handle a coal shovel, he worked on Sundays, too, firing the boilers and looking after the steam-driven compressor that furnished ice and refrigeration for the cold storage. If I or Dwight's other friends wanted to enjoy his companionship, we had to visit with him while he worked; he was nearly always working. He would never let any of us visitors help him stoke the furnaces; he was afraid we would heap the coal up clumsily; then the smoke from the chimney jutting out above the roof would billow forth in dark clouds, and his father might see it. Dwight spread the black new coals evenly with his shovel over the blinding embers.

He wore the conventional garb of the mechanic, faded and patched blue-denim overalls and jumper, with a locomotive engineer's cap. On Sundays, Chick Gish would come up to the creamery with some of those paperback thrillers, the adventures of Nick Carter and of the Merriwell boys, and the three of us would sit around reading, with a wheelbarrow of coal handy to stash the books in if Mr. Eisenhower should happen to walk in.

Although we had known each other since early childhood, my friendship with Dwight really began that fearful morning when I rode my little pony up to the Lincoln School for the first time. I was terrified, because I had attended, the year before, the Garfield School on the north, or fashionable, side of town, where my family had lived for a while in a fancy two-story house. But in the summer my father had moved us to his ranch a mile south of town. So now I must go to the Lincoln School, where north-siders were regarded, not without reason, as outrageous snobs, and could expect a rough reception.

When I saw Dwight Eisenhower standing on the school ground, my spirits rose. Some nine months older than I—in his eighth year, I think—he was much taller. He had already a sense of responsibility that made me feel secure at his side. I latched onto him for protection. He and his younger brother Roy were the only ones I knew at the school. At noon I ate the lunch I had brought from home; then Dwight and Roy asked me over to their house, Mrs. Eisenhower made a place for me at the table and I ate a second lunch.

I was one grade below Dwight, but in our school two grades were usually put into the same room, under the same teacher. So we had many classes together. As a pupil he was just about average, except in history, which he loved—in that he was brilliant. A voracious reader, he would read anything. Paper-backed novels of frontier adventures were among his favorites. I lent him my copies of *Tom Sawyer* and *Huckleberry Finn* and he was enchanted.

He had a few fights in grade school—what boy didn't? Most of them were harmless, bloodless scuffles. I recall one, however, which made something of a sensation. As in most schools, there was a bully boy among us. Let's call him Jack. His idea of fun was to jump on the back of some smaller boy and ride him down on his face. One day this bully made the mistake of jumping on Roy Eisenhower. Jack gave him an extra shove at the end of the ride, grinding his face into the muddy cinders and scratching it badly. Roy's face was really messed up.

Dwight took up for his brother, confronted the bully, and words flew hot and heavy while the rest of us boys ganged around. Someone—I think it was Barney Parker—put a chip on Jack's shoulder and prompted him to dare Dwight to knock it off.

Jack said, "I dare you to knock it off."

Something happened so quickly that none of the eyewitnesses could agree what it was. But Dwight knocked the chip off and bloodied Jack's nose, all with one fast, hard lick. Jack, the bully, was gentled down and Dwight became a hero to the smaller boys, including myself.

Dwight and I had known each other from infancy, because our parents had been friends for many years before we were born. Near my grandfather's homestead, between the towns of Hope and Navarre, in Dickinson County, Kansas, about eighteen miles southeast of Abilene, was the farm of Jacob Eisenhower, who had migrated from Pennsylvania. I remember that he spoke with a German accent.

On this farm Dwight's father, David Jacob

Eisenhower, was reared. David grew up, left the farm and set up a tinshop at Hope. He married Ida Stover, one of my mother's best friends. The two oldest boys, Arthur and Edgar, were born at Hope.

The tinshop was not a success, and David Eisenhower took a job with the M. K. & T. railroad as a tinsmith. He moved his family to Denison, Texas, where Dwight was born on October 14, 1890.

Dwight's father was applying himself, meanwhile, to a course in stationary steam engineering with the International Correspondence School. He received a diploma, which was duly framed and hung on the dining-room wall of the Eisenhower home at Abilene after David settled his family there in 1891, having become chief engineer of the Belle Springs Creamery.

For twenty years Dwight Eisenhower's life revolved around the home, the school and the creamery. His three younger brothers, Roy, Earl and Milton, were born at Abilene. All six boys achieved a remarkable degree of success, each in his chosen field. Their success can be attributed, I believe, partly to the strict training they received from their parents, who taught them to work, but also partly to the galling indifference with which they were treated by some of the "best people" in town. Abilene had changed rapidly from a hell-roaring frontier outpost to a sedate little city where only the well-to-do had social position. The Eisenhower boys, who didn't count in the eyes of the self-important, made up their minds to "be somebody."

No family in town, however, was more respectable than the Eisenhowers, who practiced all the standard civic virtues. They were peace-loving, honest, sober, industrious. Their only failing was the lack of money; not that they actually suffered from want, but there was nothing left over for luxuries.

Mrs. Eisenhower was a sandy-haired little woman, always busy, always smiling. She believed in working her boys hard to keep them out of mischief. Their father, a dark, austere man with a heavy mustache, believed in working them hard so they would learn to make a living. He was one of the River Brethren, originally Dunkards, who believed in simplicity of dress and quietness of manner and speech.

Whatever the religious convictions of the boys may have been, they did not talk about them. I never knew any of the family to attend the River Brethren church; they seemed to have organized a schismatic branch of their own. Every Sunday afternoon about fifteen people would gather at the Eisenhower house. There was a small organ and

the group would sing and pray for hours—at least it seemed that long to me. I would get so restless, if I happened to be visiting Dwight, that he would sneak me out before his father noticed my fidgetings and gave me a whack—Mr. Eisenhower would as soon whack me as one of his own sons. Then we would go down to the Rock Island stock pens and play follow-the-leader on the high gates and fences.

Mr. Eisenhower, though taciturn, had, I think, an unusually free and independent mind. Two years after Dwight had gone to West Point, I was an up-and-coming young insurance agent with a good buggy. Although I was a Democrat, when Election Day rolled around some Republican clients of mine offered me ten dollars to go pick up the members of their party who had not voted yet and carry them to the polls. Among the missing faithful Republicans was David Eisenhower. I drove up to the creamery at five o'clock, his quitting time. He didn't seem eager to accompany me, demurred that he had on dirty clothes and would have to go all the way home to change. Finally, however, he found a clean jumper and put it on. I carried him to the voting place and waited for him. That was in 1912, the year the Democrats ran Woodrow Wilson, long of Princeton University, against William Howard Taft and Theodore Roosevelt.

Mr. Eisenhower came out of the place, climbed into the buggy and sat a while in thought as we jogged along. At last he spoke. "I don't think women belong in politics, but they should have the vote if they want it." A pause. Then, "I think that college professor should make a pretty good President."

I do not refer to Dwight as "Ike," because, in spite of the statement made in various books and articles that he was called "Ike" throughout his boyhood, I never heard that nickname applied to him until our reunion in 1941. Then everybody called him "Ike."

Some of his biographers, perhaps in an attempt to explain his prowess as a soldier, have pictured him as a country-town bully who went about picking fights, a boy who was fast with his dukes, trimming down other hoodlums who aspired to the championship.

When Dwight entered high school I lost my school-ground contact with him, as I was in the grade below. But I generally met him right after school hours, which was the customary time for settling any arguments that had come up during the day, and I can't recall that he had a single fight in his first two years of high school. For the next two years—1908–10—I saw Dwight only at

Christmas and during the summers, as I was attending Wentworth Military Academy at Lexington, Missouri, 200 miles away, but I never heard of his having a fight during that period. He was by nature quiet, serious, shy, not given to boasting or bragging. It is not true, either, that he was a drinker of hard liquor, a card sharper, or a chaser of girls who were talked about.

One of our mutual friends, Charles Gish—who now lives at Gravois Mills, Missouri—was somewhat gayer than the rest of us. He liked to play pool, would take a drink, knew a bit about poker, would bet or gamble on anything, was interested in girls and crazy about hunting and fishing. "Chick," as we called him, was, like myself, a close friend of Dwight. The others in our group were the Lucier boys—Big, Little and Middle-Sized Frenchy—Claude Weickel and Dave Brightbill. Often the bunch of us would go to the creamery where Dwight fired the boilers on Sundays and play cards with him, mostly games called pitch and hearts. Gish tried to teach us what little he knew about poker, but it didn't take. A few pennies changed hands during the games of hearts. That was the extent of Dwight's boyhood gambling.

As for girls, although he seemed interested in them, and would have an occasional date, he simply had little time for them. When he returned from West Point in uniform, he did, I am told, cut quite a swath among the ladies. But that is another story.

Most of the phony tales about Dwight's youth that have found their way into print originated, no doubt, with people of fertile imagination who knew him slightly, or at a distance, or not at all. Even some of his own brothers, because of the wide range in their ages, hardly knew him intimately. Milton, for instance, nine years his junior, is very close to him nowadays, but he was still a little boy when Dwight left home for West Point.

The statement has been made, and often repeated, that he first planned to enter Annapolis, not West Point. If that is so, he never said anything to me about it. He did make it clear that he sought the West Point cadetship solely as the means of getting an education; it never occurred to him, then, that he might want to stay in the Army.

Of all the weird fabrications that have been published, perhaps the strangest is the dramatic tale about how Dwight was attacked by blood-poisoning, and the ruthless doctor insisted on amputating his leg, Dwight said no, he would rather die, and his big brother slept stretched across the bedroom doorsill so that the doctor could not make a surprise attack and capture the leg. Just as Dwight was at the point of death, however—so goes the tale—the leg miraculously healed of itself. Here is what really happened:

On Friday nights, since there was nothing else to do, we boys had the habit of going to meet the ten-o'clock train. One evening we got up a rather rough game of tag on the depot platform. Dwight stumbled while dodging and ripped his best Sunday pants on some projection, also the skin of his knee. The wound on his knee didn't bother him, but the damage to his pants worried him a lot.

The next day, a hot Saturday, we went down to my father's ranch on the Smoky Hill River to try our hand at building a boat. There was no breeze, and down between the wooded banks it was stifling. Dwight suggested that we drop the boat project and take a swim. (The only instance that I remember when he dropped any project before it was finished.) He plunged, with his wound, into the filthy river, which served as a sewer for several Kansas towns.

He was not at school on Monday. Roy told me the leg had swollen up and was painful. I saw him from the school ground at recess, limping from the house to the privy. At noon I went with Roy across the street to visit him. His mother had propped him up on a bed and he was waiting for Doctor Conkling. I was still there when the doctor arrived. He looked at the leg and said, "Um. . . . We'll have to stop it before it gets to the groin or it might become dangerous."

He painted three stripes around the leg with carbolic acid, using a ball of cotton and tweezers as applicator, and after each stripe he applied alcohol to soften the sting. I held the acid, Roy held the alcohol, and Mrs. Eisenhower held Dwight's hand. He never uttered a sound when the acid burned him, but he did make the most horrible faces.

Finally, the doctor smeared the wound with a black salve, ghastly-looking stuff, explaining to Roy and me that it was "made from a dead fish in Russia."

After a day or two in bed, Dwight limped back to school.

One evening at Fort Sam in 1941, Dwight Eisenhower was talking with a group of his friends, and one of them asked him how he could stand up, day after day, under long hours of work and still have enough "go" left in him to play an occasional game of golf.

"Well," he replied, winking at me, "I guess I am pretty rugged; but, then, you know, I was born in Texas and used to be a cowboy."

He meant to leave the impression that he had been a cowboy in Texas; the wink was for me because I knew he had been a cowboy in Kansas.

During a couple of summers before he left for West Point—he was eighteen and nineteen years old—he worked on my father's ranches. One was a mile south of the Eisenhower home, on a bend of the Smoky Hill River. The other, thirty miles south on the headwaters of Holland Creek, was strictly a grass ranch. In the spring, after the grass was well started, we would drive 300 or 400 head of cattle from the Abilene ranch to the south ranch. In this herd we would have old cows with young calves, yearlings and a few four-year-old steers that had failed to feed out for market.

Anyone who has driven cattle will understand how difficult it is to drive a herd made up of such stock. The cows and calves were draggy, the steers and yearlings were frisky and raring to go. The "point man" had the most important job on this drive. He was the pace-setter. He couldn't go to sleep or even doze. He had to have eyes in the back of his head. My dad picked Dwight Eisenhower for this job because, although the least experienced of all the hands, a tenderfoot, he was the most dependable.

Dwight had to hold back the leaders and watch the rear for the stragglers. The cows would stop for the calves to nurse, and no amount of prodding could get them going. He had to keep a sharp eye for watering places, meadows for the cattle to graze in, groves where they could rest in the cool shade. Riding point was a lonesome job. I rode a pretty fast mare, and was therefore a "side rider." I patrolled one side from front to rear, and thus had a chance to ride up and visit with Dwight once in a while.

We used heavy gear. Our saddles were heavy Pueblos. Each had big saddle bags, each a rolled slicker, a lariat rope and a fifteen-foot Australian-type bullwhip. I don't recall that Dwight was an expert roper, but I do remember he could handle a bullwhip pretty well. We practiced with the bullwhip and could whip it forward and back until it cracked like a Gatling gun or a fast-firing six-gun. Our target practice with the bullwhip consisted of picking sunflowers with it as we rode along.

We started the cattle off about an hour before daybreak, to take advantage of the cool mornings, and we penned them down about dusk in the evening, at a farm some twenty miles out. This farm belonged to a member of a religious sect locally known as "Firebrands." The farmer's name was Heldstab but we called him "Hellstab" among ourselves.

Old Hellstab always knew about when to expect us, and had a big supper of nice hot victuals ready for us when we got there. We would rinse off hurriedly at the horse trough and dash for the table and stand behind our chairs while the ladies brought in all that tempting food.

When the table was fairly groaning, Mr. Heldstab would begin to intone the grace, "Now let us git down on our knees, O Lord, and give t'anks to Thee. . . ."

With a last ravenous look at the steaming dishes, we would kneel while the farmer prayed through his thick, barely riffled whiskers. Some of the older boys who were used to the farmer's ways would raise up surreptitiously from their kneeling place on the hard floor, and with eyes reverently half-closed, snatch a handful of biscuits, which they would distribute underneath the table. And we would munch them gratefully, with our heads bowed, giggling a little.

But not Dwight. He just knelt, ducked his head and never moved a muscle until the prayer came to an end. His attitude of devout immobility irked some of the boys, although it was not the expression of any obnormal piety, but plain good manners and consideration for his host—the result of strict home training. His shins caught some sharp kicks there behind the tablecloth, however. After supper, our foreman, Al Smart, an old cowhand, kidded him and said his name should be Dwight Moody, referring to the famous evangelist. So Dwight was called "Moody" that summer.

When we got up from our knees and were seated at the table, all those steaming hot biscuits and appetizing dishes were beginning to cool. But we had gone fourteen hours without food, except maybe a bologna sandwich stashed in our saddlebags, and the supper, even if it was not piping hot, seemed delicious.

Later, Dwight and I would find a retreat, and roll a "pill" and sit and smoke and talk a while. We slipped off because, in those days, young boys didn't care to have their parents catch them smoking. Dwight didn't smoke in my dad's presence either.

There was a big barn well filled with fluffy prairie hay, and there we all bedded down for the night. We were called about four in the morning, and had to dress, feed, saddle up and be ready for breakfast in fifteen minutes. Dwight was the first one up, first finished with his chores and first in to breakfast. We had those cattle moving and mooing before daylight and turned them into pasture before noon at the south ranch. And Mrs. Sprecker, wife of the ranch foreman, would ply us with good things to eat that she had been preparing for several days.

After a grand meal we might still have a few worm cases penned to doctor, and some fresh scratches to smear with a homemade mixture of axle grease, pine tar and crude carbolic acid. Among our stock were a good many of the black Aberdeen Angus breed, which does not submit tamely to handling. Doping the scores of these fighters with liquid fire didn't seem to soften their dispositions any. When they were roped and snubbed, it was the tenderfoot's job to tail them up to the snubbing post so that the rope could be removed.

It was fun for all except the man who had the steer by the tail. A man holding a fighting steer's tail must be quick to jump, or he can't get loose, and round and round he and the steer go until he can catch the fence for a quick scramble to safety. The top fence rail was the safety zone for everybody but the man who handled this chore. That man was generally Dwight, for he was fast on his feet and quick on the jump.

When our work was finally done, we would go fishing in the little creek that ran near the house. It was full of fish; we would usually come up with a string of bullhead cats. Some of them might even exceed six inches in length. The saintly Mrs. Sprecker cleaned them for us, pouring scalding water over them to get the skin off easily, and gave us for supper a mess of nice small fish.

I'm afraid we returned her kindness in shabby fashion. Among Mrs. Sprecker's domestic accomplishments was the art of making elderberry wine, which she sealed in jars and stored in an outbuilding on the ranch. Some of us found out where she kept this nectar, and a marauding expedition made off with a number of the jars, which we took down to the creek and emptied at our leisure, amid much merriment. I do not remember that anyone showed pangs of conscience. The pious "Moody" took shameless part in this foray. He shared the average youngster's delight in mischief. He was neither a goody-goody nor the tough egg that some writers made him out to be.

There was a machine shop on our ranch, pretty fully equipped, with a crank-style forge, anvil, vise, bolt threaders, drills and wood-working tools. Rainy days were shop days and we made things —all sorts of things. Dwight was mechanically-minded, handy with tools, and had lots of fun in the shop.

Sometimes we would ride the timber, looking for stray cattle, in a bend of the river, or hunt, or set out fish lines. As a hunter, however, Dwight was a total loss. The real reason for his awkwardness with a gun was, I am sure, his reluctance to kill helpless animals and birds. At home he never relished the job of beheading a chicken or butchering a hog.

When he was at Fort Sam Houston I invited him to go deer hunting with me. He said he had never cared for hunting. Then he asked me, reprovingly, "What has any poor little deer done to you, that you should want to kill it?" And he wound up with such a stern lecture on the useless destruction of wild life that I was sorry I had suggested a hunting party. He made me feel like a bloodthirsty savage.

But away back in those other years, shortly before he was to leave Abilene for West Point, Dwight had surprised me by announcing that he would like to go hunting once before he left. So we went hunting, Dwight, Charlie Gish and I, in the woods along the river. "And a fine day it was," Gish now recalls. "We had your two small dogs with us." These were fox terriers, Trixie and Cappy, both excellent hunters.

The dogs "treed" something in a long pipe that had been part of a sand dredge. Charlie, thinking it was a rabbit, reached down into the pipe. He let out a yell and pulled loose with a badly bitten hand. "I still have the marks on my right hand," he tells me.

Running through the pipe was a linked conveyor chain with flat paddles on it. We yanked the chain with all our might and two big fat possums came rolling out. One of them sulled— played possum—at once. We had to sick the dogs on the other before it sulled. Then we sacked them alive in a gunny sack that we used for a game bag and carried them to an old darky named Simpson, who cooked in the Home Rule Café. We told him to have them ready a couple of Sundays later.

Simpson, a specialist in Southern-style dishes, took the possums to his home and fed them on skim milk. When the big day finally came, he lined a big dishpan with plenty of dough, bedded the possums down in sweet potatoes and other fixings, put a lid of dough over all, and baked them in the café oven. Our dinner was scheduled for the evening before Dwight was to leave Abilene for West Point.

In order to celebrate the occasion with suitable pomp, I had commandeered my father's new rubber-tired surrey, which had a let-down top, and his finest trotting horse, Sunday School Bill. We had another horse, not quite so good, named Everyday Bill. It was quite a handsome rig, especially since I spent hours washing and polishing the surrey.

Charlie Gish's folks, who were away on a visit, had told us we could have our feast at their home. Mrs. Gish, before leaving, baked us a cake and garnished the table with all sorts of dainty trimmings.

We had ordered by mail a double case of beer from Kansas City. ("That was Dick Bros. Beer," writes Gish. "We sure had a time that day, and, remember, I fell down the steps in the house and skinned my face up.")

Seven of us met at the Gish home about ten or eleven o'clock in the morning and proceeded to drink a few appetizers. Besides the guest of honor, there were the three Lucier boys—Big, Little and Middle-Sized Frenchy—a boy who was either Dave Brightbill or Claude Weickel, Gish and myself.

Someone went with me in the rig to get the possums. Simpson spread a large dish towel on the floor, set the enormous possum pie in the center of it and pulled up the corners to make a handle, as the pan was piping hot.

The pie was delivered without mishap, although I remember being worried for a second because some of the juice spilled over onto the nice clean floor mat of my father's surrey.

Big Frenchy was chosen to do the carving and serving. He broke the top crust, reached in a fork and held up a possum. Little Frenchy said, "Looks just like a cat, doesn't he?" That remark took the edge off our appetites, with the result that quite a bit of the pie was left untouched.

After we had feasted our fill, we climbed aboard the surrey and took in the town. The beer and the food had raised our spirits and voices to a pretty high, and loud, pitch. We went to see the afternoon train come in. Then we drove around the block—the block being the one that faced Broadway between Second and Third streets—at least a dozen times. We even hollered at the girls—the ones we knew—although we did not ordinarily have the nerve.

All in all, it was a glorious evening. And the next morning at four o'clock, Dwight Eisenhower left Abilene on the eastbound fast mail.

THE DEVIL IN THE DESERT

by Paul Horgan

PAUL HORGAN was born in Buffalo in 1903 and moved to Albuquerque with his family while he was still attending school. His first glimpse of the New Mexico landscape was a thrilling experience for him, and gradually won out over his Eastern background. He studied singing at the Eastman School of Music in Rochester and wrote a prize-winning novel, *The Fault of Angels* (1933), about Rochester musical circles. But most of his writing has been about the Southwest, where he has lived since 1926. "The Devil in the Desert" grew out of an historical incident he read about while doing research for his definitive book on the Rio Grande.

MAY 6, 1950

ONE summer morning almost a hundred years ago in the town of Brownsville, near the mouth of the Rio Grande on the Gulf of Mexico, Father Pierre awoke before dawn in great distress.

"Yesterday," he said to himself bitterly; "I should have told him yesterday."

He listened in the dark of his room, whose little window was just showing the first pearly ghost of day over the gulf. Yes, he could hear what he dreaded to hear. Deep in the house were sounds of footsteps moving about. Father Pierre could tell where those steps went, and what their maker was doing. Now he was in the study taking up certain printed materials—a breviary, a missal, a handful of ornately printed blanks for baptisms, marriages and First Communions which could be filled in as occasion required. The footsteps receded toward the refectory, and there a battered leather knapsack soon was being filled with a cheese, two loaves of bread, a little sack of dried meal, a flask of red wine and a jug of water. Presently a distant door opened and closed, and the footsteps went across the paved garden to the side door of the sacristy in the church, where another leather case would be stocked with sacred vessels, holy oils, communion wafers and a set of vestments made in France of thin silk from Lyons.

The sacristy door sounded again, and Father Pierre knew that the next stage of all these preparations for a journey would move out beyond the rectory and the church to the ragged field where, in a corral, the two priests of the parish kept their horses. There, he knew, Pancho, the eight-year-old gelding that was the color of rusty weeds along the river, was going to be captured after an absurd moment of delicacy and apprehension, saddled and brought back to the courtyard, where the saddlebags and knapsacks were waiting. By then it would be light enough outdoors to see where you were going. It would be time to go.

From the sounds which he could hear and the activities which he could imagine, Father Pierre knew all over again something of the formidable man who was getting ready to depart. If those footsteps sounded like those of an old man, trotting and tentative, yet there was in them a stubborn force. There was plain contempt for human comfort in the noise he made before dawn when others might be sleeping; but he seemed to say that if one man could get up to make all that noise in the name of God, then any other should be glad to awaken to it.

Father Pierre knew there was grim joy in the world that morning for his friend and colleague, Father Louis Bellefontaine. He knew also that Father Louis tried to control a capacity for anger which could flare as quickly and as madly as a cat's. In the new stone rectory the two men lived together harmoniously, for the most part. It took much government of their natural temperaments to make this possible, for over everything lay the difficulty that Father Pierre, who was many years the younger, was the pastor; while Father Louis, who had come from France a generation before Father Pierre, was the assistant, and so, subject to the orders of his junior. But they made jokes about this, as they did about Father Pierre's polished education. Father Louis knew only his God, his duties and what he had learned from hard contests with nature. He knew it was proper for a fine gentleman like Father Pierre to be his superior; and he would wrinkle his old face with shrewd estimate and relish of silken details when Father Pierre was busy with narratives about life at home—which meant France, where one day

526

without doubt the younger priest would be consecrated a bishop. But Father Louis never envied his superior anything, for he knew that in his own work he was a great master—a master of the distance, the heat, the fatigue; the menace of time in slow travel; the harsh vegetation of the brush desert and the murderous Indian, whose soul was within him, but not yet formed; the fears, hopes and needs of the Christian families who lived so widely separated along the inland course of the Rio Grande. For thirty years Father Louis had ridden, mostly alone, and twice a year, on his journeys up the river.

He always undertook them with a sense not only of duty but of escape. Nowhere else did he feel so close to God as alone in the hard brush country riding to bring comfort, news and the Sacraments to some family in a jacal hidden by solitude and open to the hot sky. The older he grew, the more Father Louis longed for his escapes from town and parish. The more infirm he became with the years, the stronger was his sense of mission. Father Pierre would see a glow of youth come back over that sun-stung, seamed old face as time drew near for Father Louis to make his plans to go on his ride into the upriver country, which would take him from two to three months. If his eyes were dim with age, not so the vision in his mind, which showed him so much of what people wanted of him, and of what he could bring to them. If his hand now trembled so that he could hardly write down the names and the dates on one of his sacramental certificates, he could always joke about it, and assure his families that the deed was recorded in heaven, anyway. If sometimes his heart fluttered like a dusty bird in the cage of his ribs, and made him wonder what was ready to take flight, he could lie down for a few minutes and feel the thing calm down; and however unworldly he may have been, he always clamped his jaws together with sardonic satisfaction that his time had not yet quite come. He had things to do, and would do them.

Much of this was known to Father Pierre by intuition, and he recalled it as he arose this morning. He hastened, for if he was going to catch Father Louis and say to him what should have been said yesterday, and even long before that, he would have to hurry. *Do you suppose it could be,* thought Father Pierre, *that I am afraid of him? Or am I afraid for my dignity? What if he simply will not listen to me? He has pretended before this to be deaf like an old man when he has preferred not to hear me. Or do I not want to see a look of pain in his small old blue eyes? Actually, is there not a possibility that what I must tell him will shock him so that it might make him ill?*

Father Pierre shrugged angrily at his doubts and tried to answer them reasonably:

Nonsense. After all, a letter from the bishop has approved my decision and given me authority to do what is wise. Why must I heed for a second the individual feelings of anyone, myself included, when a duty is to be done? If I have been a coward for days, in spite of all my prayers for strength and enlightenment as to how best to do what needs doing, must I not be doubly strong today?

And yet as he went downstairs and out to the courtyard, where a rosy daylight seemed to emerge from the ocher limestone of the church wall and glow in the very air, Father Pierre was as never before conscious of the difference in years between him and the old man who was at this moment hauling at straps and buckles, with one knee raised against Pancho's belly to brace himself.

It was a picture, as Father Pierre could not help pausing to notice. The horse was laden, ready and patient. His summer coat was nicely brushed. His bridle was of woven horsehair. His saddle was bulky and tall, with some of the leather worn away so that the wooden forms of horn and cantle showed through. That saddle was chair and pillow, living room and cradle and crutch to Father Louis. To it he had attached many ingenious and cranky accessories, among which there was nowhere any provision for carrying a weapon. Father Louis went unarmed.

The old priest was dressed in a long homespun coat and heavy trousers. On his head was a woven-cane hat with a wide brim, under which his face peered around at Father Pierre like a crab apple underneath a shelf. His boots were high, the color of dried clay. Now, in the presence of the younger man, he redoubled his efforts at finishing his preparations. He made extra movements, to show how difficult the job was, and he completed them with a little flourish, to show how easily he overcame all. His breath went fast, making his voice dry and thin when he spoke.

"Well, Pierre, I am just about off. I hoped I'd see you before I went."

Father Pierre laughed. His heart beat. He said to himself, *Now, now, I must tell him now.* But he heard himself reply only, "How did you think anybody could sleep with all your racket?"

"Ha." It was a dry, indifferent comment. And then Father Louis looked sharply into his superior's eyes. What he saw there made him hurry. "Well, I have everything. I'll send word back to you if I meet anybody coming this way."

"Yes, do. But before you go ——"

Father Louis began to slap at his breast pockets with sudden dismay.

"Oh, Pierre, think of it. I nearly forgot my sunglasses, the new ones, you know the pair, which my niece sent to me from Vitry-le-François?"

"I have seen them, yes. They have green glass and metal rims, I believe?"

"The ones! Would you be a good angel and just get them for me? They must be in my room."

"You'll wait for me?"

"But of course."

"I'll be right back."

How could it be, and yet it was. Father Pierre, at the very point of discharging his sorry duty, was sent off on an errand by his victim. He shook his head. What did he fear so? The mere rage of Father Louis? The years of unspoken submission of the older man to the younger? The human aches which can invade the hearts even of those promised to God? He didn't know. All he could believe was that the unshaven, knobbled old man waiting down there by his packed horse, with his hands which trembled on a regular slow beat and his old blue eyes, was stronger than he. Father Pierre was tall and slender and chiseled in man's noble likeness. His soutane was always clean. His white face and dark eyes could blaze with the Holy Ghost. He had proper respect for authority, but could not now use his own.

Lifting piles of papers, and putting aside apples which had dried up and mineral specimens blanched by dust, he searched Father Louis' room for the green sunglasses with their oval lenses and tin rims. He smiled at the condition of the room. He did not find the glasses. He returned to the courtyard.

Father Louis was already in the saddle. In his hand he held the sunglasses. "I found them," he said. "I am sorry you had to go for them. Good-by, Pierre. Give me your blessing. I must be getting along now."

Through his thin old voice and his clouded eyes there spoke a boy who was off to a picnic. Father Pierre's heart sank as he looked at him. He knew now that he was not going to tell what it was his duty to tell. Chagrined at his own weakness, he lifted his hand and made the blessing of the cross, to which Father Louis bent his body.

After all these years he had a map in his head. The river came on a long diagonal, so. An old Indian trail went off northwestward at another angle, so. The farther inland, the farther apart they were from each other. There was one kind of country here by the seacoast. Presently it changed to something else. Finally, in the distance of weeks, where the map would have only faltering scratches of the pen, based on rumor and legend, lay the farthest wilderness of Father Louis' journeys. The natural limits of his endurance were determined by water. His private map had an X for the end of each stage of travel—a settlement, a farm, a creek, a spring, a water hole—and pray it was not dry.

For the first several days, on these journeys, he hardly seemed to have left home. The earth was still low and sandy, and he could read in it how epochs ago the sea itself was here, hauling and grinding the stuff of ocean bottoms where now he rode. The air was moist, and little clouds came to be and to vanish almost before his gaze. He could not closely follow the river, for it wandered and turned, in places doubling back upon itself. And so he followed the Indian trail, leaving it only to go to the isolated river farms in turn.

At such a one he might spend the night, or longer, depending upon what he found. Sometimes death approached in the family, and he gave the last Sacraments. Sometimes there were infants to baptize. In the morning under a tree on rough-hewn planks set across a pair of hogsheads he would say Mass and give Communion. He listened to the local news from Mexico across the Rio Grande—there was talk of another war between ranchers of Coahuila and the Mexican troops; it had not rained for a hundred and seventy days; robbers came over the river lately and killed four men here in Texas and stole some cattle and horses and went back across the river; a child was born in the Bolson de Mapimi who spoke, quite clearly, at three days old, of a flood that would come, but who, when further questioned, seemed to have lost the power of speech; and so on.

Father Louis, in his turn, told how things were at Brownsville, and farther up the coast at Corpus Christi and Galveston, and across the sea in France, where, under the new emperor, business was booming, and trade with Mexico was growing, as you could tell by the many ships which came from Marseille and Le Havre into the Gulf of Mexico. And then, after receiving gifts of food from such a family, the rider left the river and returned to the trail, going northwestward once more.

Days later, though the sky did not cool during the daytime, the quality of the heat changed, and was dry, as the old seacoast plain gave way to a wilderness of rolling country thickly covered with thorny brush. When he encountered it as it wandered, the river bed was rocky, and rock showed through the hard prickly ground. Everywhere he looked he saw only that endless roll of empty land.

Here, near to him, it was speckled with the colors of the olive, both green and ripe, but not with any of the grace he remembered from long ago in Southern France, where the olive trees gave a silver sweetness to the landscape. Farther away in the distance, the land rolls swam in glossy heat. Way off at the horizon there was a stripe of hazy blue where the hot white sky met the earth. Nowhere could he see a mountain, either in Mexico or in Texas.

As he rode, the country tried to hold him back. The thorns of the mesquite dragged at his boots and tore his clothes. Pancho was clever at avoiding most of the hazards, but in places they were so thick that all they could do, man and horse, was go slowly and stoutly through them. But this was nothing new. Father Louis had persisted before against the thorns and had prevailed.

As for water, there was always too much or too little. Too little when, after years of drought, certain springs he looked forward to would, as he came upon them, reveal only dried white stones. Too much when, in hot spells so violent that they could be ended only with violence, there would be a cloudburst and the heavens would fall almost solid and bring the first water, which, as it struck the baked earth, actually hissed and made cracking sounds until the desert was slaked enough to receive the water in its fissures and let it run.

When it ran in such quantity, every fingerlike draw became a torrent in which a man and a horse could easily be drowned. If he crossed one in safety, another was waiting to engulf him beyond the next roll. There was no place for shelter. When the rain stopped, the sun came back and dried everything the same day except the running arroyos, which went dry the next day. All too soon there was bitter dust that sparkled in the light and rose with the hot wind. Against it Father Louis tied across his face his great bandanna, which came from New Orleans.

And they went on, making a small shadow of horse and man moving slowly yet certainly across that huge empty map where days apart, each from the other, little clusters of human life and need clung to being and shone in Father Louis' mind and purpose like lanterns in the darkness—which usually was the first image he saw of his destination, when, by his reckoning, he knew it was time to reach another of his families.

Was this a hard journey? Very well, then, it was a hard journey. But so was the life hard which he found at the end of each stage of his travels. He had seen men grow old and die in his visits here, and their sons with their wives bring new souls to this wilderness in turn. They learned severe lessons in isolation, heat and the hostility of the animal and vegetable world. Everyone—the child, the grandfather, the husband, the wife, the youth, the horse, the maiden—worked unceasingly against dust, thorn, ignorance and scarcity from dawn to dark. The great world was but rumor here, and, by the time it came to brush deserts, mostly wrong. But a world without limits of dimension dwelt behind the eyes of all those parched brown people obedient to the natural terms of their lives. It was the world of the human soul, in which could live promises so beautiful and satisfactions so full of ease that the hardships and the betrayals of impersonal Nature could be survived, if only someone came from time to time with the greatest news in all life.

For Father Louis knew in a simple flatness of fact—fact as hard as a rock, as mysterious as water, as dazzling as light—that without God the richest life in the world was more arid than the desert; and with Him the poorest life was, after all, complete in a harmony which composed all things. To be the agent of such a composition put upon him a duty in the light of which all peril on his journeys became at worst mere inconvenience. Everyone he toiled overland to see needed and deserved that which he, at the moment, under existing circumstances, alone could bring.

In a very practical way he was still awed by the mystery of his office. And as a human being he could never deny himself the joy it gave him to see in their faces what his coming meant to his people in the harsh wilderness. They knew what he had come through. They were proud to be thought worth such labor and danger. They loved him.

His mind was active in the solitude through which he crawled day after day, mounted on Pancho. One of his favorite fancies was this: that a great triangle existed between God in heaven, and any little ranch toward which he rode through the days, and himself. It was an always-changing triangle, for one of its points was not fixed: his own. As he came nearer and nearer to his goal of the moment, the great hypotenuse between himself and God grew shorter and shorter, until at the last, when he arrived, there was a straight line with all in achieved communion. He smiled over this idea, but he respected it, too; and sometimes he would take a piece of charcoal from a fire and draw a series of pictures of what he meant, explaining it to the people he was visiting, and they would murmur and nod, and consult one another, and enjoy the notion with him, marveling.

One day at noon on the present journey, he knew he should soon see what would look like a long thin blade of cloud shadow far ahead on the earth that slowly quivered with wafts of light like those in wavering mirrors. But it was not a cloud shadow, as he had found out nearly thirty years ago. It was the distant gash of a long canyon whose yellow rock walls were stained with great stripes of slate blue. It came from the north, and far away to the south opened into the rocky trough of the Rio Grande. In its bottom were all the signs of a river but running water. Here and there were shallow pools fed by the underground flow which needed storm water to call it continuously to the surface. Father Louis always paused at such a pool for a bath. There were sores on his body from the catch of thorns through which he rode. Sometimes a needle of the brush would break off in his flesh and burrow its way under his skin. For the most part he was unaware of such an affliction, but by its comfort the warm alkaline water of the pool reminded him of the misery he had forgotten to notice.

It was usually midafternoon by the time he reached the canyon after first seeing it. Shadow was already rising up the canyon wall as the sun went lower. The place was like a palace to him, open to the brassy sky. Wrens and hawks came to look at him in their wary turns. To be below the surface of the rolling plain in the canyon was to have for a little while the luxury of privacy, somehow. He bathed, and dozed as he dried, and sat in the shade reading his breviary. He knew when it was just time to gather himself together and resume his ride in order to come by nightfall to the house and the spring of Encarnadino Guerra, where he could spend the night.

This friend was a boy of ten when Father Louis first met him. He was now the father of six children, the husband of a silent, smiling woman named Cipriana, the son of a widowed mother called Doña Luz, who, on his last visit, told Father Louis she would not live to enjoy the next one. He remembered how she sat blinking in the brilliant shade of the desert, bowing to him over and over, while a triumph of patience went over her face, eroded by time and trouble and work and pain, as she said, "At night, when everything is quiet, and I am awake and alone— for I cannot sleep much any more—something speaks to me, and tells me to be ready, and not to make any other plans."

She looked at him with hardly any light in her small eyes, and he knew she was right. When he said Mass for them that time, he thought he saw in her face some powerful, direct understanding of the Holy Sacrifice which during all her pious life had slumbered within her, but at last came clear in her whole, small, withered being.

He wondered whether through any dry, desert-like tenacity she might still be living.

But when he rode up in the arching twilight to the dwelling of the Guerras, almost the first thing they told him after their excited greeting was that Doña Luz had died early in the summer while sitting in the shade on her bench, holding her stick of ocotillo cactus which her hands had shined so smooth.

In the light of the candle lantern the family looked at him and then at one another. They were shocked by how he had changed since last year. He was stooped and he slowly trembled all the time. He had to peer at them to see them, even though he preserved a smile to make nothing of this. Burned by the wind and the sun, his face looked smaller. He breathed shallowly, with his mouth a little open. He seemed to them a very old man, all of a sudden. It was like a secret they must keep from him.

After their first start, they got busy to make his supper. The younger children lost their shyness and came from behind chairs and the edges of tables to see him, and at last climb upon him. He smelled dry and dusty to them, like the earth.

After supper he held lessons in catechism for the younger children, who tomorrow would receive their First Communions. The parents and the two older sons listened also.

After that, there was a little time left for gossip. The family's news was all of the seasons. The priest's was boiled down out of letters and newspapers from France. The Guerras already knew that the earthly love of his life was his native country, which he had not seen for over thirty years, but which still spoke in his darting eyes, his cleverness at description and in the accent with which he spoke Spanish. They listened respectfully while he made picture after picture in his talk of what he loved and missed, but they could not really see with him either the cool green fields, the ancient stone farmhouses, the lanes of poplar trees, the clear rivers; or the proud old towns, or the glorious towering cathedrals, or the silvery web of his dear city of Paris sparkling delicately in daytime, glowing in the long dusk with golden lamps and violet distances.

But they were honored simply to have him here, and stared before his marvels, and held their breath for tomorrow, when he would give them the Sacraments.

In the morning he visited the grave of Doña Luz. Everybody went with him. She was buried a little way off from the adobe house. When he saw how little earth she displaced, he nodded and smiled, as though meeting all over again her modest character which he knew so well. Guerra brought some water in an earthen vessel—not much, but enough. Father Louis took the jug and held it in both hands a moment, and gazed into it. They were all reminded of how precious water was on the earth, how it determined by its presence the very presence of life. Then he blessed it, and they all knew what this meant in terms of their daily struggle. Then, reciting prayers for the dead, he walked around the small mound of the grandmother and sprinkled the holy water upon it, and they knew he was keeping once again a promise made between heaven and earth a long time ago.

After that they returned to the house and he took them one by one and heard them confess their sins, of which, as they were contrite, he relieved them. Then, at an altar improvised against the wall where the old woman used to sit for so many hours, he said Mass, wearing his embroidered French silks and using the pewter chalice that came out of his saddlebag.

The family knelt on the ground in a straight line facing the altar. The famous triangle of Father Louis was brought into a straight line also. God and mankind were made one. As he recited the words during the offertory, "O God, who has established the nature of man in wondrous dignity, and even more wondrously has renewed it ——" Father Louis felt behind him the bodily presences of that isolated family, and an almost bitter sense of the dearness of each of their souls humbled him at his altar.

When Mass was over they returned within the house, where, at the raw table polished by countless unnoticed contacts of all the family, Father Louis sat down to fill in certificates of First Communion for the younger children. He had a flask of huisache ink and a German steel pen. Sitting as far back from the documents as he could, the better to read, he began to write. A look of disgust came on to his face as his trembling hand gave him trouble. Exclaiming impatiently, he put his left hand on his right wrist to add strength and steadiness where they were needed, but this did not help much, and when he was done, he pushed the papers toward the head of the family, saying, "Nobody ever can read my writing except God."

They all took him seriously, prouder than before of their papers.

"But that is enough, isn't it?" he demanded fiercely.

They had a merry breakfast, when everyone talked as though they would not soon again have a chance to talk, which was true; everyone except Guerra, who was going to speak of something as soon as he had built up enough silence. Finally he was ready.

"Father," he said, leaning back a trifle in his chair and half closing his eyes to disguise deep feelings, "you won't be going on anywhere else, after us, will you?"

"Oh, yes."

"Where will you go, father?"

"Why, I plan to ride from here over toward the river. I have a couple of families over there, and I may go as far as the town of San Ygnacio, to see if the priests from Mier are making visits there, as they ought to. Why?"

Guerra put his head on one side and shrugged. He did not want to say that the old man was exhausted and ought not to go so far in the pitiless country under the searing sun. It would not be polite to say the old man was older than his years, and he must be seventy anyway. He might be misunderstood if he said that everybody reached a time, after a life of hard work, when he must pause and rest and let stronger people do what needed doing. It would hardly do to show outright that he thought Father Louis should give up, and stay here, and rest a few weeks, and then perhaps Encarnadino Guerra might leave everything here in the hands of his two strong, quiet boys, and just ride with Father Louis until he saw him safely back in Brownsville.

Father Louis peered close at his younger friend and saw enough of these thoughts to stir him up.

"Eh?" he said, rapping hard with his knuckles on Guerra's skull. "What goes on in there?" He was sharp and angry. What were they all thinking? That he was a feeble old man? He knew all there was to know about that, but if anything was to be said about it, he, not they or anyone else, was the one to say it. "Mind your manners, you, boy," he said to Guerra, screwing up his small eyes until all that showed of them were two sharp blue points of light. "Eh? You have opinions, have you? Who told you to think anything! Eh? When I want you to think anything about anybody, I'll tell you. Eh? I got here, didn't I? How many times have I managed to come? And what for? Does anybody tell me to come? Or where to go? Or when? Or why? Then you keep your place, and thank God for your blessings, and for your friends, and understand that it is just as bad to hold an impolite thought as it is to say an impolite thing. Eh?" His whole body shook with passion which he tried to control. "Bad. You'd just better be careful, that's all I have to say, do you hear?"

The family was appalled at this burst of feeling. They sat with downcast eyes, fearing that it would be disrespectful to look upon Father Louis in his rage. But they had little glimpses of his unshaven face whitened with anger, and they could hear how pulse-shaken his voice was. Guerra was more Indian than anything else, and his countenance became fixed. He leaned back and took his dressing down without response. He was not even hurt by it. He knew why it came to him. He knew how much it proved him right in his concern. He admired the flare of spirit in the old man. He was at peace with himself for trying what he had tried.

The youngest child, not understanding what had taken place, now, belatedly, felt the emotion among all the older ones, and turning up her little clay-doll face she burst into wails of misery and fear, bringing her tiny creature paws to her howling mouth until she resembled the small sculptured masks of earth buried with the dead centuries ago deep in Mexico.

Father Louis roughly took her upon his lap. He bent his bristly face close to hers, cactus and blossom together, and in barely audible murmurs quieted the child and himself, which took about five minutes.

This act reclaimed them all for one another. Once again the visitor was kind and smiling, and the family without fear.

"And so, good-by for this time," said Father Louis, putting the child down and standing up. "If you will get my horse for me?"

Guerra spoke to one of the boys, who went to fetch Pancho. They all met him outside. Cipriana brought some tortillas for the saddlebag. Everyone knelt down to be blessed. The hot sunlight smote them. They had lingered long over their breakfast. It was late. Father Louis, mounted and ready, blessed them three times, and then turned and rode off to the south. After a while he looked back. They were still kneeling. The next time he looked back it was hard to see them, for at even a little distance they made the same shadow as the scrubby bushes which grew on the caked earth, and seemed just as eternally rooted there.

He had a bad morning. The sun seemed hotter to him than before. The savage brush seemed animated with spite as it clawed at his legs going by. Pancho, after all these years and a lifetime in the brush country, took it into his head to be terrified of familiar things, and from time to time without warning executed a rapid dance step to one side while throwing his head back and rolling his eyes at his rider.

"Hush, you fool!" Father Louis exclaimed at such times. "You fool!"

But he addressed himself as much as he did the horse. For the first few hours of that day's ride, he reviewed many times the loss of his temper at Guerra, and developed a masterly case, closely reasoned, lucid as only a French argument can be, compassionate with a largeness of heart, yet as logical as music in its progression, as to why it had been not only natural but actually necessary to reprove Guerra for having presumed to hold views about him. Reprove? Perhaps actually more of a scolding. Scolding? Thinking it over, possibly even a tongue-lashing. And the knuckles? The furious raps on the head? Still, how else could he be made to understand? But understand what?

It was no good. As he always did, in the end, he lost the argument with himself. He knew that after hours of exhausting search for conclusions which would excuse him for what he had done, he would at last come to the truth, which was that he had offended God and man through his lifelong besetting sins of pride, self-esteem and attempted condonement of his own shortcomings; and that there would be nothing left to do but go down upon his knees and admit how wrong he had been, and pray to be forgiven and to be granted strength once more to conquer himself.

He began his penance with a resolve not to eat or drink until nightfall.

By midafternoon, the brush grew thicker. Only occasionally did he come to a little clearing between the mesquite bushes, which rose higher than himself mounted on Pancho. In spite of his green sunglasses, the ground sparkled and glared enough to hurt his eyes. He watched for but he could not see the long pale blur which would tell him that another canyon lay ahead which he would follow until it took him, after several days, to the Rio Grande. He kept the sun on his right, for it was declining to the west in the white sky and he was going south. The day was still.

But how was this? He thought he heard a singing wind, but when he tried to notice whether he could feel the air stirring or see dust rising ahead of him, there was no sign of wind. He halted Pancho. What did he hear, then? He turned his head. Yes, he could hear something, now far ahead, now here in his very ear. He searched the undulating horizon, but he saw nothing except the wavering image of glassy heat where the white sky met the dusty earth.

As he rode on, the singing in the air became louder. It sounded like the voice of the desert heat. He shook his head, resentful of natural conditions which hid behind mystery. And then suddenly he knew, and scornfully rebuked himself for taking so long about it.

He was riding into a swarm of cicadas, and now he could see the first ones, clinging to the mesquite as they raised their shrieking song of the heat. The farther he rode, the louder they became. He bent his head under their stinging assault upon his hearing. There were thousands and millions of them. Blindly they fulfilled their natures in their collective scream of response to the sun and the desert. The very atmosphere seemed to be in flames, and the sound of the stridulating insects added to the illusion.

Father Louis had touched the desert often enough. He had smelled it. He had tasted it when its dust rose on the wind. He had seen it in every state. But never before in so real a sense had he heard it.

He was suddenly exhausted. In a clearing, a little lake of baked dust a few yards in diameter, he halted and dismounted, tying Pancho to a stout mesquite branch. Disturbed, a cloud of cicadas rose on crackling threads of flight and found another bush. The ringing song rose all about him. He could not even hear the sound of Pancho stamping his foot to shake off flies. He clapped his hands, but made barely a sound against the strident song in the air. He felt removed from himself. All desert natures combined to render him impersonal. Here, humbled not only from within but from without, he could find real contrition. He knelt down to pray.

The sunlight was brilliant in the center of the clearing, a little open room hidden by time, distance and mesquite clumps. At the west side of it there was lacy shade, cast by tall bushes. But Father Louis rejected it and knelt in the plain sunlight. He bent his head under the beat of his spirit and of the insect scream which seemed to invoke the zenith. He prayed to be forgiven for his miserable anger. He always prayed in French, the language through which he had first met God.

He was not long now at his contritions, for he knew that prayer was not so often a matter of length as of depth. Much sobered, even saddened, by his intense self-discovery, he arose wearily from his knees and went over to the shade to lie down. He went as deeply into the under boughs of the thorny mesquite as he could. He closed his eyes. At once he felt cooler, just to have the hot light shaded from his sight. Ah, this was delicious, just to lie for a few moments and gather strength to go on for the remaining hours of daylight. He felt how his limbs all went heavy on the earth as he let himself drift off to sleep.

Little coins of light fell over him through the intricate branches. Where he lay, he made solid shadow himself under the mesquite tree. He was as quiet and substantial as a rock. And if he used

Nature, it in turn used him without his knowing, for he was asleep.

He did not see, or smell, or feel what came in slow inquiry along the trackless ground, striving forward in orderly, powerful progress, flowing in a dry glitter and advancing through always-new and always-repeated thrust of form from side to side and yet ahead. It was a diamondback rattlesnake in search of shade and the cool. It came from deep in the scattered brush, and it found the heavy-sleeping man under the bushy tree. With what seemed almost conscious caution against awakening the sleeper, the snake drew closer and closer in infinite delicacy, until it lay heavily at rest in the shade of Father Louis' right shoulder, its length doubled back and forth in inert splendor.

The sleepers did not stir for a while and then Father Louis grew tense in dream, his mouth fell open and, awakening with a jerk, he sat up, lost in forgetfulness of where he was or how he came there. He stared at the white sky.

The thick snake, at the first quiver of motion beside it, drew instantly into its coil and shook its dozen rattles. Their song could not be heard over the general din of the cicadas.

"Ah, yes," sighed Father Louis, as he discovered where he was, and why, and whither he was going. He put his hand to his brow and sank roughly back to the earth to take a few more minutes of rest. The snake struck him in the shoulder, and struck him again. Its coils turned dust into liquid light as they lashed. The strikes came like blows made by the thick, powerful arm of a young man.

"What then?" said Father Louis at the sudden stabbing pain, and the blows that shook him. He first thought of mesquite thorns on a springy branch; they were long and, as he had often said, sharp as fangs, and they could fester if not treated. It occurred to him that this would be troublesome now, as he could hardly reach his own shoulder to wash, cut open the skin and dig out the thorns if they had broken to stay in the flesh.

But he turned to see the branch which had attacked him, and saw the snake instead. The snake was retreating. He could see its eye with its glaring drop of light. His heart began to beat hard. He had a surge of rage. He wanted to kill the snake, and actually rose to one knee and scraped the ground with his hands for something to attack with—a rock, a club of dead wood, anything—but he could find nothing. He sank down again, and out of habit in any crisis brought his hands flat together with crossed thumbs in the attitude of prayer.

"No, no; no anger," he beseeched of himself

with his eyes shut. He had just endured and come through the storm of his own pride, and he must not now create another. He opened his eyes and looked after the snake, and saw it where it paused half in, half out of the dappled shade of the next bush.

"Go," he said to it.

What he meant by this came to be more and more clear through calm and struggle in the next hour or so. The snake, as though it heard him, resumed in infinite slowness the gliding flow of its retreat until it was lost to sight among the hot thickets where the insects still sang and sang.

"Yes, go," he repeated bitterly; and was ashamed to discover that he was weeping. It was the humanity in him which wept because death was coming. He fell over upon his face and put his cracked and dusty hands over his eyes. His mouth was open and took into itself the loose acid earth with his breath. His tears ran down his fingers. His heart was pounding rapidly upon the ground. It seemed to shake the earth. It told Father Louis that he was afraid.

Afraid? Of what? he thought. *Afraid of death? But I have dealt with it all my life and I have robbed it of its terrors for those who knew how to die. Is death the only victory of life? Or do we have to defeat life in its own terms? That depends. It depends upon whether sin is ever outside oneself or always within. Yes, this is a very interesting matter.*

He made himself lie quietly without thought for a moment. If perhaps he conserved his energy he might by natural vitality, by pure goodness, defeat the murder which had been dealt him by the desert. He forced himself to relax, and promised that in a little while his head would be clearer, his heart would calm itself, and moving with infinite caution he would arise, mount his horse and go slowly, steadily, cleverly, toward the long evening, and come to the canyon where there must be a familiar trickle of water. A cool night with much prayer, a stout will, and tomorrow he would go forward and by the end of the day come to friends who would know how to make poultices and feed him and recover him to the use and enjoyment of many more years of duty, work and acquired merit.

But the poison worked rapidly, and he felt it charging his mind with throbbing pain which confused him. Shining blades went across his vision behind his eyes like spokes of a great wheel. He was dazzled by their power. When he raised his head they took it with them, rolling and rolling until he fell down again upon the ground with his cheek cut by little pebbles of gypsum. He tried to

speak and to say, "Let me not live for vanity, though, Lord."

Questions now became academic, for he went blind in his inner vision, and lay trembling involuntarily as the terrible message which had been stricken into him traveled the course of his blood and reached him everywhere within.

Tied to his mesquite tree, Pancho stamped and waited. Presently Father Louis believed that he awoke.

His mind was working sharply and with, it seemed to him, exquisite new ease and clarity. He saw all his thoughts in crystal depths of cold fresh water. He knew he was in the mesquite thicket, and what had happened to him, and he possessed this knowledge with a beauty of feeling which all his life he had known in the state of grace, after receiving or administering the Sacraments. It was more than mere physical well-being. It was a sense of delivery from the ordinary guilt of his own clay, and the exasperating weight of the world. It was the real meaning of communion with all that lay beyond himself. In such a state, truth needed no seeking and no definition. It was here, within, and it was there, without. It was everywhere. When all was known, there could be no astonishment.

He was therefore not astonished now when right before him, lying at ease in the light of the sun, was the snake, gazing at him with piercing sweetness.

He spoke to it. "I do not hate you. It is enough that I recognize you."

The snake replied, "That is my damnation."

"Yes," said Father Louis, "for when evil is recognized, all other powers move together to defeat it."

"And yet they never do defeat it, do they? How do you explain that?"

"Ah. You and I do not see it in quite the same way. You conceive of the possible death of evil as being one final end, after which only goodness will survive."

"I do."

"That is your vanity. For the fact is that evil must be done to death over and over again, with every act of life. One might even say that this repeated act is a very condition for the survival of life itself. For only by acts of growth can more life be made, and if all evil, all acts of death, were ended once and for all, there would be nothing left for the soul to triumph over in repeated acts of growth."

The snake sighed despondently and said, "Do you not permit me a comparable purpose and privilege? That is, of triumphing repeatedly over all acts of good—that is, of life—until only I remain?"

"I permit you your established role, but I do not admit the possibility of your triumphing repeatedly over all acts of life. I must point out that, historically, your premise is untenable."

"And yet I have played a part in every human life."

"Oh, admittedly. We are not discussing the fact that your powers exist; only the fact that they have their limits."

The snake smiled. "This? From you?" it asked with ironic politeness.

"What do you mean, sir?"

"If my powers have their limits, then how is it that I have killed you? What greater power is there than that?"

Father Louis passed his hand across his face to hide his amusement. "You have betrayed the weakness of your whole position," he replied. "For it appears to be impossible for you to know that the death of matter is of no importance, except to other matter. The materialist can see only destruction as the logical end of his powers. I, and my brothers, and my children, know that beyond matter lies spirit, and that it is there where answers are found, and truths become commonplace, and such efforts as yours, so restless, so ingenious, so full of torturing vanity, are seen for what they really are."

The snake frowned for a moment, but then shook off its irritation and said, again with politeness, even with charm and appeal, which Father Louis was the first to admit, "Everyone must do that which his nature dictates."

"There again," said Father Louis with assumed gravity, "there is much behind the formation of that nature which you do not take into account."

"Oh, come. After all, I am a snake, I came from snakes, I do a snake's work. How could I behave like anything but a snake?"

"The outer form is hardly the point. You can assume any form you choose, I believe?"

The snake hesitated before answering. A gleam of admiration went through its expression, and it marveled frankly for a moment at the astuteness of Father Louis.

"I must say, even if we are enemies, you force me to admire and like you," it said.

"Thank you," said Father Louis. "Viewed abstractly, you have great and beautiful qualities of your own."

"Do you really think so?"

"Oh, yes, I do. But I must add that they seem to me less important, in the end, than they do to you."

"You can also be very rude, you know."

"I do not think of it that way," said Father Louis mildly. "Finally, it doesn't matter how things are said or done, it is what things are said or done. For example, I really believe you can do things far more expertly than I can. But when we come to what things, there I have you."

The snake looked far from pleased.

Father Louis resumed, "I can't assume any form, for example, as you can. I remain always what I am, a man, an old man, a dirty old man when water is scarce or I am busy, an old man full of pride and sin and vanity and all the rest of it; but nobody is ever in doubt as to what I mean or as to what I think life means, and with all my mistakes in style and good form, the garden I scratch keeps growing."

"And I?"

"And you, sometimes you are a snake, and sometimes a whisper, and again, a daydream, a lump in the blood, a sweet face, an ambition, a scheme for making money, a task for an army. Sometimes you can even be a man and disarm everyone entirely who cannot see your heart. But someone there is who always sees. Goodness is often performed without the slightest knowledge of its doing. But evil is always known."

"Yes, I think more people know me than the other thing."

"But don't congratulate yourself upon that," said Father Louis, "for it means always one of your uncountable defeats when you are known."

Father Louis saw that the snake would have to grow angry unless the subject was changed. The snake changed it. "I wonder," it mused, "why I ever came to you today."

Father Louis shrugged. "Sooner or later, we would have come together," he said.

"Did you expect me?"

"I've been expecting you all my life; though not exactly in this particular guise. You came to me in my sleep, like an evil dream."

"All I wanted was a little comfort. It was so hot. So dry."

Father Louis smiled in delight. "You see? For comfort, even you have to appeal to the powers of goodness."

"Why did you let me go?"

"I had no weapon."

"You could have stamped upon me."

"I do not believe in killing."

"Yet I am your enemy."

"Yes, you are. But I believe there are greater ways to dispose of you than in revenge."

"You do not have much time left, you know. Just think of all the time you would have left if I had not come to you. If you had seen me and killed me first."

"Yes, I have thought of that. But you speak as though time were my property. It is not. How can I count it? Or know how much of it is my share?"

The snake scowled and looked from side to side evasively. Unwillingly, against its own comfort, it asked, "Who else can decide your share? Where do you get it? What do you refer to?"

The snake began uneasily to bring its coils together. There was anguish in its movement, slow as it was. It seemed to be obeying desire which was hurtful and yet impossible to deny.

"You do not really want to hear," said Father Louis tenderly.

"Oh, yes, I do; tell me," said the snake with broken breath, already suffering under the answer which it demanded.

Father Louis bent over the snake with compassion. There was torture in the creature, as with glittering sweet power it besought Father Louis to answer.

"Very well, my poor sinner," said Father Louis gravely. "I, and all creatures, draw our share of time in this life from God, our Father in heaven."

At these words the snake, with the speed of lightning, knew convulsion in its dread coils, and with mouth wide open and fangs exposed, struck again and again at the earth, where the dust rose like particles of gold and silver. Father Louis regarded it with pity as its paroxysm of hatred and chagrin spent itself.

At last, gasping softly and stretched out in exhaustion, the snake said sorrowfully, "And so it is not by my will that you die now?"

"No."

"I was only the means?"

"Only the means."

"Your hour was designated elsewhere?"

Father Louis looked upward. His face was radiant. "My hour was fixed by our Heavenly Father."

The snake closed its eyes and shuddered reminiscently. Then it said, "And my hour?"

"You will die in your bodily form by His will."

"I do not want to die."

"But you will live in your quality of evil by His will."

"You're sure?"

"Yes. But you will live only on earth, no matter what form you assume."

The snake grew pale. "Oh, no."

"Yes," said Father Louis as his argument drew to its close, "for there can be no evil in heaven."

The snake lay with its mouth open, its tongue like a little tongue of fire, flickering in despair, its eyes staring without sight. It was vanquished,

destroyed, made trivial. Father Louis shook his head over it and wished it might not have suffered. Then he felt his brow, where the diamondlike lucidity of the past quarter of an hour seemed to be clouding over. His skull was cracking under blows that beat and beat there. How could he feel so bad after feeling so well?

"And now you must excuse me," he said uncertainly to the snake. "I have things to do, and, actually, I do not feel too well. Thank you, if you will just go now," and he looked to see if the snake was leaving, but the snake was already gone.

The battering pains in his head brought Father Louis from vision to consciousness.

"Oh, my God, my God," he said devoutly and with much effort, even with modesty, representing his trouble to Him whose suffering he had dwelt upon so deeply in a lifetime.

He looked around. The air seemed entirely silent. This was because there was a ringing in his head so bewildering that he could no longer hear the myriad insects at their screaming celebration of the heat.

He saw Pancho tied to the tree. "No, you must not stay with me," he said, and tried to stand up. He could hardly stand, for his legs were weak as paralysis crept into them. And so he crawled across the open place among the thickets until he could hold to his stirrup, haul himself up and lean with his head on the saddle for a moment.

"You need not die here, tied to a tree," he said. "Let me get my things, and you may go."

He fumbled with the buckles and straps until he was able to haul the saddle off the horse. It fell to the ground. He worked at the bridle until he had freed it enough to pull it off over Pancho's head. The horsehair bridle hung from the thorny tree and trailed in the dust.

"Huya! Huya!" cried Father Louis, waving his hand at Pancho to make him trot away, as so often he had done after unsaddling the horse at the corral at Brownsville. But Pancho simply stood and regarded him.

"Very well, very well; in your own time, then," he said, and went down to his hands and knees, fondling a pouch on the saddle. Out of it into his hands came the objects he wished to hold once more. Holding them to his breast, he crawled back to his fatal shade across the clearing. The sun was almost down.

"My soul doth magnify the Lord," he murmured in Latin while pains like blades pierced him through and through. Even the heavy washing waves of death could not erase entirely from his foundering mind the terrible privilege of knowing in a final hour what saints might have endured. "And my spirit has rejoiced in God my savior," he said, without knowing he spoke. But he brought a lifetime of prayer with him to death's door, and in a little while it entered there with him.

Pancho late the next evening finished finding his way through the brush back to the house of Encarnadino Guerra. The family saw that he was without his saddle and bridle. Guerra and his big sons went searching, and, though they persevered for days, found nothing in that wilderness of repeated clump and glaring shadow and lost sameness. They had to give up. Later that year, when surveyors from an expedition of the United States Army came by his place on their way to Brownsville, Guerra told them the news, and asked them to see that it reached the proper authorities, along with the horse Pancho which he hoped they would take with them.

And then one day eight years afterward, Guerra was on his way to San Ygnacio on the Rio Grande to see his new grandson, born to the household of his oldest boy, who now lived there. Coming into a small clearing in the brush, he found quite by accident what he had looked for long ago. There was not much left, for the desert earth and sky were voracious. Coyotes and blowing sand, vultures and beating sunlight and wind had worked with the years on flesh and leather, French silk, parchment and homespun. Reverently Guerra took up the few bones that had not been scattered, and the few hard things that still stayed by them: the pewter chalice, a rosary of small sea shells, three American silver dollars, the pair of green sunglasses, and, from a mesquite tree where it hung now off the ground, the horsehair bridle.

When he could, he made the journey to Brownsville, bringing the relics of his old friend with him. He found his way to Father Pierre Arnoud.

"How these things speak to us!" said Father Pierre, after hearing the end of the story that had begun eight years before. He looked at Guerra and saw that this was a man who had lost a dear friend, who would understand anything said to him in the name of Father Louis. He added, "I am leaving soon for France. Do you know where that is?"

"Yes. He used to tell us much about it."

Father Pierre was making ready to obey a summons to return home to receive the dignity of bishop of a French diocese.

"I am going there to assume new work," he said. "These things, this sacrifice," he said, indi-

cating what Guerra had brought, "will help me to do it better."

Guerra nodded.

"We will bury him here in the churchyard," continued Father Pierre, "and you must be present. As you were his friend, and have served him so well, now I would like to ask your permission to keep this."

He held up the little string of seashells.

"Yes," said Guerra, accepting with simplicity the power to dispose.

"I wonder how he died," murmured Father Pierre. "Indians? A heart attack?"

"Not Indians."

"Why not?"

"They would not have let the horse go."

"True. What then?"

Guerra made a gesture with his mouth, putting his lips forward as though he would point to a place far from there and long ago. He saw the clearing in the thorny brush again, and he knew its nature, all of it.

"I think I know."

"How could you possibly?"

"He did not die suddenly."

"No?"

"No. He had time to free his horse."

"True."

"If he thought he could have saved himself, he would have come with the horse."

"Undoubtedly."

"But he did not come. He stayed. That means he knew there wasn't any use."

"Yes?"

"Where I found him was just like the place where it would happen."

"What would happen?"

With his hand Guerra made in the air a slow, sinuous motion from side to side in an unmistakable imitation.

"No!" said Father Pierre. "A snake?"

Guerra nodded. "I think so," he said.

Father Pierre shuddered at the nature of that fate, and then presently he kindled at the memory of an old weakness and an old strength.

"Do you know? I will tell you something," he said. "Our dear friend was an old man, tired and ill, when he went on that last journey. For days before he left, I was supposed to tell him that he could not go. I tried and I tried. But I could not tell him. Even on the last morning I could not give the order." Father Pierre put his hands together in emotion. "What could I have saved him from? From dying at his work? That is how we—all of us—want to die when our time comes."

He looked earnestly at Guerra, but if he thought he would find the abstract pardon of life there, he was mistaken. Guerra simply looked back at him with the impersonal judgment of the world.

"No, I could not give the order," resumed Father Pierre. "And do you know? I am sure he knew what I had to say. He would not let me say it. He gave the orders. Just to prove it, he even sent me upstairs to find his green sunglasses. I went, and I did not find them. When I came down again, there they were; he had them all the time."

Guerra laughed out loud at the crankiness this recalled, and what it meant. He bent over, took up the pair of green glass spectacles with their rusted tin rims and, with a gleam of meaning, handed them to Father Pierre.

"Then keep these also," he said.

"Thank you," said the bishop-elect soberly.

INDEX